THE SANDMAN

BOOK ONE

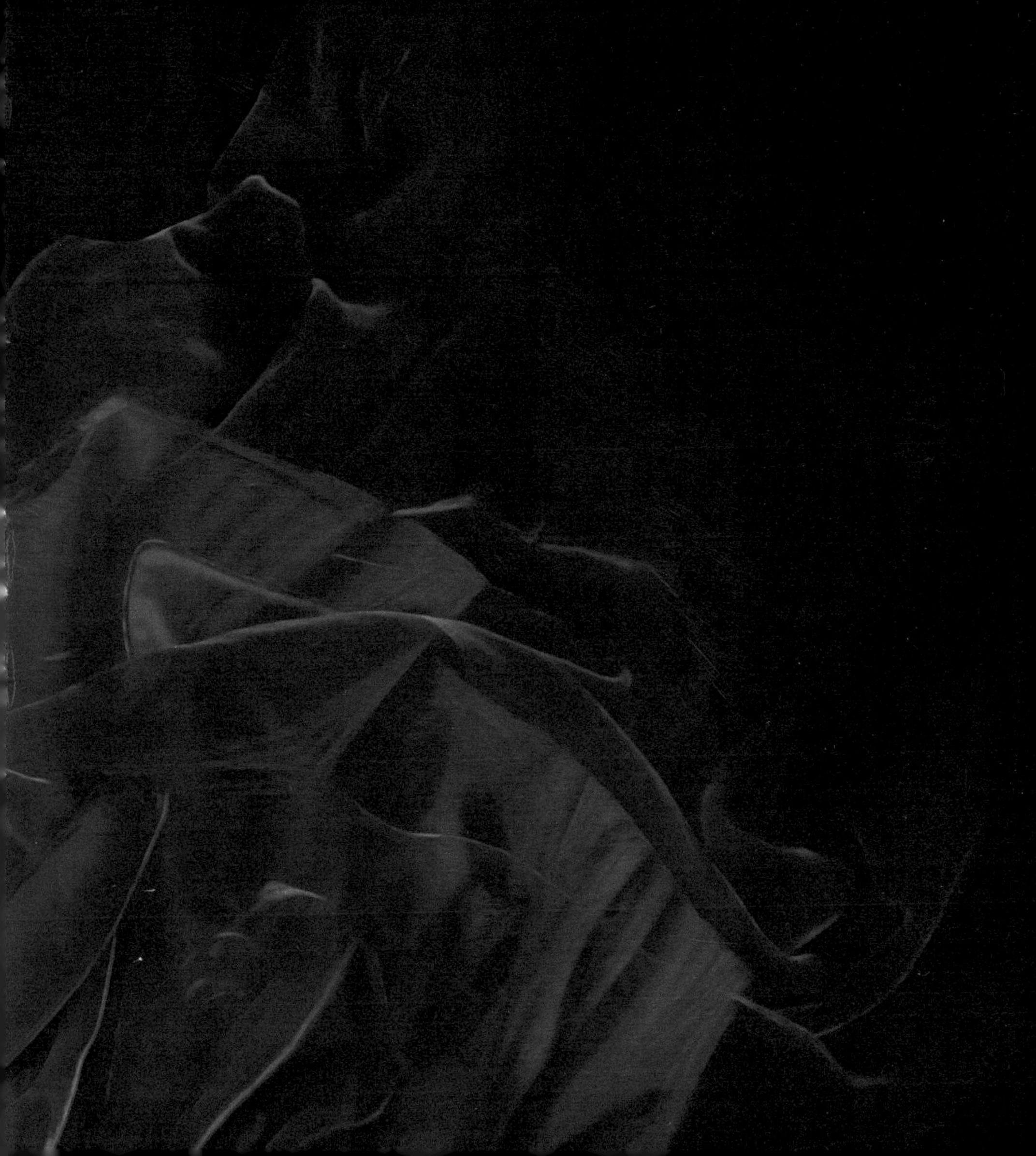

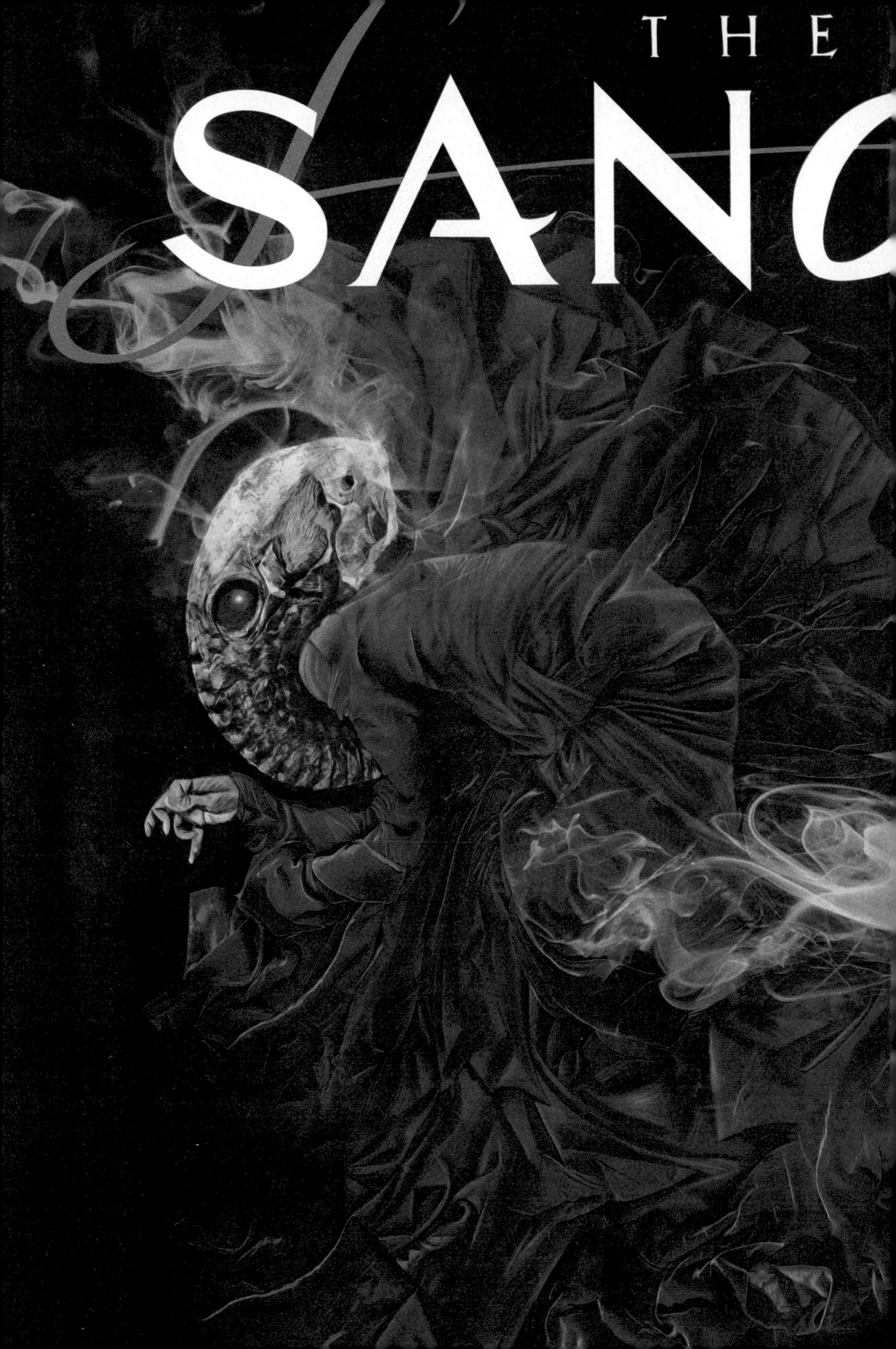
THE
SAN

MAN

BOOK ONE

NEIL GAIMAN
writer

SAM KIETH ∫ **MIKE DRINGENBERG** ∫ **MALCOLM JONES III**
CHRIS BACHALO ∫ **MICHAEL ZULLI** ∫ **STEVE PARKHOUSE**
KELLEY JONES ∫ **CHARLES VESS** ∫ **COLLEEN DORAN**
artists

DANIEL VOZZO ∫ **STEVE OLIFF**
colorists

TODD KLEIN
letterer

DAVE MCKEAN
collection cover and original series covers

SANDMAN based on characters created by
GAIMAN, KIETH, and DRINGENBERG

KAREN BERGER Editor – Original Series
ART YOUNG Associate Editor – Original Series
TOM PEYER Assistant Editor – Original Series
CHRIS CONROY & ROBIN WILDMAN Editors – Collected Edition
STEVE COOK Design Director – Books
MEGEN BELLERSEN Publication Design
SUZANNAH ROWNTREE & EMILY ELMER Publication Production

MARIE JAVINS Editor-in-Chief, DC Comics

DANIEL CHERRY III Senior VP – General Manager
JIM LEE Publisher & Chief Creative Officer
DON FALLETTI VP – Manufacturing Operations & Workflow Management
LAWRENCE GANEM VP – Talent Services
ALISON GILL Senior VP – Manufacturing & Operations
JEFFREY KAUFMAN VP – Editorial Strategy & Programming
NICK J. NAPOLITANO VP – Manufacturing Administration & Design
NANCY SPEARS VP – Revenue

THE SANDMAN BOOK ONE

DC Comics, 2900 West Alameda Ave., Burbank, CA 91505
Printed by LSC Communications, Owensville, MO, USA. 3/4/22. First Printing.
ISBN: 978-1-77951-517-9

Library of Congress Cataloging-in-Publication Data is available.

For Dave Dickson: oldest friend.
—**Neil Gaiman**

To my wife Kathy, my pal Tim, and to everyone in jail.
—**Sam Kieth**

To friends and lovers. To Sam, Malcolm, and Neil; may your talents
never dim. You made working on this book an indescribable pleasure.
To Karen, Tom, and Art (without whom this book would not have been
possible), thanks for the time and your super-human patience. Special
thanks to Beth, Matte, Sigal, the incomparable Barbara Brandt (a.k.a.
Victoria), Rachel, Sean F., Shawn S., Mimi, Gigi, Heather, Yann,
Brantski, Mai Li, Bernie Wrightson (for Cain and Abel),
and, as ever, to Cinnamon.
—**Mike Dringenberg**

To Little Malcolm.
—**Malcolm Jones III**

But where shall wisdom be found? And where is the place of
understanding? Man knoweth not the price thereof; neither is it found
in the land of the living...for the price of wisdom is above rubies.
—*The Book of Job*, chapter 28, verses 12, 13, 18

D is for lots of things.
—John Dee, All Fool's Day 1989

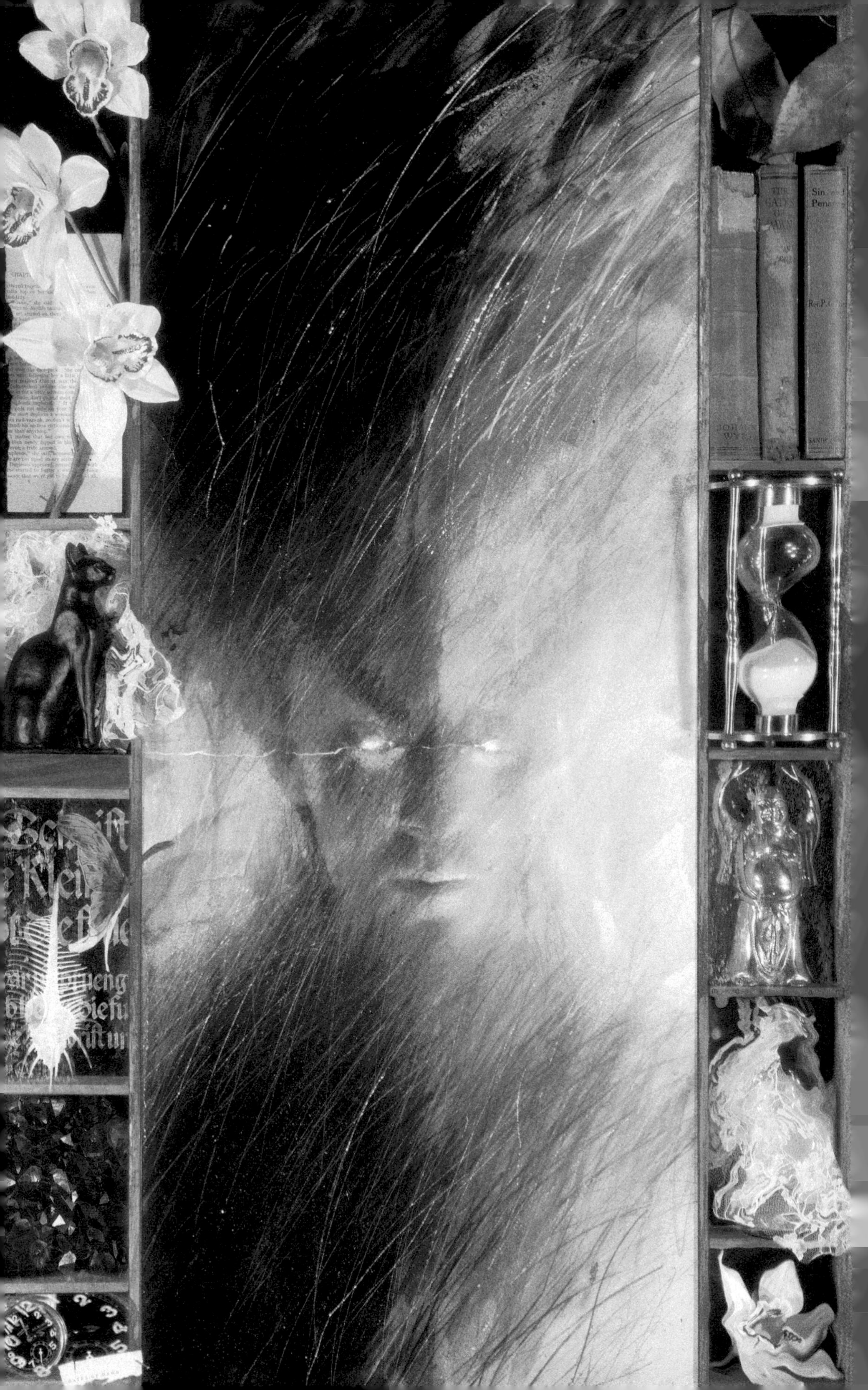

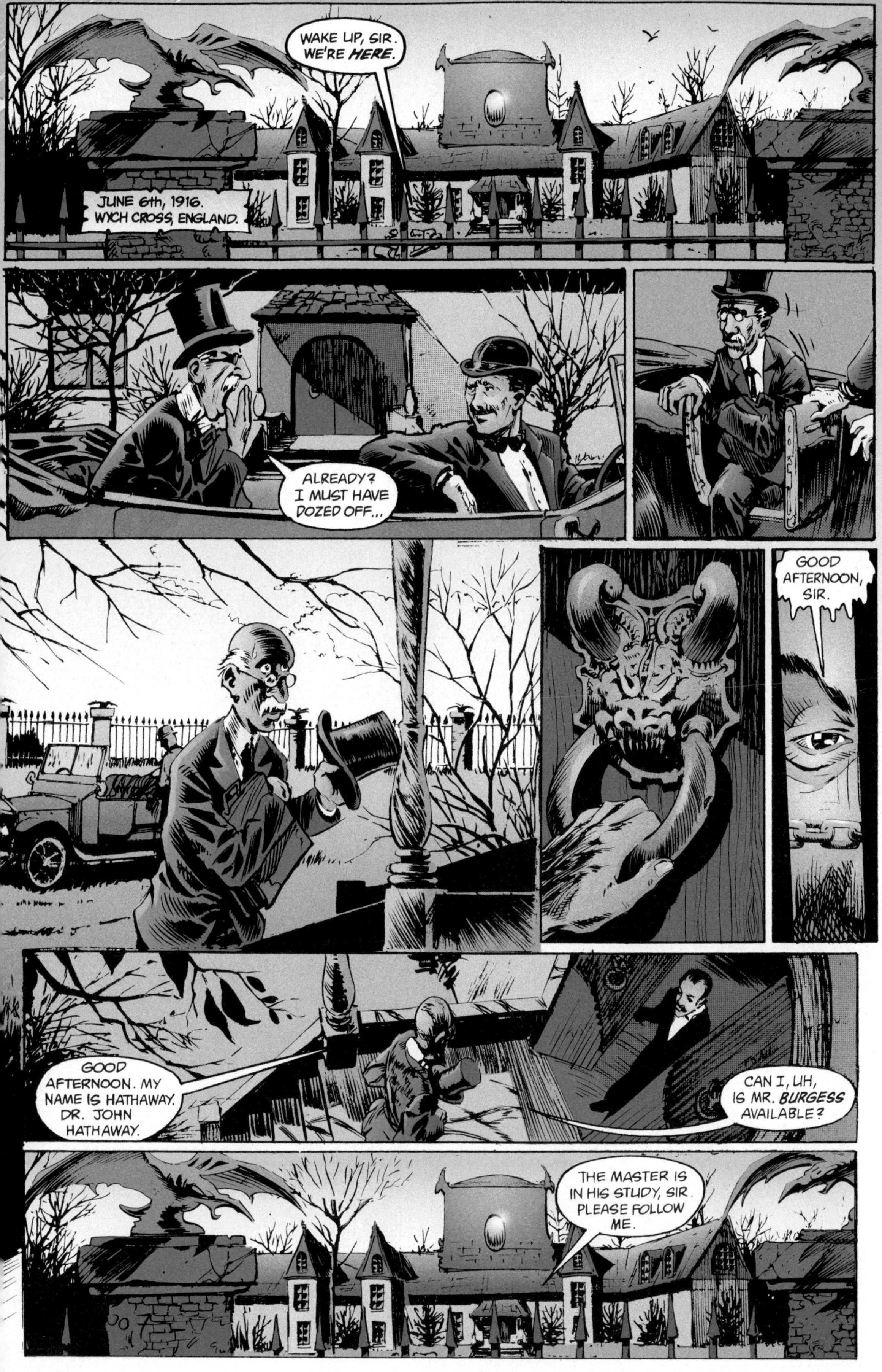
JUNE 6th, 1916.
WYCH CROSS, ENGLAND.
WAKE UP, SIR. WE'RE HERE.
ALREADY? I MUST HAVE DOZED OFF...
GOOD AFTERNOON, SIR.
GOOD AFTERNOON. MY NAME IS HATHAWAY. DR. JOHN HATHAWAY.
CAN I, UH, IS MR. BURGESS AVAILABLE?
THE MASTER IS IN HIS STUDY, SIR. PLEASE FOLLOW ME.

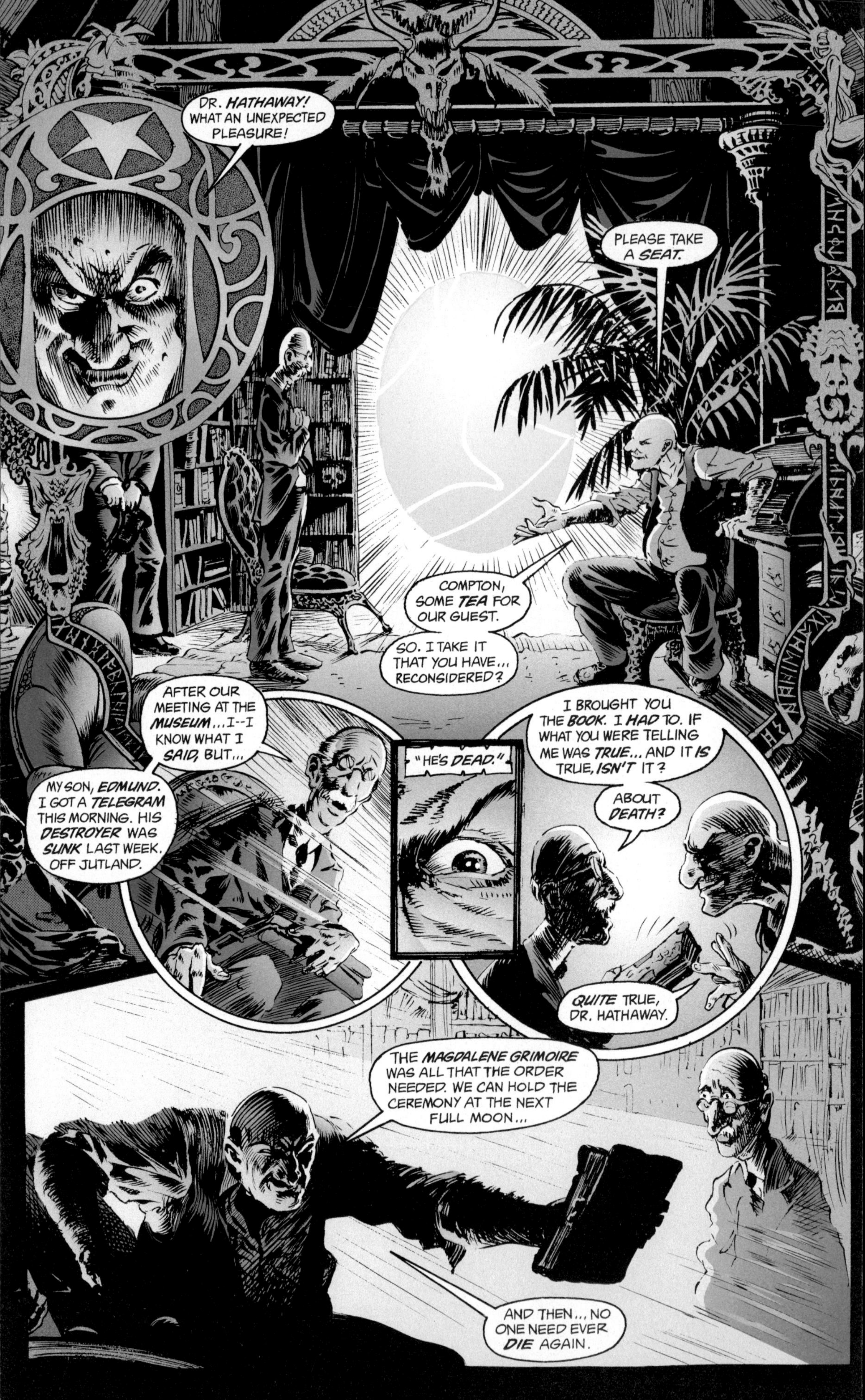
DR. HATHAWAY! WHAT AN UNEXPECTED PLEASURE!
PLEASE TAKE A SEAT.
COMPTON, SOME TEA FOR OUR GUEST.
SO. I TAKE IT THAT YOU HAVE... RECONSIDERED?
AFTER OUR MEETING AT THE MUSEUM... I--I KNOW WHAT I SAID, BUT...
MY SON, EDMUND. I GOT A TELEGRAM THIS MORNING. HIS DESTROYER WAS SUNK LAST WEEK, OFF JUTLAND.
"HE'S DEAD."
I BROUGHT YOU THE BOOK. I HAD TO. IF WHAT YOU WERE TELLING ME WAS TRUE... AND IT IS TRUE, ISN'T IT?
ABOUT DEATH?
QUITE TRUE, DR. HATHAWAY.
THE MAGDALENE GRIMOIRE WAS ALL THAT THE ORDER NEEDED. WE CAN HOLD THE CEREMONY AT THE NEXT FULL MOON...
AND THEN... NO ONE NEED EVER DIE AGAIN.

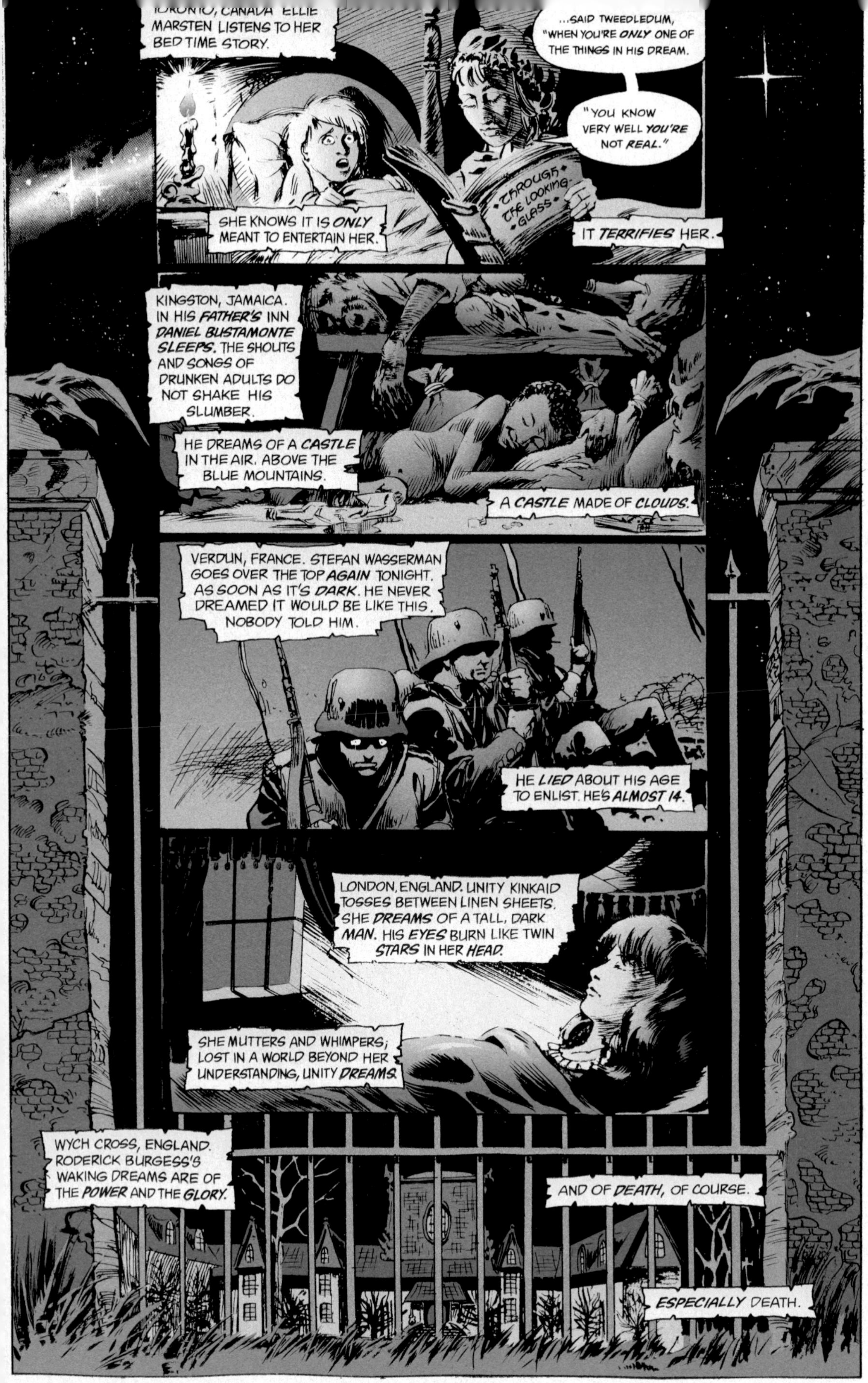
TORONTO, CANADA. ELLIE MARSTEN LISTENS TO HER BED TIME STORY.
...SAID TWEEDLEDUM, "WHEN YOU'RE ONLY ONE OF THE THINGS IN HIS DREAM.
"YOU KNOW VERY WELL YOU'RE NOT REAL."
THROUGH THE LOOKING-GLASS
SHE KNOWS IT IS ONLY MEANT TO ENTERTAIN HER.
IT TERRIFIES HER.
KINGSTON, JAMAICA. IN HIS FATHER'S INN DANIEL BUSTAMONTE SLEEPS. THE SHOUTS AND SONGS OF DRUNKEN ADULTS DO NOT SHAKE HIS SLUMBER.
HE DREAMS OF A CASTLE IN THE AIR, ABOVE THE BLUE MOUNTAINS.
A CASTLE MADE OF CLOUDS.
VERDUN, FRANCE. STEFAN WASSERMAN GOES OVER THE TOP AGAIN TONIGHT. AS SOON AS IT'S DARK. HE NEVER DREAMED IT WOULD BE LIKE THIS. NOBODY TOLD HIM.
HE LIED ABOUT HIS AGE TO ENLIST. HE'S ALMOST 14.
LONDON, ENGLAND. UNITY KINKAID TOSSES BETWEEN LINEN SHEETS. SHE DREAMS OF A TALL, DARK MAN. HIS EYES BURN LIKE TWIN STARS IN HER HEAD.
SHE MUTTERS AND WHIMPERS; LOST IN A WORLD BEYOND HER UNDERSTANDING, UNITY DREAMS.
WYCH CROSS, ENGLAND. RODERICK BURGESS'S WAKING DREAMS ARE OF THE POWER AND THE GLORY.
AND OF DEATH, OF COURSE.
ESPECIALLY DEATH.

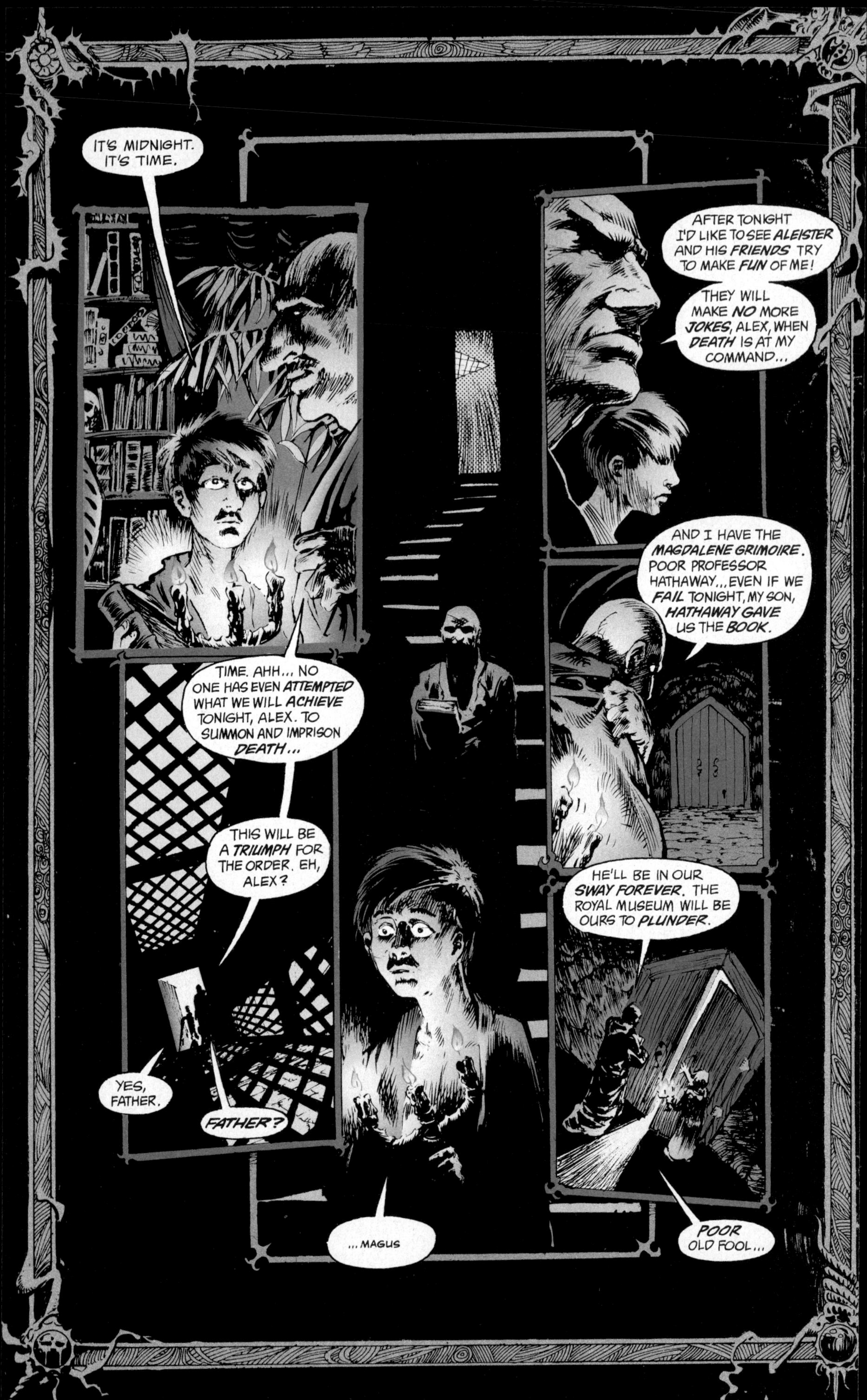
IT'S MIDNIGHT. IT'S TIME.
AFTER TONIGHT I'D LIKE TO SEE ALEISTER AND HIS FRIENDS TRY TO MAKE FUN OF ME!
THEY WILL MAKE NO MORE JOKES, ALEX, WHEN DEATH IS AT MY COMMAND...
TIME. AHH... NO ONE HAS EVEN ATTEMPTED WHAT WE WILL ACHIEVE TONIGHT, ALEX. TO SUMMON AND IMPRISON DEATH...
AND I HAVE THE MAGDALENE GRIMOIRE. POOR PROFESSOR HATHAWAY... EVEN IF WE FAIL TONIGHT, MY SON, HATHAWAY GAVE US THE BOOK.
THIS WILL BE A TRIUMPH FOR THE ORDER. EH, ALEX?
HE'LL BE IN OUR SWAY FOREVER. THE ROYAL MUSEUM WILL BE OURS TO PLUNDER.
YES, FATHER.
FATHER?
...MAGUS
POOR OLD FOOL...

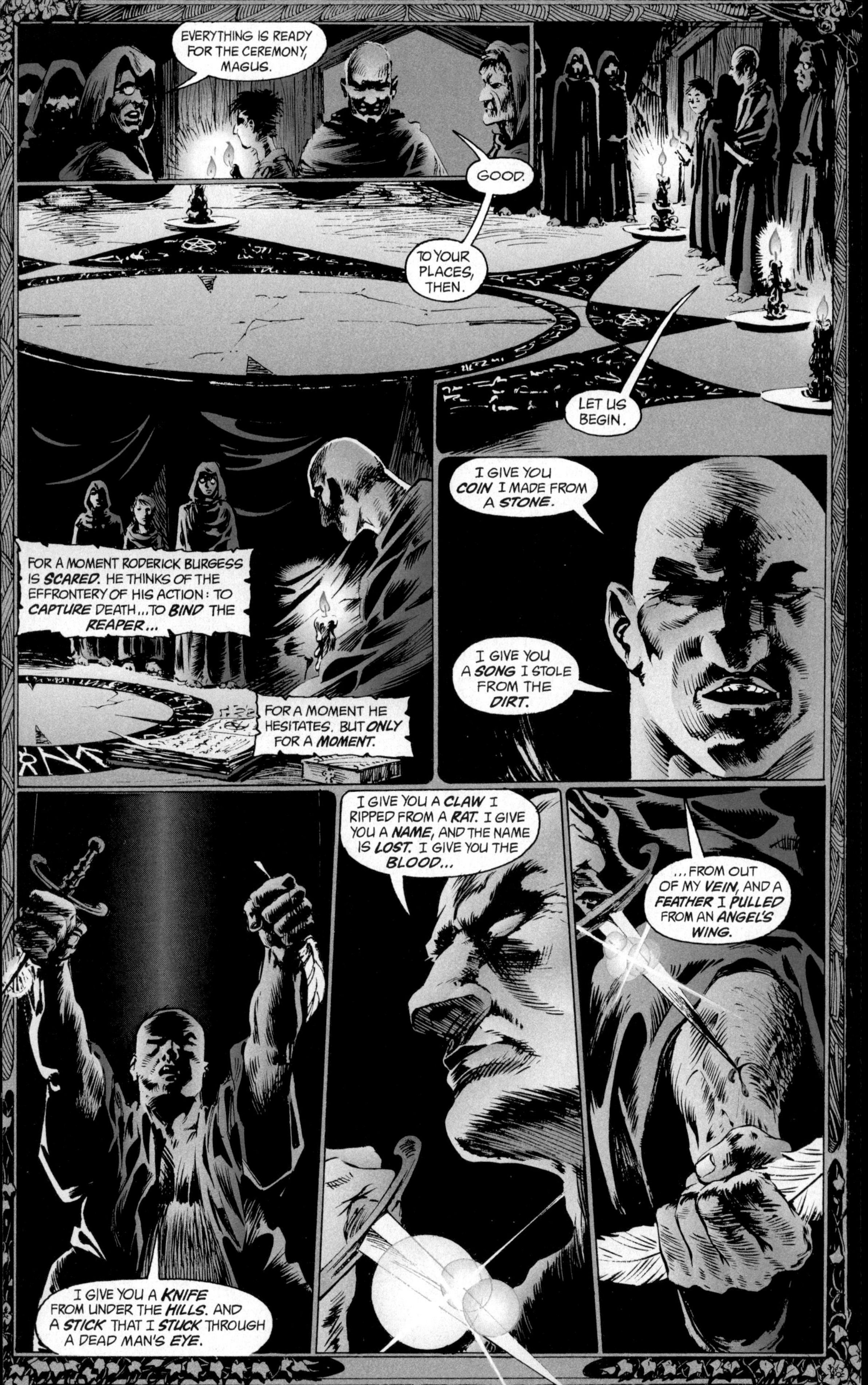

EVERYTHING IS READY FOR THE CEREMONY, MAGUS.
GOOD.
TO YOUR PLACES, THEN.
LET US BEGIN.
FOR A MOMENT RODERICK BURGESS IS SCARED. HE THINKS OF THE EFFRONTERY OF HIS ACTION: TO CAPTURE DEATH... TO BIND THE REAPER...
FOR A MOMENT HE HESITATES. BUT ONLY FOR A MOMENT.
I GIVE YOU COIN I MADE FROM A STONE.
I GIVE YOU A SONG I STOLE FROM THE DIRT.
I GIVE YOU A KNIFE FROM UNDER THE HILLS. AND A STICK THAT I STUCK THROUGH A DEAD MAN'S EYE.
I GIVE YOU A CLAW I RIPPED FROM A RAT. I GIVE YOU A NAME, AND THE NAME IS LOST. I GIVE YOU THE BLOOD...
...FROM OUT OF MY VEIN, AND A FEATHER I PULLED FROM AN ANGEL'S WING.

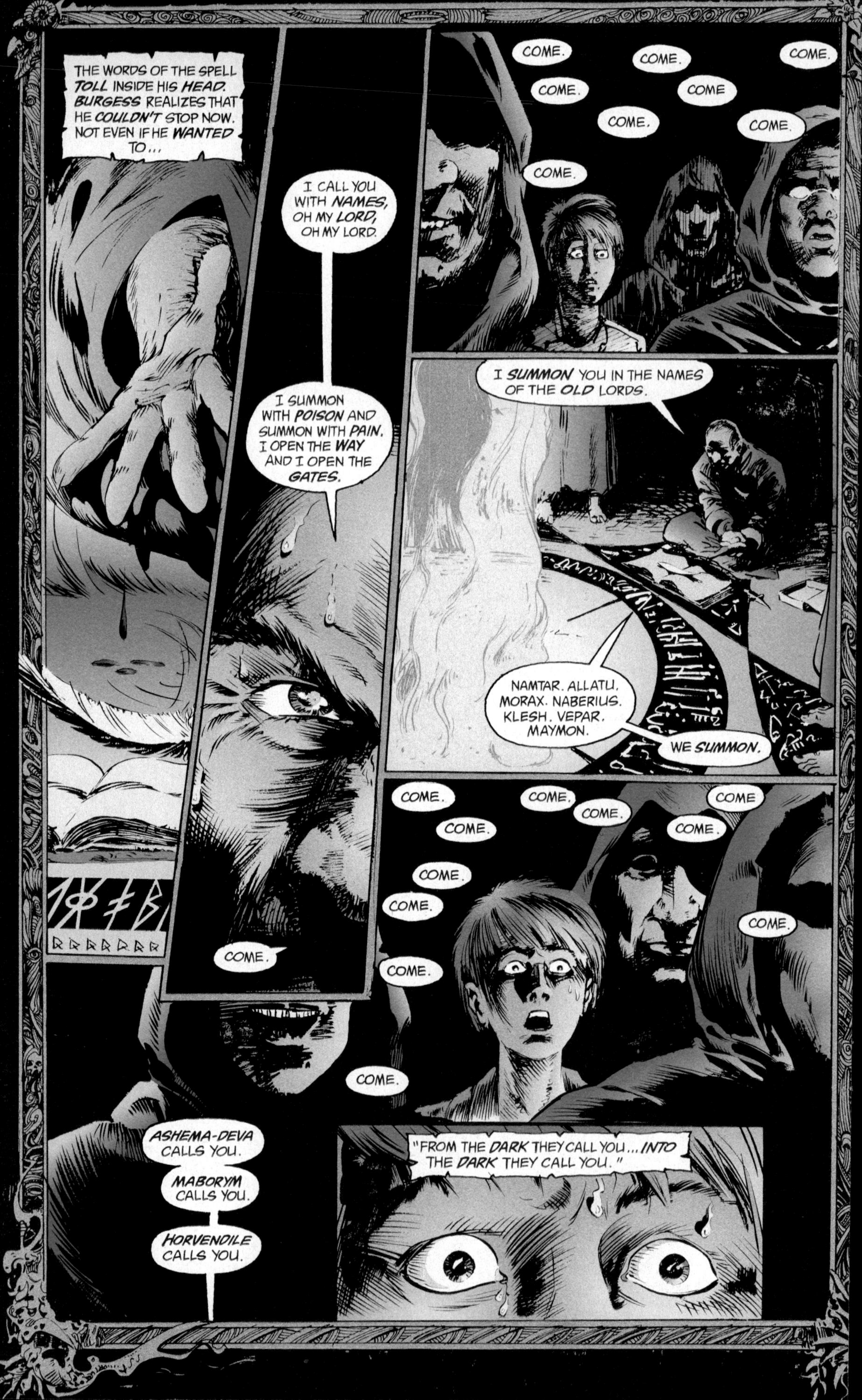

THE WORDS OF THE SPELL TOLL INSIDE HIS HEAD. BURGESS REALIZES THAT HE COULDN'T STOP NOW. NOT EVEN IF HE WANTED TO...
I CALL YOU WITH NAMES, OH MY LORD, OH MY LORD.
I SUMMON WITH POISON AND SUMMON WITH PAIN. I OPEN THE WAY AND I OPEN THE GATES.
COME.
COME.
COME.
COME.
COME
COME.
COME.
COME.
I SUMMON YOU IN THE NAMES OF THE OLD LORDS.
NAMTAR. ALLATU. MORAX. NABERIUS. KLESH. VEPAR. MAYMON.
WE SUMMON.
COME.
COME.
COME.
COME.
COME
COME.
COME.
COME.
COME.
COME.
COME.
ASHEMA-DEVA CALLS YOU.
MABORYM CALLS YOU.
HORVENDILE CALLS YOU.
"FROM THE DARK THEY CALL YOU... INTO THE DARK THEY CALL YOU."

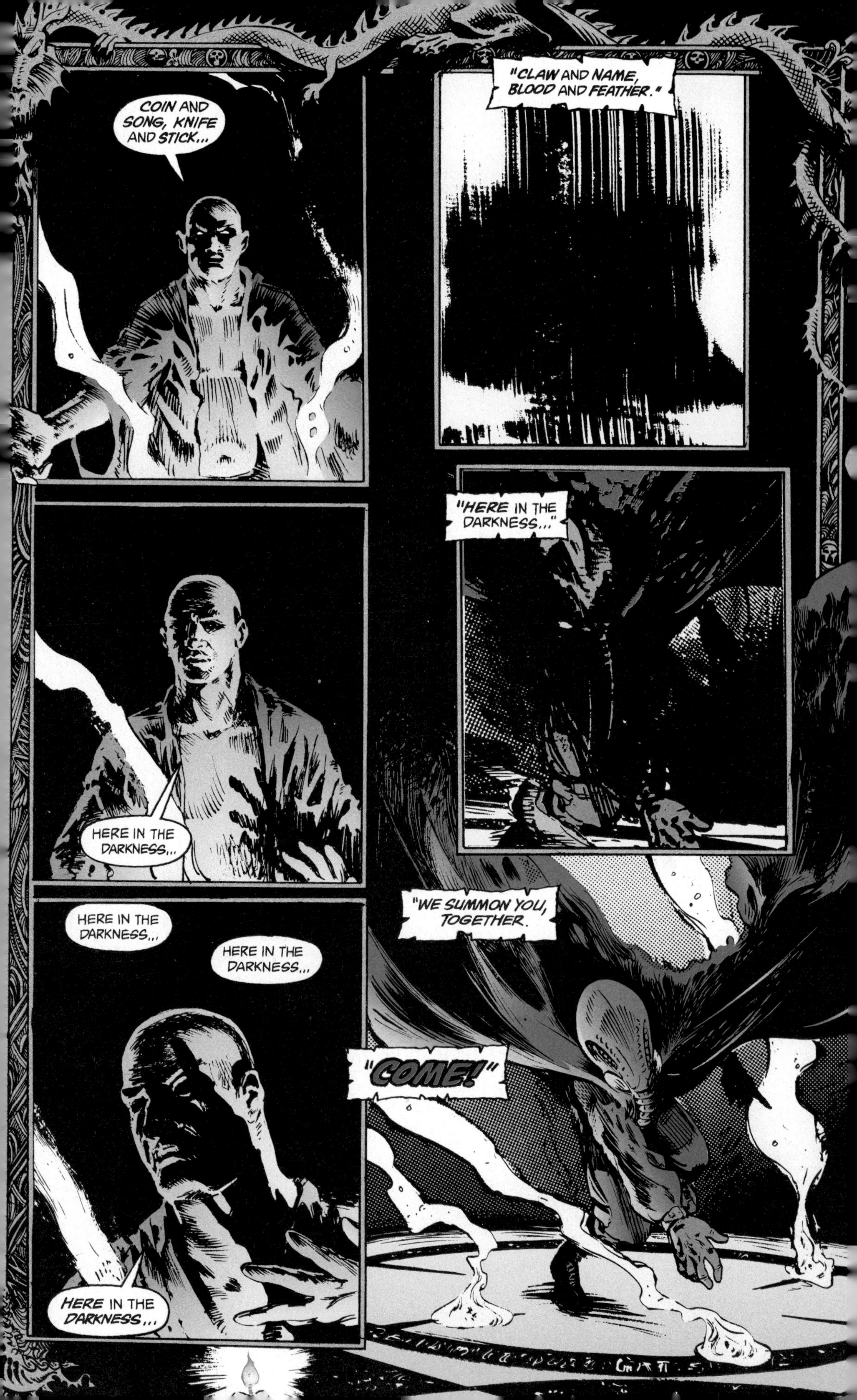

COIN AND SONG, KNIFE AND STICK...
"CLAW AND NAME, BLOOD AND FEATHER."
HERE IN THE DARKNESS...
"HERE IN THE DARKNESS..."
HERE IN THE DARKNESS...
HERE IN THE DARKNESS...
HERE IN THE DARKNESS...
"WE SUMMON YOU, TOGETHER.
"COME!"

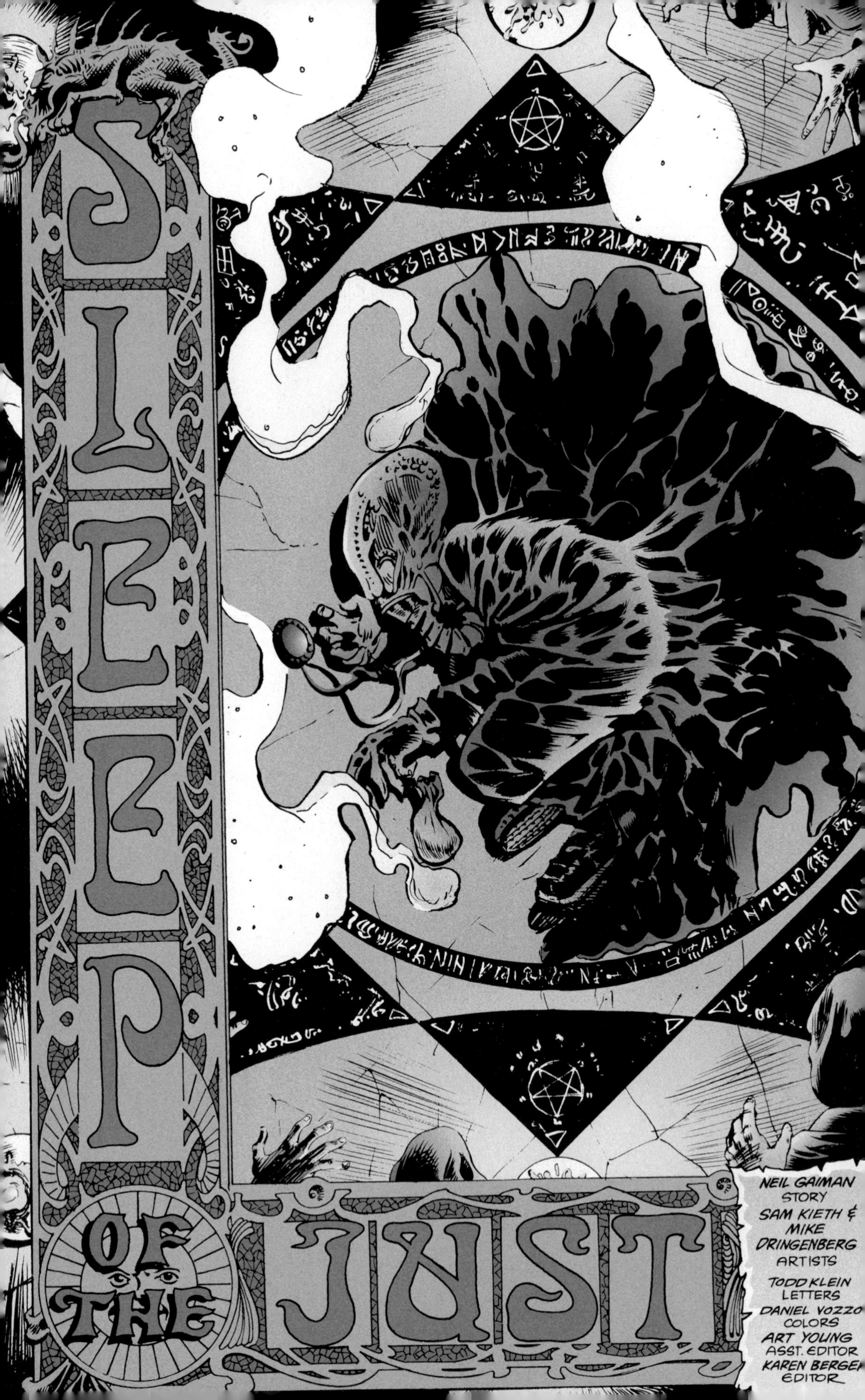
SLEEP OF THE JUST
NEIL GAIMAN
STORY
SAM KIETH &
MIKE
DRINGENBERG
ARTISTS
TODD KLEIN
LETTERS
DANIEL VOZZO
COLORS
ART YOUNG
ASST. EDITOR
KAREN BERGER
EDITOR

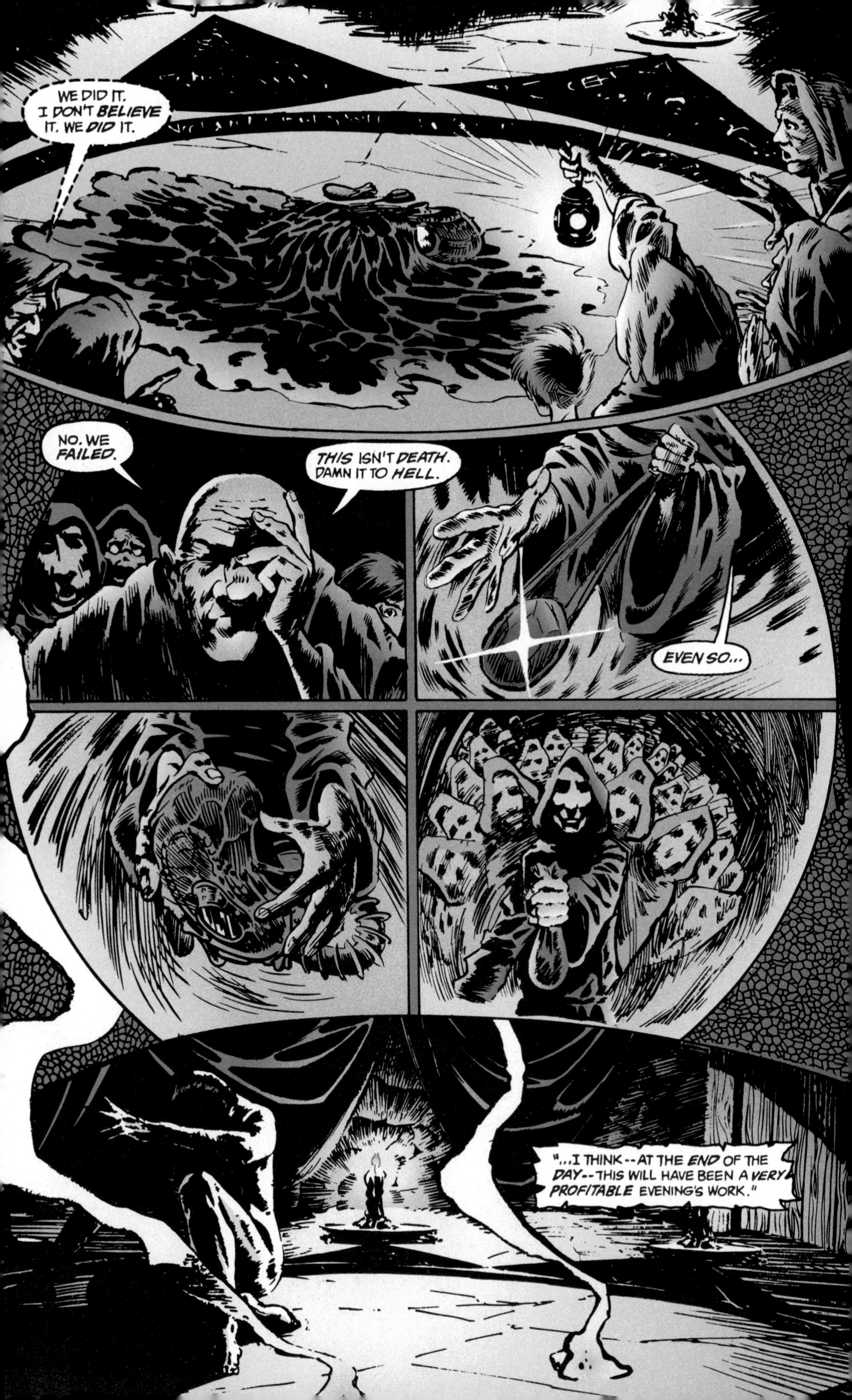
WE DID IT. I DON'T BELIEVE IT. WE DID IT.
NO. WE FAILED.
THIS ISN'T DEATH. DAMN IT TO HELL.
EVEN SO...
"...I THINK--AT THE END OF THE DAY--THIS WILL HAVE BEEN A VERY PROFITABLE EVENING'S WORK."

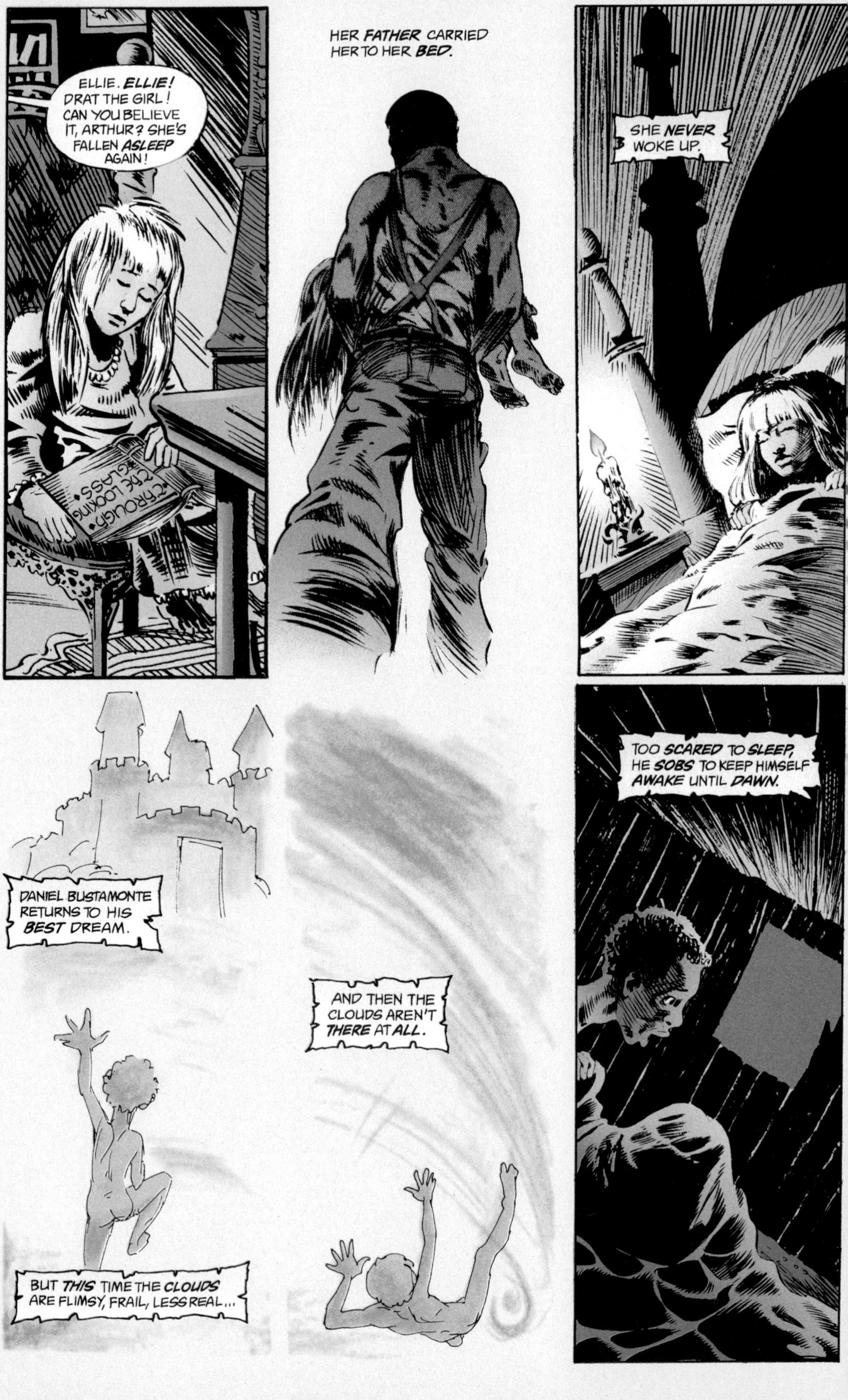
ELLIE. ELLIE! DRAT THE GIRL! CAN YOU BELIEVE IT, ARTHUR? SHE'S FALLEN ASLEEP AGAIN!
THROUGH THE LOOKING GLASS
HER FATHER CARRIED HER TO HER BED.
SHE NEVER WOKE UP.
DANIEL BUSTAMONTE RETURNS TO HIS BEST DREAM.
BUT THIS TIME THE CLOUDS ARE FLIMSY, FRAIL, LESS REAL...
AND THEN THE CLOUDS AREN'T THERE AT ALL.
TOO SCARED TO SLEEP, HE SOBS TO KEEP HIMSELF AWAKE UNTIL DAWN.

STEFAN'S CASE IS *NEW* TO THE DOCTORS. THEY THOUGHT THEY'D SEEN *EVERY* FORM OF *SHELL-SHOCK*.

HOW LONG CAN A BOY GO WITHOUT *SLEEPING*? WHEN DO THE *NIGHTMARES* SNEAK *OUT* INTO THE DAYLIGHT?

THE *MORPHINE* IS PROVING *USELESS*.

IT'S *SAD*.

STEFAN WASSERMAN WENT OVER THE *TOP*.

UNITY KINKAID FINDS IT HARDER AND HARDER TO STAY *AWAKE*.

SHE NOW SLEEPS FOR ALMOST TWENTY HOURS A DAY.

SHE USED TO *DREAM*; TO *SHIFT* IN HER SLEEP, MUTTERING AND SIGHING, *LOCKED* IN HALF-REMEMBERED *FANTASIES...*

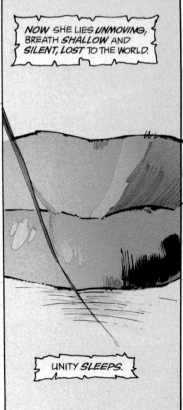

NOW SHE LIES *UNMOVING*, BREATH *SHALLOW* AND *SILENT, LOST* TO THE WORLD.

UNITY *SLEEPS*.

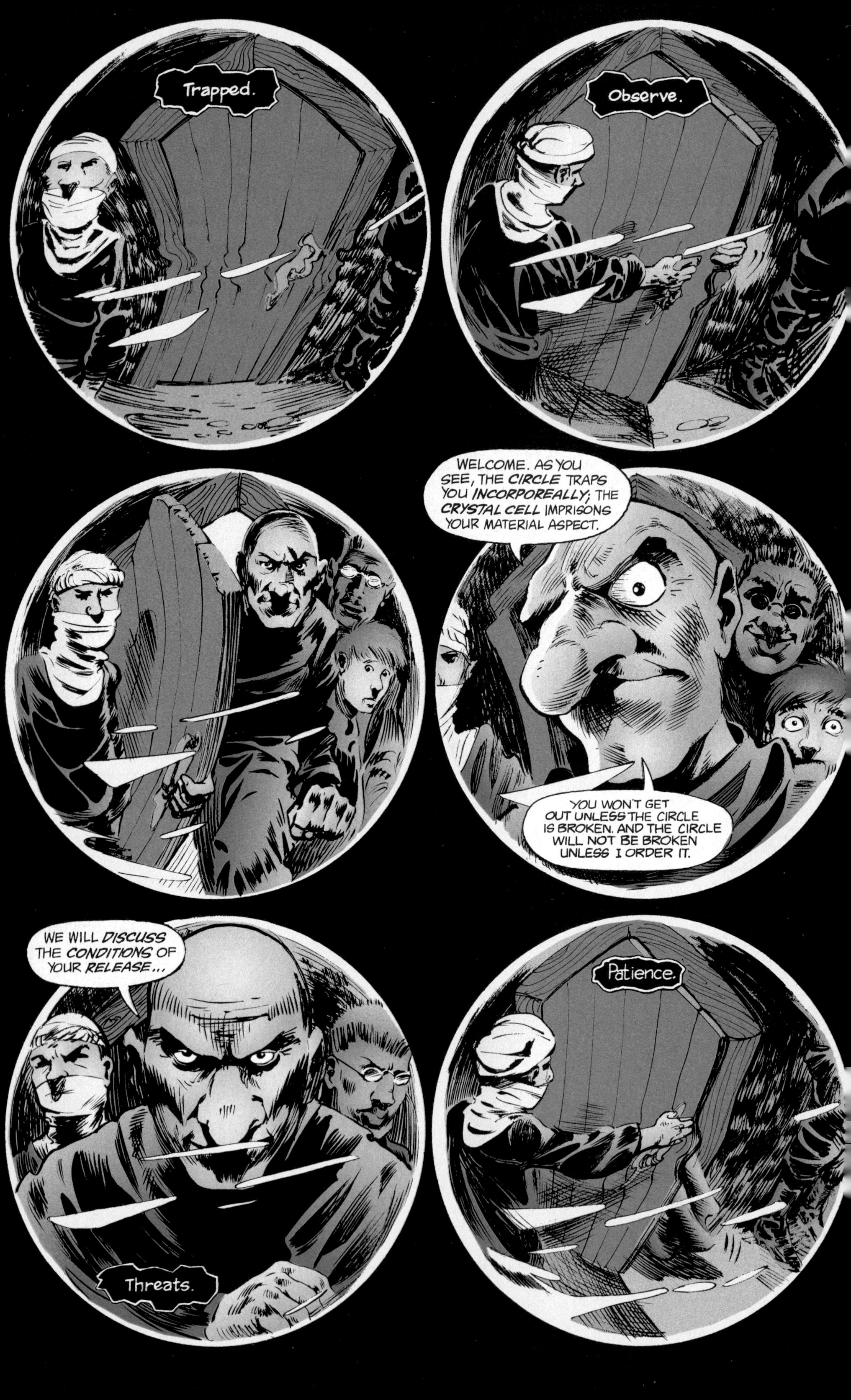

Trapped.
Observe.
WELCOME. AS YOU SEE, THE CIRCLE TRAPS YOU INCORPOREALLY; THE CRYSTAL CELL IMPRISONS YOUR MATERIAL ASPECT.
YOU WON'T GET OUT UNLESS THE CIRCLE IS BROKEN. AND THE CIRCLE WILL NOT BE BROKEN UNLESS I ORDER IT.
WE WILL DISCUSS THE CONDITIONS OF YOUR RELEASE...
Threats.
Patience.

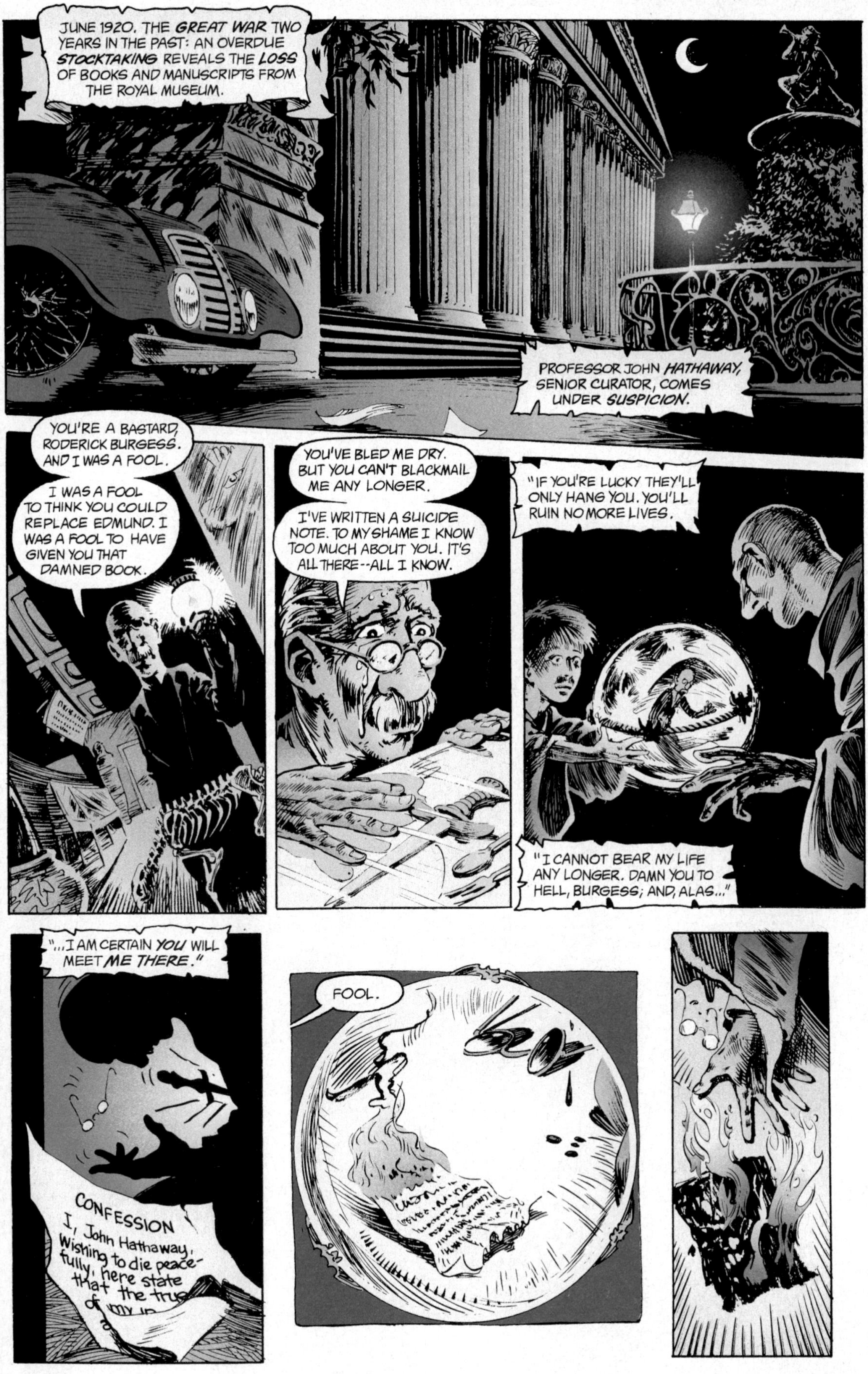

JUNE 1920. THE GREAT WAR TWO YEARS IN THE PAST: AN OVERDUE STOCKTAKING REVEALS THE LOSS OF BOOKS AND MANUSCRIPTS FROM THE ROYAL MUSEUM.
PROFESSOR JOHN HATHAWAY, SENIOR CURATOR, COMES UNDER SUSPICION.
YOU'RE A BASTARD, RODERICK BURGESS. AND I WAS A FOOL.
I WAS A FOOL TO THINK YOU COULD REPLACE EDMUND. I WAS A FOOL TO HAVE GIVEN YOU THAT DAMNED BOOK.
YOU'VE BLED ME DRY. BUT YOU CAN'T BLACKMAIL ME ANY LONGER.
I'VE WRITTEN A SUICIDE NOTE. TO MY SHAME I KNOW TOO MUCH ABOUT YOU. IT'S ALL THERE--ALL I KNOW.
"IF YOU'RE LUCKY THEY'LL ONLY HANG YOU. YOU'LL RUIN NO MORE LIVES.
"I CANNOT BEAR MY LIFE ANY LONGER. DAMN YOU TO HELL, BURGESS; AND, ALAS..."
"...I AM CERTAIN YOU WILL MEET ME THERE."
CONFESSION
I, John Hathaway, Wishing to die peacefully, here state that the tru
FOOL.

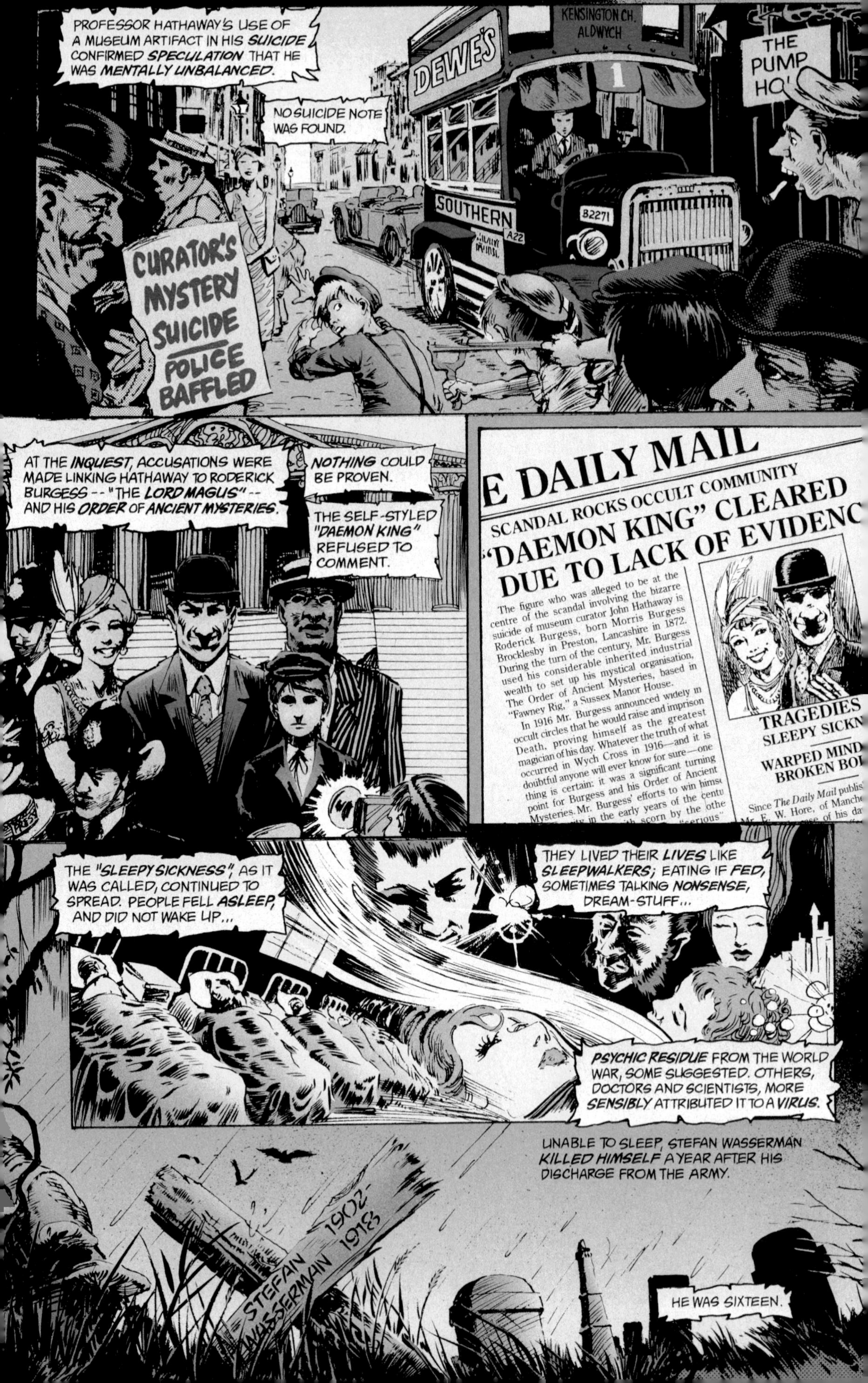
PROFESSOR HATHAWAY'S USE OF A MUSEUM ARTIFACT IN HIS SUICIDE CONFIRMED SPECULATION THAT HE WAS MENTALLY UNBALANCED.
NO SUICIDE NOTE WAS FOUND.
KENSINGTON CH. ALDWYCH
DEWE'S
1
SOUTHERN
B2271
THE PUMP HO
CURATOR'S MYSTERY SUICIDE
POLICE BAFFLED
AT THE INQUEST, ACCUSATIONS WERE MADE LINKING HATHAWAY TO RODERICK BURGESS -- "THE LORD MAGUS" -- AND HIS ORDER OF ANCIENT MYSTERIES.
NOTHING COULD BE PROVEN.
THE SELF-STYLED "DAEMON KING" REFUSED TO COMMENT.
E DAILY MAIL
SCANDAL ROCKS OCCULT COMMUNITY
"DAEMON KING" CLEARED DUE TO LACK OF EVIDENC
The figure who was alleged to be at the centre of the scandal involving the bizarre suicide of museum curator John Hathaway is Roderick Burgess, born Morris Burgess Brocklesby in Preston, Lancashire in 1872. During the turn of the century, Mr. Burgess used his considerable inherited industrial wealth to set up his mystical organisation, The Order of Ancient Mysteries, based in "Fawney Rig," a Sussex Manor House.
In 1916 Mr. Burgess announced widely in occult circles that he would raise and imprison Death, proving himself as the greatest magician of his day. Whatever the truth of what occurred in Wych Cross in 1916—and it is doubtful anyone will ever know for sure—one thing is certain: it was a significant turning point for Burgess and his Order of Ancient Mysteries. Mr. Burgess' efforts to win himse
TRAGEDIES SLEEPY SICKN
WARPED MIND BROKEN BO
Since The Daily Mail publis
THE "SLEEPY SICKNESS", AS IT WAS CALLED, CONTINUED TO SPREAD. PEOPLE FELL ASLEEP, AND DID NOT WAKE UP...
THEY LIVED THEIR LIVES LIKE SLEEPWALKERS; EATING IF FED, SOMETIMES TALKING NONSENSE, DREAM-STUFF...
PSYCHIC RESIDUE FROM THE WORLD WAR, SOME SUGGESTED. OTHERS, DOCTORS AND SCIENTISTS, MORE SENSIBLY ATTRIBUTED IT TO A VIRUS.
UNABLE TO SLEEP, STEFAN WASSERMAN KILLED HIMSELF A YEAR AFTER HIS DISCHARGE FROM THE ARMY.
STEFAN WASSERMAN 1902-1918
HE WAS SIXTEEN.

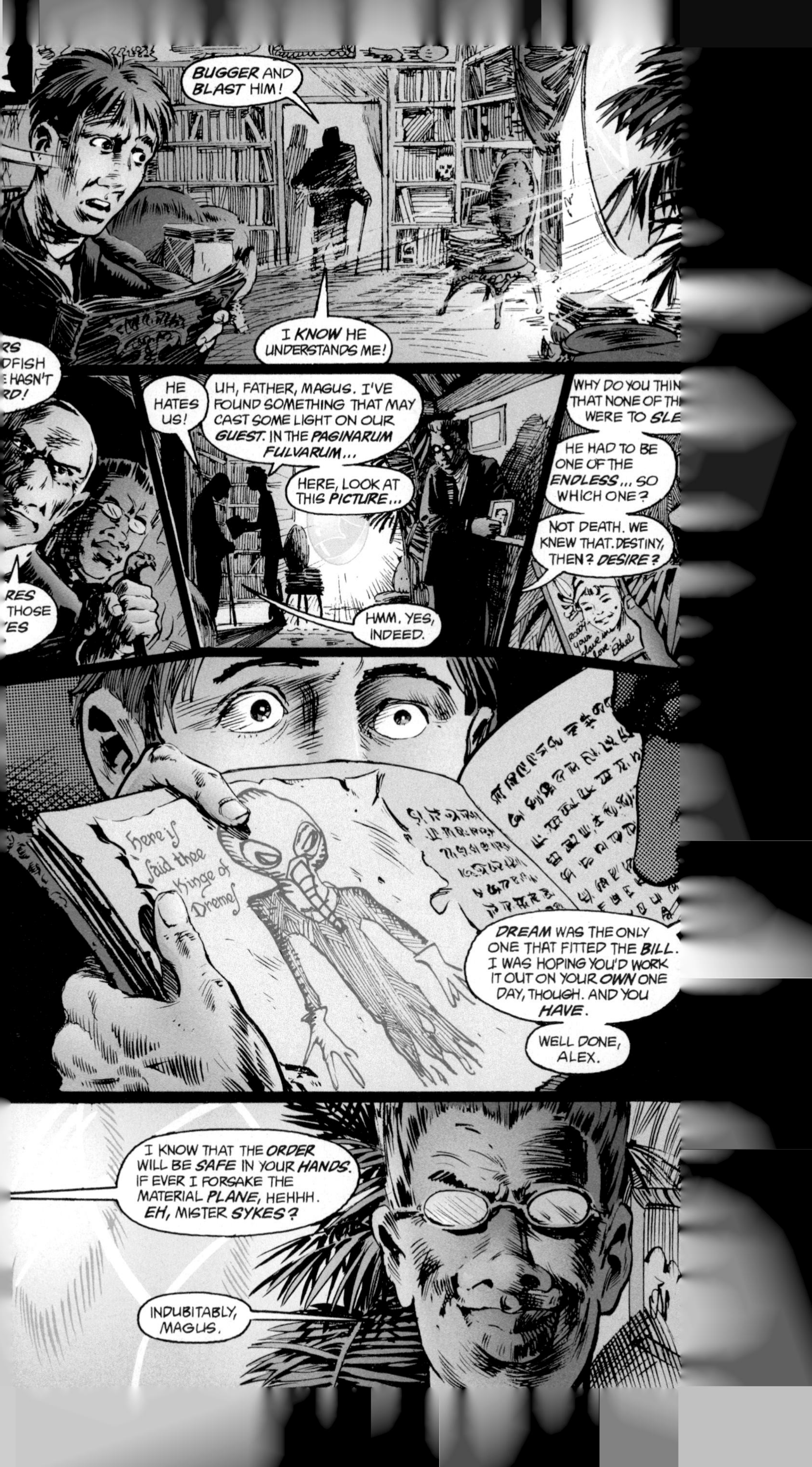
BUGGER AND BLAST HIM!
I KNOW HE UNDERSTANDS ME!
HE HATES US!
UH, FATHER, MAGUS. I'VE FOUND SOMETHING THAT MAY CAST SOME LIGHT ON OUR GUEST. IN THE PAGINARUM FULVARUM...
HERE, LOOK AT THIS PICTURE...
HMM. YES, INDEED.
WHY DO YOU THIN THAT NONE OF TH WERE TO SLE
HE HAD TO BE ONE OF THE ENDLESS... SO WHICH ONE?
NOT DEATH. WE KNEW THAT. DESTINY, THEN? DESIRE?
Here is said thee Kinge of Dremes
DREAM WAS THE ONLY ONE THAT FITTED THE BILL. I WAS HOPING YOU'D WORK IT OUT ON YOUR OWN ONE DAY, THOUGH. AND YOU HAVE.
WELL DONE, ALEX.
I KNOW THAT THE ORDER WILL BE SAFE IN YOUR HANDS. IF EVER I FORSAKE THE MATERIAL PLANE, HEHHH. EH, MISTER SYKES?
INDUBITABLY, MAGUS.

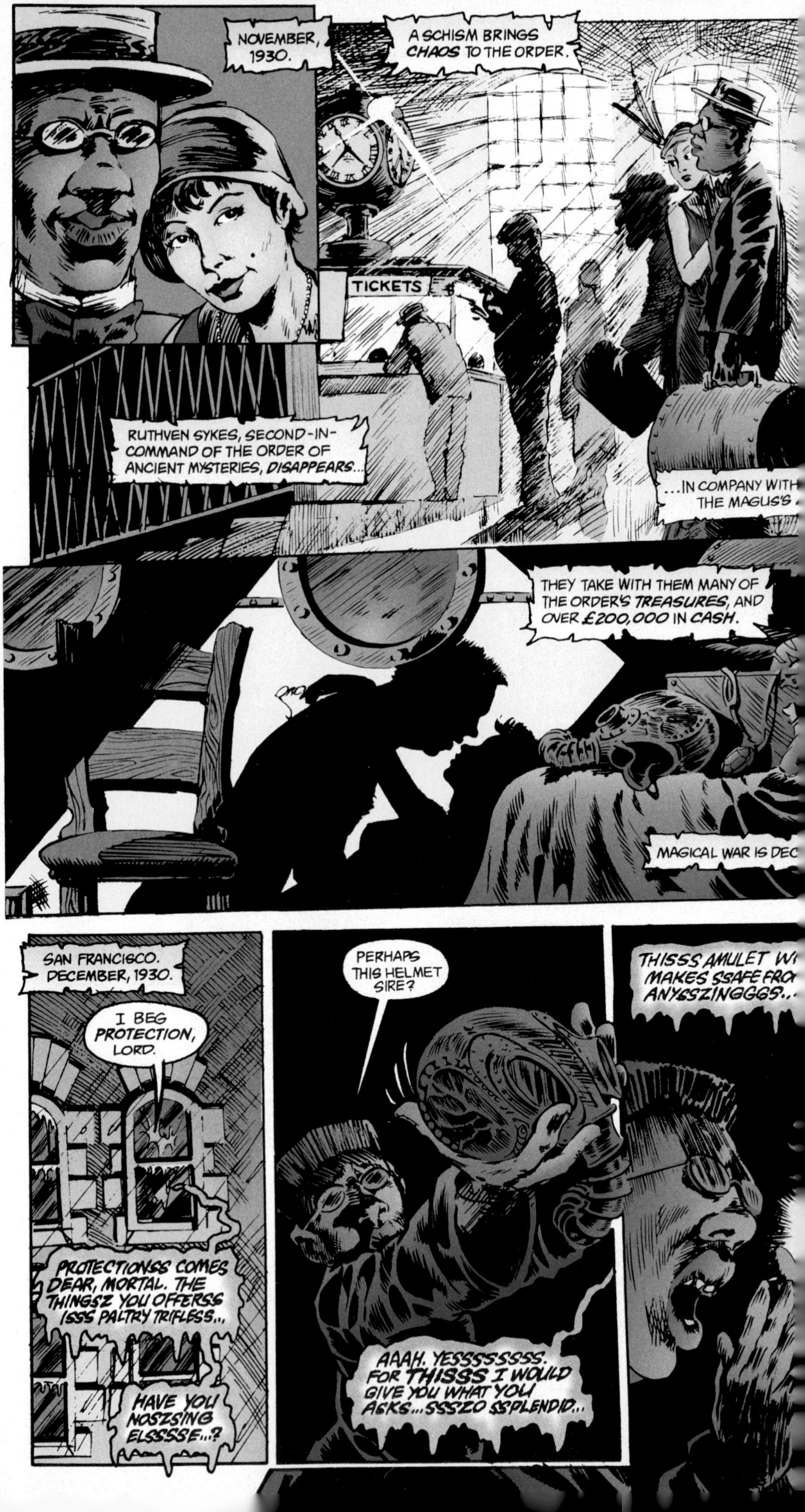
NOVEMBER, 1930.
A SCHISM BRINGS CHAOS TO THE ORDER.
TICKETS
RUTHVEN SYKES, SECOND-IN-COMMAND OF THE ORDER OF ANCIENT MYSTERIES, DISAPPEARS...
...IN COMPANY WITH THE
THEY TAKE WITH THEM MANY OF THE ORDER'S TREASURES, AND OVER £200,000 IN CASH.
MAGICAL WAR IS
SAN FRANCISCO. DECEMBER, 1930.
I BEG PROTECTION, LORD.
PROTECTIONSS COMES DEAR, MORTAL. THE THINGSZ YOU OFFERSS ISSS PALTRY TRIFLESS...
HAVE YOU NOSZSING ELSSSSE...?
PERHAPS THIS HELMET SIRE?
AAAH. YESSSSSSSS. FOR THISSS I WOULD GIVE YOU WHAT YOU ASKS...SSSZO SSPLENDID...
THISSS AMULET
MAKES
ANYSSZINGGGS...

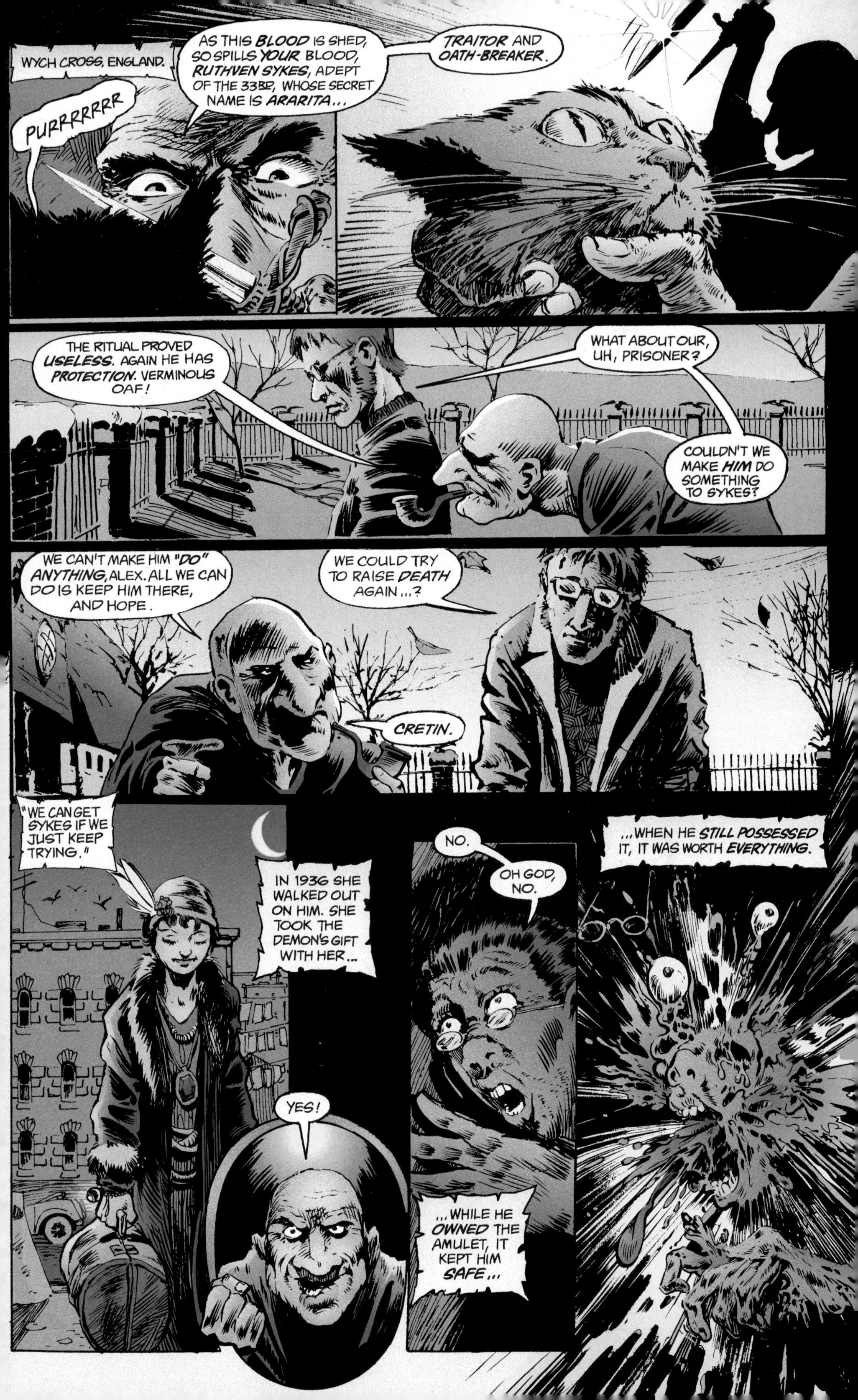
WYCH CROSS, ENGLAND.
PURRRRRRR
AS THIS BLOOD IS SHED, SO SPILLS YOUR BLOOD, RUTHVEN SYKES, ADEPT OF THE 33RD, WHOSE SECRET NAME IS ARARITA...
TRAITOR AND OATH-BREAKER.
THE RITUAL PROVED USELESS. AGAIN HE HAS PROTECTION. VERMINOUS OAF!
WHAT ABOUT OUR, UH, PRISONER?
COULDN'T WE MAKE HIM DO SOMETHING TO SYKES?
WE CAN'T MAKE HIM "DO" ANYTHING, ALEX. ALL WE CAN DO IS KEEP HIM THERE, AND HOPE.
WE COULD TRY TO RAISE DEATH AGAIN...?
CRETIN.
"WE CAN GET SYKES IF WE JUST KEEP TRYING."
IN 1936 SHE WALKED OUT ON HIM. SHE TOOK THE DEMON'S GIFT WITH HER...
YES!
NO.
OH GOD, NO.
...WHILE HE OWNED THE AMULET, IT KEPT HIM SAFE...
...WHEN HE STILL POSSESSED IT, IT WAS WORTH EVERYTHING.

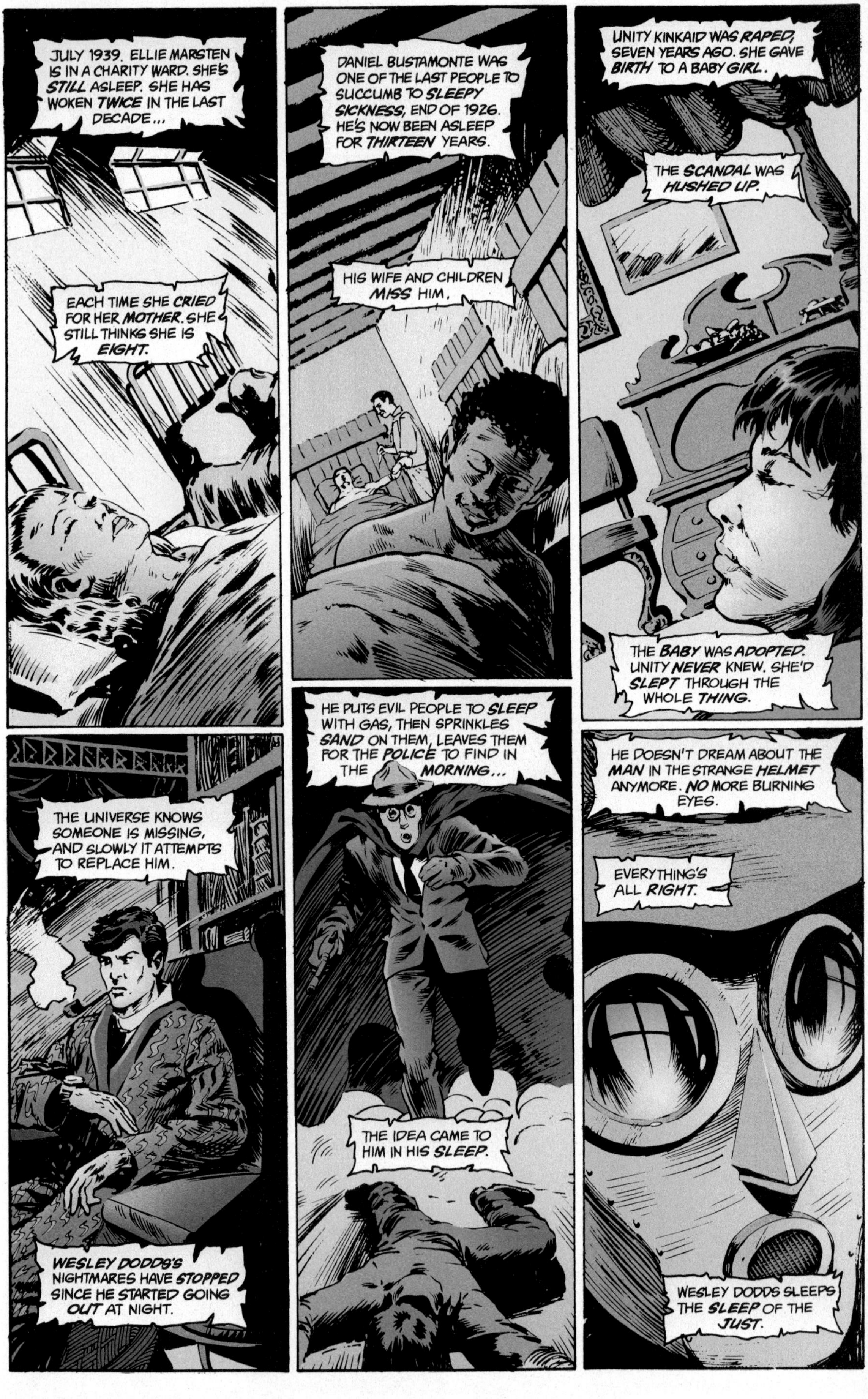
JULY 1939. ELLIE MARSTEN IS IN A CHARITY WARD. SHE'S STILL ASLEEP. SHE HAS WOKEN TWICE IN THE LAST DECADE...
EACH TIME SHE CRIED FOR HER MOTHER. SHE STILL THINKS SHE IS EIGHT.
DANIEL BUSTAMONTE WAS ONE OF THE LAST PEOPLE TO SUCCUMB TO SLEEPY SICKNESS, END OF 1926. HE'S NOW BEEN ASLEEP FOR THIRTEEN YEARS.
HIS WIFE AND CHILDREN MISS HIM.
UNITY KINKAID WAS RAPED, SEVEN YEARS AGO. SHE GAVE BIRTH TO A BABY GIRL.
THE SCANDAL WAS HUSHED UP.
THE BABY WAS ADOPTED. UNITY NEVER KNEW. SHE'D SLEPT THROUGH THE WHOLE THING.
THE UNIVERSE KNOWS SOMEONE IS MISSING, AND SLOWLY IT ATTEMPTS TO REPLACE HIM.
WESLEY DODDS'S NIGHTMARES HAVE STOPPED SINCE HE STARTED GOING OUT AT NIGHT.
HE PUTS EVIL PEOPLE TO SLEEP WITH GAS, THEN SPRINKLES SAND ON THEM, LEAVES THEM FOR THE POLICE TO FIND IN THE MORNING...
THE IDEA CAME TO HIM IN HIS SLEEP.
HE DOESN'T DREAM ABOUT THE MAN IN THE STRANGE HELMET ANYMORE. NO MORE BURNING EYES.
EVERYTHING'S ALL RIGHT.
WESLEY DODDS SLEEPS THE SLEEP OF THE JUST.

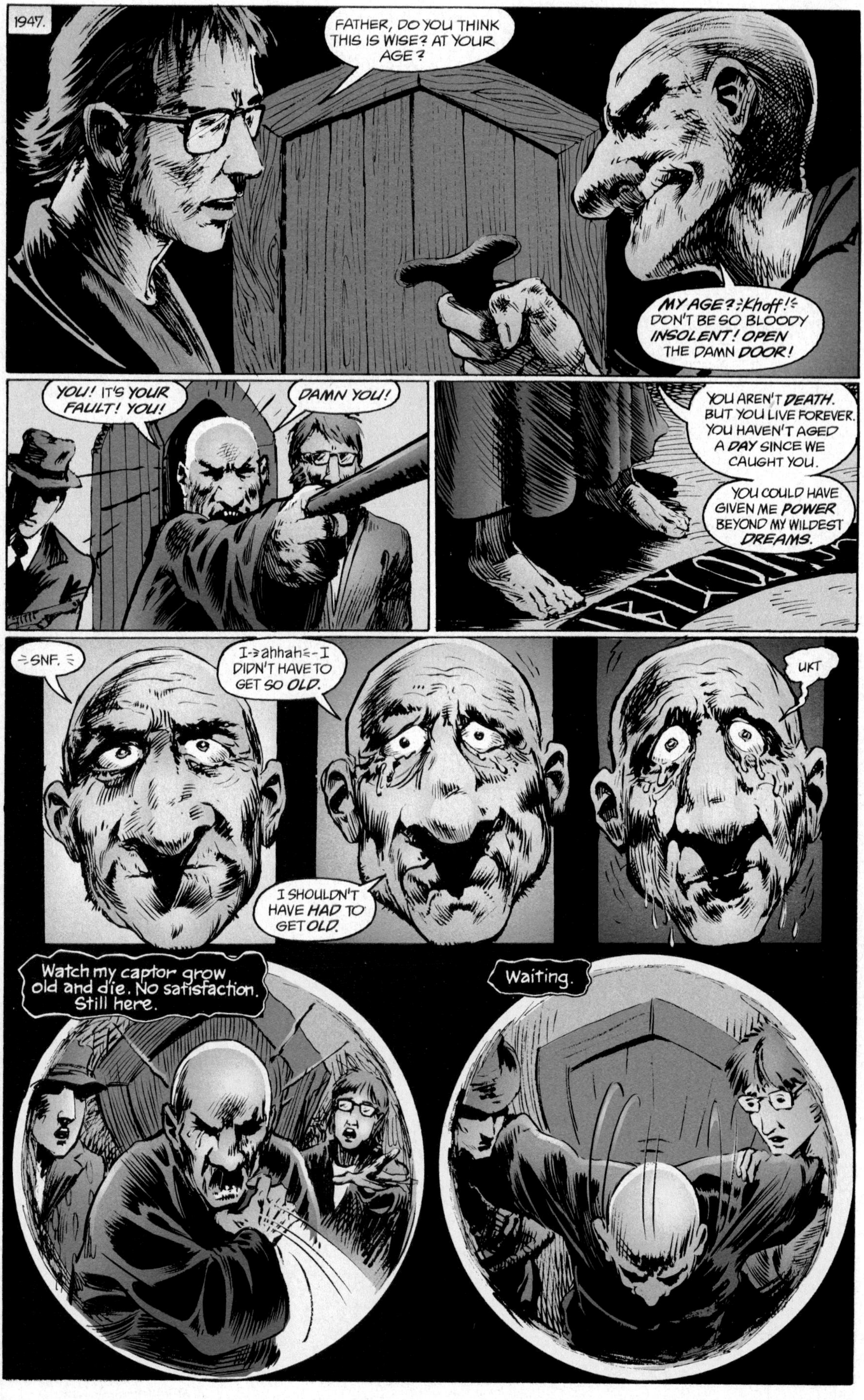
1947.
FATHER, DO YOU THINK THIS IS WISE? AT YOUR AGE?
MY AGE? Khoff! DON'T BE SO BLOODY INSOLENT! OPEN THE DAMN DOOR!
YOU! IT'S YOUR FAULT! YOU!
DAMN YOU!
YOU AREN'T DEATH. BUT YOU LIVE FOREVER. YOU HAVEN'T AGED A DAY SINCE WE CAUGHT YOU.
YOU COULD HAVE GIVEN ME POWER BEYOND MY WILDEST DREAMS.
SNF.
I- ahhah -I DIDN'T HAVE TO GET SO OLD.
I SHOULDN'T HAVE HAD TO GET OLD.
UKT
Watch my captor grow old and die. No satisfaction. Still here.
Waiting.

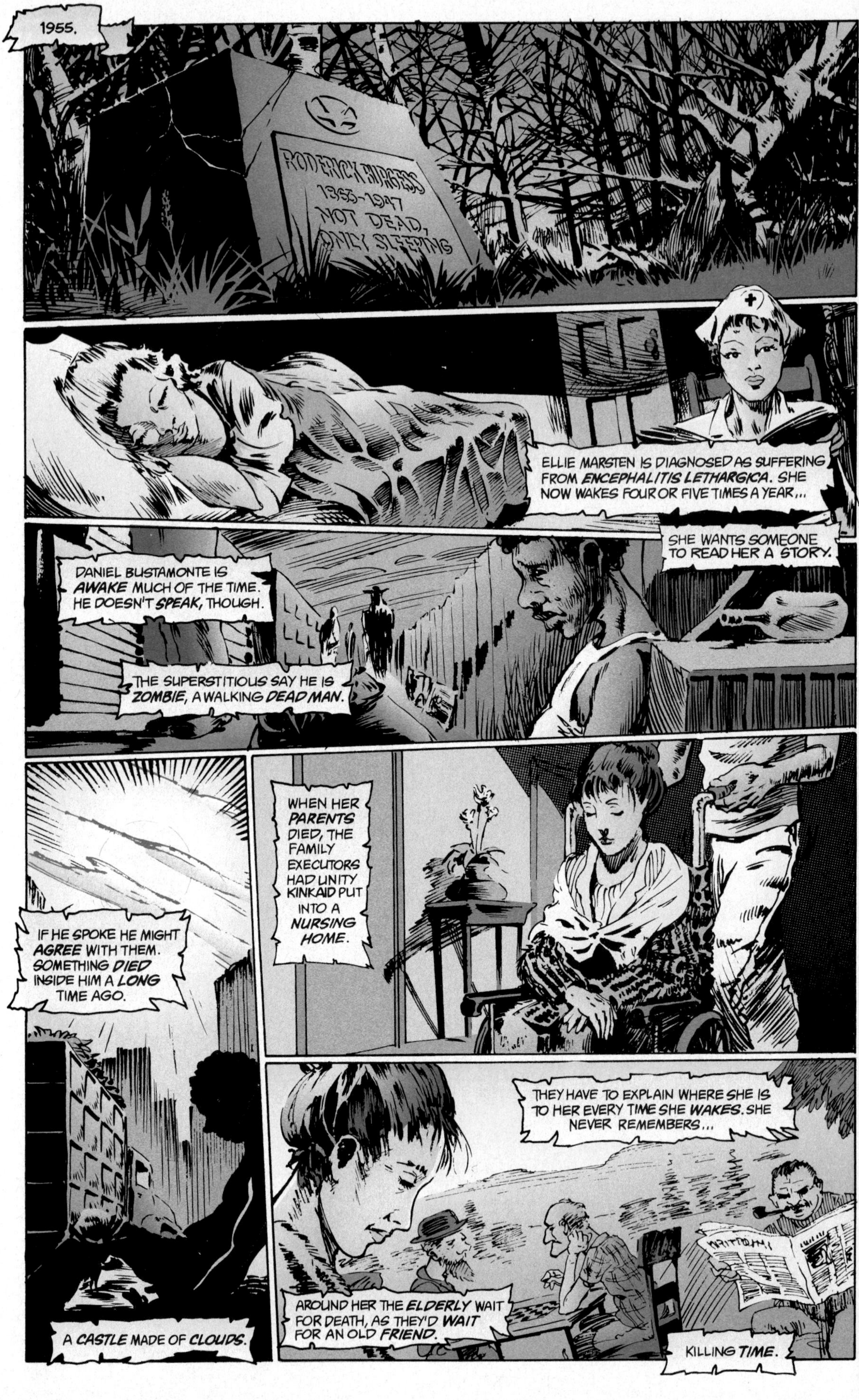
1955.
RODERICK BURGESS
1863-1947
NOT DEAD,
ONLY SLEEPING
ELLIE MARSTEN IS DIAGNOSED AS SUFFERING FROM ENCEPHALITIS LETHARGICA. SHE NOW WAKES FOUR OR FIVE TIMES A YEAR...
SHE WANTS SOMEONE TO READ HER A STORY.
DANIEL BUSTAMONTE IS AWAKE MUCH OF THE TIME. HE DOESN'T SPEAK, THOUGH.
THE SUPERSTITIOUS SAY HE IS ZOMBIE, A WALKING DEAD MAN.
IF HE SPOKE HE MIGHT AGREE WITH THEM. SOMETHING DIED INSIDE HIM A LONG TIME AGO.
A CASTLE MADE OF CLOUDS.
WHEN HER PARENTS DIED, THE FAMILY EXECUTORS HAD UNITY KINKAID PUT INTO A NURSING HOME.
THEY HAVE TO EXPLAIN WHERE SHE IS TO HER EVERY TIME SHE WAKES. SHE NEVER REMEMBERS...
AROUND HER THE ELDERLY WAIT FOR DEATH, AS THEY'D WAIT FOR AN OLD FRIEND.
KILLING TIME.

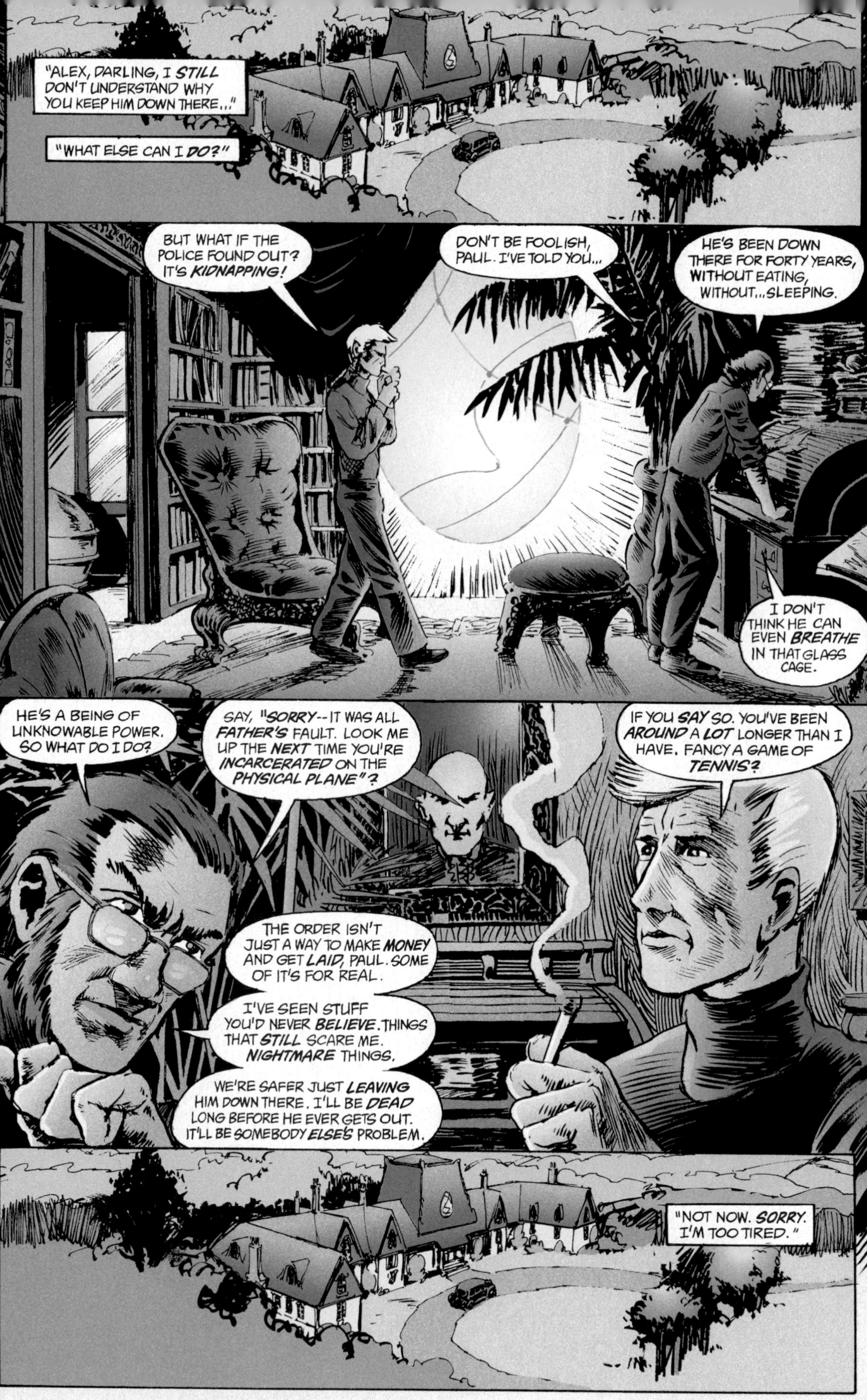
"ALEX, DARLING, I STILL DON'T UNDERSTAND WHY YOU KEEP HIM DOWN THERE..."
"WHAT ELSE CAN I DO?"
BUT WHAT IF THE POLICE FOUND OUT? IT'S KIDNAPPING!
DON'T BE FOOLISH, PAUL. I'VE TOLD YOU...
HE'S BEEN DOWN THERE FOR FORTY YEARS, WITHOUT EATING, WITHOUT...SLEEPING.
I DON'T THINK HE CAN EVEN BREATHE IN THAT GLASS CAGE.
HE'S A BEING OF UNKNOWABLE POWER. SO WHAT DO I DO?
SAY, "SORRY--IT WAS ALL FATHER'S FAULT. LOOK ME UP THE NEXT TIME YOU'RE INCARCERATED ON THE PHYSICAL PLANE"?
IF YOU SAY SO. YOU'VE BEEN AROUND A LOT LONGER THAN I HAVE. FANCY A GAME OF TENNIS?
THE ORDER ISN'T JUST A WAY TO MAKE MONEY AND GET LAID, PAUL. SOME OF IT'S FOR REAL.
I'VE SEEN STUFF YOU'D NEVER BELIEVE. THINGS THAT STILL SCARE ME. NIGHTMARE THINGS.
WE'RE SAFER JUST LEAVING HIM DOWN THERE. I'LL BE DEAD LONG BEFORE HE EVER GETS OUT. IT'LL BE SOMEBODY ELSE'S PROBLEM.
"NOT NOW. SORRY. I'M TOO TIRED."

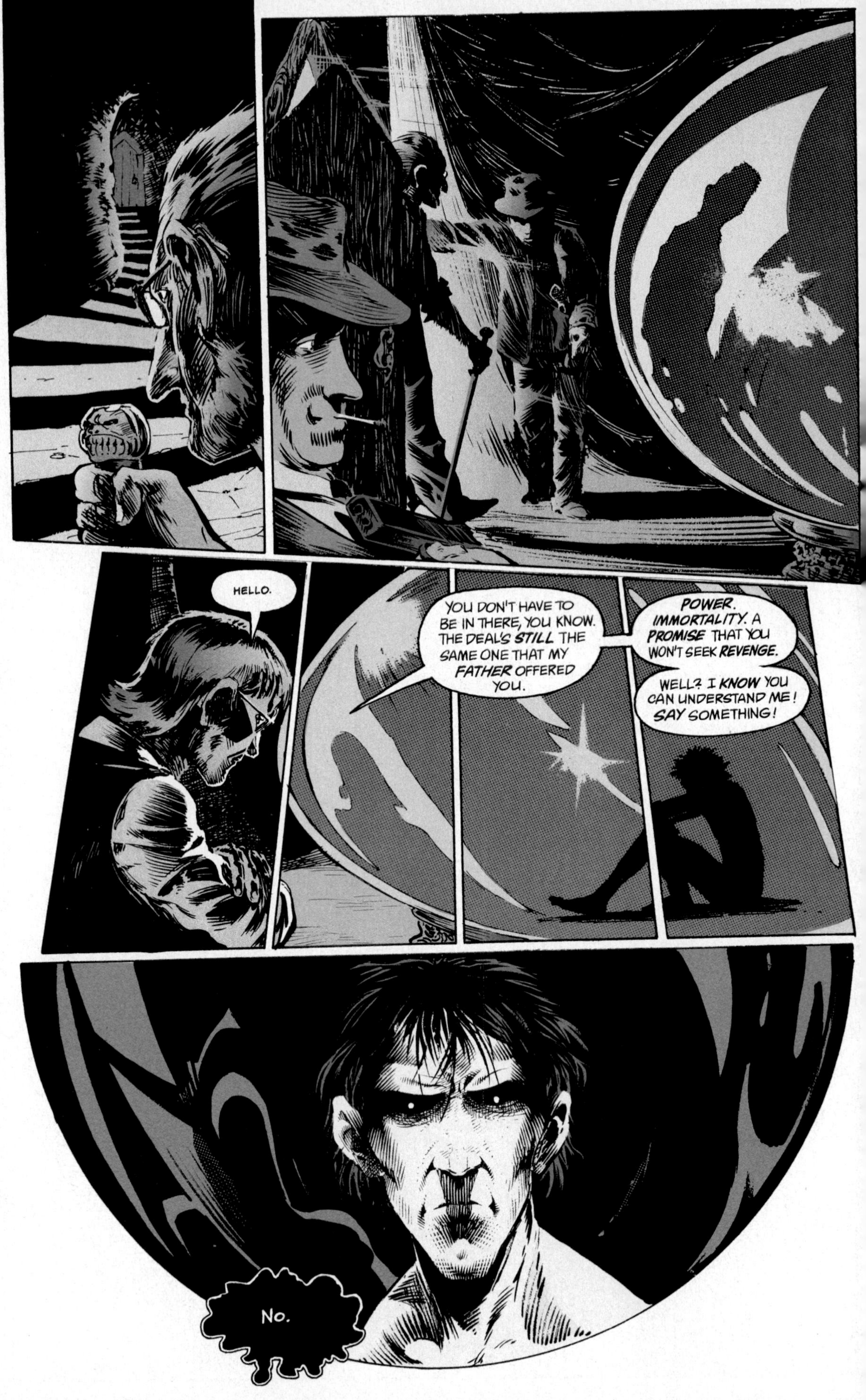
HELLO.
YOU DON'T HAVE TO BE IN THERE, YOU KNOW. THE DEAL'S STILL THE SAME ONE THAT MY FATHER OFFERED YOU.
POWER. IMMORTALITY. A PROMISE THAT YOU WON'T SEEK REVENGE.
WELL? I KNOW YOU CAN UNDERSTAND ME! SAY SOMETHING!
No.

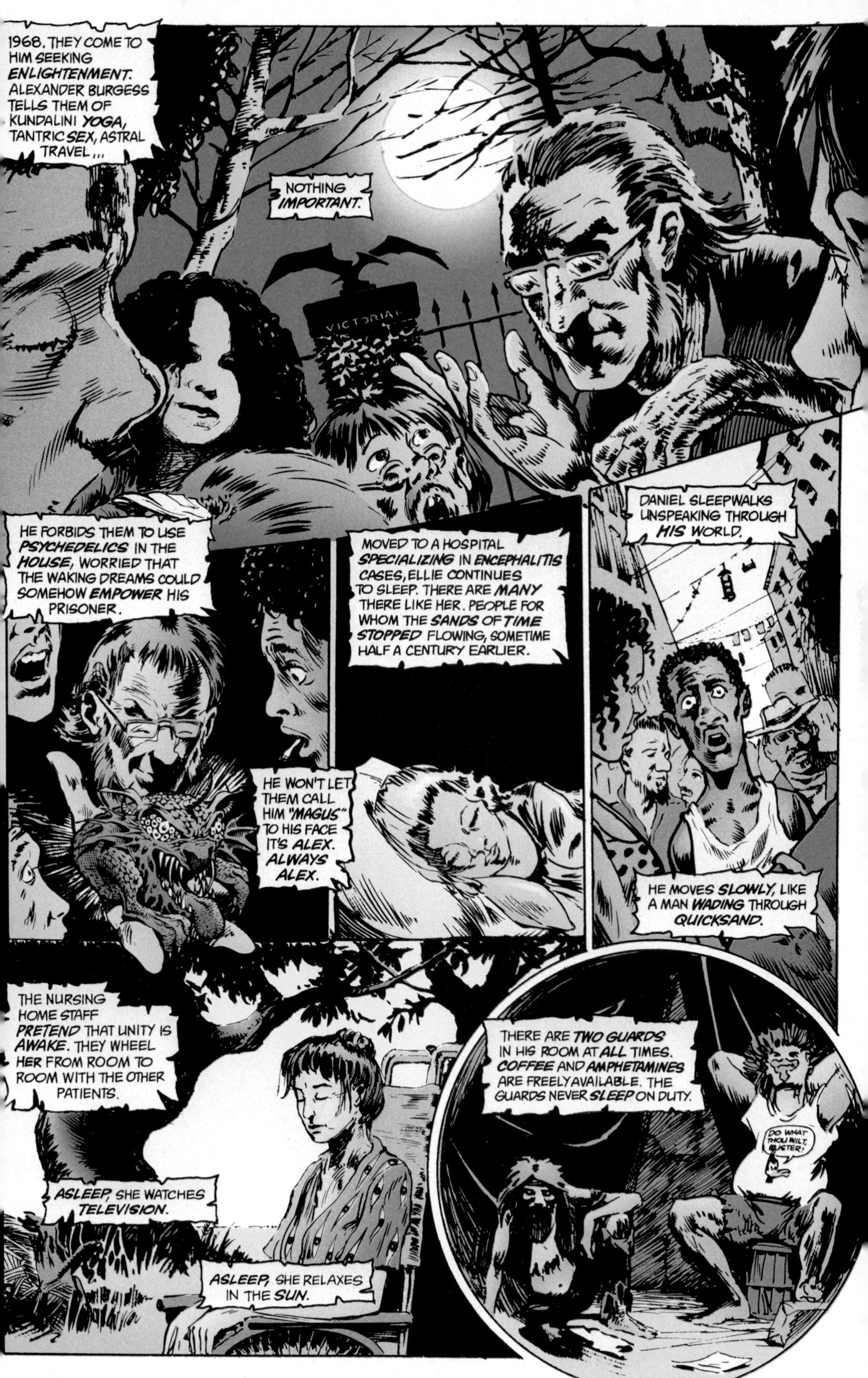
1968. THEY COME TO HIM SEEKING ENLIGHTENMENT. ALEXANDER BURGESS TELLS THEM OF KUNDALINI YOGA, TANTRIC SEX, ASTRAL TRAVEL...
NOTHING IMPORTANT.
VICTORIA
HE FORBIDS THEM TO USE PSYCHEDELICS IN THE HOUSE, WORRIED THAT THE WAKING DREAMS COULD SOMEHOW EMPOWER HIS PRISONER.
HE WON'T LET THEM CALL HIM "MAGUS" TO HIS FACE. IT'S ALEX. ALWAYS ALEX.
MOVED TO A HOSPITAL SPECIALIZING IN ENCEPHALITIS CASES, ELLIE CONTINUES TO SLEEP. THERE ARE MANY THERE LIKE HER. PEOPLE FOR WHOM THE SANDS OF TIME STOPPED FLOWING, SOMETIME HALF A CENTURY EARLIER.
DANIEL SLEEPWALKS UNSPEAKING THROUGH HIS WORLD.
HE MOVES SLOWLY, LIKE A MAN WADING THROUGH QUICKSAND.
THE NURSING HOME STAFF PRETEND THAT UNITY IS AWAKE. THEY WHEEL HER FROM ROOM TO ROOM WITH THE OTHER PATIENTS.
ASLEEP, SHE WATCHES TELEVISION.
ASLEEP, SHE RELAXES IN THE SUN.
THERE ARE TWO GUARDS IN HIS ROOM AT ALL TIMES. COFFEE AND AMPHETAMINES ARE FREELY AVAILABLE. THE GUARDS NEVER SLEEP ON DUTY.
DO WHAT THOU WILT, BUSTER!

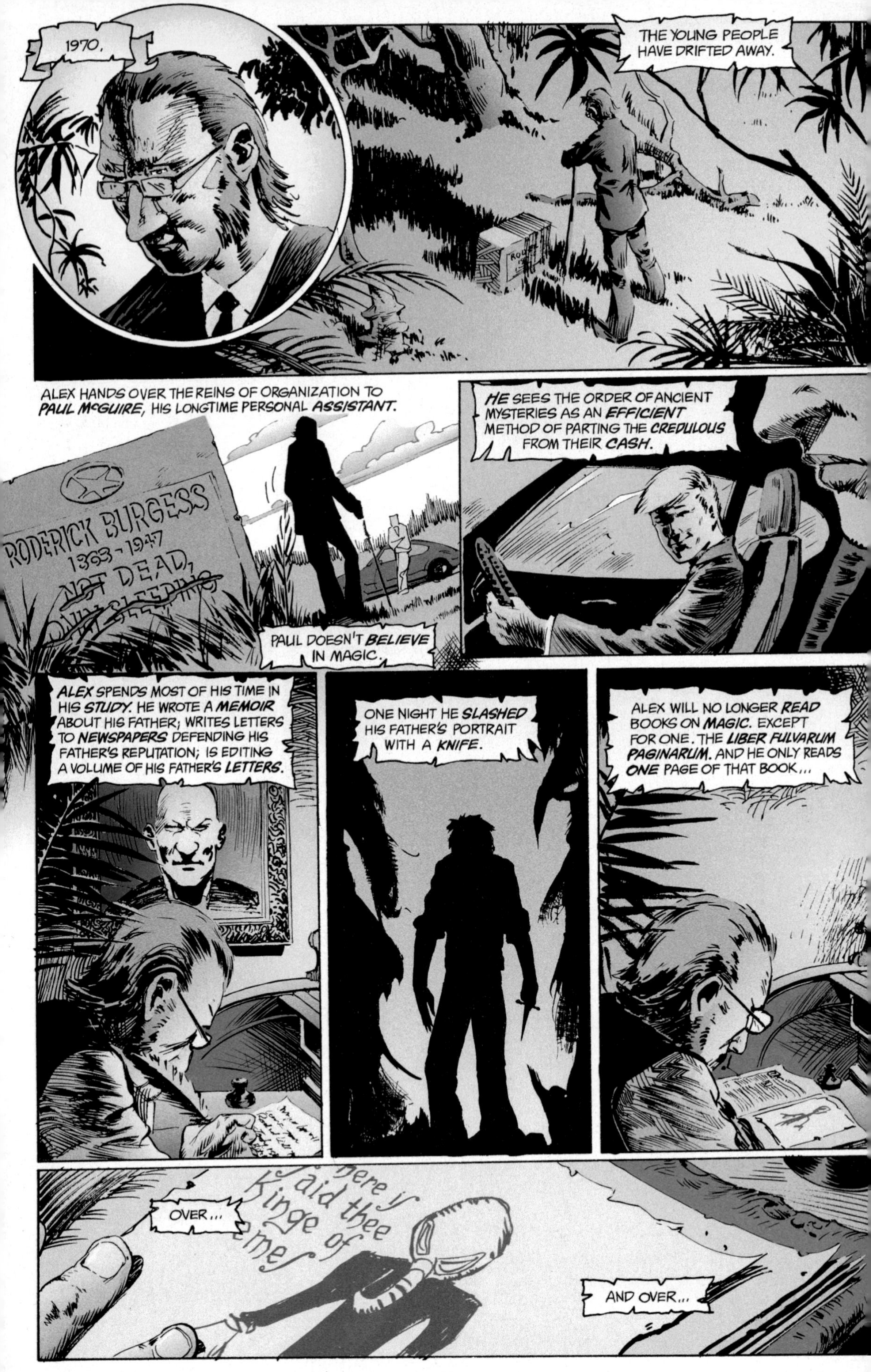

1970.
THE YOUNG PEOPLE HAVE DRIFTED AWAY.
ALEX HANDS OVER THE REINS OF ORGANIZATION TO PAUL McGUIRE, HIS LONGTIME PERSONAL ASSISTANT.
RODERICK BURGESS
1863 - 1947
NOT DEAD,
PAUL DOESN'T BELIEVE IN MAGIC.
HE SEES THE ORDER OF ANCIENT MYSTERIES AS AN EFFICIENT METHOD OF PARTING THE CREDULOUS FROM THEIR CASH.
ALEX SPENDS MOST OF HIS TIME IN HIS STUDY. HE WROTE A MEMOIR ABOUT HIS FATHER; WRITES LETTERS TO NEWSPAPERS DEFENDING HIS FATHER'S REPUTATION; IS EDITING A VOLUME OF HIS FATHER'S LETTERS.
ONE NIGHT HE SLASHED HIS FATHER'S PORTRAIT WITH A KNIFE.
ALEX WILL NO LONGER READ BOOKS ON MAGIC. EXCEPT FOR ONE. THE LIBER FULVARUM PAGINARUM. AND HE ONLY READS ONE PAGE OF THAT BOOK...
OVER...
AND OVER...

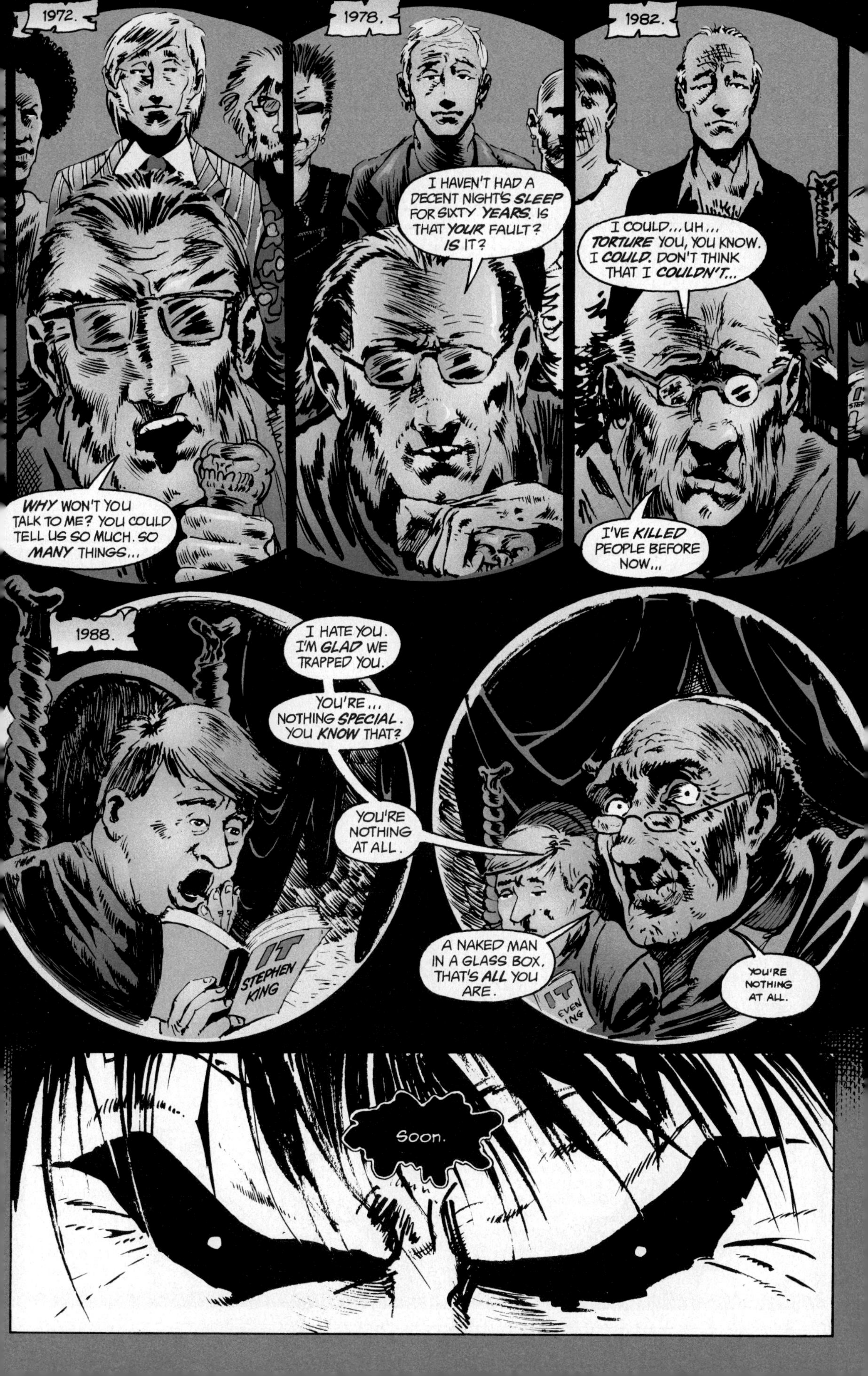
1972.
WHY WON'T YOU TALK TO ME? YOU COULD TELL US SO MUCH. SO MANY THINGS...
1978.
I HAVEN'T HAD A DECENT NIGHT'S SLEEP FOR SIXTY YEARS. IS THAT YOUR FAULT? IS IT?
1982.
I COULD... UH... TORTURE YOU, YOU KNOW. I COULD. DON'T THINK THAT I COULDN'T...
I'VE KILLED PEOPLE BEFORE NOW...
1988.
I HATE YOU. I'M GLAD WE TRAPPED YOU.
YOU'RE... NOTHING SPECIAL. YOU KNOW THAT?
YOU'RE NOTHING AT ALL.
IT
STEPHEN KING
A NAKED MAN IN A GLASS BOX. THAT'S ALL YOU ARE.
YOU'RE NOTHING AT ALL.
Soon.

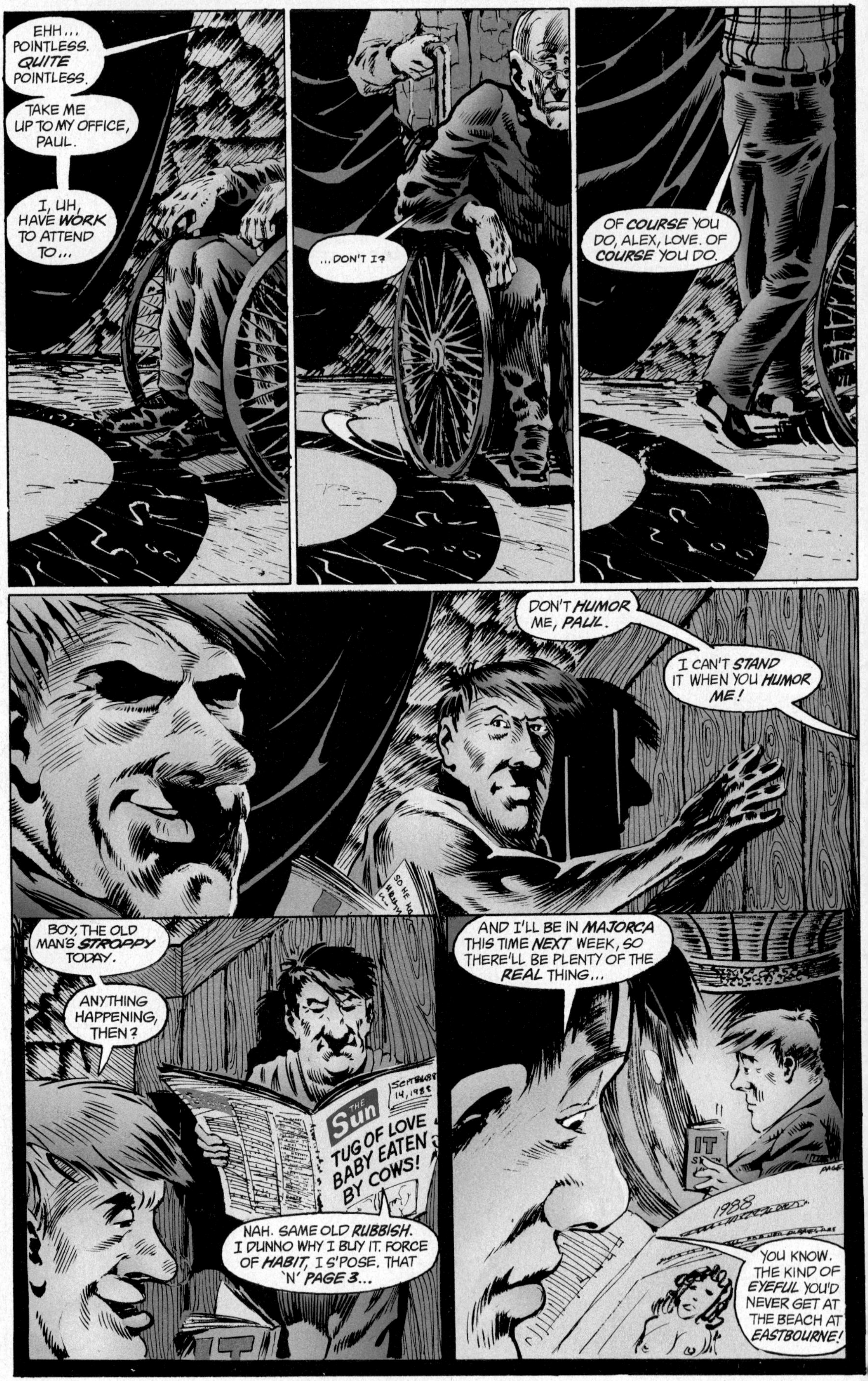
EHH... POINTLESS. QUITE POINTLESS.
TAKE ME UP TO MY OFFICE, PAUL.
I, UH, HAVE WORK TO ATTEND TO...
...DON'T I?
OF COURSE YOU DO, ALEX, LOVE. OF COURSE YOU DO.
DON'T HUMOR ME, PAUL.
I CAN'T STAND IT WHEN YOU HUMOR ME!
BOY, THE OLD MAN'S STROPPY TODAY.
ANYTHING HAPPENING, THEN?
THE Sun
TUG OF LOVE BABY EATEN BY COWS!
NAH. SAME OLD RUBBISH. I DUNNO WHY I BUY IT. FORCE OF HABIT, I S'POSE. THAT 'N' PAGE 3...
AND I'LL BE IN MAJORCA THIS TIME NEXT WEEK, SO THERE'LL BE PLENTY OF THE REAL THING...
1988
YOU KNOW. THE KIND OF EYEFUL YOU'D NEVER GET AT THE BEACH AT EASTBOURNE!

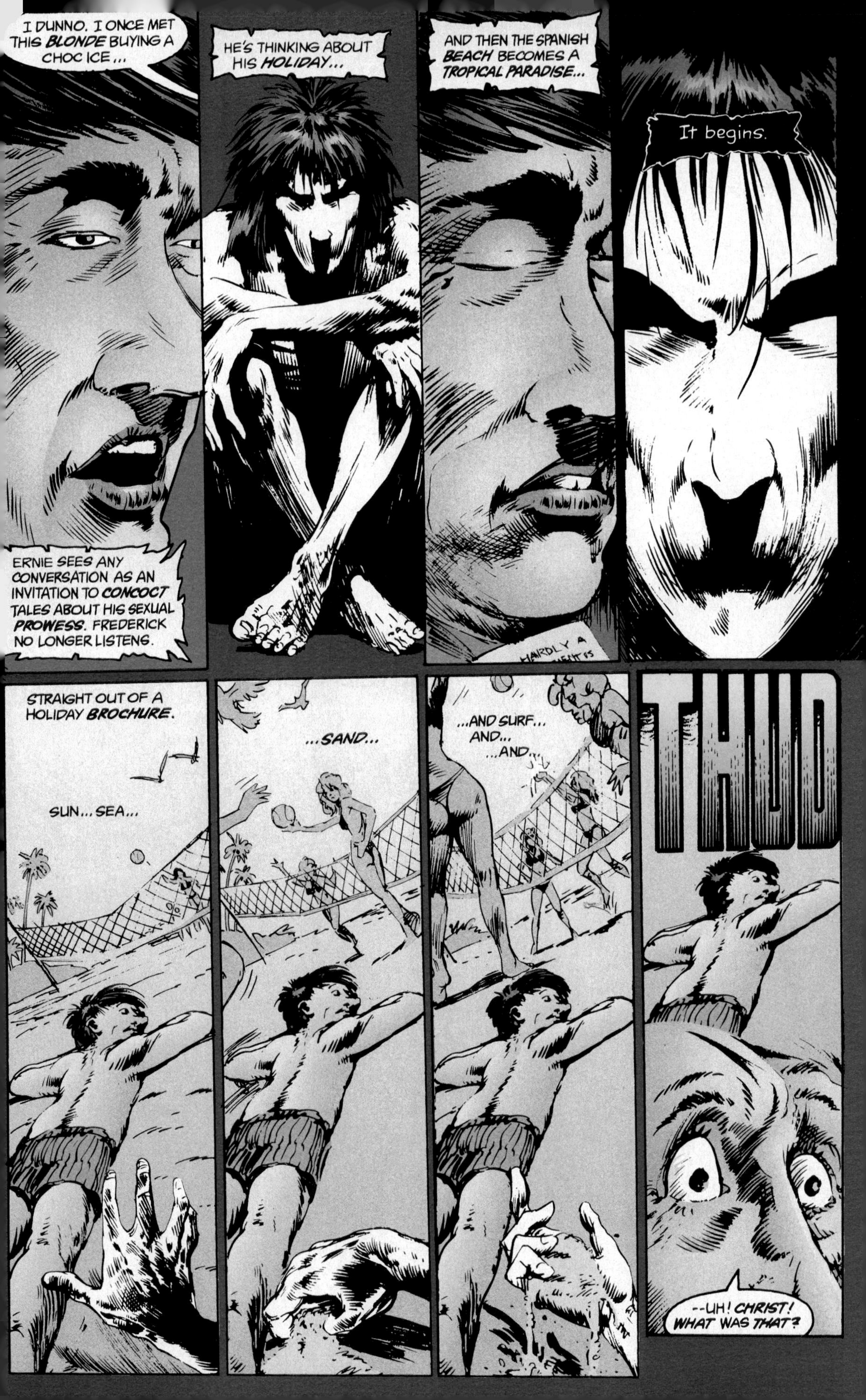
I DUNNO. I ONCE MET THIS BLONDE BUYING A CHOC ICE...
ERNIE SEES ANY CONVERSATION AS AN INVITATION TO CONCOCT TALES ABOUT HIS SEXUAL PROWESS. FREDERICK NO LONGER LISTENS.
HE'S THINKING ABOUT HIS HOLIDAY...
AND THEN THE SPANISH BEACH BECOMES A TROPICAL PARADISE...
It begins.
STRAIGHT OUT OF A HOLIDAY BROCHURE.
SUN... SEA...
...SAND...
...AND SURF... AND... ...AND...
THUD
--UH! CHRIST! WHAT WAS THAT?

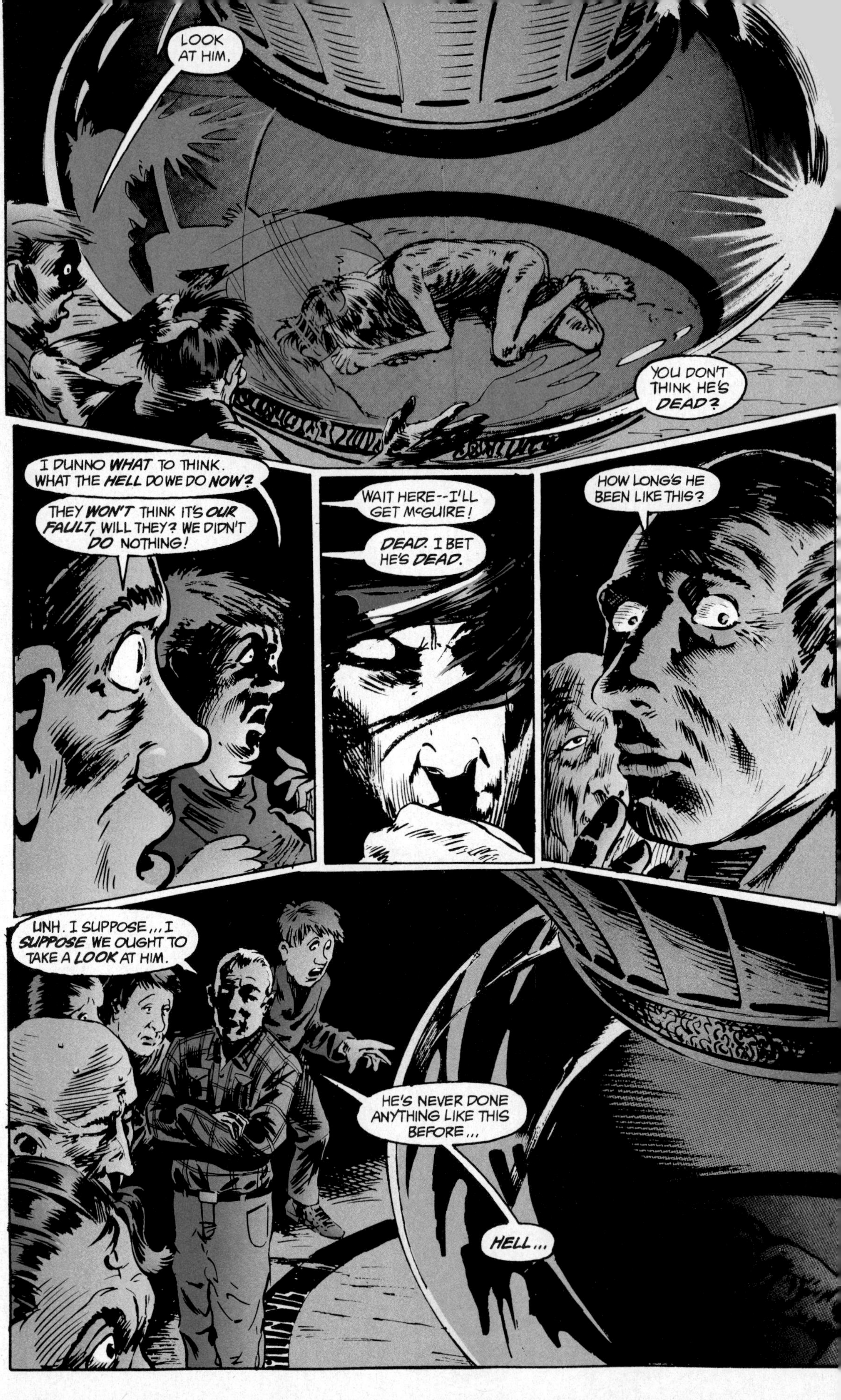
LOOK AT HIM.
YOU DON'T THINK HE'S DEAD?
I DUNNO WHAT TO THINK. WHAT THE HELL DO WE DO NOW?
THEY WON'T THINK IT'S OUR FAULT, WILL THEY? WE DIDN'T DO NOTHING!
WAIT HERE--I'LL GET McGUIRE!
DEAD. I BET HE'S DEAD.
HOW LONG'S HE BEEN LIKE THIS?
UNH. I SUPPOSE... I SUPPOSE WE OUGHT TO TAKE A LOOK AT HIM.
HE'S NEVER DONE ANYTHING LIKE THIS BEFORE...
HELL...

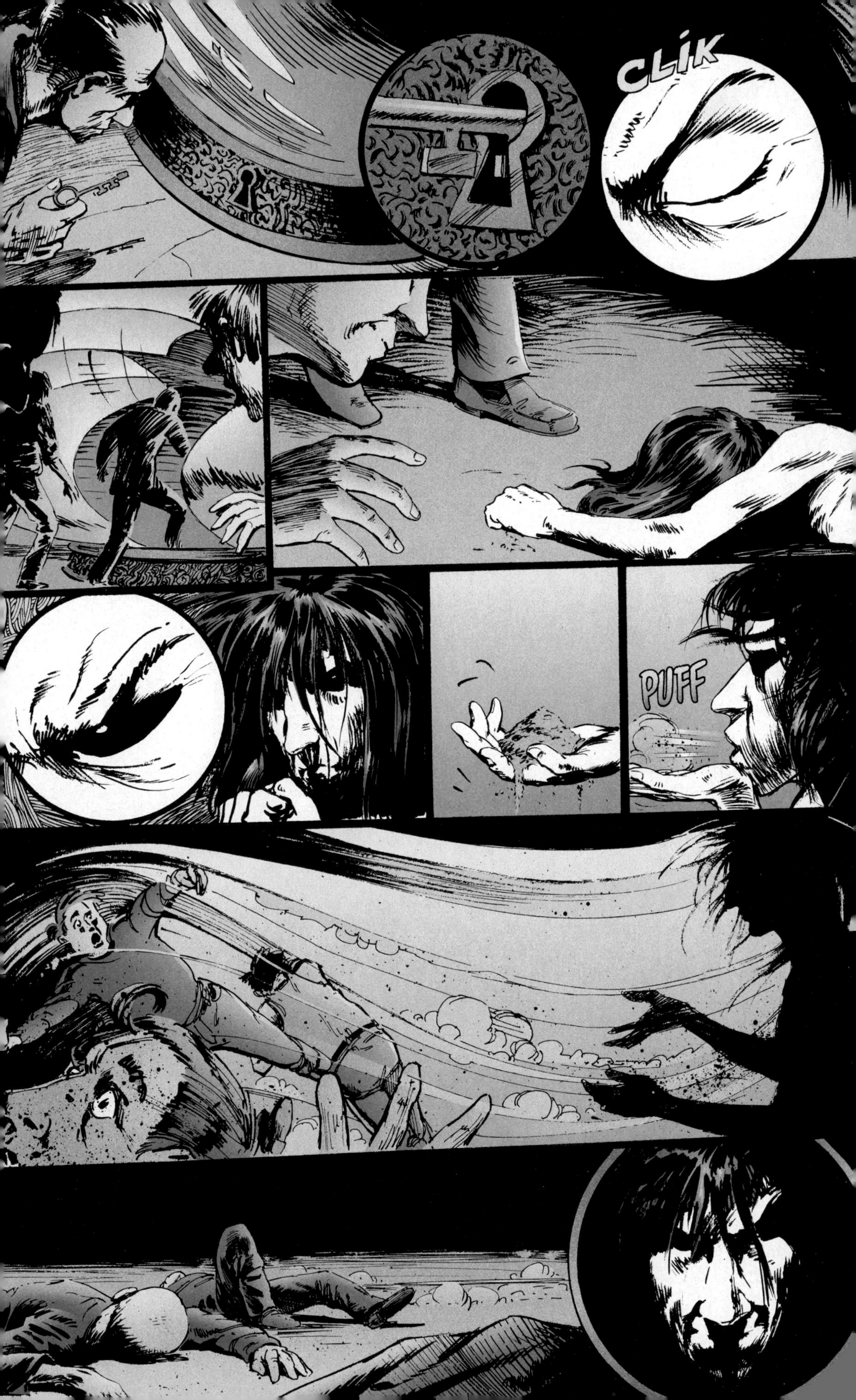
CLIK
PUFF

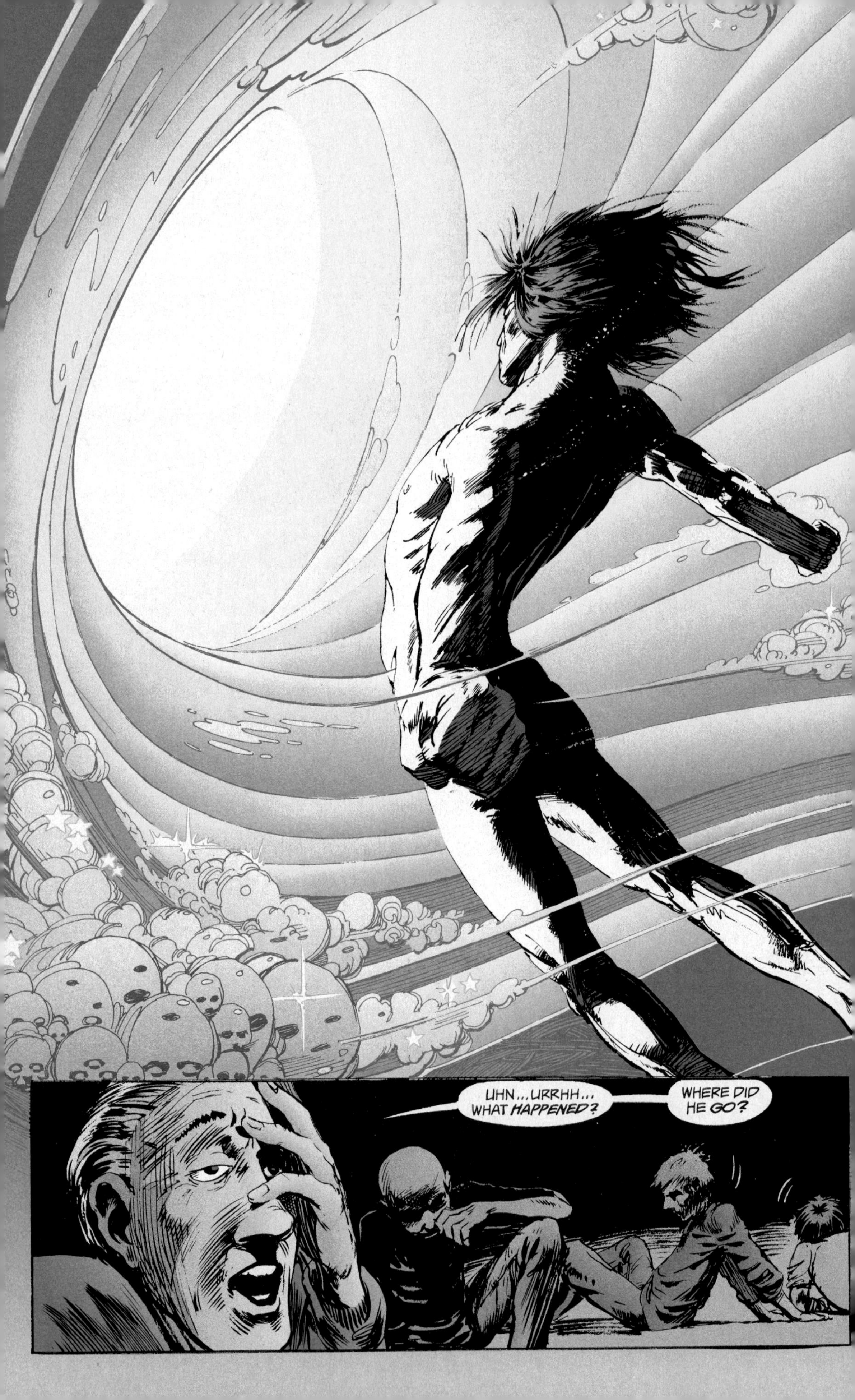
UHN... URRHH... WHAT HAPPENED?
WHERE DID HE GO?

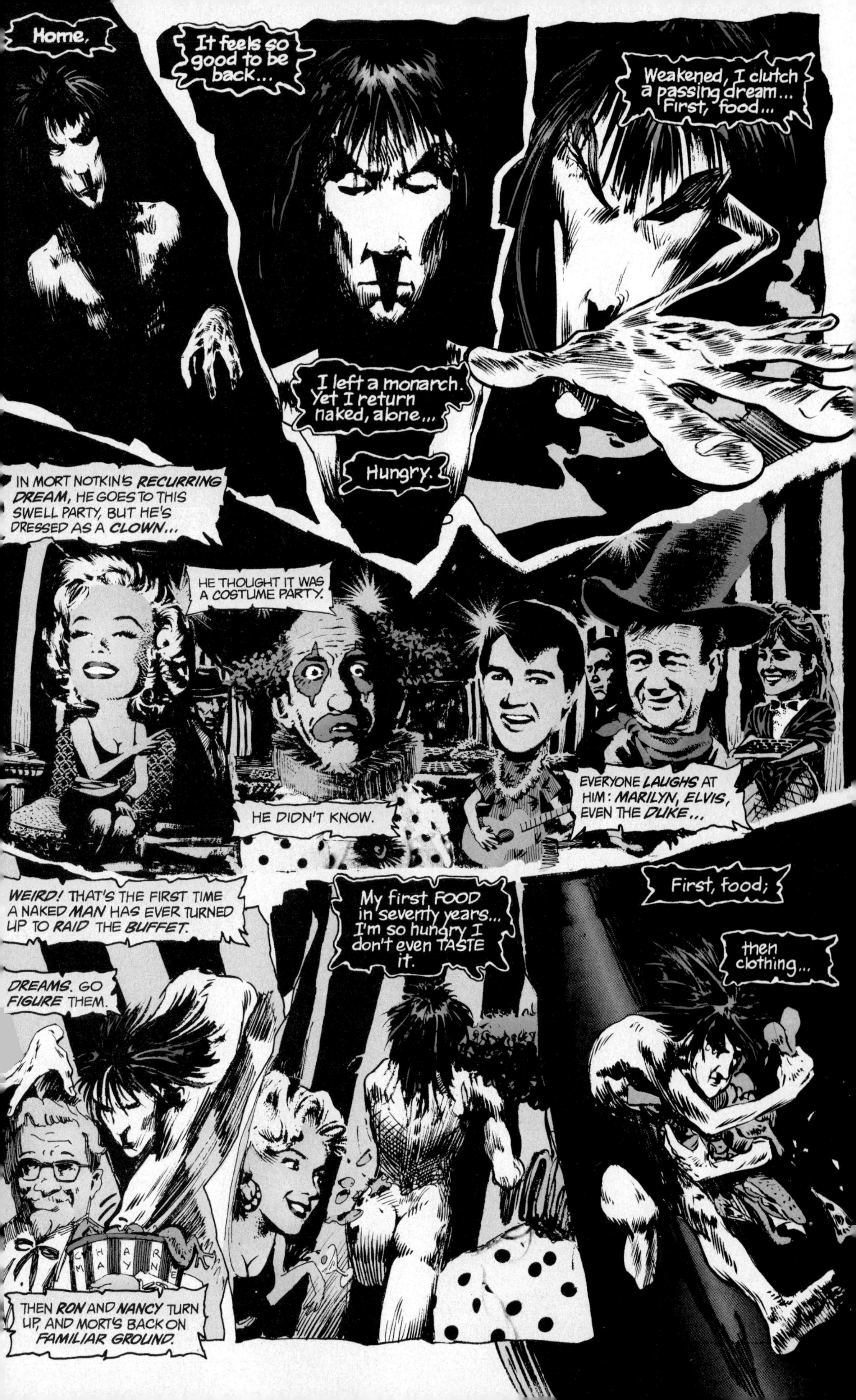
Home,
It feels so good to be back...
Weakened, I clutch a passing dream... First, food...
I left a monarch. Yet I return naked, alone...
Hungry.
IN MORT NOTKIN'S RECURRING DREAM, HE GOES TO THIS SWELL PARTY, BUT HE'S DRESSED AS A CLOWN...
HE THOUGHT IT WAS A COSTUME PARTY.
HE DIDN'T KNOW.
EVERYONE LAUGHS AT HIM: MARILYN, ELVIS, EVEN THE DUKE...
WEIRD! THAT'S THE FIRST TIME A NAKED MAN HAS EVER TURNED UP TO RAID THE BUFFET.
DREAMS. GO FIGURE THEM.
THEN RON AND NANCY TURN UP, AND MORT'S BACK ON FAMILIAR GROUND.
My first FOOD in seventy years... I'm so hungry I don't even TASTE it.
First, food;
then clothing...

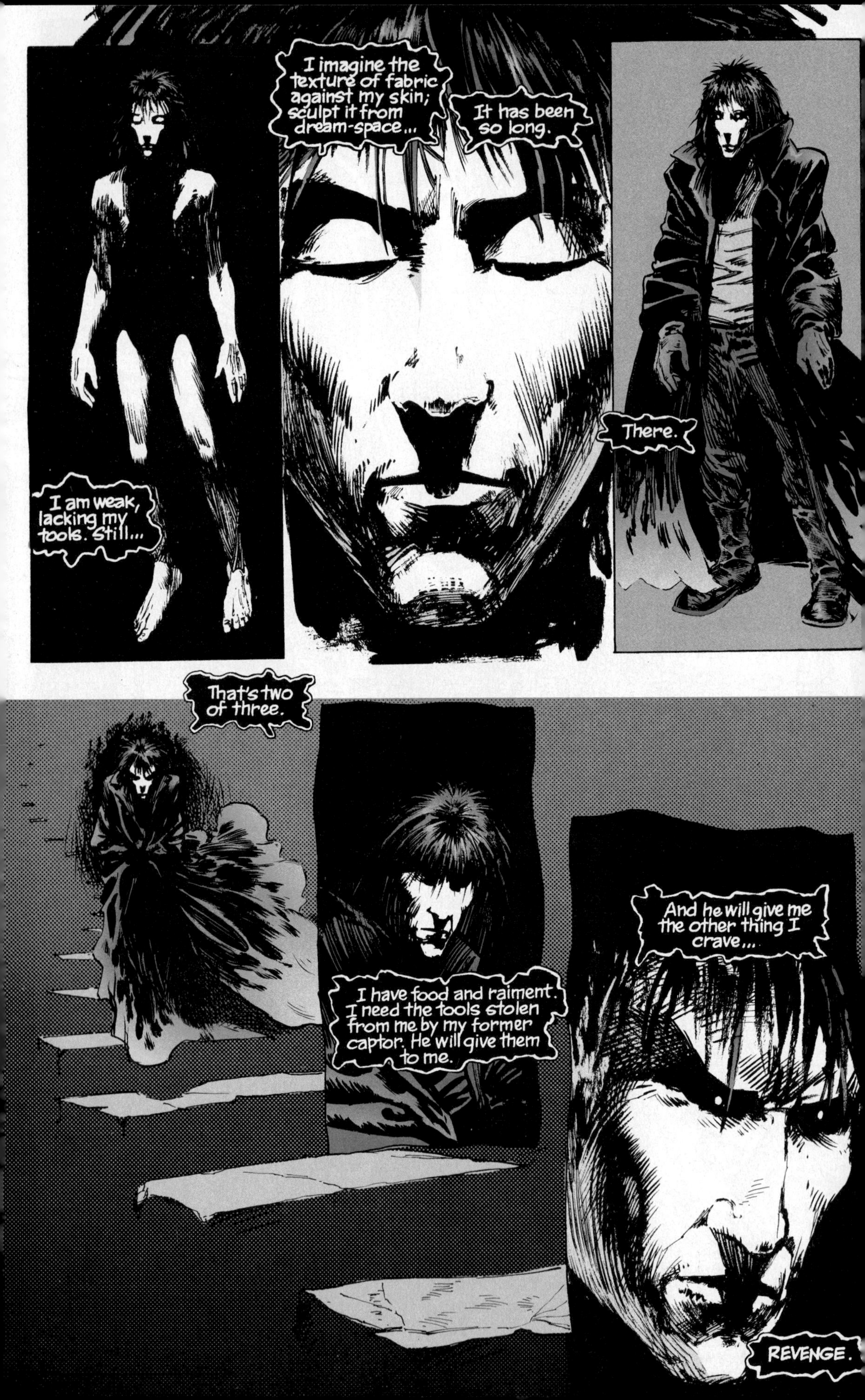
I am weak, lacking my tools. Still...
I imagine the texture of fabric against my skin; sculpt it from dream-space...
It has been so long.
There.
That's two of three.
I have food and raiment. I need the tools stolen from me by my former captor. He will give them to me.
And he will give me the other thing I crave...
REVENGE.

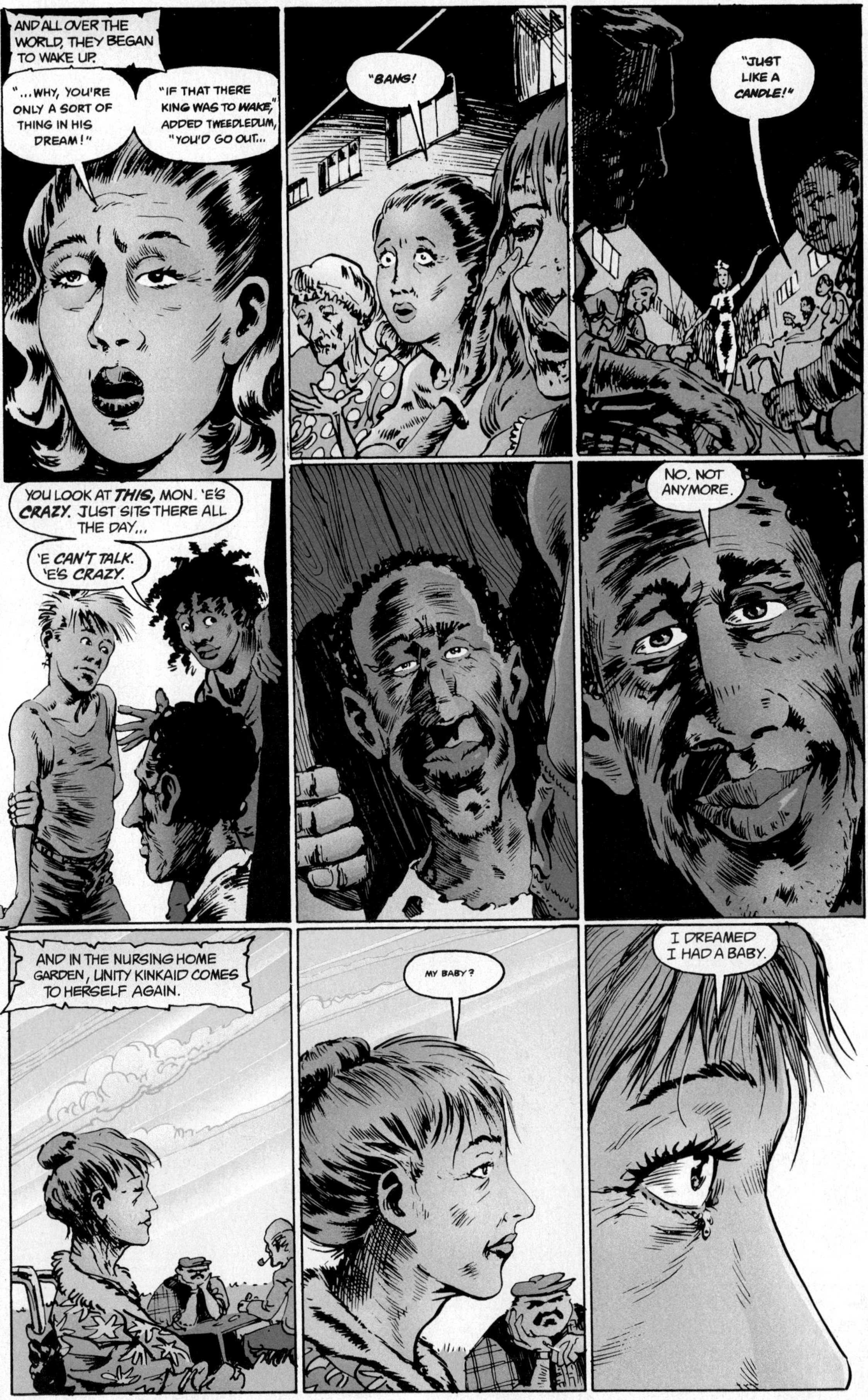

AND ALL OVER THE WORLD, THEY BEGAN TO WAKE UP.
"...WHY, YOU'RE ONLY A SORT OF THING IN HIS DREAM!"
"IF THAT THERE KING WAS TO WAKE," ADDED TWEEDLEDUM, "YOU'D GO OUT...
"BANG!
"JUST LIKE A CANDLE!"
YOU LOOK AT THIS, MON. 'E'S CRAZY. JUST SITS THERE ALL THE DAY...
'E CAN'T TALK. 'E'S CRAZY.
NO. NOT ANYMORE.
AND IN THE NURSING HOME GARDEN, UNITY KINKAID COMES TO HERSELF AGAIN.
MY BABY?
I DREAMED I HAD A BABY.

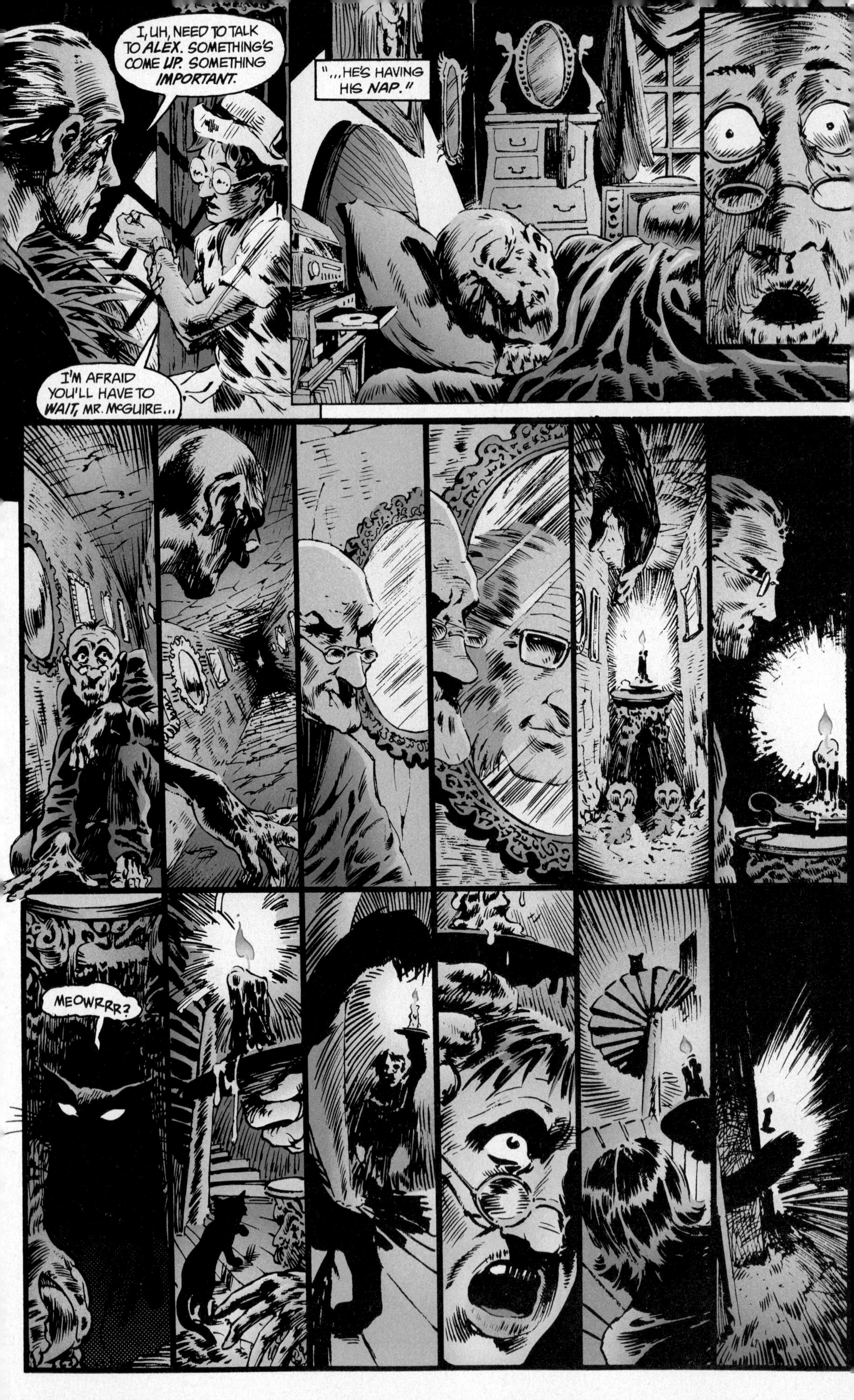
I, UH, NEED TO TALK TO ALEX. SOMETHING'S COME UP. SOMETHING IMPORTANT.
I'M AFRAID YOU'LL HAVE TO WAIT, MR. McGUIRE...
"...HE'S HAVING HIS NAP."
MEOWRRR?

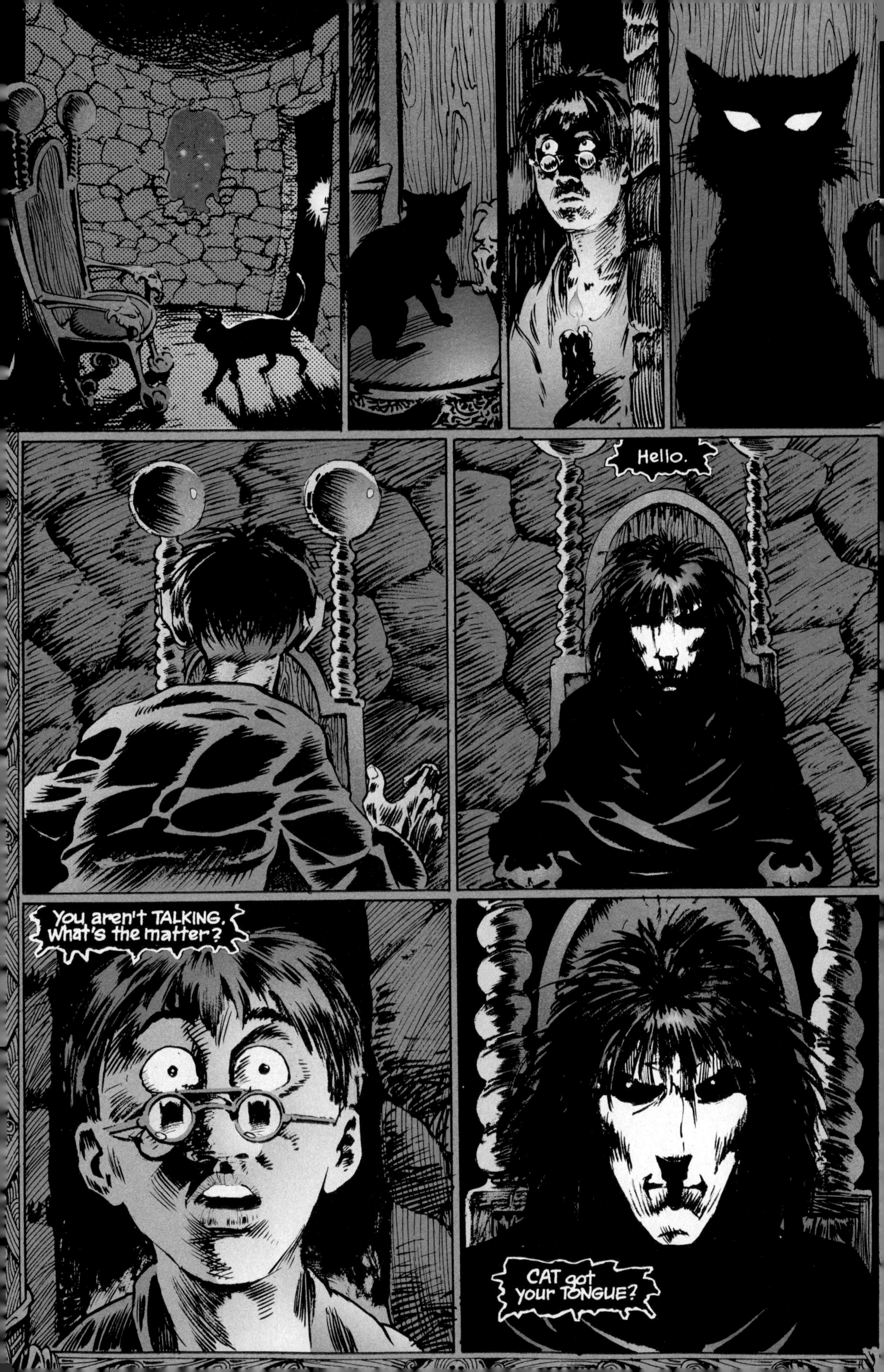
Hello.
You aren't TALKING. What's the matter?
CAT got your TONGUE?

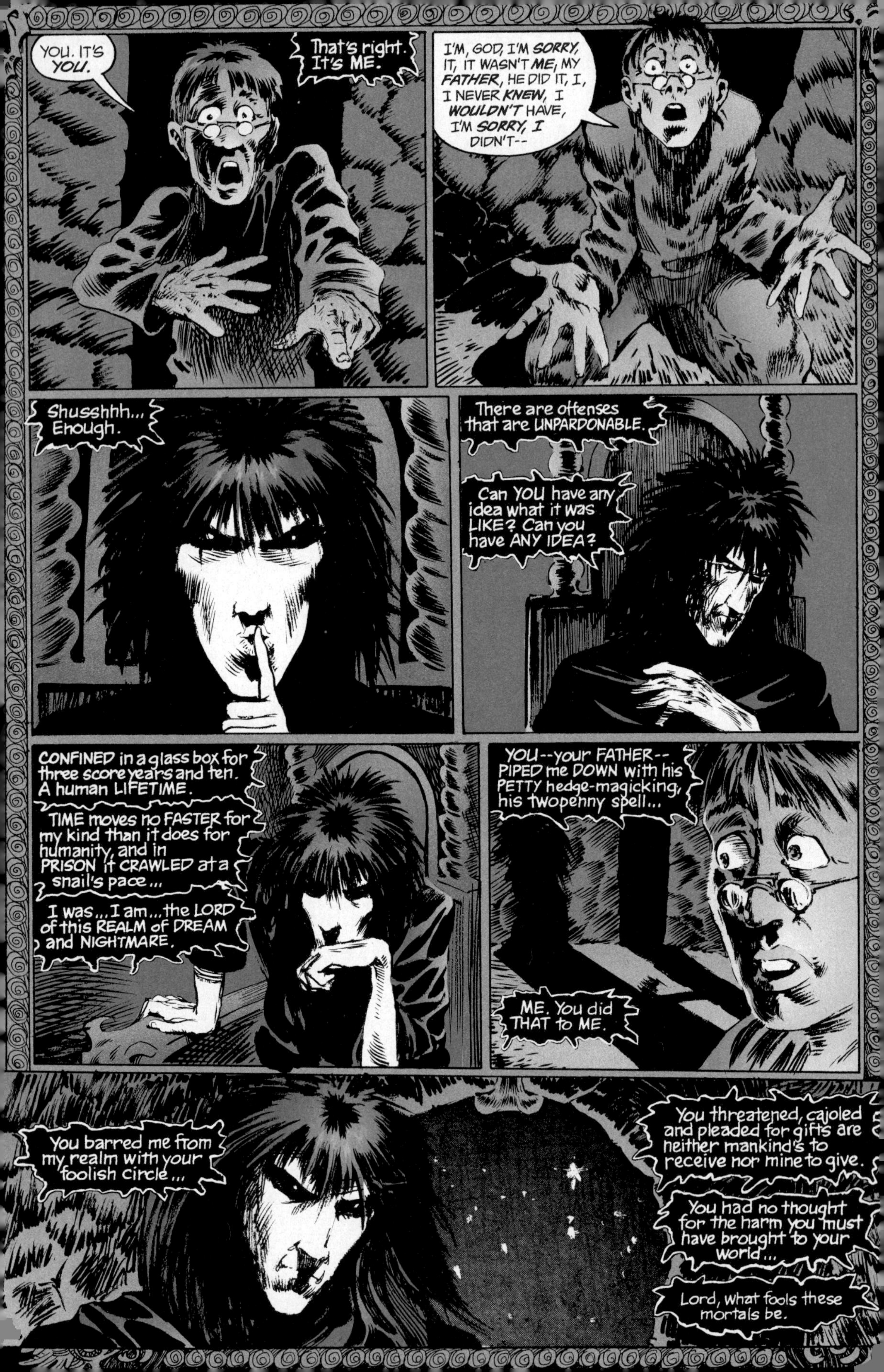

YOU. IT'S YOU.
That's right. It's ME.
I'M, GOD, I'M SORRY, IT, IT WASN'T ME, MY FATHER, HE DID IT, I, I NEVER KNEW, I WOULDN'T HAVE, I'M SORRY, I DIDN'T--
Shusshhh... Enough.
There are offenses that are UNPARDONABLE.
Can YOU have any idea what it was LIKE? Can you have ANY IDEA?
CONFINED in a glass box for three score years and ten. A human LIFETIME.
TIME moves no FASTER for my kind than it does for humanity, and in PRISON it CRAWLED at a snail's pace...
I was... I am... the LORD of this REALM of DREAM and NIGHTMARE.
YOU--your FATHER--PIPED me DOWN with his PETTY hedge-magicking, his twopenny spell...
ME. You did THAT to ME.
You barred me from my realm with your foolish circle...
You threatened, cajoled and pleaded for gifts are neither mankind's to receive nor mine to give.
You had no thought for the harm you must have brought to your world...
Lord, what fools these mortals be.

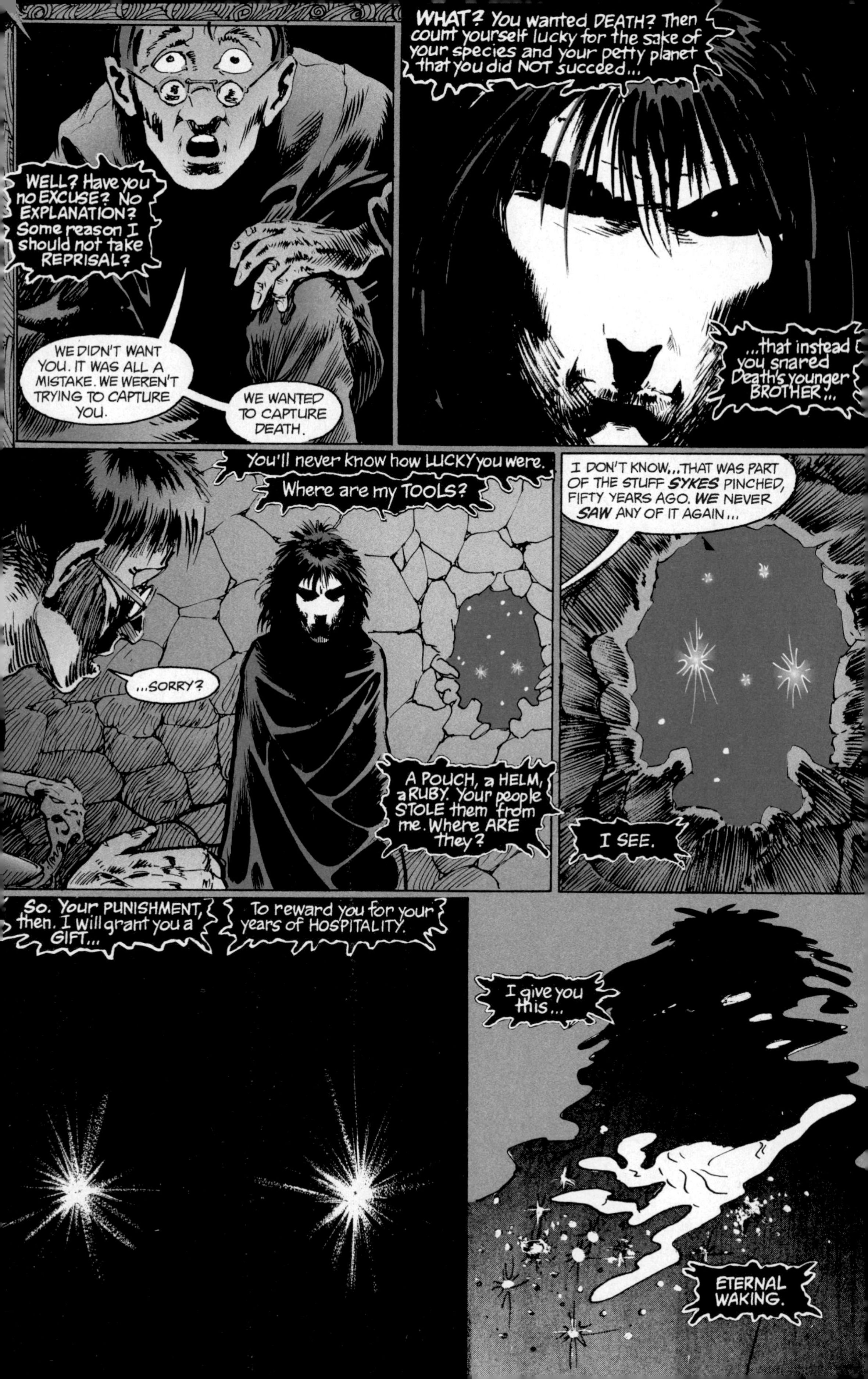
WELL? Have you no EXCUSE? No EXPLANATION? Some reason I should not take REPRISAL?
WE DIDN'T WANT YOU. IT WAS ALL A MISTAKE. WE WEREN'T TRYING TO CAPTURE YOU.
WE WANTED TO CAPTURE DEATH.
WHAT? You wanted DEATH? Then count yourself lucky for the sake of your species and your petty planet that you did NOT succeed...
...that instead you snared Death's younger BROTHER...
You'll never know how LUCKY you were.
Where are my TOOLS?
...SORRY?
A POUCH, a HELM, a RUBY. Your people STOLE them from me. Where ARE they?
I DON'T KNOW...THAT WAS PART OF THE STUFF SYKES PINCHED, FIFTY YEARS AGO. WE NEVER SAW ANY OF IT AGAIN...
I SEE.
So. Your PUNISHMENT, then. I will grant you a GIFT...
To reward you for your years of HOSPITALITY.
I give you this...
ETERNAL WAKING.

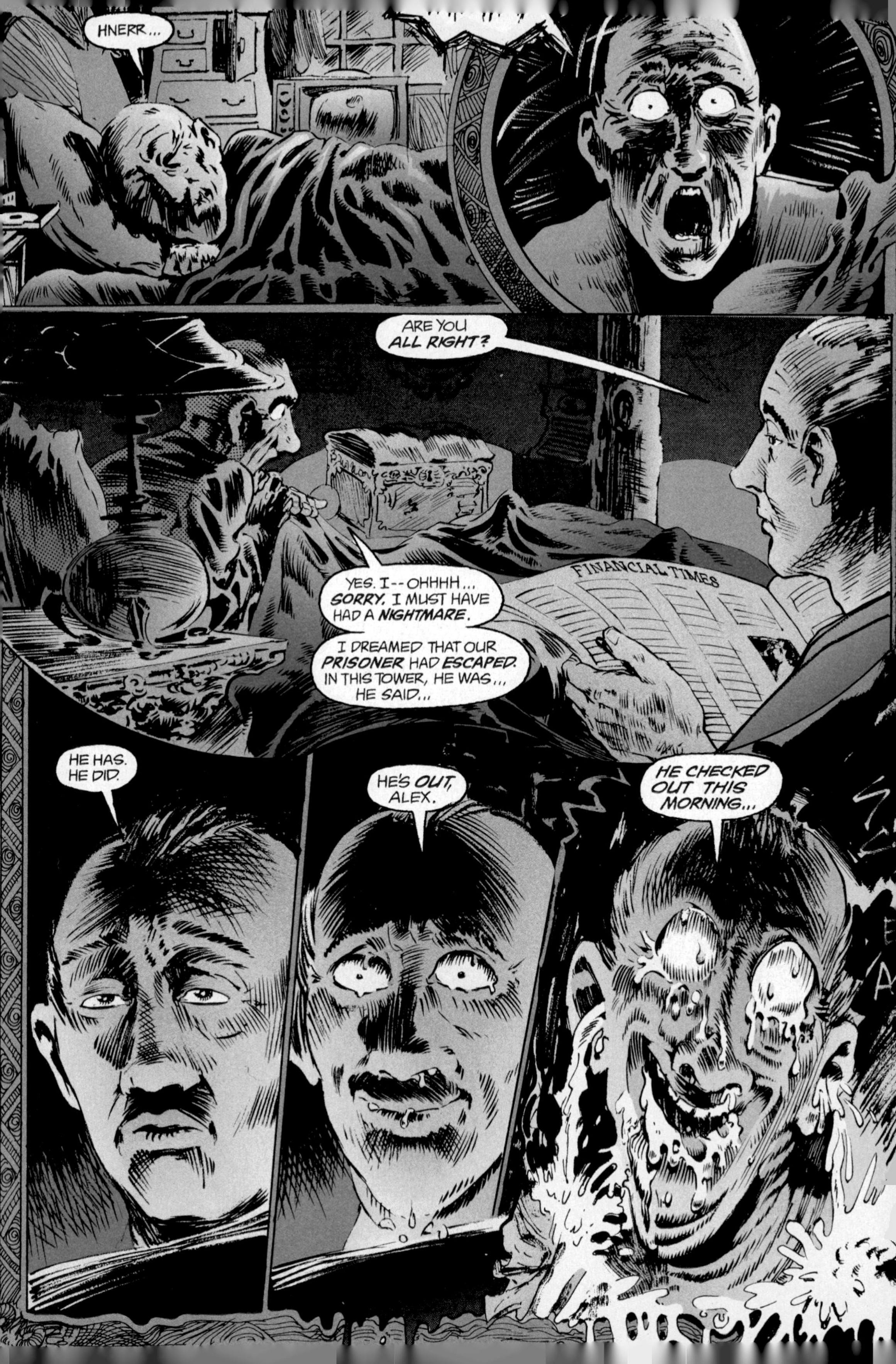
HNERR...
ARE YOU ALL RIGHT?
YES. I--OHHHH... SORRY. I MUST HAVE HAD A NIGHTMARE.
I DREAMED THAT OUR PRISONER HAD ESCAPED. IN THIS TOWER, HE WAS... HE SAID...
FINANCIAL TIMES
HE HAS. HE DID.
HE'S OUT, ALEX.
HE CHECKED OUT THIS MORNING...

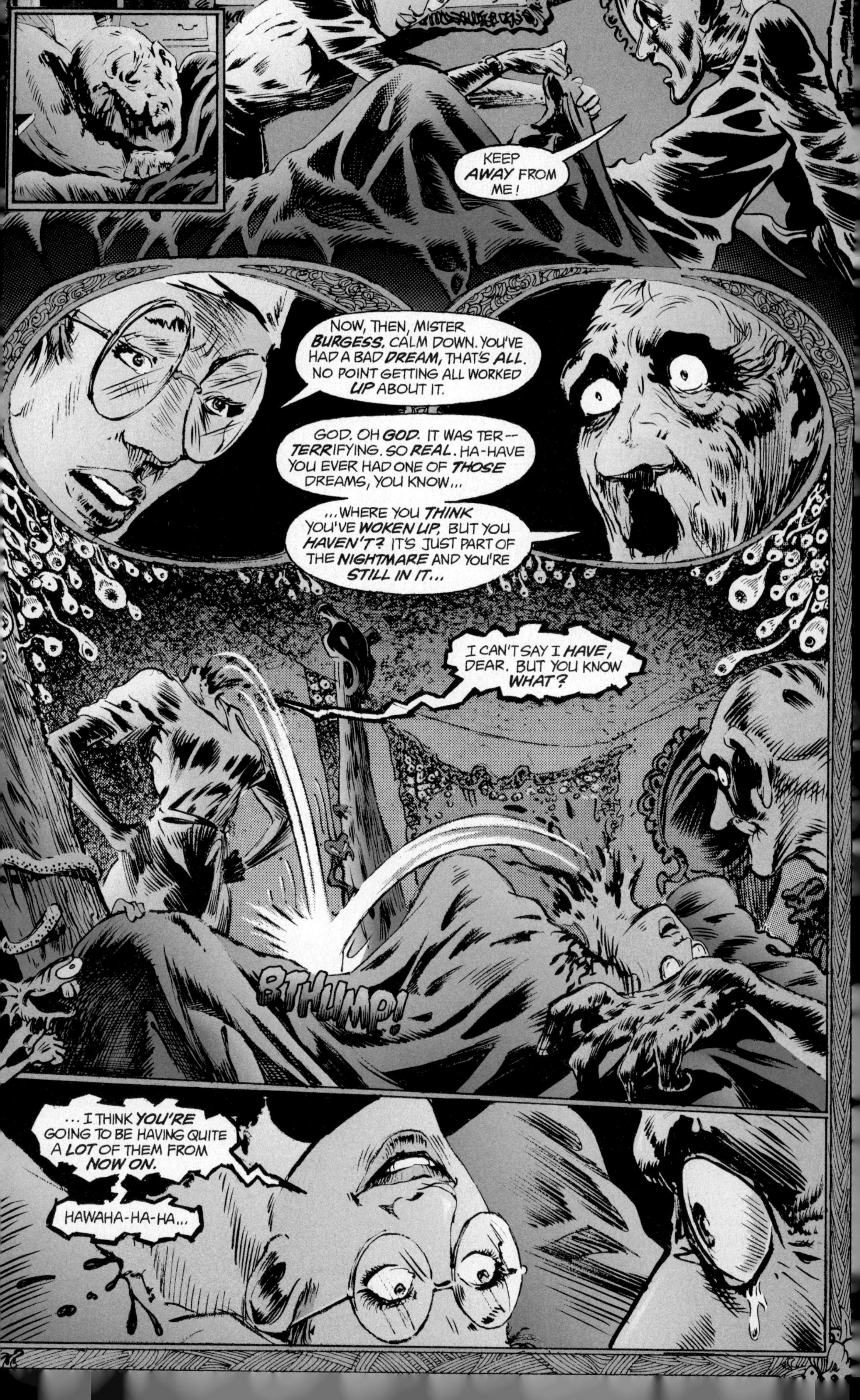
KEEP AWAY FROM ME!
NOW, THEN, MISTER BURGESS, CALM DOWN. YOU'VE HAD A BAD DREAM, THAT'S ALL. NO POINT GETTING ALL WORKED UP ABOUT IT.
GOD, OH GOD. IT WAS TER-- TERRIFYING. SO REAL. HA-HAVE YOU EVER HAD ONE OF THOSE DREAMS, YOU KNOW...
...WHERE YOU THINK YOU'VE WOKEN UP, BUT YOU HAVEN'T? IT'S JUST PART OF THE NIGHTMARE AND YOU'RE STILL IN IT...
I CAN'T SAY I HAVE, DEAR. BUT YOU KNOW WHAT?
BTHUMP!
... I THINK YOU'RE GOING TO BE HAVING QUITE A LOT OF THEM FROM NOW ON.
HAWAHA-HA-HA...

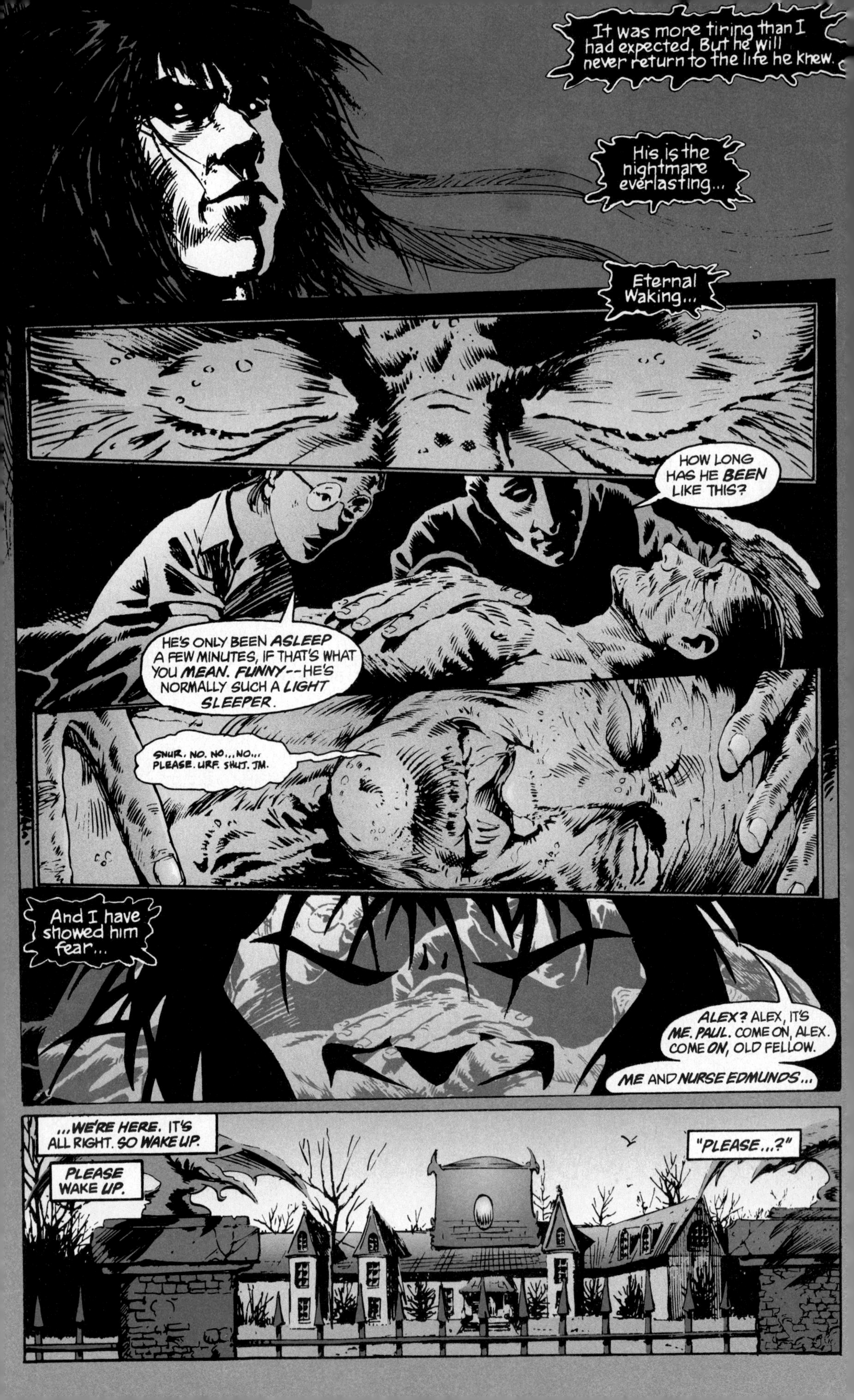
It was more tiring than I had expected, But he will never return to the life he knew.
His is the nightmare everlasting...
Eternal Waking...
HOW LONG HAS HE BEEN LIKE THIS?
HE'S ONLY BEEN ASLEEP A FEW MINUTES, IF THAT'S WHAT YOU MEAN. FUNNY--HE'S NORMALLY SUCH A LIGHT SLEEPER.
SNUR. NO. NO...NO... PLEASE. URF. SHUT. JM.
And I have showed him fear...
ALEX? ALEX, IT'S ME. PAUL. COME ON, ALEX. COME ON, OLD FELLOW.
ME AND NURSE EDMUNDS...
...WE'RE HERE. IT'S ALL RIGHT. SO WAKE UP.
PLEASE WAKE UP.
"PLEASE...?"

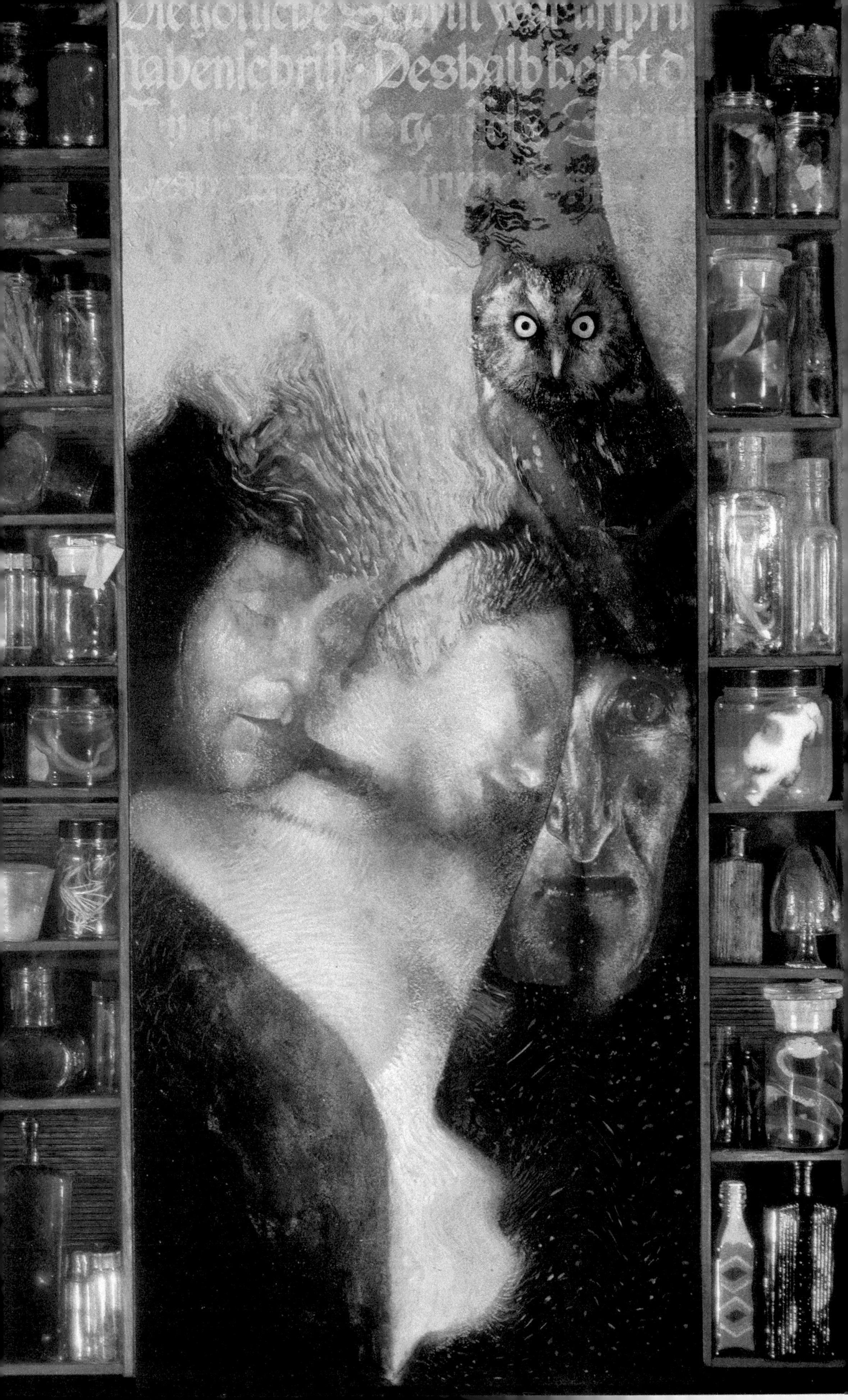

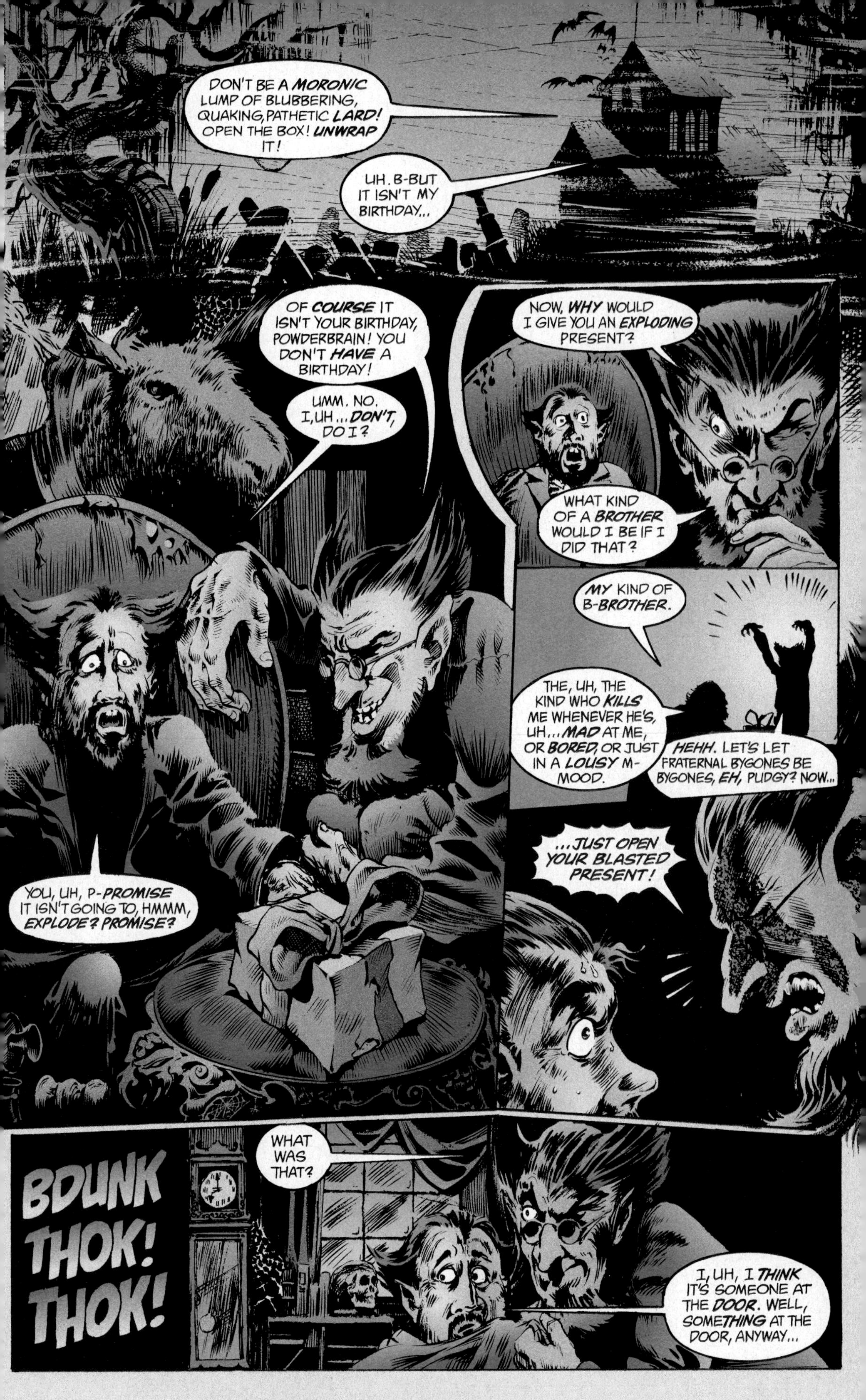
DON'T BE A MORONIC LUMP OF BLUBBERING, QUAKING, PATHETIC LARD! OPEN THE BOX! UNWRAP IT!
UH. B-BUT IT ISN'T MY BIRTHDAY...
OF COURSE IT ISN'T YOUR BIRTHDAY, POWDERBRAIN! YOU DON'T HAVE A BIRTHDAY!
UMM. NO. I, UH... DON'T, DO I?
YOU, UH, P-PROMISE IT ISN'T GOING TO, HMMM, EXPLODE? PROMISE?
NOW, WHY WOULD I GIVE YOU AN EXPLODING PRESENT?
WHAT KIND OF A BROTHER WOULD I BE IF I DID THAT?
MY KIND OF B-BROTHER.
THE, UH, THE KIND WHO KILLS ME WHENEVER HE'S, UH... MAD AT ME, OR BORED, OR JUST IN A LOUSY M-MOOD.
HEHH. LET'S LET FRATERNAL BYGONES BE BYGONES, EH, PUDGY? NOW...
...JUST OPEN YOUR BLASTED PRESENT!
BDUNK
THOK!
THOK!
WHAT WAS THAT?
I, UH, I THINK IT'S SOMEONE AT THE DOOR. WELL, SOMETHING AT THE DOOR, ANYWAY...

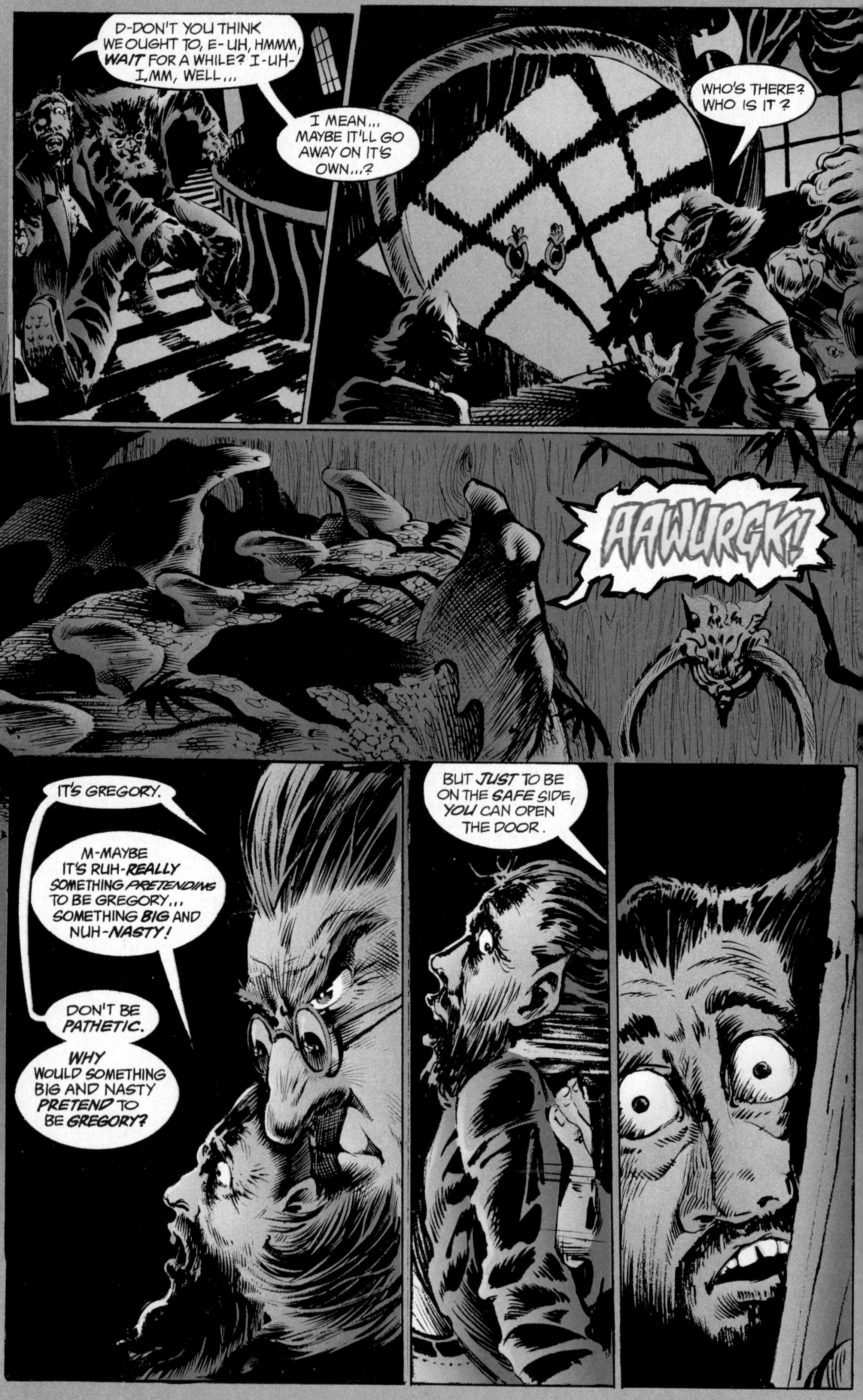
D-DON'T YOU THINK WE OUGHT TO, E-UH, HMMM, WAIT FOR A WHILE? I-UH- I,MM, WELL...
I MEAN... MAYBE IT'LL GO AWAY ON IT'S OWN...?
WHO'S THERE? WHO IS IT?
AAWURGK!
IT'S GREGORY.
M-MAYBE IT'S RUH-REALLY SOMETHING PRETENDING TO BE GREGORY... SOMETHING BIG AND NUH-NASTY!
DON'T BE PATHETIC.
WHY WOULD SOMETHING BIG AND NASTY PRETEND TO BE GREGORY?
BUT JUST TO BE ON THE SAFE SIDE, YOU CAN OPEN THE DOOR.

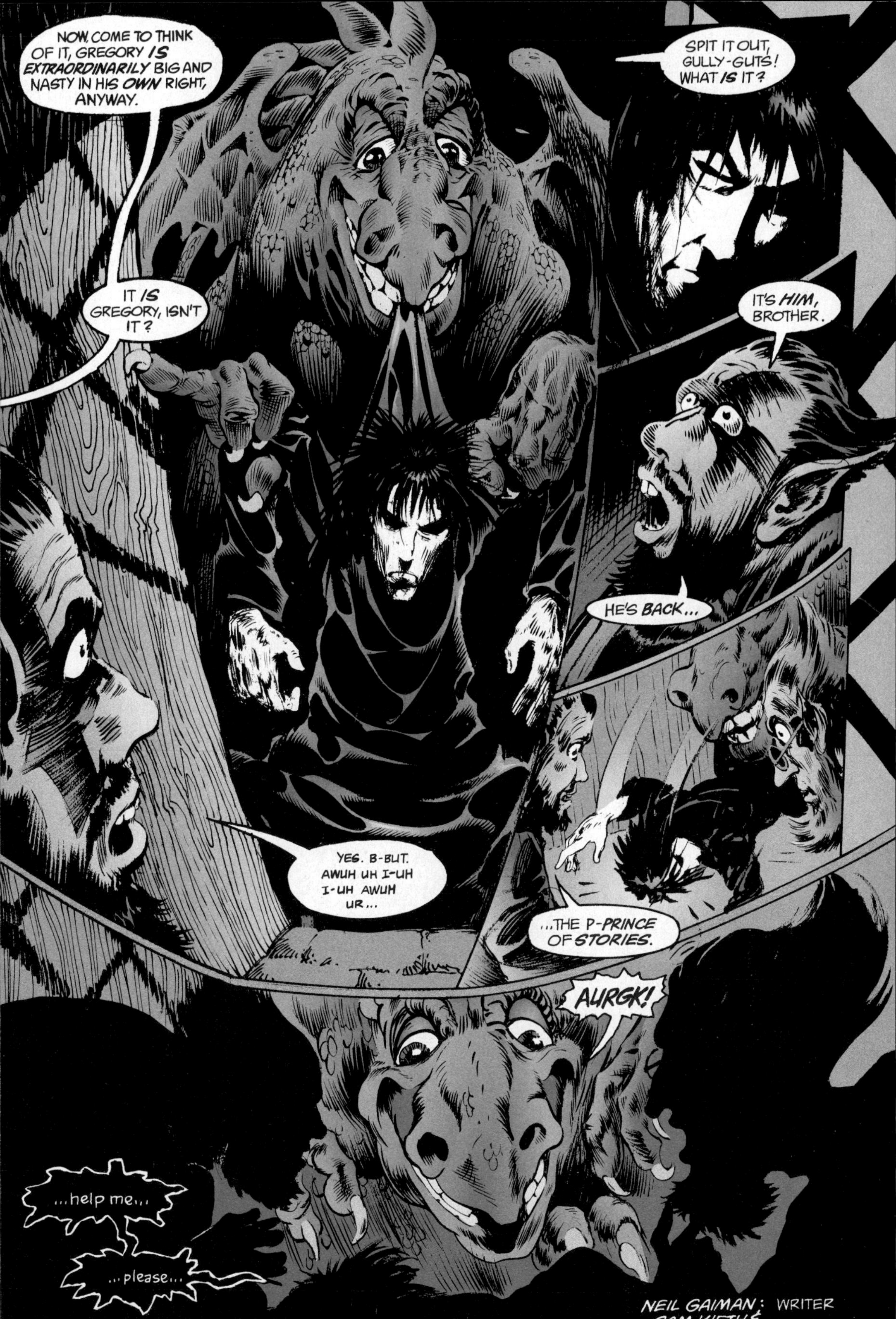
NOW, COME TO THINK OF IT, GREGORY IS EXTRAORDINARILY BIG AND NASTY IN HIS OWN RIGHT, ANYWAY.
SPIT IT OUT, GULLY-GUTS! WHAT IS IT?
IT IS GREGORY, ISN'T IT?
IT'S HIM, BROTHER.
HE'S BACK...
YES. B-BUT. AWUH UH I-UH I-UH AWUH UR...
...THE P-PRINCE OF STORIES.
AURGK!
...help me...
...please...

IMPERFECT HOSTS

NEIL GAIMAN: WRITER
SAM KIETH & MIKE DRINGENBERG: ARTISTS
TODD KLEIN: LETTERER
DANIEL VOZZO: COLORIST
ART YOUNG: ASST. EDITOR
KAREN BERGER: EDITOR

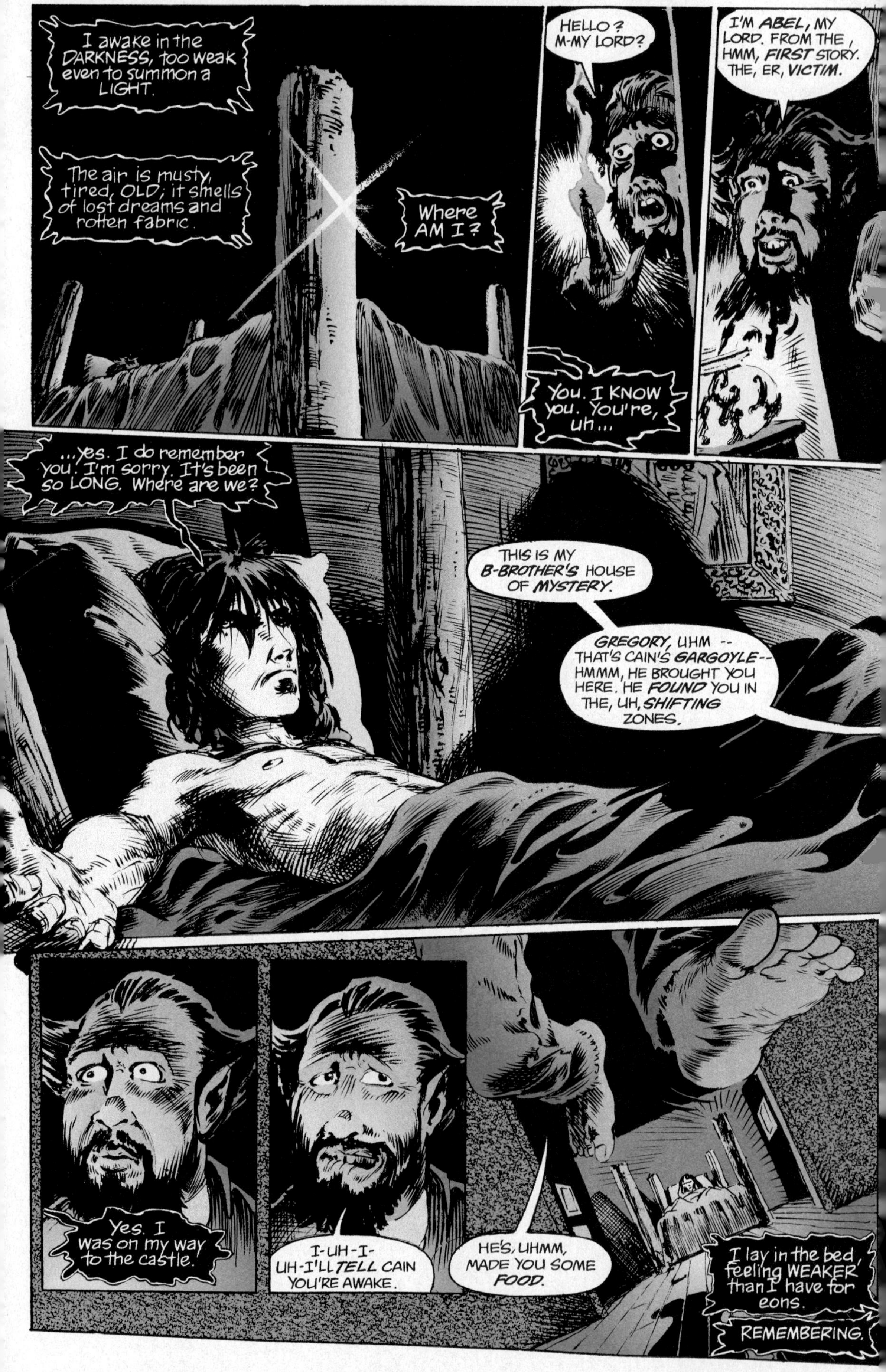

I awake in the DARKNESS, too weak even to summon a LIGHT.
The air is musty, tired, OLD; it smells of lost dreams and rotten fabric.
Where AM I?
HELLO? M-MY LORD?
You. I KNOW you. You're, uh...
I'M ABEL, MY LORD. FROM THE, HMM, FIRST STORY. THE, ER, VICTIM.
...yes. I do remember you. I'm sorry. It's been so LONG. Where are we?
THIS IS MY B-BROTHER'S HOUSE OF MYSTERY.
GREGORY, UHM -- THAT'S CAIN'S GARGOYLE -- HMMM, HE BROUGHT YOU HERE. HE FOUND YOU IN THE, UH, SHIFTING ZONES.
Yes. I was on my way to the castle.
I-UH-I-UH-I'LL TELL CAIN YOU'RE AWAKE.
HE'S, UHMM, MADE YOU SOME FOOD.
I lay in the bed, feeling WEAKER than I have for eons.
REMEMBERING.

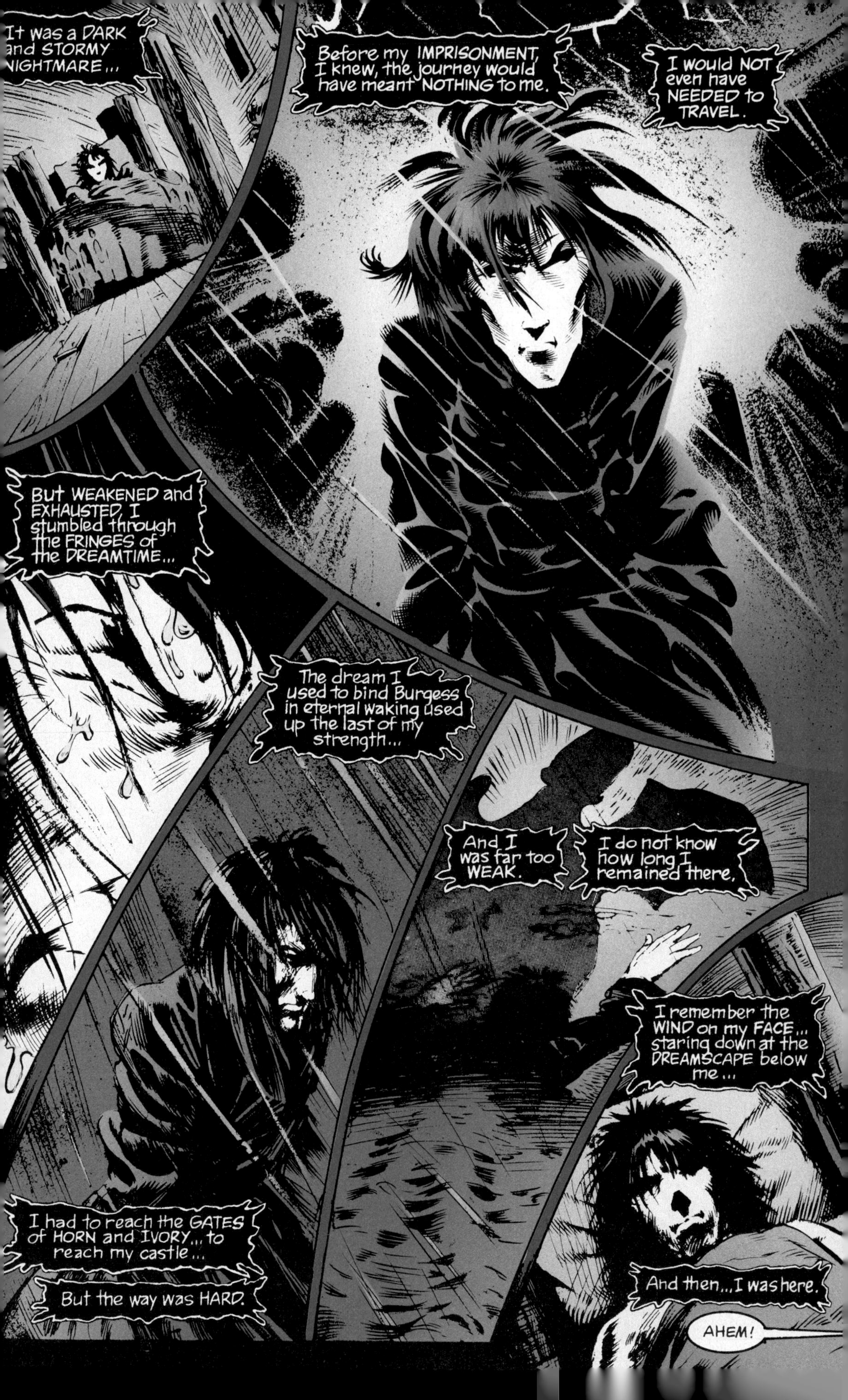

It was a DARK and STORMY NIGHTMARE...
Before my IMPRISONMENT, I knew, the journey would have meant NOTHING to me.
I would NOT even have NEEDED to TRAVEL.
But WEAKENED and EXHAUSTED, I stumbled through the FRINGES of the DREAMTIME...
The dream I used to bind Burgess in eternal waking used up the last of my strength...
I had to reach the GATES of HORN and IVORY... to reach my castle...
But the way was HARD.
And I was far too WEAK.
I do not know how long I remained there,
I remember the WIND on my FACE... staring down at the DREAMSCAPE below me...
And then... I was here.
AHEM!

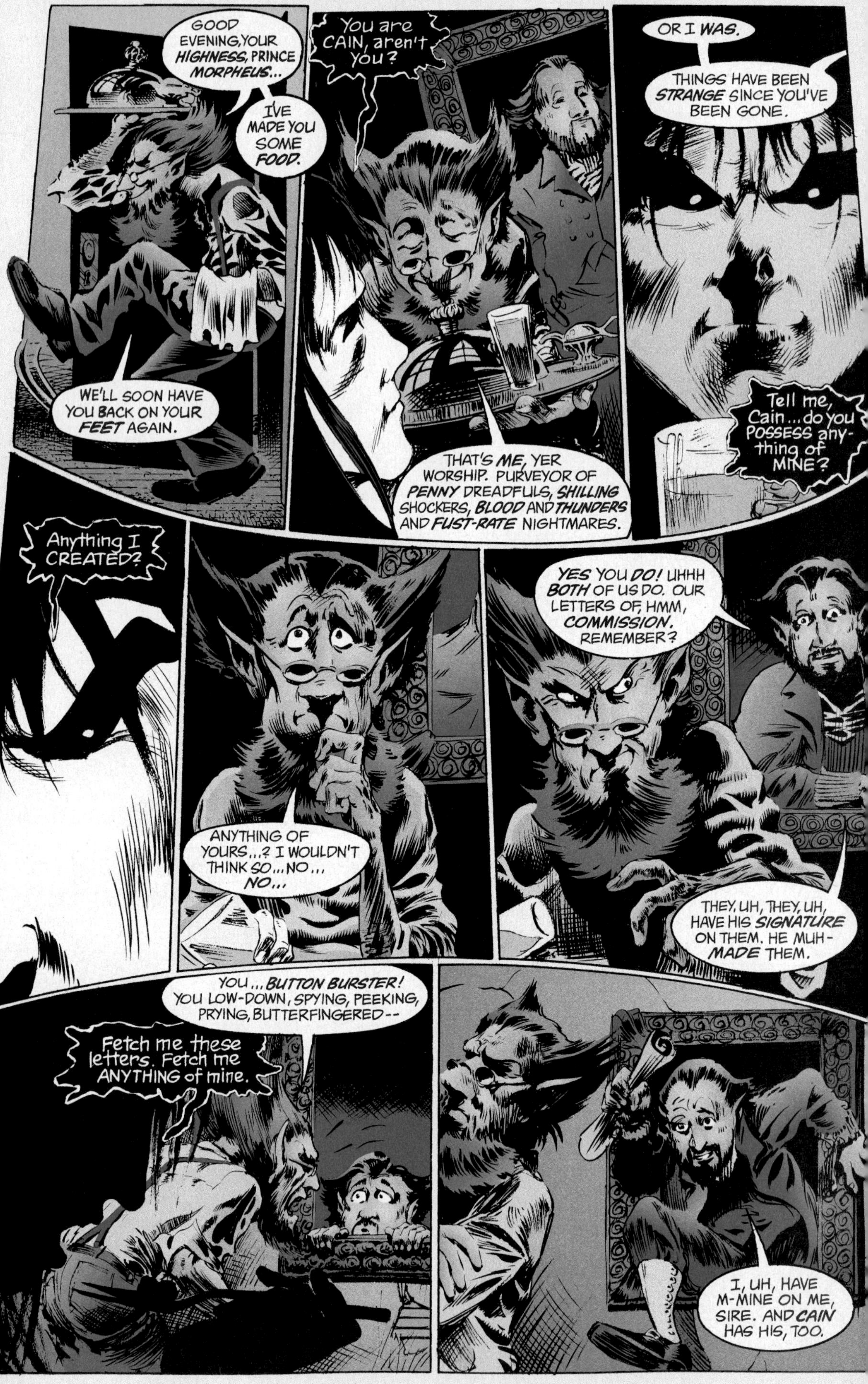
GOOD EVENING, YOUR HIGHNESS, PRINCE MORPHEUS...
I'VE MADE YOU SOME FOOD.
WE'LL SOON HAVE YOU BACK ON YOUR FEET AGAIN.
You are CAIN, aren't you?
THAT'S ME, YER WORSHIP. PURVEYOR OF PENNY DREADFULS, SHILLING SHOCKERS, BLOOD AND THUNDERS AND FUST-RATE NIGHTMARES.
OR I WAS.
THINGS HAVE BEEN STRANGE SINCE YOU'VE BEEN GONE.
Tell me, Cain... do you POSSESS anything of MINE?
Anything I CREATED?
ANYTHING OF YOURS...? I WOULDN'T THINK SO... NO... NO...
YES YOU DO! UHHH BOTH OF US DO. OUR LETTERS OF, HMM, COMMISSION. REMEMBER?
THEY, UH, THEY, UH, HAVE HIS SIGNATURE ON THEM. HE MUH-MADE THEM.
YOU... BUTTON BURSTER! YOU LOW-DOWN, SPYING, PEEKING, PRYING, BUTTERFINGERED--
Fetch me these letters. Fetch me ANYTHING of mine.
I, UH, HAVE M-MINE ON ME, SIRE. AND CAIN HAS HIS, TOO.

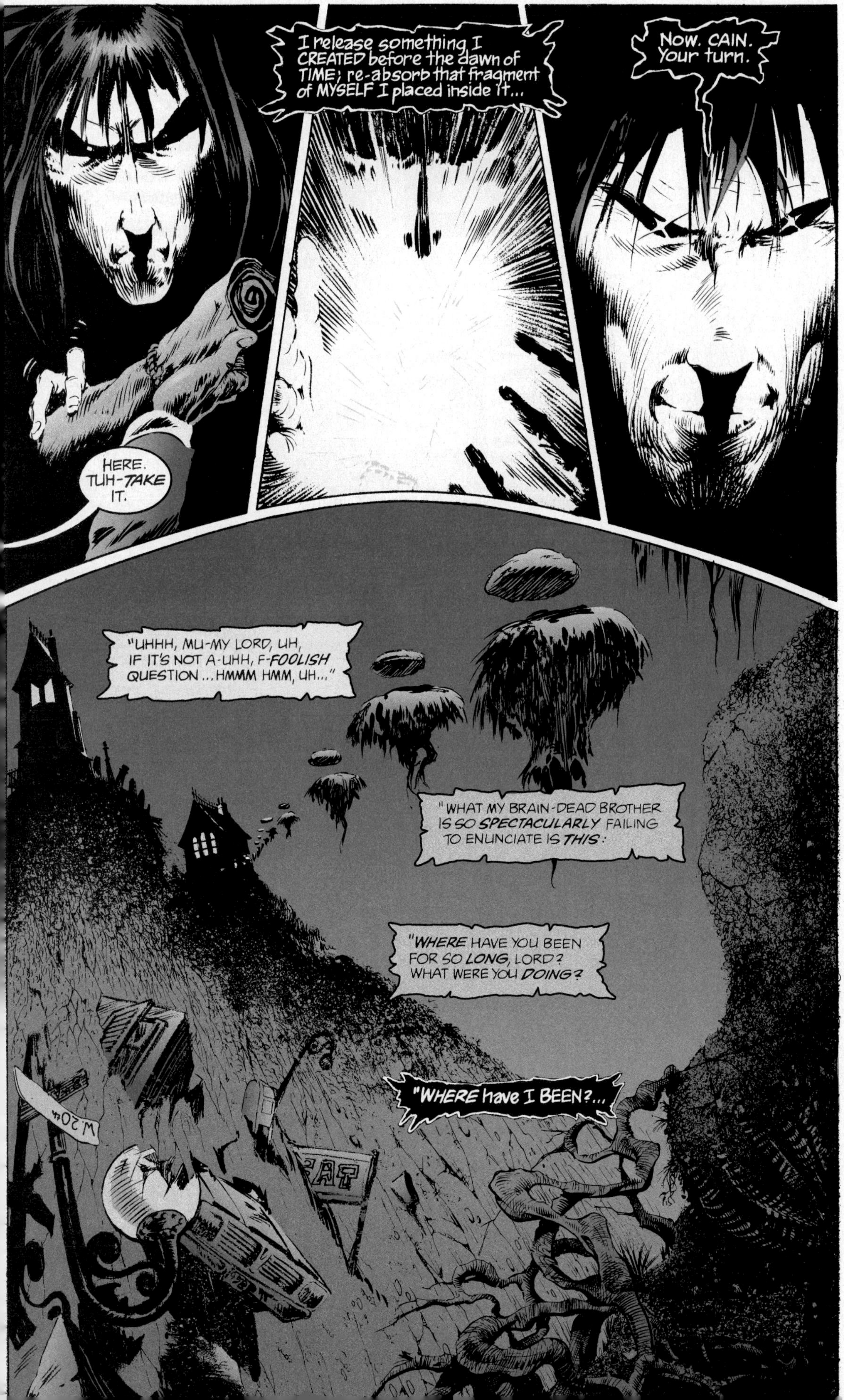
HERE. TUH-TAKE IT.
I release something I CREATED before the dawn of TIME; re-absorb that fragment of MYSELF I placed inside it...
Now. CAIN. Your turn.
"UHHH, MU-MY LORD, UH, IF IT'S NOT A-UHH, F-FOOLISH QUESTION ... HMMM HMM, UH..."
"WHAT MY BRAIN-DEAD BROTHER IS SO SPECTACULARLY FAILING TO ENUNCIATE IS THIS:
"WHERE HAVE YOU BEEN FOR SO LONG, LORD? WHAT WERE YOU DOING?
"WHERE have I BEEN?...
W. 204

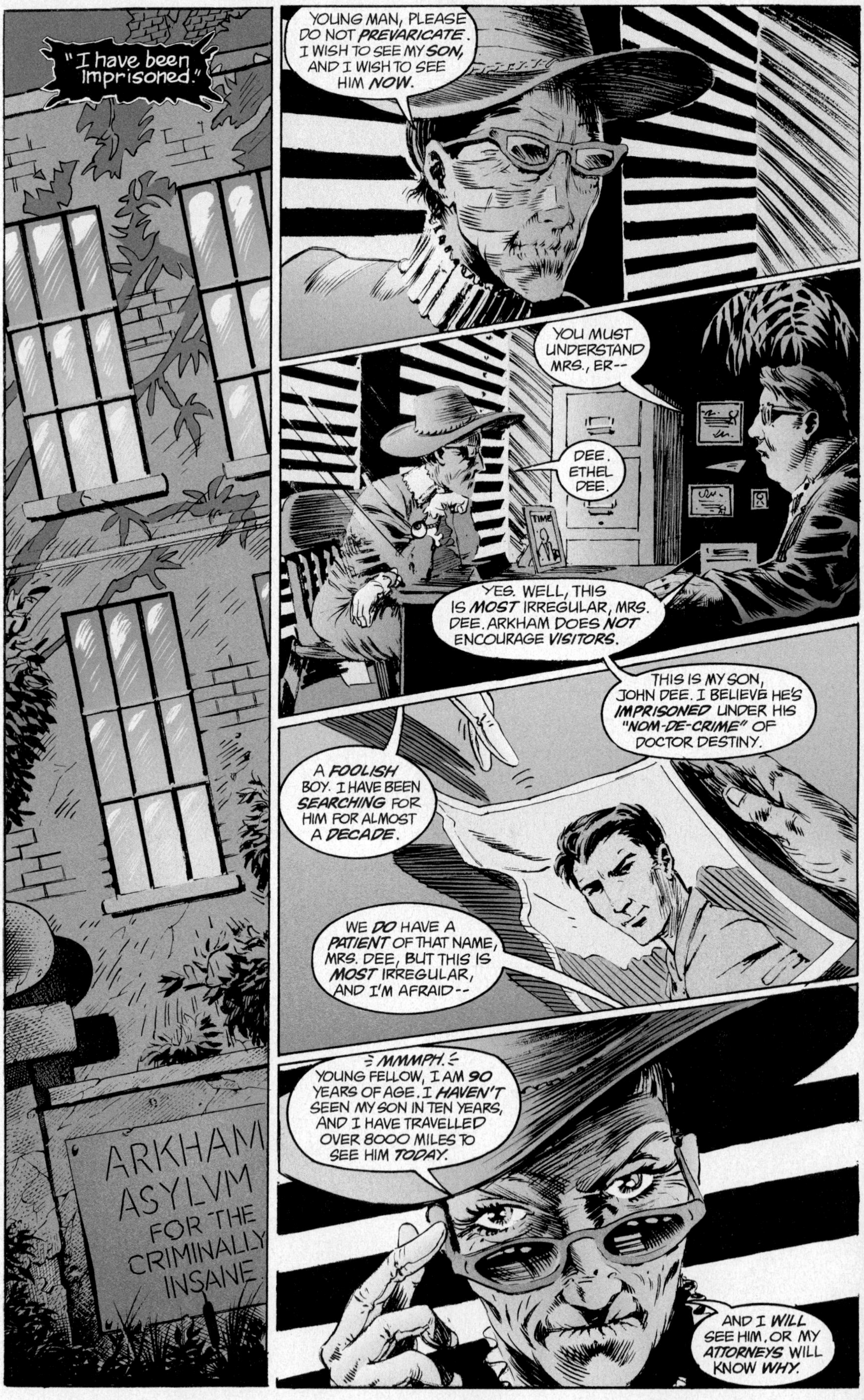
"I have been imprisoned."
ARKHAM ASYLUM FOR THE CRIMINALLY INSANE
YOUNG MAN, PLEASE DO NOT PREVARICATE. I WISH TO SEE MY SON, AND I WISH TO SEE HIM NOW.
YOU MUST UNDERSTAND MRS., ER--
DEE. ETHEL DEE.
YES. WELL, THIS IS MOST IRREGULAR, MRS. DEE. ARKHAM DOES NOT ENCOURAGE VISITORS.
THIS IS MY SON, JOHN DEE. I BELIEVE HE'S IMPRISONED UNDER HIS "NOM-DE-CRIME" OF DOCTOR DESTINY.
A FOOLISH BOY. I HAVE BEEN SEARCHING FOR HIM FOR ALMOST A DECADE.
WE DO HAVE A PATIENT OF THAT NAME, MRS. DEE, BUT THIS IS MOST IRREGULAR, AND I'M AFRAID--
MMMPH.
YOUNG FELLOW, I AM 90 YEARS OF AGE. I HAVEN'T SEEN MY SON IN TEN YEARS, AND I HAVE TRAVELLED OVER 8000 MILES TO SEE HIM TODAY.
AND I WILL SEE HIM, OR MY ATTORNEYS WILL KNOW WHY.

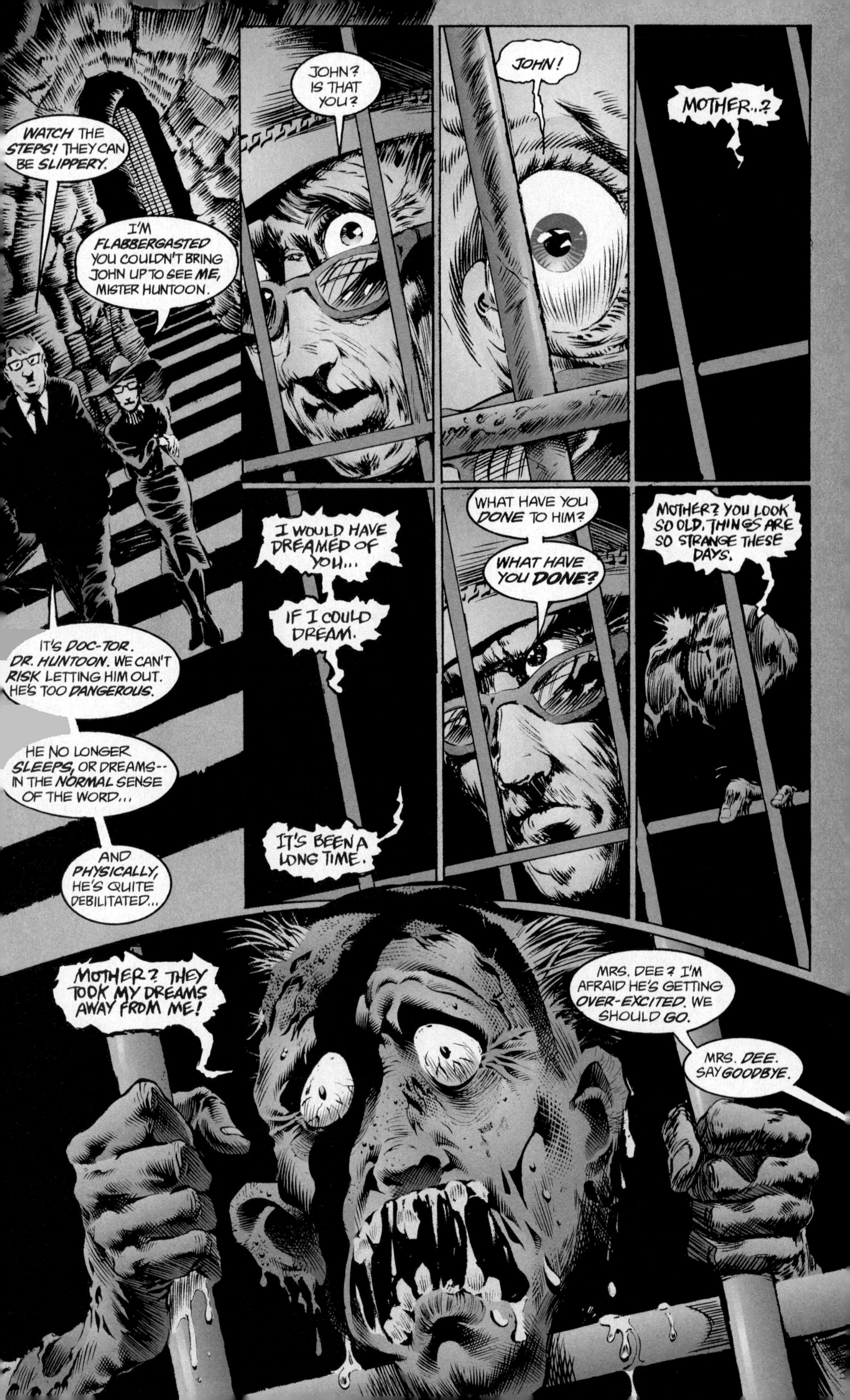
WATCH THE STEPS! THEY CAN BE SLIPPERY.
I'M FLABBERGASTED YOU COULDN'T BRING JOHN UP TO SEE ME, MISTER HUNTOON.
IT'S DOC-TOR. DR. HUNTOON. WE CAN'T RISK LETTING HIM OUT. HE'S TOO DANGEROUS.
HE NO LONGER SLEEPS, OR DREAMS-- IN THE NORMAL SENSE OF THE WORD...
AND PHYSICALLY, HE'S QUITE DEBILITATED...
JOHN? IS THAT YOU?
JOHN!
MOTHER...?
I WOULD HAVE DREAMED OF YOU...
IF I COULD DREAM.
IT'S BEEN A LONG TIME.
WHAT HAVE YOU DONE TO HIM?
WHAT HAVE YOU DONE?
MOTHER? YOU LOOK SO OLD. THINGS ARE SO STRANGE THESE DAYS.
MOTHER? THEY TOOK MY DREAMS AWAY FROM ME!
MRS. DEE? I'M AFRAID HE'S GETTING OVER-EXCITED. WE SHOULD GO.
MRS. DEE. SAY GOODBYE.

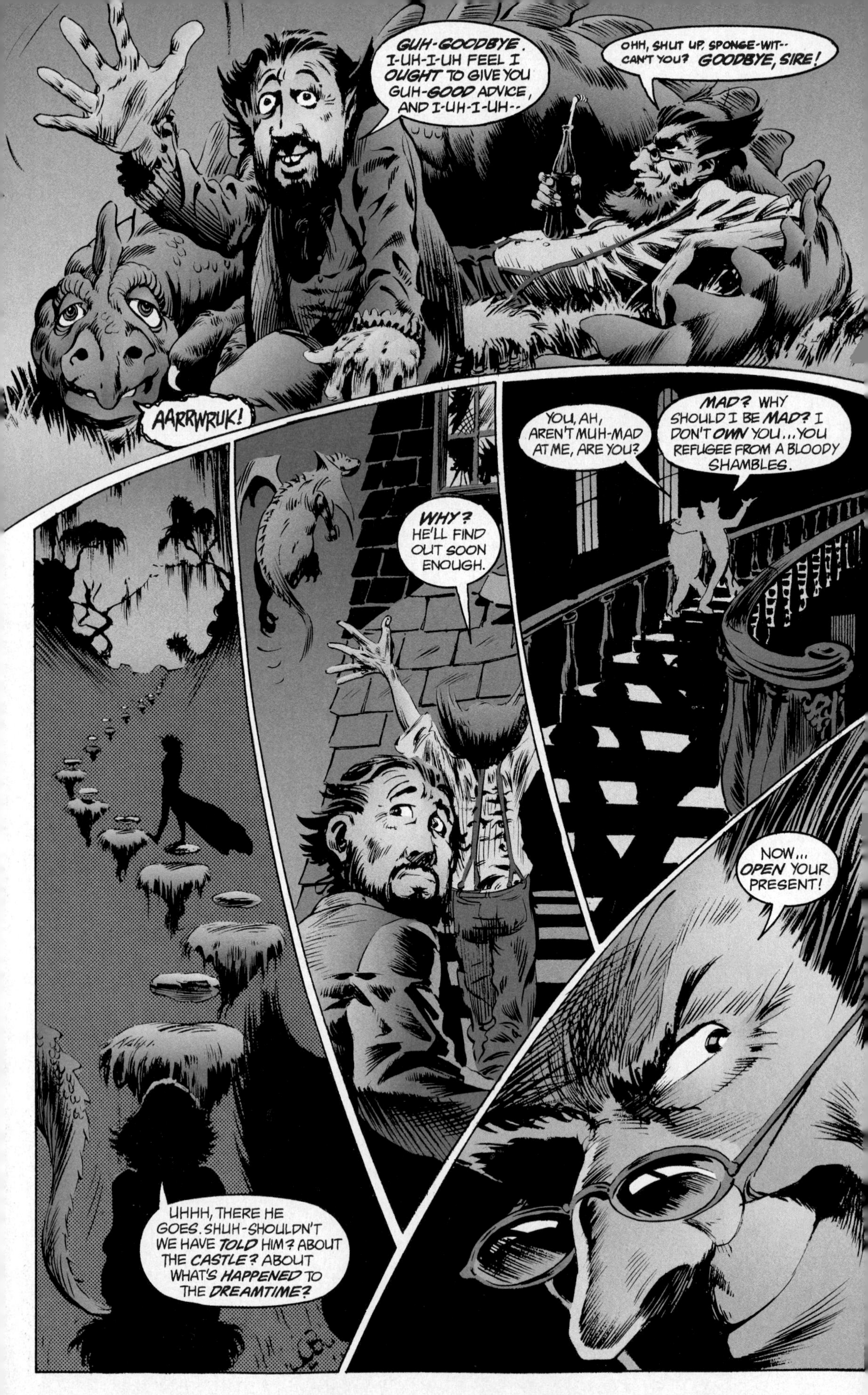
GUH-GOODBYE. I-UH-I-UH FEEL I OUGHT TO GIVE YOU GUH-GOOD ADVICE, AND I-UH-I-UH--
OHH, SHUT UP, SPONGE-WIT-- CAN'T YOU? GOODBYE, SIRE!
AARRWRUK!
UHHH, THERE HE GOES. SHUH-SHOULDN'T WE HAVE TOLD HIM? ABOUT THE CASTLE? ABOUT WHAT'S HAPPENED TO THE DREAMTIME?
WHY? HE'LL FIND OUT SOON ENOUGH.
YOU, AH, AREN'T MUH-MAD AT ME, ARE YOU?
MAD? WHY SHOULD I BE MAD? I DON'T OWN YOU... YOU REFUGEE FROM A BLOODY SHAMBLES.
NOW... OPEN YOUR PRESENT!

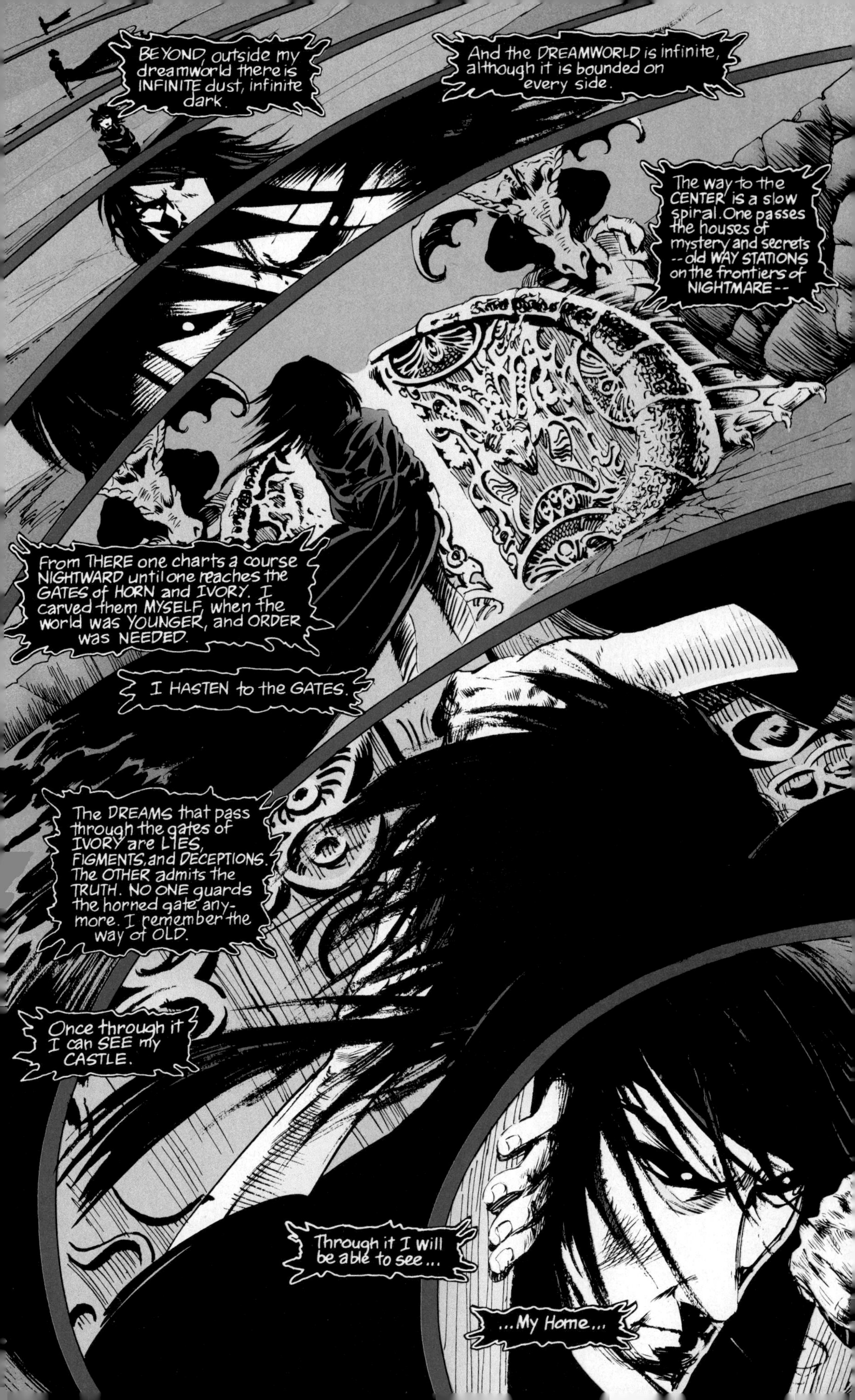
BEYOND, outside my dreamworld there is INFINITE dust, infinite dark.
And the DREAMWORLD is infinite, although it is bounded on every side.
The way to the CENTER is a slow spiral. One passes the houses of mystery and secrets --old WAY STATIONS on the frontiers of NIGHTMARE--
From THERE one charts a course NIGHTWARD until one reaches the GATES of HORN and IVORY. I carved them MYSELF, when the world was YOUNGER, and ORDER was NEEDED.
I HASTEN to the GATES.
The DREAMS that pass through the gates of IVORY are LIES, FIGMENTS, and DECEPTIONS. The OTHER admits the TRUTH. NO ONE guards the horned gate any-more. I remember the way of OLD.
Once through it I can SEE my CASTLE.
Through it I will be able to see...
...My Home...

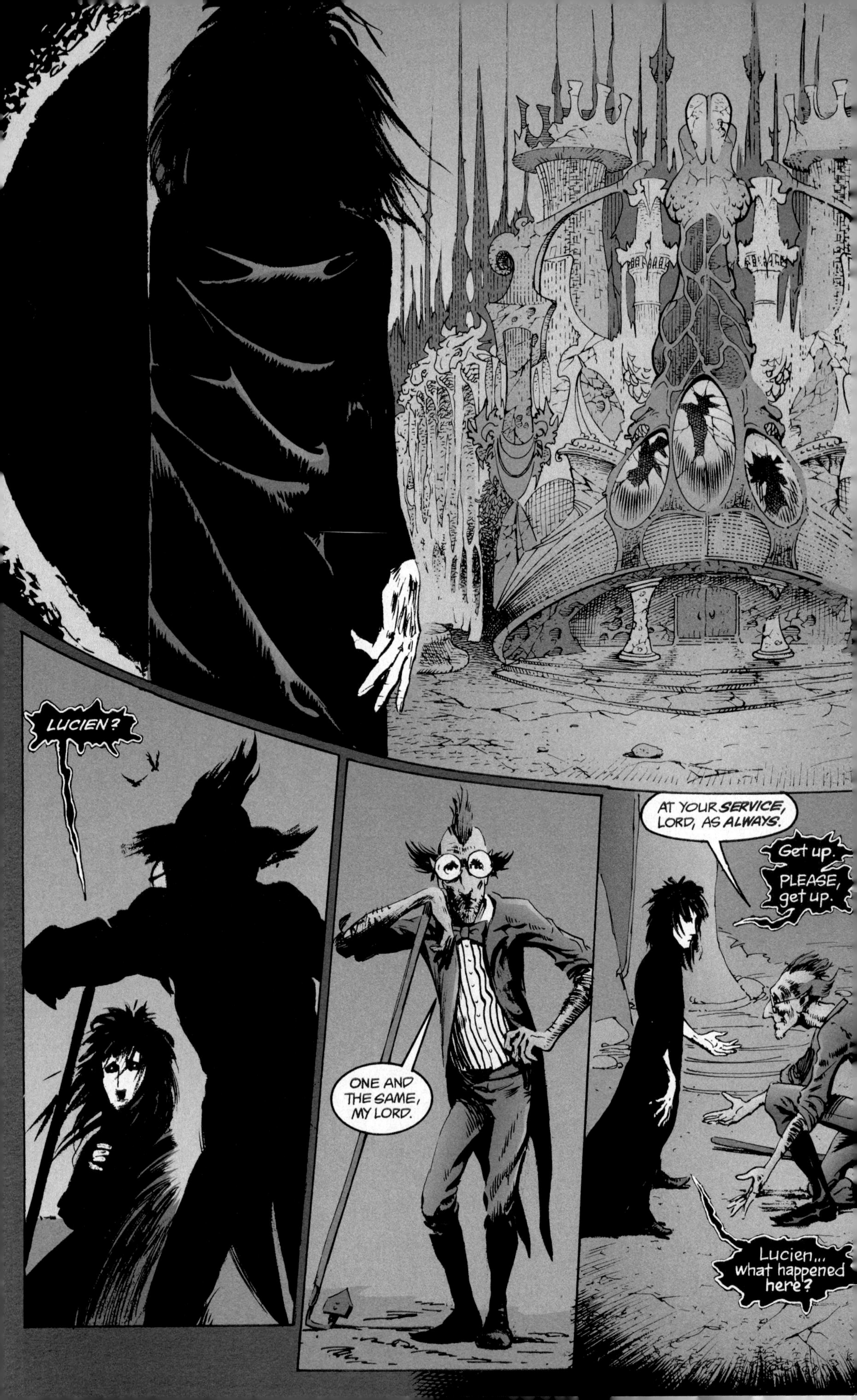
LUCIEN?
ONE AND THE SAME, MY LORD.
AT YOUR SERVICE, LORD, AS ALWAYS.
Get up.
PLEASE, get up.
Lucien... what happened here?

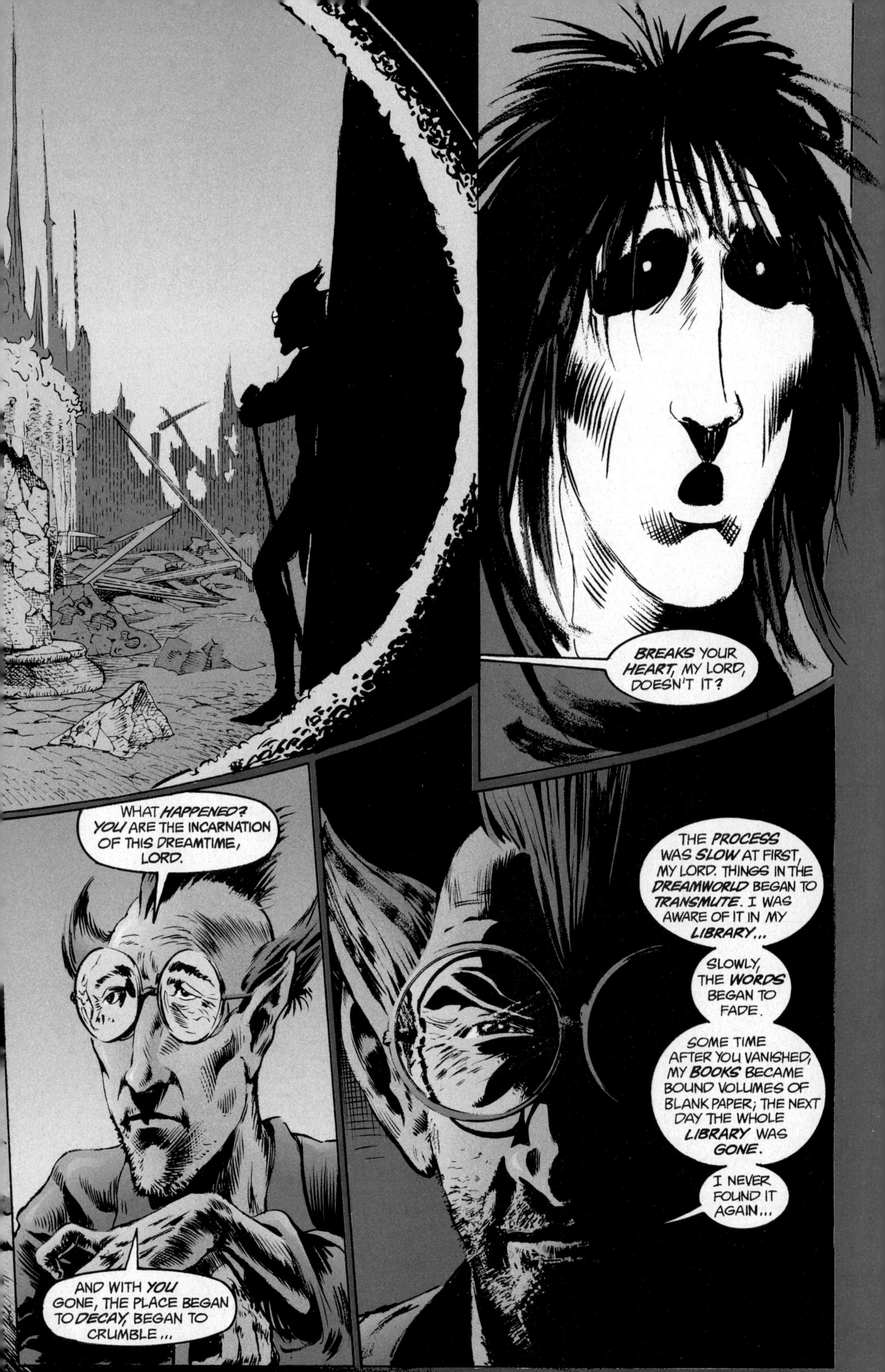
BREAKS YOUR HEART, MY LORD, DOESN'T IT?
WHAT HAPPENED? YOU ARE THE INCARNATION OF THIS DREAMTIME, LORD.
AND WITH YOU GONE, THE PLACE BEGAN TO DECAY, BEGAN TO CRUMBLE...
THE PROCESS WAS SLOW AT FIRST, MY LORD. THINGS IN THE DREAMWORLD BEGAN TO TRANSMUTE. I WAS AWARE OF IT IN MY LIBRARY...
SLOWLY, THE WORDS BEGAN TO FADE.
SOME TIME AFTER YOU VANISHED, MY BOOKS BECAME BOUND VOLUMES OF BLANK PAPER; THE NEXT DAY THE WHOLE LIBRARY WAS GONE.
I NEVER FOUND IT AGAIN...

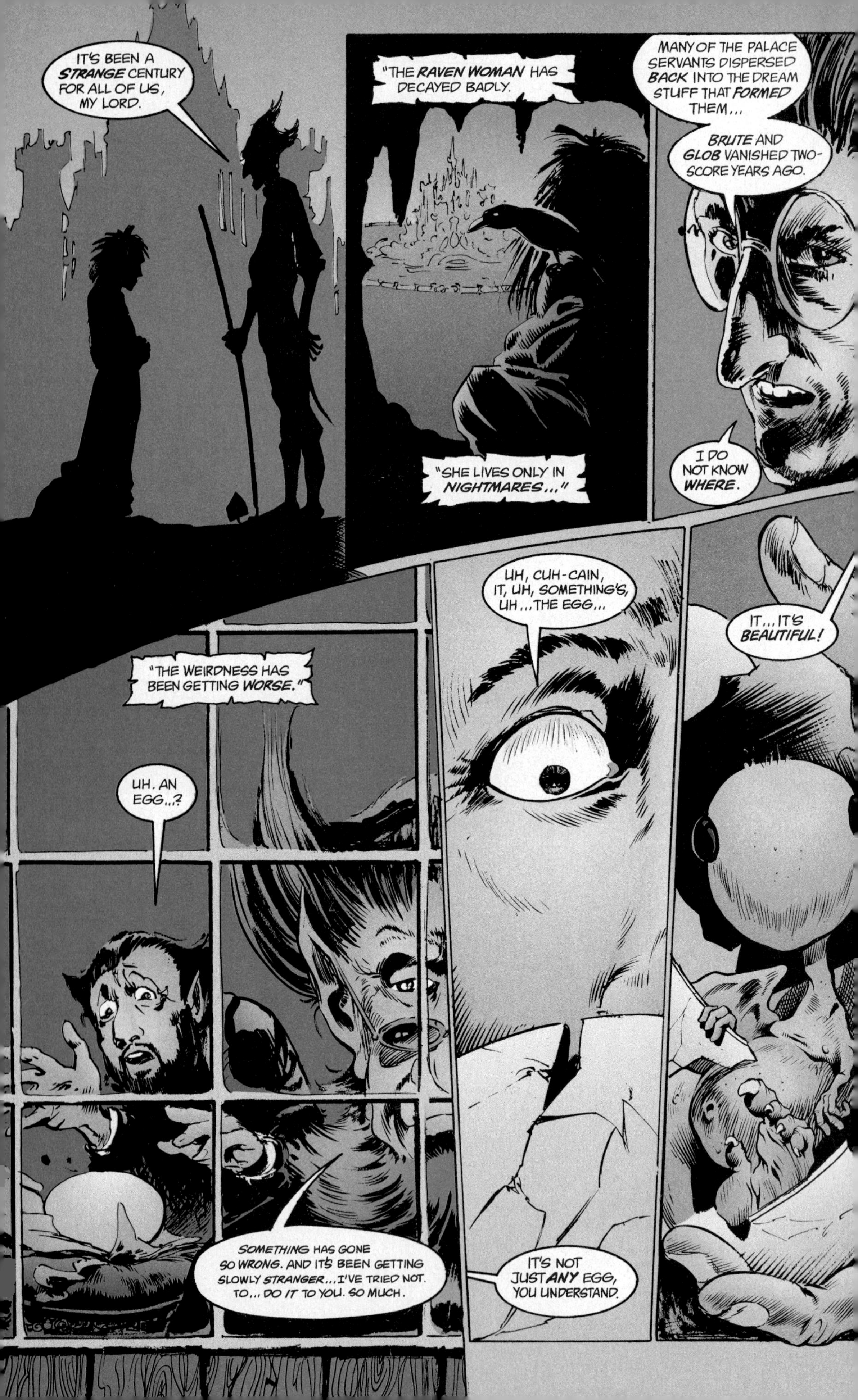
IT'S BEEN A STRANGE CENTURY FOR ALL OF US, MY LORD.
"THE RAVEN WOMAN HAS DECAYED BADLY.
"SHE LIVES ONLY IN NIGHTMARES..."
MANY OF THE PALACE SERVANTS DISPERSED BACK INTO THE DREAM STUFF THAT FORMED THEM...
BRUTE AND GLOB VANISHED TWO-SCORE YEARS AGO.
I DO NOT KNOW WHERE.
"THE WEIRDNESS HAS BEEN GETTING WORSE."
UH. AN EGG...?
SOMETHING HAS GONE SO WRONG. AND IT'S BEEN GETTING SLOWLY STRANGER... I'VE TRIED NOT. TO... DO IT TO YOU. SO MUCH.
UH, CUH-CAIN, IT, UH, SOMETHING'S, UH... THE EGG...
IT'S NOT JUST ANY EGG, YOU UNDERSTAND.
IT... IT'S BEAUTIFUL!

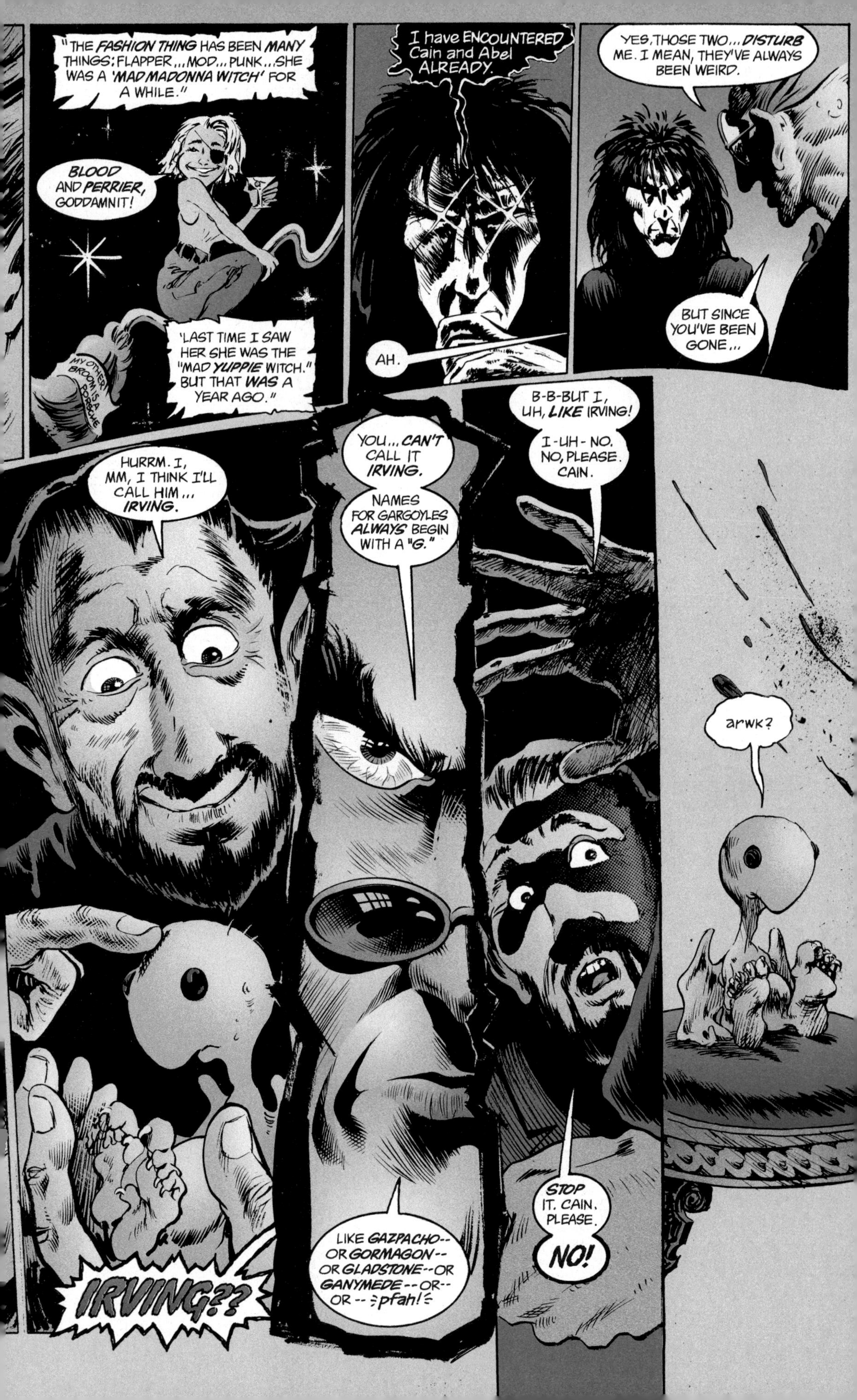
"THE FASHION THING HAS BEEN MANY THINGS: FLAPPER... MOD... PUNK... SHE WAS A 'MAD MADONNA WITCH' FOR A WHILE."
BLOOD AND PERRIER, GODDAMNIT!
'LAST TIME I SAW HER SHE WAS THE "MAD YUPPIE WITCH." BUT THAT WAS A YEAR AGO."
MY OTHER BROOM IS A PORSCHE
I have ENCOUNTERED Cain and Abel ALREADY.
AH.
YES, THOSE TWO... DISTURB ME. I MEAN, THEY'VE ALWAYS BEEN WEIRD.
BUT SINCE YOU'VE BEEN GONE...
HURRM. I, MM, I THINK I'LL CALL HIM... IRVING.
IRVING??
YOU... CAN'T CALL IT IRVING.
NAMES FOR GARGOYLES ALWAYS BEGIN WITH A "G."
LIKE GAZPACHO-- OR GORMAGON-- OR GLADSTONE--OR GANYMEDE--OR-- OR-- pfah!
B-B-BUT I, UH, LIKE IRVING!
I-UH- NO. NO, PLEASE. CAIN.
STOP IT. CAIN. PLEASE.
NO!
arwk?

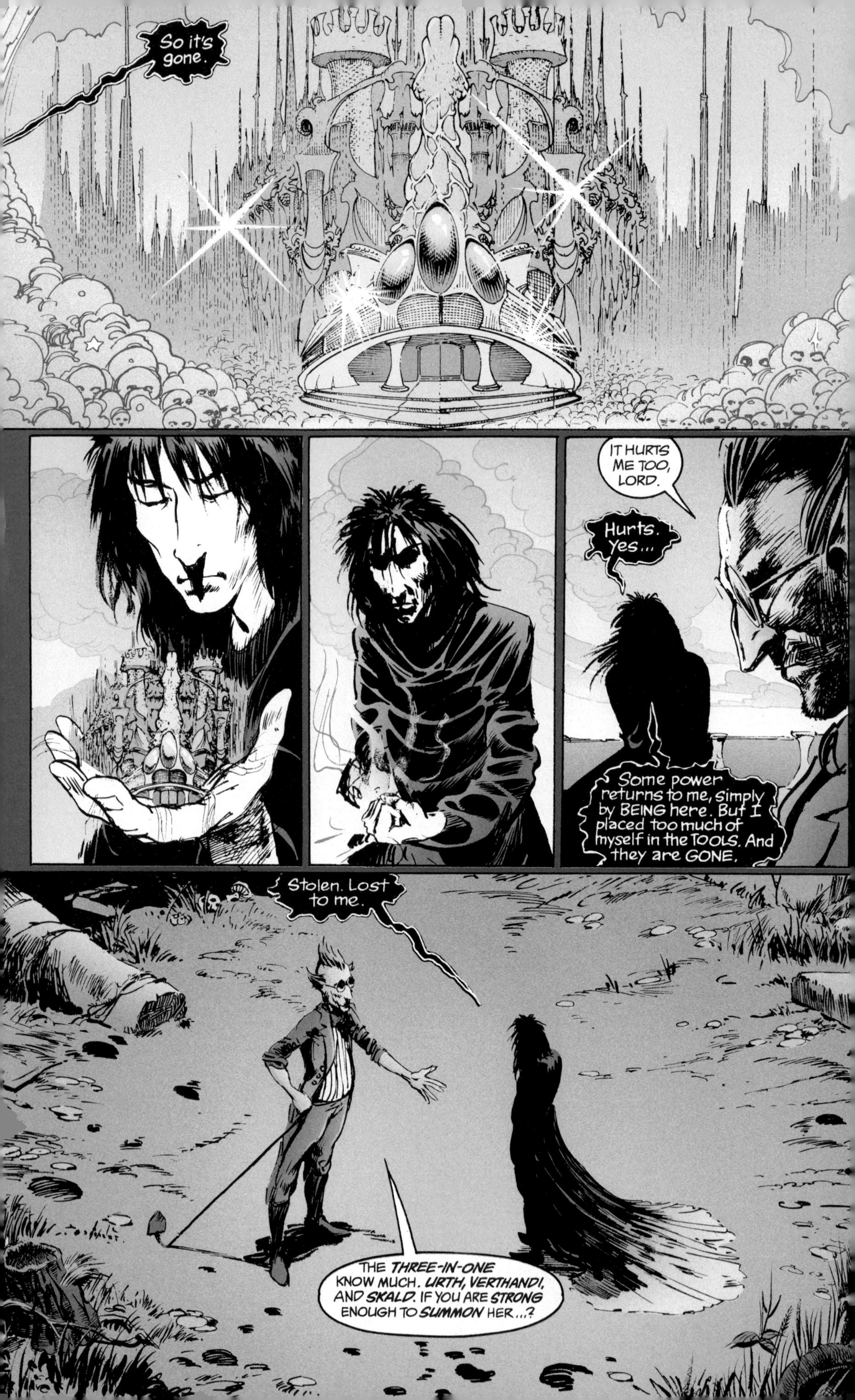
So it's gone.
IT HURTS ME TOO, LORD.
Hurts. yes...
Some power returns to me, simply by BEING here. But I placed too much of myself in the TOOLS. And they are GONE.
Stolen. Lost to me.
THE THREE-IN-ONE KNOW MUCH. URTH, VERTHANDI, AND SKALD. IF YOU ARE STRONG ENOUGH TO SUMMON HER...?

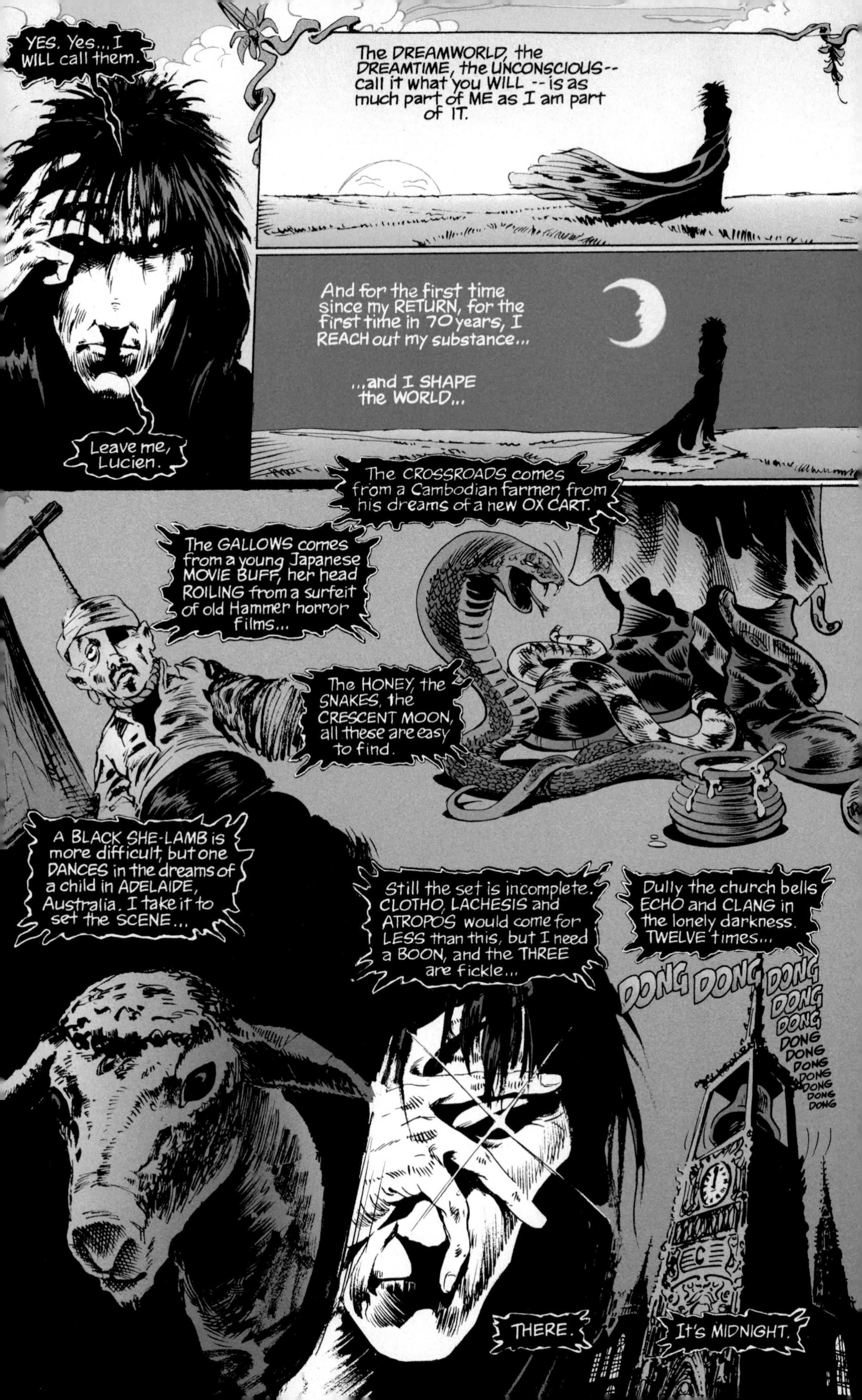
YES. Yes... I WILL call them.
The DREAMWORLD, the DREAMTIME, the UNCONSCIOUS-- call it what you WILL --is as much part of ME as I am part of IT.
And for the first time since my RETURN, for the first time in 70 years, I REACH out my substance...
...and I SHAPE the WORLD...
Leave me, Lucien.
The CROSSROADS comes from a Cambodian farmer, from his dreams of a new OX CART.
The GALLOWS comes from a young Japanese MOVIE BUFF, her head ROILING from a surfeit of old Hammer horror films...
The HONEY, the SNAKES, the CRESCENT MOON, all these are easy to find.
A BLACK SHE-LAMB is more difficult, but one DANCES in the dreams of a child in ADELAIDE, Australia. I take it to set the SCENE...
Still the set is incomplete. CLOTHO, LACHESIS and ATROPOS would come for LESS than this, but I need a BOON, and the THREE are fickle...
Dully the church bells ECHO and CLANG in the lonely darkness. TWELVE times...
DONG DONG DONG DONG DONG DONG DONG DONG DONG DONG DONG DONG
THERE.
It's MIDNIGHT.

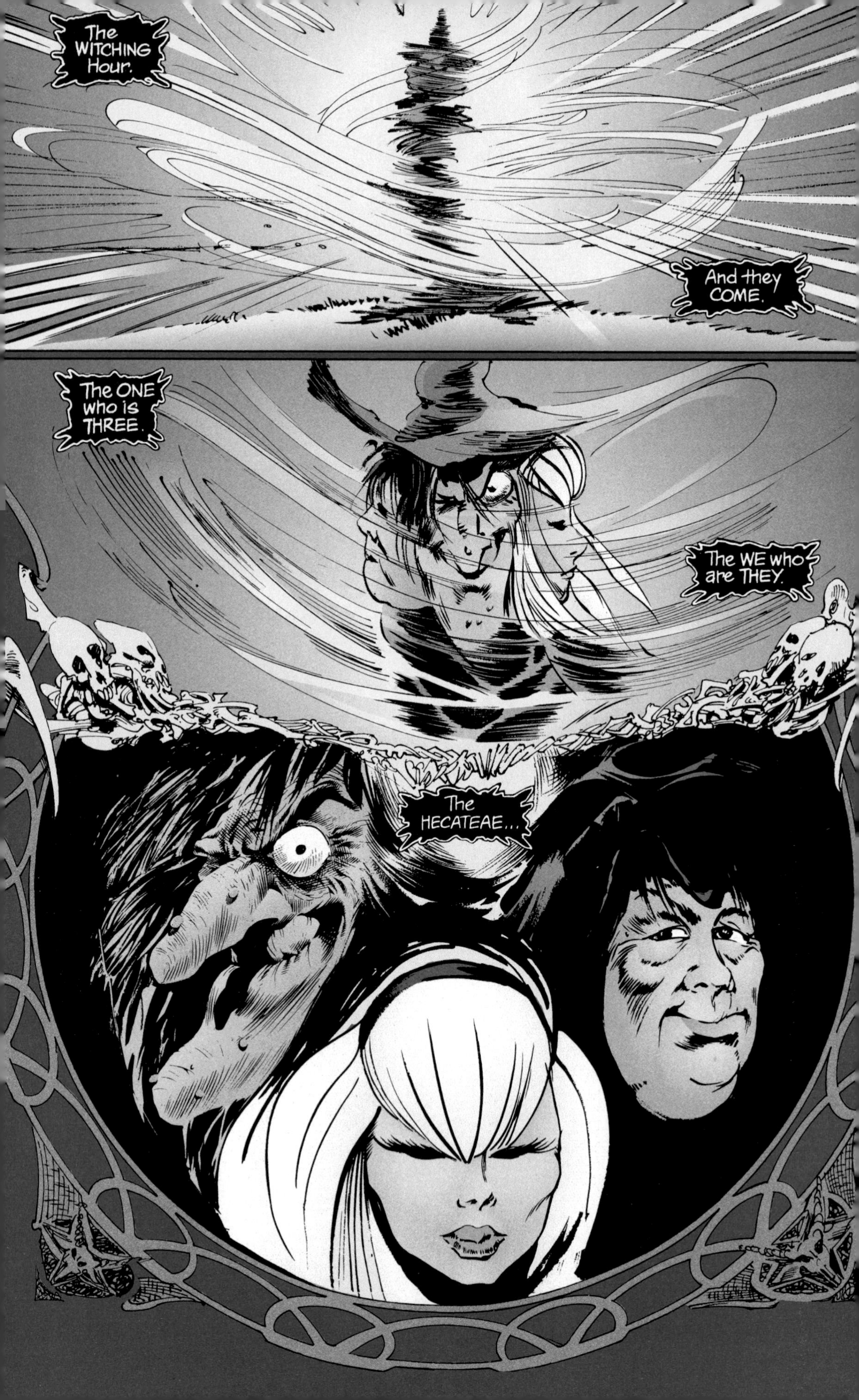
The WITCHING Hour.
And they COME.
The ONE who is THREE.
The WE who are THEY.
The HECATEAE...

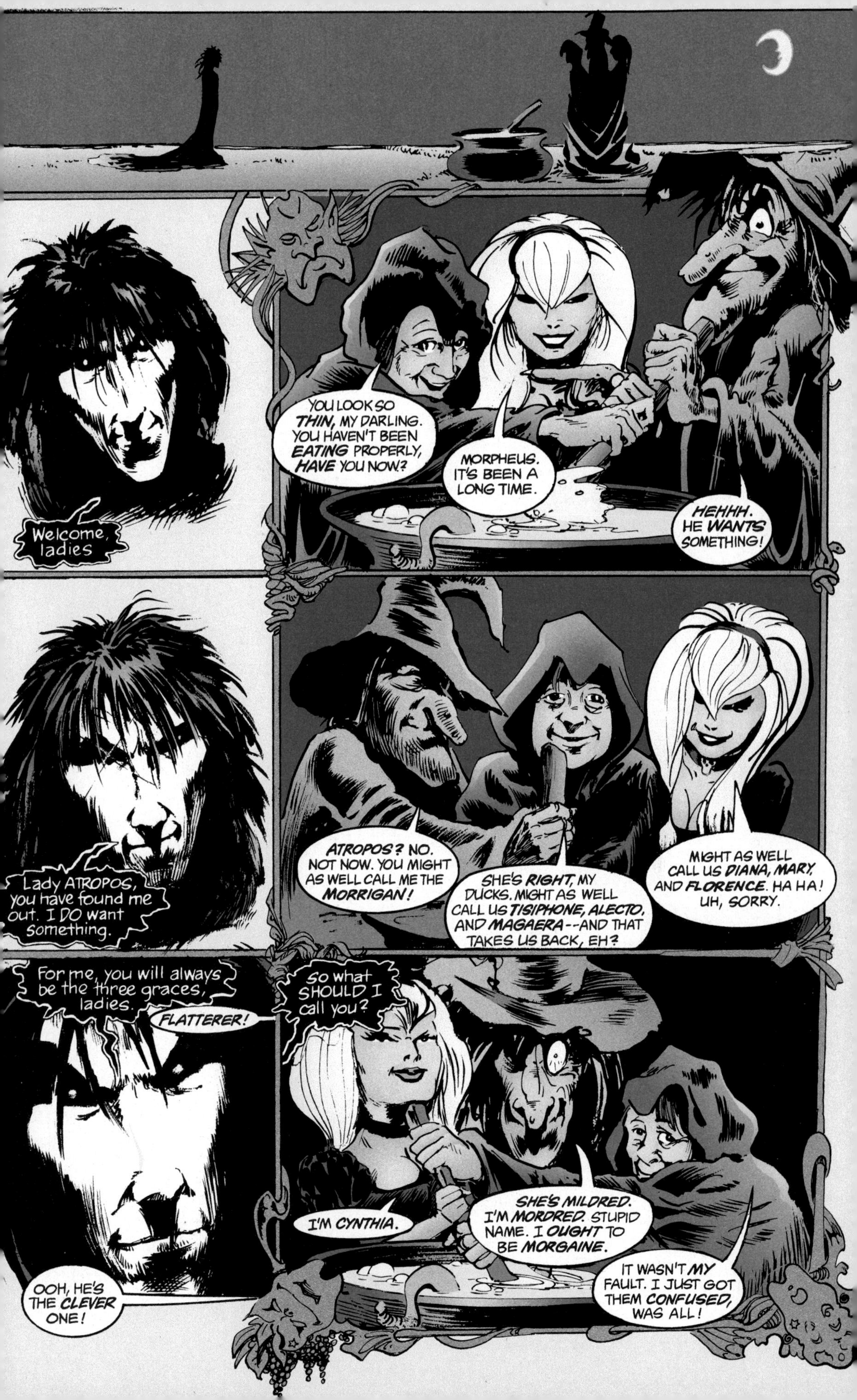

Welcome, ladies
YOU LOOK SO THIN, MY DARLING. YOU HAVEN'T BEEN EATING PROPERLY, HAVE YOU NOW?
MORPHEUS. IT'S BEEN A LONG TIME.
HEHHH. HE WANTS SOMETHING!
Lady ATROPOS, you have found me out. I DO want something.
ATROPOS? NO. NOT NOW. YOU MIGHT AS WELL CALL ME THE MORRIGAN!
SHE'S RIGHT, MY DUCKS. MIGHT AS WELL CALL US TISIPHONE, ALECTO, AND MAGAERA--AND THAT TAKES US BACK, EH?
MIGHT AS WELL CALL US DIANA, MARY, AND FLORENCE. HA HA! UH, SORRY.
For me, you will always be the three graces, ladies.
FLATTERER!
So what SHOULD I call you?
I'M CYNTHIA.
SHE'S MILDRED. I'M MORDRED. STUPID NAME. I OUGHT TO BE MORGAINE.
IT WASN'T MY FAULT. I JUST GOT THEM CONFUSED, WAS ALL!
OOH, HE'S THE CLEVER ONE!

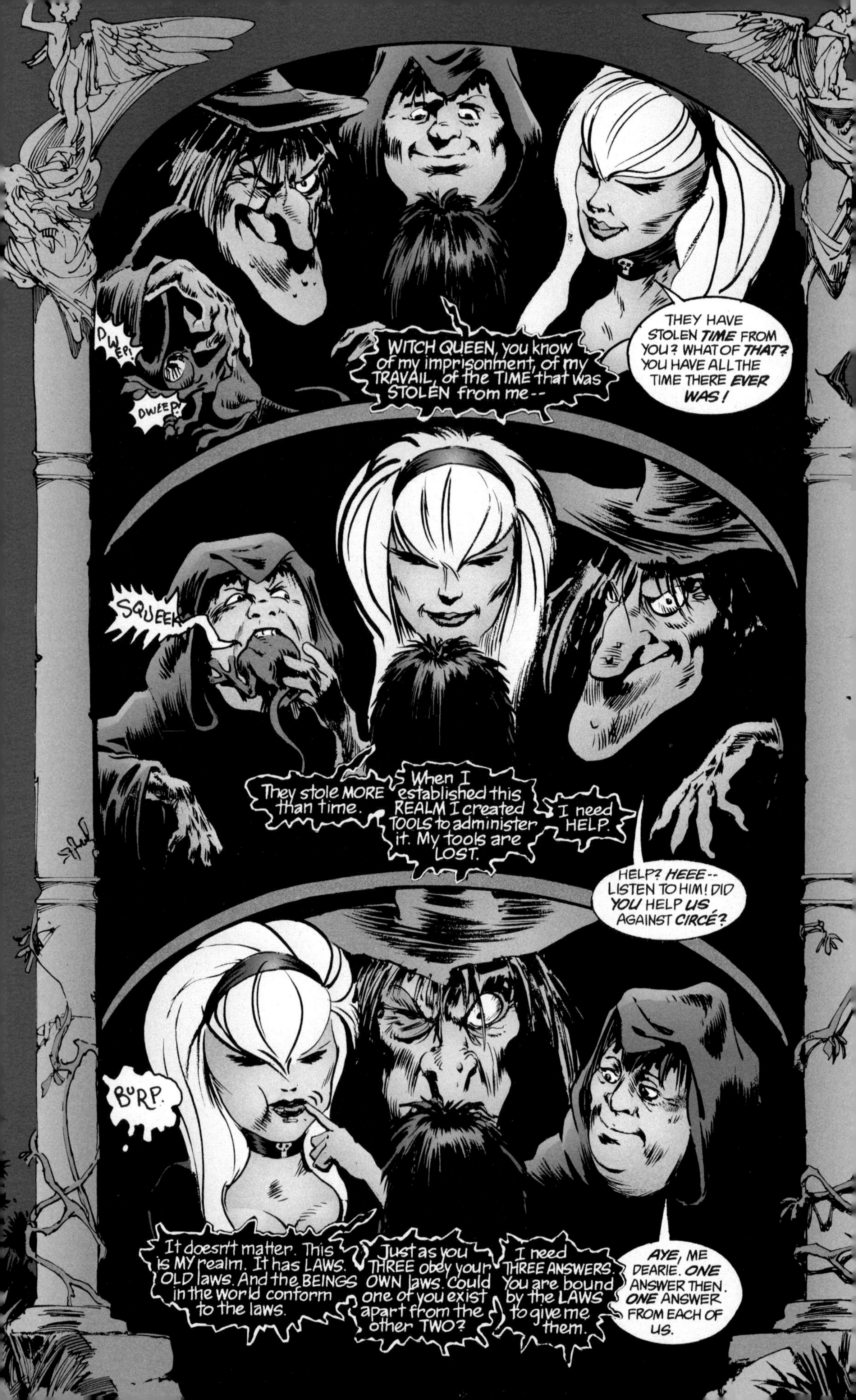
DWEEP!
DWEEP!
WITCH QUEEN, you know of my imprisonment, of my TRAVAIL, of the TIME that was STOLEN from me--
THEY HAVE STOLEN TIME FROM YOU? WHAT OF THAT? YOU HAVE ALL THE TIME THERE EVER WAS!
SQUEEK
They stole MORE than time.
When I established this REALM I created TOOLS to administer it. My tools are LOST.
I need HELP.
HELP? HEEE-- LISTEN TO HIM! DID YOU HELP US AGAINST CIRCÉ?
BURP.
It doesn't matter. This is MY realm. It has LAWS. OLD laws. And the BEINGS in the world conform to the laws.
Just as you THREE obey your OWN laws. Could one of you exist apart from the other TWO?
I need THREE ANSWERS. You are bound by the LAWS to give me them.
AYE, ME DEARIE. ONE ANSWER THEN. ONE ANSWER FROM EACH OF US.

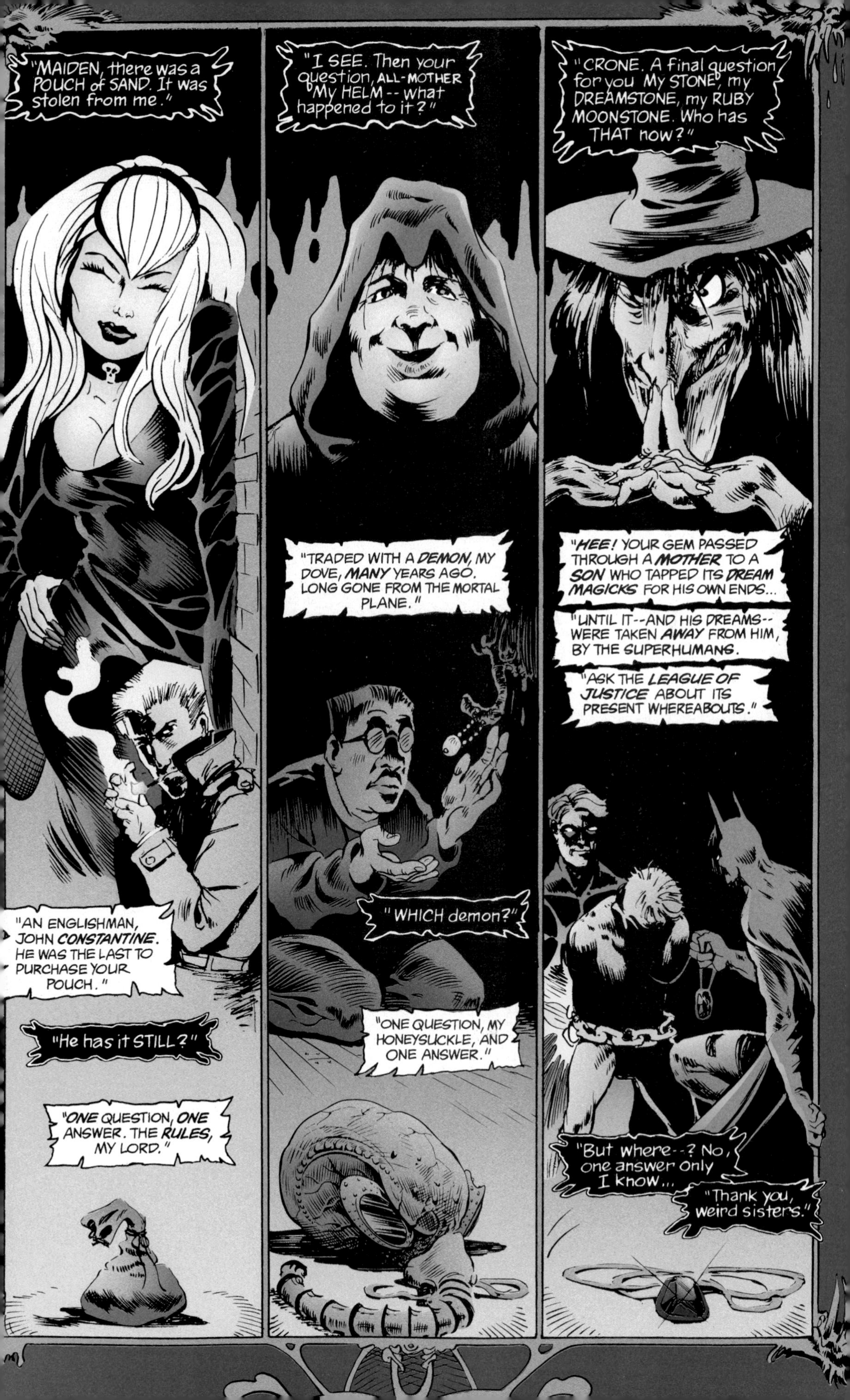
"MAIDEN, there was a POUCH of SAND. It was stolen from me."
"AN ENGLISHMAN, JOHN CONSTANTINE. HE WAS THE LAST TO PURCHASE YOUR POUCH."
"He has it STILL?"
"ONE QUESTION, ONE ANSWER. THE RULES, MY LORD."
"I SEE. Then your question, ALL-MOTHER My HELM -- what happened to it?"
"TRADED WITH A DEMON, MY DOVE, MANY YEARS AGO. LONG GONE FROM THE MORTAL PLANE."
"WHICH demon?"
"ONE QUESTION, MY HONEYSUCKLE, AND ONE ANSWER."
"CRONE. A final question for you My STONE, my DREAMSTONE, my RUBY MOONSTONE. Who has THAT now?"
"HEE! YOUR GEM PASSED THROUGH A MOTHER TO A SON WHO TAPPED ITS DREAM MAGICKS FOR HIS OWN ENDS...
"UNTIL IT--AND HIS DREAMS--WERE TAKEN AWAY FROM HIM, BY THE SUPERHUMANS.
"ASK THE LEAGUE OF JUSTICE ABOUT ITS PRESENT WHEREABOUTS."
"But where--? No, one answer only I know...
"Thank you, weird sisters."

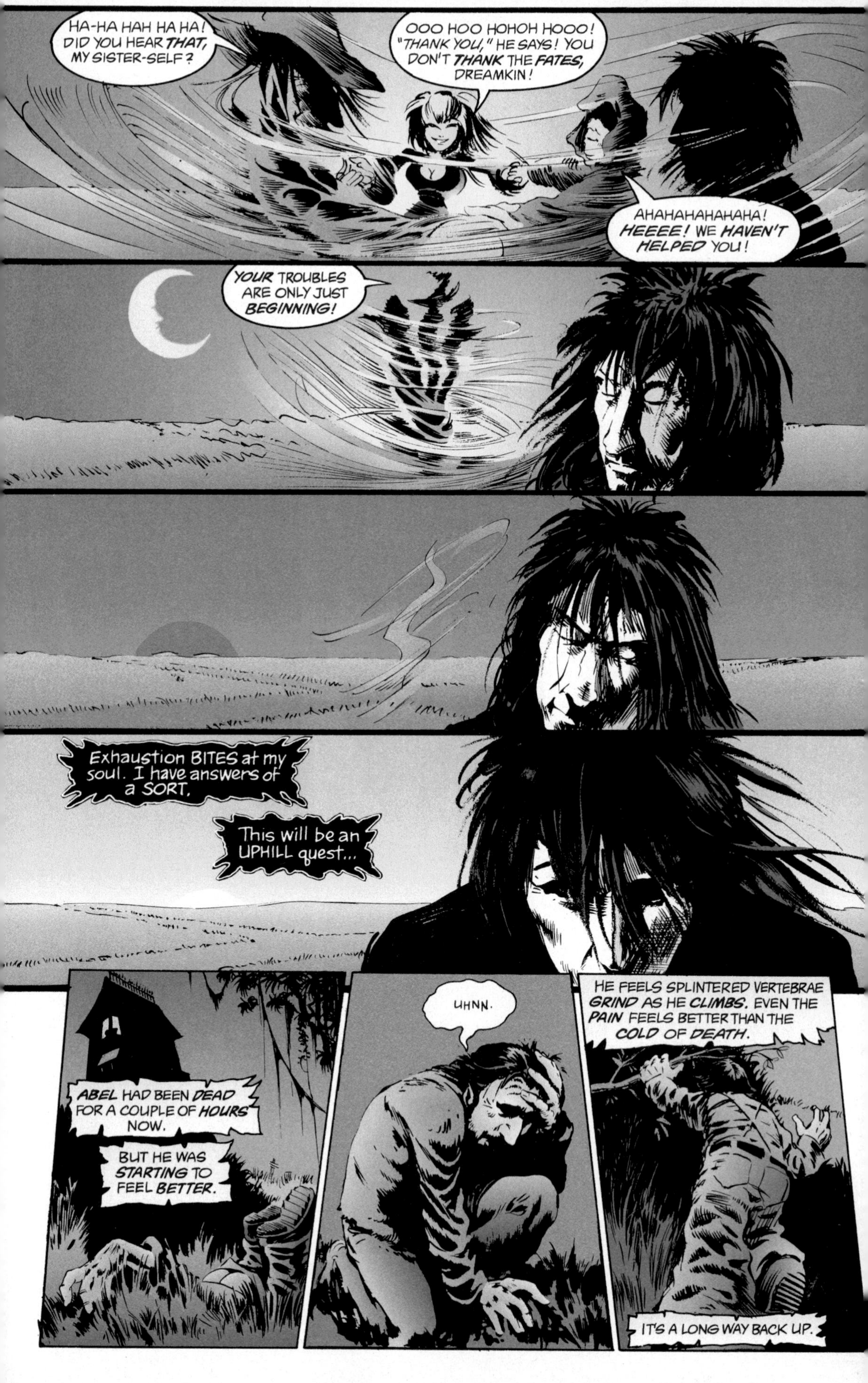
HA-HA HAH HA HA! DID YOU HEAR THAT, MY SISTER-SELF?
OOO HOO HOHOH HOOO! "THANK YOU," HE SAYS! YOU DON'T THANK THE FATES, DREAMKIN!
AHAHAHAHAHAHA! HEEEE! WE HAVEN'T HELPED YOU!
YOUR TROUBLES ARE ONLY JUST BEGINNING!
Exhaustion BITES at my soul. I have answers of a SORT.
This will be an UPHILL quest...
ABEL HAD BEEN DEAD FOR A COUPLE OF HOURS NOW.
BUT HE WAS STARTING TO FEEL BETTER.
UHNN.
HE FEELS SPLINTERED VERTEBRAE GRIND AS HE CLIMBS. EVEN THE PAIN FEELS BETTER THAN THE COLD OF DEATH.
IT'S A LONG WAY BACK UP.

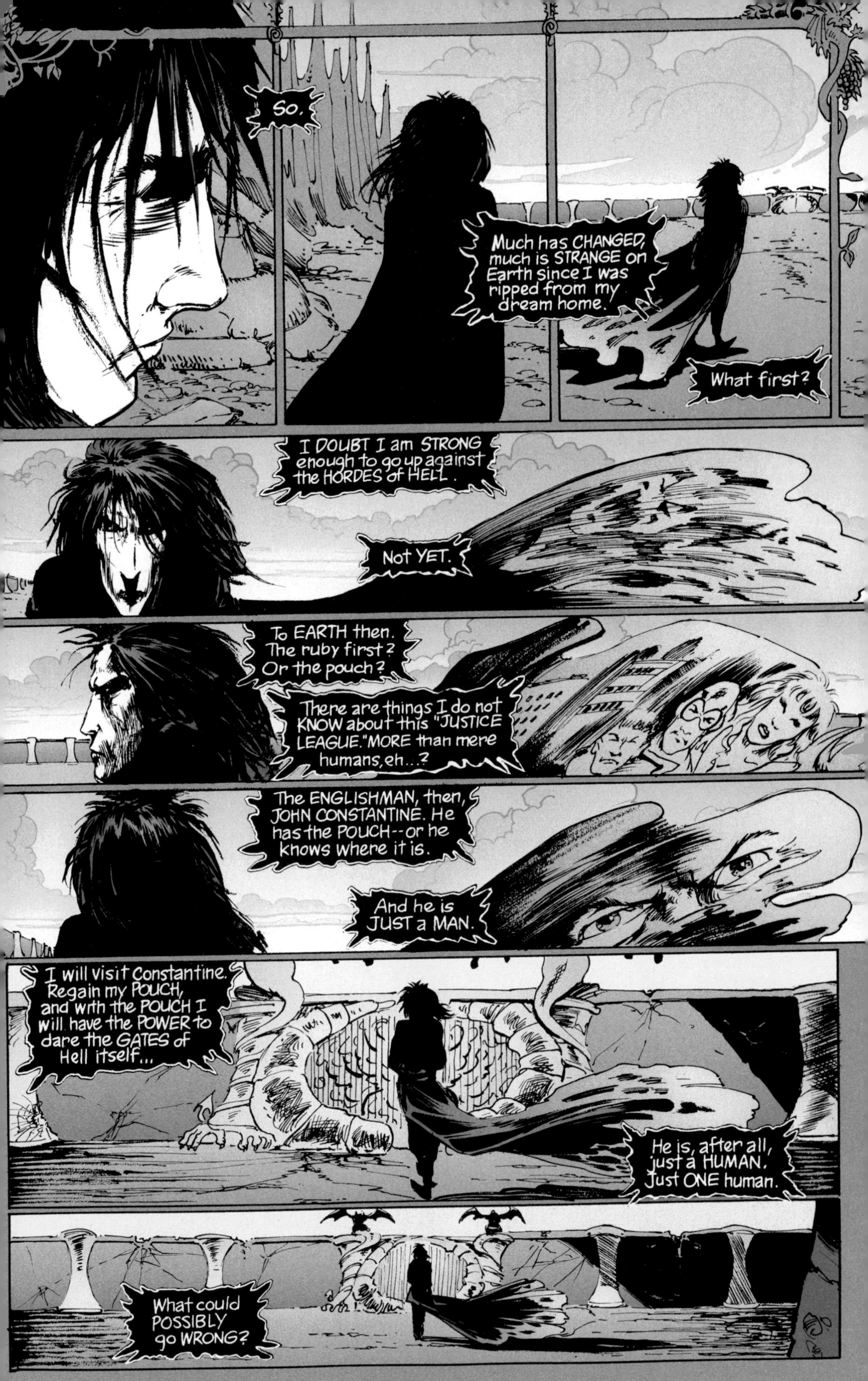
So.
Much has CHANGED, much is STRANGE on Earth since I was ripped from my dream home.
What first?
I DOUBT I am STRONG enough to go up against the HORDES of HELL.
Not YET.
To EARTH then. The ruby first? Or the pouch?
There are things I do not KNOW about this "JUSTICE LEAGUE." MORE than mere humans, eh...?
The ENGLISHMAN, then, JOHN CONSTANTINE. He has the POUCH--or he knows where it is.
And he is JUST a MAN.
I will visit Constantine. Regain my POUCH, and with the POUCH I will have the POWER to dare the GATES of Hell itself...
He is, after all, just a HUMAN. Just ONE human.
What could POSSIBLY go WRONG?

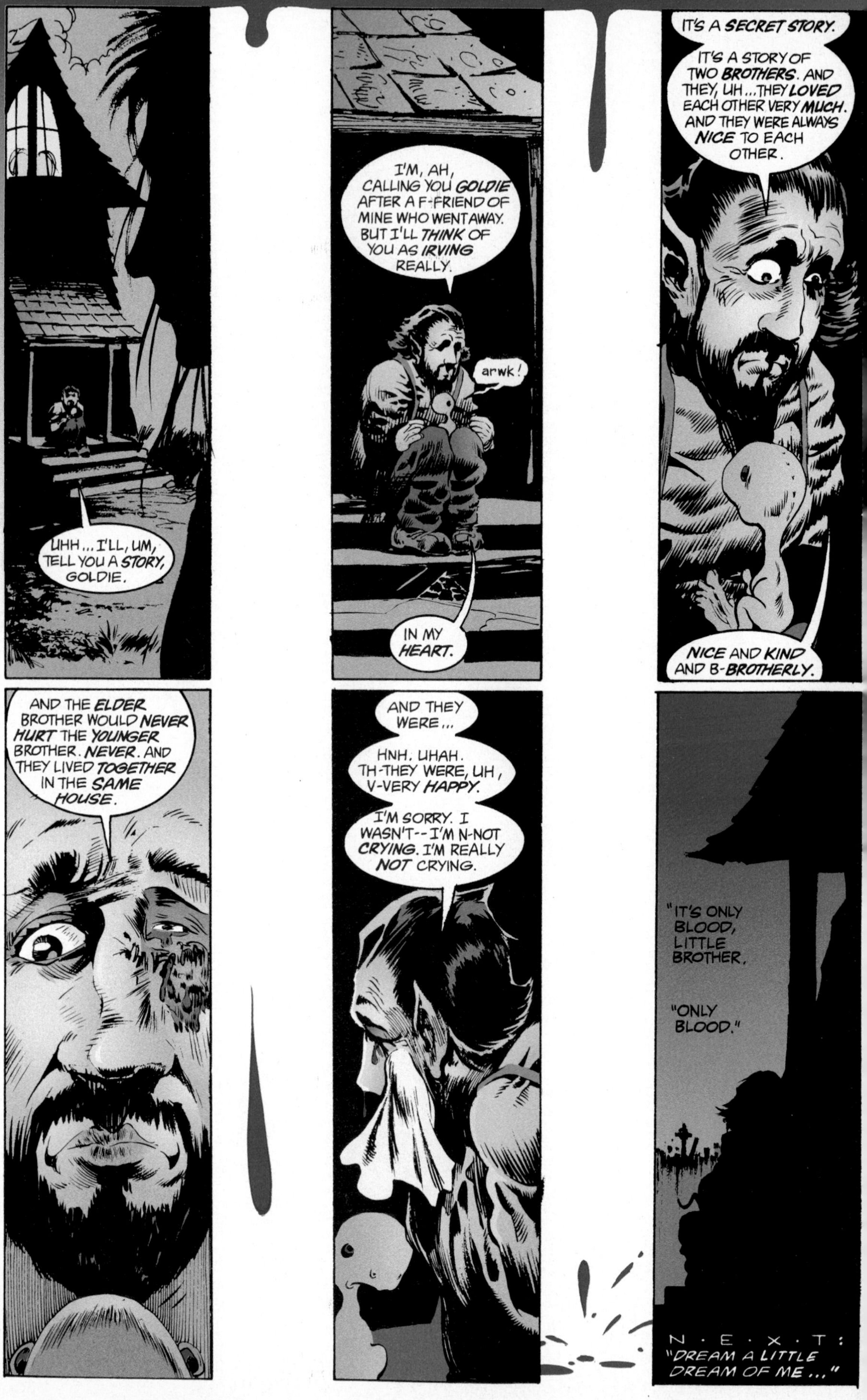
UHH... I'LL, UM, TELL YOU A STORY, GOLDIE.
I'M, AH, CALLING YOU GOLDIE AFTER A F-FRIEND OF MINE WHO WENT AWAY. BUT I'LL THINK OF YOU AS IRVING REALLY.
arwk!
IN MY HEART.
IT'S A SECRET STORY.
IT'S A STORY OF TWO BROTHERS. AND THEY, UH... THEY LOVED EACH OTHER VERY MUCH. AND THEY WERE ALWAYS NICE TO EACH OTHER.
NICE AND KIND AND B-BROTHERLY.
AND THE ELDER BROTHER WOULD NEVER HURT THE YOUNGER BROTHER. NEVER. AND THEY LIVED TOGETHER IN THE SAME HOUSE.
AND THEY WERE...
HNH. UHAH. TH-THEY WERE, UH, V-VERY HAPPY.
I'M SORRY. I WASN'T-- I'M N-NOT CRYING. I'M REALLY NOT CRYING.
"IT'S ONLY BLOOD, LITTLE BROTHER.
"ONLY BLOOD."
N·E·X·T: "DREAM A LITTLE DREAM OF ME..."

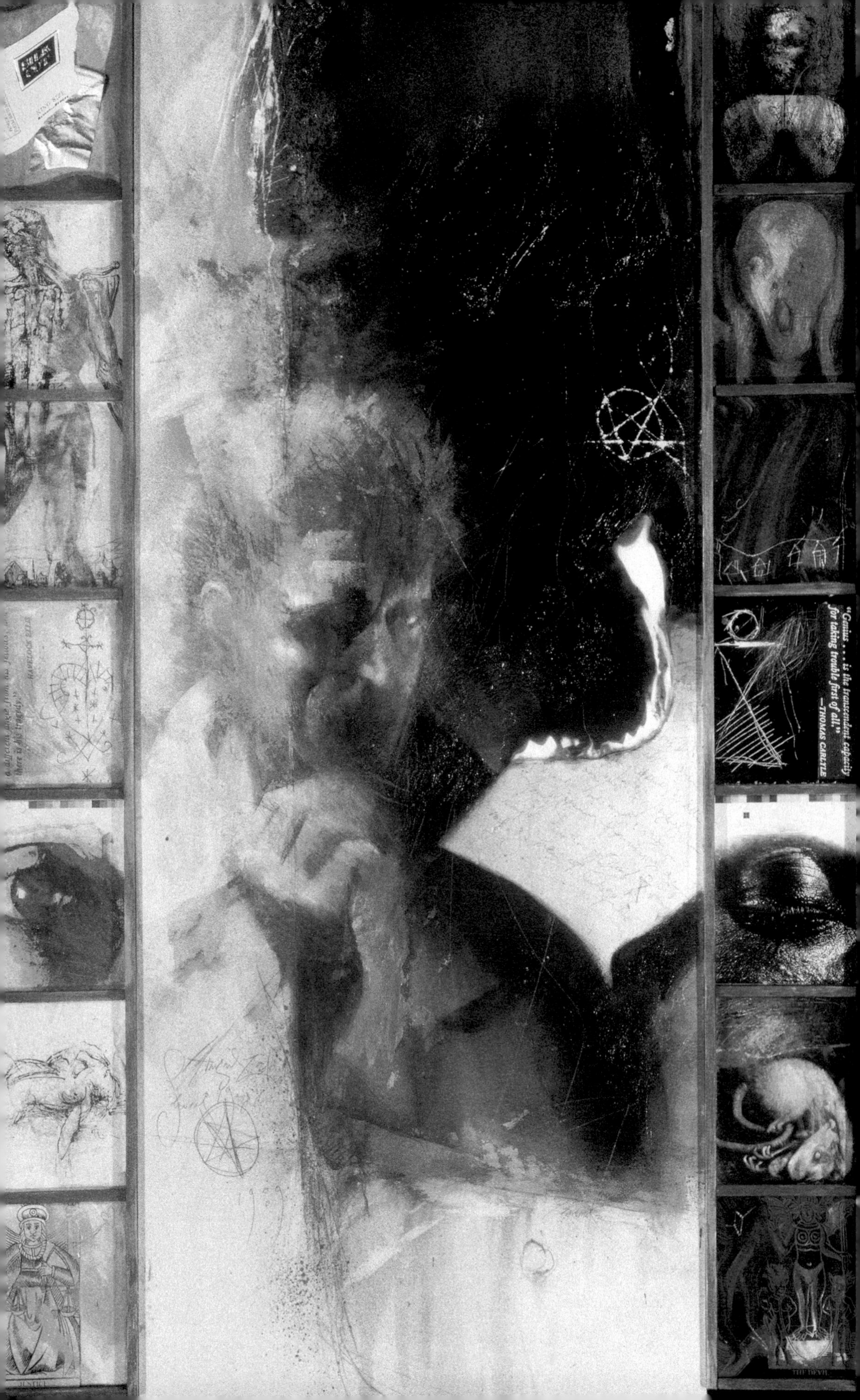
"Genius . . . is the transcendent capacity for taking trouble first of all."
—THOMAS CARLYLE

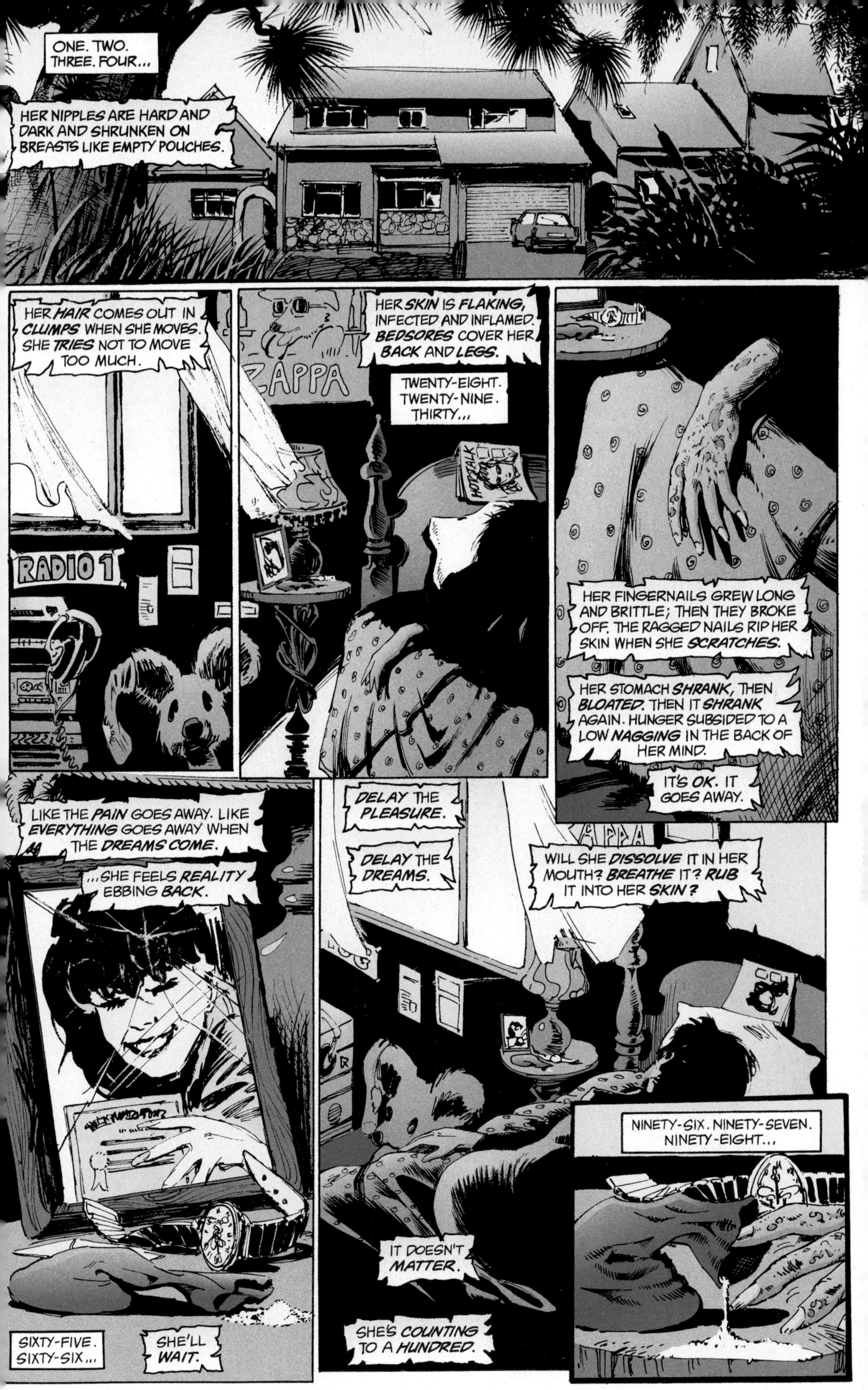

ONE. TWO. THREE. FOUR...
HER NIPPLES ARE HARD AND DARK AND SHRUNKEN ON BREASTS LIKE EMPTY POUCHES.
HER HAIR COMES OUT IN CLUMPS WHEN SHE MOVES. SHE TRIES NOT TO MOVE TOO MUCH.
RADIO 1
HER SKIN IS FLAKING, INFECTED AND INFLAMED. BEDSORES COVER HER BACK AND LEGS.
ZAPPA
TWENTY-EIGHT. TWENTY-NINE. THIRTY...
HER FINGERNAILS GREW LONG AND BRITTLE; THEN THEY BROKE OFF. THE RAGGED NAILS RIP HER SKIN WHEN SHE SCRATCHES.
HER STOMACH SHRANK, THEN BLOATED. THEN IT SHRANK AGAIN. HUNGER SUBSIDED TO A LOW NAGGING IN THE BACK OF HER MIND.
IT'S OK. IT GOES AWAY.
LIKE THE PAIN GOES AWAY. LIKE EVERYTHING GOES AWAY WHEN THE DREAMS COME.
...SHE FEELS REALITY EBBING BACK.
SIXTY-FIVE. SIXTY-SIX...
SHE'LL WAIT.
DELAY THE PLEASURE.
DELAY THE DREAMS.
WILL SHE DISSOLVE IT IN HER MOUTH? BREATHE IT? RUB IT INTO HER SKIN?
IT DOESN'T MATTER.
SHE'S COUNTING TO A HUNDRED.
NINETY-SIX. NINETY-SEVEN. NINETY-EIGHT...

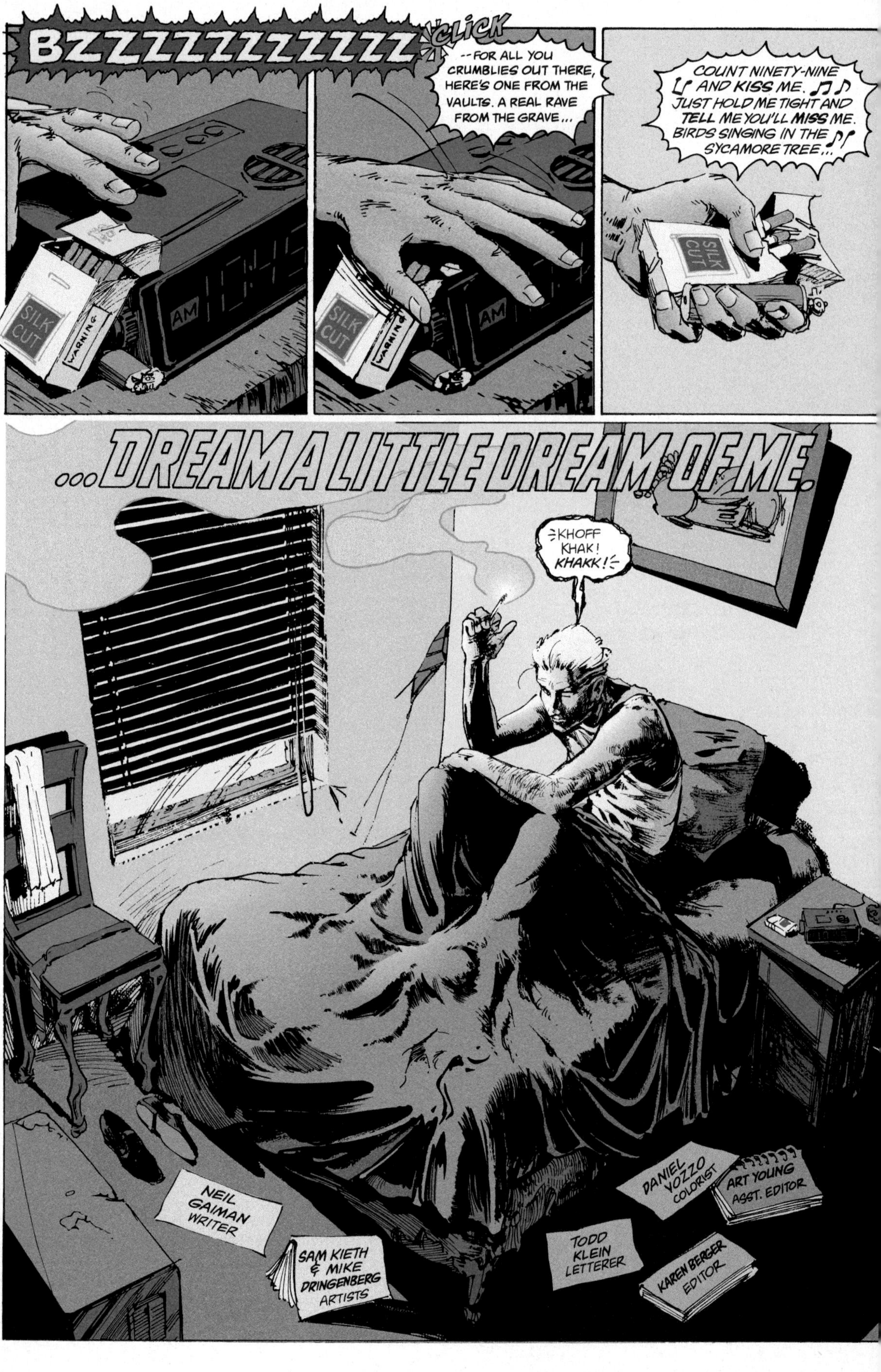
BZZZZZZZZZZZZ
CLICK
--FOR ALL YOU CRUMBLIES OUT THERE, HERE'S ONE FROM THE VAULTS. A REAL RAVE FROM THE GRAVE...
COUNT NINETY-NINE AND KISS ME. JUST HOLD ME TIGHT AND TELL ME YOU'LL MISS ME. BIRDS SINGING IN THE SYCAMORE TREE...
...DREAM A LITTLE DREAM OF ME.
KHOFF KHAK! KHAKK!
NEIL GAIMAN WRITER
SAM KIETH & MIKE DRINGENBERG ARTISTS
DANIEL VOZZO COLORIST
TODD KLEIN LETTERER
ART YOUNG ASST. EDITOR
KAREN BERGER EDITOR

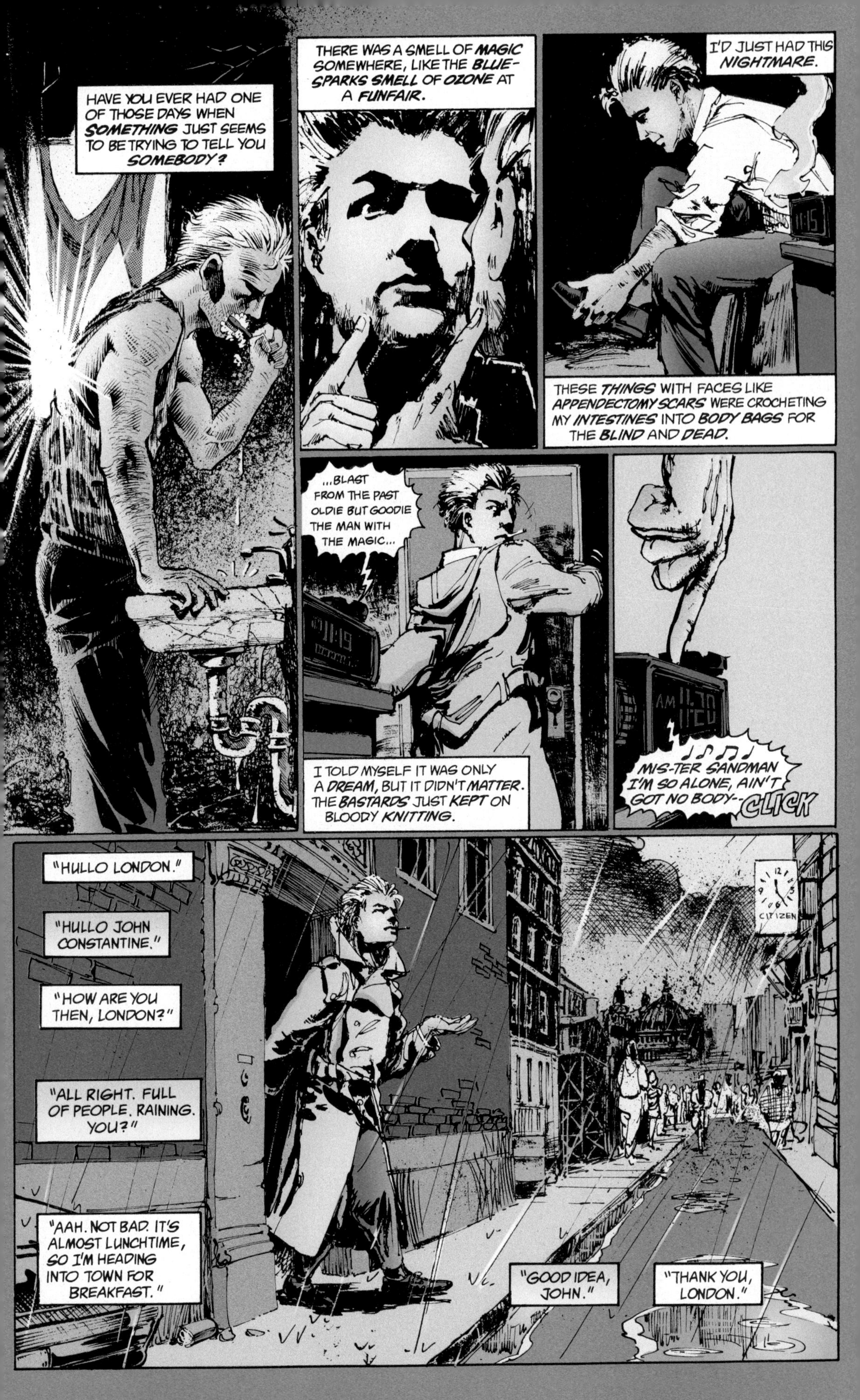
HAVE YOU EVER HAD ONE OF THOSE DAYS WHEN SOMETHING JUST SEEMS TO BE TRYING TO TELL YOU SOMEBODY?
THERE WAS A SMELL OF MAGIC SOMEWHERE, LIKE THE BLUE-SPARKS SMELL OF OZONE AT A FUNFAIR.
I'D JUST HAD THIS NIGHTMARE.
THESE THINGS WITH FACES LIKE APPENDECTOMY SCARS WERE CROCHETING MY INTESTINES INTO BODY BAGS FOR THE BLIND AND DEAD.
...BLAST FROM THE PAST OLDIE BUT GOODIE THE MAN WITH THE MAGIC...
I TOLD MYSELF IT WAS ONLY A DREAM, BUT IT DIDN'T MATTER. THE BASTARDS JUST KEPT ON BLOODY KNITTING.
AM 11:20
MIS-TER SANDMAN I'M SO ALONE, AIN'T GOT NO BODY--
CLICK
"HULLO LONDON."
"HULLO JOHN CONSTANTINE."
"HOW ARE YOU THEN, LONDON?"
"ALL RIGHT. FULL OF PEOPLE. RAINING. YOU?"
"AAH. NOT BAD. IT'S ALMOST LUNCHTIME, SO I'M HEADING INTO TOWN FOR BREAKFAST."
CITIZEN
"GOOD IDEA, JOHN."
"THANK YOU, LONDON."

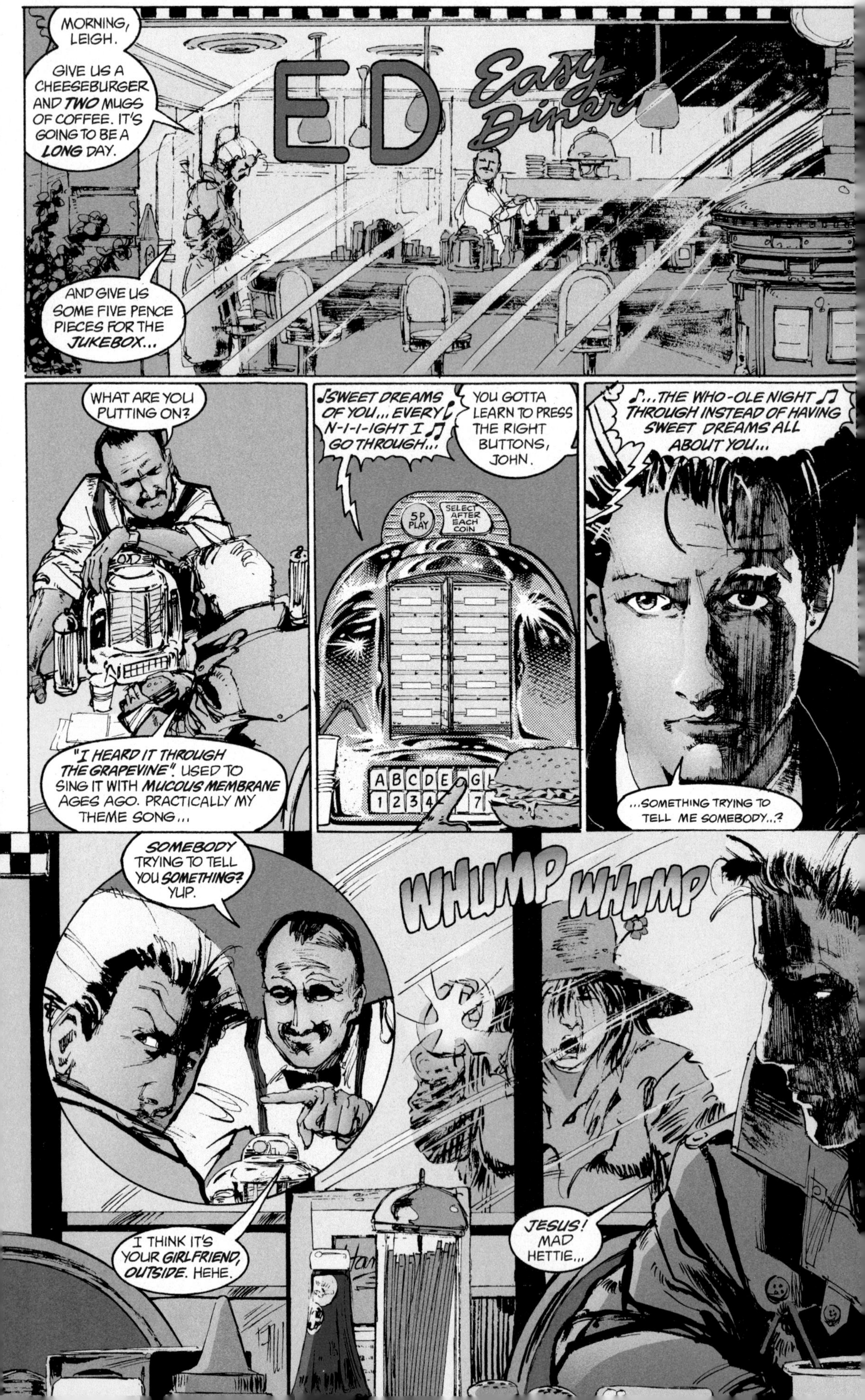
MORNING, LEIGH.
GIVE US A CHEESEBURGER AND TWO MUGS OF COFFEE. IT'S GOING TO BE A LONG DAY.
ED
Easy Diner
AND GIVE US SOME FIVE PENCE PIECES FOR THE JUKEBOX...
WHAT ARE YOU PUTTING ON?
"I HEARD IT THROUGH THE GRAPEVINE". USED TO SING IT WITH MUCOUS MEMBRANE AGES AGO. PRACTICALLY MY THEME SONG...
♪SWEET DREAMS OF YOU... EVERY N-I-I-IGHT I GO THROUGH...♪
YOU GOTTA LEARN TO PRESS THE RIGHT BUTTONS, JOHN.
5P PLAY
SELECT AFTER EACH COIN
♪...THE WHO-OLE NIGHT THROUGH INSTEAD OF HAVING SWEET DREAMS ALL ABOUT YOU...♪
...SOMETHING TRYING TO TELL ME SOMEBODY...?
SOMEBODY TRYING TO TELL YOU SOMETHING? YUP.
I THINK IT'S YOUR GIRLFRIEND, OUTSIDE. HEHE.
WHUMP WHUMP
JESUS! MAD HETTIE...

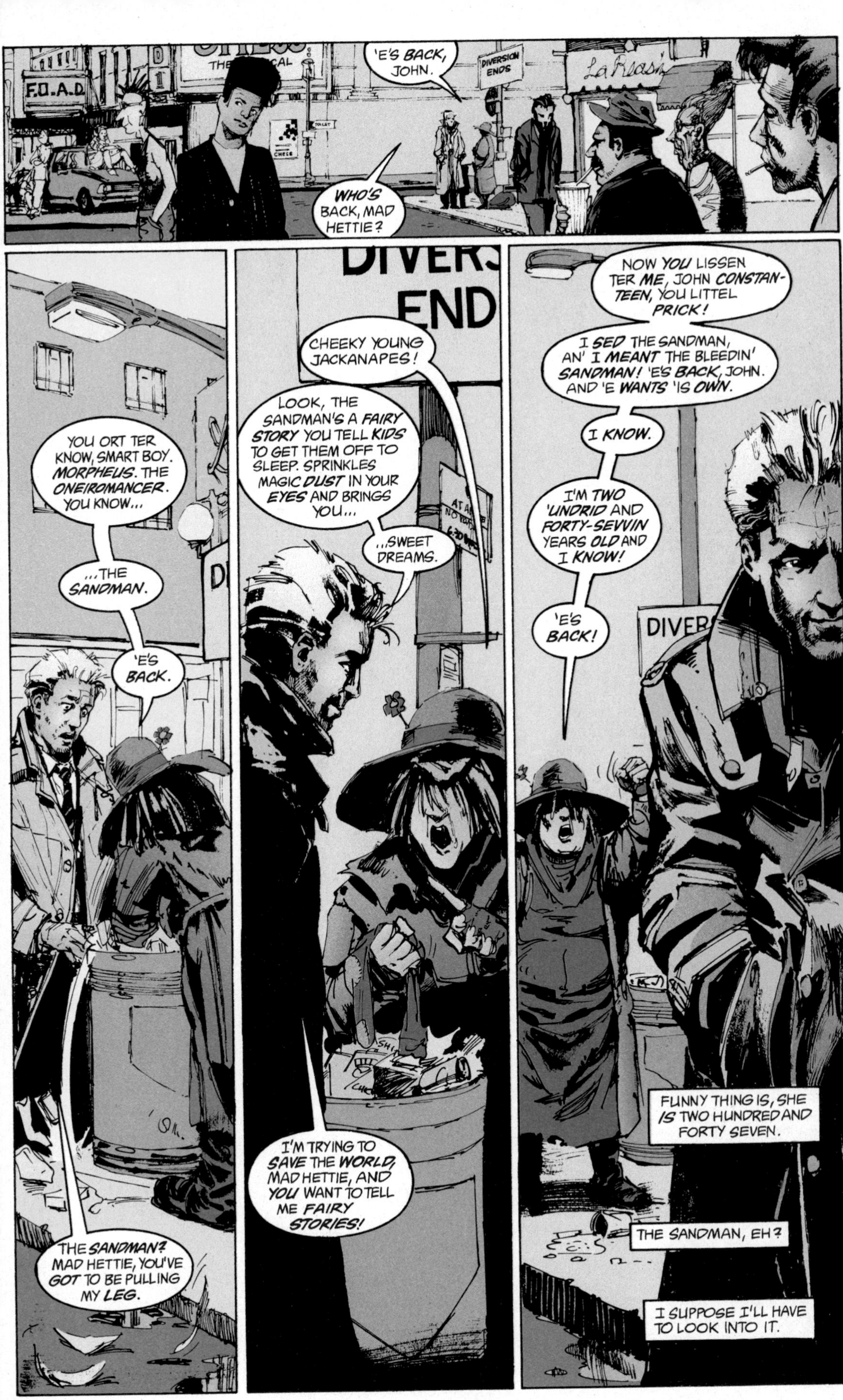
F.O.A.D
DIVERSION ENDS
'E'S BACK, JOHN.
WHO'S BACK, MAD HETTIE?
YOU ORT TER KNOW, SMART BOY. MORPHEUS. THE ONEIROMANCER. YOU KNOW...
...THE SANDMAN.
'E'S BACK.
THE SANDMAN? MAD HETTIE, YOU'VE GOT TO BE PULLING MY LEG.
CHEEKY YOUNG JACKANAPES!
LOOK, THE SANDMAN'S A FAIRY STORY YOU TELL KIDS TO GET THEM OFF TO SLEEP. SPRINKLES MAGIC DUST IN YOUR EYES AND BRINGS YOU...
...SWEET DREAMS.
I'M TRYING TO SAVE THE WORLD, MAD HETTIE, AND YOU WANT TO TELL ME FAIRY STORIES!
NOW YOU LISSEN TER ME, JOHN CONSTAN-TEEN, YOU LITTEL PRICK!
I SED THE SANDMAN, AN' I MEANT THE BLEEDIN' SANDMAN! 'E'S BACK, JOHN. AND 'E WANTS 'IS OWN.
I KNOW.
I'M TWO 'UNDRID AND FORTY-SEVVIN YEARS OLD AND I KNOW!
'E'S BACK!
FUNNY THING IS, SHE IS TWO HUNDRED AND FORTY SEVEN.
THE SANDMAN, EH?
I SUPPOSE I'LL HAVE TO LOOK INTO IT.

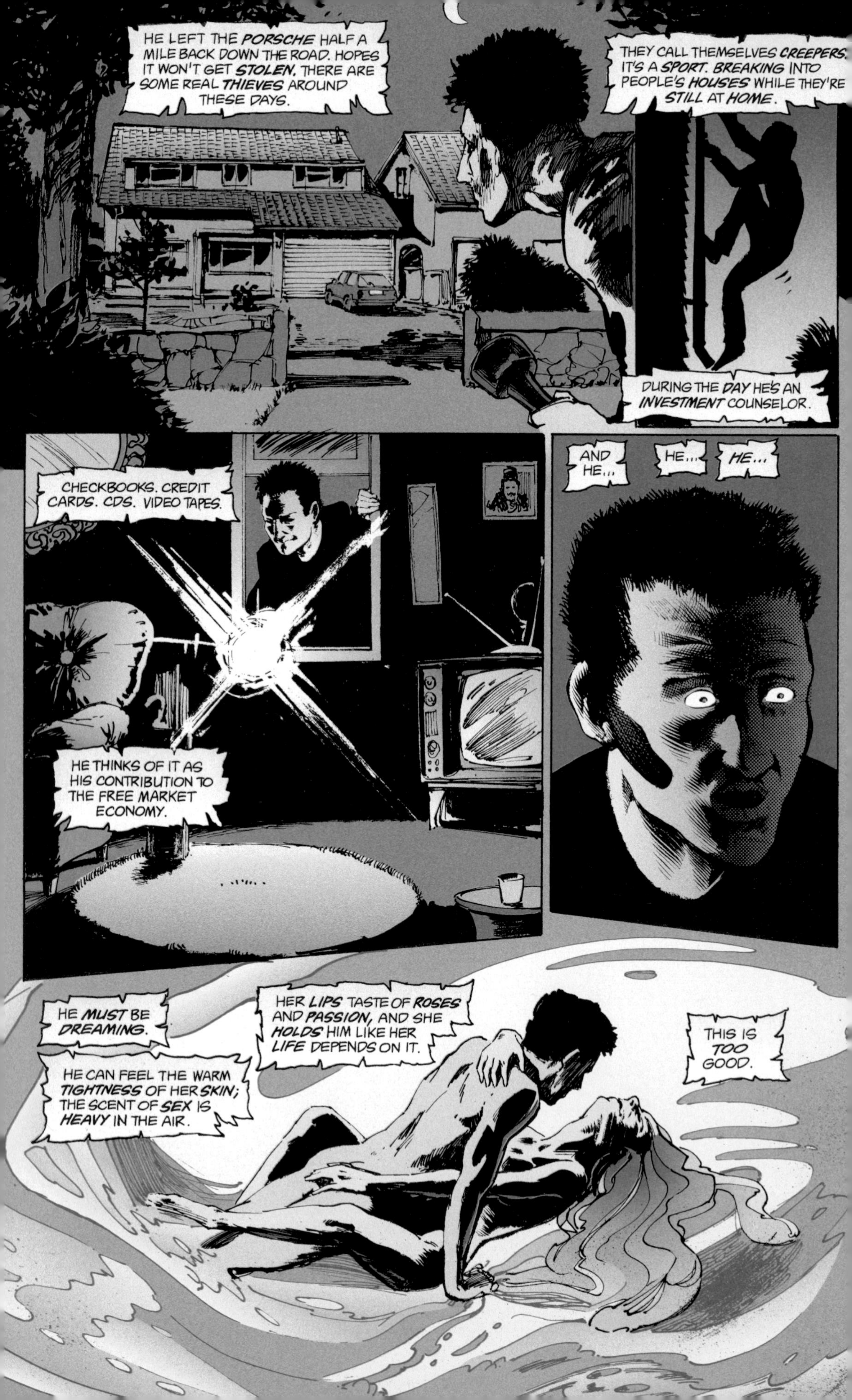

HE LEFT THE PORSCHE HALF A MILE BACK DOWN THE ROAD. HOPES IT WON'T GET STOLEN. THERE ARE SOME REAL THIEVES AROUND THESE DAYS.
THEY CALL THEMSELVES CREEPERS. IT'S A SPORT. BREAKING INTO PEOPLE'S HOUSES WHILE THEY'RE STILL AT HOME.
DURING THE DAY HE'S AN INVESTMENT COUNSELOR.
CHECKBOOKS. CREDIT CARDS. CDS. VIDEO TAPES.
HE THINKS OF IT AS HIS CONTRIBUTION TO THE FREE MARKET ECONOMY.
AND HE...
HE...
HE...
HE MUST BE DREAMING.
HER LIPS TASTE OF ROSES AND PASSION, AND SHE HOLDS HIM LIKE HER LIFE DEPENDS ON IT.
THIS IS TOO GOOD.
HE CAN FEEL THE WARM TIGHTNESS OF HER SKIN; THE SCENT OF SEX IS HEAVY IN THE AIR.

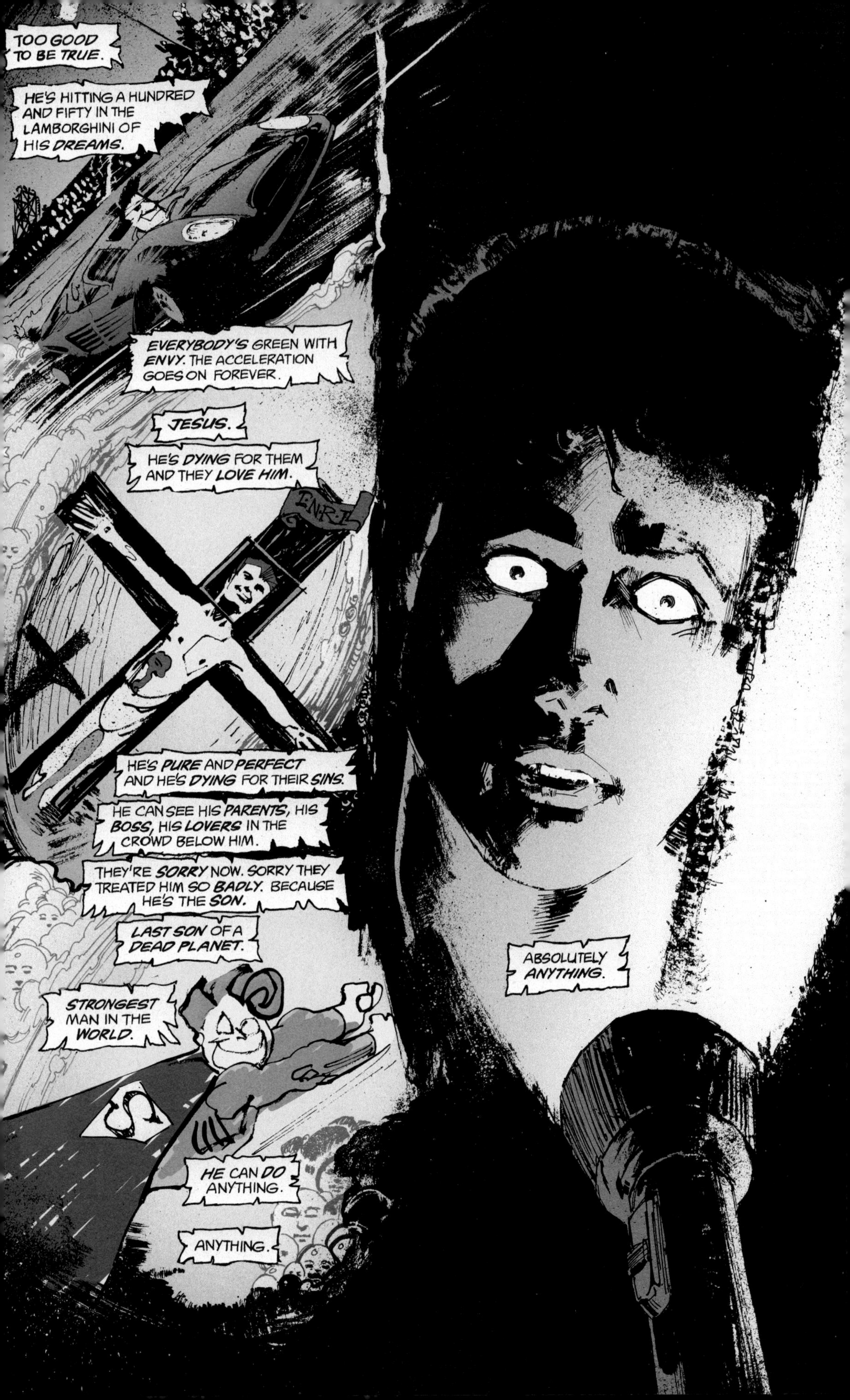
TOO GOOD TO BE TRUE.
HE'S HITTING A HUNDRED AND FIFTY IN THE LAMBORGHINI OF HIS DREAMS.
EVERYBODY'S GREEN WITH ENVY. THE ACCELERATION GOES ON FOREVER.
JESUS.
HE'S DYING FOR THEM AND THEY LOVE HIM.
I.N.R.I.
HE'S PURE AND PERFECT AND HE'S DYING FOR THEIR SINS.
HE CAN SEE HIS PARENTS, HIS BOSS, HIS LOVERS IN THE CROWD BELOW HIM.
THEY'RE SORRY NOW. SORRY THEY TREATED HIM SO BADLY. BECAUSE HE'S THE SON.
LAST SON OF A DEAD PLANET.
STRONGEST MAN IN THE WORLD.
HE CAN DO ANYTHING.
ANYTHING.
ABSOLUTELY ANYTHING.

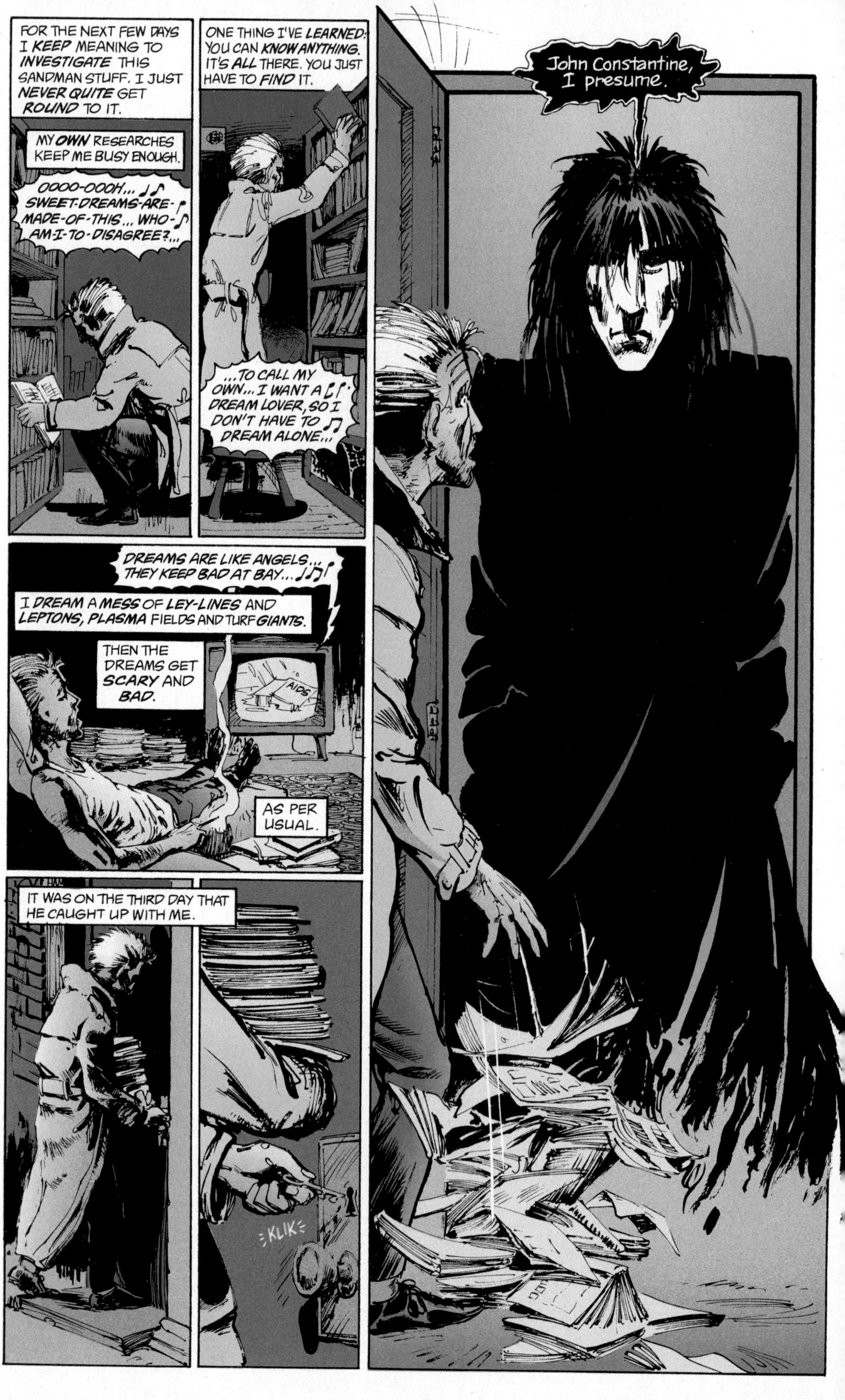
FOR THE NEXT FEW DAYS I KEEP MEANING TO INVESTIGATE THIS SANDMAN STUFF. I JUST NEVER QUITE GET ROUND TO IT.
MY OWN RESEARCHES KEEP ME BUSY ENOUGH.
OOOO-OOOH... SWEET-DREAMS-ARE-MADE-OF-THIS... WHO-AM-I-TO-DISAGREE?...
ONE THING I'VE LEARNED: YOU CAN KNOW ANYTHING. IT'S ALL THERE. YOU JUST HAVE TO FIND IT.
...TO CALL MY OWN... I WANT A DREAM LOVER, SO I DON'T HAVE TO DREAM ALONE...
DREAMS ARE LIKE ANGELS... THEY KEEP BAD AT BAY...
I DREAM A MESS OF LEY-LINES AND LEPTONS, PLASMA FIELDS AND TURF GIANTS.
THEN THE DREAMS GET SCARY AND BAD.
AIDS
AS PER USUAL.
IT WAS ON THE THIRD DAY THAT HE CAUGHT UP WITH ME.
KLIK
John Constantine, I presume.

WELL, I'M *NOT* DOCTOR *LIVINGSTONE*, PAL. HEH.

SORRY. LITTLE JOKE.

VERY LITTLE.

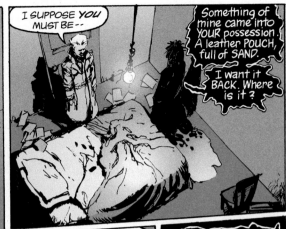

I SUPPOSE *YOU* MUST BE--

Something of mine came into *YOUR* possession. A leather POUCH, full of SAND.

I want it BACK. Where is it?

THAT *POUCH?* THAT WAS *YEARS* AGO. *YEAH*, I BOUGHT IT IN A *GARAGE* SALE IN *SAN FRANCISCO*.

I KNEW IT WAS *POWERFUL*. BUT I NEVER EVEN MANAGED TO GET THE *DRAWSTRINGS* OPEN...

WHERE IS IT NOW?

I HAVEN'T SEEN IT FOR *AGES*. BUT THE ODDS ARE IT'S DOWN IN CHAS' *LOCK-UP*, WITH ME STUFF FROM... *PADDINGTON. AND* FROM THE NOTTINGHILL PLACE.

AND THE EAST CROYDON FLAT BEFORE THAT...

Let us retrieve it, then.

I *HOPE* YOU DON'T EXPECT ME TO GO ON *PUBLIC TRANSPORT* WITH *YOU* DRESSED LIKE *THAT*.

BE *DEAD* EMBARRASSING.

Is this better?

...AUHH.

I OUGHT TO INTRODUCE YOU TO THE BIG *GREEN* BLOKE, YOU'D *LIKE* HIM.

HE HASN'T GOT A SENSE OF HUMOR *EITHER*.

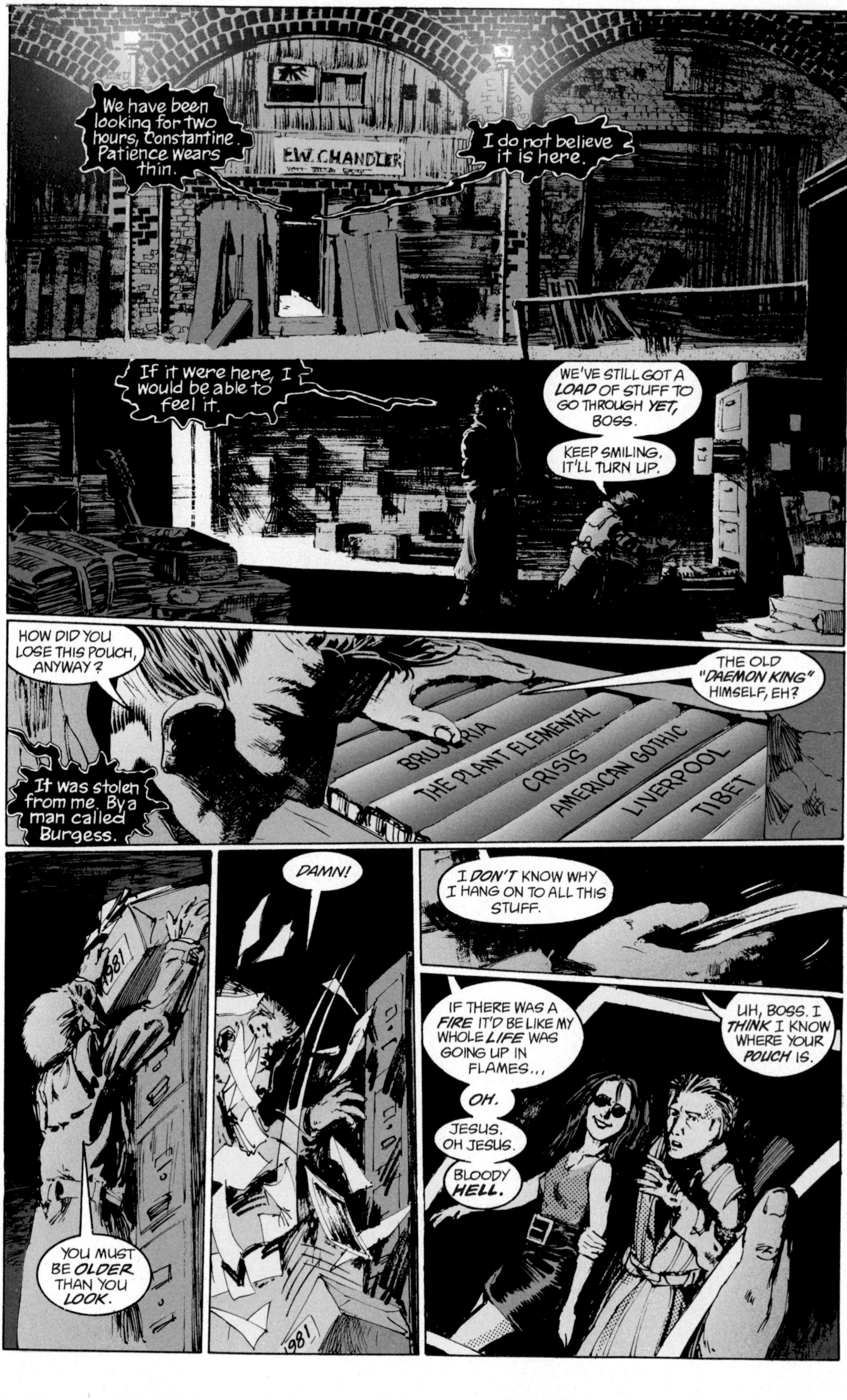
We have been looking for two hours, Constantine. Patience wears thin.
F.W. CHANDLER
I do not believe it is here.
If it were here, I would be able to feel it.
WE'VE STILL GOT A LOAD OF STUFF TO GO THROUGH YET, BOSS.
KEEP SMILING. IT'LL TURN UP.
HOW DID YOU LOSE THIS POUCH, ANYWAY?
THE OLD "DAEMON KING" HIMSELF, EH?
It was stolen from me. By a man called Burgess.
BRUJERIA
THE PLANT ELEMENTAL
CRISIS
AMERICAN GOTHIC
LIVERPOOL
TIBET
1981
YOU MUST BE OLDER THAN YOU LOOK.
DAMN!
1981
I DON'T KNOW WHY I HANG ON TO ALL THIS STUFF.
IF THERE WAS A FIRE IT'D BE LIKE MY WHOLE LIFE WAS GOING UP IN FLAMES...
UH, BOSS. I THINK I KNOW WHERE YOUR POUCH IS.
OH.
JESUS. OH JESUS.
BLOODY HELL.

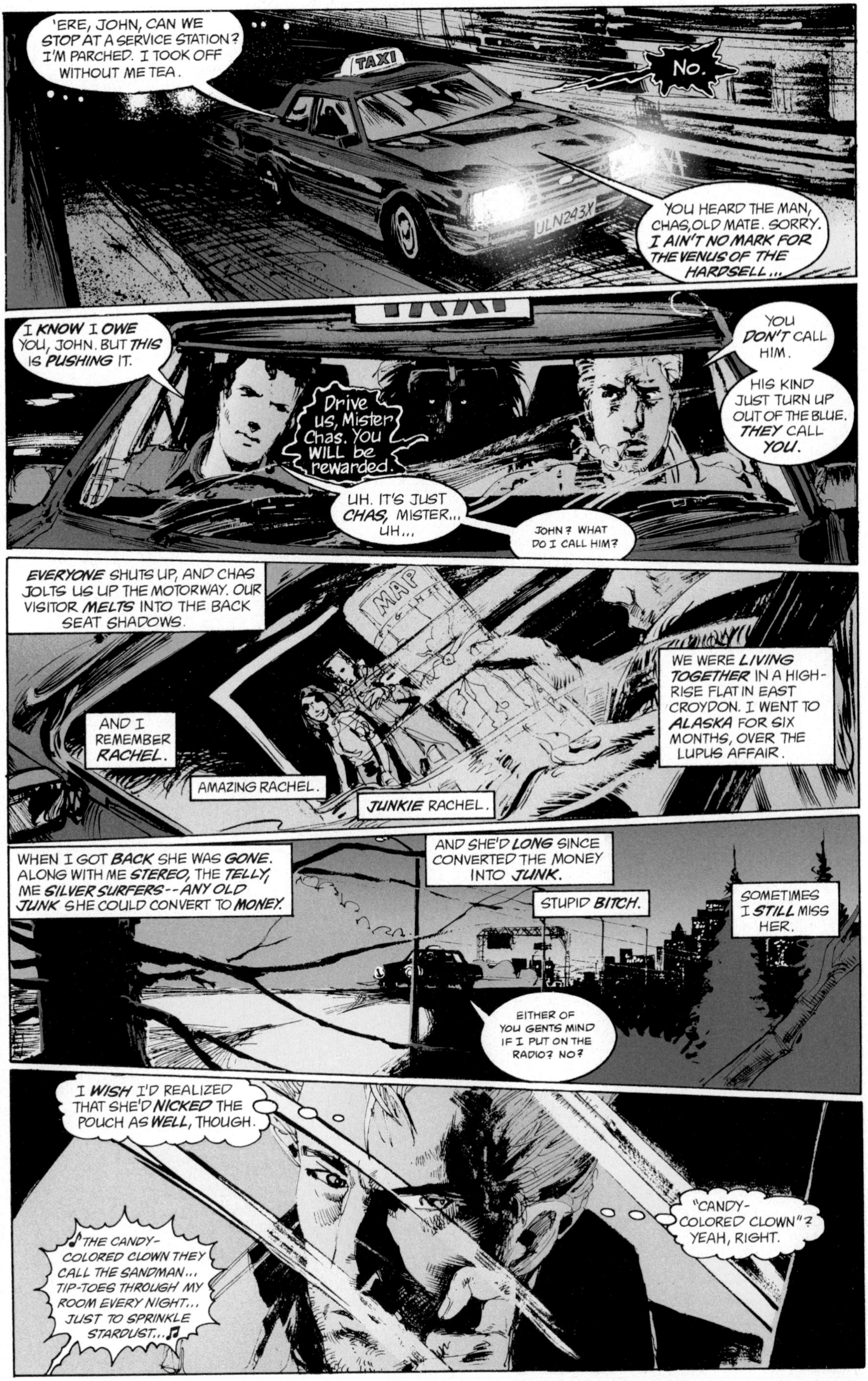
'ERE, JOHN, CAN WE STOP AT A SERVICE STATION? I'M PARCHED. I TOOK OFF WITHOUT ME TEA.
No.
ULN243X
YOU HEARD THE MAN, CHAS, OLD MATE. SORRY. I AIN'T NO MARK FOR THE VENUS OF THE HARDSELL...
TAXI
I KNOW I OWE YOU, JOHN. BUT THIS IS PUSHING IT.
Drive us, Mister Chas. You WILL be rewarded.
YOU DON'T CALL HIM.
HIS KIND JUST TURN UP OUT OF THE BLUE. THEY CALL YOU.
UH. IT'S JUST CHAS, MISTER... UH...
JOHN? WHAT DO I CALL HIM?
EVERYONE SHUTS UP, AND CHAS JOLTS US UP THE MOTORWAY. OUR VISITOR MELTS INTO THE BACK SEAT SHADOWS.
MAP
WE WERE LIVING TOGETHER IN A HIGH-RISE FLAT IN EAST CROYDON. I WENT TO ALASKA FOR SIX MONTHS, OVER THE LUPUS AFFAIR.
AND I REMEMBER RACHEL.
AMAZING RACHEL.
JUNKIE RACHEL.
WHEN I GOT BACK SHE WAS GONE. ALONG WITH ME STEREO, THE TELLY, ME SILVER SURFERS--ANY OLD JUNK SHE COULD CONVERT TO MONEY.
AND SHE'D LONG SINCE CONVERTED THE MONEY INTO JUNK.
STUPID BITCH.
SOMETIMES I STILL MISS HER.
EITHER OF YOU GENTS MIND IF I PUT ON THE RADIO? NO?
I WISH I'D REALIZED THAT SHE'D NICKED THE POUCH AS WELL, THOUGH.
♪THE CANDY-COLORED CLOWN THEY CALL THE SANDMAN... TIP-TOES THROUGH MY ROOM EVERY NIGHT... JUST TO SPRINKLE STARDUST...♫
"CANDY-COLORED CLOWN"? YEAH, RIGHT.

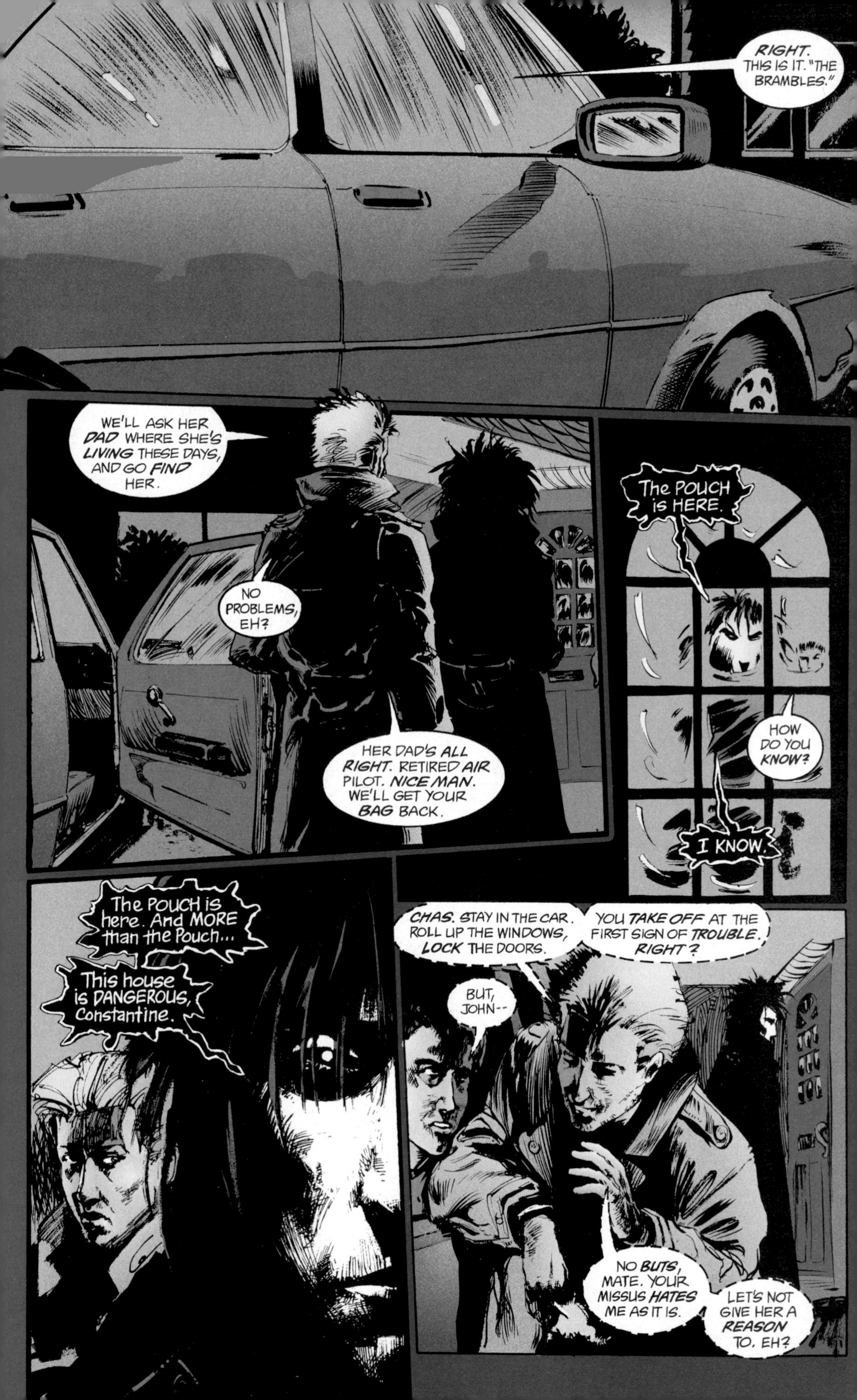
RIGHT. THIS IS IT. "THE BRAMBLES."
WE'LL ASK HER DAD WHERE SHE'S LIVING THESE DAYS, AND GO FIND HER.
NO PROBLEMS, EH?
HER DAD'S ALL RIGHT. RETIRED AIR PILOT. NICE MAN. WE'LL GET YOUR BAG BACK.
The POUCH is HERE.
HOW DO YOU KNOW?
I KNOW.
The POUCH is here. And MORE than the Pouch...
This house is DANGEROUS, Constantine.
CHAS. STAY IN THE CAR. ROLL UP THE WINDOWS, LOCK THE DOORS.
YOU TAKE OFF AT THE FIRST SIGN OF TROUBLE. RIGHT?
BUT, JOHN--
NO BUTS, MATE. YOUR MISSUS HATES ME AS IT IS.
LET'S NOT GIVE HER A REASON TO. EH?

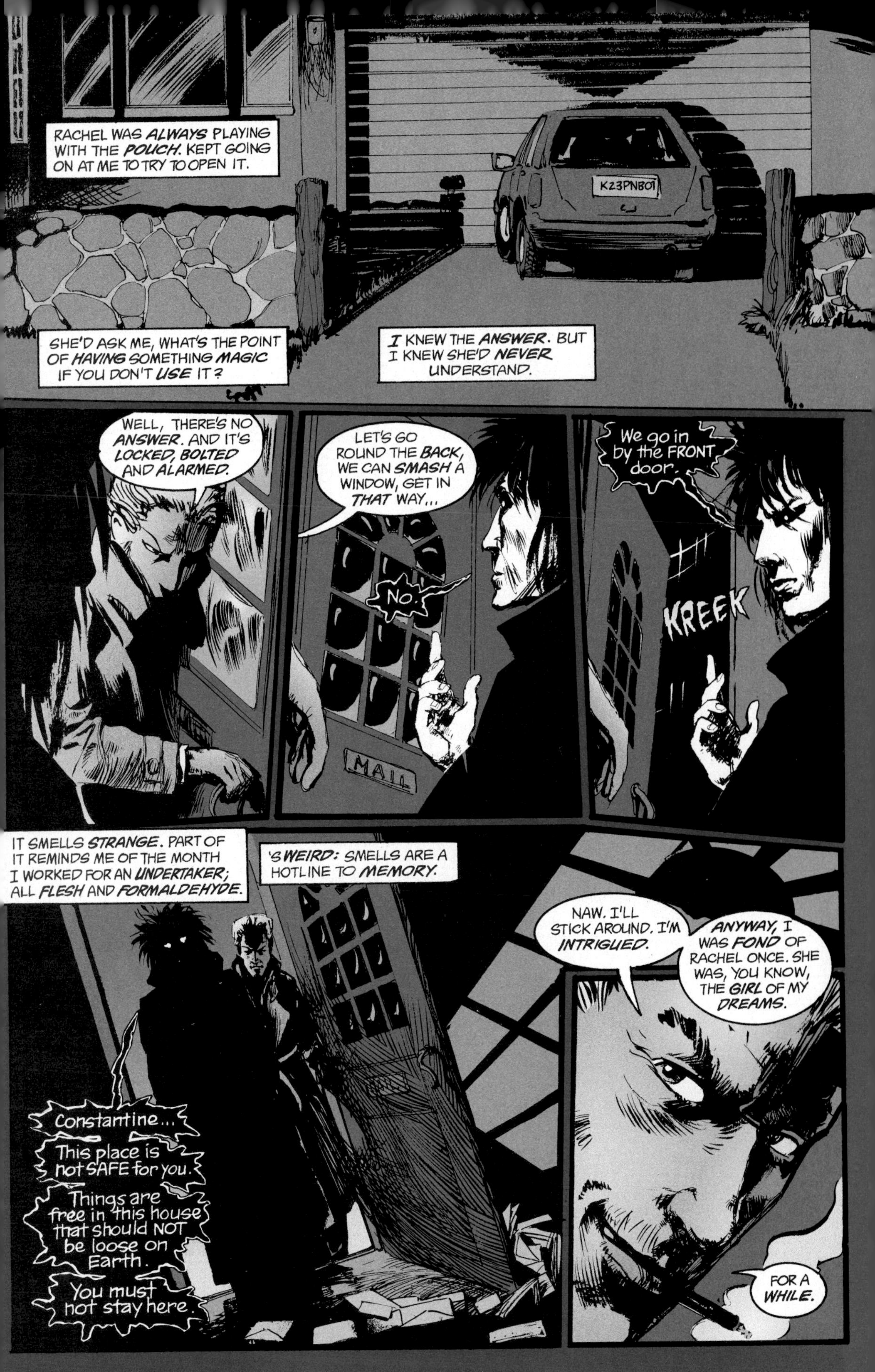

RACHEL WAS ALWAYS PLAYING WITH THE POUCH. KEPT GOING ON AT ME TO TRY TO OPEN IT.
K23PNB01
SHE'D ASK ME, WHAT'S THE POINT OF HAVING SOMETHING MAGIC IF YOU DON'T USE IT?
I KNEW THE ANSWER. BUT I KNEW SHE'D NEVER UNDERSTAND.
WELL, THERE'S NO ANSWER. AND IT'S LOCKED, BOLTED AND ALARMED.
LET'S GO ROUND THE BACK, WE CAN SMASH A WINDOW, GET IN THAT WAY...
No.
MAIL
We go in by the FRONT door.
KREEK
IT SMELLS STRANGE. PART OF IT REMINDS ME OF THE MONTH I WORKED FOR AN UNDERTAKER; ALL FLESH AND FORMALDEHYDE.
'S WEIRD: SMELLS ARE A HOTLINE TO MEMORY.
Constantine...
This place is not SAFE for you.
Things are free in this house that should NOT be loose on Earth.
You must not stay here.
NAW. I'LL STICK AROUND. I'M INTRIGUED.
ANYWAY, I WAS FOND OF RACHEL ONCE. SHE WAS, YOU KNOW, THE GIRL OF MY DREAMS.
FOR A WHILE.

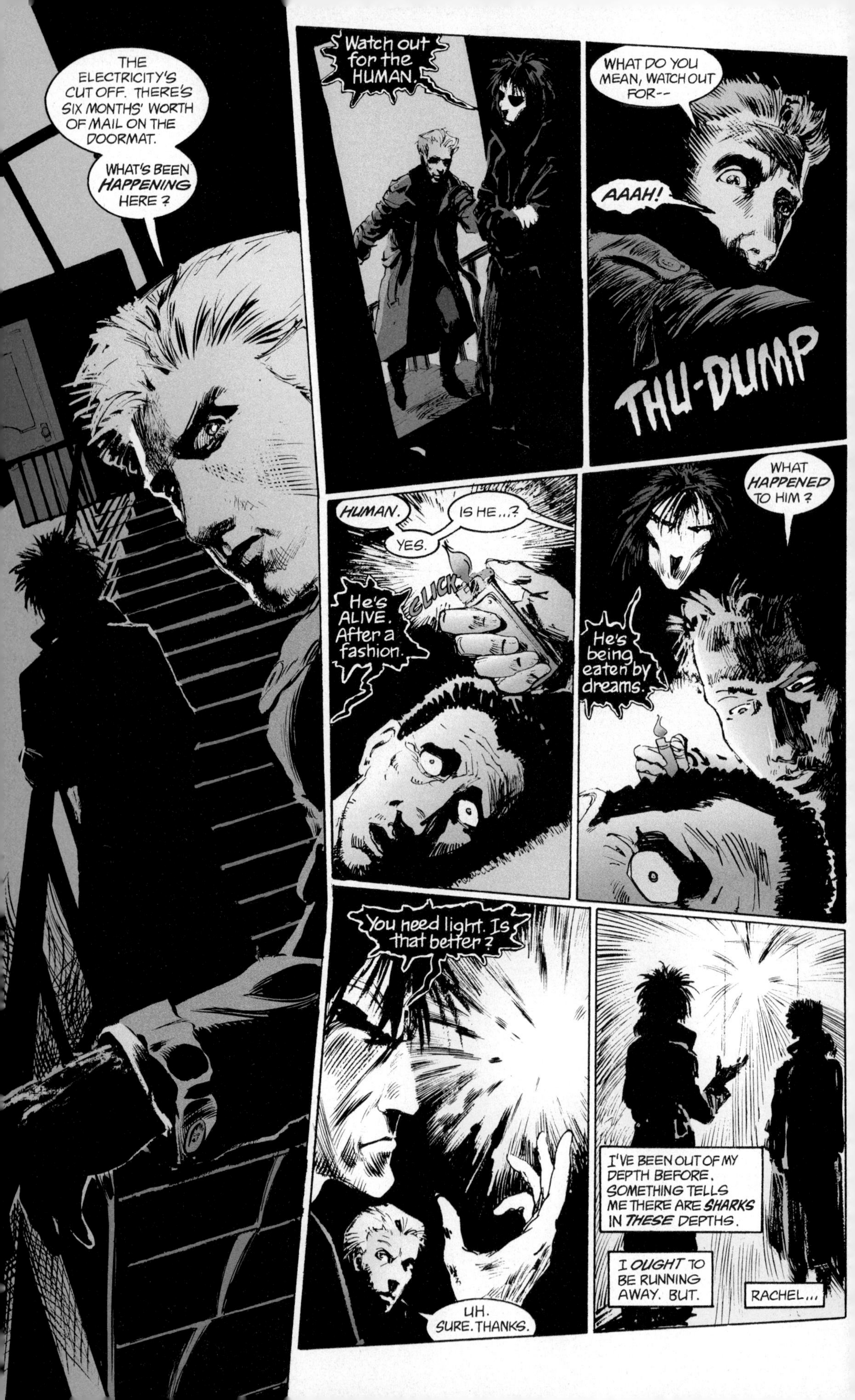

THE ELECTRICITY'S CUT OFF. THERE'S SIX MONTHS' WORTH OF MAIL ON THE DOORMAT.
WHAT'S BEEN HAPPENING HERE ?
Watch out for the HUMAN.
WHAT DO YOU MEAN, WATCH OUT FOR--
AAAH!
THU-DUMP
HUMAN.
IS HE...?
YES.
CLICK
He's ALIVE. After a fashion.
WHAT HAPPENED TO HIM ?
He's being eaten by dreams.
You need light. Is that better ?
UH. SURE. THANKS.
I'VE BEEN OUT OF MY DEPTH BEFORE. SOMETHING TELLS ME THERE ARE SHARKS IN THESE DEPTHS.
I OUGHT TO BE RUNNING AWAY. BUT.
RACHEL...

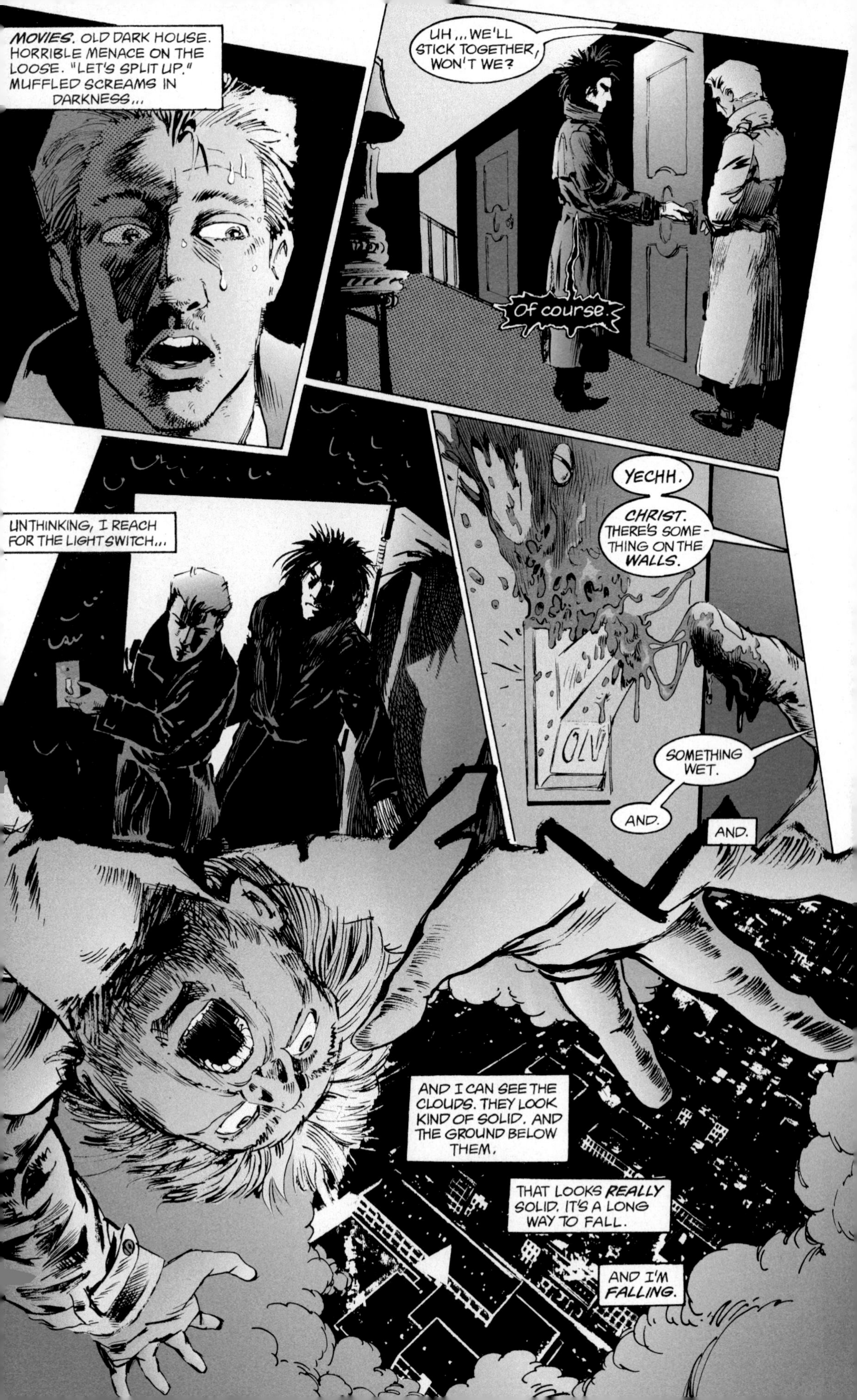

MOVIES. OLD DARK HOUSE. HORRIBLE MENACE ON THE LOOSE. "LET'S SPLIT UP." MUFFLED SCREAMS IN DARKNESS...
UH... WE'LL STICK TOGETHER, WON'T WE?
Of course.
UNTHINKING, I REACH FOR THE LIGHTSWITCH...
YECHH.
CHRIST. THERE'S SOMETHING ON THE WALLS.
SOMETHING WET.
AND.
AND.
AND I CAN SEE THE CLOUDS. THEY LOOK KIND OF SOLID. AND THE GROUND BELOW THEM.
THAT LOOKS REALLY SOLID. IT'S A LONG WAY TO FALL.
AND I'M FALLING.

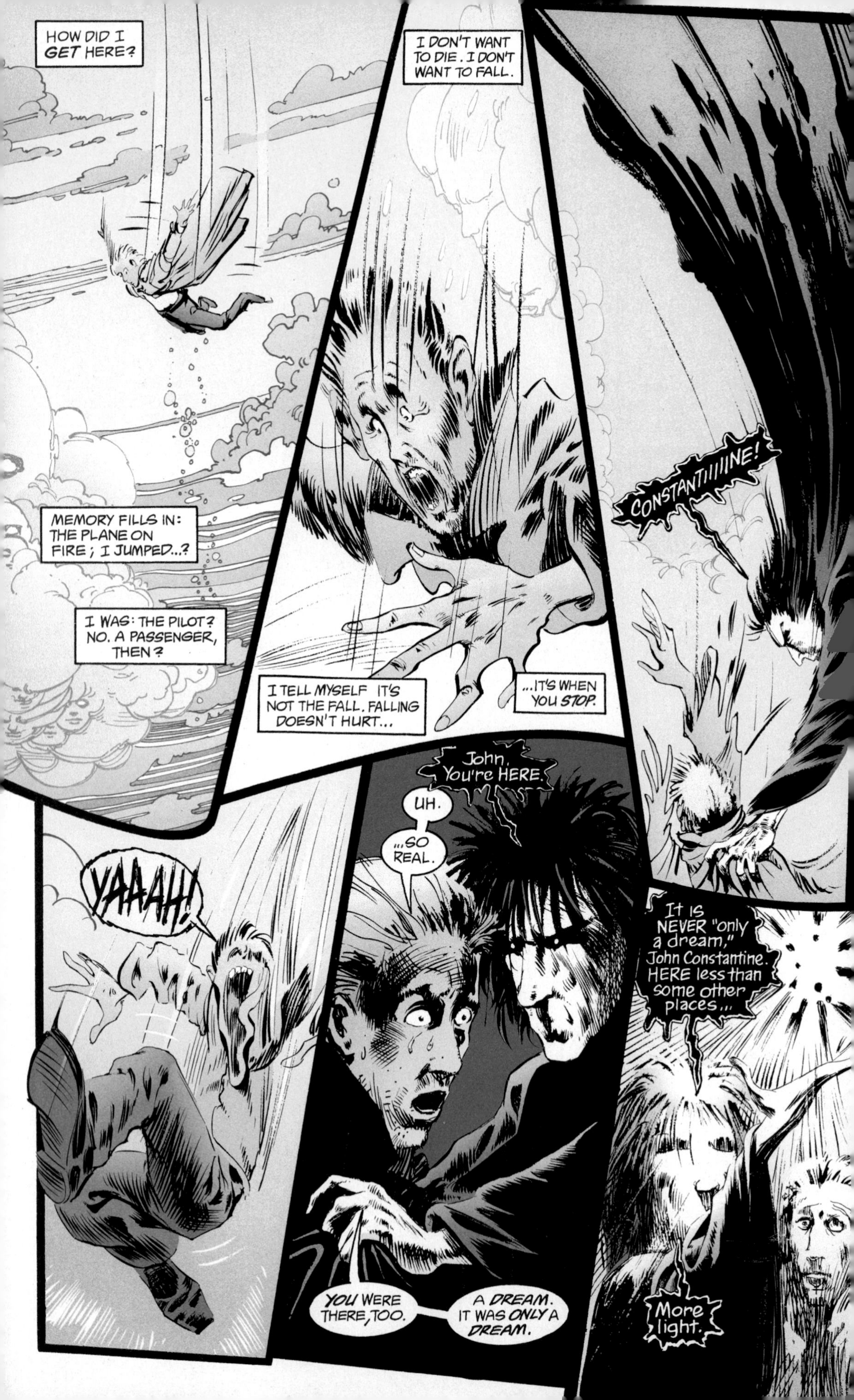
HOW DID I GET HERE?
MEMORY FILLS IN: THE PLANE ON FIRE; I JUMPED...?
I WAS: THE PILOT? NO. A PASSENGER, THEN?
I DON'T WANT TO DIE. I DON'T WANT TO FALL.
I TELL MYSELF IT'S NOT THE FALL. FALLING DOESN'T HURT...
...IT'S WHEN YOU STOP.
CONSTANTIIIIIINE!
YAAAH!
John. You're HERE.
UH.
...SO REAL.
YOU WERE THERE, TOO.
A DREAM. IT WAS ONLY A DREAM.
It is NEVER "only a dream," John Constantine. HERE less than some other places...
More light.

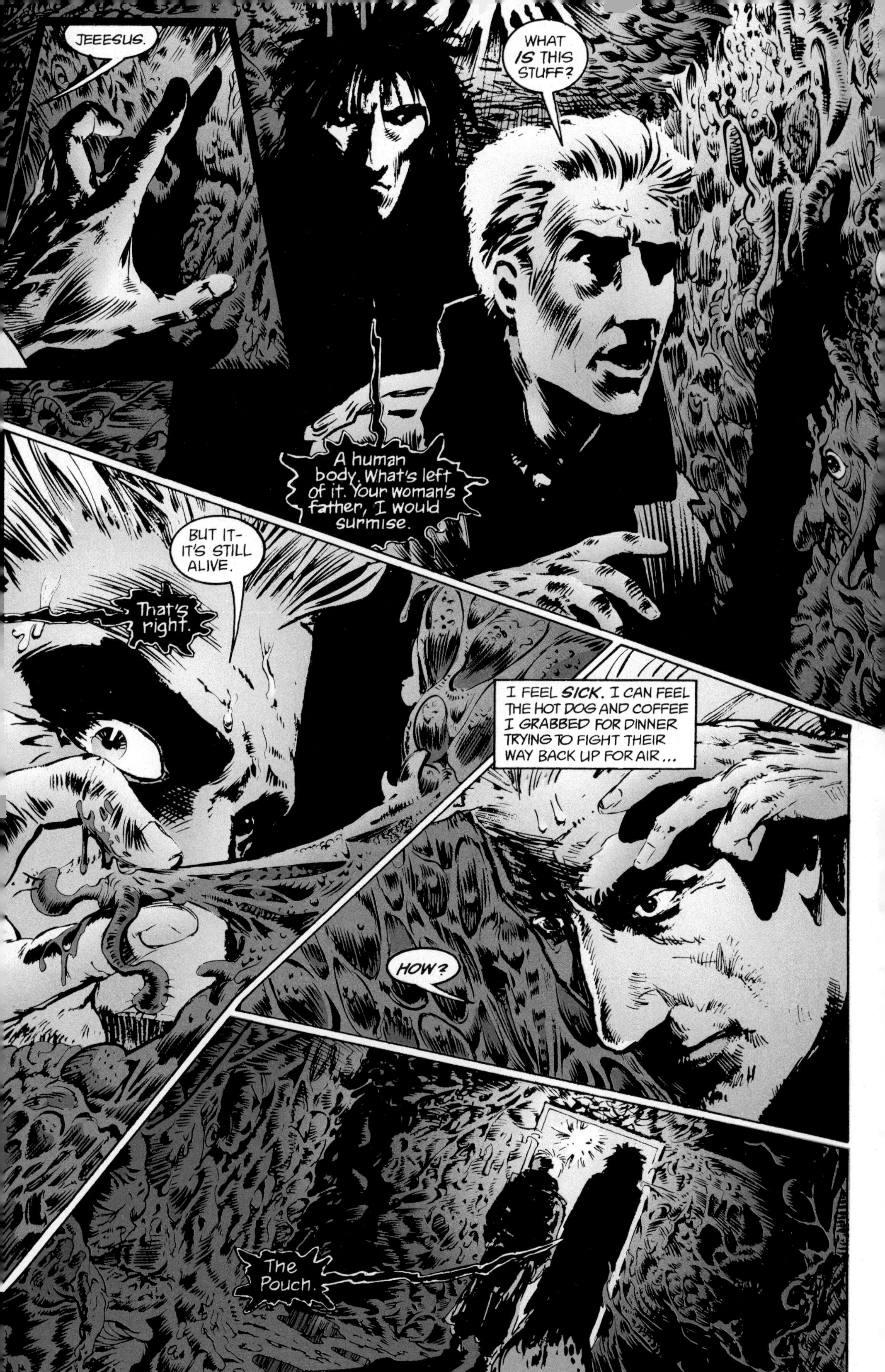
JEEESUS.
WHAT IS THIS STUFF?
A human body. What's left of it. Your woman's father, I would surmise.
BUT IT- IT'S STILL ALIVE.
That's right.
I FEEL SICK. I CAN FEEL THE HOT DOG AND COFFEE I GRABBED FOR DINNER TRYING TO FIGHT THEIR WAY BACK UP FOR AIR...
HOW?
The Pouch.

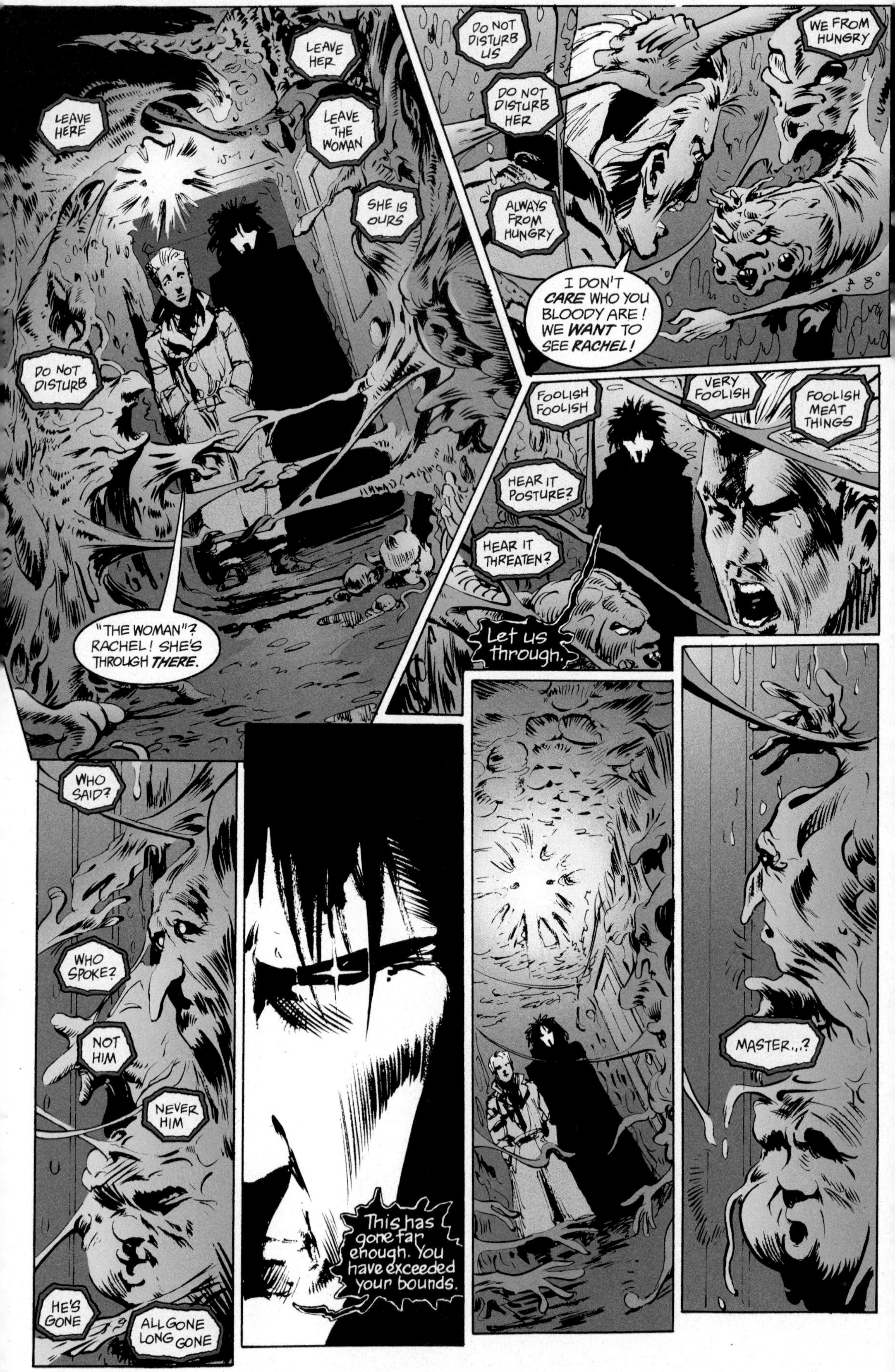
LEAVE HERE
LEAVE HER
LEAVE THE WOMAN
SHE IS OURS
DO NOT DISTURB
"THE WOMAN"? RACHEL! SHE'S THROUGH THERE.
DO NOT DISTURB US
DO NOT DISTURB HER
WE FROM HUNGRY
ALWAYS FROM HUNGRY
I DON'T CARE WHO YOU BLOODY ARE! WE WANT TO SEE RACHEL!
FOOLISH FOOLISH
VERY FOOLISH
FOOLISH MEAT THINGS
HEAR IT POSTURE?
HEAR IT THREATEN?
Let us through.
WHO SAID?
WHO SPOKE?
NOT HIM
NEVER HIM
HE'S GONE
ALL GONE LONG GONE
This has gone far enough. You have exceeded your bounds.
MASTER...?

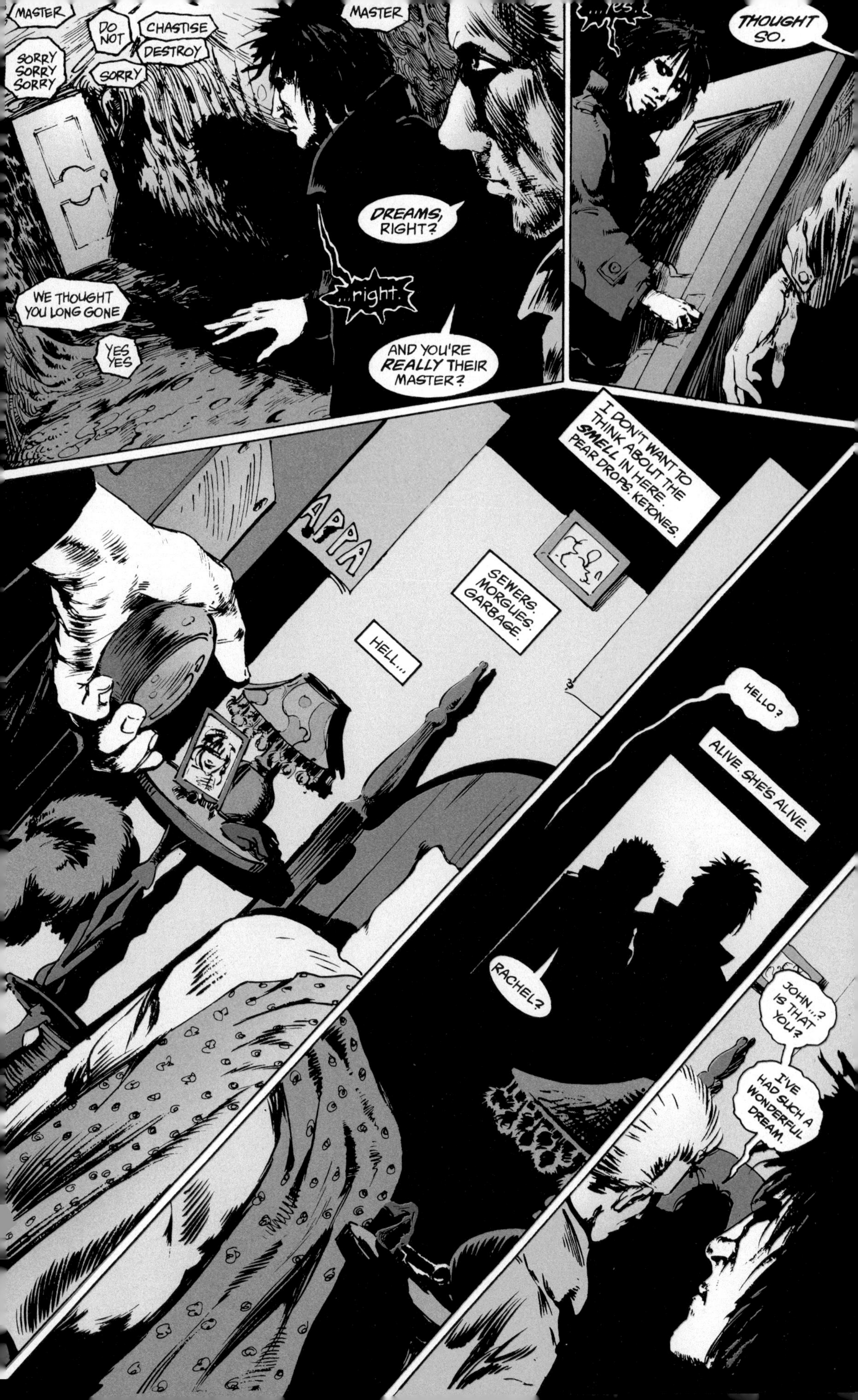
MASTER
SORRY SORRY SORRY
DO NOT
CHASTISE
DESTROY
SORRY
MASTER
WE THOUGHT YOU LONG GONE
YES YES
DREAMS, RIGHT?
...right.
AND YOU'RE REALLY THEIR MASTER?
...yes.
THOUGHT SO.
I DON'T WANT TO THINK ABOUT THE SMELL IN HERE. PEAR DROPS. KETONES.
SEWERS. MORGUES. GARBAGE.
HELL...
APPA
HELLO?
ALIVE. SHE'S ALIVE.
RACHEL?
JOHN...? IS THAT YOU?
I'VE HAD SUCH A WONDERFUL DREAM.

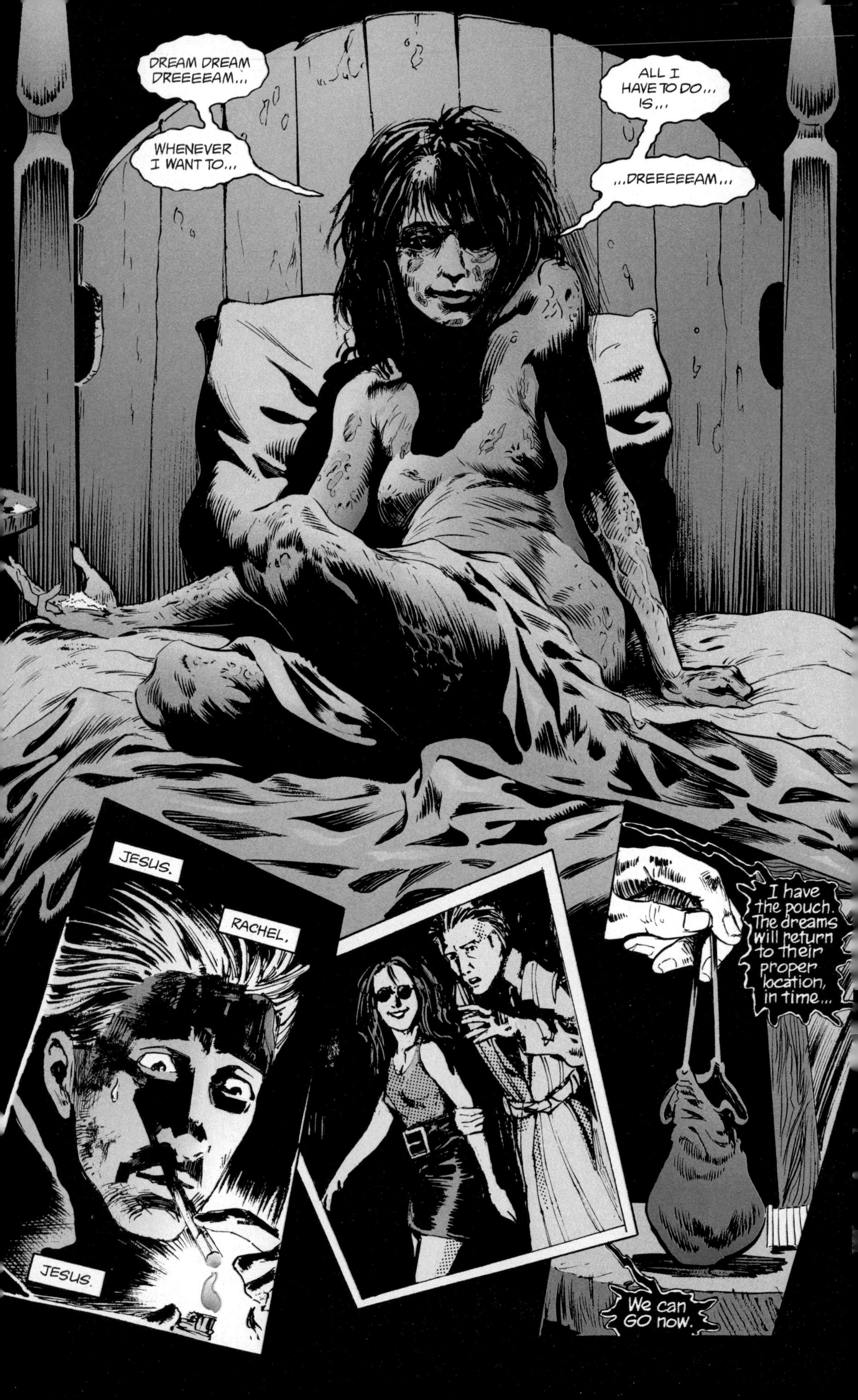
DREAM DREAM DREEEEAM...
WHENEVER I WANT TO...
ALL I HAVE TO DO... IS...
...DREEEEEAM...
JESUS.
RACHEL.
JESUS.
I have the pouch. The dreams will return to their proper location, in time...
We can GO now.

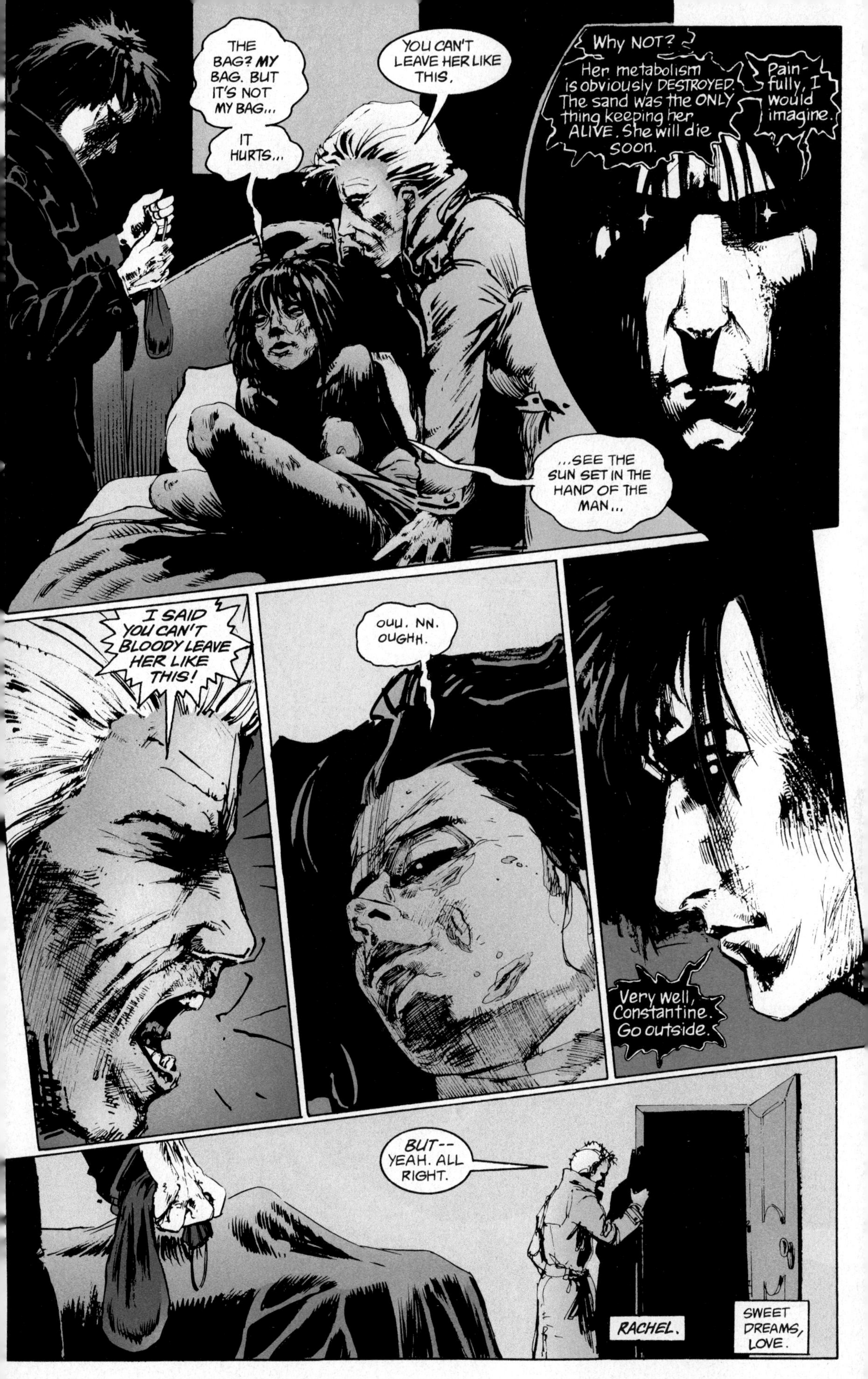
THE BAG? MY BAG. BUT IT'S NOT MY BAG...
IT HURTS...
YOU CAN'T LEAVE HER LIKE THIS.
Why NOT?
Her metabolism is obviously DESTROYED. The sand was the ONLY thing keeping her ALIVE. She will die soon.
Painfully, I would imagine.
...SEE THE SUN SET IN THE HAND OF THE MAN...
I SAID YOU CAN'T BLOODY LEAVE HER LIKE THIS!
OUU. NN. OUGHH.
Very well, Constantine. Go outside.
BUT-- YEAH. ALL RIGHT.
RACHEL.
SWEET DREAMS, LOVE.

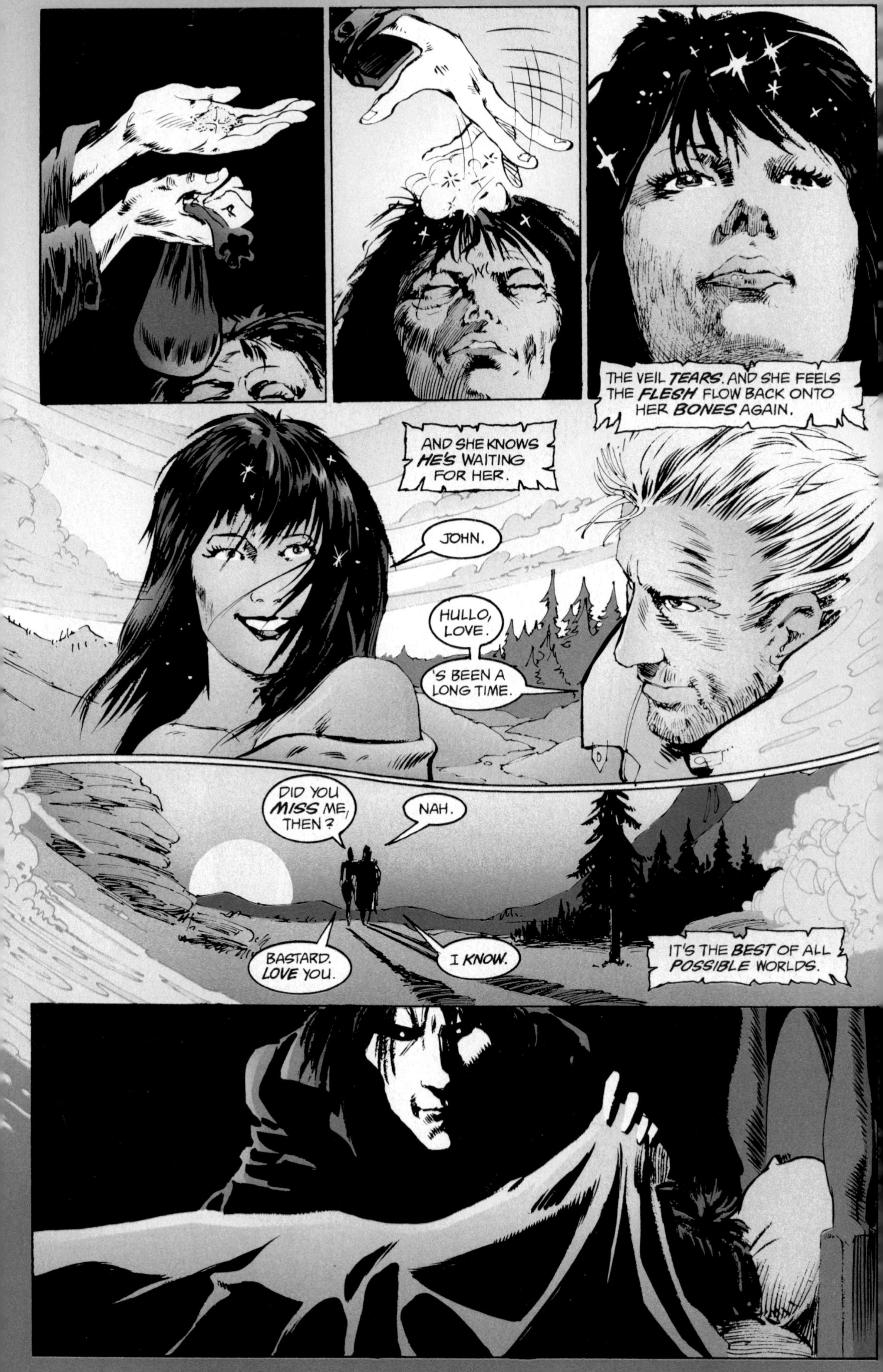

THE VEIL TEARS. AND SHE FEELS THE FLESH FLOW BACK ONTO HER BONES AGAIN.
AND SHE KNOWS HE'S WAITING FOR HER.
JOHN.
HULLO, LOVE.
'S BEEN A LONG TIME.
DID YOU MISS ME, THEN?
NAH.
BASTARD. LOVE YOU.
I KNOW.
IT'S THE BEST OF ALL POSSIBLE WORLDS.

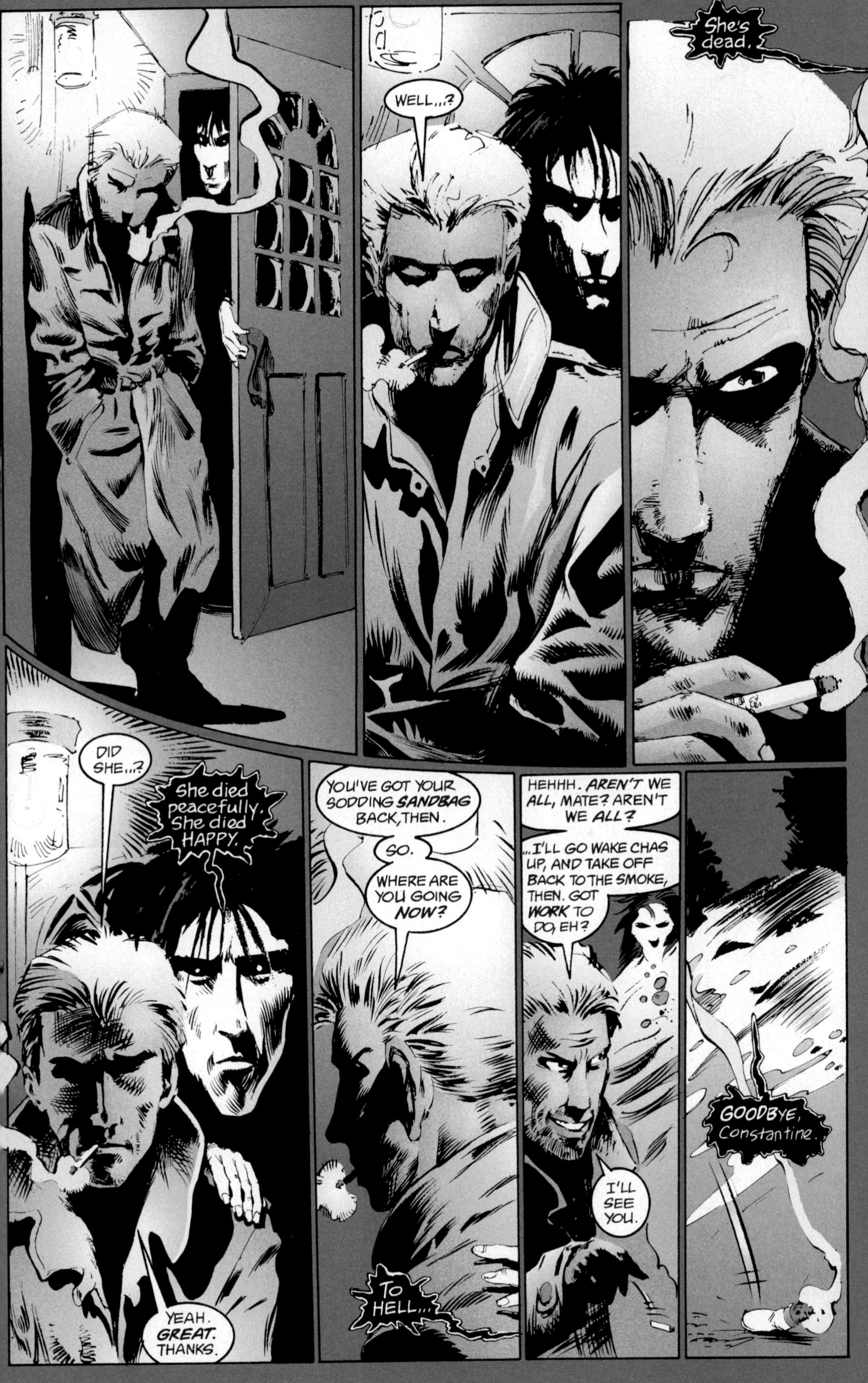
WELL...?
She's dead.
DID SHE...?
She died peacefully. She died HAPPY.
YEAH. GREAT. THANKS.
YOU'VE GOT YOUR SODDING SANDBAG BACK, THEN.
SO.
WHERE ARE YOU GOING NOW?
TO HELL...
HEHHH. AREN'T WE ALL, MATE? AREN'T WE ALL?
...I'LL GO WAKE CHAS UP, AND TAKE OFF BACK TO THE SMOKE, THEN. GOT WORK TO DO, EH?
I'LL SEE YOU.
GOODBYE, Constantine.

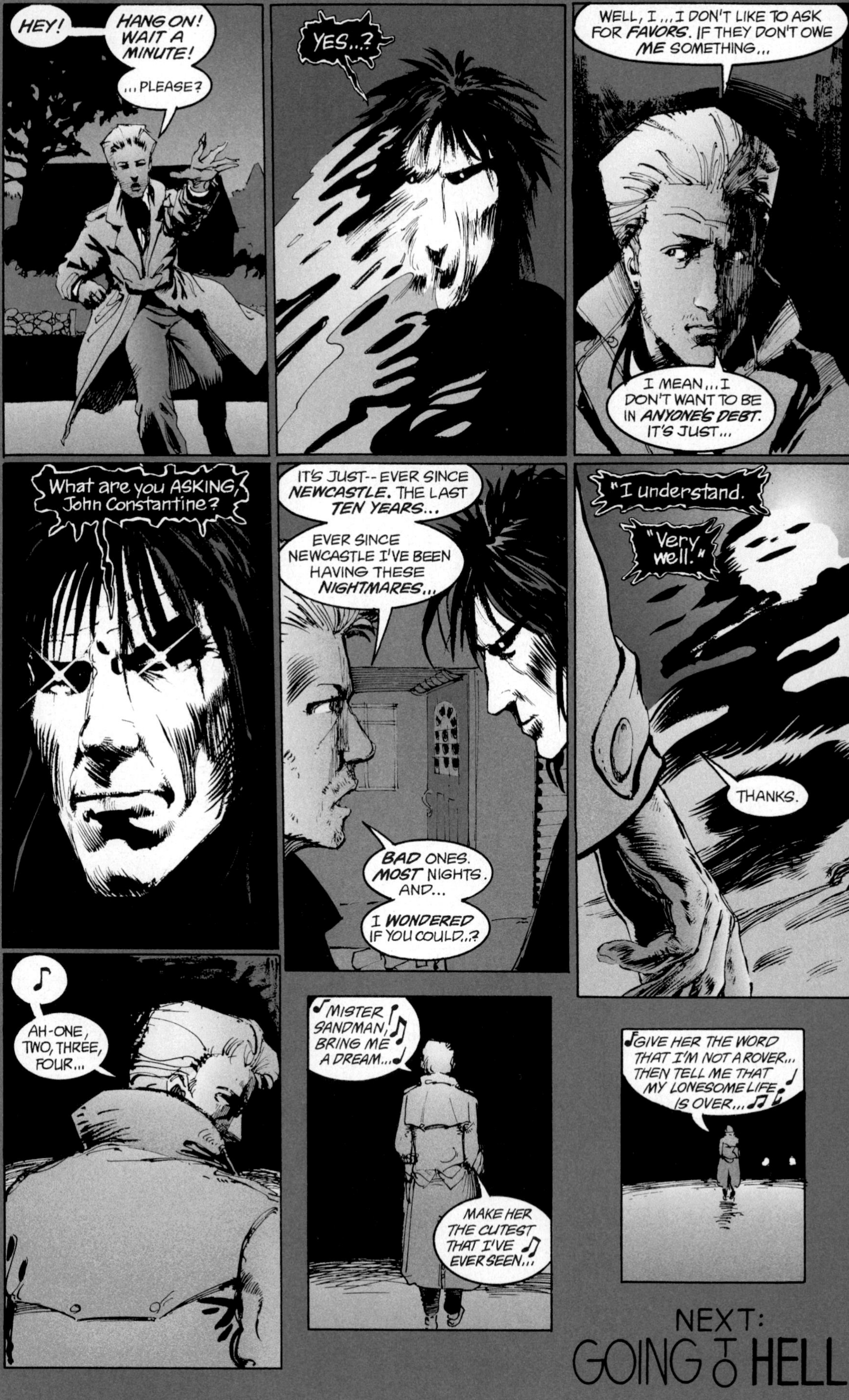
HEY!
HANG ON! WAIT A MINUTE!
...PLEASE?
YES...?
WELL, I...I DON'T LIKE TO ASK FOR FAVORS. IF THEY DON'T OWE ME SOMETHING...
I MEAN...I DON'T WANT TO BE IN ANYONE'S DEBT. IT'S JUST...
What are you ASKING, John Constantine?
IT'S JUST-- EVER SINCE NEWCASTLE. THE LAST TEN YEARS...
EVER SINCE NEWCASTLE I'VE BEEN HAVING THESE NIGHTMARES...
BAD ONES. MOST NIGHTS. AND...
I WONDERED IF YOU COULD...?
"I understand.
"Very well."
THANKS.
♪
AH-ONE, TWO, THREE, FOUR...
♪ MISTER SANDMAN, BRING ME A DREAM... ♪
MAKE HER THE CUTEST THAT I'VE EVER SEEN... ♪
♪ GIVE HER THE WORD THAT I'M NOT A ROVER... THEN TELL ME THAT MY LONESOME LIFE IS OVER... ♪

NEXT:
GOING TO HELL

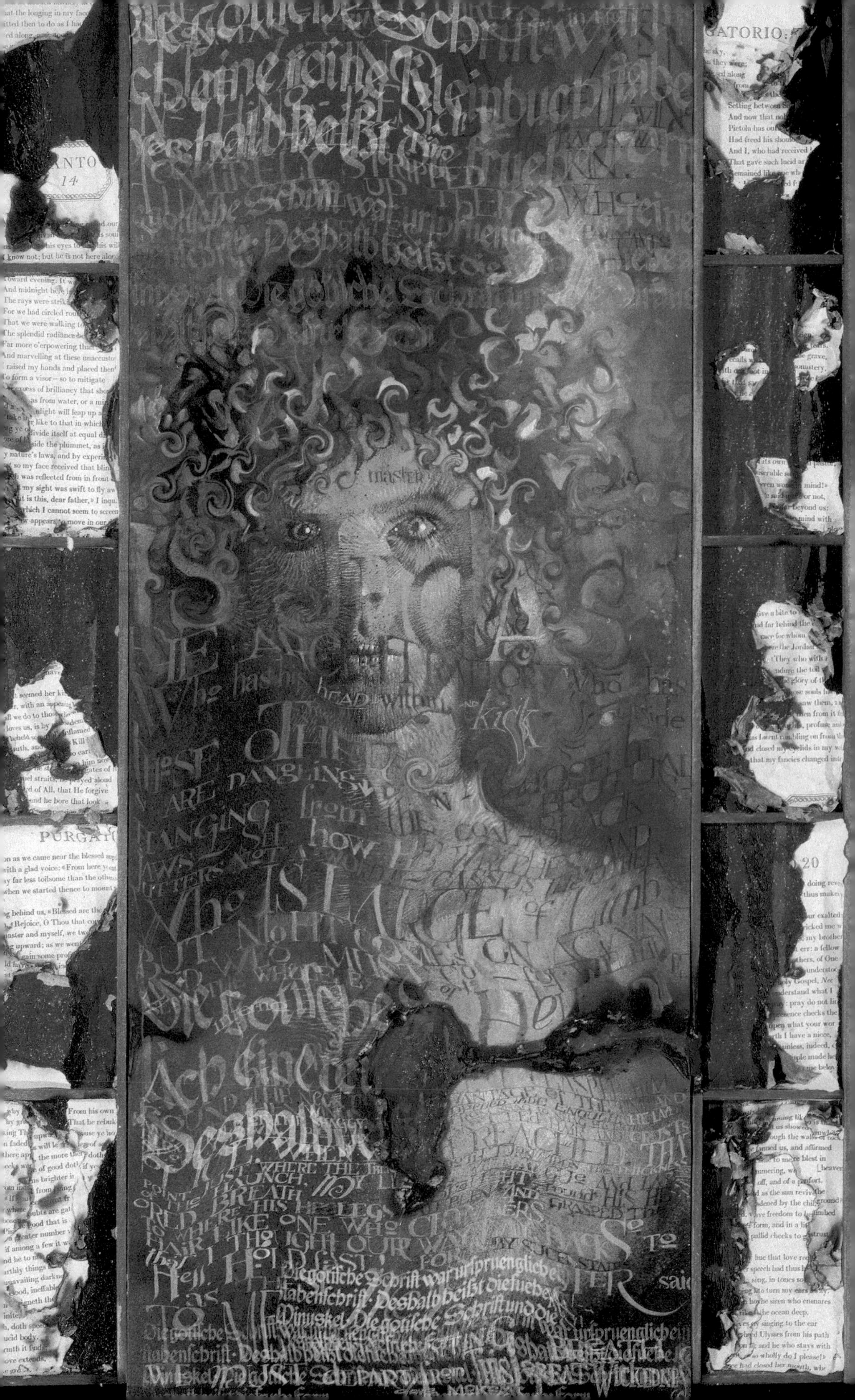
master
kick

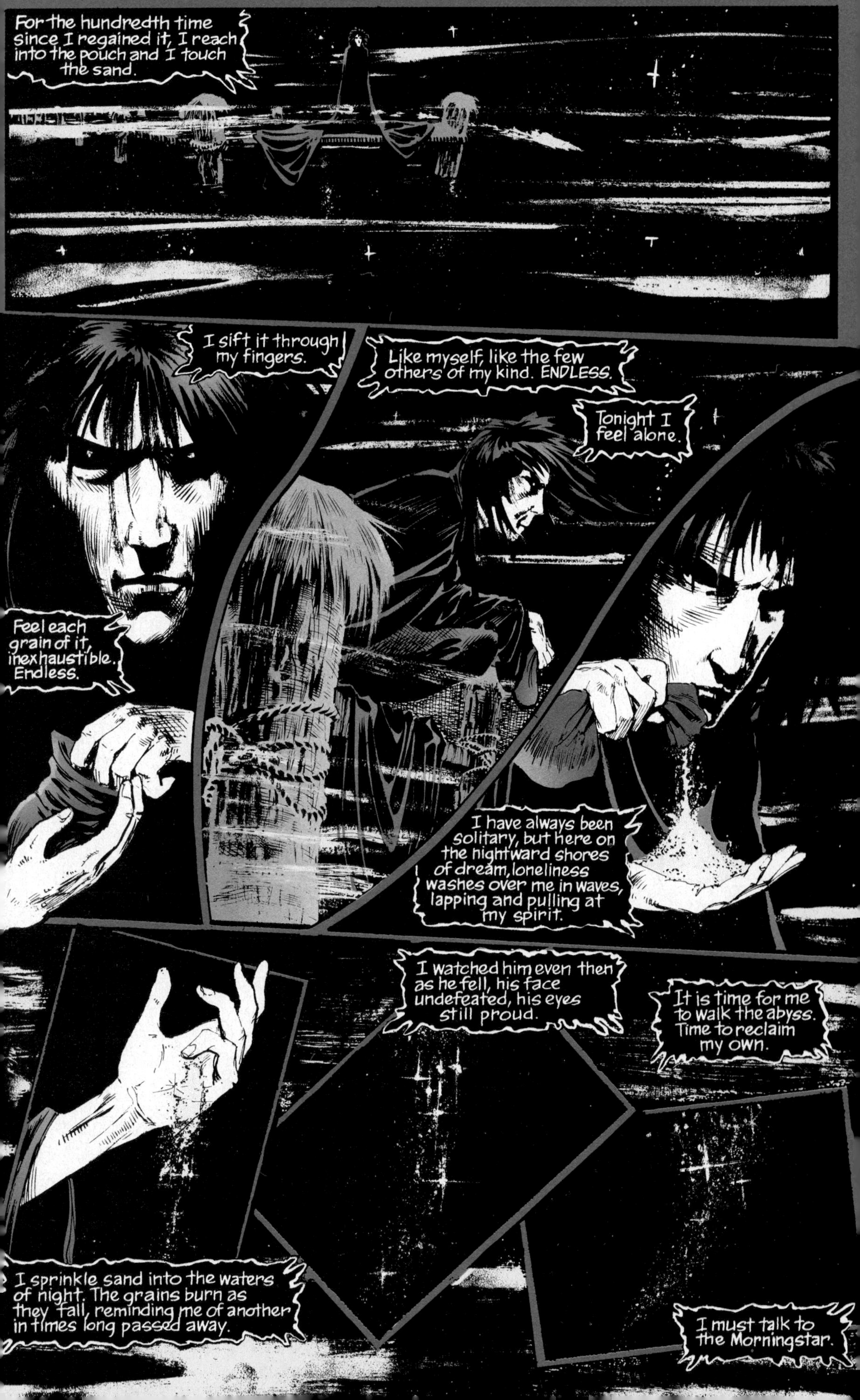
For the hundredth time since I regained it, I reach into the pouch and I touch the sand.
I sift it through my fingers.
Feel each grain of it, inexhaustible. Endless.
Like myself, like the few others of my kind. ENDLESS.
Tonight I feel alone.
I have always been solitary, but here on the nightward shores of dream, loneliness washes over me in waves, lapping and pulling at my spirit.
I sprinkle sand into the waters of night. The grains burn as they fall, reminding me of another in times long passed away.
I watched him even then as he fell, his face undefeated, his eyes still proud.
It is time for me to walk the abyss. Time to reclaim my own.
I must talk to the Morningstar.

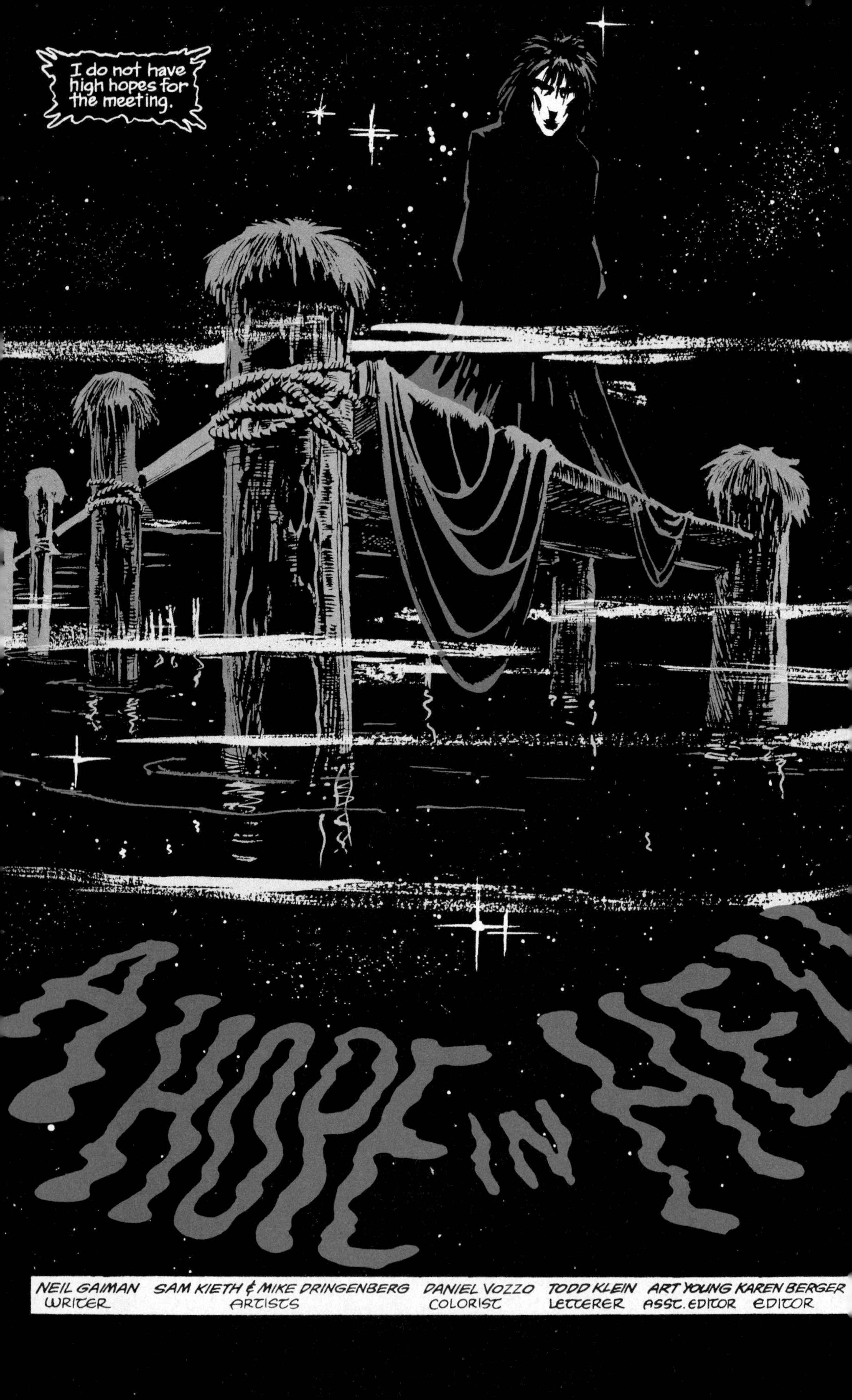
I do not have high hopes for the meeting.
NEIL GAIMAN WRITER
SAM KIETH & MIKE DRINGENBERG ARTISTS
DANIEL VOZZO COLORIST
TODD KLEIN LETTERER
ART YOUNG ASST. EDITOR
KAREN BERGER EDITOR

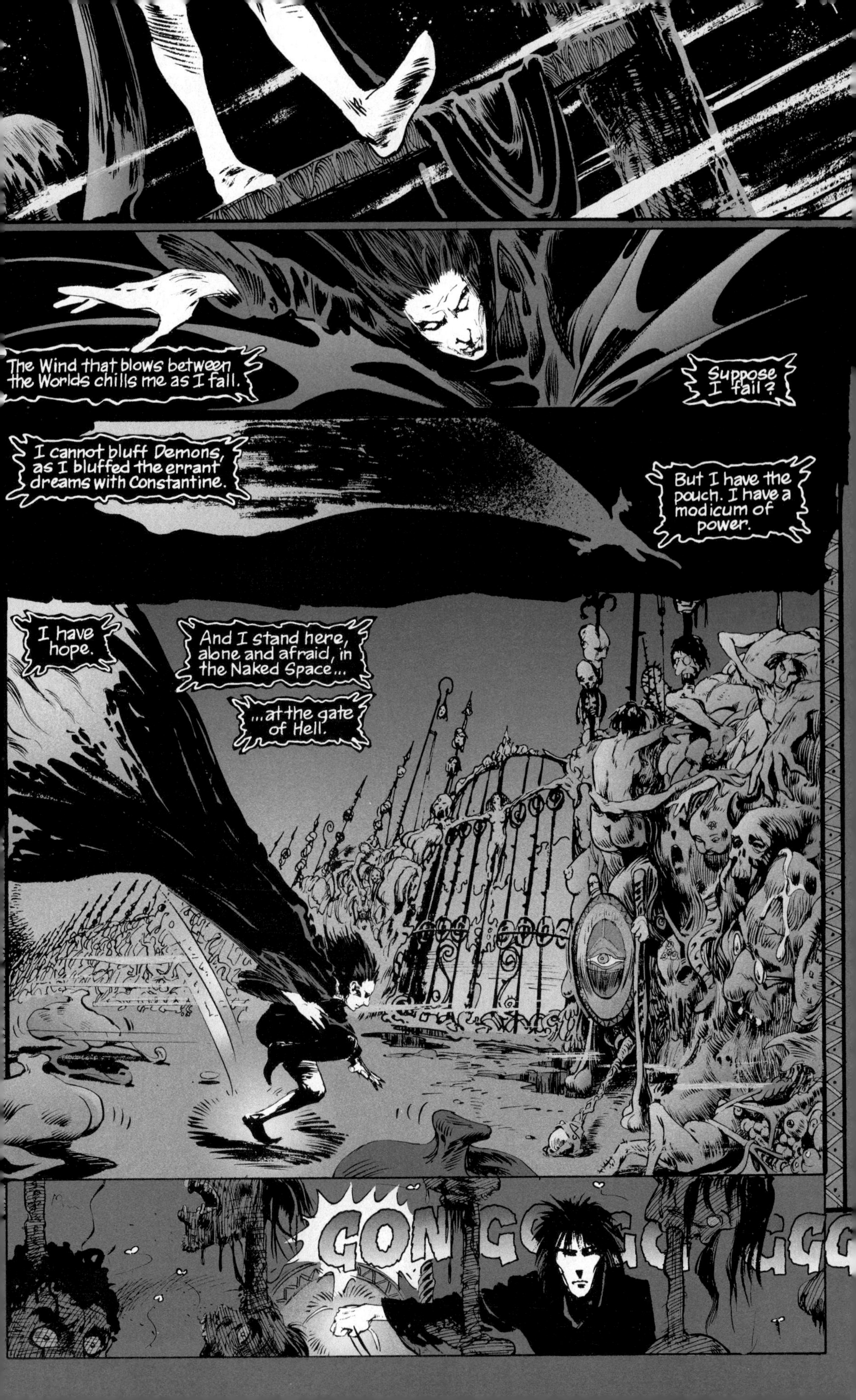
The Wind that blows between the Worlds chills me as I fall.
Suppose I fail?
I cannot bluff Demons, as I bluffed the errant dreams with Constantine.
But I have the pouch. I have a modicum of power.
I have hope.
And I stand here, alone and afraid, in the Naked Space...
...at the gate of Hell.
GON

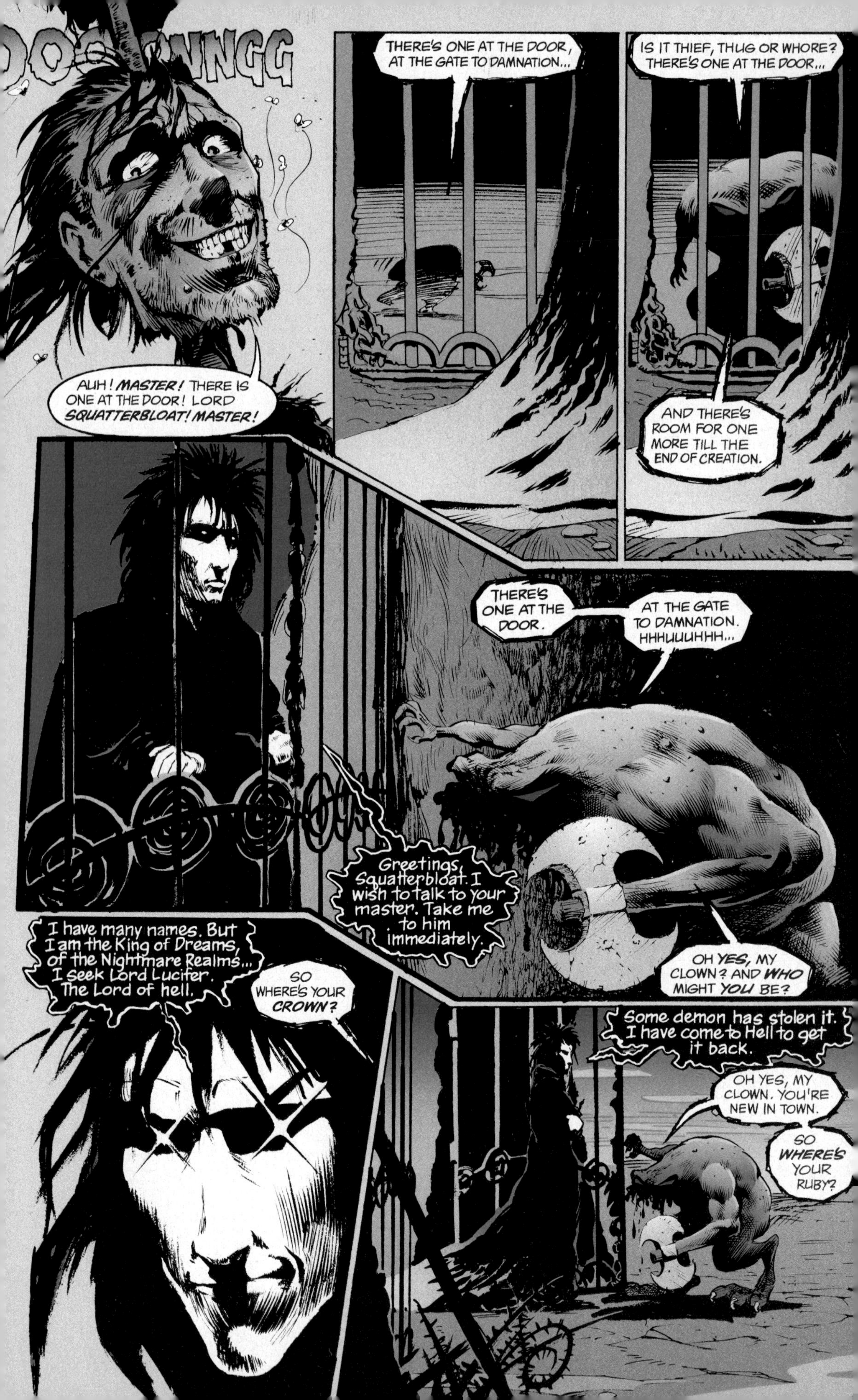
DOOONNGG
THERE'S ONE AT THE DOOR, AT THE GATE TO DAMNATION...
IS IT THIEF, THUG OR WHORE? THERE'S ONE AT THE DOOR...
AUH! MASTER! THERE IS ONE AT THE DOOR! LORD SQUATTERBLOAT! MASTER!
AND THERE'S ROOM FOR ONE MORE TILL THE END OF CREATION.
THERE'S ONE AT THE DOOR.
AT THE GATE TO DAMNATION. HHHUUUHHH...
Greetings, Squatterbloat. I wish to talk to your master. Take me to him immediately.
OH YES, MY CLOWN? AND WHO MIGHT YOU BE?
I have many names. But I am the King of Dreams, of the Nightmare Realms... I seek Lord Lucifer. The Lord of hell.
SO WHERE'S YOUR CROWN?
Some demon has stolen it. I have come to Hell to get it back.
OH YES, MY CLOWN. YOU'RE NEW IN TOWN.
SO WHERE'S YOUR RUBY?

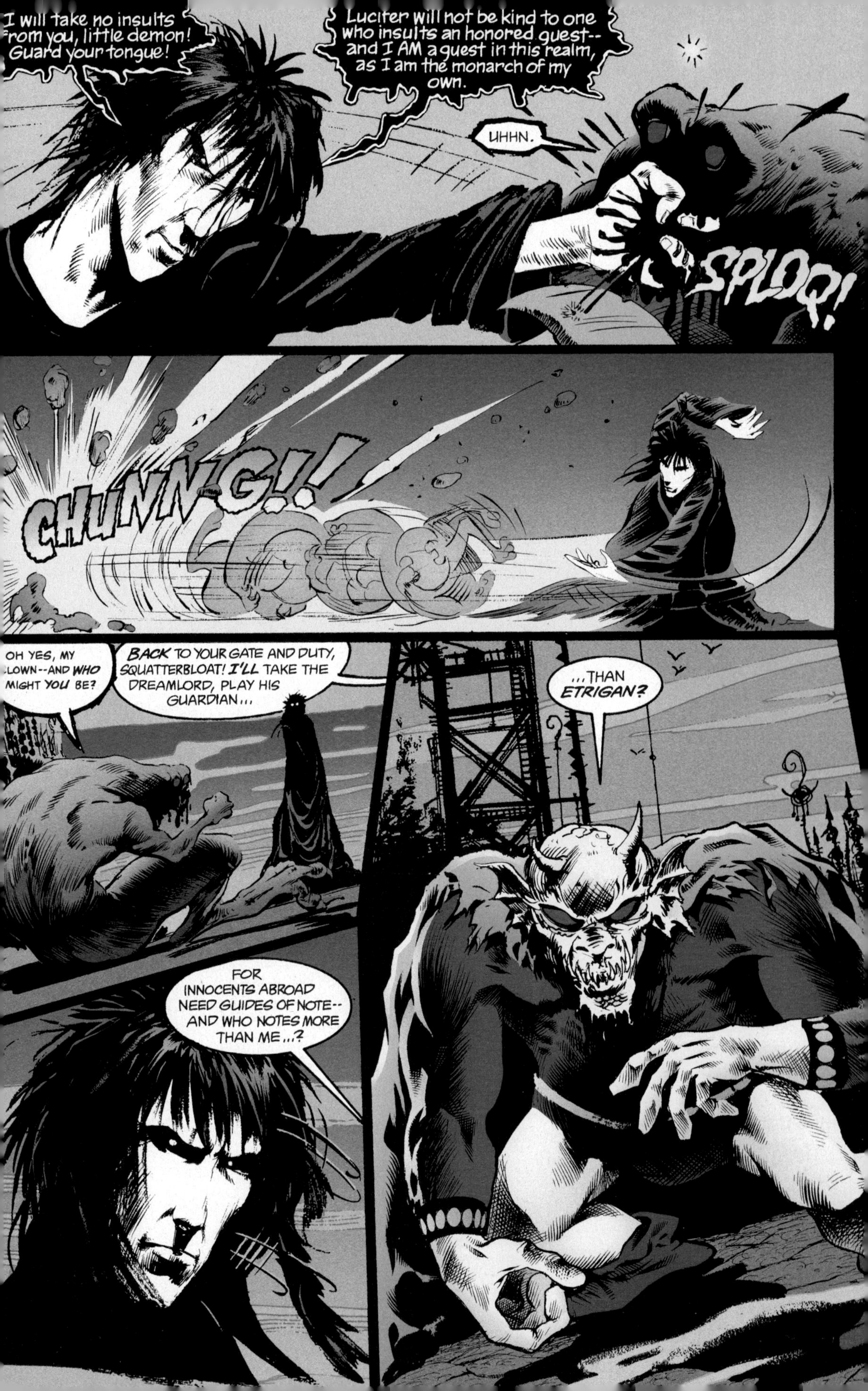
I will take no insults from you, little demon! Guard your tongue!
Lucifer will not be kind to one who insults an honored guest-- and I AM a guest in this realm, as I am the monarch of my own.
UHHN.
SPLOQ!
CHUNNG!!
OH YES, MY CLOWN--AND WHO MIGHT YOU BE?
BACK TO YOUR GATE AND DUTY, SQUATTERBLOAT! I'LL TAKE THE DREAMLORD, PLAY HIS GUARDIAN...
...THAN ETRIGAN?
FOR INNOCENTS ABROAD NEED GUIDES OF NOTE-- AND WHO NOTES MORE THAN ME...?

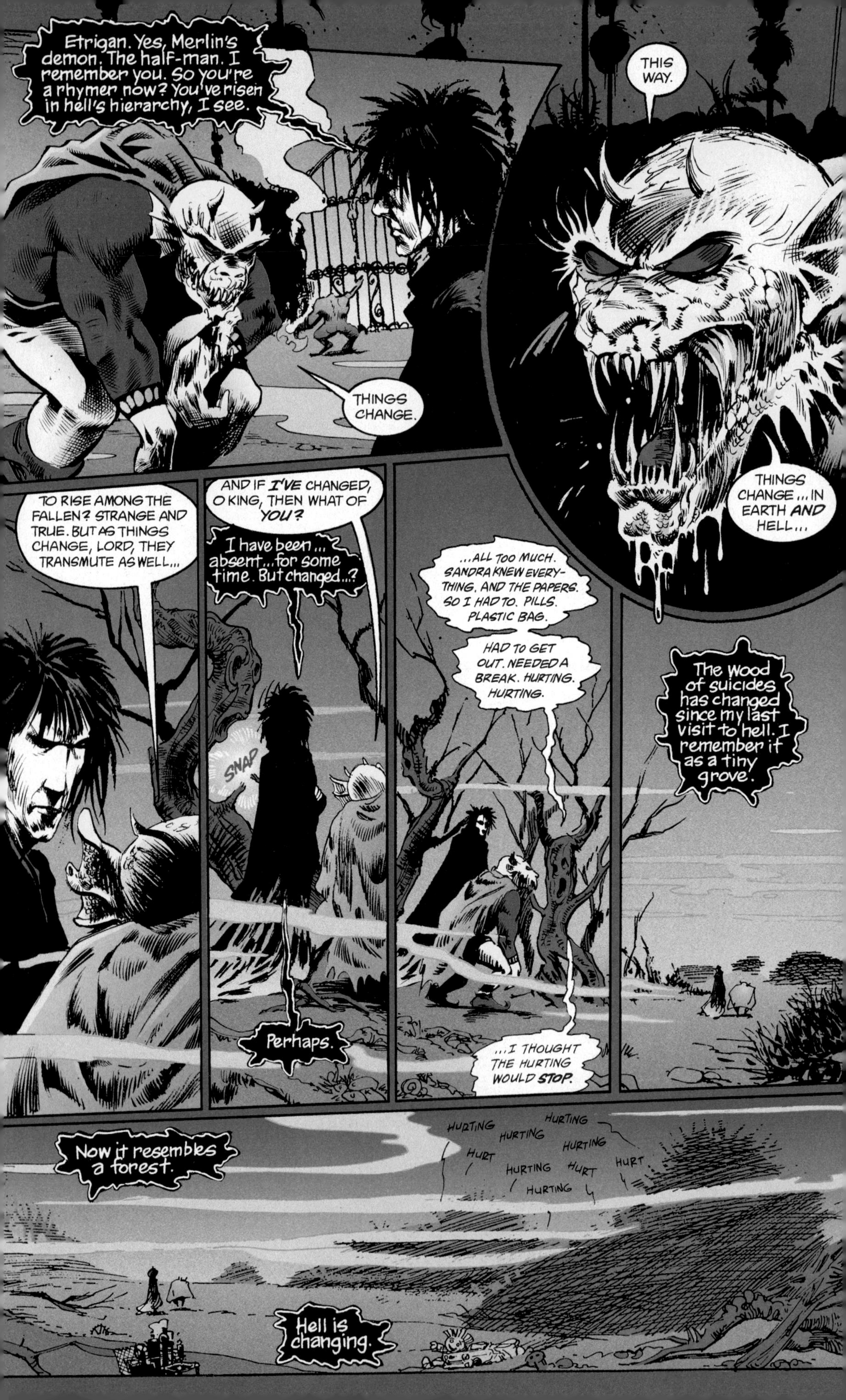

Etrigan. Yes, Merlin's demon. The half-man. I remember you. So you're a rhymer now? You've risen in hell's hierarchy, I see.
THINGS CHANGE.
THIS WAY.
THINGS CHANGE... IN EARTH AND HELL...
TO RISE AMONG THE FALLEN? STRANGE AND TRUE. BUT AS THINGS CHANGE, LORD, THEY TRANSMUTE AS WELL...
AND IF I'VE CHANGED, O KING, THEN WHAT OF YOU?
I have been... absent... for some time. But changed...?
SNAP
Perhaps.
...ALL TOO MUCH. SANDRA KNEW EVERYTHING. AND THE PAPERS. SO I HAD TO. PILLS. PLASTIC BAG.
HAD TO GET OUT. NEEDED A BREAK. HURTING. HURTING.
...I THOUGHT THE HURTING WOULD STOP.
The wood of suicides has changed since my last visit to hell. I remember it as a tiny grove.
Now it resembles a forest.
HURTING
HURTING
HURTING
HURTING
HURT
HURTING
HURT
HURT
HURTING
Hell is changing.

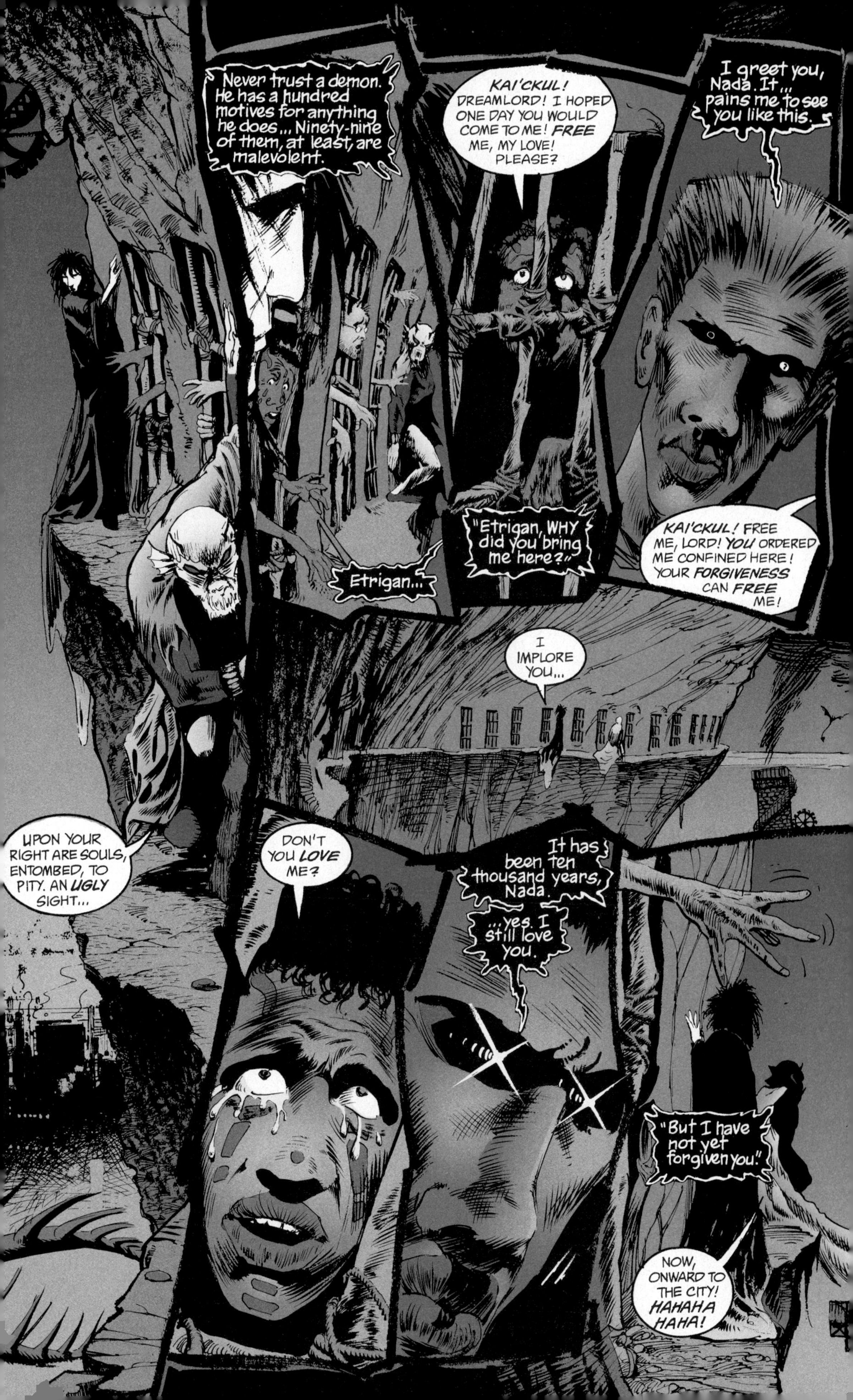
Never trust a demon. He has a hundred motives for anything he does... Ninety-nine of them, at least, are malevolent.
KAI'CKUL! DREAMLORD! I HOPED ONE DAY YOU WOULD COME TO ME! FREE ME, MY LOVE! PLEASE?
I greet you, Nada. It... pains me to see you like this.
Etrigan...
"Etrigan, WHY did you bring me here?"
KAI'CKUL! FREE ME, LORD! YOU ORDERED ME CONFINED HERE! YOUR FORGIVENESS CAN FREE ME!
I IMPLORE YOU...
UPON YOUR RIGHT ARE SOULS, ENTOMBED, TO PITY. AN UGLY SIGHT...
DON'T YOU LOVE ME?
It has been ten thousand years, Nada.
...yes. I still love you.
"But I have not yet forgiven you."
NOW, ONWARD TO THE CITY! HAHAHA HAHA!

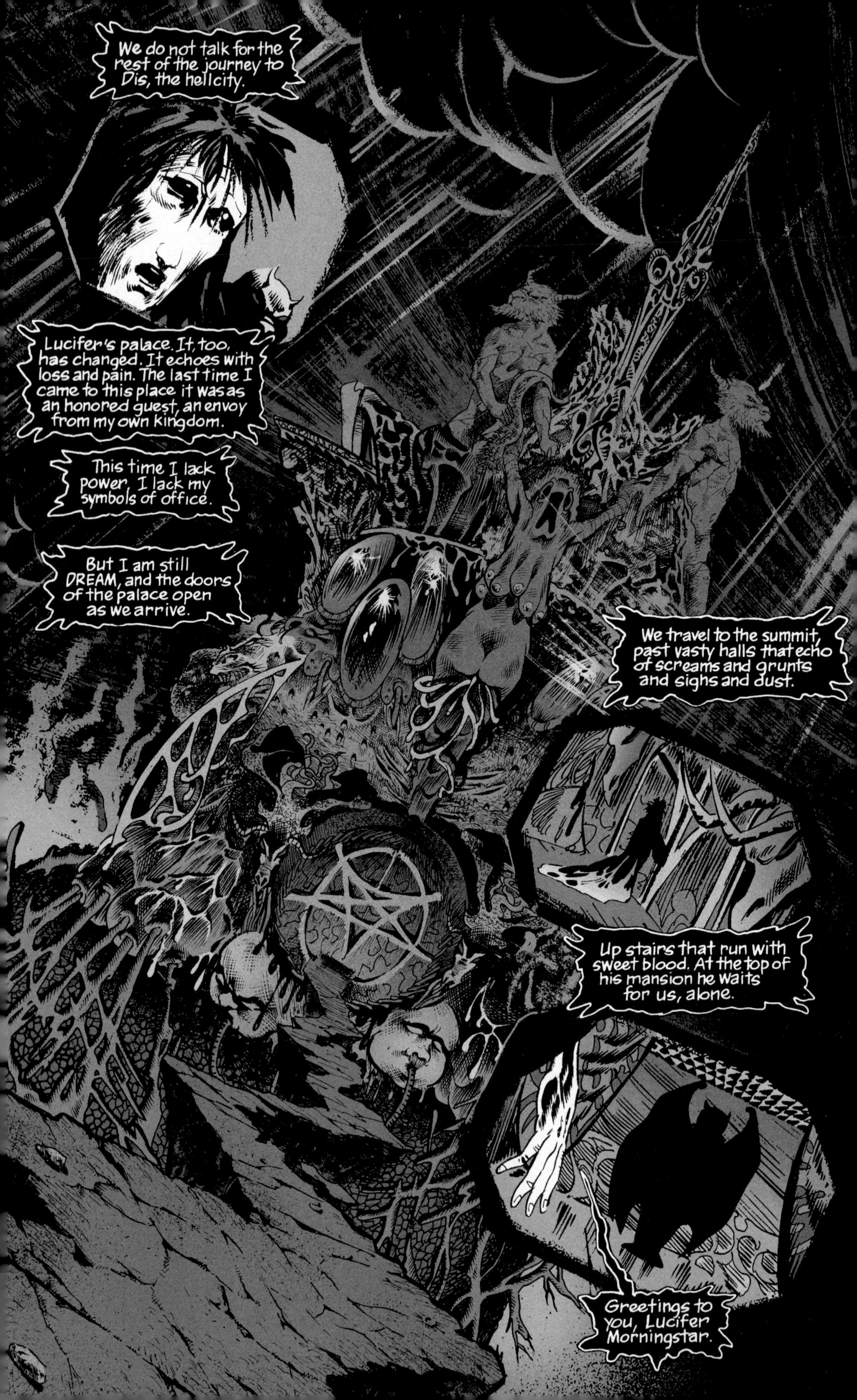
We do not talk for the rest of the journey to Dis, the hellcity.
Lucifer's palace. It, too, has changed. It echoes with loss and pain. The last time I came to this place it was as an honored guest, an envoy from my own kingdom.
This time I lack power, I lack my symbols of office.
But I am still DREAM, and the doors of the palace open as we arrive.
We travel to the summit, past vasty halls that echo of screams and grunts and sighs and dust.
Up stairs that run with sweet blood. At the top of his mansion he waits for us, alone.
Greetings to you, Lucifer Morningstar.

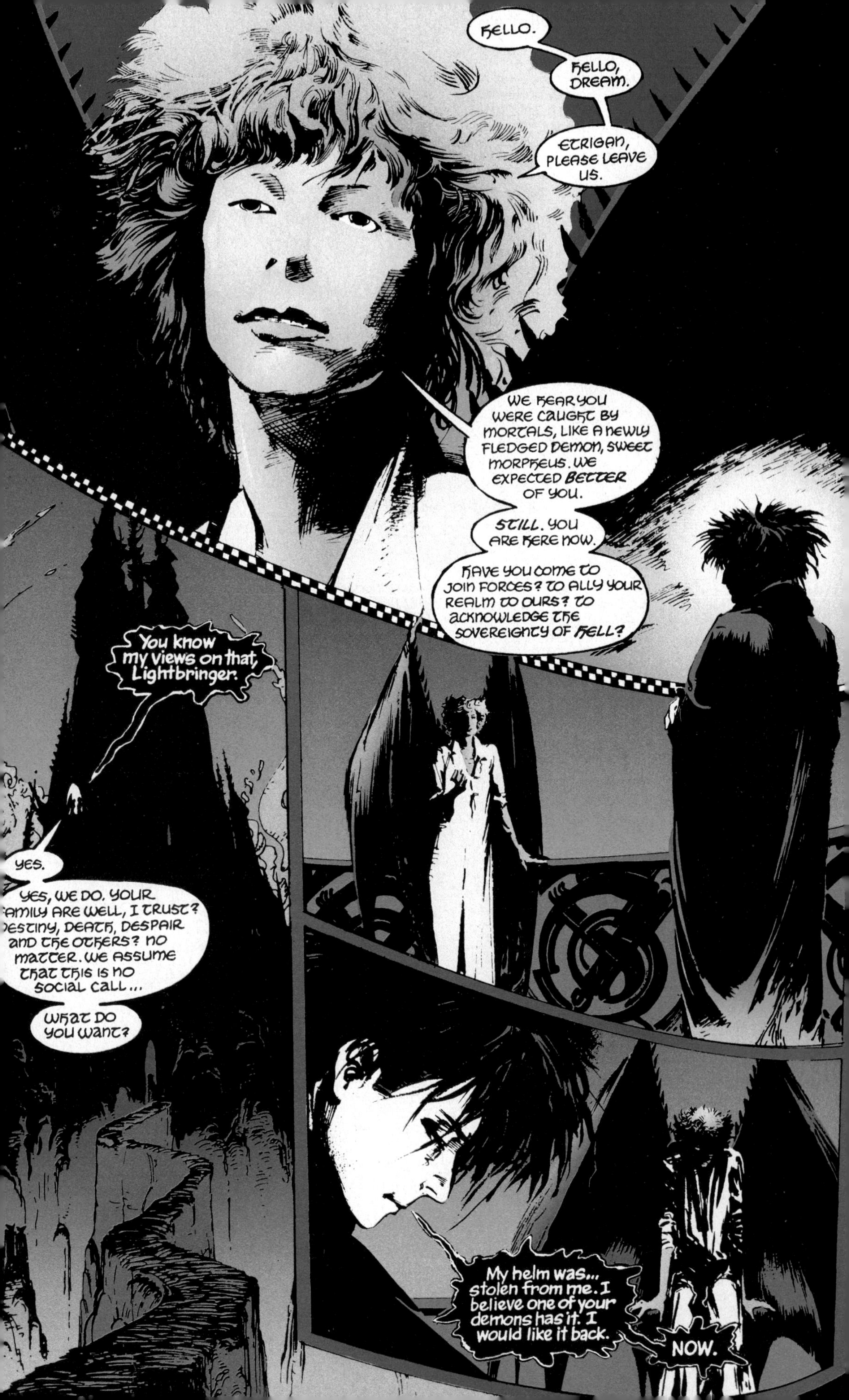
HELLO.
HELLO, DREAM.
ETRIGAN, PLEASE LEAVE US.
WE HEAR YOU WERE CAUGHT BY MORTALS, LIKE A NEWLY FLEDGED DEMON, SWEET MORPHEUS. WE EXPECTED BETTER OF YOU.
STILL. YOU ARE HERE NOW.
HAVE YOU COME TO JOIN FORCES? TO ALLY YOUR REALM TO OURS? TO ACKNOWLEDGE THE SOVEREIGNTY OF HELL?
You know my views on that, Lightbringer.
YES.
YES, WE DO. YOUR FAMILY ARE WELL, I TRUST? DESTINY, DEATH, DESPAIR AND THE OTHERS? NO MATTER. WE ASSUME THAT THIS IS NO SOCIAL CALL...
WHAT DO YOU WANT?
My helm was... stolen from me. I believe one of your demons has it. I would like it back.
NOW.

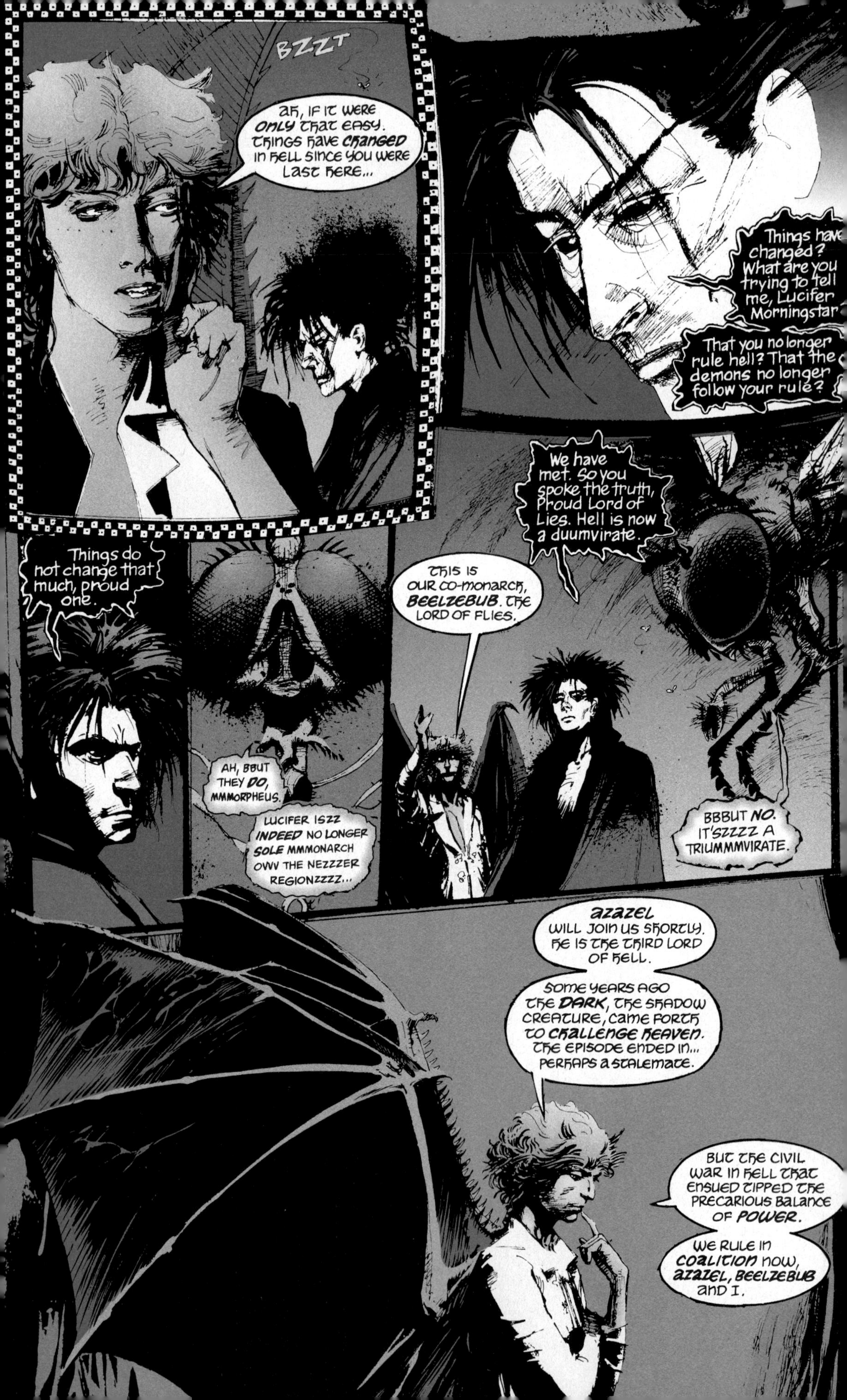
BZZT
AH, IF IT WERE ONLY THAT EASY. THINGS HAVE CHANGED IN HELL SINCE YOU WERE LAST HERE...
Things have changed? What are you trying to tell me, Lucifer Morningstar?
That you no longer rule hell? That the demons no longer follow your rule?
Things do not change that much, proud one.
AH, BBUT THEY DO, MMMORPHEUS.
LUCIFER ISZZ INDEED NO LONGER SOLE MMMONARCH OVVV THE NEZZZER REGIONZZZZ...
THIS IS OUR CO-MONARCH, BEELZEBUB. THE LORD OF FLIES.
We have met. So you spoke the truth, Proud Lord of Lies. Hell is now a duumvirate.
BBBUT NO. IT'SZZZZ A TRIUMMMVIRATE.
AZAZEL WILL JOIN US SHORTLY. HE IS THE THIRD LORD OF HELL.
SOME YEARS AGO THE DARK, THE SHADOW CREATURE, CAME FORTH TO CHALLENGE HEAVEN. THE EPISODE ENDED IN... PERHAPS A STALEMATE.
BUT THE CIVIL WAR IN HELL THAT ENSUED TIPPED THE PRECARIOUS BALANCE OF POWER.
WE RULE IN COALITION NOW, AZAZEL, BEELZEBUB AND I.

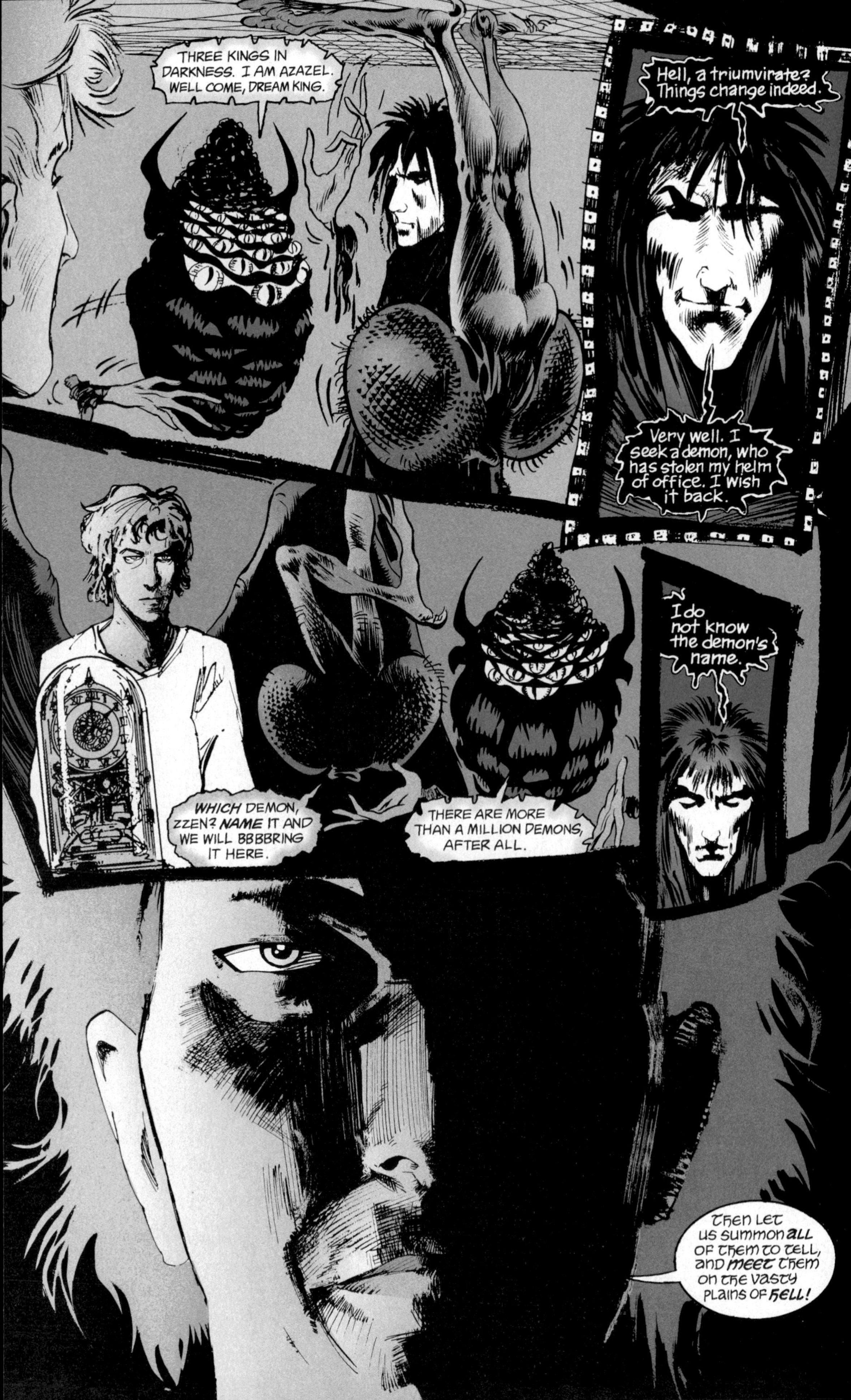
THREE KINGS IN DARKNESS. I AM AZAZEL. WELL COME, DREAM KING.
Hell, a triumvirate? Things change indeed.
Very well. I seek a demon, who has stolen my helm of office. I wish it back.
WHICH DEMON, ZZEN? NAME IT AND WE WILL BBBBRING IT HERE.
THERE ARE MORE THAN A MILLION DEMONS, AFTER ALL.
I do not know the demon's name.
THEN LET US SUMMON ALL OF THEM TO TELL, AND MEET THEM ON THE VASTY PLAINS OF HELL!

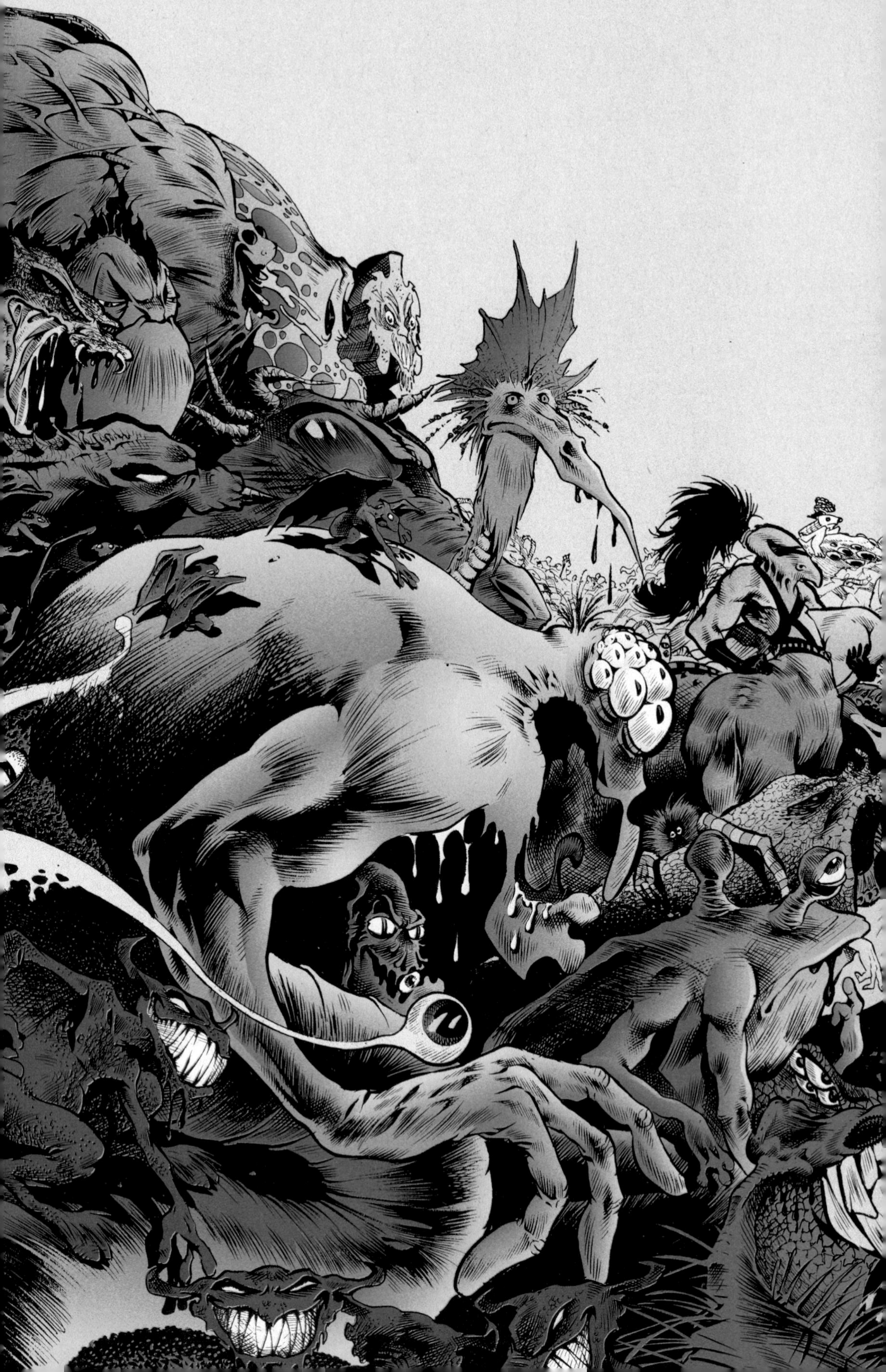

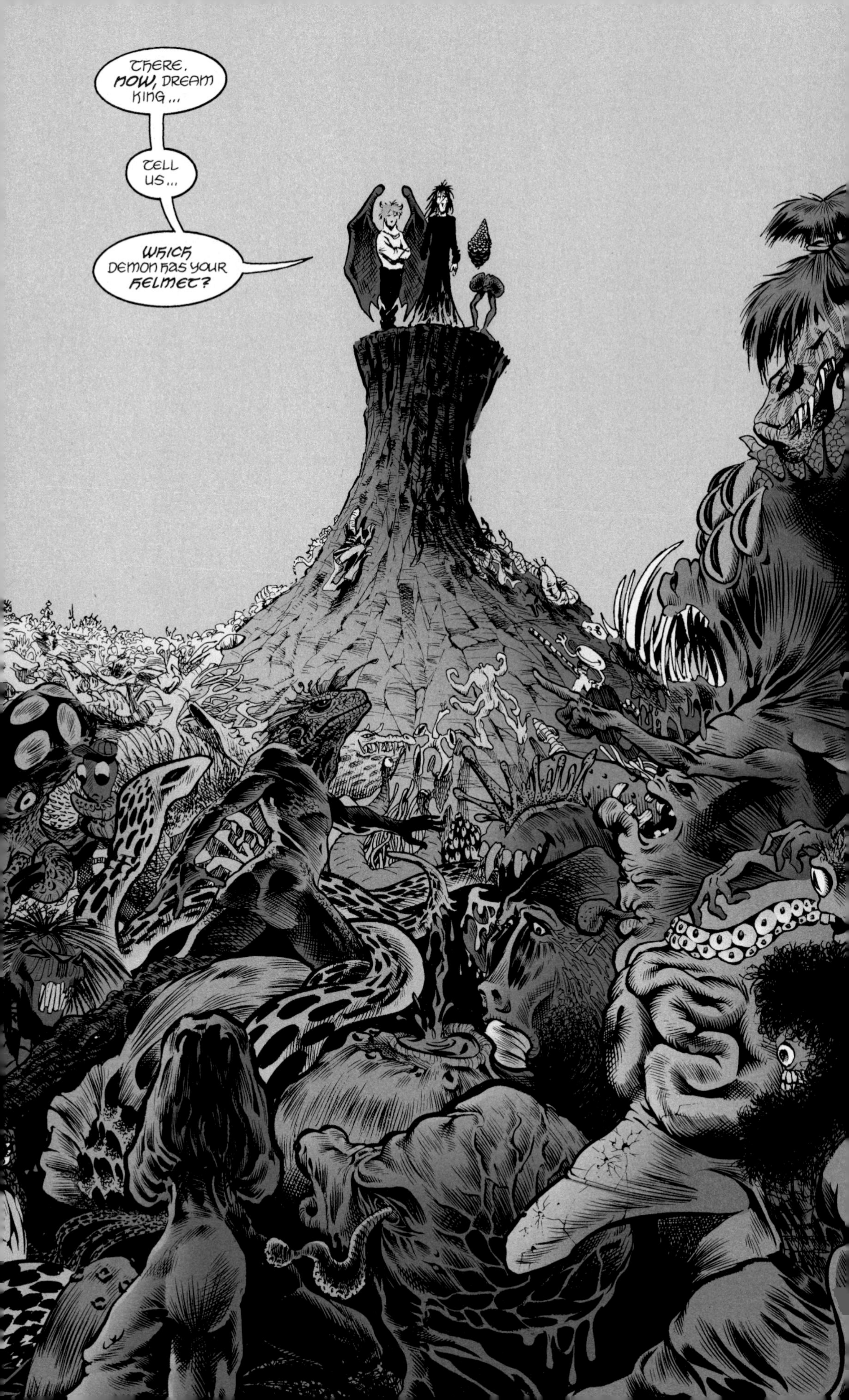
THERE. NOW, DREAM KING...
TELL US...
WHICH DEMON HAS YOUR HELMET?

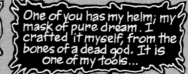

I look at the demons. Some I recognize from nightmares. Others have passed through the dreamworld in the past. But there are so many...

One of you has my helm; my mask of pure dream. I crafted it myself, from the bones of a dead god. It is one of my tools...

Ah.

That one.

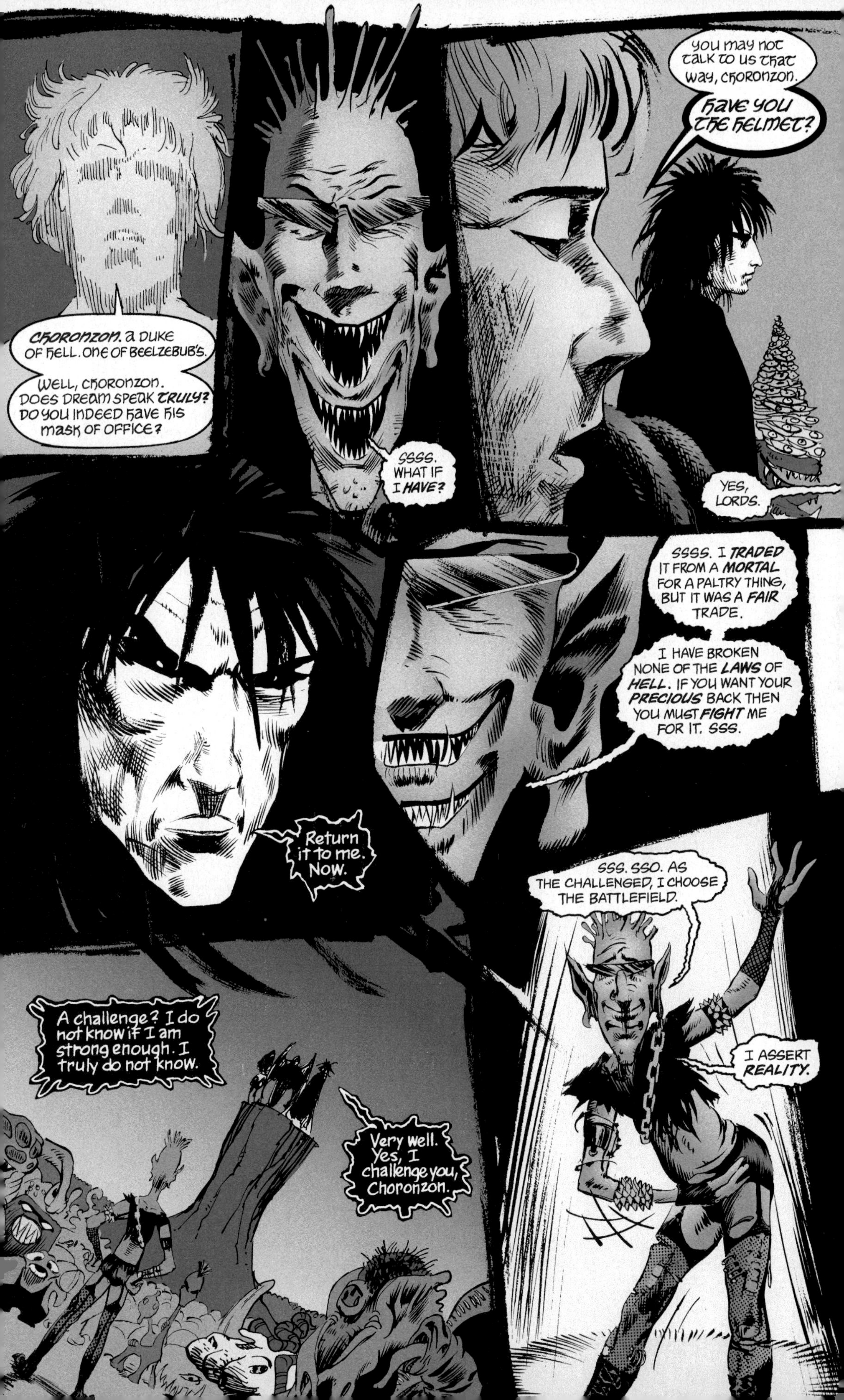
CHORONZON. A DUKE OF HELL. ONE OF BEELZEBUB'S.
WELL, CHORONZON. DOES DREAM SPEAK TRULY? DO YOU INDEED HAVE HIS MASK OF OFFICE?
SSSS. WHAT IF I HAVE?
YOU MAY NOT TALK TO US THAT WAY, CHORONZON.
HAVE YOU THE HELMET?
YES, LORDS.
SSSS. I TRADED IT FROM A MORTAL FOR A PALTRY THING, BUT IT WAS A FAIR TRADE.
I HAVE BROKEN NONE OF THE LAWS OF HELL. IF YOU WANT YOUR PRECIOUS BACK THEN YOU MUST FIGHT ME FOR IT. SSS.
Return it to me. Now.
SSS. SSO. AS THE CHALLENGED, I CHOOSE THE BATTLEFIELD.
I ASSERT REALITY.
A challenge? I do not know if I am strong enough. I truly do not know.
Very well. Yes, I challenge you, Choronzon.

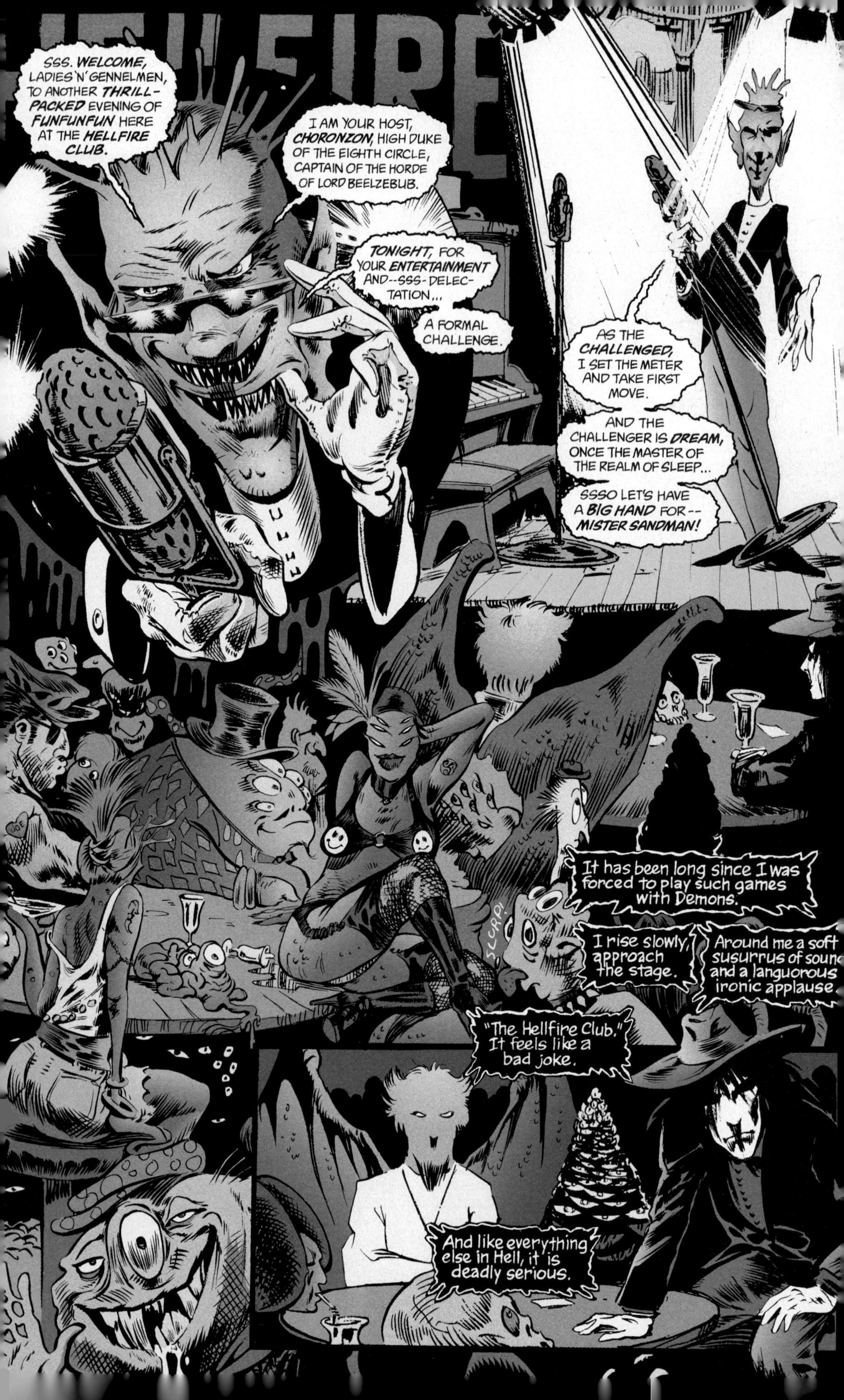

HELLFIRE
SSS. WELCOME, LADIES 'N' GENNELMEN, TO ANOTHER THRILL-PACKED EVENING OF FUNFUNFUN HERE AT THE HELLFIRE CLUB.
I AM YOUR HOST, CHORONZON, HIGH DUKE OF THE EIGHTH CIRCLE, CAPTAIN OF THE HORDE OF LORD BEELZEBUB.
TONIGHT, FOR YOUR ENTERTAINMENT AND--SSS-DELECTATION...
A FORMAL CHALLENGE.
AS THE CHALLENGED, I SET THE METER AND TAKE FIRST MOVE.
AND THE CHALLENGER IS DREAM, ONCE THE MASTER OF THE REALM OF SLEEP...
SSSO LET'S HAVE A BIG HAND FOR-- MISTER SANDMAN!
It has been long since I was forced to play such games with Demons.
I rise slowly, approach the stage.
Around me a soft susurrus of soun and a languorous ironic applause.
SLURP!
"The Hellfire Club." It feels like a bad joke.
And like everything else in Hell, it is deadly serious.

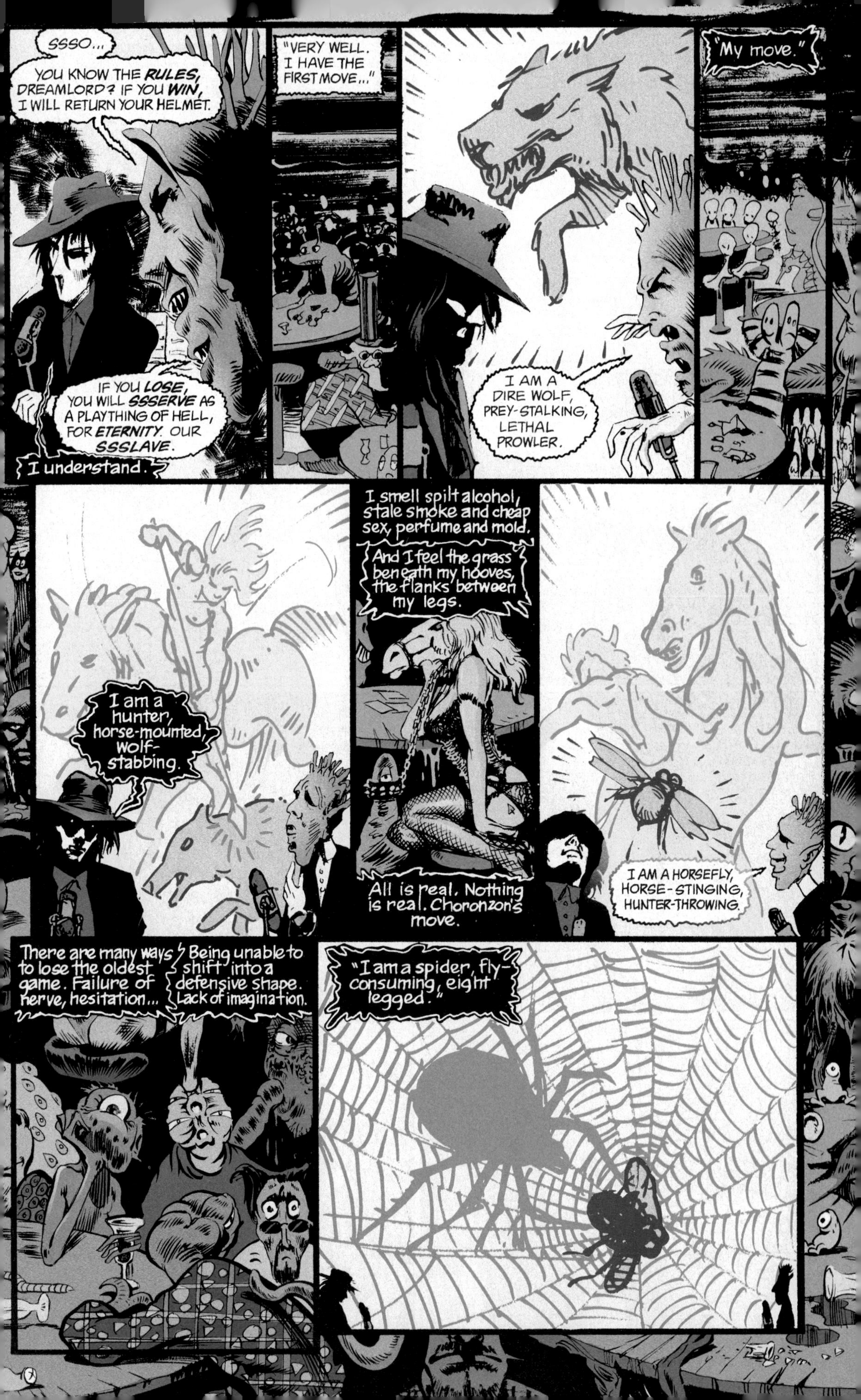

SSSO...
YOU KNOW THE RULES, DREAMLORD? IF YOU WIN, I WILL RETURN YOUR HELMET.
IF YOU LOSE, YOU WILL SSSERVE AS A PLAYTHING OF HELL, FOR ETERNITY. OUR SSSLAVE.
I understand.
"VERY WELL. I HAVE THE FIRST MOVE..."
I AM A DIRE WOLF, PREY-STALKING, LETHAL PROWLER.
"My move."
I am a hunter, horse-mounted, wolf-stabbing.
I smell spilt alcohol, stale smoke and cheap sex, perfume and mold.
And I feel the grass beneath my hooves, the flanks between my legs.
All is real. Nothing is real. Choronzon's move.
I AM A HORSEFLY, HORSE-STINGING, HUNTER-THROWING.
There are many ways to lose the oldest game. Failure of nerve, hesitation...
Being unable to shift into a defensive shape. Lack of imagination.
"I am a spider, fly-consuming, eight legged."

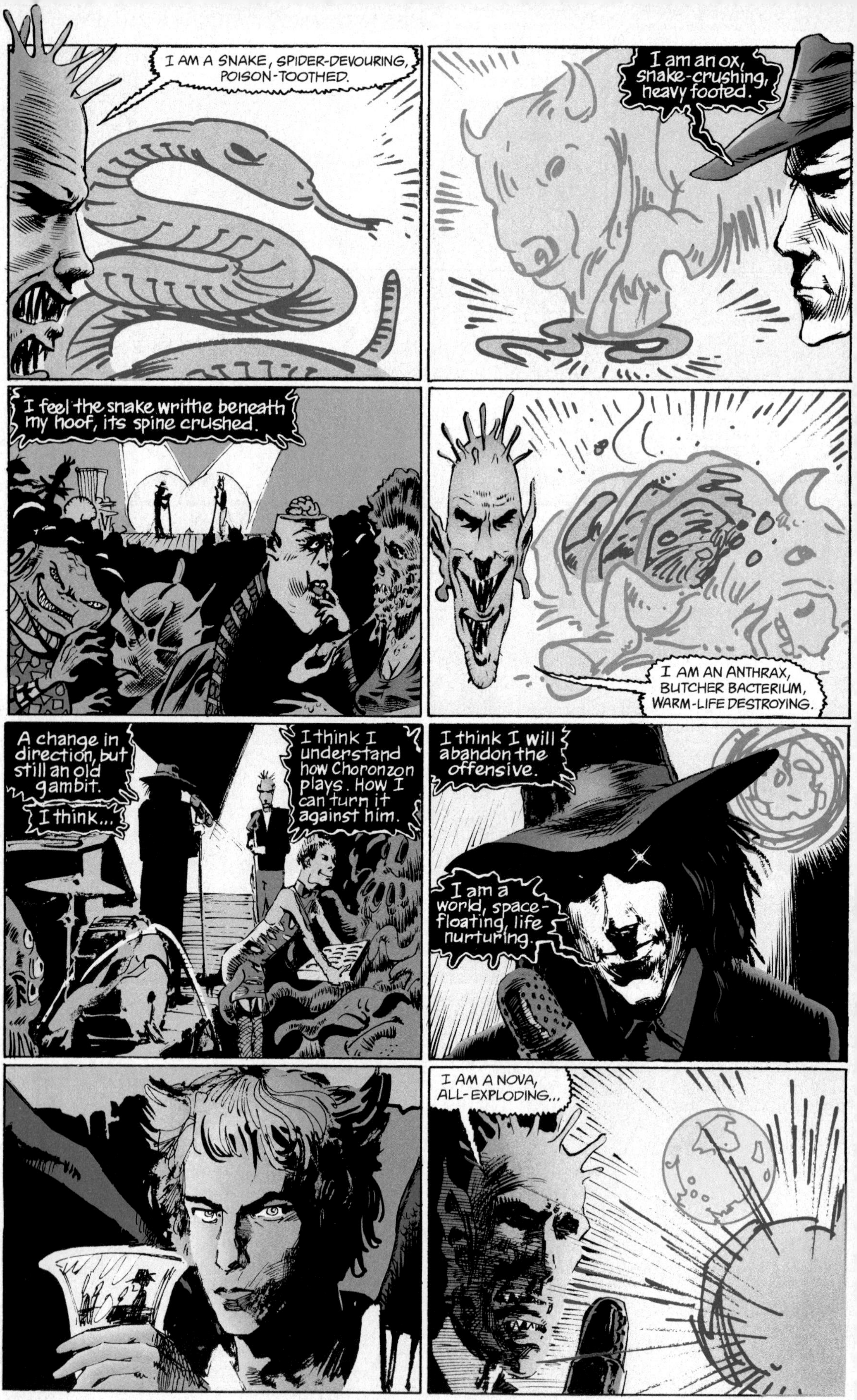
I AM A SNAKE, SPIDER-DEVOURING, POISON-TOOTHED.
I am an ox, snake-crushing, heavy footed.
I feel the snake writhe beneath my hoof, its spine crushed.
I AM AN ANTHRAX, BUTCHER BACTERIUM, WARM-LIFE DESTROYING.
A change in direction, but still an old gambit.
I think...
I think I understand how Choronzon plays. How I can turn it against him.
I think I will abandon the offensive.
I am a world, space-floating, life nurturing.
I AM A NOVA, ALL-EXPLODING...

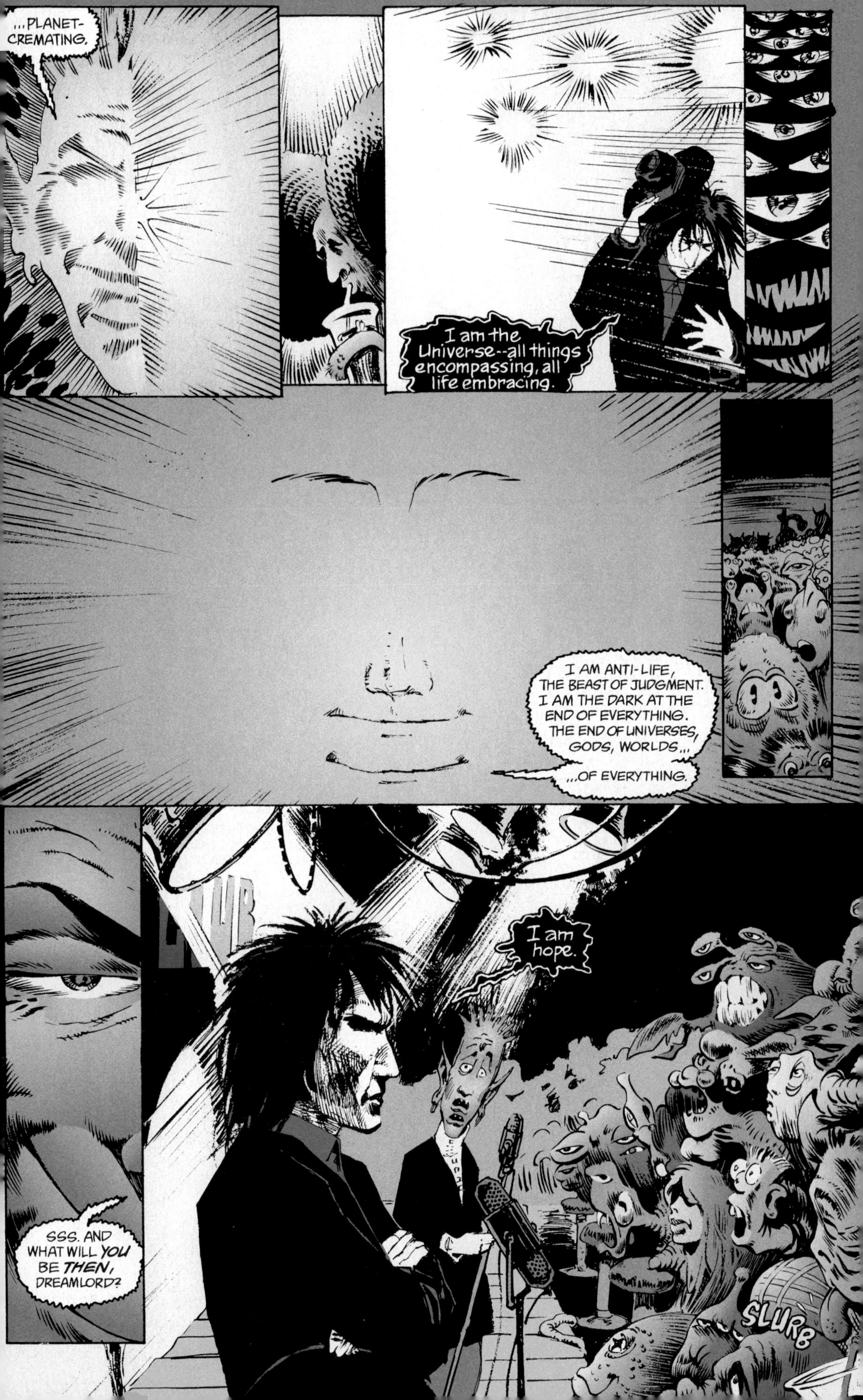
...PLANET-CREMATING.
I am the Universe--all things encompassing, all life embracing.
I AM ANTI-LIFE, THE BEAST OF JUDGMENT. I AM THE DARK AT THE END OF EVERYTHING. THE END OF UNIVERSES, GODS, WORLDS...
...OF EVERYTHING.
I am hope.
SSS. AND WHAT WILL YOU BE THEN, DREAMLORD?
SLURB

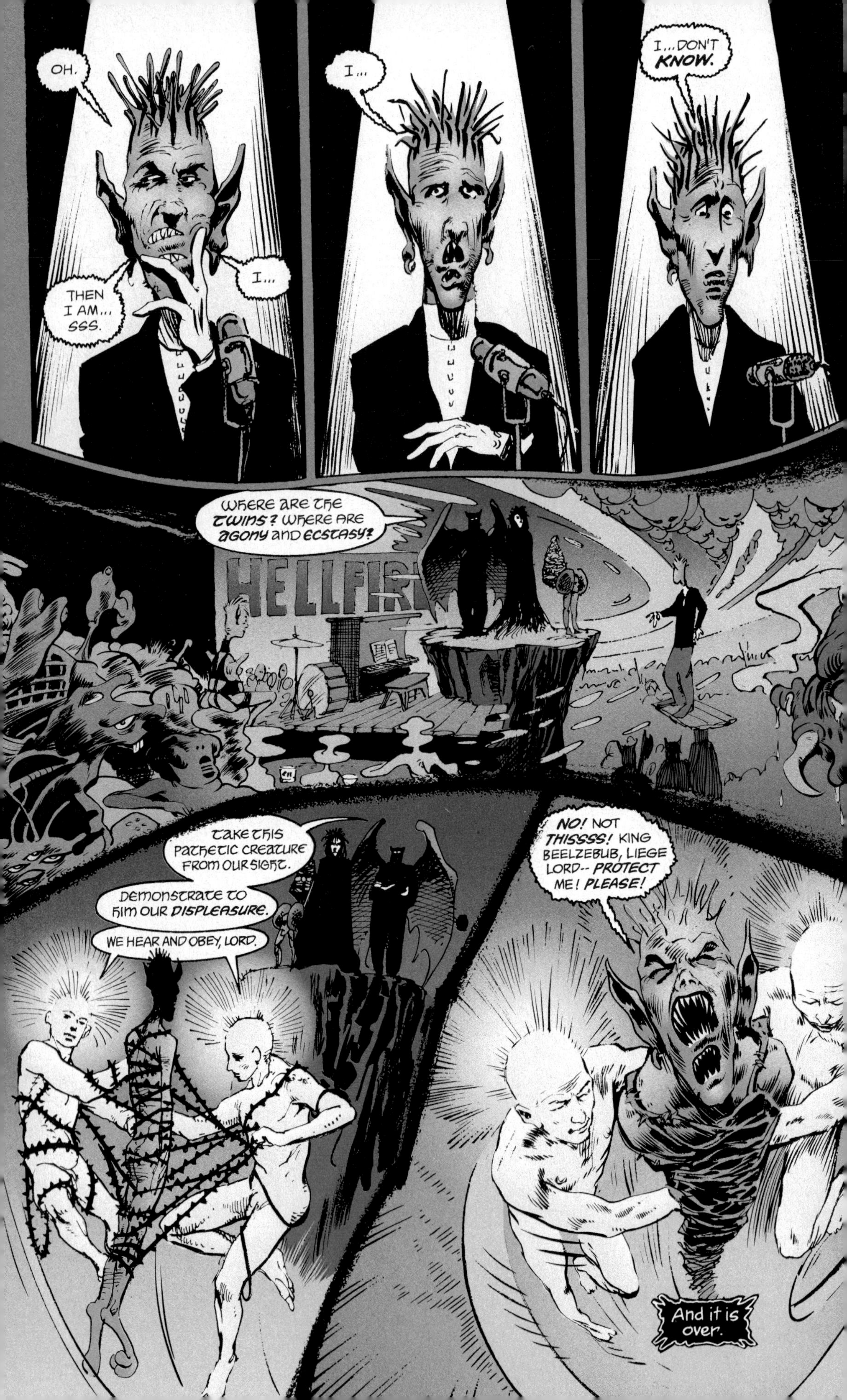

OH.
I...
THEN I AM... SSS.
I...
I... DON'T KNOW.
WHERE ARE THE TWINS? WHERE ARE AGONY AND ECSTASY?
HELLFIRE
TAKE THIS PATHETIC CREATURE FROM OUR SIGHT.
DEMONSTRATE TO HIM OUR DISPLEASURE.
WE HEAR AND OBEY, LORD.
NO! NOT THISSSS! KING BEELZEBUB, LIEGE LORD-- PROTECT ME! PLEASE!
And it is over.

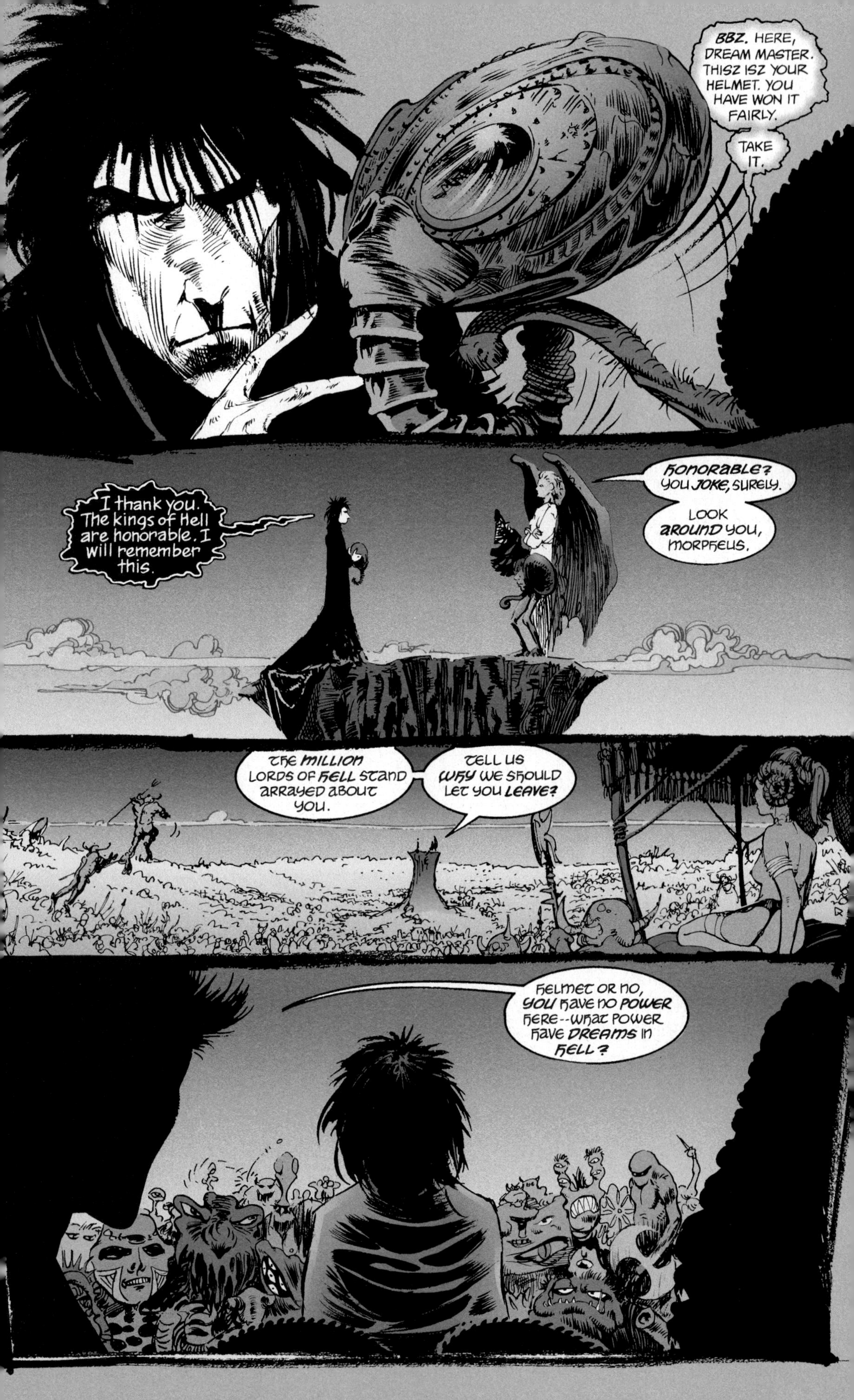
BBZ. HERE, DREAM MASTER. THISZ ISZ YOUR HELMET. YOU HAVE WON IT FAIRLY.
TAKE IT.
I thank you. The kings of Hell are honorable. I will remember this.
HONORABLE? YOU JOKE, SURELY.
LOOK AROUND YOU, MORPHEUS.
THE MILLION LORDS OF HELL STAND ARRAYED ABOUT YOU.
TELL US WHY WE SHOULD LET YOU LEAVE?
HELMET OR NO, YOU HAVE NO POWER HERE--WHAT POWER HAVE DREAMS IN HELL?

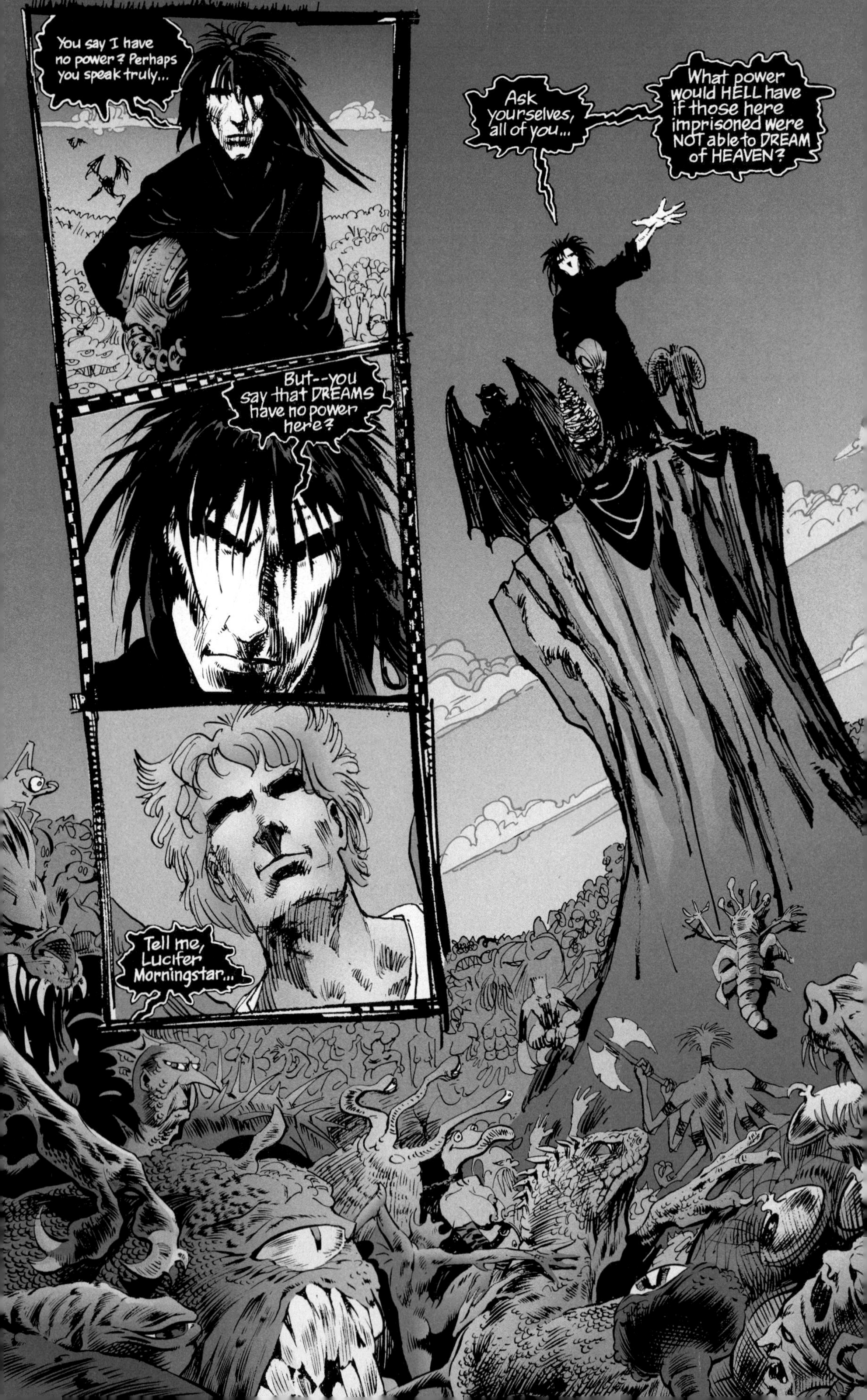
You say I have no power? Perhaps you speak truly...
But--you say that DREAMS have no power here?
Tell me, Lucifer Morningstar...
Ask yourselves, all of you...
What power would HELL have if those here imprisoned were NOT able to DREAM of HEAVEN?

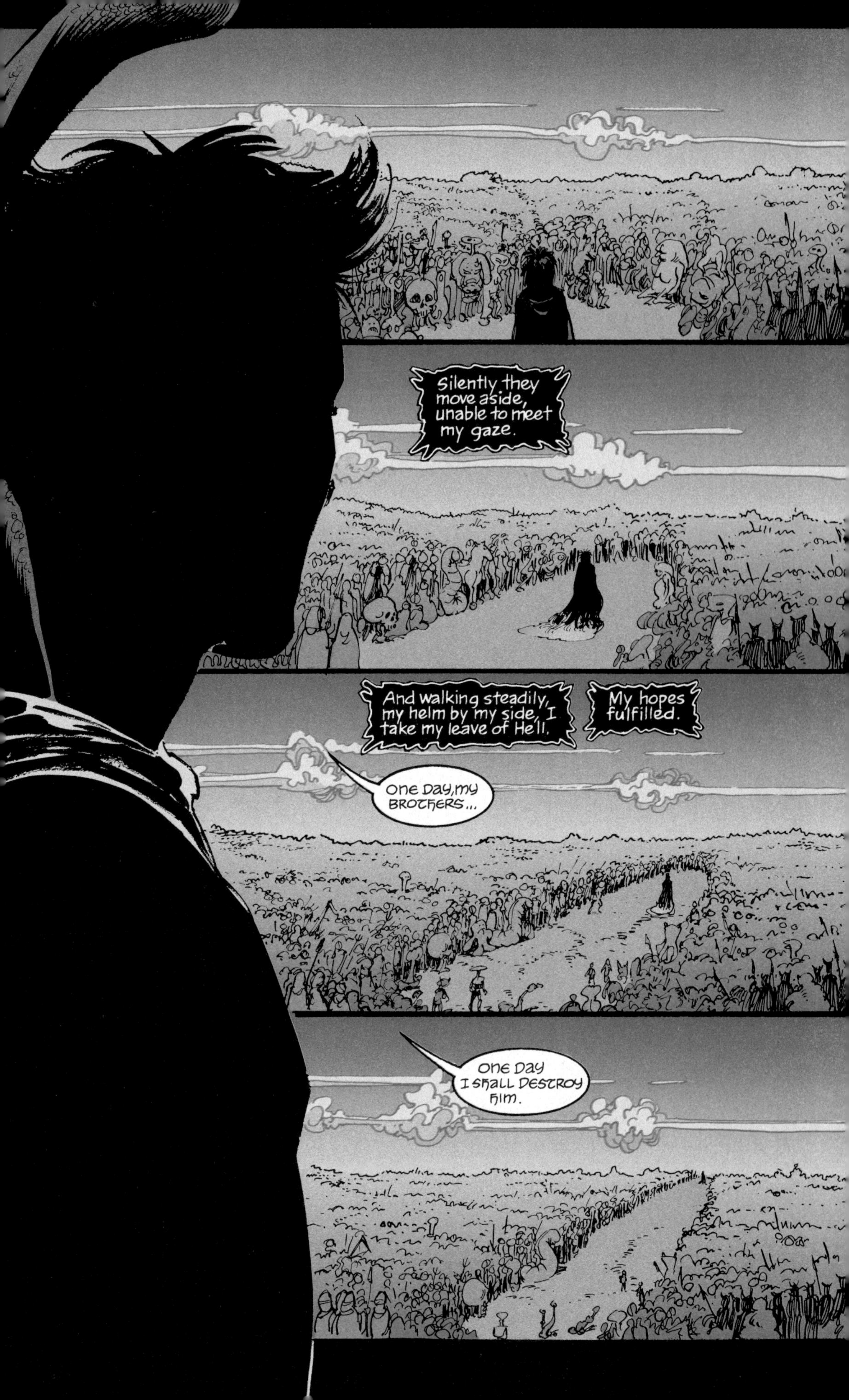
Silently they move aside, unable to meet my gaze.
And walking steadily, my helm by my side, I take my leave of Hell.
My hopes fulfilled.
One Day, my BROTHERS...
One Day I SHALL DESTROY HIM.

EPILOGUE

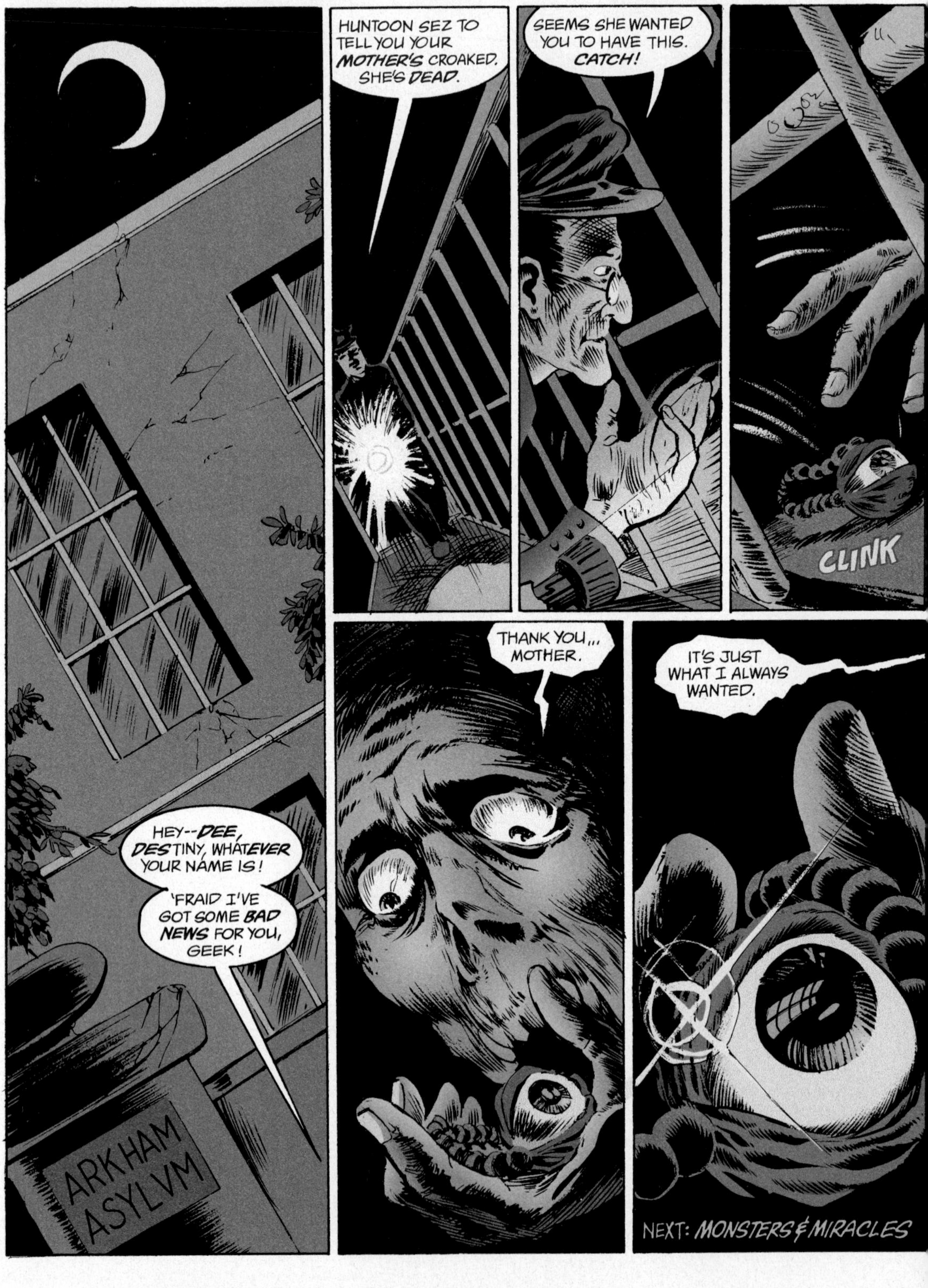
HUNTOON SEZ TO TELL YOU YOUR MOTHER'S CROAKED. SHE'S DEAD.
SEEMS SHE WANTED YOU TO HAVE THIS. CATCH!
CLINK
HEY--DEE, DESTINY, WHATEVER YOUR NAME IS!
'FRAID I'VE GOT SOME BAD NEWS FOR YOU, GEEK!
ARKHAM ASYLVM
THANK YOU... MOTHER.
IT'S JUST WHAT I ALWAYS WANTED.
NEXT: MONSTERS & MIRACLES

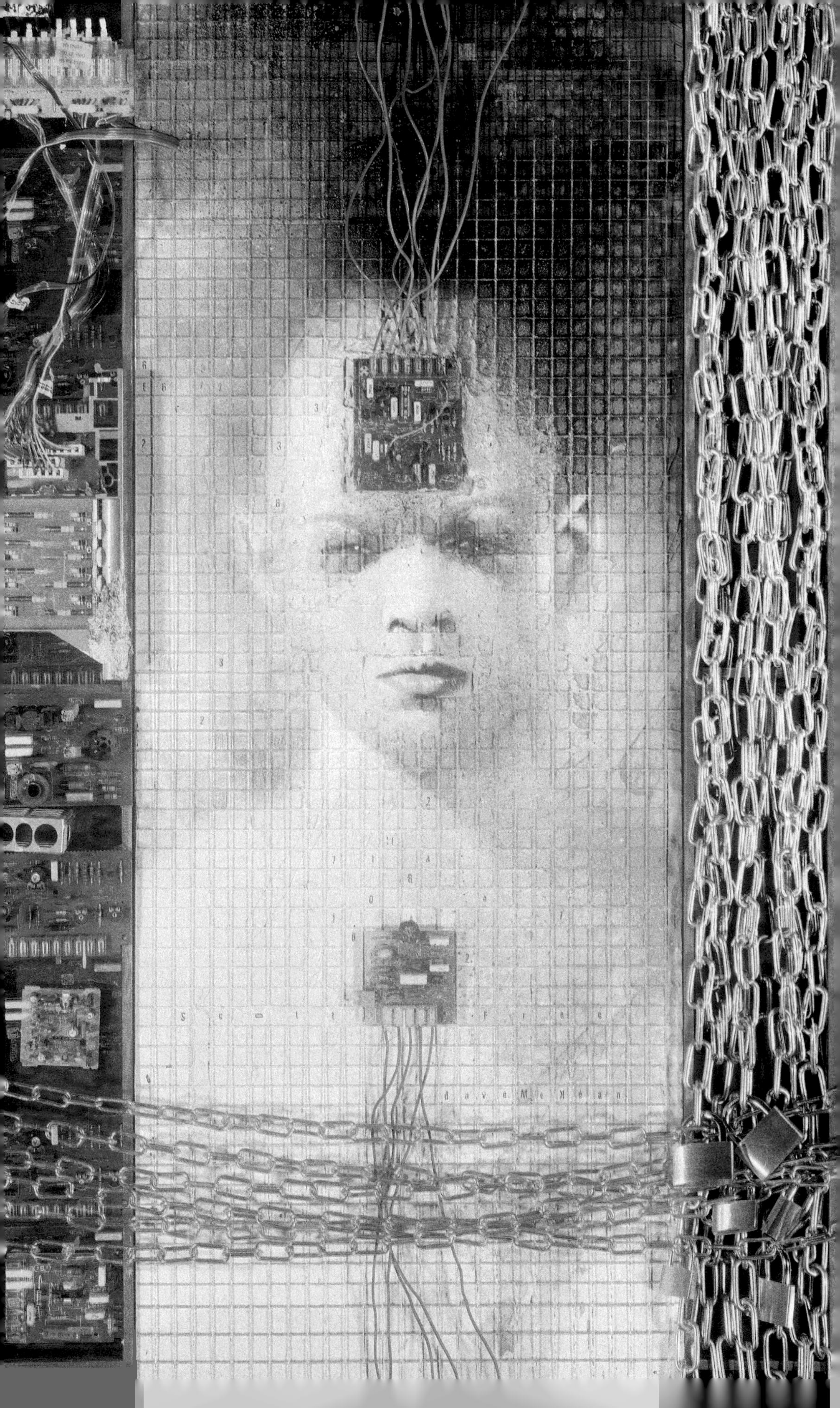

S c o t t F r e e
d a v e M c K e a n

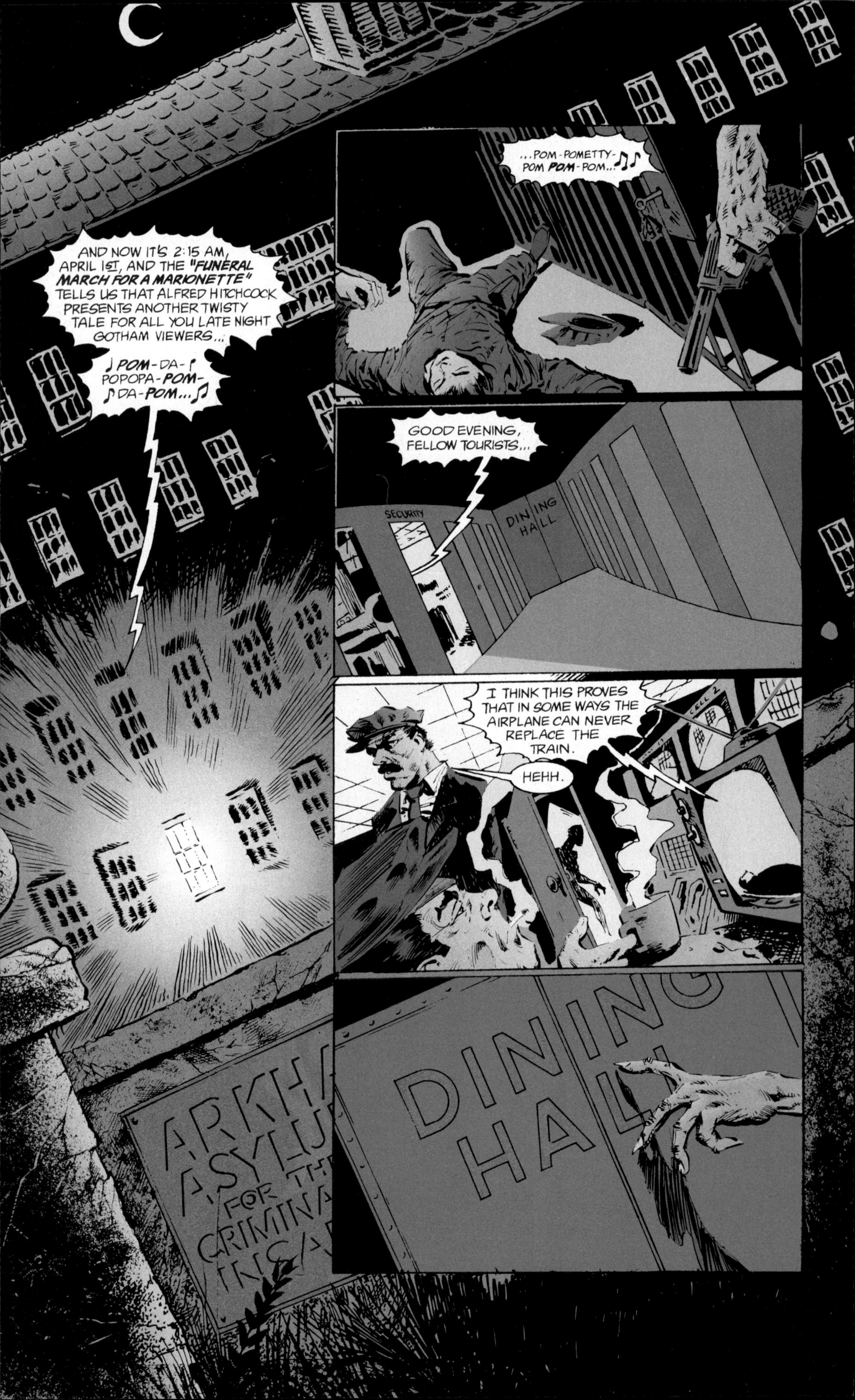
AND NOW IT'S 2:15 AM, APRIL 1ST, AND THE "FUNERAL MARCH FOR A MARIONETTE" TELLS US THAT ALFRED HITCHCOCK PRESENTS ANOTHER TWISTY TALE FOR ALL YOU LATE NIGHT GOTHAM VIEWERS...
POM-DA-POPOPA-POM-DA-POM...
...POM-POMETTY-POM POM-POM...
GOOD EVENING, FELLOW TOURISTS...
SECURITY
DINING HALL
I THINK THIS PROVES THAT IN SOME WAYS THE AIRPLANE CAN NEVER REPLACE THE TRAIN.
HEHH.
CELL 2
DINING HALL

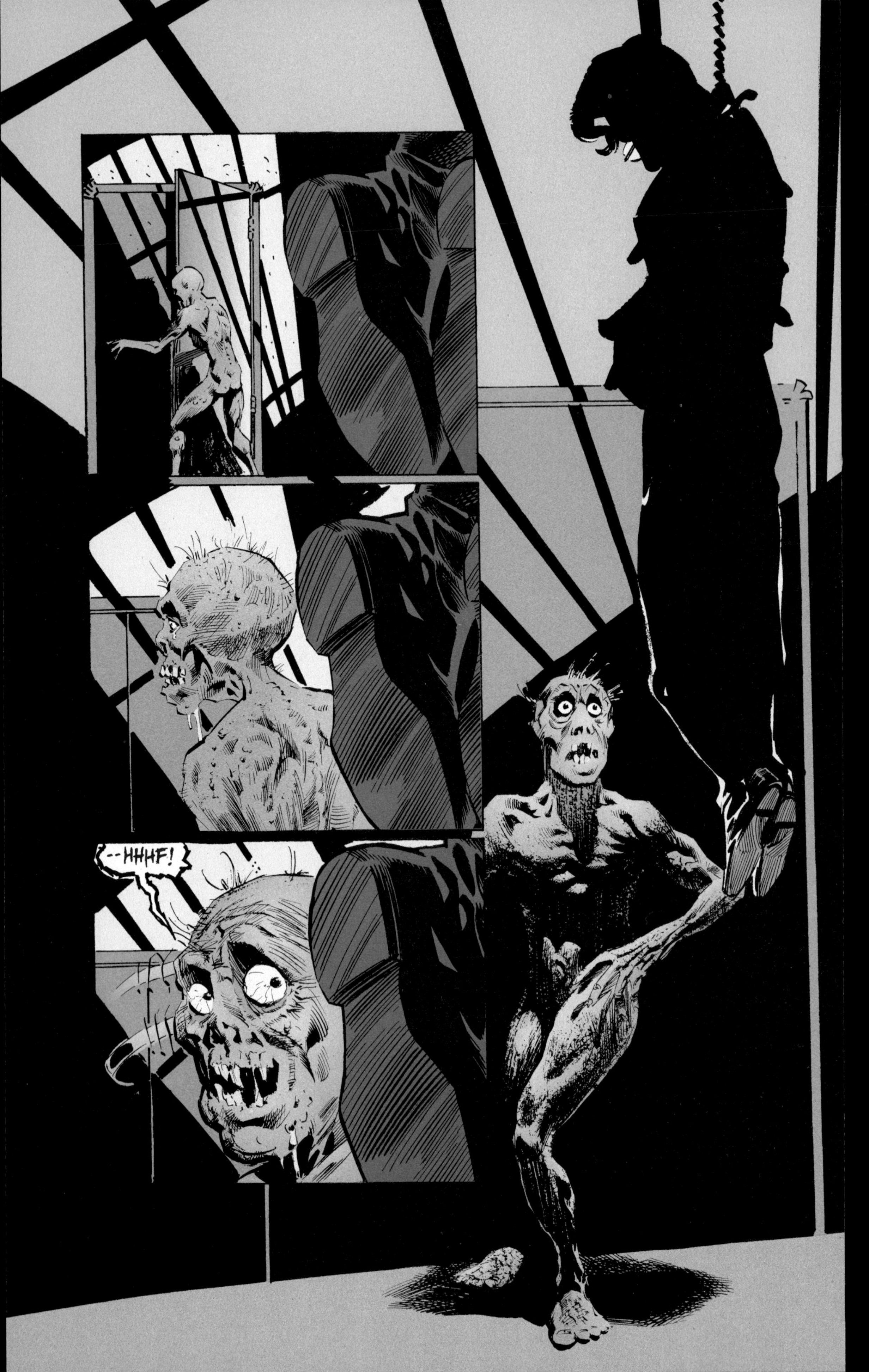
--HHHF!

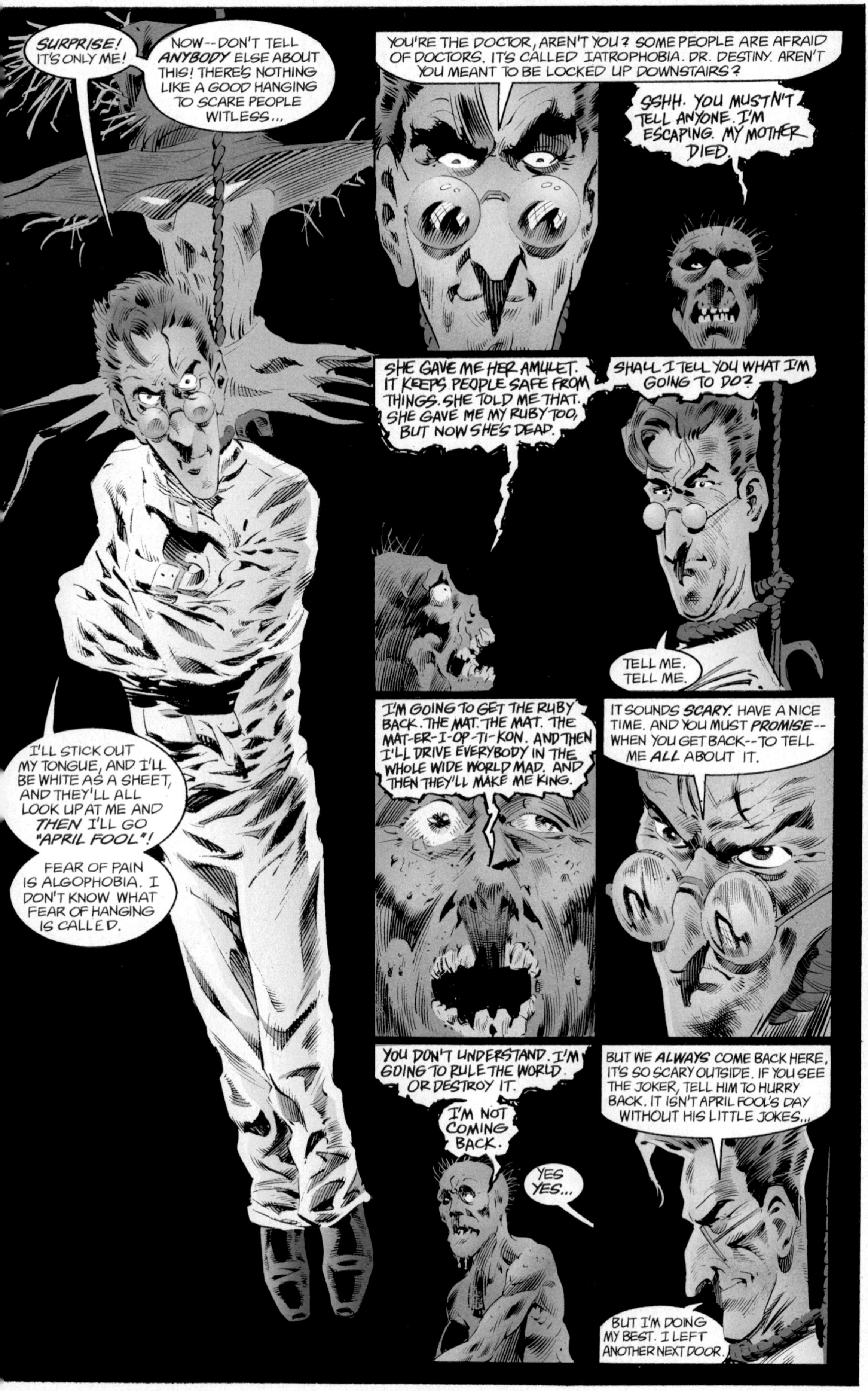
SURPRISE! IT'S ONLY ME!
NOW--DON'T TELL ANYBODY ELSE ABOUT THIS! THERE'S NOTHING LIKE A GOOD HANGING TO SCARE PEOPLE WITLESS...
I'LL STICK OUT MY TONGUE, AND I'LL BE WHITE AS A SHEET, AND THEY'LL ALL LOOK UP AT ME AND THEN I'LL GO "APRIL FOOL"!
FEAR OF PAIN IS ALGOPHOBIA. I DON'T KNOW WHAT FEAR OF HANGING IS CALLED.
YOU'RE THE DOCTOR, AREN'T YOU? SOME PEOPLE ARE AFRAID OF DOCTORS. IT'S CALLED IATROPHOBIA. DR. DESTINY. AREN'T YOU MEANT TO BE LOCKED UP DOWNSTAIRS?
SSHH. YOU MUSTN'T TELL ANYONE. I'M ESCAPING. MY MOTHER DIED.
SHE GAVE ME HER AMULET. IT KEEPS PEOPLE SAFE FROM THINGS. SHE TOLD ME THAT. SHE GAVE ME MY RUBY TOO, BUT NOW SHE'S DEAD.
SHALL I TELL YOU WHAT I'M GOING TO DO?
TELL ME. TELL ME.
I'M GOING TO GET THE RUBY BACK. THE MAT. THE MAT. THE MAT-ER-I-OP-TI-KON. AND THEN I'LL DRIVE EVERYBODY IN THE WHOLE WIDE WORLD MAD. AND THEN THEY'LL MAKE ME KING.
IT SOUNDS SCARY. HAVE A NICE TIME. AND YOU MUST PROMISE--WHEN YOU GET BACK--TO TELL ME ALL ABOUT IT.
YOU DON'T UNDERSTAND. I'M GOING TO RULE THE WORLD. OR DESTROY IT.
I'M NOT COMING BACK.
YES YES...
BUT WE ALWAYS COME BACK HERE. IT'S SO SCARY OUTSIDE. IF YOU SEE THE JOKER, TELL HIM TO HURRY BACK. IT ISN'T APRIL FOOL'S DAY WITHOUT HIS LITTLE JOKES...
BUT I'M DOING MY BEST. I LEFT ANOTHER NEXT DOOR.

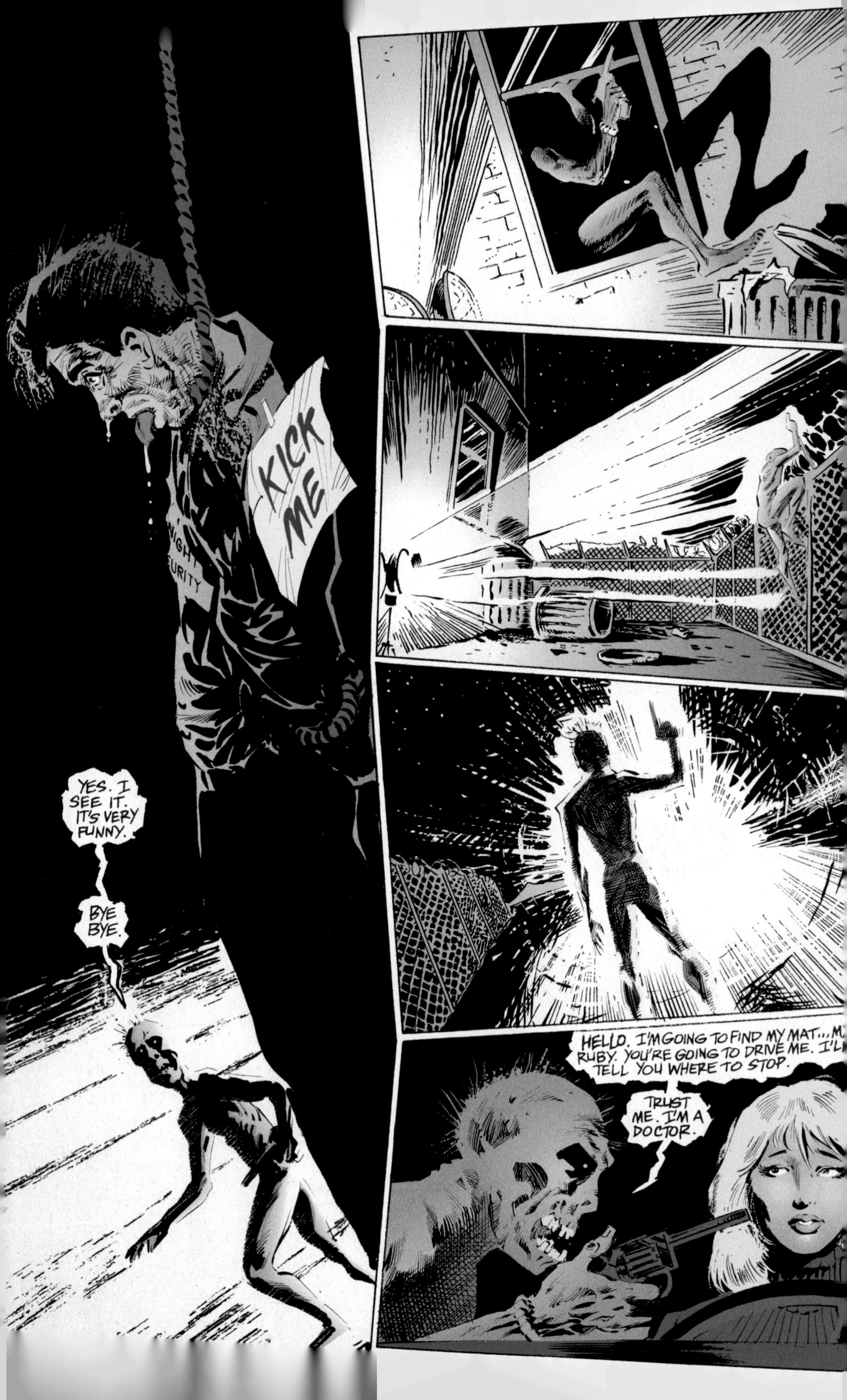
KICK ME
NIGHT SECURITY
YES. I SEE IT. IT'S VERY FUNNY.
BYE BYE.
HELLO. I'M GOING TO FIND MY MAT... M RUBY. YOU'RE GOING TO DRIVE ME. I'L TELL YOU WHERE TO STOP.
TRUST ME. I'M A DOCTOR.

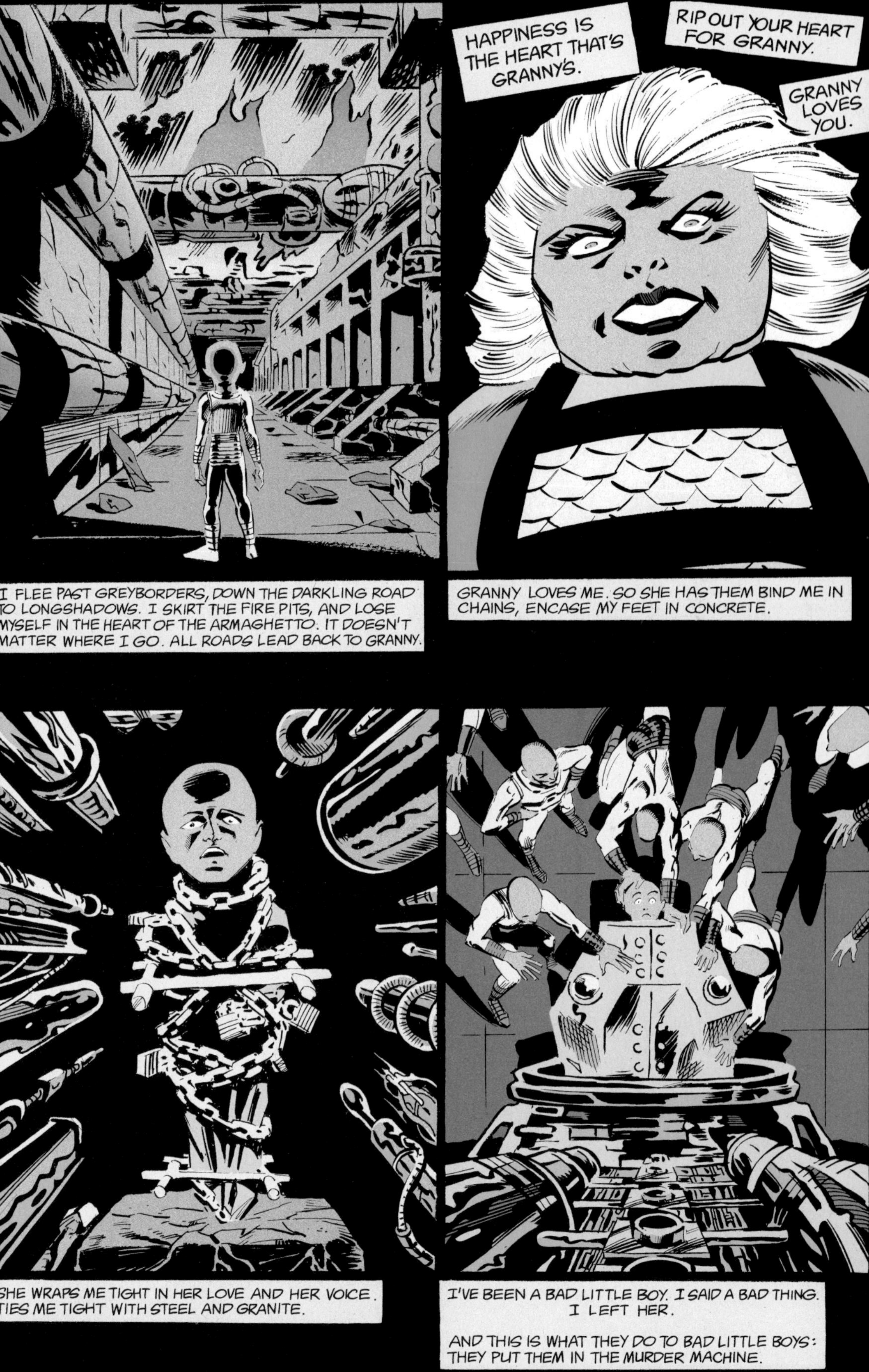
I FLEE PAST GREYBORDERS, DOWN THE DARKLING ROAD TO LONGSHADOWS. I SKIRT THE FIRE PITS, AND LOSE MYSELF IN THE HEART OF THE ARMAGHETTO. IT DOESN'T MATTER WHERE I GO. ALL ROADS LEAD BACK TO GRANNY.
HAPPINESS IS THE HEART THAT'S GRANNY'S.
RIP OUT YOUR HEART FOR GRANNY.
GRANNY LOVES YOU.
GRANNY LOVES ME. SO SHE HAS THEM BIND ME IN CHAINS, ENCASE MY FEET IN CONCRETE.
SHE WRAPS ME TIGHT IN HER LOVE AND HER VOICE TIES ME TIGHT WITH STEEL AND GRANITE.
I'VE BEEN A BAD LITTLE BOY. I SAID A BAD THING. I LEFT HER.
AND THIS IS WHAT THEY DO TO BAD LITTLE BOYS: THEY PUT THEM IN THE MURDER MACHINE.

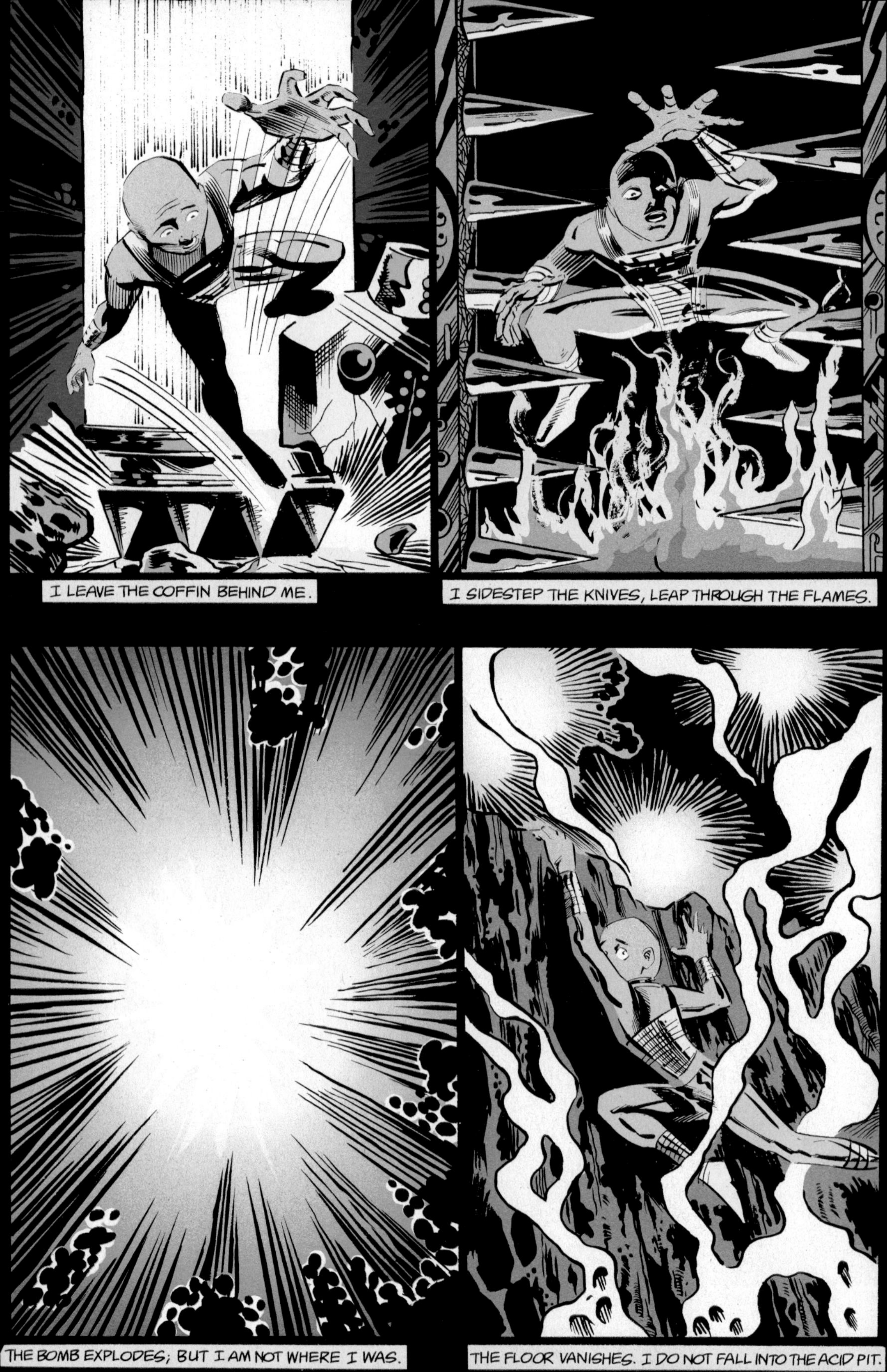
I LEAVE THE COFFIN BEHIND ME.
I SIDESTEP THE KNIVES, LEAP THROUGH THE FLAMES.
THE BOMB EXPLODES; BUT I AM NOT WHERE I WAS.
THE FLOOR VANISHES. I DO NOT FALL INTO THE ACID PIT.

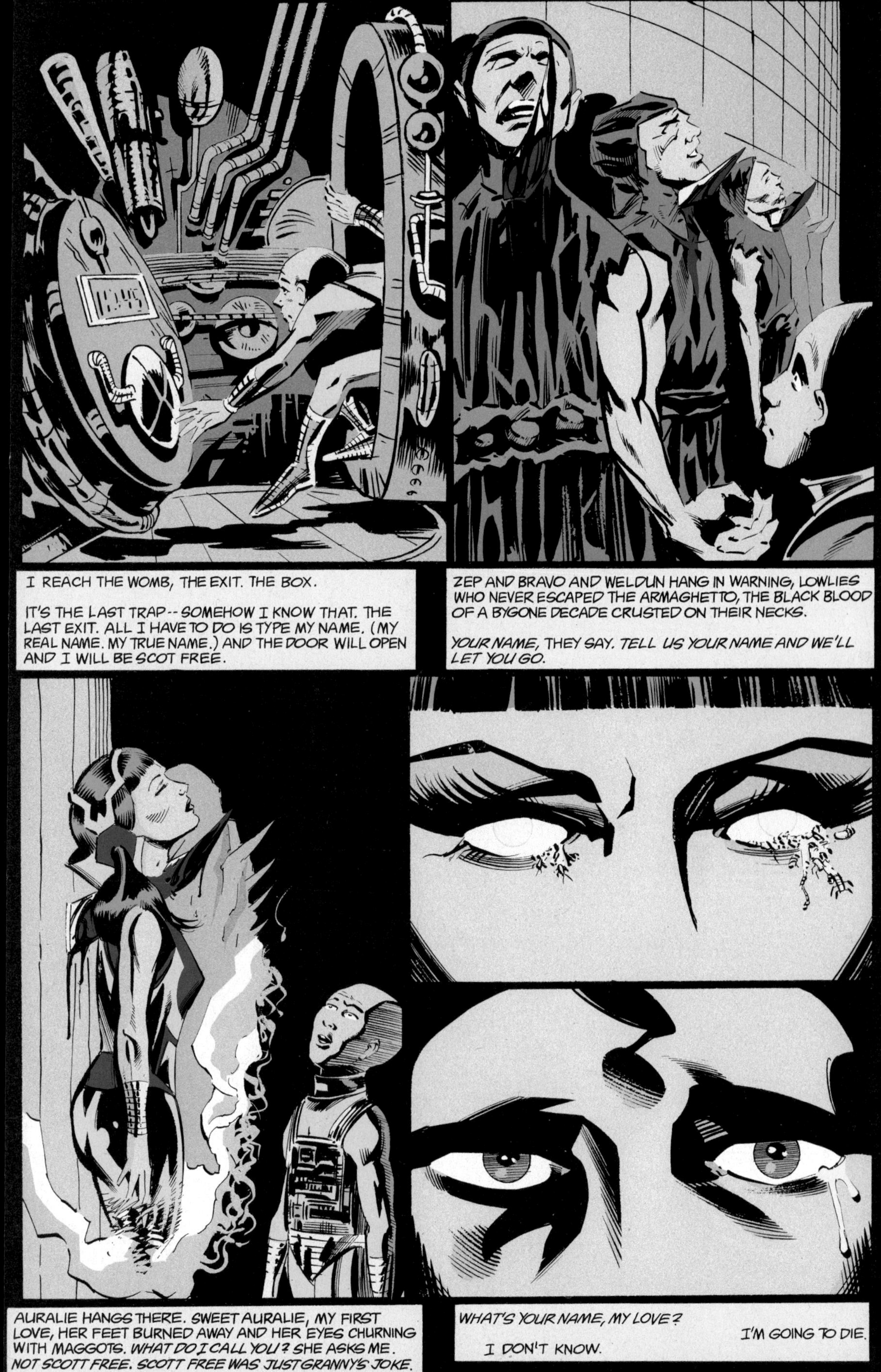
I REACH THE WOMB, THE EXIT. THE BOX.
IT'S THE LAST TRAP-- SOMEHOW I KNOW THAT. THE LAST EXIT. ALL I HAVE TO DO IS TYPE MY NAME. (MY REAL NAME. MY TRUE NAME.) AND THE DOOR WILL OPEN AND I WILL BE SCOT FREE.
ZEP AND BRAVO AND WELDUN HANG IN WARNING, LOWLIES WHO NEVER ESCAPED THE ARMAGHETTO, THE BLACK BLOOD OF A BYGONE DECADE CRUSTED ON THEIR NECKS.
YOUR NAME, THEY SAY. TELL US YOUR NAME AND WE'LL LET YOU GO.
AURALIE HANGS THERE. SWEET AURALIE, MY FIRST LOVE, HER FEET BURNED AWAY AND HER EYES CHURNING WITH MAGGOTS. WHAT DO I CALL YOU? SHE ASKS ME. NOT SCOTT FREE. SCOTT FREE WAS JUST GRANNY'S JOKE.
WHAT'S YOUR NAME, MY LOVE?
I DON'T KNOW.
I'M GOING TO DIE.

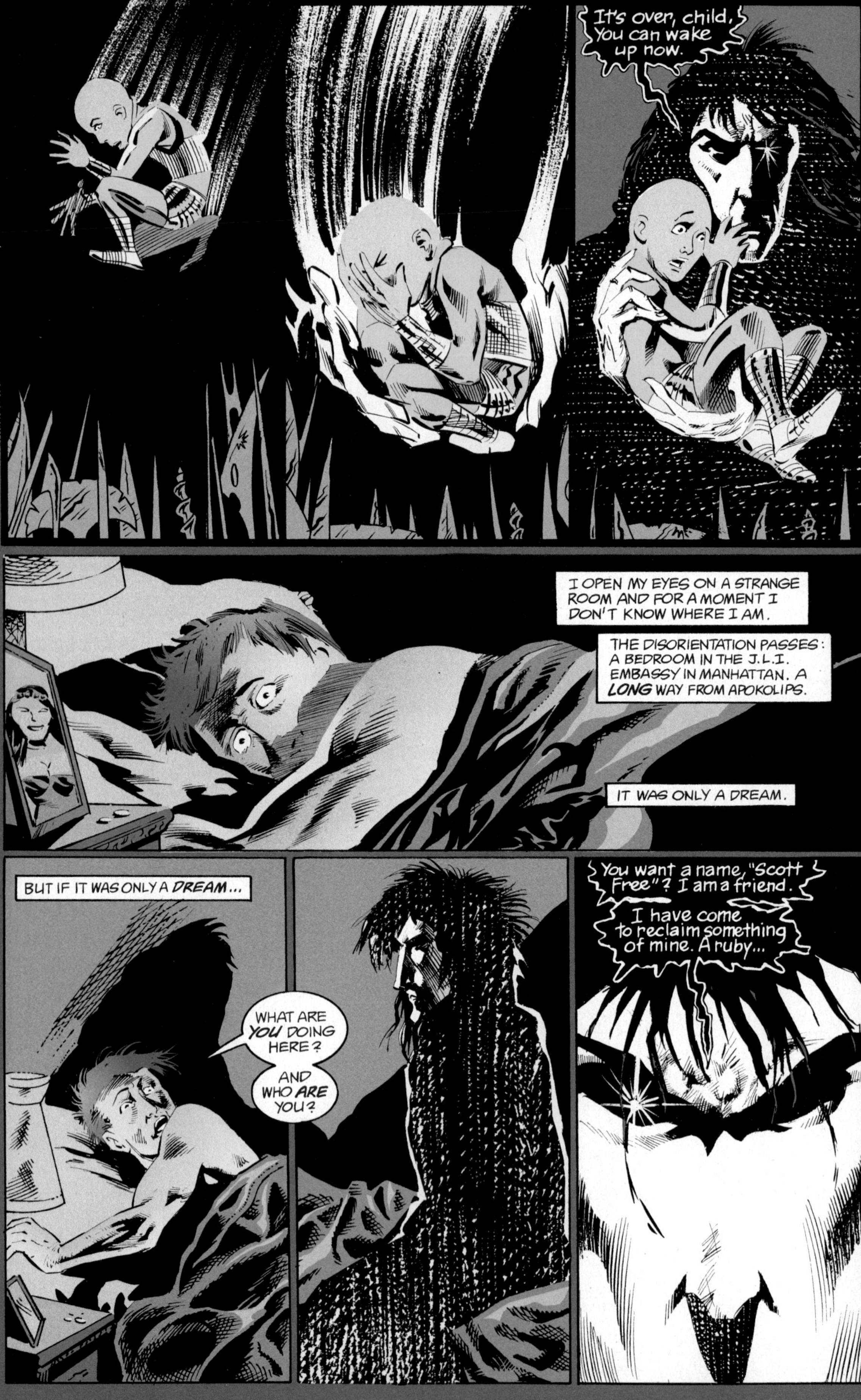
It's over, child. You can wake up now.
I OPEN MY EYES ON A STRANGE ROOM AND FOR A MOMENT I DON'T KNOW WHERE I AM.
THE DISORIENTATION PASSES: A BEDROOM IN THE J.L.I. EMBASSY IN MANHATTAN. A LONG WAY FROM APOKOLIPS.
IT WAS ONLY A DREAM.
BUT IF IT WAS ONLY A DREAM...
WHAT ARE YOU DOING HERE?
AND WHO ARE YOU?
You want a name, "Scott Free"? I am a friend.
I have come to reclaim something of mine. A ruby...

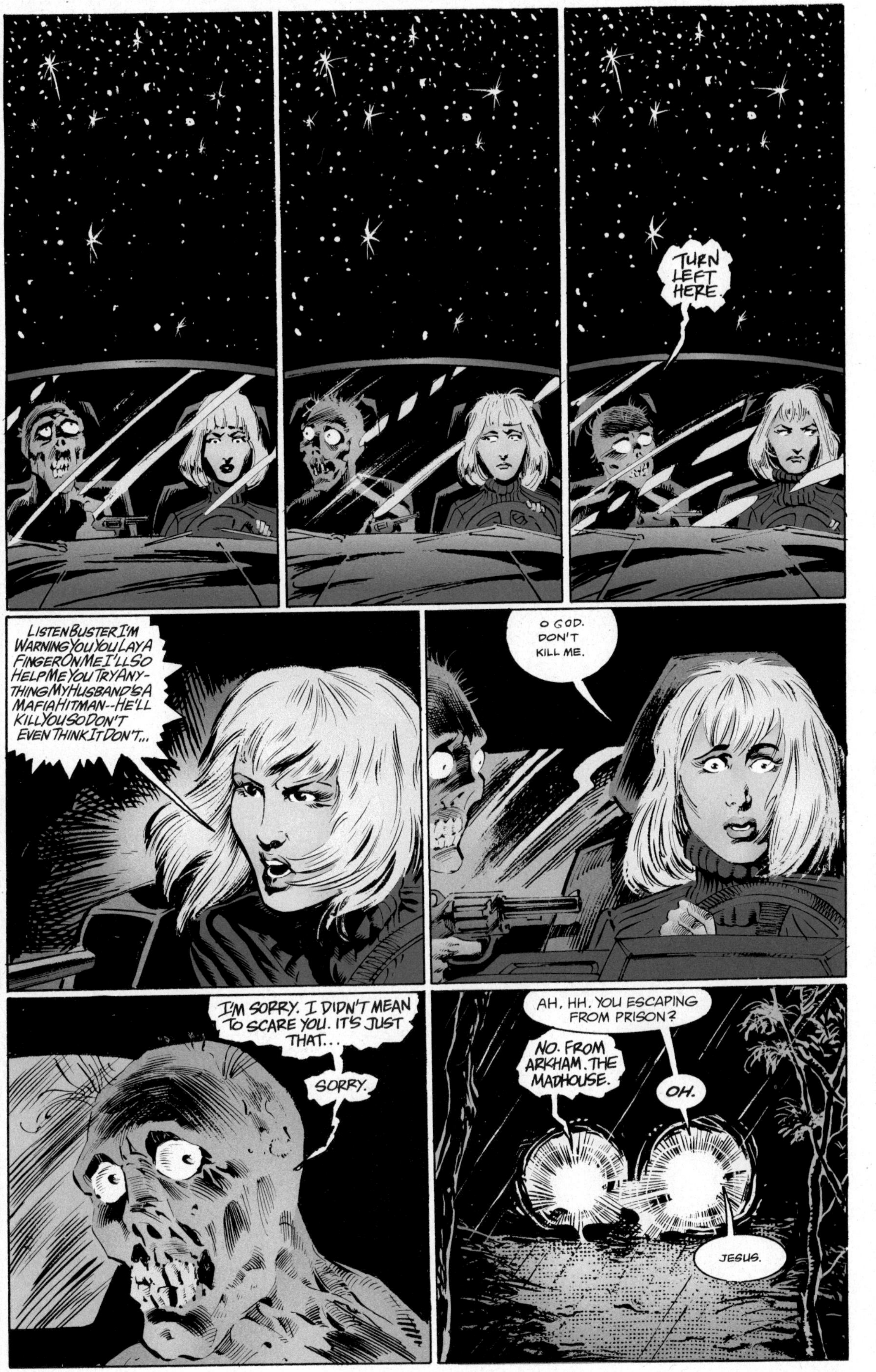
TURN LEFT HERE.
LISTEN BUSTER I'M WARNING YOU YOU LAY A FINGER ON ME I'LL SO HELP ME YOU TRY ANYTHING MY HUSBAND'S A MAFIA HITMAN--HE'LL KILL YOU SO DON'T EVEN THINK IT DON'T...
O GOD. DON'T KILL ME.
I'M SORRY. I DIDN'T MEAN TO SCARE YOU. IT'S JUST THAT...
SORRY.
AH, HH. YOU ESCAPING FROM PRISON?
NO. FROM ARKHAM. THE MADHOUSE.
OH.
JESUS.

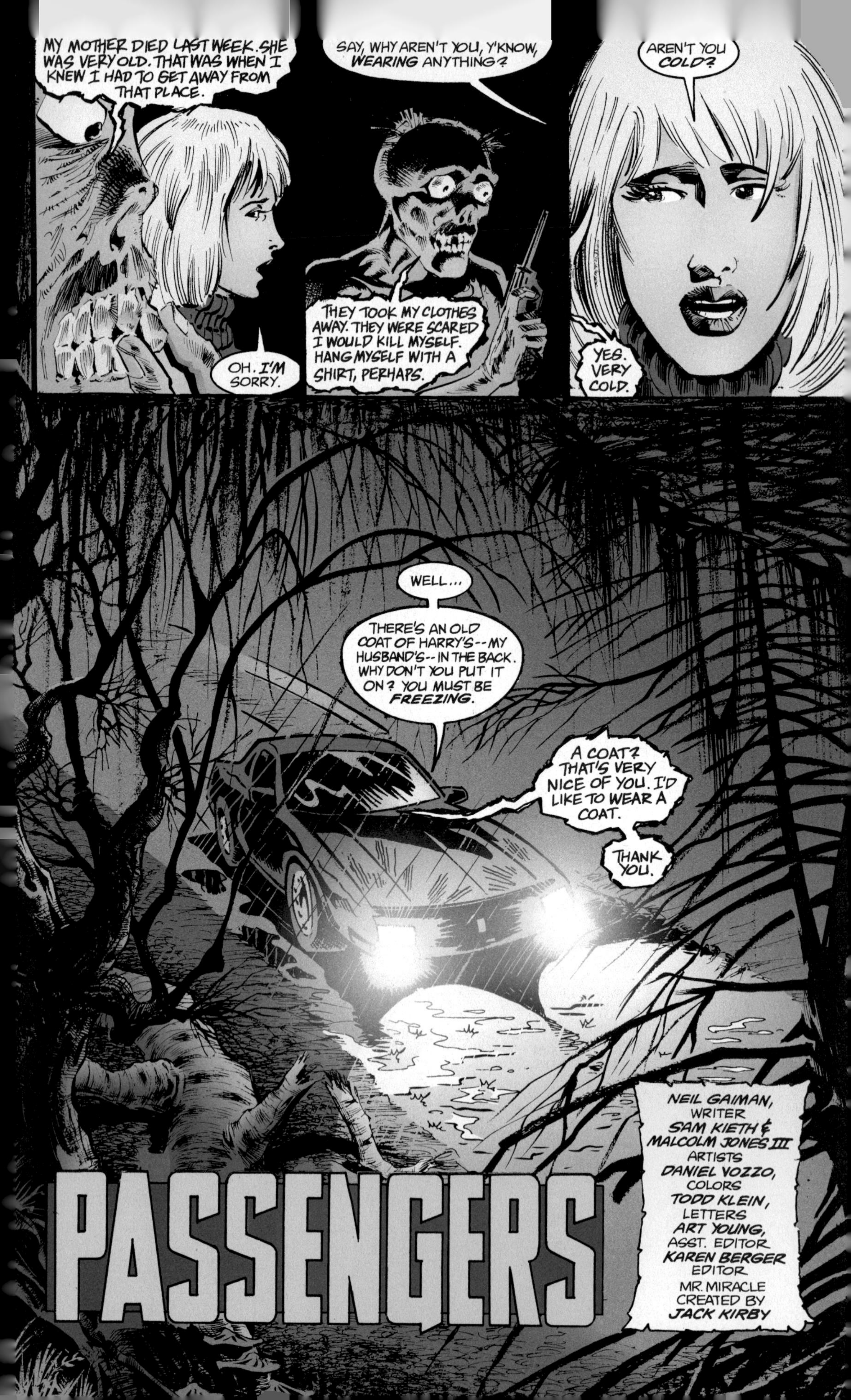
MY MOTHER DIED LAST WEEK. SHE WAS VERY OLD. THAT WAS WHEN I KNEW I HAD TO GET AWAY FROM THAT PLACE.
OH. I'M SORRY.
SAY, WHY AREN'T YOU, Y'KNOW, WEARING ANYTHING?
THEY TOOK MY CLOTHES AWAY. THEY WERE SCARED I WOULD KILL MYSELF. HANG MYSELF WITH A SHIRT, PERHAPS.
AREN'T YOU COLD?
YES. VERY COLD.
WELL...
THERE'S AN OLD COAT OF HARRY'S-- MY HUSBAND'S-- IN THE BACK. WHY DON'T YOU PUT IT ON? YOU MUST BE FREEZING.
A COAT? THAT'S VERY NICE OF YOU. I'D LIKE TO WEAR A COAT.
THANK YOU.
PASSENGERS
NEIL GAIMAN, WRITER
SAM KIETH & MALCOLM JONES III ARTISTS
DANIEL VOZZO, COLORS
TODD KLEIN, LETTERS
ART YOUNG, ASST. EDITOR
KAREN BERGER EDITOR
MR. MIRACLE CREATED BY JACK KIRBY

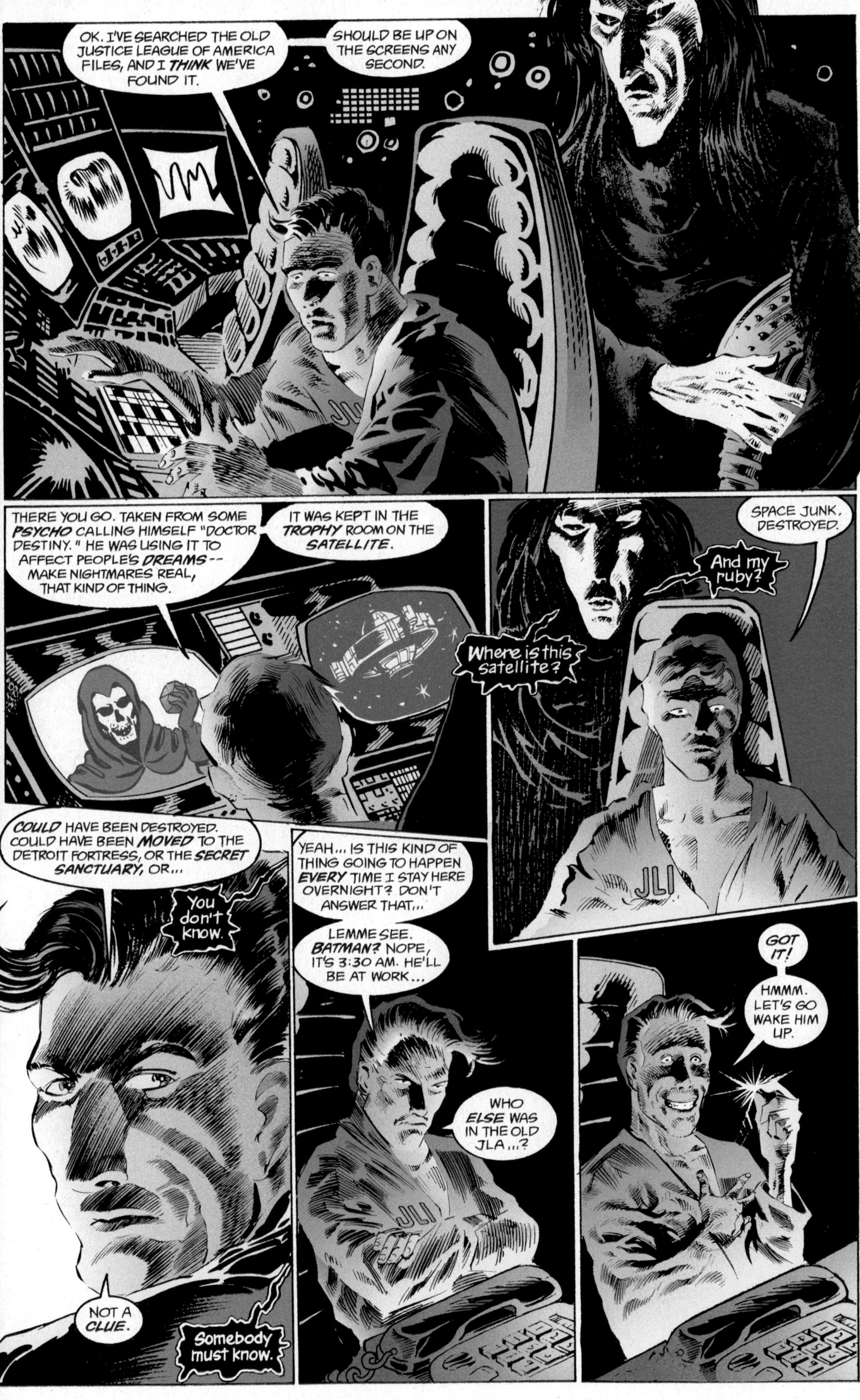
OK. I'VE SEARCHED THE OLD JUSTICE LEAGUE OF AMERICA FILES, AND I THINK WE'VE FOUND IT.
SHOULD BE UP ON THE SCREENS ANY SECOND.
THERE YOU GO. TAKEN FROM SOME PSYCHO CALLING HIMSELF "DOCTOR DESTINY." HE WAS USING IT TO AFFECT PEOPLE'S DREAMS -- MAKE NIGHTMARES REAL, THAT KIND OF THING.
IT WAS KEPT IN THE TROPHY ROOM ON THE SATELLITE.
Where is this satellite?
SPACE JUNK. DESTROYED.
And my ruby?
COULD HAVE BEEN DESTROYED. COULD HAVE BEEN MOVED TO THE DETROIT FORTRESS, OR THE SECRET SANCTUARY, OR...
You don't know.
NOT A CLUE.
Somebody must know.
YEAH... IS THIS KIND OF THING GOING TO HAPPEN EVERY TIME I STAY HERE OVERNIGHT? DON'T ANSWER THAT...
LEMME SEE. BATMAN? NOPE, IT'S 3:30 AM. HE'LL BE AT WORK...
WHO ELSE WAS IN THE OLD JLA...?
GOT IT!
HMMM. LET'S GO WAKE HIM UP.

WHAT'S YOUR NAME?

ROSEMARY.

ROSEMARY...

THAT'S FOR REMEMBERING...

SO WHAT SHOULD I CALL YOU?

I USED TO CALL MYSELF... DESTINY. DOCTOR DESTINY.

IT WASN'T MY NAME. MY MOTHER CALLED ME JOHN. JOHNNY BOY. DREAM BOY.

I WAS A REAL DOCTOR. NOT A MEDICAL ONE. A SCIENTIST ONE. NOW I'M JUST DR. DEE. DR... JOHN... DEE...

JOHN... I'VE GOT SOME SANDWICHES, IN A LUNCH-PAIL BEHIND MY SEAT, IF YOU'RE HUNGRY...?

NO. NO THANK YOU. I'M NEVER VERY HUNGRY ANY MORE...

LOOK, JOHN, I'M A NURSE. YOU CAN TELL ME, I WON'T FREAK. IS IT THE BIG A?

BIG A?

NIGHT OF THE LIVING DEAD

PLUS CO-HIT:
ZOMBY WOOF

AIDS.

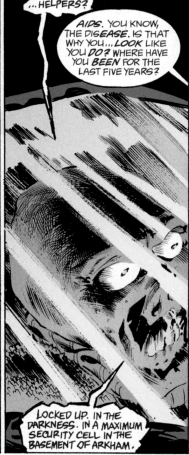

...HELPERS?

AIDS. YOU KNOW, THE DISEASE. IS THAT WHY YOU... LOOK LIKE YOU DO? WHERE HAVE YOU BEEN FOR THE LAST FIVE YEARS?

LOCKED UP. IN THE DARKNESS. IN A MAXIMUM SECURITY CELL IN THE BASEMENT OF ARKHAM.

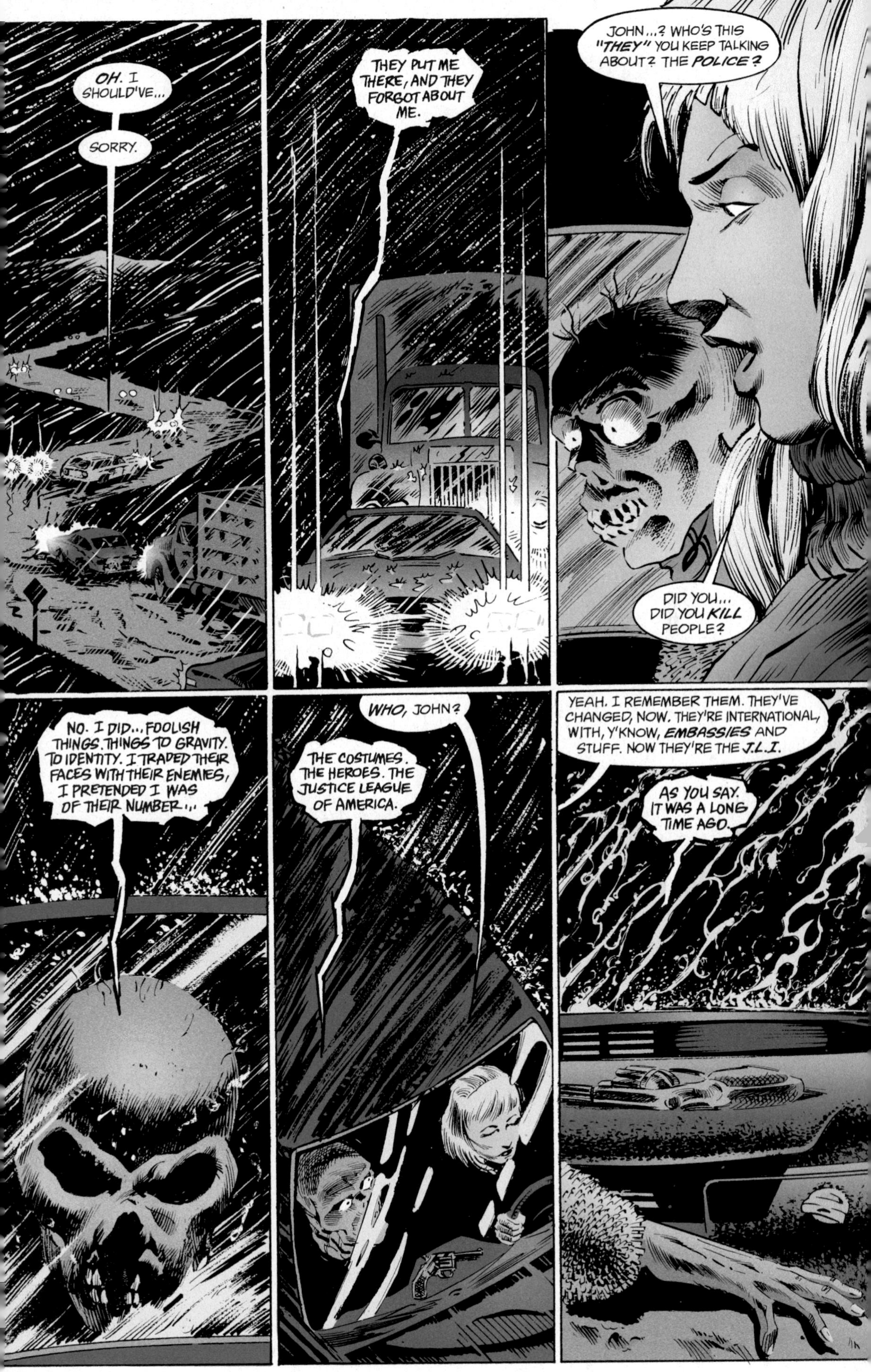
OH. I SHOULD'VE...
SORRY.
THEY PUT ME THERE, AND THEY FORGOT ABOUT ME.
JOHN...? WHO'S THIS "THEY" YOU KEEP TALKING ABOUT? THE POLICE?
DID YOU... DID YOU KILL PEOPLE?
NO. I DID... FOOLISH THINGS. THINGS TO GRAVITY. TO IDENTITY. I TRADED THEIR FACES WITH THEIR ENEMIES, I PRETENDED I WAS OF THEIR NUMBER...
WHO, JOHN?
THE COSTUMES. THE HEROES. THE JUSTICE LEAGUE OF AMERICA.
YEAH. I REMEMBER THEM. THEY'VE CHANGED, NOW. THEY'RE INTERNATIONAL, WITH, Y'KNOW, EMBASSIES AND STUFF. NOW THEY'RE THE J.L.I.
AS YOU SAY. IT WAS A LONG TIME AGO.

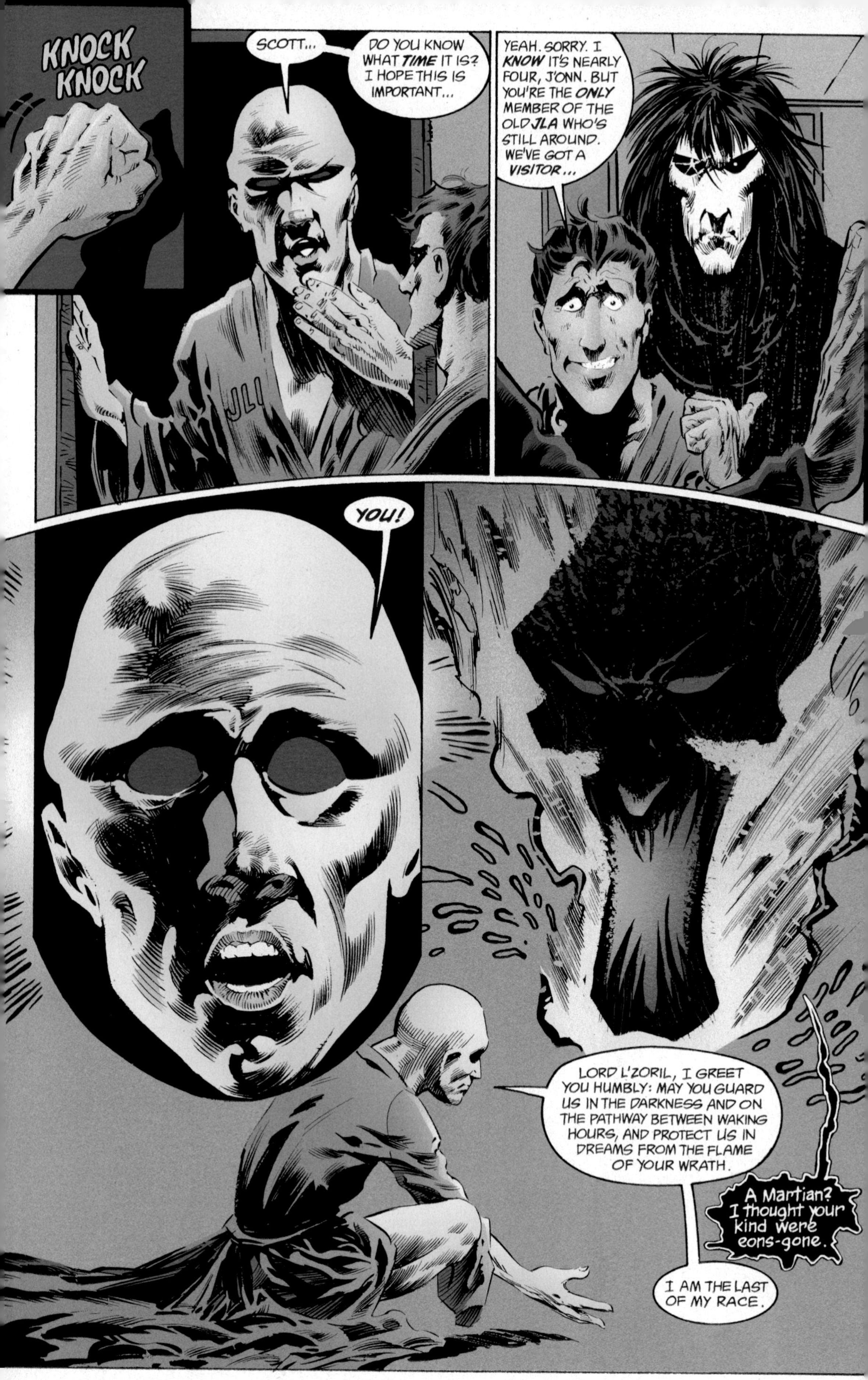
KNOCK KNOCK
SCOTT...
DO YOU KNOW WHAT TIME IT IS? I HOPE THIS IS IMPORTANT...
JLI
YEAH. SORRY. I KNOW IT'S NEARLY FOUR, J'ONN. BUT YOU'RE THE ONLY MEMBER OF THE OLD JLA WHO'S STILL AROUND. WE'VE GOT A VISITOR...
YOU!
LORD L'ZORIL, I GREET YOU HUMBLY: MAY YOU GUARD US IN THE DARKNESS AND ON THE PATHWAY BETWEEN WAKING HOURS, AND PROTECT US IN DREAMS FROM THE FLAME OF YOUR WRATH.
A Martian? I thought your kind were eons-gone.
I AM THE LAST OF MY RACE.

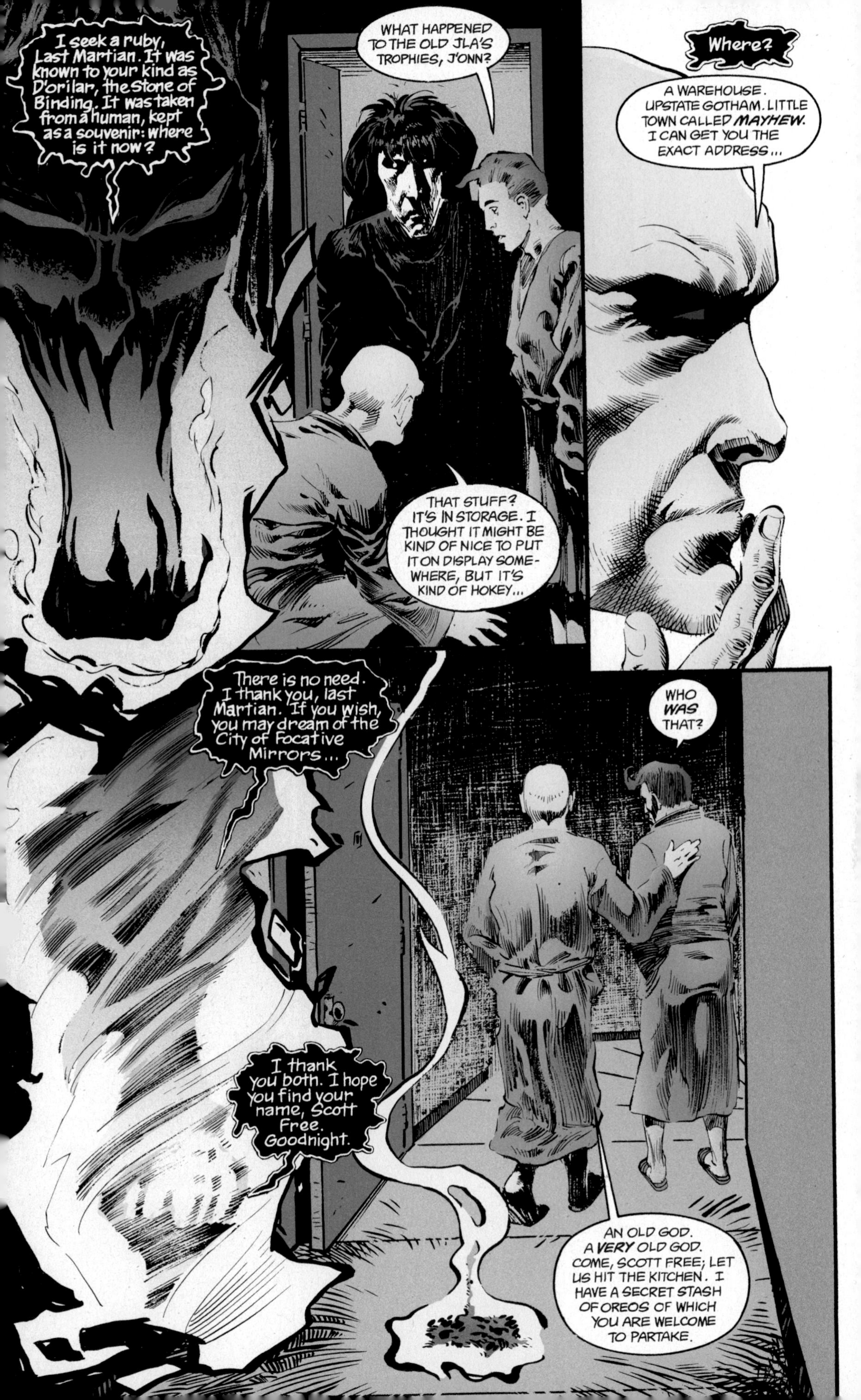
I seek a ruby, Last Martian. It was known to your kind as D'orilar, the Stone of Binding. It was taken from a human, kept as a souvenir: where is it now?
WHAT HAPPENED TO THE OLD JLA'S TROPHIES, J'ONN?
THAT STUFF? IT'S IN STORAGE. I THOUGHT IT MIGHT BE KIND OF NICE TO PUT IT ON DISPLAY SOME-WHERE, BUT IT'S KIND OF HOKEY...
Where?
A WAREHOUSE. UPSTATE GOTHAM. LITTLE TOWN CALLED MAYHEW. I CAN GET YOU THE EXACT ADDRESS...
There is no need. I thank you, last Martian. If you wish, you may dream of the City of Focative Mirrors...
I thank you both. I hope you find your name, Scott Free. Goodnight.
WHO WAS THAT?
AN OLD GOD. A VERY OLD GOD. COME, SCOTT FREE; LET US HIT THE KITCHEN. I HAVE A SECRET STASH OF OREOS OF WHICH YOU ARE WELCOME TO PARTAKE.

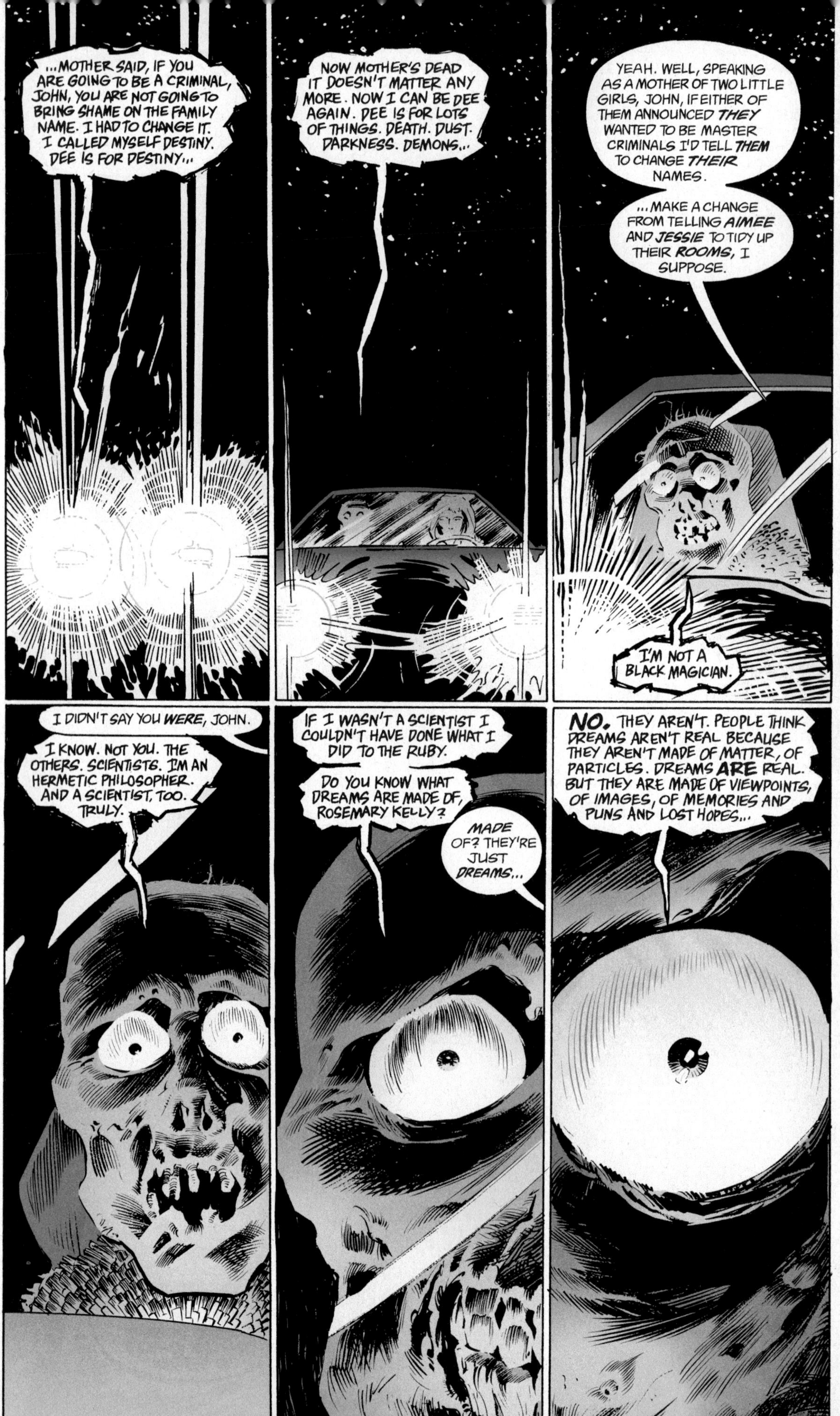
...MOTHER SAID, IF YOU ARE GOING TO BE A CRIMINAL, JOHN, YOU ARE NOT GOING TO BRING SHAME ON THE FAMILY NAME. I HAD TO CHANGE IT. I CALLED MYSELF DESTINY. DEE IS FOR DESTINY...
NOW MOTHER'S DEAD IT DOESN'T MATTER ANY MORE. NOW I CAN BE DEE AGAIN. DEE IS FOR LOTS OF THINGS. DEATH. DUST. DARKNESS. DEMONS...
YEAH. WELL, SPEAKING AS A MOTHER OF TWO LITTLE GIRLS, JOHN, IF EITHER OF THEM ANNOUNCED THEY WANTED TO BE MASTER CRIMINALS I'D TELL THEM TO CHANGE THEIR NAMES.
...MAKE A CHANGE FROM TELLING AIMEE AND JESSIE TO TIDY UP THEIR ROOMS, I SUPPOSE.
I'M NOT A BLACK MAGICIAN.
I DIDN'T SAY YOU WERE, JOHN.
I KNOW. NOT YOU. THE OTHERS. SCIENTISTS. I'M AN HERMETIC PHILOSOPHER. AND A SCIENTIST, TOO. TRULY.
IF I WASN'T A SCIENTIST I COULDN'T HAVE DONE WHAT I DID TO THE RUBY.
DO YOU KNOW WHAT DREAMS ARE MADE OF, ROSEMARY KELLY?
MADE OF? THEY'RE JUST DREAMS...
NO. THEY AREN'T. PEOPLE THINK DREAMS AREN'T REAL BECAUSE THEY AREN'T MADE OF MATTER, OF PARTICLES. DREAMS ARE REAL. BUT THEY ARE MADE OF VIEWPOINTS, OF IMAGES, OF MEMORIES AND PUNS AND LOST HOPES...

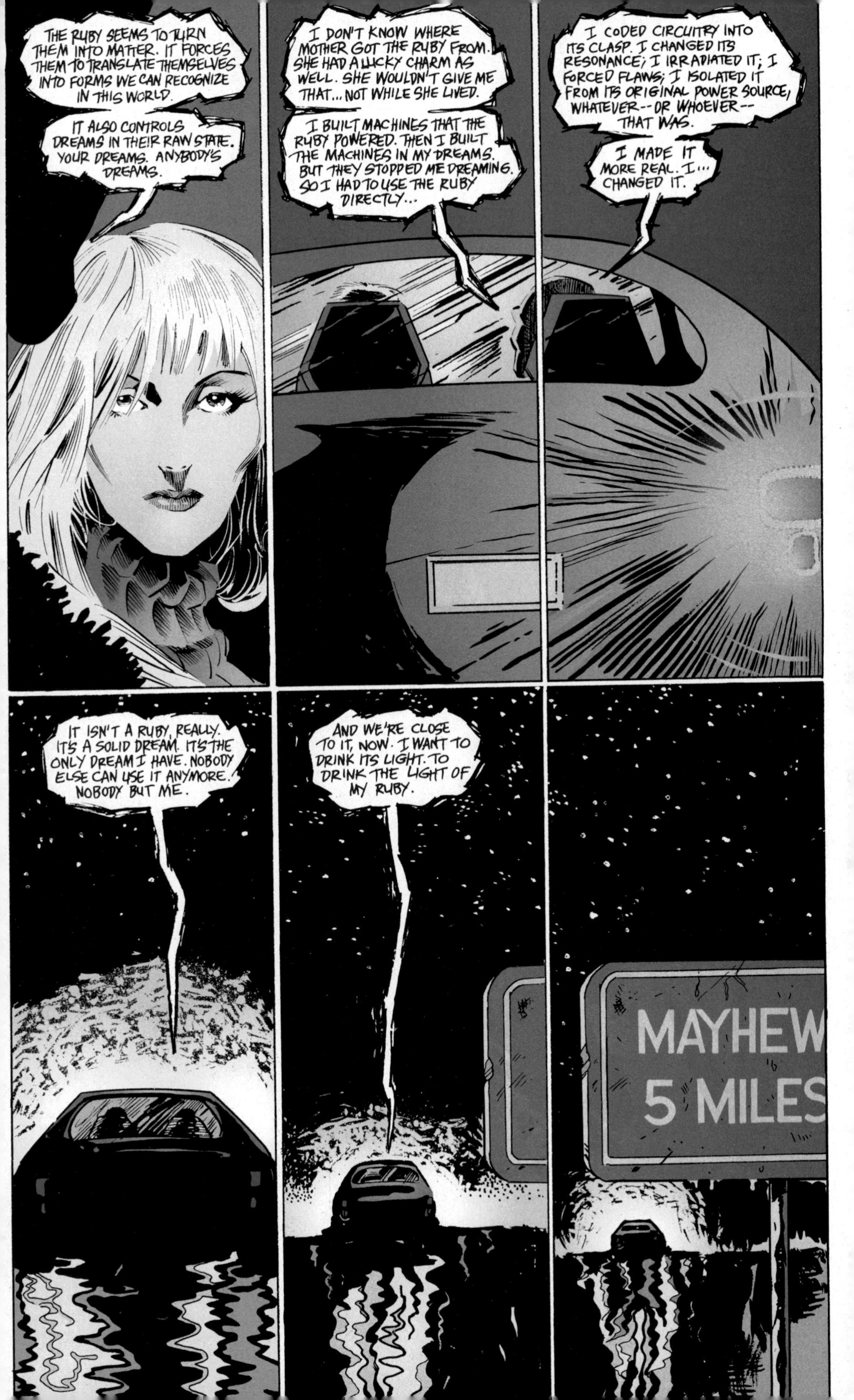
THE RUBY SEEMS TO TURN THEM INTO MATTER. IT FORCES THEM TO TRANSLATE THEMSELVES INTO FORMS WE CAN RECOGNIZE IN THIS WORLD.
IT ALSO CONTROLS DREAMS IN THEIR RAW STATE. YOUR DREAMS. ANYBODY'S DREAMS.
I DON'T KNOW WHERE MOTHER GOT THE RUBY FROM. SHE HAD A LUCKY CHARM AS WELL. SHE WOULDN'T GIVE ME THAT... NOT WHILE SHE LIVED.
I BUILT MACHINES THAT THE RUBY POWERED. THEN I BUILT THE MACHINES IN MY DREAMS. BUT THEY STOPPED ME DREAMING. SO I HAD TO USE THE RUBY DIRECTLY...
I CODED CIRCUITRY INTO ITS CLASP. I CHANGED ITS RESONANCE; I IRRADIATED IT; I FORCED FLAWS; I ISOLATED IT FROM ITS ORIGINAL POWER SOURCE, WHATEVER--OR WHOEVER--THAT WAS.
I MADE IT MORE REAL. I... CHANGED IT.
IT ISN'T A RUBY, REALLY. IT'S A SOLID DREAM. IT'S THE ONLY DREAM I HAVE. NOBODY ELSE CAN USE IT ANYMORE. NOBODY BUT ME.
AND WE'RE CLOSE TO IT, NOW. I WANT TO DRINK ITS LIGHT. TO DRINK THE LIGHT OF MY RUBY.
MAYHEW
5 MILES

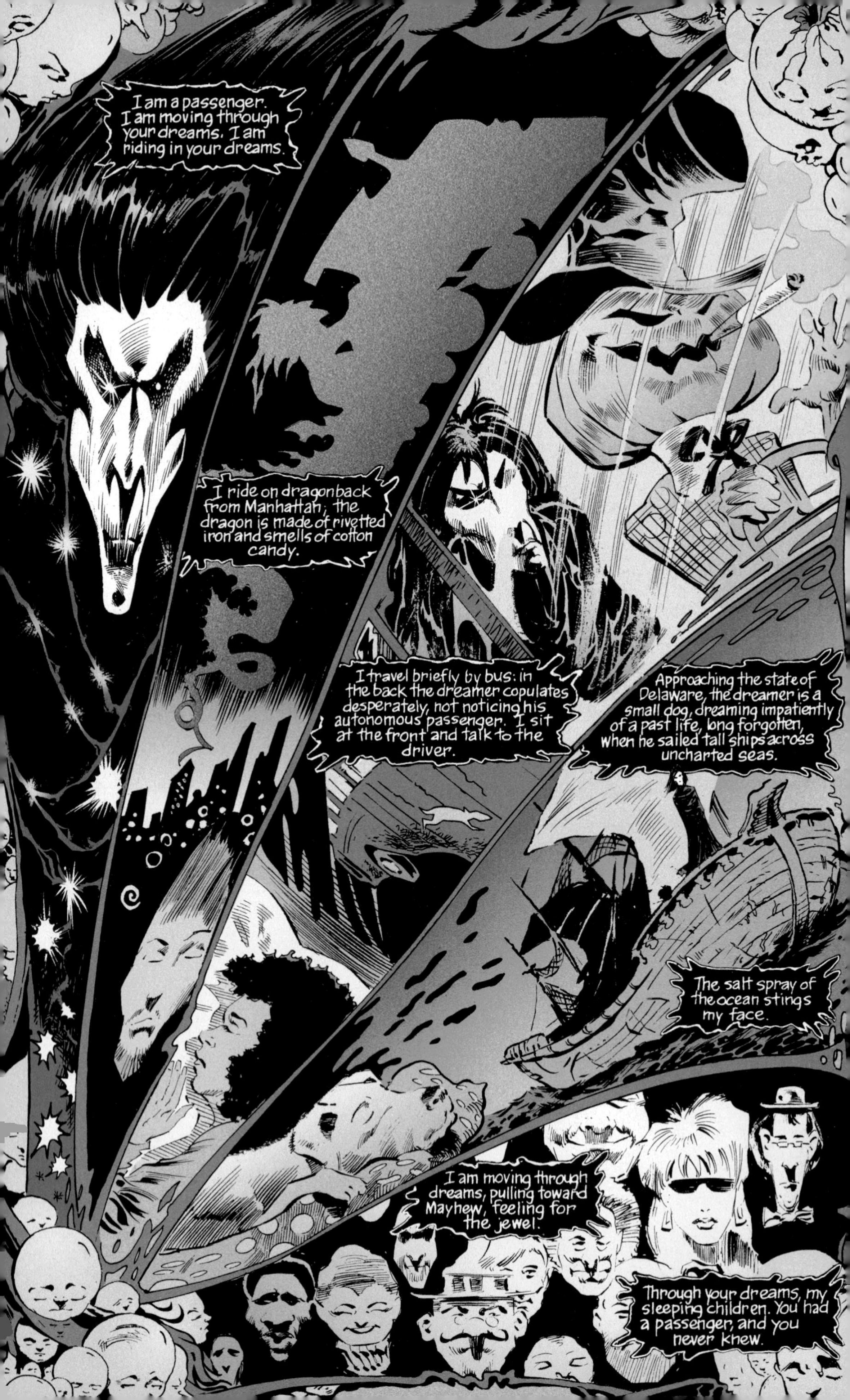
I am a passenger. I am moving through your dreams. I am riding in your dreams.
I ride on dragonback from Manhattan; the dragon is made of rivetted iron and smells of cotton candy.
I travel briefly by bus: in the back the dreamer copulates desperately, not noticing his autonomous passenger. I sit at the front and talk to the driver.
Approaching the state of Delaware, the dreamer is a small dog, dreaming impatiently of a past life, long forgotten, when he sailed tall ships across uncharted seas.
The salt spray of the ocean stings my face.
I am moving through dreams, pulling toward Mayhew, feeling for the jewel.
Through your dreams, my sleeping children. You had a passenger, and you never knew.

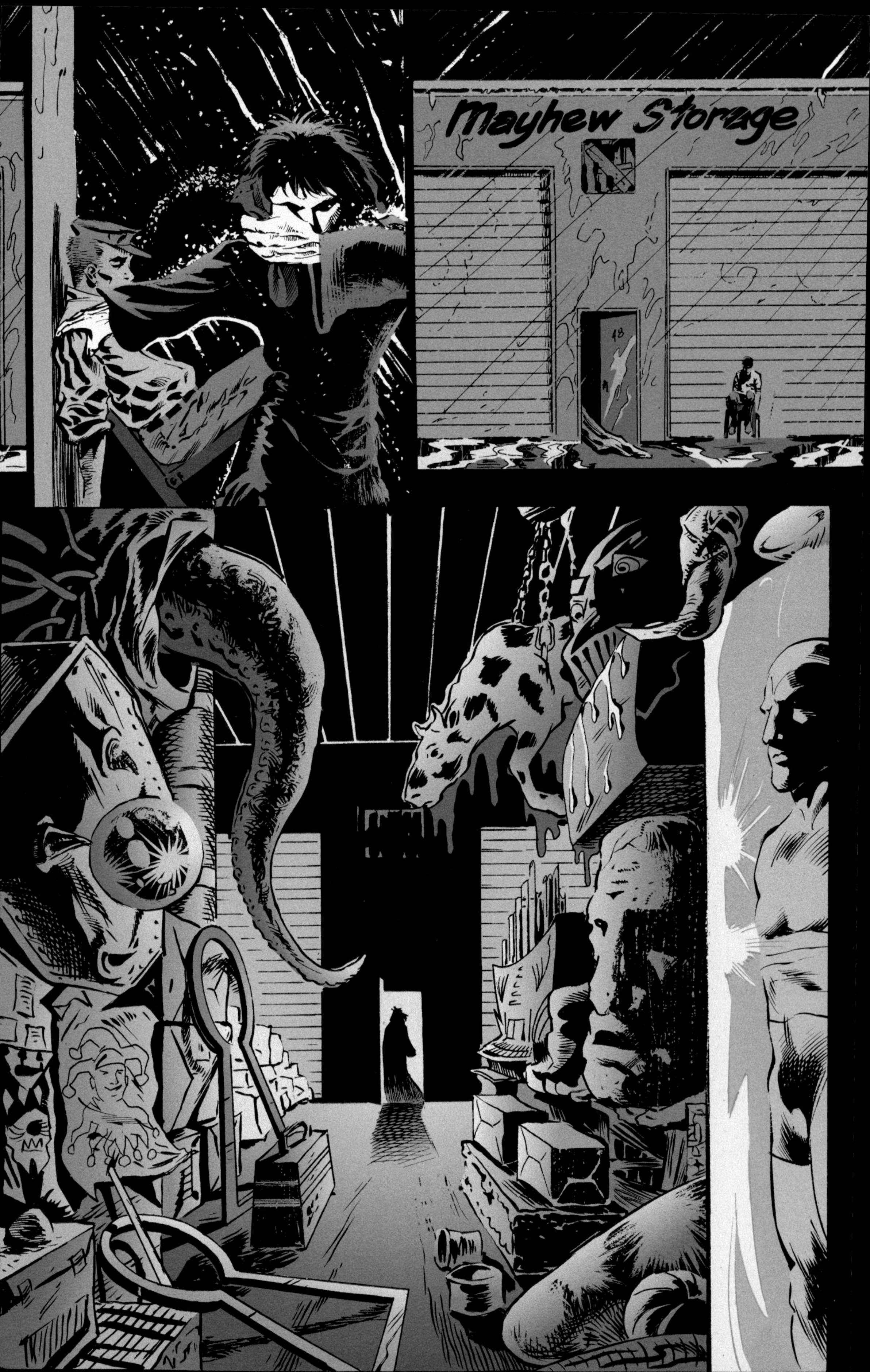
Mayhew Storage
48

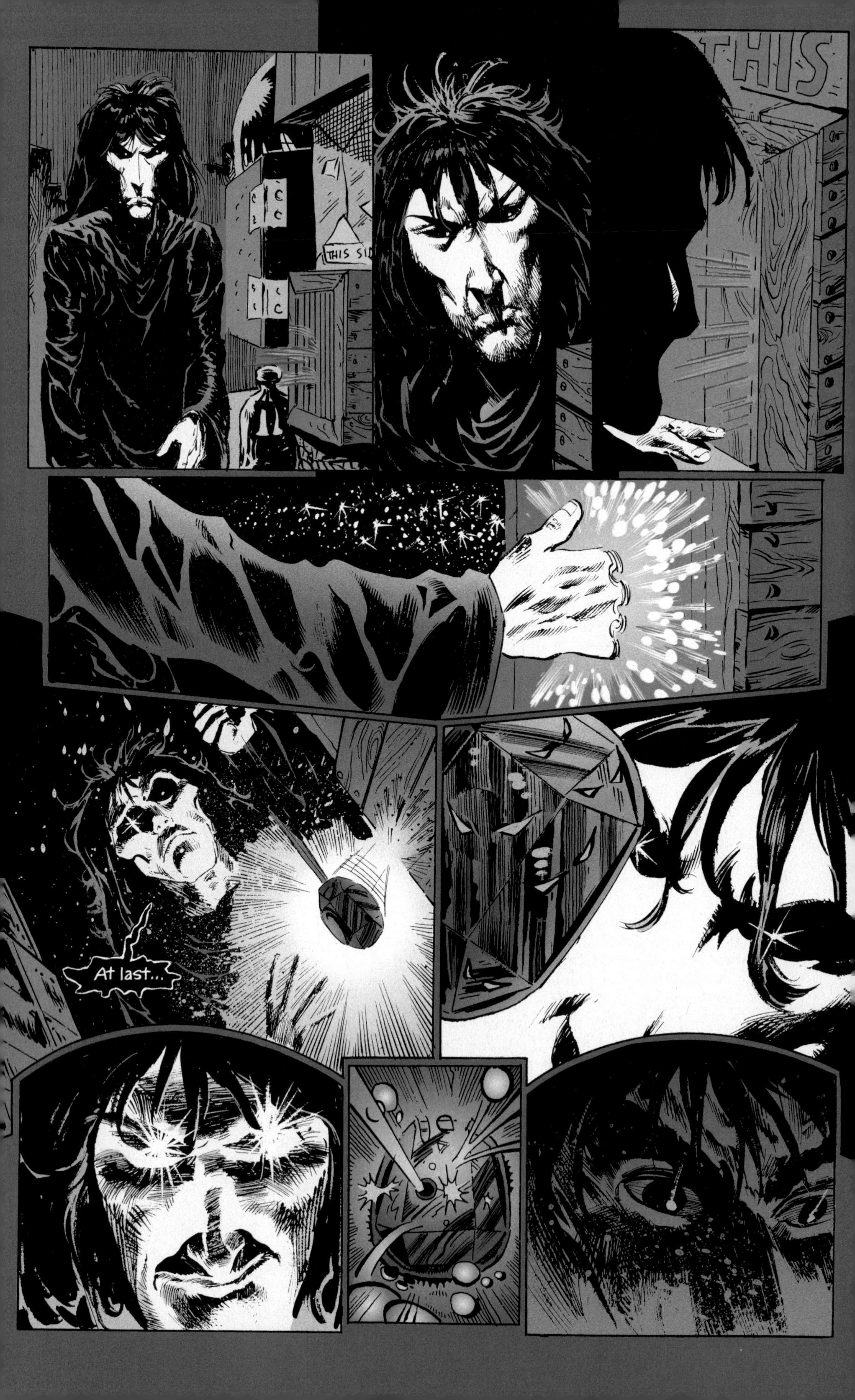
THIS SI
THIS
At last...

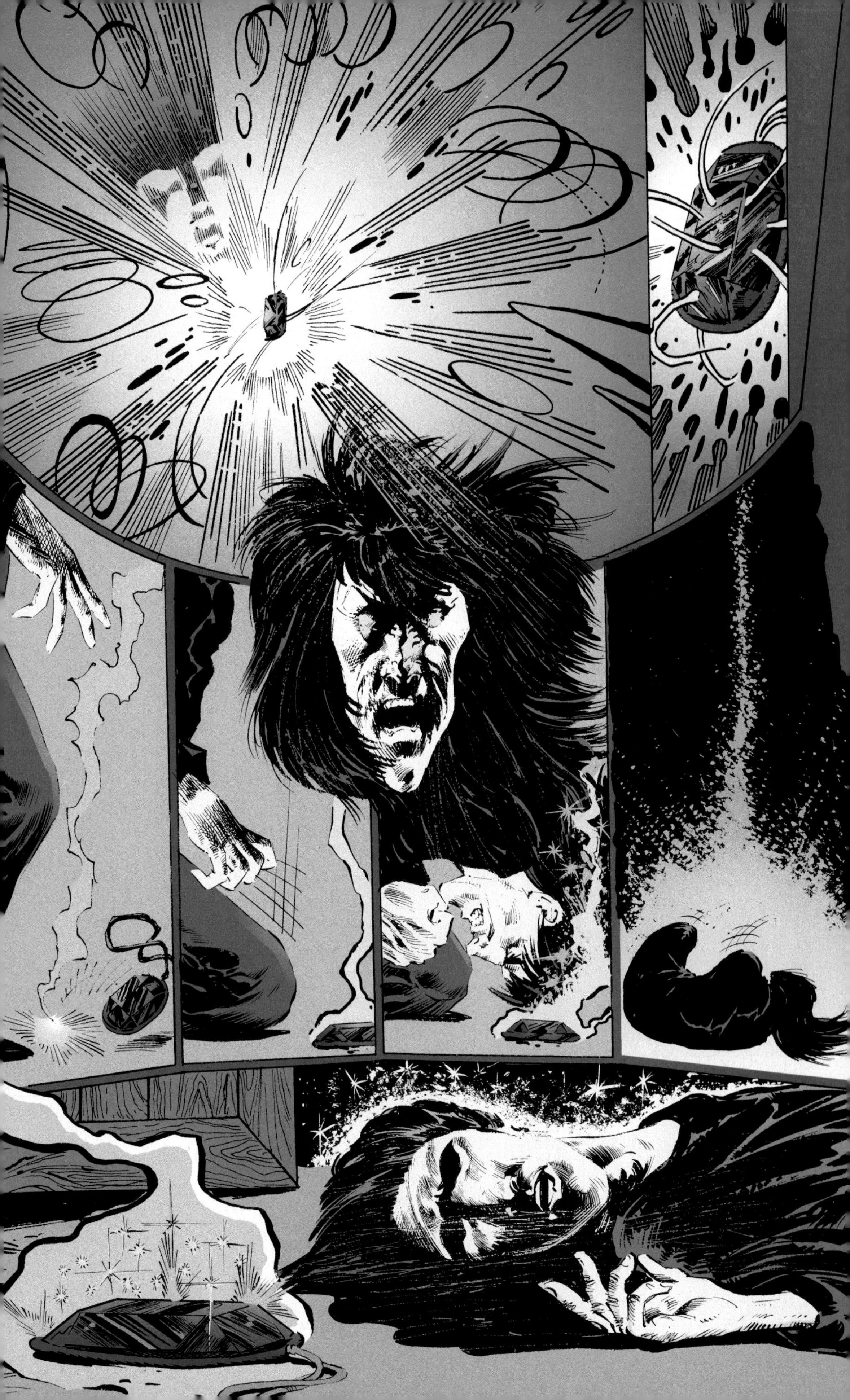

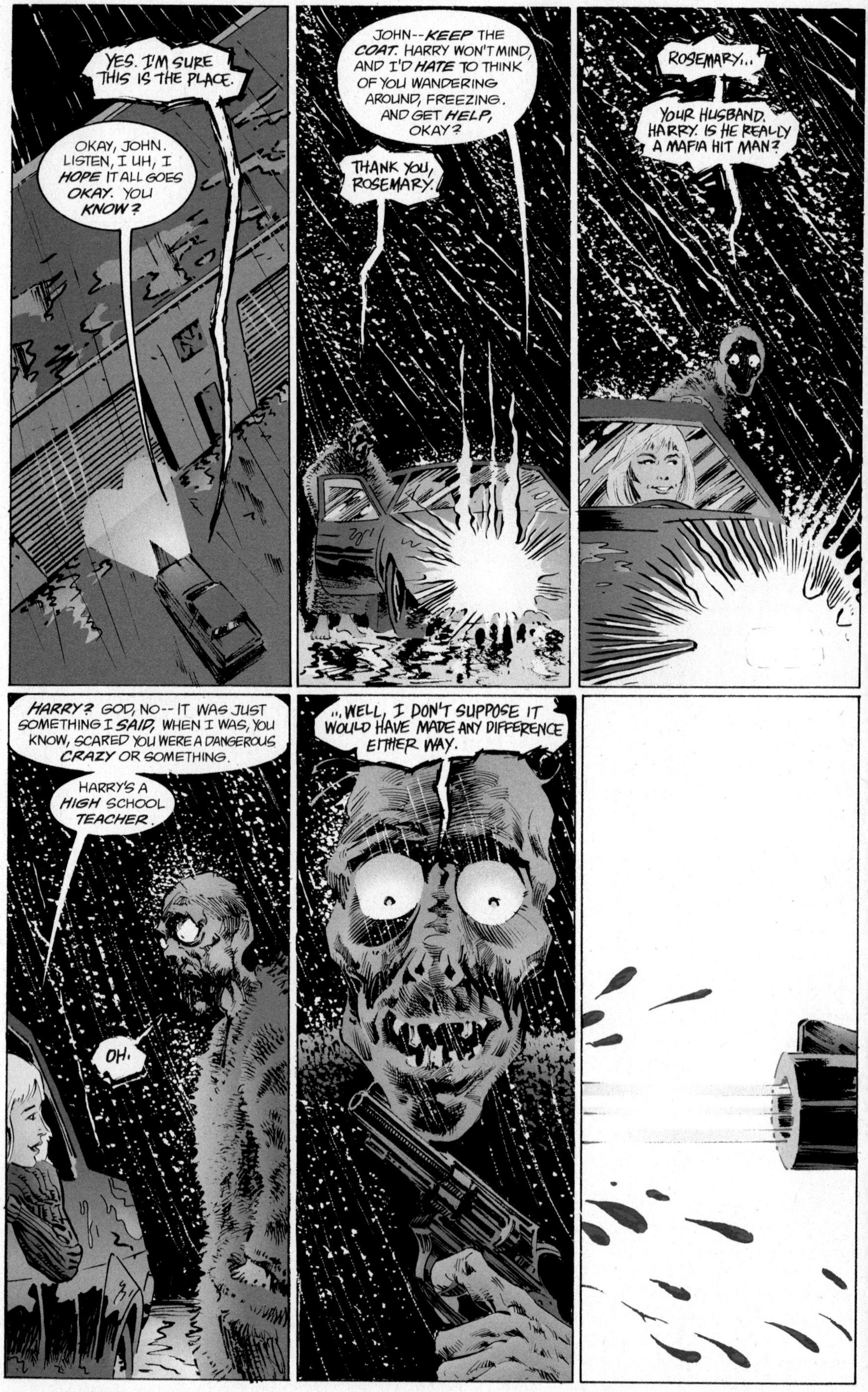
YES. I'M SURE THIS IS THE PLACE.
OKAY, JOHN. LISTEN, I UH, I HOPE IT ALL GOES OKAY. YOU KNOW?
JOHN--KEEP THE COAT. HARRY WON'T MIND, AND I'D HATE TO THINK OF YOU WANDERING AROUND, FREEZING. AND GET HELP, OKAY?
THANK YOU, ROSEMARY.
ROSEMARY...
YOUR HUSBAND. HARRY. IS HE REALLY A MAFIA HIT MAN?
HARRY? GOD, NO--IT WAS JUST SOMETHING I SAID, WHEN I WAS, YOU KNOW, SCARED YOU WERE A DANGEROUS CRAZY OR SOMETHING.
HARRY'S A HIGH SCHOOL TEACHER.
OH.
...WELL, I DON'T SUPPOSE IT WOULD HAVE MADE ANY DIFFERENCE EITHER WAY.

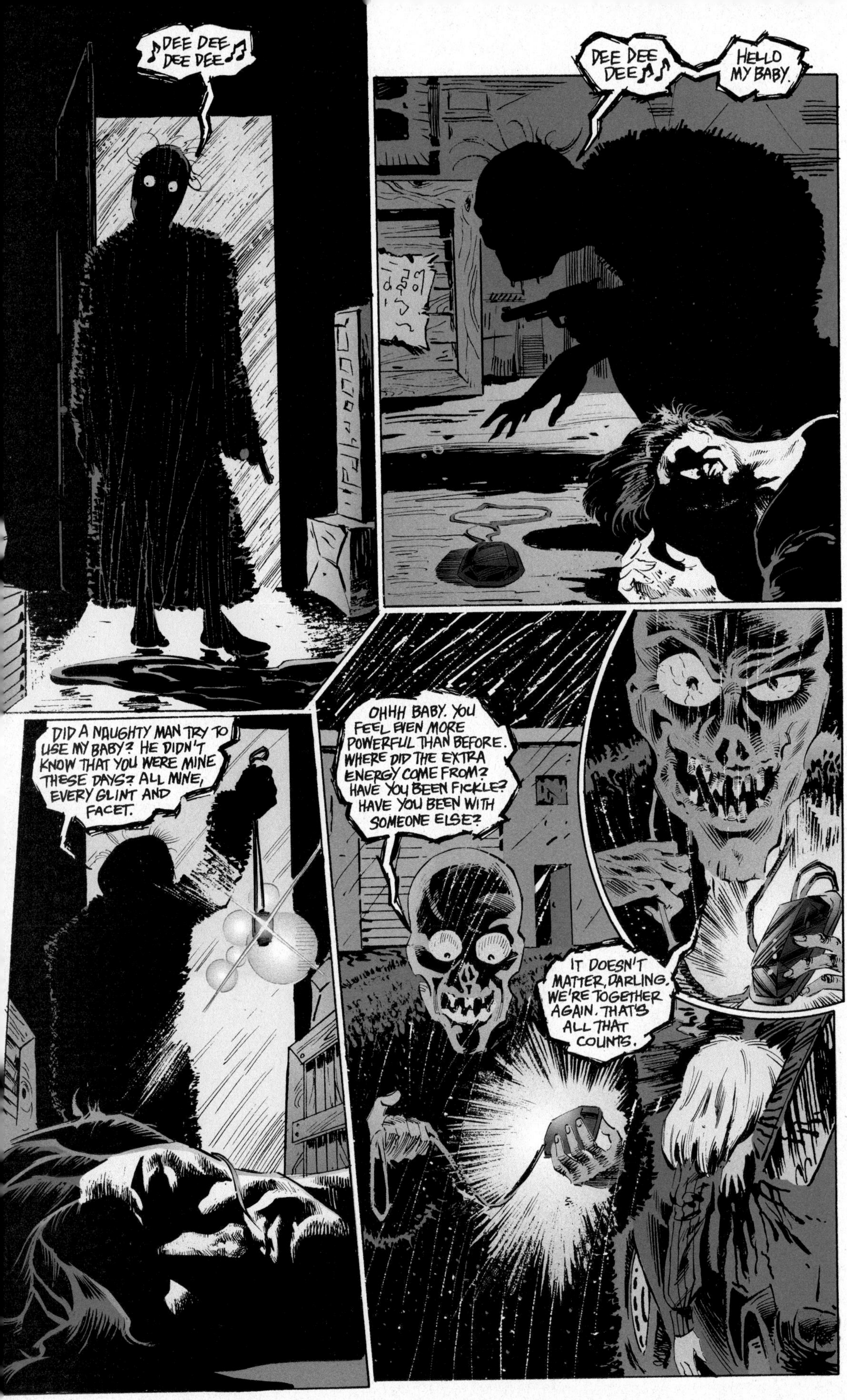
♪DEE DEE DEE DEE♫
DEE DEE DEE♪♪
HELLO MY BABY.
DID A NAUGHTY MAN TRY TO USE MY BABY? HE DIDN'T KNOW THAT YOU WERE MINE THESE DAYS? ALL MINE, EVERY GLINT AND FACET.
OHHH BABY. YOU FEEL EVEN MORE POWERFUL THAN BEFORE. WHERE DID THE EXTRA ENERGY COME FROM? HAVE YOU BEEN FICKLE? HAVE YOU BEEN WITH SOMEONE ELSE?
IT DOESN'T MATTER, DARLING. WE'RE TOGETHER AGAIN. THAT'S ALL THAT COUNTS.

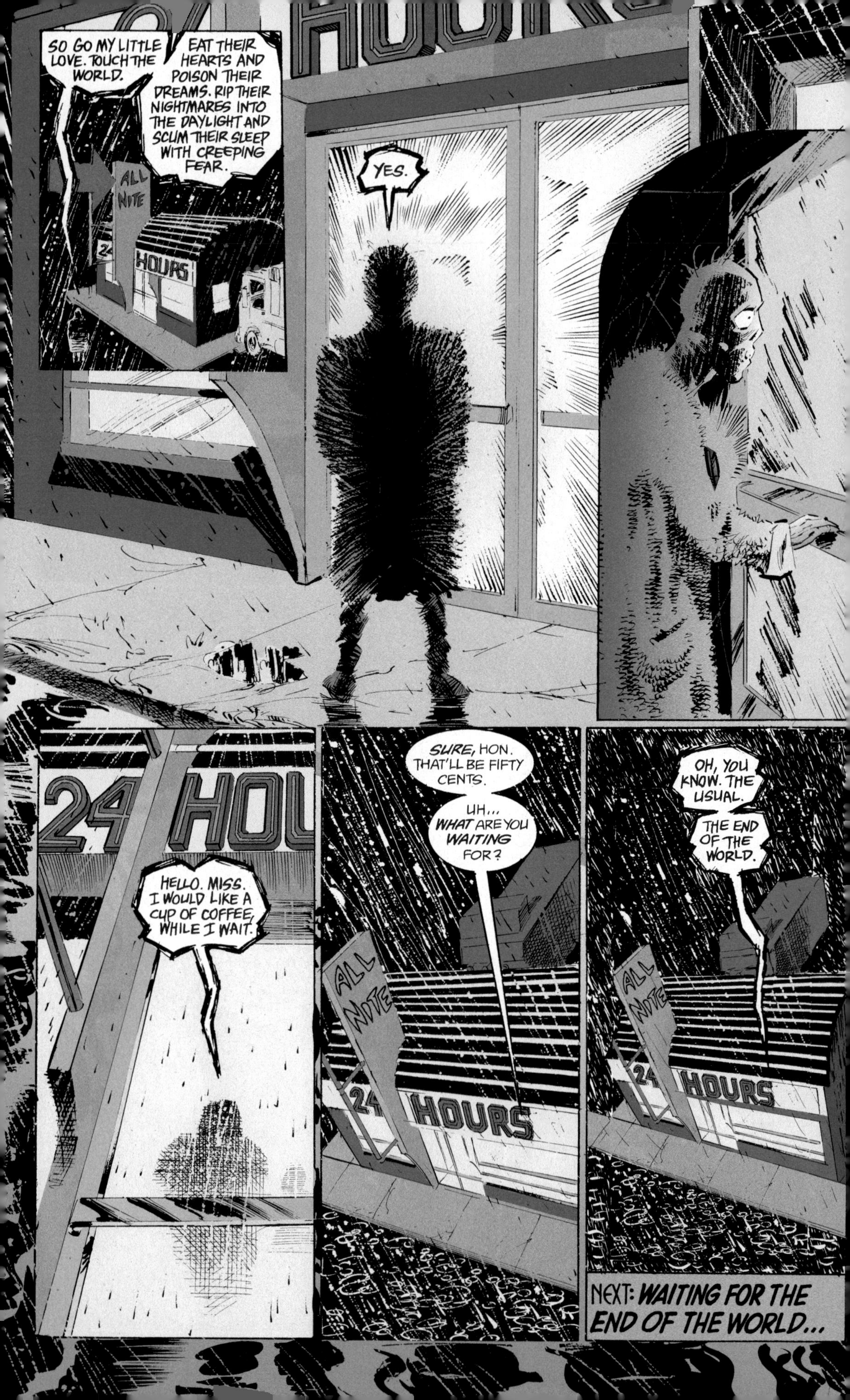
SO GO MY LITTLE LOVE. TOUCH THE WORLD.
EAT THEIR HEARTS AND POISON THEIR DREAMS. RIP THEIR NIGHTMARES INTO THE DAYLIGHT AND SCUM THEIR SLEEP WITH CREEPING FEAR.
ALL NITE
24 HOURS
YES.
24 HOURS
HELLO. MISS. I WOULD LIKE A CUP OF COFFEE, WHILE I WAIT.
SURE, HON. THAT'LL BE FIFTY CENTS.
UH... WHAT ARE YOU WAITING FOR?
ALL NITE
24 HOURS
OH, YOU KNOW. THE USUAL.
THE END OF THE WORLD.
ALL NITE
24 HOURS
NEXT: WAITING FOR THE END OF THE WORLD...

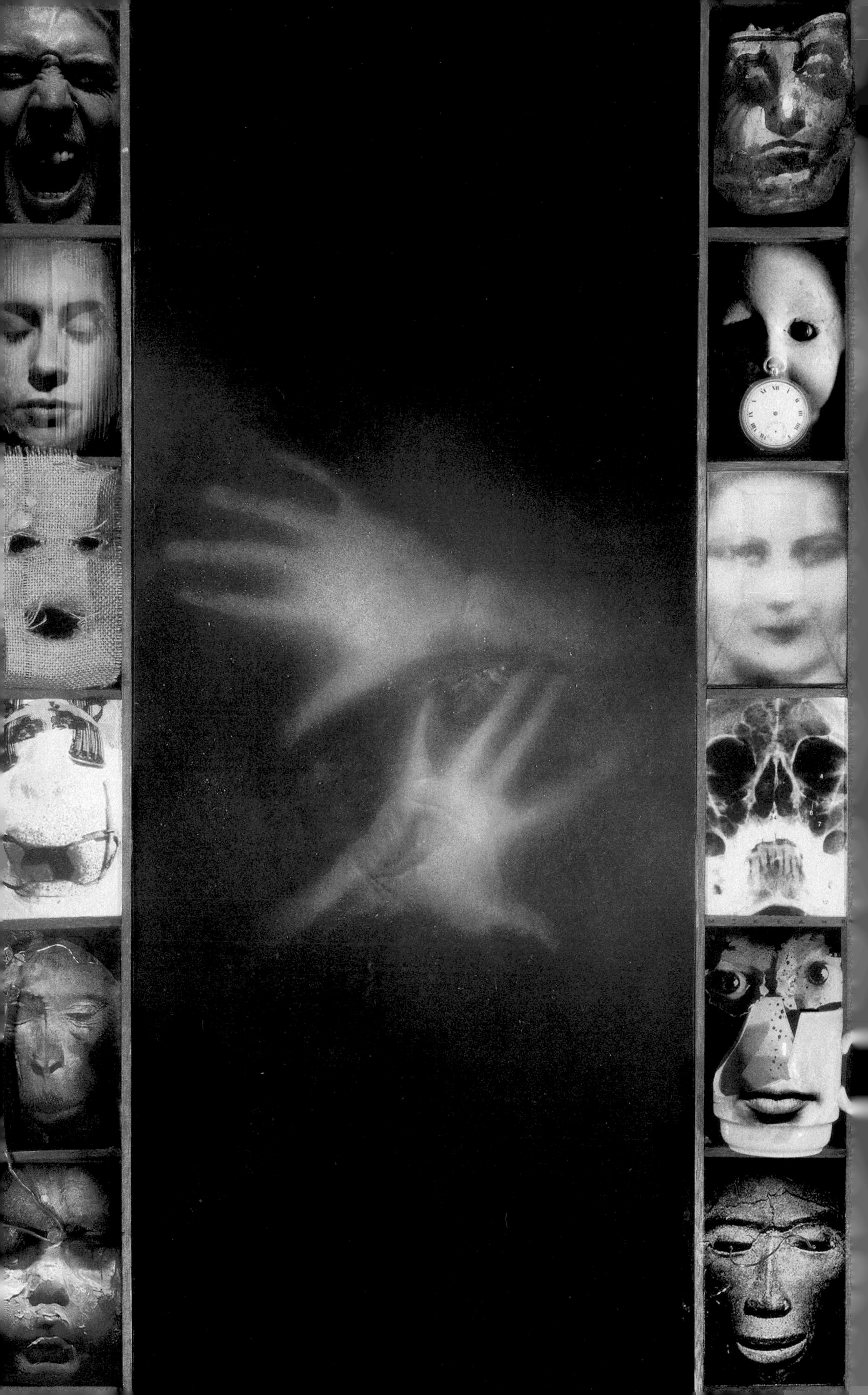

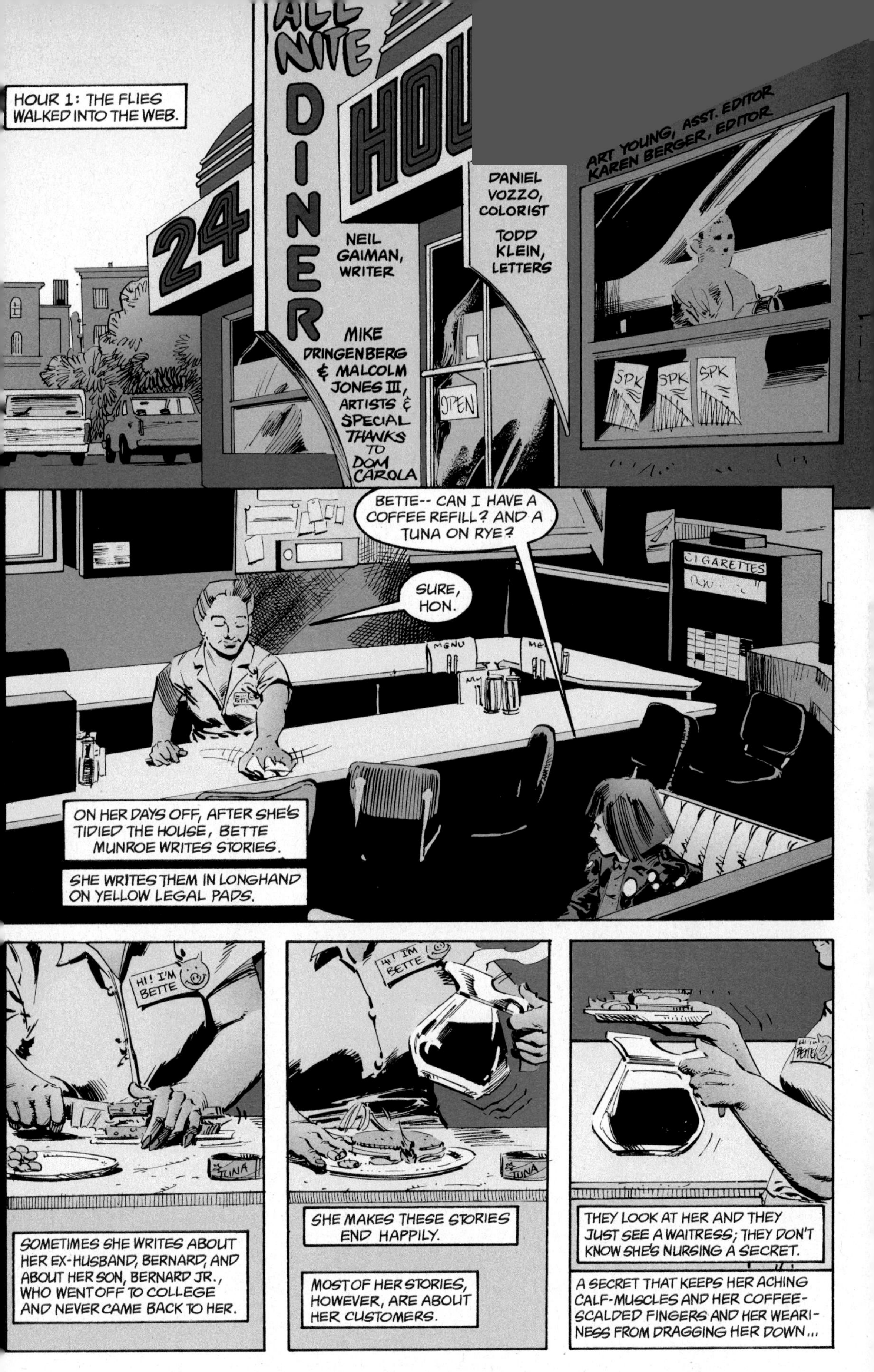

HOUR 1: THE FLIES WALKED INTO THE WEB.
ALL NITE
DINER
24 HOU
NEIL GAIMAN, WRITER
MIKE DRINGENBERG & MALCOLM JONES III, ARTISTS & SPECIAL THANKS TO DOM CAROLA
DANIEL VOZZO, COLORIST
TODD KLEIN, LETTERS
ART YOUNG, ASST. EDITOR
KAREN BERGER, EDITOR
OPEN
SPK
SPK
SPK
BETTE-- CAN I HAVE A COFFEE REFILL? AND A TUNA ON RYE?
SURE, HON.
CIGARETTES
MENU
ON HER DAYS OFF, AFTER SHE'S TIDIED THE HOUSE, BETTE MUNROE WRITES STORIES.
SHE WRITES THEM IN LONGHAND ON YELLOW LEGAL PADS.
HI! I'M BETTE
TUNA
SOMETIMES SHE WRITES ABOUT HER EX-HUSBAND, BERNARD, AND ABOUT HER SON, BERNARD JR., WHO WENT OFF TO COLLEGE AND NEVER CAME BACK TO HER.
HI! I'M BETTE
TUNA
SHE MAKES THESE STORIES END HAPPILY.
MOST OF HER STORIES, HOWEVER, ARE ABOUT HER CUSTOMERS.
THEY LOOK AT HER AND THEY JUST SEE A WAITRESS; THEY DON'T KNOW SHE'S NURSING A SECRET.
A SECRET THAT KEEPS HER ACHING CALF-MUSCLES AND HER COFFEE-SCALDED FINGERS AND HER WEARINESS FROM DRAGGING HER DOWN...

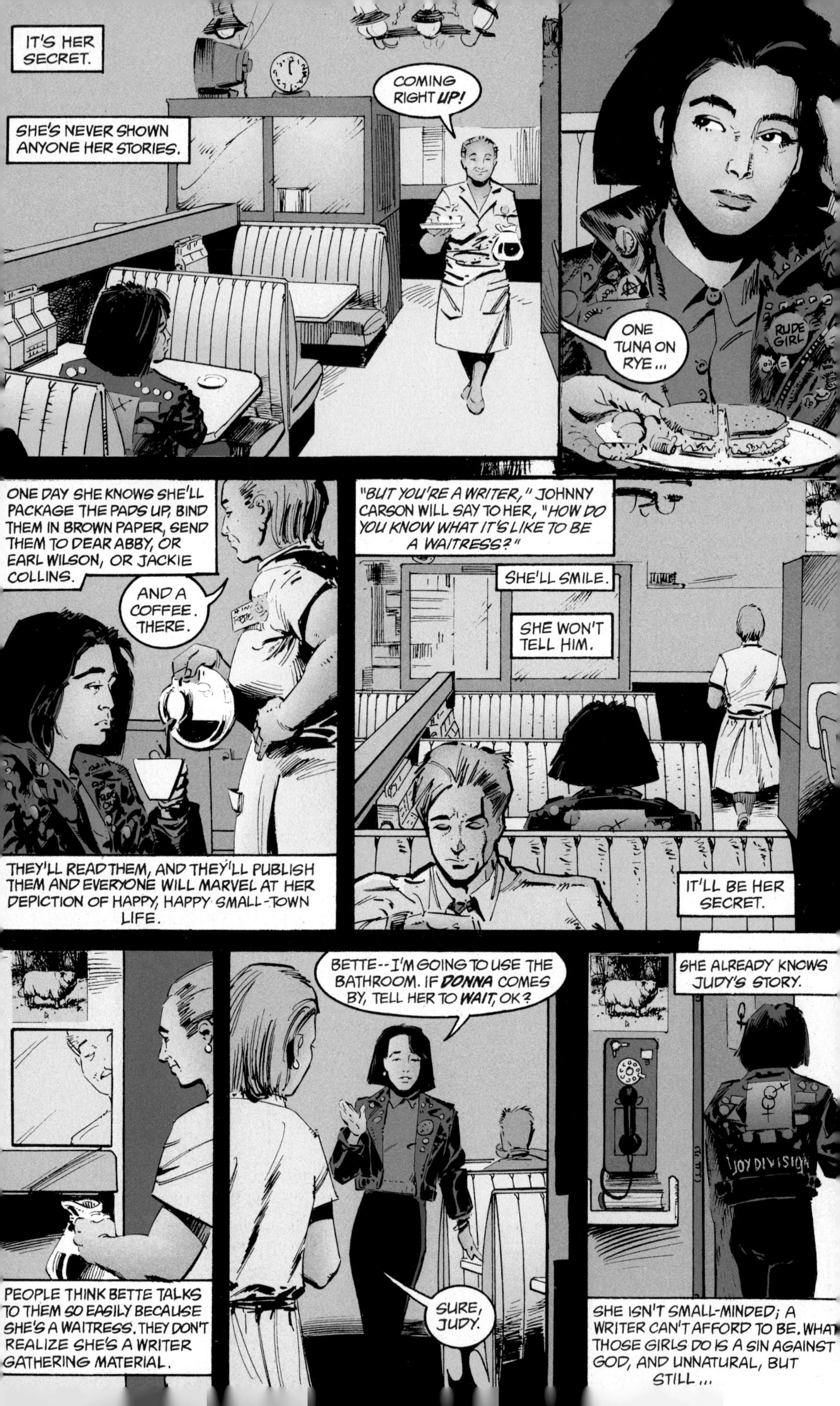
IT'S HER SECRET.
SHE'S NEVER SHOWN ANYONE HER STORIES.
COMING RIGHT UP!
ONE TUNA ON RYE...
RUDE GIRL
ONE DAY SHE KNOWS SHE'LL PACKAGE THE PADS UP, BIND THEM IN BROWN PAPER, SEND THEM TO DEAR ABBY, OR EARL WILSON, OR JACKIE COLLINS.
AND A COFFEE. THERE.
THEY'LL READ THEM, AND THEY'LL PUBLISH THEM AND EVERYONE WILL MARVEL AT HER DEPICTION OF HAPPY, HAPPY SMALL-TOWN LIFE.
"BUT YOU'RE A WRITER," JOHNNY CARSON WILL SAY TO HER, "HOW DO YOU KNOW WHAT IT'S LIKE TO BE A WAITRESS?"
SHE'LL SMILE.
SHE WON'T TELL HIM.
IT'LL BE HER SECRET.
PEOPLE THINK BETTE TALKS TO THEM SO EASILY BECAUSE SHE'S A WAITRESS. THEY DON'T REALIZE SHE'S A WRITER GATHERING MATERIAL.
BETTE--I'M GOING TO USE THE BATHROOM. IF DONNA COMES BY, TELL HER TO WAIT, OK?
SURE, JUDY.
SHE ALREADY KNOWS JUDY'S STORY.
JOY DIVISION
SHE ISN'T SMALL-MINDED; A WRITER CAN'T AFFORD TO BE. WHAT THOSE GIRLS DO IS A SIN AGAINST GOD, AND UNNATURAL, BUT STILL...

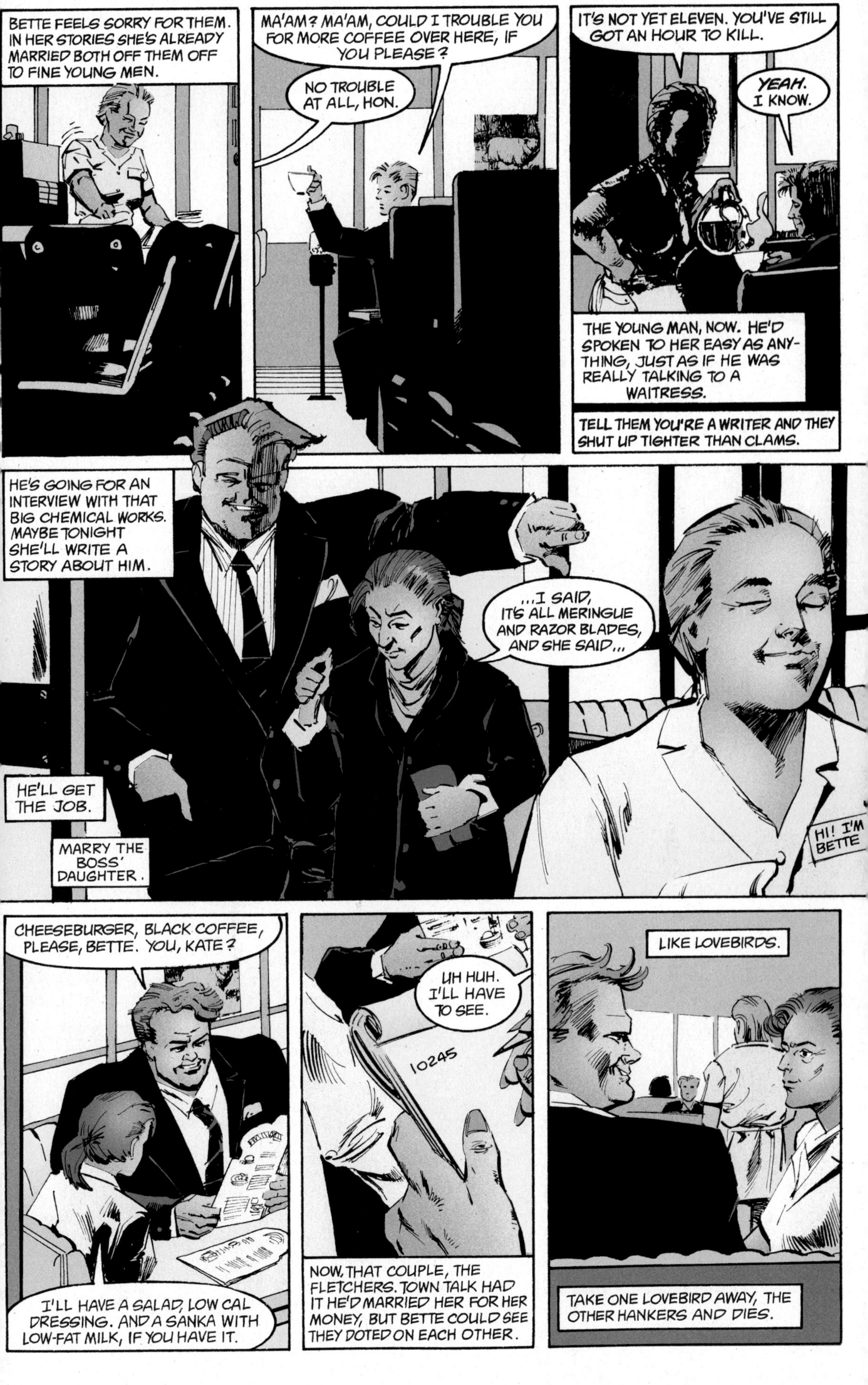
BETTE FEELS SORRY FOR THEM. IN HER STORIES SHE'S ALREADY MARRIED BOTH OFF THEM OFF TO FINE YOUNG MEN.
MA'AM? MA'AM, COULD I TROUBLE YOU FOR MORE COFFEE OVER HERE, IF YOU PLEASE?
NO TROUBLE AT ALL, HON.
IT'S NOT YET ELEVEN. YOU'VE STILL GOT AN HOUR TO KILL.
YEAH. I KNOW.
THE YOUNG MAN, NOW. HE'D SPOKEN TO HER EASY AS ANYTHING, JUST AS IF HE WAS REALLY TALKING TO A WAITRESS.
TELL THEM YOU'RE A WRITER AND THEY SHUT UP TIGHTER THAN CLAMS.
HE'S GOING FOR AN INTERVIEW WITH THAT BIG CHEMICAL WORKS. MAYBE TONIGHT SHE'LL WRITE A STORY ABOUT HIM.
...I SAID, IT'S ALL MERINGUE AND RAZOR BLADES, AND SHE SAID...
HE'LL GET THE JOB.
MARRY THE BOSS' DAUGHTER.
HI! I'M BETTE
CHEESEBURGER, BLACK COFFEE, PLEASE, BETTE. YOU, KATE?
I'LL HAVE A SALAD, LOW CAL DRESSING. AND A SANKA WITH LOW-FAT MILK, IF YOU HAVE IT.
UH HUH. I'LL HAVE TO SEE.
10245
NOW, THAT COUPLE, THE FLETCHERS. TOWN TALK HAD IT HE'D MARRIED HER FOR HER MONEY, BUT BETTE COULD SEE THEY DOTED ON EACH OTHER.
LIKE LOVEBIRDS.
TAKE ONE LOVEBIRD AWAY, THE OTHER HANKERS AND DIES.

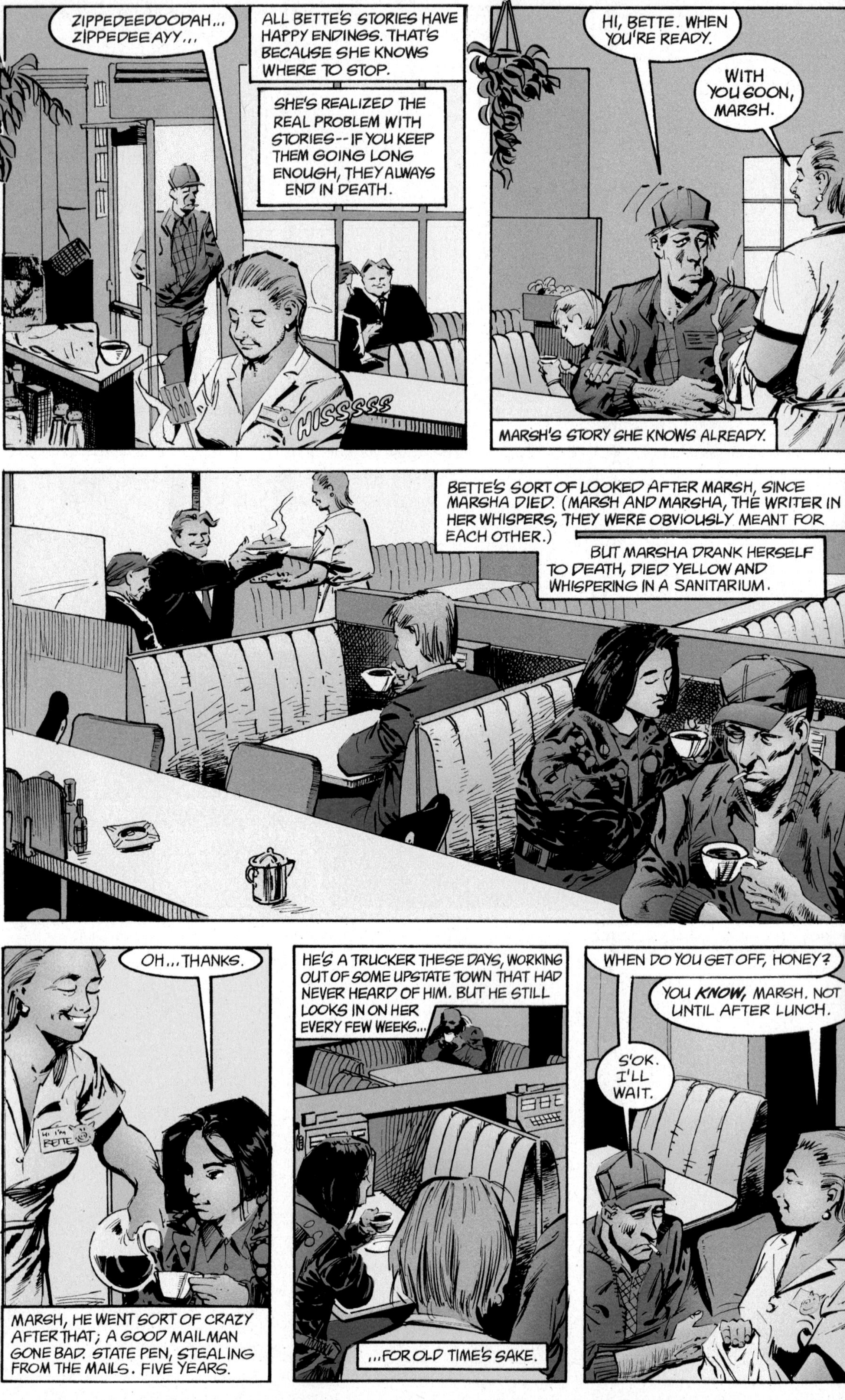
ZIPPEDEEDOODAH... ZIPPEDEE AYY...
ALL BETTE'S STORIES HAVE HAPPY ENDINGS. THAT'S BECAUSE SHE KNOWS WHERE TO STOP.
SHE'S REALIZED THE REAL PROBLEM WITH STORIES--IF YOU KEEP THEM GOING LONG ENOUGH, THEY ALWAYS END IN DEATH.
HISSSSS
HI, BETTE. WHEN YOU'RE READY.
WITH YOU SOON, MARSH.
MARSH'S STORY SHE KNOWS ALREADY.
BETTE'S SORT OF LOOKED AFTER MARSH, SINCE MARSHA DIED. (MARSH AND MARSHA, THE WRITER IN HER WHISPERS, THEY WERE OBVIOUSLY MEANT FOR EACH OTHER.)
BUT MARSHA DRANK HERSELF TO DEATH, DIED YELLOW AND WHISPERING IN A SANITARIUM.
OH... THANKS.
HI I'M BETTE
MARSH, HE WENT SORT OF CRAZY AFTER THAT; A GOOD MAILMAN GONE BAD. STATE PEN, STEALING FROM THE MAILS. FIVE YEARS.
HE'S A TRUCKER THESE DAYS, WORKING OUT OF SOME UPSTATE TOWN THAT HAD NEVER HEARD OF HIM. BUT HE STILL LOOKS IN ON HER EVERY FEW WEEKS...
...FOR OLD TIME'S SAKE.
WHEN DO YOU GET OFF, HONEY?
YOU KNOW, MARSH. NOT UNTIL AFTER LUNCH.
S'OK. I'LL WAIT.

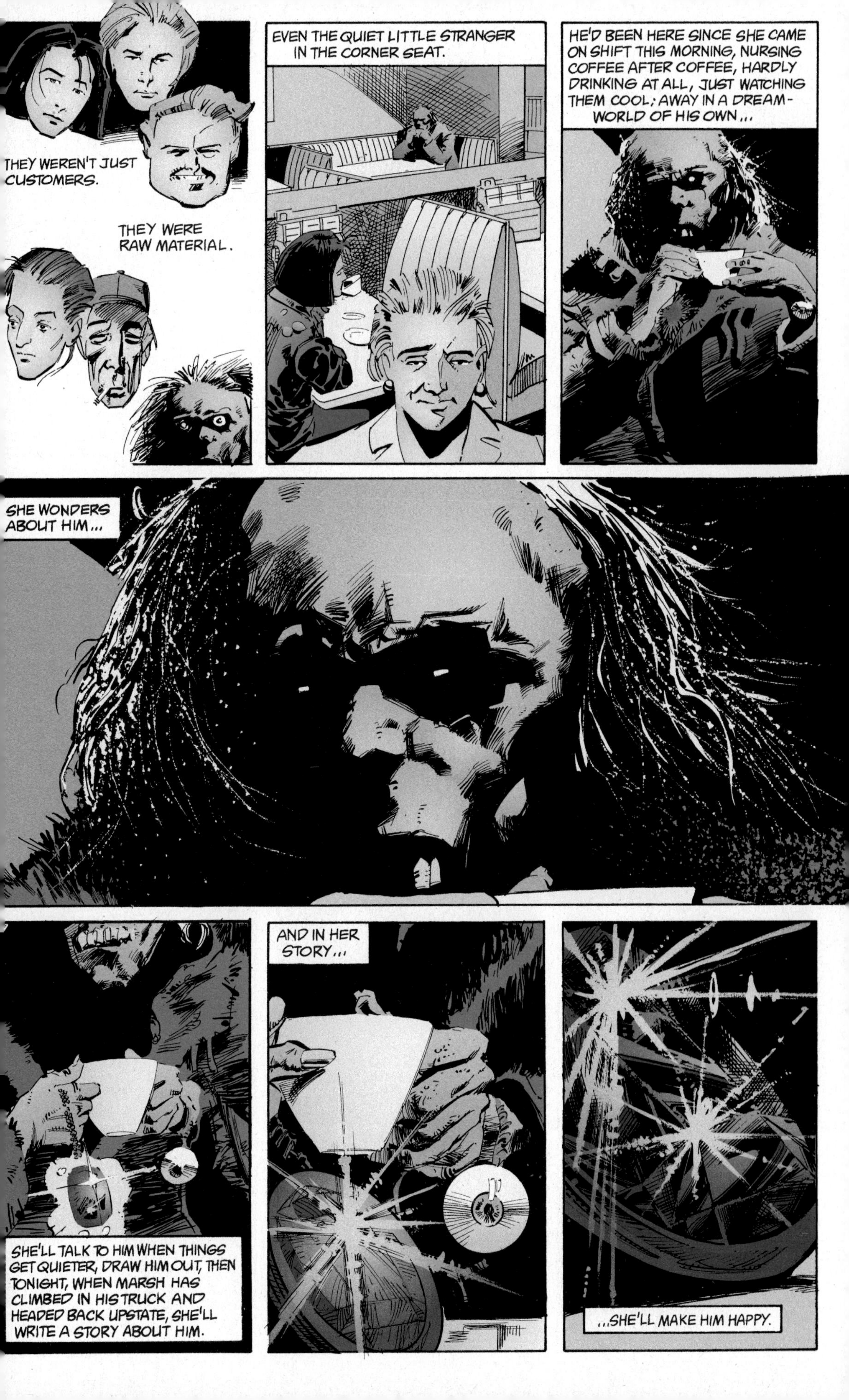
THEY WEREN'T JUST CUSTOMERS.
THEY WERE RAW MATERIAL.
EVEN THE QUIET LITTLE STRANGER IN THE CORNER SEAT.
HE'D BEEN HERE SINCE SHE CAME ON SHIFT THIS MORNING, NURSING COFFEE AFTER COFFEE, HARDLY DRINKING AT ALL, JUST WATCHING THEM COOL; AWAY IN A DREAM-WORLD OF HIS OWN...
SHE WONDERS ABOUT HIM...
SHE'LL TALK TO HIM WHEN THINGS GET QUIETER, DRAW HIM OUT, THEN TONIGHT, WHEN MARSH HAS CLIMBED IN HIS TRUCK AND HEADED BACK UPSTATE, SHE'LL WRITE A STORY ABOUT HIM.
AND IN HER STORY...
...SHE'LL MAKE HIM HAPPY.

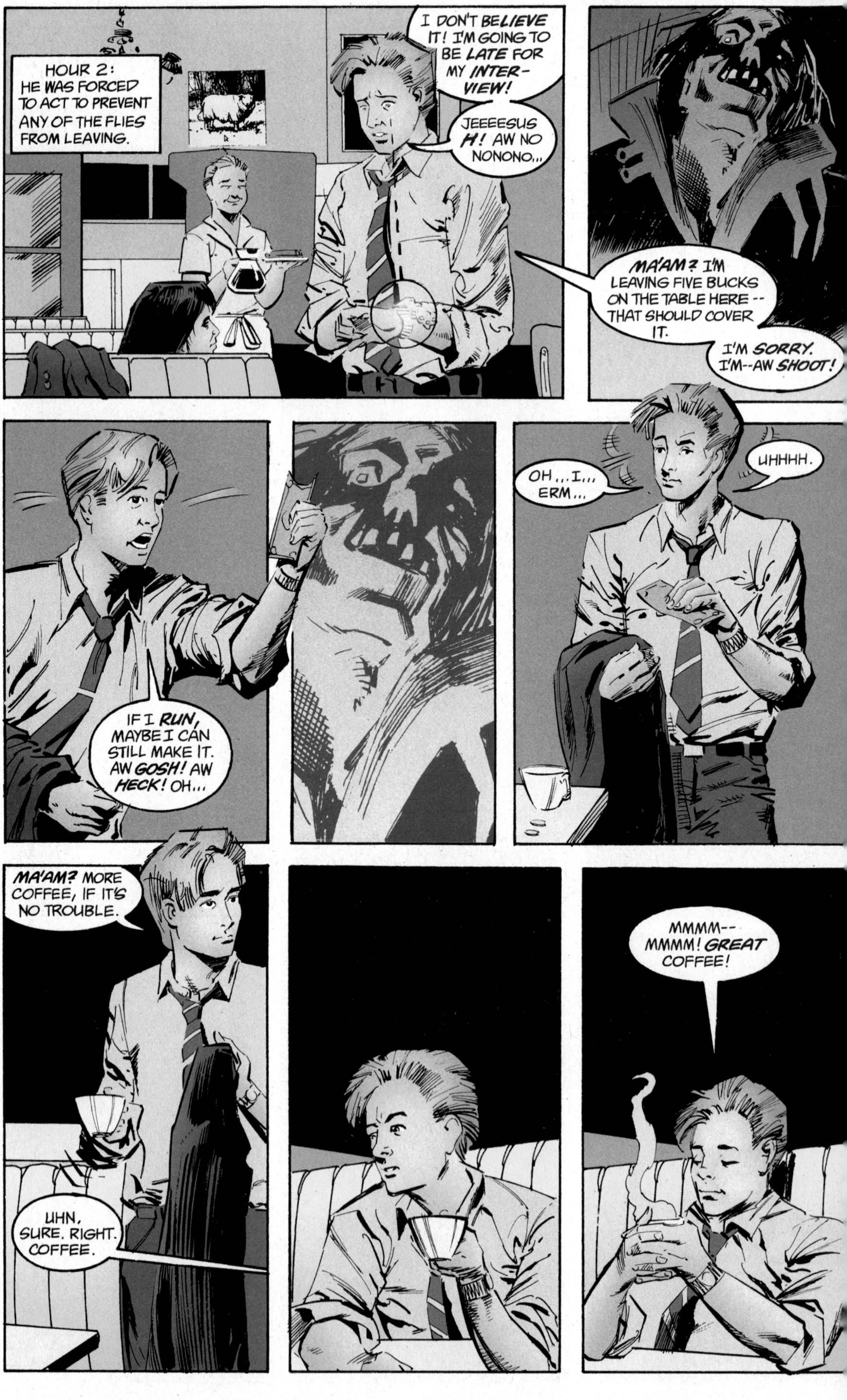

HOUR 2: HE WAS FORCED TO ACT TO PREVENT ANY OF THE FLIES FROM LEAVING.
I DON'T BELIEVE IT! I'M GOING TO BE LATE FOR MY INTER-VIEW!
JEEEESUS H! AW NO NONONO...
MA'AM? I'M LEAVING FIVE BUCKS ON THE TABLE HERE -- THAT SHOULD COVER IT.
I'M SORRY. I'M--AW SHOOT!
IF I RUN, MAYBE I CAN STILL MAKE IT. AW GOSH! AW HECK! OH...
OH ... I ... ERM ...
UHHHH.
MA'AM? MORE COFFEE, IF IT'S NO TROUBLE.
UHN, SURE. RIGHT. COFFEE.
MMMM-- MMMM! GREAT COFFEE!

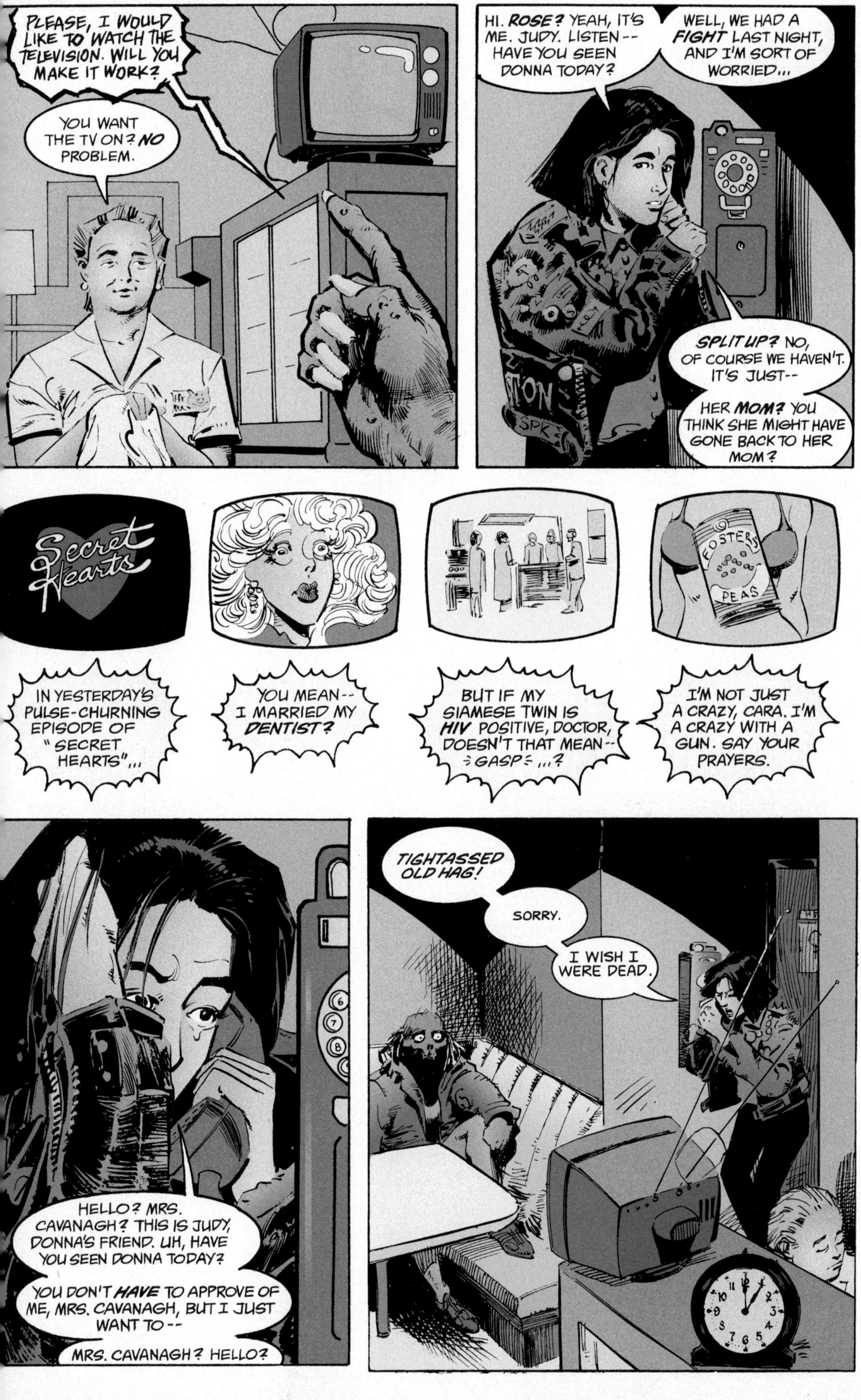
PLEASE, I WOULD LIKE TO WATCH THE TELEVISION. WILL YOU MAKE IT WORK?
YOU WANT THE TV ON? NO PROBLEM.
HI. ROSE? YEAH, IT'S ME. JUDY. LISTEN -- HAVE YOU SEEN DONNA TODAY?
WELL, WE HAD A FIGHT LAST NIGHT, AND I'M SORT OF WORRIED...
SPLIT UP? NO, OF COURSE WE HAVEN'T. IT'S JUST--
HER MOM? YOU THINK SHE MIGHT HAVE GONE BACK TO HER MOM?
Secret Hearts
FOSTERS PEAS
IN YESTERDAY'S PULSE-CHURNING EPISODE OF "SECRET HEARTS"...
YOU MEAN-- I MARRIED MY DENTIST?
BUT IF MY SIAMESE TWIN IS HIV POSITIVE, DOCTOR, DOESN'T THAT MEAN-- ≑GASP≑ ...?
I'M NOT JUST A CRAZY, CARA. I'M A CRAZY WITH A GUN. SAY YOUR PRAYERS.
HELLO? MRS. CAVANAGH? THIS IS JUDY, DONNA'S FRIEND. UH, HAVE YOU SEEN DONNA TODAY?
YOU DON'T HAVE TO APPROVE OF ME, MRS. CAVANAGH, BUT I JUST WANT TO --
MRS. CAVANAGH? HELLO?
TIGHTASSED OLD HAG!
SORRY.
I WISH I WERE DEAD.

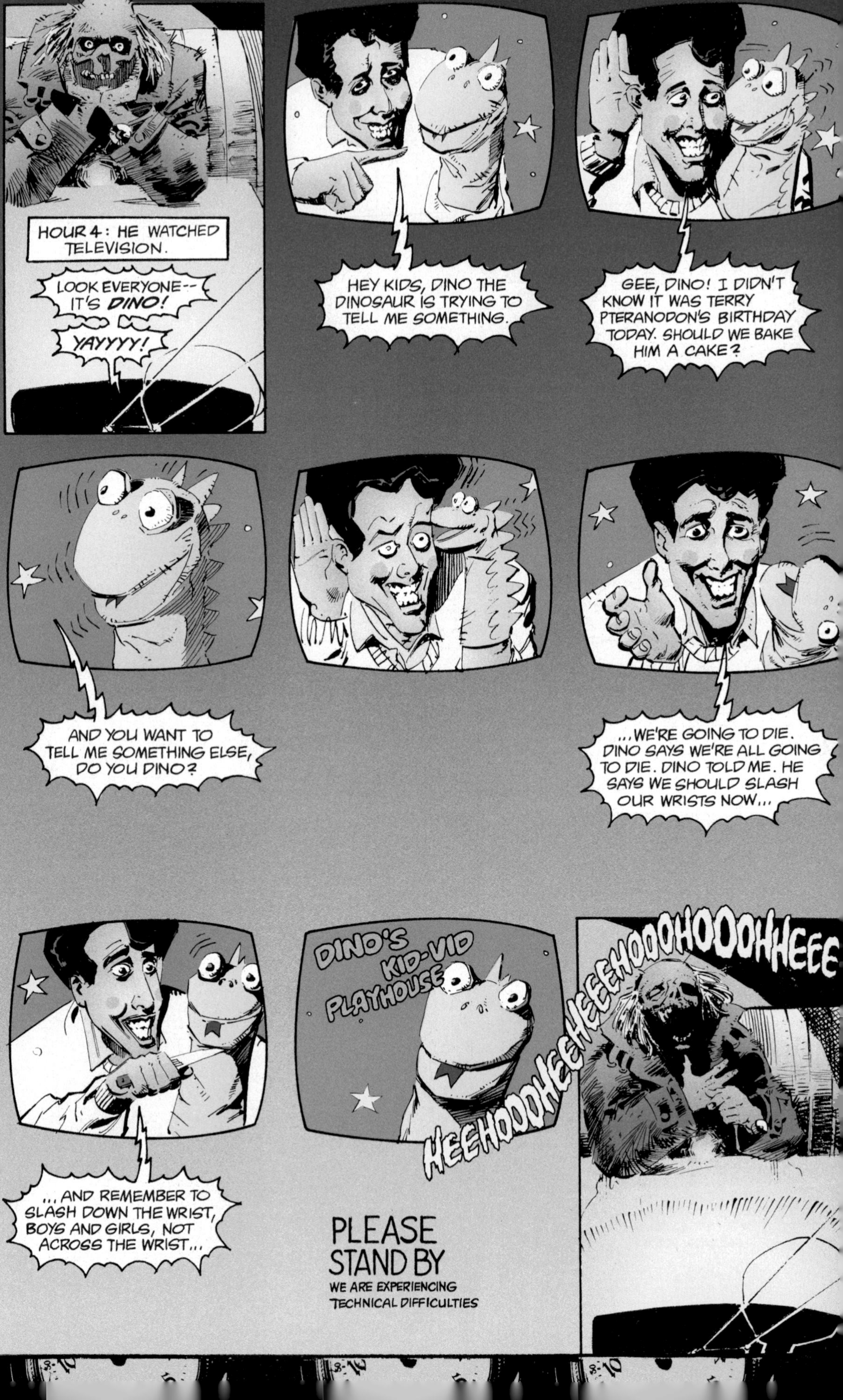
HOUR 4: HE WATCHED TELEVISION.
LOOK EVERYONE-- IT'S DINO!
YAYYYY!
HEY KIDS, DINO THE DINOSAUR IS TRYING TO TELL ME SOMETHING.
GEE, DINO! I DIDN'T KNOW IT WAS TERRY PTERANODON'S BIRTHDAY TODAY. SHOULD WE BAKE HIM A CAKE?
AND YOU WANT TO TELL ME SOMETHING ELSE, DO YOU DINO?
...WE'RE GOING TO DIE. DINO SAYS WE'RE ALL GOING TO DIE. DINO TOLD ME. HE SAYS WE SHOULD SLASH OUR WRISTS NOW...
...AND REMEMBER TO SLASH DOWN THE WRIST, BOYS AND GIRLS, NOT ACROSS THE WRIST...
DINO'S KID-VID PLAYHOUSE
PLEASE STAND BY
WE ARE EXPERIENCING TECHNICAL DIFFICULTIES
HEEHOOOHEEHEEEHEEEHOOOHOOOOHHEEE

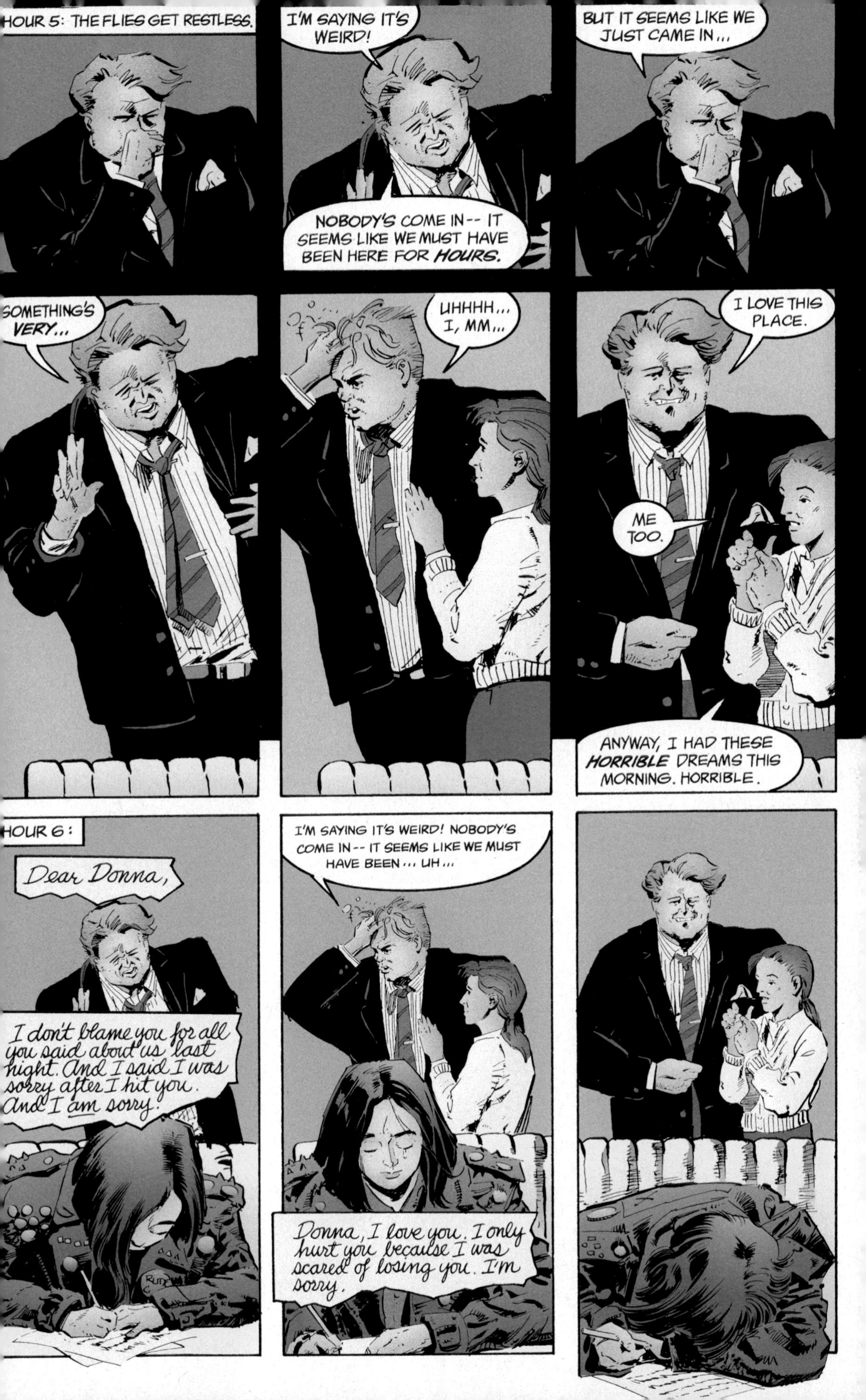
HOUR 5: THE FLIES GET RESTLESS.
I'M SAYING IT'S WEIRD!
NOBODY'S COME IN-- IT SEEMS LIKE WE MUST HAVE BEEN HERE FOR HOURS.
BUT IT SEEMS LIKE WE JUST CAME IN...
SOMETHING'S VERY...
UHHHH... I, MM...
I LOVE THIS PLACE.
ME TOO.
ANYWAY, I HAD THESE HORRIBLE DREAMS THIS MORNING. HORRIBLE.
HOUR 6:
Dear Donna,
I don't blame you for all you said about us last night. And I said I was sorry after I hit you. And I am sorry.
I'M SAYING IT'S WEIRD! NOBODY'S COME IN-- IT SEEMS LIKE WE MUST HAVE BEEN... UH...
Donna, I love you. I only hurt you because I was scared of losing you. I'm sorry.

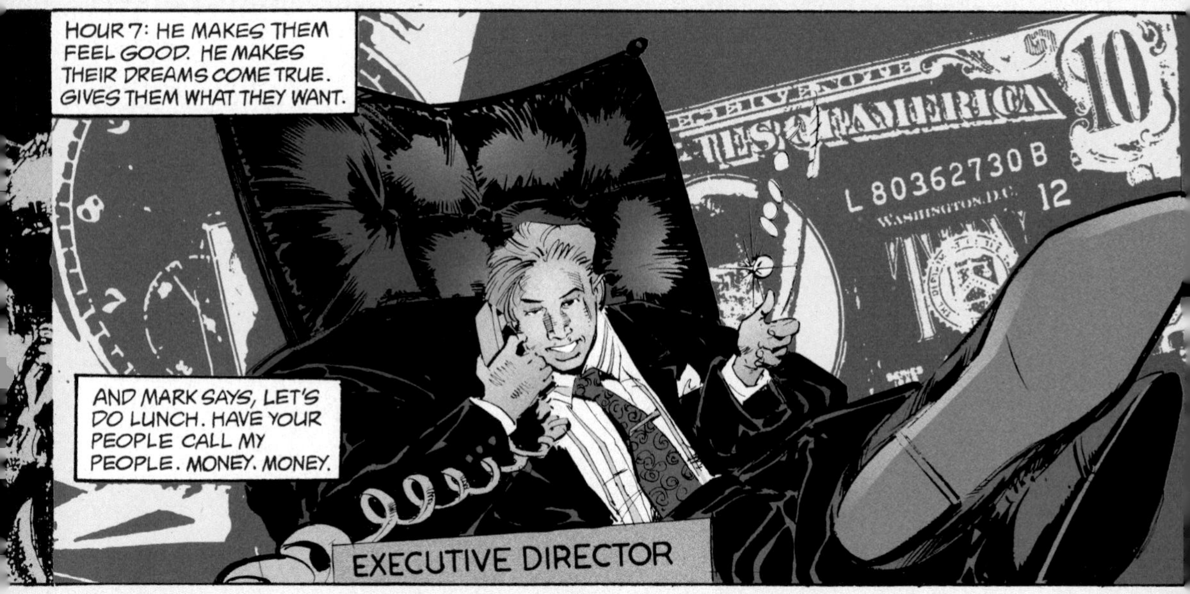
HOUR 7: HE MAKES THEM FEEL GOOD. HE MAKES THEIR DREAMS COME TRUE. GIVES THEM WHAT THEY WANT.
L 80362730 B
12
10
AND MARK SAYS, LET'S DO LUNCH. HAVE YOUR PEOPLE CALL MY PEOPLE. MONEY. MONEY.
EXECUTIVE DIRECTOR

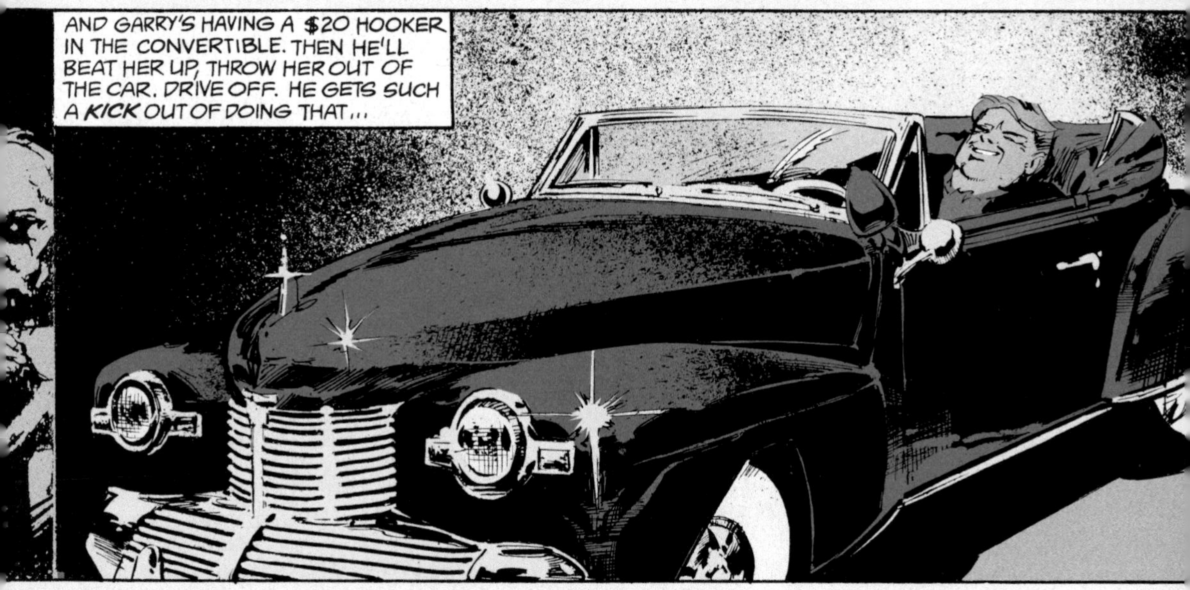
AND GARRY'S HAVING A $20 HOOKER IN THE CONVERTIBLE. THEN HE'LL BEAT HER UP, THROW HER OUT OF THE CAR. DRIVE OFF. HE GETS SUCH A *KICK* OUT OF DOING THAT...

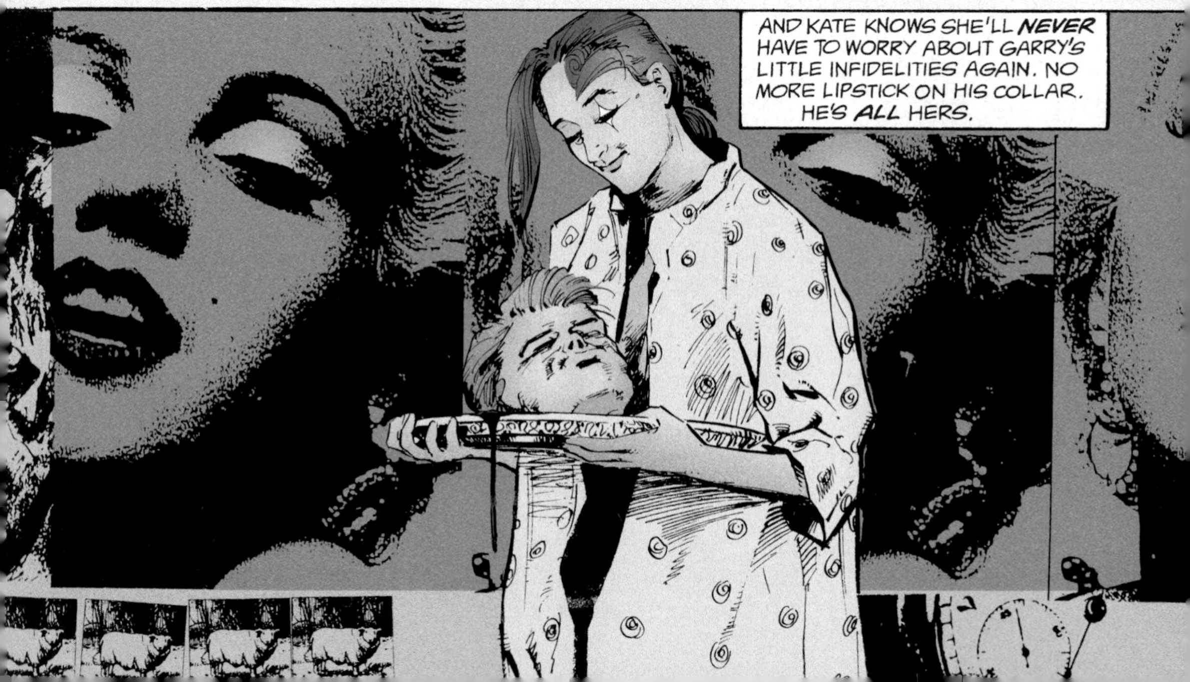
AND KATE KNOWS SHE'LL *NEVER* HAVE TO WORRY ABOUT GARRY'S LITTLE INFIDELITIES AGAIN. NO MORE LIPSTICK ON HIS COLLAR. HE'S *ALL* HERS.

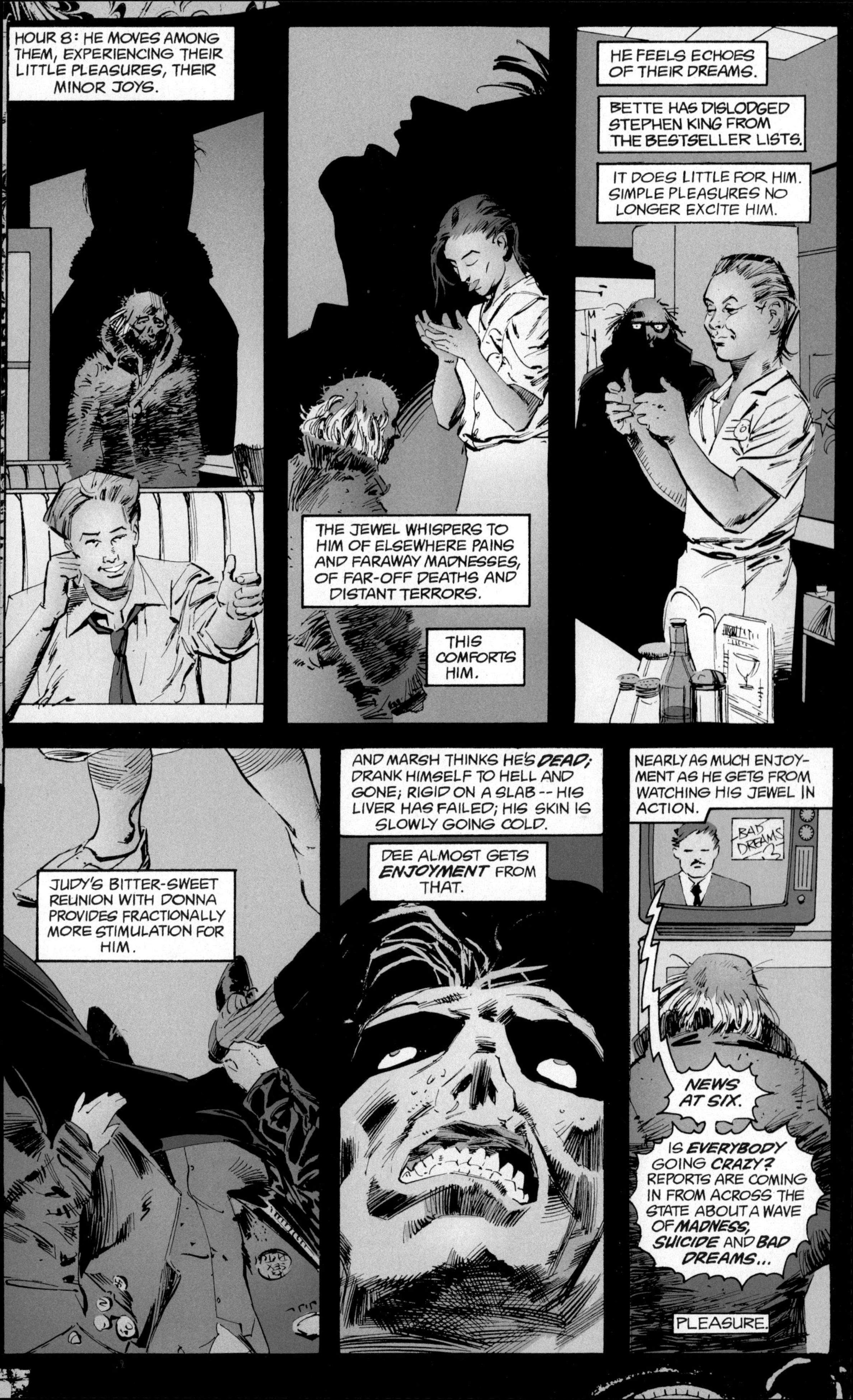
HOUR 8: HE MOVES AMONG THEM, EXPERIENCING THEIR LITTLE PLEASURES, THEIR MINOR JOYS.
THE JEWEL WHISPERS TO HIM OF ELSEWHERE PAINS AND FARAWAY MADNESSES, OF FAR-OFF DEATHS AND DISTANT TERRORS.
THIS COMFORTS HIM.
HE FEELS ECHOES OF THEIR DREAMS.
BETTE HAS DISLODGED STEPHEN KING FROM THE BESTSELLER LISTS.
IT DOES LITTLE FOR HIM. SIMPLE PLEASURES NO LONGER EXCITE HIM.
JUDY'S BITTER-SWEET REUNION WITH DONNA PROVIDES FRACTIONALLY MORE STIMULATION FOR HIM.
AND MARSH THINKS HE'S DEAD; DRANK HIMSELF TO HELL AND GONE; RIGID ON A SLAB -- HIS LIVER HAS FAILED; HIS SKIN IS SLOWLY GOING COLD.
DEE ALMOST GETS ENJOYMENT FROM THAT.
NEARLY AS MUCH ENJOYMENT AS HE GETS FROM WATCHING HIS JEWEL IN ACTION.
BAD DREAMS
NEWS AT SIX.
IS EVERYBODY GOING CRAZY? REPORTS ARE COMING IN FROM ACROSS THE STATE ABOUT A WAVE OF MADNESS, SUICIDE AND BAD DREAMS...
PLEASURE.

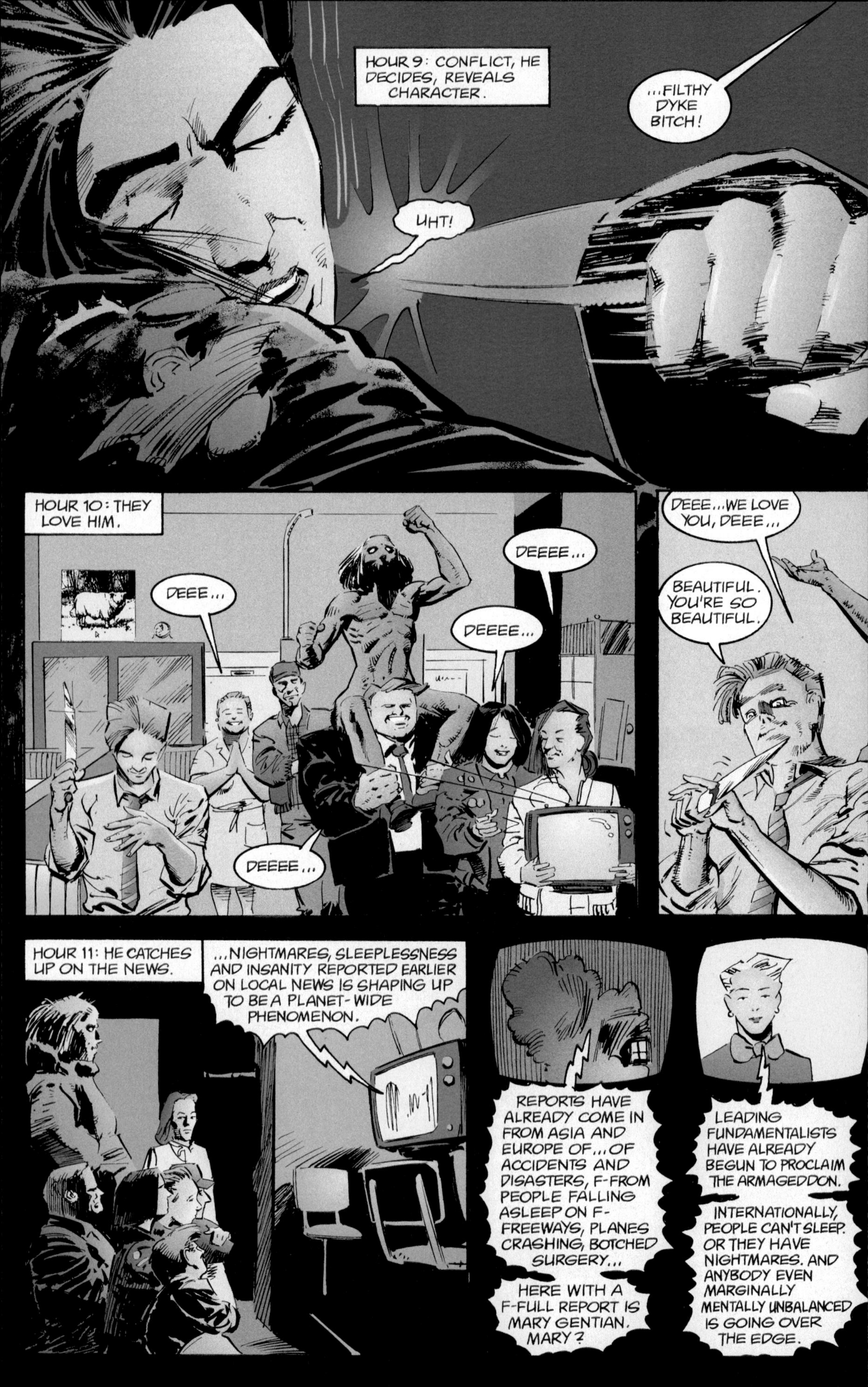
HOUR 9: CONFLICT, HE DECIDES, REVEALS CHARACTER.
...FILTHY DYKE BITCH!
UHT!
HOUR 10: THEY LOVE HIM.
DEEE...
DEEEE...
DEEEE...
DEEEE...
DEEE...WE LOVE YOU, DEEE...
BEAUTIFUL. YOU'RE SO BEAUTIFUL.
HOUR 11: HE CATCHES UP ON THE NEWS.
...NIGHTMARES, SLEEPLESSNESS AND INSANITY REPORTED EARLIER ON LOCAL NEWS IS SHAPING UP TO BE A PLANET-WIDE PHENOMENON.
REPORTS HAVE ALREADY COME IN FROM ASIA AND EUROPE OF... OF ACCIDENTS AND DISASTERS, F-FROM PEOPLE FALLING ASLEEP ON F-FREEWAYS, PLANES CRASHING, BOTCHED SURGERY...
HERE WITH A F-FULL REPORT IS MARY GENTIAN. MARY?
LEADING FUNDAMENTALISTS HAVE ALREADY BEGUN TO PROCLAIM THE ARMAGEDDON.
INTERNATIONALLY, PEOPLE CAN'T SLEEP. OR THEY HAVE NIGHTMARES. AND ANYBODY EVEN MARGINALLY MENTALLY UNBALANCED IS GOING OVER THE EDGE.

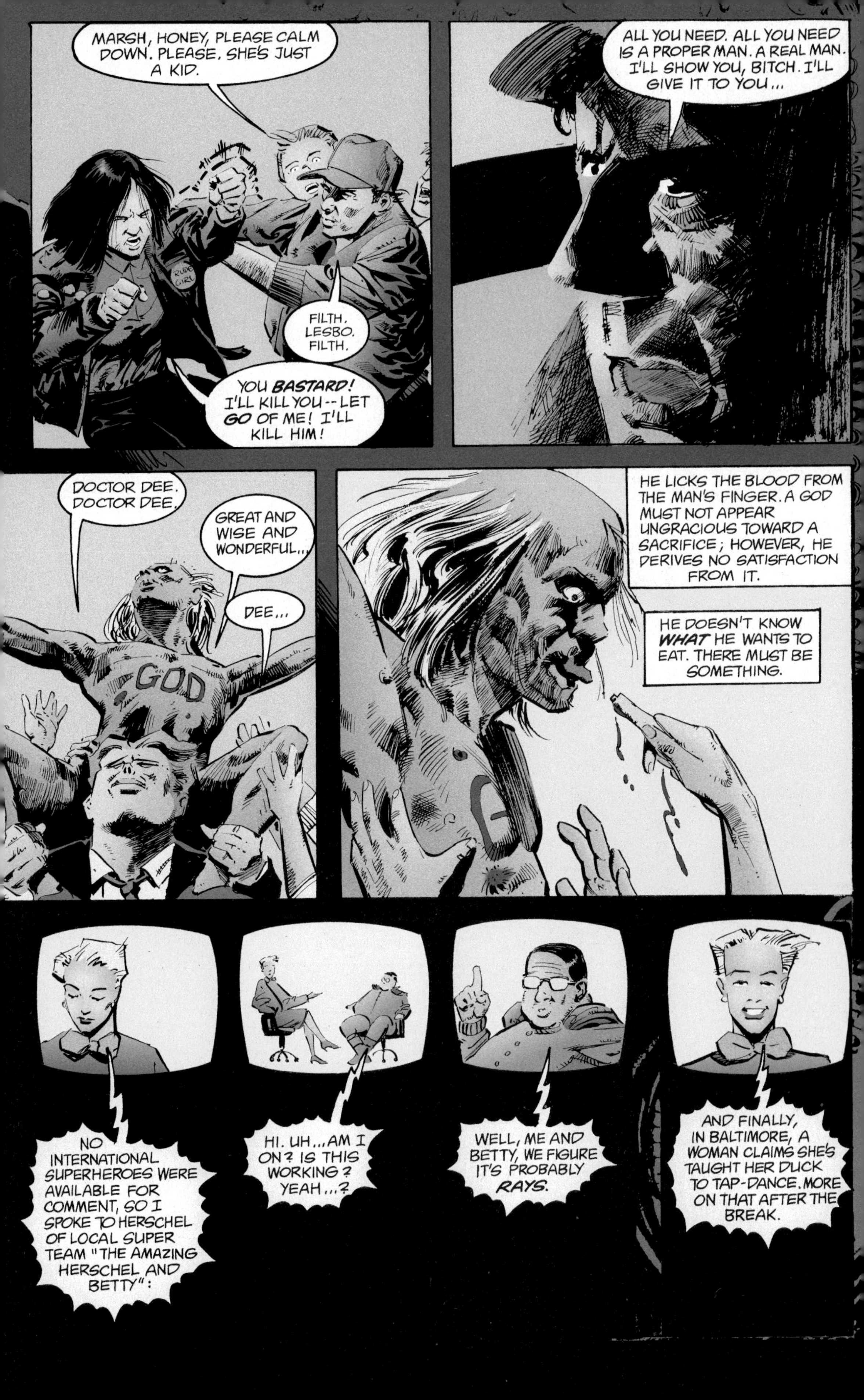

MARSH, HONEY, PLEASE CALM DOWN. PLEASE. SHE'S JUST A KID.
RUDE GIRL
FILTH. LESBO. FILTH.
YOU BASTARD! I'LL KILL YOU -- LET GO OF ME! I'LL KILL HIM!
ALL YOU NEED. ALL YOU NEED IS A PROPER MAN. A REAL MAN. I'LL SHOW YOU, BITCH. I'LL GIVE IT TO YOU...
DOCTOR DEE. DOCTOR DEE.
GREAT AND WISE AND WONDERFUL...
DEE...
GOD
HE LICKS THE BLOOD FROM THE MAN'S FINGER. A GOD MUST NOT APPEAR UNGRACIOUS TOWARD A SACRIFICE; HOWEVER, HE DERIVES NO SATISFACTION FROM IT.
HE DOESN'T KNOW WHAT HE WANTS TO EAT. THERE MUST BE SOMETHING.
NO INTERNATIONAL SUPERHEROES WERE AVAILABLE FOR COMMENT, SO I SPOKE TO HERSCHEL OF LOCAL SUPER TEAM "THE AMAZING HERSCHEL AND BETTY":
HI. UH...AM I ON? IS THIS WORKING? YEAH...?
WELL, ME AND BETTY, WE FIGURE IT'S PROBABLY RAYS.
AND FINALLY, IN BALTIMORE, A WOMAN CLAIMS SHE'S TAUGHT HER DUCK TO TAP-DANCE. MORE ON THAT AFTER THE BREAK.

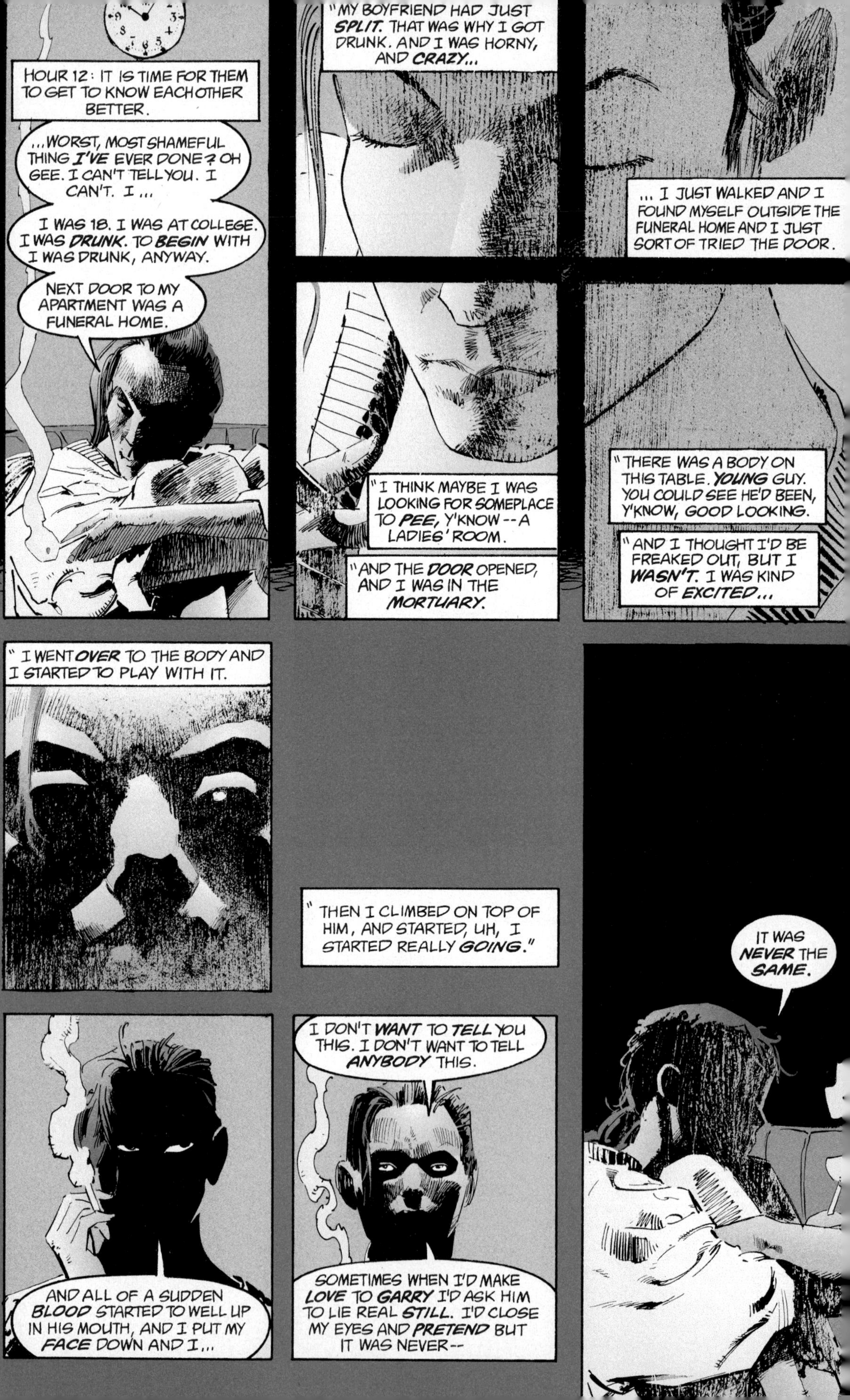
HOUR 12: IT IS TIME FOR THEM TO GET TO KNOW EACH OTHER BETTER.
...WORST, MOST SHAMEFUL THING I'VE EVER DONE? OH GEE. I CAN'T TELL YOU. I CAN'T. I...
I WAS 18. I WAS AT COLLEGE. I WAS DRUNK. TO BEGIN WITH I WAS DRUNK, ANYWAY.
NEXT DOOR TO MY APARTMENT WAS A FUNERAL HOME.
"MY BOYFRIEND HAD JUST SPLIT. THAT WAS WHY I GOT DRUNK. AND I WAS HORNY, AND CRAZY...
... I JUST WALKED AND I FOUND MYSELF OUTSIDE THE FUNERAL HOME AND I JUST SORT OF TRIED THE DOOR.
"I THINK MAYBE I WAS LOOKING FOR SOMEPLACE TO PEE, Y'KNOW -- A LADIES' ROOM.
"AND THE DOOR OPENED, AND I WAS IN THE MORTUARY.
"THERE WAS A BODY ON THIS TABLE. YOUNG GUY. YOU COULD SEE HE'D BEEN, Y'KNOW, GOOD LOOKING.
"AND I THOUGHT I'D BE FREAKED OUT, BUT I WASN'T. I WAS KIND OF EXCITED...
" I WENT OVER TO THE BODY AND I STARTED TO PLAY WITH IT.
" THEN I CLIMBED ON TOP OF HIM, AND STARTED, UH, I STARTED REALLY GOING."
AND ALL OF A SUDDEN BLOOD STARTED TO WELL UP IN HIS MOUTH, AND I PUT MY FACE DOWN AND I...
I DON'T WANT TO TELL YOU THIS. I DON'T WANT TO TELL ANYBODY THIS.
SOMETIMES WHEN I'D MAKE LOVE TO GARRY I'D ASK HIM TO LIE REAL STILL. I'D CLOSE MY EYES AND PRETEND BUT IT WAS NEVER--
IT WAS NEVER THE SAME.

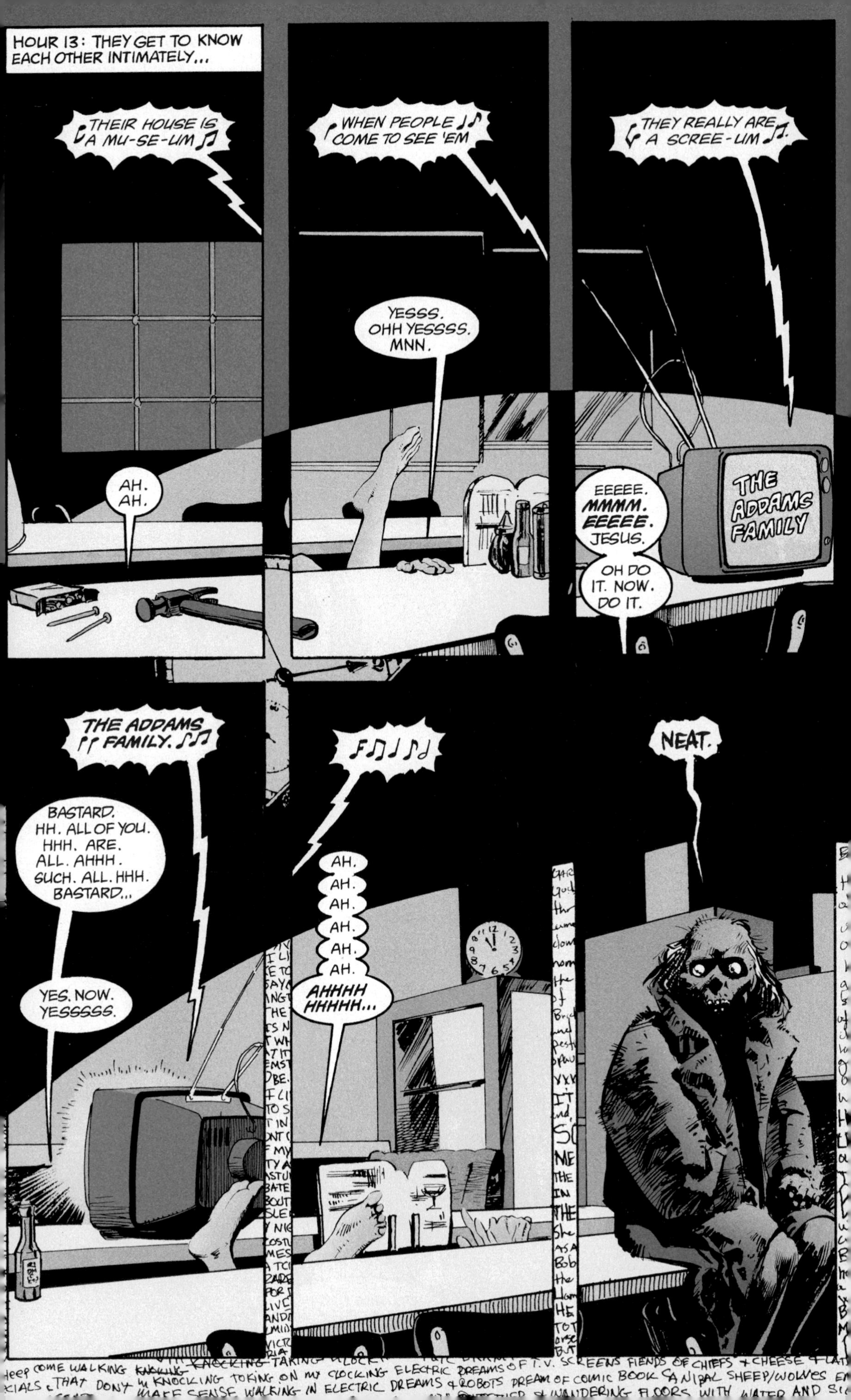

HOUR 13: THEY GET TO KNOW EACH OTHER INTIMATELY...
THEIR HOUSE IS A MU-SE-UM
AH. AH.
WHEN PEOPLE COME TO SEE 'EM
YESSS. OHH YESSSS. MNN.
THEY REALLY ARE A SCREE-UM
THE ADDAMS FAMILY
EEEEE. MMMM. EEEEE. JESUS.
OH DO IT. NOW. DO IT.
THE ADDAMS FAMILY.
BASTARD. HH. ALL OF YOU. HHH. ARE. ALL. AHHH. SUCH. ALL. HHH. BASTARD...
YES. NOW. YESSSSS.
AH. AH. AH. AH. AH. AH.
AHHHH HHHHH...
NEAT.

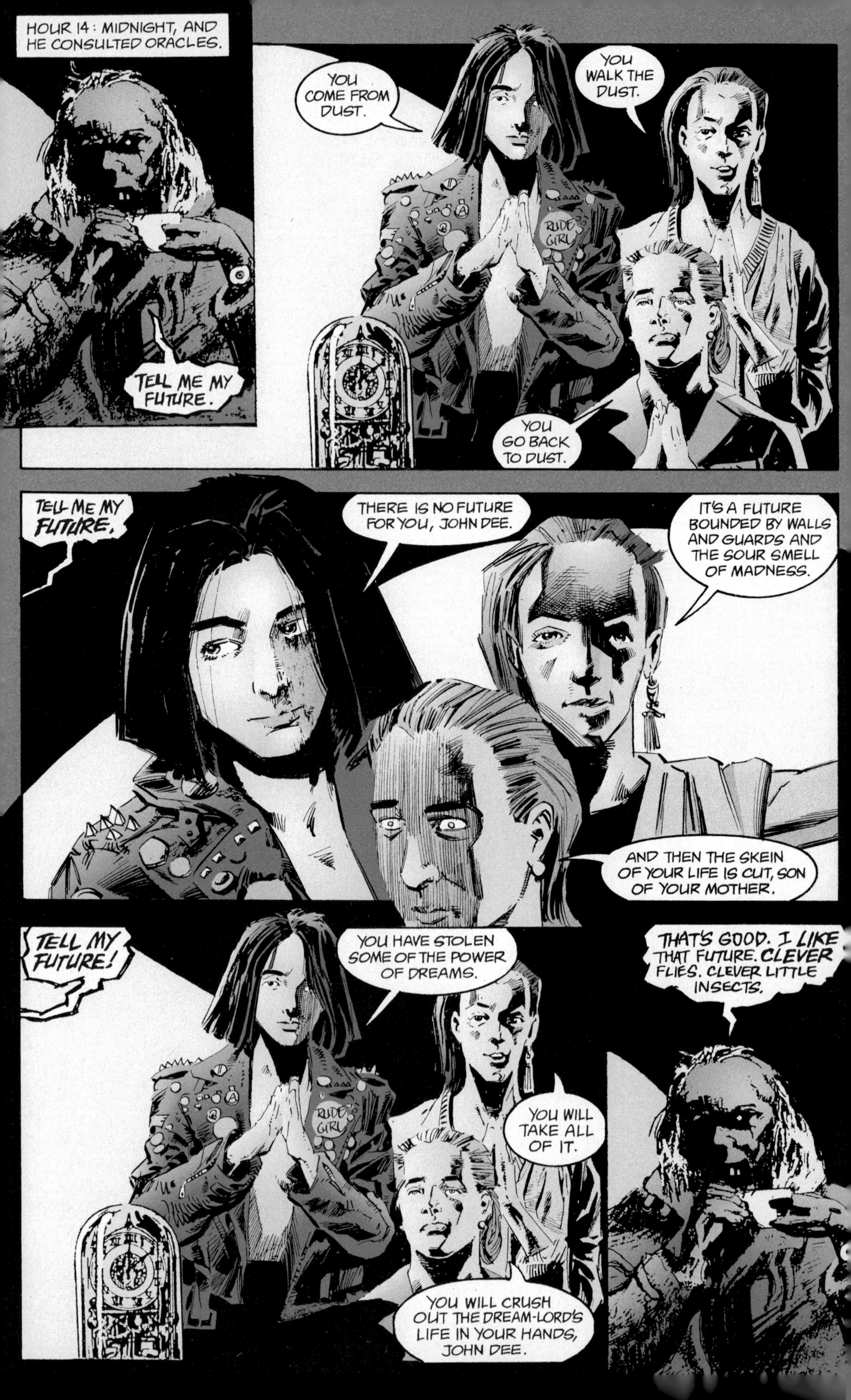
HOUR 14: MIDNIGHT, AND HE CONSULTED ORACLES.
TELL ME MY FUTURE.
YOU COME FROM DUST.
YOU WALK THE DUST.
YOU GO BACK TO DUST.
TELL ME MY FUTURE.
THERE IS NO FUTURE FOR YOU, JOHN DEE.
IT'S A FUTURE BOUNDED BY WALLS AND GUARDS AND THE SOUR SMELL OF MADNESS.
AND THEN THE SKEIN OF YOUR LIFE IS CUT, SON OF YOUR MOTHER.
TELL MY FUTURE!
YOU HAVE STOLEN SOME OF THE POWER OF DREAMS.
YOU WILL TAKE ALL OF IT.
YOU WILL CRUSH OUT THE DREAM-LORD'S LIFE IN YOUR HANDS, JOHN DEE.
THAT'S GOOD. I LIKE THAT FUTURE. CLEVER FLIES. CLEVER LITTLE INSECTS.
RUDE GIRL
RUDE GIRL

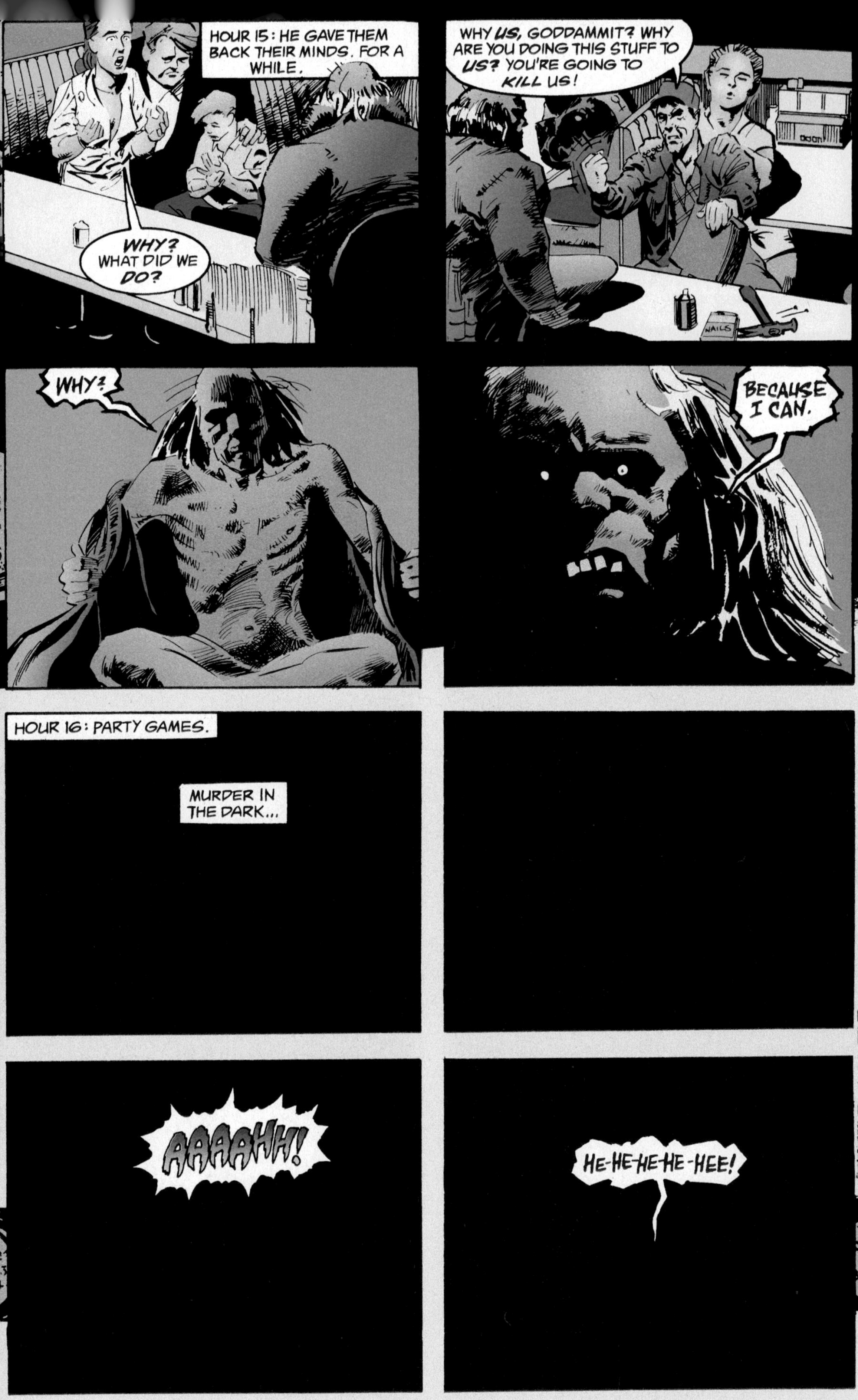
HOUR 15: HE GAVE THEM BACK THEIR MINDS. FOR A WHILE.
WHY? WHAT DID WE DO?
WHY US, GODDAMMIT? WHY ARE YOU DOING THIS STUFF TO US? YOU'RE GOING TO KILL US!
NAILS
WHY?
BECAUSE I CAN.
HOUR 16: PARTY GAMES.
MURDER IN THE DARK...
AAAAHH!
HE-HE-HE-HE-HEE!

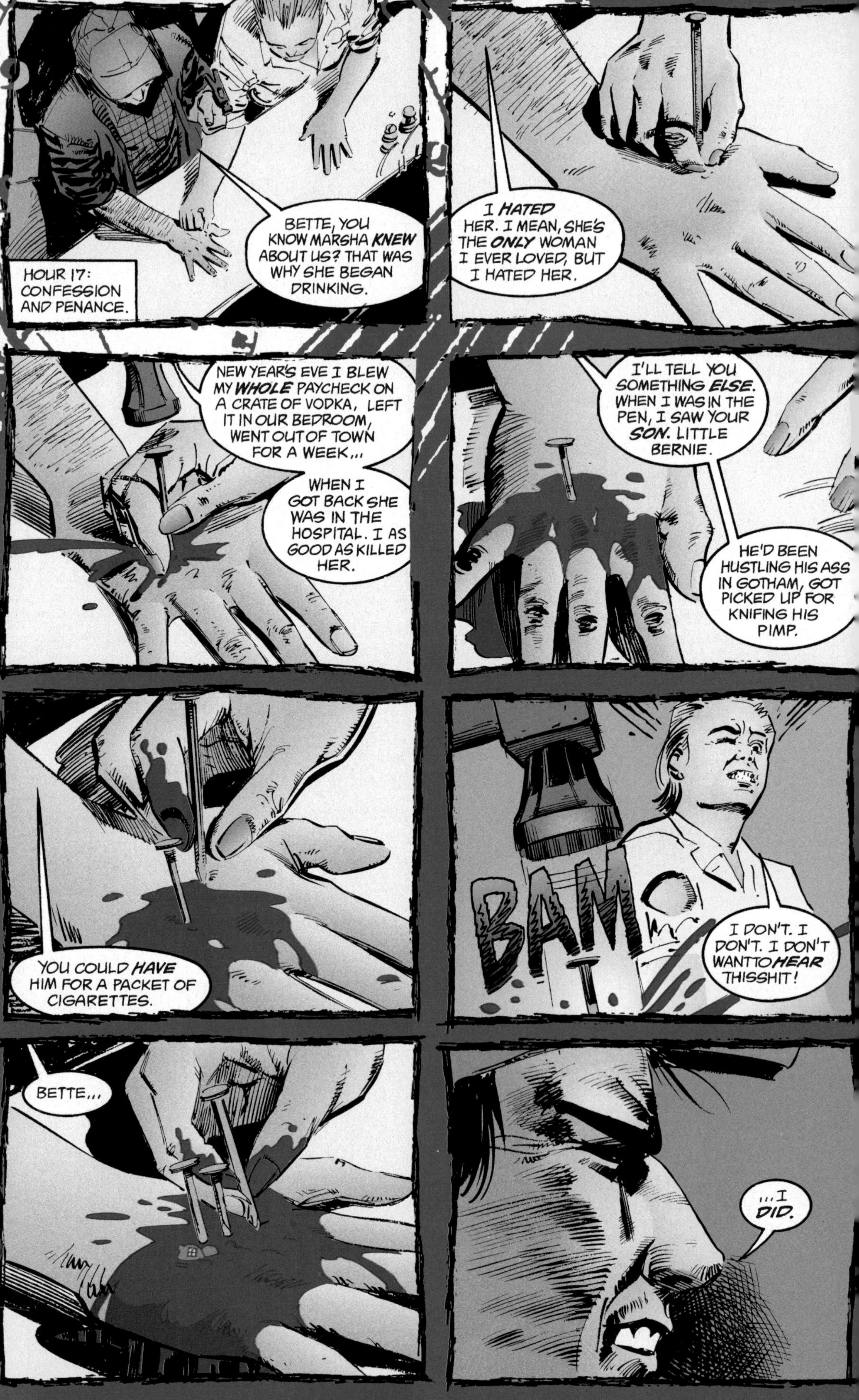
HOUR 17: CONFESSION AND PENANCE.
BETTE, YOU KNOW MARSHA KNEW ABOUT US? THAT WAS WHY SHE BEGAN DRINKING.
I HATED HER. I MEAN, SHE'S THE ONLY WOMAN I EVER LOVED, BUT I HATED HER.
NEW YEAR'S EVE I BLEW MY WHOLE PAYCHECK ON A CRATE OF VODKA, LEFT IT IN OUR BEDROOM, WENT OUT OF TOWN FOR A WEEK...
WHEN I GOT BACK SHE WAS IN THE HOSPITAL. I AS GOOD AS KILLED HER.
I'LL TELL YOU SOMETHING ELSE. WHEN I WAS IN THE PEN, I SAW YOUR SON. LITTLE BERNIE.
HE'D BEEN HUSTLING HIS ASS IN GOTHAM, GOT PICKED UP FOR KNIFING HIS PIMP.
YOU COULD HAVE HIM FOR A PACKET OF CIGARETTES.
BAM
I DON'T. I DON'T. I DON'T WANTTO HEAR THISSHIT!
BETTE...
...I DID.

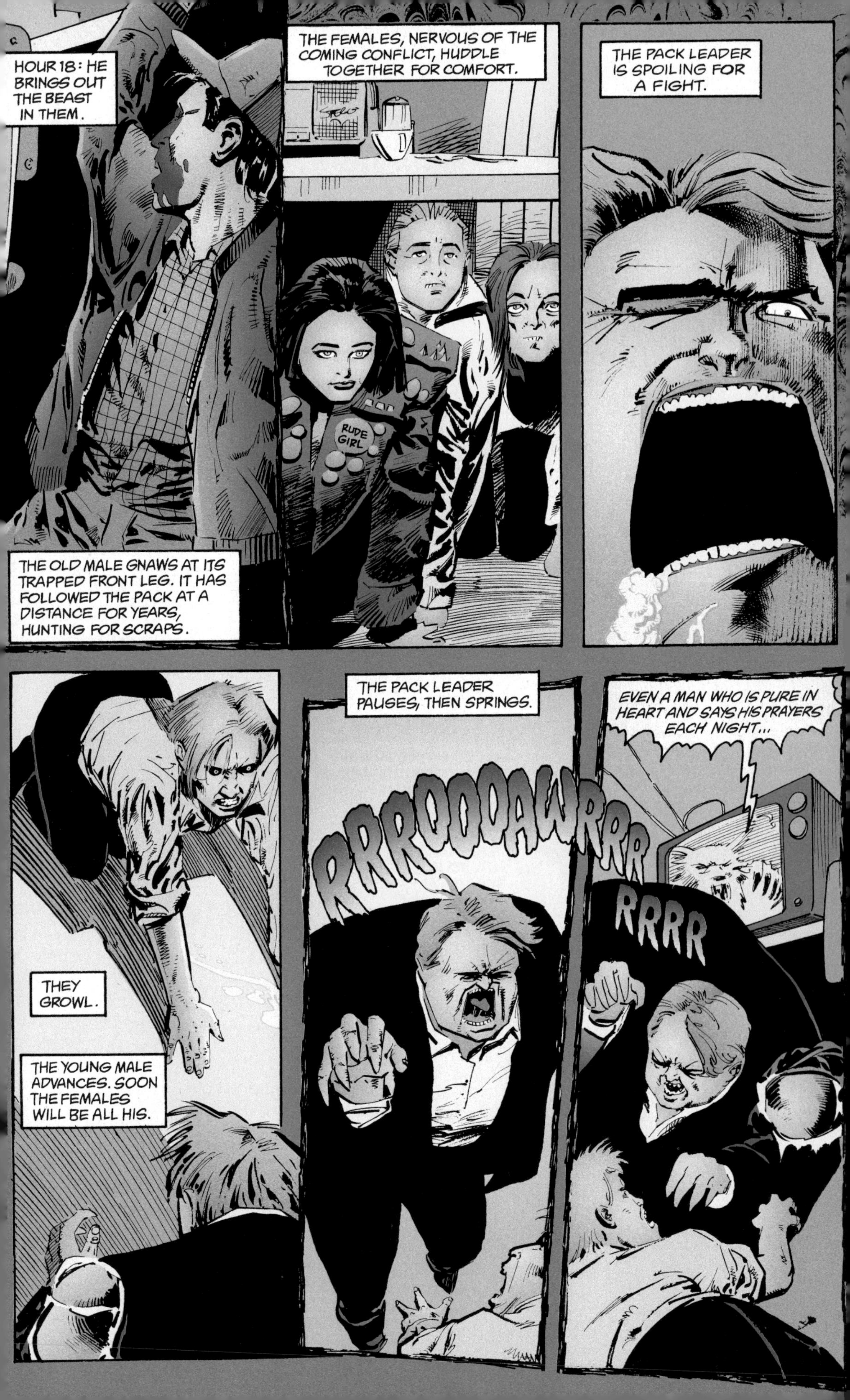
HOUR 18: HE BRINGS OUT THE BEAST IN THEM.
THE OLD MALE GNAWS AT ITS TRAPPED FRONT LEG. IT HAS FOLLOWED THE PACK AT A DISTANCE FOR YEARS, HUNTING FOR SCRAPS.
THE FEMALES, NERVOUS OF THE COMING CONFLICT, HUDDLE TOGETHER FOR COMFORT.
RUDE GIRL
THE PACK LEADER IS SPOILING FOR A FIGHT.
THEY GROWL.
THE YOUNG MALE ADVANCES. SOON THE FEMALES WILL BE ALL HIS.
THE PACK LEADER PAUSES, THEN SPRINGS.
RRROOOAWRRR
EVEN A MAN WHO IS PURE IN HEART AND SAYS HIS PRAYERS EACH NIGHT...
RRRR

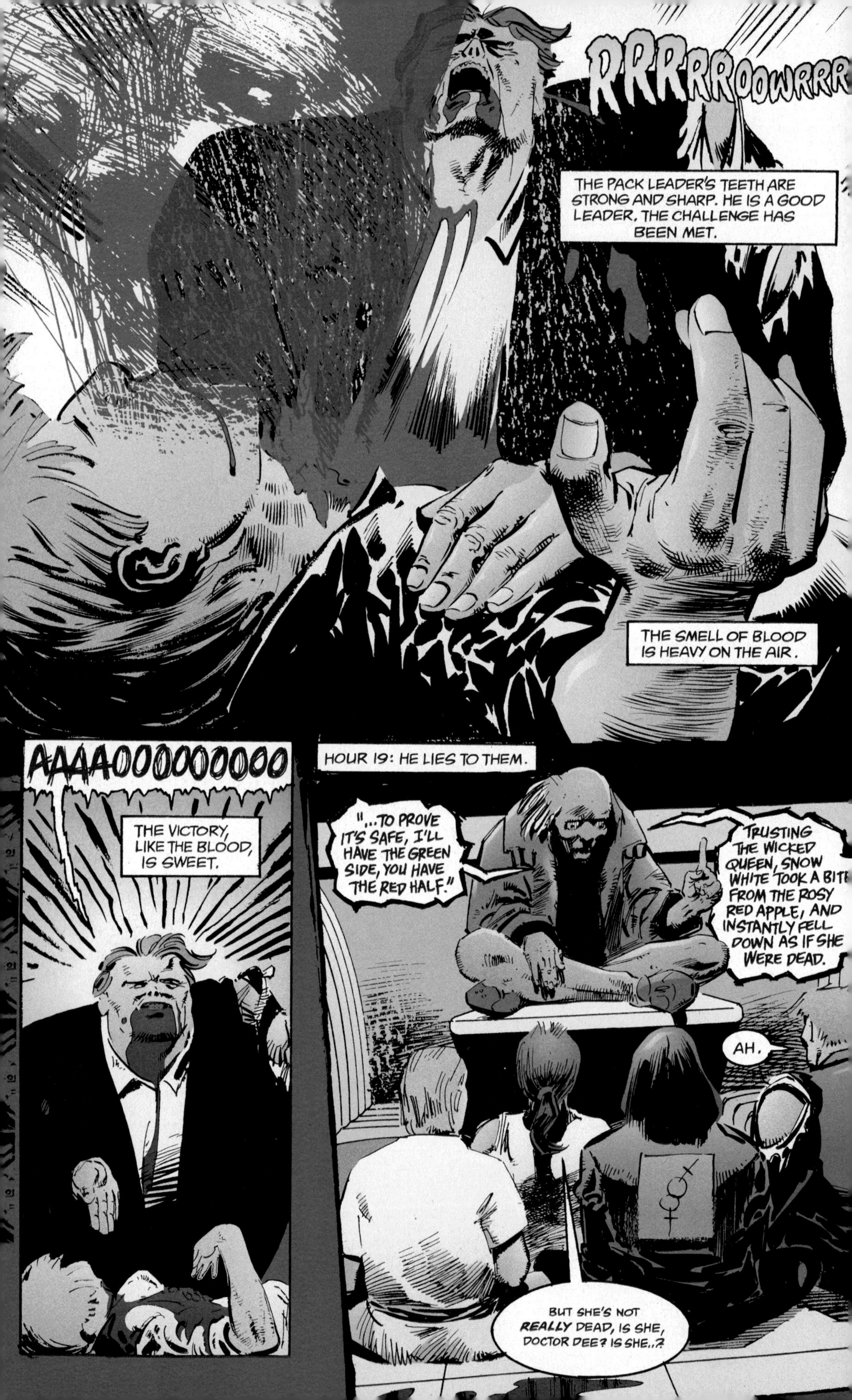
RRRRROOWRRR
THE PACK LEADER'S TEETH ARE STRONG AND SHARP. HE IS A GOOD LEADER. THE CHALLENGE HAS BEEN MET.
THE SMELL OF BLOOD IS HEAVY ON THE AIR.
AAAAOOOOOOOOO
THE VICTORY, LIKE THE BLOOD, IS SWEET.
HOUR 19: HE LIES TO THEM.
"...TO PROVE IT'S SAFE, I'LL HAVE THE GREEN SIDE, YOU HAVE THE RED HALF."
TRUSTING THE WICKED QUEEN, SNOW WHITE TOOK A BITE FROM THE ROSY RED APPLE, AND INSTANTLY FELL DOWN AS IF SHE WERE DEAD.
AH.
BUT SHE'S NOT REALLY DEAD, IS SHE, DOCTOR DEE? IS SHE..?

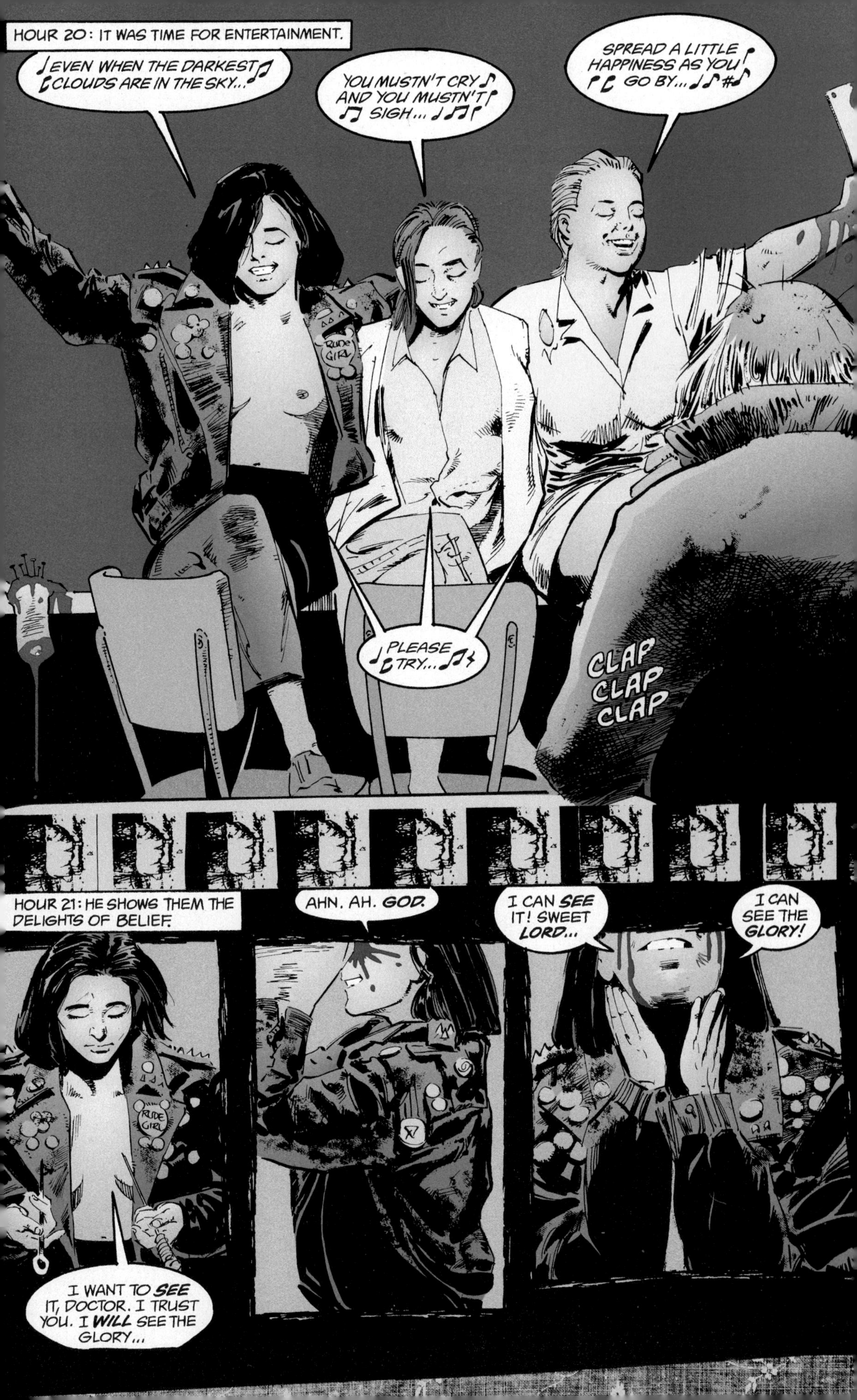
HOUR 20: IT WAS TIME FOR ENTERTAINMENT.
EVEN WHEN THE DARKEST CLOUDS ARE IN THE SKY...
YOU MUSTN'T CRY AND YOU MUSTN'T SIGH...
SPREAD A LITTLE HAPPINESS AS YOU GO BY...
PLEASE TRY...
CLAP CLAP CLAP
HOUR 21: HE SHOWS THEM THE DELIGHTS OF BELIEF.
I WANT TO SEE IT, DOCTOR. I TRUST YOU. I WILL SEE THE GLORY...
AHN. AH. GOD.
I CAN SEE IT! SWEET LORD...
I CAN SEE THE GLORY!

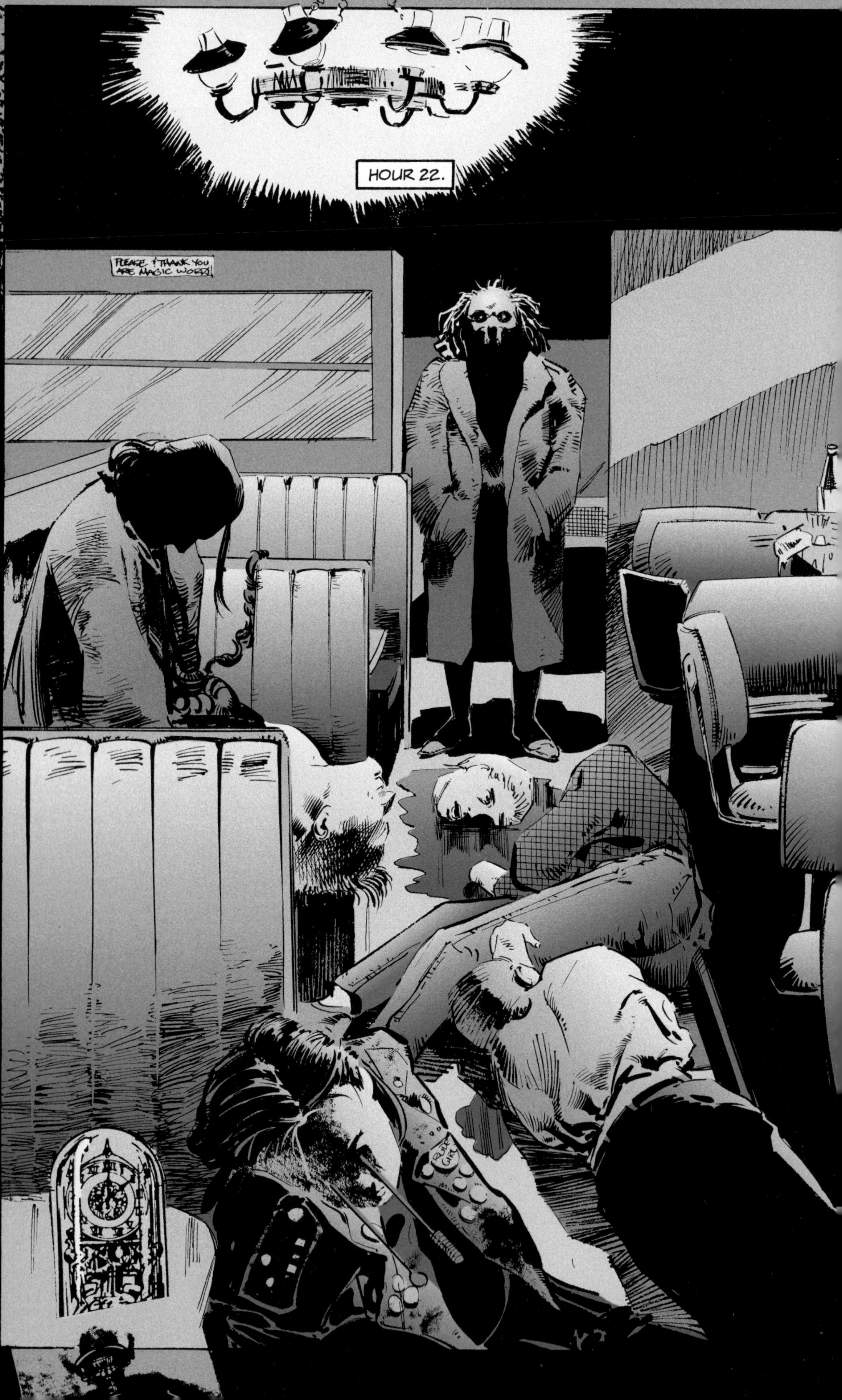

HOUR 22.
PLEASE & THANK YOU ARE MAGIC WORDS

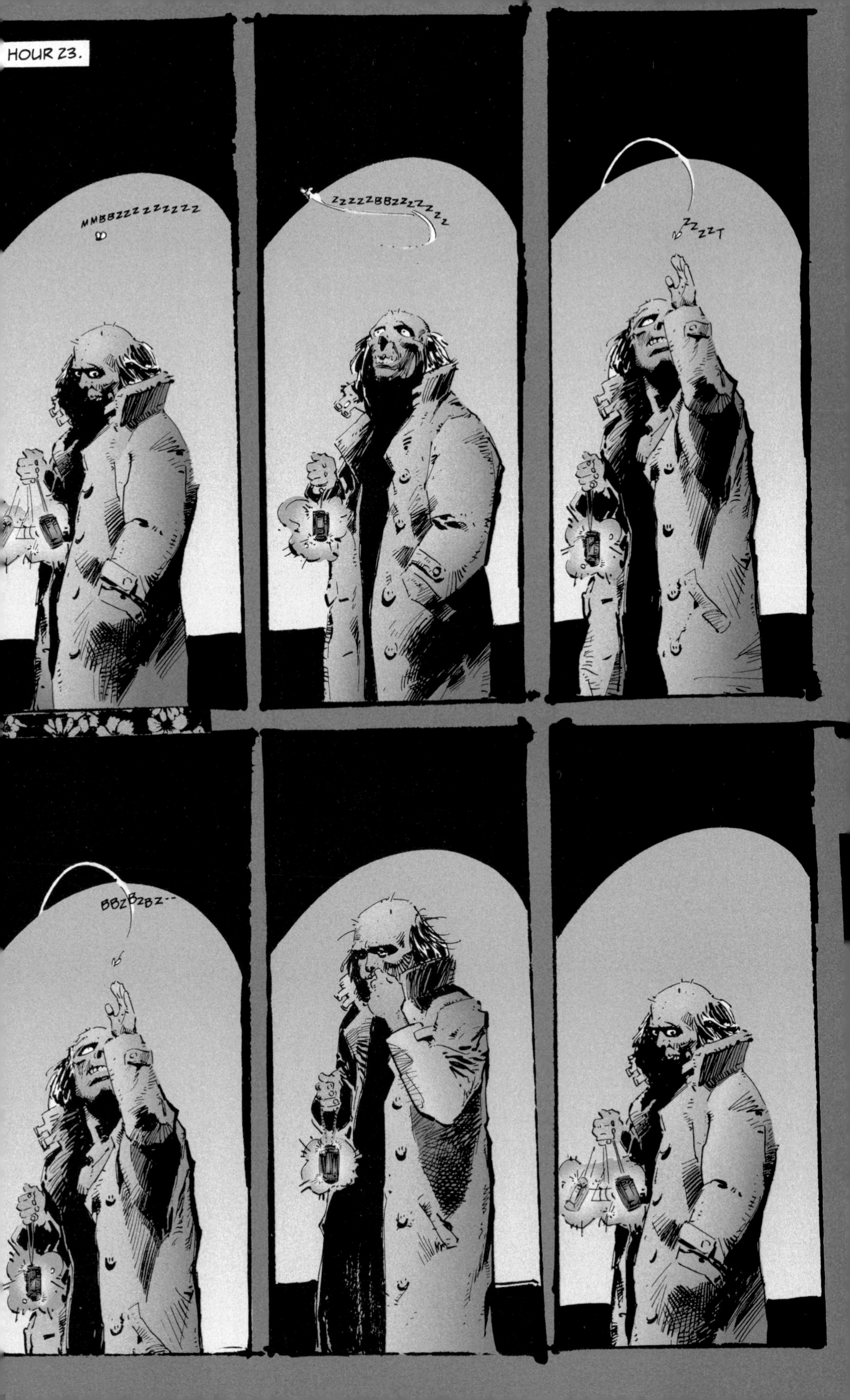
HOUR 23.
MMBBZZZZZZZZZZZ
ZZZZZBBZZZZZZZ
ZZZZT
BBZBZBZ--

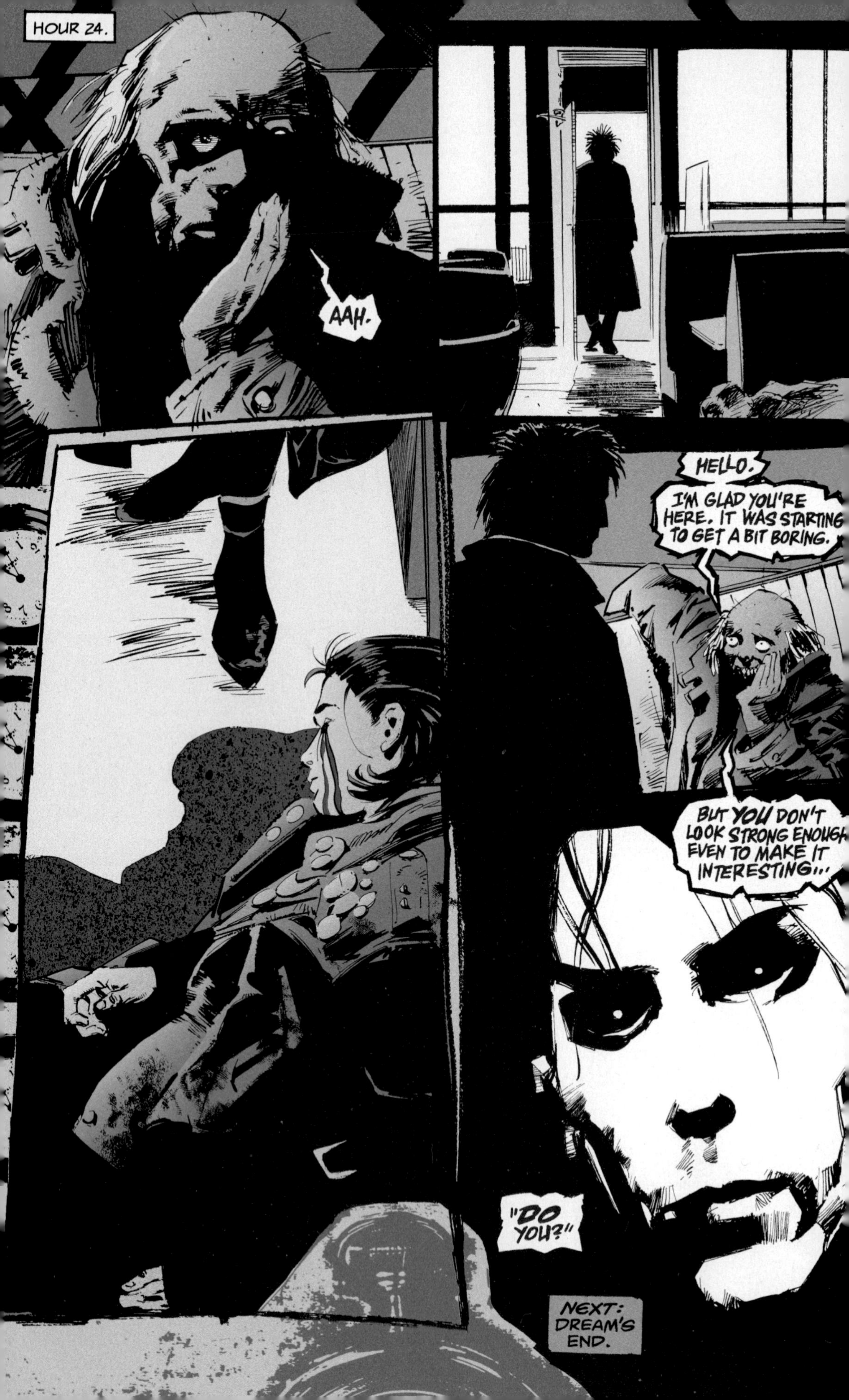
HOUR 24.
AAH.
HELLO.
I'M GLAD YOU'RE HERE. IT WAS STARTING TO GET A BIT BORING.
BUT YOU DON'T LOOK STRONG ENOUGH EVEN TO MAKE IT INTERESTING...
"DO YOU?"
NEXT: DREAM'S END.

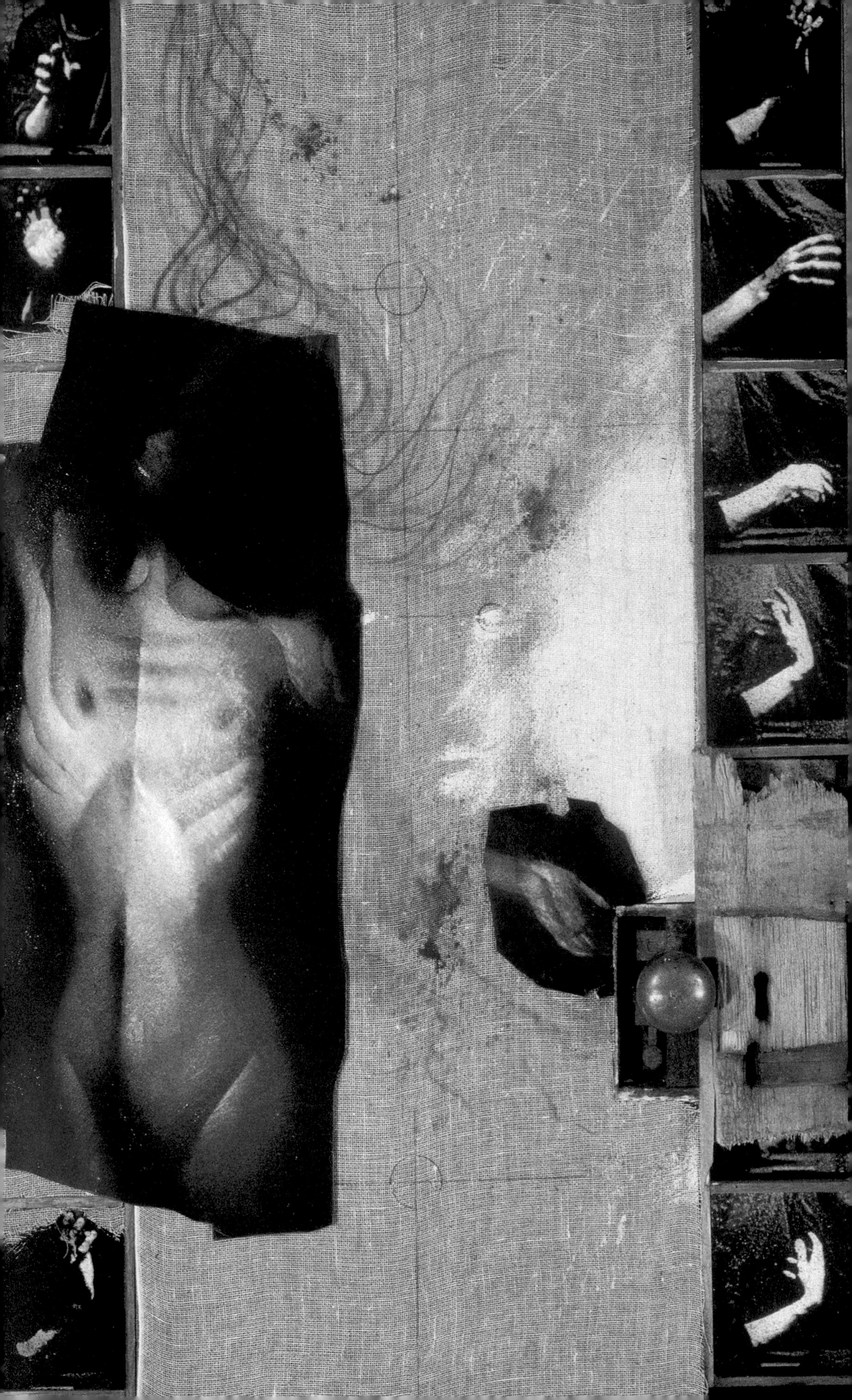

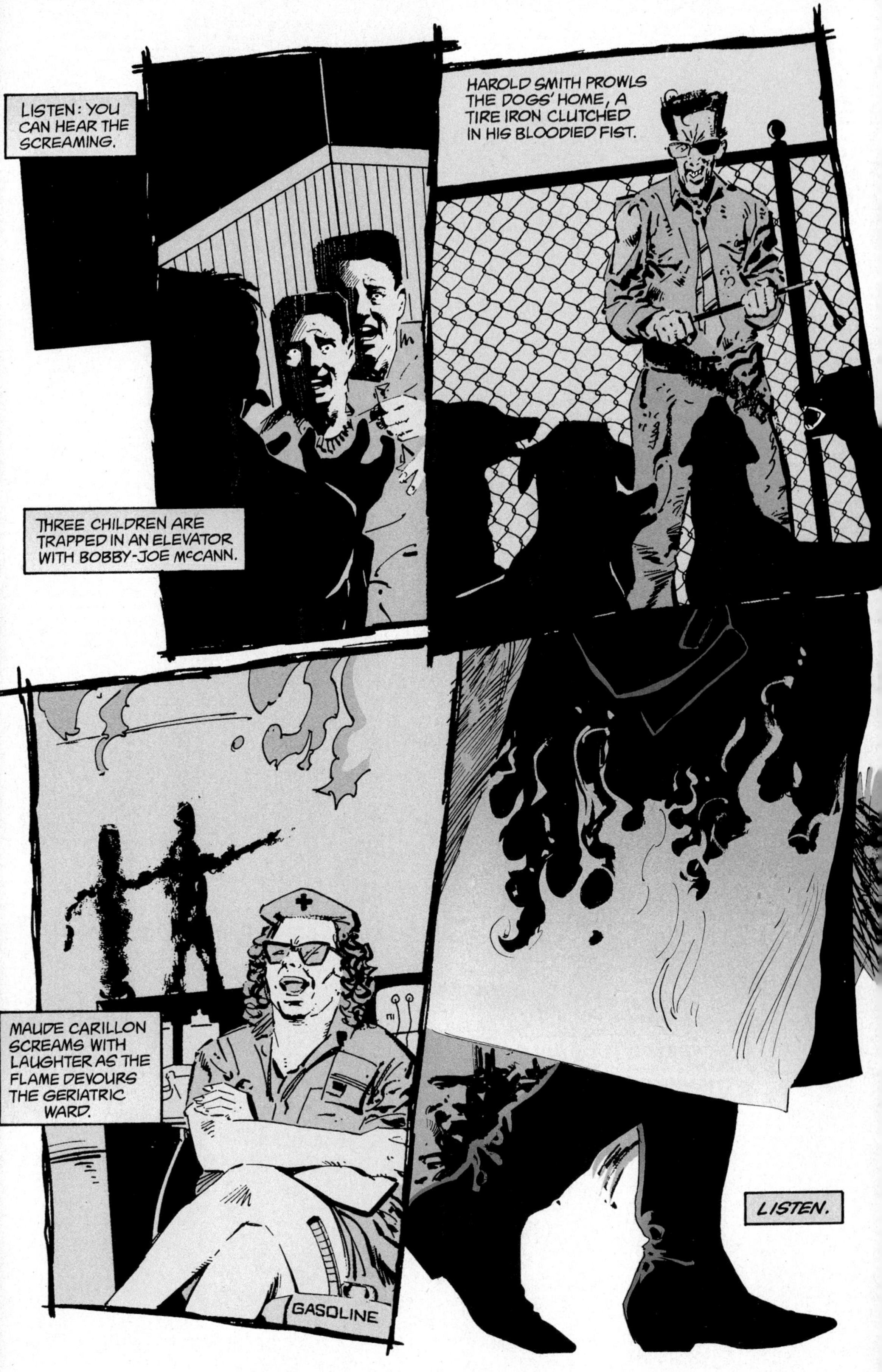

LISTEN: YOU CAN HEAR THE SCREAMING.
THREE CHILDREN ARE TRAPPED IN AN ELEVATOR WITH BOBBY-JOE McCANN.
HAROLD SMITH PROWLS THE DOGS' HOME, A TIRE IRON CLUTCHED IN HIS BLOODIED FIST.
MAUDE CARILLON SCREAMS WITH LAUGHTER AS THE FLAME DEVOURS THE GERIATRIC WARD.
GASOLINE
LISTEN.

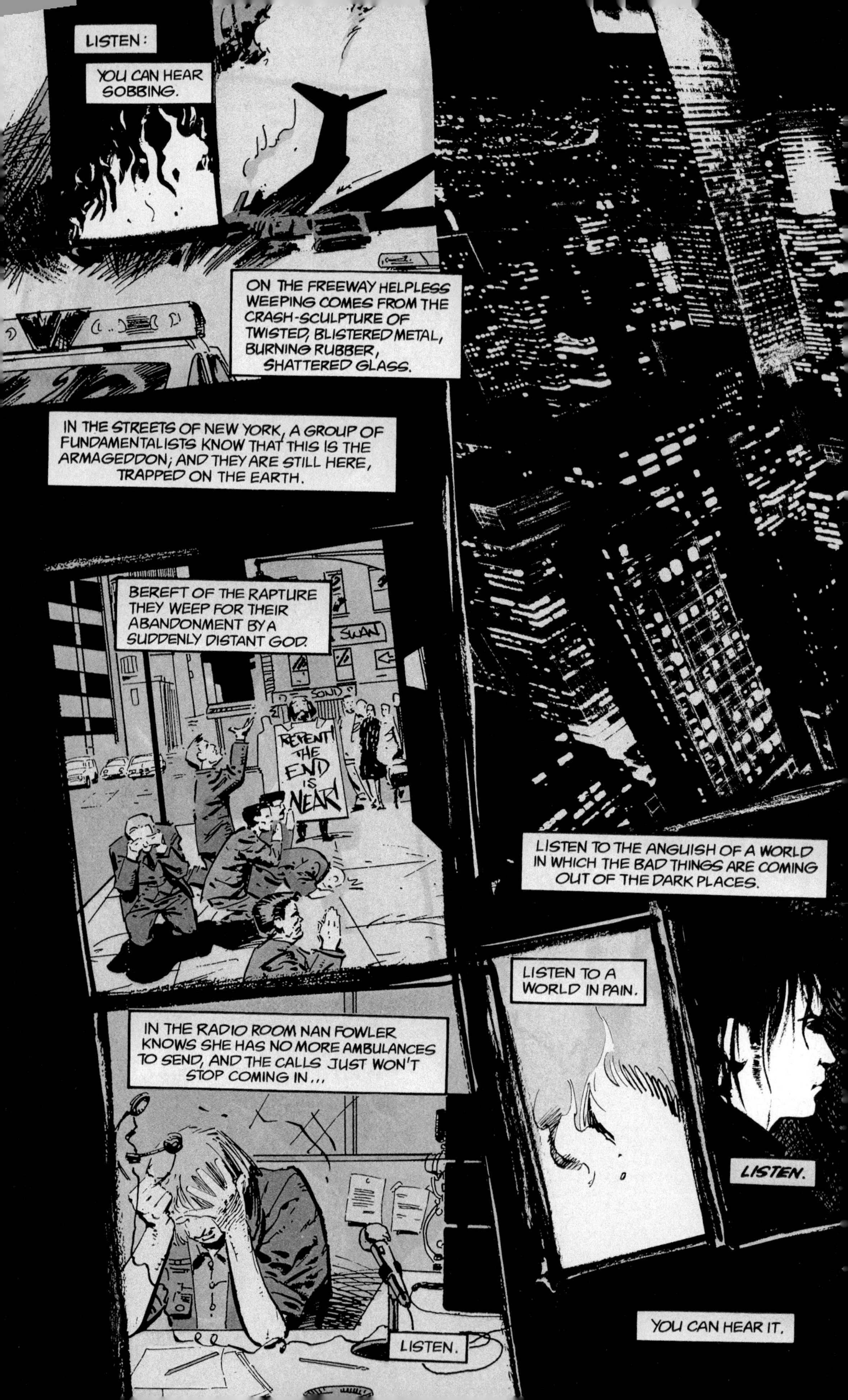
LISTEN:
YOU CAN HEAR SOBBING.
ON THE FREEWAY HELPLESS WEEPING COMES FROM THE CRASH-SCULPTURE OF TWISTED, BLISTERED METAL, BURNING RUBBER, SHATTERED GLASS.
IN THE STREETS OF NEW YORK, A GROUP OF FUNDAMENTALISTS KNOW THAT THIS IS THE ARMAGEDDON; AND THEY ARE STILL HERE, TRAPPED ON THE EARTH.
BEREFT OF THE RAPTURE THEY WEEP FOR THEIR ABANDONMENT BY A SUDDENLY DISTANT GOD.
SWAN
REPENT! THE END IS NEAR!
IN THE RADIO ROOM NAN FOWLER KNOWS SHE HAS NO MORE AMBULANCES TO SEND, AND THE CALLS JUST WON'T STOP COMING IN...
LISTEN.
LISTEN TO THE ANGUISH OF A WORLD IN WHICH THE BAD THINGS ARE COMING OUT OF THE DARK PLACES.
LISTEN TO A WORLD IN PAIN.
LISTEN.
YOU CAN HEAR IT.

SOUND

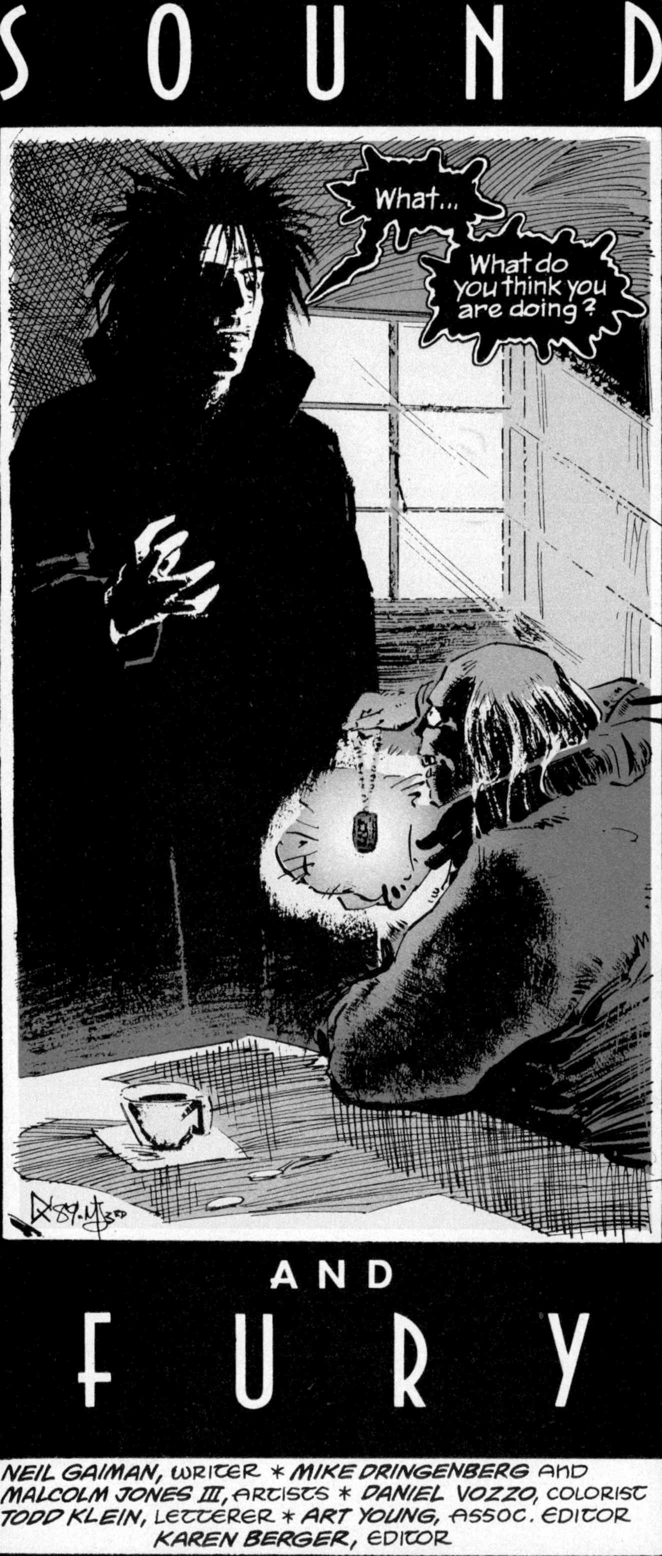
What...
What do you think you are doing?

AND FURY

NEIL GAIMAN, WRITER * MIKE DRINGENBERG AND MALCOLM JONES III, ARTISTS * DANIEL VOZZO, COLORIST TODD KLEIN, LETTERER * ART YOUNG, ASSOC. EDITOR KAREN BERGER, EDITOR

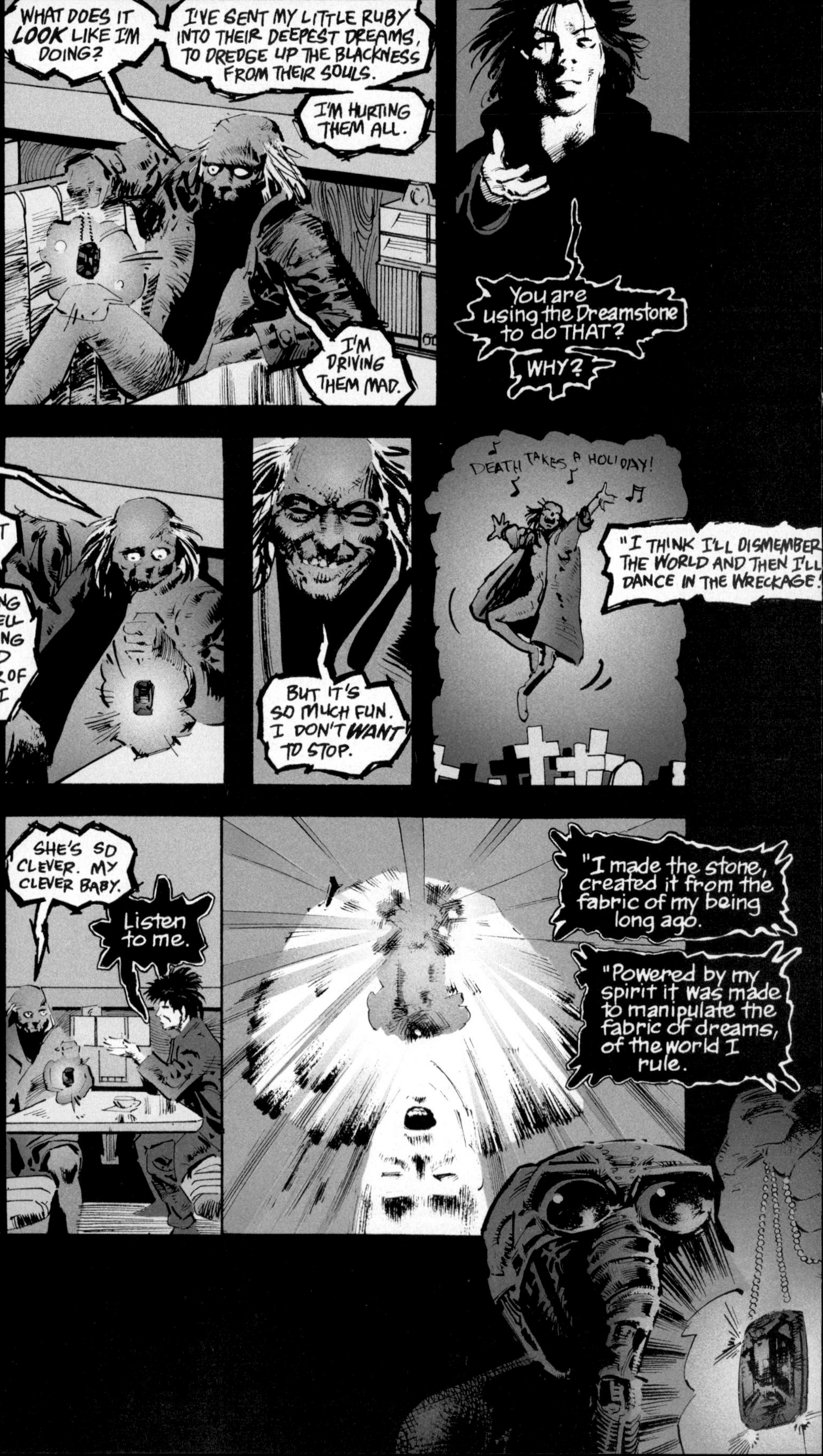
WHAT DOES IT LOOK LIKE I'M DOING?
I'VE SENT MY LITTLE RUBY INTO THEIR DEEPEST DREAMS, TO DREDGE UP THE BLACKNESS FROM THEIR SOULS.
I'M HURTING THEM ALL.
I'M DRIVING THEM MAD.
You are using the Dreamstone to do THAT?
WHY?
MMMM. HMM.
REVENGE, POSSIBLY. THAT AND DREAMS OF POWER.
IN THE BEGINNING I THOUGHT I'D TELL THEM I WAS DOING THIS AND THEY'D MAKE ME RULER OF THE WORLD IF I STOPPED...
BUT IT'S SO MUCH FUN. I DON'T WANT TO STOP.
DEATH TAKES A HOLIDAY!
"I THINK I'LL DISMEMBER THE WORLD AND THEN I'LL DANCE IN THE WRECKAGE!
SHE'S SO CLEVER. MY CLEVER BABY.
Listen to me.
"I made the stone, created it from the fabric of my being long ago.
"Powered by my spirit it was made to manipulate the fabric of dreams, of the world I rule.

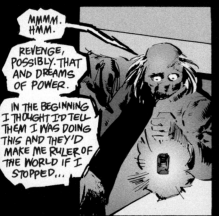

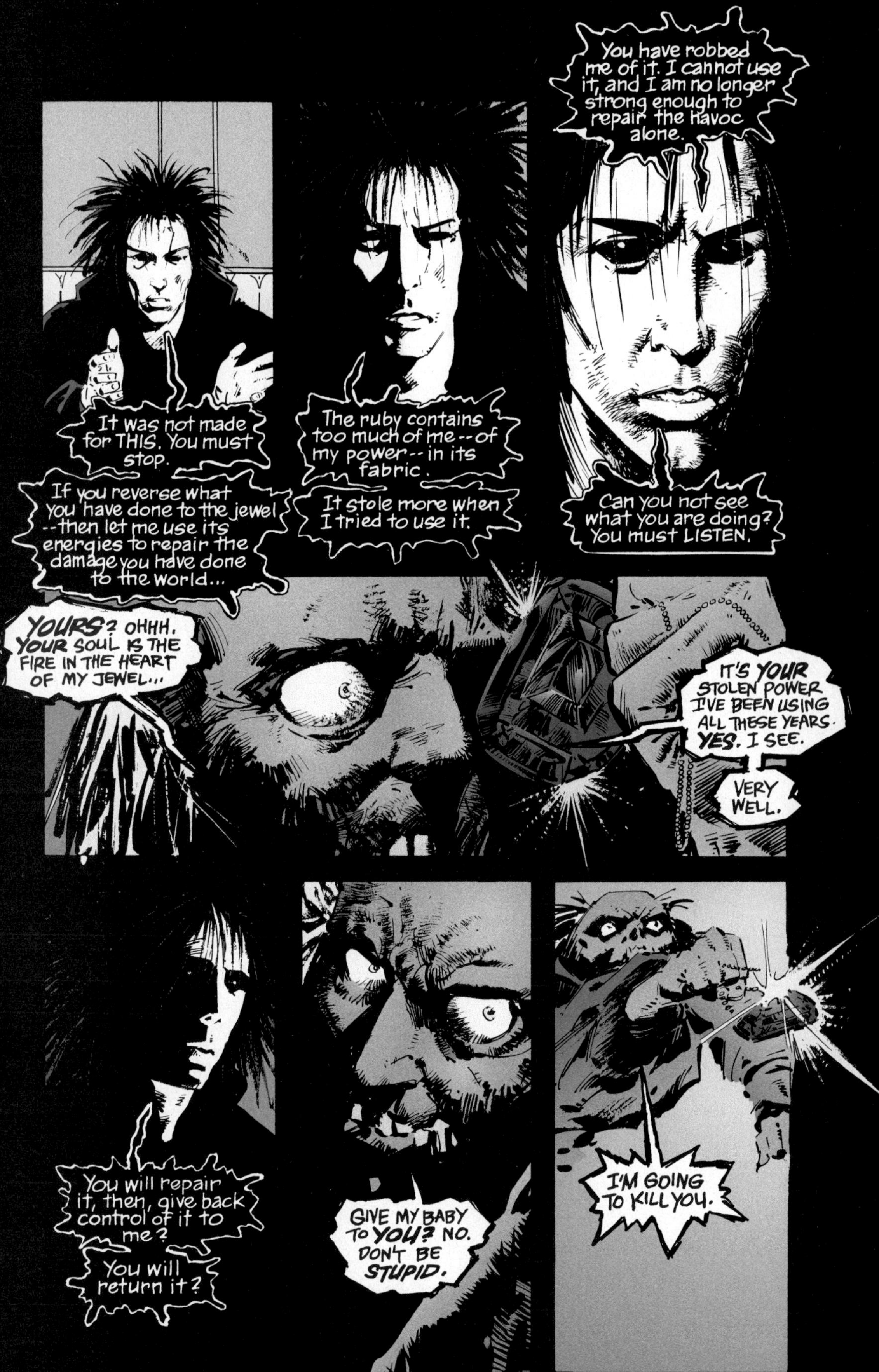

It was not made for THIS. You must stop.
If you reverse what you have done to the jewel --then let me use its energies to repair the damage you have done to the world...
The ruby contains too much of me--of my power--in its fabric.
It stole more when I tried to use it.
You have robbed me of it. I cannot use it, and I am no longer strong enough to repair the havoc alone.
Can you not see what you are doing? You must LISTEN.
YOURS? OHHH. YOUR SOUL IS THE FIRE IN THE HEART OF MY JEWEL...
IT'S YOUR STOLEN POWER I'VE BEEN USING ALL THESE YEARS. YES. I SEE.
VERY WELL.
You will repair it, then, give back control of it to me?
You will return it?
GIVE MY BABY TO YOU? NO. DON'T BE STUPID.
I'M GOING TO KILL YOU.

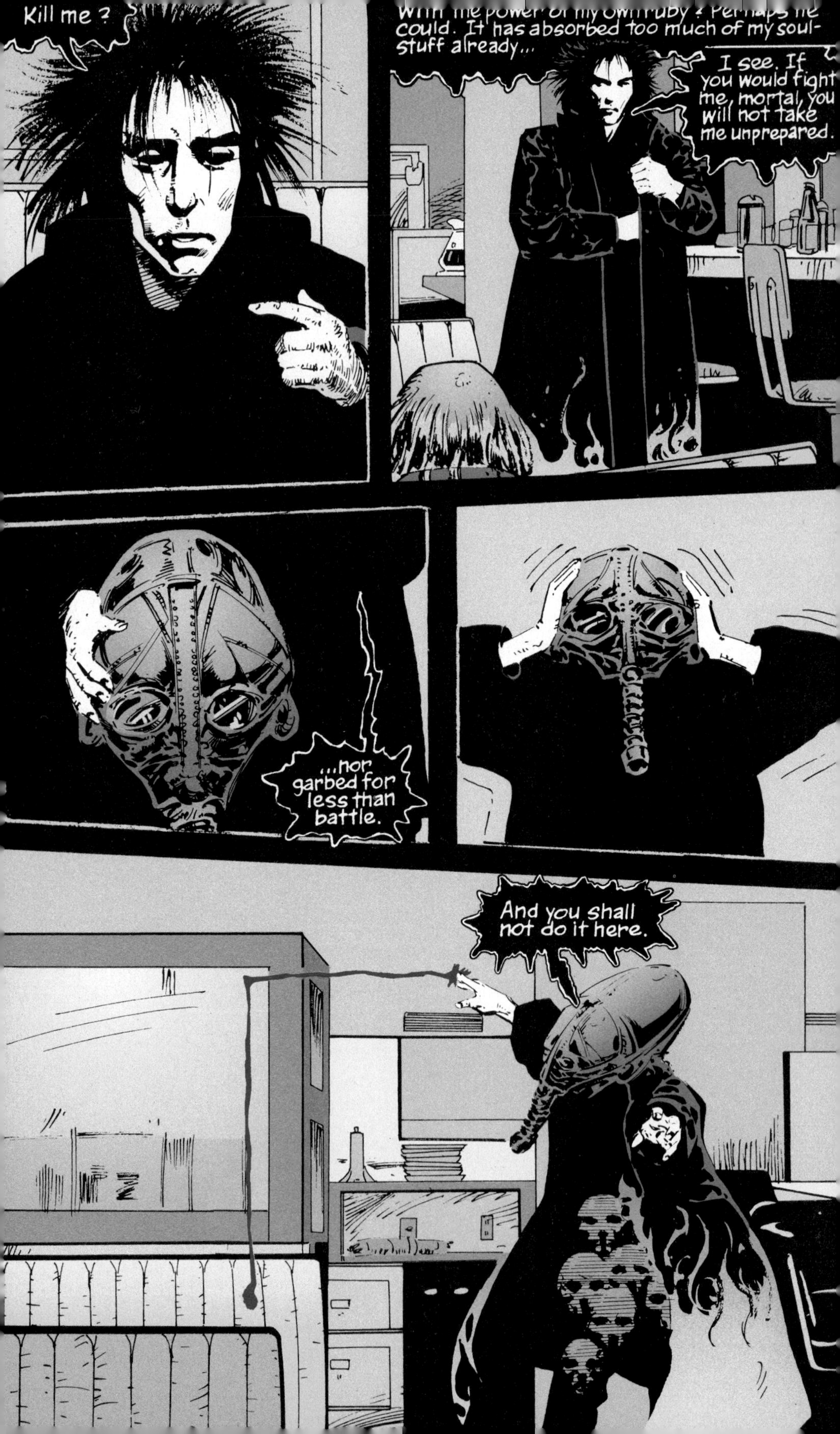
Kill me?
With the power of my own ruby? Perhaps he could. It has absorbed too much of my soul-stuff already...
I see. If you would fight me, mortal, you will not take me unprepared.
...nor garbed for less than battle.
And you shall not do it here.

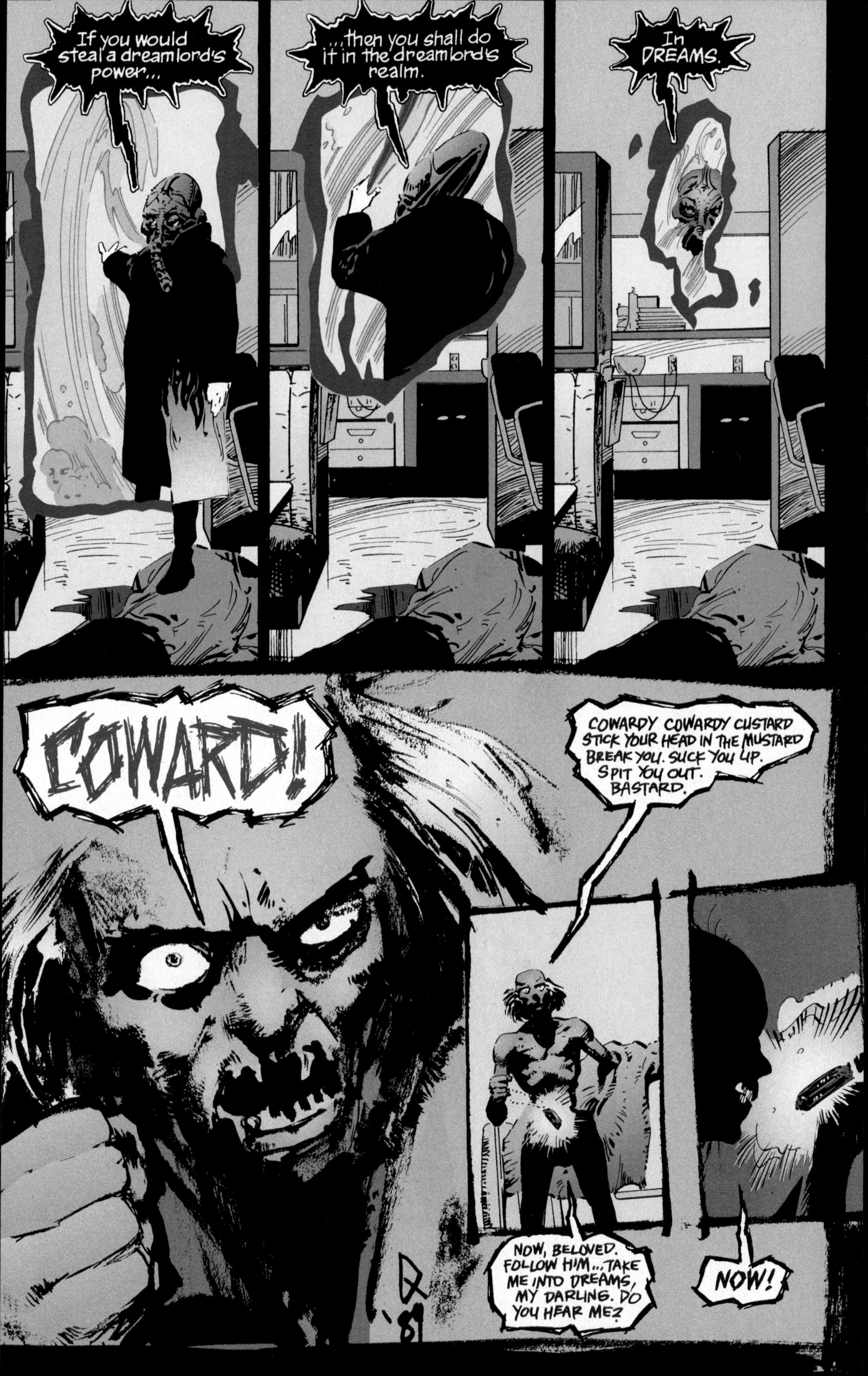
If you would steal a dreamlord's power...
...then you shall do it in the dreamlord's realm.
In DREAMS.
COWARD!
COWARDY COWARDY CUSTARD STICK YOUR HEAD IN THE MUSTARD BREAK YOU. SUCK YOU UP. SPIT YOU OUT. BASTARD.
NOW, BELOVED. FOLLOW HIM... TAKE ME INTO DREAMS, MY DARLING. DO YOU HEAR ME?
NOW!

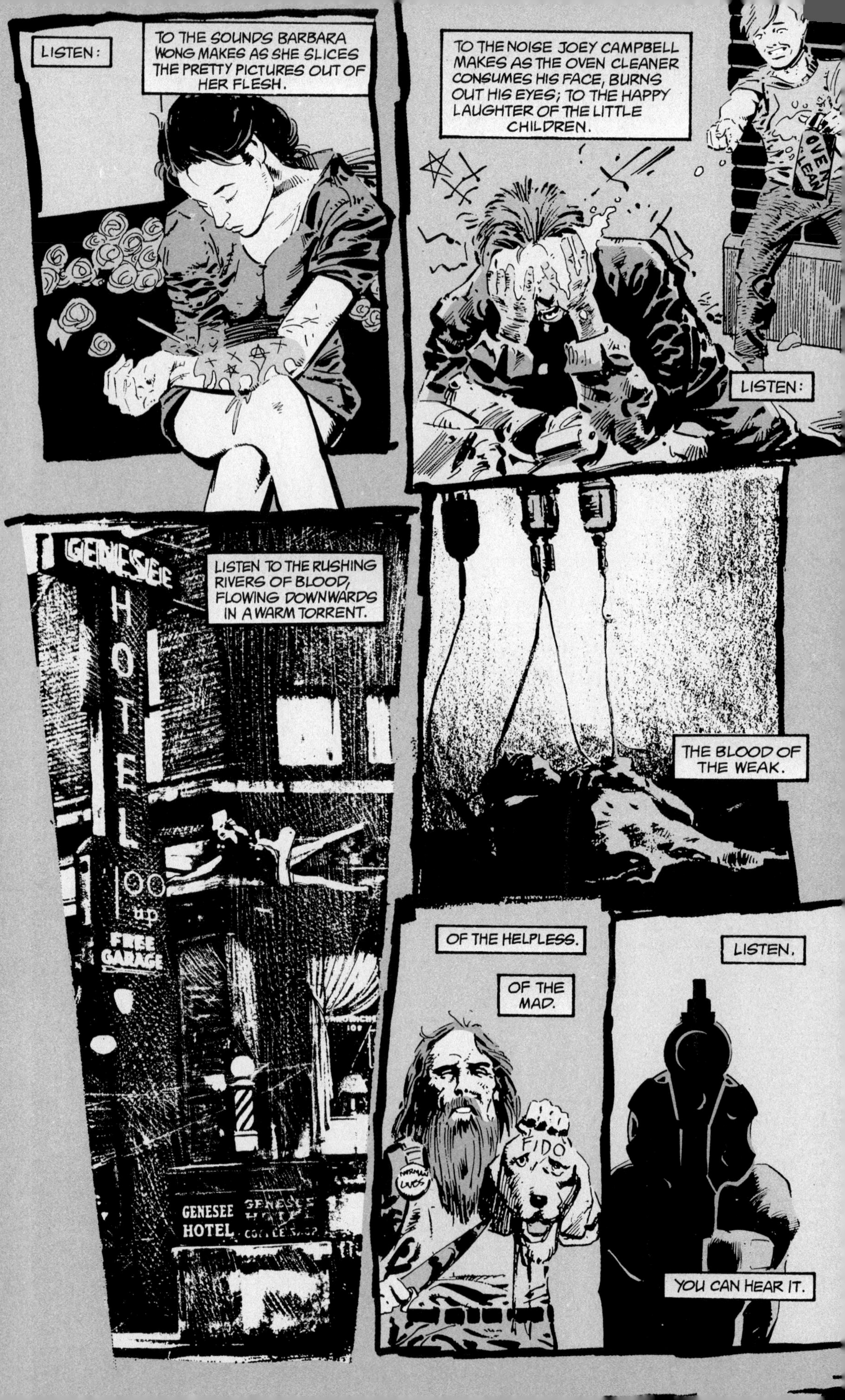
LISTEN:
TO THE SOUNDS BARBARA WONG MAKES AS SHE SLICES THE PRETTY PICTURES OUT OF HER FLESH.
TO THE NOISE JOEY CAMPBELL MAKES AS THE OVEN CLEANER CONSUMES HIS FACE, BURNS OUT HIS EYES; TO THE HAPPY LAUGHTER OF THE LITTLE CHILDREN.
LISTEN:
GENESEE
HOTEL
FREE GARAGE
LISTEN TO THE RUSHING RIVERS OF BLOOD, FLOWING DOWNWARDS IN A WARM TORRENT.
GENESEE HOTEL
THE BLOOD OF THE WEAK.
OF THE HELPLESS.
OF THE MAD.
FIDO
LISTEN.
YOU CAN HEAR IT.

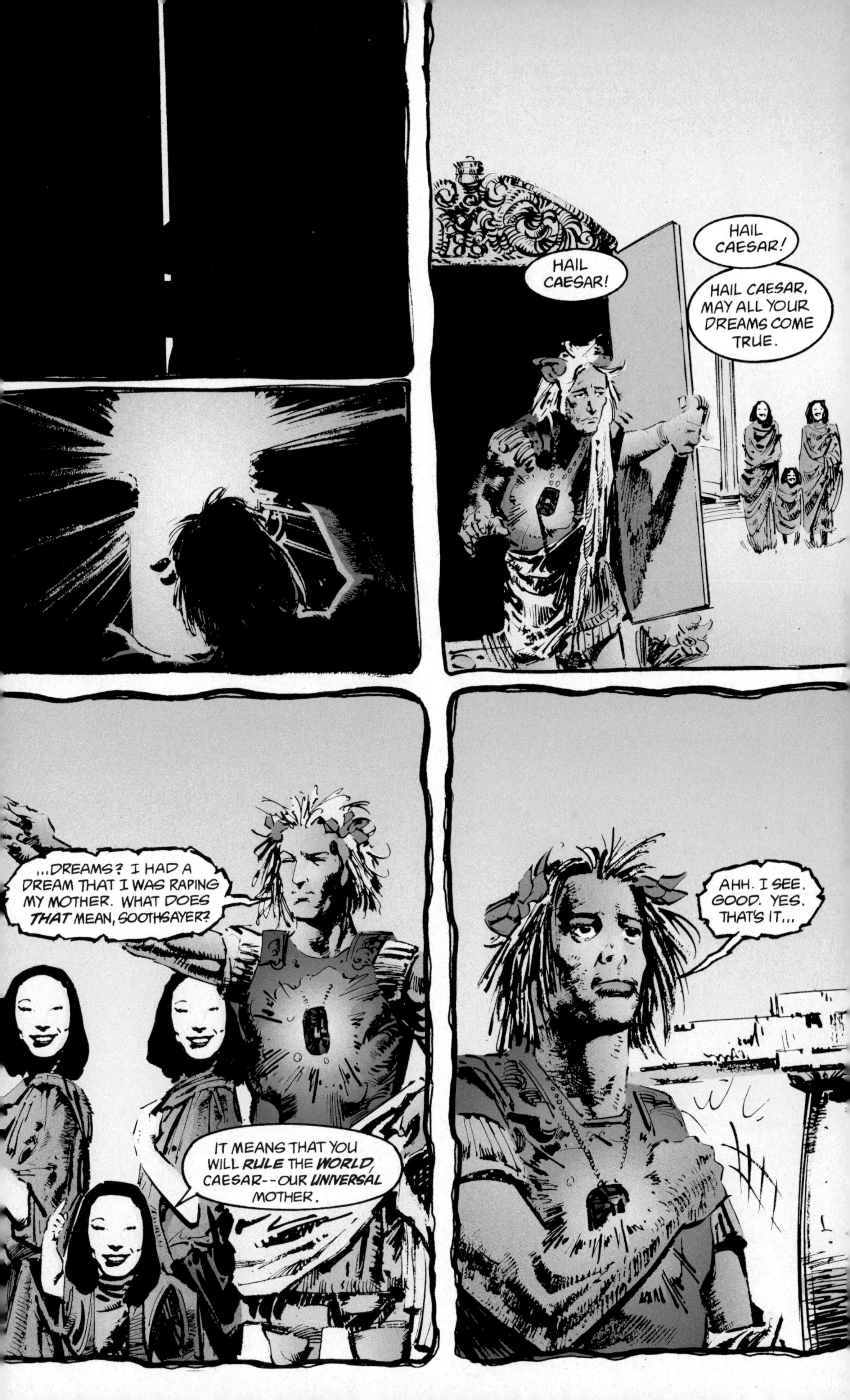
HAIL CAESAR!
HAIL CAESAR!
HAIL CAESAR, MAY ALL YOUR DREAMS COME TRUE.
...DREAMS? I HAD A DREAM THAT I WAS RAPING MY MOTHER. WHAT DOES THAT MEAN, SOOTHSAYER?
IT MEANS THAT YOU WILL RULE THE WORLD, CAESAR--OUR UNIVERSAL MOTHER.
AHH. I SEE. GOOD. YES. THAT'S IT...

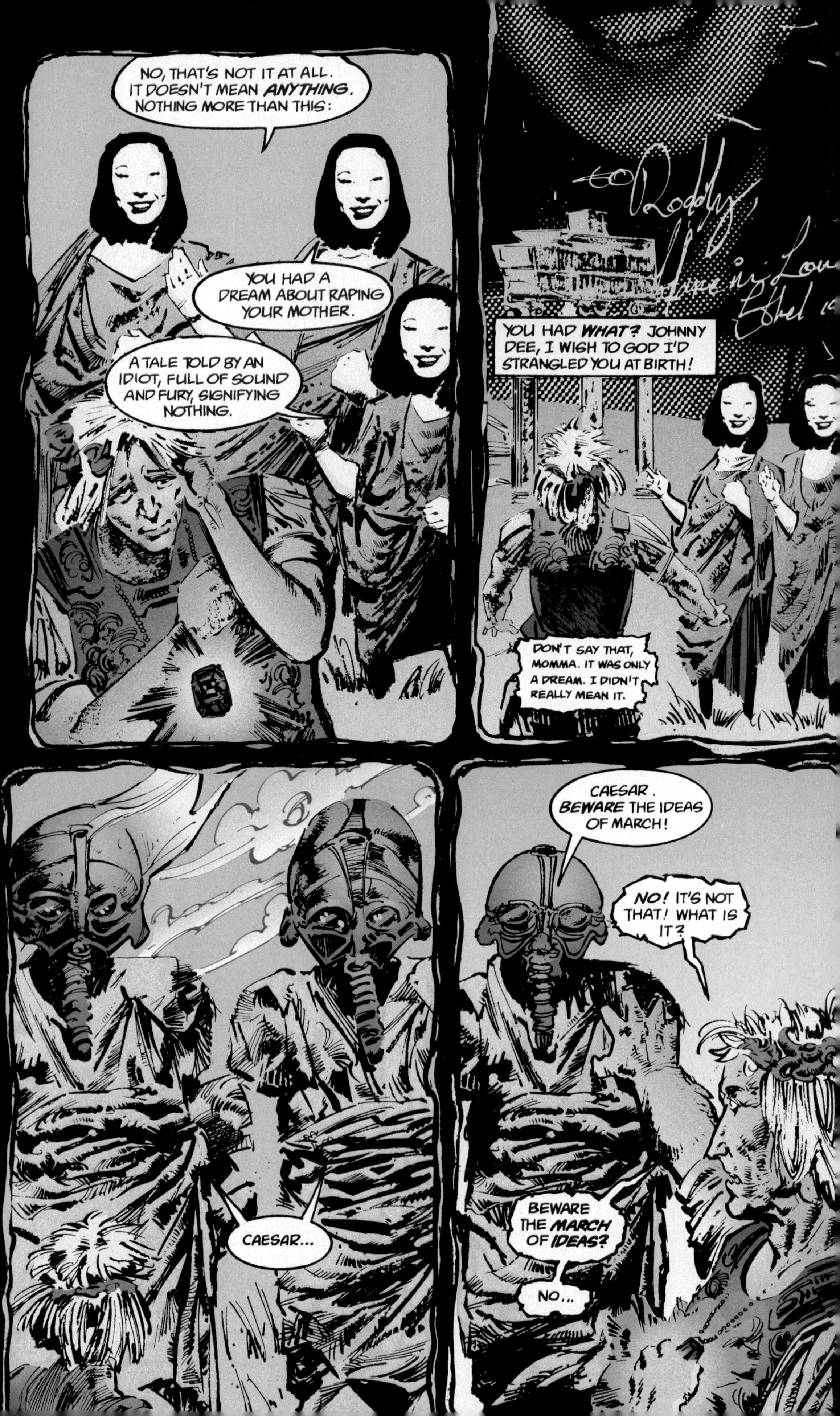
NO, THAT'S NOT IT AT ALL. IT DOESN'T MEAN ANYTHING. NOTHING MORE THAN THIS:
YOU HAD A DREAM ABOUT RAPING YOUR MOTHER.
A TALE TOLD BY AN IDIOT, FULL OF SOUND AND FURY, SIGNIFYING NOTHING.
YOU HAD WHAT? JOHNNY DEE, I WISH TO GOD I'D STRANGLED YOU AT BIRTH!
DON'T SAY THAT, MOMMA. IT WAS ONLY A DREAM. I DIDN'T REALLY MEAN IT.
CAESAR...
CAESAR. BEWARE THE IDEAS OF MARCH!
NO! IT'S NOT THAT! WHAT IS IT?
BEWARE THE MARCH OF IDEAS?
NO...

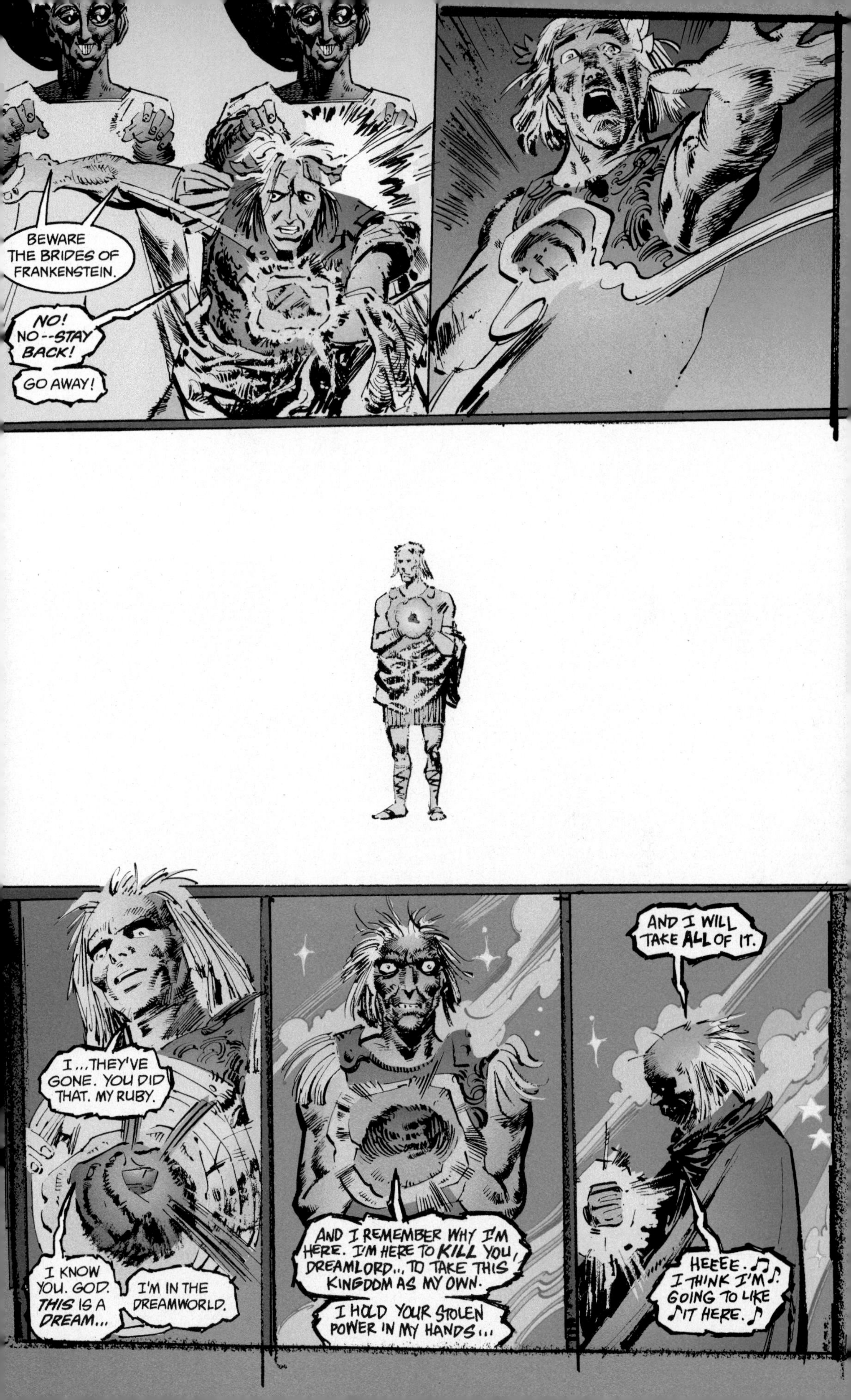
BEWARE THE BRIDES OF FRANKENSTEIN.
NO! NO--STAY BACK!
GO AWAY!
I...THEY'VE GONE. YOU DID THAT. MY RUBY.
I KNOW YOU. GOD. THIS IS A DREAM...
I'M IN THE DREAMWORLD.
AND I REMEMBER WHY I'M HERE. I'M HERE TO KILL YOU, DREAMLORD... TO TAKE THIS KINGDOM AS MY OWN.
I HOLD YOUR STOLEN POWER IN MY HANDS...
AND I WILL TAKE ALL OF IT.
HEEEE. ♫ I THINK I'M ♪ GOING TO LIKE ♪ IT HERE. ♪

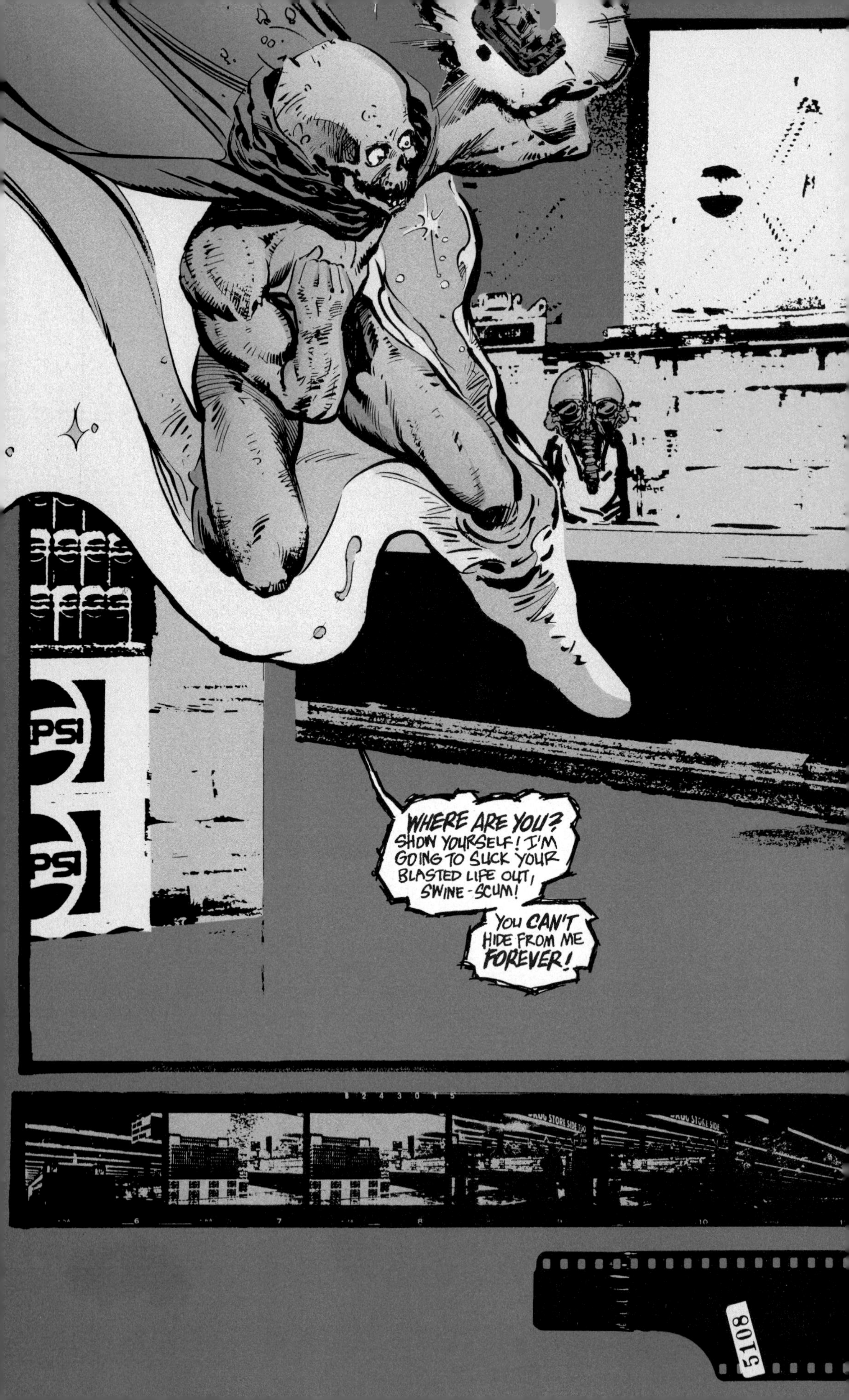

WHERE ARE YOU? SHOW YOURSELF! I'M GOING TO SUCK YOUR BLASTED LIFE OUT, SWINE-SCUM!
YOU CAN'T HIDE FROM ME FOREVER!
PSI
PSI
5108

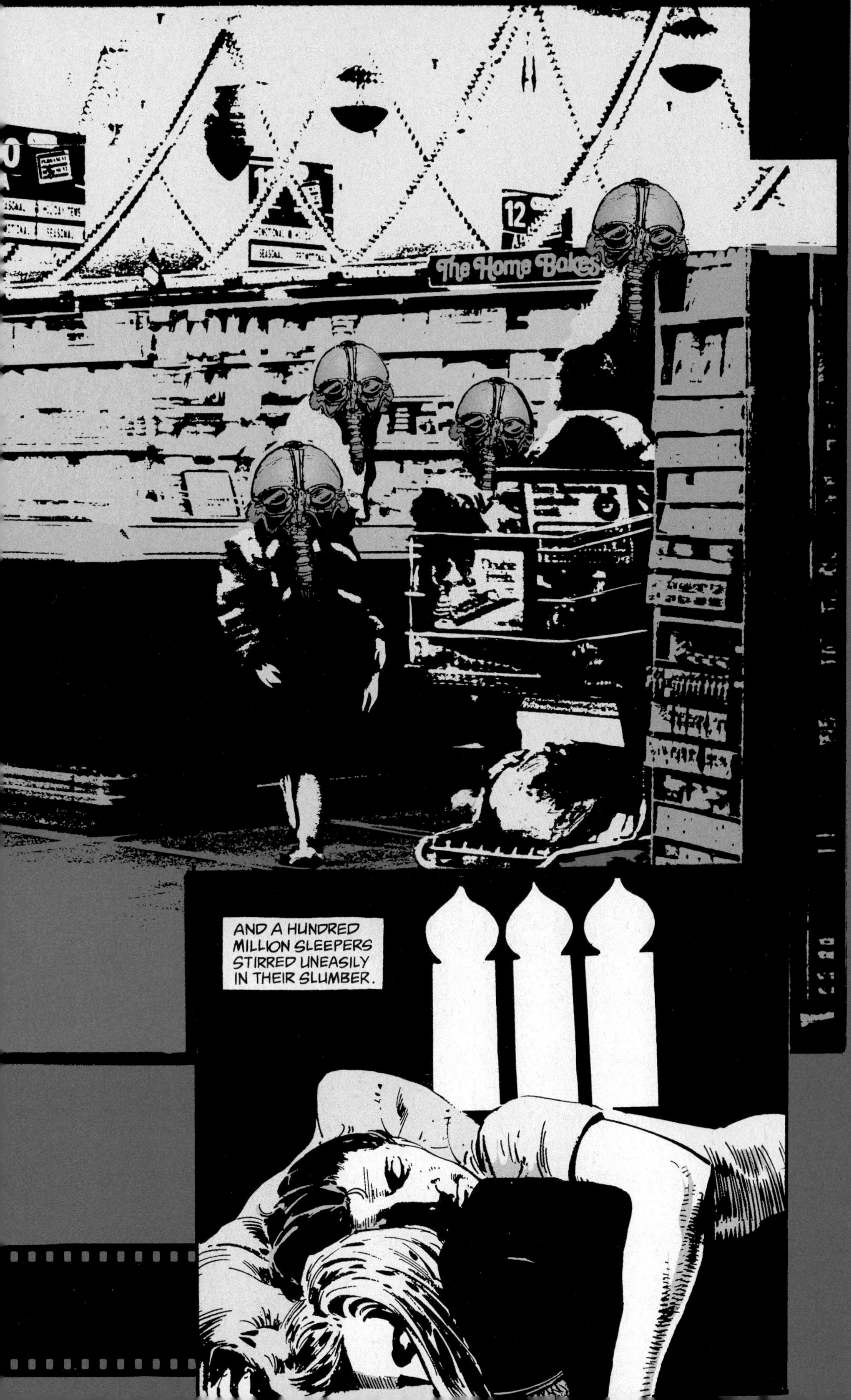
The Home Bakes
AND A HUNDRED MILLION SLEEPERS STIRRED UNEASILY IN THEIR SLUMBER.

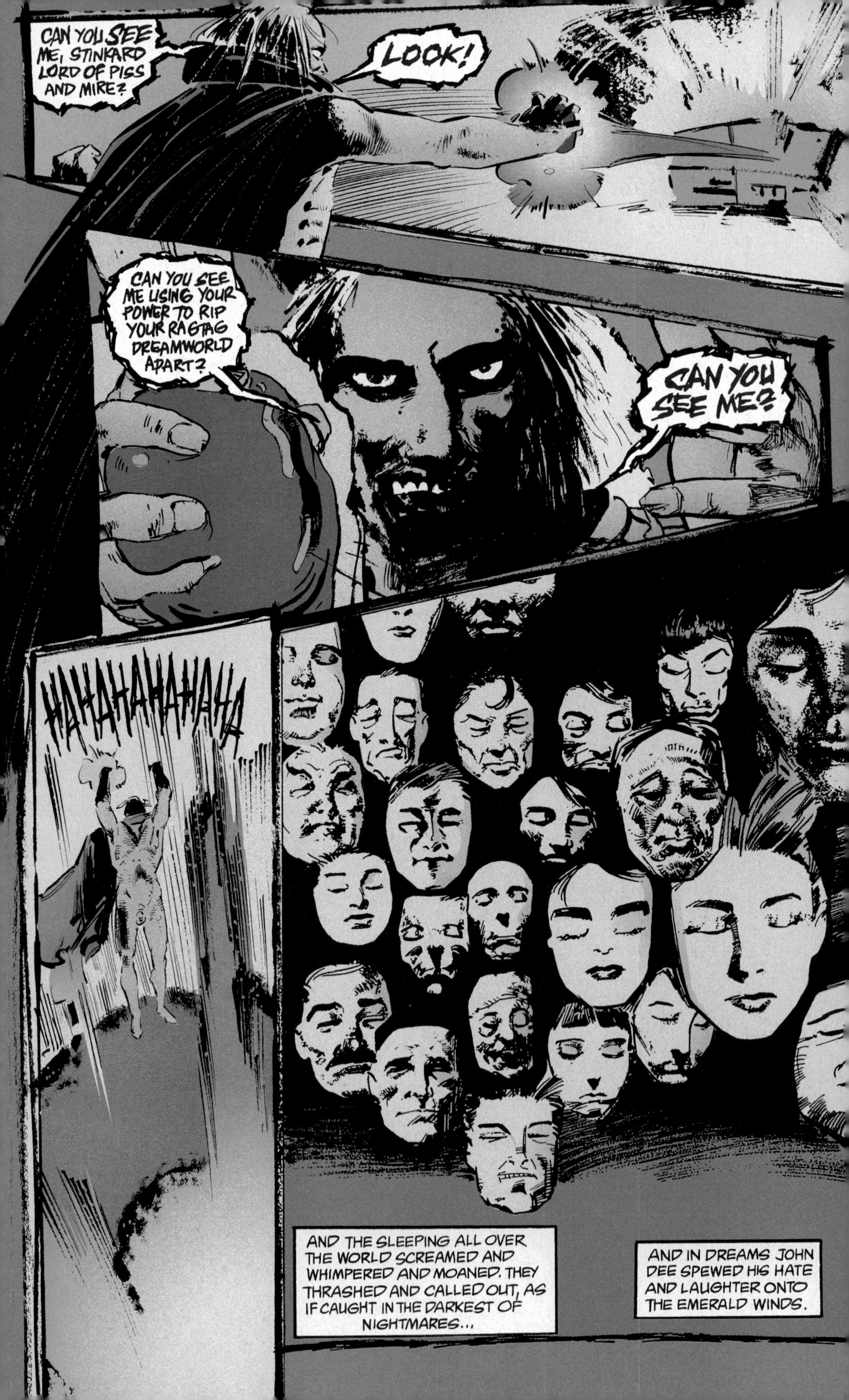
CAN YOU SEE ME, STINKARD LORD OF PISS AND MIRE?
LOOK!
CAN YOU SEE ME USING YOUR POWER TO RIP YOUR RAGTAG DREAMWORLD APART?
CAN YOU SEE ME?
HAHAHAHAHAHAHA
AND THE SLEEPING ALL OVER THE WORLD SCREAMED AND WHIMPERED AND MOANED. THEY THRASHED AND CALLED OUT, AS IF CAUGHT IN THE DARKEST OF NIGHTMARES...
AND IN DREAMS JOHN DEE SPEWED HIS HATE AND LAUGHTER ONTO THE EMERALD WINDS.

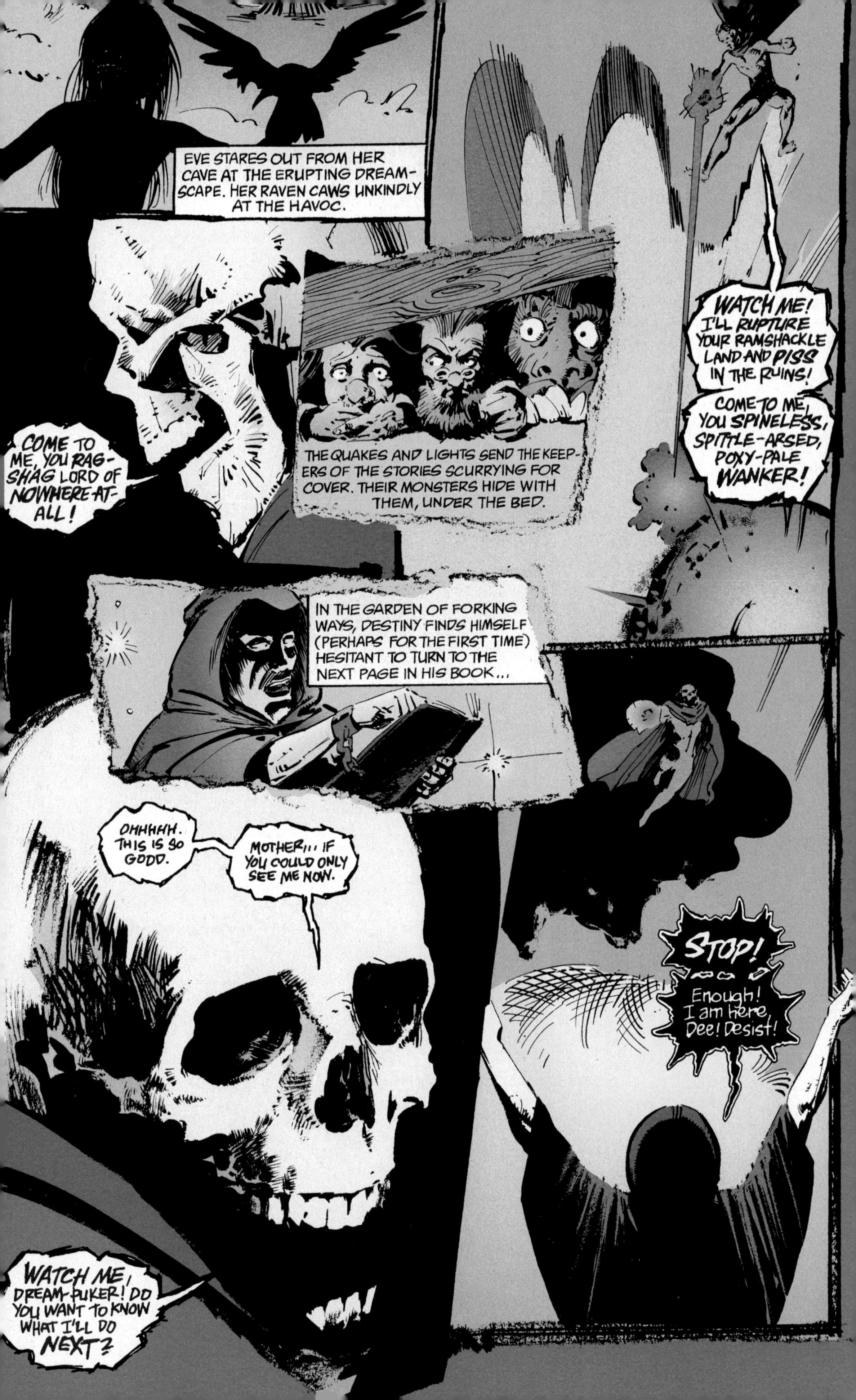
EVE STARES OUT FROM HER CAVE AT THE ERUPTING DREAM-SCAPE. HER RAVEN CAWS UNKINDLY AT THE HAVOC.
WATCH ME! I'LL RUPTURE YOUR RAMSHACKLE LAND AND PISS IN THE RUINS!
COME TO ME, YOU SPINELESS, SPITTLE-ARSED, POXY-PALE WANKER!
COME TO ME, YOU RAG-SHAG LORD OF NOWHERE-AT-ALL!
THE QUAKES AND LIGHTS SEND THE KEEPERS OF THE STORIES SCURRYING FOR COVER. THEIR MONSTERS HIDE WITH THEM, UNDER THE BED.
IN THE GARDEN OF FORKING WAYS, DESTINY FINDS HIMSELF (PERHAPS FOR THE FIRST TIME) HESITANT TO TURN TO THE NEXT PAGE IN HIS BOOK...
OHHHHH. THIS IS SO GOOD.
MOTHER... IF YOU COULD ONLY SEE ME NOW.
STOP!
Enough! I am here, Dee! Desist!
WATCH ME, DREAM-PUKER! DO YOU WANT TO KNOW WHAT I'LL DO NEXT?

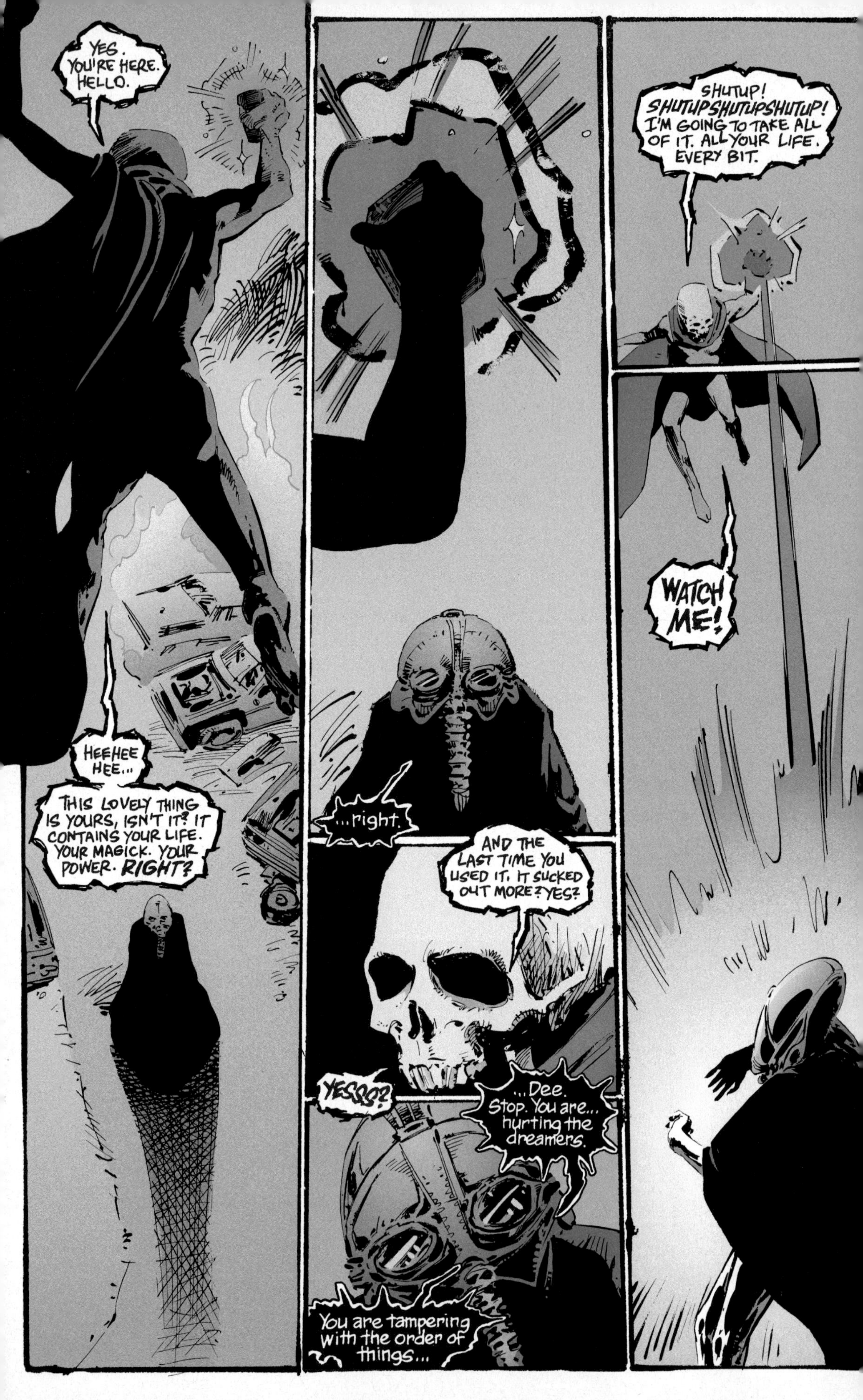
YES. YOU'RE HERE. HELLO.
HEEHEE HEE...
THIS LOVELY THING IS YOURS, ISN'T IT? IT CONTAINS YOUR LIFE. YOUR MAGICK. YOUR POWER. RIGHT?
...right.
AND THE LAST TIME YOU USED IT, IT SUCKED OUT MORE? YES?
YESSS?
...Dee. Stop. You are... hurting the dreamers.
You are tampering with the order of things...
SHUTUP! SHUTUPSHUTUPSHUTUP! I'M GOING TO TAKE ALL OF IT. ALL YOUR LIFE. EVERY BIT.
WATCH ME!

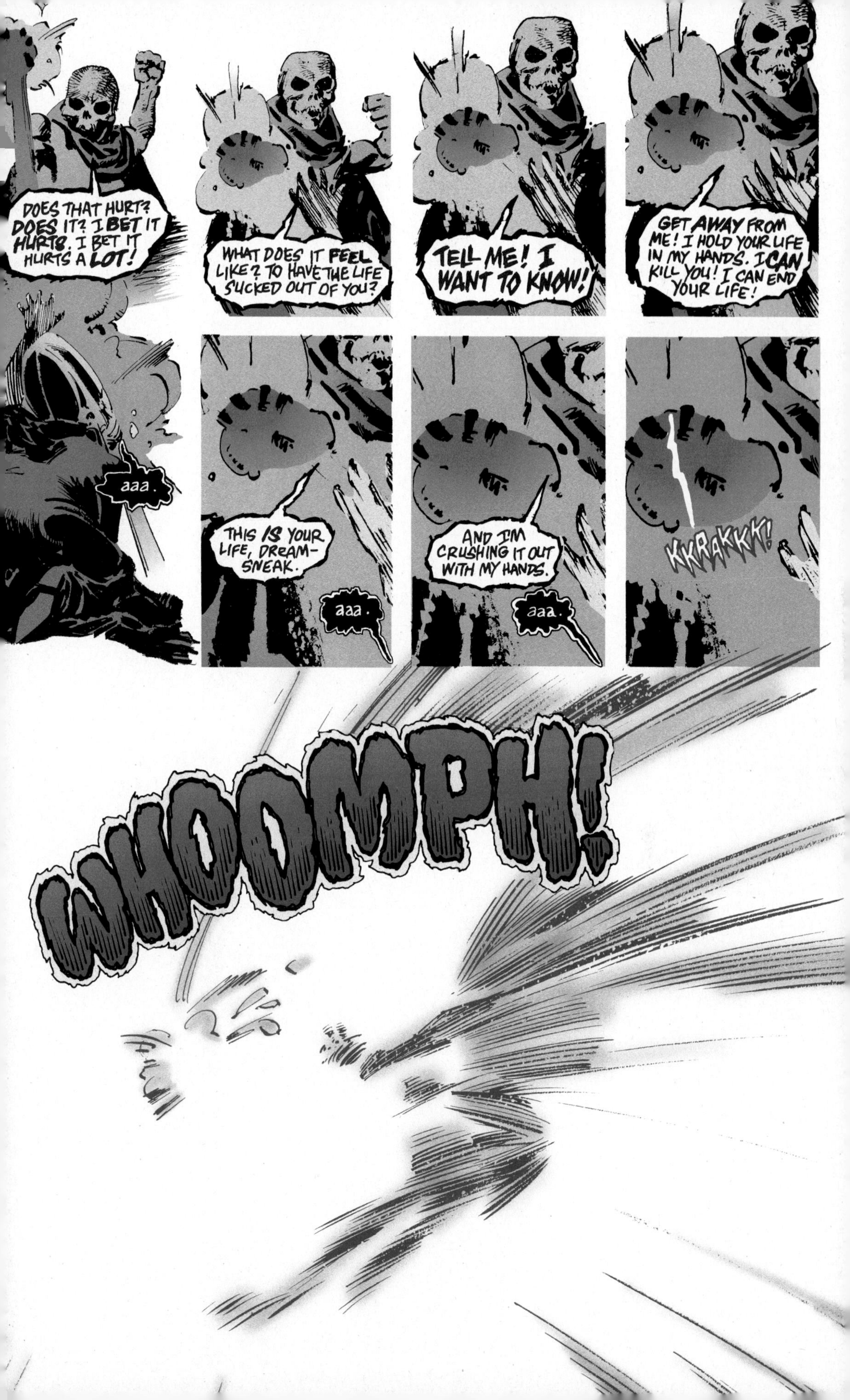
DOES THAT HURT? DOES IT? I BET IT HURTS. I BET IT HURTS A LOT!
WHAT DOES IT FEEL LIKE? TO HAVE THE LIFE SUCKED OUT OF YOU?
TELL ME! I WANT TO KNOW!
GET AWAY FROM ME! I HOLD YOUR LIFE IN MY HANDS. I CAN KILL YOU! I CAN END YOUR LIFE!
aaa.
THIS IS YOUR LIFE, DREAM-SNEAK.
aaa.
AND I'M CRUSHING IT OUT WITH MY HANDS.
aaa.
KKRAKKK!
WHOOMPH!

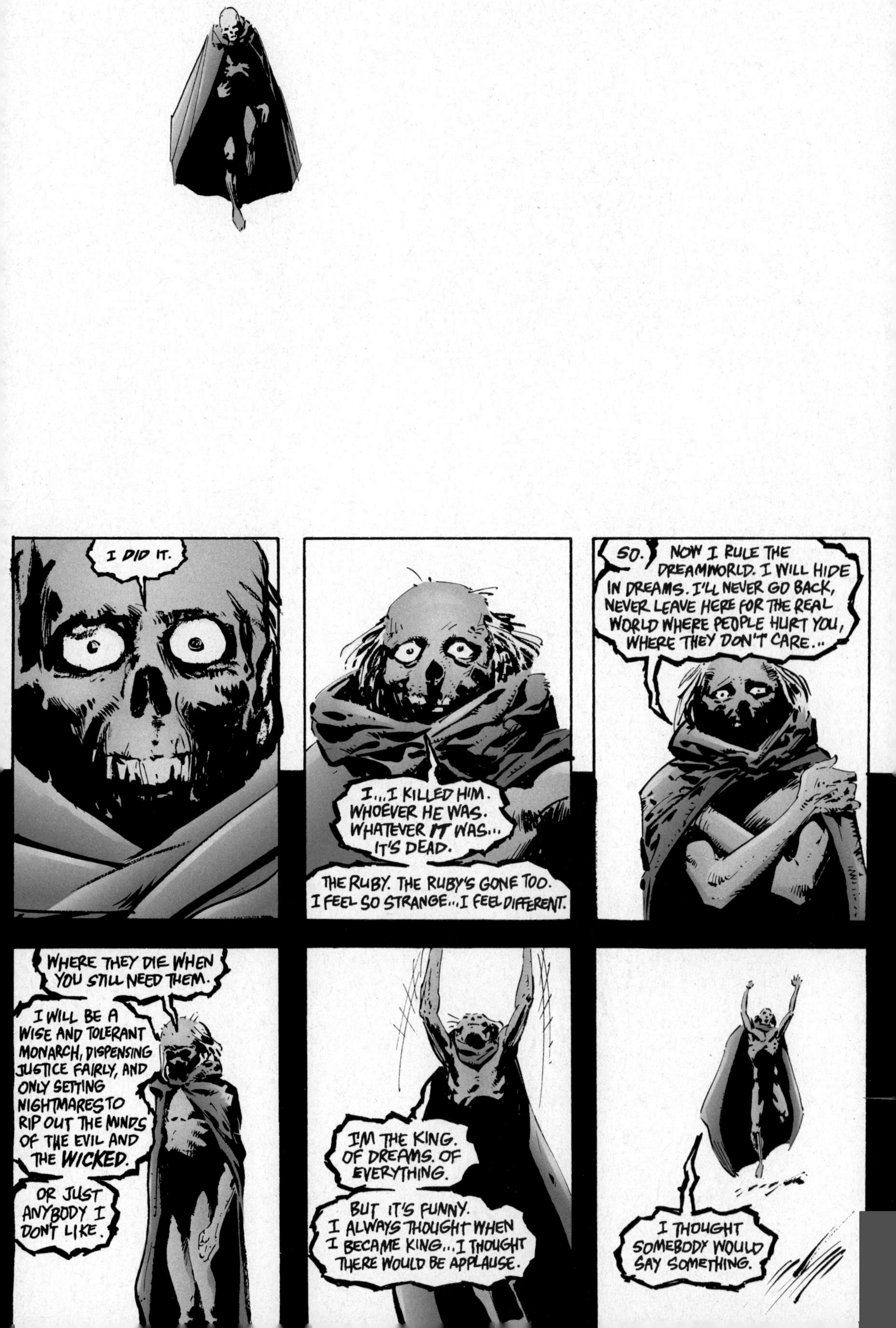
I DID IT.
I...I KILLED HIM. WHOEVER HE WAS. WHATEVER IT WAS... IT'S DEAD.
THE RUBY. THE RUBY'S GONE TOO. I FEEL SO STRANGE... I FEEL DIFFERENT.
SO.
NOW I RULE THE DREAMWORLD. I WILL HIDE IN DREAMS. I'LL NEVER GO BACK, NEVER LEAVE HERE FOR THE REAL WORLD WHERE PEOPLE HURT YOU, WHERE THEY DON'T CARE...
WHERE THEY DIE WHEN YOU STILL NEED THEM.
I WILL BE A WISE AND TOLERANT MONARCH, DISPENSING JUSTICE FAIRLY, AND ONLY SETTING NIGHTMARES TO RIP OUT THE MINDS OF THE EVIL AND THE WICKED.
OR JUST ANYBODY I DON'T LIKE.
I'M THE KING. OF DREAMS. OF EVERYTHING.
BUT IT'S FUNNY. I ALWAYS THOUGHT WHEN I BECAME KING... I THOUGHT THERE WOULD BE APPLAUSE.
I THOUGHT SOMEBODY WOULD SAY SOMETHING.

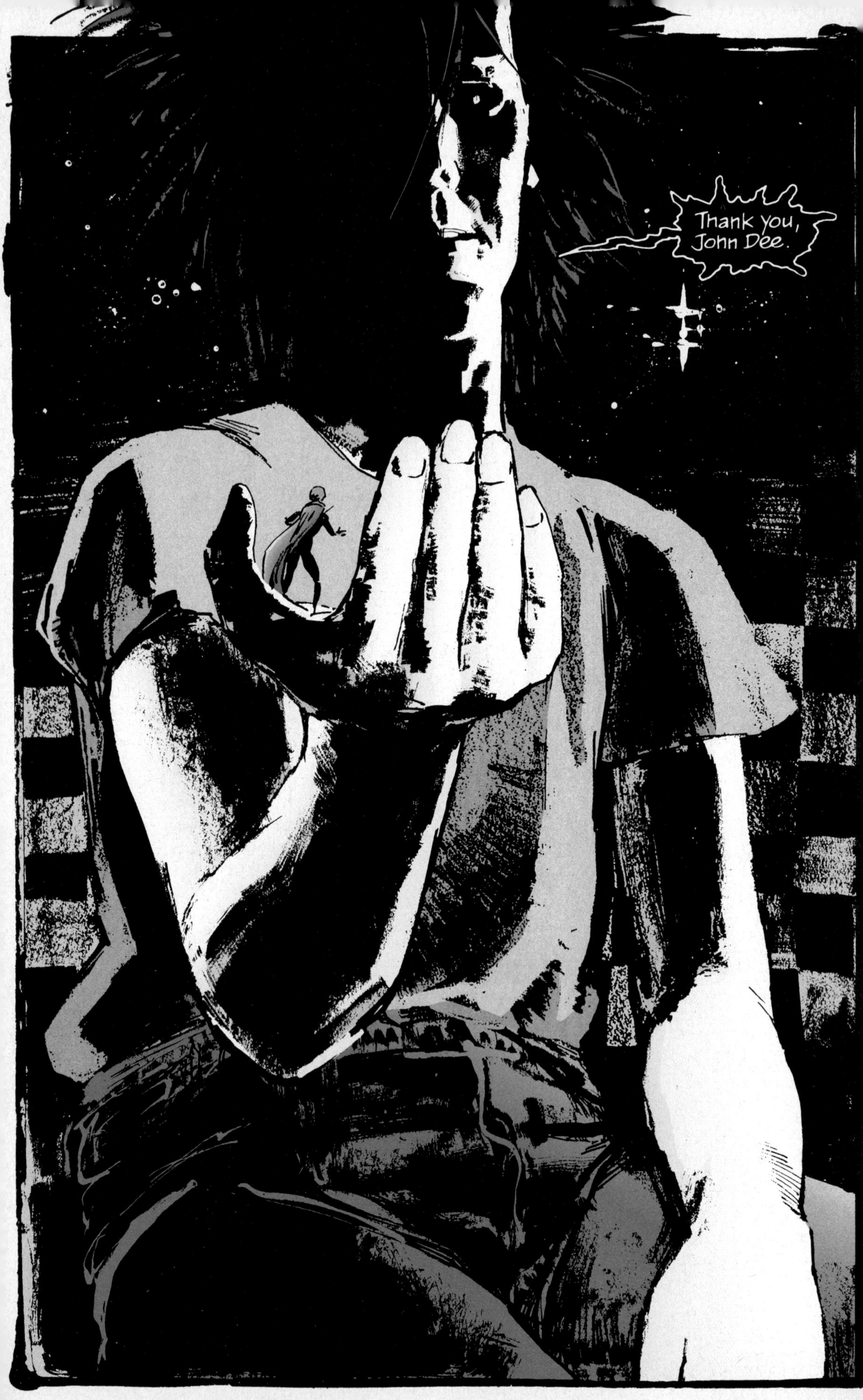
Thank you, John Dee.

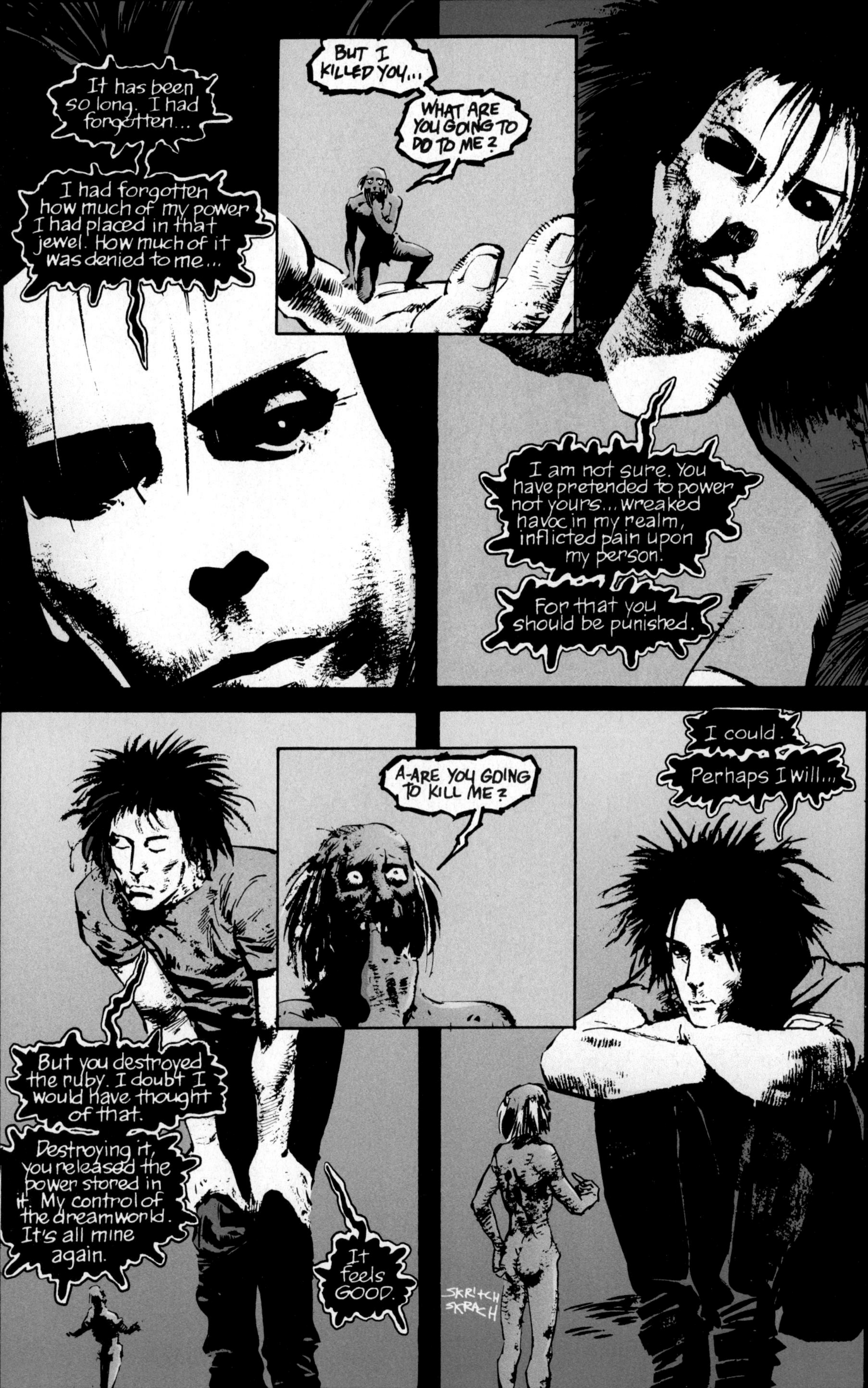
It has been so long. I had forgotten...
I had forgotten how much of my power I had placed in that jewel. How much of it was denied to me...
BUT I KILLED YOU...
WHAT ARE YOU GOING TO DO TO ME?
I am not sure. You have pretended to power not yours... wreaked havoc in my realm, inflicted pain upon my person.
For that you should be punished.
But you destroyed the ruby. I doubt I would have thought of that.
Destroying it, you released the power stored in it. My control of the dreamworld. It's all mine again.
It feels GOOD.
A-ARE YOU GOING TO KILL ME?
I could.
Perhaps I will...
SKR!TCH SKRACH

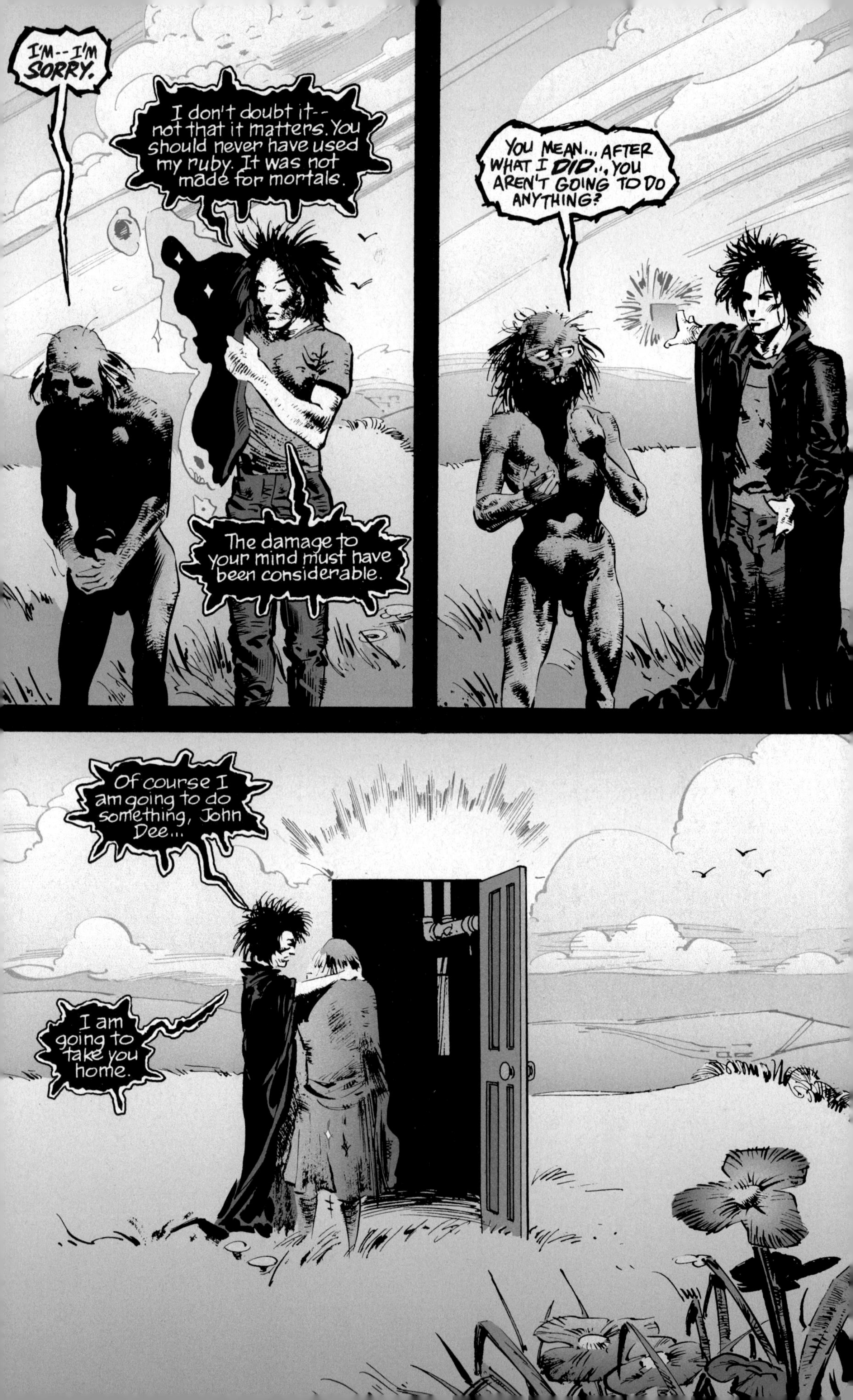
I'M-- I'M SORRY.
I don't doubt it-- not that it matters. You should never have used my ruby. It was not made for mortals.
The damage to your mind must have been considerable.
YOU MEAN... AFTER WHAT I DID..., YOU AREN'T GOING TO DO ANYTHING?
Of course I am going to do something, John Dee...
I am going to take you home.

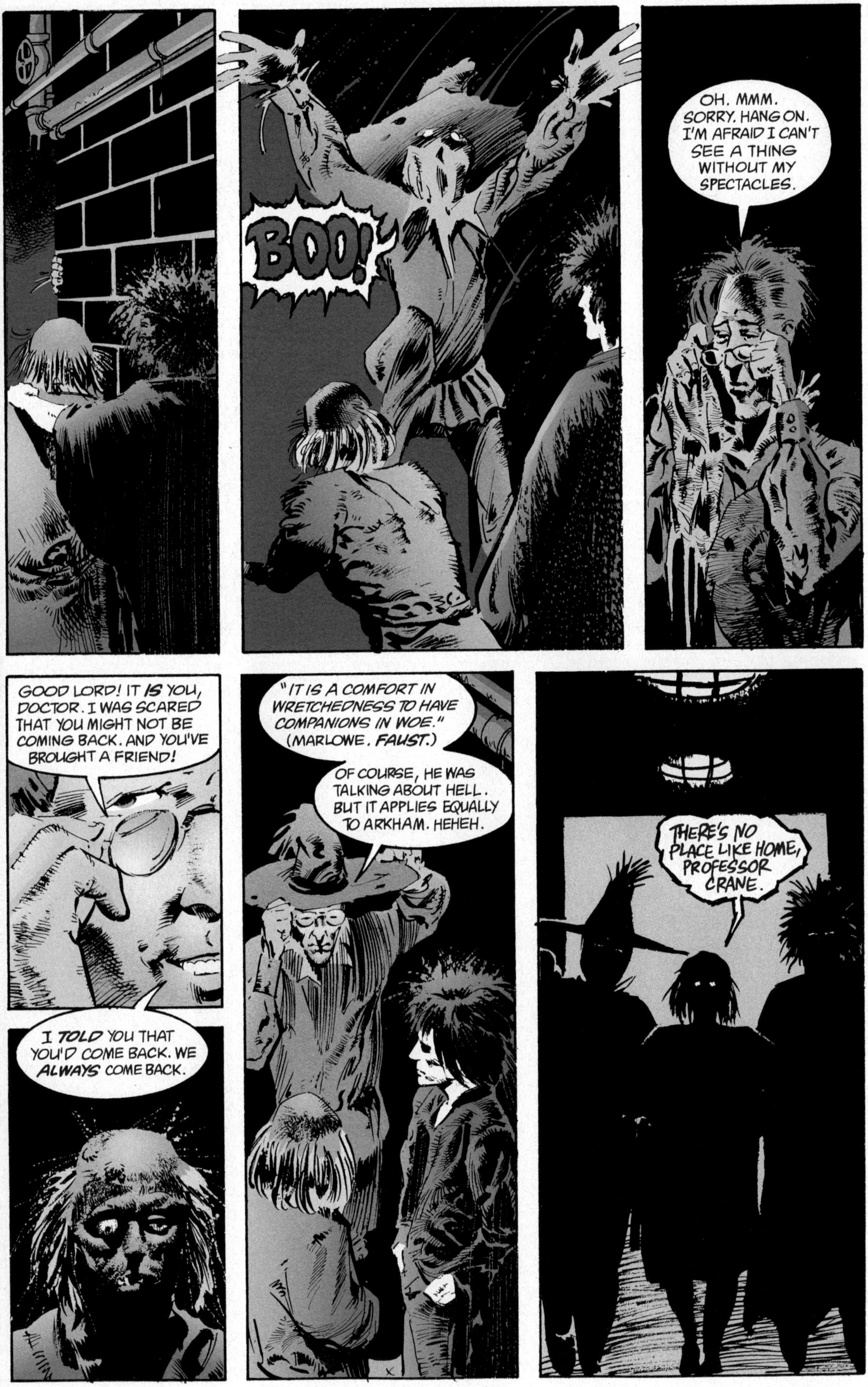

BOO!
OH. MMM. SORRY. HANG ON. I'M AFRAID I CAN'T SEE A THING WITHOUT MY SPECTACLES.
GOOD LORD! IT IS YOU, DOCTOR. I WAS SCARED THAT YOU MIGHT NOT BE COMING BACK. AND YOU'VE BROUGHT A FRIEND!
I TOLD YOU THAT YOU'D COME BACK. WE ALWAYS COME BACK.
"IT IS A COMFORT IN WRETCHEDNESS TO HAVE COMPANIONS IN WOE." (MARLOWE. FAUST.)
OF COURSE, HE WAS TALKING ABOUT HELL. BUT IT APPLIES EQUALLY TO ARKHAM. HEHEH.
THERE'S NO PLACE LIKE HOME, PROFESSOR CRANE.

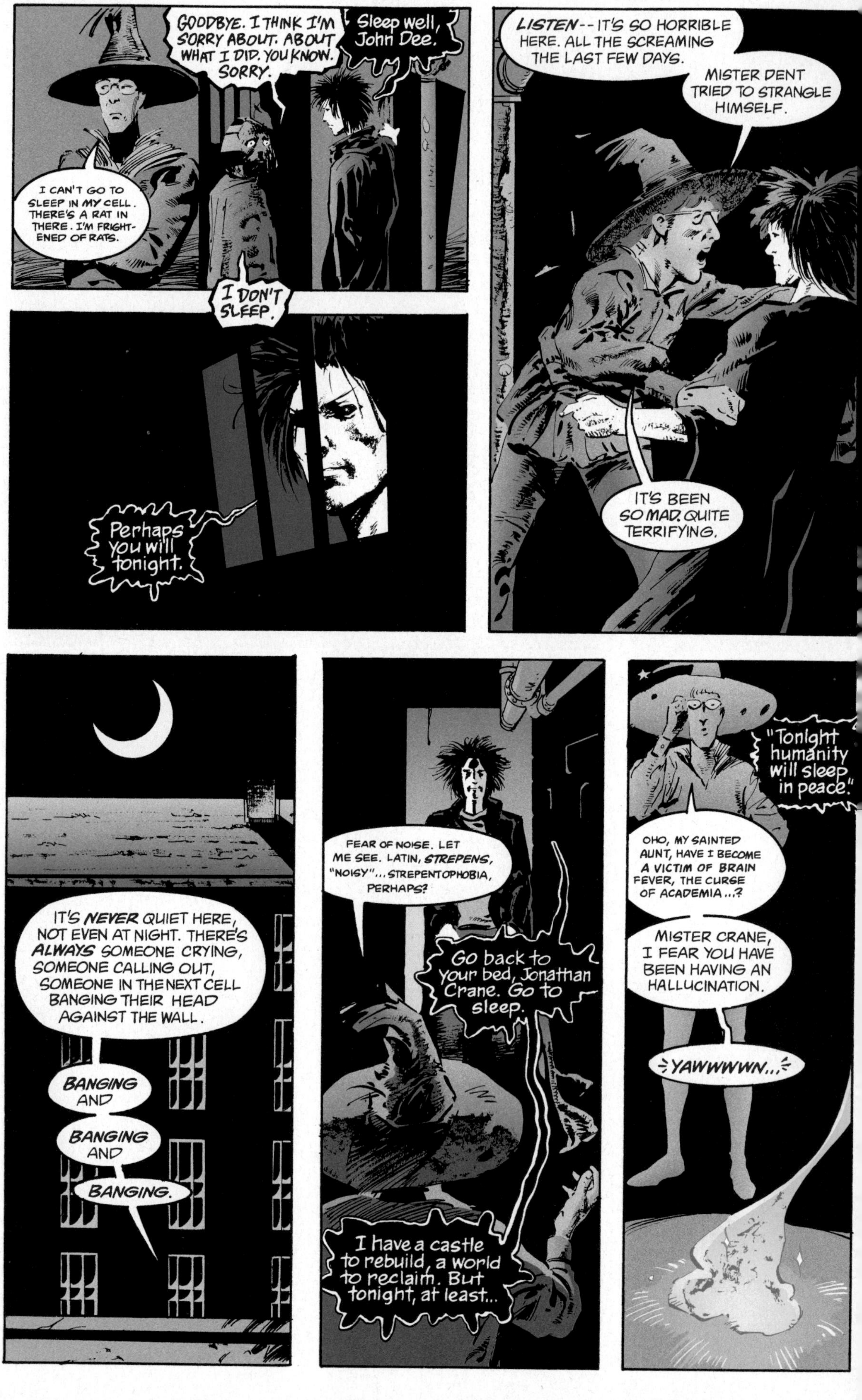
GOODBYE. I THINK I'M SORRY ABOUT. ABOUT WHAT I DID. YOU KNOW. SORRY.
Sleep well, John Dee.
I CAN'T GO TO SLEEP IN MY CELL. THERE'S A RAT IN THERE. I'M FRIGHTENED OF RATS.
I DON'T SLEEP.
Perhaps you will tonight.
LISTEN-- IT'S SO HORRIBLE HERE. ALL THE SCREAMING THE LAST FEW DAYS.
MISTER DENT TRIED TO STRANGLE HIMSELF.
IT'S BEEN SO MAD. QUITE TERRIFYING.
IT'S NEVER QUIET HERE, NOT EVEN AT NIGHT. THERE'S ALWAYS SOMEONE CRYING, SOMEONE CALLING OUT, SOMEONE IN THE NEXT CELL BANGING THEIR HEAD AGAINST THE WALL.
BANGING AND
BANGING AND
BANGING.
FEAR OF NOISE. LET ME SEE. LATIN, STREPENS, "NOISY"... STREPENTOPHOBIA, PERHAPS?
Go back to your bed, Jonathan Crane. Go to sleep.
I have a castle to rebuild, a world to reclaim. But tonight, at least...
"Tonight humanity will sleep in peace."
OHO, MY SAINTED AUNT, HAVE I BECOME A VICTIM OF BRAIN FEVER, THE CURSE OF ACADEMIA...?
MISTER CRANE, I FEAR YOU HAVE BEEN HAVING AN HALLUCINATION.
YAWWWWN...

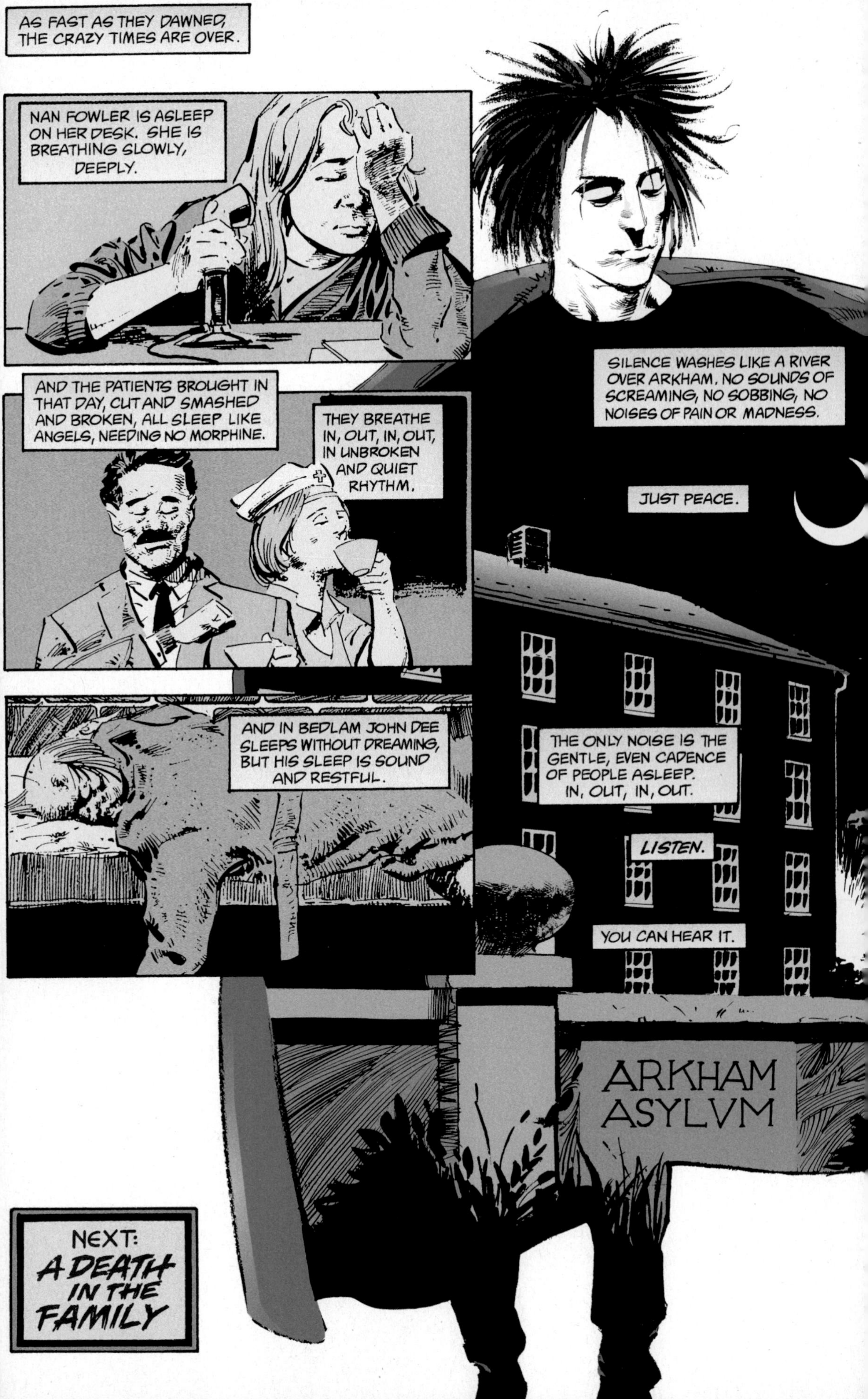
AS FAST AS THEY DAWNED, THE CRAZY TIMES ARE OVER.
NAN FOWLER IS ASLEEP ON HER DESK. SHE IS BREATHING SLOWLY, DEEPLY.
AND THE PATIENTS BROUGHT IN THAT DAY, CUT AND SMASHED AND BROKEN, ALL SLEEP LIKE ANGELS, NEEDING NO MORPHINE.
THEY BREATHE IN, OUT, IN, OUT, IN UNBROKEN AND QUIET RHYTHM.
AND IN BEDLAM JOHN DEE SLEEPS WITHOUT DREAMING, BUT HIS SLEEP IS SOUND AND RESTFUL.
SILENCE WASHES LIKE A RIVER OVER ARKHAM. NO SOUNDS OF SCREAMING, NO SOBBING, NO NOISES OF PAIN OR MADNESS.
JUST PEACE.
THE ONLY NOISE IS THE GENTLE, EVEN CADENCE OF PEOPLE ASLEEP. IN, OUT, IN, OUT.
LISTEN.
YOU CAN HEAR IT.
ARKHAM ASYLVM
NEXT: A DEATH IN THE FAMILY

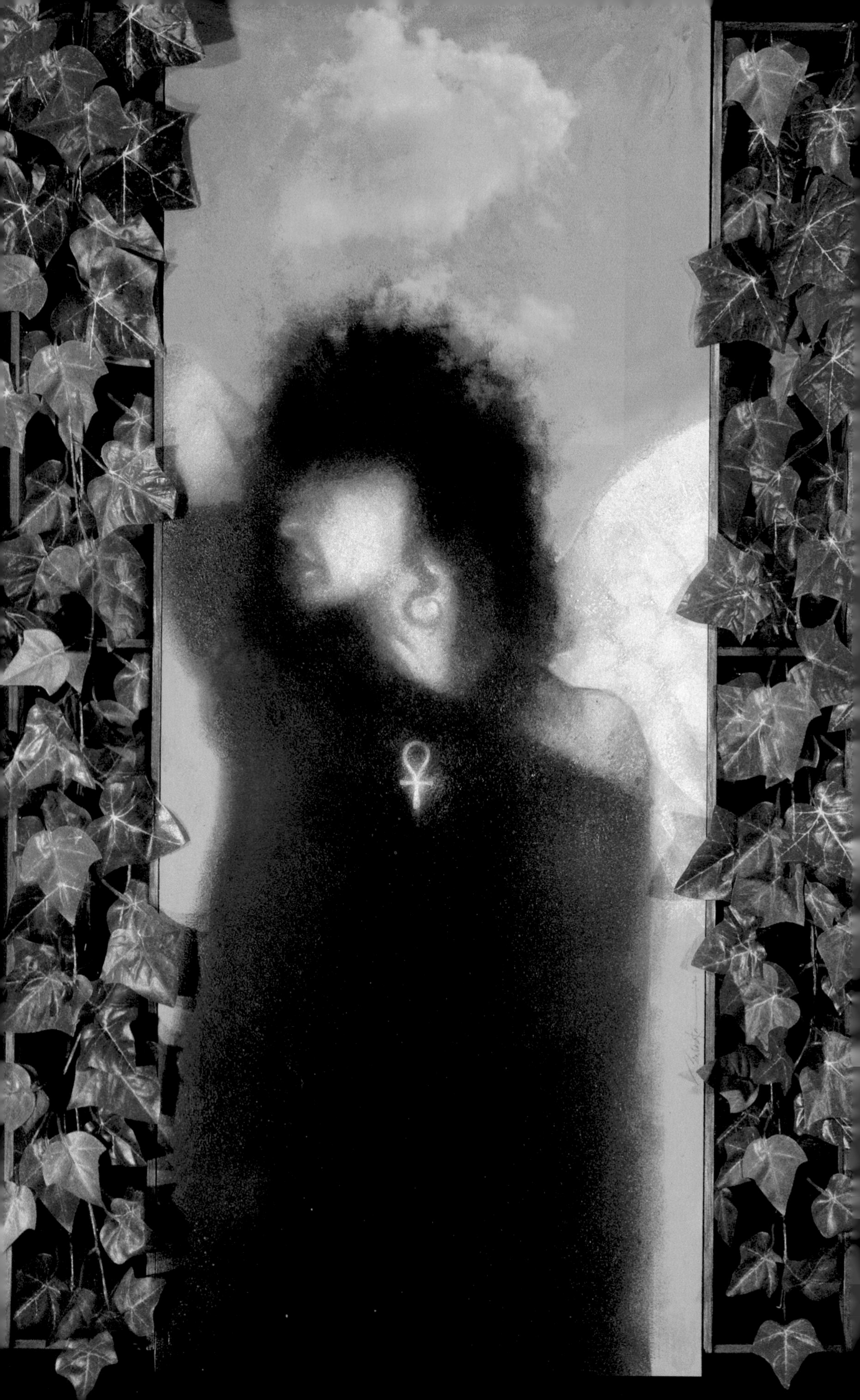

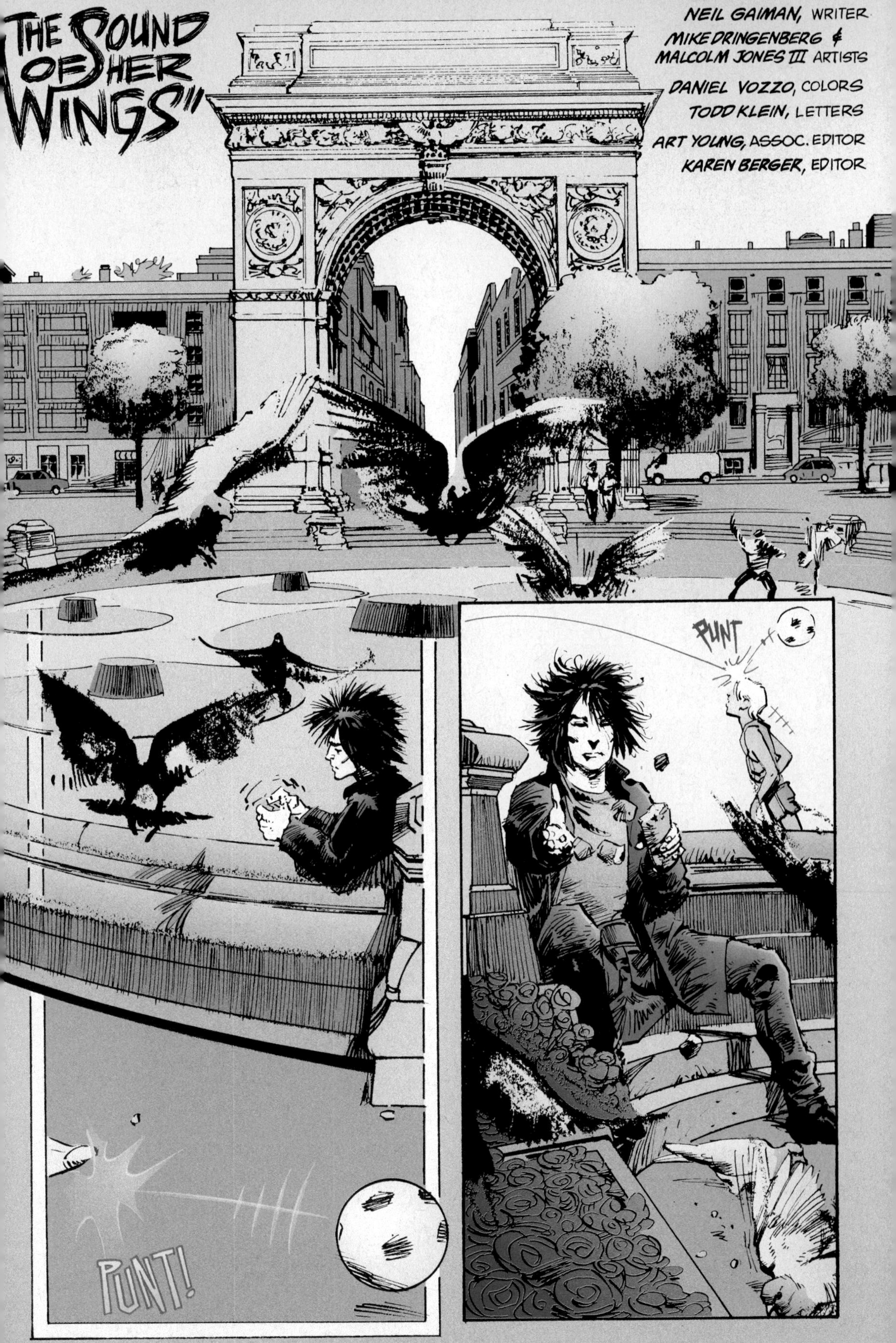

"THE SOUND OF HER WINGS"
NEIL GAIMAN, WRITER
MIKE DRINGENBERG & MALCOLM JONES III ARTISTS
DANIEL VOZZO, COLORS
TODD KLEIN, LETTERS
ART YOUNG, ASSOC. EDITOR
KAREN BERGER, EDITOR
PUNT!
PUNT

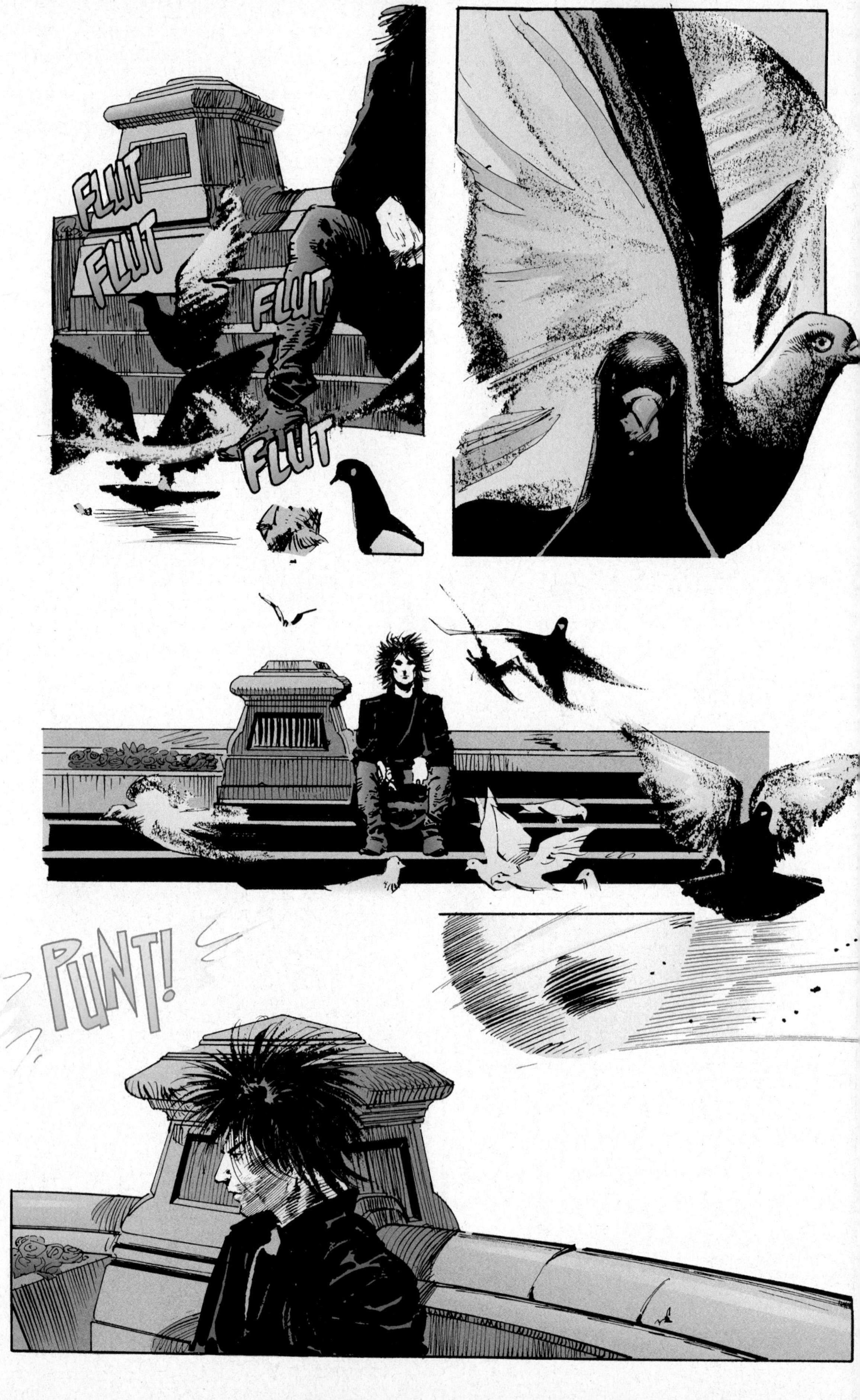
FLUT
FLUT
FLUT
FLUT
PUNT!

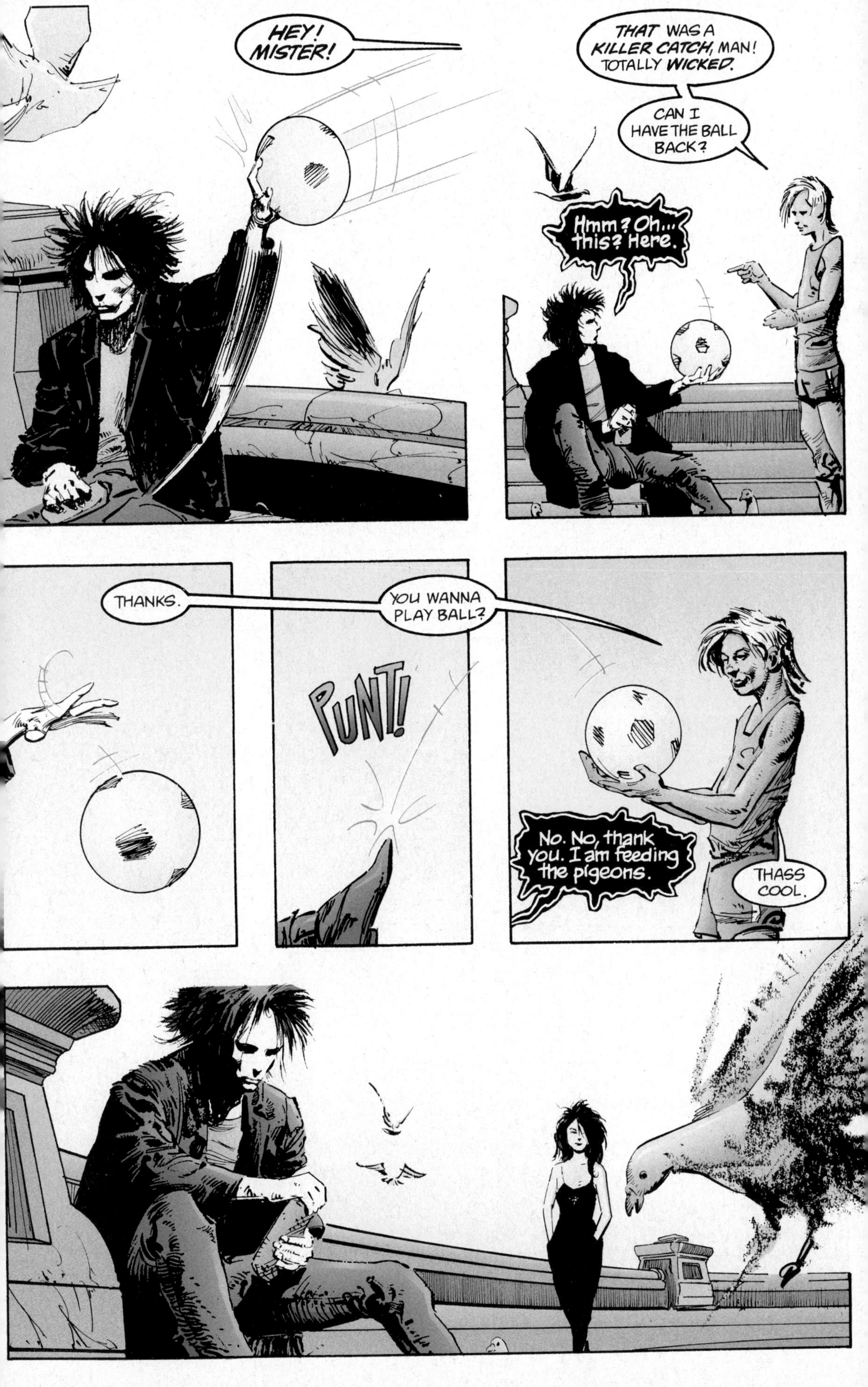
HEY! MISTER!
THAT WAS A KILLER CATCH, MAN! TOTALLY WICKED.
CAN I HAVE THE BALL BACK?
Hmm? Oh... this? Here.
THANKS.
YOU WANNA PLAY BALL?
PUNT!
No. No, thank you. I am feeding the pigeons.
THASS COOL.

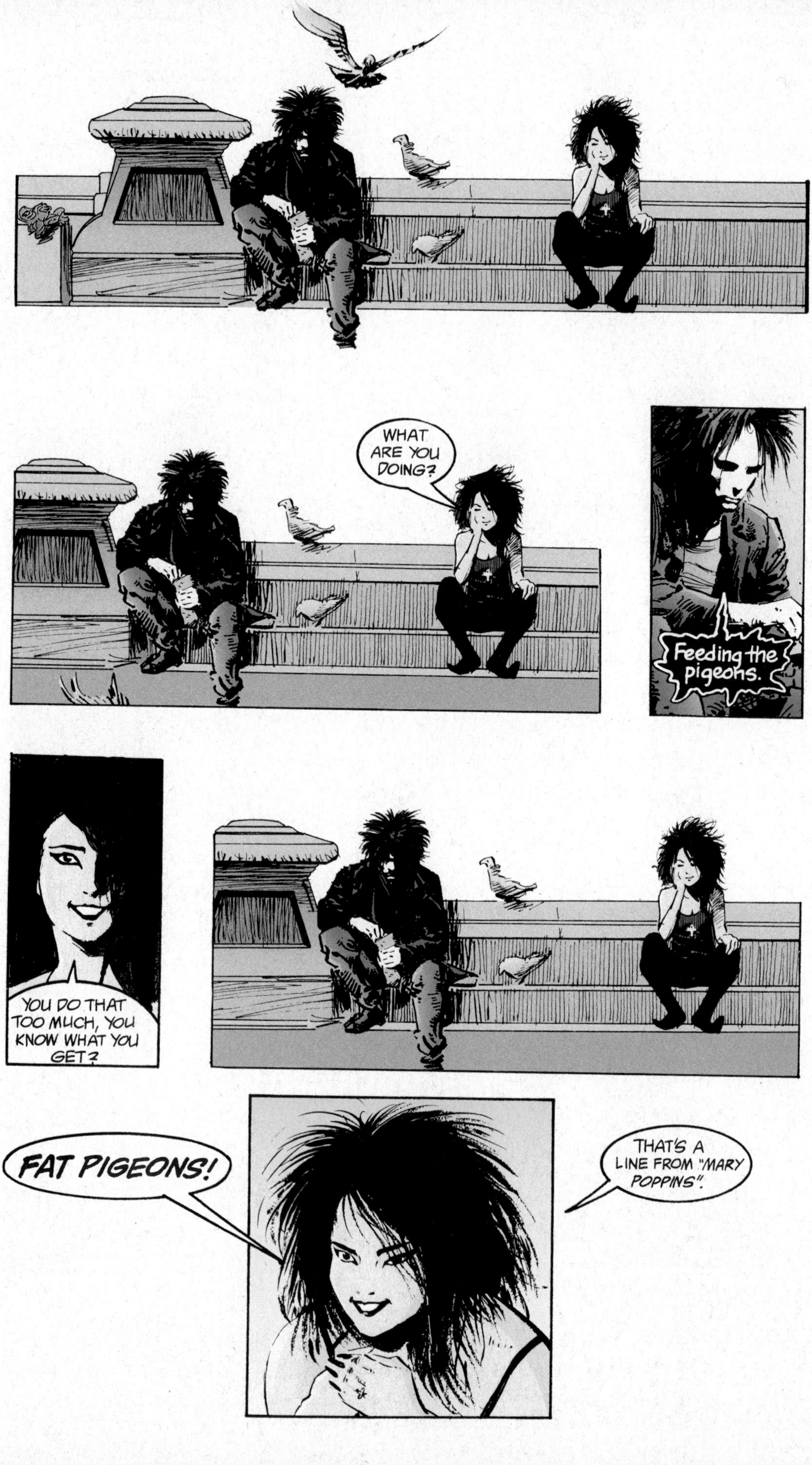

WHAT ARE YOU DOING?
Feeding the pigeons.
YOU DO THAT TOO MUCH, YOU KNOW WHAT YOU GET?
FAT PIGEONS!
THAT'S A LINE FROM "MARY POPPINS".

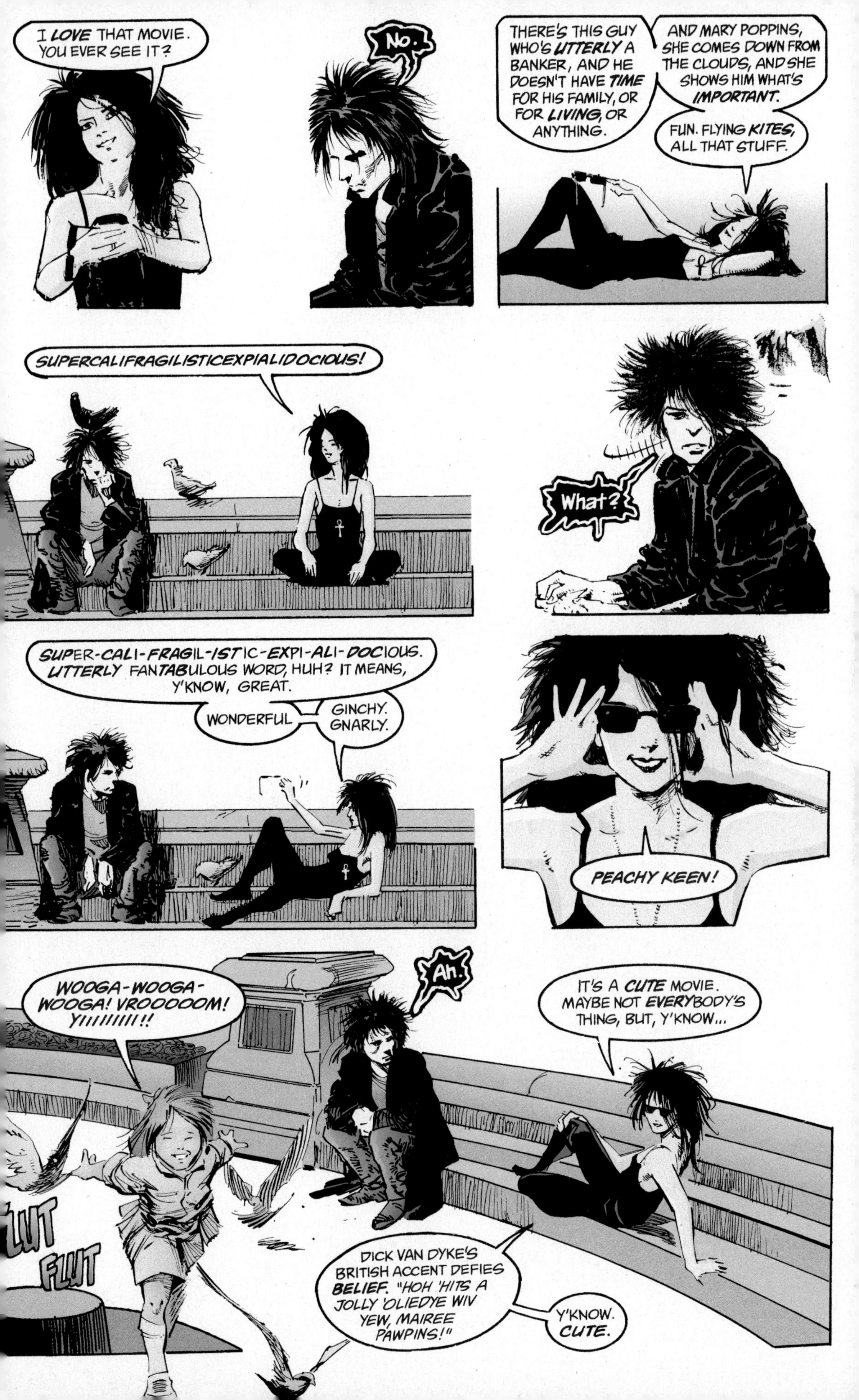
I LOVE THAT MOVIE. YOU EVER SEE IT?
No.
THERE'S THIS GUY WHO'S UTTERLY A BANKER, AND HE DOESN'T HAVE TIME FOR HIS FAMILY, OR FOR LIVING, OR ANYTHING.
AND MARY POPPINS, SHE COMES DOWN FROM THE CLOUDS, AND SHE SHOWS HIM WHAT'S IMPORTANT.
FUN. FLYING KITES, ALL THAT STUFF.
SUPERCALIFRAGILISTICEXPIALIDOCIOUS!
What?
SUPER-CALI-FRAGIL-ISTIC-EXPI-ALI-DOCIOUS. UTTERLY FANTABULOUS WORD, HUH? IT MEANS, Y'KNOW, GREAT.
WONDERFUL
GINCHY. GNARLY.
PEACHY KEEN!
WOOGA-WOOGA-WOOGA! VROOOOOM! YIIIIIIIII!!
Ah.
IT'S A CUTE MOVIE. MAYBE NOT EVERYBODY'S THING, BUT, Y'KNOW...
FLUT
FLUT
DICK VAN DYKE'S BRITISH ACCENT DEFIES BELIEF. "HOH 'HITS A JOLLY 'OLIEDYE WIV YEW, MAIREE PAWPINS!"
Y'KNOW. CUTE.

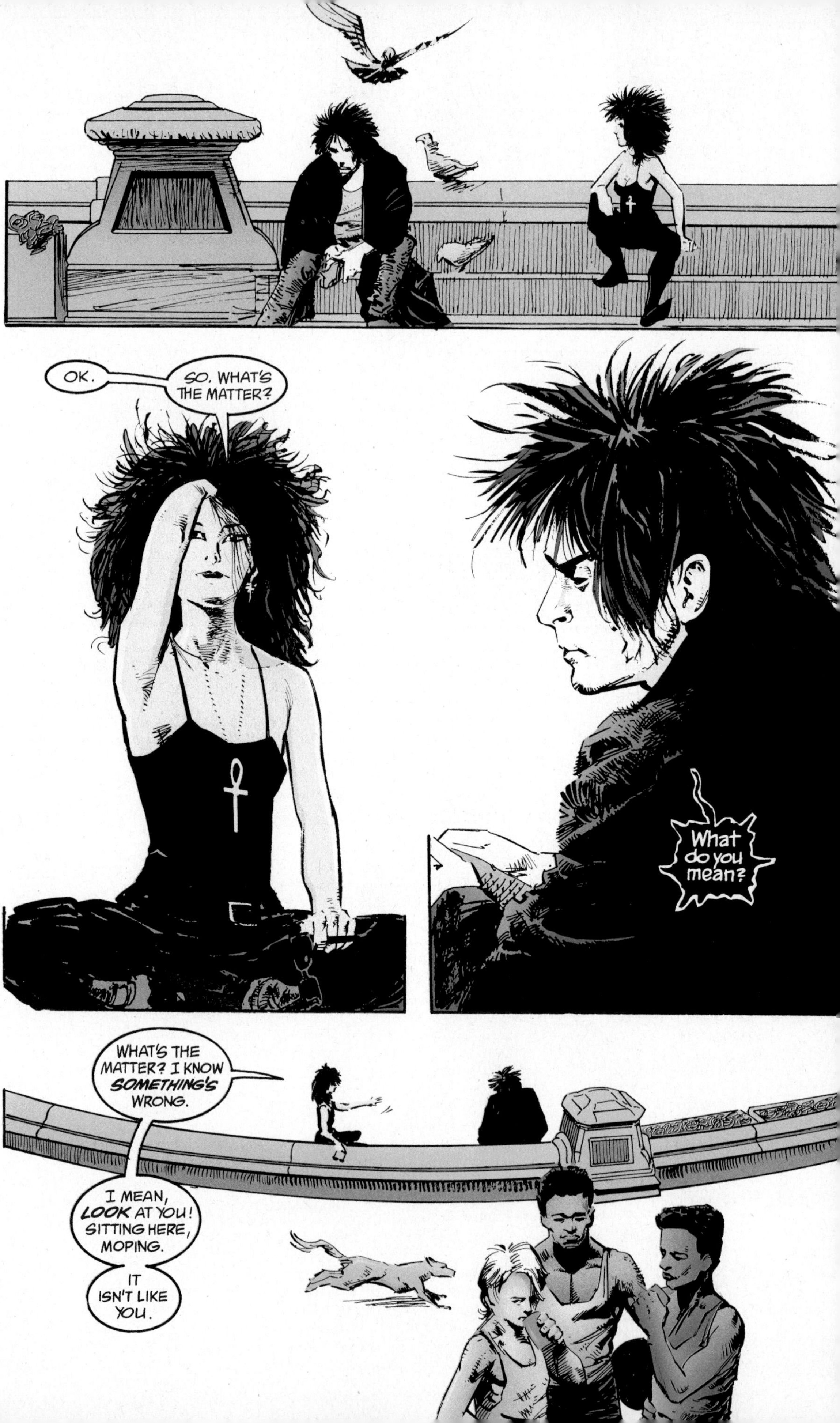
OK.
SO, WHAT'S THE MATTER?
What do you mean?
WHAT'S THE MATTER? I KNOW *SOMETHING'S* WRONG.
I MEAN, *LOOK* AT YOU! SITTING HERE, MOPING.
IT ISN'T LIKE YOU.

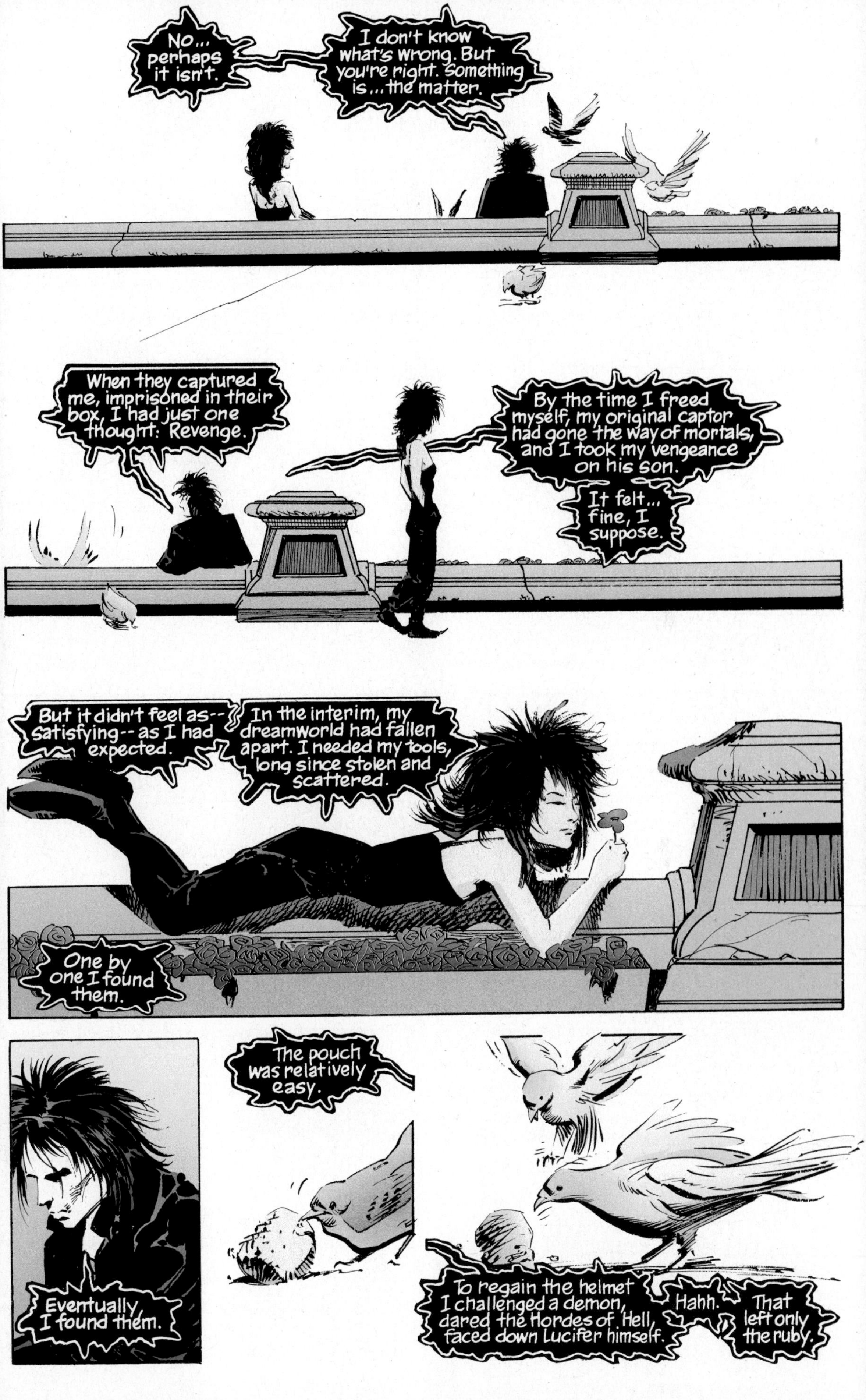
No... perhaps it isn't.
I don't know what's wrong. But you're right. Something is... the matter.
When they captured me, imprisoned in their box, I had just one thought: Revenge.
By the time I freed myself, my original captor had gone the way of mortals, and I took my vengeance on his son.
It felt... fine, I suppose.
But it didn't feel as-- satisfying-- as I had expected.
In the interim, my dreamworld had fallen apart. I needed my tools, long since stolen and scattered.
One by one I found them.
Eventually, I found them.
The pouch was relatively easy.
To regain the helmet I challenged a demon, dared the Hordes of Hell, faced down Lucifer himself.
Hahh.
That left only the ruby.

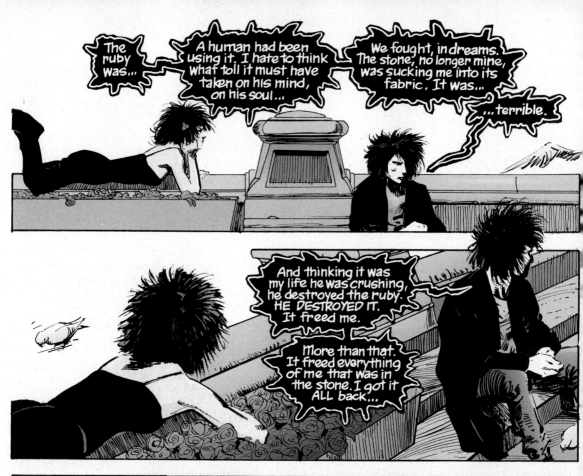

The ruby was...

A human had been using it. I hate to think what toll it must have taken on his mind, on his soul...

We fought, in dreams. The stone, no longer mine, was sucking me into its fabric. It was...

...terrible.

And thinking it was my life he was crushing, he destroyed the ruby. HE DESTROYED IT. It freed me.

More than that. It freed everything of me that was in the stone. I got it ALL back...

I was more powerful than I had been in eons. I returned the human to the madhouse...

You see, until then I'd been driven. I'd had a true quest, a purpose beyond my function--and then, suddenly, the quest was over.

I felt...drained. Disappointed. Let down.

Does that make sense? I had been sure that as soon as I had everything back I'd feel good. But inside I felt worse than when I started.

I feel like... nothing.

There. You asked.

I'm sorry. Maybe I don't have an answer.

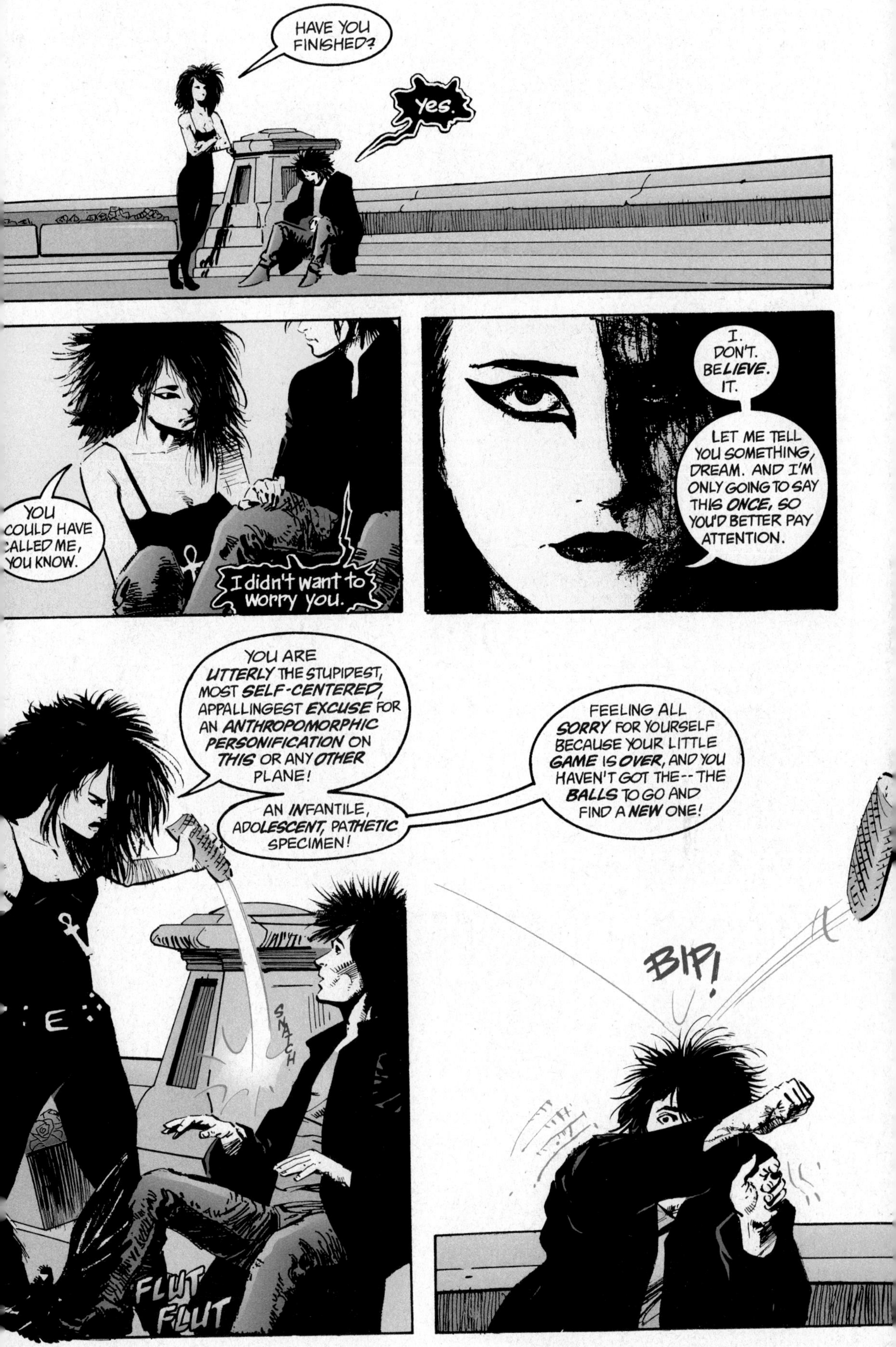

HAVE YOU FINISHED?
Yes.
YOU COULD HAVE CALLED ME, YOU KNOW.
I didn't want to worry you.
I. DON'T. BELIEVE. IT.
LET ME TELL YOU SOMETHING, DREAM. AND I'M ONLY GOING TO SAY THIS ONCE, SO YOU'D BETTER PAY ATTENTION.
YOU ARE UTTERLY THE STUPIDEST, MOST SELF-CENTERED, APPALLINGEST EXCUSE FOR AN ANTHROPOMORPHIC PERSONIFICATION ON THIS OR ANY OTHER PLANE!
AN INFANTILE, ADOLESCENT, PATHETIC SPECIMEN!
FEELING ALL SORRY FOR YOURSELF BECAUSE YOUR LITTLE GAME IS OVER, AND YOU HAVEN'T GOT THE--THE BALLS TO GO AND FIND A NEW ONE!
SNATCH
FLUT
FLUT
BIP!

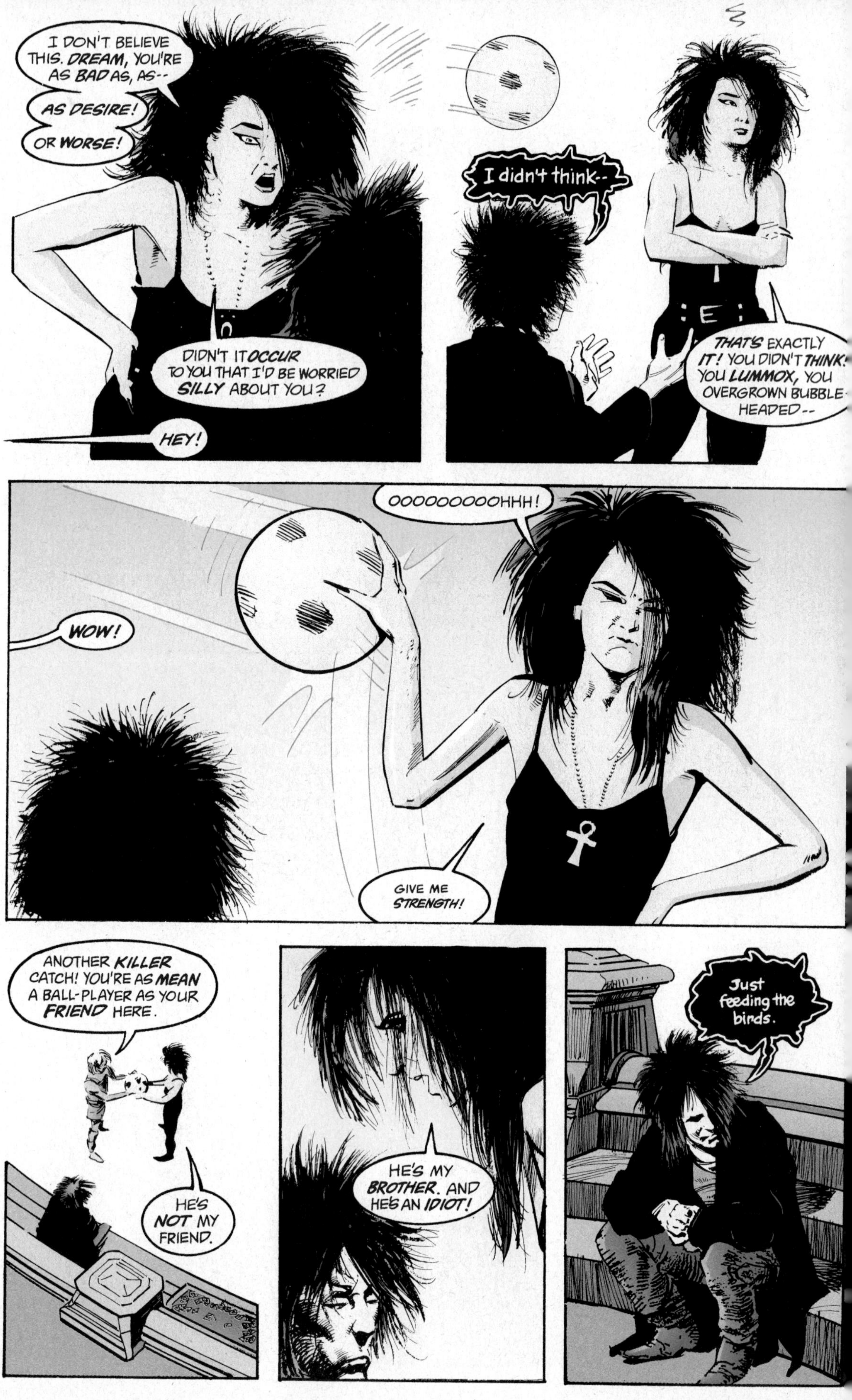

I DON'T BELIEVE THIS. DREAM, YOU'RE AS BAD AS, AS--
AS DESIRE!
OR WORSE!
DIDN'T IT OCCUR TO YOU THAT I'D BE WORRIED SILLY ABOUT YOU?
HEY!
I didn't think--
THAT'S EXACTLY IT! YOU DIDN'T THINK! YOU LUMMOX, YOU OVERGROWN BUBBLE-HEADED--
OOOOOOOOOHHH!
WOW!
GIVE ME STRENGTH!
ANOTHER KILLER CATCH! YOU'RE AS MEAN A BALL-PLAYER AS YOUR FRIEND HERE.
HE'S NOT MY FRIEND.
HE'S MY BROTHER. AND HE'S AN IDIOT!
Just feeding the birds.

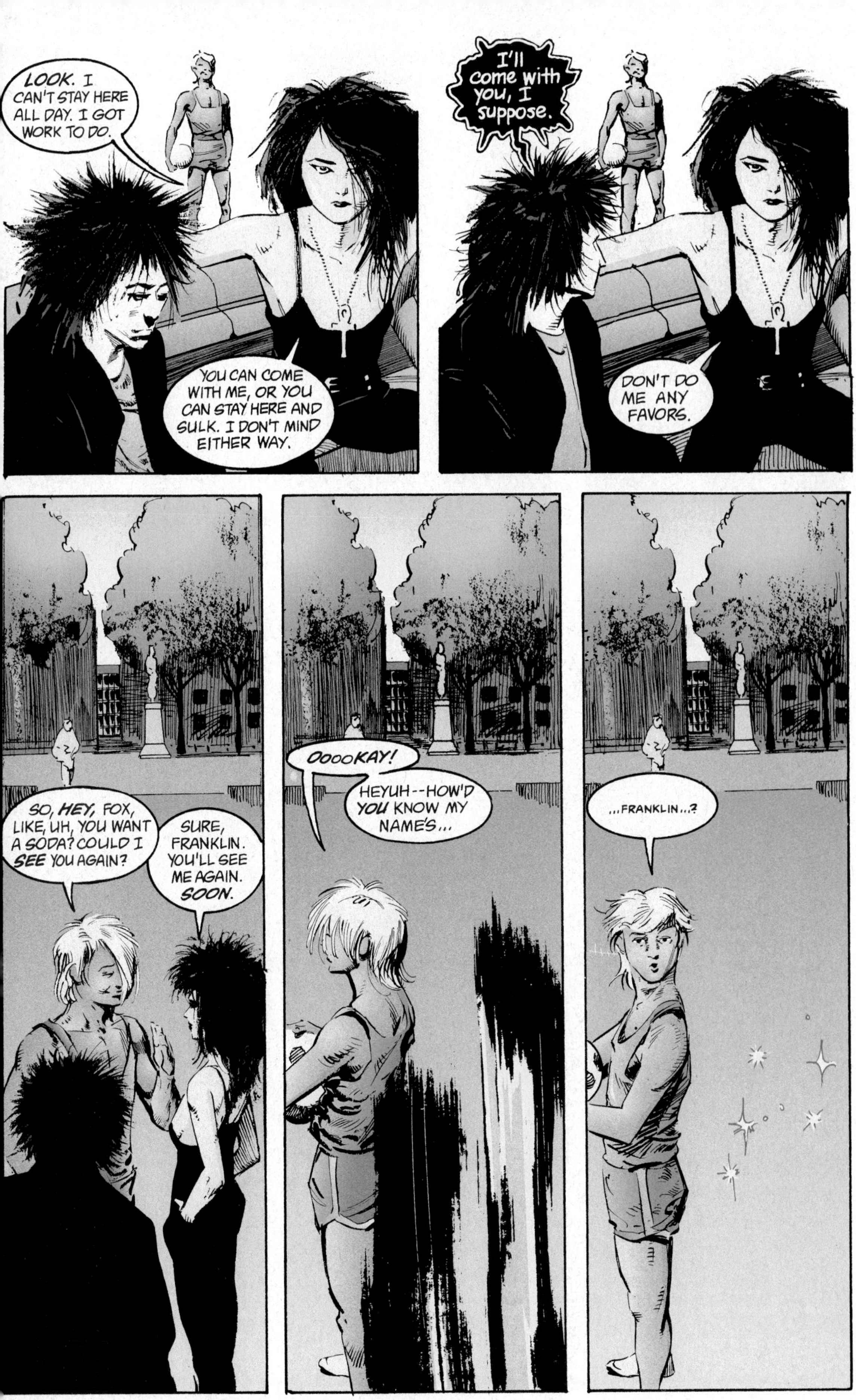
LOOK. I CAN'T STAY HERE ALL DAY. I GOT WORK TO DO.
YOU CAN COME WITH ME, OR YOU CAN STAY HERE AND SULK. I DON'T MIND EITHER WAY.
I'll come with you, I suppose.
DON'T DO ME ANY FAVORS.
SO, HEY, FOX, LIKE, UH, YOU WANT A SODA? COULD I SEE YOU AGAIN?
SURE, FRANKLIN. YOU'LL SEE ME AGAIN. SOON.
OOOOKAY!
HEYUH--HOW'D YOU KNOW MY NAME'S...
...FRANKLIN...?

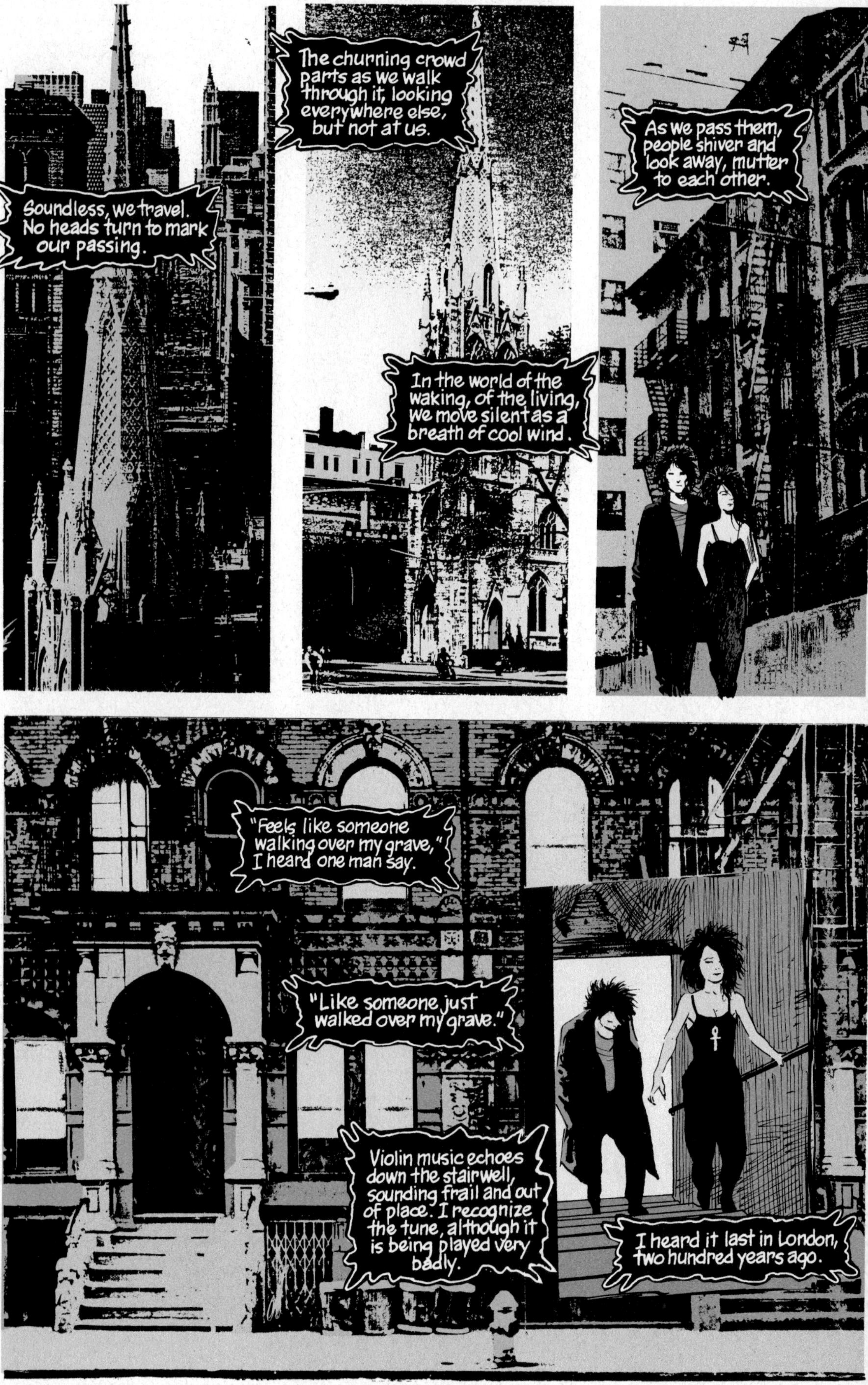
Soundless, we travel. No heads turn to mark our passing.
The churning crowd parts as we walk through it, looking everywhere else, but not at us.
In the world of the waking, of the living, we move silent as a breath of cool wind.
As we pass them, people shiver and look away, mutter to each other.
"Feels like someone walking over my grave," I heard one man say.
"Like someone just walked over my grave."
Violin music echoes down the stairwell, sounding frail and out of place. I recognize the tune, although it is being played very badly.
I heard it last in London, two hundred years ago.

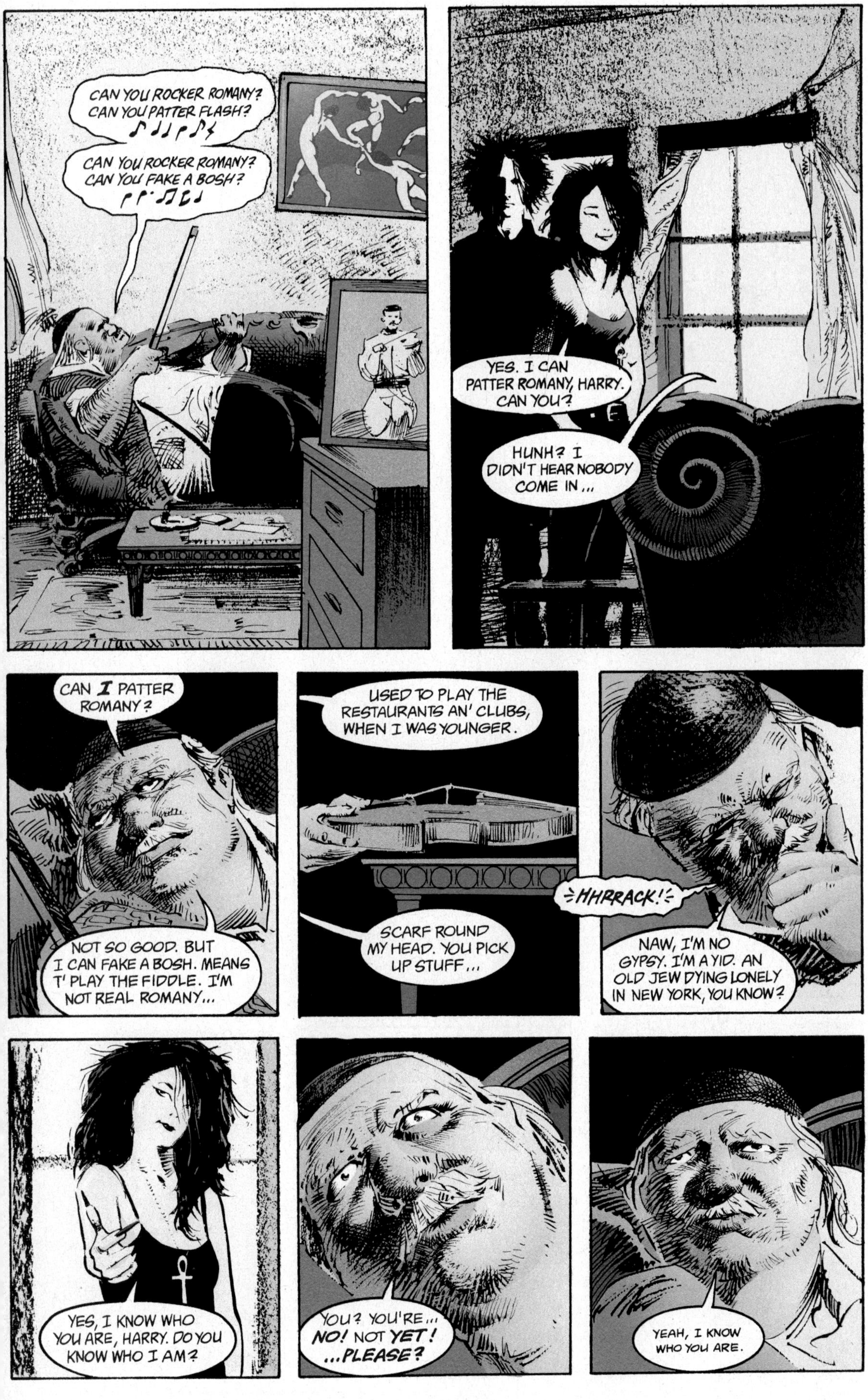
CAN YOU ROCKER ROMANY? CAN YOU PATTER FLASH?
CAN YOU ROCKER ROMANY? CAN YOU FAKE A BOSH?
YES. I CAN PATTER ROMANY, HARRY. CAN YOU?
HUNH? I DIDN'T HEAR NOBODY COME IN...
CAN I PATTER ROMANY?
NOT SO GOOD. BUT I CAN FAKE A BOSH. MEANS T' PLAY THE FIDDLE. I'M NOT REAL ROMANY...
USED TO PLAY THE RESTAURANTS AN' CLUBS, WHEN I WAS YOUNGER.
SCARF ROUND MY HEAD. YOU PICK UP STUFF...
HHRRACK!
NAW, I'M NO GYPSY. I'M A YID. AN OLD JEW DYING LONELY IN NEW YORK, YOU KNOW?
YES, I KNOW WHO YOU ARE, HARRY. DO YOU KNOW WHO I AM?
YOU? YOU'RE... NO! NOT YET! ...PLEASE?
YEAH, I KNOW WHO YOU ARE.

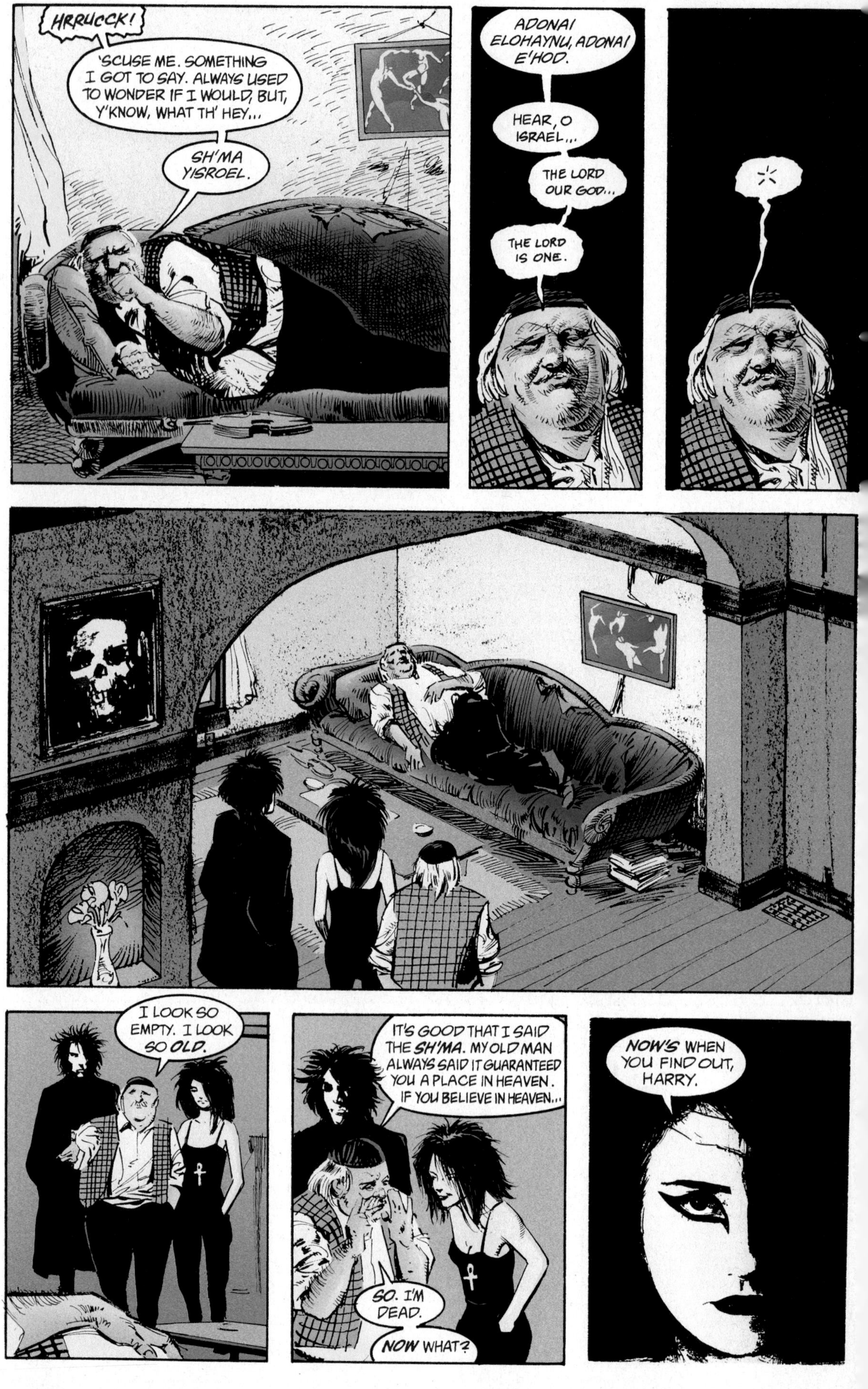
HRRUCCK!
'SCUSE ME. SOMETHING I GOT TO SAY. ALWAYS USED TO WONDER IF I WOULD, BUT, Y'KNOW, WHAT TH' HEY...
SH'MA YISROEL.
ADONAI ELOHAYNU, ADONAI E'HOD.
HEAR, O ISRAEL...
THE LORD OUR GOD...
THE LORD IS ONE.
I LOOK SO EMPTY. I LOOK SO OLD.
IT'S GOOD THAT I SAID THE SH'MA. MY OLD MAN ALWAYS SAID IT GUARANTEED YOU A PLACE IN HEAVEN. IF YOU BELIEVE IN HEAVEN...
SO. I'M DEAD.
NOW WHAT?
NOW'S WHEN YOU FIND OUT, HARRY.

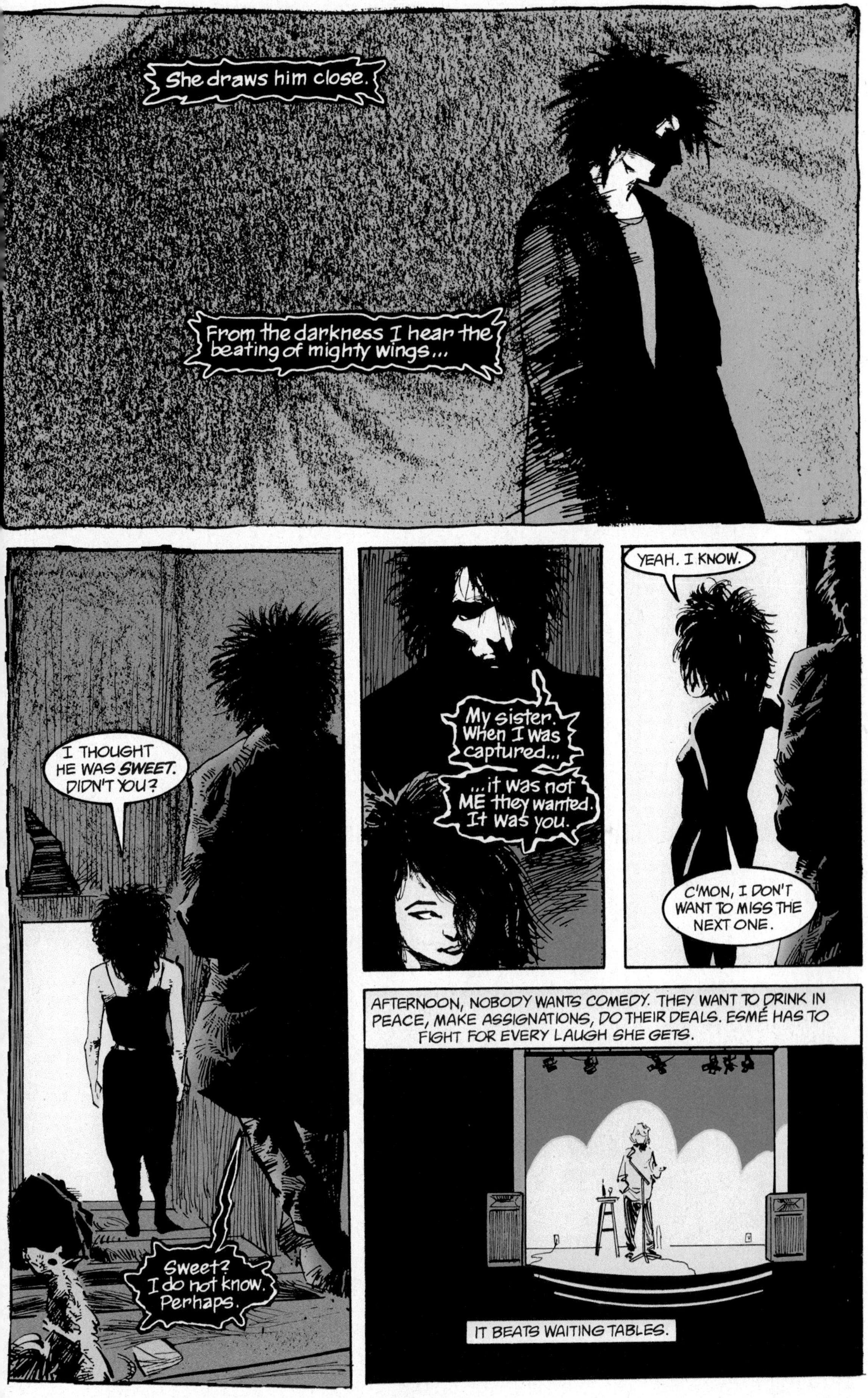
She draws him close.
From the darkness I hear the beating of mighty wings...
I THOUGHT HE WAS SWEET. DIDN'T YOU?
Sweet? I do not know. Perhaps.
My sister. When I was captured...
...it was not ME they wanted. It was you.
YEAH. I KNOW.
C'MON, I DON'T WANT TO MISS THE NEXT ONE.
AFTERNOON, NOBODY WANTS COMEDY. THEY WANT TO DRINK IN PEACE, MAKE ASSIGNATIONS, DO THEIR DEALS. ESMÉ HAS TO FIGHT FOR EVERY LAUGH SHE GETS.
IT BEATS WAITING TABLES.

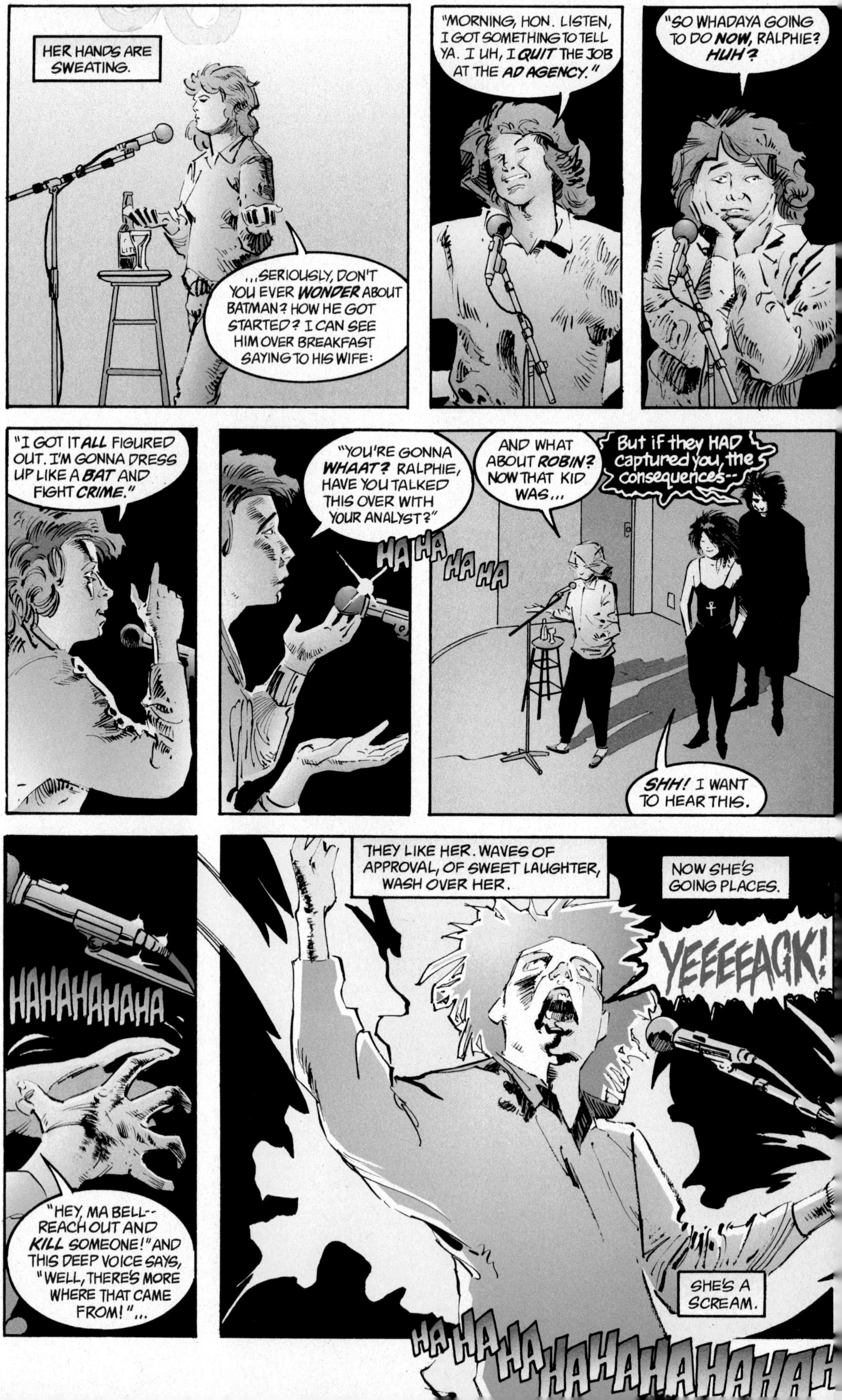
HER HANDS ARE SWEATING.
...SERIOUSLY, DON'T YOU EVER WONDER ABOUT BATMAN? HOW HE GOT STARTED? I CAN SEE HIM OVER BREAKFAST SAYING TO HIS WIFE:
"MORNING, HON. LISTEN, I GOT SOMETHING TO TELL YA. I UH, I QUIT THE JOB AT THE AD AGENCY."
"SO WHADAYA GOING TO DO NOW, RALPHIE? HUH?
"I GOT IT ALL FIGURED OUT. I'M GONNA DRESS UP LIKE A BAT AND FIGHT CRIME."
"YOU'RE GONNA WHAAT? RALPHIE, HAVE YOU TALKED THIS OVER WITH YOUR ANALYST?"
HA HA HA HA
AND WHAT ABOUT ROBIN? NOW THAT KID WAS...
But if they HAD captured you, the consequences--
SHH! I WANT TO HEAR THIS.
HAHAHAHAHA
"HEY, MA BELL-- REACH OUT AND KILL SOMEONE!" AND THIS DEEP VOICE SAYS, "WELL, THERE'S MORE WHERE THAT CAME FROM!"...
THEY LIKE HER. WAVES OF APPROVAL, OF SWEET LAUGHTER, WASH OVER HER.
NOW SHE'S GOING PLACES.
YEEEEAGK!
SHE'S A SCREAM.
HA HA HA HAHAHAHAHAHAH

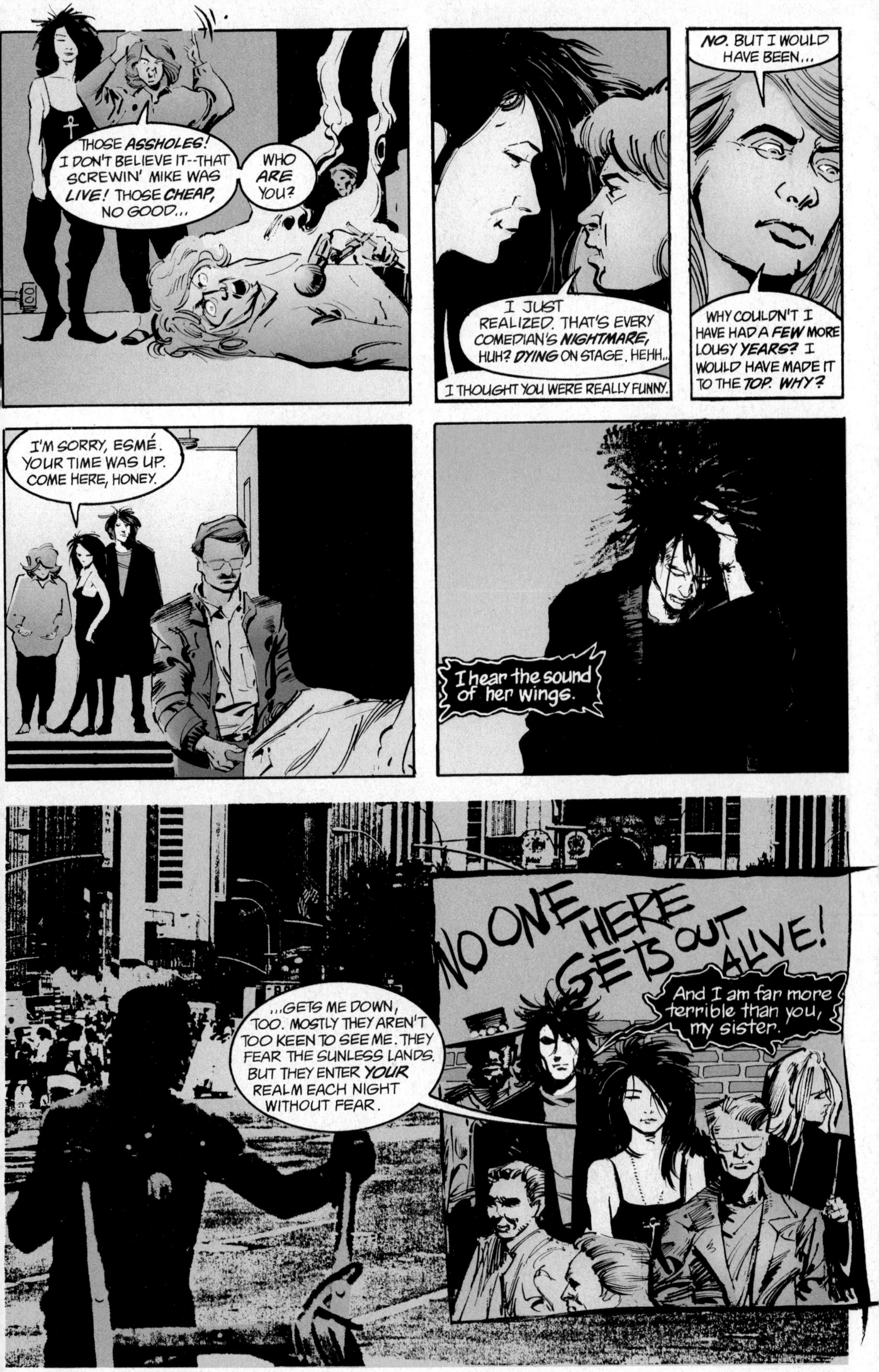
THOSE ASSHOLES! I DON'T BELIEVE IT--THAT SCREWIN' MIKE WAS LIVE! THOSE CHEAP, NO GOOD...
WHO ARE YOU?
I JUST REALIZED. THAT'S EVERY COMEDIAN'S NIGHTMARE, HUH? DYING ON STAGE. HEHH...
I THOUGHT YOU WERE REALLY FUNNY.
NO. BUT I WOULD HAVE BEEN...
WHY COULDN'T I HAVE HAD A FEW MORE LOUSY YEARS? I WOULD HAVE MADE IT TO THE TOP. WHY?
I'M SORRY, ESMÉ. YOUR TIME WAS UP. COME HERE, HONEY.
I hear the sound of her wings.
...GETS ME DOWN, TOO. MOSTLY THEY AREN'T TOO KEEN TO SEE ME. THEY FEAR THE SUNLESS LANDS. BUT THEY ENTER YOUR REALM EACH NIGHT WITHOUT FEAR.
NO ONE HERE GETS OUT ALIVE!
And I am far more terrible than you, my sister.

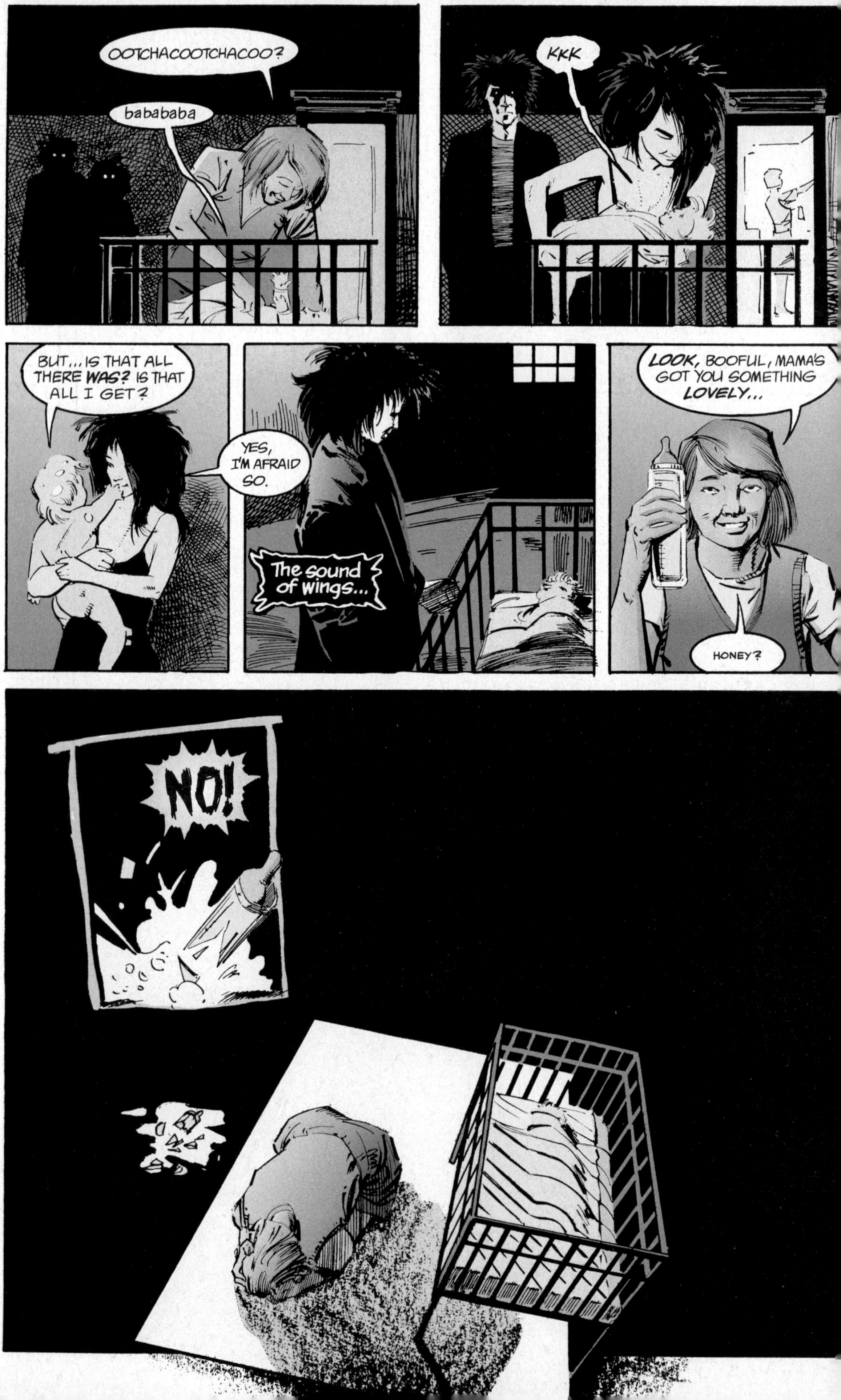
OOTCHACOOTCHACOO?
bababababa
KKK
BUT... IS THAT ALL THERE WAS? IS THAT ALL I GET?
YES, I'M AFRAID SO.
The sound of wings...
LOOK, BOOFUL, MAMA'S GOT YOU SOMETHING LOVELY...
HONEY?
NO!

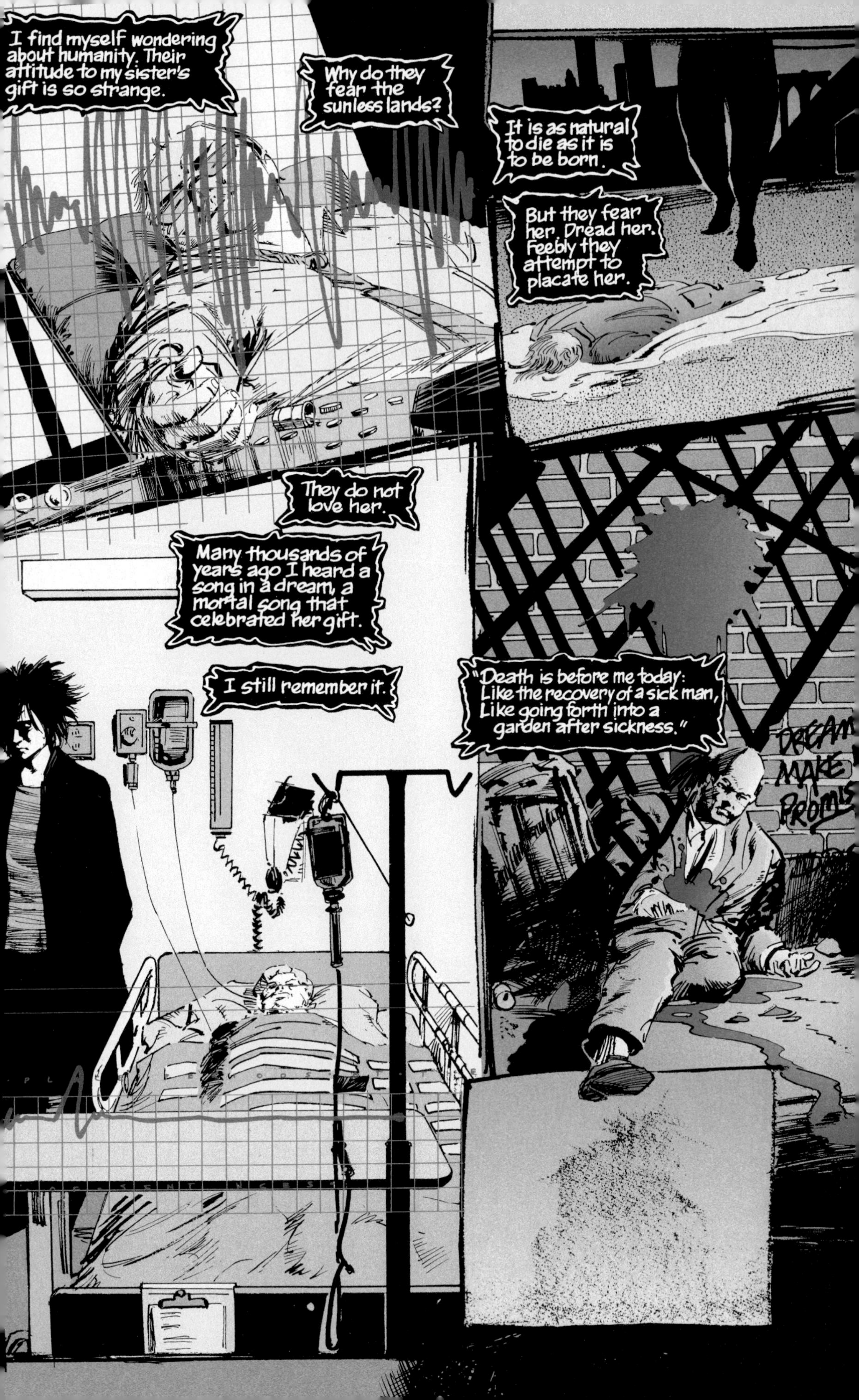
I find myself wondering about humanity. Their attitude to my sister's gift is so strange.
Why do they fear the sunless lands?
It is as natural to die as it is to be born.
But they fear her. Dread her. Feebly they attempt to placate her.
They do not love her.
Many thousands of years ago I heard a song in a dream, a mortal song that celebrated her gift.
I still remember it.
"Death is before me today: Like the recovery of a sick man, Like going forth into a garden after sickness."
DREAM
MAKE

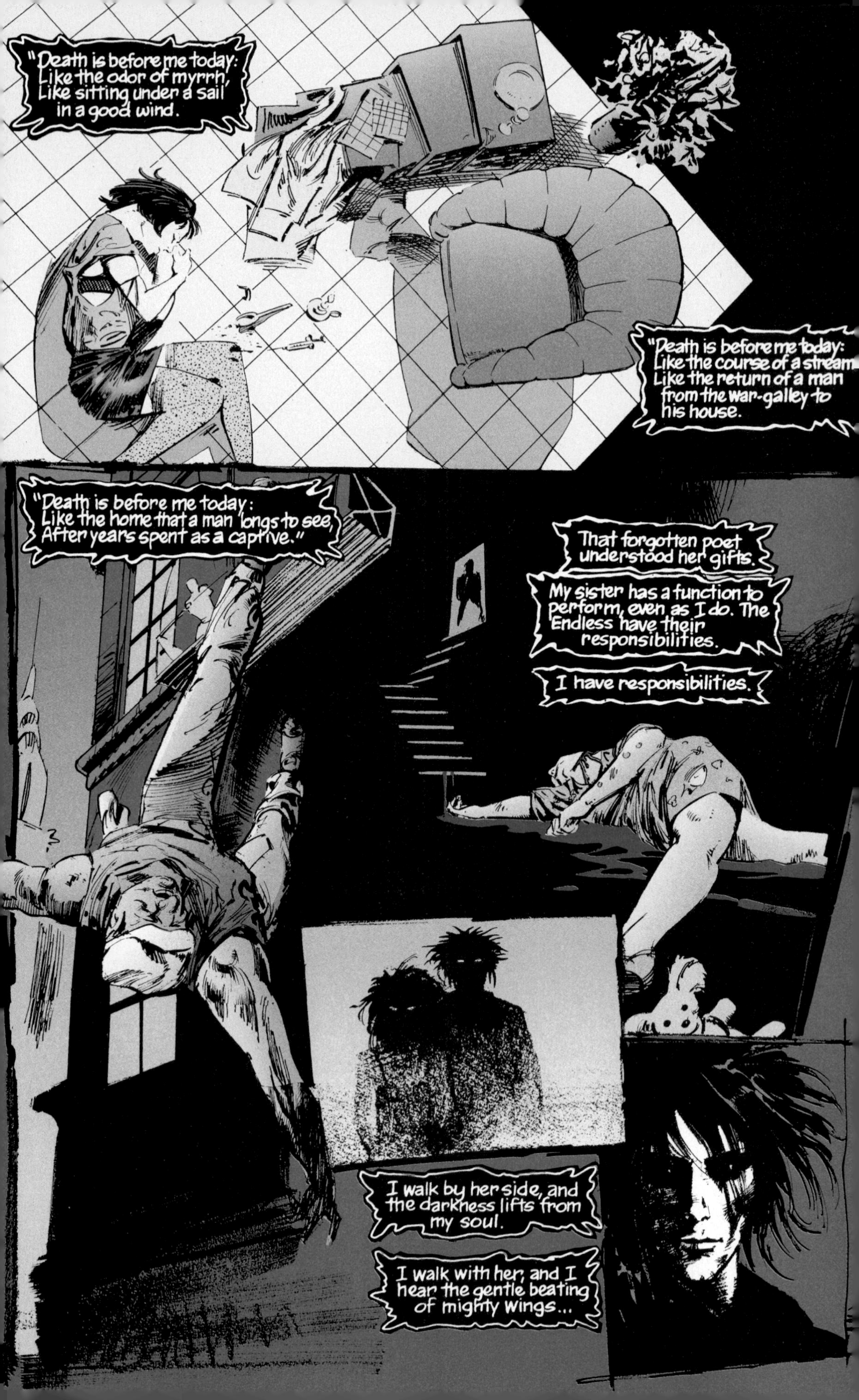
"Death is before me today: Like the odor of myrrh, Like sitting under a sail in a good wind.
"Death is before me today: Like the course of a stream Like the return of a man from the war-galley to his house.
"Death is before me today: Like the home that a man longs to see, After years spent as a captive."
That forgotten poet understood her gifts.
My sister has a function to perform, even as I do. The Endless have their responsibilities.
I have responsibilities.
I walk by her side, and the darkness lifts from my soul.
I walk with her, and I hear the gentle beating of mighty wings...

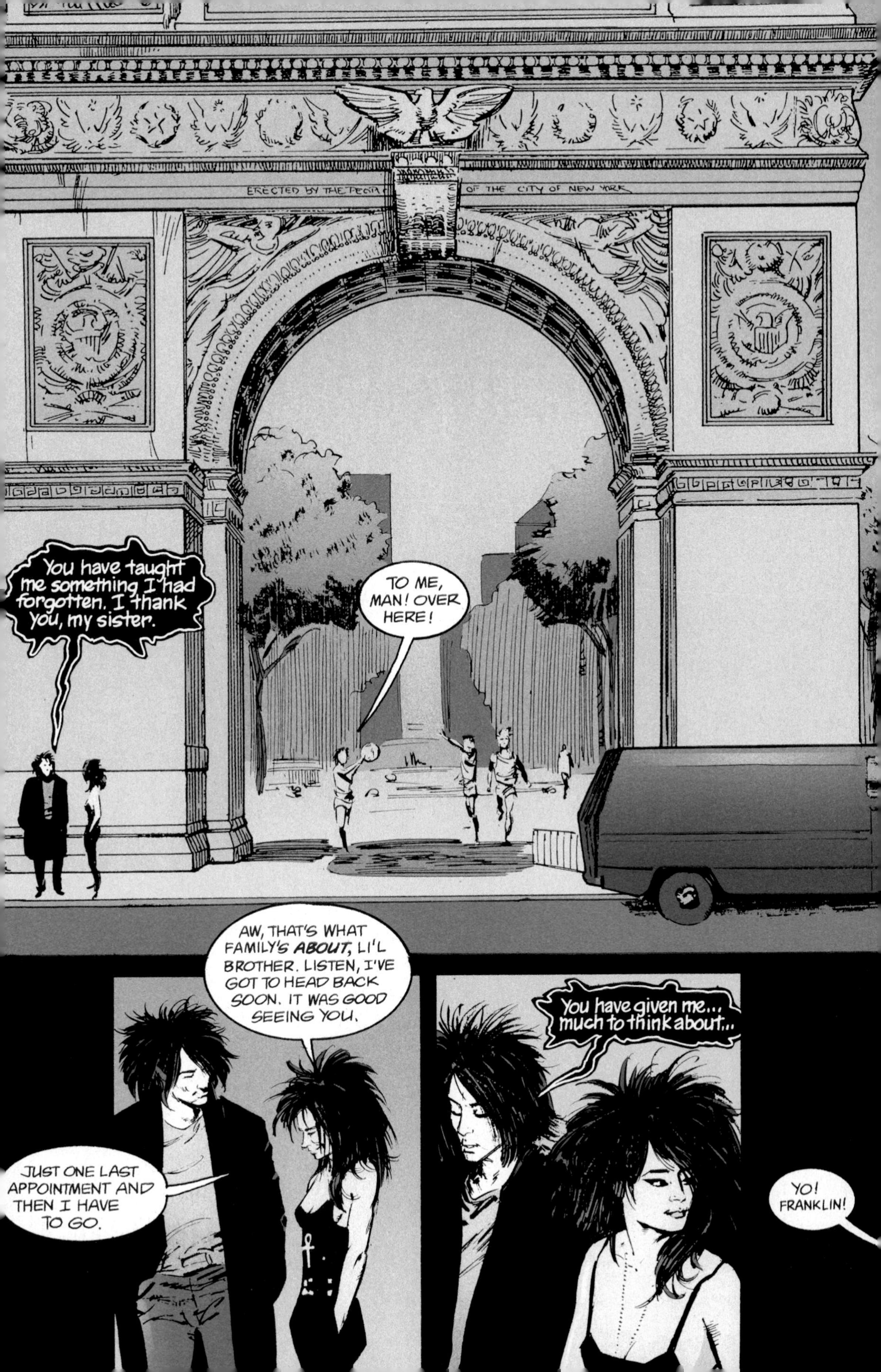
ERECTED BY THE PEOPLE OF THE CITY OF NEW YORK
You have taught me something I had forgotten. I thank you, my sister.
TO ME, MAN! OVER HERE!
AW, THAT'S WHAT FAMILY'S ABOUT, LI'L BROTHER. LISTEN, I'VE GOT TO HEAD BACK SOON. IT WAS GOOD SEEING YOU.
JUST ONE LAST APPOINTMENT AND THEN I HAVE TO GO.
You have given me... much to think about...
YO! FRANKLIN!

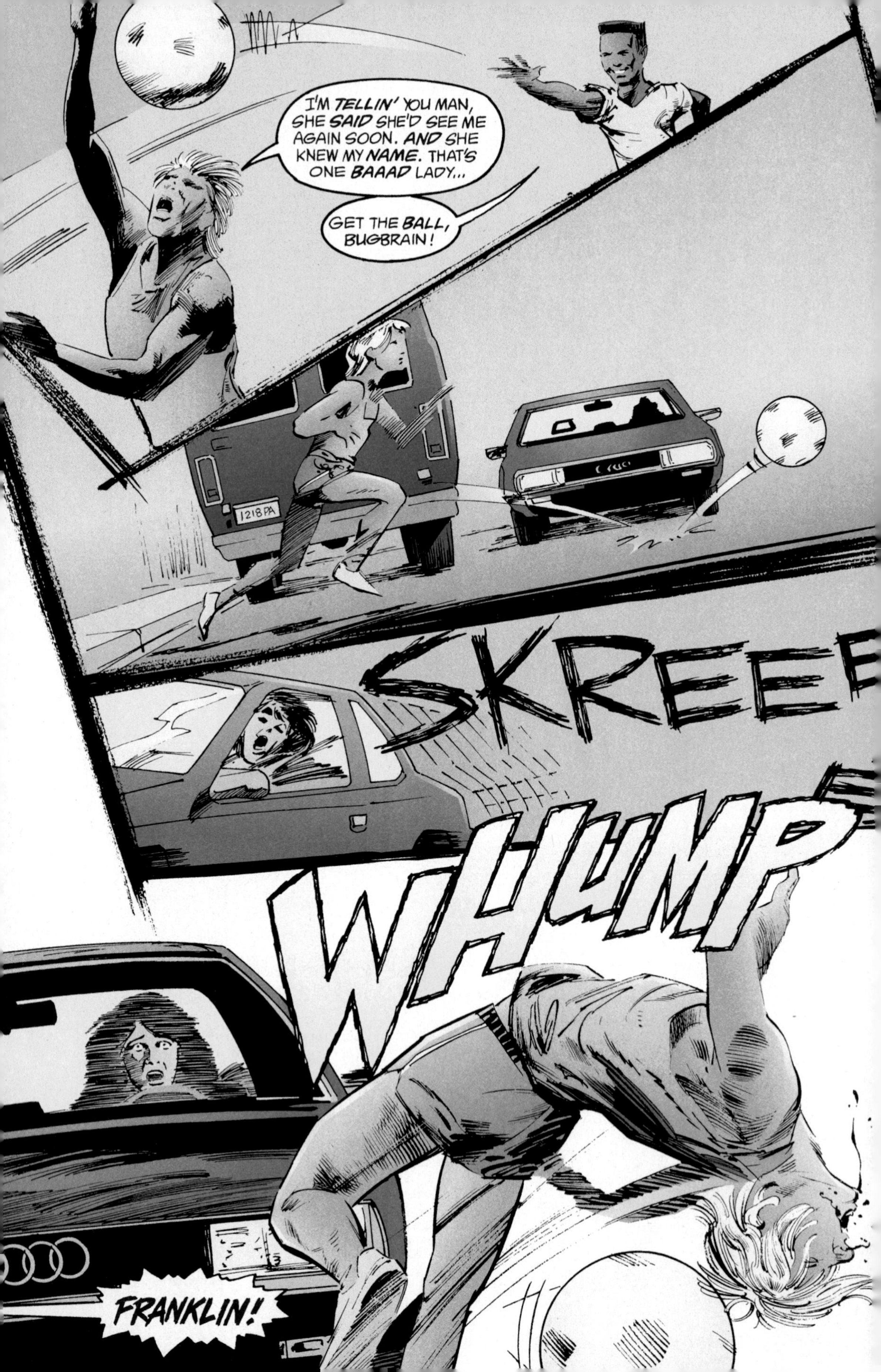
I'M TELLIN' YOU MAN, SHE SAID SHE'D SEE ME AGAIN SOON. AND SHE KNEW MY NAME. THAT'S ONE BAAAD LADY...
GET THE BALL, BUGBRAIN!
1218 PA
SKREEE
WHUMP
FRANKLIN!

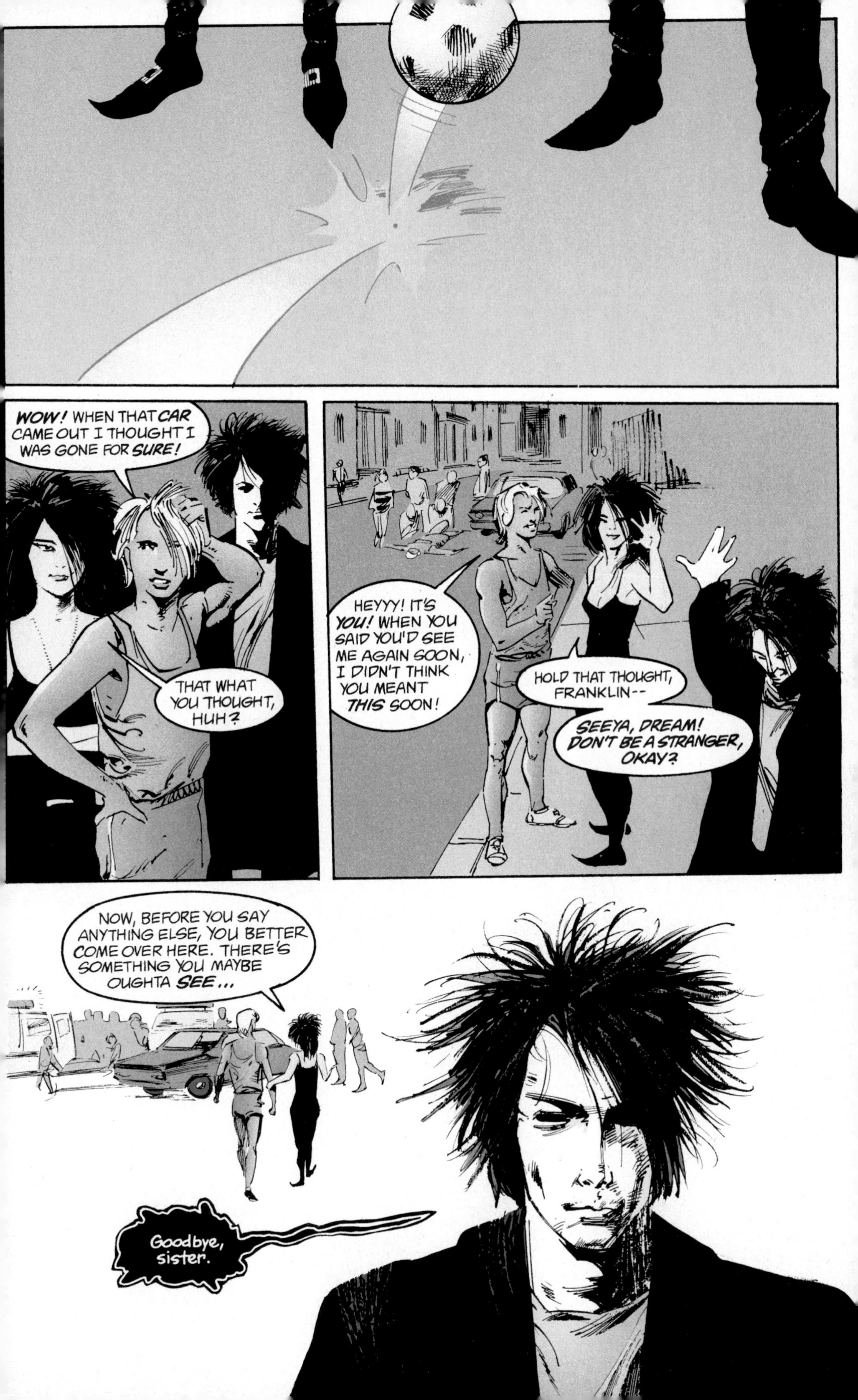
WOW! WHEN THAT CAR CAME OUT I THOUGHT I WAS GONE FOR SURE!
THAT WHAT YOU THOUGHT, HUH?
HEYYY! IT'S YOU! WHEN YOU SAID YOU'D SEE ME AGAIN SOON, I DIDN'T THINK YOU MEANT THIS SOON!
HOLD THAT THOUGHT, FRANKLIN--
SEEYA, DREAM! DON'T BE A STRANGER, OKAY?
NOW, BEFORE YOU SAY ANYTHING ELSE, YOU BETTER COME OVER HERE. THERE'S SOMETHING YOU MAYBE OUGHTA SEE...
Goodbye, sister.

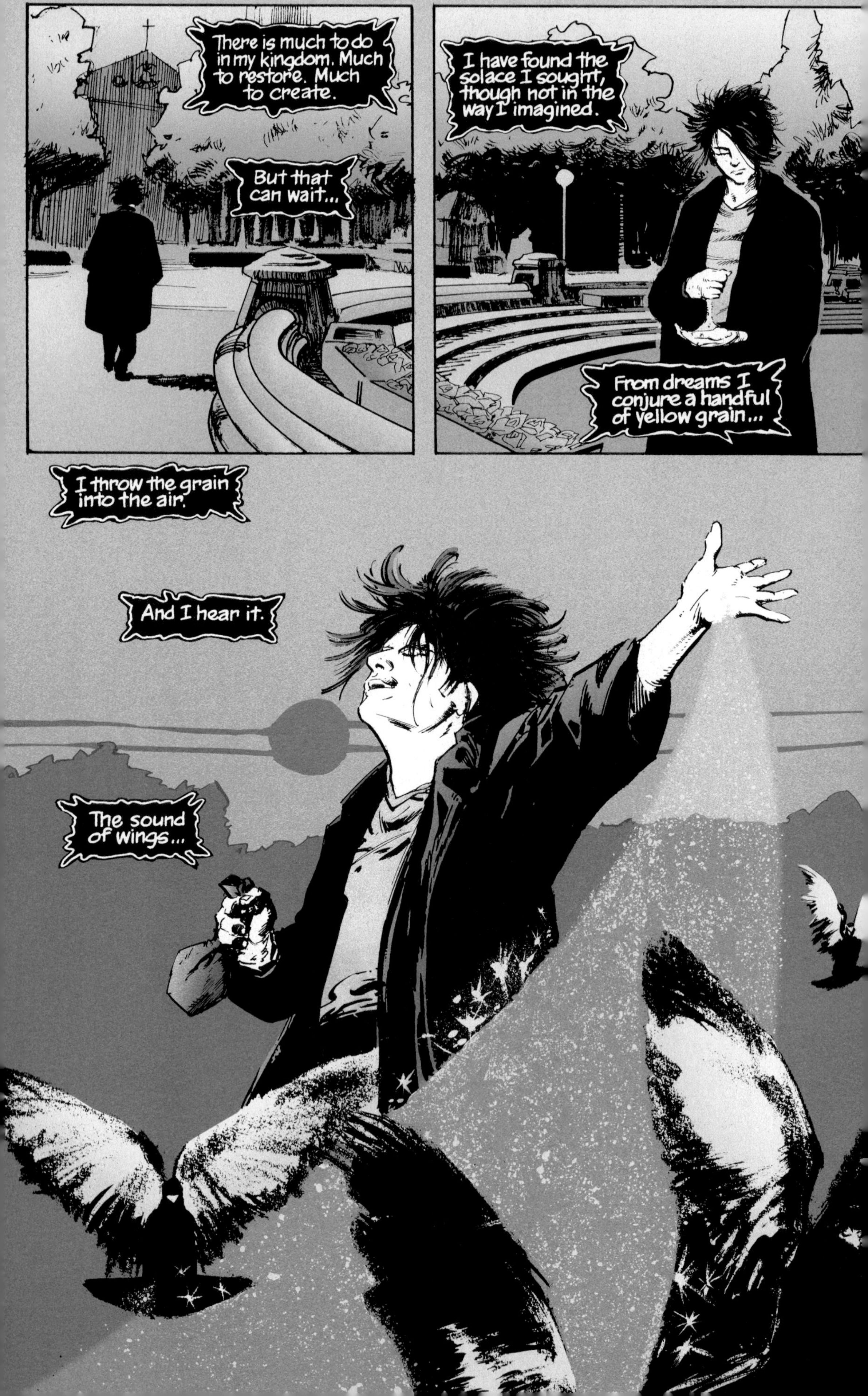
There is much to do in my kingdom. Much to restore. Much to create.
But that can wait...
I have found the solace I sought, though not in the way I imagined.
From dreams I conjure a handful of yellow grain...
I throw the grain into the air.
And I hear it.
The sound of wings...

Dreams and visions are infused into men for
their advantage and instruction...
—Artemidoros at Daldus, *Oneirocritica*, second century AD

Dreams are weird and stupid and they scare me.
—Rose Walker, April 1990

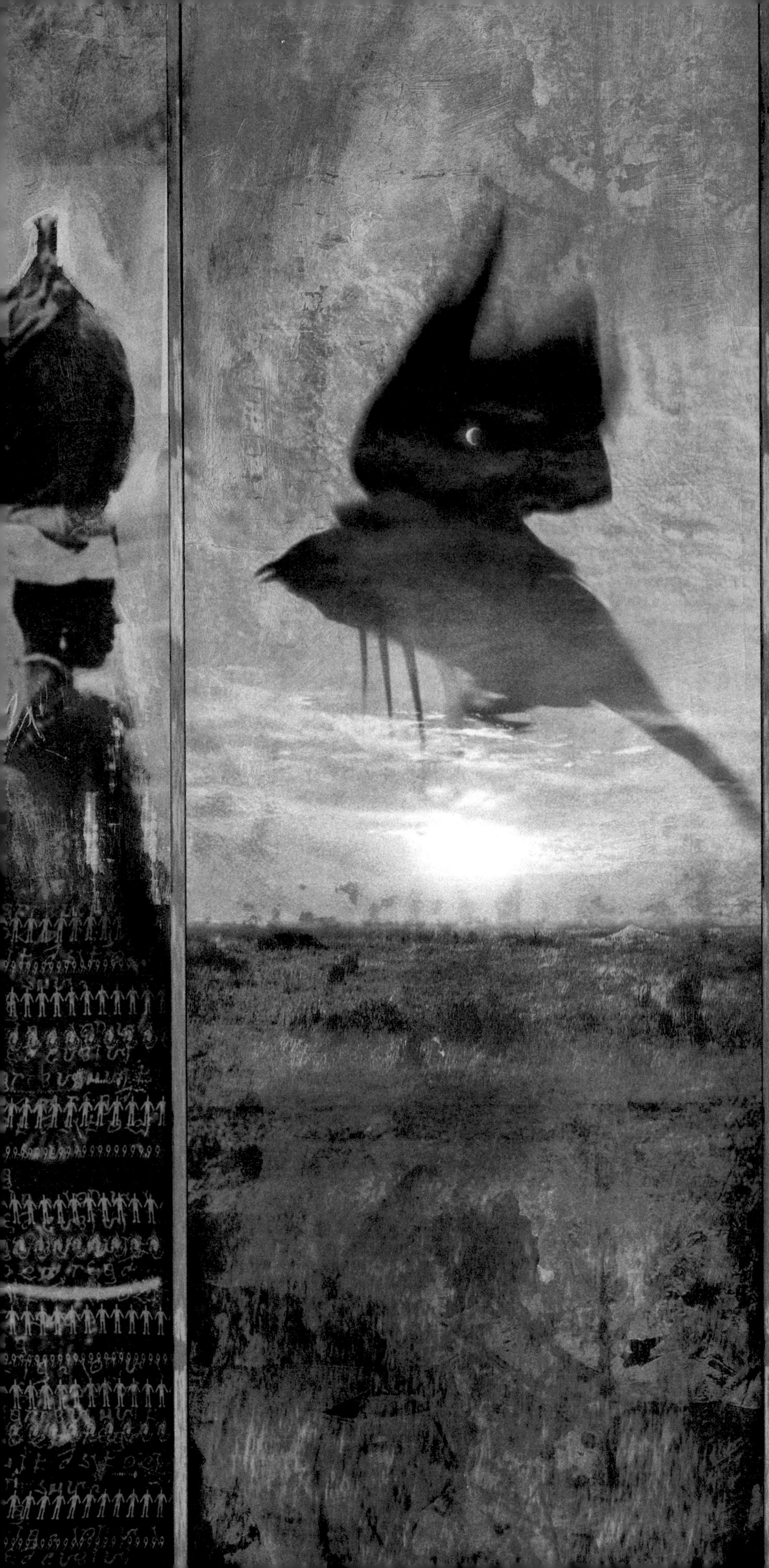

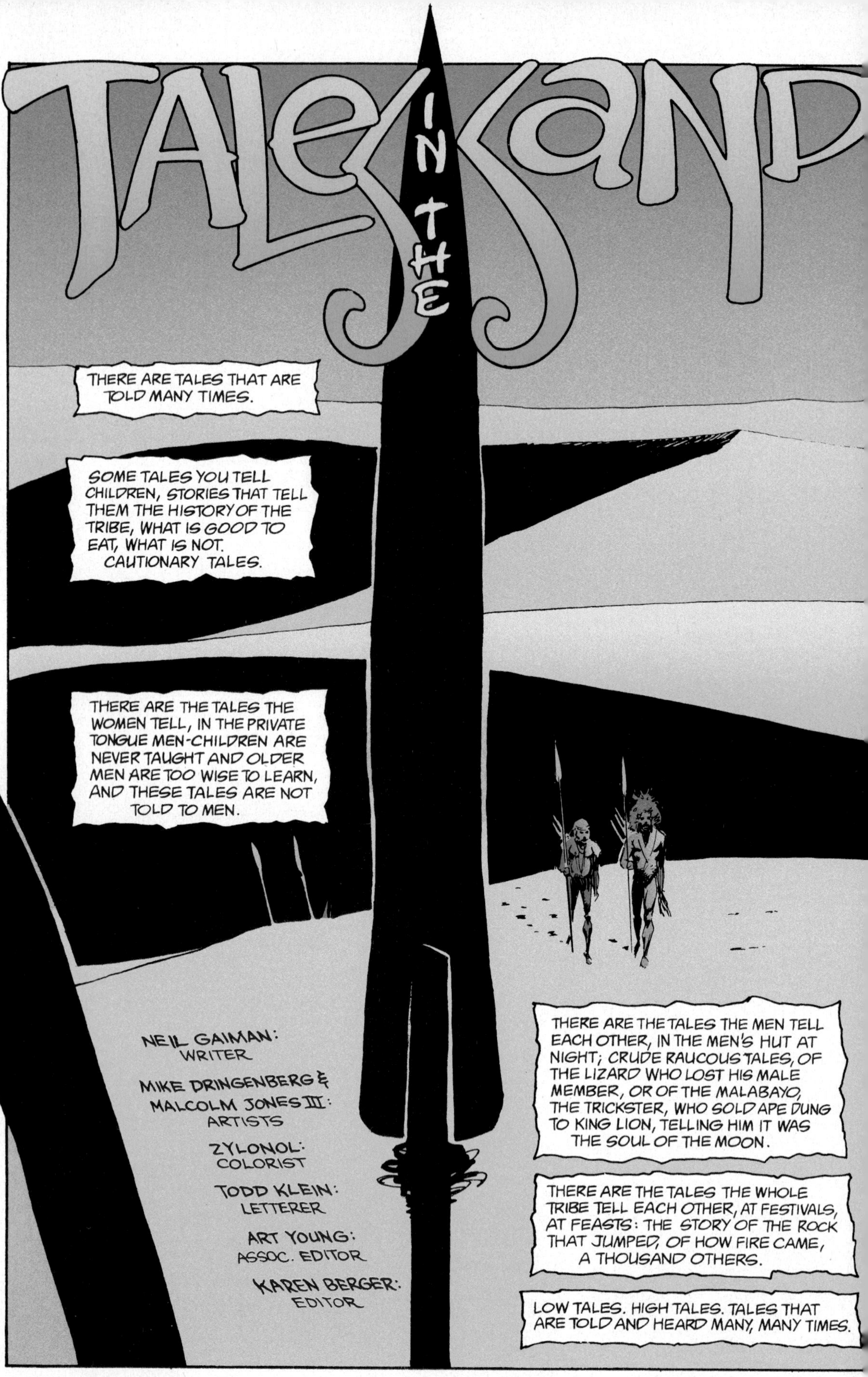
TALES IN THE SAND
THERE ARE TALES THAT ARE TOLD MANY TIMES.
SOME TALES YOU TELL CHILDREN, STORIES THAT TELL THEM THE HISTORY OF THE TRIBE, WHAT IS GOOD TO EAT, WHAT IS NOT. CAUTIONARY TALES.
THERE ARE THE TALES THE WOMEN TELL, IN THE PRIVATE TONGUE MEN-CHILDREN ARE NEVER TAUGHT AND OLDER MEN ARE TOO WISE TO LEARN, AND THESE TALES ARE NOT TOLD TO MEN.
NEIL GAIMAN: WRITER
MIKE DRINGENBERG & MALCOLM JONES III: ARTISTS
ZYLONOL: COLORIST
TODD KLEIN: LETTERER
ART YOUNG: ASSOC. EDITOR
KAREN BERGER: EDITOR
THERE ARE THE TALES THE MEN TELL EACH OTHER, IN THE MEN'S HUT AT NIGHT; CRUDE RAUCOUS TALES, OF THE LIZARD WHO LOST HIS MALE MEMBER, OR OF THE MALABAYO, THE TRICKSTER, WHO SOLD APE DUNG TO KING LION, TELLING HIM IT WAS THE SOUL OF THE MOON.
THERE ARE THE TALES THE WHOLE TRIBE TELL EACH OTHER, AT FESTIVALS, AT FEASTS: THE STORY OF THE ROCK THAT JUMPED, OF HOW FIRE CAME, A THOUSAND OTHERS.
LOW TALES. HIGH TALES. TALES THAT ARE TOLD AND HEARD MANY, MANY TIMES.

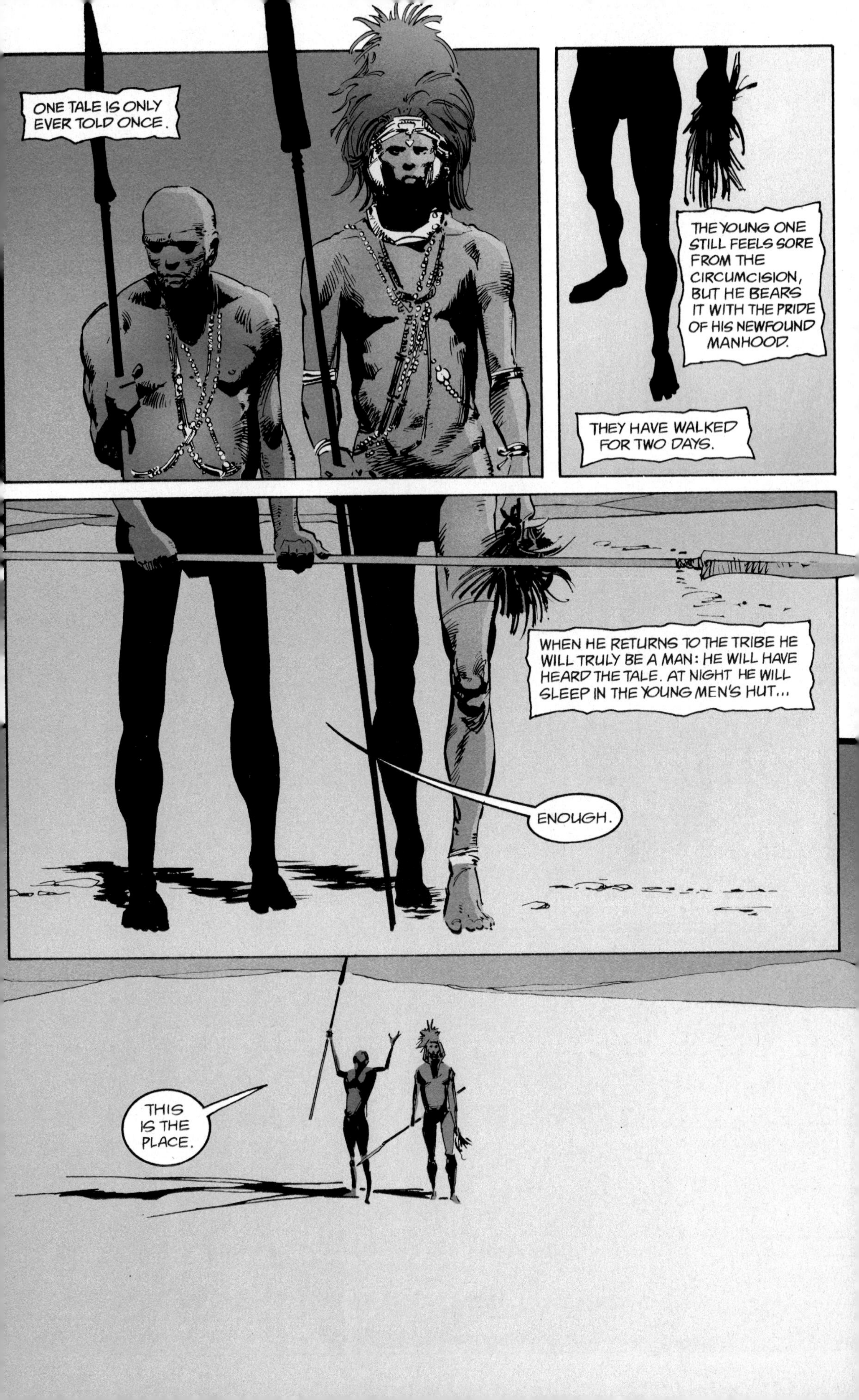
ONE TALE IS ONLY EVER TOLD ONCE.
THE YOUNG ONE STILL FEELS SORE FROM THE CIRCUMCISION, BUT HE BEARS IT WITH THE PRIDE OF HIS NEWFOUND MANHOOD.
THEY HAVE WALKED FOR TWO DAYS.
WHEN HE RETURNS TO THE TRIBE HE WILL TRULY BE A MAN: HE WILL HAVE HEARD THE TALE. AT NIGHT HE WILL SLEEP IN THE YOUNG MEN'S HUT...
ENOUGH.
THIS IS THE PLACE.

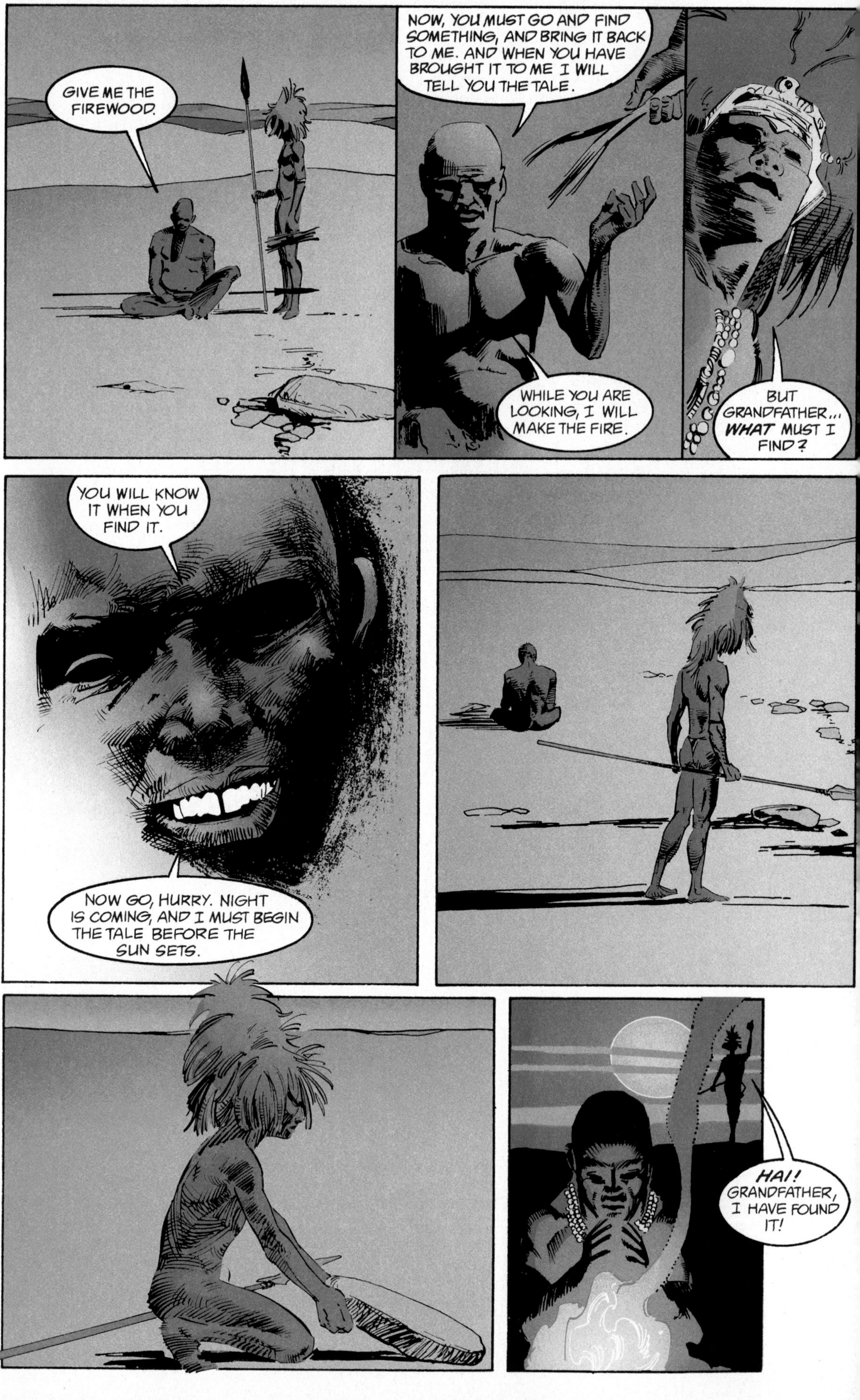
GIVE ME THE FIREWOOD.
NOW, YOU MUST GO AND FIND SOMETHING, AND BRING IT BACK TO ME. AND WHEN YOU HAVE BROUGHT IT TO ME I WILL TELL YOU THE TALE.
WHILE YOU ARE LOOKING, I WILL MAKE THE FIRE.
BUT GRANDFATHER... WHAT MUST I FIND?
YOU WILL KNOW IT WHEN YOU FIND IT.
NOW GO, HURRY. NIGHT IS COMING, AND I MUST BEGIN THE TALE BEFORE THE SUN SETS.
HAI! GRANDFATHER, I HAVE FOUND IT!

BUT WHAT IS IT?

GIVE IT TO ME.

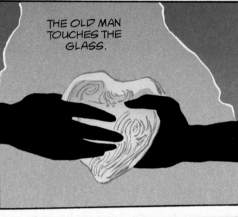

THE OLD MAN TOUCHES THE GLASS.

HE REMEMBERS, FLEETINGLY, THE TIME HIS MOTHER'S BROTHER TOOK HIM OUT TO THIS PLACE, SENT HIM TO FIND A SIMILAR SHARD...

AND THEN HE BEGINS TO TELL THE TALE.

THIS GLASS WAS ONCE PART OF A CITY. IF YOU LOOK AROUND IN THIS PLACE YOU WILL FIND OTHER SHARDS LIKE IT.

IT IS FORBIDDEN TO TAKE THEM FROM THIS PLACE.

I WILL TELL YOU OF THAT CITY, AND OF HOW IT WAS LOST TO US...

AND ONE DAY, IF YOU LIVE LONG ENOUGH, YOU WILL BRING ONE OTHER OUT HERE, AND TELL HIM THE TALE.

FOR THIS IS THE WAY IT HAS ALWAYS BEEN. EACH OF US HEARS THE TALE ONCE, IN THIS PLACE. AND EACH OF US TELLS THE STORY ONCE IN THIS PLACE...

...IF GRANDMOTHER DEATH SPARES US LONG ENOUGH TO TELL IT...

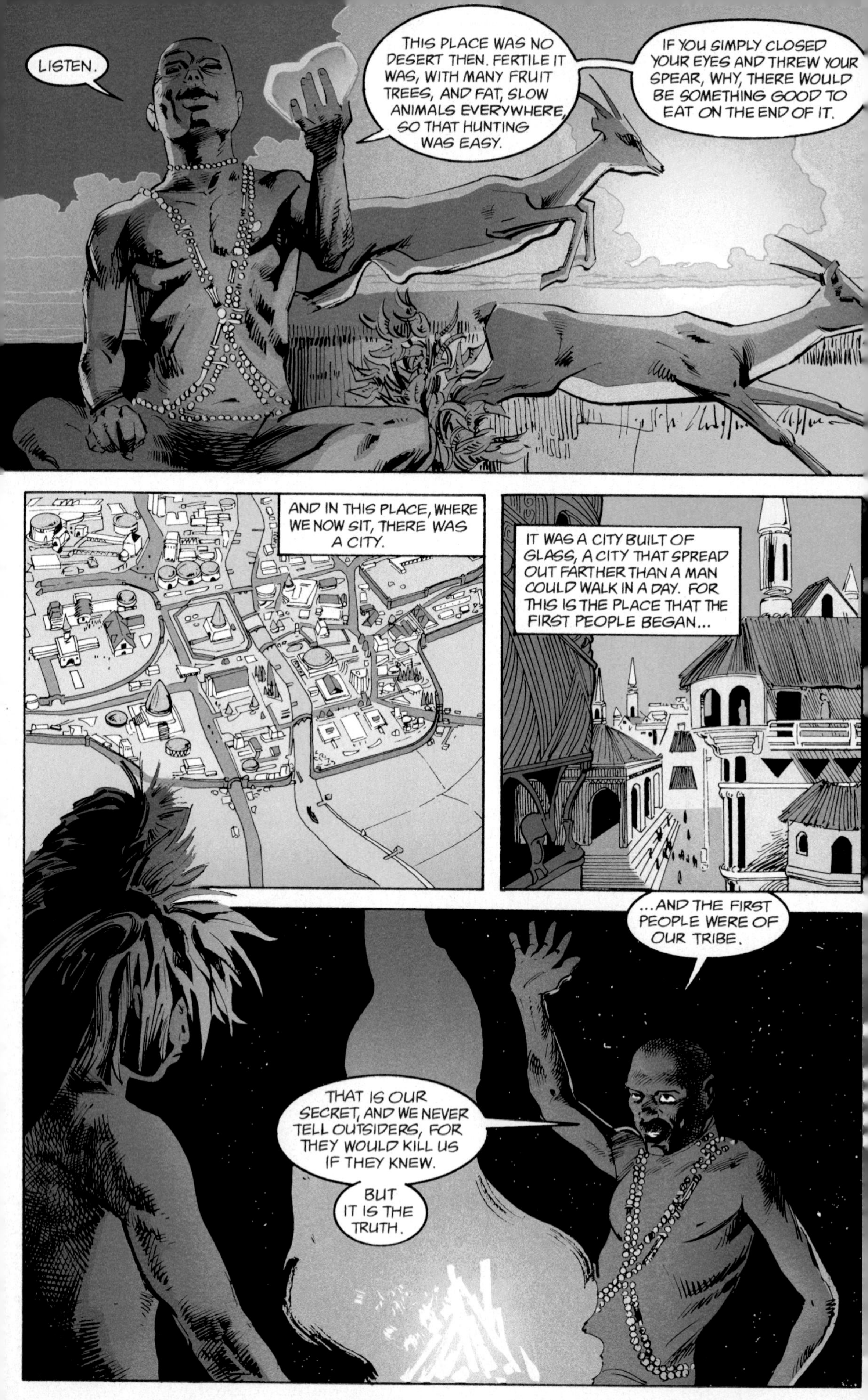
LISTEN.
THIS PLACE WAS NO DESERT THEN. FERTILE IT WAS, WITH MANY FRUIT TREES, AND FAT, SLOW ANIMALS EVERYWHERE, SO THAT HUNTING WAS EASY.
IF YOU SIMPLY CLOSED YOUR EYES AND THREW YOUR SPEAR, WHY, THERE WOULD BE SOMETHING GOOD TO EAT ON THE END OF IT.
AND IN THIS PLACE, WHERE WE NOW SIT, THERE WAS A CITY.
IT WAS A CITY BUILT OF GLASS, A CITY THAT SPREAD OUT FARTHER THAN A MAN COULD WALK IN A DAY. FOR THIS IS THE PLACE THAT THE FIRST PEOPLE BEGAN...
...AND THE FIRST PEOPLE WERE OF OUR TRIBE.
THAT IS OUR SECRET, AND WE NEVER TELL OUTSIDERS, FOR THEY WOULD KILL US IF THEY KNEW.
BUT IT IS THE TRUTH.

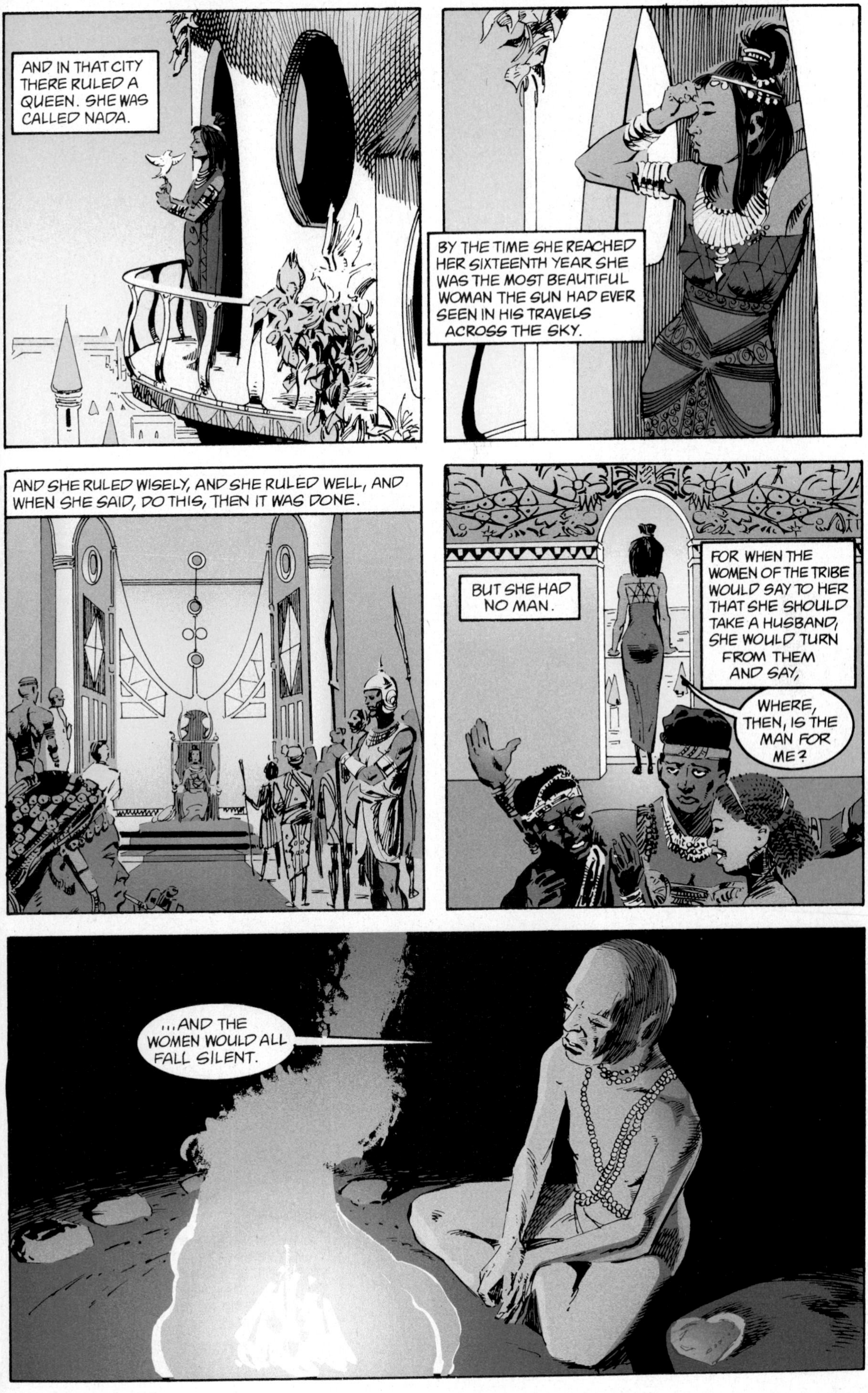
AND IN THAT CITY THERE RULED A QUEEN. SHE WAS CALLED NADA.
BY THE TIME SHE REACHED HER SIXTEENTH YEAR SHE WAS THE MOST BEAUTIFUL WOMAN THE SUN HAD EVER SEEN IN HIS TRAVELS ACROSS THE SKY.
AND SHE RULED WISELY, AND SHE RULED WELL, AND WHEN SHE SAID, DO THIS, THEN IT WAS DONE.
BUT SHE HAD NO MAN.
FOR WHEN THE WOMEN OF THE TRIBE WOULD SAY TO HER THAT SHE SHOULD TAKE A HUSBAND, SHE WOULD TURN FROM THEM AND SAY,
WHERE, THEN, IS THE MAN FOR ME?
...AND THE WOMEN WOULD ALL FALL SILENT.

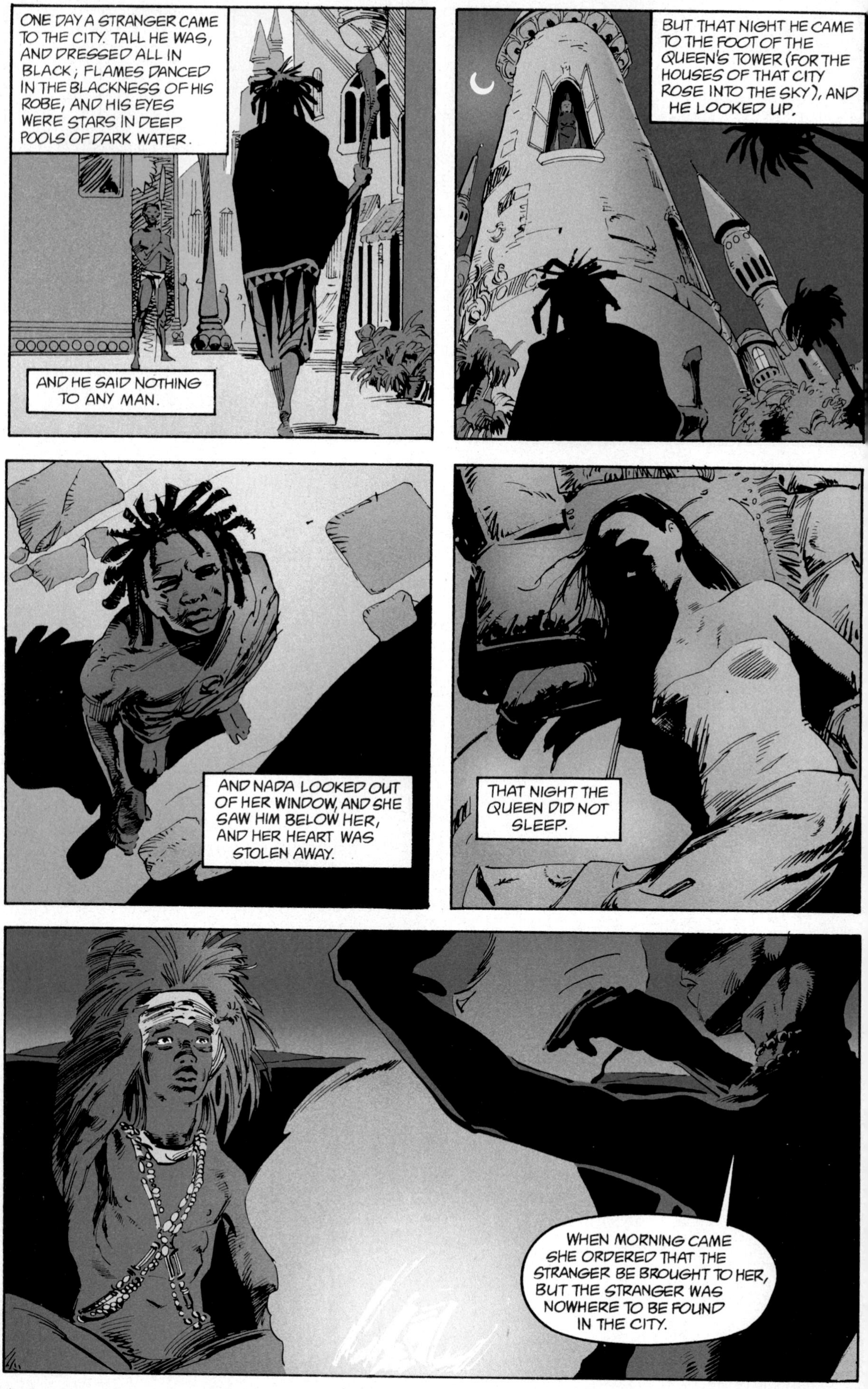
ONE DAY A STRANGER CAME TO THE CITY. TALL HE WAS, AND DRESSED ALL IN BLACK; FLAMES DANCED IN THE BLACKNESS OF HIS ROBE, AND HIS EYES WERE STARS IN DEEP POOLS OF DARK WATER.
AND HE SAID NOTHING TO ANY MAN.
BUT THAT NIGHT HE CAME TO THE FOOT OF THE QUEEN'S TOWER (FOR THE HOUSES OF THAT CITY ROSE INTO THE SKY), AND HE LOOKED UP.
AND NADA LOOKED OUT OF HER WINDOW, AND SHE SAW HIM BELOW HER, AND HER HEART WAS STOLEN AWAY.
THAT NIGHT THE QUEEN DID NOT SLEEP.
WHEN MORNING CAME SHE ORDERED THAT THE STRANGER BE BROUGHT TO HER, BUT THE STRANGER WAS NOWHERE TO BE FOUND IN THE CITY.

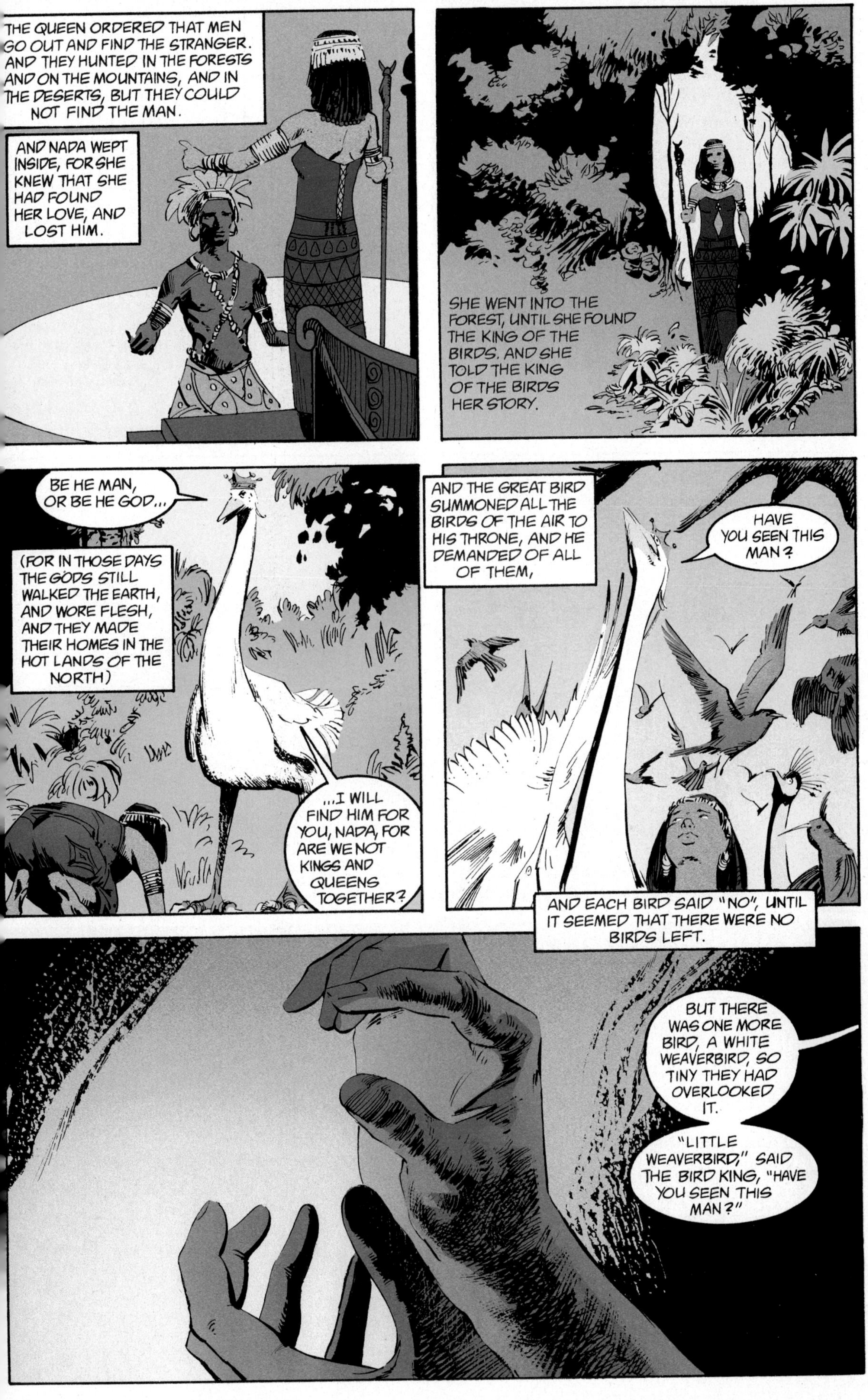
THE QUEEN ORDERED THAT MEN GO OUT AND FIND THE STRANGER. AND THEY HUNTED IN THE FORESTS AND ON THE MOUNTAINS, AND IN THE DESERTS, BUT THEY COULD NOT FIND THE MAN.
AND NADA WEPT INSIDE, FOR SHE KNEW THAT SHE HAD FOUND HER LOVE, AND LOST HIM.
SHE WENT INTO THE FOREST, UNTIL SHE FOUND THE KING OF THE BIRDS. AND SHE TOLD THE KING OF THE BIRDS HER STORY.
BE HE MAN, OR BE HE GOD...
(FOR IN THOSE DAYS THE GODS STILL WALKED THE EARTH, AND WORE FLESH, AND THEY MADE THEIR HOMES IN THE HOT LANDS OF THE NORTH)
...I WILL FIND HIM FOR YOU, NADA, FOR ARE WE NOT KINGS AND QUEENS TOGETHER?
AND THE GREAT BIRD SUMMONED ALL THE BIRDS OF THE AIR TO HIS THRONE, AND HE DEMANDED OF ALL OF THEM,
HAVE YOU SEEN THIS MAN?
AND EACH BIRD SAID "NO", UNTIL IT SEEMED THAT THERE WERE NO BIRDS LEFT.
BUT THERE WAS ONE MORE BIRD, A WHITE WEAVERBIRD, SO TINY THEY HAD OVERLOOKED IT.
"LITTLE WEAVERBIRD," SAID THE BIRD KING, "HAVE YOU SEEN THIS MAN?"

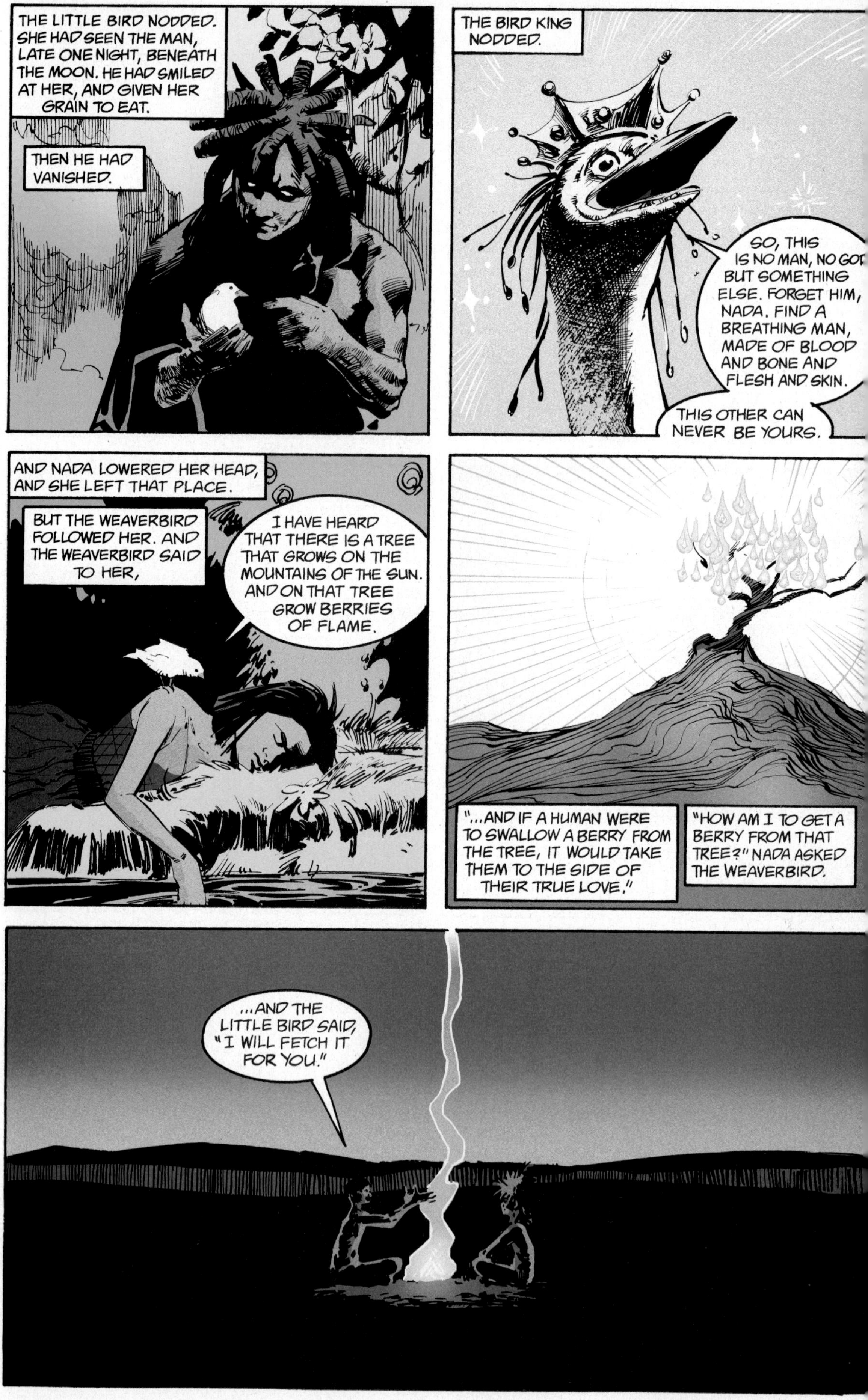
THE LITTLE BIRD NODDED. SHE HAD SEEN THE MAN, LATE ONE NIGHT, BENEATH THE MOON. HE HAD SMILED AT HER, AND GIVEN HER GRAIN TO EAT.
THEN HE HAD VANISHED.
THE BIRD KING NODDED.
SO, THIS IS NO MAN, NO GOD BUT SOMETHING ELSE. FORGET HIM, NADA. FIND A BREATHING MAN, MADE OF BLOOD AND BONE AND FLESH AND SKIN.
THIS OTHER CAN NEVER BE YOURS.
AND NADA LOWERED HER HEAD, AND SHE LEFT THAT PLACE.
BUT THE WEAVERBIRD FOLLOWED HER. AND THE WEAVERBIRD SAID TO HER,
I HAVE HEARD THAT THERE IS A TREE THAT GROWS ON THE MOUNTAINS OF THE SUN. AND ON THAT TREE GROW BERRIES OF FLAME.
"...AND IF A HUMAN WERE TO SWALLOW A BERRY FROM THE TREE, IT WOULD TAKE THEM TO THE SIDE OF THEIR TRUE LOVE."
"HOW AM I TO GET A BERRY FROM THAT TREE?" NADA ASKED THE WEAVERBIRD.
...AND THE LITTLE BIRD SAID, "I WILL FETCH IT FOR YOU."

THE LITTLE BIRD FLEW UP INTO THE SKY. IT FLEW SO HIGH IT VANISHED FROM SIGHT, WHILE THE QUEEN WAITED BELOW.

FOR A DAY SHE WAITED, AND AT THE END OF THE DAY SHE SAW A TINY SPECK IN THE SKY ABOVE HER.

IT WAS THE WEAVERBIRD, BUT IT HAD BEEN BURNT A DEEP BROWN BY THE HEAT OF THE SUN, AND IN ITS BEAK IT CARRIED A BERRY FROM THE TREES THAT GROW ON THE MOUNTAINS OF THE SUN.

(THAT IS WHY TO THIS DAY THE WEAVERBIRD IS BROWN.)

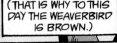

THE WEAVERBIRD DROPPED THE FLAMING BERRY OF THE SUN-TREE ON THE GROUND IN FRONT OF NADA, AND THE QUEEN PICKED UP THE WEAVER-BIRD, AND SAID TO IT...

FOR WHAT YOU HAVE DONE, NO ONE OF THIS LAND WILL EVER HARM YOU OR YOUR KIND, LITTLE BIRD.

SO IT IS FORBIDDEN TO EAT WEAVERBIRD FLESH, OR TO HARM A WEAVERBIRD, AND THAT IS WHY WE LET THEM WEAVE THEIR NESTS IN OUR VILLAGES.

AND NADA WENT BACK TO HER PALACE...

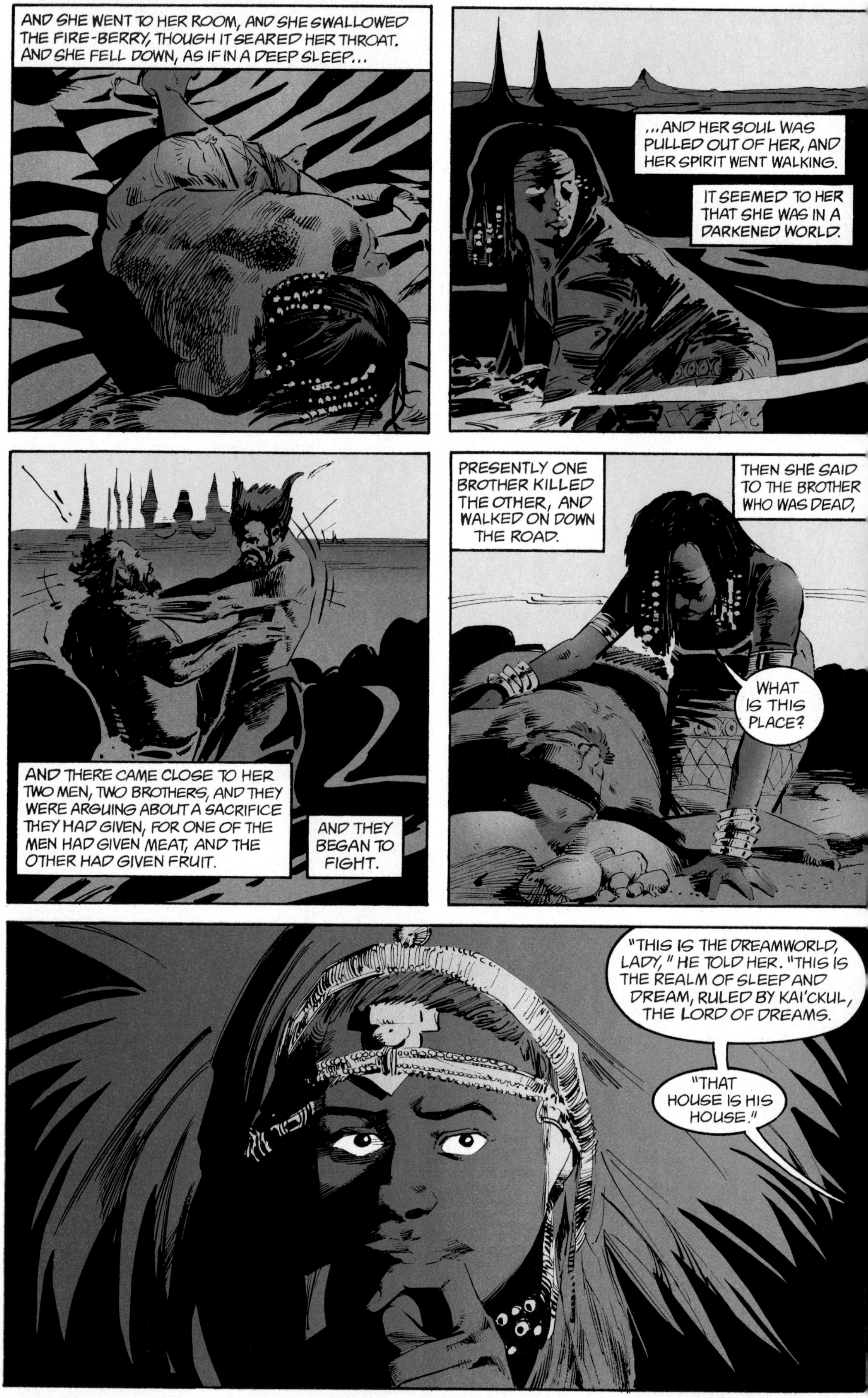
AND SHE WENT TO HER ROOM, AND SHE SWALLOWED THE FIRE-BERRY, THOUGH IT SEARED HER THROAT. AND SHE FELL DOWN, AS IF IN A DEEP SLEEP...
...AND HER SOUL WAS PULLED OUT OF HER, AND HER SPIRIT WENT WALKING.
IT SEEMED TO HER THAT SHE WAS IN A DARKENED WORLD.
AND THERE CAME CLOSE TO HER TWO MEN, TWO BROTHERS, AND THEY WERE ARGUING ABOUT A SACRIFICE THEY HAD GIVEN, FOR ONE OF THE MEN HAD GIVEN MEAT, AND THE OTHER HAD GIVEN FRUIT.
AND THEY BEGAN TO FIGHT.
PRESENTLY ONE BROTHER KILLED THE OTHER, AND WALKED ON DOWN THE ROAD.
THEN SHE SAID TO THE BROTHER WHO WAS DEAD,
WHAT IS THIS PLACE?
"THIS IS THE DREAMWORLD, LADY," HE TOLD HER. "THIS IS THE REALM OF SLEEP AND DREAM, RULED BY KAI'CKUL, THE LORD OF DREAMS.
"THAT HOUSE IS HIS HOUSE."

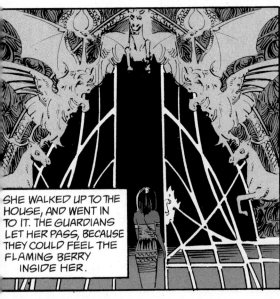

SHE WALKED UP TO THE HOUSE, AND WENT IN TO IT. THE GUARDIANS LET HER PASS, BECAUSE THEY COULD FEEL THE FLAMING BERRY INSIDE HER.

IN THE THRONE ROOM SHE SAW KAI'CKUL, THE DREAM LORD, ON HIS THRONE, AND HIS HEAD WAS HIDDEN. HE SAID TO HER,

Who are you? Why have you come here?

I SEEK A STRANGER, FOR I LOVE HIM. FLAMES DANCE IN THE BLACKNESS OF HIS ROBE, AND HIS EYES ARE STARS IN POOLS OF DEEP WATER.

HE CAME TO MY TOWER ONE NIGHT, AND LOOKED UP AT ME, BUT HE SAID NOTHING.

AT THIS, KAI'CKUL REMOVED HIS HELMET, AND SHE SAW BEFORE HER THE STRANGER WHO HAD STOOD BENEATH HER HOUSE IN THE CITY OF GLASS.

AND HER HEART SANK WITHIN HER, FOR SHE HAD CONFESSED HER LOVE TO ONE OF THE ENDLESS, WHO ARE NOT GODS, AND WILL NEVER DIE LIKE GODS.

AND IN THE TWIN STARS OF HIS EYES SHE SAW HE LOVED HER TOO.

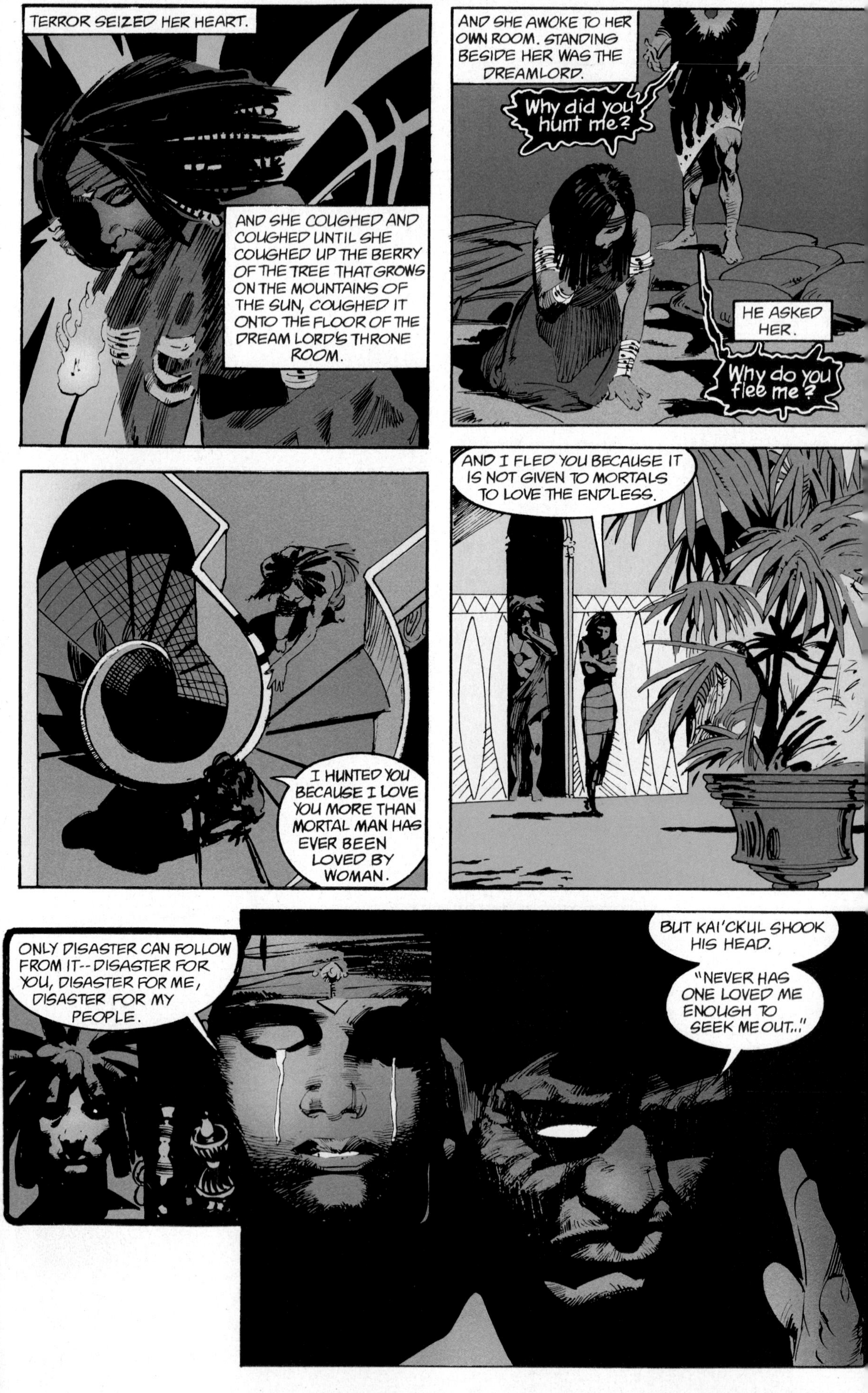
TERROR SEIZED HER HEART.
AND SHE COUGHED AND COUGHED UNTIL SHE COUGHED UP THE BERRY OF THE TREE THAT GROWS ON THE MOUNTAINS OF THE SUN, COUGHED IT ONTO THE FLOOR OF THE DREAM LORD'S THRONE ROOM.
AND SHE AWOKE TO HER OWN ROOM. STANDING BESIDE HER WAS THE DREAMLORD.
Why did you hunt me?
HE ASKED HER.
Why do you flee me?
I HUNTED YOU BECAUSE I LOVE YOU MORE THAN MORTAL MAN HAS EVER BEEN LOVED BY WOMAN.
AND I FLED YOU BECAUSE IT IS NOT GIVEN TO MORTALS TO LOVE THE ENDLESS.
ONLY DISASTER CAN FOLLOW FROM IT-- DISASTER FOR YOU, DISASTER FOR ME, DISASTER FOR MY PEOPLE.
BUT KAI'CKUL SHOOK HIS HEAD.
"NEVER HAS ONE LOVED ME ENOUGH TO SEEK ME OUT..."

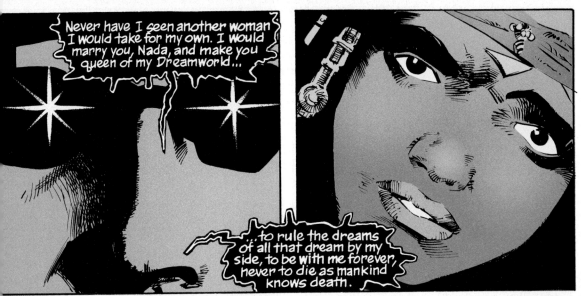

Never have I seen another woman I would take for my own. I would marry you, Nada, and make you queen of my Dreamworld...

...to rule the dreams of all that dream by my side, to be with me forever, never to die as mankind knows death.

And this I swear by the ruby on my chest.

AND AT THIS NADA WAS DEATHLY AFRAID, FOR THOUGH SHE LOVED HIM, SHE KNEW THIS WAS NOT MEANT TO BE, AND SHE COULD NOT COUNTENANCE HIS DESTRUCTION, AND HERS.

FOR LOVE IS NO PART OF THE DREAM-WORLD. LOVE BELONGS TO DESIRE, AND DESIRE IS ALWAYS CRUEL.

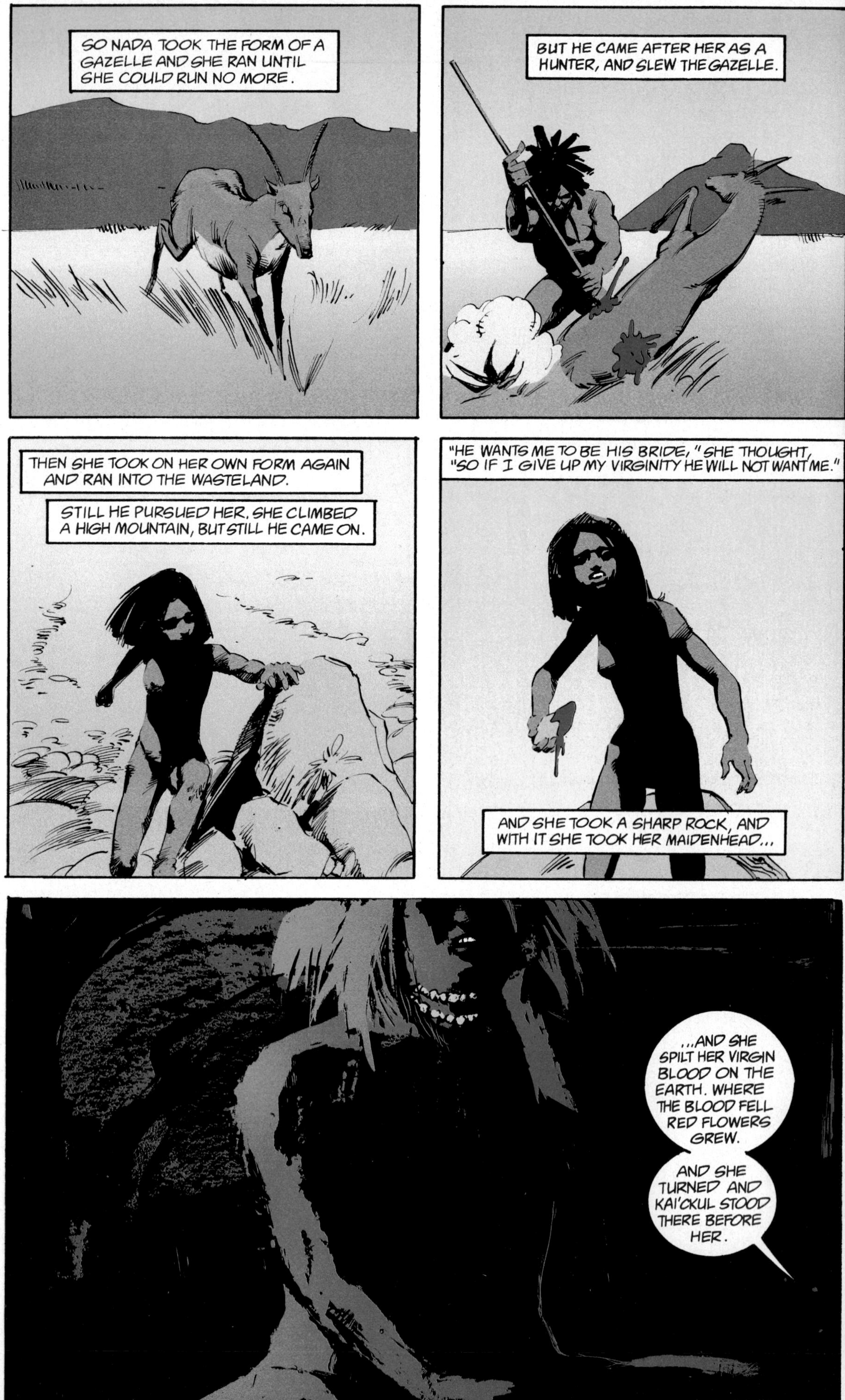
SO NADA TOOK THE FORM OF A GAZELLE AND SHE RAN UNTIL SHE COULD RUN NO MORE.
BUT HE CAME AFTER HER AS A HUNTER, AND SLEW THE GAZELLE.
THEN SHE TOOK ON HER OWN FORM AGAIN AND RAN INTO THE WASTELAND.
STILL HE PURSUED HER. SHE CLIMBED A HIGH MOUNTAIN, BUT STILL HE CAME ON.
"HE WANTS ME TO BE HIS BRIDE," SHE THOUGHT, "SO IF I GIVE UP MY VIRGINITY HE WILL NOT WANT ME."
AND SHE TOOK A SHARP ROCK, AND WITH IT SHE TOOK HER MAIDENHEAD...
...AND SHE SPILT HER VIRGIN BLOOD ON THE EARTH. WHERE THE BLOOD FELL RED FLOWERS GREW.
AND SHE TURNED AND KAI'CKUL STOOD THERE BEFORE HER.

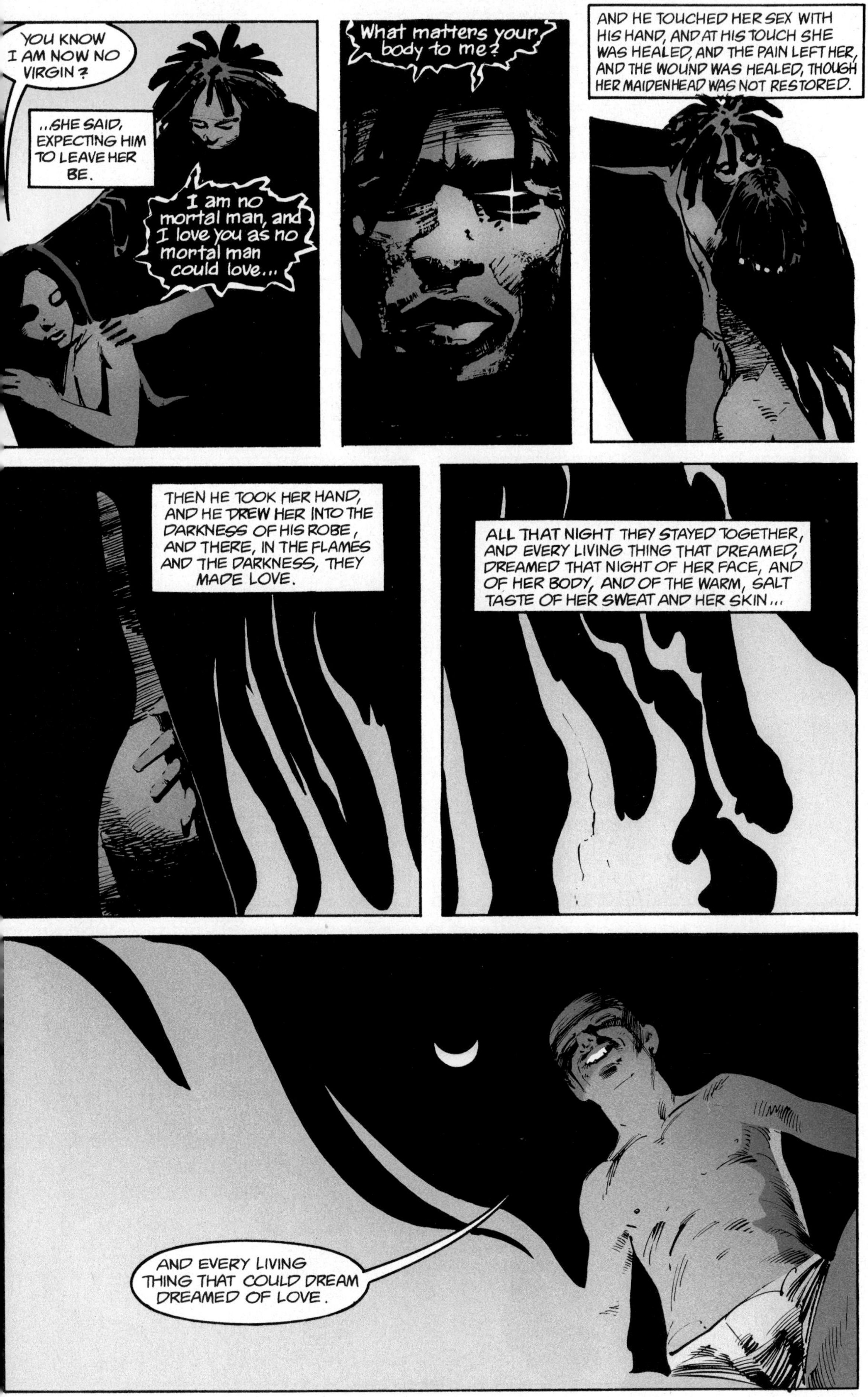
YOU KNOW I AM NOW NO VIRGIN?
...SHE SAID, EXPECTING HIM TO LEAVE HER BE.
I am no mortal man, and I love you as no mortal man could love...
What matters your body to me?
AND HE TOUCHED HER SEX WITH HIS HAND, AND AT HIS TOUCH SHE WAS HEALED, AND THE PAIN LEFT HER, AND THE WOUND WAS HEALED, THOUGH HER MAIDENHEAD WAS NOT RESTORED.
THEN HE TOOK HER HAND, AND HE DREW HER INTO THE DARKNESS OF HIS ROBE, AND THERE, IN THE FLAMES AND THE DARKNESS, THEY MADE LOVE.
ALL THAT NIGHT THEY STAYED TOGETHER, AND EVERY LIVING THING THAT DREAMED, DREAMED THAT NIGHT OF HER FACE, AND OF HER BODY, AND OF THE WARM, SALT TASTE OF HER SWEAT AND HER SKIN...
AND EVERY LIVING THING THAT COULD DREAM DREAMED OF LOVE.

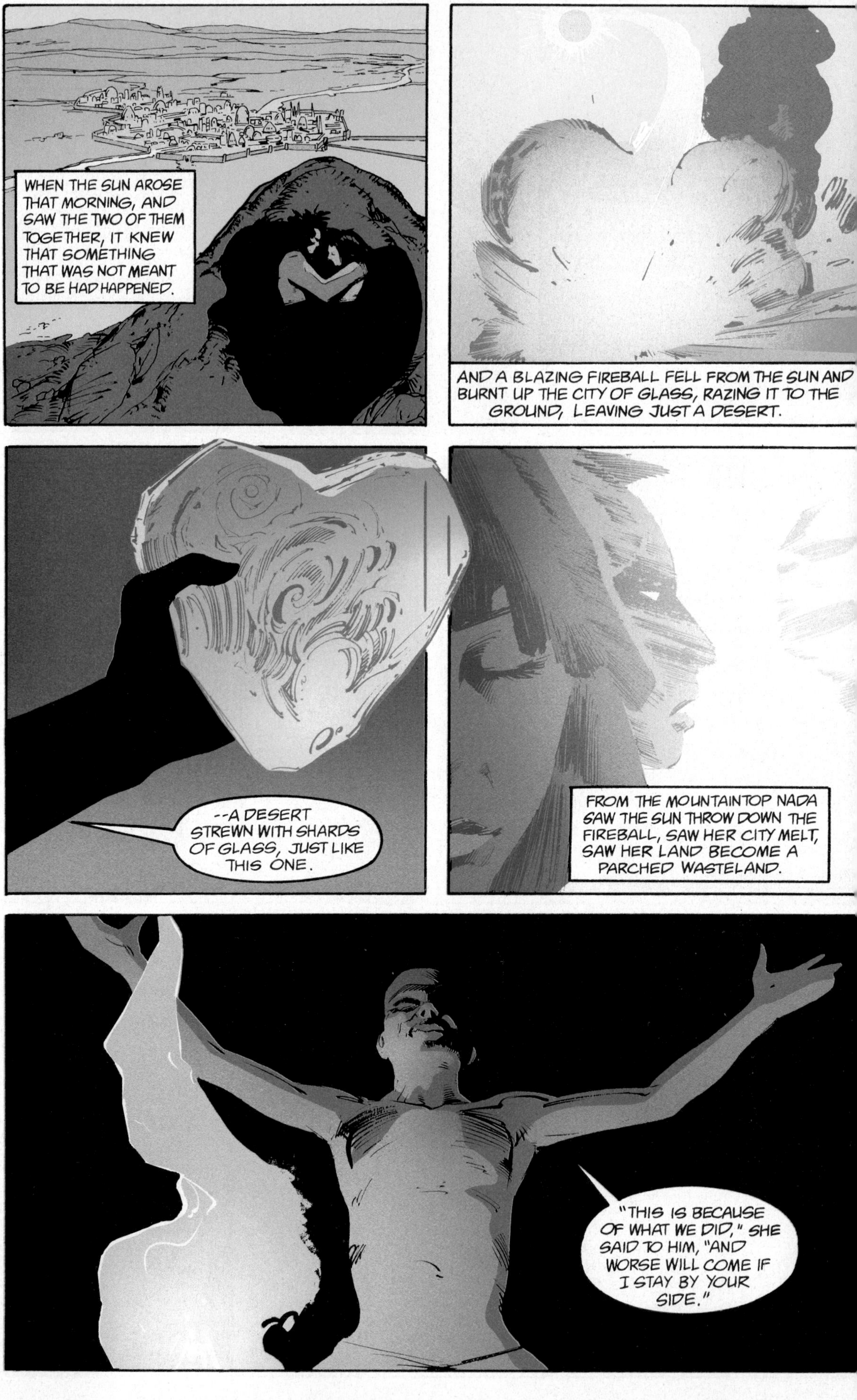
WHEN THE SUN AROSE THAT MORNING, AND SAW THE TWO OF THEM TOGETHER, IT KNEW THAT SOMETHING THAT WAS NOT MEANT TO BE HAD HAPPENED.
AND A BLAZING FIREBALL FELL FROM THE SUN AND BURNT UP THE CITY OF GLASS, RAZING IT TO THE GROUND, LEAVING JUST A DESERT.
--A DESERT STREWN WITH SHARDS OF GLASS, JUST LIKE THIS ONE.
FROM THE MOUNTAINTOP NADA SAW THE SUN THROW DOWN THE FIREBALL, SAW HER CITY MELT, SAW HER LAND BECOME A PARCHED WASTELAND.
"THIS IS BECAUSE OF WHAT WE DID," SHE SAID TO HIM, "AND WORSE WILL COME IF I STAY BY YOUR SIDE."

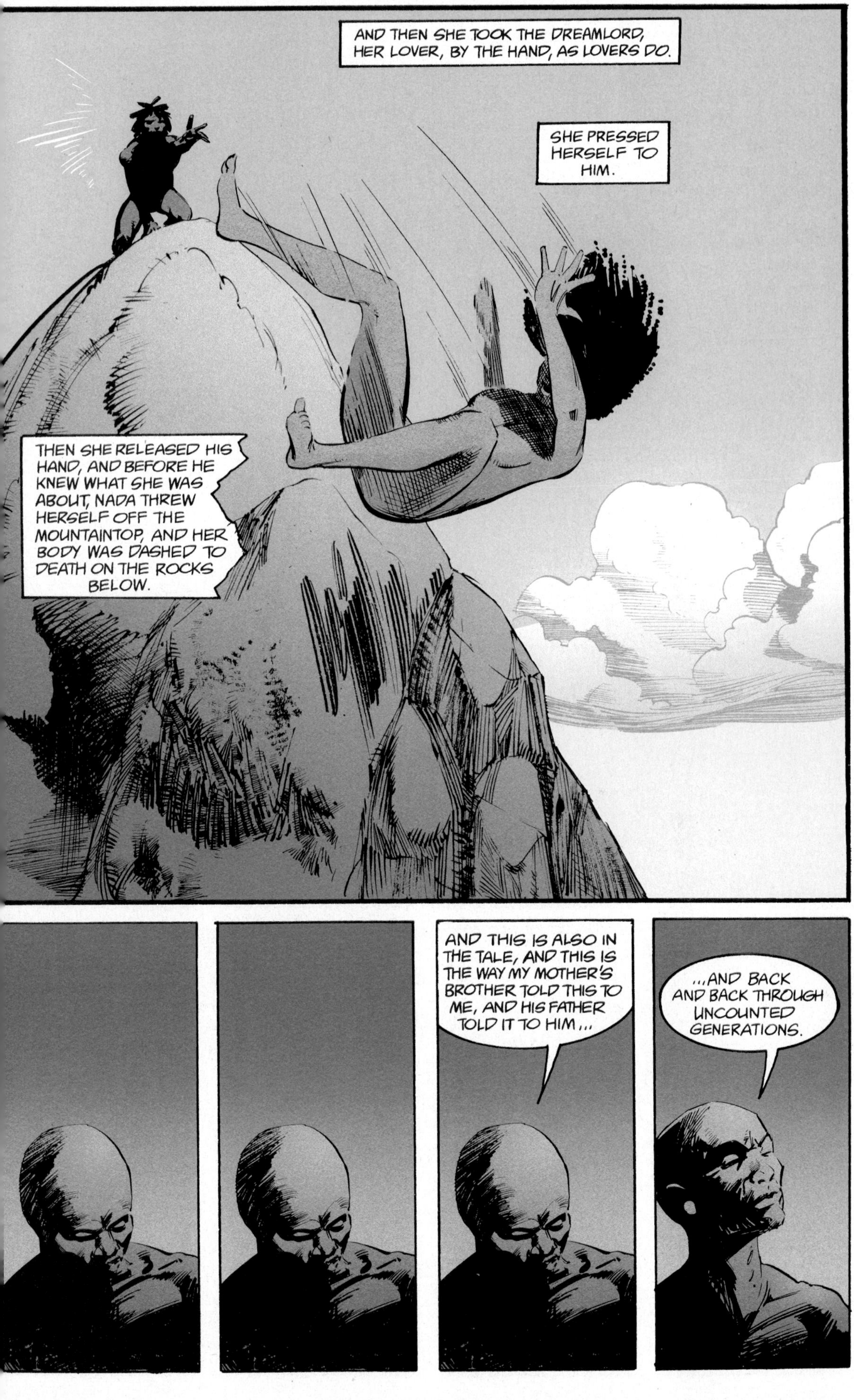
AND THEN SHE TOOK THE DREAMLORD, HER LOVER, BY THE HAND, AS LOVERS DO.
SHE PRESSED HERSELF TO HIM.
THEN SHE RELEASED HIS HAND, AND BEFORE HE KNEW WHAT SHE WAS ABOUT, NADA THREW HERSELF OFF THE MOUNTAINTOP, AND HER BODY WAS DASHED TO DEATH ON THE ROCKS BELOW.
AND THIS IS ALSO IN THE TALE, AND THIS IS THE WAY MY MOTHER'S BROTHER TOLD THIS TO ME, AND HIS FATHER TOLD IT TO HIM...
...AND BACK AND BACK THROUGH UNCOUNTED GENERATIONS.

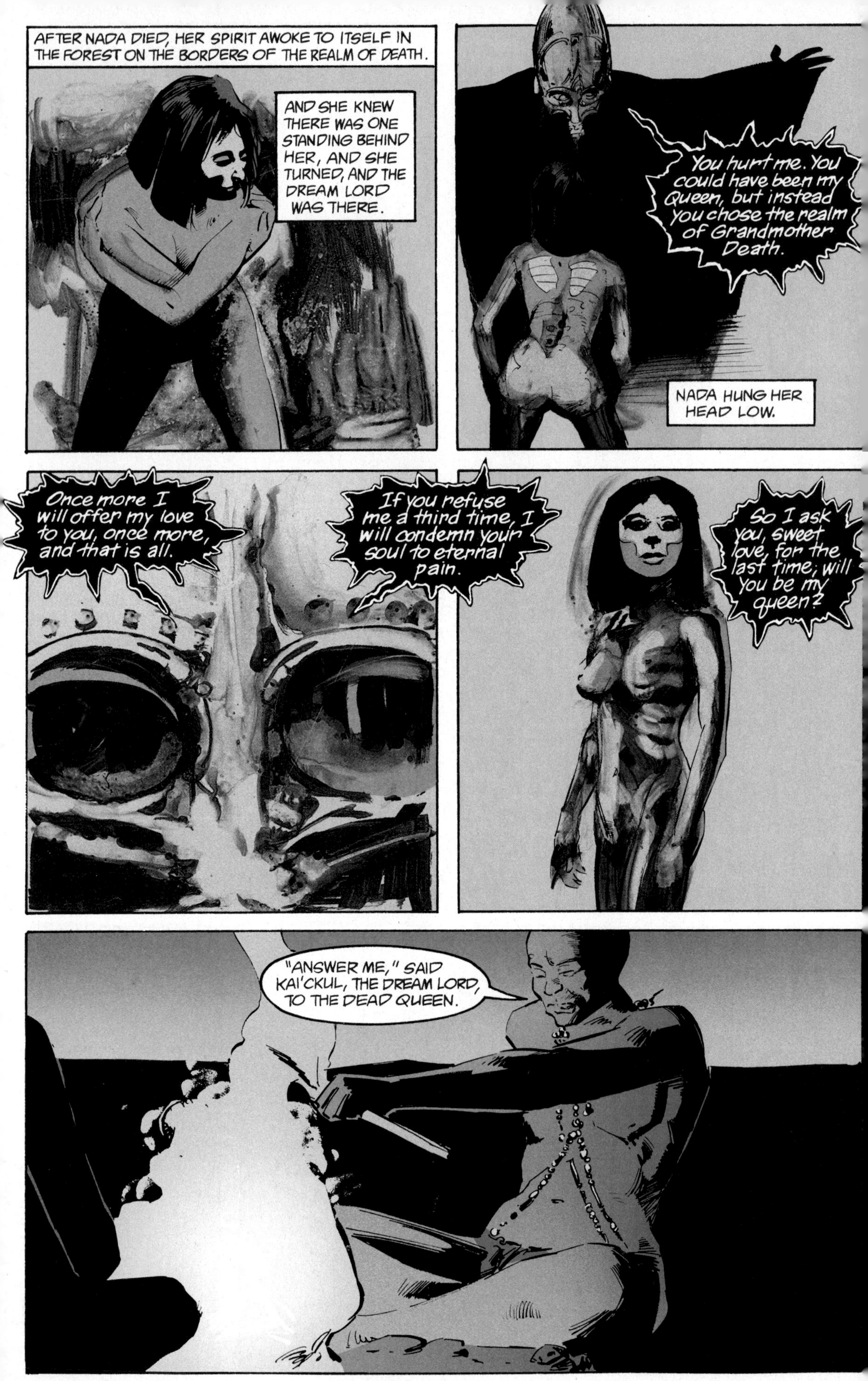
AFTER NADA DIED, HER SPIRIT AWOKE TO ITSELF IN THE FOREST ON THE BORDERS OF THE REALM OF DEATH.
AND SHE KNEW THERE WAS ONE STANDING BEHIND HER, AND SHE TURNED, AND THE DREAM LORD WAS THERE.
You hurt me. You could have been my Queen, but instead you chose the realm of Grandmother Death.
NADA HUNG HER HEAD LOW.
Once more I will offer my love to you, once more, and that is all.
If you refuse me a third time, I will condemn your soul to eternal pain.
So I ask you, sweet love, for the last time; will you be my queen?
"ANSWER ME," SAID KAI'CKUL, THE DREAM LORD, TO THE DEAD QUEEN.

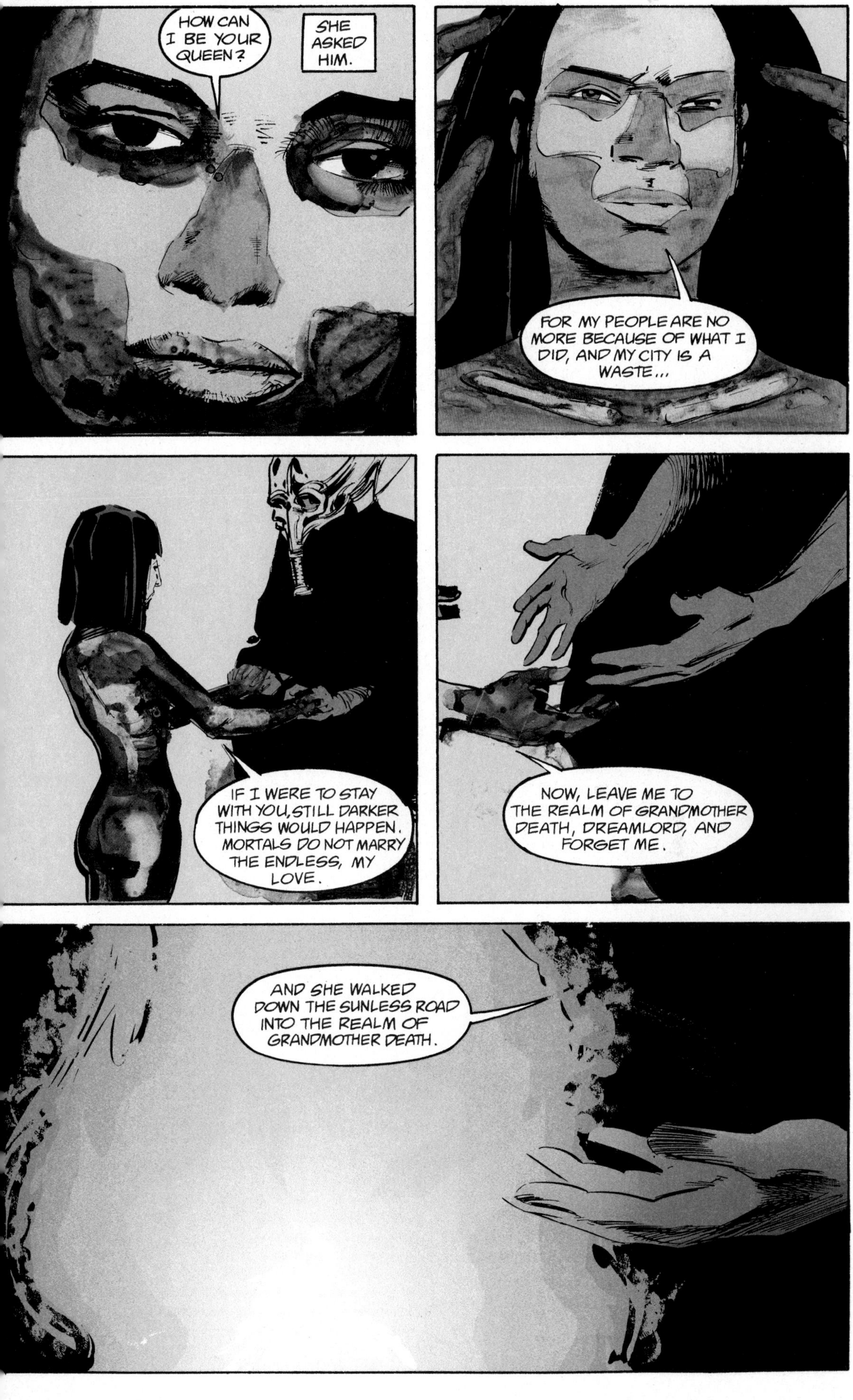
HOW CAN I BE YOUR QUEEN?
SHE ASKED HIM.
FOR MY PEOPLE ARE NO MORE BECAUSE OF WHAT I DID, AND MY CITY IS A WASTE...
IF I WERE TO STAY WITH YOU, STILL DARKER THINGS WOULD HAPPEN. MORTALS DO NOT MARRY THE ENDLESS, MY LOVE.
NOW, LEAVE ME TO THE REALM OF GRANDMOTHER DEATH, DREAMLORD, AND FORGET ME.
AND SHE WALKED DOWN THE SUNLESS ROAD INTO THE REALM OF GRANDMOTHER DEATH.

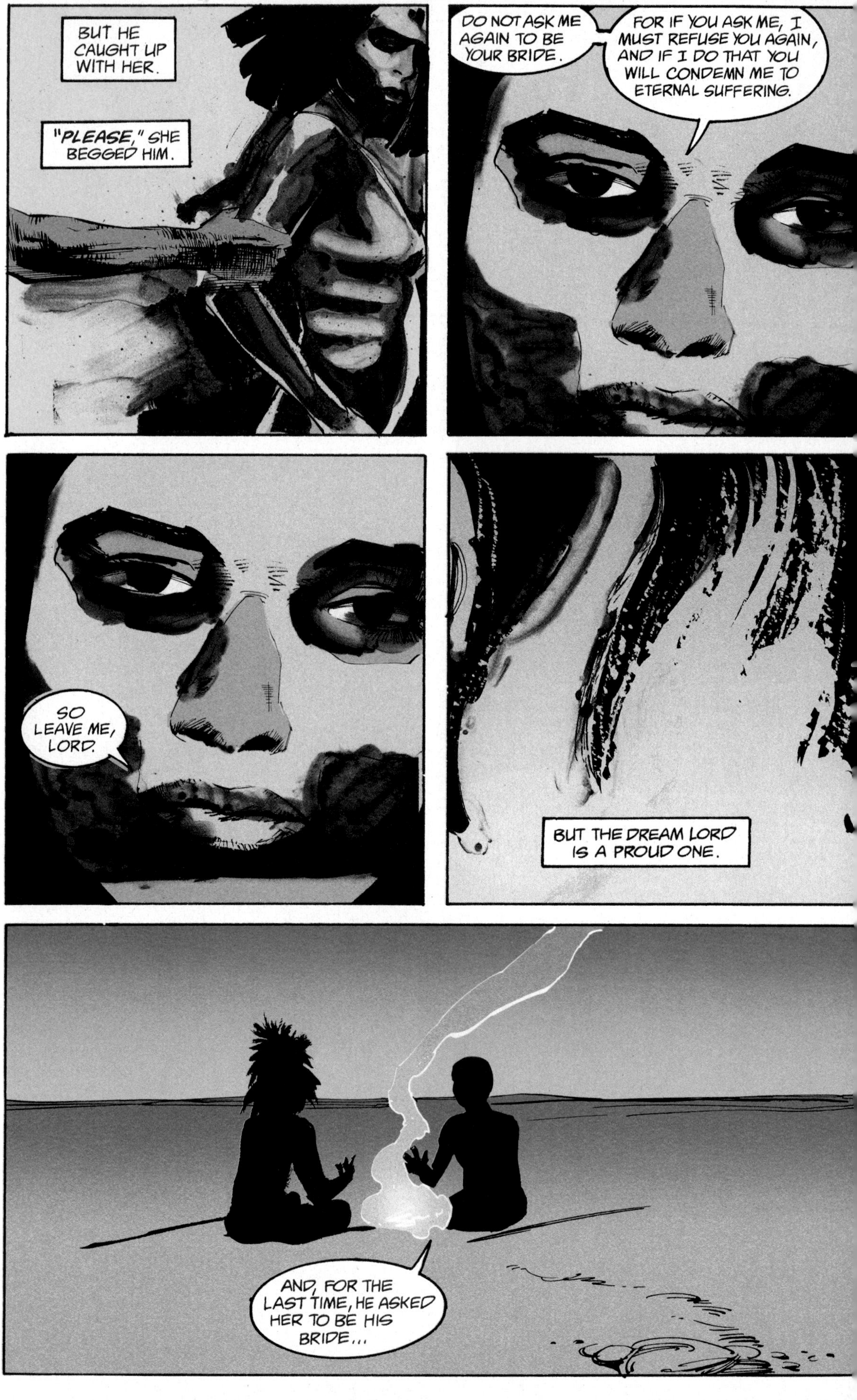
BUT HE CAUGHT UP WITH HER.
"PLEASE," SHE BEGGED HIM.
DO NOT ASK ME AGAIN TO BE YOUR BRIDE.
FOR IF YOU ASK ME, I MUST REFUSE YOU AGAIN, AND IF I DO THAT YOU WILL CONDEMN ME TO ETERNAL SUFFERING.
SO LEAVE ME, LORD.
BUT THE DREAM LORD IS A PROUD ONE.
AND, FOR THE LAST TIME, HE ASKED HER TO BE HIS BRIDE...

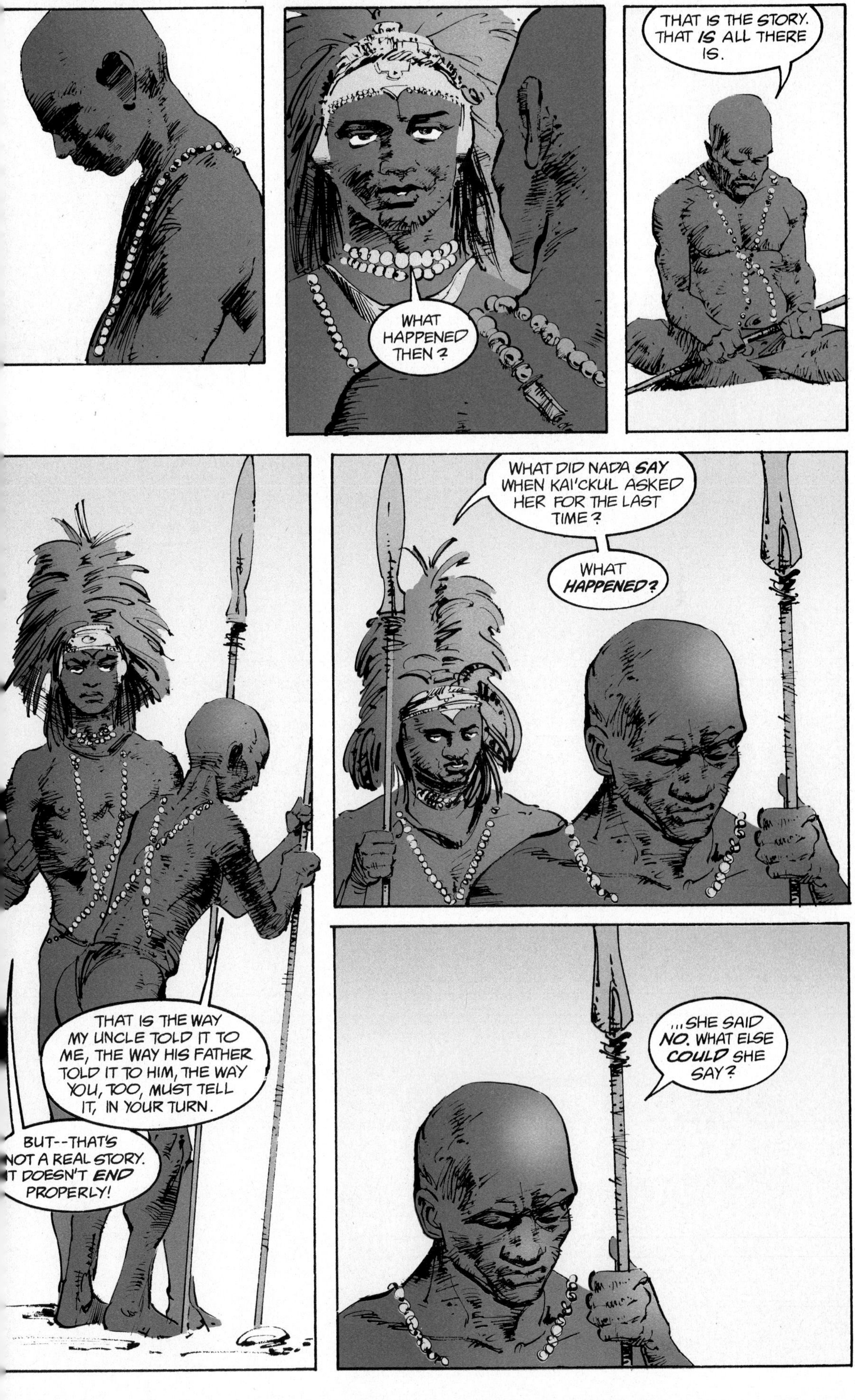
WHAT HAPPENED THEN?
THAT IS THE STORY. THAT IS ALL THERE IS.
THAT IS THE WAY MY UNCLE TOLD IT TO ME, THE WAY HIS FATHER TOLD IT TO HIM, THE WAY YOU, TOO, MUST TELL IT, IN YOUR TURN.
BUT--THAT'S NOT A REAL STORY. IT DOESN'T END PROPERLY!
WHAT DID NADA SAY WHEN KAI'CKUL ASKED HER FOR THE LAST TIME?
WHAT HAPPENED?
...SHE SAID NO. WHAT ELSE COULD SHE SAY?

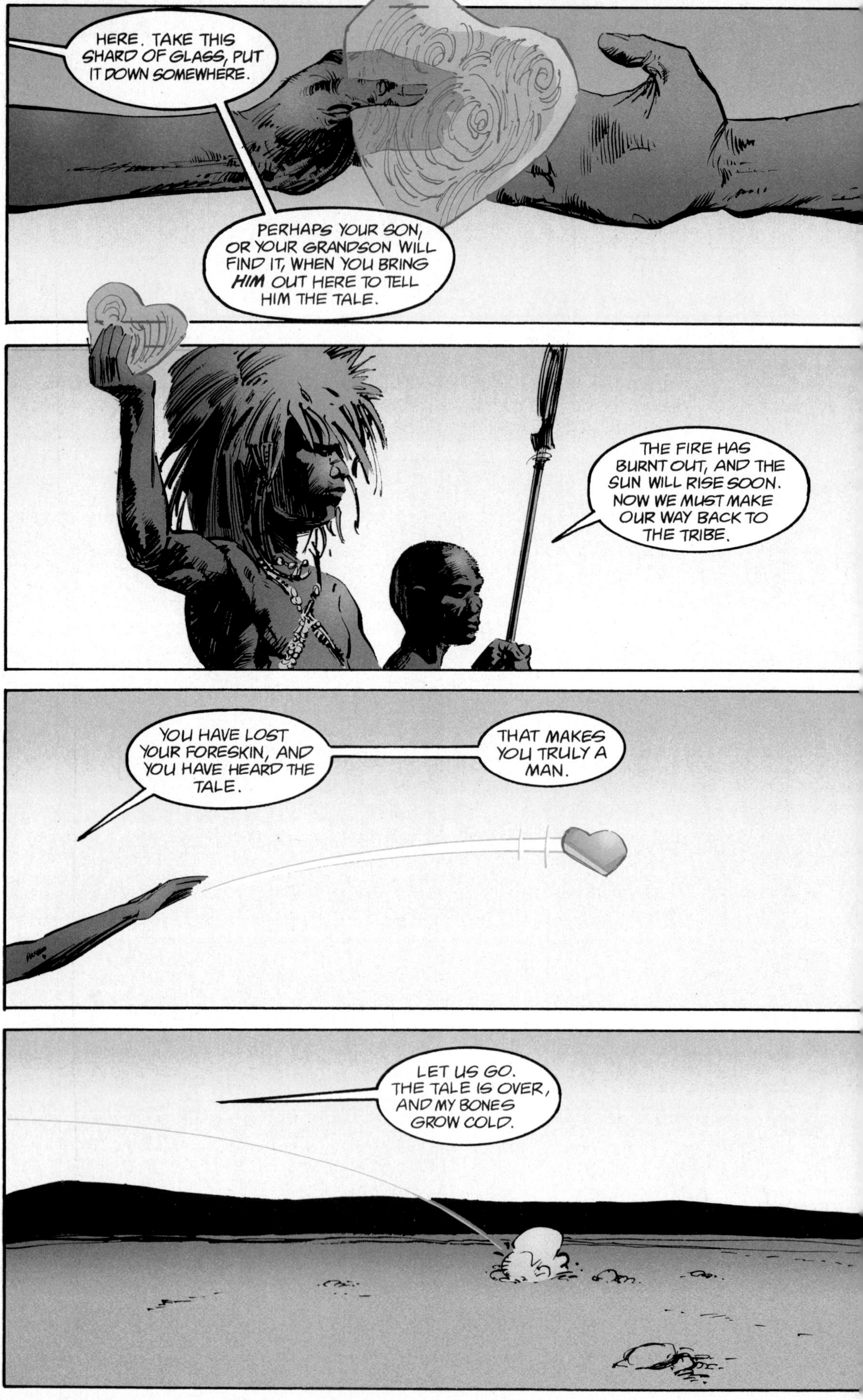
HERE. TAKE THIS SHARD OF GLASS, PUT IT DOWN SOMEWHERE.
PERHAPS YOUR SON, OR YOUR GRANDSON WILL FIND IT, WHEN YOU BRING HIM OUT HERE TO TELL HIM THE TALE.
THE FIRE HAS BURNT OUT, AND THE SUN WILL RISE SOON. NOW WE MUST MAKE OUR WAY BACK TO THE TRIBE.
YOU HAVE LOST YOUR FORESKIN, AND YOU HAVE HEARD THE TALE.
THAT MAKES YOU TRULY A MAN.
LET US GO. THE TALE IS OVER, AND MY BONES GROW COLD.

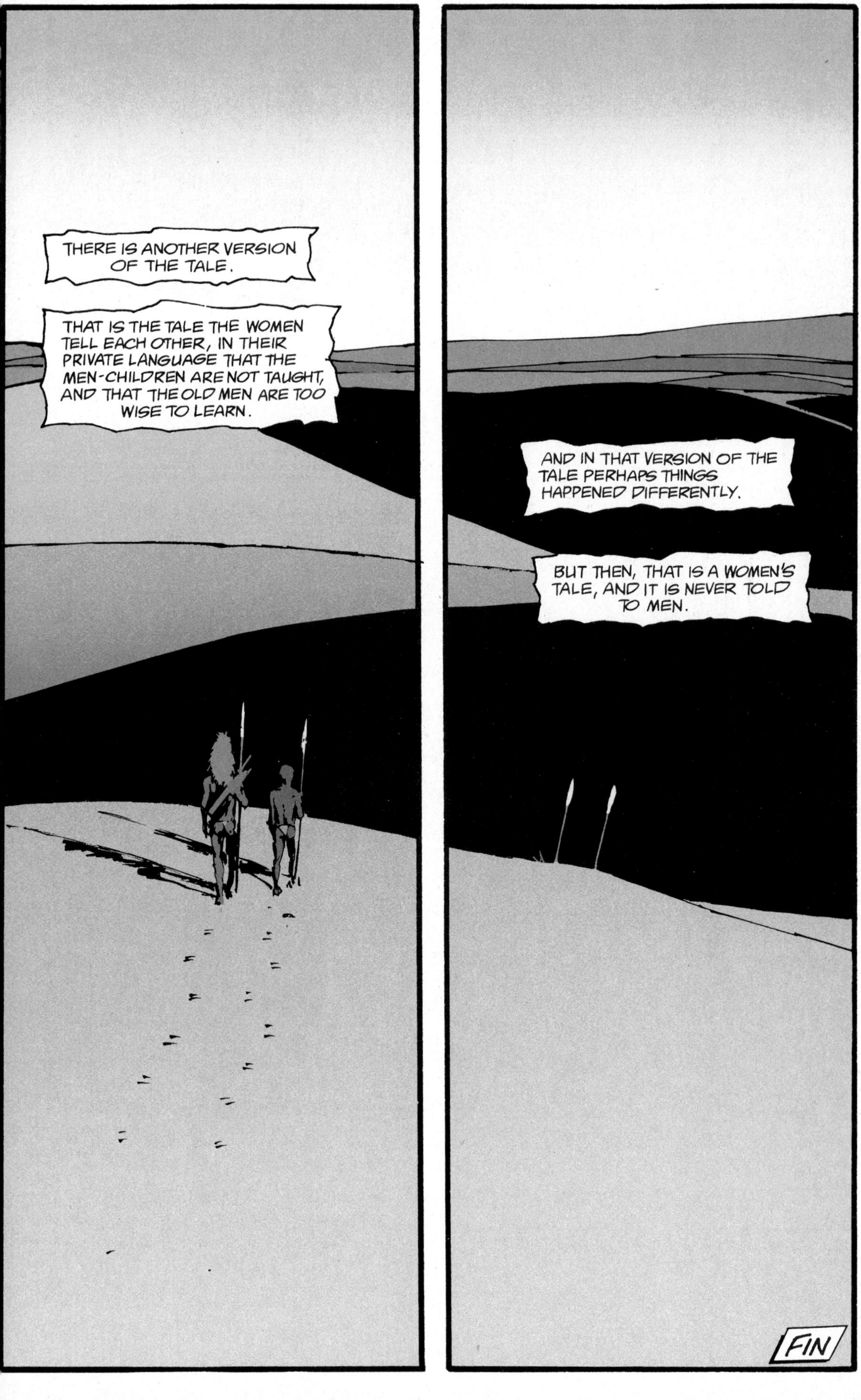
THERE IS ANOTHER VERSION OF THE TALE.
THAT IS THE TALE THE WOMEN TELL EACH OTHER, IN THEIR PRIVATE LANGUAGE THAT THE MEN-CHILDREN ARE NOT TAUGHT, AND THAT THE OLD MEN ARE TOO WISE TO LEARN.
AND IN THAT VERSION OF THE TALE PERHAPS THINGS HAPPENED DIFFERENTLY.
BUT THEN, THAT IS A WOMEN'S TALE, AND IT IS NEVER TOLD TO MEN.
FIN

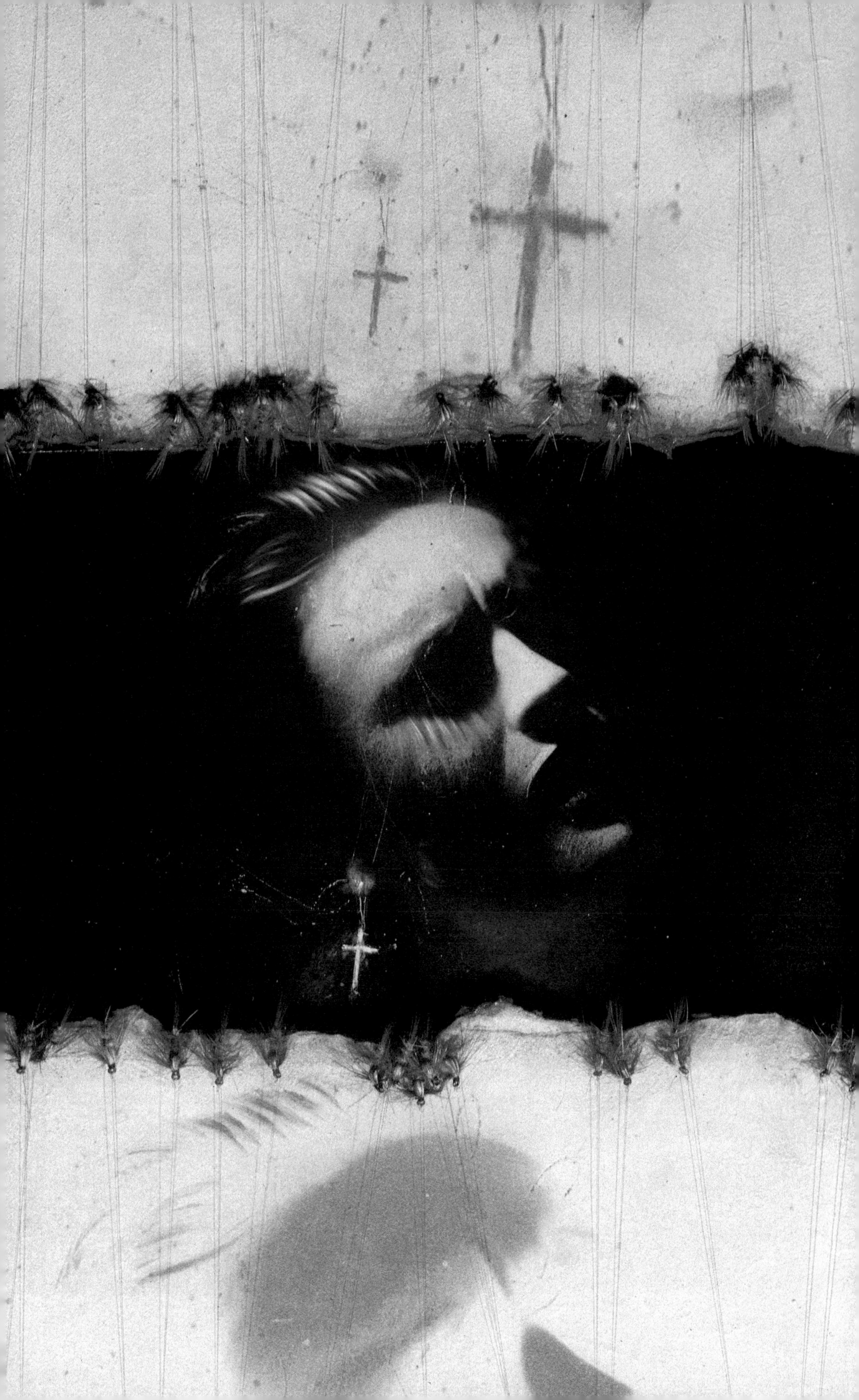

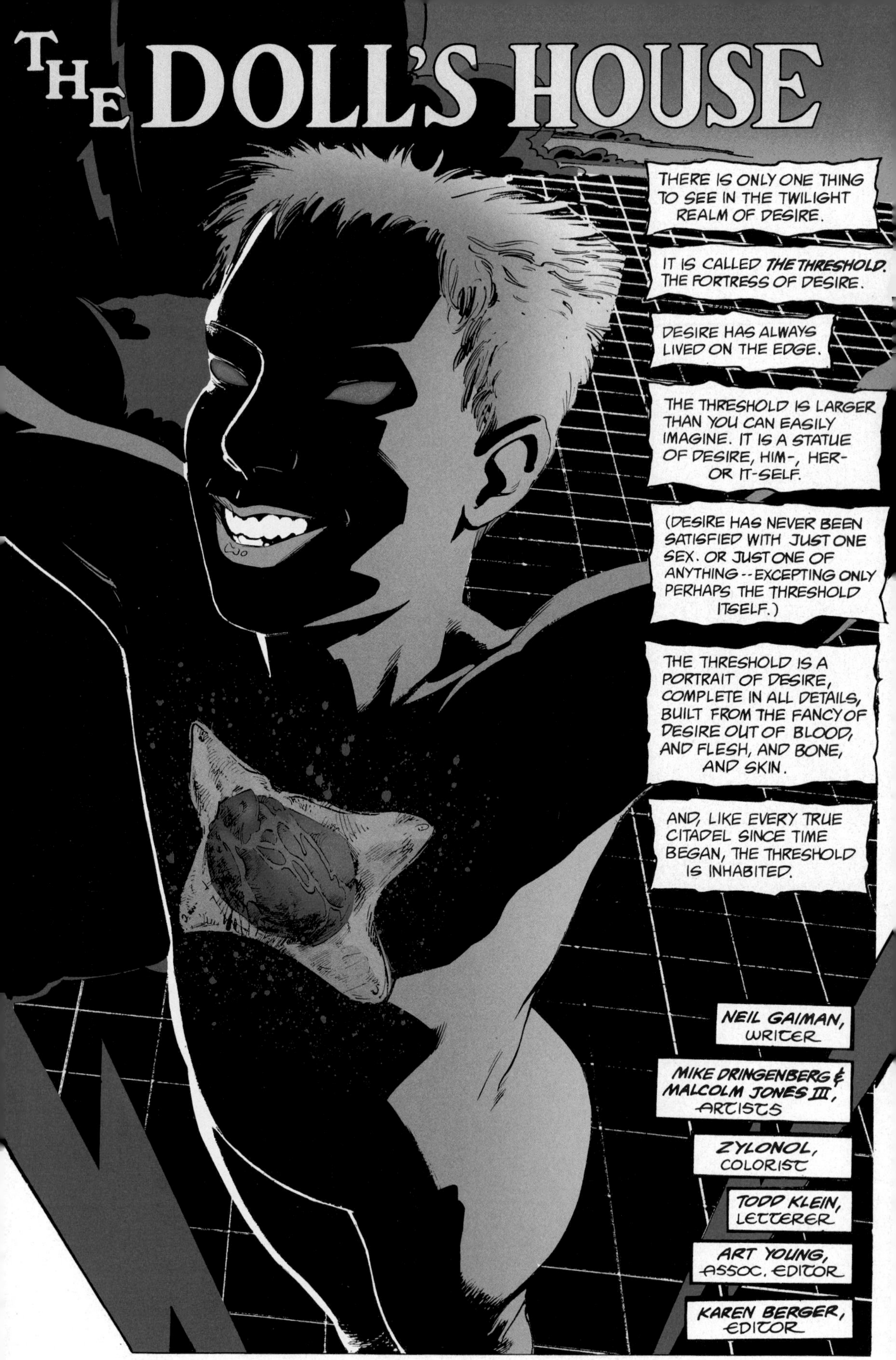
THE DOLL'S HOUSE
THERE IS ONLY ONE THING TO SEE IN THE TWILIGHT REALM OF DESIRE.
IT IS CALLED THE THRESHOLD. THE FORTRESS OF DESIRE.
DESIRE HAS ALWAYS LIVED ON THE EDGE.
THE THRESHOLD IS LARGER THAN YOU CAN EASILY IMAGINE. IT IS A STATUE OF DESIRE, HIM-, HER- OR IT-SELF.
(DESIRE HAS NEVER BEEN SATISFIED WITH JUST ONE SEX. OR JUST ONE OF ANYTHING -- EXCEPTING ONLY PERHAPS THE THRESHOLD ITSELF.)
THE THRESHOLD IS A PORTRAIT OF DESIRE, COMPLETE IN ALL DETAILS, BUILT FROM THE FANCY OF DESIRE OUT OF BLOOD, AND FLESH, AND BONE, AND SKIN.
AND, LIKE EVERY TRUE CITADEL SINCE TIME BEGAN, THE THRESHOLD IS INHABITED.
NEIL GAIMAN, WRITER
MIKE DRINGENBERG & MALCOLM JONES III, ARTISTS
ZYLONOL, COLORIST
TODD KLEIN, LETTERER
ART YOUNG, ASSOC. EDITOR
KAREN BERGER, EDITOR

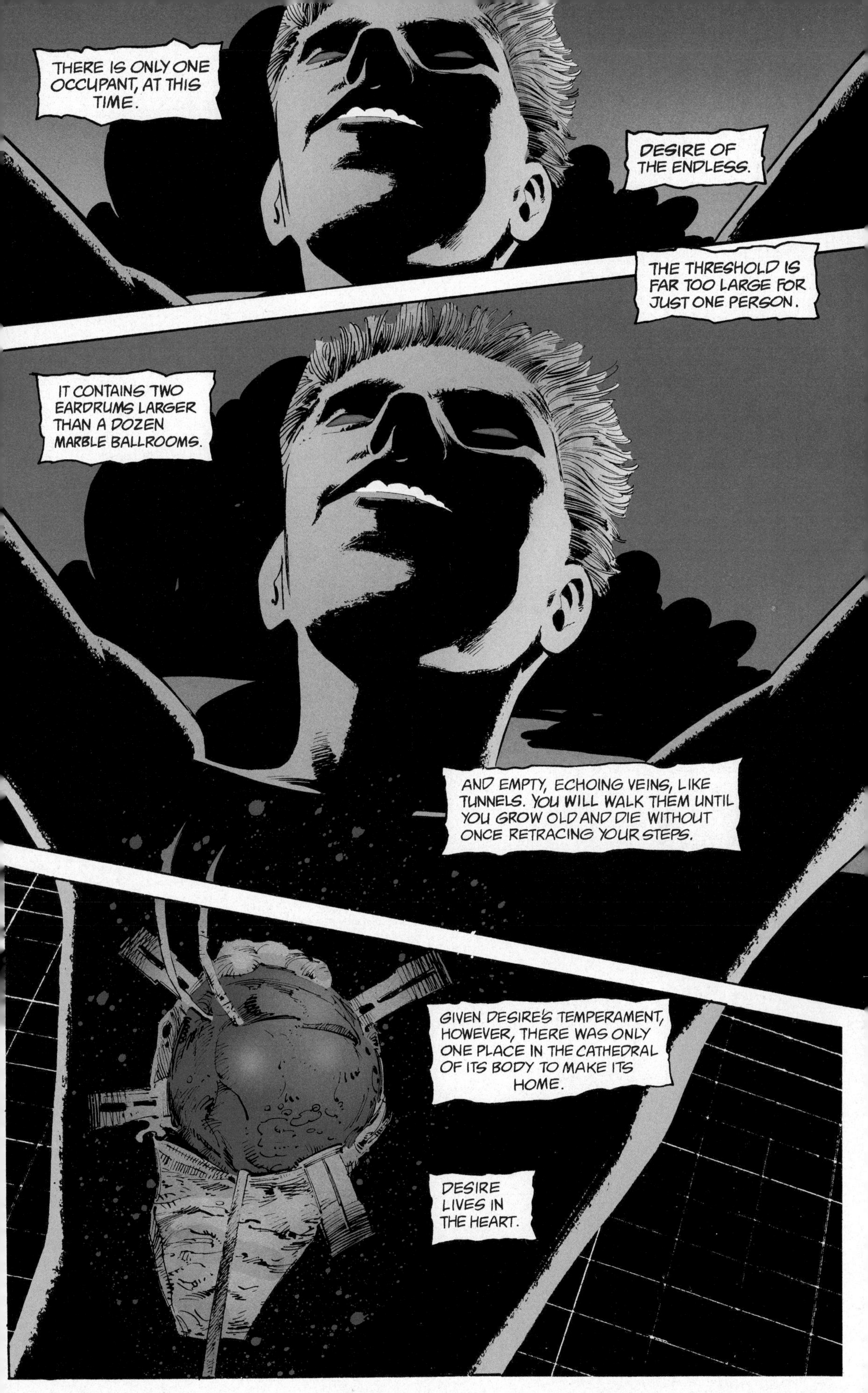
THERE IS ONLY ONE OCCUPANT, AT THIS TIME.
DESIRE OF THE ENDLESS.
THE THRESHOLD IS FAR TOO LARGE FOR JUST ONE PERSON.
IT CONTAINS TWO EARDRUMS LARGER THAN A DOZEN MARBLE BALLROOMS.
AND EMPTY, ECHOING VEINS, LIKE TUNNELS. YOU WILL WALK THEM UNTIL YOU GROW OLD AND DIE WITHOUT ONCE RETRACING YOUR STEPS.
GIVEN DESIRE'S TEMPERAMENT, HOWEVER, THERE WAS ONLY ONE PLACE IN THE CATHEDRAL OF ITS BODY TO MAKE ITS HOME.
DESIRE LIVES IN THE HEART.

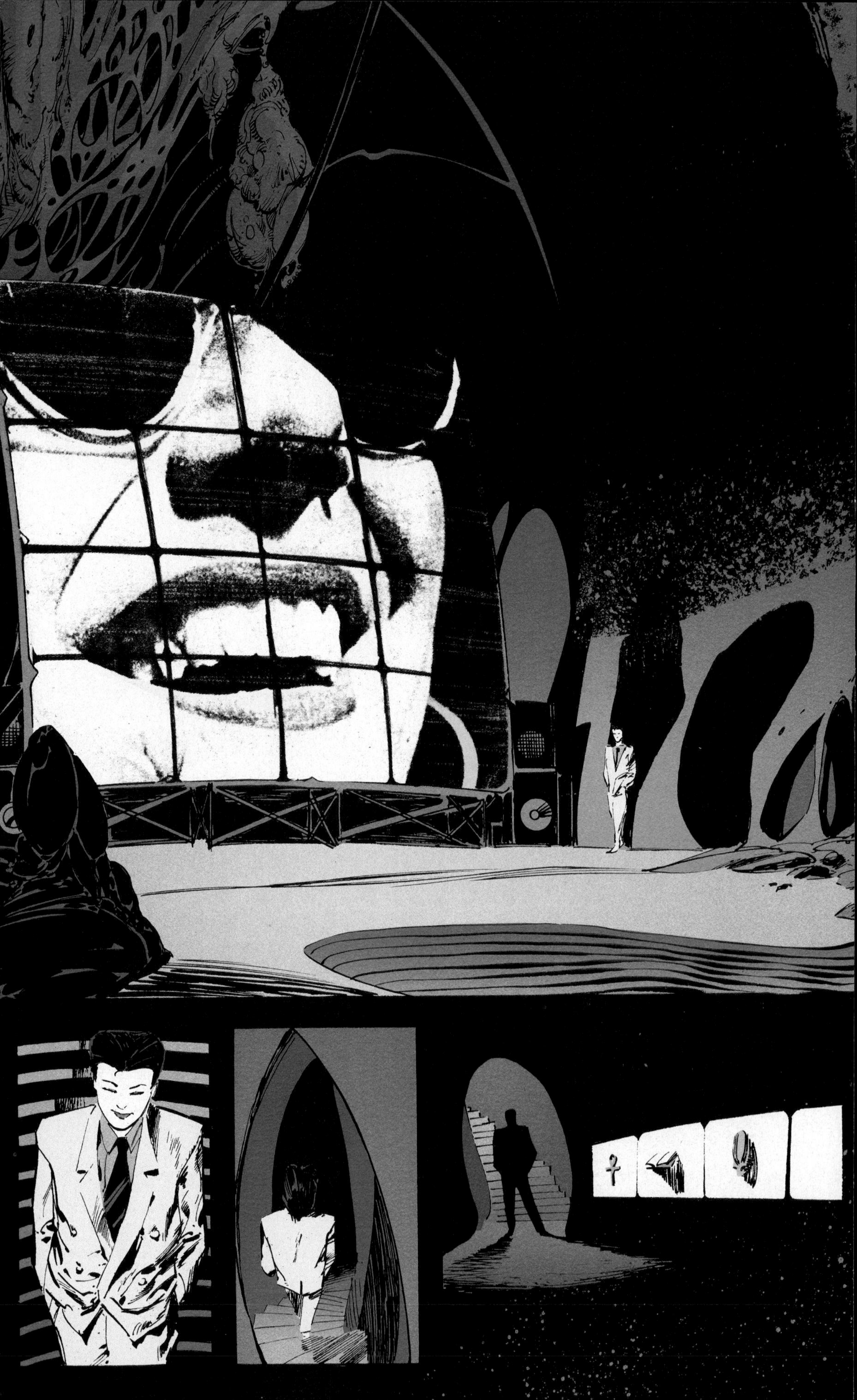

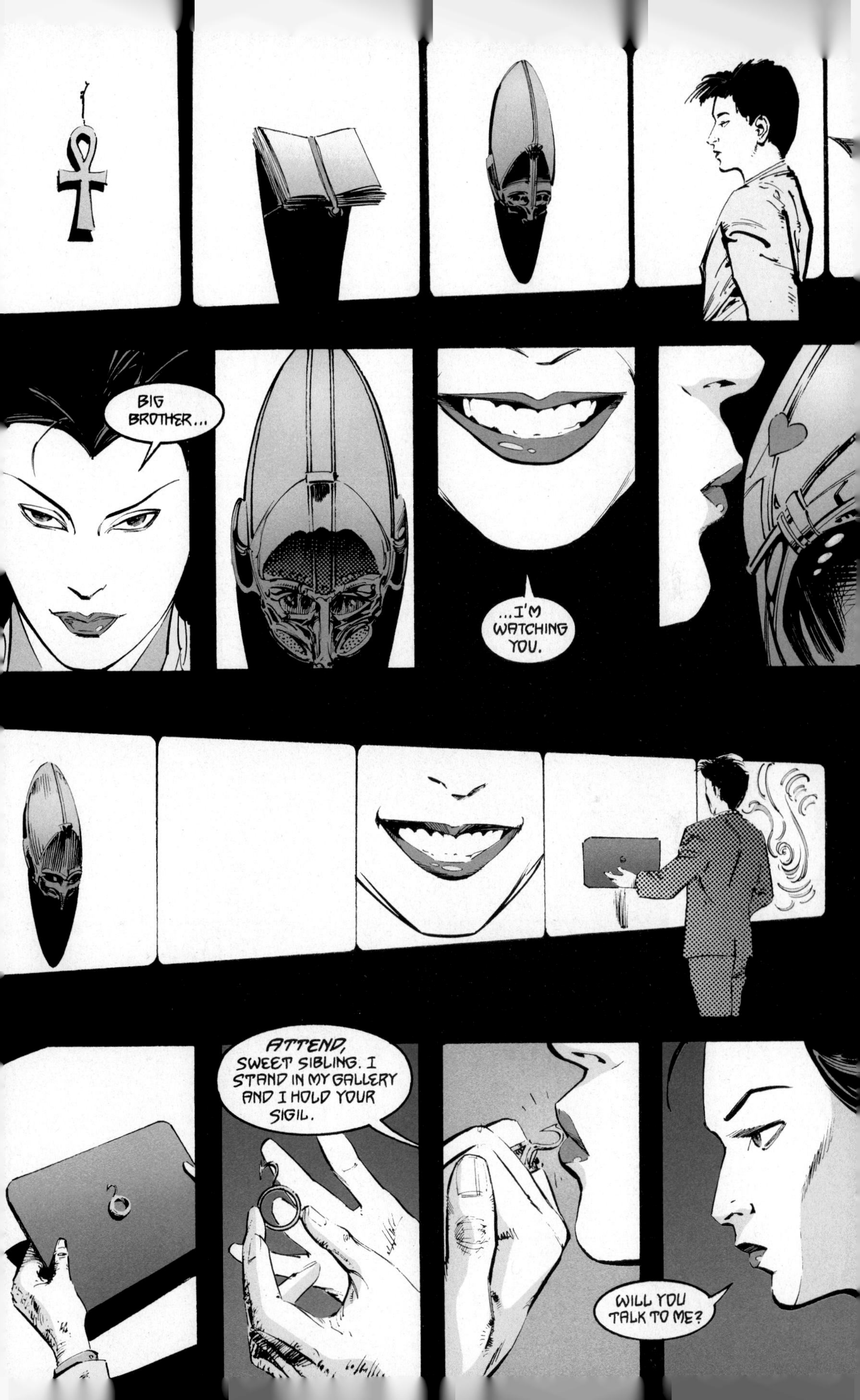
BIG BROTHER...
...I'M WATCHING YOU.
ATTEND, SWEET SIBLING. I STAND IN MY GALLERY AND I HOLD YOUR SIGIL.
WILL YOU TALK TO ME?

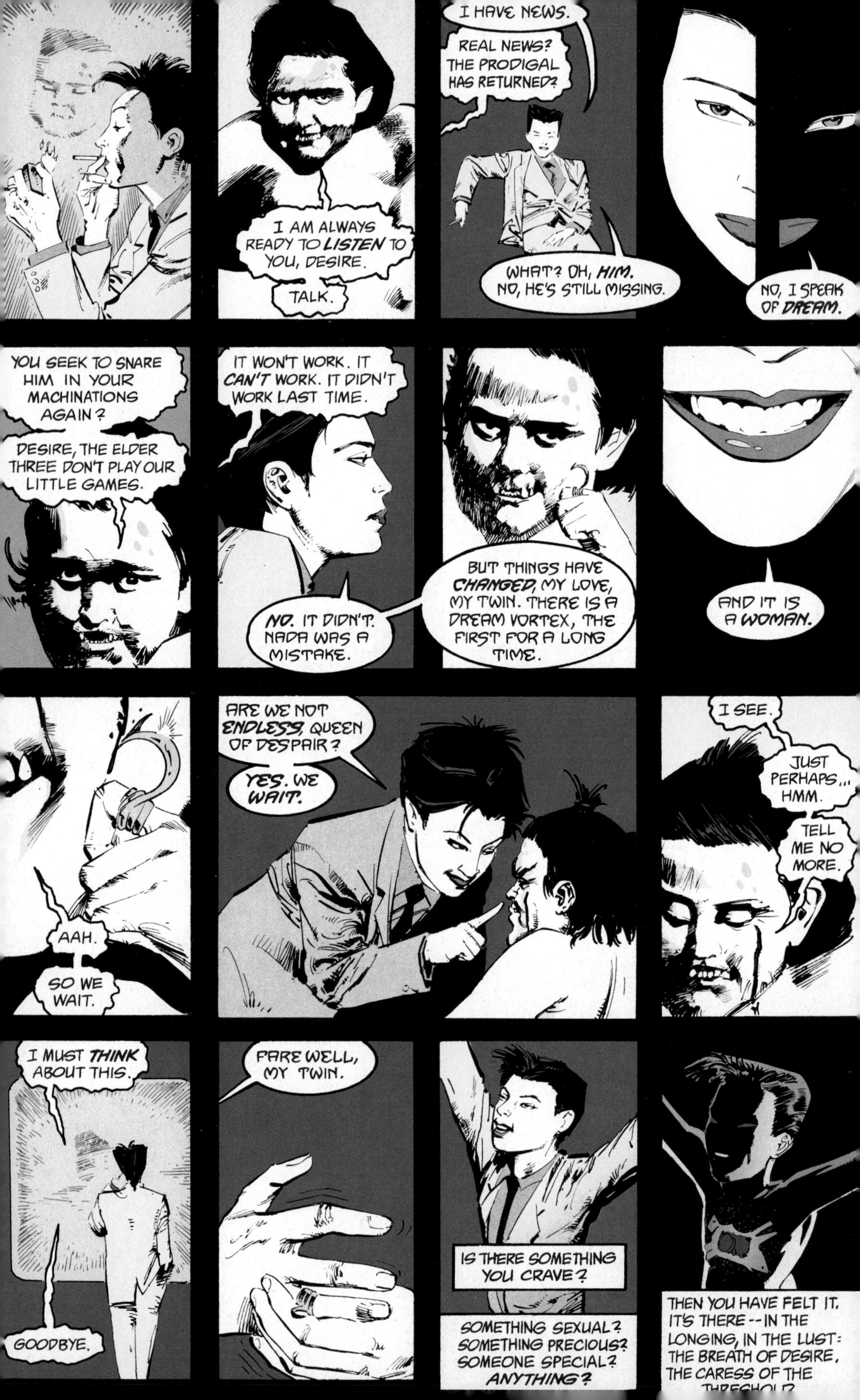
I AM ALWAYS READY TO LISTEN TO YOU, DESIRE.
TALK.
I HAVE NEWS.
REAL NEWS? THE PRODIGAL HAS RETURNED?
WHAT? OH, HIM. NO, HE'S STILL MISSING.
NO, I SPEAK OF DREAM.
YOU SEEK TO SNARE HIM IN YOUR MACHINATIONS AGAIN?
DESIRE, THE ELDER THREE DON'T PLAY OUR LITTLE GAMES.
IT WON'T WORK. IT CAN'T WORK. IT DIDN'T WORK LAST TIME.
NO. IT DIDN'T. NADA WAS A MISTAKE.
BUT THINGS HAVE CHANGED, MY LOVE, MY TWIN. THERE IS A DREAM VORTEX, THE FIRST FOR A LONG TIME.
AND IT IS A WOMAN.
AAH.
SO WE WAIT.
ARE WE NOT ENDLESS, QUEEN OF DESPAIR?
YES. WE WAIT.
I SEE.
JUST PERHAPS... HMM.
TELL ME NO MORE.
I MUST THINK ABOUT THIS.
GOODBYE.
FAREWELL, MY TWIN.
IS THERE SOMETHING YOU CRAVE?
SOMETHING SEXUAL? SOMETHING PRECIOUS? SOMEONE SPECIAL? ANYTHING?
THEN YOU HAVE FELT IT. IT'S THERE--IN THE LONGING, IN THE LUST: THE BREATH OF DESIRE, THE CARESS OF THE

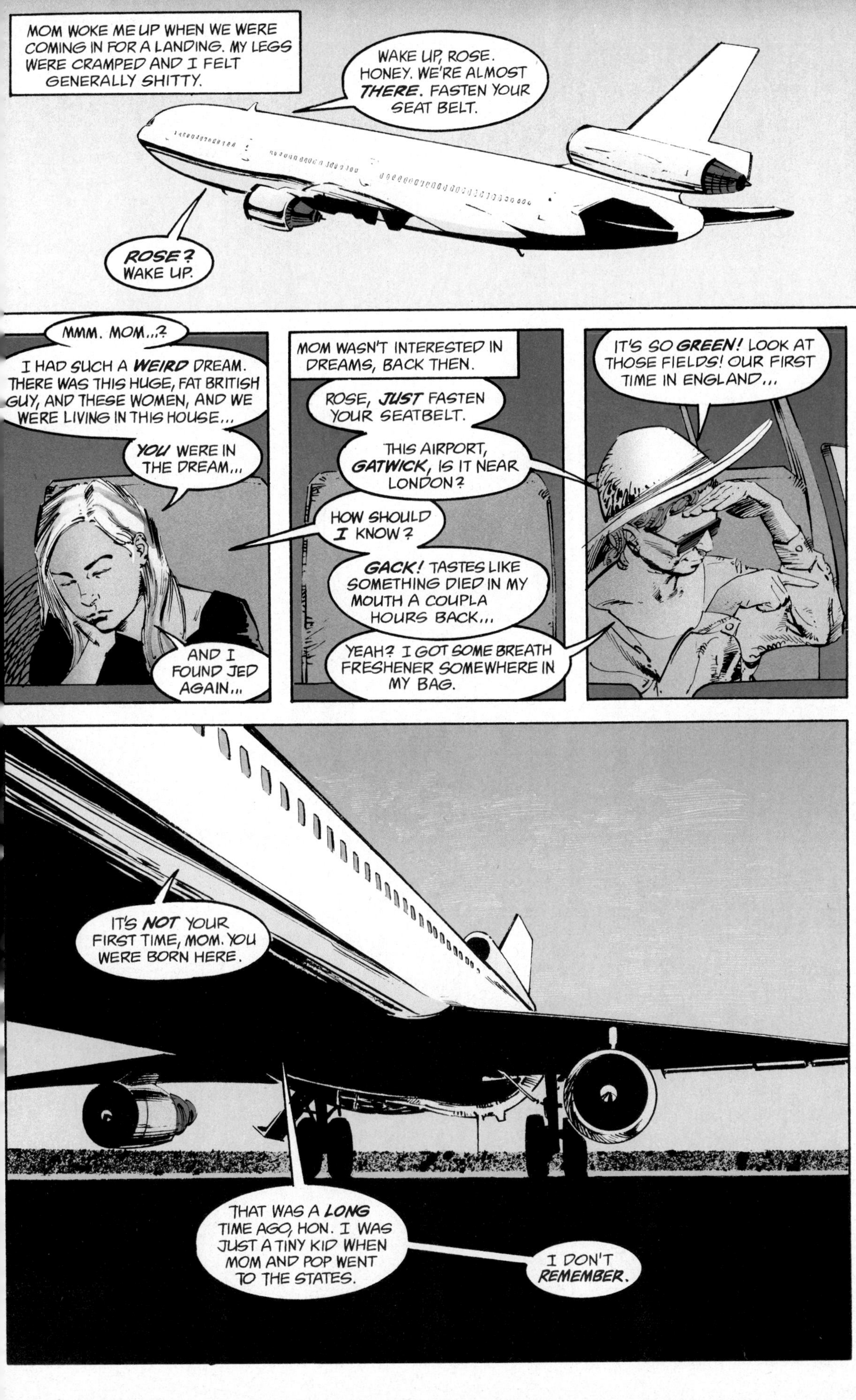

MOM WOKE ME UP WHEN WE WERE COMING IN FOR A LANDING. MY LEGS WERE CRAMPED AND I FELT GENERALLY SHITTY.
WAKE UP, ROSE. HONEY. WE'RE ALMOST THERE. FASTEN YOUR SEAT BELT.
ROSE? WAKE UP.
MMM. MOM...?
I HAD SUCH A WEIRD DREAM. THERE WAS THIS HUGE, FAT BRITISH GUY, AND THESE WOMEN, AND WE WERE LIVING IN THIS HOUSE...
YOU WERE IN THE DREAM...
AND I FOUND JED AGAIN...
MOM WASN'T INTERESTED IN DREAMS, BACK THEN.
ROSE, JUST FASTEN YOUR SEATBELT.
THIS AIRPORT, GATWICK, IS IT NEAR LONDON?
HOW SHOULD I KNOW?
GACK! TASTES LIKE SOMETHING DIED IN MY MOUTH A COUPLA HOURS BACK...
YEAH? I GOT SOME BREATH FRESHENER SOMEWHERE IN MY BAG.
IT'S SO GREEN! LOOK AT THOSE FIELDS! OUR FIRST TIME IN ENGLAND...
IT'S NOT YOUR FIRST TIME, MOM. YOU WERE BORN HERE.
THAT WAS A LONG TIME AGO, HON. I WAS JUST A TINY KID WHEN MOM AND POP WENT TO THE STATES.
I DON'T REMEMBER.

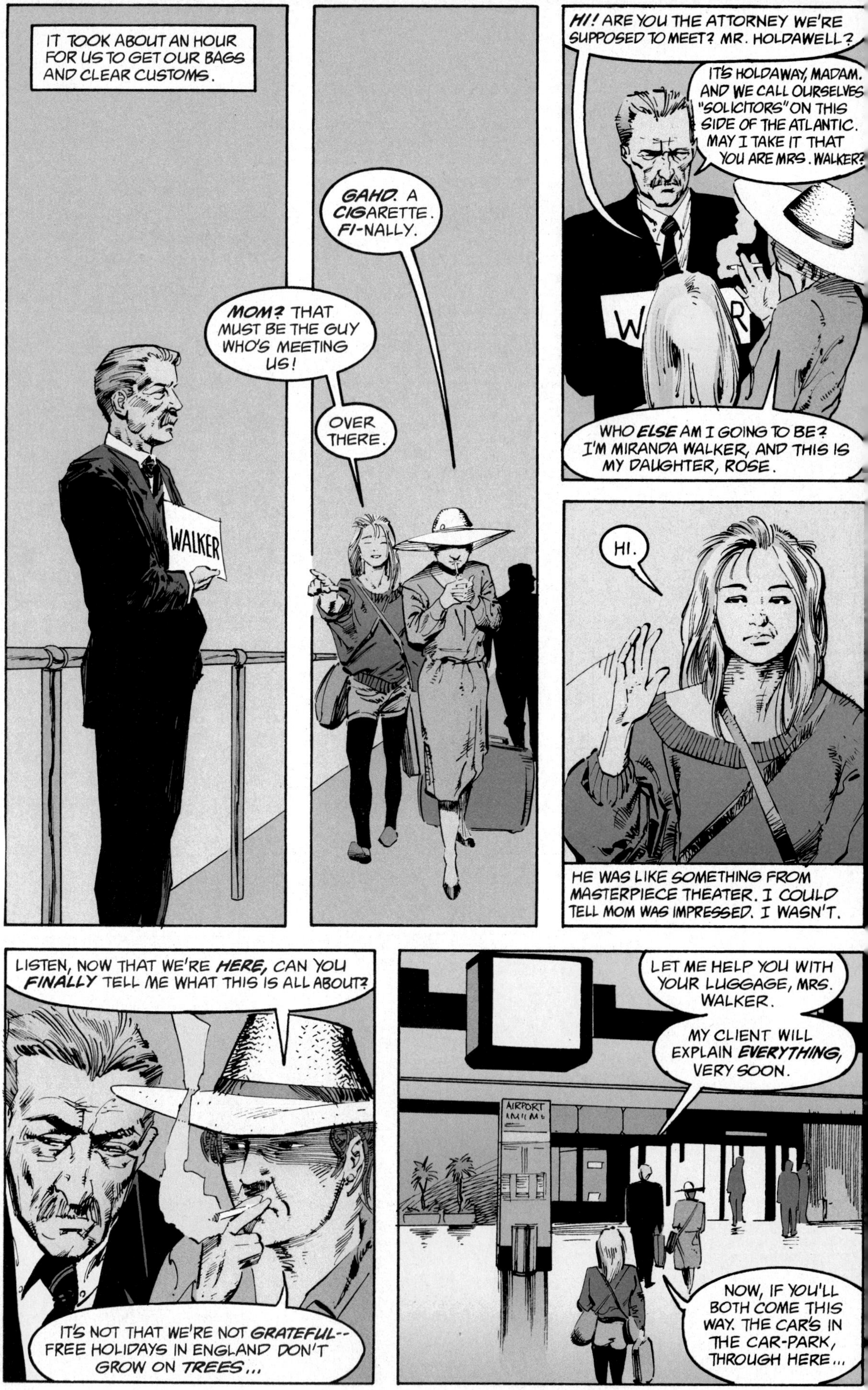
IT TOOK ABOUT AN HOUR FOR US TO GET OUR BAGS AND CLEAR CUSTOMS.
WALKER
GAHD. A CIGARETTE. FI-NALLY.
MOM? THAT MUST BE THE GUY WHO'S MEETING US!
OVER THERE.
HI! ARE YOU THE ATTORNEY WE'RE SUPPOSED TO MEET? MR. HOLDAWELL?
IT'S HOLDAWAY, MADAM. AND WE CALL OURSELVES "SOLICITORS" ON THIS SIDE OF THE ATLANTIC. MAY I TAKE IT THAT YOU ARE MRS. WALKER?
WHO ELSE AM I GOING TO BE? I'M MIRANDA WALKER, AND THIS IS MY DAUGHTER, ROSE.
HI.
HE WAS LIKE SOMETHING FROM MASTERPIECE THEATER. I COULD TELL MOM WAS IMPRESSED. I WASN'T.
LISTEN, NOW THAT WE'RE HERE, CAN YOU FINALLY TELL ME WHAT THIS IS ALL ABOUT?
IT'S NOT THAT WE'RE NOT GRATEFUL-- FREE HOLIDAYS IN ENGLAND DON'T GROW ON TREES...
LET ME HELP YOU WITH YOUR LUGGAGE, MRS. WALKER.
MY CLIENT WILL EXPLAIN EVERYTHING, VERY SOON.
AIRPORT
NOW, IF YOU'LL BOTH COME THIS WAY. THE CAR'S IN THE CAR-PARK, THROUGH HERE...

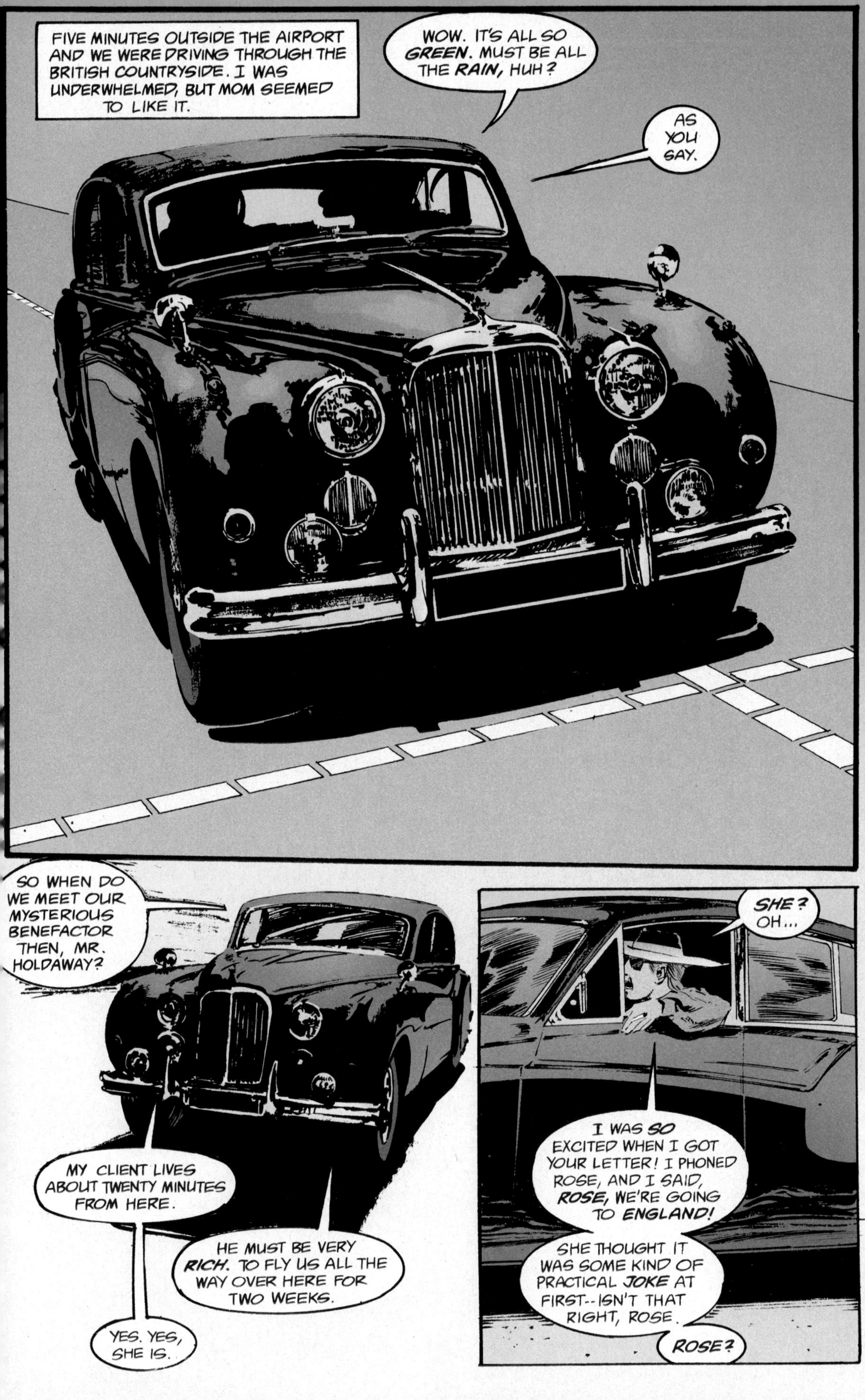
FIVE MINUTES OUTSIDE THE AIRPORT AND WE WERE DRIVING THROUGH THE BRITISH COUNTRYSIDE. I WAS UNDERWHELMED, BUT MOM SEEMED TO LIKE IT.
WOW. IT'S ALL SO GREEN. MUST BE ALL THE RAIN, HUH?
AS YOU SAY.
SO WHEN DO WE MEET OUR MYSTERIOUS BENEFACTOR THEN, MR. HOLDAWAY?
MY CLIENT LIVES ABOUT TWENTY MINUTES FROM HERE.
HE MUST BE VERY RICH. TO FLY US ALL THE WAY OVER HERE FOR TWO WEEKS.
YES. YES, SHE IS.
SHE? OH...
I WAS SO EXCITED WHEN I GOT YOUR LETTER! I PHONED ROSE, AND I SAID, ROSE, WE'RE GOING TO ENGLAND!
SHE THOUGHT IT WAS SOME KIND OF PRACTICAL JOKE AT FIRST--ISN'T THAT RIGHT, ROSE.
ROSE?

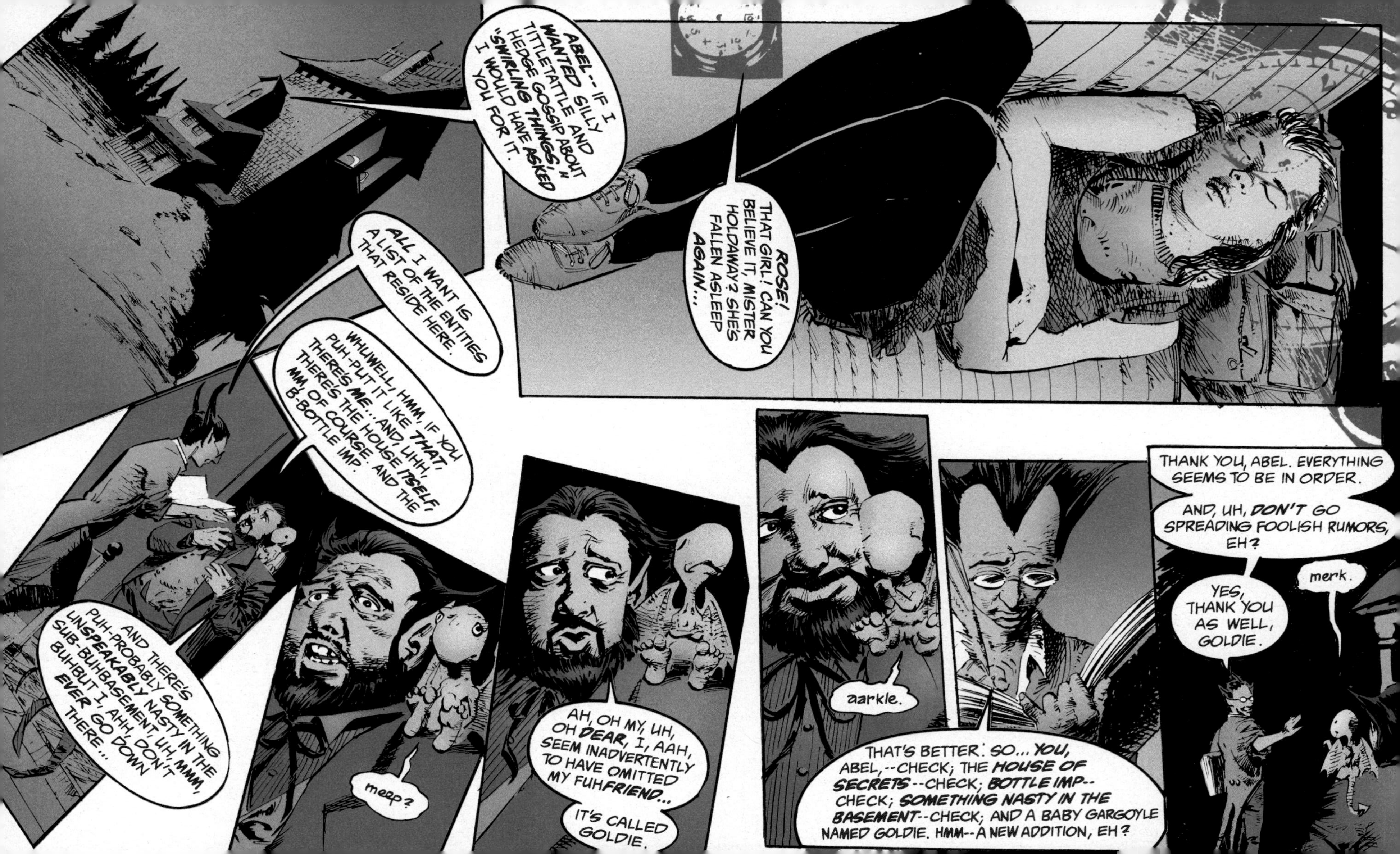
ABEL-- IF I WANTED SILLY TITTLETATTLE AND HEDGE GOSSIP ABOUT "SWIRLING THINGS," I WOULD HAVE ASKED YOU FOR IT.
ROSE! THAT GIRL! CAN YOU BELIEVE IT, MISTER HOLDAWAY? SHE'S FALLEN ASLEEP AGAIN...
ALL I WANT IS A LIST OF THE ENTITIES THAT RESIDE HERE.
WHUWELL, HMM, IF YOU PUH-PUT IT LIKE THAT, THERE'S ME... AND, UHH, THERE'S THE HOUSE ITSELF, MM, OF COURSE. AND THE B-BOTTLE IMP.
AND THERE'S PUH-PROBABLY SOMETHING UNSPEAKABLY NASTY IN THE SUB-BUHBASEMENT, UH, MMM, BUHBUT I, AHH, DON'T EVER GO DOWN THERE...
meep?
AH, OH MY, UH, OH DEAR, I, AAH, SEEM INADVERTENTLY TO HAVE OMITTED MY FUHFRIEND...
IT'S CALLED GOLDIE.
aarkle.
THAT'S BETTER. SO... YOU, ABEL, --CHECK; THE HOUSE OF SECRETS--CHECK; BOTTLE IMP--CHECK; SOMETHING NASTY IN THE BASEMENT--CHECK; AND A BABY GARGOYLE NAMED GOLDIE. HMM--A NEW ADDITION, EH?
THANK YOU, ABEL. EVERYTHING SEEMS TO BE IN ORDER.
AND, UH, DON'T GO SPREADING FOOLISH RUMORS, EH?
YES, THANK YOU AS WELL, GOLDIE.
merk.

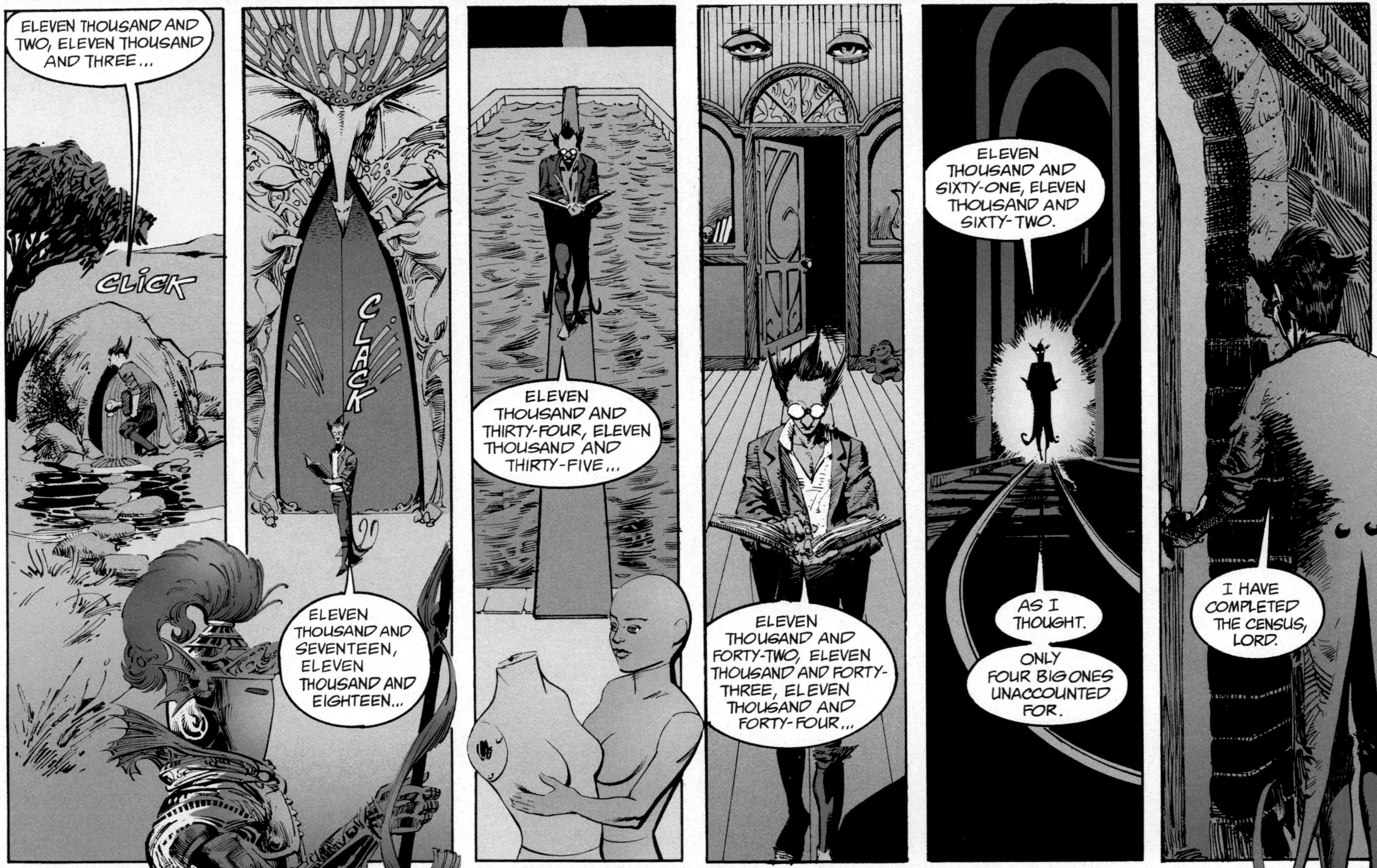
ELEVEN THOUSAND AND TWO, ELEVEN THOUSAND AND THREE...
CLICK
CLACK
ELEVEN THOUSAND AND SEVENTEEN, ELEVEN THOUSAND AND EIGHTEEN...
ELEVEN THOUSAND AND THIRTY-FOUR, ELEVEN THOUSAND AND THIRTY-FIVE...
ELEVEN THOUSAND AND FORTY-TWO, ELEVEN THOUSAND AND FORTY-THREE, ELEVEN THOUSAND AND FORTY-FOUR...
ELEVEN THOUSAND AND SIXTY-ONE, ELEVEN THOUSAND AND SIXTY-TWO.
AS I THOUGHT.
ONLY FOUR BIG ONES UNACCOUNTED FOR.
I HAVE COMPLETED THE CENSUS, LORD.

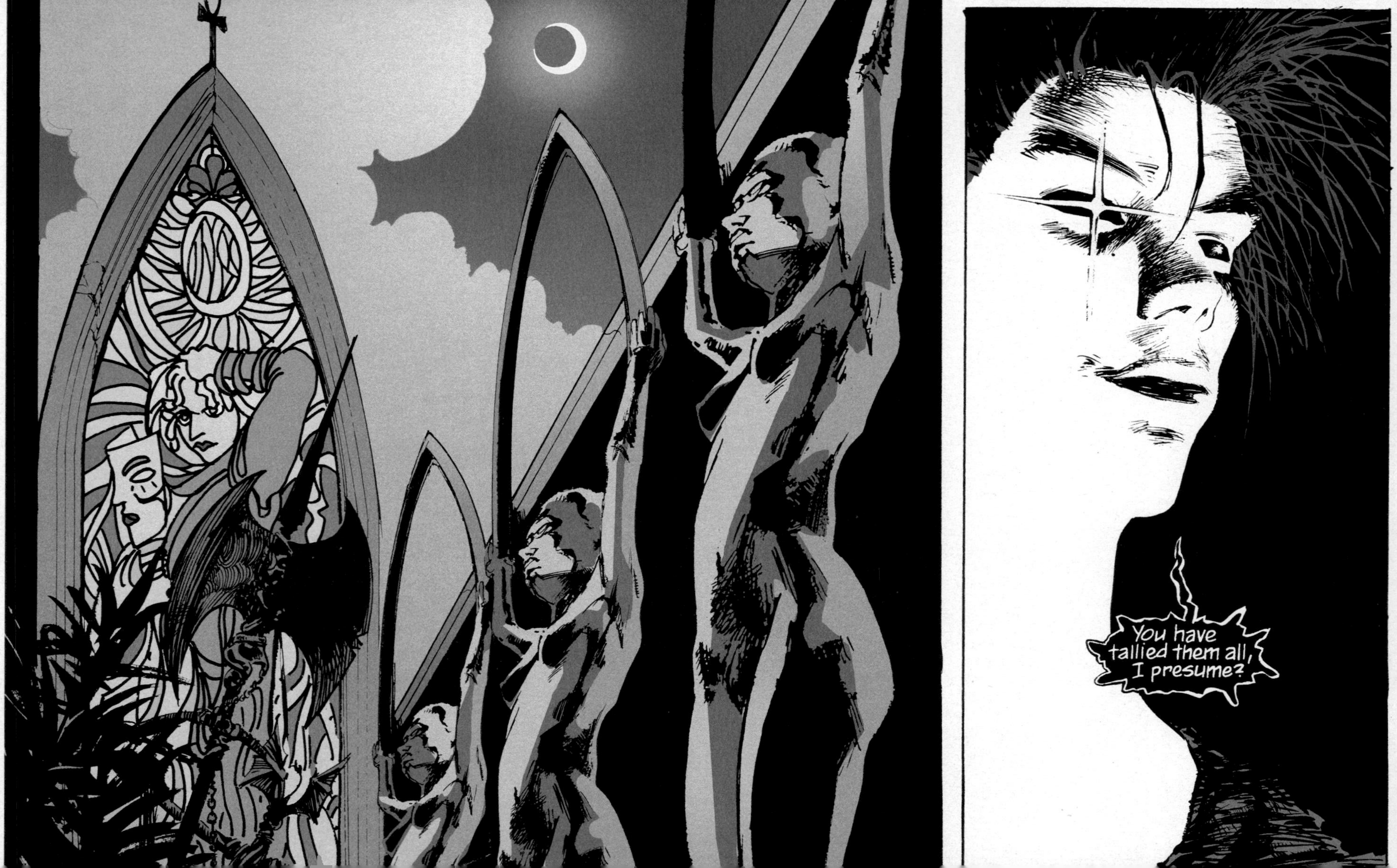
You have tallied them all, I presume?

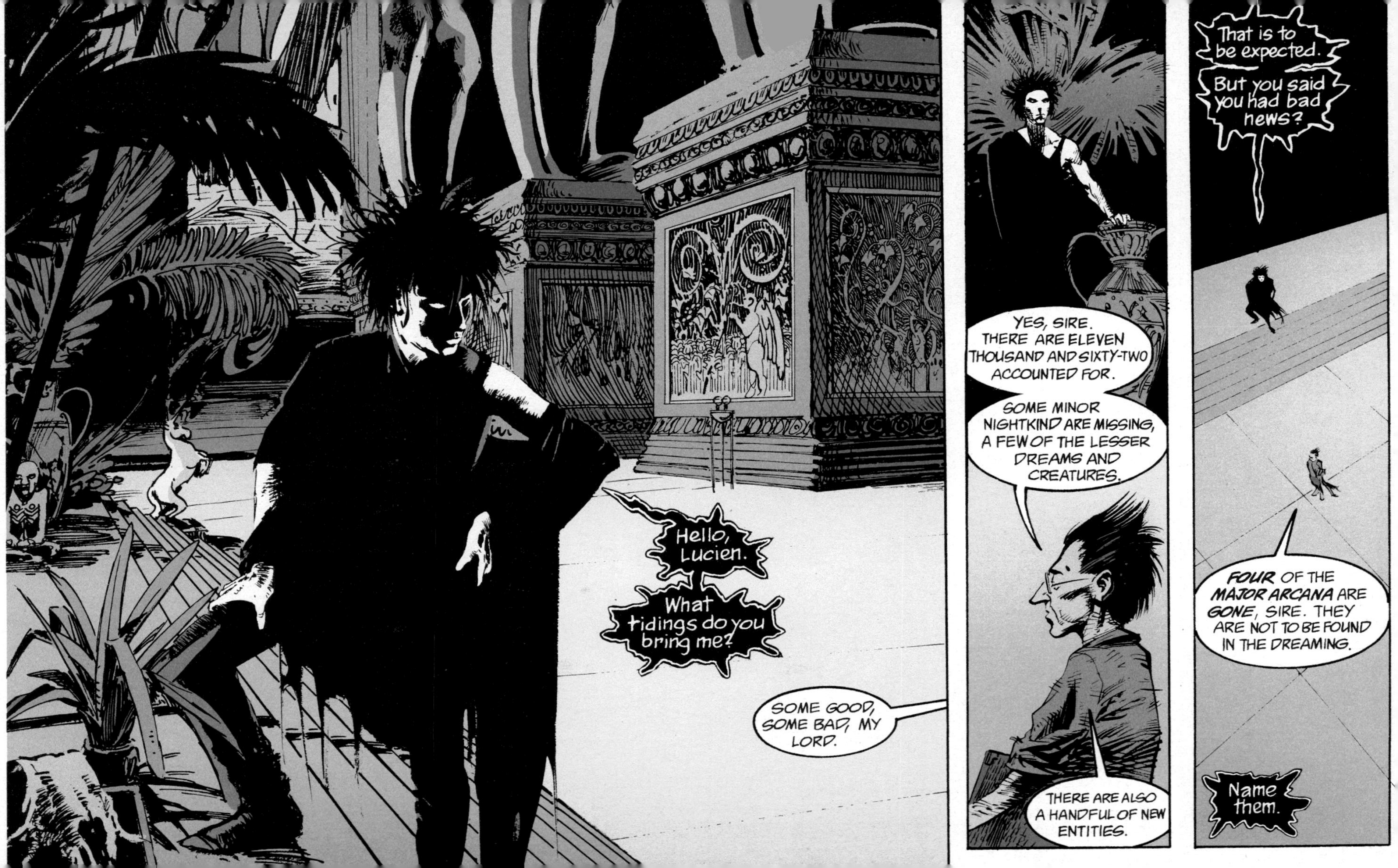
Hello, Lucien.
What tidings do you bring me?
SOME GOOD, SOME BAD, MY LORD.
YES, SIRE. THERE ARE ELEVEN THOUSAND AND SIXTY-TWO ACCOUNTED FOR.
SOME MINOR NIGHTKIND ARE MISSING, A FEW OF THE LESSER DREAMS AND CREATURES.
THERE ARE ALSO A HANDFUL OF NEW ENTITIES.
That is to be expected.
But you said you had bad news?
FOUR OF THE MAJOR ARCANA ARE GONE, SIRE. THEY ARE NOT TO BE FOUND IN THE DREAMING.
Name them.

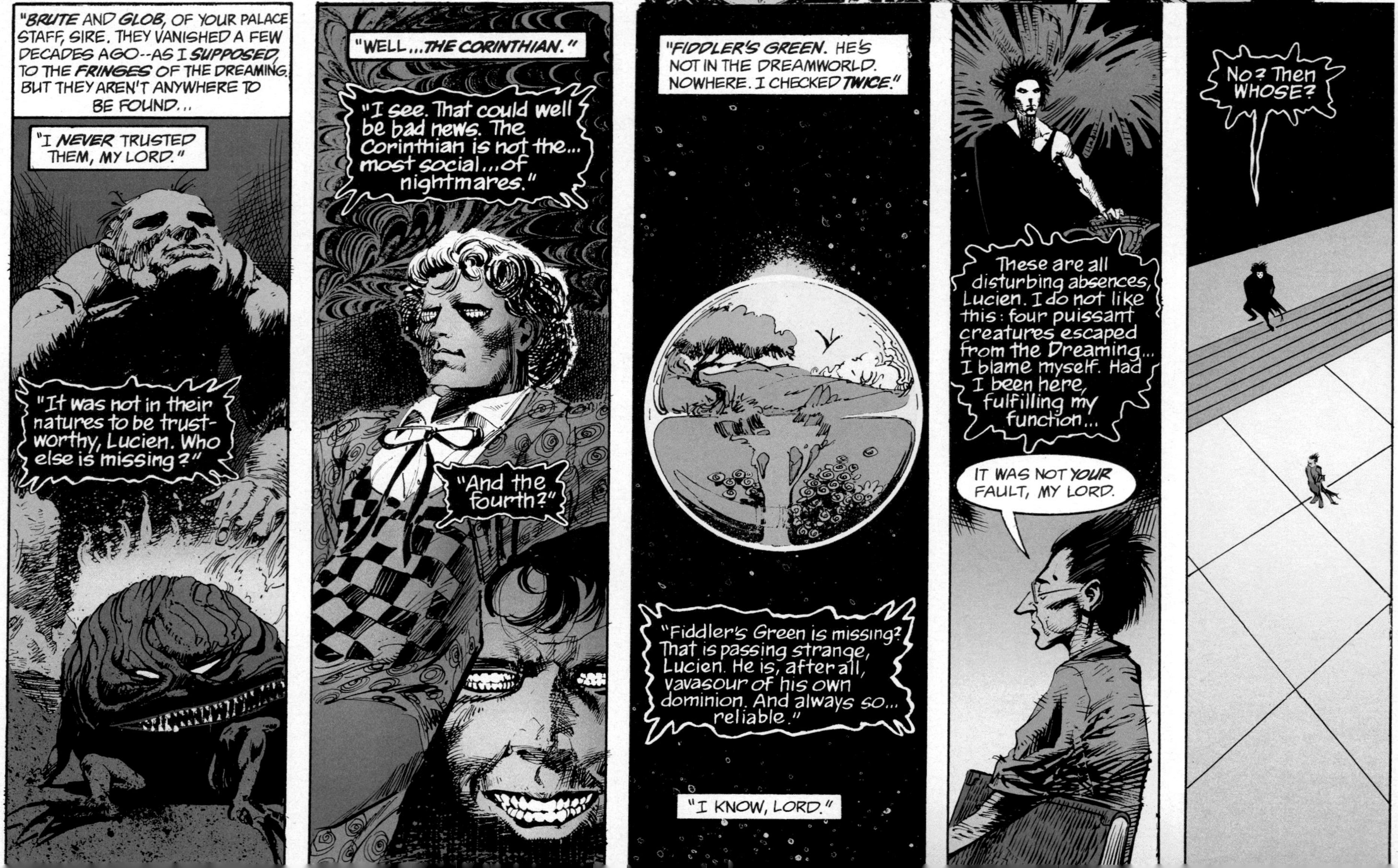
"BRUTE AND GLOB, OF YOUR PALACE STAFF, SIRE. THEY VANISHED A FEW DECADES AGO--AS I SUPPOSED, TO THE FRINGES OF THE DREAMING. BUT THEY AREN'T ANYWHERE TO BE FOUND...
"I NEVER TRUSTED THEM, MY LORD."
"It was not in their natures to be trust-worthy, Lucien. Who else is missing?"
"WELL...THE CORINTHIAN."
"I see. That could well be bad news. The Corinthian is not the... most social...of nightmares."
"And the fourth?"
"FIDDLER'S GREEN. HE'S NOT IN THE DREAMWORLD. NOWHERE. I CHECKED TWICE."
"Fiddler's Green is missing? That is passing strange, Lucien. He is, after all, vavasour of his own dominion. And always so... reliable."
"I KNOW, LORD."
These are all disturbing absences, Lucien. I do not like this: four puissant creatures escaped from the Dreaming... I blame myself. Had I been here, fulfilling my function...
IT WAS NOT YOUR FAULT, MY LORD.
No? Then WHOSE?

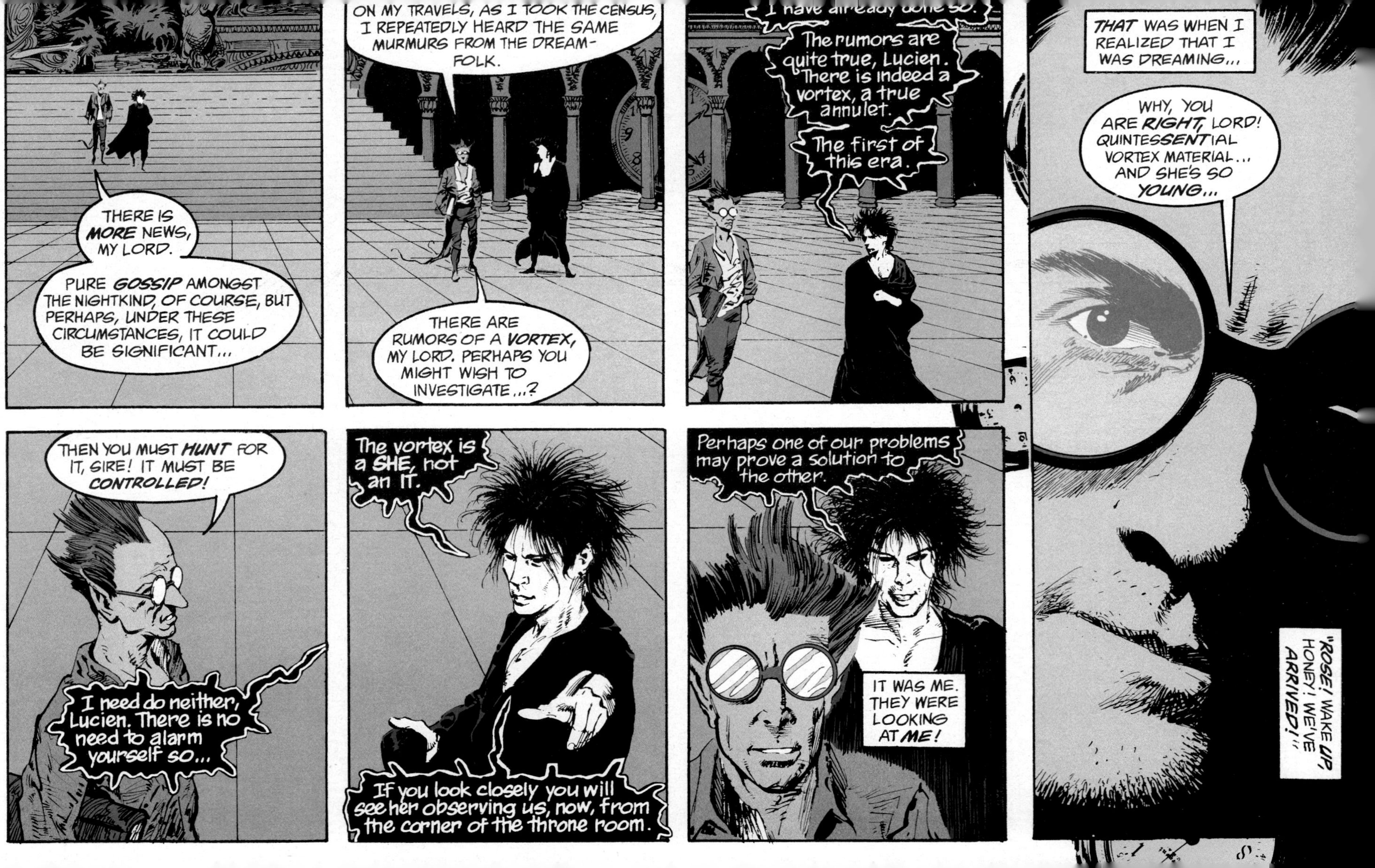

THERE IS MORE NEWS, MY LORD.
PURE GOSSIP AMONGST THE NIGHTKIND, OF COURSE, BUT PERHAPS, UNDER THESE CIRCUMSTANCES, IT COULD BE SIGNIFICANT...
ON MY TRAVELS, AS I TOOK THE CENSUS, I REPEATEDLY HEARD THE SAME MURMURS FROM THE DREAM-FOLK.
THERE ARE RUMORS OF A VORTEX, MY LORD. PERHAPS YOU MIGHT WISH TO INVESTIGATE...?
The rumors are quite true, Lucien. There is indeed a vortex, a true annulet.
The first of this era.
THEN YOU MUST HUNT FOR IT, SIRE! IT MUST BE CONTROLLED!
I need do neither, Lucien. There is no need to alarm yourself so...
The vortex is a SHE, not an IT.
If you look closely you will see her observing us, now, from the corner of the throne room.
Perhaps one of our problems may prove a solution to the other.
IT WAS ME. THEY WERE LOOKING AT ME!
THAT WAS WHEN I REALIZED THAT I WAS DREAMING...
WHY, YOU ARE RIGHT, LORD! QUINTESSENTIAL VORTEX MATERIAL... AND SHE'S SO YOUNG...
"ROSE! WAKE UP, HONEY! WE'VE ARRIVED!"

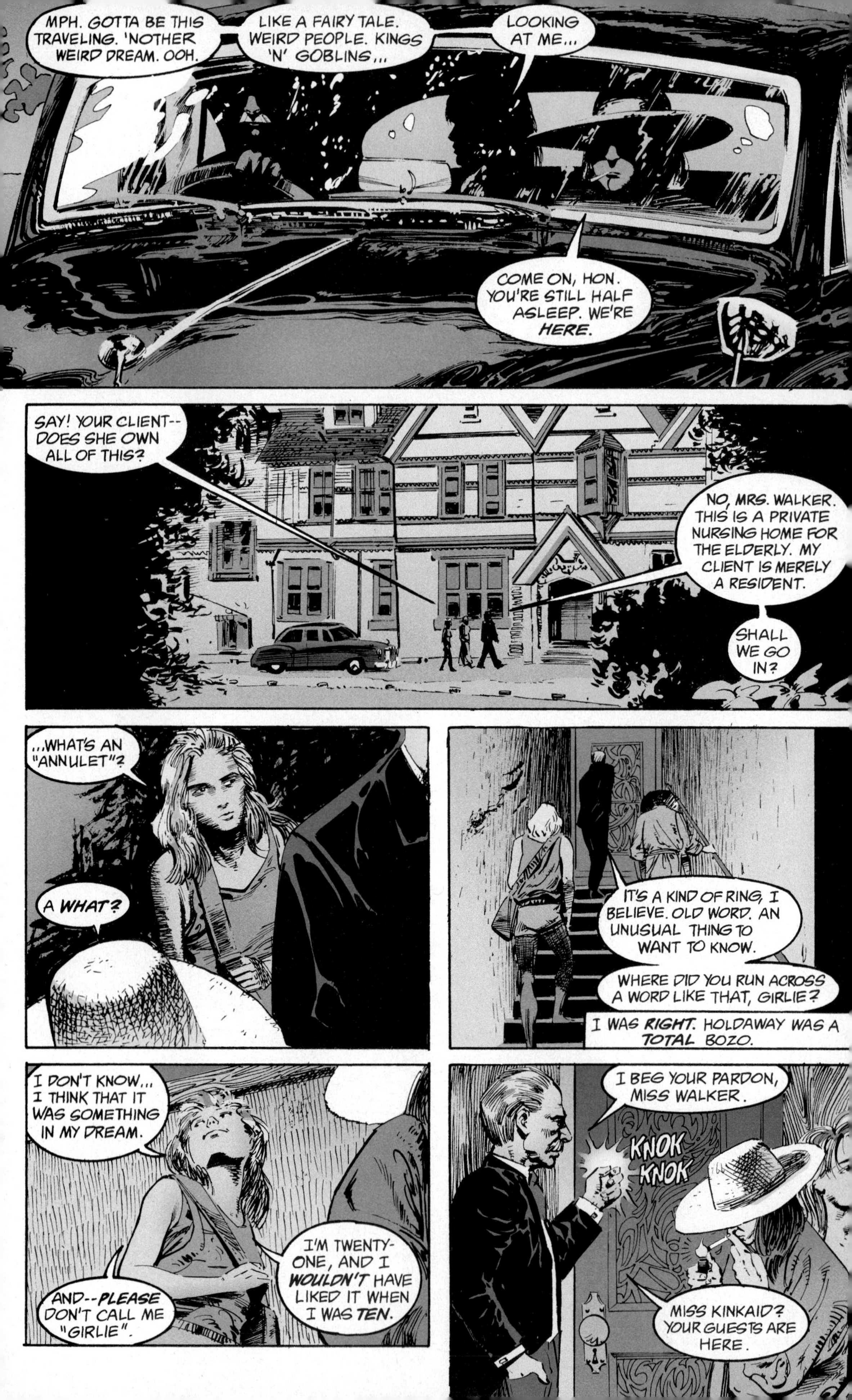
MPH. GOTTA BE THIS TRAVELING. 'NOTHER WEIRD DREAM. OOH.
LIKE A FAIRY TALE. WEIRD PEOPLE. KINGS 'N' GOBLINS...
LOOKING AT ME...
COME ON, HON. YOU'RE STILL HALF ASLEEP. WE'RE **HERE**.
SAY! YOUR CLIENT-- DOES SHE OWN ALL OF THIS?
NO, MRS. WALKER. THIS IS A PRIVATE NURSING HOME FOR THE ELDERLY. MY CLIENT IS MERELY A RESIDENT.
SHALL WE GO IN?
...WHAT'S AN "ANNULET"?
A **WHAT?**
IT'S A KIND OF RING, I BELIEVE. OLD WORD. AN UNUSUAL THING TO WANT TO KNOW.
WHERE DID YOU RUN ACROSS A WORD LIKE THAT, GIRLIE?
I WAS **RIGHT**. HOLDAWAY WAS A **TOTAL** BOZO.
I DON'T KNOW... I THINK THAT IT WAS SOMETHING IN MY DREAM.
AND--**PLEASE** DON'T CALL ME "GIRLIE".
I'M TWENTY-ONE, AND I **WOULDN'T** HAVE LIKED IT WHEN I WAS **TEN**.
I BEG YOUR PARDON, MISS WALKER.
KNOK KNOK
MISS KINKAID? YOUR GUESTS ARE HERE.

PLEASE COME IN! IT ISN'T LOCKED.

I DON'T KNOW WHAT I WAS EXPECTING. NOT HER. SHE LOOKED LOST, AND FRAGILE, LIKE A LITTLE CHINA DOLL.

AND WEIRDLY FAMILIAR, AND I DIDN'T KNOW WHY.

HELLO. YOU'RE MIRANDA WALKER. AND YOU MUST BE ROSE. COME OVER HERE, DARLING. BOTH OF YOU. LET ME LOOK AT YOU.

I'M UNITY. UNITY KINKAID.

YES. OH YES.

PLEASE, BOTH OF YOU, SIT NEXT TO ME.

THIS... THIS IS MY ROOM. I THOUGHT BRIEFLY ABOUT MOVING OUT, BUT THE BEDFORD SQUARE HOUSE WAS SOLD A LONG TIME AGO, AND I'VE LIVED HERE SO LONG.

OVER THIRTY YEARS, THEY TELL ME.

I WANTED TO SEE YOU BOTH, YOU SEE, AND I THOUGHT PERHAPS IF IT WERE ALL EXPLAINED TO YOU FIRST YOU... YOU MIGHT NOT HAVE BEEN WILLING TO COME.

AND I COULDN'T HAVE BORNE THAT.

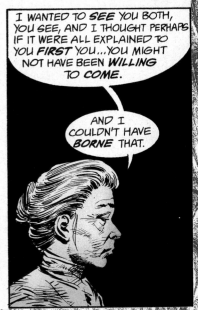

THAT'S ALL I HAVE LEFT OF THE OLD HOUSE. HOLDAWAYS HELD ONTO IT WHEN THE FURNITURE WAS SOLD, ALONG WITH A FEW PERSONAL POSSESSIONS.

I'M SORRY ABOUT ALL THIS RIGMAROLE. IT WAS MY OWN FAULT.

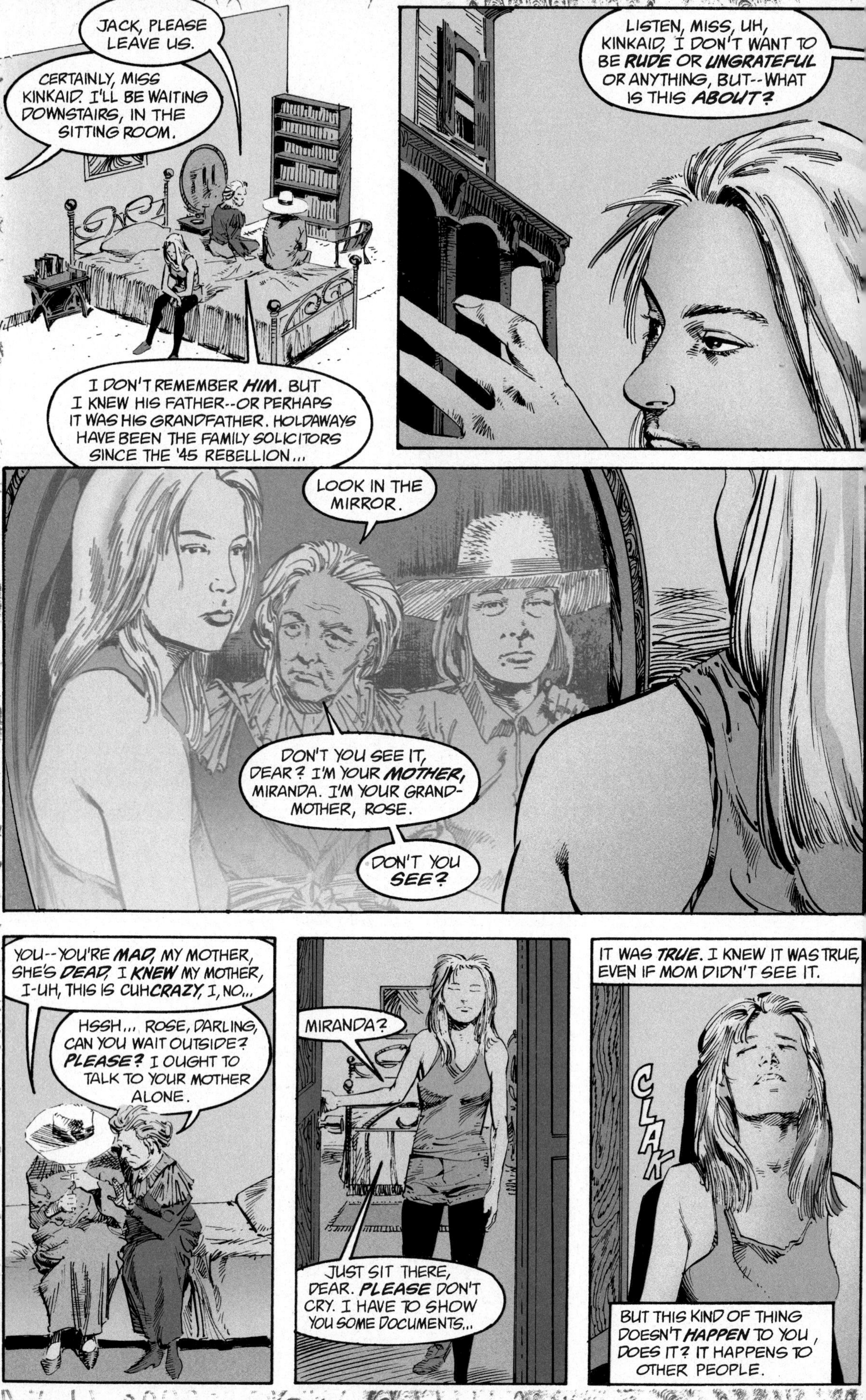
JACK, PLEASE LEAVE US.
CERTAINLY, MISS KINKAID. I'LL BE WAITING DOWNSTAIRS, IN THE SITTING ROOM.
I DON'T REMEMBER HIM. BUT I KNEW HIS FATHER--OR PERHAPS IT WAS HIS GRANDFATHER. HOLDAWAYS HAVE BEEN THE FAMILY SOLICITORS SINCE THE '45 REBELLION...
LISTEN, MISS, UH, KINKAID, I DON'T WANT TO BE RUDE OR UNGRATEFUL OR ANYTHING, BUT--WHAT IS THIS ABOUT?
LOOK IN THE MIRROR.
DON'T YOU SEE IT, DEAR? I'M YOUR MOTHER, MIRANDA. I'M YOUR GRAND-MOTHER, ROSE.
DON'T YOU SEE?
YOU--YOU'RE MAD, MY MOTHER, SHE'S DEAD, I KNEW MY MOTHER, I-UH, THIS IS CUHCRAZY, I, NO...
HSSH... ROSE, DARLING, CAN YOU WAIT OUTSIDE? PLEASE? I OUGHT TO TALK TO YOUR MOTHER ALONE.
MIRANDA?
JUST SIT THERE, DEAR. PLEASE DON'T CRY. I HAVE TO SHOW YOU SOME DOCUMENTS...
IT WAS TRUE. I KNEW IT WAS TRUE, EVEN IF MOM DIDN'T SEE IT.
CLAK
BUT THIS KIND OF THING DOESN'T HAPPEN TO YOU, DOES IT? IT HAPPENS TO OTHER PEOPLE.

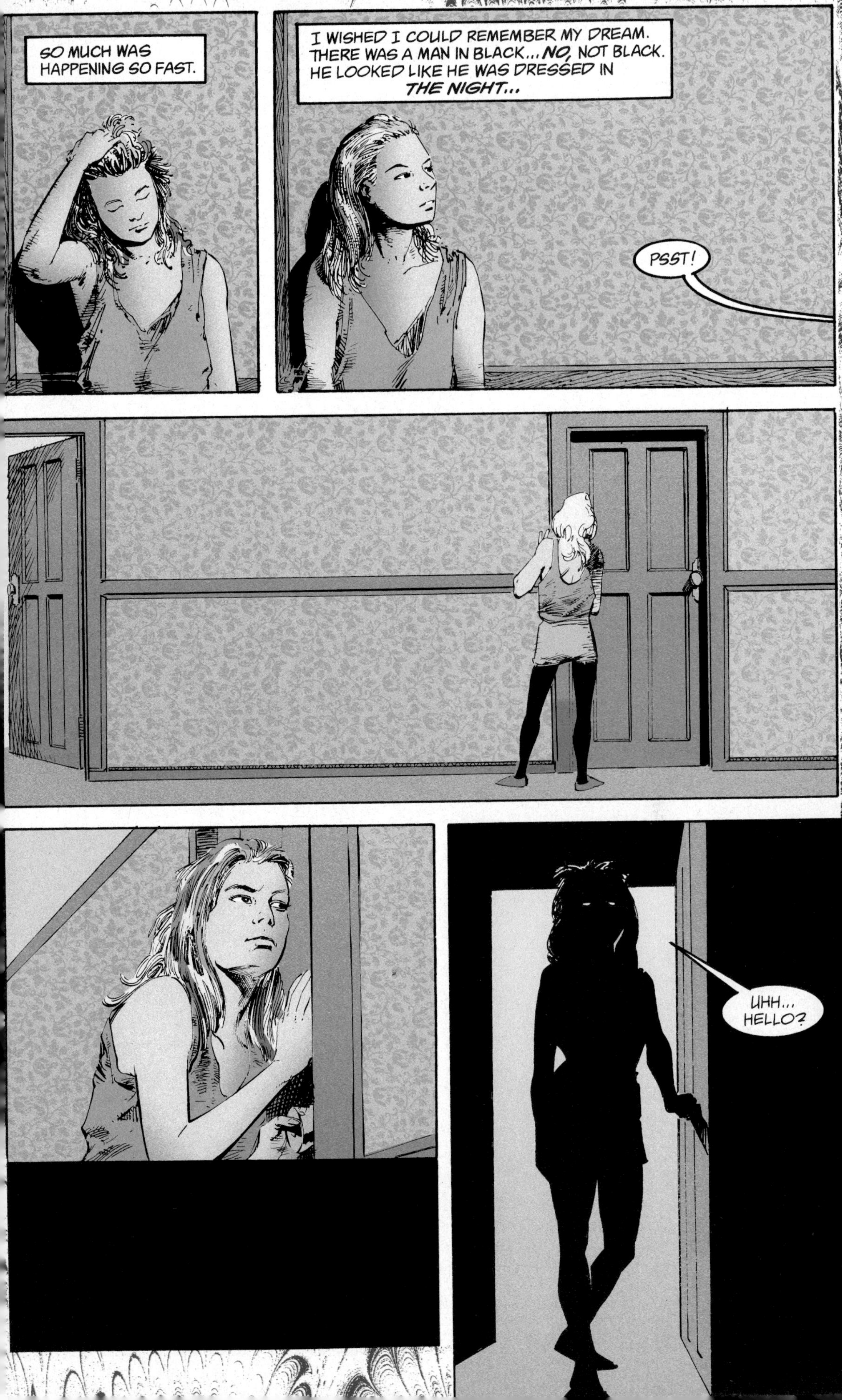
SO MUCH WAS HAPPENING SO FAST.
I WISHED I COULD REMEMBER MY DREAM. THERE WAS A MAN IN BLACK... NO, NOT BLACK. HE LOOKED LIKE HE WAS DRESSED IN THE NIGHT...
PSST!
UHH... HELLO?

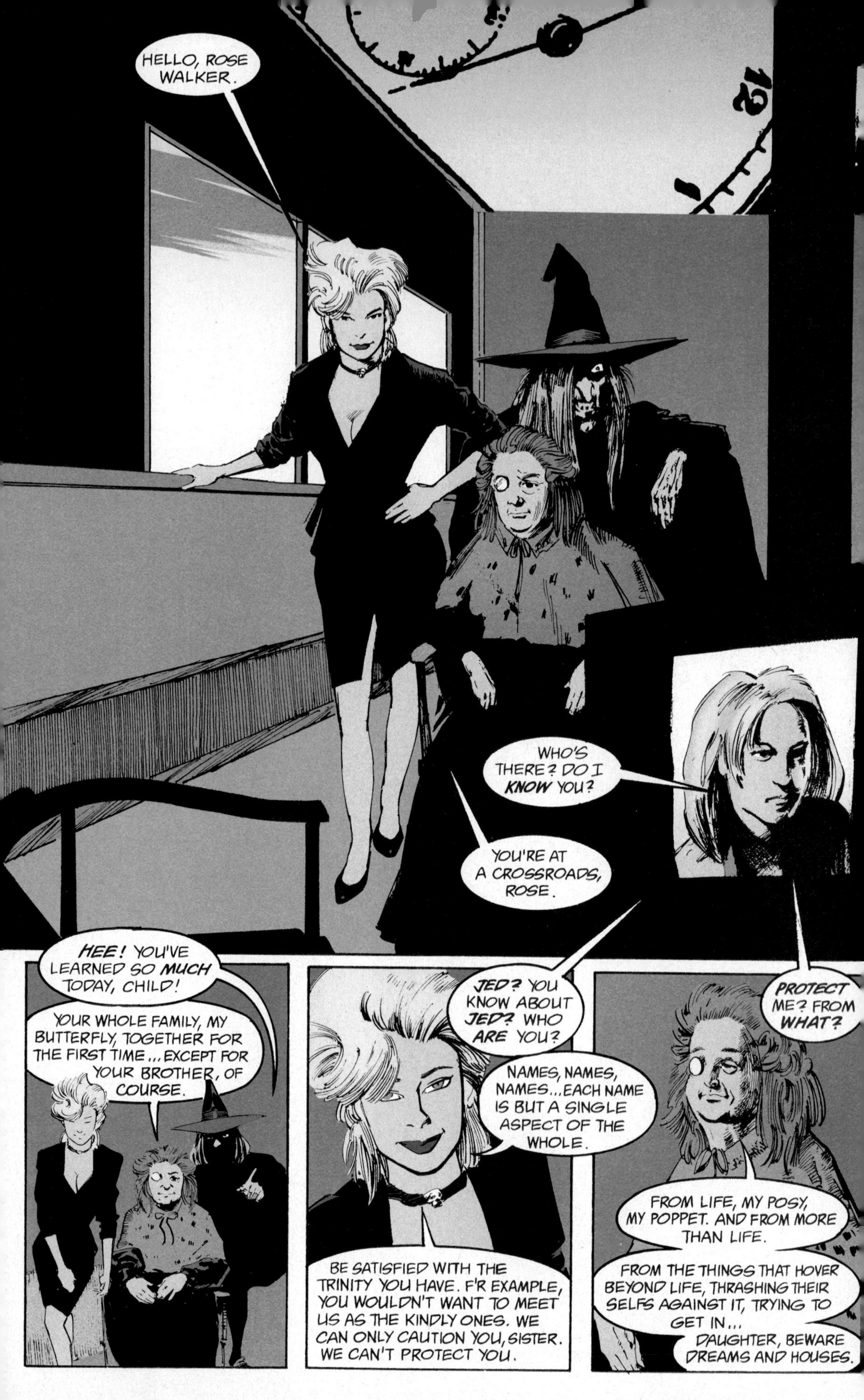
HELLO, ROSE WALKER.
WHO'S THERE? DO I KNOW YOU?
YOU'RE AT A CROSSROADS, ROSE.
HEE! YOU'VE LEARNED SO MUCH TODAY, CHILD!
YOUR WHOLE FAMILY, MY BUTTERFLY, TOGETHER FOR THE FIRST TIME... EXCEPT FOR YOUR BROTHER, OF COURSE.
JED? YOU KNOW ABOUT JED? WHO ARE YOU?
NAMES, NAMES, NAMES... EACH NAME IS BUT A SINGLE ASPECT OF THE WHOLE.
BE SATISFIED WITH THE TRINITY YOU HAVE. F'R EXAMPLE, YOU WOULDN'T WANT TO MEET US AS THE KINDLY ONES. WE CAN ONLY CAUTION YOU, SISTER. WE CAN'T PROTECT YOU.
PROTECT ME? FROM WHAT?
FROM LIFE, MY POSY, MY POPPET. AND FROM MORE THAN LIFE.
FROM THE THINGS THAT HOVER BEYOND LIFE, THRASHING THEIR SELFS AGAINST IT, TRYING TO GET IN...
DAUGHTER, BEWARE DREAMS AND HOUSES.

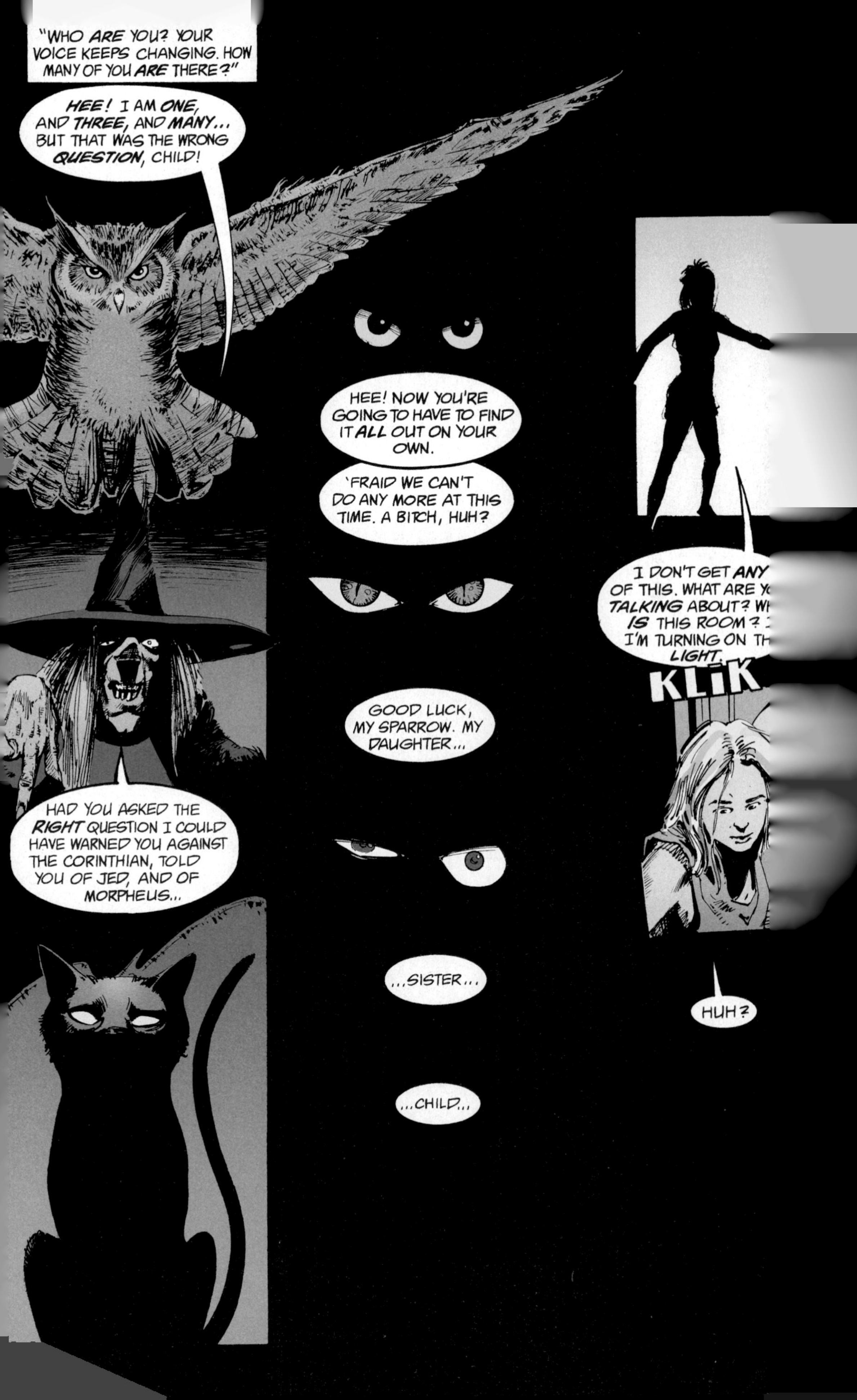
"WHO ARE YOU? YOUR VOICE KEEPS CHANGING. HOW MANY OF YOU ARE THERE?"
HEE! I AM ONE, AND THREE, AND MANY... BUT THAT WAS THE WRONG QUESTION, CHILD!
HAD YOU ASKED THE RIGHT QUESTION I COULD HAVE WARNED YOU AGAINST THE CORINTHIAN, TOLD YOU OF JED, AND OF MORPHEUS...
HEE! NOW YOU'RE GOING TO HAVE TO FIND IT ALL OUT ON YOUR OWN.
'FRAID WE CAN'T DO ANY MORE AT THIS TIME. A BITCH, HUH?
GOOD LUCK, MY SPARROW. MY DAUGHTER...
...SISTER...
...CHILD...
I DON'T GET ANY OF THIS. WHAT ARE TALKING ABOUT? IS THIS ROOM? I'M TURNING ON LIGHT.
KLIK
HUH?

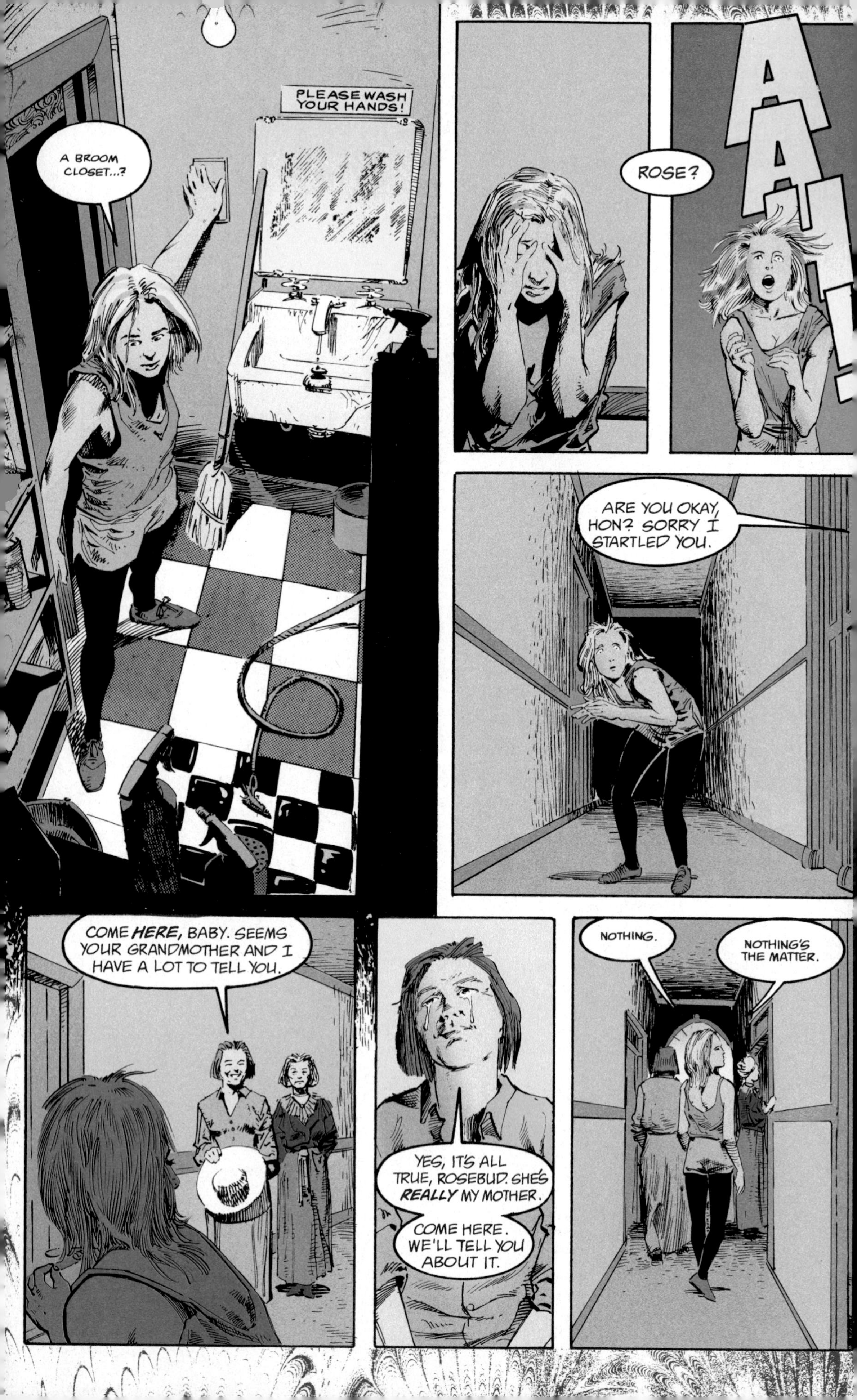
PLEASE WASH YOUR HANDS!
A BROOM CLOSET...?
ROSE?
AAH!!
ARE YOU OKAY, HON? SORRY I STARTLED YOU.
COME HERE, BABY. SEEMS YOUR GRANDMOTHER AND I HAVE A LOT TO TELL YOU.
YES, IT'S ALL TRUE, ROSEBUD. SHE'S REALLY MY MOTHER.
COME HERE. WE'LL TELL YOU ABOUT IT.
NOTHING.
NOTHING'S THE MATTER.

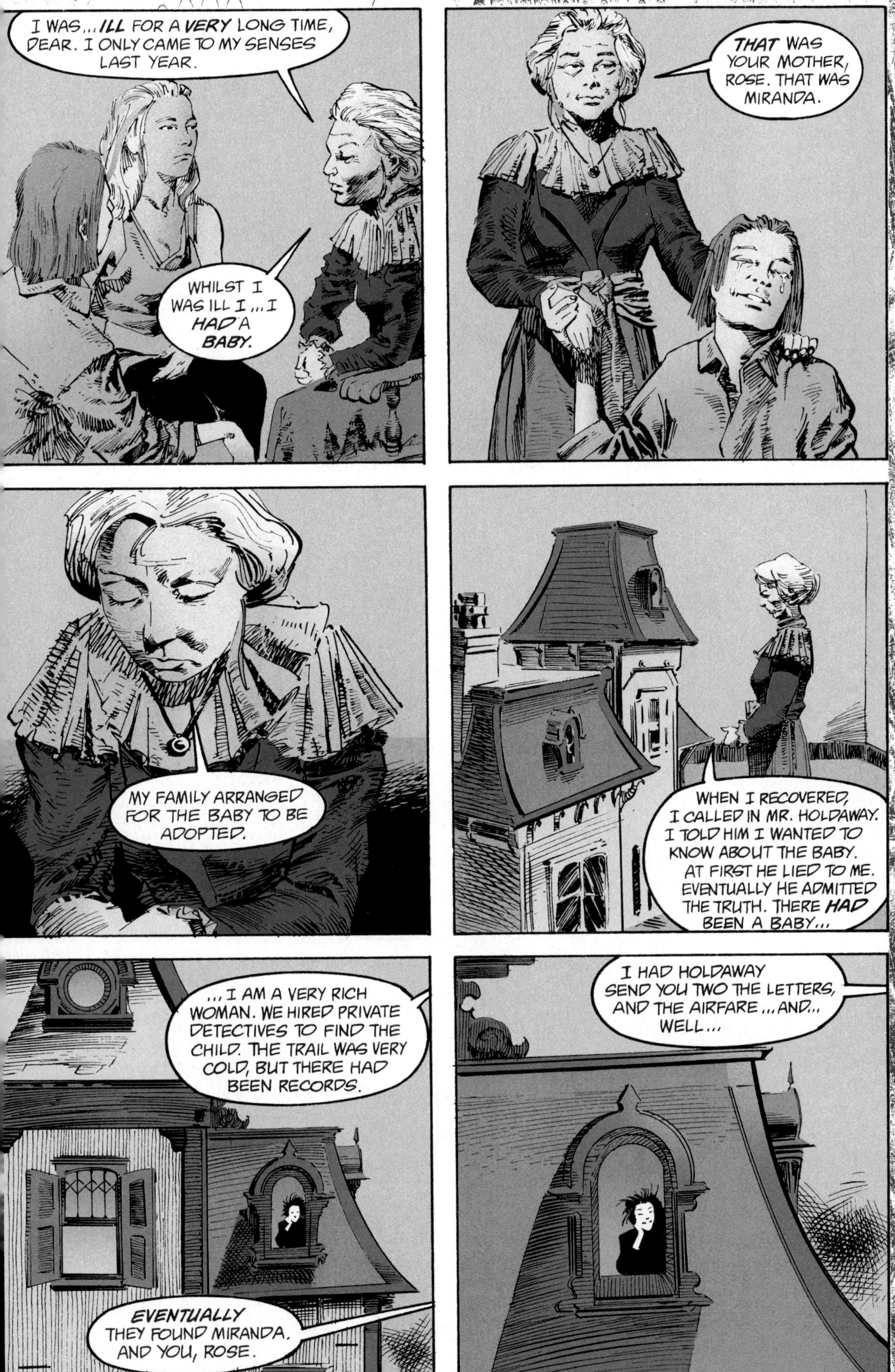
I WAS... ILL FOR A VERY LONG TIME, DEAR. I ONLY CAME TO MY SENSES LAST YEAR.
WHILST I WAS ILL I... I HAD A BABY.
THAT WAS YOUR MOTHER, ROSE. THAT WAS MIRANDA.
MY FAMILY ARRANGED FOR THE BABY TO BE ADOPTED.
WHEN I RECOVERED, I CALLED IN MR. HOLDAWAY. I TOLD HIM I WANTED TO KNOW ABOUT THE BABY. AT FIRST HE LIED TO ME. EVENTUALLY HE ADMITTED THE TRUTH. THERE HAD BEEN A BABY...
...I AM A VERY RICH WOMAN. WE HIRED PRIVATE DETECTIVES TO FIND THE CHILD. THE TRAIL WAS VERY COLD, BUT THERE HAD BEEN RECORDS.
EVENTUALLY THEY FOUND MIRANDA, AND YOU, ROSE.
I HAD HOLDAWAY SEND YOU TWO THE LETTERS, AND THE AIRFARE... AND... WELL...

...HERE YOU ARE.

THE WHOLE FAMILY. TOGETHER FOR THE FIRST TIME.

NOT JED, THOUGH. I *WONDERED*-- HAD MOM *TOLD* HER ABOUT JED?

I'M ALMOST NINETY, ROSE. BUT I'VE ONLY REALLY *LIVED* FOR ABOUT SEVENTEEN YEARS. IN A FUNNY WAY, I'M YOUNGER THAN *YOU*...

I...I SHOULD *GIVE* YOU SOMETHING, SHOULDN'T I? HERE. SOMETHING FOR YOU. A *RING*.

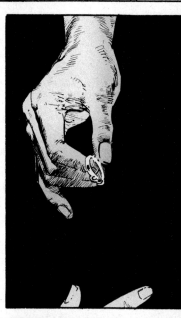

THE ANNULET...?

WHAT?

IT'S ALL COMING TRUE, ISN'T IT? MY DREAMS...

WHAT ARE YOU *TALKING* ABOUT, ROSEBUD?

WHAT'S *HAPPENING* TO ME, MOM? THE WOMAN IN THE HALL CLOSET. SHE KNEW ABOUT *JED*. SHE SAID I SHOULD BEWARE OF THE CORINTHIAN...

WHAT'S "*THE CORINTHIAN*"?

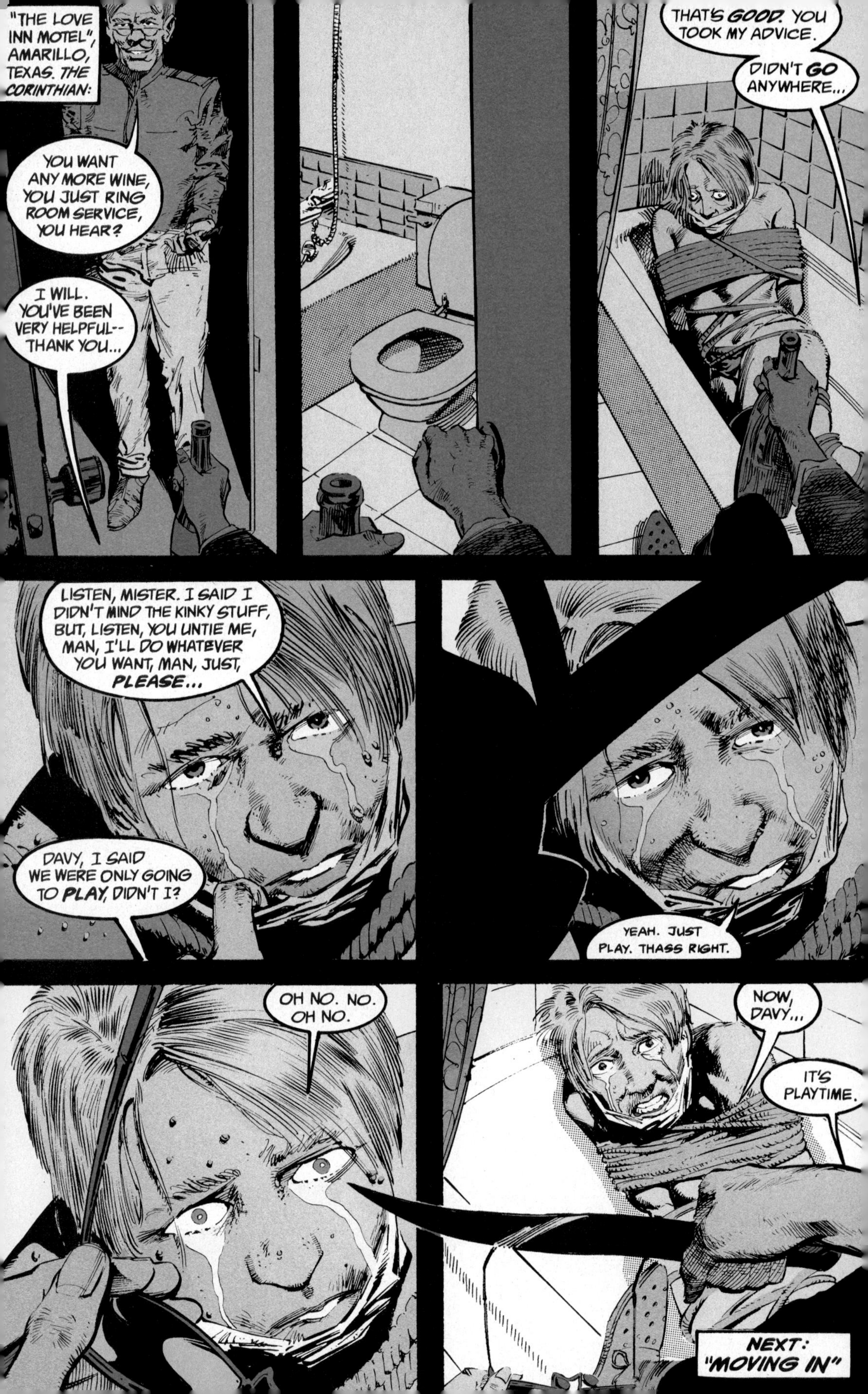
"THE LOVE INN MOTEL", AMARILLO, TEXAS. THE CORINTHIAN:
YOU WANT ANY MORE WINE, YOU JUST RING ROOM SERVICE, YOU HEAR?
I WILL. YOU'VE BEEN VERY HELPFUL-- THANK YOU...
THAT'S GOOD. YOU TOOK MY ADVICE.
DIDN'T GO ANYWHERE...
LISTEN, MISTER. I SAID I DIDN'T MIND THE KINKY STUFF, BUT, LISTEN, YOU UNTIE ME, MAN, I'LL DO WHATEVER YOU WANT, MAN, JUST, PLEASE...
DAVY, I SAID WE WERE ONLY GOING TO PLAY, DIDN'T I?
YEAH. JUST PLAY. THASS RIGHT.
OH NO. NO. OH NO.
NOW, DAVY...
IT'S PLAYTIME.
NEXT: "MOVING IN"

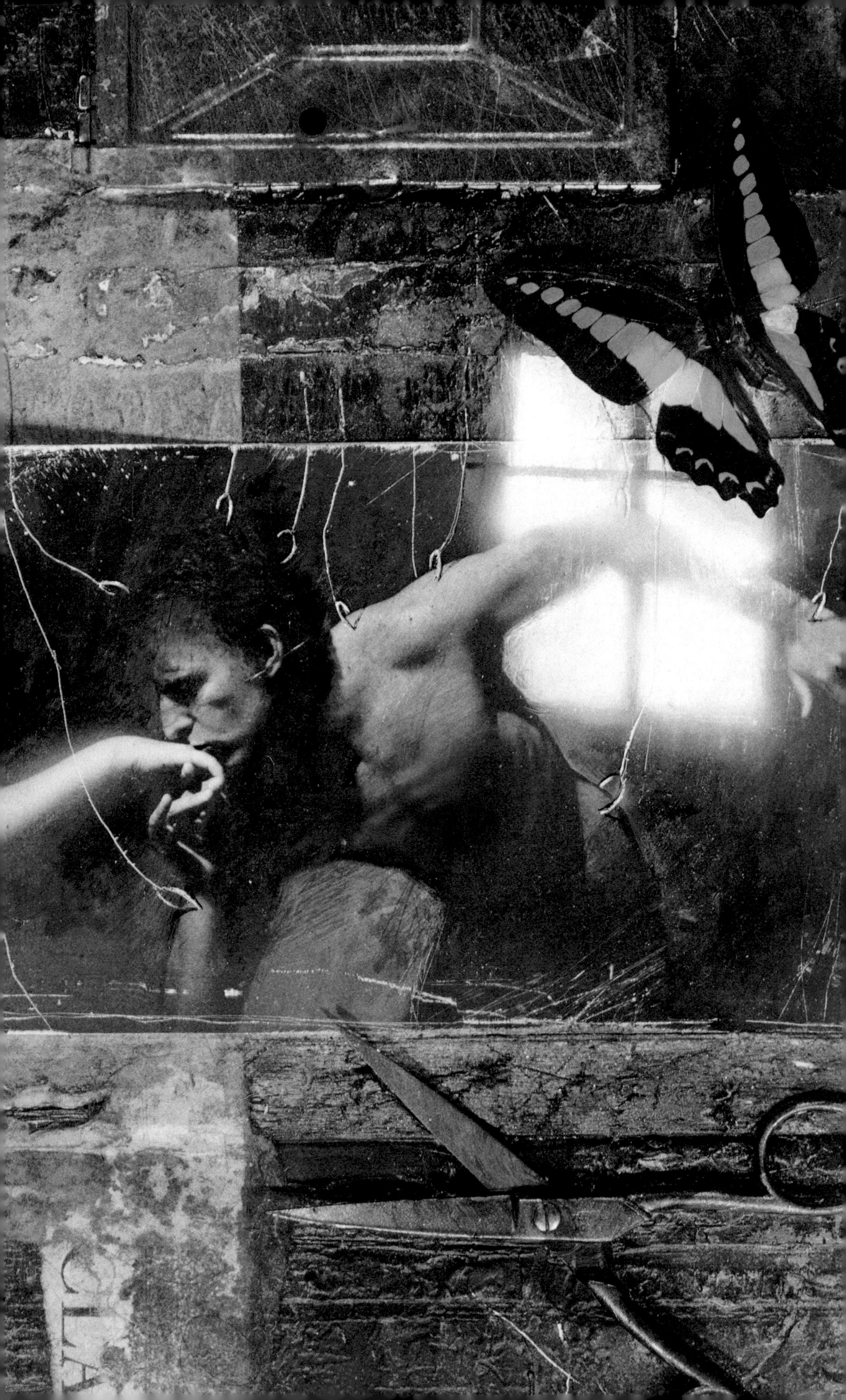

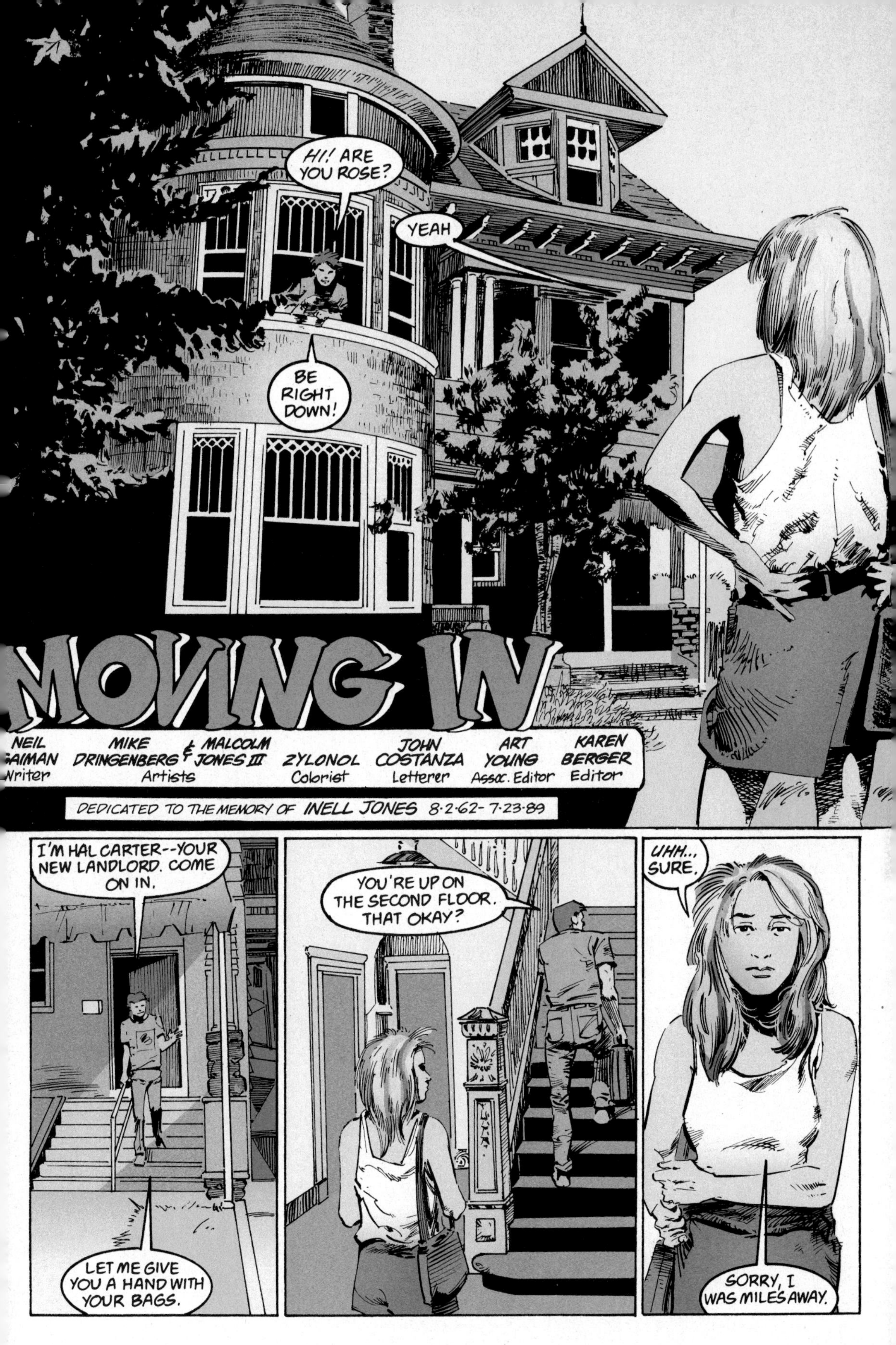
HI! ARE YOU ROSE?
YEAH
BE RIGHT DOWN!
MOVING IN
NEIL GAIMAN Writer
MIKE DRINGENBERG & MALCOLM JONES III Artists
ZYLONOL Colorist
JOHN COSTANZA Letterer
ART YOUNG Assoc. Editor
KAREN BERGER Editor
DEDICATED TO THE MEMORY OF INELL JONES 8·2·62–7·23·89
I'M HAL CARTER--YOUR NEW LANDLORD. COME ON IN.
LET ME GIVE YOU A HAND WITH YOUR BAGS.
YOU'RE UP ON THE SECOND FLOOR. THAT OKAY?
UHH... SURE.
SORRY, I WAS MILES AWAY.

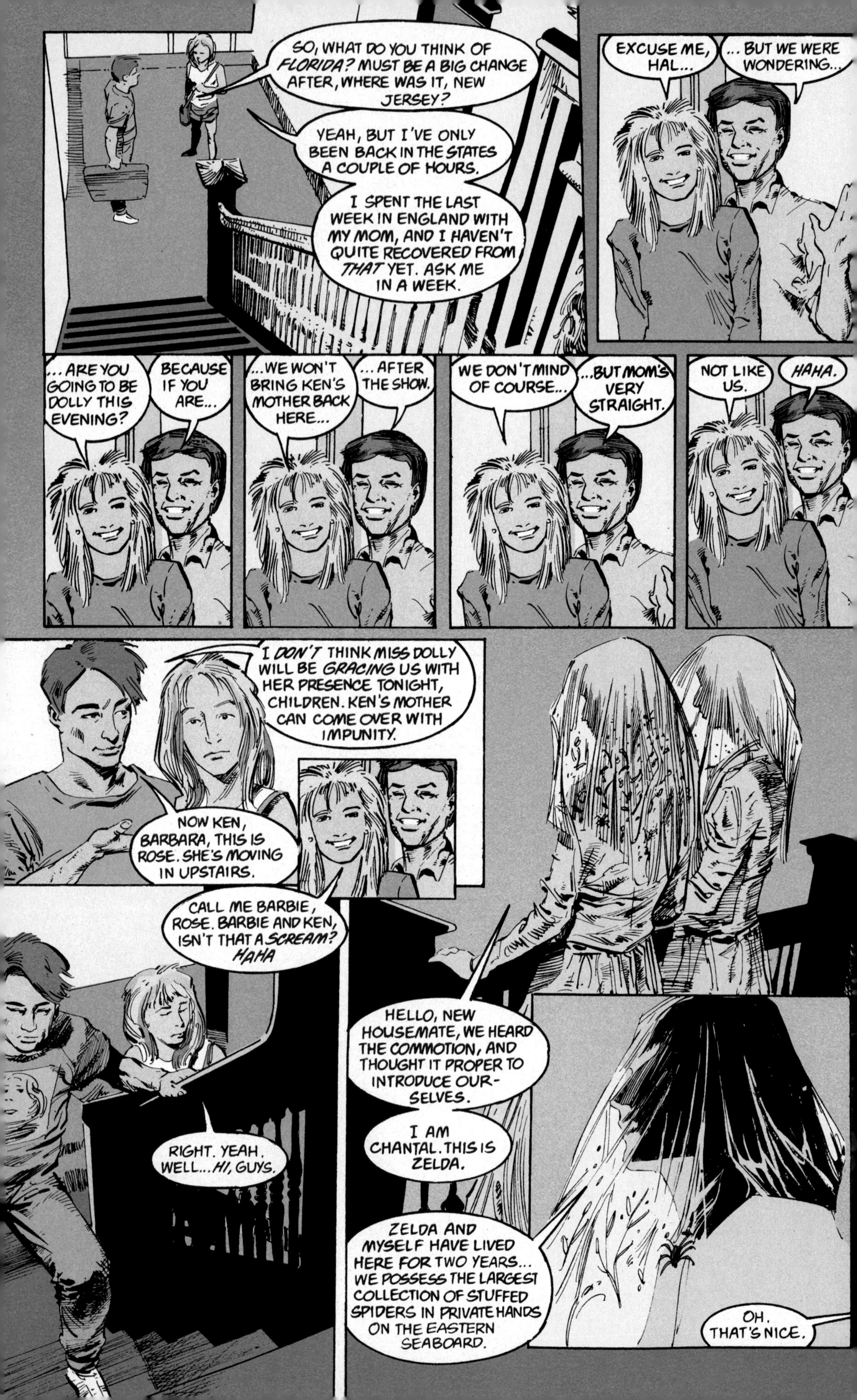

SO, WHAT DO YOU THINK OF *FLORIDA?* MUST BE A BIG CHANGE AFTER, WHERE WAS IT, NEW JERSEY?
YEAH, BUT I'VE ONLY BEEN BACK IN THE STATES A COUPLE OF HOURS.
I SPENT THE LAST WEEK IN ENGLAND WITH MY MOM, AND I HAVEN'T QUITE RECOVERED FROM *THAT* YET. ASK ME IN A WEEK.
EXCUSE ME, HAL...
... BUT WE WERE WONDERING...
... ARE YOU GOING TO BE DOLLY THIS EVENING?
BECAUSE IF YOU ARE...
...WE WON'T BRING KEN'S MOTHER BACK HERE...
... AFTER THE SHOW.
WE DON'T MIND OF COURSE...
...BUT MOM'S VERY STRAIGHT.
NOT LIKE US.
HAHA.
I *DON'T* THINK MISS DOLLY WILL BE *GRACING* US WITH HER PRESENCE TONIGHT, CHILDREN. KEN'S MOTHER CAN COME OVER WITH IMPUNITY.
NOW KEN, BARBARA, THIS IS ROSE. SHE'S MOVING IN UPSTAIRS.
CALL ME BARBIE, ROSE. BARBIE AND KEN, ISN'T THAT A *SCREAM?* *HAHA*
RIGHT. YEAH. WELL...*HI,* GUYS.
HELLO, NEW HOUSEMATE, WE HEARD THE COMMOTION, AND THOUGHT IT PROPER TO INTRODUCE OURSELVES.
I AM CHANTAL. THIS IS ZELDA.
ZELDA AND MYSELF HAVE LIVED HERE FOR TWO YEARS... WE POSSESS THE LARGEST COLLECTION OF STUFFED SPIDERS IN PRIVATE HANDS ON THE EASTERN SEABOARD.
OH. THAT'S NICE.

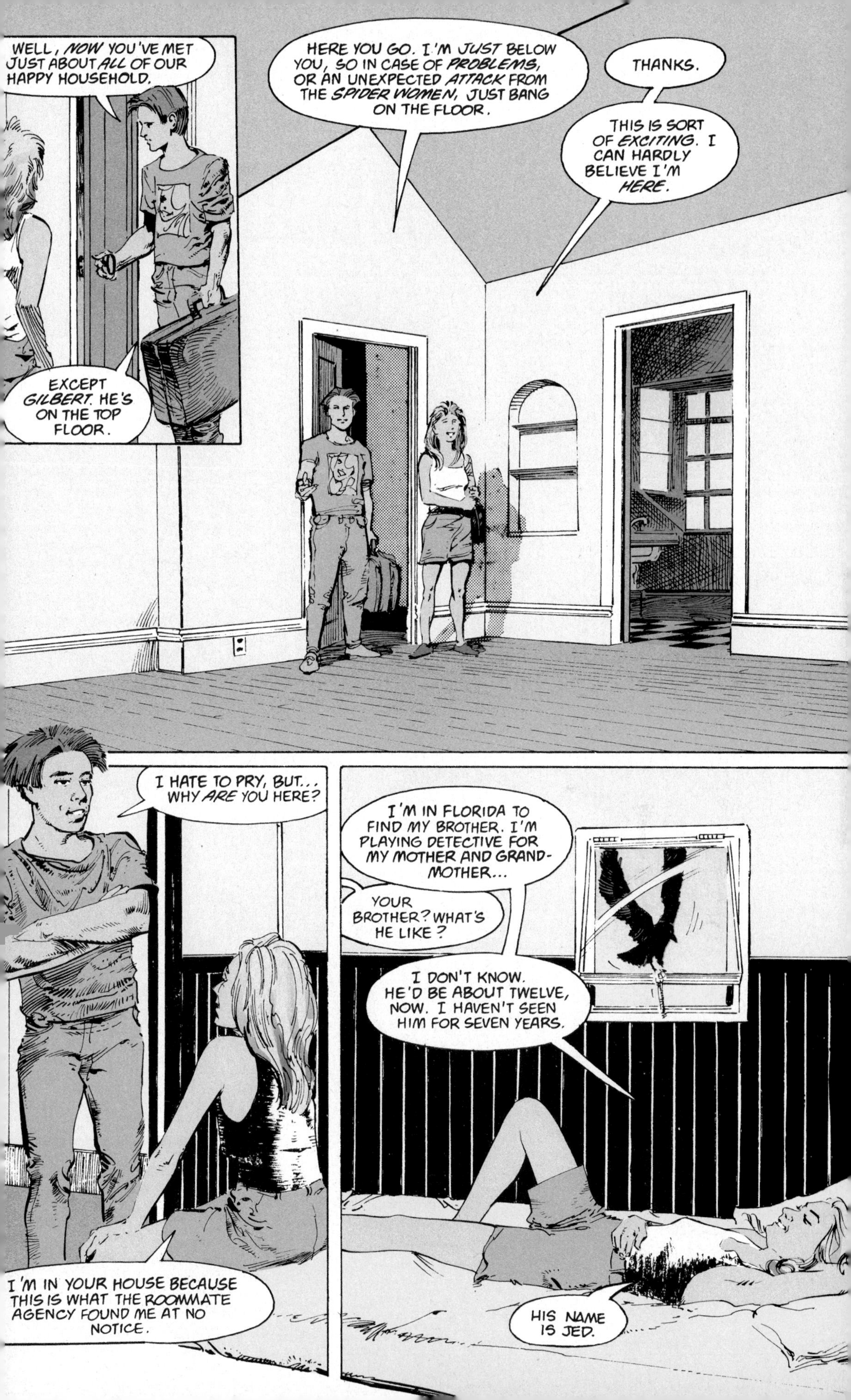
WELL, NOW YOU'VE MET JUST ABOUT ALL OF OUR HAPPY HOUSEHOLD.
EXCEPT GILBERT. HE'S ON THE TOP FLOOR.
HERE YOU GO. I'M JUST BELOW YOU, SO IN CASE OF PROBLEMS, OR AN UNEXPECTED ATTACK FROM THE SPIDER WOMEN, JUST BANG ON THE FLOOR.
THANKS.
THIS IS SORT OF EXCITING. I CAN HARDLY BELIEVE I'M HERE.
I HATE TO PRY, BUT... WHY ARE YOU HERE?
I'M IN YOUR HOUSE BECAUSE THIS IS WHAT THE ROOMMATE AGENCY FOUND ME AT NO NOTICE.
I'M IN FLORIDA TO FIND MY BROTHER. I'M PLAYING DETECTIVE FOR MY MOTHER AND GRAND-MOTHER...
YOUR BROTHER? WHAT'S HE LIKE?
I DON'T KNOW. HE'D BE ABOUT TWELVE, NOW. I HAVEN'T SEEN HIM FOR SEVEN YEARS.
HIS NAME IS JED.

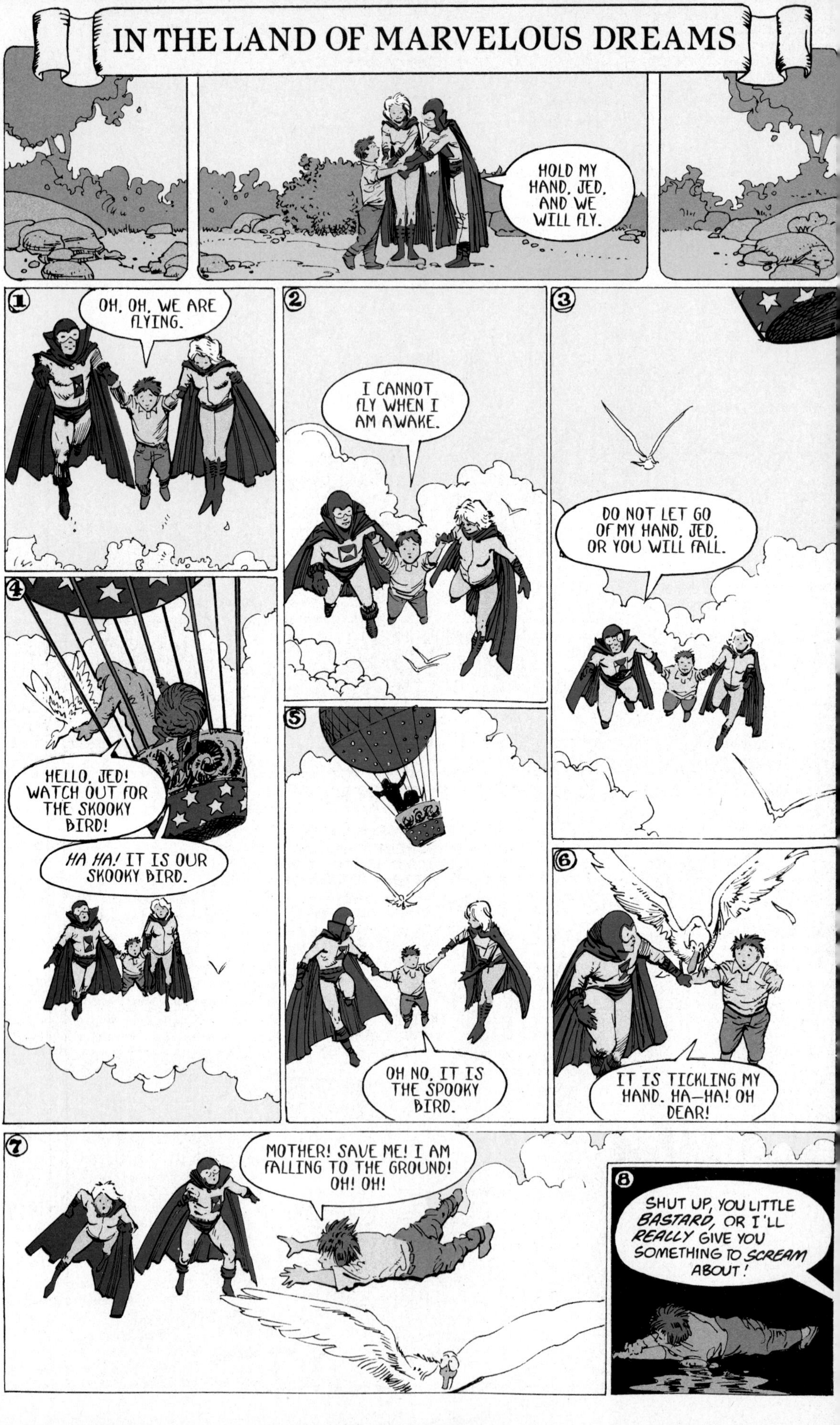
IN THE LAND OF MARVELOUS DREAMS
HOLD MY HAND, JED, AND WE WILL FLY.
1
OH, OH, WE ARE FLYING.
2
I CANNOT FLY WHEN I AM AWAKE.
3
DO NOT LET GO OF MY HAND, JED, OR YOU WILL FALL.
4
HELLO, JED! WATCH OUT FOR THE SKOOKY BIRD!
HA HA! IT IS OUR SKOOKY BIRD.
5
OH NO, IT IS THE SPOOKY BIRD.
6
IT IS TICKLING MY HAND. HA-HA! OH DEAR!
7
MOTHER! SAVE ME! I AM FALLING TO THE GROUND! OH! OH!
8
SHUT UP, YOU LITTLE BASTARD, OR I'LL REALLY GIVE YOU SOMETHING TO SCREAM ABOUT!

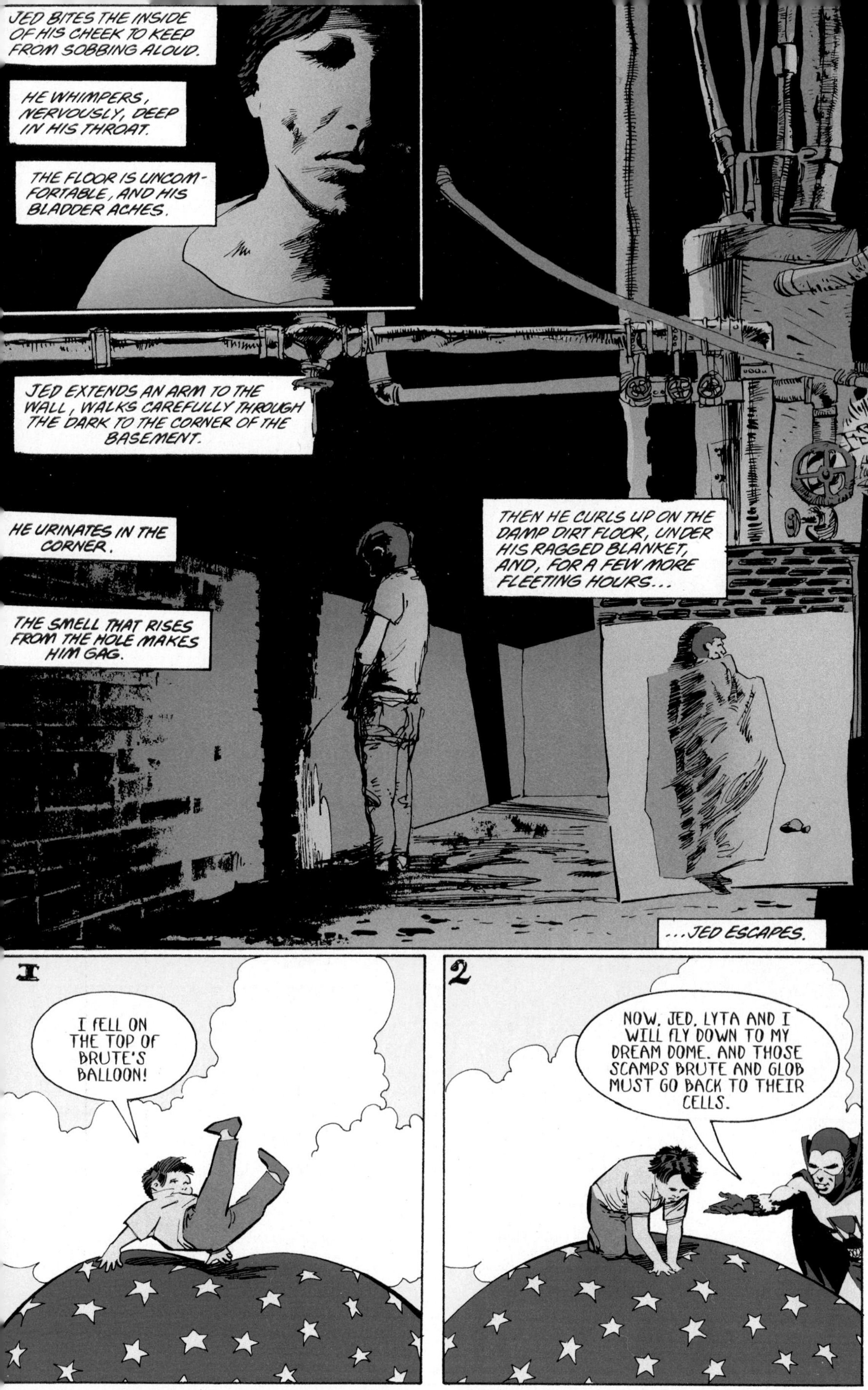

JED BITES THE INSIDE OF HIS CHEEK TO KEEP FROM SOBBING ALOUD.
HE WHIMPERS, NERVOUSLY, DEEP IN HIS THROAT.
THE FLOOR IS UNCOMFORTABLE, AND HIS BLADDER ACHES.
JED EXTENDS AN ARM TO THE WALL, WALKS CAREFULLY THROUGH THE DARK TO THE CORNER OF THE BASEMENT.
HE URINATES IN THE CORNER.
THE SMELL THAT RISES FROM THE HOLE MAKES HIM GAG.
THEN HE CURLS UP ON THE DAMP DIRT FLOOR, UNDER HIS RAGGED BLANKET, AND, FOR A FEW MORE FLEETING HOURS...
...JED ESCAPES.
1
I FELL ON THE TOP OF BRUTE'S BALLOON!
2
NOW, JED, LYTA AND I WILL FLY DOWN TO MY DREAM DOME. AND THOSE SCAMPS BRUTE AND GLOB MUST GO BACK TO THEIR CELLS.

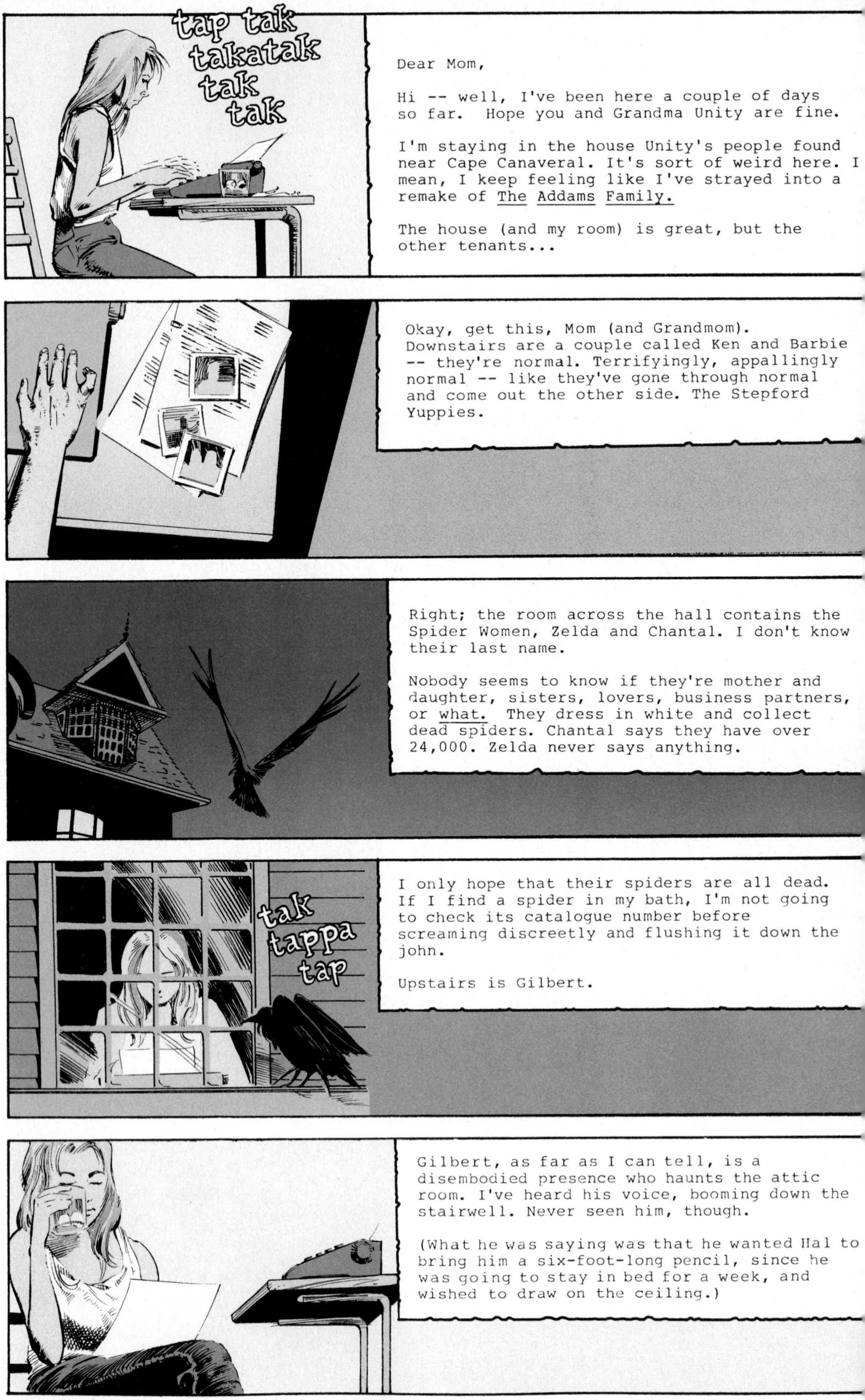
tap tak takatak tak tak
Dear Mom,
Hi -- well, I've been here a couple of days so far. Hope you and Grandma Unity are fine.
I'm staying in the house Unity's people found near Cape Canaveral. It's sort of weird here. I mean, I keep feeling like I've strayed into a remake of The Addams Family.
The house (and my room) is great, but the other tenants...
Okay, get this, Mom (and Grandmom). Downstairs are a couple called Ken and Barbie -- they're normal. Terrifyingly, appallingly normal -- like they've gone through normal and come out the other side. The Stepford Yuppies.
Right; the room across the hall contains the Spider Women, Zelda and Chantal. I don't know their last name.
Nobody seems to know if they're mother and daughter, sisters, lovers, business partners, or what. They dress in white and collect dead spiders. Chantal says they have over 24,000. Zelda never says anything.
I only hope that their spiders are all dead. If I find a spider in my bath, I'm not going to check its catalogue number before screaming discreetly and flushing it down the john.
Upstairs is Gilbert.
tak tappa tap
Gilbert, as far as I can tell, is a disembodied presence who haunts the attic room. I've heard his voice, booming down the stairwell. Never seen him, though.
(What he was saying was that he wanted Hal to bring him a six-foot-long pencil, since he was going to stay in bed for a week, and wished to draw on the ceiling.)

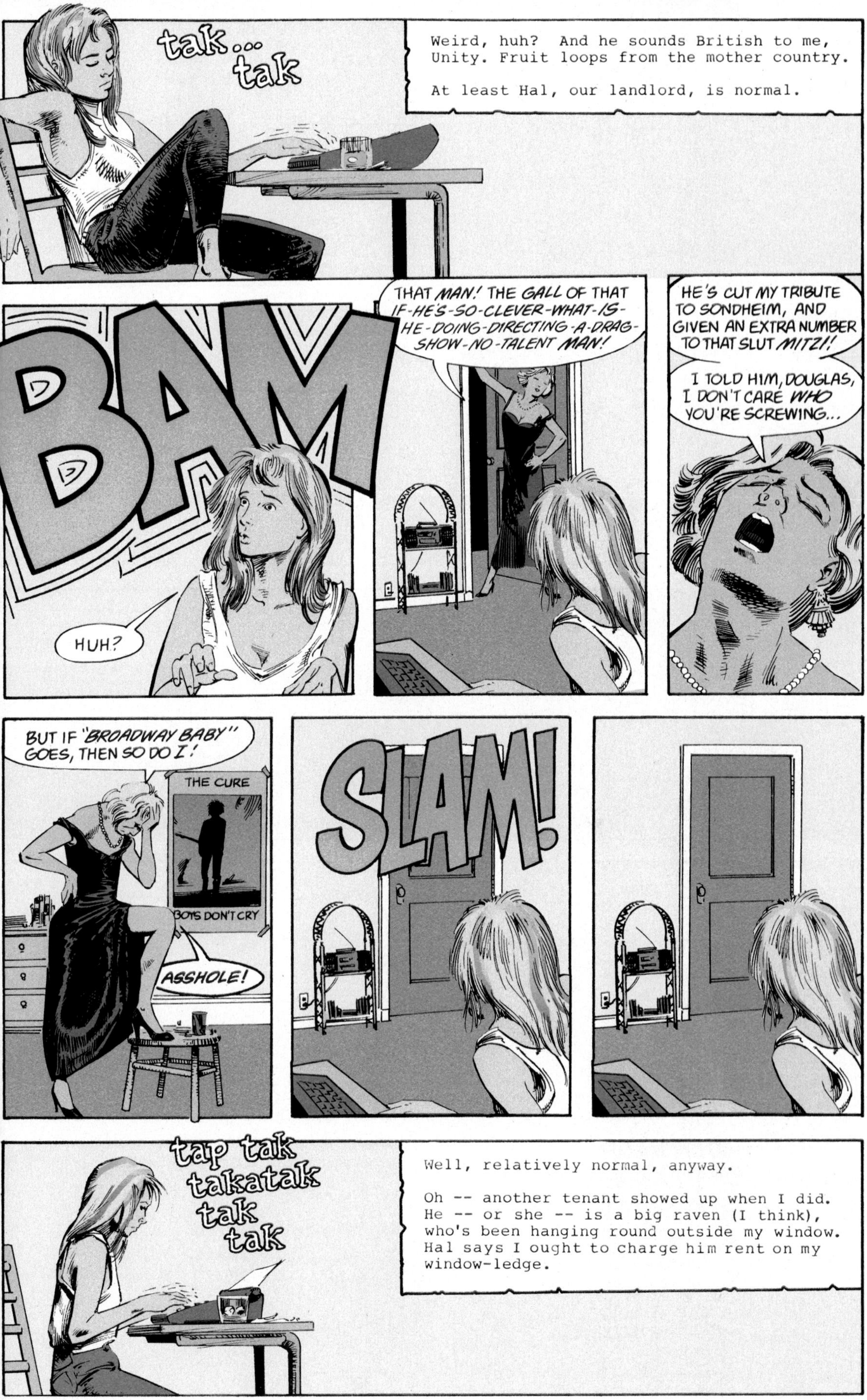
tak... tak
Weird, huh? And he sounds British to me, Unity. Fruit loops from the mother country.
At least Hal, our landlord, is normal.
BAM
HUH?
THAT MAN! THE GALL OF THAT IF-HE'S-SO-CLEVER-WHAT-IS-HE-DOING-DIRECTING-A-DRAG-SHOW-NO-TALENT MAN!
HE'S CUT MY TRIBUTE TO SONDHEIM, AND GIVEN AN EXTRA NUMBER TO THAT SLUT MITZI!
I TOLD HIM, DOUGLAS, I DON'T CARE WHO YOU'RE SCREWING...
BUT IF "BROADWAY BABY" GOES, THEN SO DO I!
THE CURE
BOYS DON'T CRY
ASSHOLE!
SLAM!
tap tak takatak tak tak
Well, relatively normal, anyway.
Oh -- another tenant showed up when I did. He -- or she -- is a big raven (I think), who's been hanging round outside my window. Hal says I ought to charge him rent on my window-ledge.

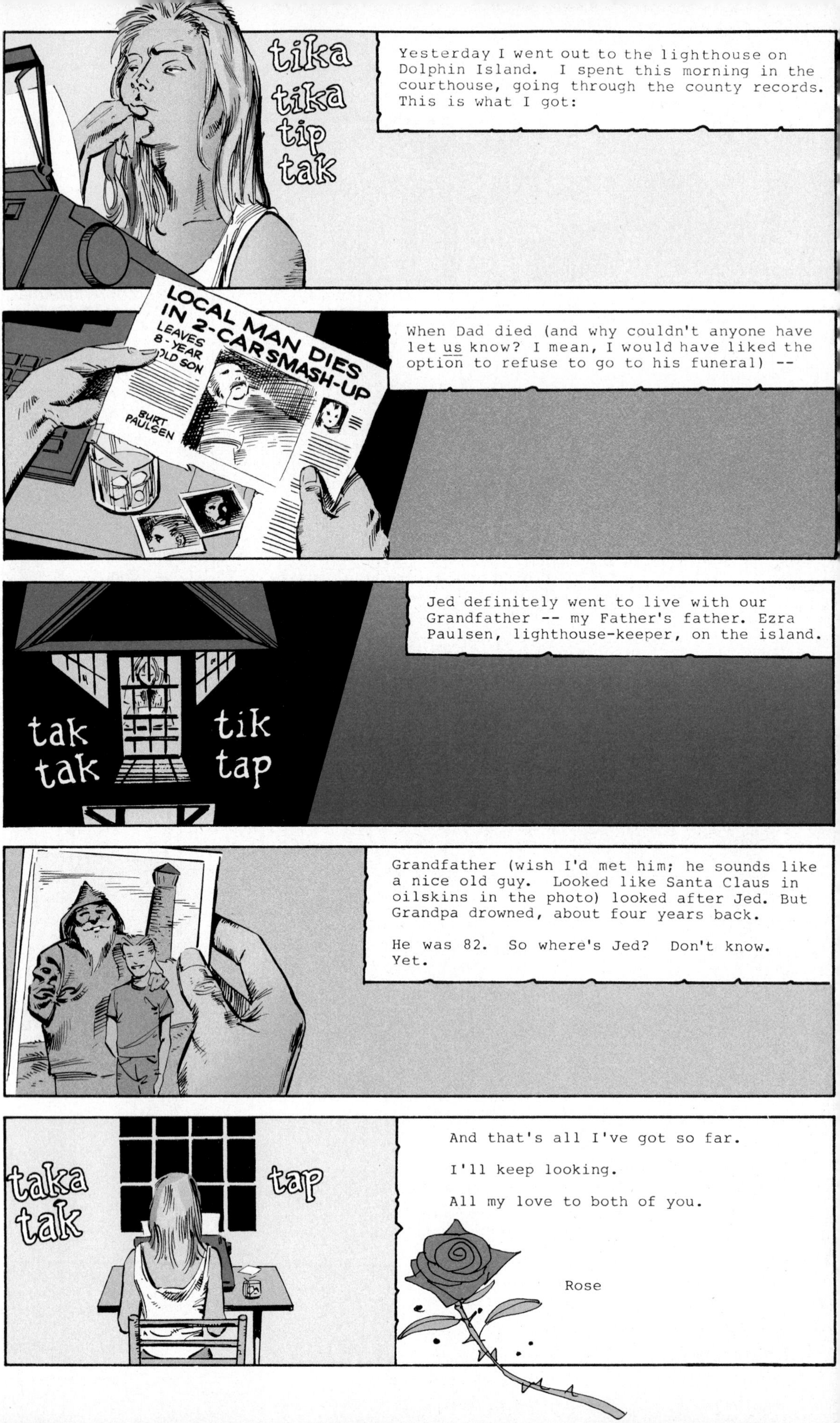
tika tika tip tak
Yesterday I went out to the lighthouse on Dolphin Island. I spent this morning in the courthouse, going through the county records. This is what I got:
LOCAL MAN DIES IN 2-CAR SMASH-UP
LEAVES 8-YEAR OLD SON
BURT PAULSEN
When Dad died (and why couldn't anyone have let us know? I mean, I would have liked the option to refuse to go to his funeral) --
Jed definitely went to live with our Grandfather -- my Father's father. Ezra Paulsen, lighthouse-keeper, on the island.
tak tak tik tap
Grandfather (wish I'd met him; he sounds like a nice old guy. Looked like Santa Claus in oilskins in the photo) looked after Jed. But Grandpa drowned, about four years back.
He was 82. So where's Jed? Don't know. Yet.
taka tak tap
And that's all I've got so far.
I'll keep looking.
All my love to both of you.
Rose

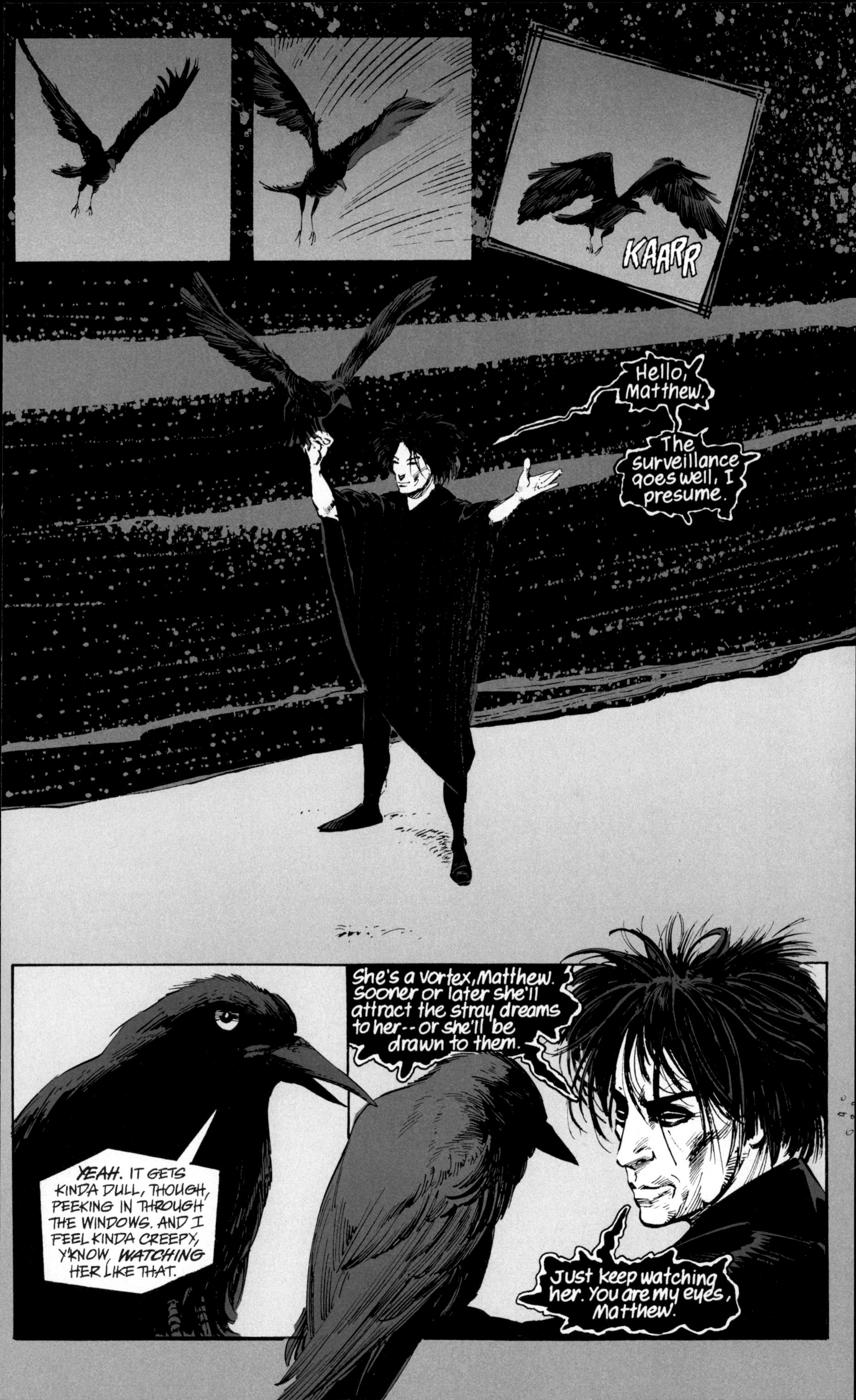
KAARR
Hello, Matthew.
The surveillance goes well, I presume.
YEAH. IT GETS KINDA DULL, THOUGH, PEEKING IN THROUGH THE WINDOWS. AND I FEEL KINDA CREEPY, Y'KNOW, WATCHING HER LIKE THAT.
She's a vortex, Matthew. Sooner or later she'll attract the stray dreams to her-- or she'll be drawn to them.
Just keep watching her. You are my eyes, Matthew.

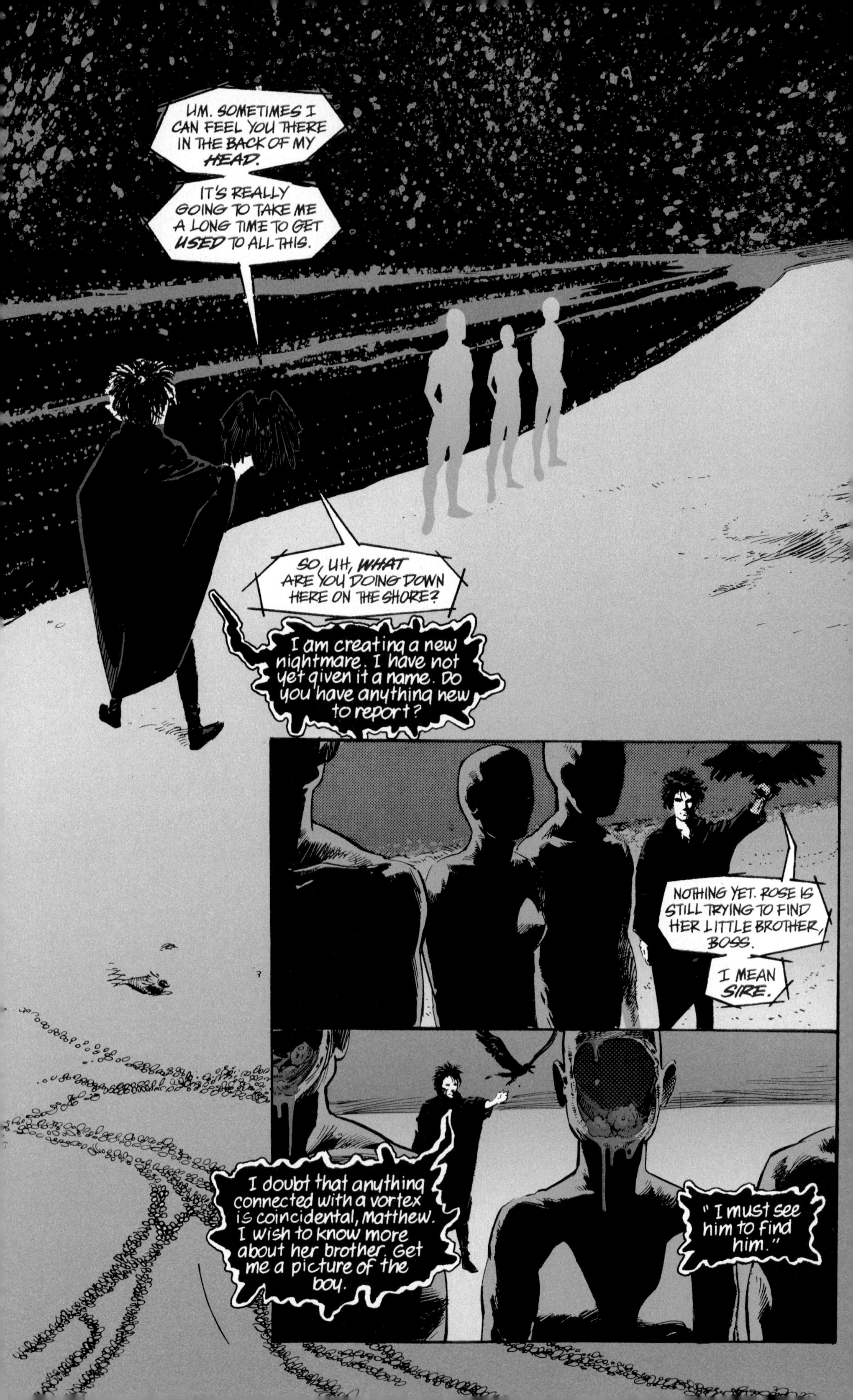
UM. SOMETIMES I CAN FEEL YOU THERE IN THE BACK OF MY HEAD.
IT'S REALLY GOING TO TAKE ME A LONG TIME TO GET USED TO ALL THIS.
SO, UH, WHAT ARE YOU DOING DOWN HERE ON THE SHORE?
I am creating a new nightmare. I have not yet given it a name. Do you have anything new to report?
NOTHING YET. ROSE IS STILL TRYING TO FIND HER LITTLE BROTHER, BOSS.
I MEAN SIRE.
I doubt that anything connected with a vortex is coincidental, matthew. I wish to know more about her brother. Get me a picture of the boy.
"I must see him to find him."

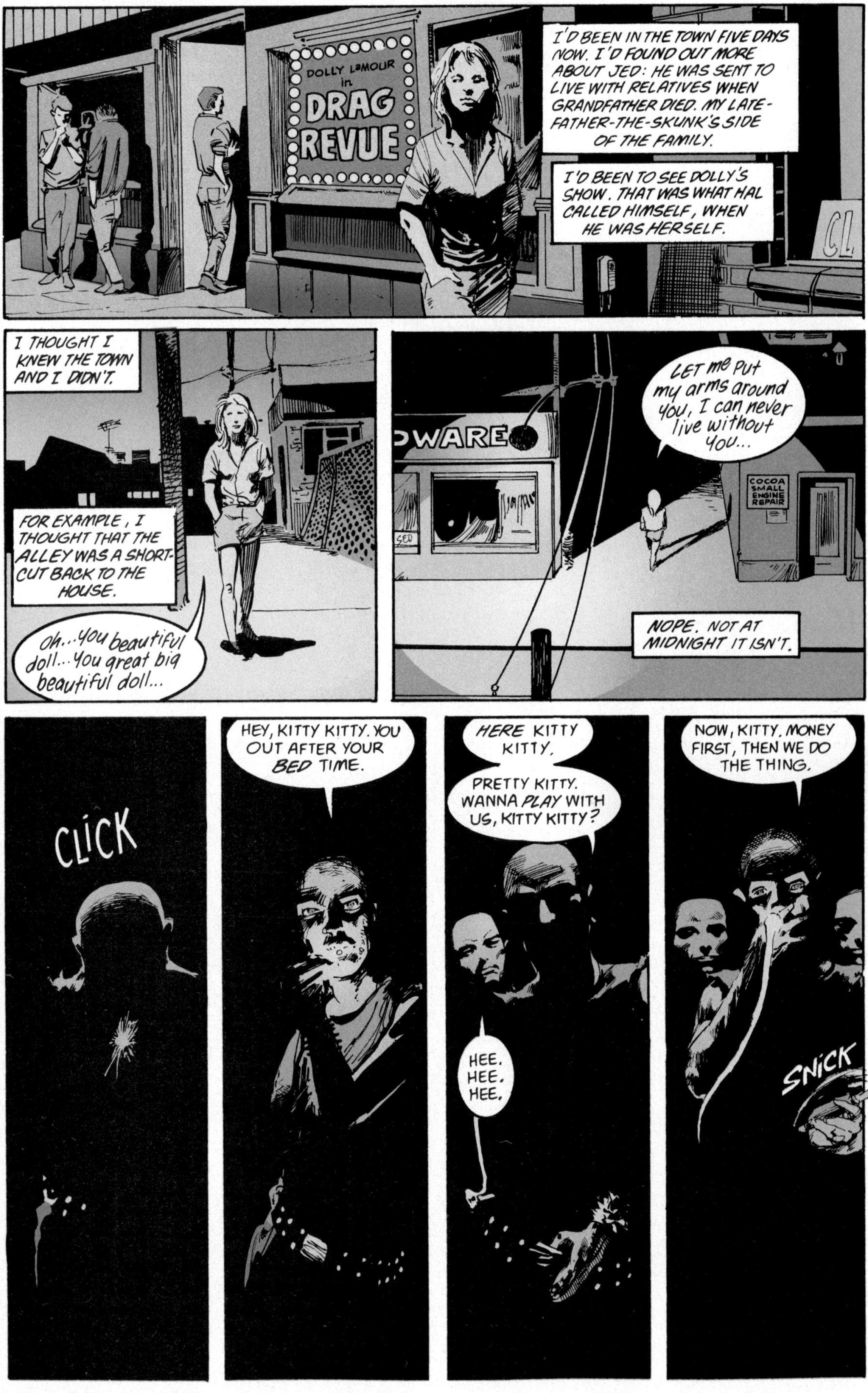
DOLLY LaMOUR in DRAG REVUE
I'D BEEN IN THE TOWN FIVE DAYS NOW. I'D FOUND OUT MORE ABOUT JED: HE WAS SENT TO LIVE WITH RELATIVES WHEN GRANDFATHER DIED. MY LATE-FATHER-THE-SKUNK'S SIDE OF THE FAMILY.
I'D BEEN TO SEE DOLLY'S SHOW. THAT WAS WHAT HAL CALLED HIMSELF, WHEN HE WAS HERSELF.
I THOUGHT I KNEW THE TOWN AND I DIDN'T.
FOR EXAMPLE, I THOUGHT THAT THE ALLEY WAS A SHORT-CUT BACK TO THE HOUSE.
Oh...You beautiful doll...You great big beautiful doll...
LET ME PUT MY ARMS AROUND YOU, I CAN NEVER LIVE WITHOUT YOU...
COCOA SMALL ENGINE REPAIR
NOPE. NOT AT MIDNIGHT IT ISN'T.
CLICK
HEY, KITTY KITTY. YOU OUT AFTER YOUR BED TIME.
HERE KITTY KITTY.
PRETTY KITTY. WANNA PLAY WITH US, KITTY KITTY?
HEE. HEE. HEE.
NOW, KITTY. MONEY FIRST, THEN WE DO THE THING.
SNICK

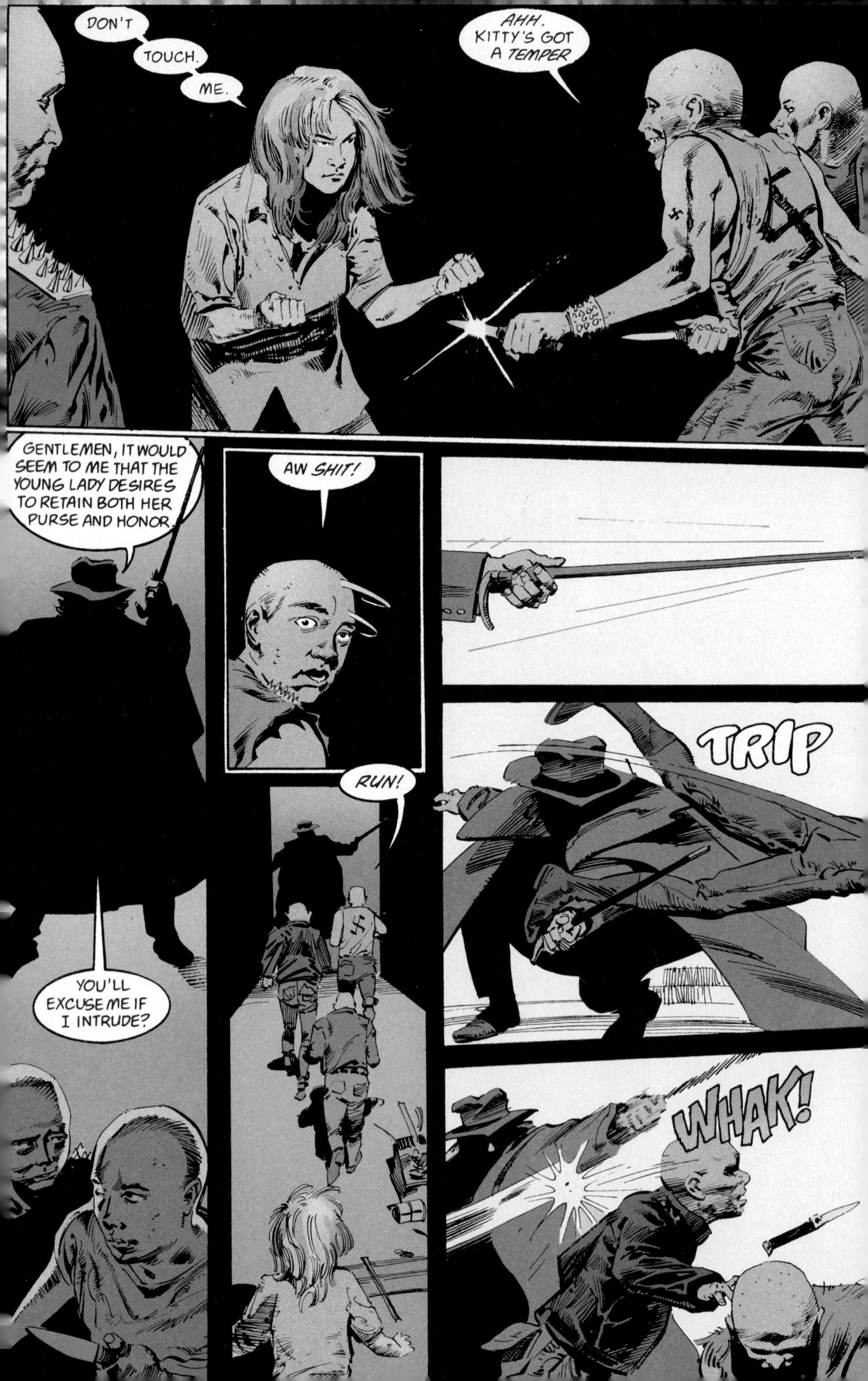
DON'T
TOUCH.
ME.
AHH. KITTY'S GOT A *TEMPER*
GENTLEMEN, IT WOULD SEEM TO ME THAT THE YOUNG LADY DESIRES TO RETAIN BOTH HER PURSE AND HONOR.
YOU'LL EXCUSE ME IF I INTRUDE?
AW *SHIT!*
RUN!
TRIP
WHAK!

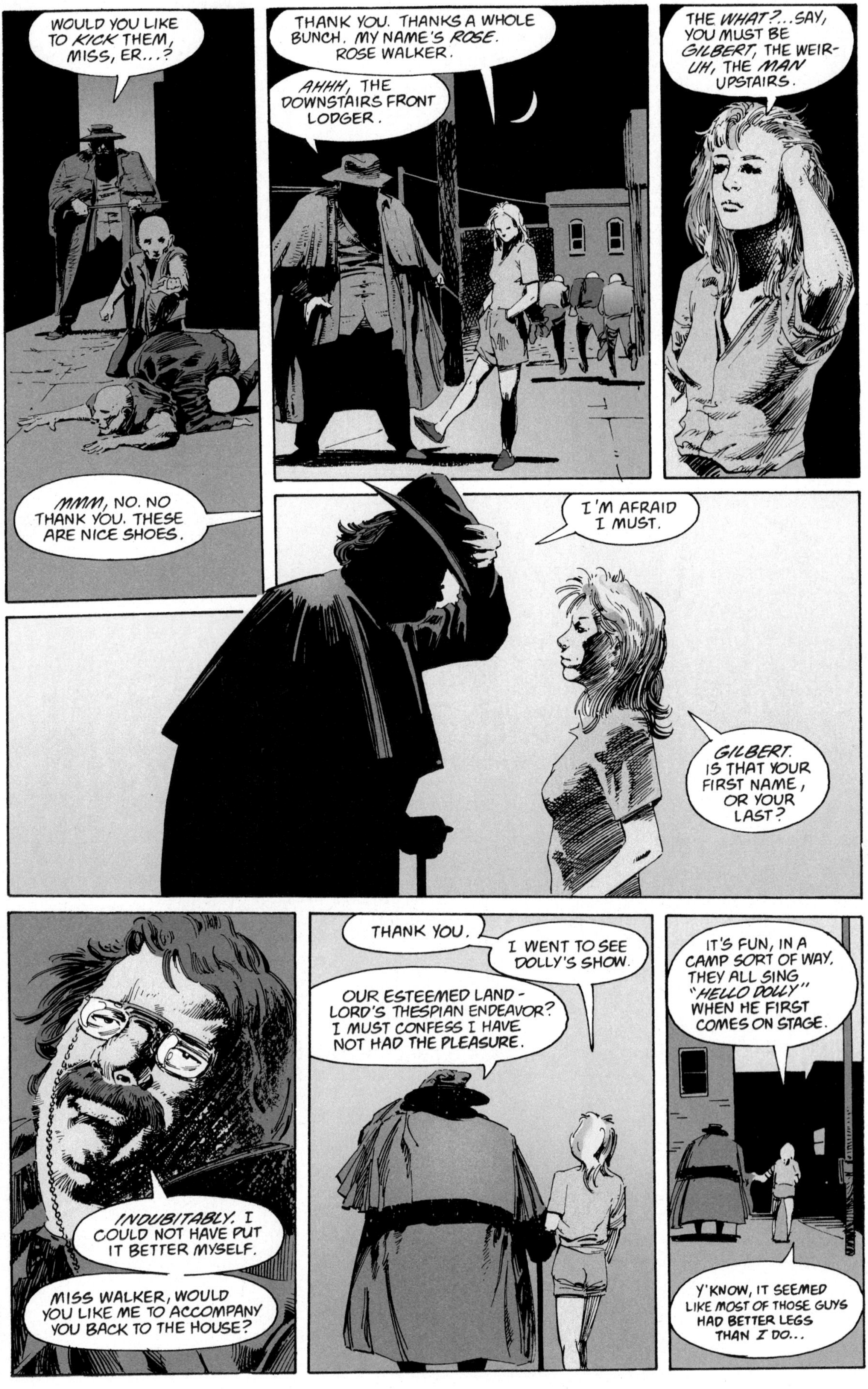

WOULD YOU LIKE TO *KICK* THEM, MISS, ER...?
THANK YOU. THANKS A WHOLE BUNCH. MY NAME'S *ROSE*. ROSE WALKER.
AHHH, THE DOWNSTAIRS FRONT LODGER.
THE *WHAT?*...SAY, YOU MUST BE *GILBERT*, THE WEIR- UH, THE *MAN* UPSTAIRS.
MMM, NO. NO THANK YOU. THESE ARE NICE SHOES.
I'M AFRAID I MUST.
GILBERT. IS THAT YOUR FIRST NAME, OR YOUR LAST?
INDUBITABLY. I COULD NOT HAVE PUT IT BETTER MYSELF.
MISS WALKER, WOULD YOU LIKE ME TO ACCOMPANY YOU BACK TO THE HOUSE?
THANK YOU.
I WENT TO SEE DOLLY'S SHOW.
OUR ESTEEMED LAND-LORD'S THESPIAN ENDEAVOR? I MUST CONFESS I HAVE NOT HAD THE PLEASURE.
IT'S FUN, IN A CAMP SORT OF WAY. THEY ALL SING "*HELLO DOLLY*" WHEN HE FIRST COMES ON STAGE.
Y'KNOW, IT SEEMED LIKE MOST OF THOSE GUYS HAD BETTER LEGS THAN *I* DO...

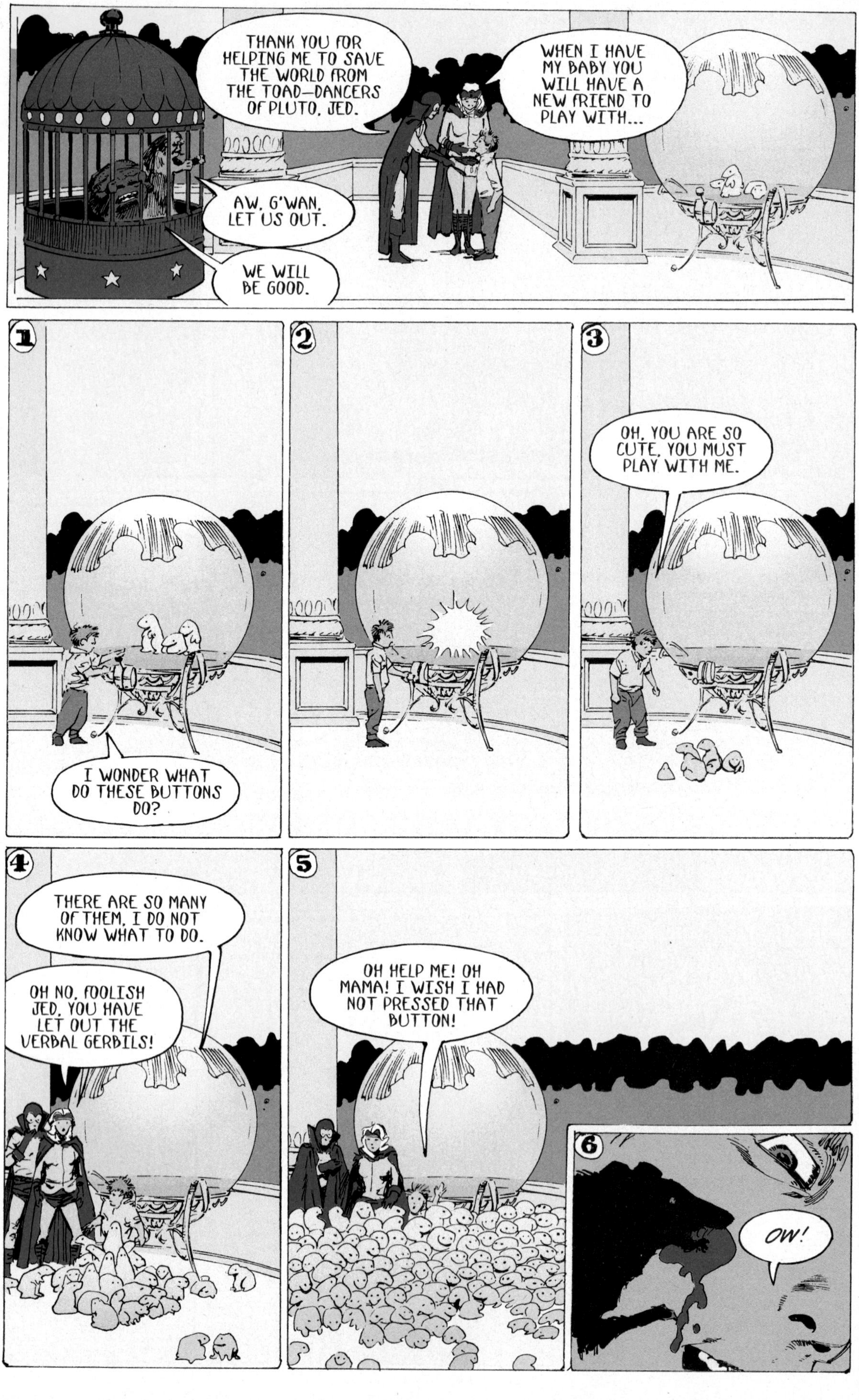
THANK YOU FOR HELPING ME TO SAVE THE WORLD FROM THE TOAD-DANCERS OF PLUTO, JED.
AW, G'WAN, LET US OUT.
WE WILL BE GOOD.
WHEN I HAVE MY BABY YOU WILL HAVE A NEW FRIEND TO PLAY WITH...
1
I WONDER WHAT DO THESE BUTTONS DO?
2
3
OH, YOU ARE SO CUTE, YOU MUST PLAY WITH ME.
4
THERE ARE SO MANY OF THEM, I DO NOT KNOW WHAT TO DO.
OH NO, FOOLISH JED, YOU HAVE LET OUT THE VERBAL GERBILS!
5
OH HELP ME! OH MAMA! I WISH I HAD NOT PRESSED THAT BUTTON!
6
OW!

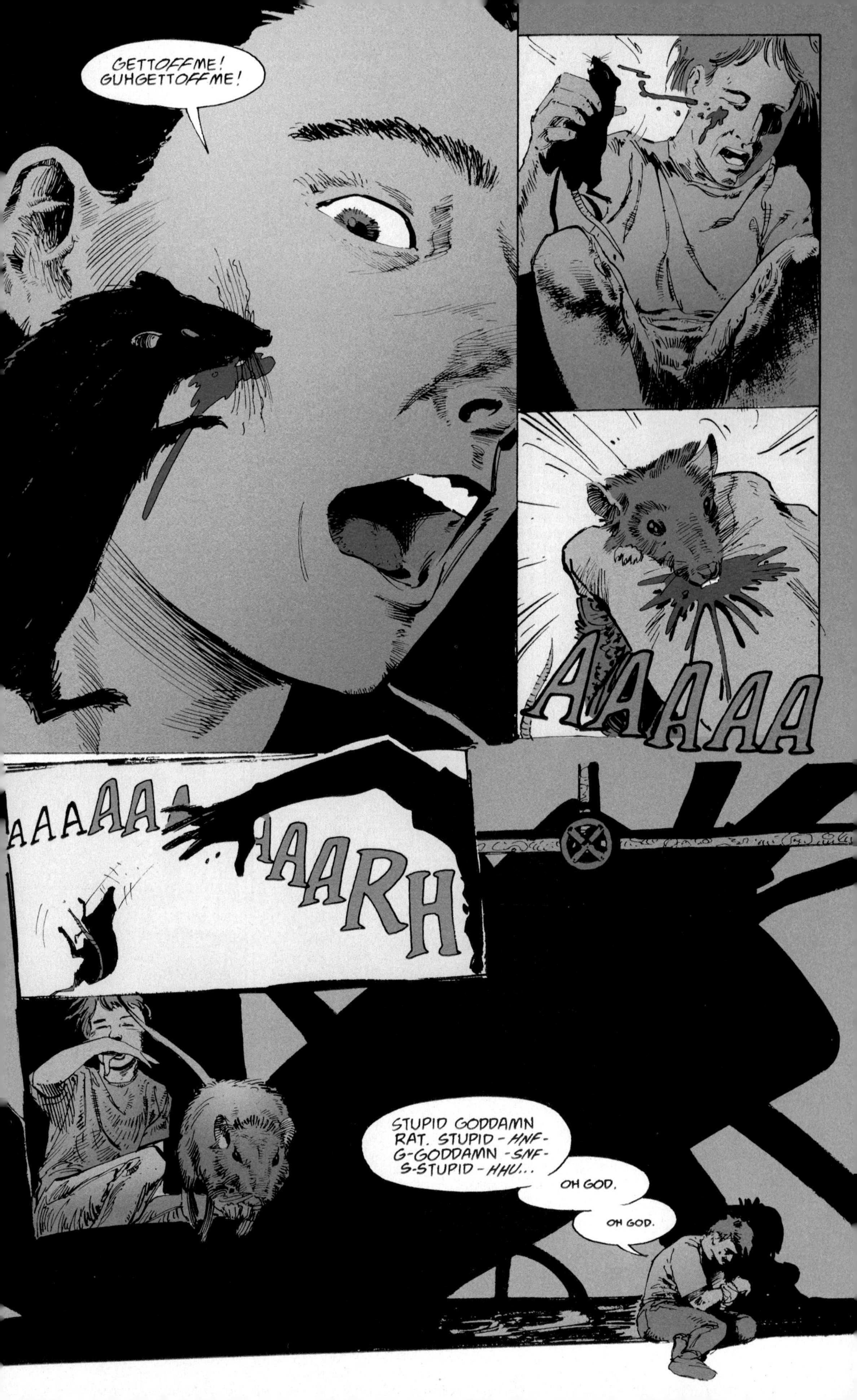
GETTOFFME! GUHGETTOFFME!
AAAAAA
AAAAAAAAARH
STUPID GODDAMN RAT. STUPID -HNF- G-GODDAMN -SNF- S-STUPID -HHU...
OH GOD.
OH GOD.

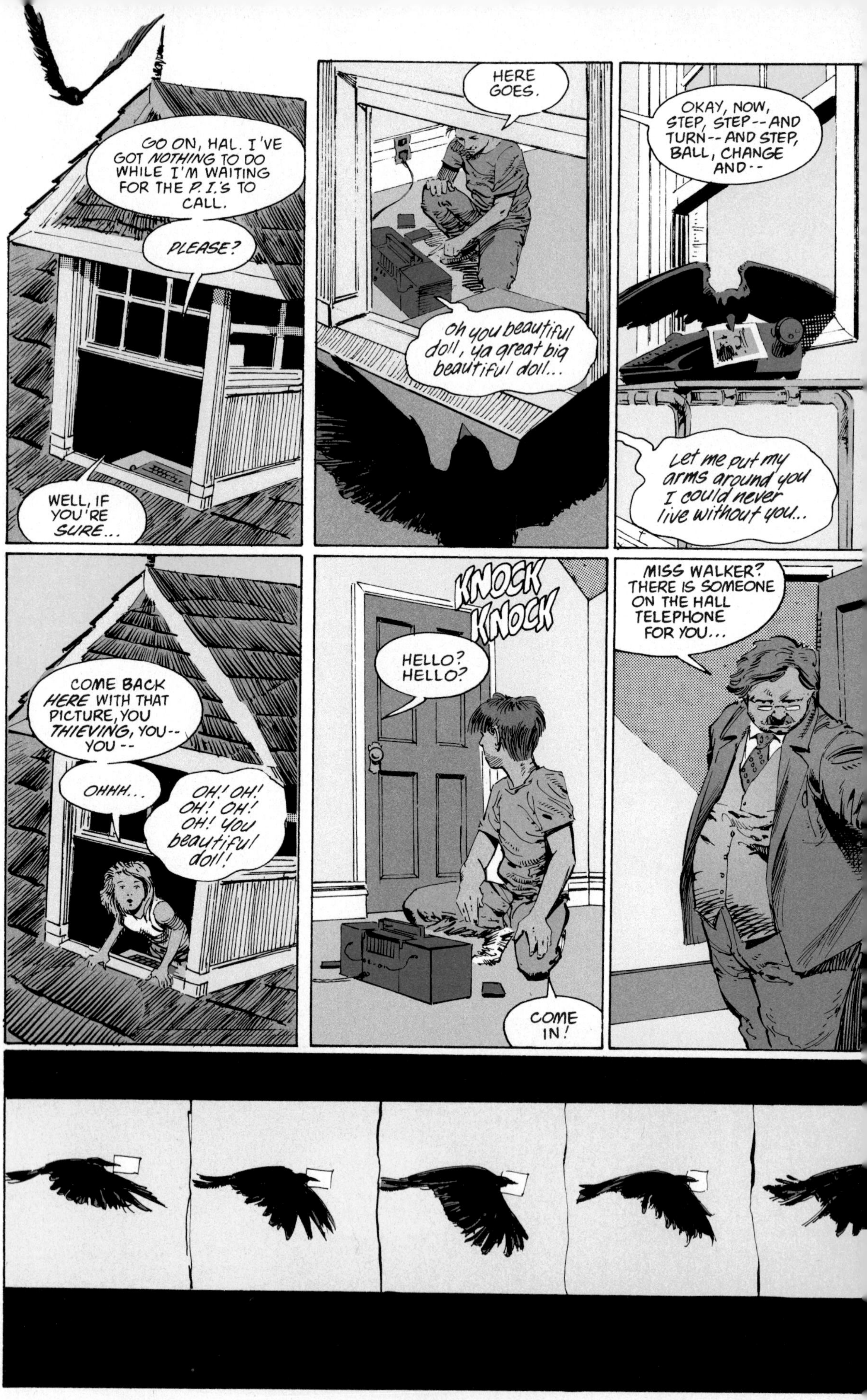
GO ON, HAL. I'VE GOT *NOTHING* TO DO WHILE I'M WAITING FOR THE *P.I.'S* TO CALL.
PLEASE?
WELL, IF YOU'RE *SURE*...
HERE GOES.
oh you beautiful doll, ya great big beautiful doll...
OKAY, NOW, STEP, STEP--AND TURN--AND STEP, BALL, CHANGE AND--
Let me put my arms around you I could never live without you...
COME BACK *HERE* WITH THAT PICTURE, YOU *THIEVING*, YOU--YOU--
OHHH...
OH! OH! OH! OH! OH! You beautiful doll!
KNOCK KNOCK
HELLO? HELLO?
COME IN!
MISS WALKER? THERE IS SOMEONE ON THE HALL TELEPHONE FOR YOU...

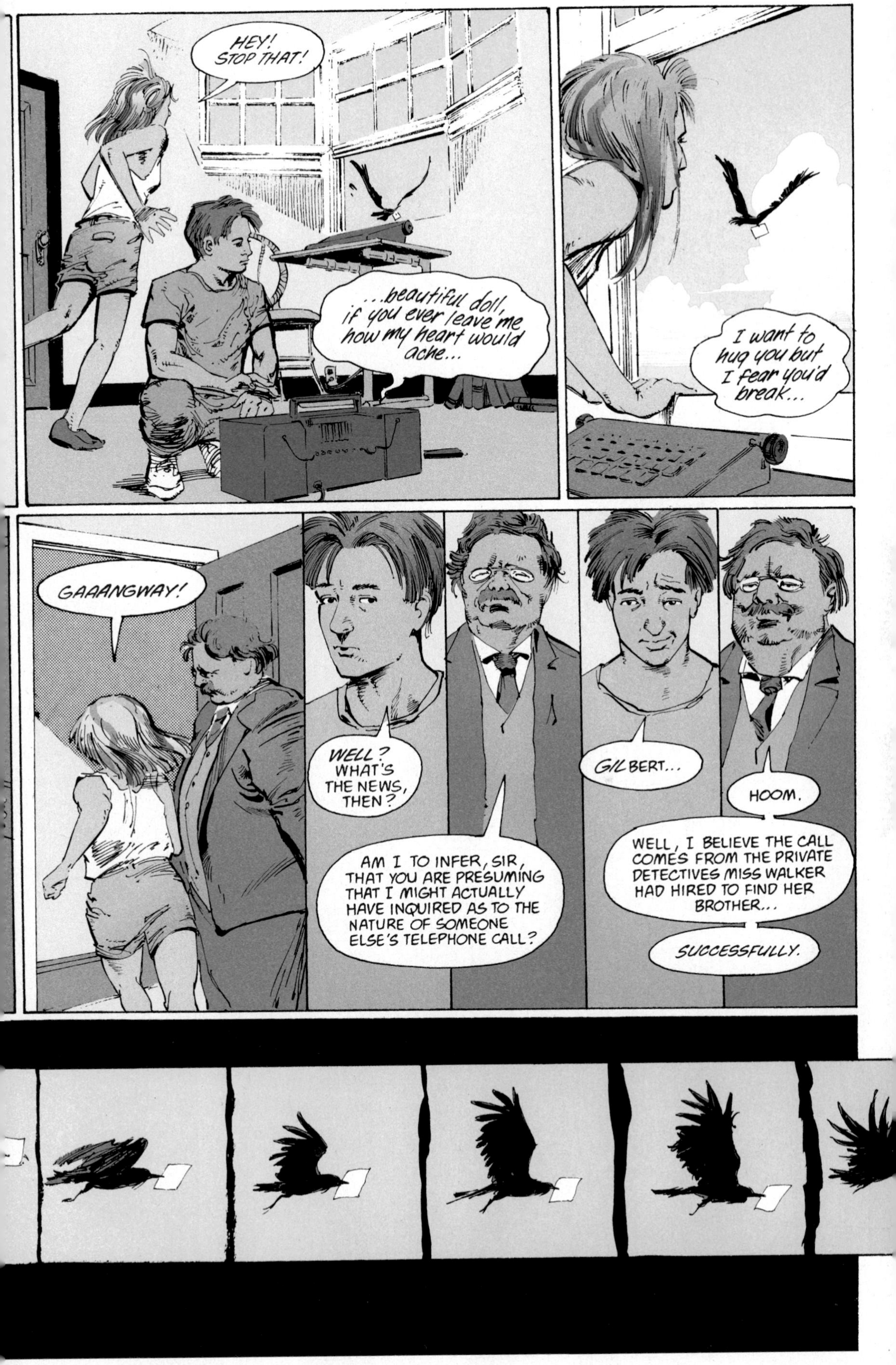
HEY! STOP THAT!
...beautiful doll, if you ever leave me how my heart would ache...
I want to hug you but I fear you'd break...
GAAANGWAY!
WELL? WHAT'S THE NEWS, THEN?
AM I TO INFER, SIR, THAT YOU ARE PRESUMING THAT I MIGHT ACTUALLY HAVE INQUIRED AS TO THE NATURE OF SOMEONE ELSE'S TELEPHONE CALL?
GILBERT...
HOOM.
WELL, I BELIEVE THE CALL COMES FROM THE PRIVATE DETECTIVES MISS WALKER HAD HIRED TO FIND HER BROTHER...
SUCCESSFULLY.

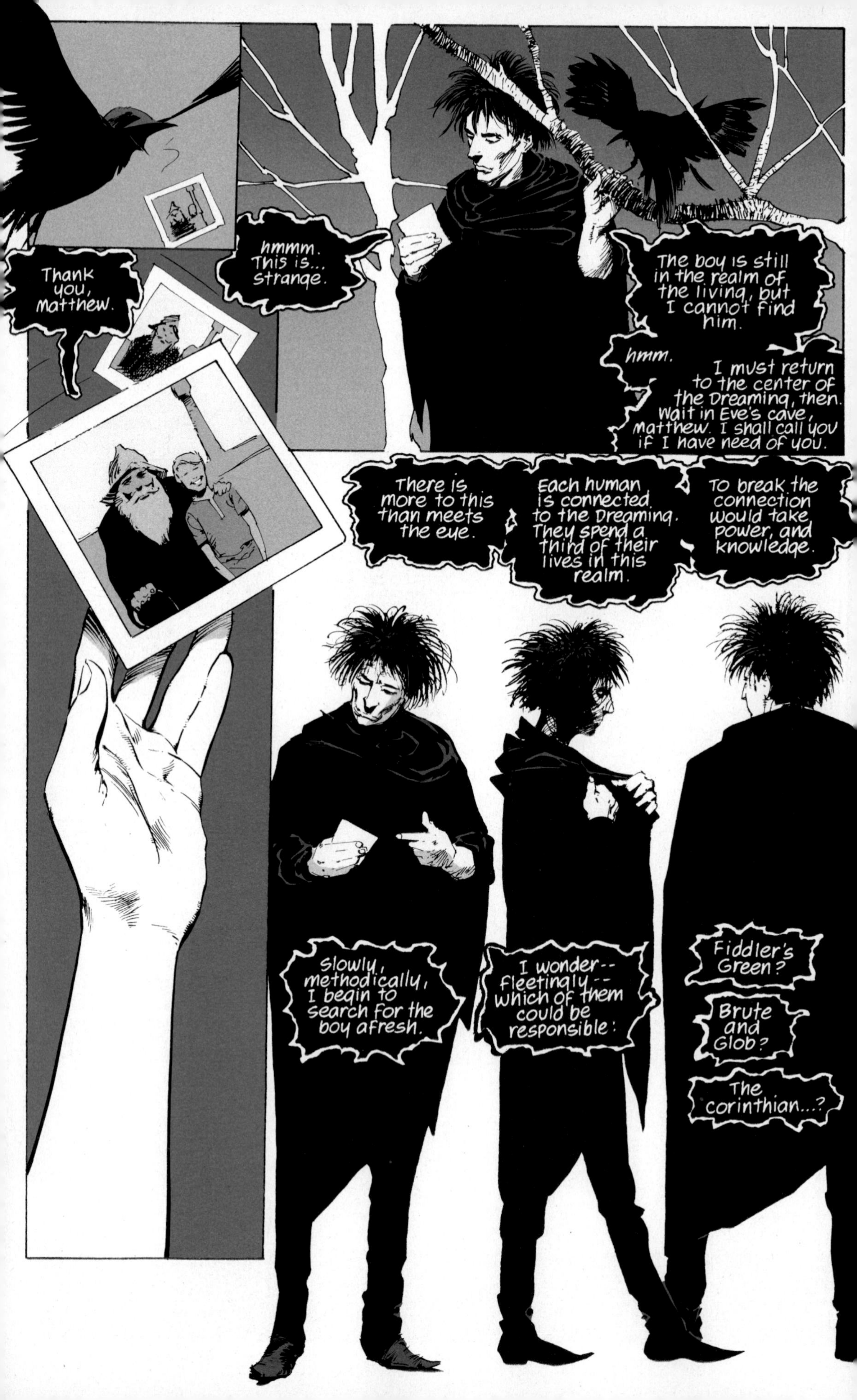
Thank you, Matthew.
hmmm. This is... strange.
The boy is still in the realm of the living, but I cannot find him.
hmm.
I must return to the center of the Dreaming, then. Wait in Eve's cave, Matthew. I shall call you if I have need of you.
There is more to this than meets the eye.
Each human is connected to the Dreaming. They spend a third of their lives in this realm.
To break the connection would take power, and knowledge.
Slowly, methodically, I begin to search for the boy afresh.
I wonder-- fleetingly-- which of them could be responsible:
Fiddler's Green?
Brute and Glob?
The Corinthian...?

THE YELLOWHAMMER MOTEL, BIRMINGHAM, ALABAMA.

THE CORINTHIAN.

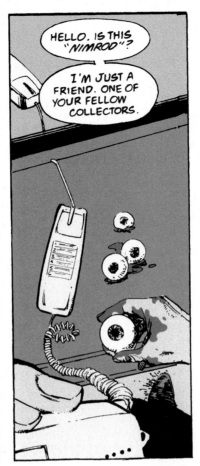

HELLO. IS THIS "NIMROD"?

I'M JUST A FRIEND. ONE OF YOUR FELLOW COLLECTORS.

I'VE HEARD ON THE GRAPEVINE ABOUT SOME KIND OF GET-TOGETHER...?

FOR PEOPLE WHO SHARE OUR SPECIALIZED INTERESTS.

UH HUH.

SHUMF SCHROMP SCHOMF

I DON'T NEED TO WRITE IT DOWN. I DON'T FORGET THINGS. SHOOT.

OKAY. THAT'S THIS WEEKEND, THEN?

I'LL BE FREE. SO WHERE EXACTLY?

GEORGIA, HUH? NICE STATE.

SURE I KNOW THAT TOWN. I KNOW AMERICA LIKE THE BACK OF MY HAND.

I'M PART OF THE AMERICAN DREAM.

SHUMF SCHROMP SCHOMF

A NAME TO REGISTER UNDER? PUT ME DOWN AS THE CORINTHIAN.

WELL, THAT'S VERY KIND OF YOU TO SAY SO. I ADMIRE YOUR WORK AS WELL.

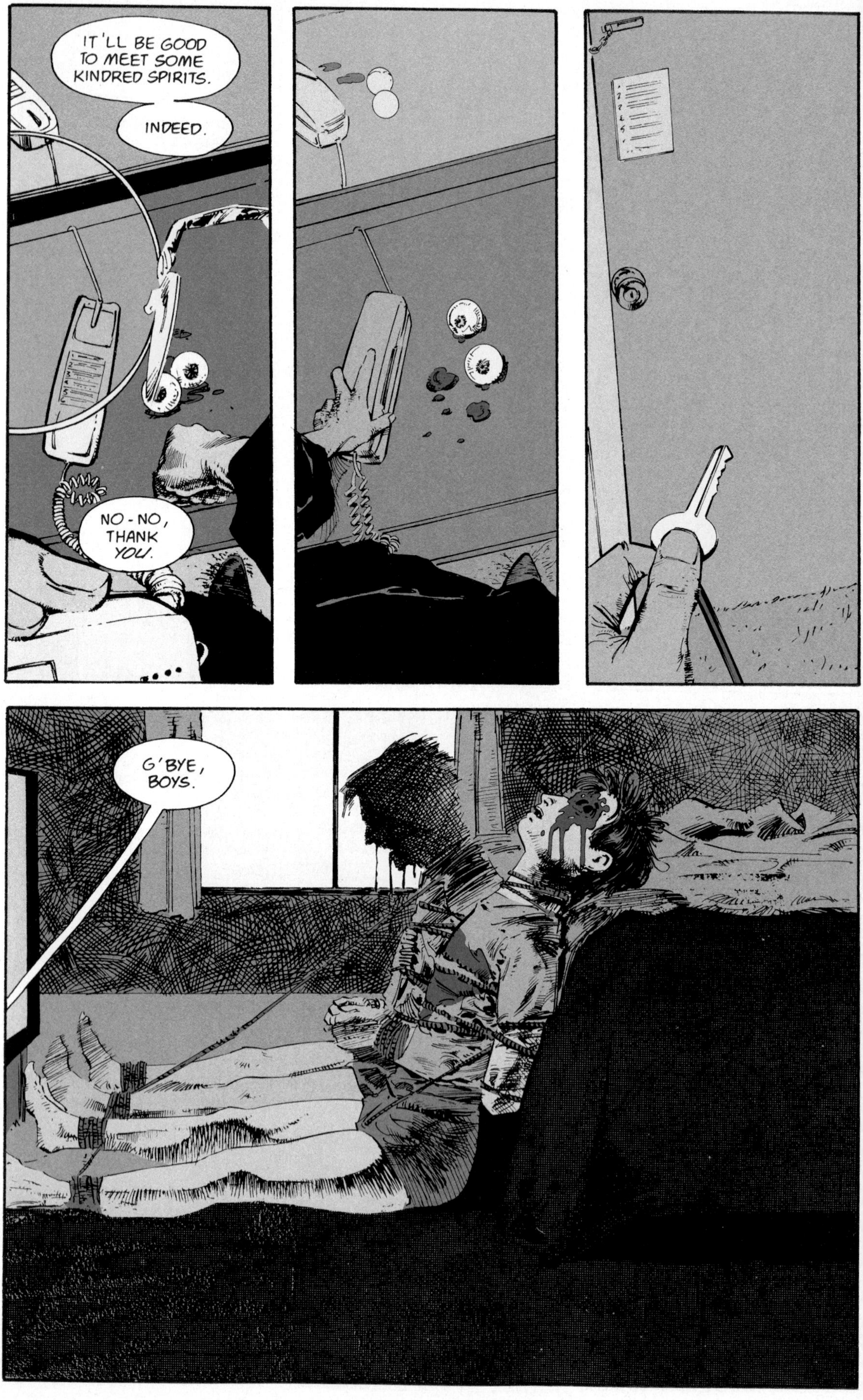
IT'LL BE GOOD TO MEET SOME KINDRED SPIRITS.
INDEED.
NO-NO, THANK YOU.
G'BYE, BOYS.

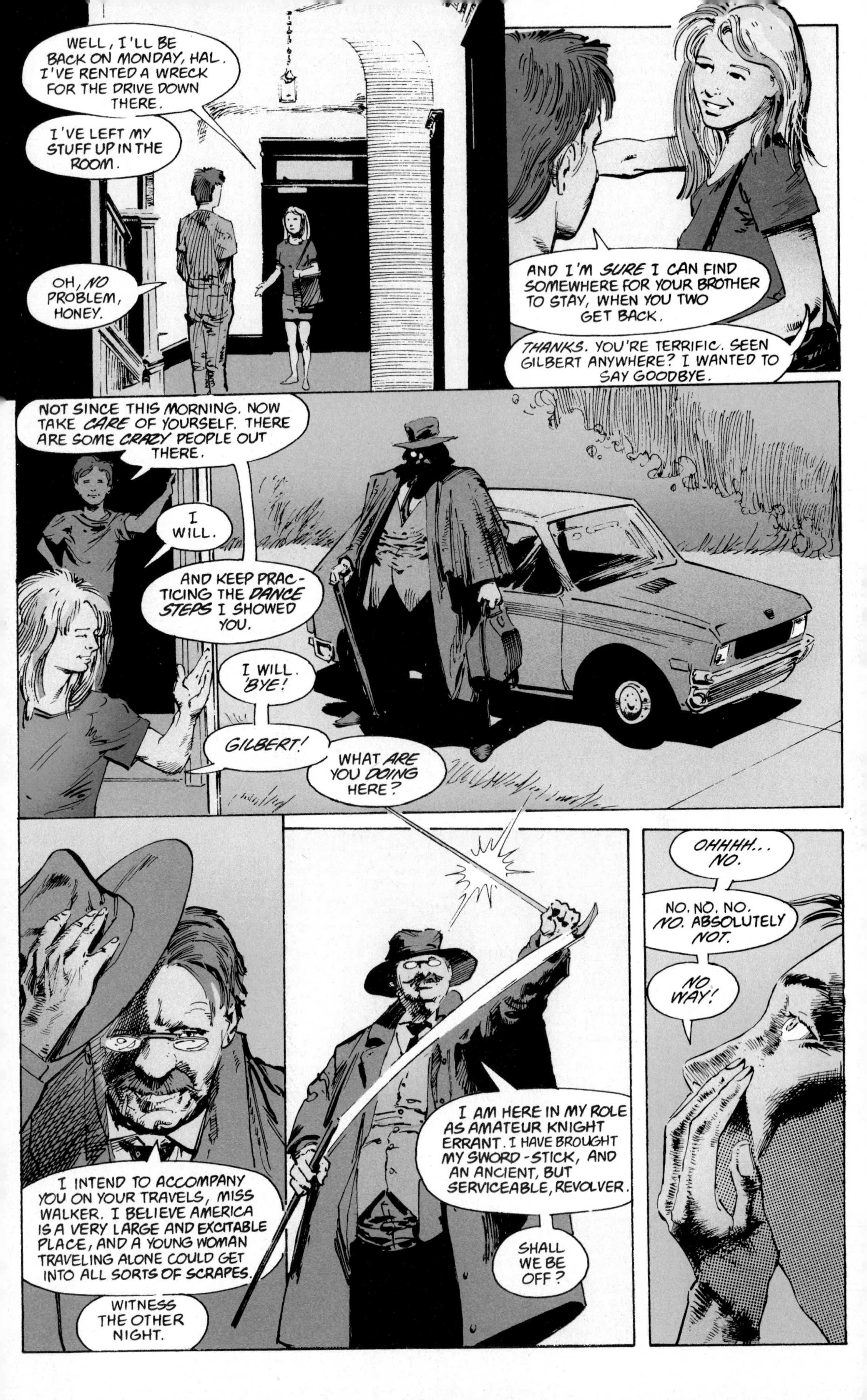

WELL, I'LL BE BACK ON MONDAY, HAL. I'VE RENTED A WRECK FOR THE DRIVE DOWN THERE.
I'VE LEFT MY STUFF UP IN THE ROOM.
OH, NO PROBLEM, HONEY.
AND I'M SURE I CAN FIND SOMEWHERE FOR YOUR BROTHER TO STAY, WHEN YOU TWO GET BACK.
THANKS. YOU'RE TERRIFIC. SEEN GILBERT ANYWHERE? I WANTED TO SAY GOODBYE.
NOT SINCE THIS MORNING. NOW TAKE CARE OF YOURSELF. THERE ARE SOME CRAZY PEOPLE OUT THERE.
I WILL.
AND KEEP PRACTICING THE DANCE STEPS I SHOWED YOU.
I WILL. 'BYE!
GILBERT!
WHAT ARE YOU DOING HERE?
I INTEND TO ACCOMPANY YOU ON YOUR TRAVELS, MISS WALKER. I BELIEVE AMERICA IS A VERY LARGE AND EXCITABLE PLACE, AND A YOUNG WOMAN TRAVELING ALONE COULD GET INTO ALL SORTS OF SCRAPES.
WITNESS THE OTHER NIGHT.
I AM HERE IN MY ROLE AS AMATEUR KNIGHT ERRANT. I HAVE BROUGHT MY SWORD-STICK, AND AN ANCIENT, BUT SERVICEABLE, REVOLVER.
SHALL WE BE OFF?
OHHHH... NO.
NO. NO. NO. NO. ABSOLUTELY NOT.
NO WAY!

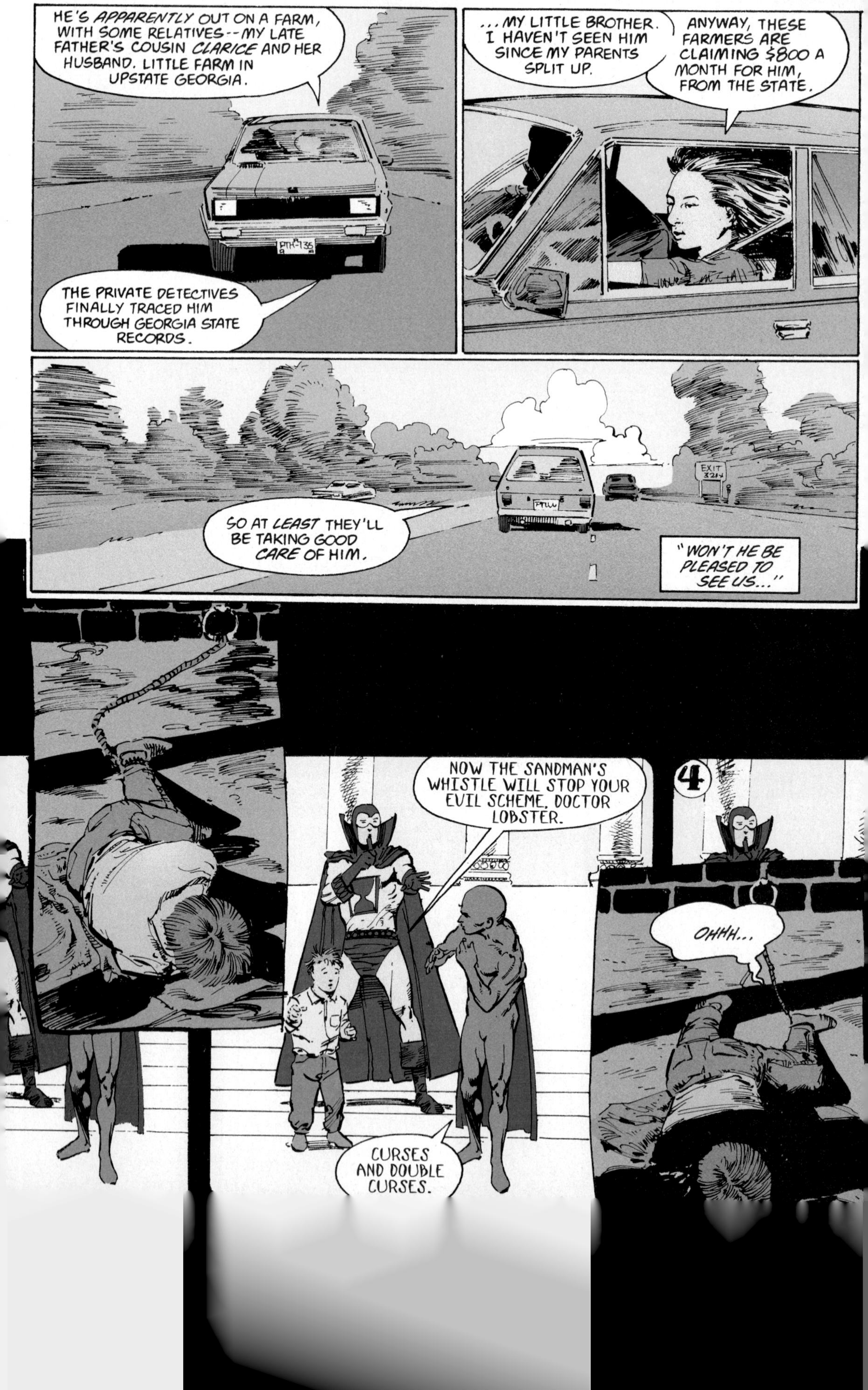
HE'S APPARENTLY OUT ON A FARM, WITH SOME RELATIVES--MY LATE FATHER'S COUSIN CLARICE AND HER HUSBAND. LITTLE FARM IN UPSTATE GEORGIA.
THE PRIVATE DETECTIVES FINALLY TRACED HIM THROUGH GEORGIA STATE RECORDS.
...MY LITTLE BROTHER. I HAVEN'T SEEN HIM SINCE MY PARENTS SPLIT UP.
ANYWAY, THESE FARMERS ARE CLAIMING $800 A MONTH FOR HIM, FROM THE STATE.
SO AT LEAST THEY'LL BE TAKING GOOD CARE OF HIM.
EXIT
"WON'T HE BE PLEASED TO SEE US..."
NOW THE SANDMAN'S WHISTLE WILL STOP YOUR EVIL SCHEME, DOCTOR LOBSTER.
CURSES AND DOUBLE CURSES.
4
OHHH...

Found him.

How dare they?

HOW DARE THEY?

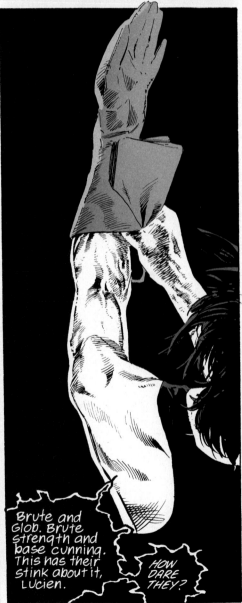

Brute and Glob. Brute strength and base cunning. This has their stink about it, Lucien.

HOW DARE THEY?

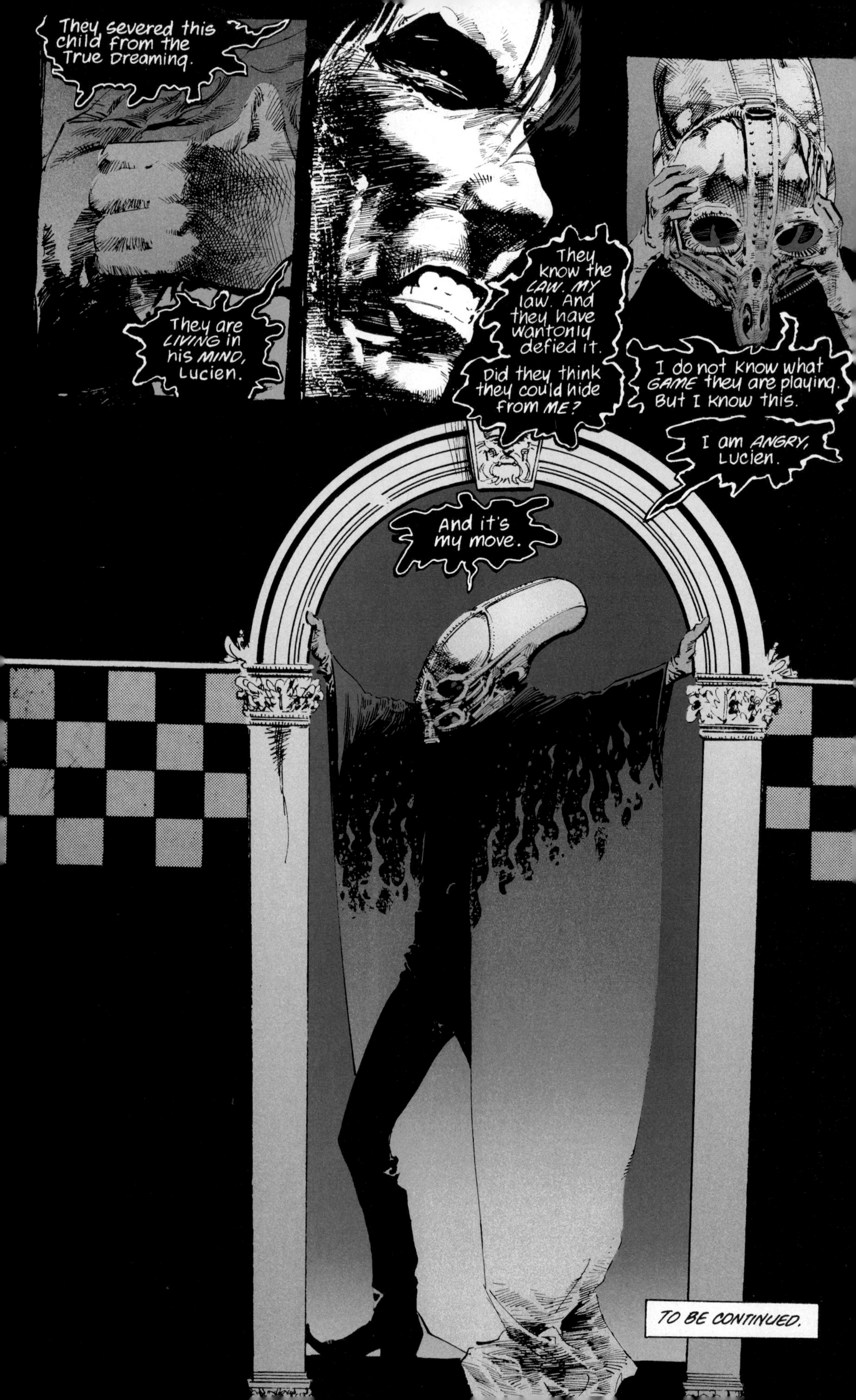
They severed this child from the True Dreaming.
They are LIVING in his MIND, Lucien.
They know the LAW. MY law. And they have wantonly defied it.
Did they think they could hide from ME?
I do not know what GAME they are playing. But I know this.
I am ANGRY, Lucien.
And it's my move.
TO BE CONTINUED.

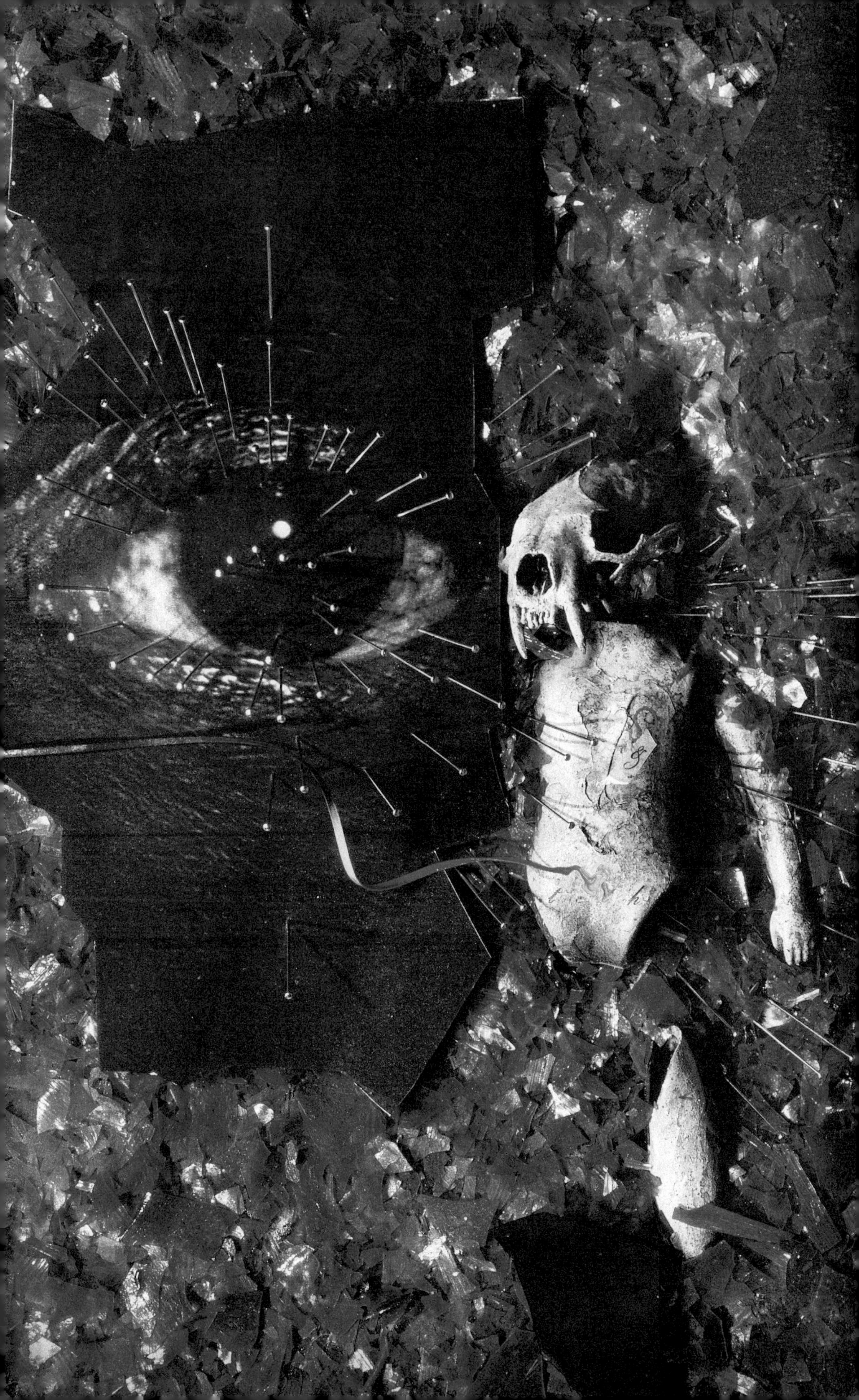

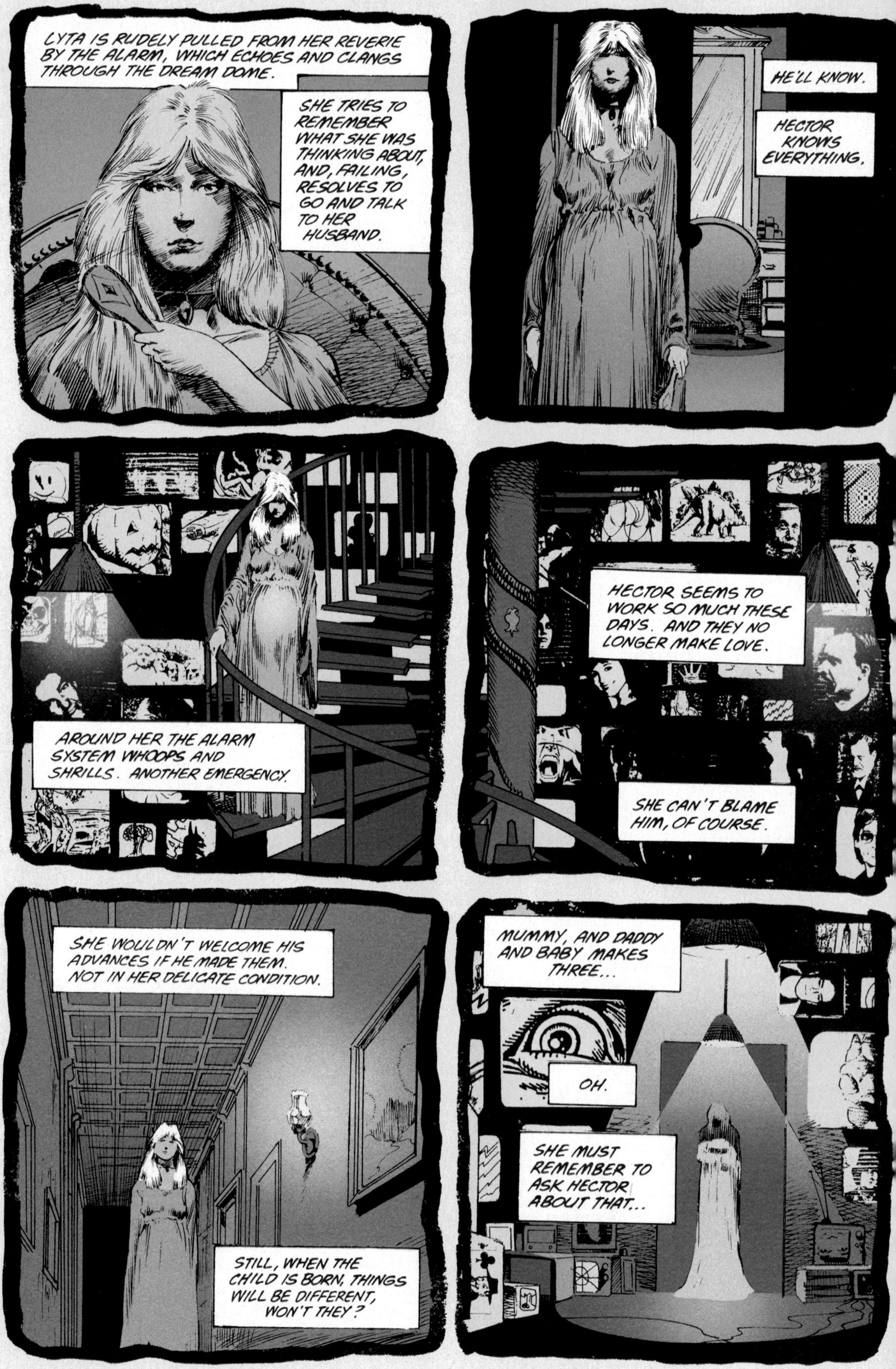
LYTA IS RUDELY PULLED FROM HER REVERIE BY THE ALARM, WHICH ECHOES AND CLANGS THROUGH THE DREAM DOME.
SHE TRIES TO REMEMBER WHAT SHE WAS THINKING ABOUT, AND, FAILING, RESOLVES TO GO AND TALK TO HER HUSBAND.
HE'LL KNOW.
HECTOR KNOWS EVERYTHING.
AROUND HER THE ALARM SYSTEM WHOOPS AND SHRILLS. ANOTHER EMERGENCY.
HECTOR SEEMS TO WORK SO MUCH THESE DAYS. AND THEY NO LONGER MAKE LOVE.
SHE CAN'T BLAME HIM, OF COURSE.
SHE WOULDN'T WELCOME HIS ADVANCES IF HE MADE THEM. NOT IN HER DELICATE CONDITION.
STILL, WHEN THE CHILD IS BORN, THINGS WILL BE DIFFERENT, WON'T THEY?
MUMMY, AND DADDY AND BABY MAKES THREE...
OH.
SHE MUST REMEMBER TO ASK HECTOR ABOUT THAT...

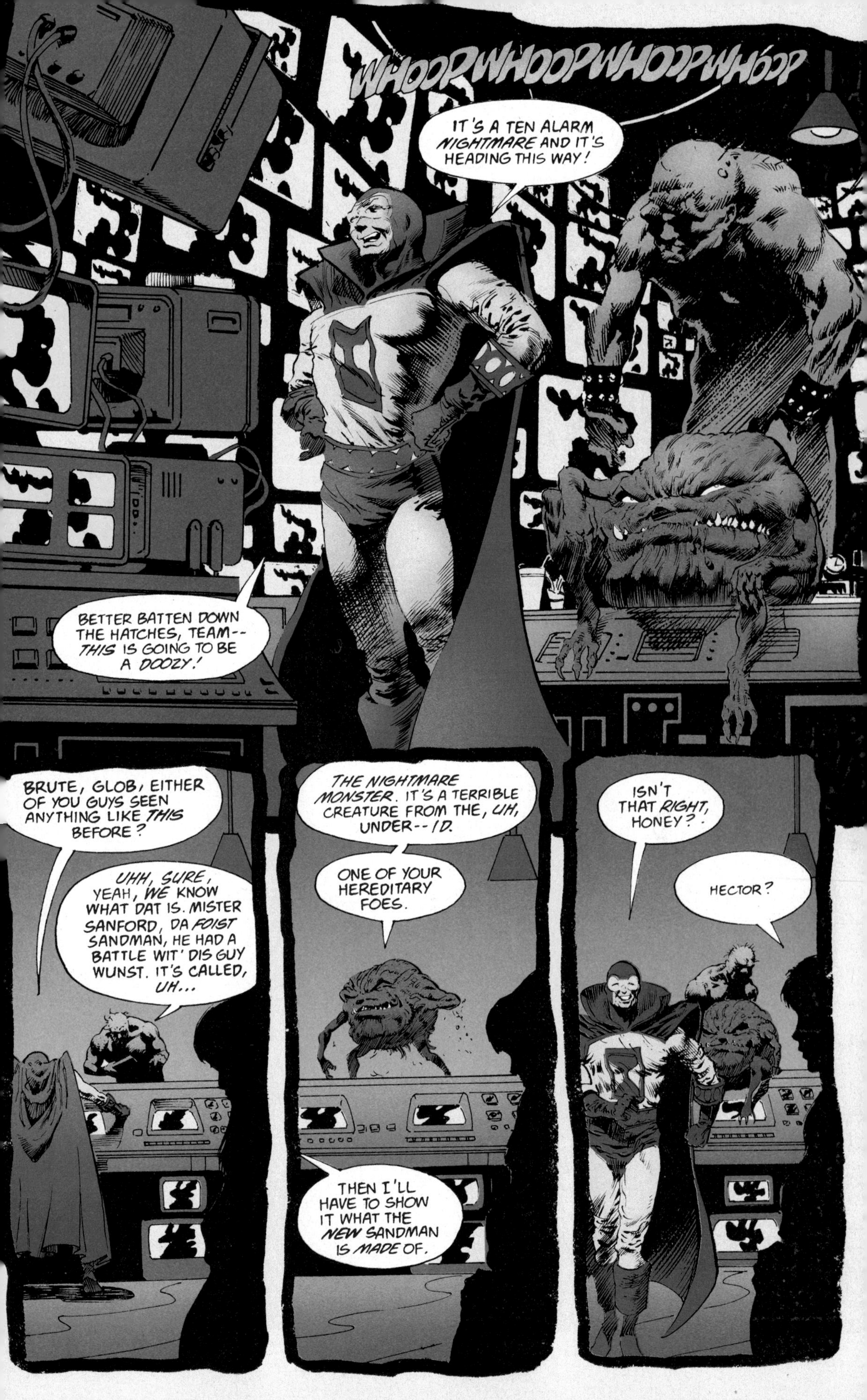
WHOOPWHOOPWHOOPWHOOP
IT'S A TEN ALARM NIGHTMARE AND IT'S HEADING THIS WAY!
BETTER BATTEN DOWN THE HATCHES, TEAM-- THIS IS GOING TO BE A DOOZY!
BRUTE, GLOB, EITHER OF YOU GUYS SEEN ANYTHING LIKE THIS BEFORE?
UHH, SURE, YEAH, WE KNOW WHAT DAT IS. MISTER SANFORD, DA FOIST SANDMAN, HE HAD A BATTLE WIT' DIS GUY WUNST. IT'S CALLED, UH...
THE NIGHTMARE MONSTER. IT'S A TERRIBLE CREATURE FROM THE, UH, UNDER--ID.
ONE OF YOUR HEREDITARY FOES.
THEN I'LL HAVE TO SHOW IT WHAT THE NEW SANDMAN IS MADE OF.
ISN'T THAT RIGHT, HONEY?
HECTOR?

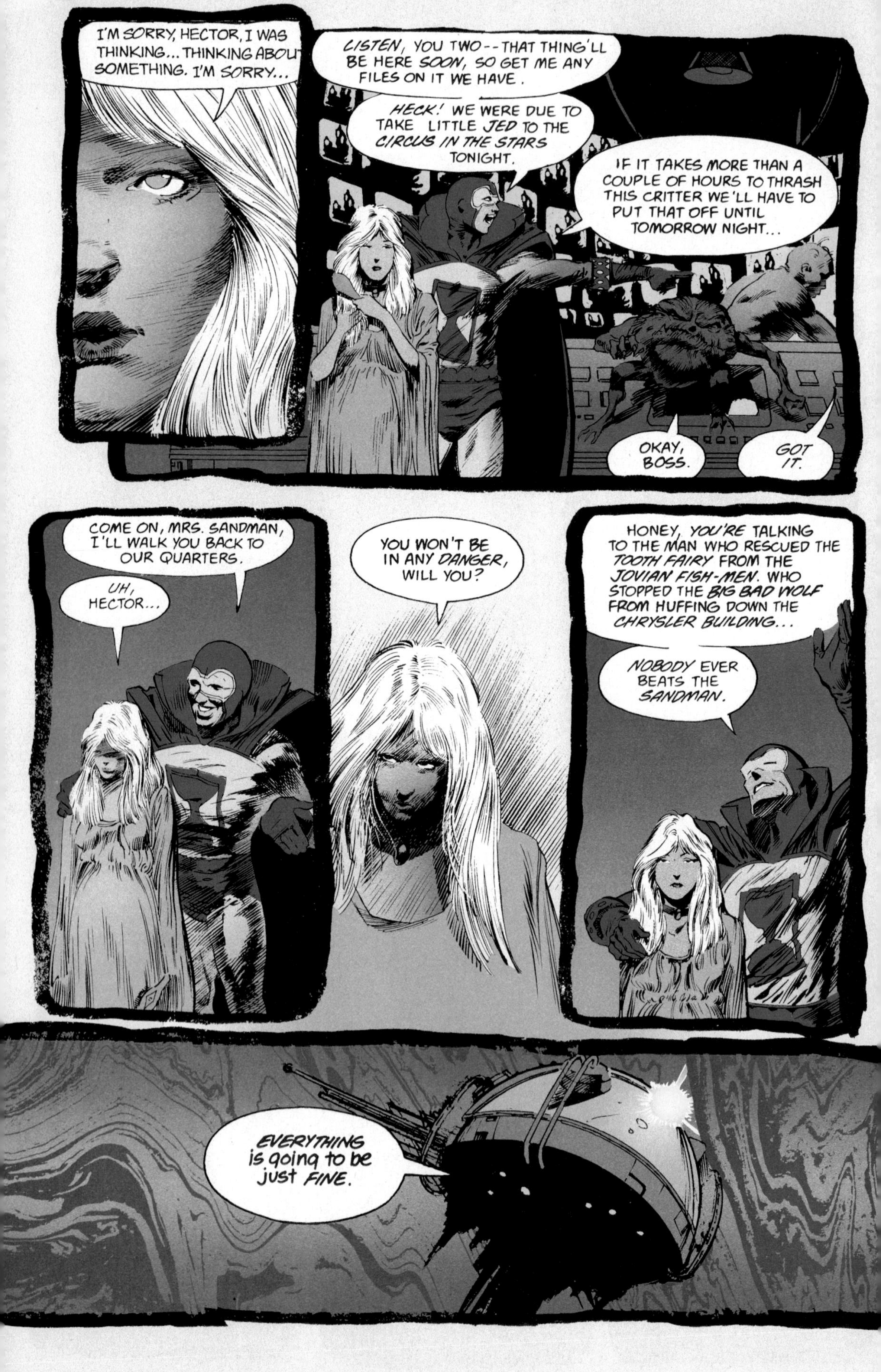
I'M SORRY, HECTOR, I WAS THINKING... THINKING ABOUT SOMETHING. I'M SORRY...
LISTEN, YOU TWO--THAT THING'LL BE HERE SOON, SO GET ME ANY FILES ON IT WE HAVE.
HECK! WE WERE DUE TO TAKE LITTLE JED TO THE CIRCUS IN THE STARS TONIGHT.
IF IT TAKES MORE THAN A COUPLE OF HOURS TO THRASH THIS CRITTER WE'LL HAVE TO PUT THAT OFF UNTIL TOMORROW NIGHT...
OKAY, BOSS.
GOT IT.
COME ON, MRS. SANDMAN, I'LL WALK YOU BACK TO OUR QUARTERS.
UH, HECTOR...
YOU WON'T BE IN ANY DANGER, WILL YOU?
HONEY, YOU'RE TALKING TO THE MAN WHO RESCUED THE TOOTH FAIRY FROM THE JOVIAN FISH-MEN. WHO STOPPED THE BIG BAD WOLF FROM HUFFING DOWN THE CHRYSLER BUILDING...
NOBODY EVER BEATS THE SANDMAN.
EVERYTHING is going to be just FINE.

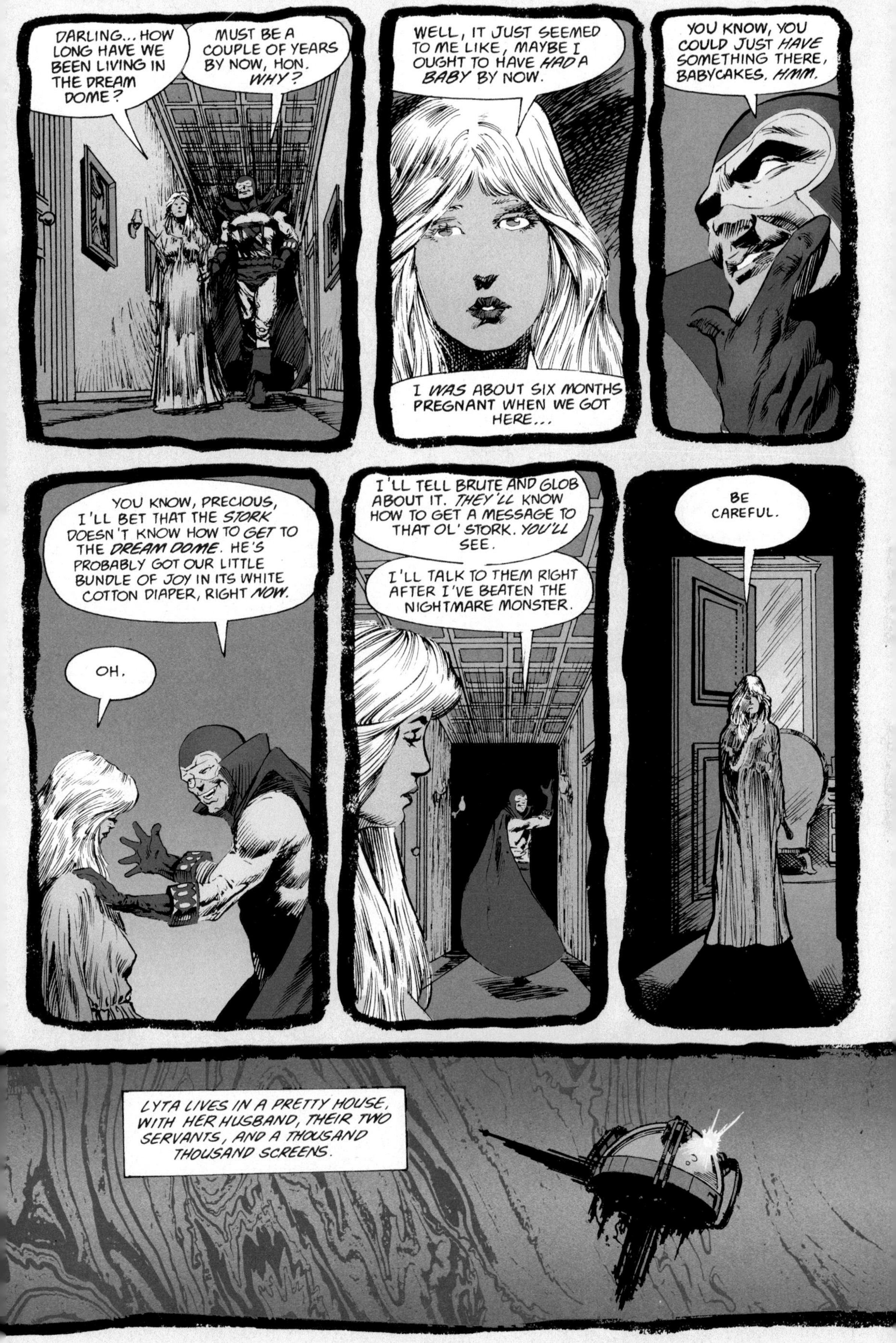
DARLING... HOW LONG HAVE WE BEEN LIVING IN THE DREAM DOME?
MUST BE A COUPLE OF YEARS BY NOW, HON. WHY?
WELL, IT JUST SEEMED TO ME LIKE, MAYBE I OUGHT TO HAVE HAD A BABY BY NOW.
I WAS ABOUT SIX MONTHS PREGNANT WHEN WE GOT HERE...
YOU KNOW, YOU COULD JUST HAVE SOMETHING THERE, BABYCAKES. HMM.
YOU KNOW, PRECIOUS, I'LL BET THAT THE STORK DOESN'T KNOW HOW TO GET TO THE DREAM DOME. HE'S PROBABLY GOT OUR LITTLE BUNDLE OF JOY IN ITS WHITE COTTON DIAPER, RIGHT NOW.
OH.
I'LL TELL BRUTE AND GLOB ABOUT IT. THEY'LL KNOW HOW TO GET A MESSAGE TO THAT OL' STORK. YOU'LL SEE.
I'LL TALK TO THEM RIGHT AFTER I'VE BEATEN THE NIGHTMARE MONSTER.
BE CAREFUL.
LYTA LIVES IN A PRETTY HOUSE, WITH HER HUSBAND, THEIR TWO SERVANTS, AND A THOUSAND THOUSAND SCREENS.

PLAYING HOUSE

NEIL GAIMAN • CHRIS BACHALO • MALCOLM JONES • ZYLONOL • JOHN COSTANZA • ART YOUNG • KAREN BERGER
writer • guest penciller • inker • colorist • letterer • assoc. editor • editor

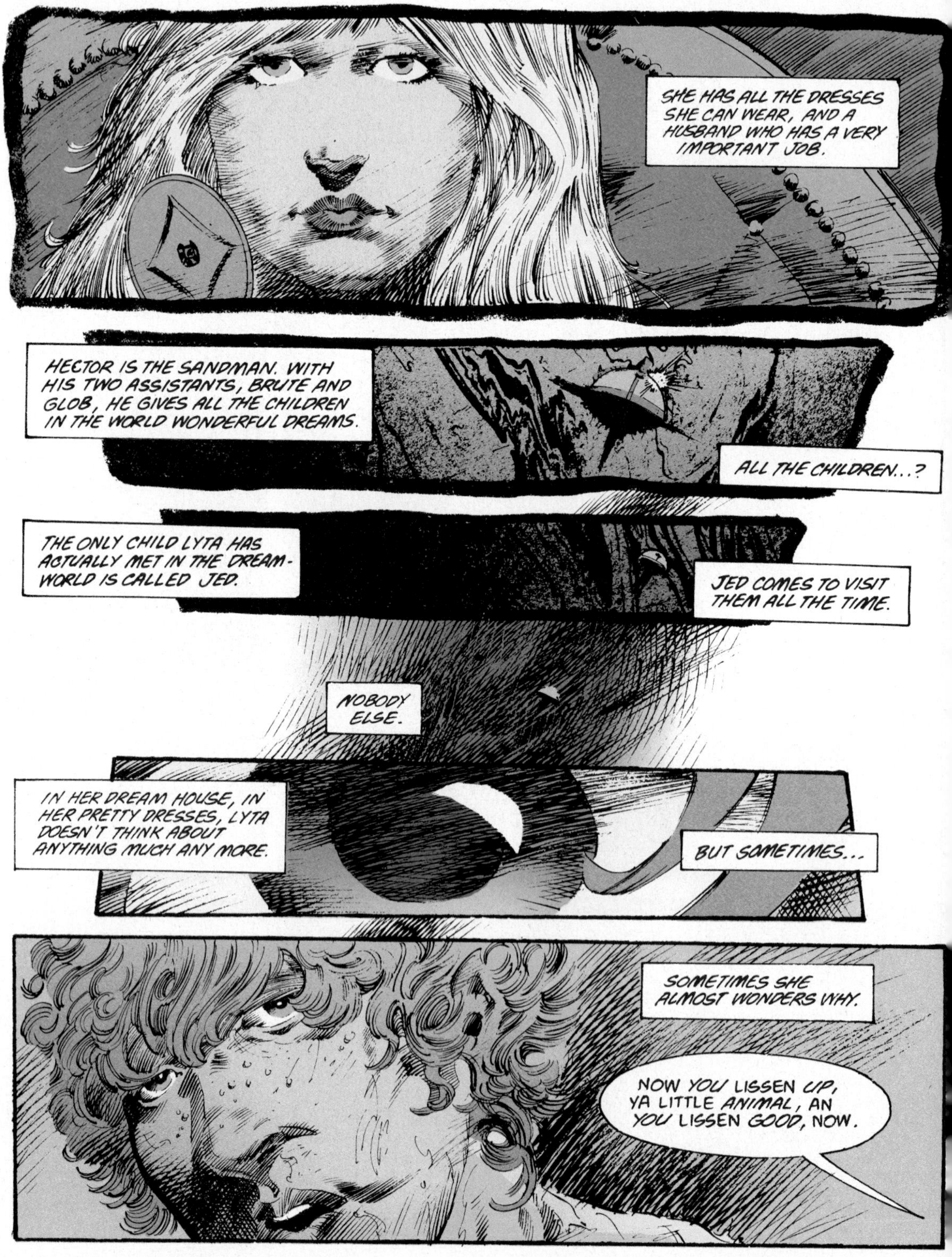
SHE HAS ALL THE DRESSES SHE CAN WEAR, AND A HUSBAND WHO HAS A VERY IMPORTANT JOB.
HECTOR IS THE SANDMAN. WITH HIS TWO ASSISTANTS, BRUTE AND GLOB, HE GIVES ALL THE CHILDREN IN THE WORLD WONDERFUL DREAMS.
ALL THE CHILDREN...?
THE ONLY CHILD LYTA HAS ACTUALLY MET IN THE DREAM-WORLD IS CALLED JED.
JED COMES TO VISIT THEM ALL THE TIME.
NOBODY ELSE.
IN HER DREAM HOUSE, IN HER PRETTY DRESSES, LYTA DOESN'T THINK ABOUT ANYTHING MUCH ANY MORE.
BUT SOMETIMES...
SOMETIMES SHE ALMOST WONDERS WHY.
NOW YOU LISSEN UP, YA LITTLE ANIMAL, AN YOU LISSEN GOOD, NOW.

NEXT WEEK, SOMEONE'S GOING TO COME FROM THE WELFARE DEPARTMENT TO SEE HOW YOU'RE *DOIN'.*

SEE IF THEY'RE GETTIN' THEIR *MONEY'S WORTH* OUTTA YA.

SO WE'RE GONNA *CLEAN* YA *UP,* AND BRING YA UP OUTTA THE CELLAR. AND *YOU'RE* GONNA SHOW HER BARNABY JUNIOR'S ROOM AND MAKE OUT IT'S YOURS, AND TELL HER HOW WELL WE FEED YOU AND ALL.

AND *NONE* OF YOUR *LYING* OR *CARRYING ON,* BOY.

FEEL *THIS? HUH? DO YA?*

OOG.

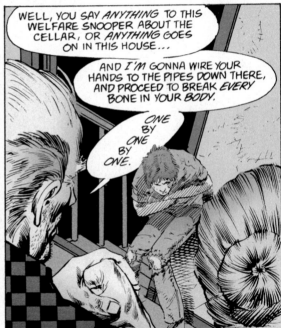

WELL, YOU SAY *ANYTHING* TO THIS WELFARE SNOOPER ABOUT THE CELLAR, OR *ANYTHING* GOES ON IN THIS HOUSE...

AND *I'M* GONNA WIRE YOUR HANDS TO THE PIPES DOWN THERE, AND PROCEED TO BREAK *EVERY* BONE IN YOUR *BODY.*

ONE BY ONE BY ONE.

NOW *GIT!*

CLARICE AND BARNABY RECEIVE $800 A MONTH FROM THE STATE FOR JED. THREE YEARS AGO HE RAN AWAY.

SINCE THEN HE'S BEEN LOCKED IN THE BASEMENT.

BARNABY AND CLARICE SEE IT AS PROTECTING THEIR INVESTMENT. THEY KNOW IT'S IMPORTANT TO KEEP JED SAFE...

THEY JUST COULDN'T TELL YOU WHY.

WHAT'S KEEPING THIS DUMB NIGHTMARE MONSTER, *HUH*, BRUTE, OLD PAL?

DUH. I DUNNO, BOSS.

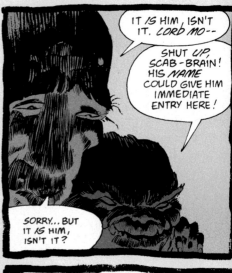

IT *IS* HIM, ISN'T IT. *LORD MO--*

SHUT *UP*, SCAB-BRAIN! HIS *NAME* COULD GIVE HIM IMMEDIATE ENTRY HERE!

SORRY... BUT IT *IS* HIM, ISN'T IT?

WHO ELSE?

SO FAR THE BARRIERS ARE HOLDING. IF HE BREAKS THEM HE KILLS THE KID, AND HE CAN'T DO THAT. *RULES*.

SO IT BUYS US A LITTLE TIME WHILE HE WORMS HIS WAY IN.

I'M *BEGINNING* TO THINK WE SHOULD HAVE STUCK WITH THE *LAST* ONE. HALL'S EVEN DUMBER THAN SANFORD WAS.

IT TAKES SOME DOING, BUT HE IS.

SAY, GUYS, DO YOU THINK THIS NIGHTMARE MONSTER'S GOING TO BE A TOUGHER BATTLE THAN THE SKELETON MEN FROM PLUTO?

DO YOU?

DO YOU?

I am coming.

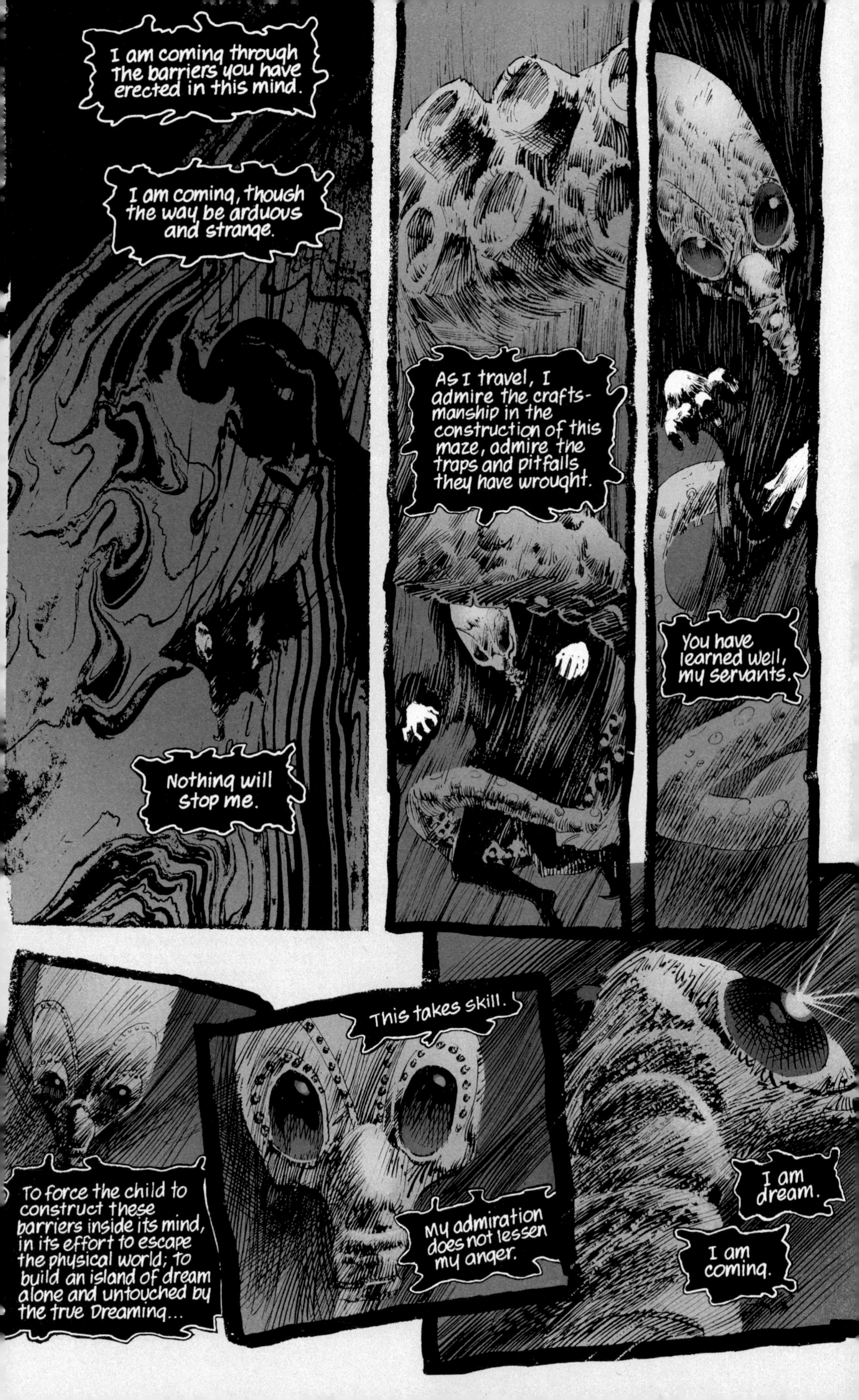
I am coming through the barriers you have erected in this mind.
I am coming, though the way be arduous and strange.
Nothing will stop me.
As I travel, I admire the crafts-manship in the construction of this maze, admire the traps and pitfalls they have wrought.
You have learned well, my servants.
To force the child to construct these barriers inside its mind, in its effort to escape the physical world; to build an island of dream alone and untouched by the true Dreaming...
This takes skill.
My admiration does not lessen my anger.
I am dream.
I am coming.

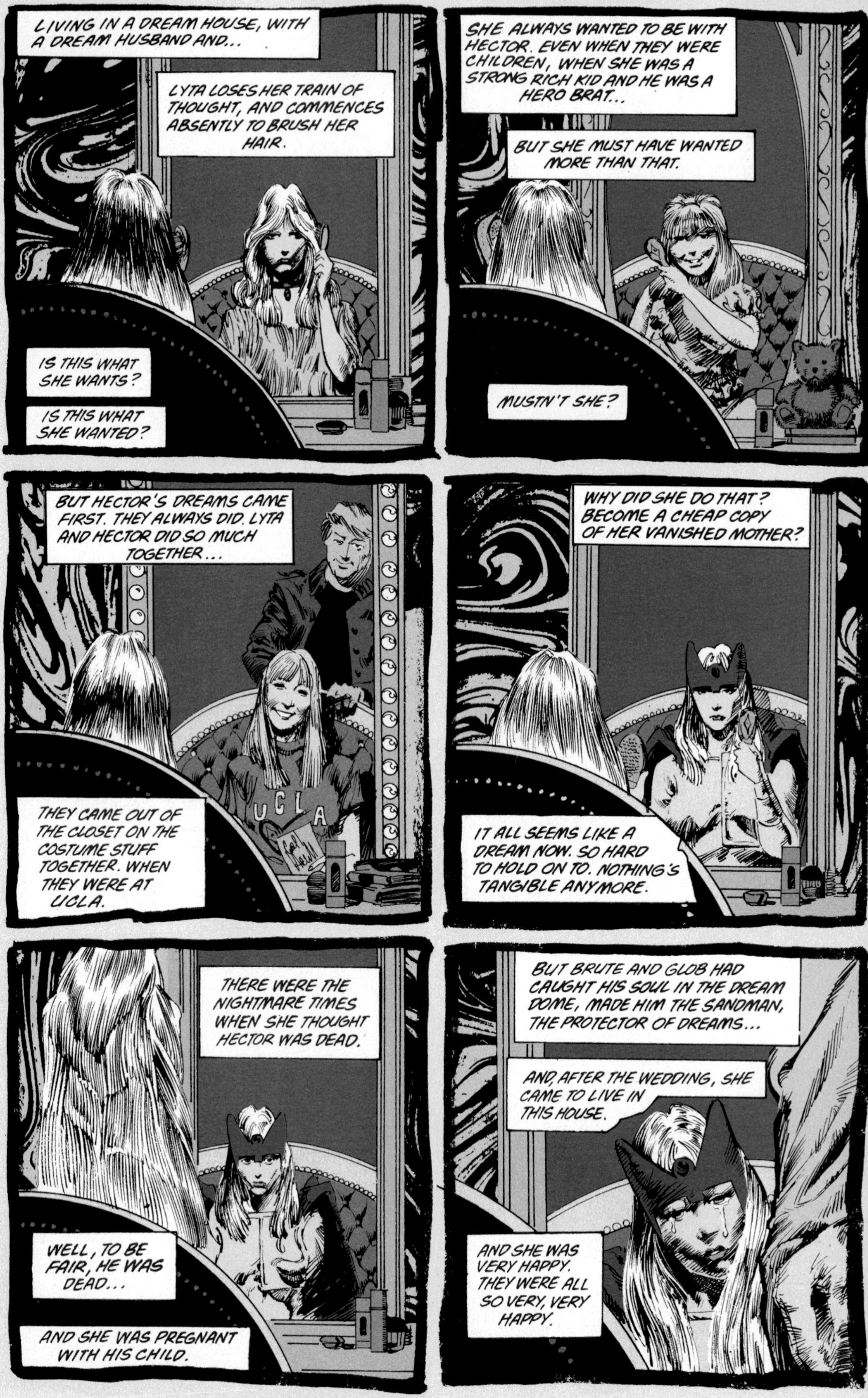
LIVING IN A DREAM HOUSE, WITH A DREAM HUSBAND AND...
LYTA LOSES HER TRAIN OF THOUGHT, AND COMMENCES ABSENTLY TO BRUSH HER HAIR.
IS THIS WHAT SHE WANTS?
IS THIS WHAT SHE WANTED?
SHE ALWAYS WANTED TO BE WITH HECTOR. EVEN WHEN THEY WERE CHILDREN, WHEN SHE WAS A STRONG RICH KID AND HE WAS A HERO BRAT...
BUT SHE MUST HAVE WANTED MORE THAN THAT.
MUSTN'T SHE?
BUT HECTOR'S DREAMS CAME FIRST. THEY ALWAYS DID. LYTA AND HECTOR DID SO MUCH TOGETHER...
THEY CAME OUT OF THE CLOSET ON THE COSTUME STUFF TOGETHER. WHEN THEY WERE AT UCLA.
UCLA
WHY DID SHE DO THAT? BECOME A CHEAP COPY OF HER VANISHED MOTHER?
IT ALL SEEMS LIKE A DREAM NOW. SO HARD TO HOLD ON TO. NOTHING'S TANGIBLE ANYMORE.
THERE WERE THE NIGHTMARE TIMES WHEN SHE THOUGHT HECTOR WAS DEAD.
WELL, TO BE FAIR, HE WAS DEAD...
AND SHE WAS PREGNANT WITH HIS CHILD.
BUT BRUTE AND GLOB HAD CAUGHT HIS SOUL IN THE DREAM DOME, MADE HIM THE SANDMAN, THE PROTECTOR OF DREAMS...
AND, AFTER THE WEDDING, SHE CAME TO LIVE IN THIS HOUSE.
AND SHE WAS VERY HAPPY. THEY WERE ALL SO VERY, VERY HAPPY.

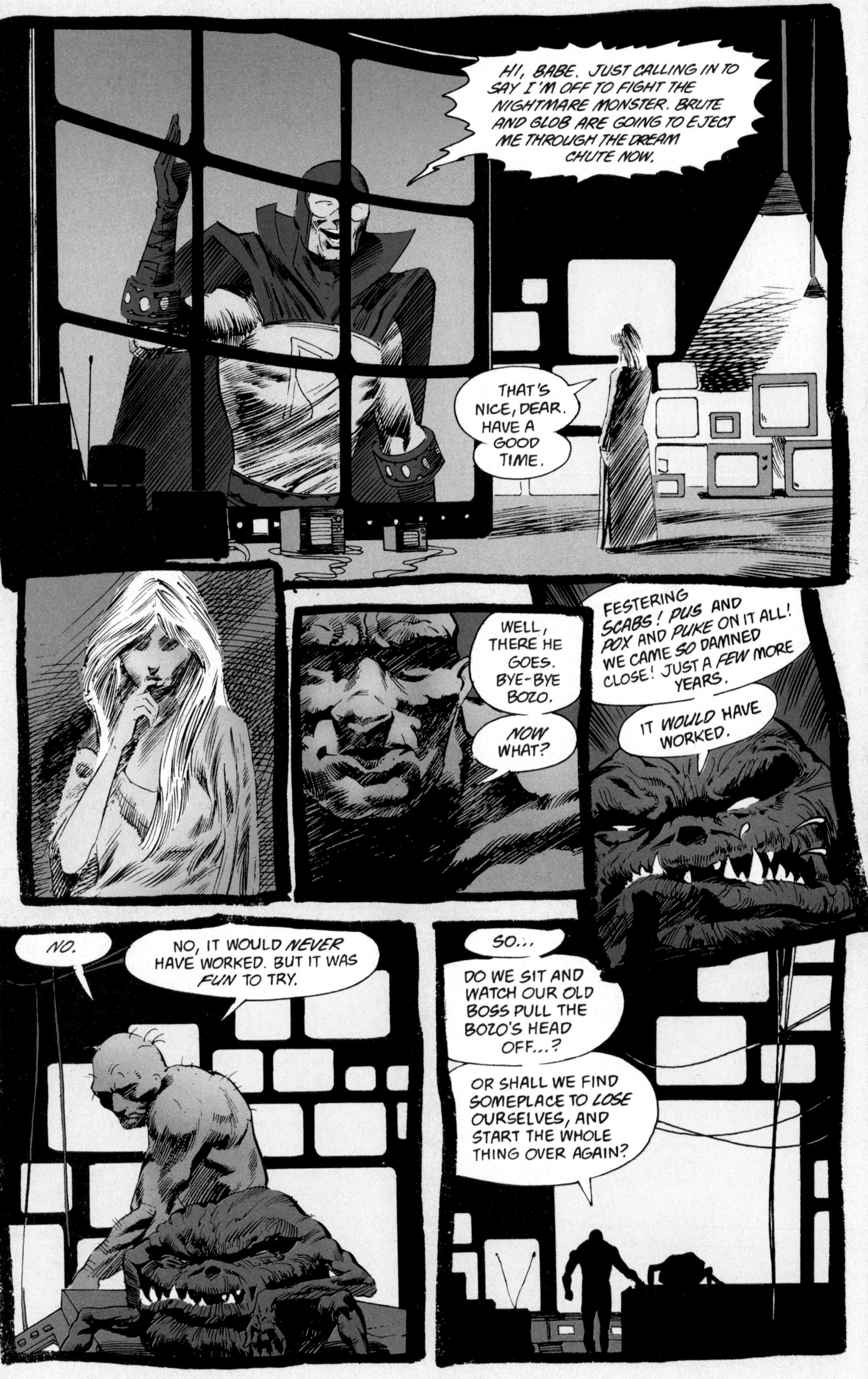
HI, BABE. JUST CALLING IN TO SAY I'M OFF TO FIGHT THE NIGHTMARE MONSTER. BRUTE AND GLOB ARE GOING TO EJECT ME THROUGH THE DREAM CHUTE NOW.
THAT'S NICE, DEAR. HAVE A GOOD TIME.
WELL, THERE HE GOES. BYE-BYE BOZO.
NOW WHAT?
FESTERING SCABS! PUS AND POX AND PUKE ON IT ALL! WE CAME SO DAMNED CLOSE! JUST A FEW MORE YEARS.
IT WOULD HAVE WORKED.
NO.
NO, IT WOULD NEVER HAVE WORKED. BUT IT WAS FUN TO TRY.
SO...
DO WE SIT AND WATCH OUR OLD BOSS PULL THE BOZO'S HEAD OFF...?
OR SHALL WE FIND SOMEPLACE TO LOSE OURSELVES, AND START THE WHOLE THING OVER AGAIN?

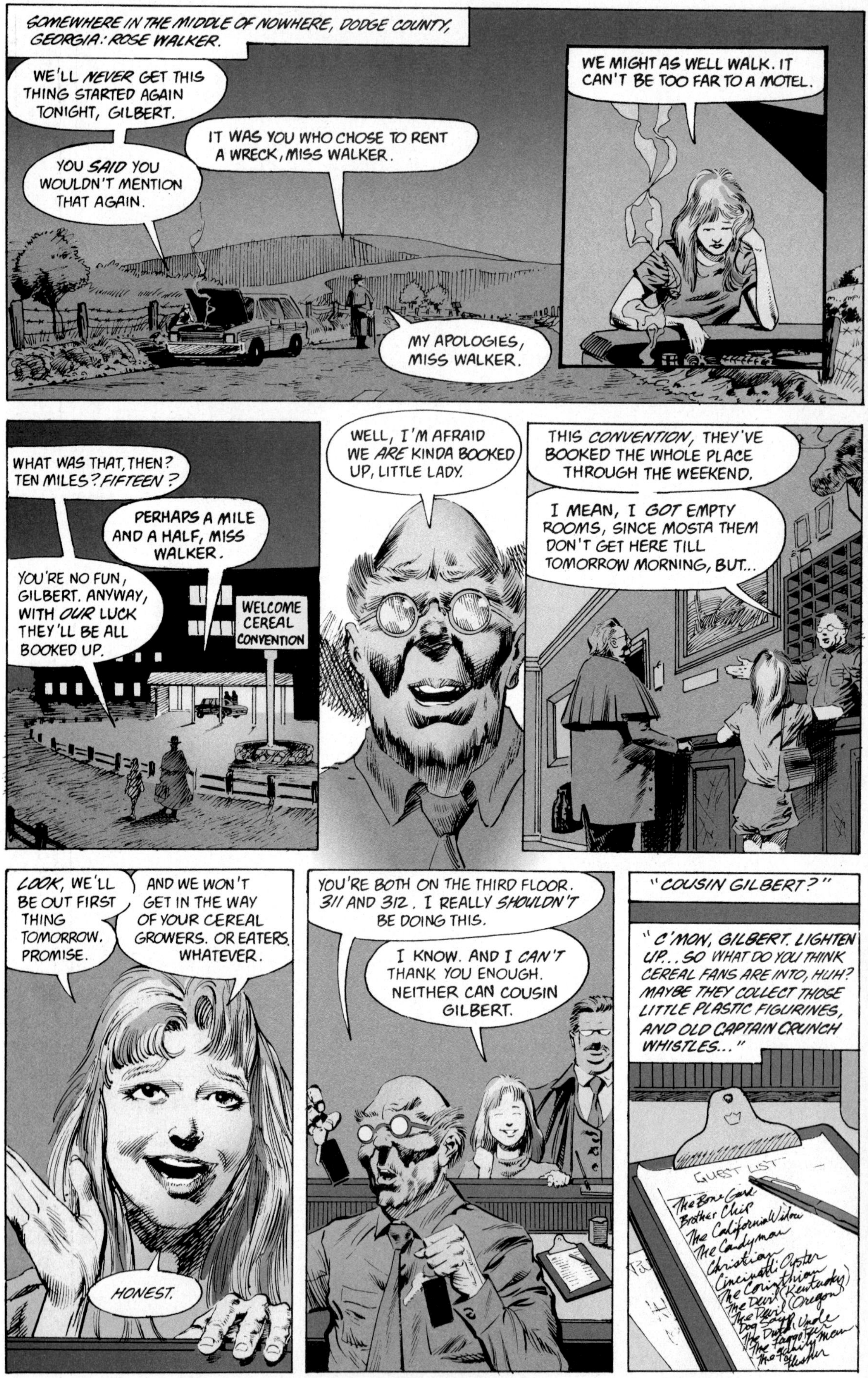
SOMEWHERE IN THE MIDDLE OF NOWHERE, DODGE COUNTY, GEORGIA: ROSE WALKER.
WE'LL NEVER GET THIS THING STARTED AGAIN TONIGHT, GILBERT.
IT WAS YOU WHO CHOSE TO RENT A WRECK, MISS WALKER.
YOU SAID YOU WOULDN'T MENTION THAT AGAIN.
MY APOLOGIES, MISS WALKER.
WE MIGHT AS WELL WALK. IT CAN'T BE TOO FAR TO A MOTEL.
WHAT WAS THAT, THEN? TEN MILES? FIFTEEN?
PERHAPS A MILE AND A HALF, MISS WALKER.
YOU'RE NO FUN, GILBERT. ANYWAY, WITH OUR LUCK THEY'LL BE ALL BOOKED UP.
WELCOME CEREAL CONVENTION
WELL, I'M AFRAID WE ARE KINDA BOOKED UP, LITTLE LADY.
THIS CONVENTION, THEY'VE BOOKED THE WHOLE PLACE THROUGH THE WEEKEND.
I MEAN, I GOT EMPTY ROOMS, SINCE MOSTA THEM DON'T GET HERE TILL TOMORROW MORNING, BUT...
LOOK, WE'LL BE OUT FIRST THING TOMORROW. PROMISE.
AND WE WON'T GET IN THE WAY OF YOUR CEREAL GROWERS. OR EATERS. WHATEVER.
HONEST.
YOU'RE BOTH ON THE THIRD FLOOR. 311 AND 312. I REALLY SHOULDN'T BE DOING THIS.
I KNOW. AND I CAN'T THANK YOU ENOUGH. NEITHER CAN COUSIN GILBERT.
"COUSIN GILBERT?"
"C'MON, GILBERT. LIGHTEN UP... SO WHAT DO YOU THINK CEREAL FANS ARE INTO, HUH? MAYBE THEY COLLECT THOSE LITTLE PLASTIC FIGURINES, AND OLD CAPTAIN CRUNCH WHISTLES..."
GUEST LIST
The Bone Card
Brother Chip
The California Widow
The Candyman
Christian
Cincinatti Oyster
The Corinthian
The Devil (Kentucky)
The Devil (Oregon)
Dog Soup
The Dutch Uncle

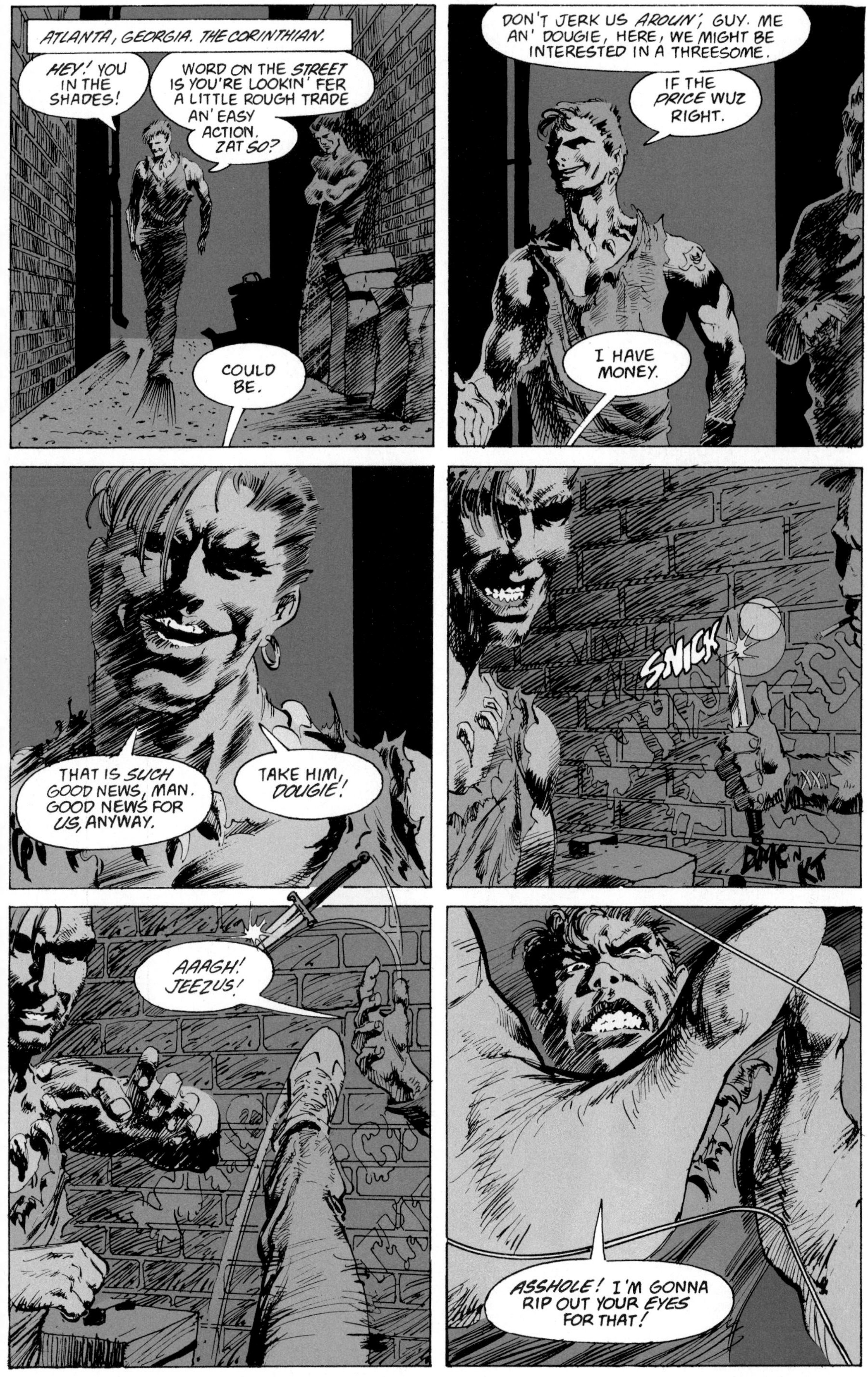
ATLANTA, GEORGIA. THE CORINTHIAN.
HEY! YOU IN THE SHADES!
WORD ON THE STREET IS YOU'RE LOOKIN' FER A LITTLE ROUGH TRADE AN' EASY ACTION. ZAT SO?
COULD BE.
DON'T JERK US AROUN', GUY. ME AN' DOUGIE, HERE, WE MIGHT BE INTERESTED IN A THREESOME.
IF THE PRICE WUZ RIGHT.
I HAVE MONEY.
THAT IS SUCH GOOD NEWS, MAN. GOOD NEWS FOR US, ANYWAY.
TAKE HIM, DOUGIE!
SNICK
AAAGH! JEEZUS!
ASSHOLE! I'M GONNA RIP OUT YOUR EYES FOR THAT!

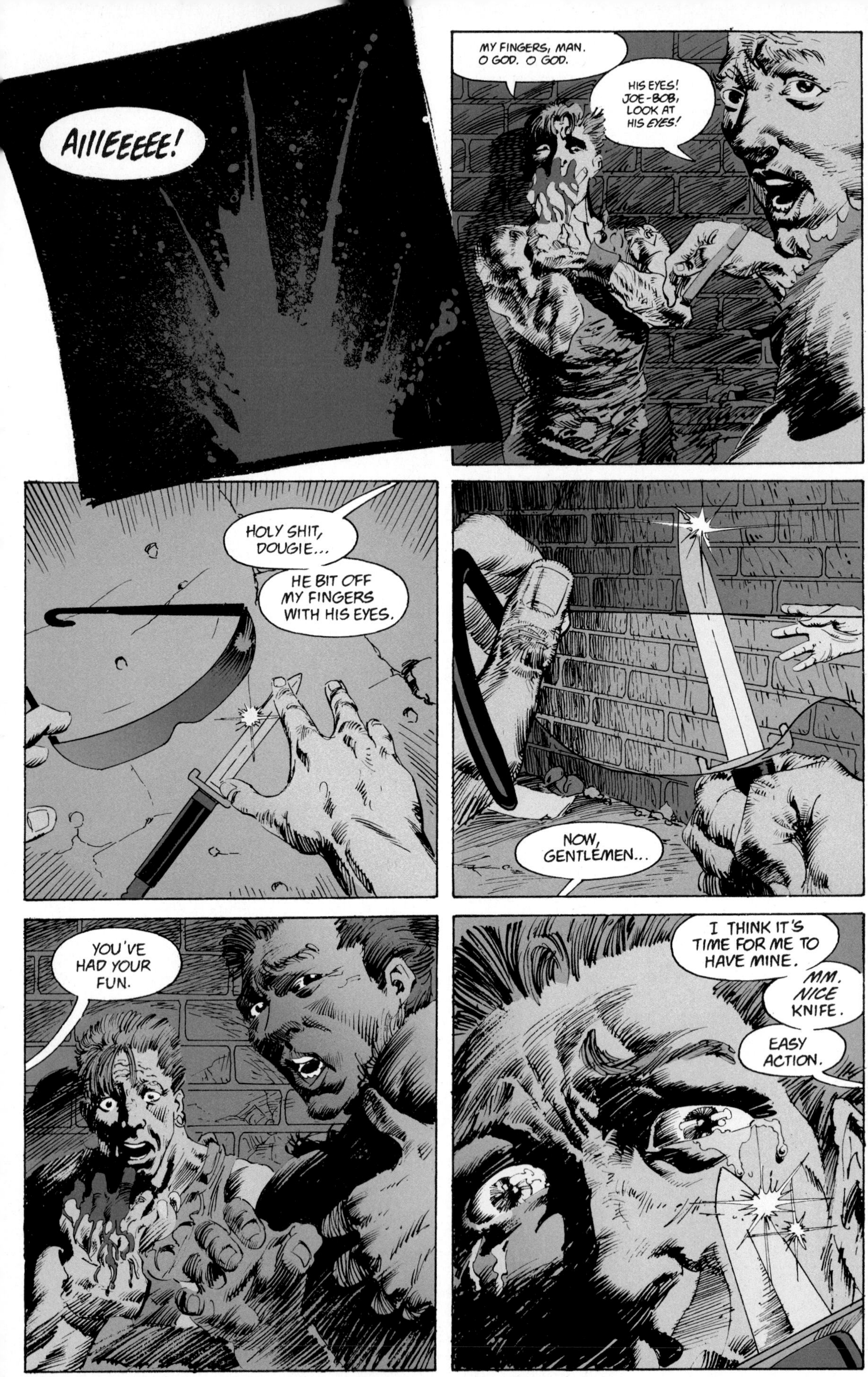
AIIIEEEEE!
MY FINGERS, MAN. O GOD. O GOD.
HIS EYES! JOE-BOB, LOOK AT HIS EYES!
HOLY SHIT, DOUGIE...
HE BIT OFF MY FINGERS WITH HIS EYES.
NOW, GENTLEMEN...
YOU'VE HAD YOUR FUN.
I THINK IT'S TIME FOR ME TO HAVE MINE.
MM. NICE KNIFE.
EASY ACTION.

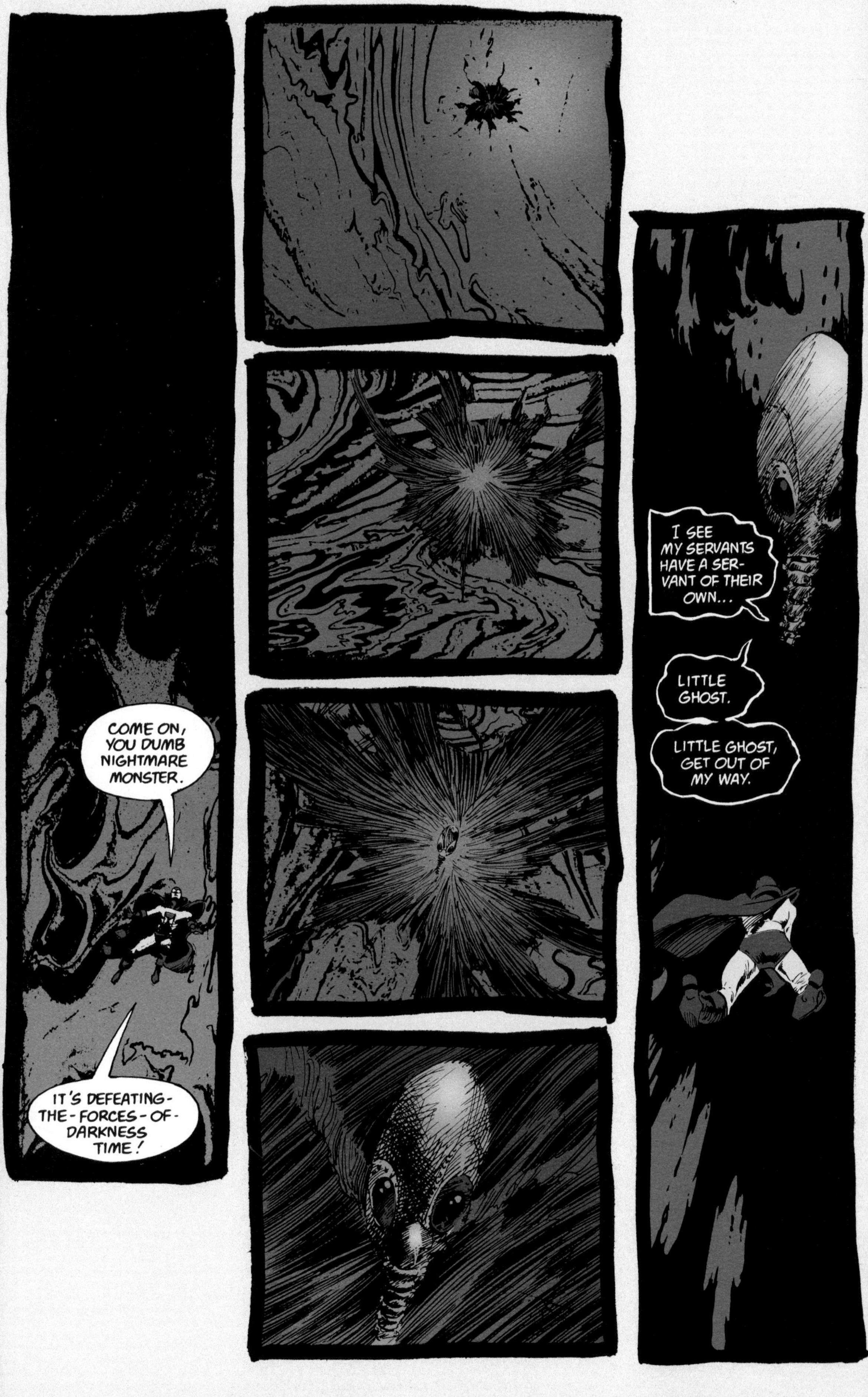
COME ON, YOU DUMB NIGHTMARE MONSTER.
IT'S DEFEATING-THE-FORCES-OF-DARKNESS TIME!
I SEE MY SERVANTS HAVE A SER-VANT OF THEIR OWN...
LITTLE GHOST.
LITTLE GHOST, GET OUT OF MY WAY.

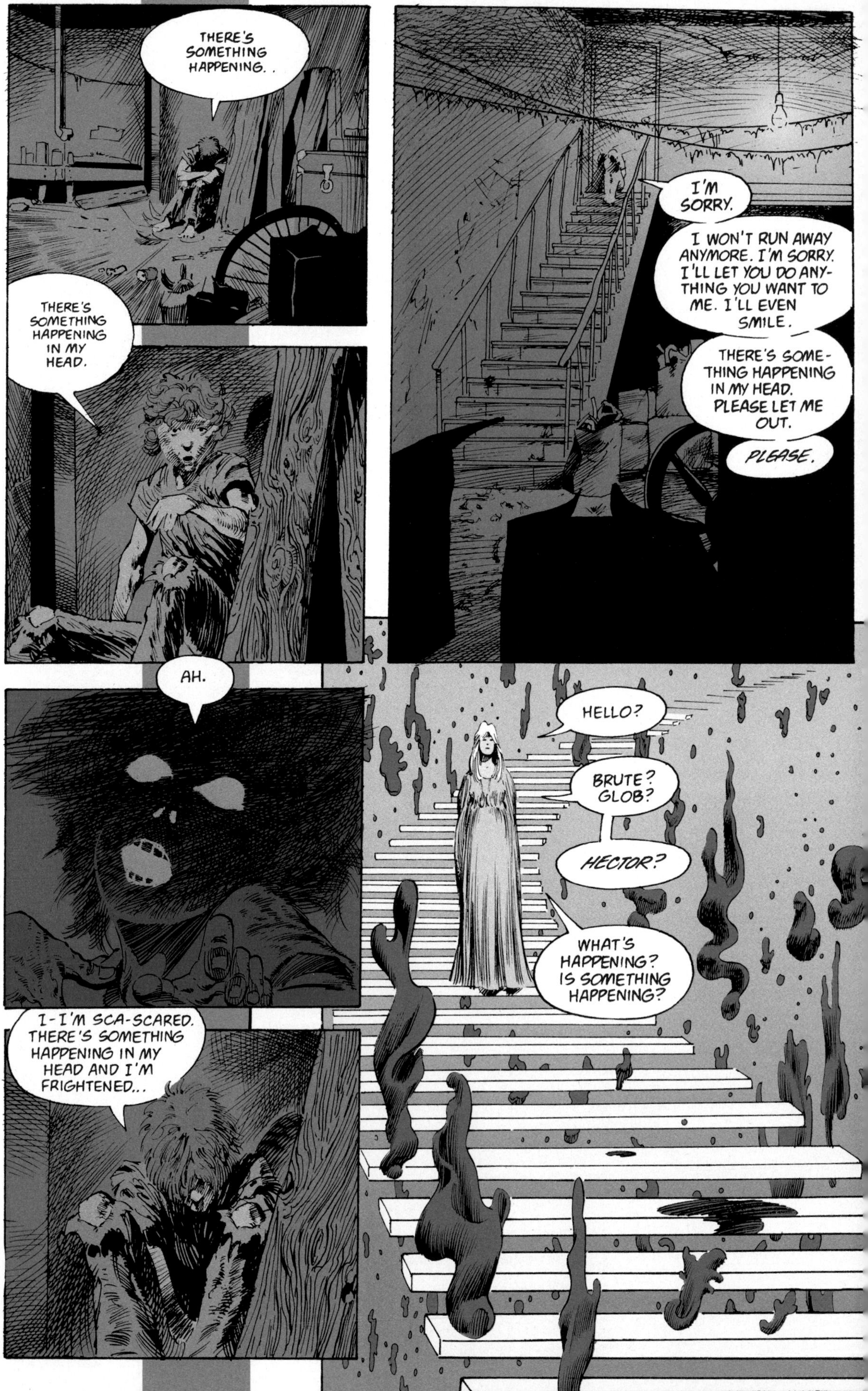
THERE'S SOMETHING HAPPENING. .
THERE'S SOMETHING HAPPENING IN MY HEAD.
I'M SORRY.
I WON'T RUN AWAY ANYMORE. I'M SORRY. I'LL LET YOU DO ANYTHING YOU WANT TO ME. I'LL EVEN SMILE.
THERE'S SOMETHING HAPPENING IN MY HEAD. PLEASE LET ME OUT.
PLEASE.
AH.
I-I'M SCA-SCARED. THERE'S SOMETHING HAPPENING IN MY HEAD AND I'M FRIGHTENED...
HELLO?
BRUTE? GLOB?
HECTOR?
WHAT'S HAPPENING? IS SOMETHING HAPPENING?

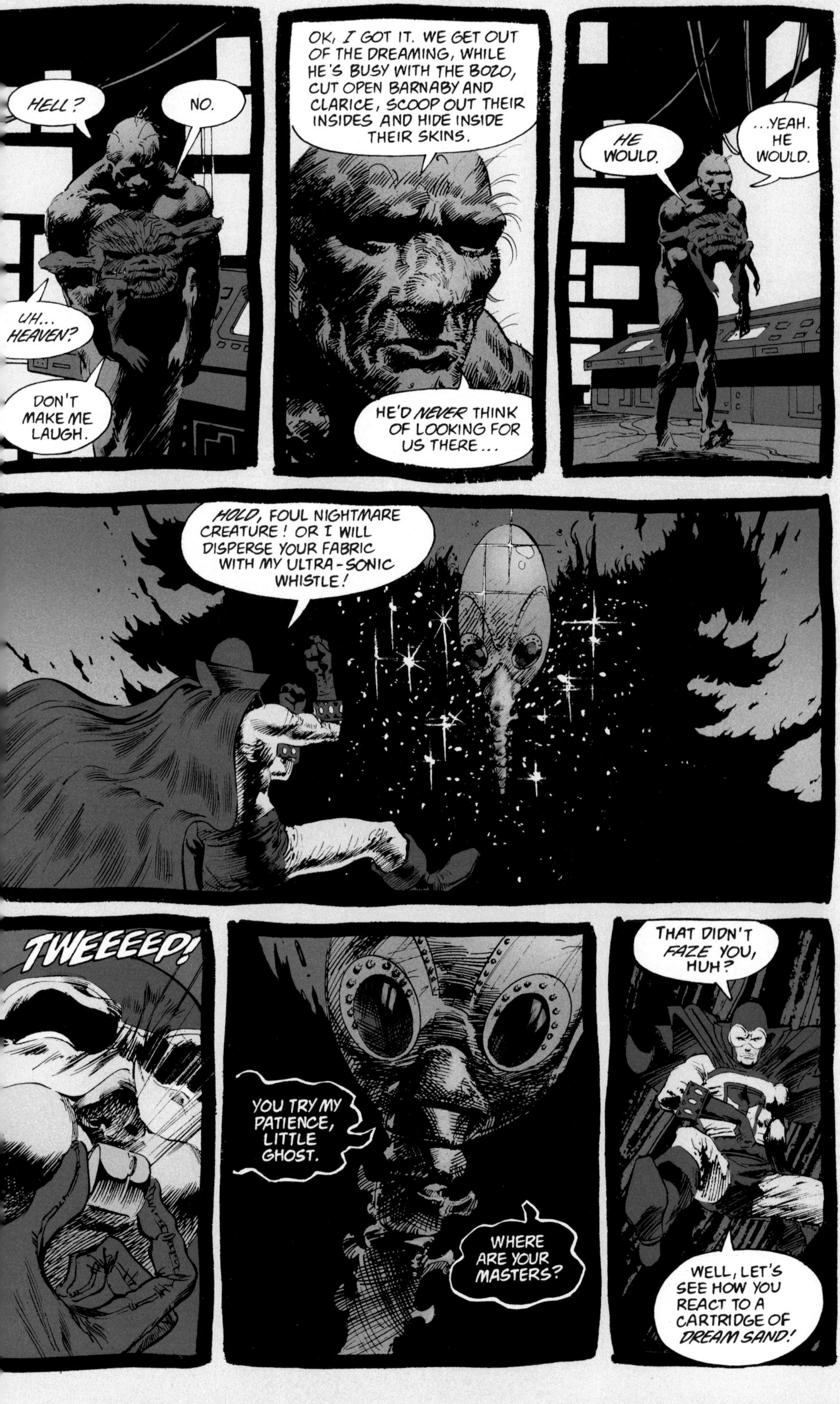
HELL?
NO.
UH... HEAVEN?
DON'T MAKE ME LAUGH.
OK, I GOT IT. WE GET OUT OF THE DREAMING, WHILE HE'S BUSY WITH THE BOZO, CUT OPEN BARNABY AND CLARICE, SCOOP OUT THEIR INSIDES AND HIDE INSIDE THEIR SKINS.
HE'D NEVER THINK OF LOOKING FOR US THERE...
HE WOULD.
...YEAH. HE WOULD.
HOLD, FOUL NIGHTMARE CREATURE! OR I WILL DISPERSE YOUR FABRIC WITH MY ULTRA-SONIC WHISTLE!
TWEEEEEP!
YOU TRY MY PATIENCE, LITTLE GHOST.
WHERE ARE YOUR MASTERS?
THAT DIDN'T FAZE YOU, HUH?
WELL, LET'S SEE HOW YOU REACT TO A CARTRIDGE OF DREAM SAND!

I CAN FEEL THEM, HIDING IN THAT PLACE. GET OUT OF MY WAY.

MONSTER, YOU SHALL NEVER GET PAST *ME.*

AND WHO ARE YOU...?

I AM THE *SANDMAN,* GUARDIAN OF THE DREAMS OF MEN, *PROTECTOR* AGAINST WICKED NIGHTMARES, *LORD* OF THE *DREAM DOME,* AND *FRIEND* OF *CHILDREN* EVERYWHERE!

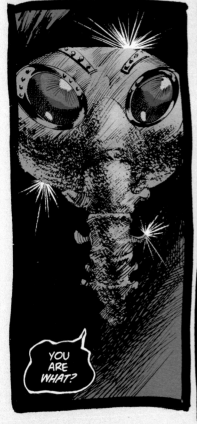

YOU ARE *WHAT?*

HRR.

HRR.

HRRRAAHH.

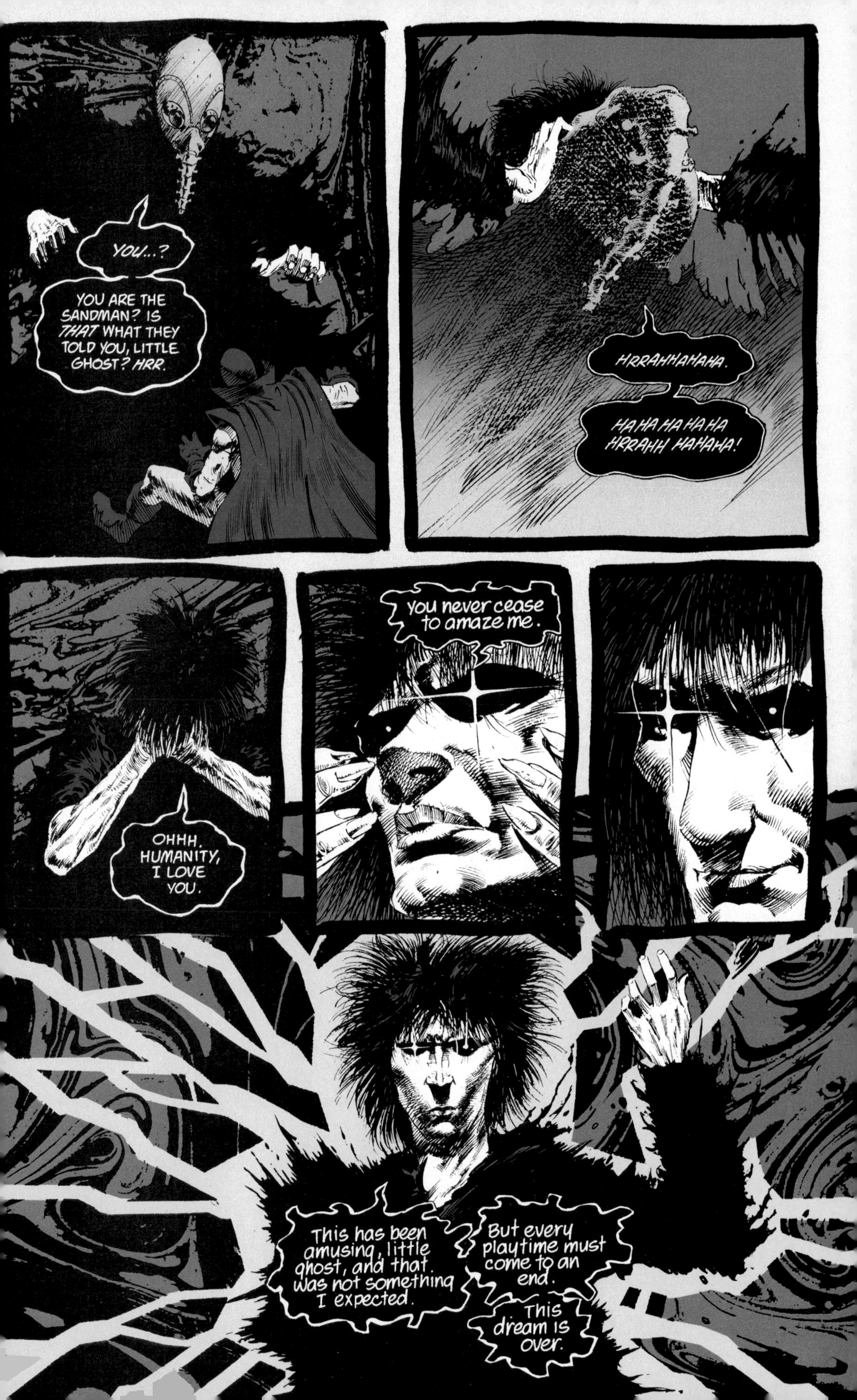
YOU..?
YOU ARE THE SANDMAN? IS THAT WHAT THEY TOLD YOU, LITTLE GHOST? HRR.
HRRAHHAHAHA.
HAHA HAHAHA HRRAHH HAHAHA!
OHHH. HUMANITY, I LOVE YOU.
You never cease to amaze me.
This has been amusing, little ghost, and that was not something I expected.
But every playtime must come to an end.
This dream is over.

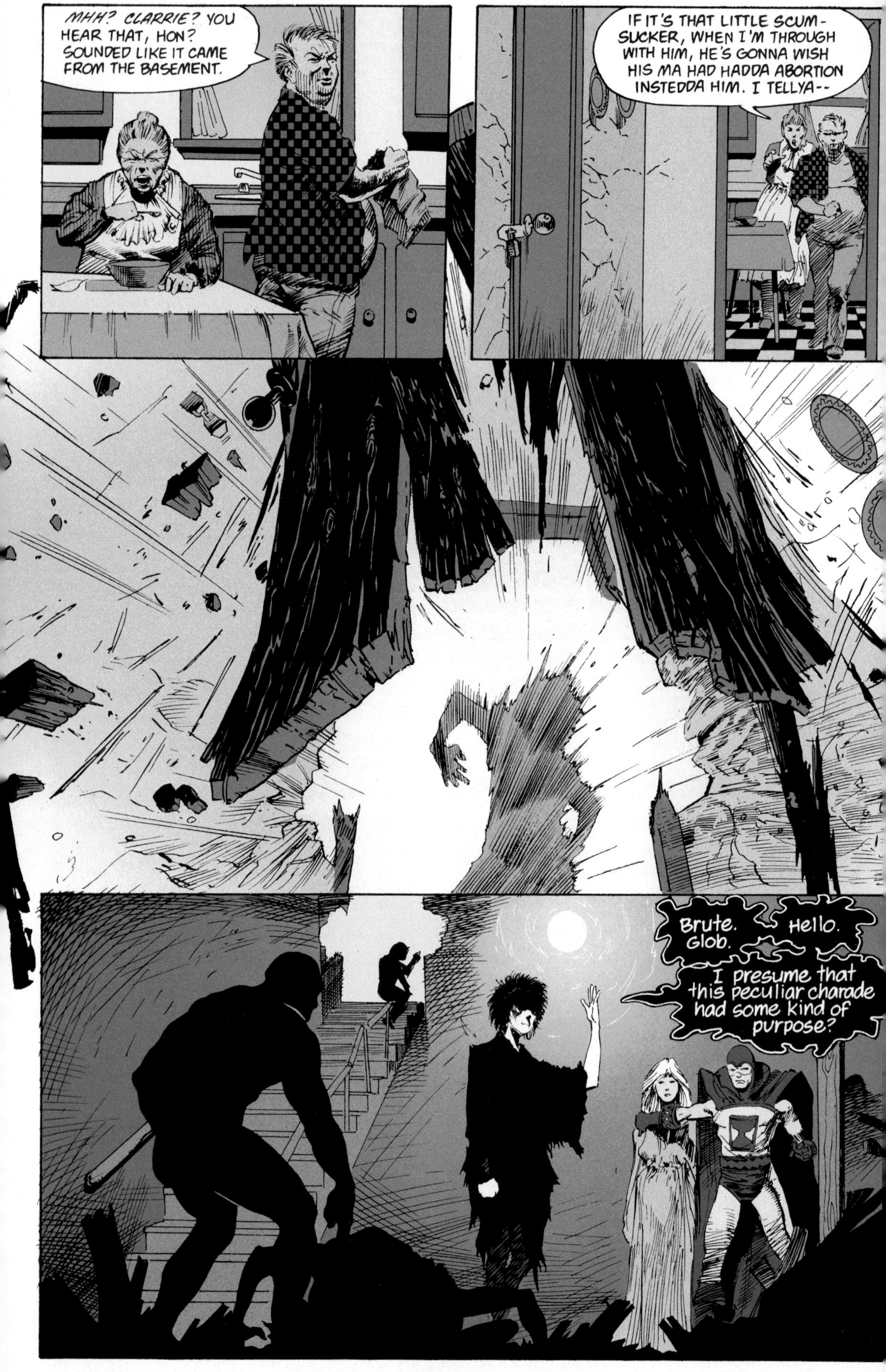
MHH? CLARRIE? YOU HEAR THAT, HON? SOUNDED LIKE IT CAME FROM THE BASEMENT.
IF IT'S THAT LITTLE SCUM-SUCKER, WHEN I'M THROUGH WITH HIM, HE'S GONNA WISH HIS MA HAD HADDA ABORTION INSTEDDA HIM. I TELLYA--
Brute. Glob.
Hello.
I presume that this peculiar charade had some kind of purpose?

OHSHITOH-
SHITOHSHITOH-
SHITOHSHITOH-
SHITOHSHIT-
OH...

Well?

I am waiting for an explanation.

WELL, YOU WERE WAY OUT OF THE PICTURE, LORD. SO WE THOUGHT, HELL, YOU'D OBVIOUSLY BE AWAY FOR A WHILE, PERHAPS FOR A REAL *LONG* WHILE, SO WE COULD MAYBE MAKE OUR *OWN* DREAM KING. ONE *WE'D* BE RUNNING...

"WE HID IN THE KID'S DREAMS, AND WALLED IT OFF FROM THE REST OF THE DREAMING. THEN WE BEGAN TO MAKE A SAND-MAN."

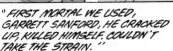

"FIRST MORTAL WE USED, GARRETT SANFORD, HE CRACKED UP, KILLED HIMSELF. COULDN'T TAKE THE STRAIN.''

WE THOUGHT, OKAY, NEXT TIME WE GET SOMEONE WHO'S DEAD TO START WITH.

SO WE HOOKED THE BOZO, TOLD HIM HE WAS THE NEW SANDMAN, AND HE BROUGHT HIS WIFE ALONG.

BUT THEN YOU PLAYED YOUR GET-OUT-OF-JAIL-FREE CARD, KIND OF EARLIER THAN WE EXPECTED. AND...

WELL...

HERE WE ALL ARE.

WHAT HAPPENS NOW?

I will clean up the mess you have created.

As for you two...

I doubt that either of you will enjoy the next few thousand years very much.

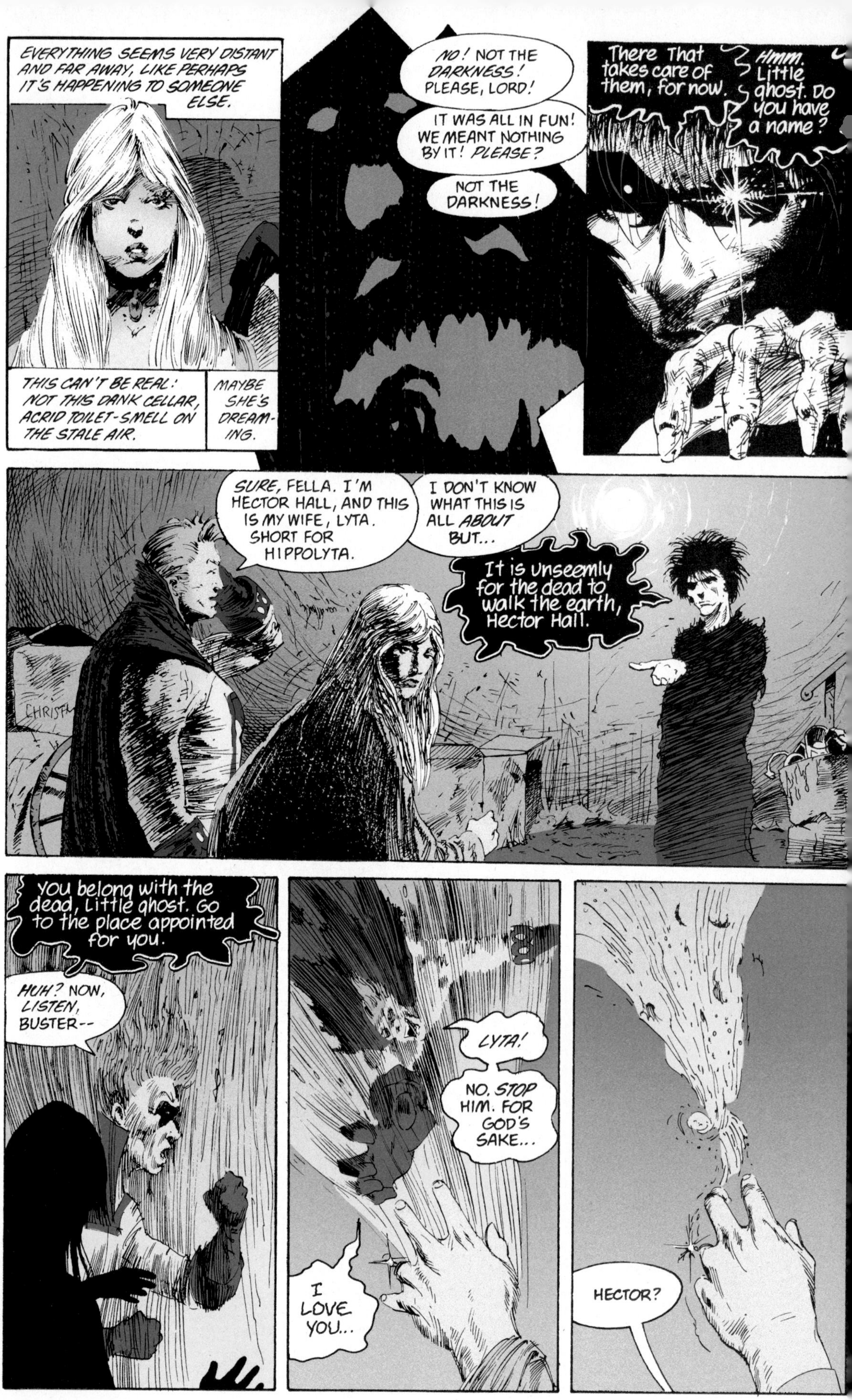
EVERYTHING SEEMS VERY DISTANT AND FAR AWAY, LIKE PERHAPS IT'S HAPPENING TO SOMEONE ELSE.
THIS CAN'T BE REAL: NOT THIS DANK CELLAR, ACRID TOILET-SMELL ON THE STALE AIR.
MAYBE SHE'S DREAMING.
NO! NOT THE DARKNESS! PLEASE, LORD!
IT WAS ALL IN FUN! WE MEANT NOTHING BY IT! PLEASE?
NOT THE DARKNESS!
There That takes care of them, for now.
Hmm. Little ghost. Do you have a name?
SURE, FELLA. I'M HECTOR HALL, AND THIS IS MY WIFE, LYTA. SHORT FOR HIPPOLYTA.
I DON'T KNOW WHAT THIS IS ALL ABOUT BUT...
It is unseemly for the dead to walk the earth, Hector Hall.
CHRISTM
You belong with the dead, Little ghost. Go to the place appointed for you.
HUH? NOW, LISTEN, BUSTER--
LYTA!
NO. STOP HIM. FOR GOD'S SAKE...
I LOVE YOU...
HECTOR?

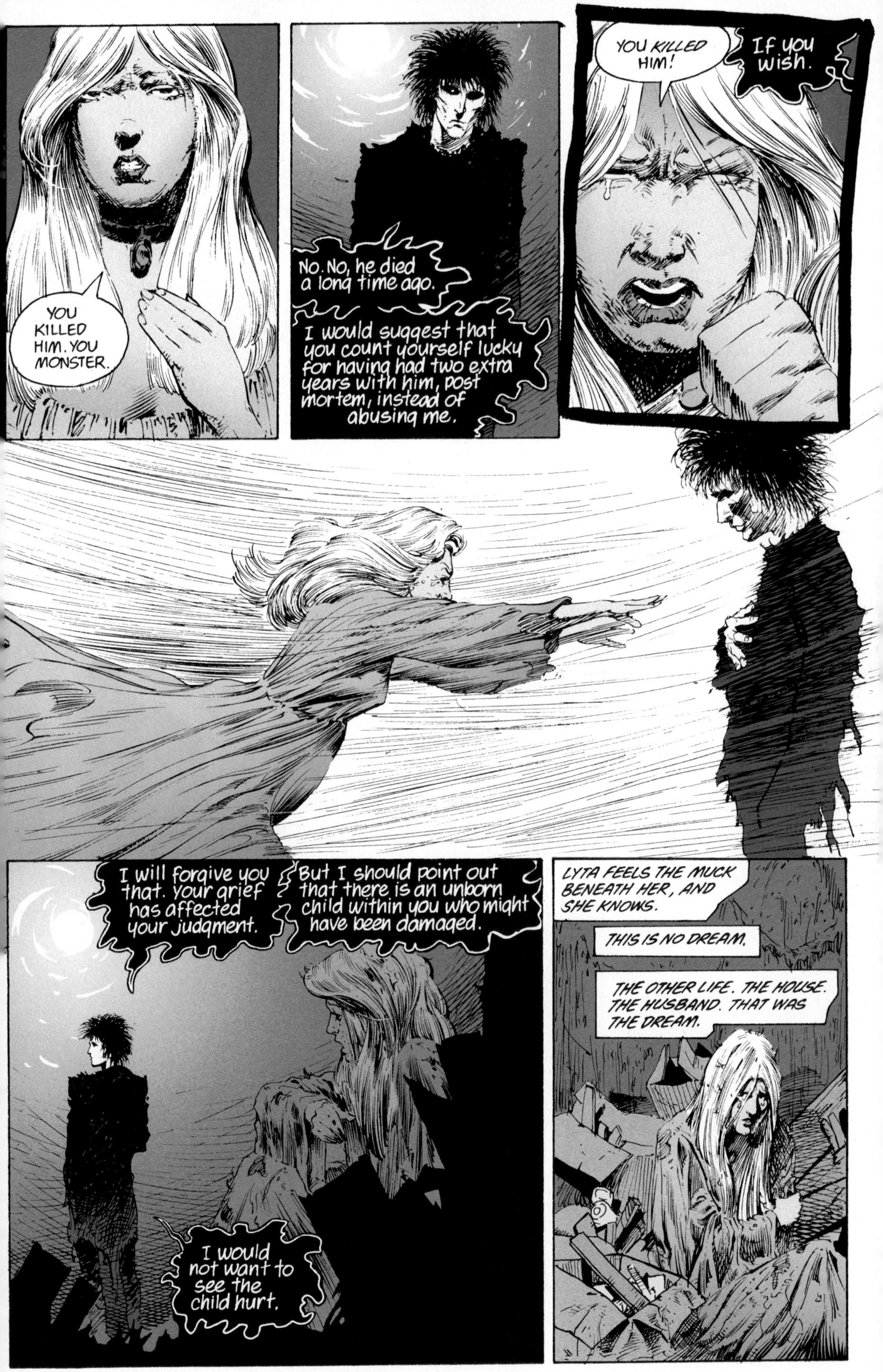
YOU KILLED HIM. YOU MONSTER.
No. No, he died a long time ago.
I would suggest that you count yourself lucky for having had two extra years with him, post mortem, instead of abusing me.
YOU KILLED HIM!
If you wish.
I will forgive you that. Your grief has affected your judgment.
But I should point out that there is an unborn child within you who might have been damaged.
I would not want to see the child hurt.
LYTA FEELS THE MUCK BENEATH HER, AND SHE KNOWS.
THIS IS NO DREAM.
THE OTHER LIFE. THE HOUSE. THE HUSBAND. THAT WAS THE DREAM.

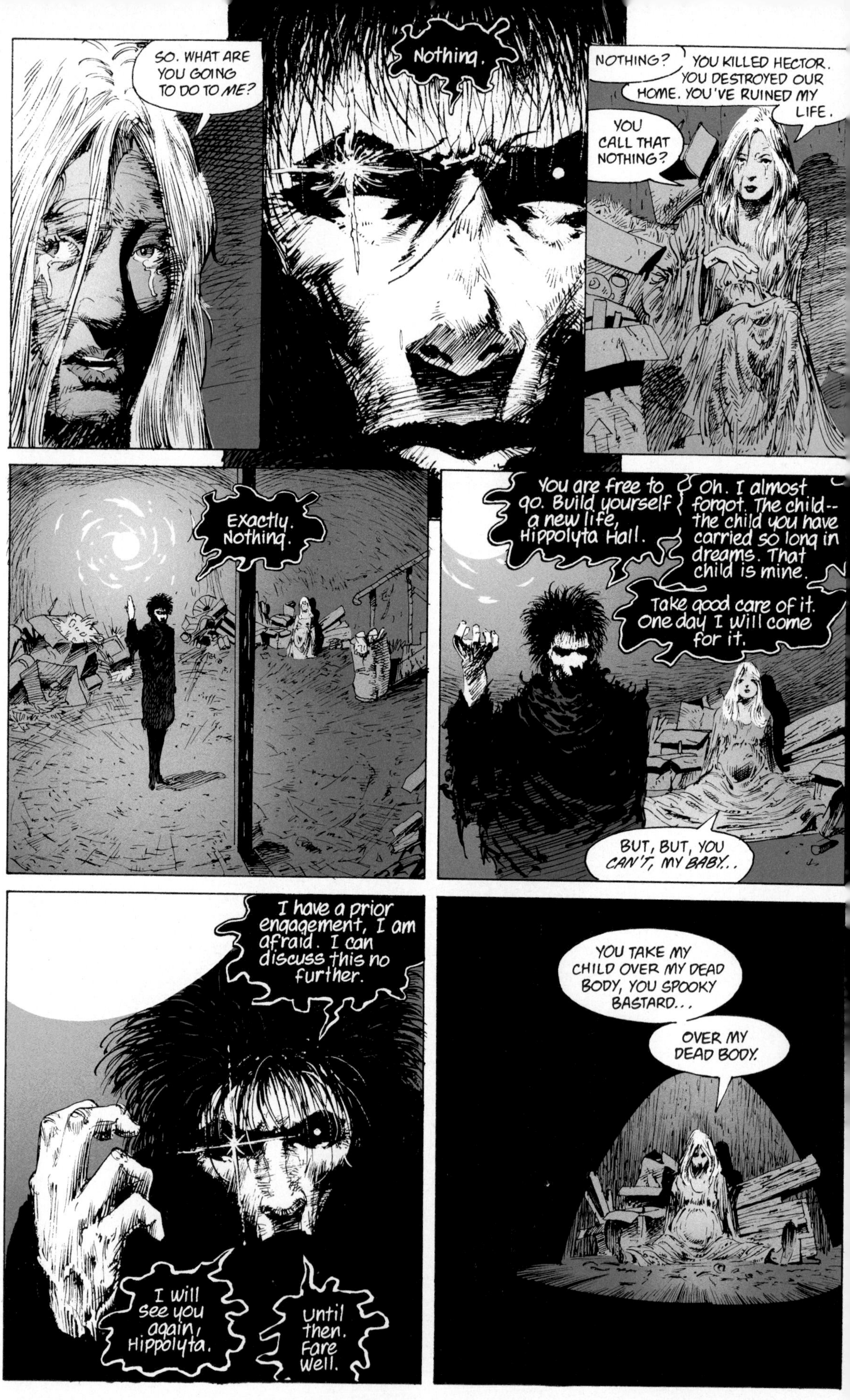
SO. WHAT ARE YOU GOING TO DO TO ME?
Nothing.
NOTHING?
YOU KILLED HECTOR. YOU DESTROYED OUR HOME. YOU'VE RUINED MY LIFE.
YOU CALL THAT NOTHING?
Exactly. Nothing.
You are free to go. Build yourself a new life, Hippolyta Hall.
Oh. I almost forgot. The child--the child you have carried so long in dreams. That child is mine.
Take good care of it. One day I will come for it.
BUT, BUT, YOU CAN'T, MY BABY...
I have a prior engagement, I am afraid. I can discuss this no further.
I will see you again, Hippolyta.
Until then. Fare well.
YOU TAKE MY CHILD OVER MY DEAD BODY, YOU SPOOKY BASTARD...
OVER MY DEAD BODY.

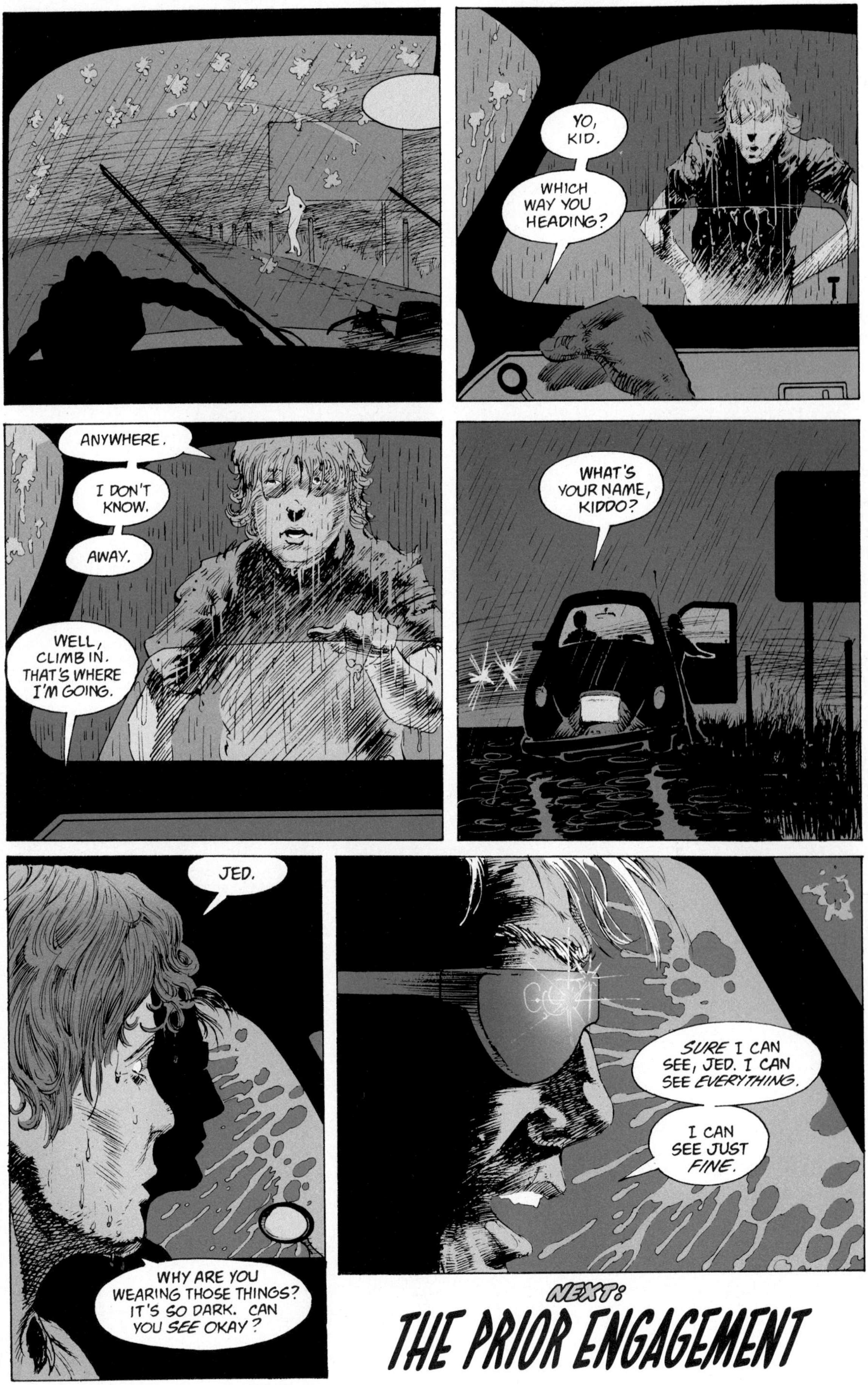
YO, KID.
WHICH WAY YOU HEADING?
ANYWHERE.
I DON'T KNOW.
AWAY.
WELL, CLIMB IN. THAT'S WHERE I'M GOING.
WHAT'S YOUR NAME, KIDDO?
JED.
WHY ARE YOU WEARING THOSE THINGS? IT'S SO DARK. CAN YOU *SEE* OKAY?
SURE I CAN SEE, JED. I CAN SEE *EVERYTHING*.
I CAN SEE JUST *FINE*.
NEXT:
THE PRIOR ENGAGEMENT

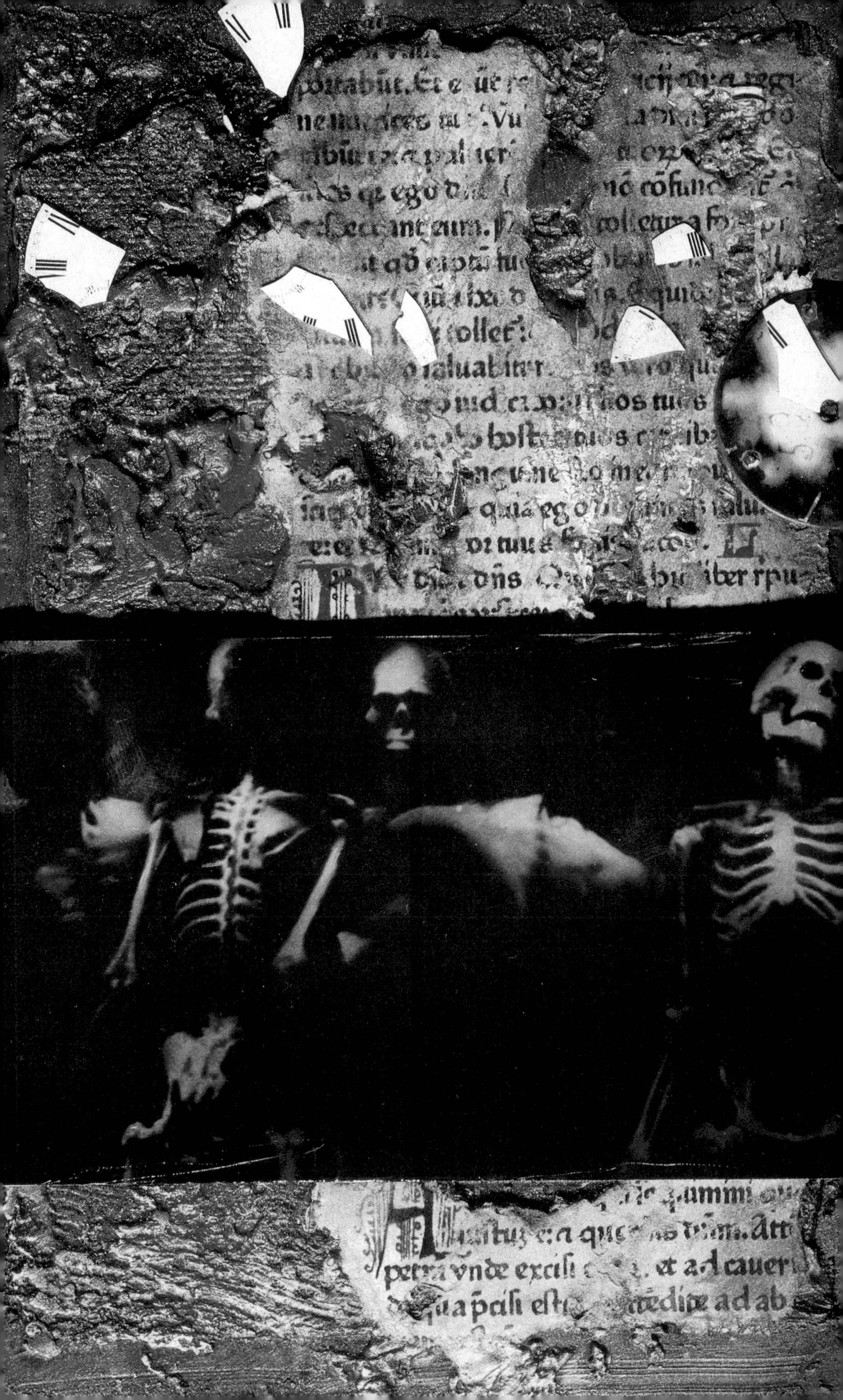

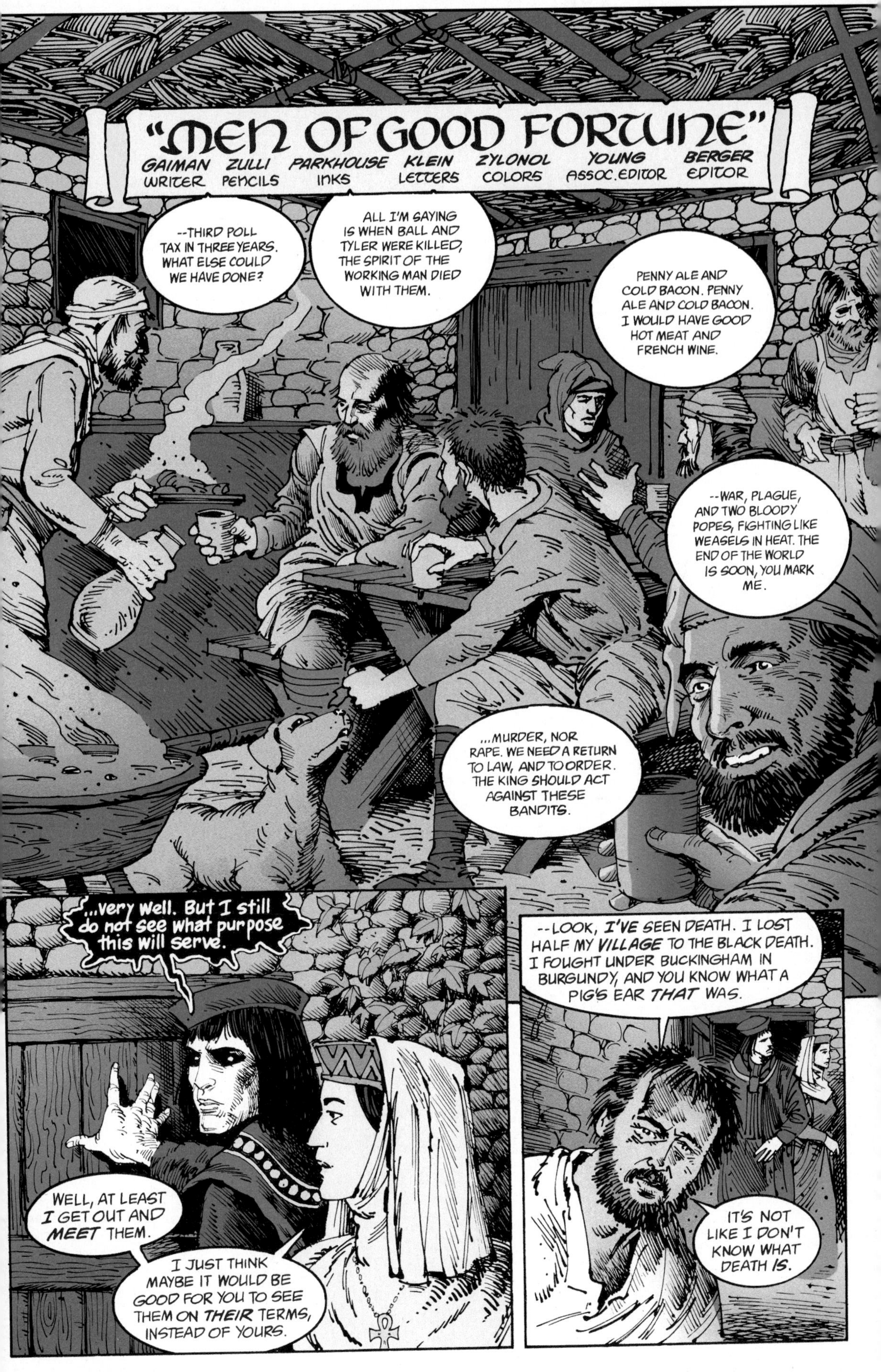
"MEN OF GOOD FORTUNE"
GAIMAN WRITER
ZULLI PENCILS
PARKHOUSE INKS
KLEIN LETTERS
ZYLONOL COLORS
YOUNG ASSOC. EDITOR
BERGER EDITOR
--THIRD POLL TAX IN THREE YEARS. WHAT ELSE COULD WE HAVE DONE?
ALL I'M SAYING IS WHEN BALL AND TYLER WERE KILLED, THE SPIRIT OF THE WORKING MAN DIED WITH THEM.
PENNY ALE AND COLD BACON. PENNY ALE AND COLD BACON. I WOULD HAVE GOOD HOT MEAT AND FRENCH WINE.
--WAR, PLAGUE, AND TWO BLOODY POPES, FIGHTING LIKE WEASELS IN HEAT. THE END OF THE WORLD IS SOON, YOU MARK ME.
...MURDER, NOR RAPE. WE NEED A RETURN TO LAW, AND TO ORDER. THE KING SHOULD ACT AGAINST THESE BANDITS.
...very well. But I still do not see what purpose this will serve.
WELL, AT LEAST I GET OUT AND MEET THEM.
I JUST THINK MAYBE IT WOULD BE GOOD FOR YOU TO SEE THEM ON THEIR TERMS, INSTEAD OF YOURS.
--LOOK, I'VE SEEN DEATH. I LOST HALF MY VILLAGE TO THE BLACK DEATH. I FOUGHT UNDER BUCKINGHAM IN BURGUNDY, AND YOU KNOW WHAT A PIG'S EAR THAT WAS.
IT'S NOT LIKE I DON'T KNOW WHAT DEATH IS.

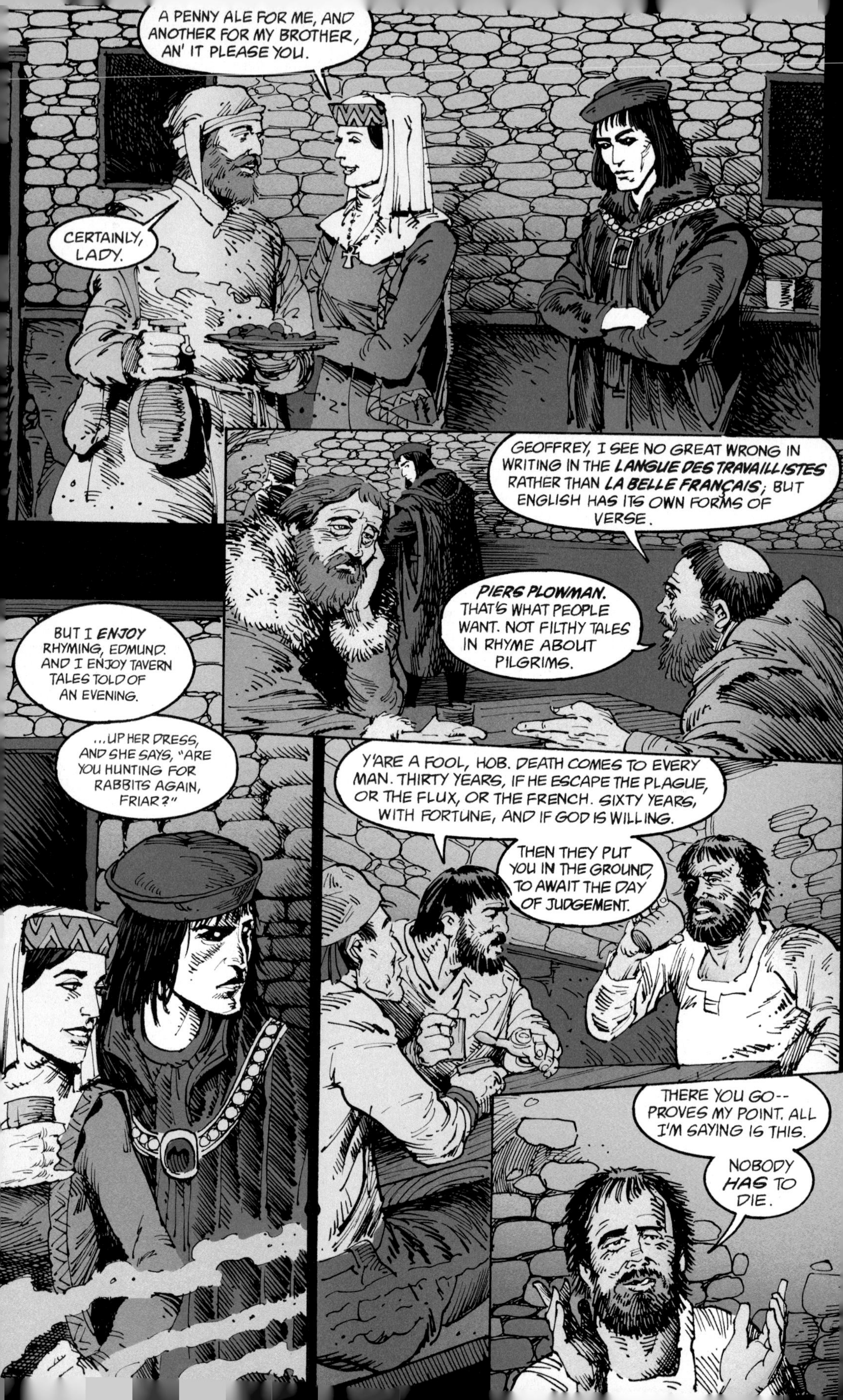
A PENNY ALE FOR ME, AND ANOTHER FOR MY BROTHER, AN' IT PLEASE YOU.
CERTAINLY, LADY.
GEOFFREY, I SEE NO GREAT WRONG IN WRITING IN THE LANGUE DES TRAVAILLISTES RATHER THAN LA BELLE FRANÇAIS; BUT ENGLISH HAS ITS OWN FORMS OF VERSE.
PIERS PLOWMAN. THAT'S WHAT PEOPLE WANT. NOT FILTHY TALES IN RHYME ABOUT PILGRIMS.
BUT I ENJOY RHYMING, EDMUND. AND I ENJOY TAVERN TALES TOLD OF AN EVENING.
...UP HER DRESS, AND SHE SAYS, "ARE YOU HUNTING FOR RABBITS AGAIN, FRIAR?"
Y'ARE A FOOL, HOB. DEATH COMES TO EVERY MAN. THIRTY YEARS, IF HE ESCAPE THE PLAGUE, OR THE FLUX, OR THE FRENCH. SIXTY YEARS, WITH FORTUNE, AND IF GOD IS WILLING.
THEN THEY PUT YOU IN THE GROUND, TO AWAIT THE DAY OF JUDGEMENT.
THERE YOU GO-- PROVES MY POINT. ALL I'M SAYING IS THIS.
NOBODY HAS TO DIE.

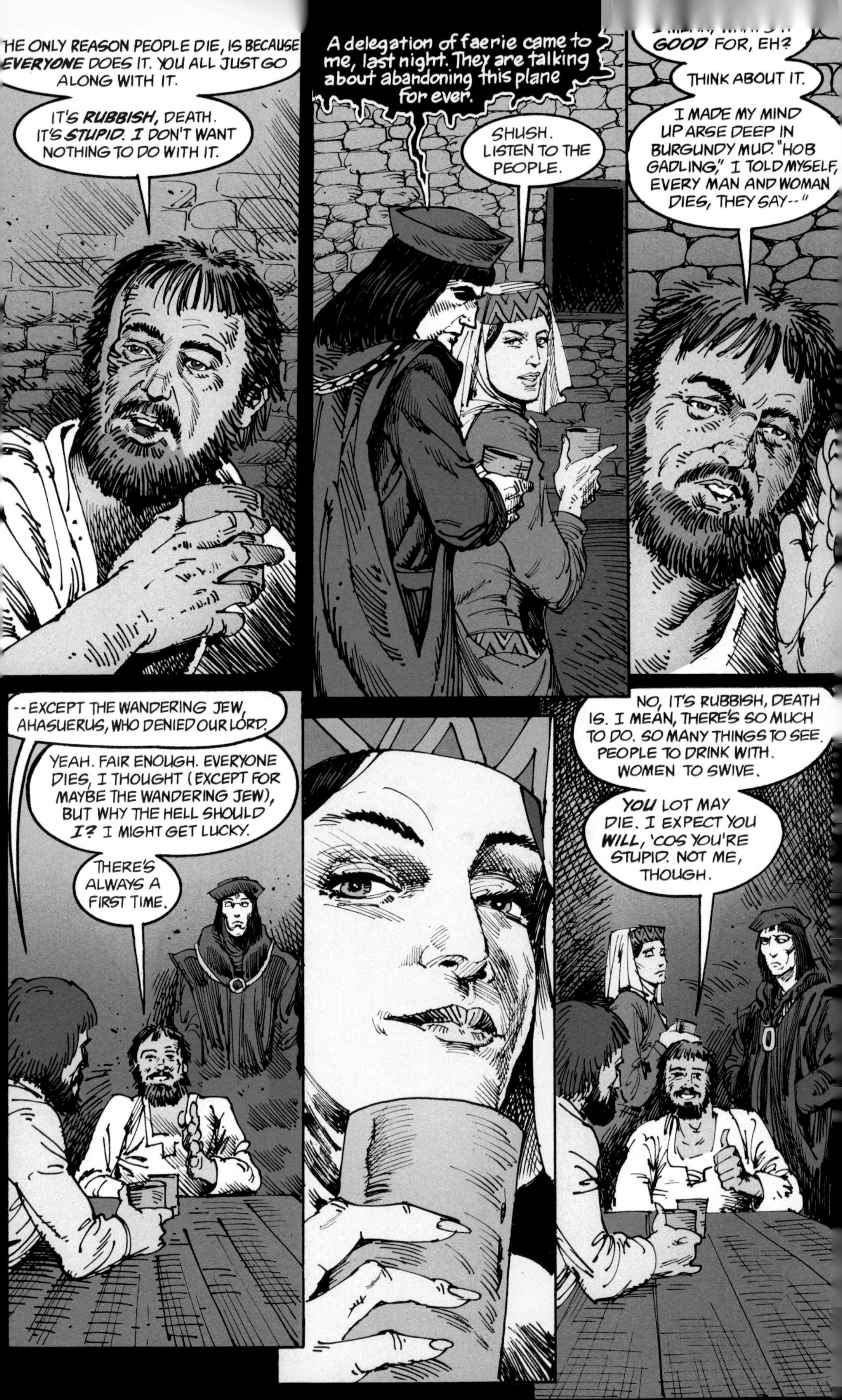
HE ONLY REASON PEOPLE DIE, IS BECAUSE EVERYONE DOES IT. YOU ALL JUST GO ALONG WITH IT.
IT'S RUBBISH, DEATH. IT'S STUPID. I DON'T WANT NOTHING TO DO WITH IT.
A delegation of faerie came to me, last night. They are talking about abandoning this plane for ever.
SHUSH. LISTEN TO THE PEOPLE.
GOOD FOR, EH?
THINK ABOUT IT.
I MADE MY MIND UP ARSE DEEP IN BURGUNDY MUD. "HOB GADLING," I TOLD MYSELF, EVERY MAN AND WOMAN DIES, THEY SAY--"
--EXCEPT THE WANDERING JEW, AHASUERUS, WHO DENIED OUR LORD.
YEAH. FAIR ENOUGH. EVERYONE DIES, I THOUGHT (EXCEPT FOR MAYBE THE WANDERING JEW), BUT WHY THE HELL SHOULD I? I MIGHT GET LUCKY.
THERE'S ALWAYS A FIRST TIME.
NO, IT'S RUBBISH, DEATH IS. I MEAN, THERE'S SO MUCH TO DO. SO MANY THINGS TO SEE. PEOPLE TO DRINK WITH. WOMEN TO SWIVE.
YOU LOT MAY DIE. I EXPECT YOU WILL, 'COS YOU'RE STUPID. NOT ME, THOUGH.

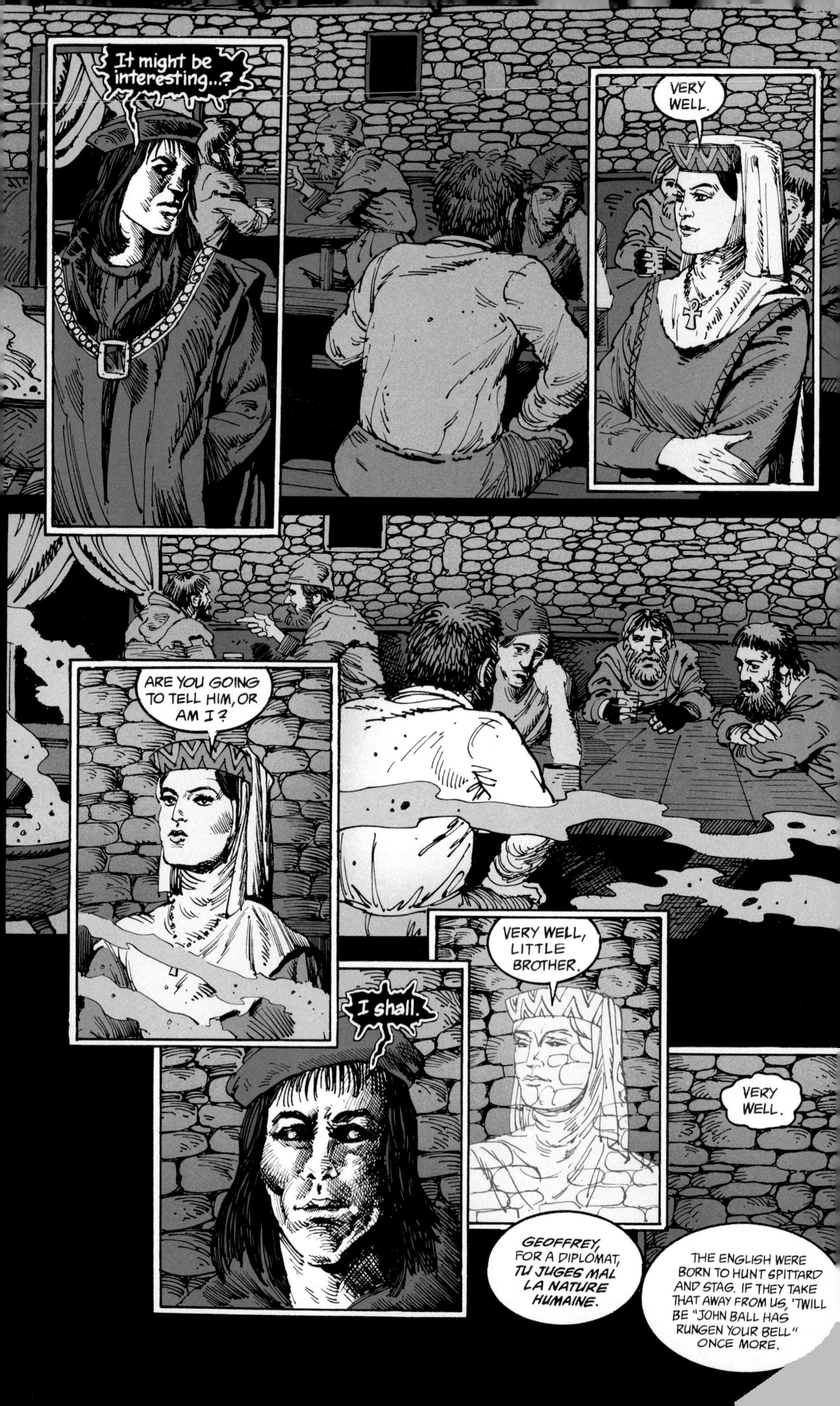
It might be interesting...?
VERY WELL.
ARE YOU GOING TO TELL HIM, OR AM I?
I shall.
VERY WELL, LITTLE BROTHER.
VERY WELL.
GEOFFREY, FOR A DIPLOMAT, TU JUGES MAL LA NATURE HUMAINE.
THE ENGLISH WERE BORN TO HUNT SPITTARD AND STAG. IF THEY TAKE THAT AWAY FROM US, 'TWILL BE "JOHN BALL HAS RUNGEN YOUR BELL" ONCE MORE.

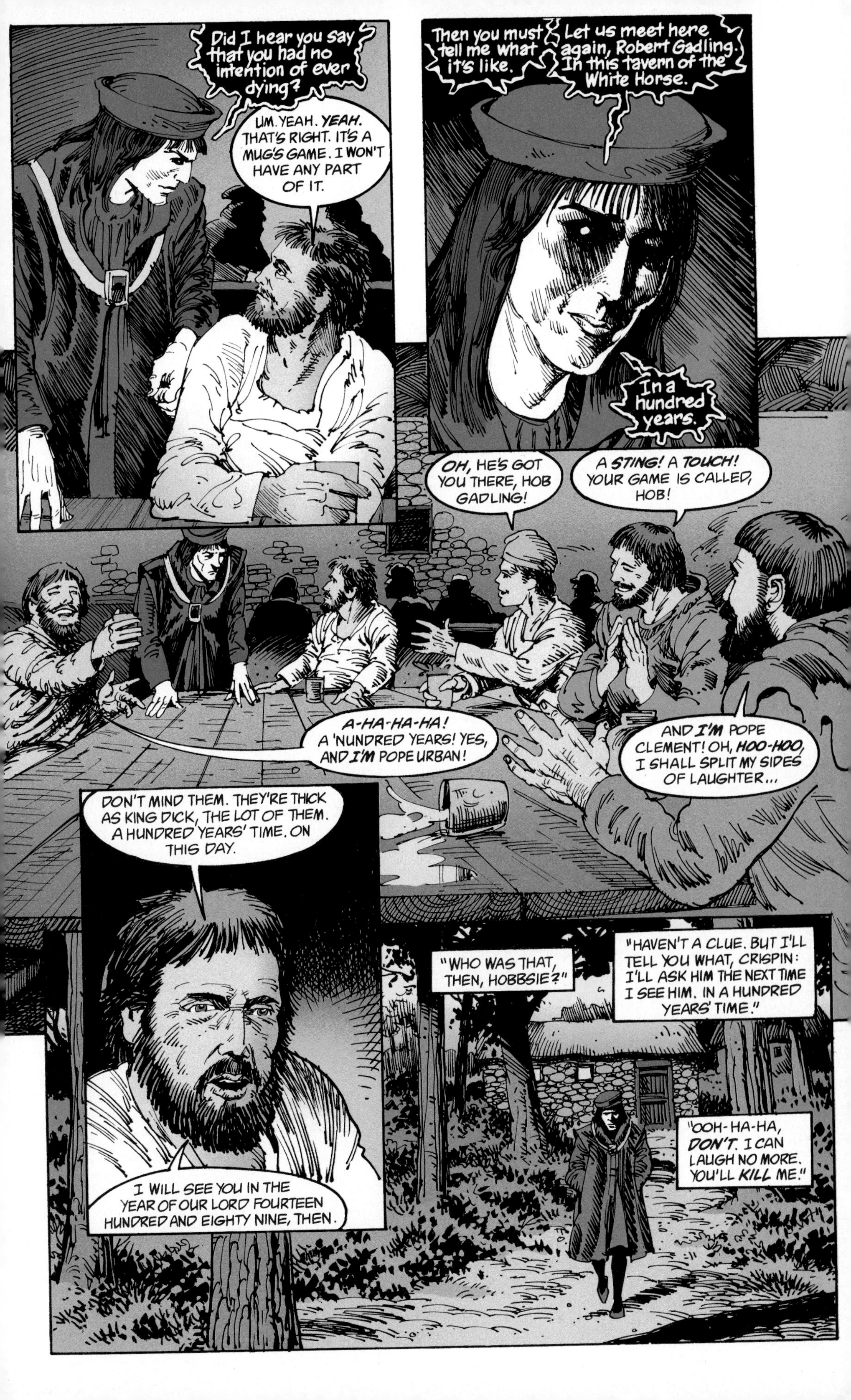
Did I hear you say that you had no intention of ever dying?
UM. YEAH. YEAH. THAT'S RIGHT. IT'S A MUG'S GAME. I WON'T HAVE ANY PART OF IT.
Then you must tell me what it's like.
Let us meet here again, Robert Gadling. In this tavern of the White Horse.
In a hundred years.
OH, HE'S GOT YOU THERE, HOB GADLING!
A STING! A TOUCH! YOUR GAME IS CALLED, HOB!
A-HA-HA-HA! A 'NUNDRED YEARS! YES, AND I'M POPE URBAN!
AND I'M POPE CLEMENT! OH, HOO-HOO, I SHALL SPLIT MY SIDES OF LAUGHTER...
DON'T MIND THEM. THEY'RE THICK AS KING DICK, THE LOT OF THEM. A HUNDRED YEARS' TIME. ON THIS DAY.
I WILL SEE YOU IN THE YEAR OF OUR LORD FOURTEEN HUNDRED AND EIGHTY NINE, THEN.
"WHO WAS THAT, THEN, HOBBSIE?"
"HAVEN'T A CLUE. BUT I'LL TELL YOU WHAT, CRISPIN: I'LL ASK HIM THE NEXT TIME I SEE HIM. IN A HUNDRED YEARS' TIME."
"OOH-HA-HA, DON'T. I CAN LAUGH NO MORE. YOU'LL KILL ME."

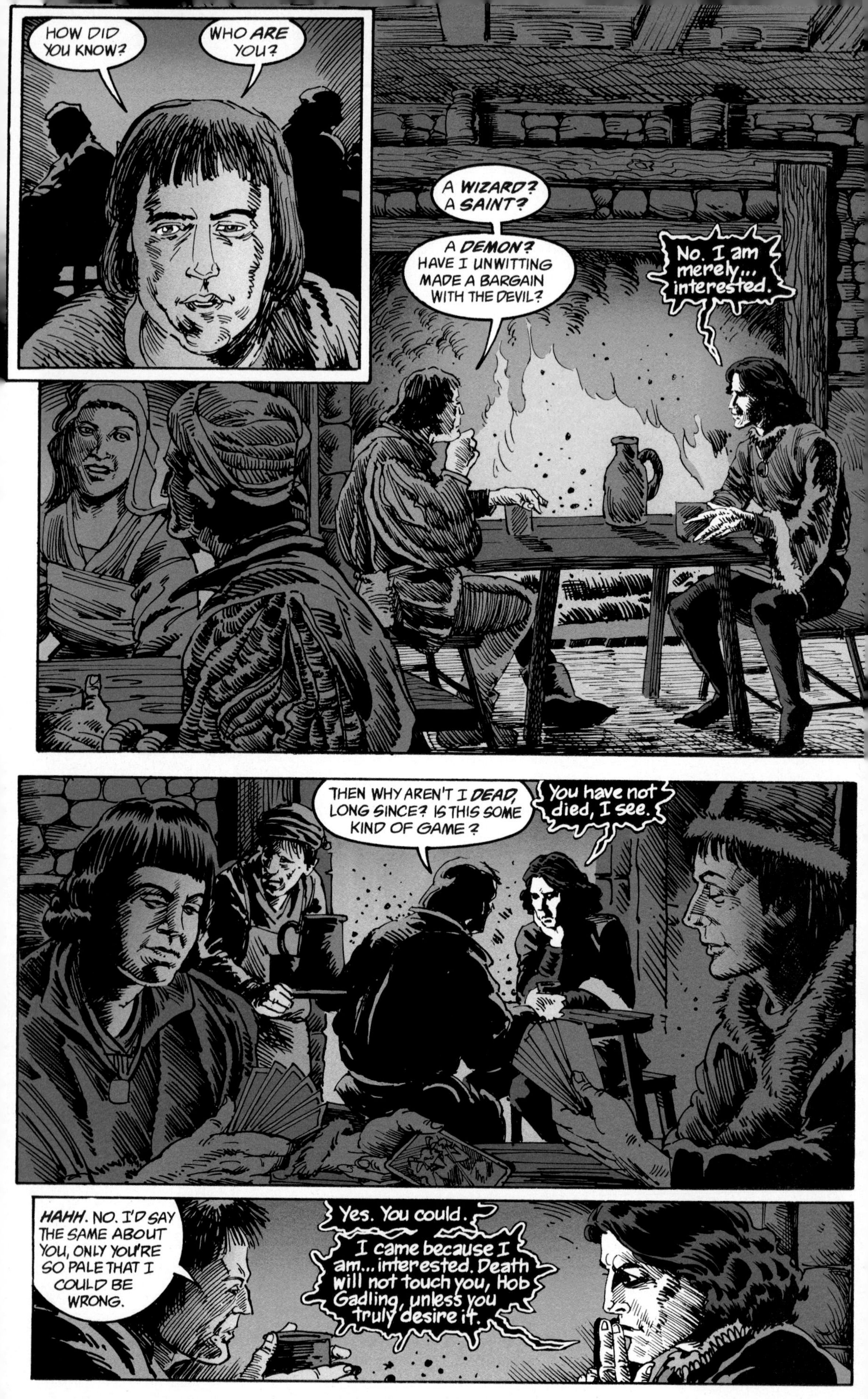
HOW DID YOU KNOW?
WHO ARE YOU?
A WIZARD? A SAINT?
A DEMON? HAVE I UNWITTING MADE A BARGAIN WITH THE DEVIL?
No. I am merely... interested.
THEN WHY AREN'T I DEAD, LONG SINCE? IS THIS SOME KIND OF GAME?
You have not died, I see.
HAHH. NO. I'D SAY THE SAME ABOUT YOU, ONLY YOU'RE SO PALE THAT I COULD BE WRONG.
Yes. You could.
I came because I am... interested. Death will not touch you, Hob Gadling, unless you truly desire it.

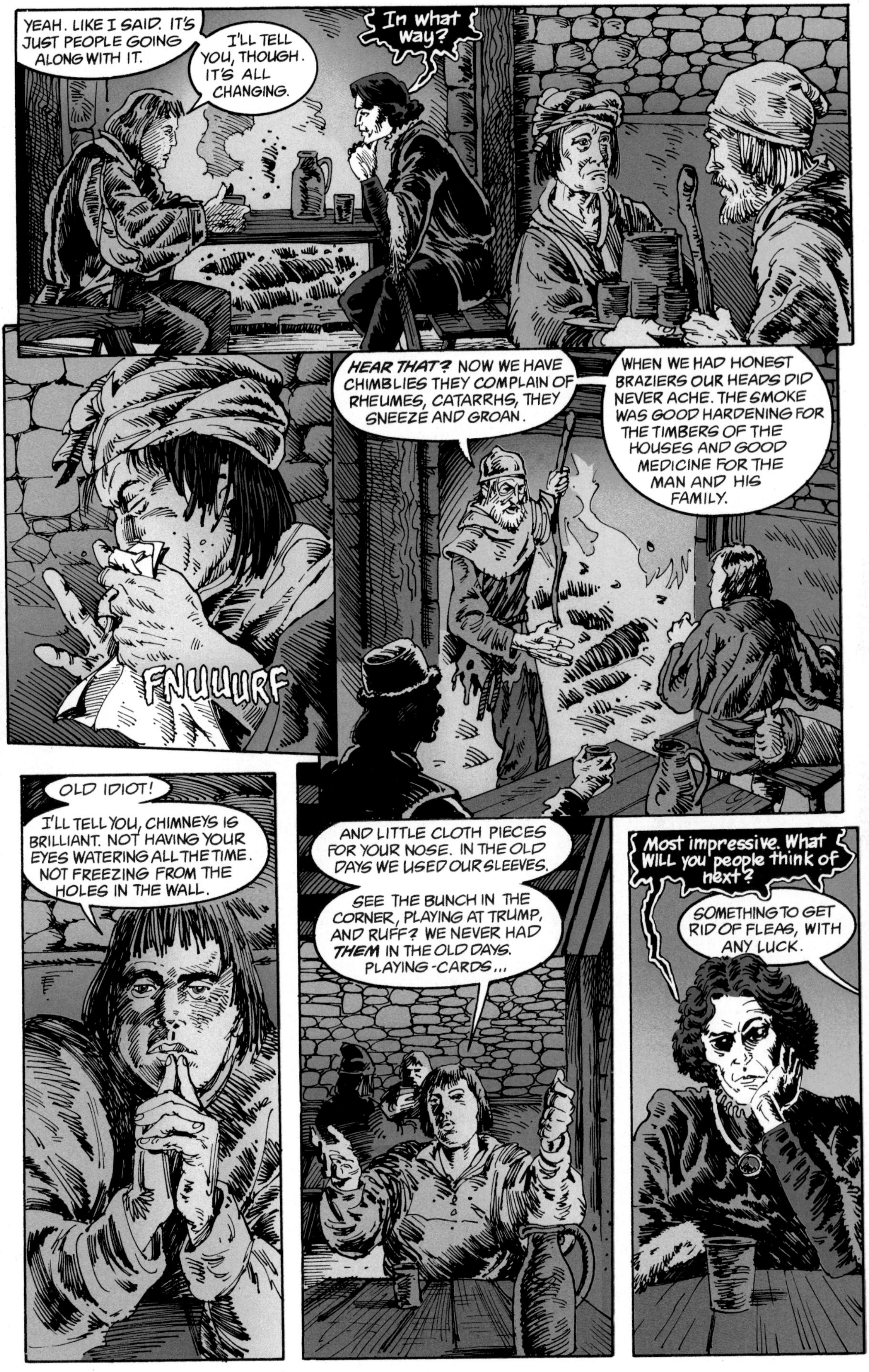

YEAH. LIKE I SAID. IT'S JUST PEOPLE GOING ALONG WITH IT.
I'LL TELL YOU, THOUGH. IT'S ALL CHANGING.
In what way?
FNUUURF
HEAR THAT? NOW WE HAVE CHIMBLIES THEY COMPLAIN OF RHEUMES, CATARRHS, THEY SNEEZE AND GROAN.
WHEN WE HAD HONEST BRAZIERS OUR HEADS DID NEVER ACHE. THE SMOKE WAS GOOD HARDENING FOR THE TIMBERS OF THE HOUSES AND GOOD MEDICINE FOR THE MAN AND HIS FAMILY.
OLD IDIOT!
I'LL TELL YOU, CHIMNEYS IS BRILLIANT. NOT HAVING YOUR EYES WATERING ALL THE TIME. NOT FREEZING FROM THE HOLES IN THE WALL.
AND LITTLE CLOTH PIECES FOR YOUR NOSE. IN THE OLD DAYS WE USED OUR SLEEVES.
SEE THE BUNCH IN THE CORNER, PLAYING AT TRUMP, AND RUFF? WE NEVER HAD THEM IN THE OLD DAYS. PLAYING-CARDS...
Most impressive. What WILL you people think of next?
SOMETHING TO GET RID OF FLEAS, WITH ANY LUCK.

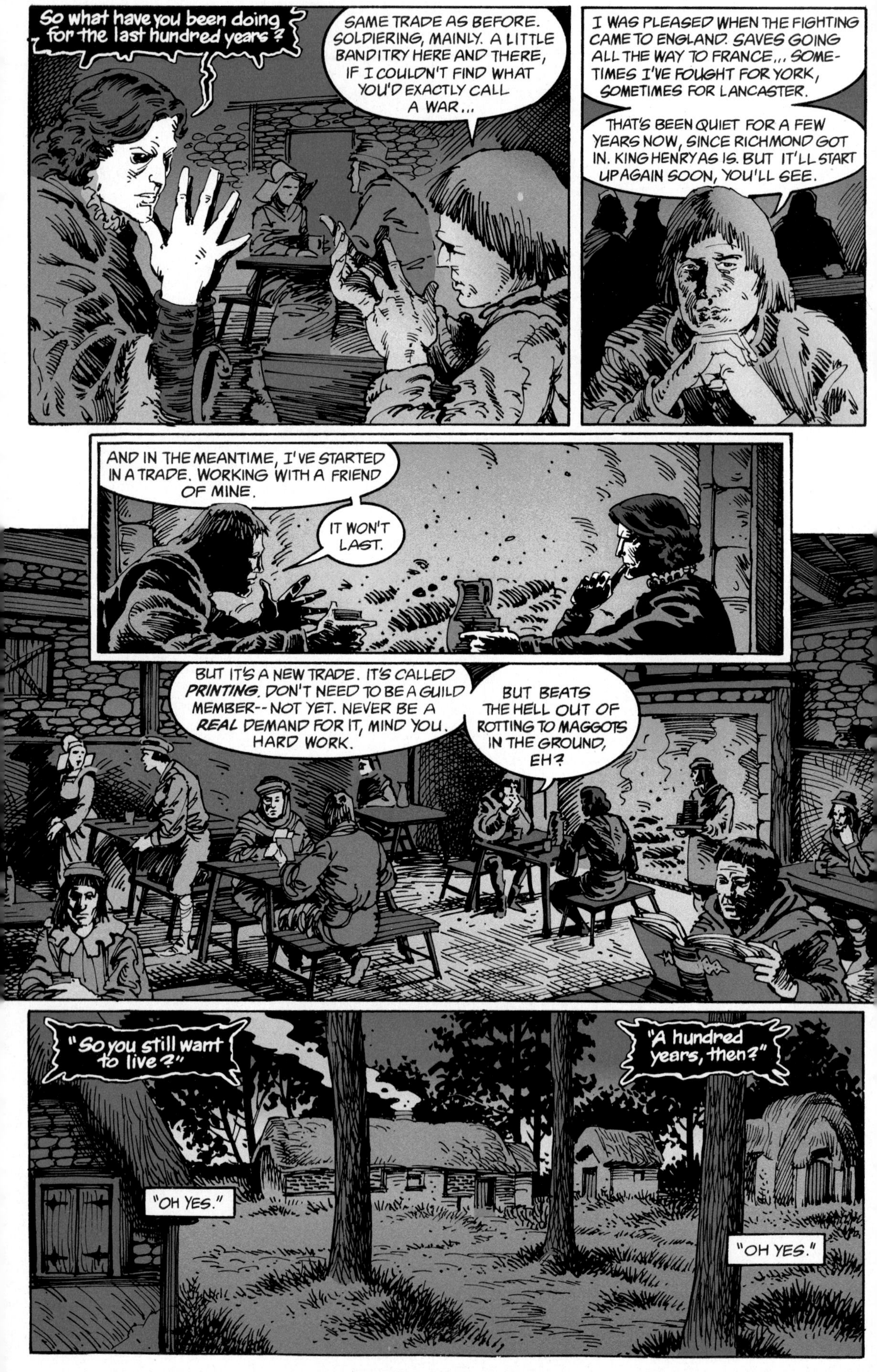
So what have you been doing for the last hundred years?
SAME TRADE AS BEFORE. SOLDIERING, MAINLY. A LITTLE BANDITRY HERE AND THERE, IF I COULDN'T FIND WHAT YOU'D EXACTLY CALL A WAR...
I WAS PLEASED WHEN THE FIGHTING CAME TO ENGLAND. SAVES GOING ALL THE WAY TO FRANCE... SOMETIMES I'VE FOUGHT FOR YORK, SOMETIMES FOR LANCASTER.
THAT'S BEEN QUIET FOR A FEW YEARS NOW, SINCE RICHMOND GOT IN. KING HENRY AS IS. BUT IT'LL START UP AGAIN SOON, YOU'LL SEE.
AND IN THE MEANTIME, I'VE STARTED IN A TRADE. WORKING WITH A FRIEND OF MINE.
IT WON'T LAST.
BUT IT'S A NEW TRADE. IT'S CALLED PRINTING. DON'T NEED TO BE A GUILD MEMBER--NOT YET. NEVER BE A REAL DEMAND FOR IT, MIND YOU. HARD WORK.
BUT BEATS THE HELL OUT OF ROTTING TO MAGGOTS IN THE GROUND, EH?
"So you still want to live?"
"OH YES."
"A hundred years, then?"
"OH YES."

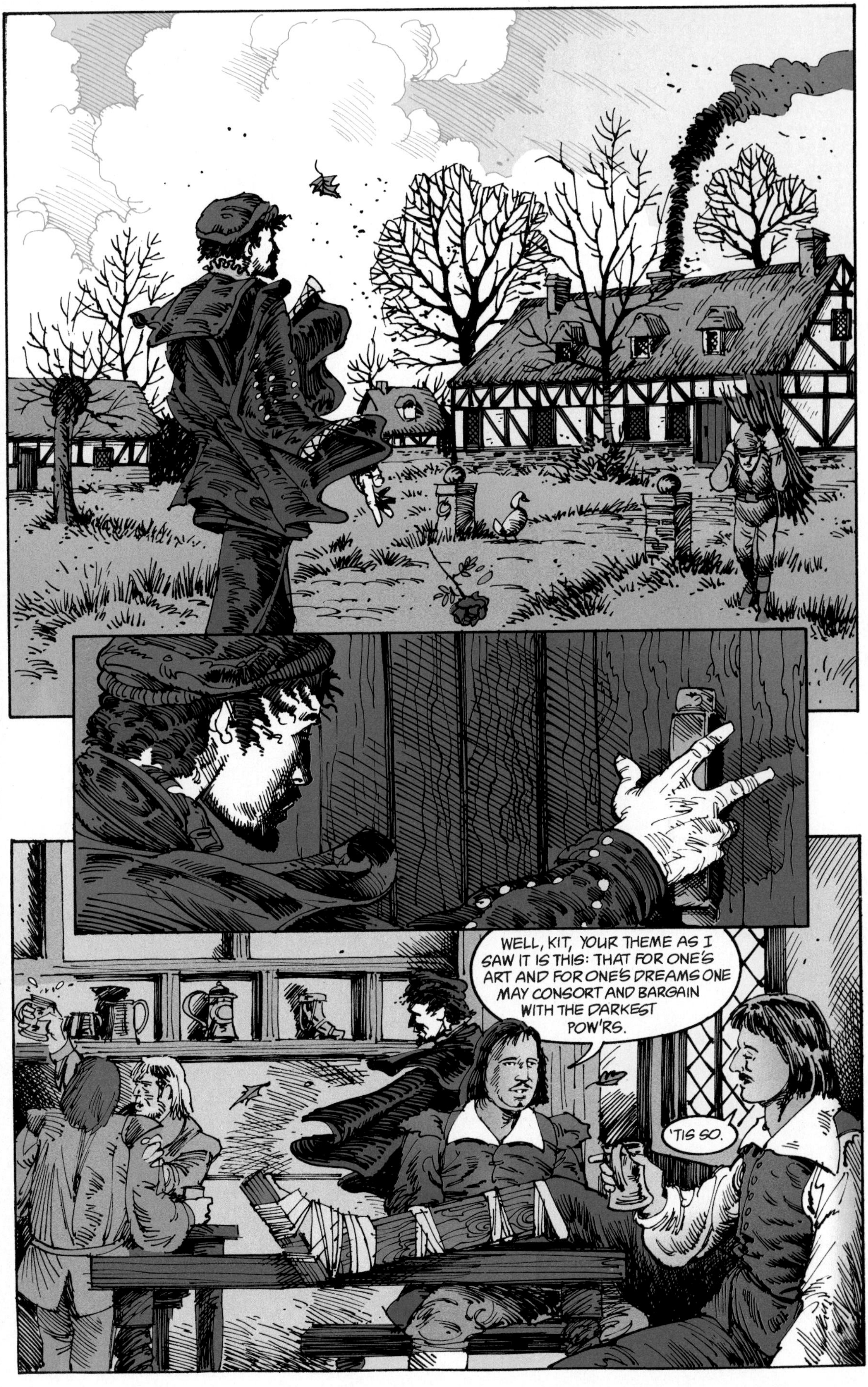
WELL, KIT, YOUR THEME AS I SAW IT IS THIS: THAT FOR ONE'S ART AND FOR ONE'S DREAMS ONE MAY CONSORT AND BARGAIN WITH THE DARKEST POW'RS.
'TIS SO.

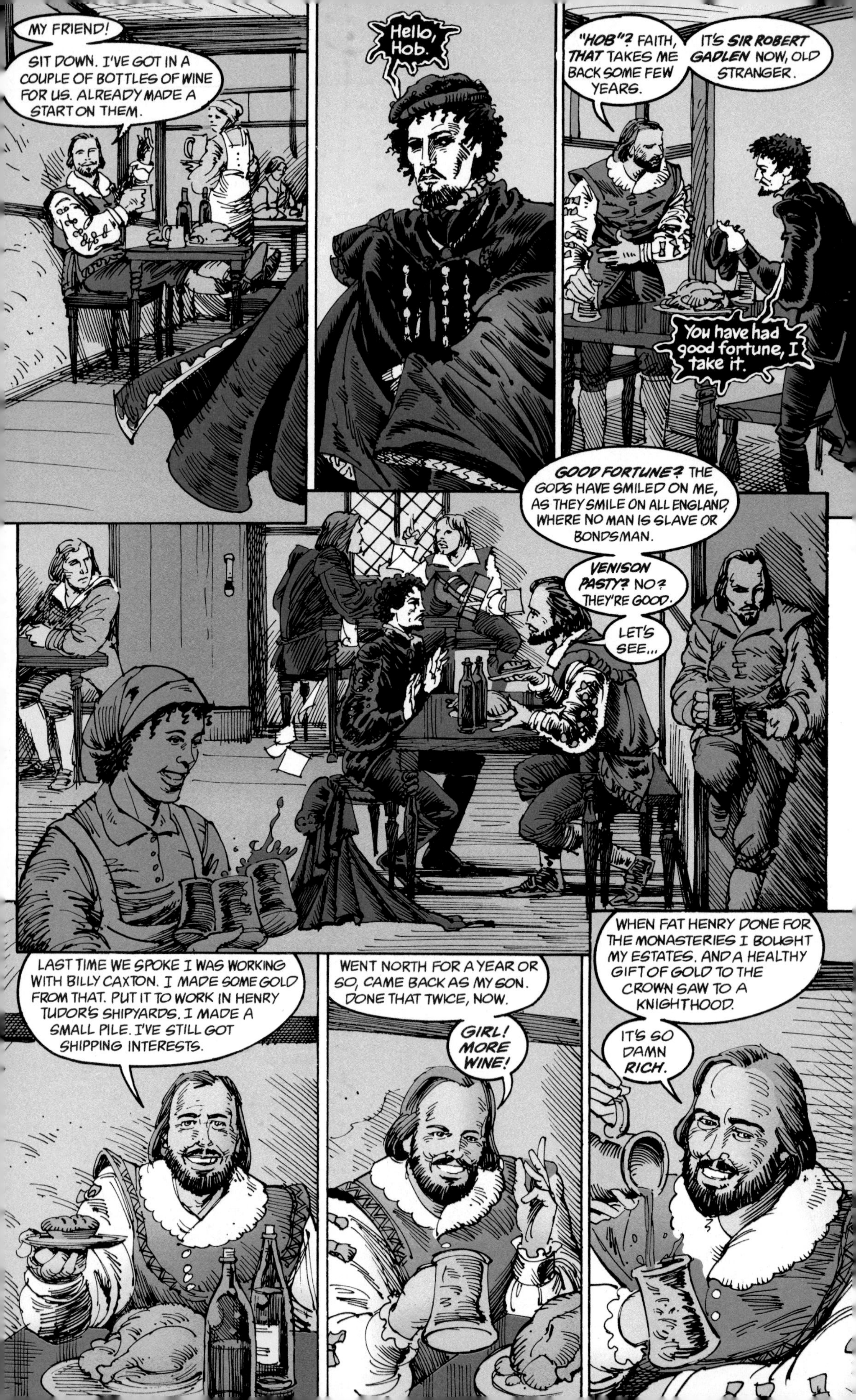
MY FRIEND!
SIT DOWN. I'VE GOT IN A COUPLE OF BOTTLES OF WINE FOR US. ALREADY MADE A START ON THEM.
Hello, Hob.
"HOB"? FAITH, THAT TAKES ME BACK SOME FEW YEARS.
IT'S SIR ROBERT GADLEN NOW, OLD STRANGER.
You have had good fortune, I take it.
GOOD FORTUNE? THE GODS HAVE SMILED ON ME, AS THEY SMILE ON ALL ENGLAND, WHERE NO MAN IS SLAVE OR BONDSMAN.
VENISON PASTY? NO? THEY'RE GOOD.
LET'S SEE...
LAST TIME WE SPOKE I WAS WORKING WITH BILLY CAXTON. I MADE SOME GOLD FROM THAT. PUT IT TO WORK IN HENRY TUDOR'S SHIPYARDS. I MADE A SMALL PILE. I'VE STILL GOT SHIPPING INTERESTS.
WENT NORTH FOR A YEAR OR SO, CAME BACK AS MY SON. DONE THAT TWICE, NOW.
GIRL! MORE WINE!
WHEN FAT HENRY DONE FOR THE MONASTERIES I BOUGHT MY ESTATES. AND A HEALTHY GIFT OF GOLD TO THE CROWN SAW TO A KNIGHTHOOD.
IT'S SO DAMN RICH.

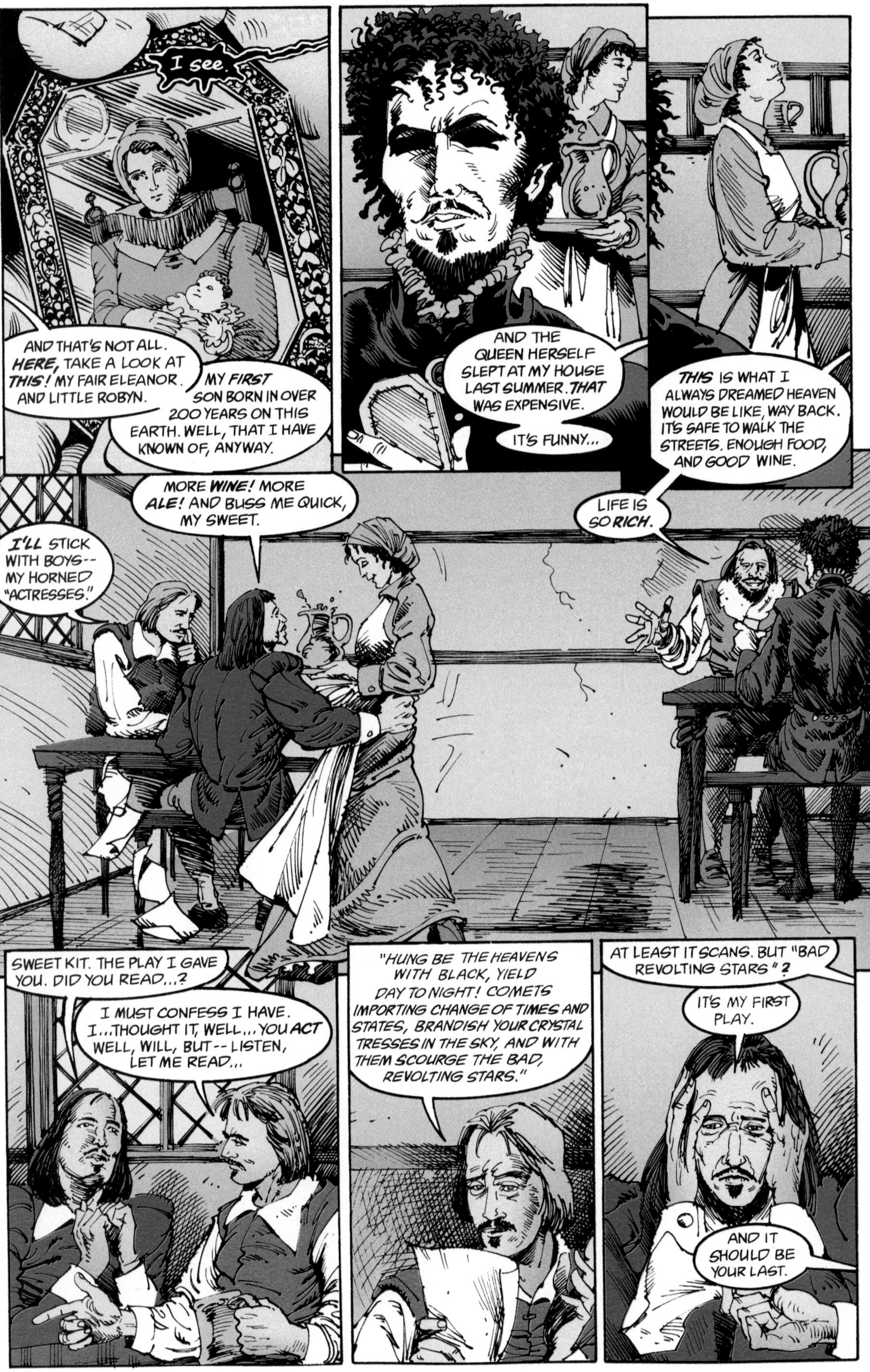
I see.
AND THAT'S NOT ALL. HERE, TAKE A LOOK AT THIS! MY FAIR ELEANOR. AND LITTLE ROBYN.
MY FIRST SON BORN IN OVER 200 YEARS ON THIS EARTH. WELL, THAT I HAVE KNOWN OF, ANYWAY.
AND THE QUEEN HERSELF SLEPT AT MY HOUSE LAST SUMMER. THAT WAS EXPENSIVE.
IT'S FUNNY...
THIS IS WHAT I ALWAYS DREAMED HEAVEN WOULD BE LIKE, WAY BACK. IT'S SAFE TO WALK THE STREETS, ENOUGH FOOD, AND GOOD WINE.
MORE WINE! MORE ALE! AND BUSS ME QUICK, MY SWEET.
LIFE IS SO RICH.
I'LL STICK WITH BOYS-- MY HORNED "ACTRESSES."
SWEET KIT. THE PLAY I GAVE YOU. DID YOU READ...?
I MUST CONFESS I HAVE. I...THOUGHT IT, WELL... YOU ACT WELL, WILL, BUT-- LISTEN, LET ME READ...
"HUNG BE THE HEAVENS WITH BLACK, YIELD DAY TO NIGHT! COMETS IMPORTING CHANGE OF TIMES AND STATES, BRANDISH YOUR CRYSTAL TRESSES IN THE SKY, AND WITH THEM SCOURGE THE BAD, REVOLTING STARS."
AT LEAST IT SCANS. BUT "BAD REVOLTING STARS"?
IT'S MY FIRST PLAY.
AND IT SHOULD BE YOUR LAST.

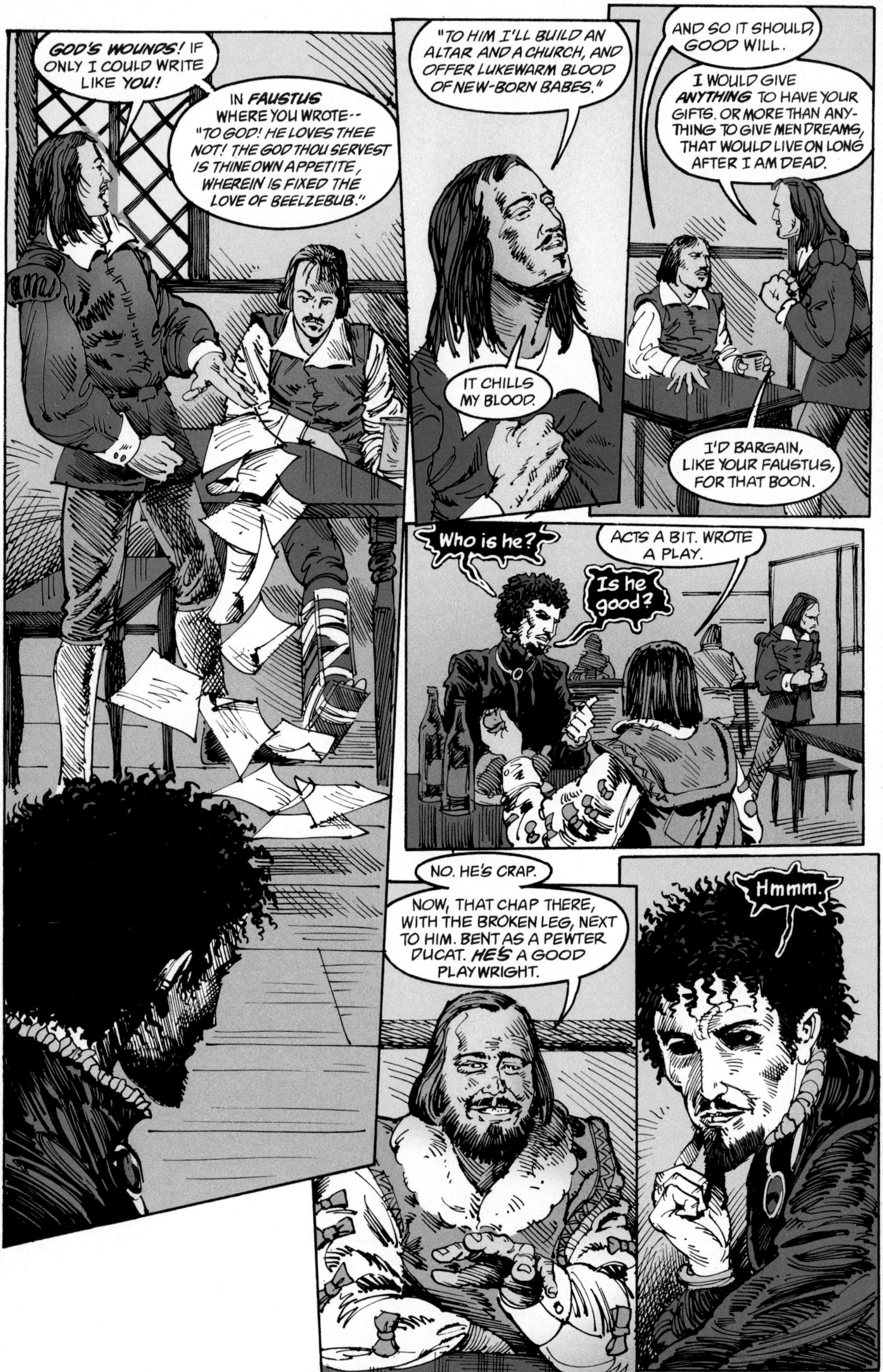
GOD'S WOUNDS! IF ONLY I COULD WRITE LIKE YOU!
IN FAUSTUS WHERE YOU WROTE-- "TO GOD! HE LOVES THEE NOT! THE GOD THOU SERVEST IS THINE OWN APPETITE, WHEREIN IS FIXED THE LOVE OF BEELZEBUB."
"TO HIM I'LL BUILD AN ALTAR AND A CHURCH, AND OFFER LUKEWARM BLOOD OF NEW-BORN BABES."
IT CHILLS MY BLOOD.
AND SO IT SHOULD, GOOD WILL.
I WOULD GIVE ANYTHING TO HAVE YOUR GIFTS. OR MORE THAN ANYTHING TO GIVE MEN DREAMS, THAT WOULD LIVE ON LONG AFTER I AM DEAD.
I'D BARGAIN, LIKE YOUR FAUSTUS, FOR THAT BOON.
Who is he?
ACTS A BIT. WROTE A PLAY.
Is he good?
NO. HE'S CRAP.
NOW, THAT CHAP THERE, WITH THE BROKEN LEG, NEXT TO HIM. BENT AS A PEWTER DUCAT. HE'S A GOOD PLAYWRIGHT.
Hmmm.

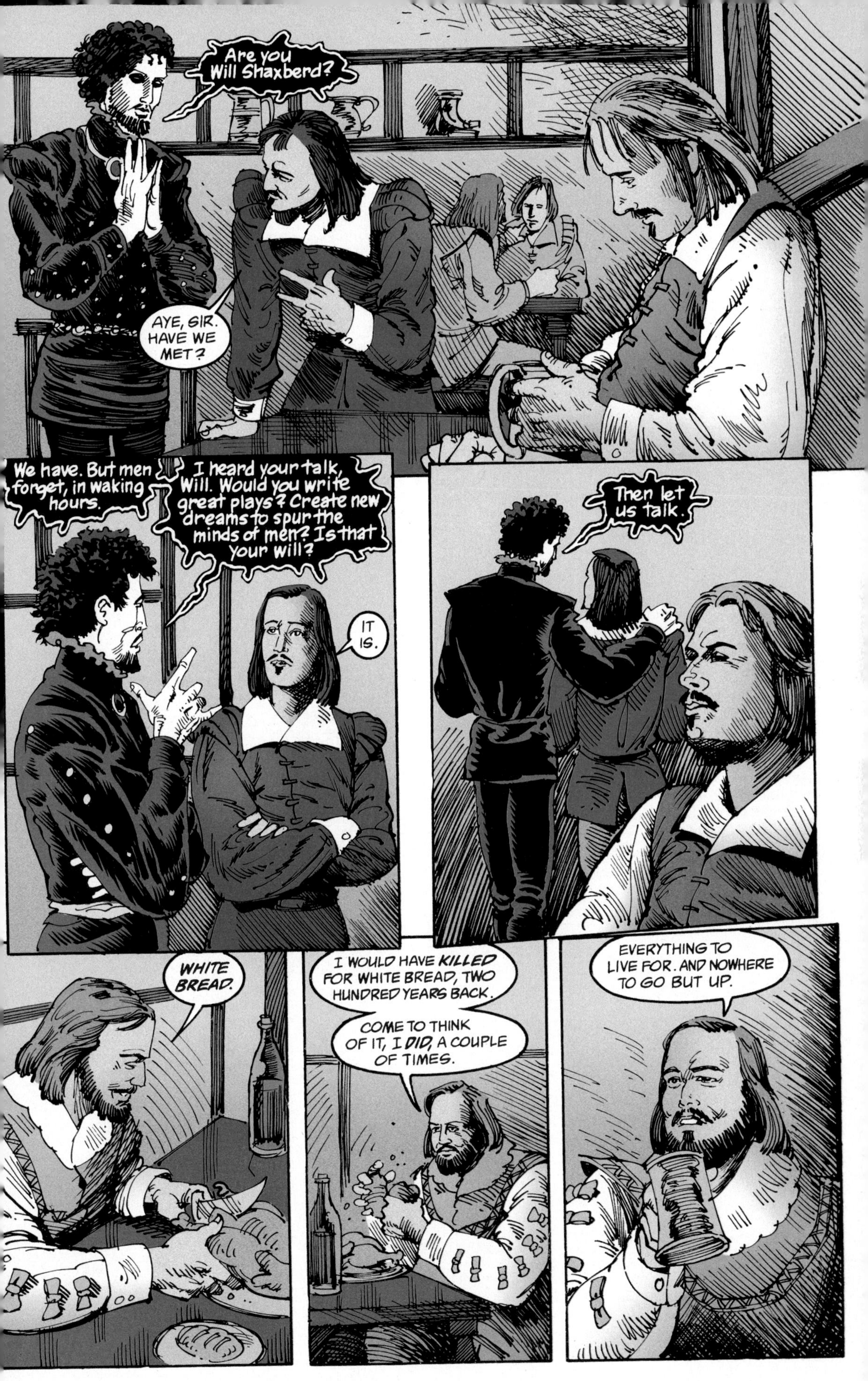
Are you Will Shaxberd?
AYE, SIR. HAVE WE MET?
We have. But men forget, in waking hours.
I heard your talk, Will. Would you write great plays? Create new dreams to spur the minds of men? Is that your will?
IT IS.
Then let us talk.
WHITE BREAD.
I WOULD HAVE KILLED FOR WHITE BREAD, TWO HUNDRED YEARS BACK.
COME TO THINK OF IT, I DID, A COUPLE OF TIMES.
EVERYTHING TO LIVE FOR. AND NOWHERE TO GO BUT UP.

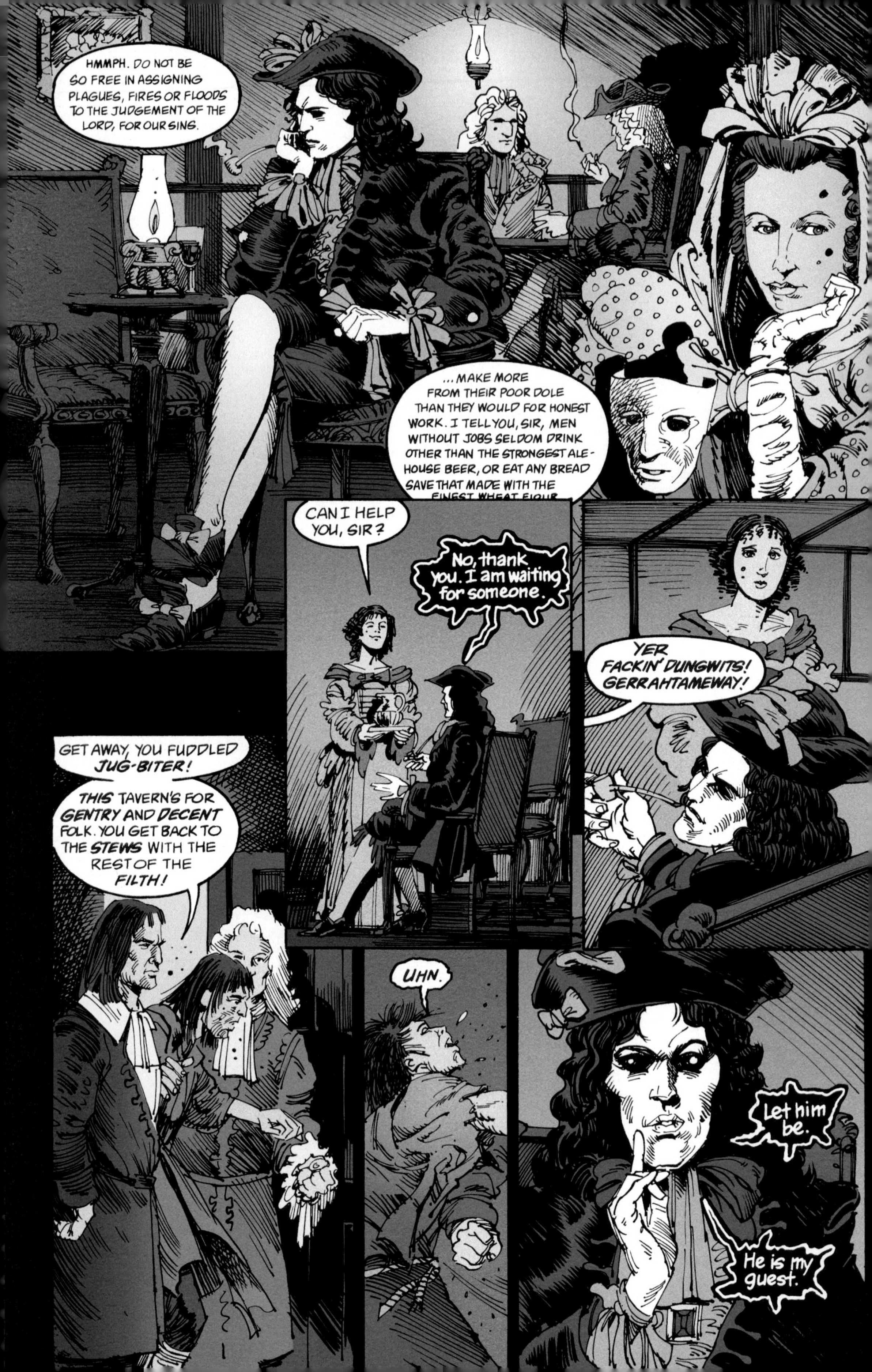
HMMPH. DO NOT BE SO FREE IN ASSIGNING PLAGUES, FIRES OR FLOODS TO THE JUDGEMENT OF THE LORD, FOR OUR SINS.
...MAKE MORE FROM THEIR POOR DOLE THAN THEY WOULD FOR HONEST WORK. I TELL YOU, SIR, MEN WITHOUT JOBS SELDOM DRINK OTHER THAN THE STRONGEST ALE-HOUSE BEER, OR EAT ANY BREAD SAVE THAT MADE WITH THE
CAN I HELP YOU, SIR?
No, thank you. I am waiting for someone.
YER FACKIN' DUNGWITS! GERRAHTAMEWAY!
GET AWAY, YOU FUDDLED JUG-BITER!
THIS TAVERN'S FOR GENTRY AND DECENT FOLK. YOU GET BACK TO THE STEWS WITH THE REST OF THE FILTH!
UHN.
Let him be.
He is my guest.

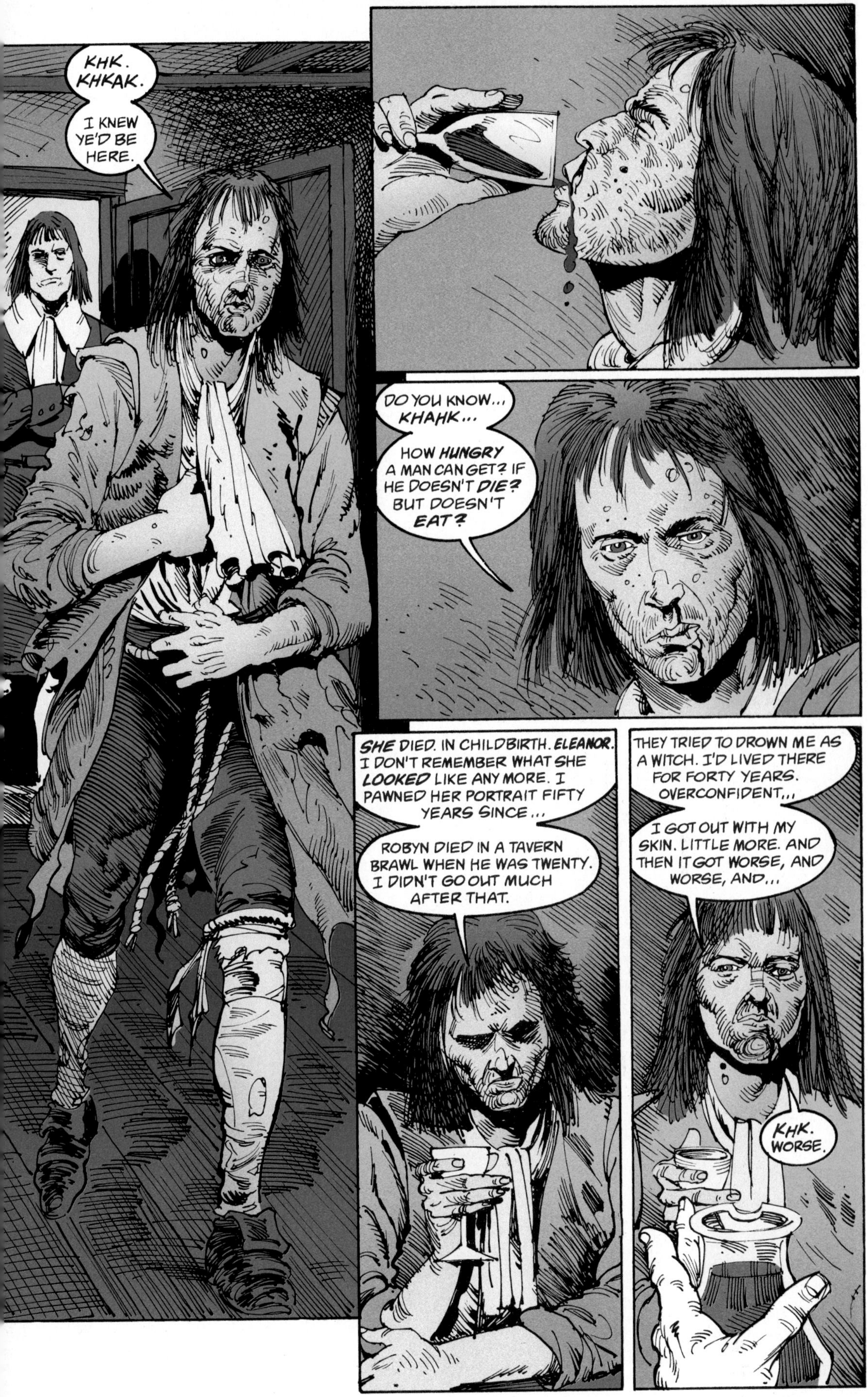
KHK. KHKAK.
I KNEW YE'D BE HERE.
DO YOU KNOW... KHAHK...
HOW HUNGRY A MAN CAN GET? IF HE DOESN'T DIE? BUT DOESN'T EAT?
SHE DIED. IN CHILDBIRTH. ELEANOR. I DON'T REMEMBER WHAT SHE LOOKED LIKE ANY MORE. I PAWNED HER PORTRAIT FIFTY YEARS SINCE...
ROBYN DIED IN A TAVERN BRAWL WHEN HE WAS TWENTY. I DIDN'T GO OUT MUCH AFTER THAT.
THEY TRIED TO DROWN ME AS A WITCH. I'D LIVED THERE FOR FORTY YEARS. OVERCONFIDENT...
I GOT OUT WITH MY SKIN. LITTLE MORE. AND THEN IT GOT WORSE, AND WORSE, AND...
KHK. WORSE.

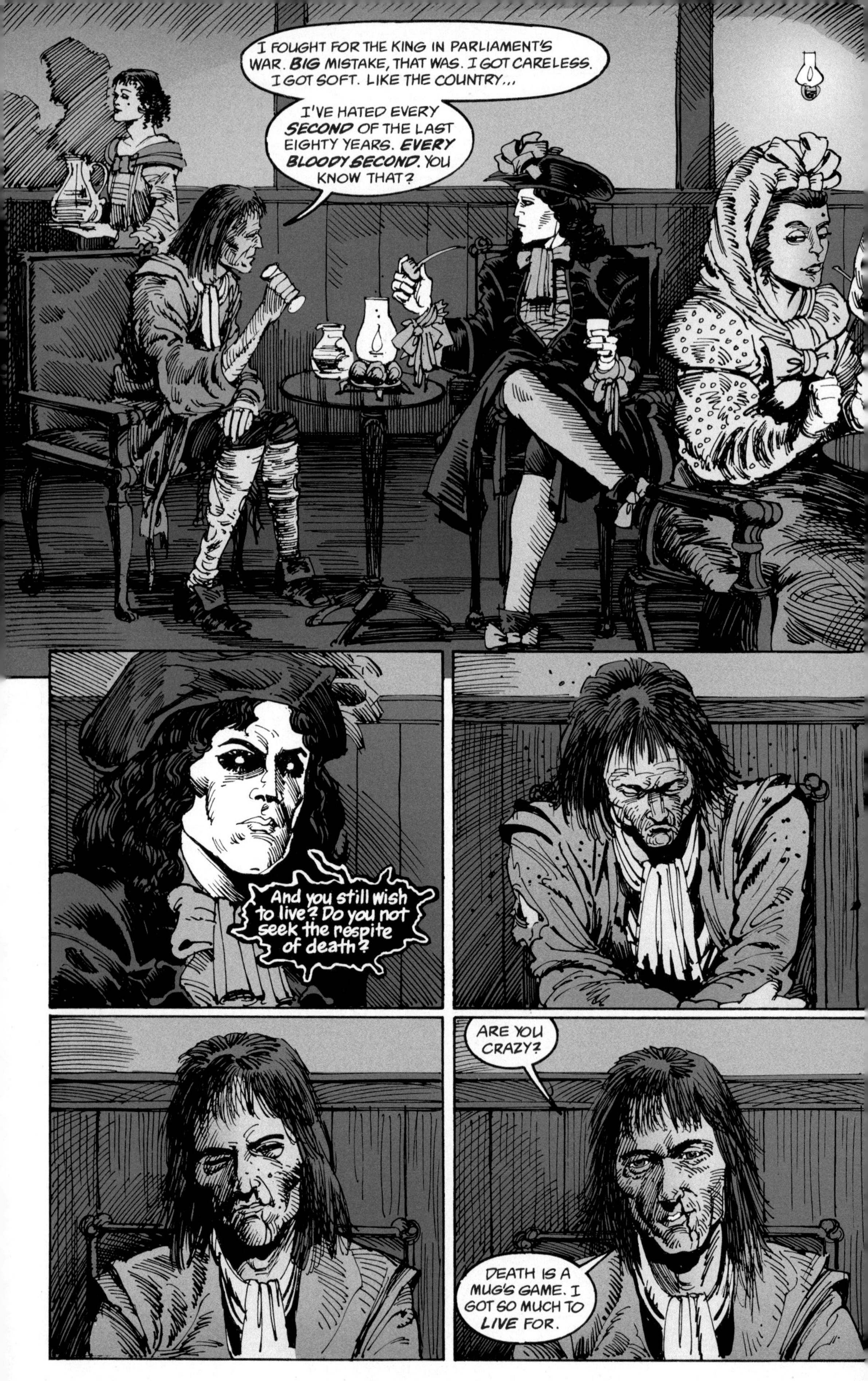
I FOUGHT FOR THE KING IN PARLIAMENT'S WAR. BIG MISTAKE, THAT WAS. I GOT CARELESS. I GOT SOFT. LIKE THE COUNTRY...
I'VE HATED EVERY SECOND OF THE LAST EIGHTY YEARS. EVERY BLOODY SECOND. YOU KNOW THAT?
And you still wish to live? Do you not seek the respite of death?
ARE YOU CRAZY?
DEATH IS A MUG'S GAME. I GOT SO MUCH TO LIVE FOR.

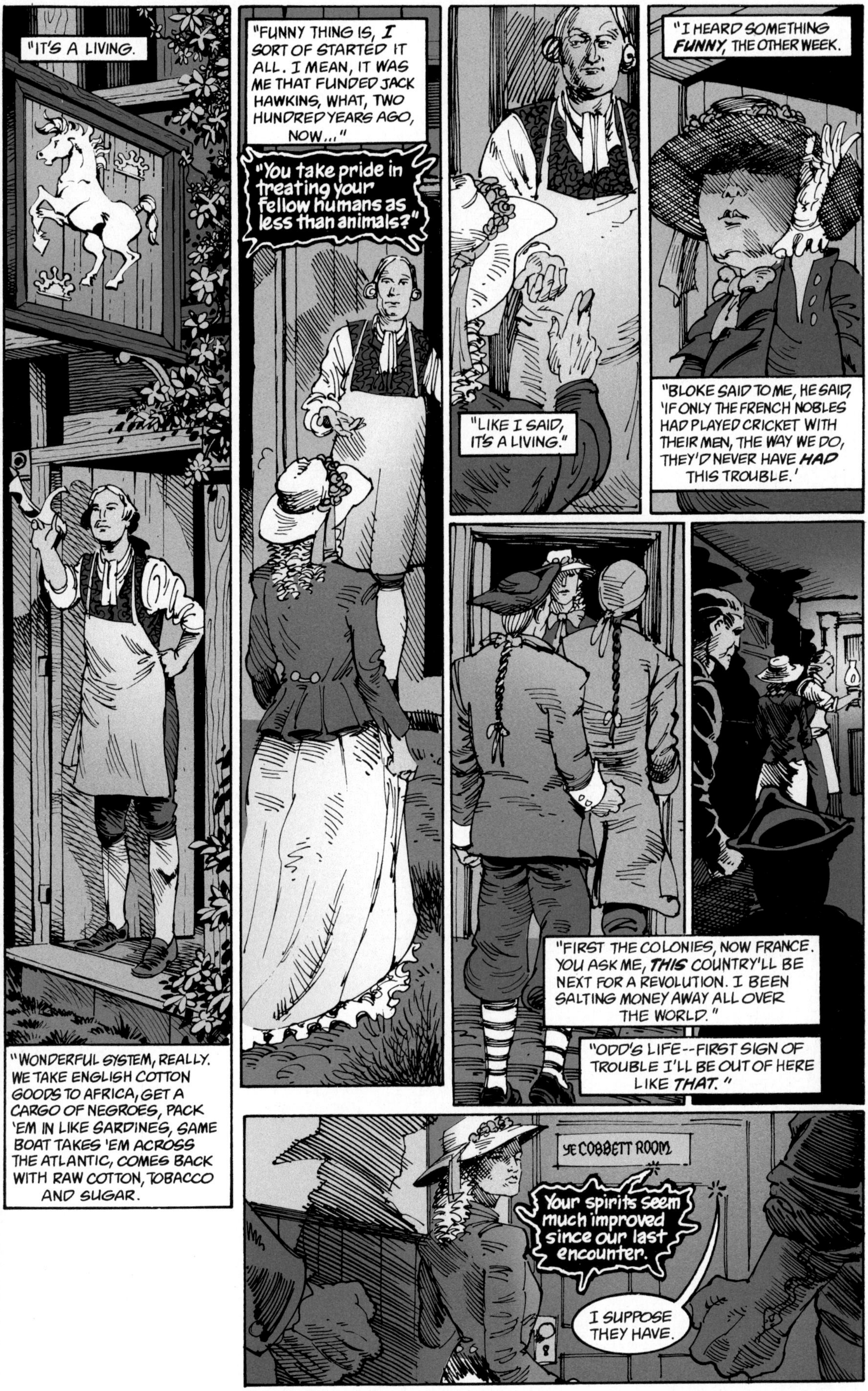

"IT'S A LIVING.
"WONDERFUL SYSTEM, REALLY. WE TAKE ENGLISH COTTON GOODS TO AFRICA, GET A CARGO OF NEGROES, PACK 'EM IN LIKE SARDINES, SAME BOAT TAKES 'EM ACROSS THE ATLANTIC, COMES BACK WITH RAW COTTON, TOBACCO AND SUGAR.
"FUNNY THING IS, I SORT OF STARTED IT ALL. I MEAN, IT WAS ME THAT FUNDED JACK HAWKINS, WHAT, TWO HUNDRED YEARS AGO, NOW..."
"You take pride in treating your fellow humans as less than animals?"
"LIKE I SAID, IT'S A LIVING."
"I HEARD SOMETHING FUNNY, THE OTHER WEEK.
"BLOKE SAID TO ME, HE SAID, 'IF ONLY THE FRENCH NOBLES HAD PLAYED CRICKET WITH THEIR MEN, THE WAY WE DO, THEY'D NEVER HAVE HAD THIS TROUBLE.'
"FIRST THE COLONIES, NOW FRANCE. YOU ASK ME, THIS COUNTRY'LL BE NEXT FOR A REVOLUTION. I BEEN SALTING MONEY AWAY ALL OVER THE WORLD."
"ODD'S LIFE--FIRST SIGN OF TROUBLE I'LL BE OUT OF HERE LIKE THAT."
YE COBBETT ROOM
Your spirits seem much improved since our last encounter.
I SUPPOSE THEY HAVE.

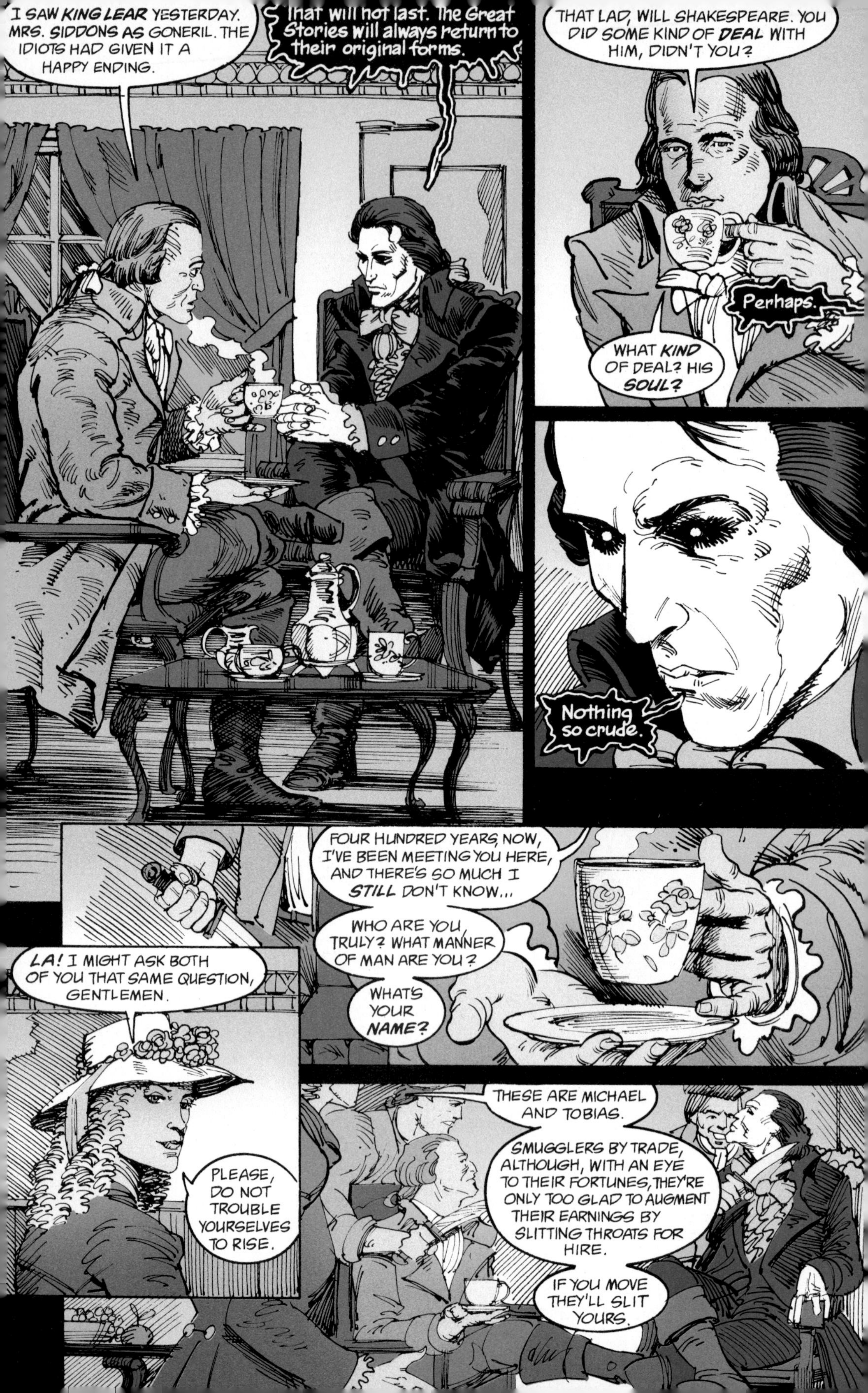
I SAW KING LEAR YESTERDAY. MRS. SIDDONS AS GONERIL. THE IDIOTS HAD GIVEN IT A HAPPY ENDING.
That will not last. The Great Stories will always return to their original forms.
THAT LAD, WILL SHAKESPEARE. YOU DID SOME KIND OF DEAL WITH HIM, DIDN'T YOU?
Perhaps.
WHAT KIND OF DEAL? HIS SOUL?
Nothing so crude.
FOUR HUNDRED YEARS, NOW, I'VE BEEN MEETING YOU HERE, AND THERE'S SO MUCH I STILL DON'T KNOW...
WHO ARE YOU, TRULY? WHAT MANNER OF MAN ARE YOU?
WHAT'S YOUR NAME?
LA! I MIGHT ASK BOTH OF YOU THAT SAME QUESTION, GENTLEMEN.
PLEASE, DO NOT TROUBLE YOURSELVES TO RISE.
THESE ARE MICHAEL AND TOBIAS.
SMUGGLERS BY TRADE, ALTHOUGH, WITH AN EYE TO THEIR FORTUNES, THEY'RE ONLY TOO GLAD TO AUGMENT THEIR EARNINGS BY SLITTING THROATS FOR HIRE.
IF YOU MOVE THEY'LL SLIT YOURS.

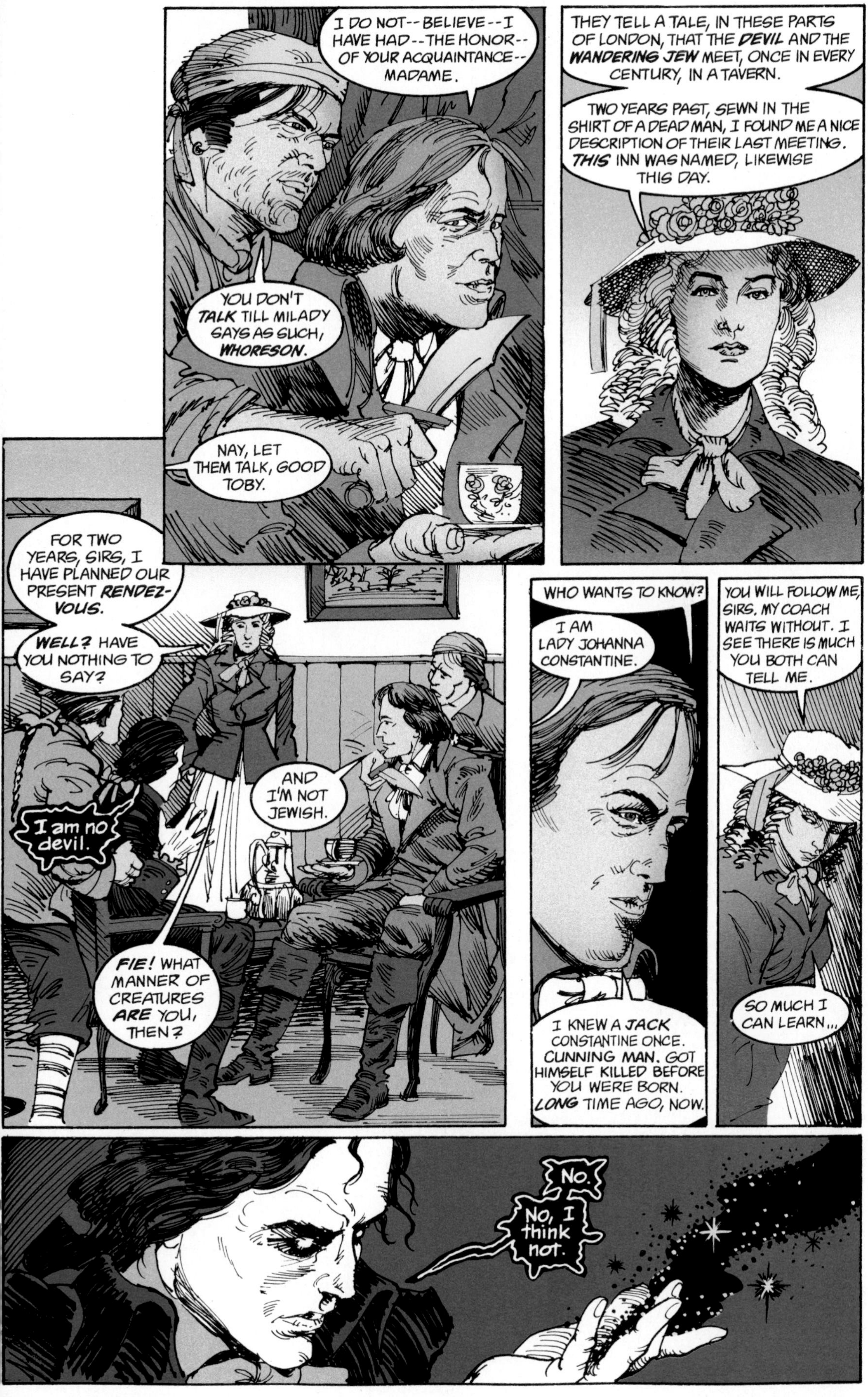
I DO NOT-- BELIEVE--I HAVE HAD--THE HONOR-- OF YOUR ACQUAINTANCE-- MADAME.
YOU DON'T TALK TILL MILADY SAYS AS SUCH, WHORESON.
NAY, LET THEM TALK, GOOD TOBY.
THEY TELL A TALE, IN THESE PARTS OF LONDON, THAT THE DEVIL AND THE WANDERING JEW MEET, ONCE IN EVERY CENTURY, IN A TAVERN.
TWO YEARS PAST, SEWN IN THE SHIRT OF A DEAD MAN, I FOUND ME A NICE DESCRIPTION OF THEIR LAST MEETING. THIS INN WAS NAMED, LIKEWISE THIS DAY.
FOR TWO YEARS, SIRS, I HAVE PLANNED OUR PRESENT RENDEZ-VOUS.
WELL? HAVE YOU NOTHING TO SAY?
I am no devil.
AND I'M NOT JEWISH.
FIE! WHAT MANNER OF CREATURES ARE YOU, THEN?
WHO WANTS TO KNOW?
I AM LADY JOHANNA CONSTANTINE.
I KNEW A JACK CONSTANTINE ONCE. CUNNING MAN. GOT HIMSELF KILLED BEFORE YOU WERE BORN. LONG TIME AGO, NOW.
YOU WILL FOLLOW ME, SIRS. MY COACH WAITS WITHOUT. I SEE THERE IS MUCH YOU BOTH CAN TELL ME.
SO MUCH I CAN LEARN...
No.
No, I think not.

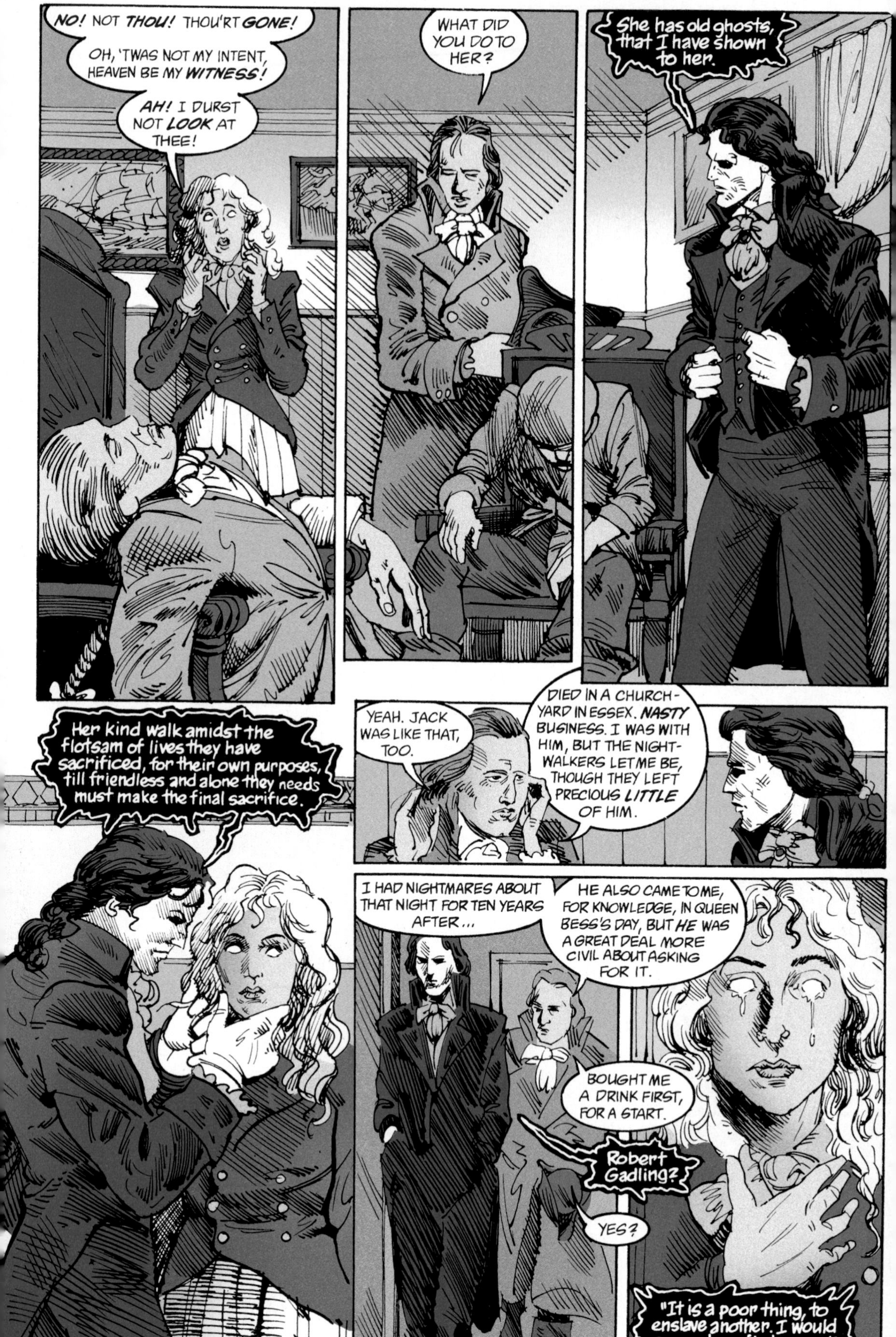
NO! NOT THOU! THOU'RT GONE!
OH, 'TWAS NOT MY INTENT, HEAVEN BE MY WITNESS!
AH! I DURST NOT LOOK AT THEE!
WHAT DID YOU DO TO HER?
She has old ghosts, that I have shown to her.
Her kind walk amidst the flotsam of lives they have sacrificed, for their own purposes, till friendless and alone they needs must make the final sacrifice.
YEAH. JACK WAS LIKE THAT, TOO.
DIED IN A CHURCH-YARD IN ESSEX. NASTY BUSINESS. I WAS WITH HIM, BUT THE NIGHT-WALKERS LET ME BE, THOUGH THEY LEFT PRECIOUS LITTLE OF HIM.
I HAD NIGHTMARES ABOUT THAT NIGHT FOR TEN YEARS AFTER...
HE ALSO CAME TO ME, FOR KNOWLEDGE, IN QUEEN BESS'S DAY, BUT HE WAS A GREAT DEAL MORE CIVIL ABOUT ASKING FOR IT.
BOUGHT ME A DRINK FIRST, FOR A START.
Robert Gadling?
YES?
"It is a poor thing, to enslave another. I would suggest you find yourself a different line of business."

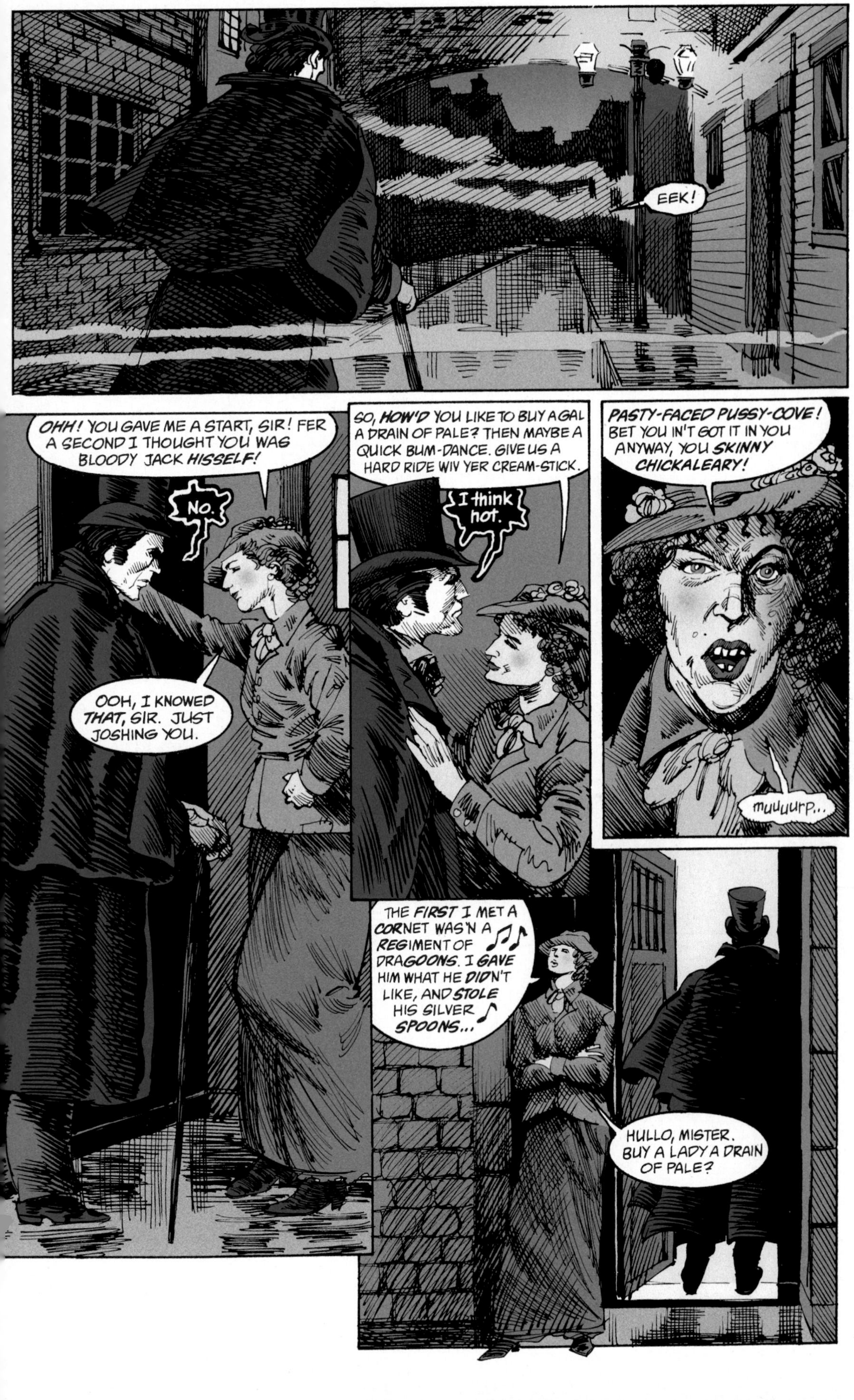
EEK!
OHH! YOU GAVE ME A START, SIR! FER A SECOND I THOUGHT YOU WAS BLOODY JACK HISSELF!
No.
OOH, I KNOWED THAT, SIR. JUST JOSHING YOU.
SO, HOW'D YOU LIKE TO BUY A GAL A DRAIN OF PALE? THEN MAYBE A QUICK BUM-DANCE. GIVE US A HARD RIDE WIV YER CREAM-STICK.
I think not.
PASTY-FACED PUSSY-COVE! BET YOU IN'T GOT IT IN YOU ANYWAY, YOU SKINNY CHICKALEARY!
muuuurp...
THE FIRST I MET A CORNET WAS'N A REGIMENT OF DRAGOONS. I GAVE HIM WHAT HE DIDN'T LIKE, AND STOLE HIS SILVER SPOONS...
HULLO, MISTER. BUY A LADY A DRAIN OF PALE?

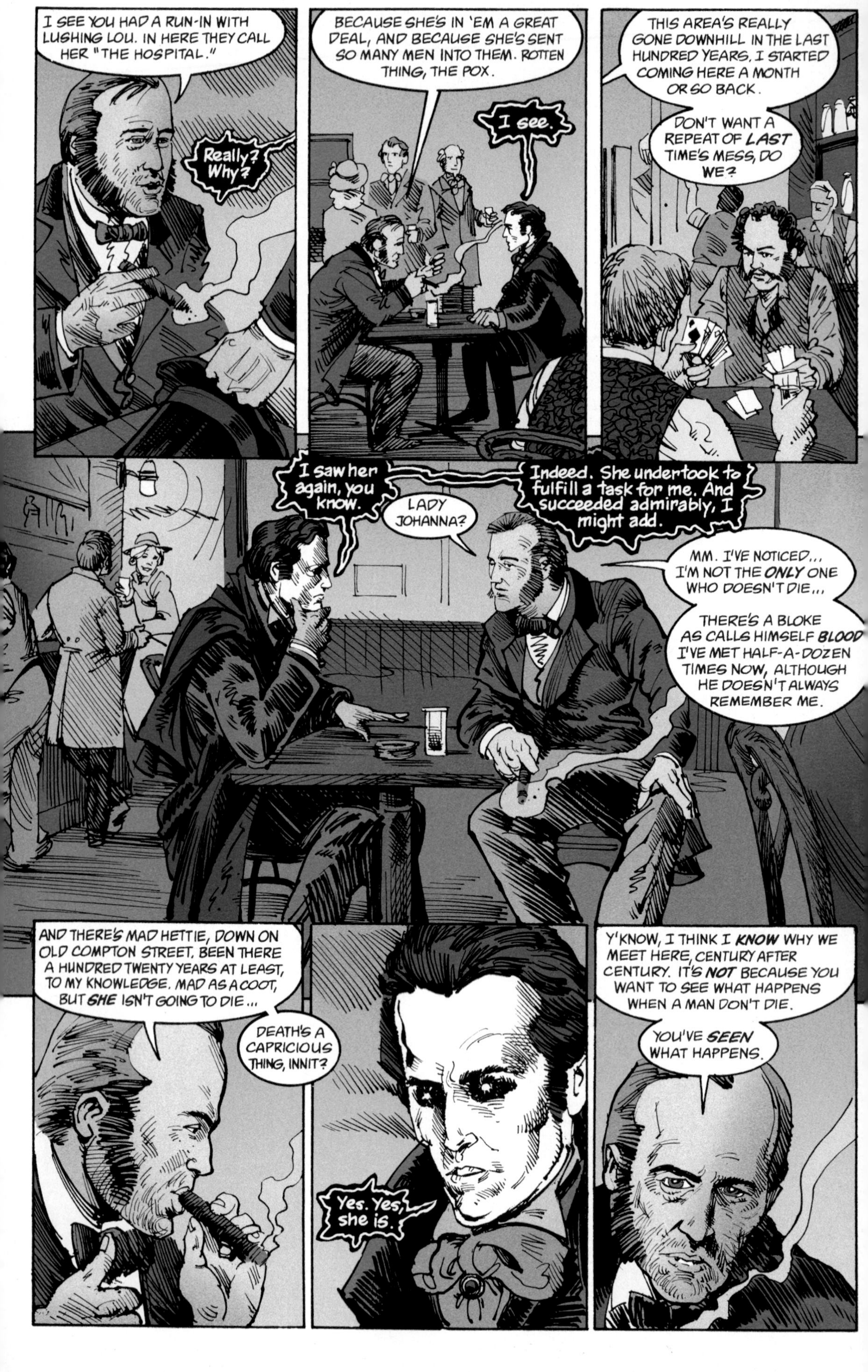
I SEE YOU HAD A RUN-IN WITH LUSHING LOU. IN HERE THEY CALL HER "THE HOSPITAL."
Really? Why?
BECAUSE SHE'S IN 'EM A GREAT DEAL, AND BECAUSE SHE'S SENT SO MANY MEN INTO THEM. ROTTEN THING, THE POX.
I see.
THIS AREA'S REALLY GONE DOWNHILL IN THE LAST HUNDRED YEARS. I STARTED COMING HERE A MONTH OR SO BACK.
DON'T WANT A REPEAT OF LAST TIME'S MESS, DO WE?
I saw her again, you know.
LADY JOHANNA?
Indeed. She undertook to fulfill a task for me. And succeeded admirably, I might add.
MM. I'VE NOTICED... I'M NOT THE ONLY ONE WHO DOESN'T DIE...
THERE'S A BLOKE AS CALLS HIMSELF BLOOD I'VE MET HALF-A-DOZEN TIMES NOW, ALTHOUGH HE DOESN'T ALWAYS REMEMBER ME.
AND THERE'S MAD HETTIE, DOWN ON OLD COMPTON STREET. BEEN THERE A HUNDRED TWENTY YEARS AT LEAST, TO MY KNOWLEDGE. MAD AS A COOT, BUT SHE ISN'T GOING TO DIE...
DEATH'S A CAPRICIOUS THING, INNIT?
Yes. Yes, she is.
Y'KNOW, I THINK I KNOW WHY WE MEET HERE, CENTURY AFTER CENTURY. IT'S NOT BECAUSE YOU WANT TO SEE WHAT HAPPENS WHEN A MAN DON'T DIE.
YOU'VE SEEN WHAT HAPPENS.

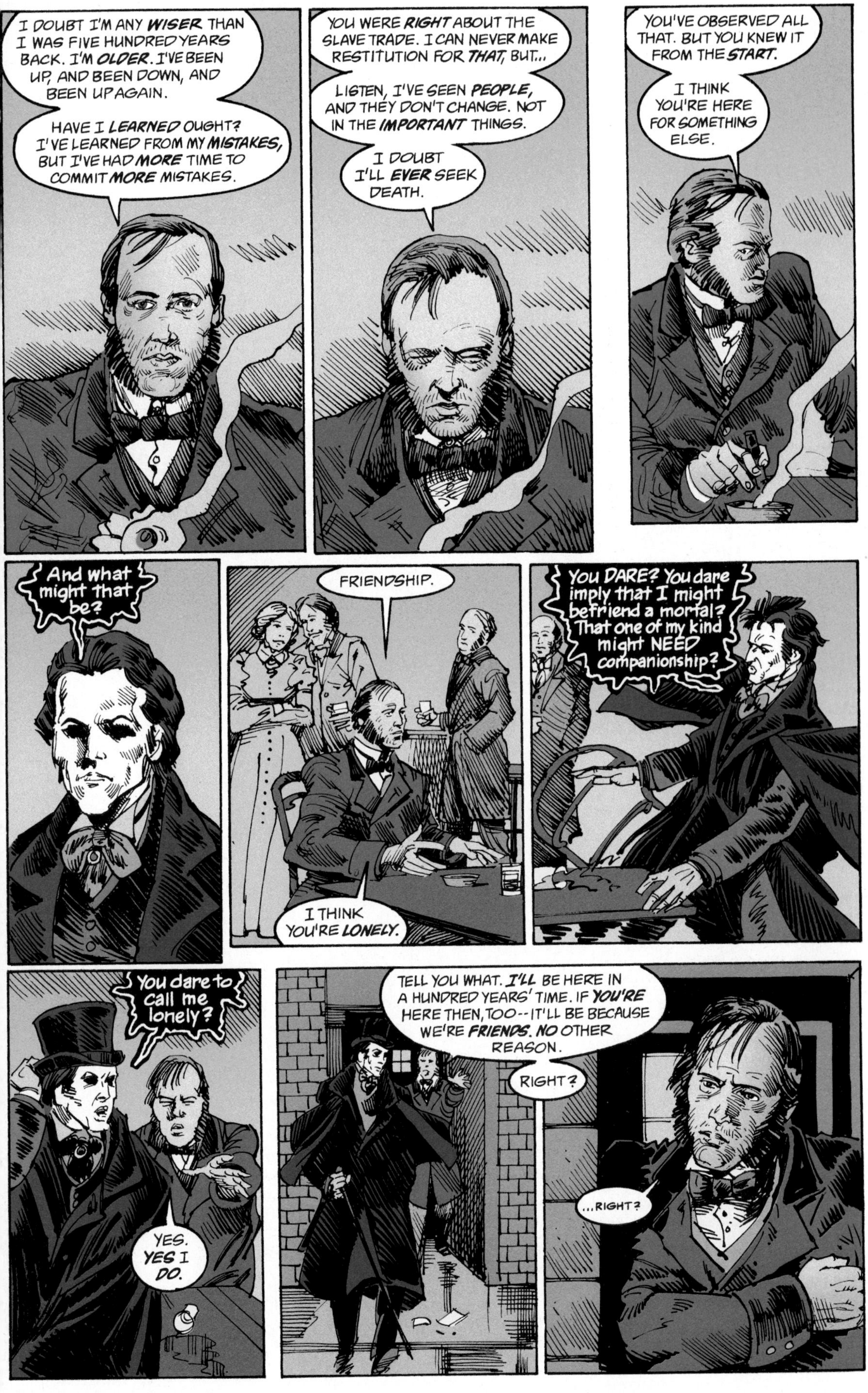
I DOUBT I'M ANY WISER THAN I WAS FIVE HUNDRED YEARS BACK. I'M OLDER. I'VE BEEN UP, AND BEEN DOWN, AND BEEN UP AGAIN.
HAVE I LEARNED OUGHT? I'VE LEARNED FROM MY MISTAKES, BUT I'VE HAD MORE TIME TO COMMIT MORE MISTAKES.
YOU WERE RIGHT ABOUT THE SLAVE TRADE. I CAN NEVER MAKE RESTITUTION FOR THAT, BUT...
LISTEN, I'VE SEEN PEOPLE, AND THEY DON'T CHANGE. NOT IN THE IMPORTANT THINGS.
I DOUBT I'LL EVER SEEK DEATH.
YOU'VE OBSERVED ALL THAT. BUT YOU KNEW IT FROM THE START.
I THINK YOU'RE HERE FOR SOMETHING ELSE.
And what might that be?
FRIENDSHIP.
I THINK YOU'RE LONELY.
You DARE? You dare imply that I might befriend a mortal? That one of my kind might NEED companionship?
You dare to call me lonely?
YES. YES I DO.
TELL YOU WHAT. I'LL BE HERE IN A HUNDRED YEARS' TIME. IF YOU'RE HERE THEN, TOO-- IT'LL BE BECAUSE WE'RE FRIENDS. NO OTHER REASON.
RIGHT?
...RIGHT?

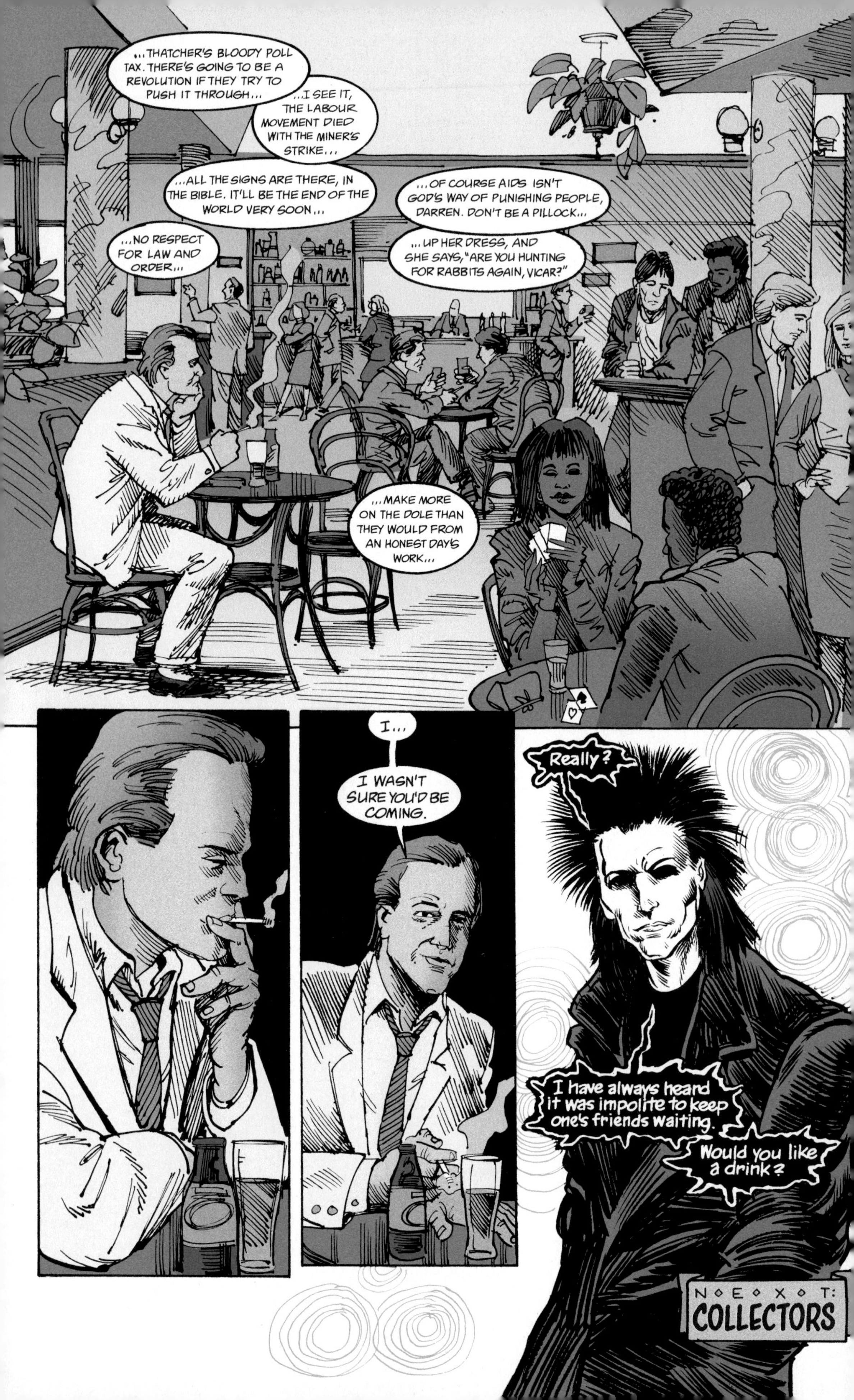
...THATCHER'S BLOODY POLL TAX. THERE'S GOING TO BE A REVOLUTION IF THEY TRY TO PUSH IT THROUGH...
...I SEE IT, THE LABOUR MOVEMENT DIED WITH THE MINER'S STRIKE...
...ALL THE SIGNS ARE THERE, IN THE BIBLE. IT'LL BE THE END OF THE WORLD VERY SOON...
...OF COURSE AIDS ISN'T GOD'S WAY OF PUNISHING PEOPLE, DARREN. DON'T BE A PILLOCK...
...NO RESPECT FOR LAW AND ORDER...
...UP HER DRESS, AND SHE SAYS, "ARE YOU HUNTING FOR RABBITS AGAIN, VICAR?"
...MAKE MORE ON THE DOLE THAN THEY WOULD FROM AN HONEST DAY'S WORK...
I...
I WASN'T SURE YOU'D BE COMING.
Really?
I have always heard it was impolite to keep one's friends waiting.
Would you like a drink?
NEXT: COLLECTORS

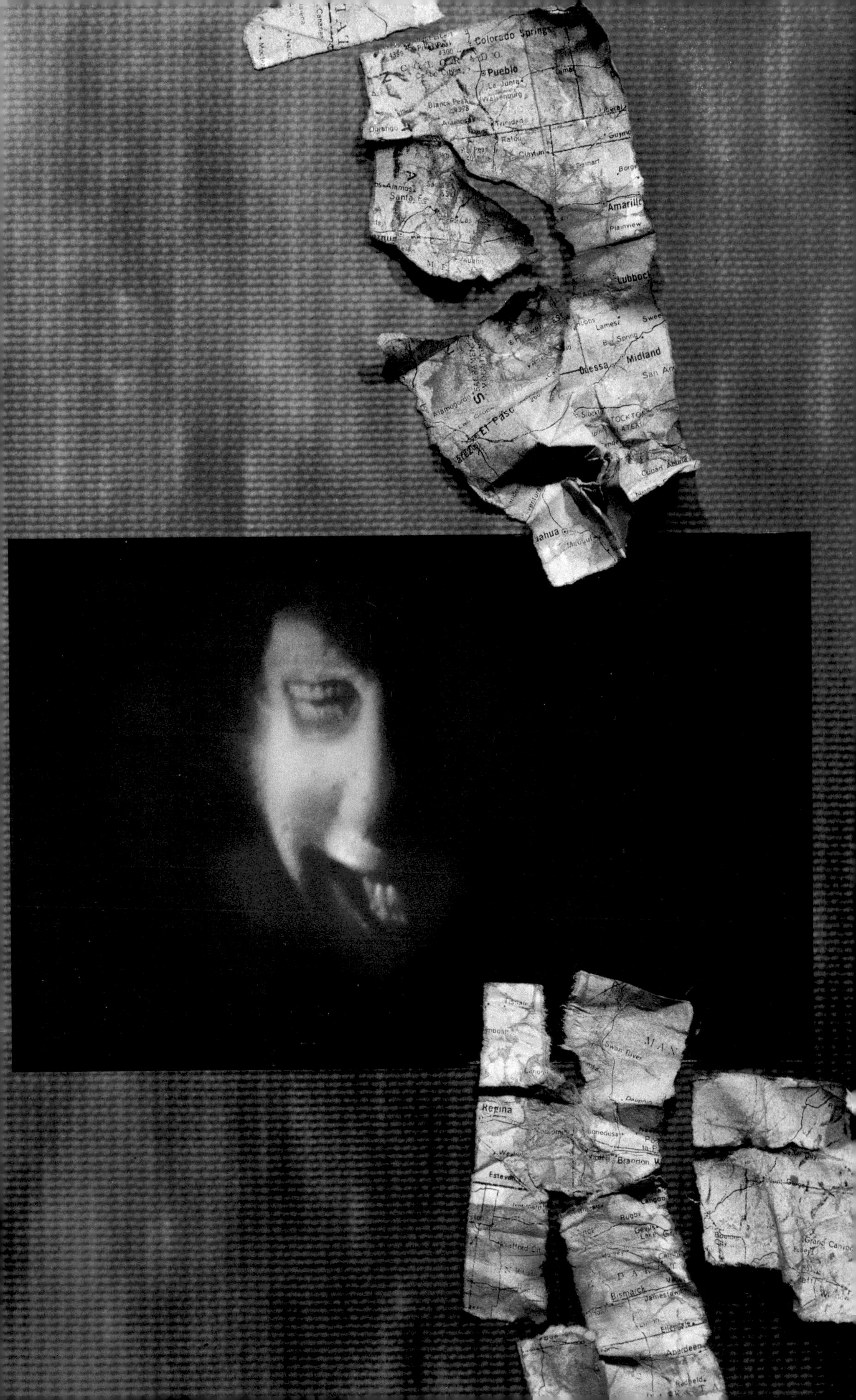
Colorado Springs
Pueblo
Santa Fe
Amarillo
Plainview
Lubbock
Lamesa
Big Spring
Odessa
Midland
Alamogordo
El Paso
Swan River
Regina
Brandon
Bismarck
Jamestown
Aberdeen
Grand Canyon

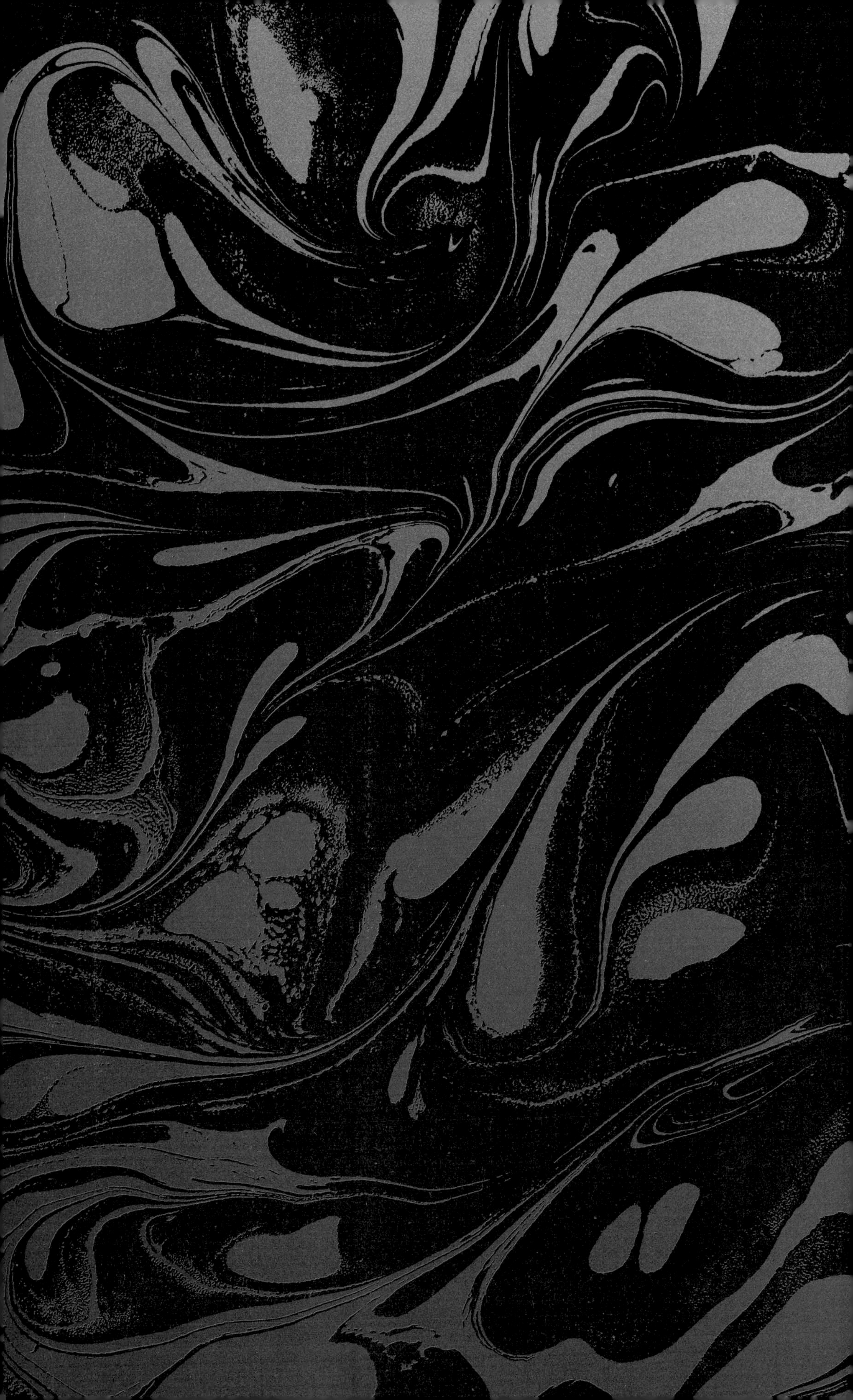

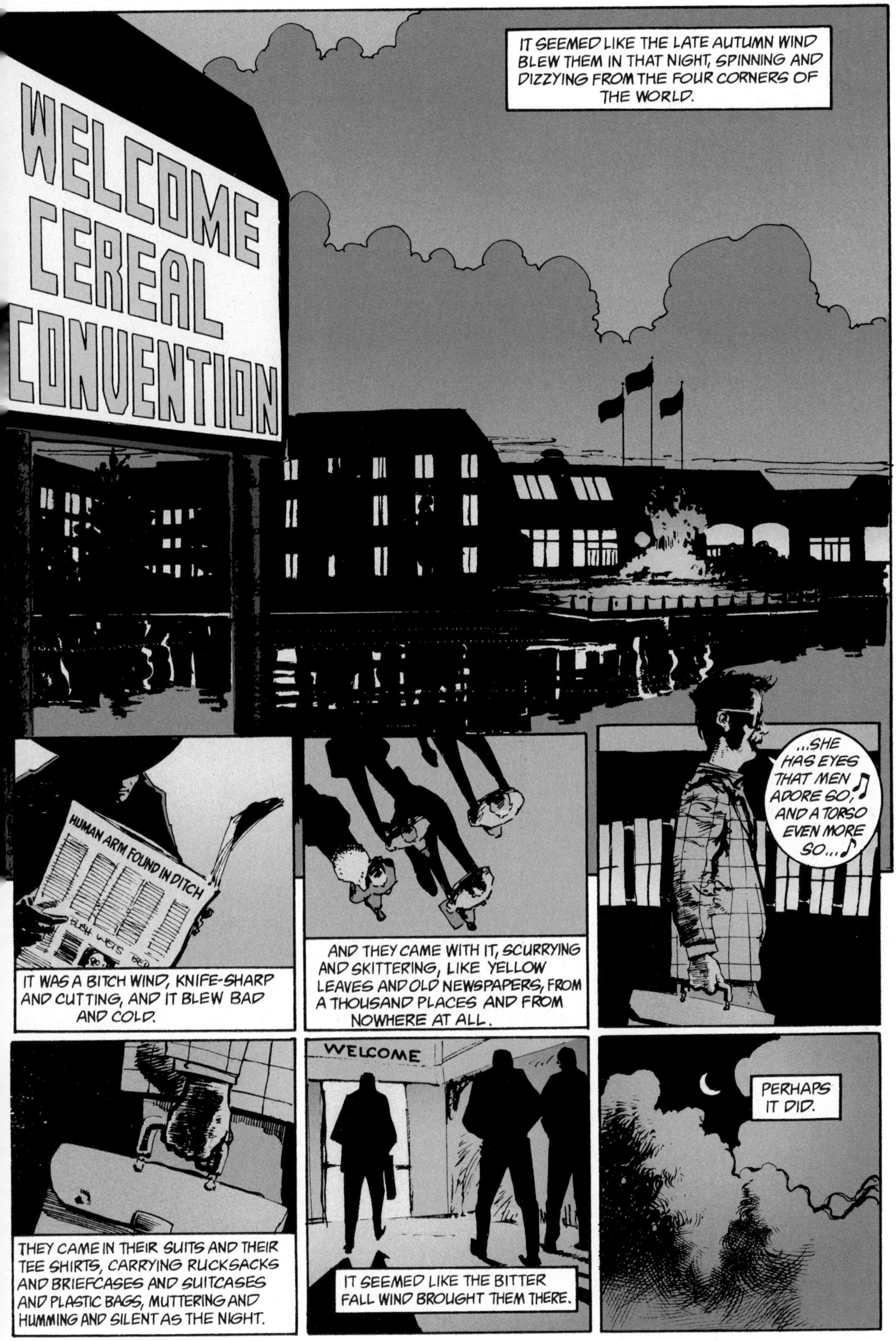
WELCOME CEREAL CONVENTION
IT SEEMED LIKE THE LATE AUTUMN WIND BLEW THEM IN THAT NIGHT, SPINNING AND DIZZYING FROM THE FOUR CORNERS OF THE WORLD.
HUMAN ARM FOUND IN DITCH
IT WAS A BITCH WIND, KNIFE-SHARP AND CUTTING, AND IT BLEW BAD AND COLD.
AND THEY CAME WITH IT, SCURRYING AND SKITTERING, LIKE YELLOW LEAVES AND OLD NEWSPAPERS, FROM A THOUSAND PLACES AND FROM NOWHERE AT ALL.
...SHE HAS EYES THAT MEN ADORE SO, AND A TORSO EVEN MORE SO...
THEY CAME IN THEIR SUITS AND THEIR TEE SHIRTS, CARRYING RUCKSACKS AND BRIEFCASES AND SUITCASES AND PLASTIC BAGS, MUTTERING AND HUMMING AND SILENT AS THE NIGHT.
WELCOME
IT SEEMED LIKE THE BITTER FALL WIND BROUGHT THEM THERE.
PERHAPS IT DID.

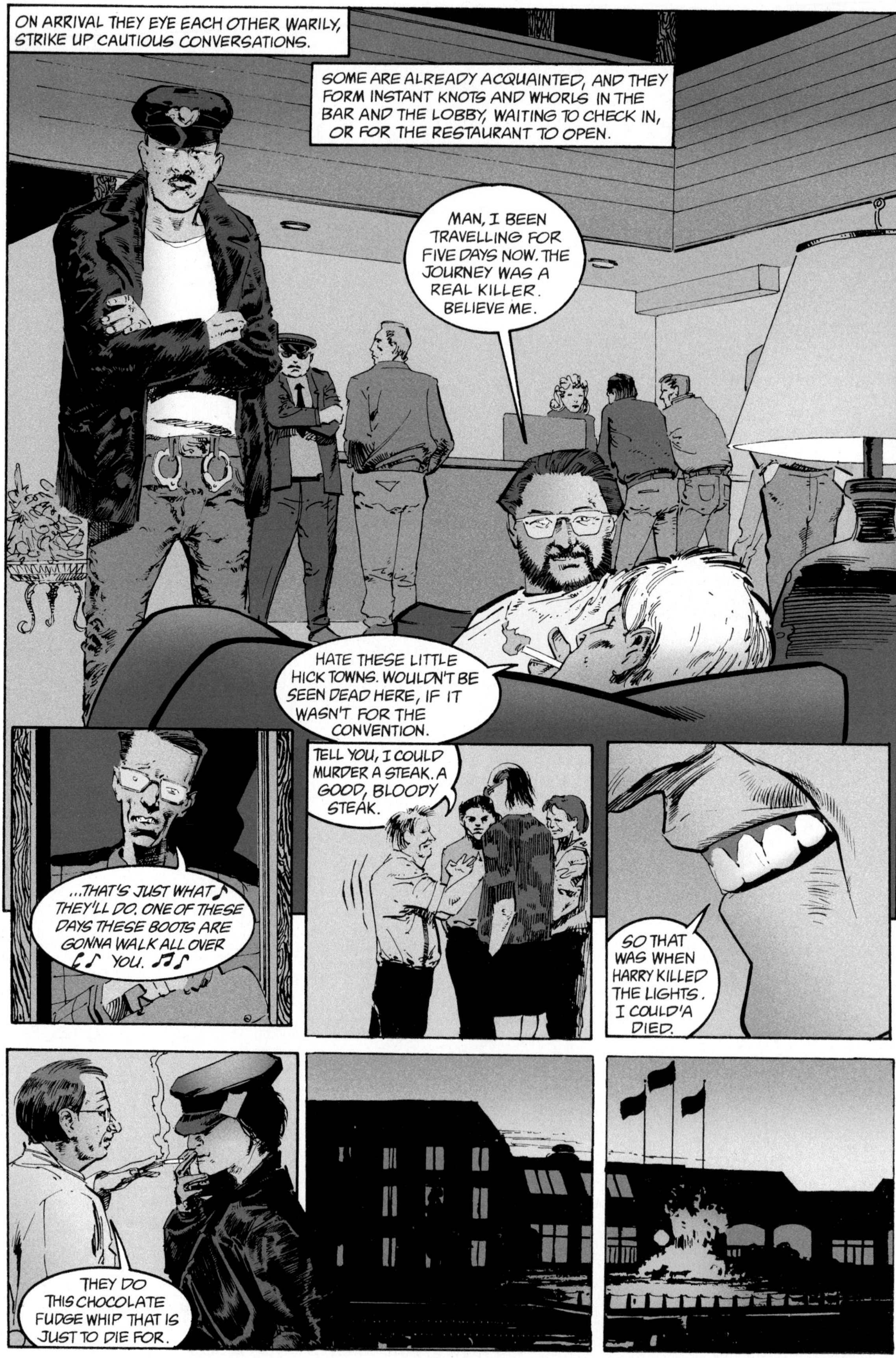
ON ARRIVAL THEY EYE EACH OTHER WARILY, STRIKE UP CAUTIOUS CONVERSATIONS.
SOME ARE ALREADY ACQUAINTED, AND THEY FORM INSTANT KNOTS AND WHORLS IN THE BAR AND THE LOBBY, WAITING TO CHECK IN, OR FOR THE RESTAURANT TO OPEN.
MAN, I BEEN TRAVELLING FOR FIVE DAYS NOW. THE JOURNEY WAS A REAL KILLER. BELIEVE ME.
HATE THESE LITTLE HICK TOWNS. WOULDN'T BE SEEN DEAD HERE, IF IT WASN'T FOR THE CONVENTION.
...THAT'S JUST WHAT ♪ THEY'LL DO. ONE OF THESE DAYS THESE BOOTS ARE GONNA WALK ALL OVER ♪♪ YOU. ♫♪
TELL YOU, I COULD MURDER A STEAK. A GOOD, BLOODY STEAK.
SO THAT WAS WHEN HARRY KILLED THE LIGHTS. I COULD'A DIED.
THEY DO THIS CHOCOLATE FUDGE WHIP THAT IS JUST TO DIE FOR.

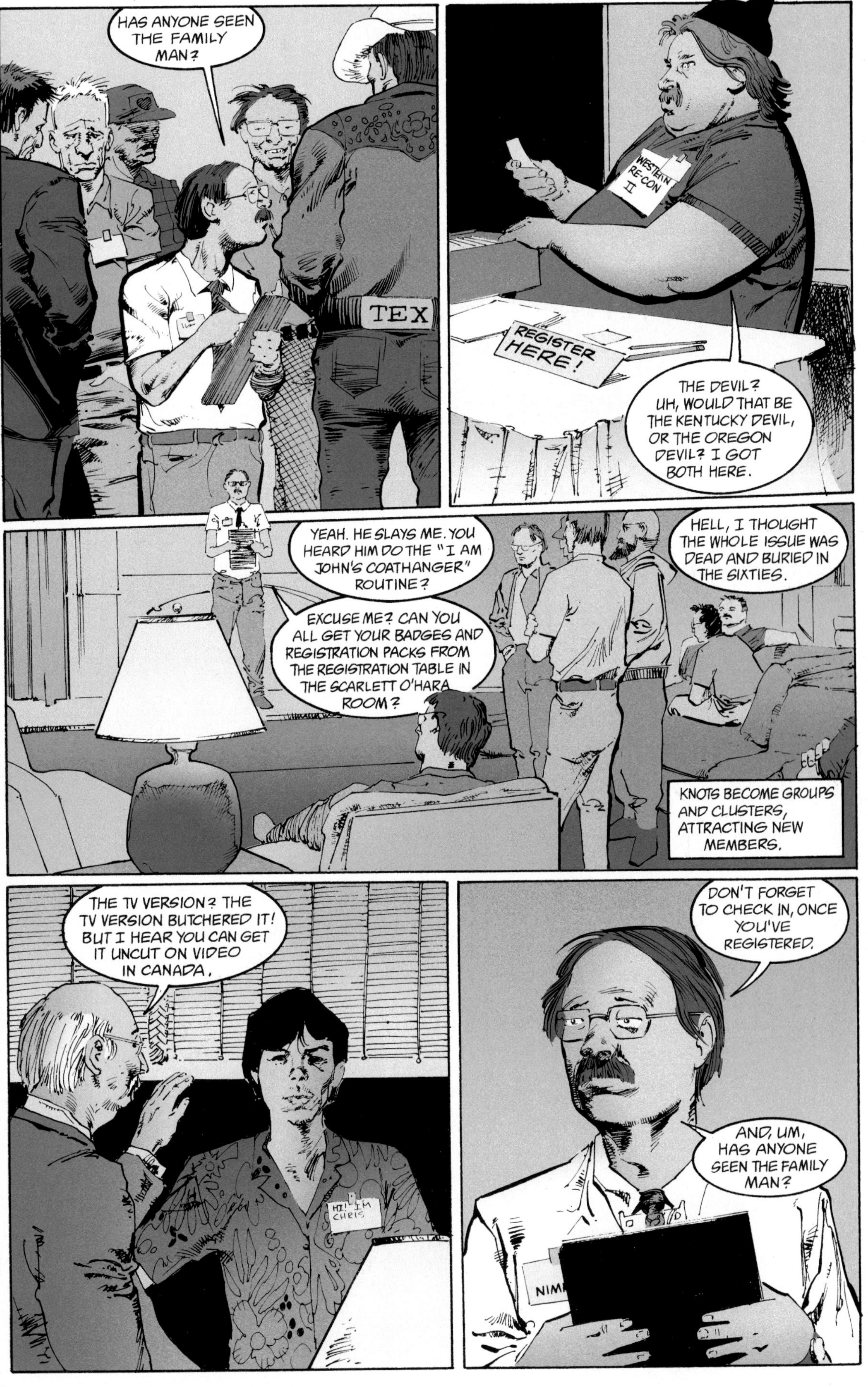
HAS ANYONE SEEN THE FAMILY MAN?
TEX
WESTERN RE-CON II
REGISTER HERE!
THE DEVIL? UH, WOULD THAT BE THE KENTUCKY DEVIL, OR THE OREGON DEVIL? I GOT BOTH HERE.
YEAH. HE SLAYS ME. YOU HEARD HIM DO THE "I AM JOHN'S COATHANGER" ROUTINE?
HELL, I THOUGHT THE WHOLE ISSUE WAS DEAD AND BURIED IN THE SIXTIES.
EXCUSE ME? CAN YOU ALL GET YOUR BADGES AND REGISTRATION PACKS FROM THE REGISTRATION TABLE IN THE SCARLETT O'HARA ROOM?
KNOTS BECOME GROUPS AND CLUSTERS, ATTRACTING NEW MEMBERS.
THE TV VERSION? THE TV VERSION BUTCHERED IT! BUT I HEAR YOU CAN GET IT UNCUT ON VIDEO IN CANADA.
HI! I'M CHRIS
DON'T FORGET TO CHECK IN, ONCE YOU'VE REGISTERED.
AND, UM, HAS ANYONE SEEN THE FAMILY MAN?

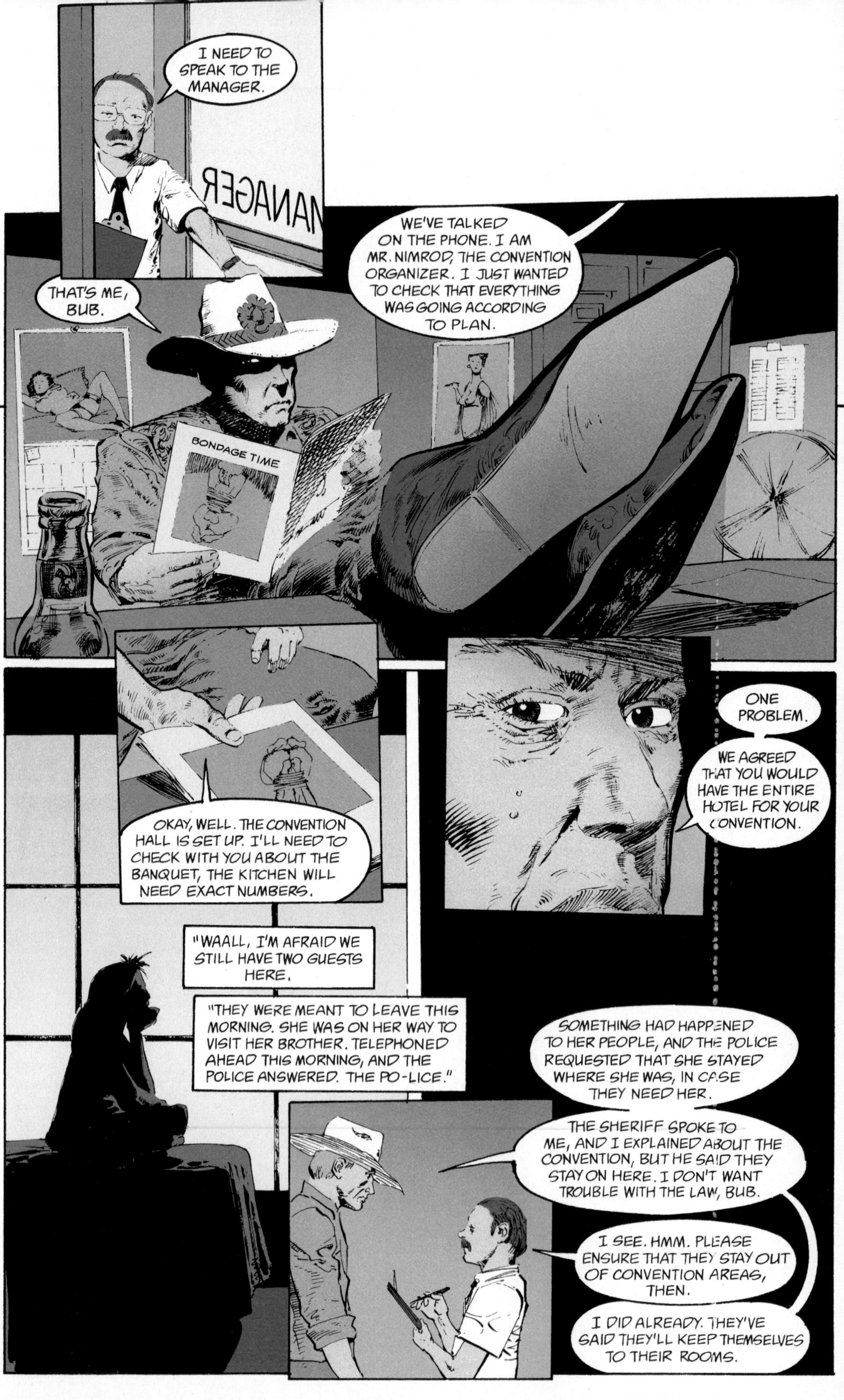
I NEED TO SPEAK TO THE MANAGER.
MANAGER
THAT'S ME, BUB.
WE'VE TALKED ON THE PHONE. I AM MR. NIMROD, THE CONVENTION ORGANIZER. I JUST WANTED TO CHECK THAT EVERYTHING WAS GOING ACCORDING TO PLAN.
BONDAGE TIME
OKAY, WELL. THE CONVENTION HALL IS SET UP. I'LL NEED TO CHECK WITH YOU ABOUT THE BANQUET, THE KITCHEN WILL NEED EXACT NUMBERS.
ONE PROBLEM.
WE AGREED THAT YOU WOULD HAVE THE ENTIRE HOTEL FOR YOUR CONVENTION.
"WAALL, I'M AFRAID WE STILL HAVE TWO GUESTS HERE.
"THEY WERE MEANT TO LEAVE THIS MORNING. SHE WAS ON HER WAY TO VISIT HER BROTHER. TELEPHONED AHEAD THIS MORNING, AND THE POLICE ANSWERED. THE PO-LICE."
SOMETHING HAD HAPPENED TO HER PEOPLE, AND THE POLICE REQUESTED THAT SHE STAYED WHERE SHE WAS, IN CASE THEY NEED HER.
THE SHERIFF SPOKE TO ME, AND I EXPLAINED ABOUT THE CONVENTION, BUT HE SAID THEY STAY ON HERE. I DON'T WANT TROUBLE WITH THE LAW, BUB.
I SEE. HMM. PLEASE ENSURE THAT THEY STAY OUT OF CONVENTION AREAS, THEN.
I DID ALREADY. THEY'VE SAID THEY'LL KEEP THEMSELVES TO THEIR ROOMS.

IN A PERFECT WORLD, ROSE WALKER WOULD BE SITTING IN THE CAR WITH HER BROTHER, JED, NEXT TO HER. GILBERT WOULD BE IN THE BACK.

THEY'D BE DRIVING BACK TO THE ROOMS ROSE RENTED, THEN SHE AND JED WOULD FLY BACK TO BOSTON.

PERFECT WORLD.

JED. ROSE. MOM. TOGETHER...

SHE HASN'T SEEN JED FOR SEVEN YEARS, SHE WAS FOURTEEN. HE WAS FIVE.

PERFECT.

SHE HAD WONDERED IF THEY'D RECOGNIZE EACH OTHER. SHE WAS SO PROUD OF HERSELF FOR TRACKING HIM DOWN.

ONE PHONE CALL. THAT'S ALL IT TOOK AND IT ALL CAME TUMBLING DOWN.

SHE PHONED AHEAD. LET THEM KNOW SHE WAS COMING.

THE POLICE ANSWERED.

PERFECT IT WOULD HAVE BEEN PERFECT IT WOULD HAVE BEEN--

PERFECT.

KNOCK KNOCK

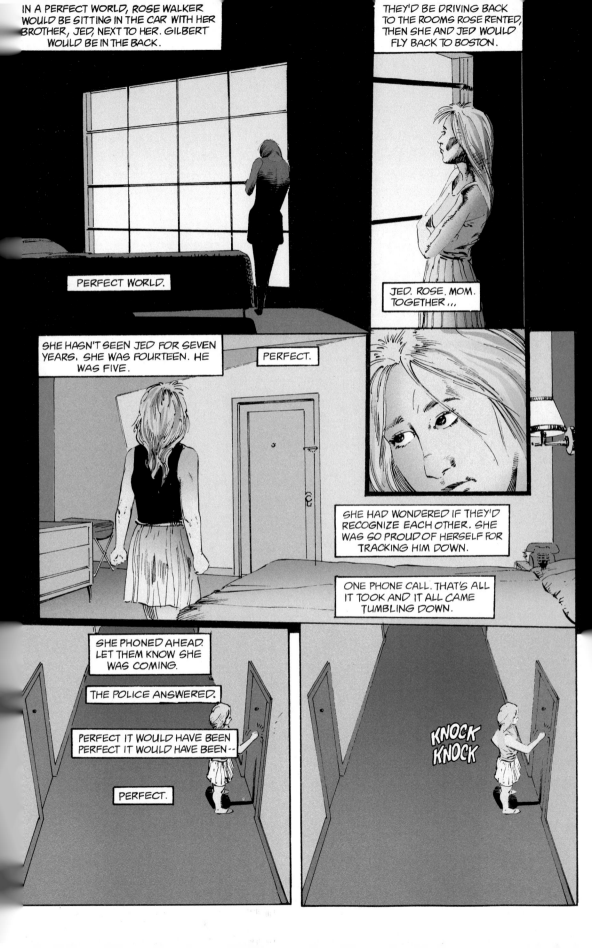

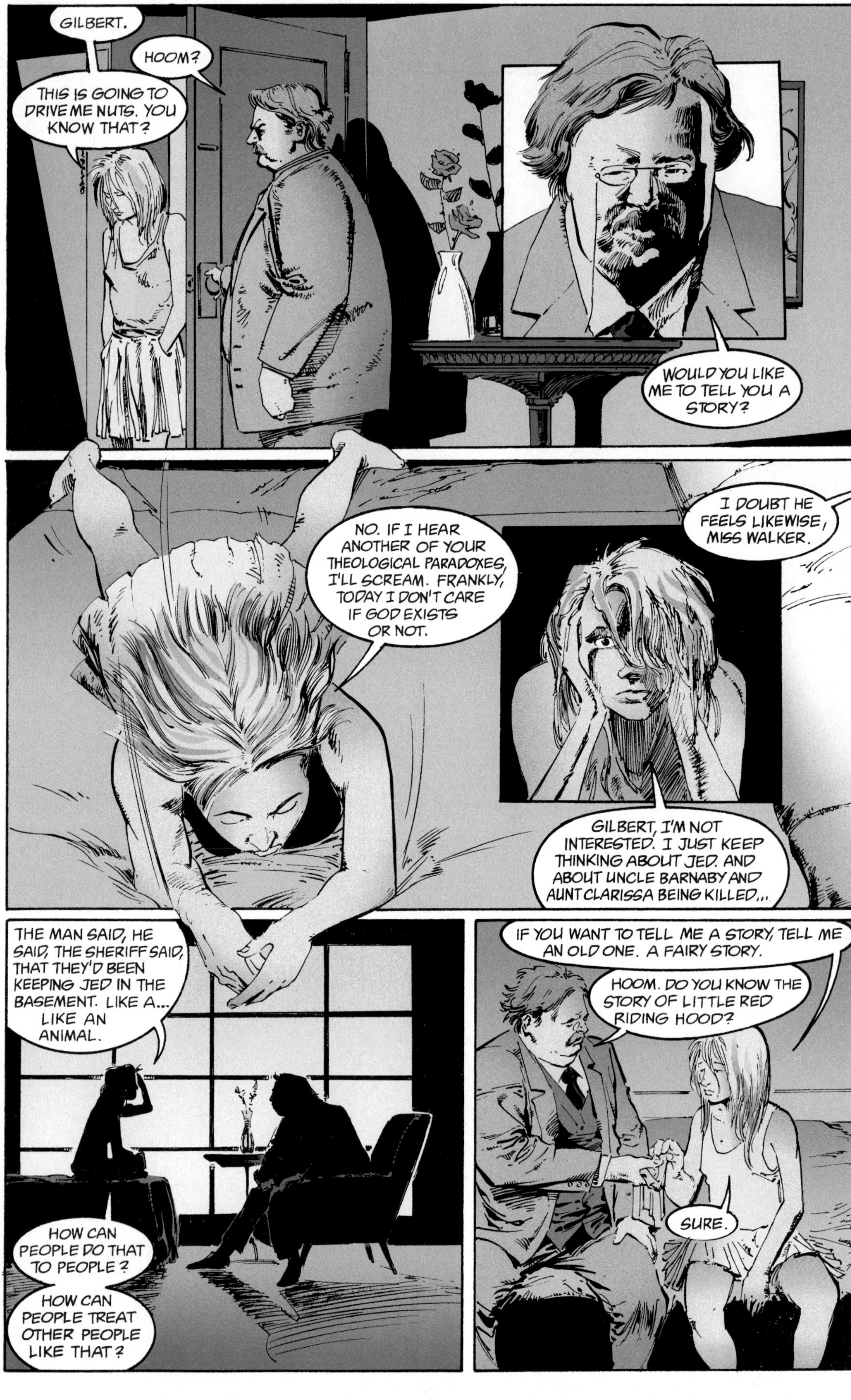
GILBERT.
HOOM?
THIS IS GOING TO DRIVE ME NUTS. YOU KNOW THAT?
WOULD YOU LIKE ME TO TELL YOU A STORY?
NO. IF I HEAR ANOTHER OF YOUR THEOLOGICAL PARADOXES, I'LL SCREAM. FRANKLY, TODAY I DON'T CARE IF GOD EXISTS OR NOT.
I DOUBT HE FEELS LIKEWISE, MISS WALKER.
GILBERT, I'M NOT INTERESTED. I JUST KEEP THINKING ABOUT JED. AND ABOUT UNCLE BARNABY AND AUNT CLARISSA BEING KILLED...
THE MAN SAID, HE SAID, THE SHERIFF SAID, THAT THEY'D BEEN KEEPING JED IN THE BASEMENT. LIKE A... LIKE AN ANIMAL.
HOW CAN PEOPLE DO THAT TO PEOPLE?
HOW CAN PEOPLE TREAT OTHER PEOPLE LIKE THAT?
IF YOU WANT TO TELL ME A STORY, TELL ME AN OLD ONE. A FAIRY STORY.
HOOM. DO YOU KNOW THE STORY OF LITTLE RED RIDING HOOD?
SURE.

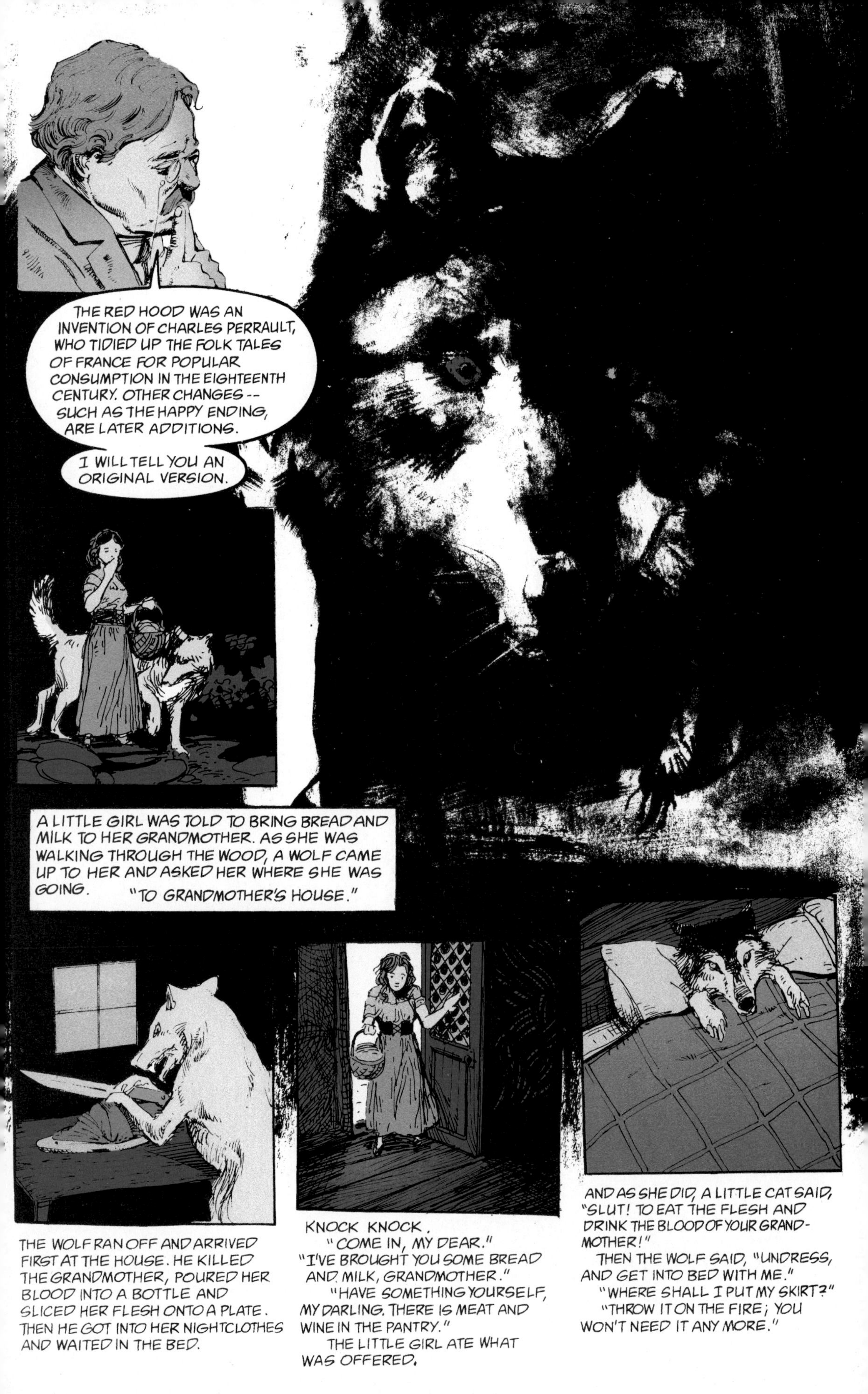
THE RED HOOD WAS AN INVENTION OF CHARLES PERRAULT, WHO TIDIED UP THE FOLK TALES OF FRANCE FOR POPULAR CONSUMPTION IN THE EIGHTEENTH CENTURY. OTHER CHANGES -- SUCH AS THE HAPPY ENDING, ARE LATER ADDITIONS.
I WILL TELL YOU AN ORIGINAL VERSION.
A LITTLE GIRL WAS TOLD TO BRING BREAD AND MILK TO HER GRANDMOTHER. AS SHE WAS WALKING THROUGH THE WOOD, A WOLF CAME UP TO HER AND ASKED HER WHERE SHE WAS GOING. "TO GRANDMOTHER'S HOUSE."
THE WOLF RAN OFF AND ARRIVED FIRST AT THE HOUSE. HE KILLED THE GRANDMOTHER, POURED HER BLOOD INTO A BOTTLE AND SLICED HER FLESH ONTO A PLATE. THEN HE GOT INTO HER NIGHTCLOTHES AND WAITED IN THE BED.
KNOCK KNOCK. "COME IN, MY DEAR." "I'VE BROUGHT YOU SOME BREAD AND MILK, GRANDMOTHER." "HAVE SOMETHING YOURSELF, MY DARLING. THERE IS MEAT AND WINE IN THE PANTRY." THE LITTLE GIRL ATE WHAT WAS OFFERED.
AND AS SHE DID, A LITTLE CAT SAID, "SLUT! TO EAT THE FLESH AND DRINK THE BLOOD OF YOUR GRANDMOTHER!" THEN THE WOLF SAID, "UNDRESS, AND GET INTO BED WITH ME." "WHERE SHALL I PUT MY SKIRT?" "THROW IT ON THE FIRE; YOU WON'T NEED IT ANY MORE."

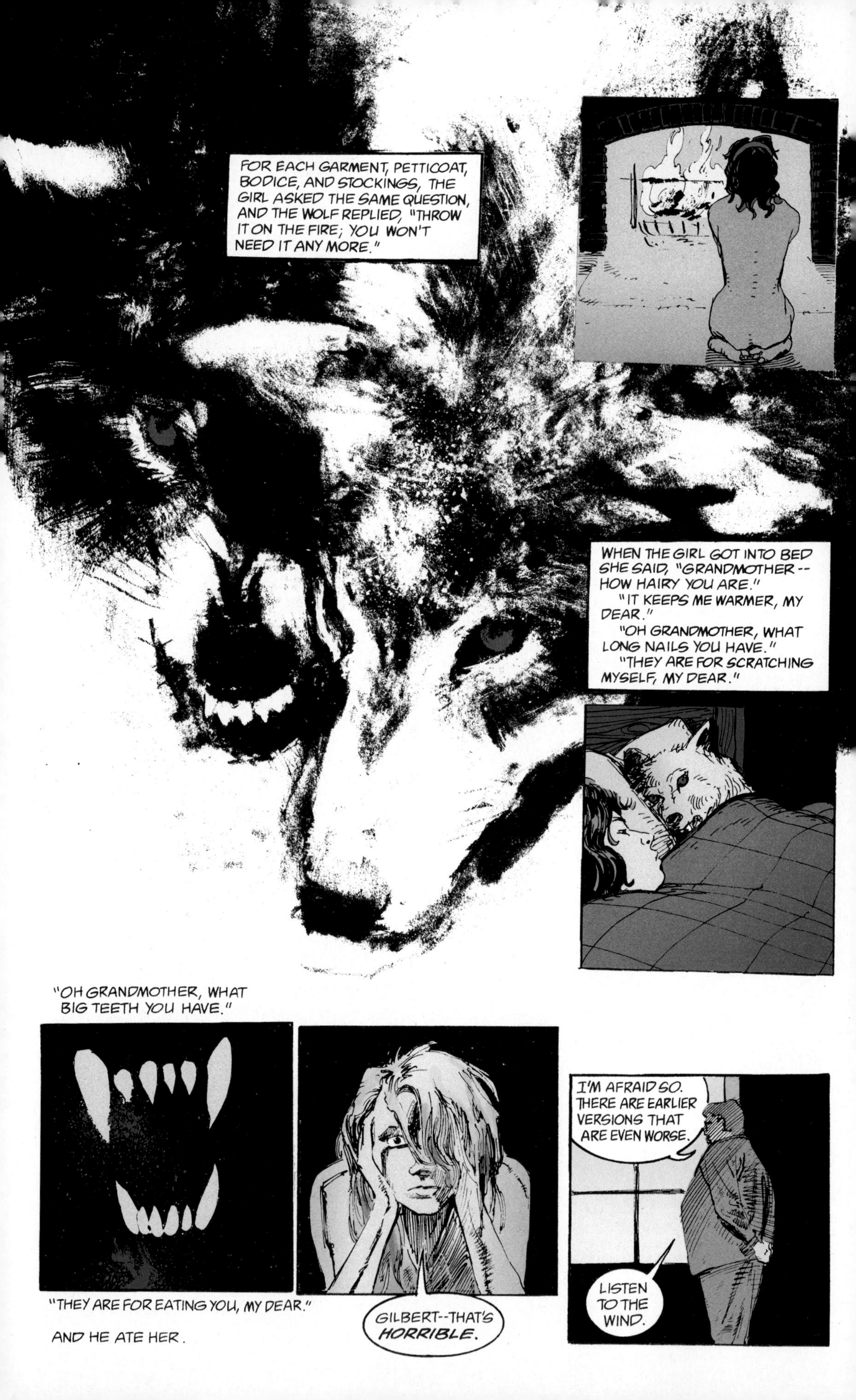
FOR EACH GARMENT, PETTICOAT, BODICE, AND STOCKINGS, THE GIRL ASKED THE SAME QUESTION, AND THE WOLF REPLIED, "THROW IT ON THE FIRE; YOU WON'T NEED IT ANY MORE."
WHEN THE GIRL GOT INTO BED SHE SAID, "GRANDMOTHER-- HOW HAIRY YOU ARE."
"IT KEEPS ME WARMER, MY DEAR."
"OH GRANDMOTHER, WHAT LONG NAILS YOU HAVE."
"THEY ARE FOR SCRATCHING MYSELF, MY DEAR."
"OH GRANDMOTHER, WHAT BIG TEETH YOU HAVE."
"THEY ARE FOR EATING YOU, MY DEAR."
AND HE ATE HER.
GILBERT--THAT'S HORRIBLE.
I'M AFRAID SO. THERE ARE EARLIER VERSIONS THAT ARE EVEN WORSE.
LISTEN TO THE WIND.

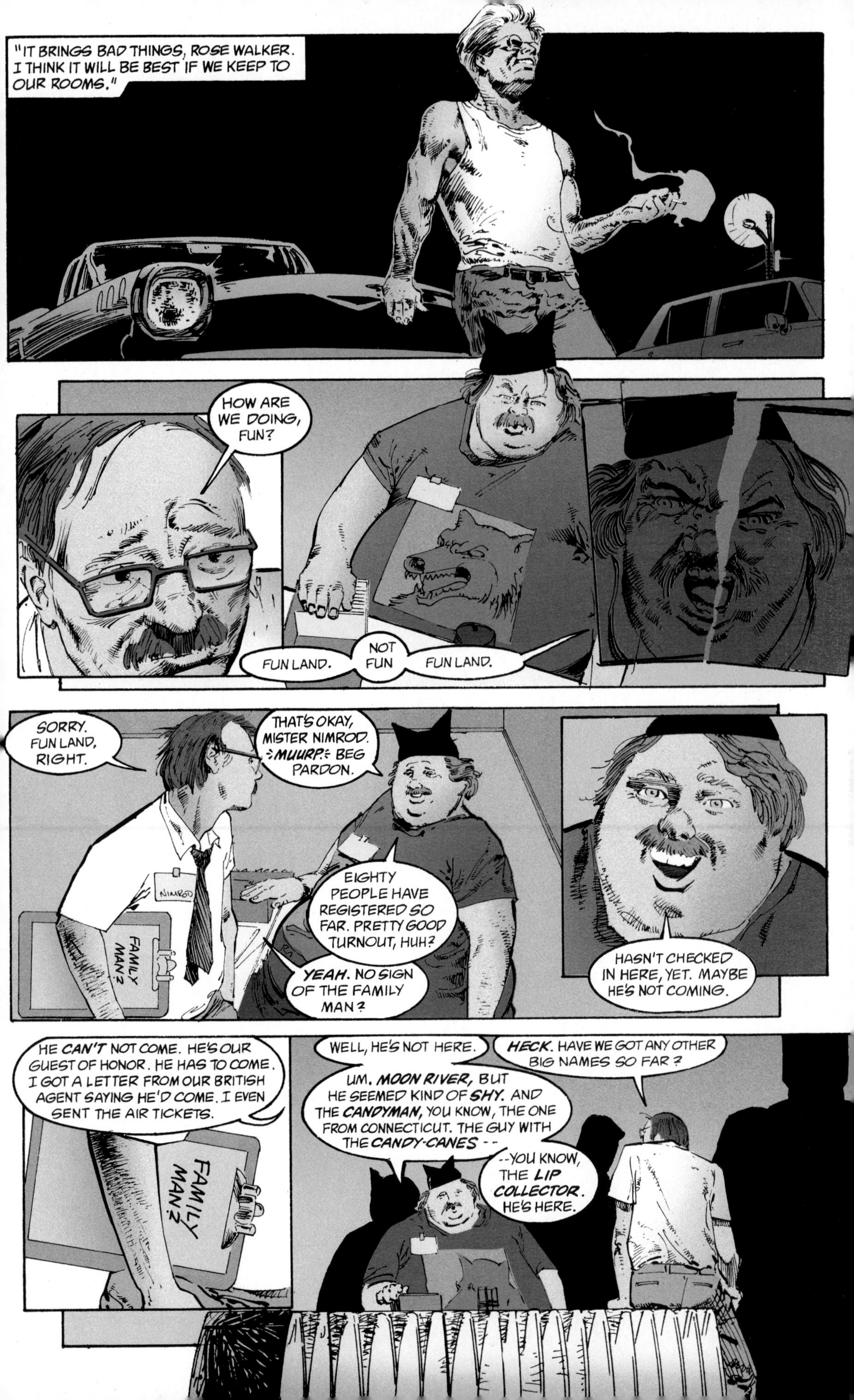
"IT BRINGS BAD THINGS, ROSE WALKER. I THINK IT WILL BE BEST IF WE KEEP TO OUR ROOMS."
HOW ARE WE DOING, FUN?
FUN LAND.
NOT FUN
FUN LAND.
SORRY. FUN LAND, RIGHT.
THAT'S OKAY, MISTER NIMROD. ÷MUURP÷ BEG PARDON.
NIMROD
EIGHTY PEOPLE HAVE REGISTERED SO FAR. PRETTY GOOD TURNOUT, HUH?
FAMILY MAN?
YEAH. NO SIGN OF THE FAMILY MAN?
HASN'T CHECKED IN HERE, YET. MAYBE HE'S NOT COMING.
HE CAN'T NOT COME. HE'S OUR GUEST OF HONOR. HE HAS TO COME. I GOT A LETTER FROM OUR BRITISH AGENT SAYING HE'D COME. I EVEN SENT THE AIR TICKETS.
FAMILY MAN?
WELL, HE'S NOT HERE.
HECK. HAVE WE GOT ANY OTHER BIG NAMES SO FAR?
UM. MOON RIVER, BUT HE SEEMED KIND OF SHY. AND THE CANDYMAN, YOU KNOW, THE ONE FROM CONNECTICUT. THE GUY WITH THE CANDY-CANES --
--YOU KNOW, THE LIP COLLECTOR. HE'S HERE.

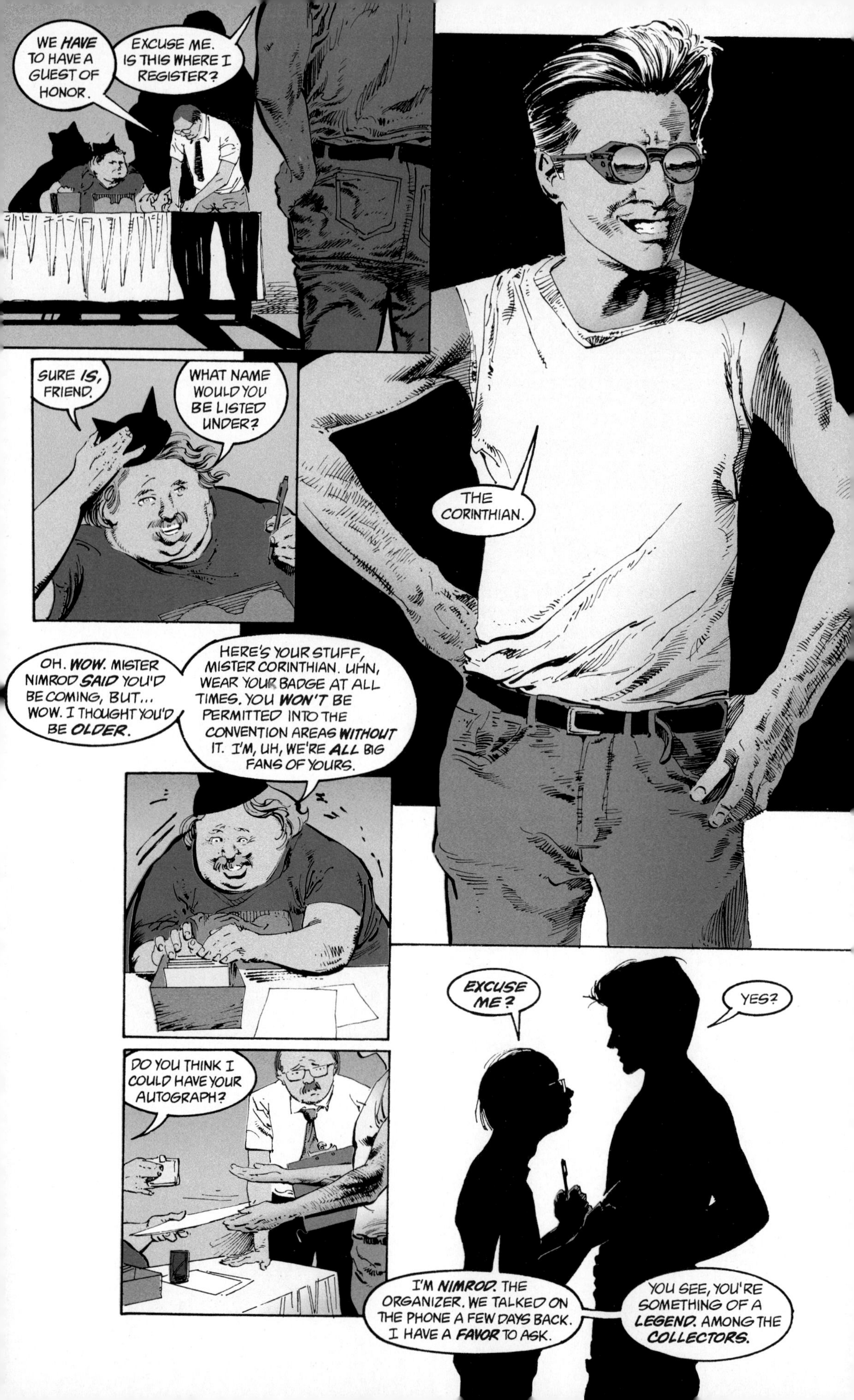
WE HAVE TO HAVE A GUEST OF HONOR.
EXCUSE ME. IS THIS WHERE I REGISTER?
SURE IS, FRIEND.
WHAT NAME WOULD YOU BE LISTED UNDER?
THE CORINTHIAN.
OH. WOW. MISTER NIMROD SAID YOU'D BE COMING, BUT... WOW. I THOUGHT YOU'D BE OLDER.
HERE'S YOUR STUFF, MISTER CORINTHIAN. UHN, WEAR YOUR BADGE AT ALL TIMES. YOU WON'T BE PERMITTED INTO THE CONVENTION AREAS WITHOUT IT. I'M, UH, WE'RE ALL BIG FANS OF YOURS.
DO YOU THINK I COULD HAVE YOUR AUTOGRAPH?
EXCUSE ME?
YES?
I'M NIMROD. THE ORGANIZER. WE TALKED ON THE PHONE A FEW DAYS BACK. I HAVE A FAVOR TO ASK.
YOU SEE, YOU'RE SOMETHING OF A LEGEND. AMONG THE COLLECTORS.

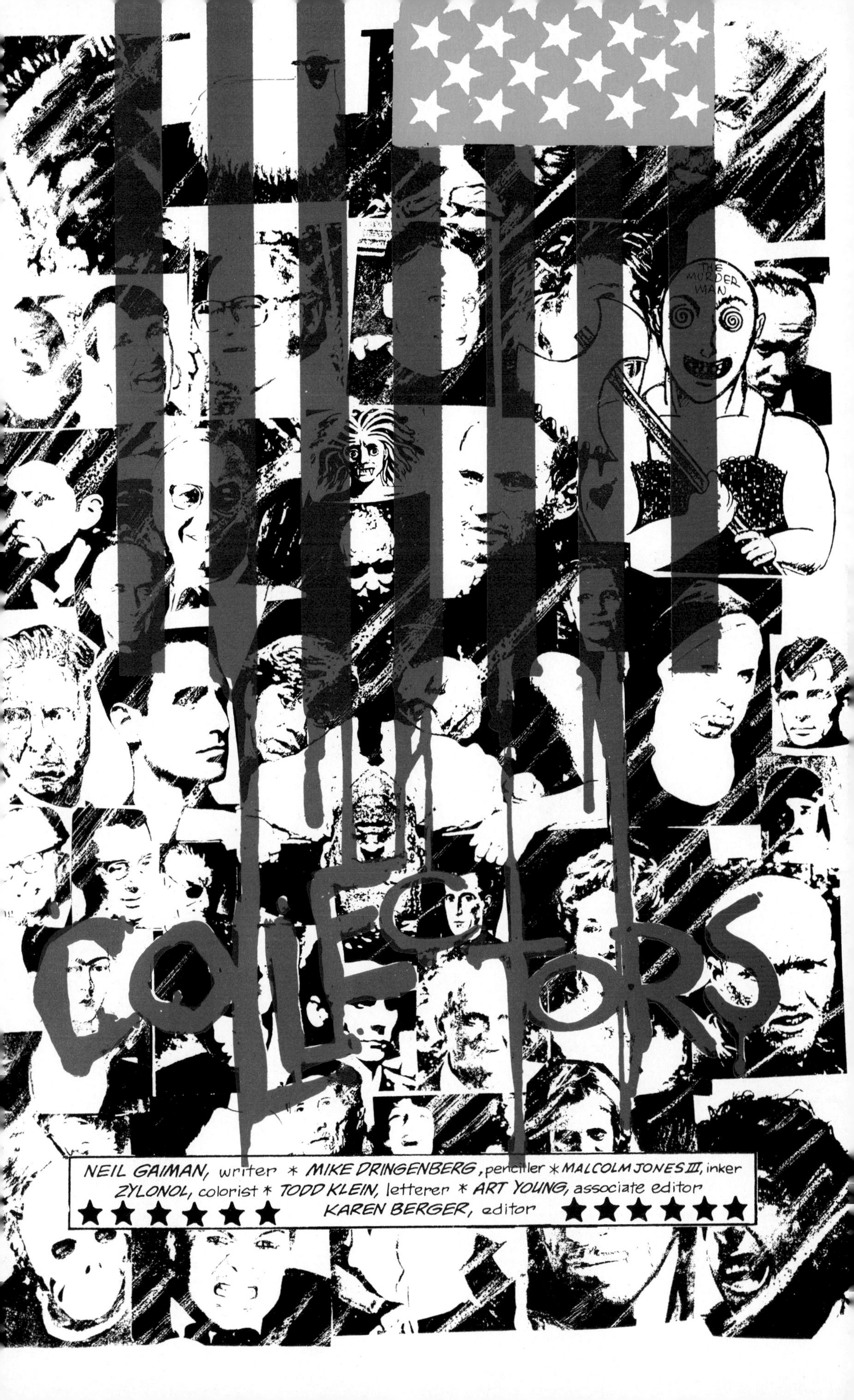
THE MURDER MAN
COLLECTORS
NEIL GAIMAN, writer * MIKE DRINGENBERG, penciller * MALCOLM JONES III, inker
ZYLONOL, colorist * TODD KLEIN, letterer * ART YOUNG, associate editor
KAREN BERGER, editor

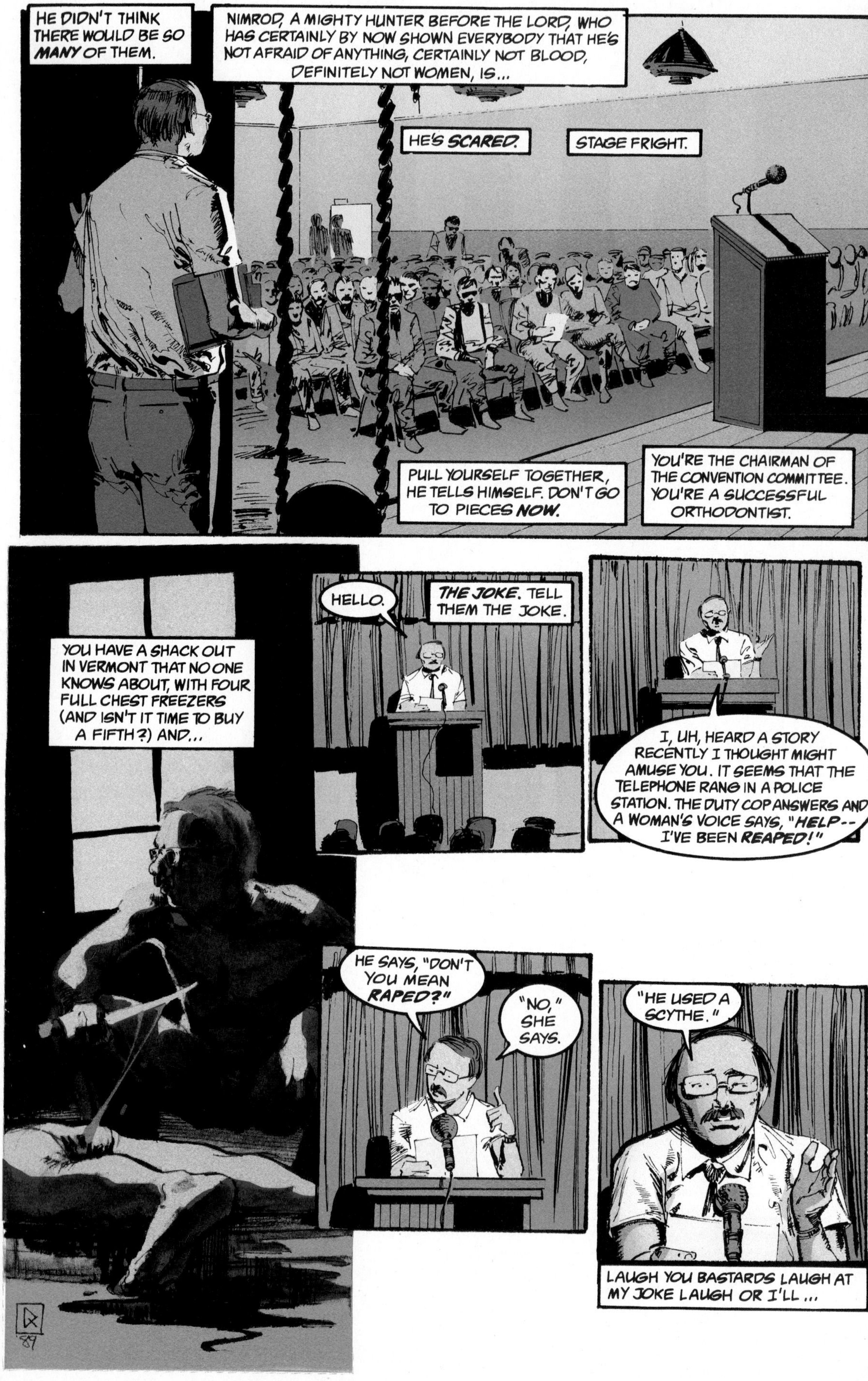

HE DIDN'T THINK THERE WOULD BE SO *MANY* OF THEM.
NIMROD, A MIGHTY HUNTER BEFORE THE LORD, WHO HAS CERTAINLY BY NOW SHOWN EVERYBODY THAT HE'S NOT AFRAID OF ANYTHING, CERTAINLY NOT BLOOD, DEFINITELY NOT WOMEN, IS...
HE'S *SCARED.*
STAGE FRIGHT.
PULL YOURSELF TOGETHER, HE TELLS HIMSELF. DON'T GO TO PIECES *NOW.*
YOU'RE THE CHAIRMAN OF THE CONVENTION COMMITTEE. YOU'RE A SUCCESSFUL ORTHODONTIST.
YOU HAVE A SHACK OUT IN VERMONT THAT NO ONE KNOWS ABOUT, WITH FOUR FULL CHEST FREEZERS (AND ISN'T IT TIME TO BUY A FIFTH?) AND...
HELLO.
THE JOKE. TELL THEM THE JOKE.
I, UH, HEARD A STORY RECENTLY I THOUGHT MIGHT AMUSE YOU. IT SEEMS THAT THE TELEPHONE RANG IN A POLICE STATION. THE DUTY COP ANSWERS AND A WOMAN'S VOICE SAYS, "*HELP--* I'VE BEEN *REAPED!*"
HE SAYS, "DON'T YOU MEAN *RAPED?*"
"NO," SHE SAYS.
"HE USED A SCYTHE."
LAUGH YOU BASTARDS LAUGH AT MY JOKE LAUGH OR I'LL...
'89

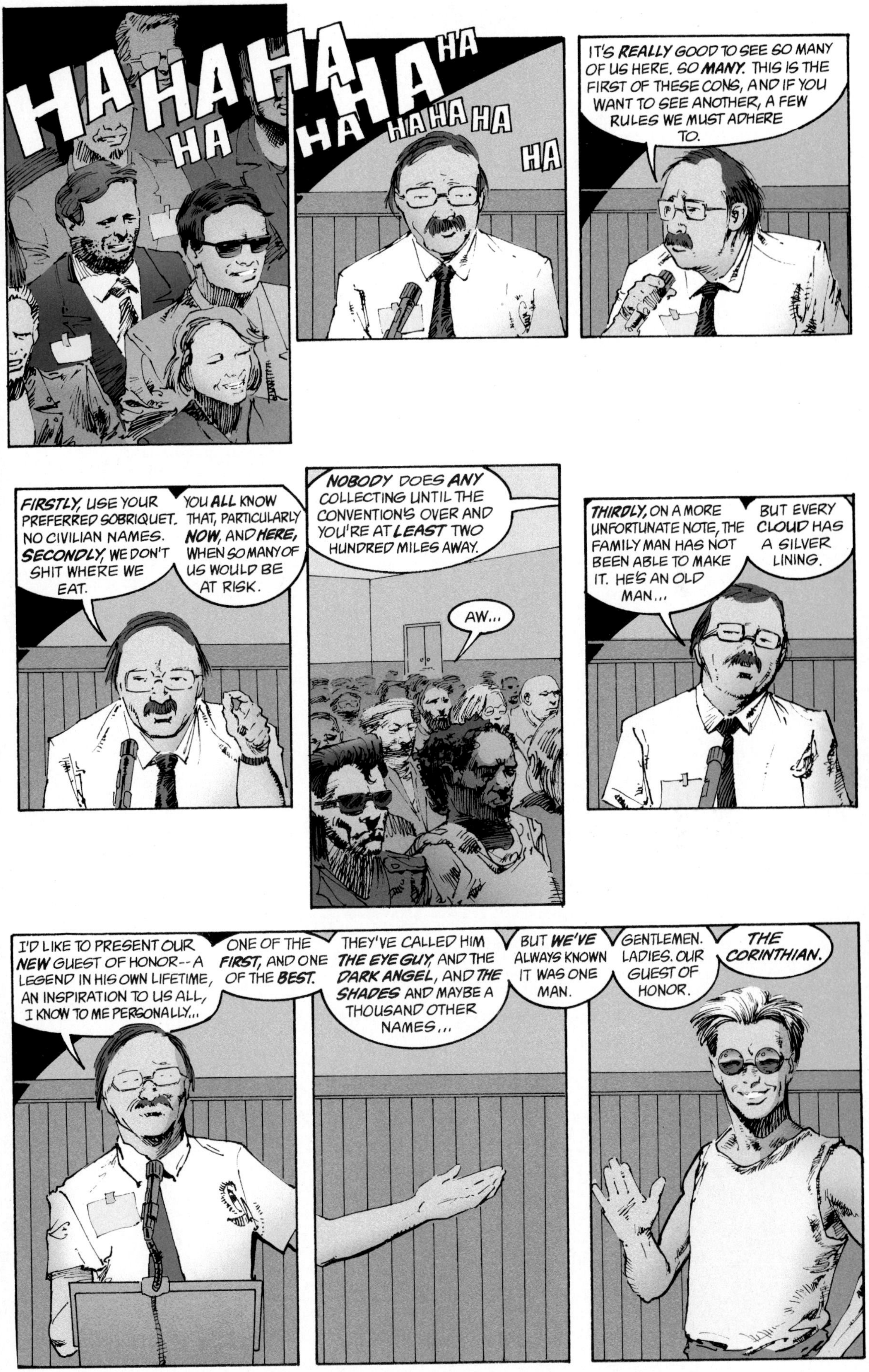
HAHAHAHAHAHA HA HA HAHAHAHA HA
IT'S REALLY GOOD TO SEE SO MANY OF US HERE. SO MANY. THIS IS THE FIRST OF THESE CONS, AND IF YOU WANT TO SEE ANOTHER, A FEW RULES WE MUST ADHERE TO.
FIRSTLY, USE YOUR PREFERRED SOBRIQUET. NO CIVILIAN NAMES. SECONDLY, WE DON'T SHIT WHERE WE EAT.
YOU ALL KNOW THAT, PARTICULARLY NOW, AND HERE, WHEN SO MANY OF US WOULD BE AT RISK.
NOBODY DOES ANY COLLECTING UNTIL THE CONVENTION'S OVER AND YOU'RE AT LEAST TWO HUNDRED MILES AWAY.
AW...
THIRDLY, ON A MORE UNFORTUNATE NOTE, THE FAMILY MAN HAS NOT BEEN ABLE TO MAKE IT. HE'S AN OLD MAN...
BUT EVERY CLOUD HAS A SILVER LINING.
I'D LIKE TO PRESENT OUR NEW GUEST OF HONOR-- A LEGEND IN HIS OWN LIFETIME, AN INSPIRATION TO US ALL, I KNOW TO ME PERSONALLY...
ONE OF THE FIRST, AND ONE OF THE BEST.
THEY'VE CALLED HIM THE EYE GUY, AND THE DARK ANGEL, AND THE SHADES AND MAYBE A THOUSAND OTHER NAMES...
BUT WE'VE ALWAYS KNOWN IT WAS ONE MAN.
GENTLEMEN. LADIES. OUR GUEST OF HONOR.
THE CORINTHIAN.

YOU KNOW WHAT'S SO *GREAT* ABOUT SOMETHING LIKE THIS?

NO.

WE'RE ALL SO *DIFFERENT*. UNITED BY OUR COMMON INTERESTS. THAT'S *GREAT*.

FILM PROGRAM

DON'T LOOK NOW 8:30
THE COLLECTOR 10:00
MANHUNTER 11:30
FROM THE LIFE OF THE MARIONETTES 1:00
IN COLD BLOOD 2:30
COMPULSION 4:00
STRAIGHT ON TILL MORNING 5:
RRY ON SCREAM!
IGHT OF THE H

SATURDAY.

WHAT'RE YOU LOOKING AT?

THE FILM PROGRAM. THEY'RE SHOWING *THE COLLECTOR*. A REMARKABLE NOVEL. WHEN I FIRST READ THAT BOOK, I THOUGHT--

--FOR THE *FIRST* TIME, I AM UNDERSTOOD.

EXCUSE ME, BUT I'VE SEEN YOU *BEFORE*, HAVEN'T I? YOU'RE THAT *DOCTOR*. WOW--TO THINK THAT *YOU'RE* A--THAT YOU'RE A COLLECTOR. *WOW.*

⸢Khoff⸣. MM. THANK YOU. *YOU* ARE?

I'M THE *BOGEYMAN*.

I'VE HEARD OF YOU. THE *NEWSPAPERS*, IN THEIR FACILE WAY, HAVE CHRISTENED ME *FLAY-BY-NIGHT*. SEVENTY-NINE.

SORRY?

"GIVE ME A NUMBER." THAT'S YOUR LINE, ISN'T IT? *SEVENTY-NINE*.

OH YEAH, RIGHT. SHE WAS, LIKE, SHE HAD THESE BEAUTIFUL EYES, LIKE PATCHES OF SKY EARLY IN THE MORNING, AND SHE SCREAMED LIKE AN ANGEL.

SAY, YOU EVER READ A MAGAZINE CALLED *CHASTE*? IT'S REALLY TERRIFIC.

I'VE HEARD OF IT.

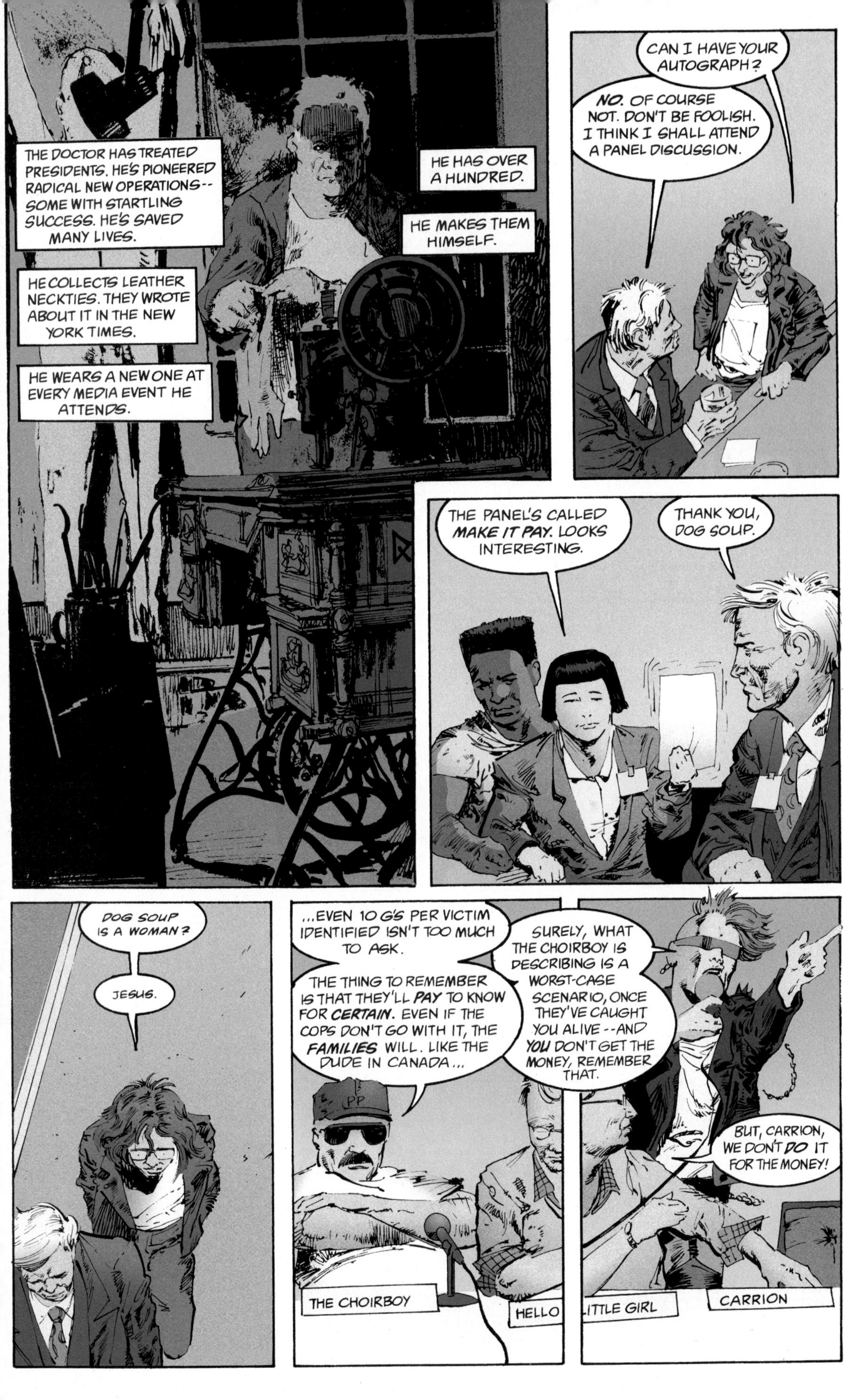
THE DOCTOR HAS TREATED PRESIDENTS. HE'S PIONEERED RADICAL NEW OPERATIONS-- SOME WITH STARTLING SUCCESS. HE'S SAVED MANY LIVES.
HE COLLECTS LEATHER NECKTIES. THEY WROTE ABOUT IT IN THE NEW YORK TIMES.
HE WEARS A NEW ONE AT EVERY MEDIA EVENT HE ATTENDS.
HE HAS OVER A HUNDRED.
HE MAKES THEM HIMSELF.
CAN I HAVE YOUR AUTOGRAPH?
NO. OF COURSE NOT. DON'T BE FOOLISH. I THINK I SHALL ATTEND A PANEL DISCUSSION.
THE PANEL'S CALLED MAKE IT PAY. LOOKS INTERESTING.
THANK YOU, DOG SOUP.
DOG SOUP IS A WOMAN?
JESUS.
...EVEN 10 G'S PER VICTIM IDENTIFIED ISN'T TOO MUCH TO ASK.
THE THING TO REMEMBER IS THAT THEY'LL PAY TO KNOW FOR CERTAIN. EVEN IF THE COPS DON'T GO WITH IT, THE FAMILIES WILL. LIKE THE DUDE IN CANADA...
SURELY, WHAT THE CHOIRBOY IS DESCRIBING IS A WORST-CASE SCENARIO, ONCE THEY'VE CAUGHT YOU ALIVE--AND YOU DON'T GET THE MONEY, REMEMBER THAT.
BUT, CARRION, WE DON'T DO IT FOR THE MONEY!
THE CHOIRBOY
HELLO LITTLE GIRL
CARRION

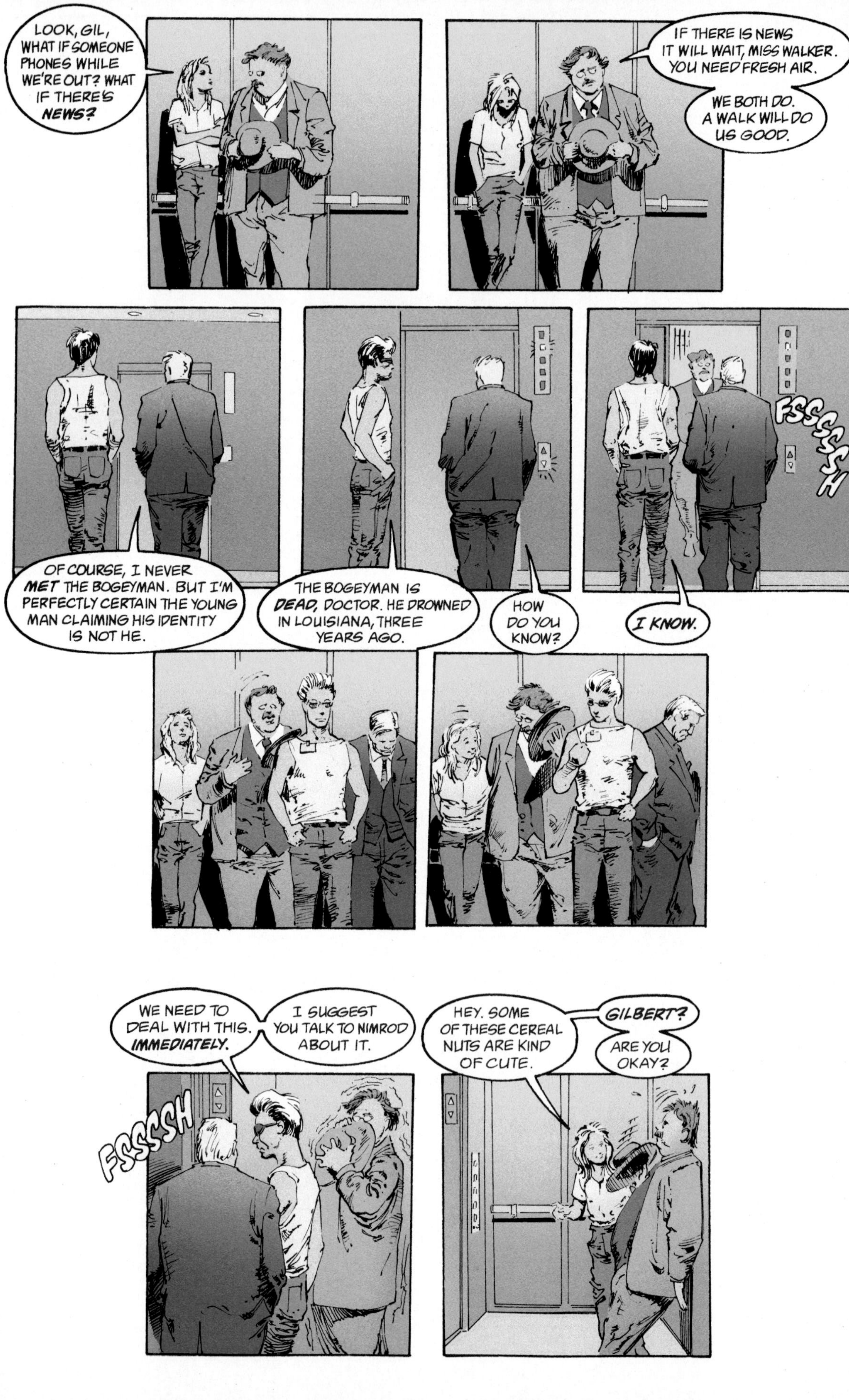

LOOK, GIL, WHAT IF SOMEONE PHONES WHILE WE'RE OUT? WHAT IF THERE'S NEWS?
IF THERE IS NEWS IT WILL WAIT, MISS WALKER. YOU NEED FRESH AIR.
WE BOTH DO. A WALK WILL DO US GOOD.
OF COURSE, I NEVER MET THE BOGEYMAN. BUT I'M PERFECTLY CERTAIN THE YOUNG MAN CLAIMING HIS IDENTITY IS NOT HE.
THE BOGEYMAN IS DEAD, DOCTOR. HE DROWNED IN LOUISIANA, THREE YEARS AGO.
HOW DO YOU KNOW?
I KNOW.
FSSSSSH
WE NEED TO DEAL WITH THIS. IMMEDIATELY.
I SUGGEST YOU TALK TO NIMROD ABOUT IT.
FSSSSH
HEY. SOME OF THESE CEREAL NUTS ARE KIND OF CUTE.
GILBERT?
ARE YOU OKAY?

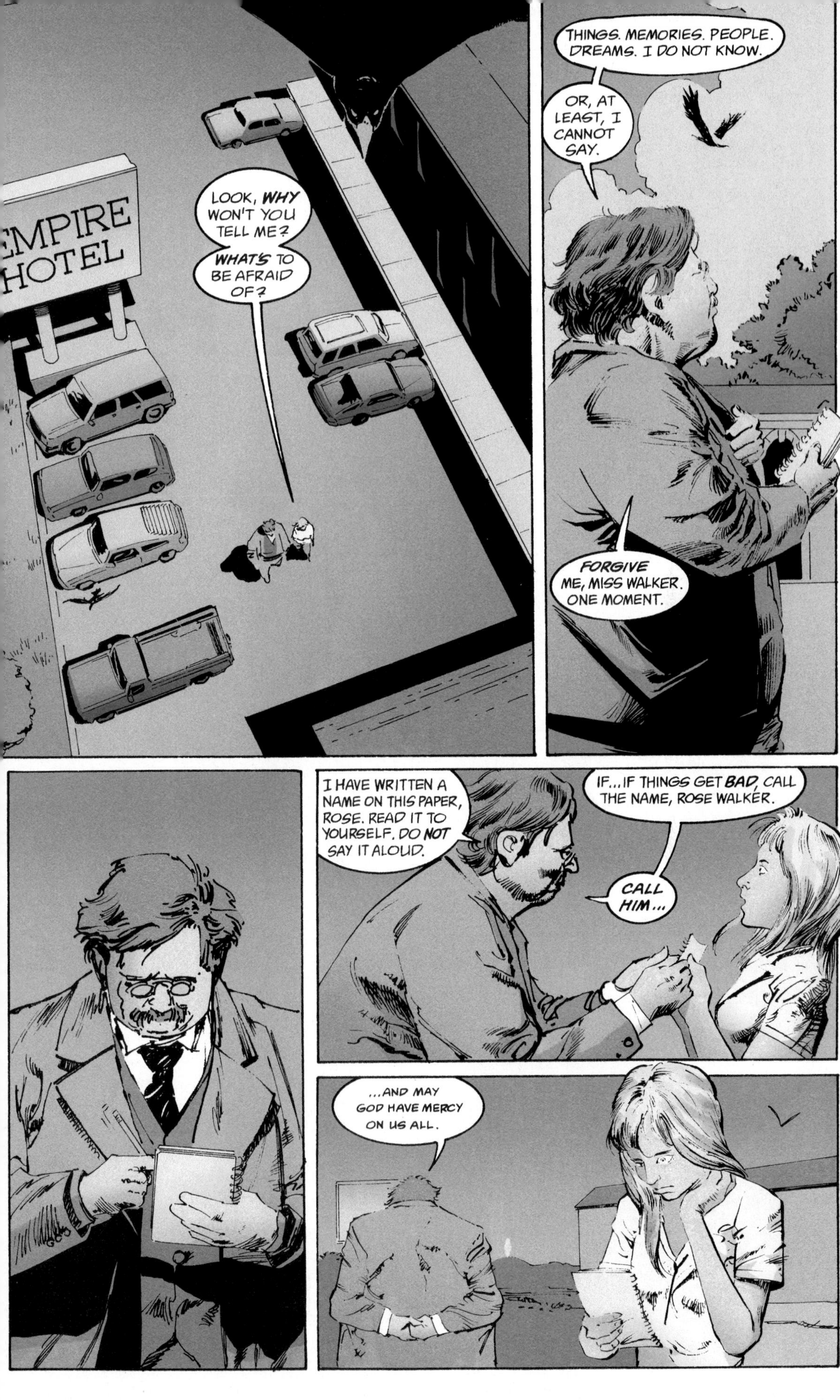

EMPIRE HOTEL
LOOK, WHY WON'T YOU TELL ME?
WHAT'S TO BE AFRAID OF?
THINGS. MEMORIES. PEOPLE. DREAMS. I DO NOT KNOW.
OR, AT LEAST, I CANNOT SAY.
FORGIVE ME, MISS WALKER. ONE MOMENT.
I HAVE WRITTEN A NAME ON THIS PAPER, ROSE. READ IT TO YOURSELF. DO NOT SAY IT ALOUD.
IF... IF THINGS GET BAD, CALL THE NAME, ROSE WALKER.
CALL HIM...
...AND MAY GOD HAVE MERCY ON US ALL.

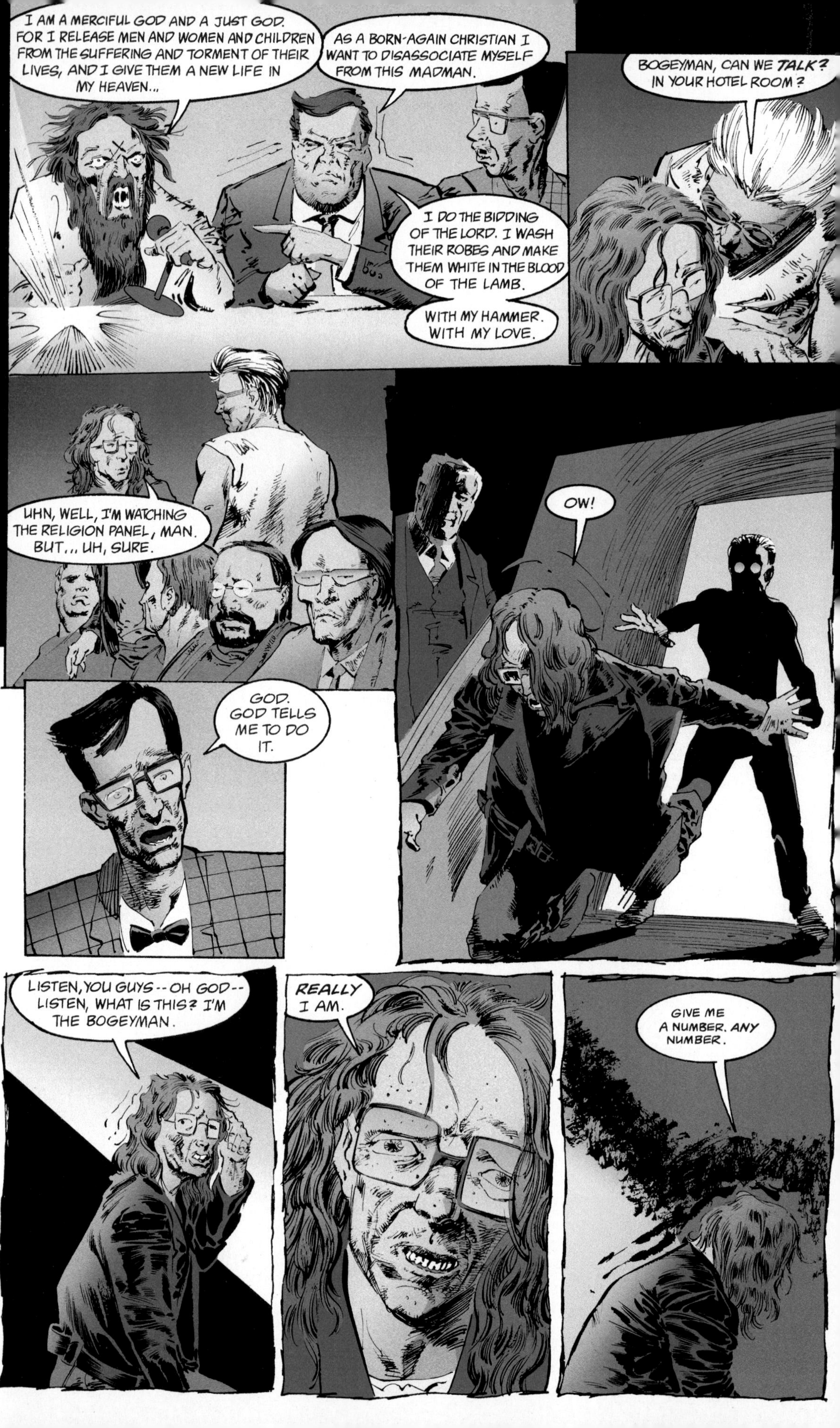
I AM A MERCIFUL GOD AND A JUST GOD. FOR I RELEASE MEN AND WOMEN AND CHILDREN FROM THE SUFFERING AND TORMENT OF THEIR LIVES, AND I GIVE THEM A NEW LIFE IN MY HEAVEN...
AS A BORN-AGAIN CHRISTIAN I WANT TO DISASSOCIATE MYSELF FROM THIS MADMAN.
I DO THE BIDDING OF THE LORD. I WASH THEIR ROBES AND MAKE THEM WHITE IN THE BLOOD OF THE LAMB.
WITH MY HAMMER. WITH MY LOVE.
BOGEYMAN, CAN WE TALK? IN YOUR HOTEL ROOM?
UHN, WELL, I'M WATCHING THE RELIGION PANEL, MAN. BUT... UH, SURE.
GOD. GOD TELLS ME TO DO IT.
OW!
LISTEN, YOU GUYS -- OH GOD -- LISTEN, WHAT IS THIS? I'M THE BOGEYMAN.
REALLY I AM.
GIVE ME A NUMBER. ANY NUMBER.

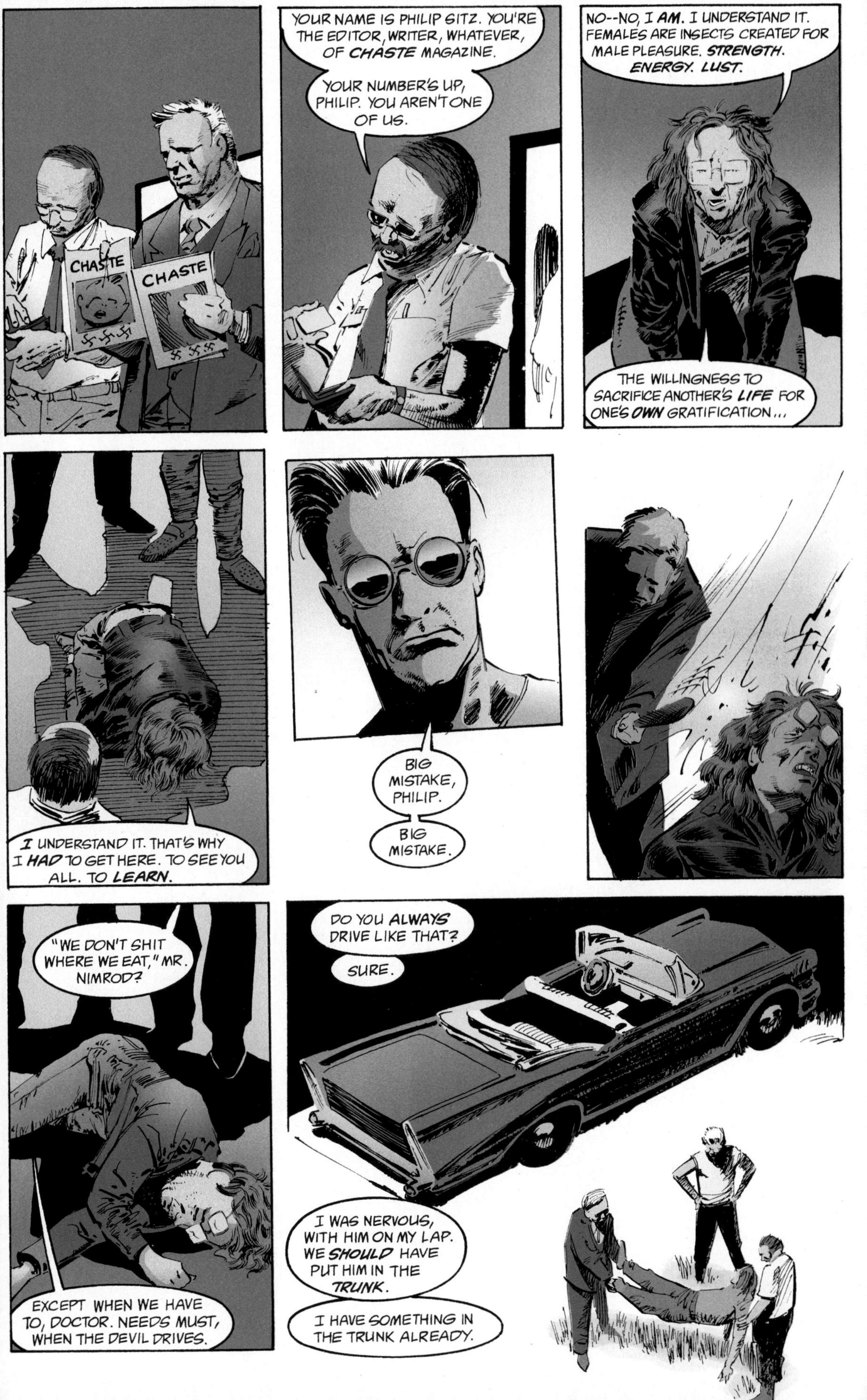
CHASTE
CHASTE
YOUR NAME IS PHILIP SITZ. YOU'RE THE EDITOR, WRITER, WHATEVER, OF CHASTE MAGAZINE.
YOUR NUMBER'S UP, PHILIP. YOU AREN'T ONE OF US.
NO--NO, I AM. I UNDERSTAND IT. FEMALES ARE INSECTS CREATED FOR MALE PLEASURE. STRENGTH. ENERGY. LUST.
THE WILLINGNESS TO SACRIFICE ANOTHER'S LIFE FOR ONE'S OWN GRATIFICATION...
I UNDERSTAND IT. THAT'S WHY I HAD TO GET HERE. TO SEE YOU ALL. TO LEARN.
BIG MISTAKE, PHILIP.
BIG MISTAKE.
"WE DON'T SHIT WHERE WE EAT," MR. NIMROD?
EXCEPT WHEN WE HAVE TO, DOCTOR. NEEDS MUST, WHEN THE DEVIL DRIVES.
DO YOU ALWAYS DRIVE LIKE THAT?
SURE.
I WAS NERVOUS, WITH HIM ON MY LAP. WE SHOULD HAVE PUT HIM IN THE TRUNK.
I HAVE SOMETHING IN THE TRUNK ALREADY.

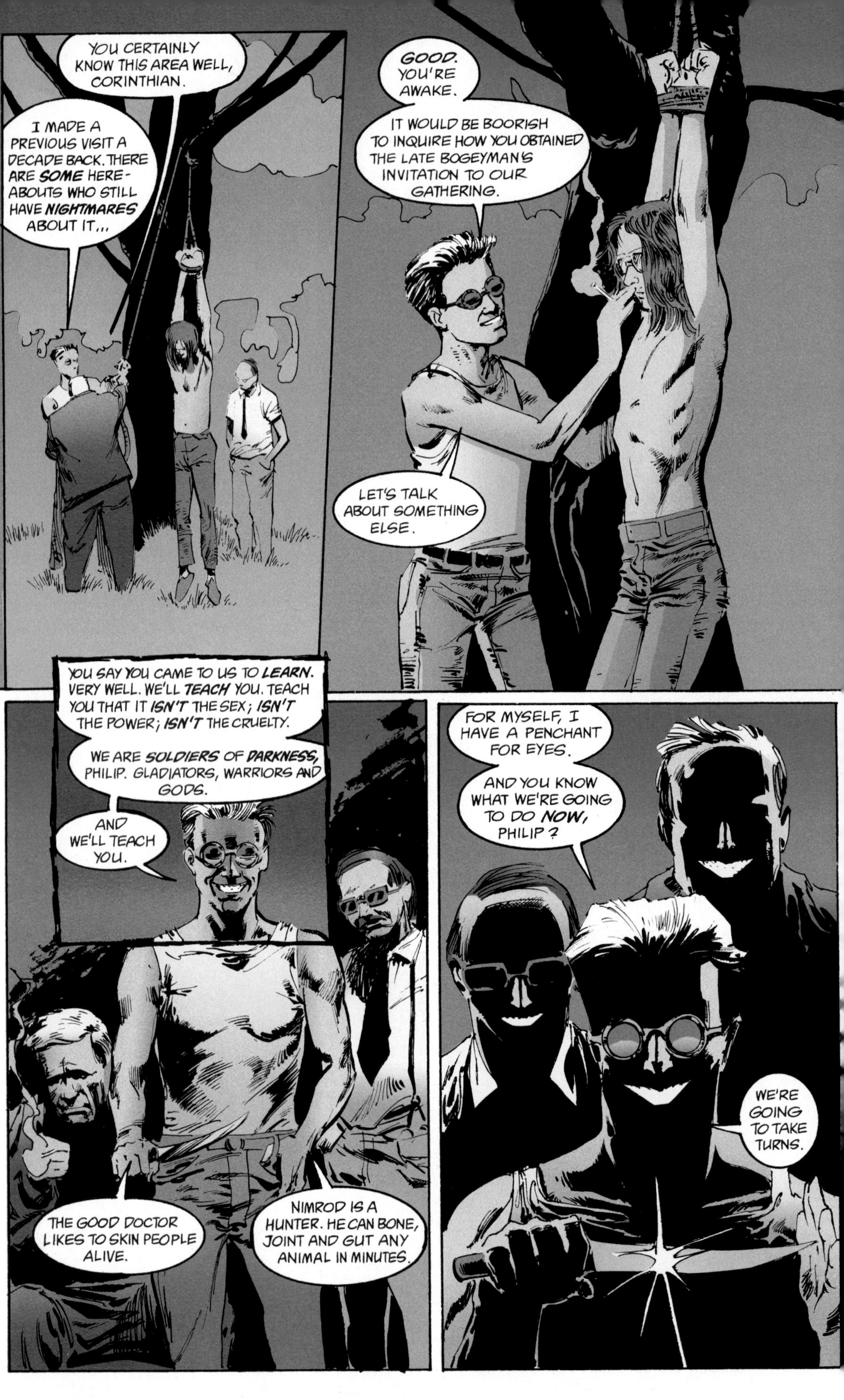
YOU CERTAINLY KNOW THIS AREA WELL, CORINTHIAN.
I MADE A PREVIOUS VISIT A DECADE BACK. THERE ARE SOME HERE-ABOUTS WHO STILL HAVE NIGHTMARES ABOUT IT...
GOOD. YOU'RE AWAKE.
IT WOULD BE BOORISH TO INQUIRE HOW YOU OBTAINED THE LATE BOGEYMAN'S INVITATION TO OUR GATHERING.
LET'S TALK ABOUT SOMETHING ELSE.
YOU SAY YOU CAME TO US TO LEARN. VERY WELL. WE'LL TEACH YOU. TEACH YOU THAT IT ISN'T THE SEX; ISN'T THE POWER; ISN'T THE CRUELTY.
WE ARE SOLDIERS OF DARKNESS, PHILIP. GLADIATORS, WARRIORS AND GODS.
AND WE'LL TEACH YOU.
THE GOOD DOCTOR LIKES TO SKIN PEOPLE ALIVE.
NIMROD IS A HUNTER. HE CAN BONE, JOINT AND GUT ANY ANIMAL IN MINUTES.
FOR MYSELF, I HAVE A PENCHANT FOR EYES.
AND YOU KNOW WHAT WE'RE GOING TO DO NOW, PHILIP?
WE'RE GOING TO TAKE TURNS.

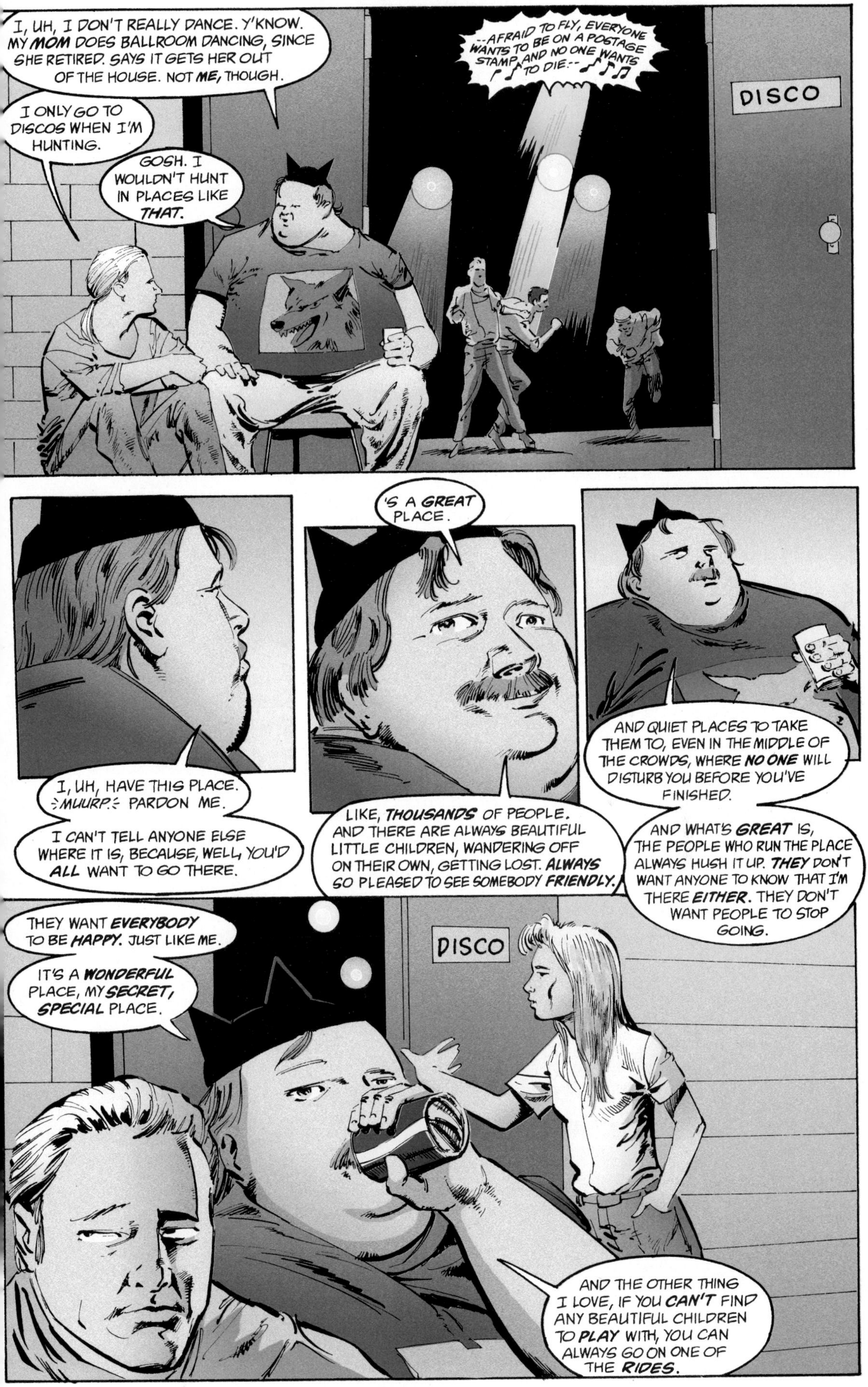
I, UH, I DON'T REALLY DANCE. Y'KNOW. MY MOM DOES BALLROOM DANCING, SINCE SHE RETIRED. SAYS IT GETS HER OUT OF THE HOUSE. NOT ME, THOUGH.
--AFRAID TO FLY, EVERYONE WANTS TO BE ON A POSTAGE STAMP, AND NO ONE WANTS TO DIE.--
DISCO
I ONLY GO TO DISCOS WHEN I'M HUNTING.
GOSH. I WOULDN'T HUNT IN PLACES LIKE THAT.
I, UH, HAVE THIS PLACE. MUURP. PARDON ME.
I CAN'T TELL ANYONE ELSE WHERE IT IS, BECAUSE, WELL, YOU'D ALL WANT TO GO THERE.
'S A GREAT PLACE.
LIKE, THOUSANDS OF PEOPLE. AND THERE ARE ALWAYS BEAUTIFUL LITTLE CHILDREN, WANDERING OFF ON THEIR OWN, GETTING LOST. ALWAYS SO PLEASED TO SEE SOMEBODY FRIENDLY.
AND QUIET PLACES TO TAKE THEM TO, EVEN IN THE MIDDLE OF THE CROWDS, WHERE NO ONE WILL DISTURB YOU BEFORE YOU'VE FINISHED.
AND WHAT'S GREAT IS, THE PEOPLE WHO RUN THE PLACE ALWAYS HUSH IT UP. THEY DON'T WANT ANYONE TO KNOW THAT I'M THERE EITHER. THEY DON'T WANT PEOPLE TO STOP GOING.
THEY WANT EVERYBODY TO BE HAPPY. JUST LIKE ME.
IT'S A WONDERFUL PLACE, MY SECRET, SPECIAL PLACE.
DISCO
AND THE OTHER THING I LOVE, IF YOU CAN'T FIND ANY BEAUTIFUL CHILDREN TO PLAY WITH, YOU CAN ALWAYS GO ON ONE OF THE RIDES.

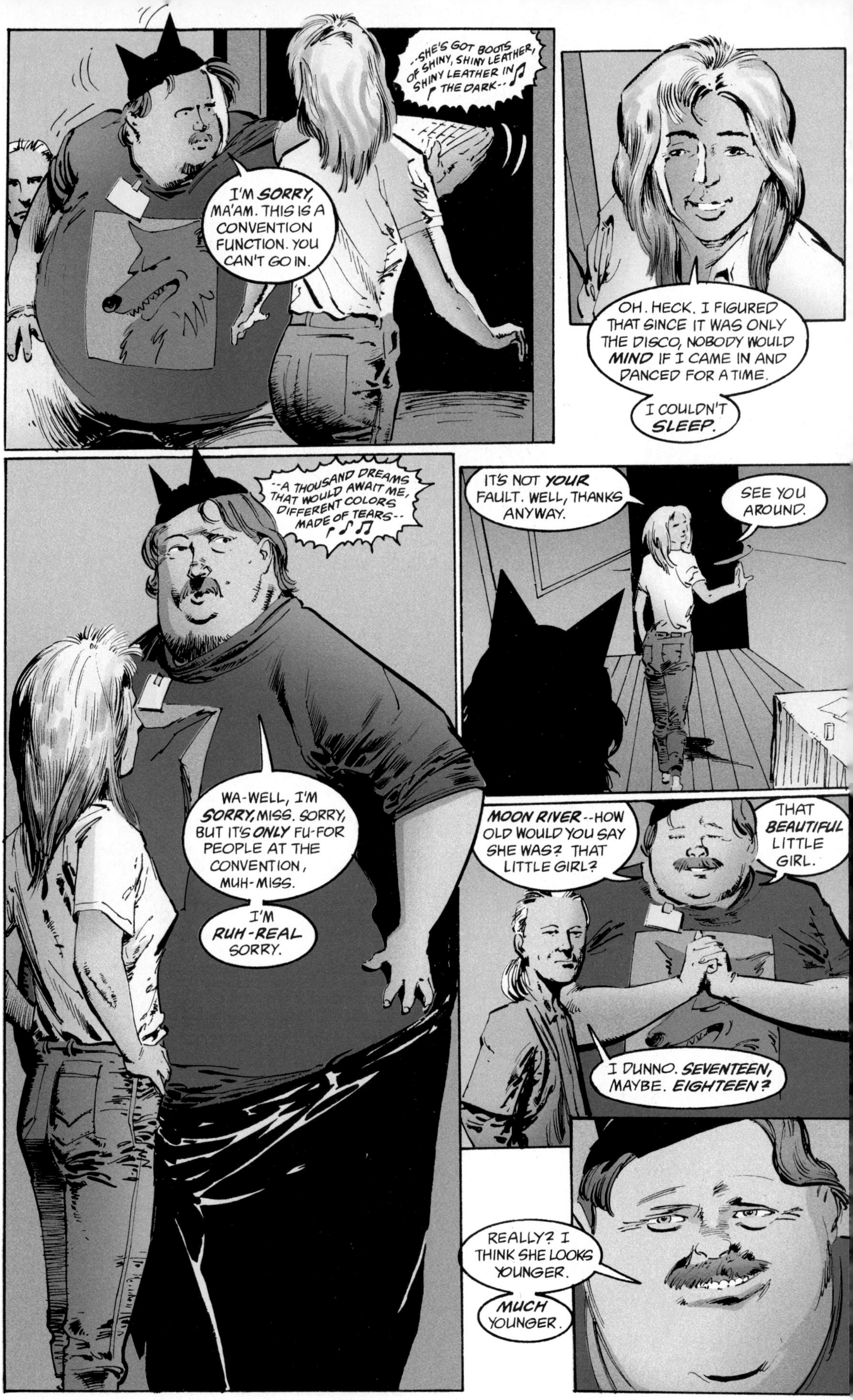
--SHE'S GOT BOOTS OF SHINY, SHINY LEATHER, SHINY LEATHER IN THE DARK--
I'M SORRY, MA'AM. THIS IS A CONVENTION FUNCTION. YOU CAN'T GO IN.
OH. HECK. I FIGURED THAT SINCE IT WAS ONLY THE DISCO, NOBODY WOULD MIND IF I CAME IN AND DANCED FOR A TIME.
I COULDN'T SLEEP.
--A THOUSAND DREAMS THAT WOULD AWAIT ME, DIFFERENT COLORS MADE OF TEARS--
WA-WELL, I'M SORRY, MISS. SORRY, BUT IT'S ONLY FU-FOR PEOPLE AT THE CONVENTION, MUH-MISS.
I'M RUH-REAL SORRY.
IT'S NOT YOUR FAULT. WELL, THANKS ANYWAY.
SEE YOU AROUND.
MOON RIVER--HOW OLD WOULD YOU SAY SHE WAS? THAT LITTLE GIRL?
THAT BEAUTIFUL LITTLE GIRL.
I DUNNO. SEVENTEEN, MAYBE. EIGHTEEN?
REALLY? I THINK SHE LOOKS YOUNGER.
MUCH YOUNGER.

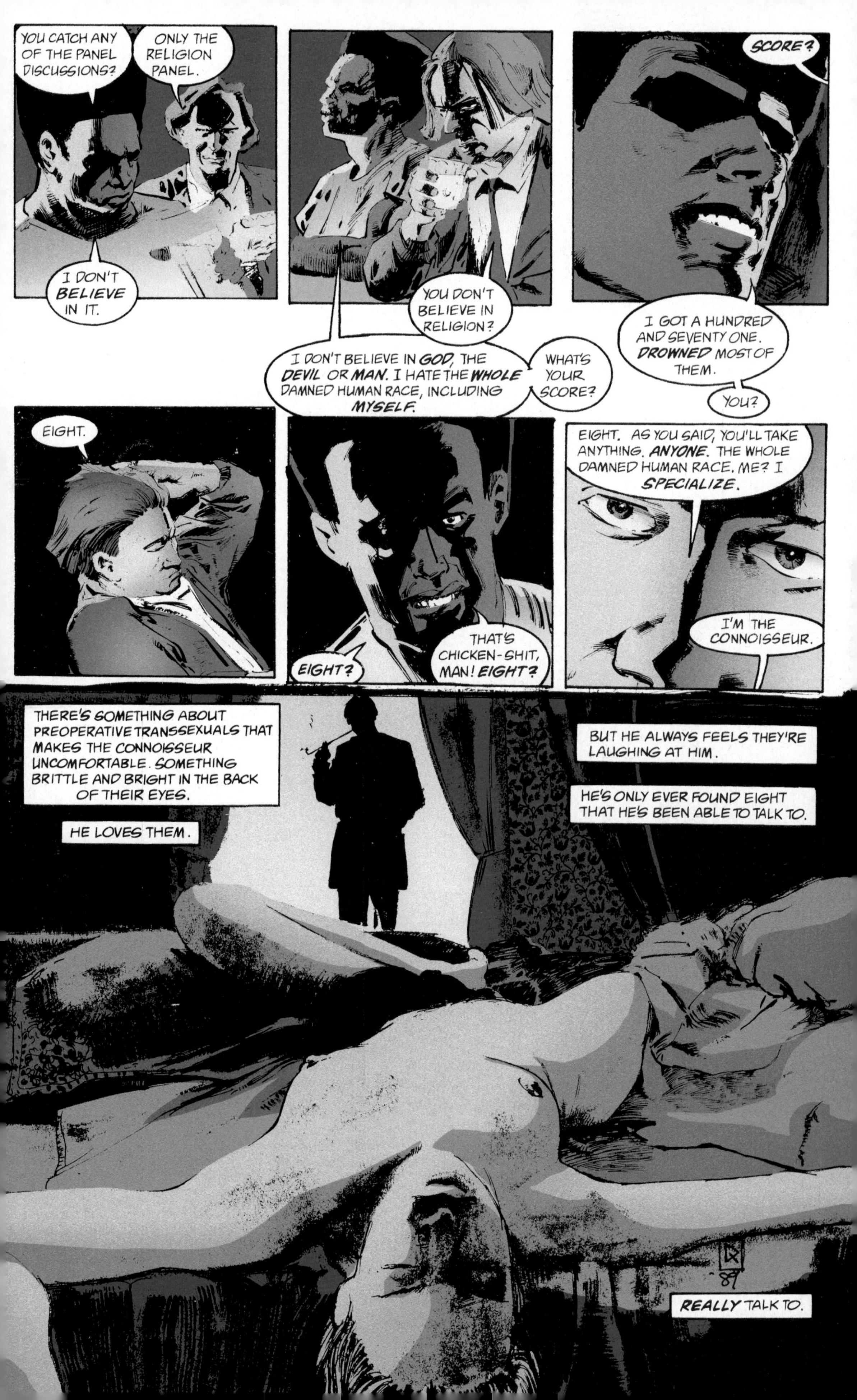

YOU CATCH ANY OF THE PANEL DISCUSSIONS?
ONLY THE RELIGION PANEL.
I DON'T BELIEVE IN IT.
YOU DON'T BELIEVE IN RELIGION?
I DON'T BELIEVE IN GOD, THE DEVIL OR MAN. I HATE THE WHOLE DAMNED HUMAN RACE, INCLUDING MYSELF.
WHAT'S YOUR SCORE?
SCORE?
I GOT A HUNDRED AND SEVENTY ONE. DROWNED MOST OF THEM.
YOU?
EIGHT.
EIGHT?
THAT'S CHICKEN-SHIT, MAN! EIGHT?
EIGHT. AS YOU SAID, YOU'LL TAKE ANYTHING. ANYONE. THE WHOLE DAMNED HUMAN RACE. ME? I SPECIALIZE.
I'M THE CONNOISSEUR.
THERE'S SOMETHING ABOUT PREOPERATIVE TRANSSEXUALS THAT MAKES THE CONNOISSEUR UNCOMFORTABLE. SOMETHING BRITTLE AND BRIGHT IN THE BACK OF THEIR EYES.
HE LOVES THEM.
BUT HE ALWAYS FEELS THEY'RE LAUGHING AT HIM.
HE'S ONLY EVER FOUND EIGHT THAT HE'S BEEN ABLE TO TALK TO.
REALLY TALK TO.

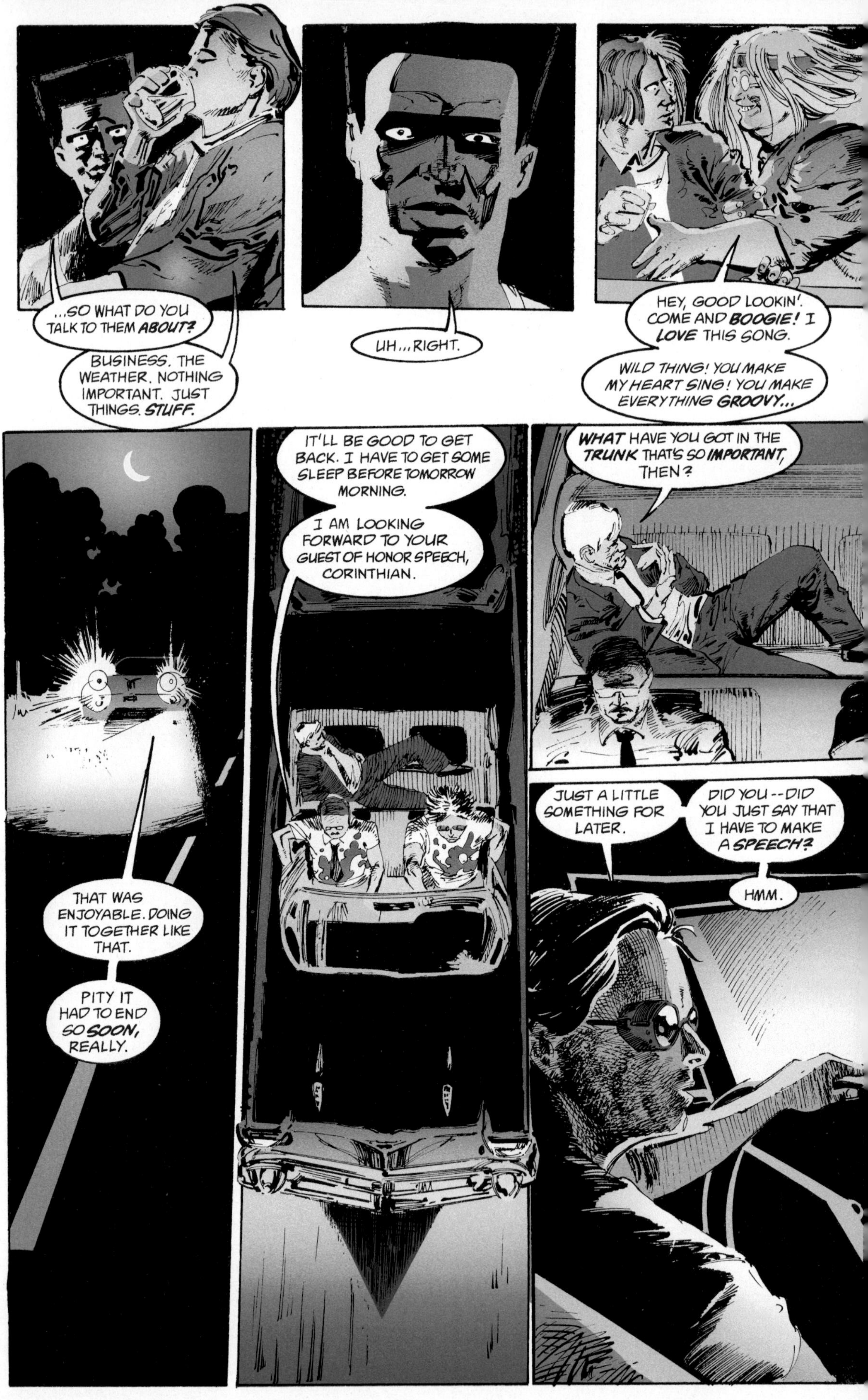

...SO WHAT DO YOU TALK TO THEM ABOUT?
BUSINESS. THE WEATHER. NOTHING IMPORTANT. JUST THINGS. STUFF.
UH...RIGHT.
HEY, GOOD LOOKIN'. COME AND BOOGIE! I LOVE THIS SONG.
WILD THING! YOU MAKE MY HEART SING! YOU MAKE EVERYTHING GROOVY...
THAT WAS ENJOYABLE. DOING IT TOGETHER LIKE THAT.
PITY IT HAD TO END SO SOON, REALLY.
IT'LL BE GOOD TO GET BACK. I HAVE TO GET SOME SLEEP BEFORE TOMORROW MORNING.
I AM LOOKING FORWARD TO YOUR GUEST OF HONOR SPEECH, CORINTHIAN.
WHAT HAVE YOU GOT IN THE TRUNK THAT'S SO IMPORTANT, THEN?
JUST A LITTLE SOMETHING FOR LATER.
DID YOU--DID YOU JUST SAY THAT I HAVE TO MAKE A SPEECH?
HMM.

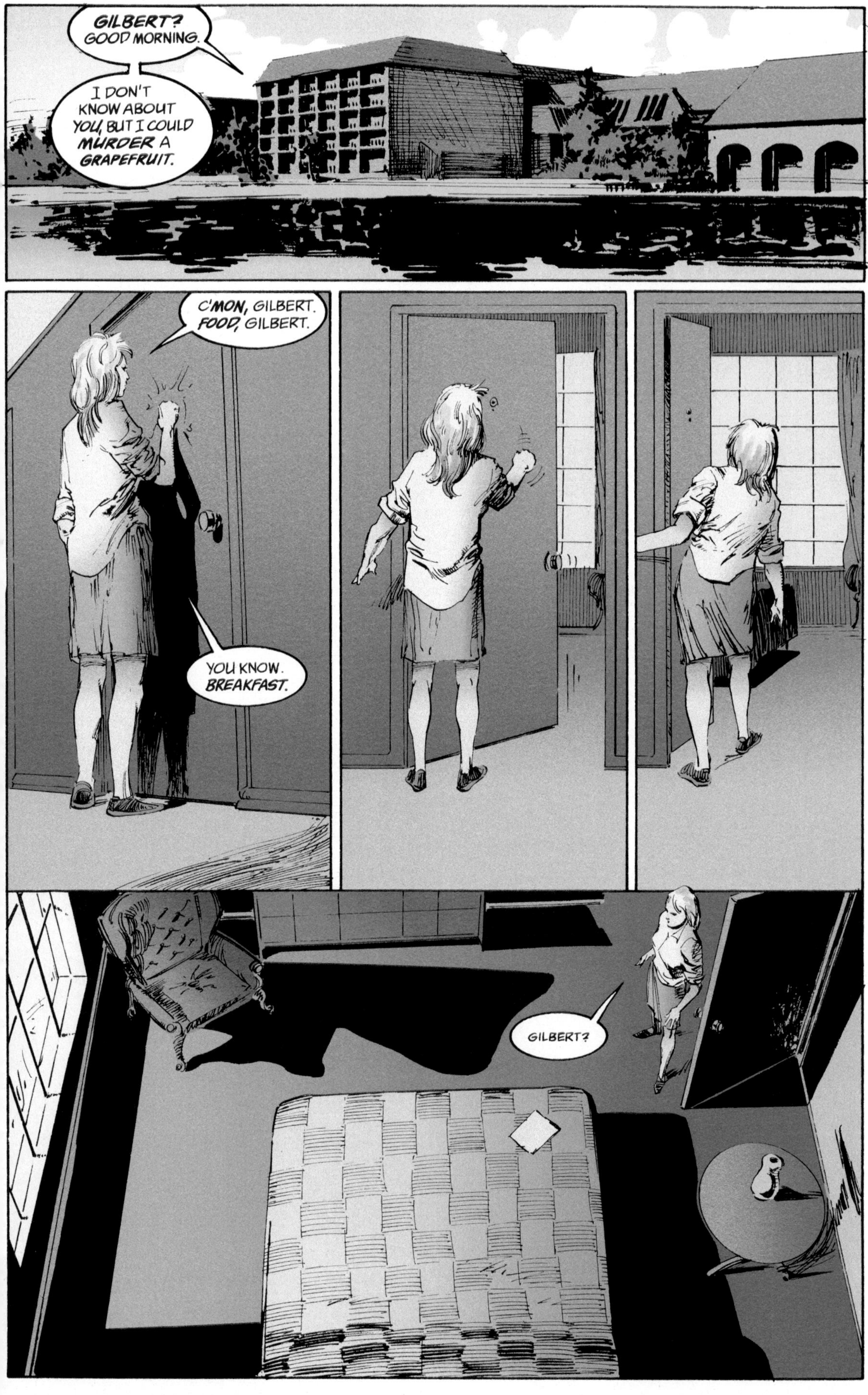
GILBERT? GOOD MORNING.
I DON'T KNOW ABOUT YOU, BUT I COULD MURDER A GRAPEFRUIT.
C'MON, GILBERT. FOOD, GILBERT.
YOU KNOW. BREAKFAST.
GILBERT?

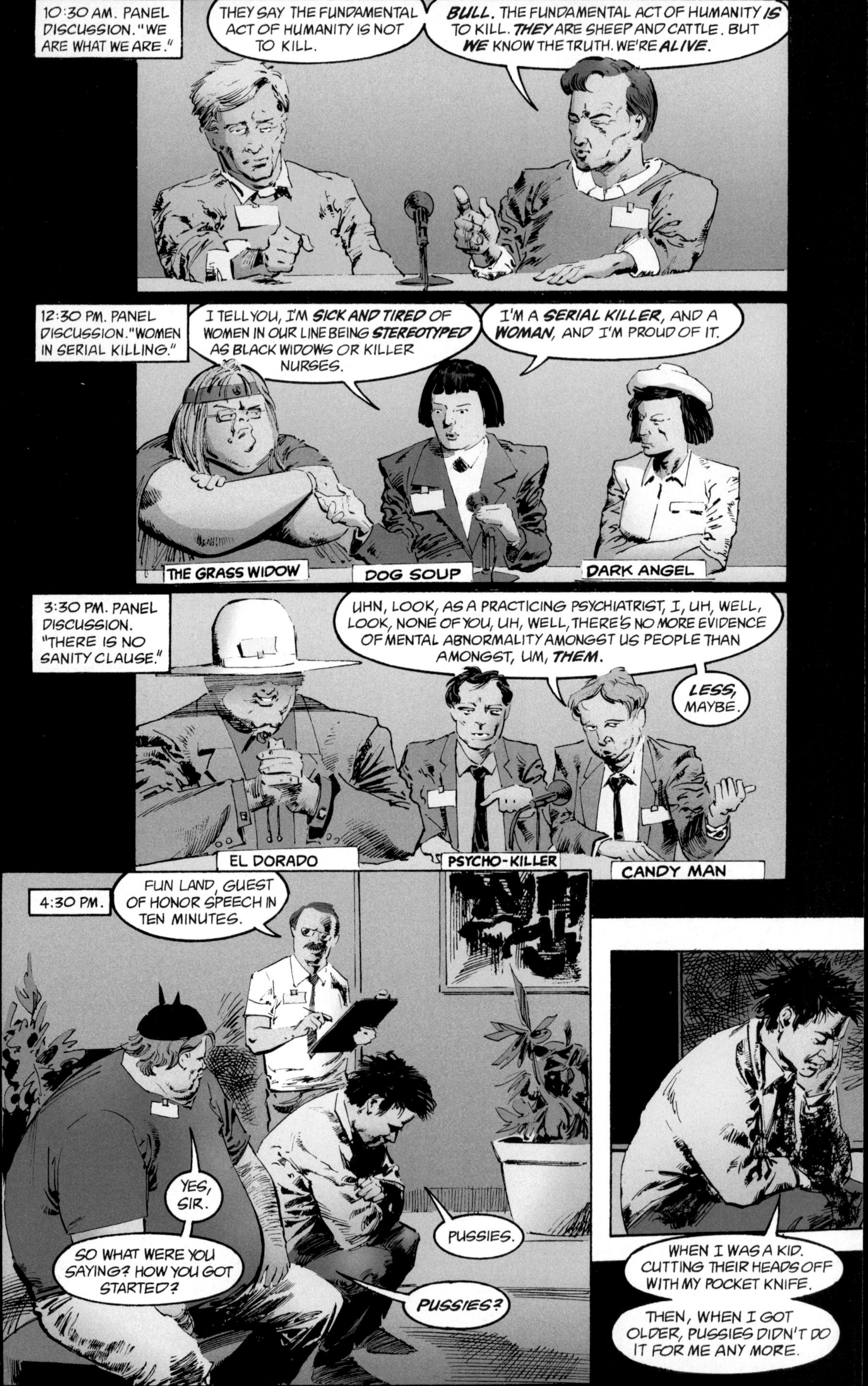

10:30 AM. PANEL DISCUSSION. "WE ARE WHAT WE ARE."
THEY SAY THE FUNDAMENTAL ACT OF HUMANITY IS NOT TO KILL.
BULL. THE FUNDAMENTAL ACT OF HUMANITY IS TO KILL. THEY ARE SHEEP AND CATTLE. BUT WE KNOW THE TRUTH. WE'RE ALIVE.
12:30 PM. PANEL DISCUSSION. "WOMEN IN SERIAL KILLING."
I TELL YOU, I'M SICK AND TIRED OF WOMEN IN OUR LINE BEING STEREOTYPED AS BLACK WIDOWS OR KILLER NURSES.
I'M A SERIAL KILLER, AND A WOMAN, AND I'M PROUD OF IT.
THE GRASS WIDOW
DOG SOUP
DARK ANGEL
3:30 PM. PANEL DISCUSSION. "THERE IS NO SANITY CLAUSE."
UHN, LOOK, AS A PRACTICING PSYCHIATRIST, I, UH, WELL, LOOK, NONE OF YOU, UH, WELL, THERE'S NO MORE EVIDENCE OF MENTAL ABNORMALITY AMONGST US PEOPLE THAN AMONGST, UM, THEM.
LESS, MAYBE.
EL DORADO
PSYCHO-KILLER
CANDY MAN
4:30 PM.
FUN LAND, GUEST OF HONOR SPEECH IN TEN MINUTES.
YES, SIR.
SO WHAT WERE YOU SAYING? HOW YOU GOT STARTED?
PUSSIES.
PUSSIES?
WHEN I WAS A KID. CUTTING THEIR HEADS OFF WITH MY POCKET KNIFE.
THEN, WHEN I GOT OLDER, PUSSIES DIDN'T DO IT FOR ME ANY MORE.

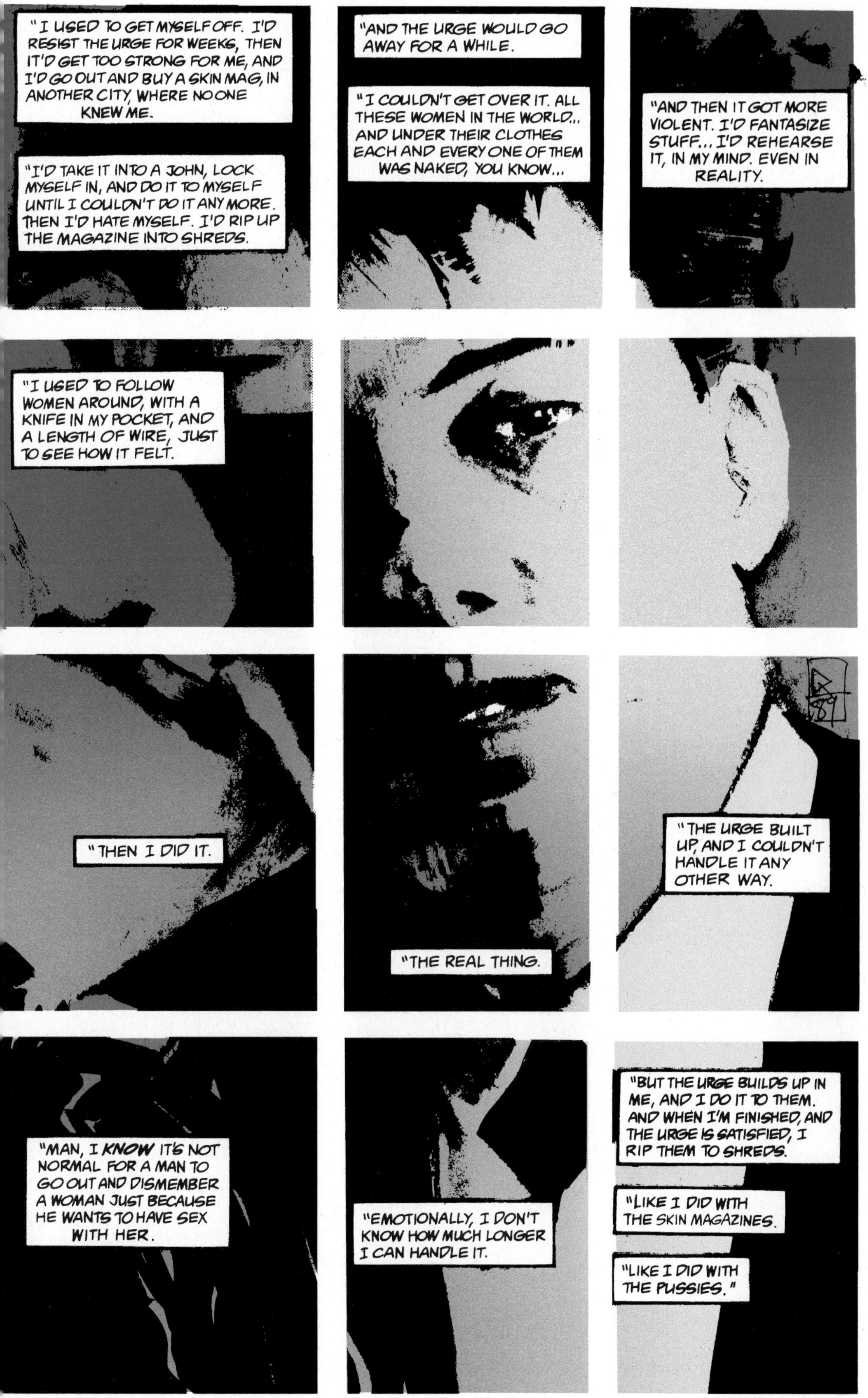
"I USED TO GET MYSELF OFF. I'D RESIST THE URGE FOR WEEKS, THEN IT'D GET TOO STRONG FOR ME, AND I'D GO OUT AND BUY A SKIN MAG, IN ANOTHER CITY, WHERE NO ONE KNEW ME.
"I'D TAKE IT INTO A JOHN, LOCK MYSELF IN, AND DO IT TO MYSELF UNTIL I COULDN'T DO IT ANY MORE. THEN I'D HATE MYSELF. I'D RIP UP THE MAGAZINE INTO SHREDS.
"AND THE URGE WOULD GO AWAY FOR A WHILE.
"I COULDN'T GET OVER IT. ALL THESE WOMEN IN THE WORLD... AND UNDER THEIR CLOTHES EACH AND EVERY ONE OF THEM WAS NAKED, YOU KNOW...
"AND THEN IT GOT MORE VIOLENT. I'D FANTASIZE STUFF... I'D REHEARSE IT, IN MY MIND. EVEN IN REALITY.
"I USED TO FOLLOW WOMEN AROUND, WITH A KNIFE IN MY POCKET, AND A LENGTH OF WIRE, JUST TO SEE HOW IT FELT.
"THEN I DID IT.
"THE REAL THING.
"THE URGE BUILT UP, AND I COULDN'T HANDLE IT ANY OTHER WAY.
"MAN, I KNOW IT'S NOT NORMAL FOR A MAN TO GO OUT AND DISMEMBER A WOMAN JUST BECAUSE HE WANTS TO HAVE SEX WITH HER.
"EMOTIONALLY, I DON'T KNOW HOW MUCH LONGER I CAN HANDLE IT.
"BUT THE URGE BUILDS UP IN ME, AND I DO IT TO THEM. AND WHEN I'M FINISHED, AND THE URGE IS SATISFIED, I RIP THEM TO SHREDS.
"LIKE I DID WITH THE SKIN MAGAZINES.
"LIKE I DID WITH THE PUSSIES."

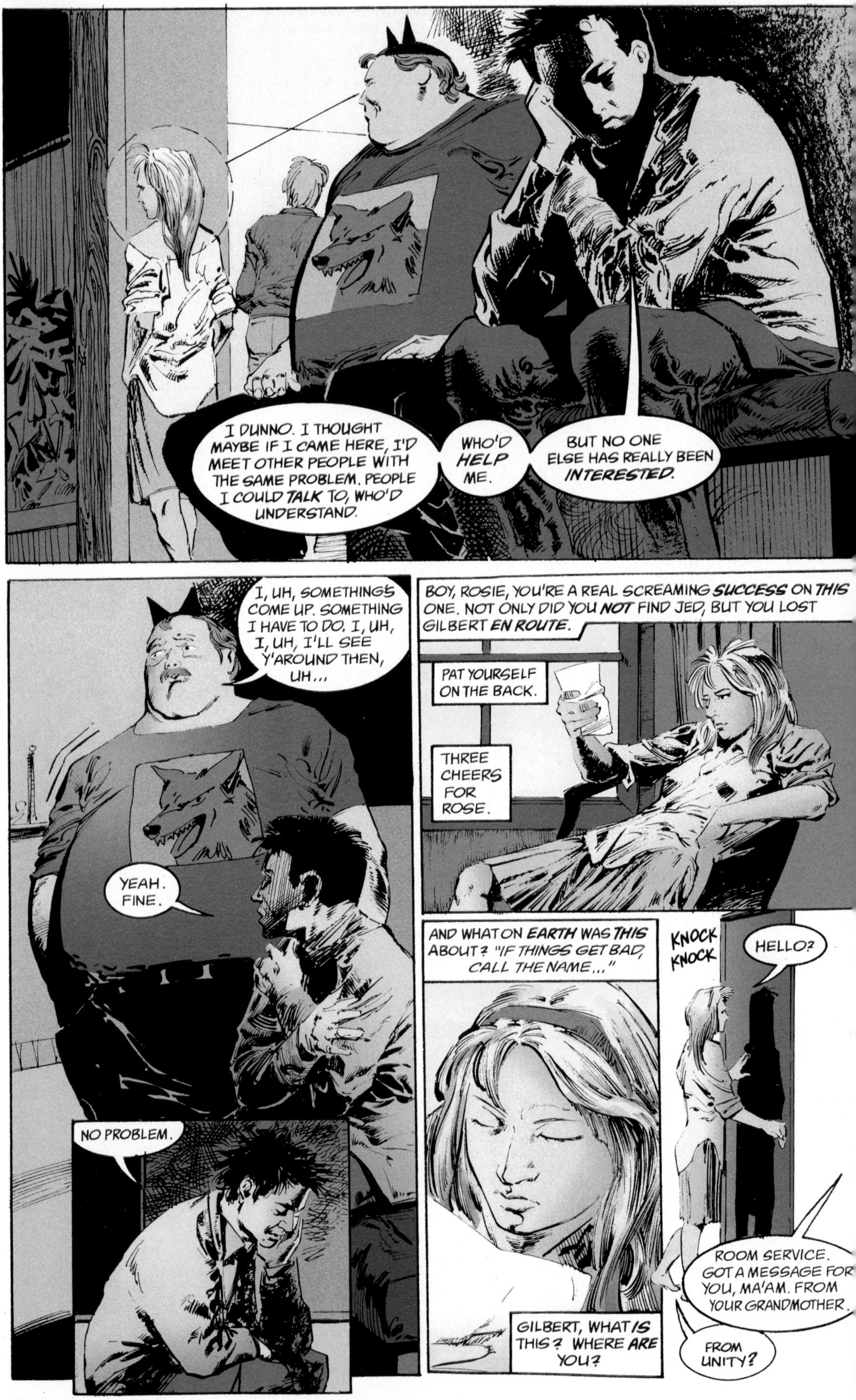
I DUNNO. I THOUGHT MAYBE IF I CAME HERE, I'D MEET OTHER PEOPLE WITH THE SAME PROBLEM. PEOPLE I COULD TALK TO, WHO'D UNDERSTAND.
WHO'D HELP ME.
BUT NO ONE ELSE HAS REALLY BEEN INTERESTED.
I, UH, SOMETHING'S COME UP. SOMETHING I HAVE TO DO. I, UH, I, UH, I'LL SEE Y'AROUND THEN, UH...
YEAH. FINE.
NO PROBLEM.
BOY, ROSIE, YOU'RE A REAL SCREAMING SUCCESS ON THIS ONE. NOT ONLY DID YOU NOT FIND JED, BUT YOU LOST GILBERT EN ROUTE.
PAT YOURSELF ON THE BACK.
THREE CHEERS FOR ROSE.
AND WHAT ON EARTH WAS THIS ABOUT? "IF THINGS GET BAD, CALL THE NAME..."
GILBERT, WHAT IS THIS? WHERE ARE YOU?
KNOCK KNOCK
HELLO?
ROOM SERVICE. GOT A MESSAGE FOR YOU, MA'AM. FROM YOUR GRANDMOTHER.
FROM UNITY?

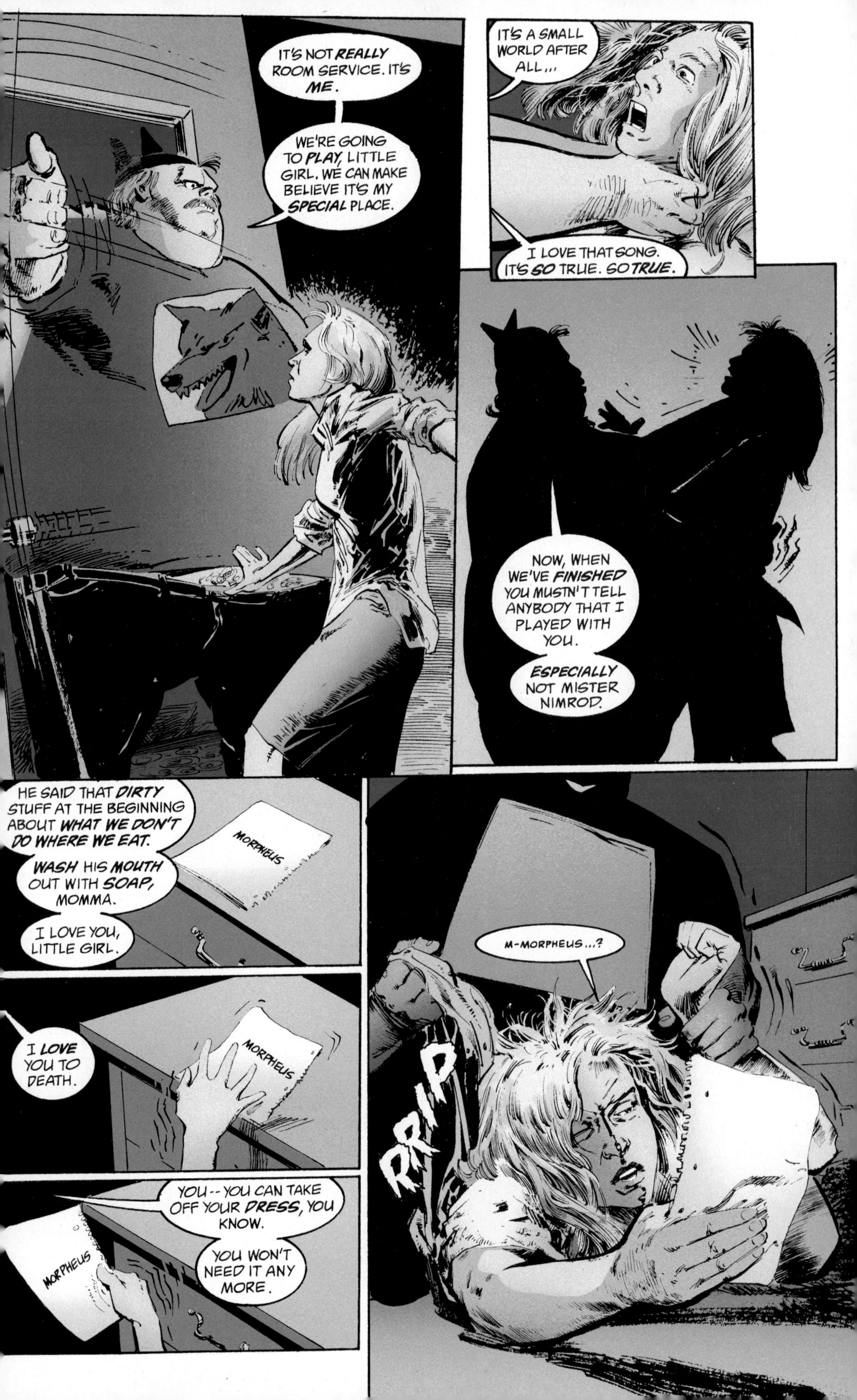
IT'S NOT REALLY ROOM SERVICE. IT'S ME.
WE'RE GOING TO PLAY, LITTLE GIRL. WE CAN MAKE BELIEVE IT'S MY SPECIAL PLACE.
IT'S A SMALL WORLD AFTER ALL...
I LOVE THAT SONG. IT'S SO TRUE. SO TRUE.
NOW, WHEN WE'VE FINISHED YOU MUSTN'T TELL ANYBODY THAT I PLAYED WITH YOU.
ESPECIALLY NOT MISTER NIMROD.
HE SAID THAT DIRTY STUFF AT THE BEGINNING ABOUT WHAT WE DON'T DO WHERE WE EAT.
MORPHEUS
WASH HIS MOUTH OUT WITH SOAP, MOMMA.
I LOVE YOU, LITTLE GIRL.
I LOVE YOU TO DEATH.
MORPHEUS
YOU -- YOU CAN TAKE OFF YOUR DRESS, YOU KNOW.
YOU WON'T NEED IT ANY MORE.
MORPHEUS
M-MORPHEUS...?
RRIP

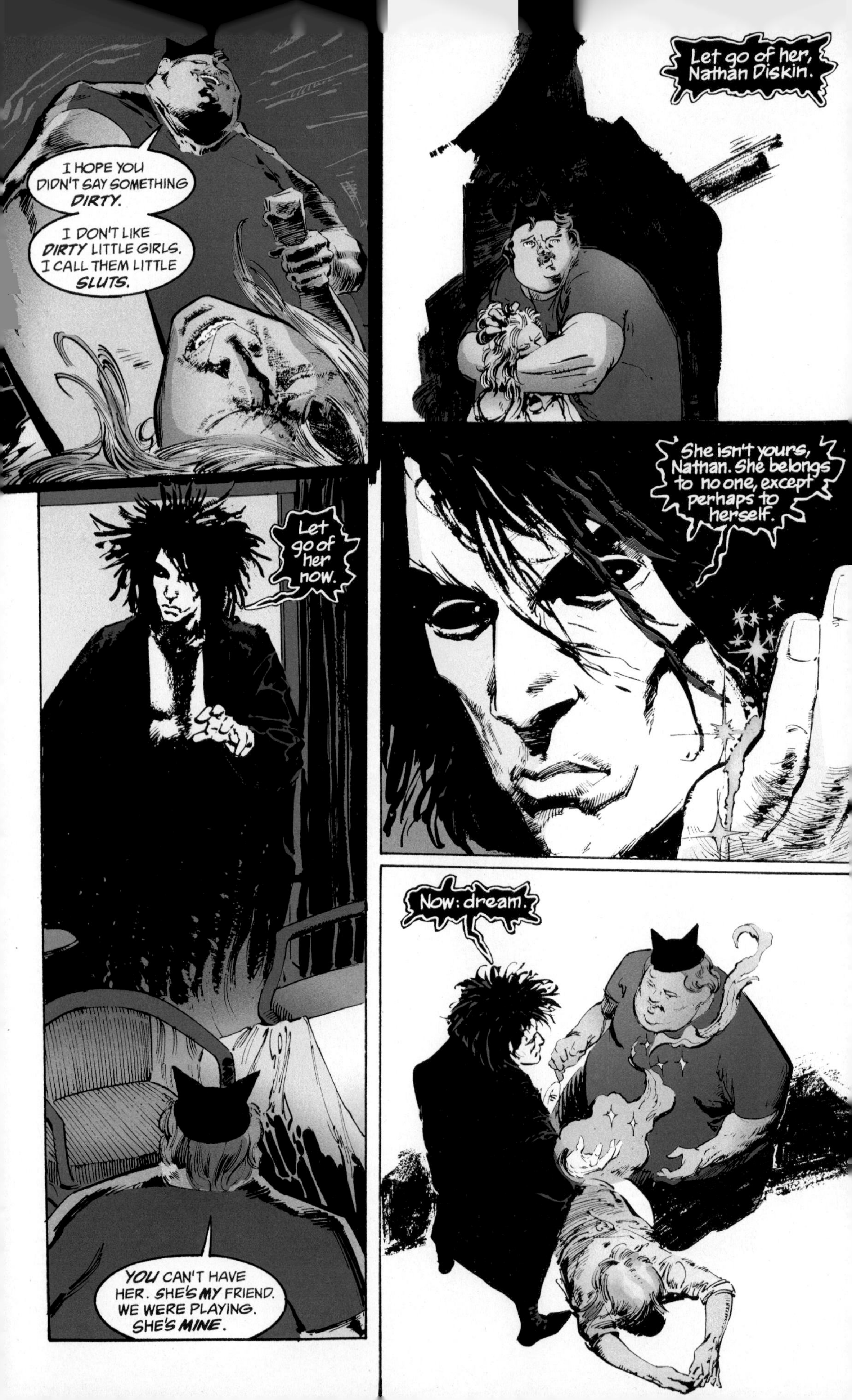
I HOPE YOU DIDN'T SAY SOMETHING DIRTY.
I DON'T LIKE DIRTY LITTLE GIRLS. I CALL THEM LITTLE SLUTS.
Let go of her, Nathan Diskin.
Let go of her now.
YOU CAN'T HAVE HER. SHE'S MY FRIEND. WE WERE PLAYING. SHE'S MINE.
She isn't yours, Nathan. She belongs to no one, except perhaps to herself.
Now: dream.

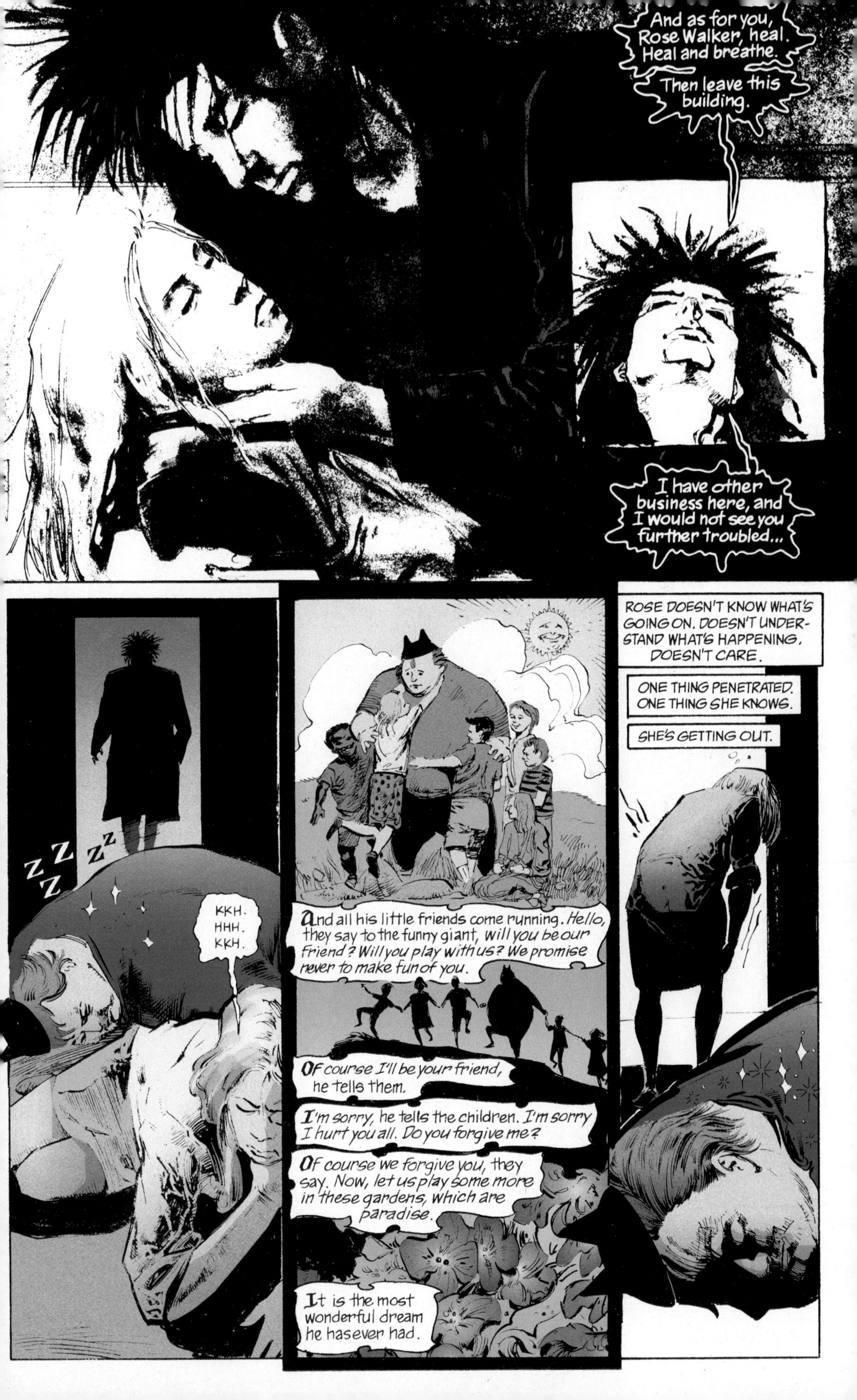
And as for you, Rose Walker, heal. Heal and breathe.
Then leave this building.
I have other business here, and I would not see you further troubled...
ZZZZZ
KKH. HHH. KKH.
And all his little friends come running. Hello, they say to the funny giant, will you be our friend? Will you play with us? We promise never to make fun of you.
Of course I'll be your friend, he tells them.
I'm sorry, he tells the children. I'm sorry I hurt you all. Do you forgive me?
Of course we forgive you, they say. Now, let us play some more in these gardens, which are paradise.
It is the most wonderful dream he has ever had.
ROSE DOESN'T KNOW WHAT'S GOING ON. DOESN'T UNDERSTAND WHAT'S HAPPENING. DOESN'T CARE.
ONE THING PENETRATED. ONE THING SHE KNOWS.
SHE'S GETTING OUT.

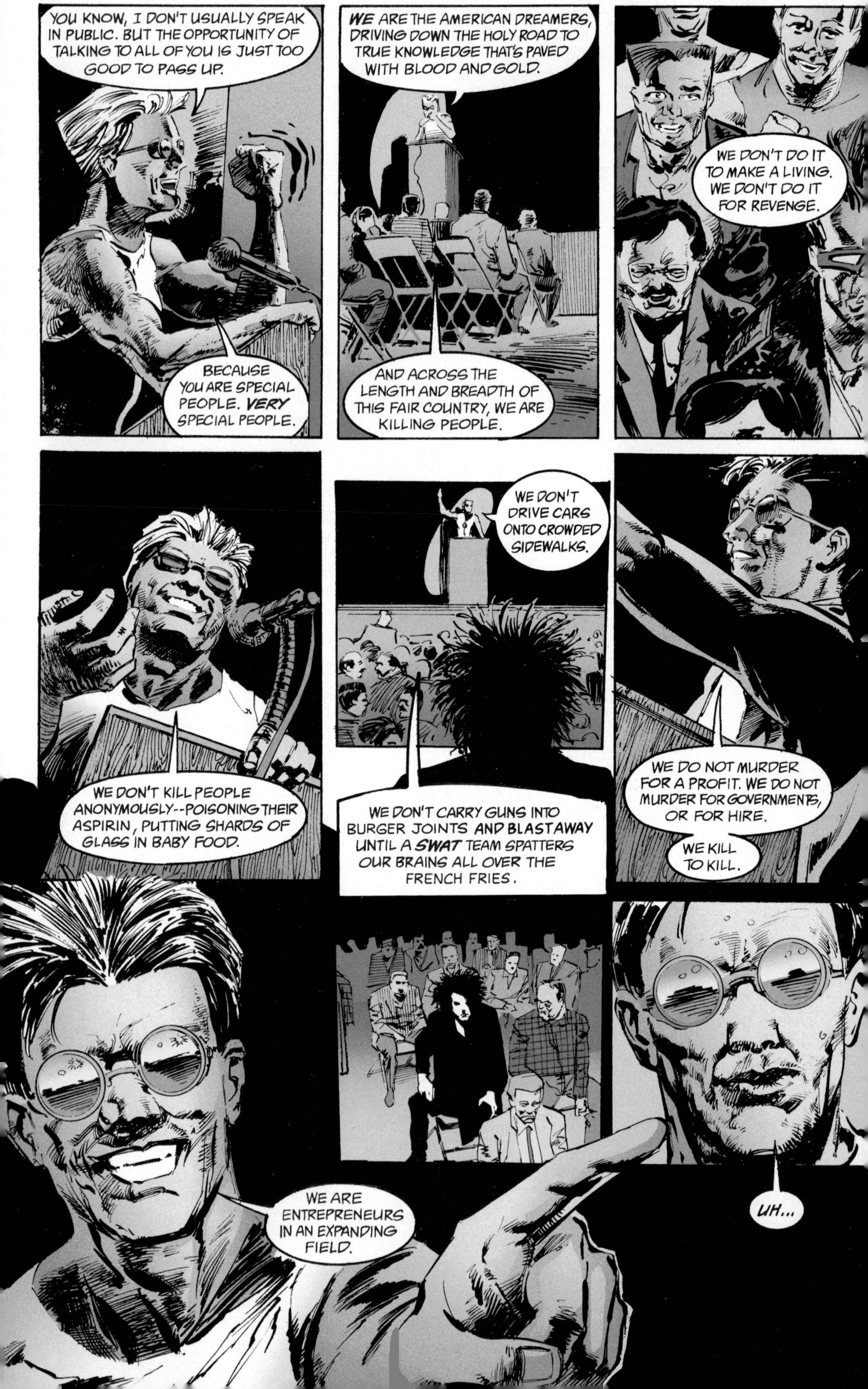
YOU KNOW, I DON'T USUALLY SPEAK IN PUBLIC. BUT THE OPPORTUNITY OF TALKING TO ALL OF YOU IS JUST TOO GOOD TO PASS UP.
BECAUSE YOU ARE SPECIAL PEOPLE. VERY SPECIAL PEOPLE.
WE ARE THE AMERICAN DREAMERS, DRIVING DOWN THE HOLY ROAD TO TRUE KNOWLEDGE THAT'S PAVED WITH BLOOD AND GOLD.
AND ACROSS THE LENGTH AND BREADTH OF THIS FAIR COUNTRY, WE ARE KILLING PEOPLE.
WE DON'T DO IT TO MAKE A LIVING. WE DON'T DO IT FOR REVENGE.
WE DON'T KILL PEOPLE ANONYMOUSLY--POISONING THEIR ASPIRIN, PUTTING SHARDS OF GLASS IN BABY FOOD.
WE DON'T DRIVE CARS ONTO CROWDED SIDEWALKS.
WE DON'T CARRY GUNS INTO BURGER JOINTS AND BLAST AWAY UNTIL A SWAT TEAM SPATTERS OUR BRAINS ALL OVER THE FRENCH FRIES.
WE DO NOT MURDER FOR A PROFIT. WE DO NOT MURDER FOR GOVERNMENTS, OR FOR HIRE.
WE KILL TO KILL.
WE ARE ENTREPRENEURS IN AN EXPANDING FIELD.
UH...

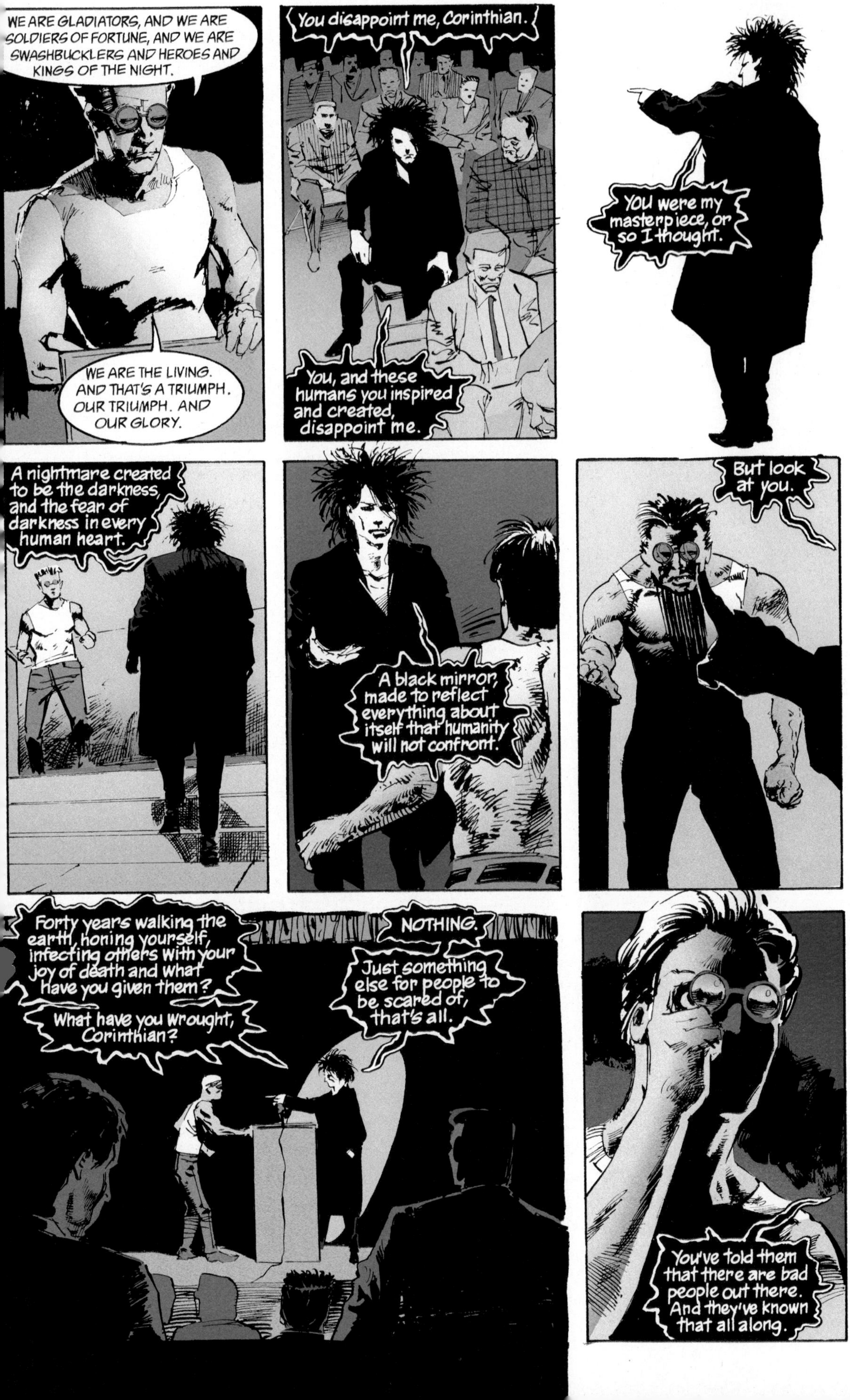
WE ARE GLADIATORS, AND WE ARE SOLDIERS OF FORTUNE, AND WE ARE SWASHBUCKLERS AND HEROES AND KINGS OF THE NIGHT.
WE ARE THE LIVING. AND THAT'S A TRIUMPH. OUR TRIUMPH. AND OUR GLORY.
You disappoint me, Corinthian.
You, and these humans you inspired and created, disappoint me.
YOU were my masterpiece, or so I thought.
A nightmare created to be the darkness, and the fear of darkness in every human heart.
A black mirror, made to reflect everything about itself that humanity will not confront.
But look at you.
Forty years walking the earth, honing yourself, infecting others with your joy of death and what have you given them?
What have you wrought, Corinthian?
NOTHING.
Just something else for people to be scared of, that's all.
You've told them that there are bad people out there. And they've known that all along.

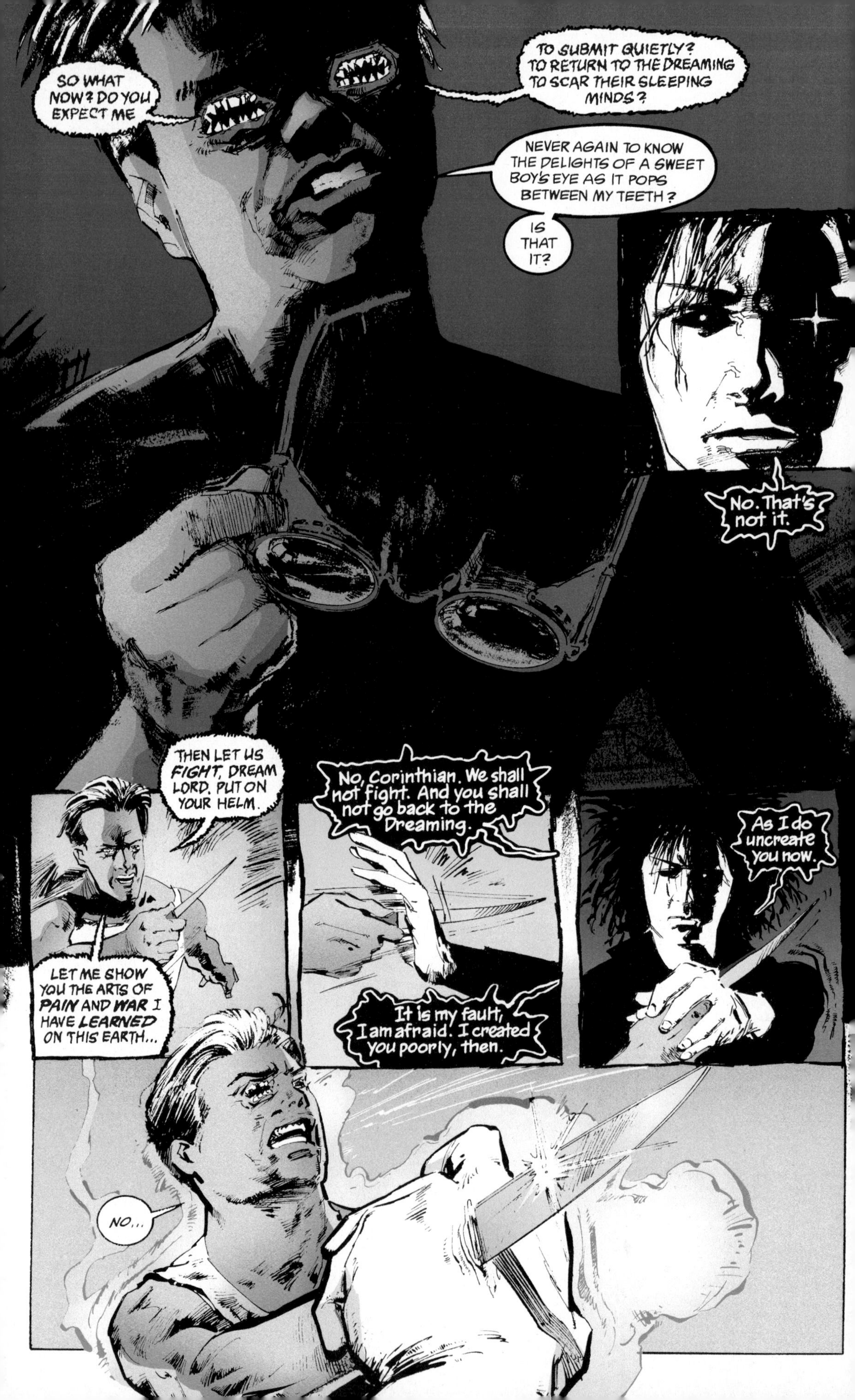
SO WHAT NOW? DO YOU EXPECT ME
TO SUBMIT QUIETLY? TO RETURN TO THE DREAMING TO SCAR THEIR SLEEPING MINDS?
NEVER AGAIN TO KNOW THE DELIGHTS OF A SWEET BOY'S EYE AS IT POPS BETWEEN MY TEETH?
IS THAT IT?
No. That's not it.
THEN LET US *FIGHT*, DREAM LORD. PUT ON YOUR HELM.
LET ME SHOW YOU THE ARTS OF *PAIN* AND *WAR* I HAVE *LEARNED* ON THIS EARTH...
No, Corinthian. We shall not fight. And you shall not go back to the Dreaming.
It is my fault, I am afraid. I created you poorly, then.
As I do uncreate you now.
NO...

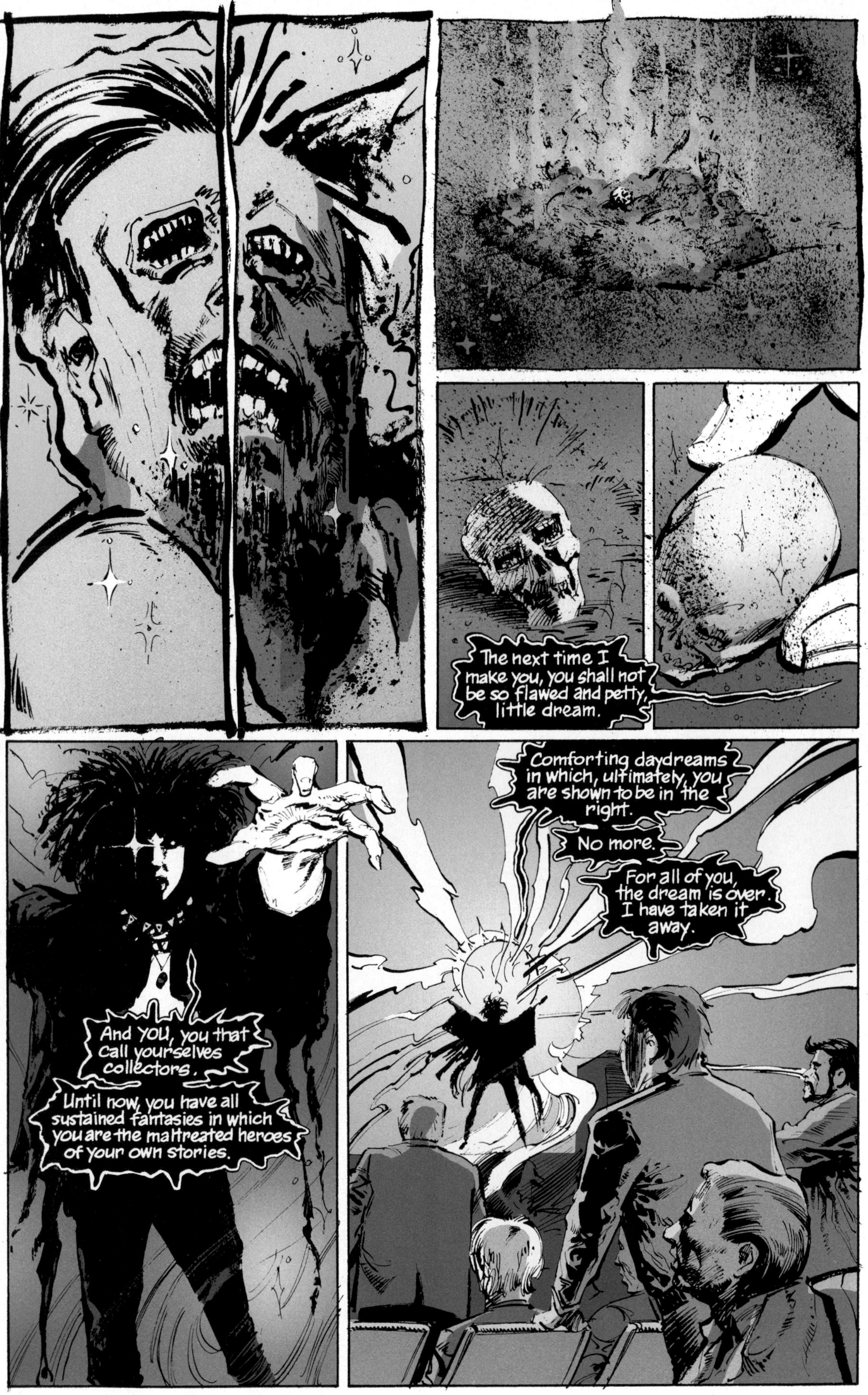
The next time I make you, you shall not be so flawed and petty, little dream.
And YOU, you that call yourselves collectors.
Until now, you have all sustained fantasies in which you are the maltreated heroes of your own stories.
Comforting daydreams in which, ultimately, you are shown to be in the right.
No more.
For all of you, the dream is over. I have taken it away.

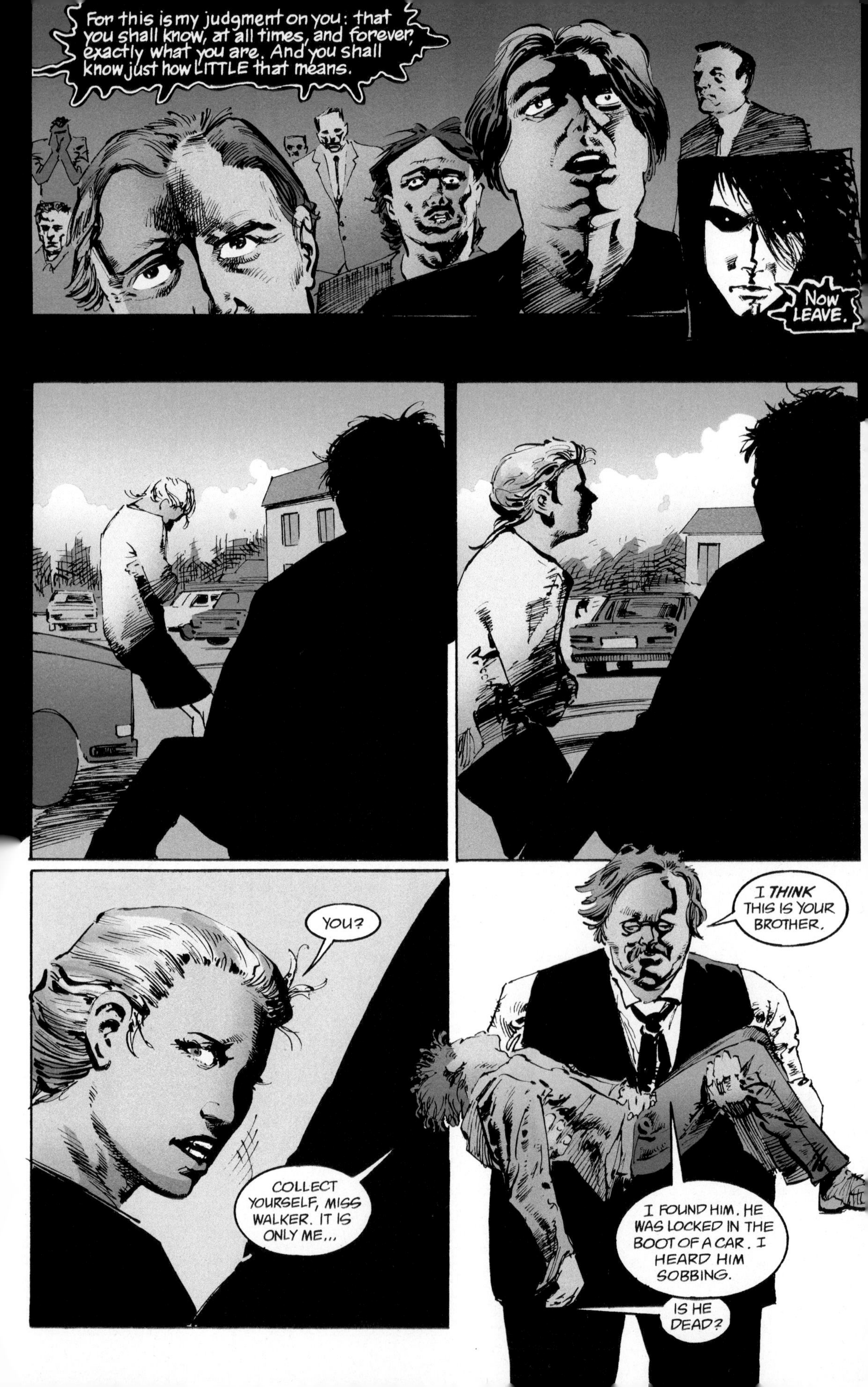
For this is my judgment on you: that you shall know, at all times, and forever, exactly what you are. And you shall know just how LITTLE that means.
Now LEAVE.
YOU?
COLLECT YOURSELF, MISS WALKER. IT IS ONLY ME...
I THINK THIS IS YOUR BROTHER.
I FOUND HIM. HE WAS LOCKED IN THE BOOT OF A CAR. I HEARD HIM SOBBING.
IS HE DEAD?

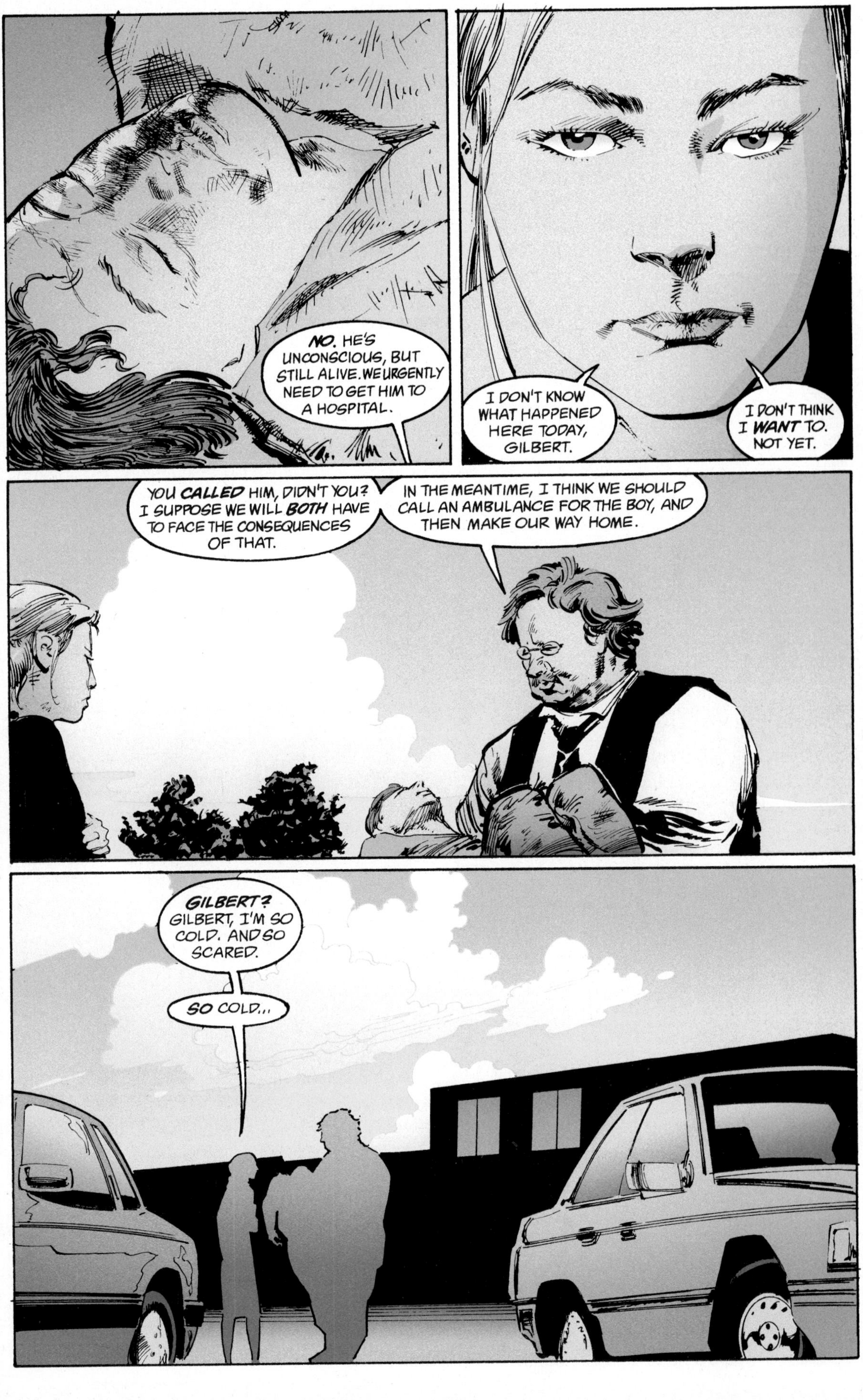

NO. HE'S UNCONSCIOUS, BUT STILL ALIVE. WE URGENTLY NEED TO GET HIM TO A HOSPITAL.
I DON'T KNOW WHAT HAPPENED HERE TODAY, GILBERT.
I DON'T THINK I WANT TO. NOT YET.
YOU CALLED HIM, DIDN'T YOU? I SUPPOSE WE WILL BOTH HAVE TO FACE THE CONSEQUENCES OF THAT.
IN THE MEANTIME, I THINK WE SHOULD CALL AN AMBULANCE FOR THE BOY, AND THEN MAKE OUR WAY HOME.
GILBERT? GILBERT, I'M SO COLD. AND SO SCARED.
SO COLD...

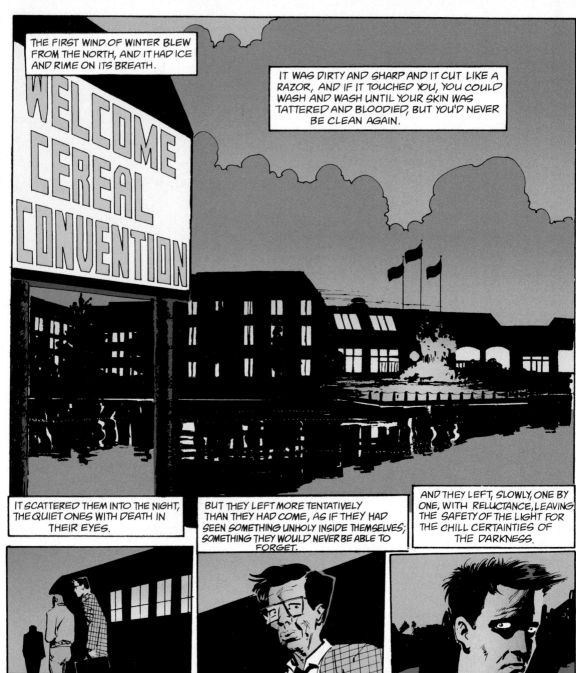

THE FIRST WIND OF WINTER BLEW FROM THE NORTH, AND IT HAD ICE AND RIME ON ITS BREATH.
WELCOME CEREAL CONVENTION
IT WAS DIRTY AND SHARP AND IT CUT LIKE A RAZOR, AND IF IT TOUCHED YOU, YOU COULD WASH AND WASH UNTIL YOUR SKIN WAS TATTERED AND BLOODIED, BUT YOU'D NEVER BE CLEAN AGAIN.
IT SCATTERED THEM INTO THE NIGHT, THE QUIET ONES WITH DEATH IN THEIR EYES.
BUT THEY LEFT MORE TENTATIVELY THAN THEY HAD COME, AS IF THEY HAD SEEN SOMETHING UNHOLY INSIDE THEMSELVES; SOMETHING THEY WOULD NEVER BE ABLE TO FORGET.
AND THEY LEFT, SLOWLY, ONE BY ONE, WITH RELUCTANCE, LEAVING THE SAFETY OF THE LIGHT FOR THE CHILL CERTAINTIES OF THE DARKNESS.
IT SEEMED LIKE THE NIGHT SUCKED THEM UP, TOOK THEM INTO ITS DARK HEART.
IT SEEMED LIKE THE DARKNESS SWALLOWED THEM...
PERHAPS IT DID.

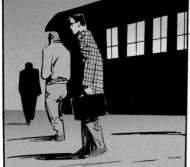

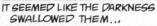

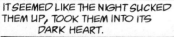

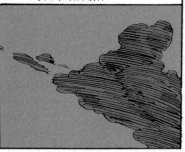

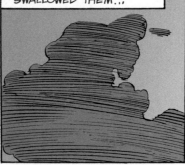

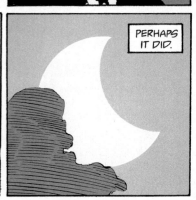

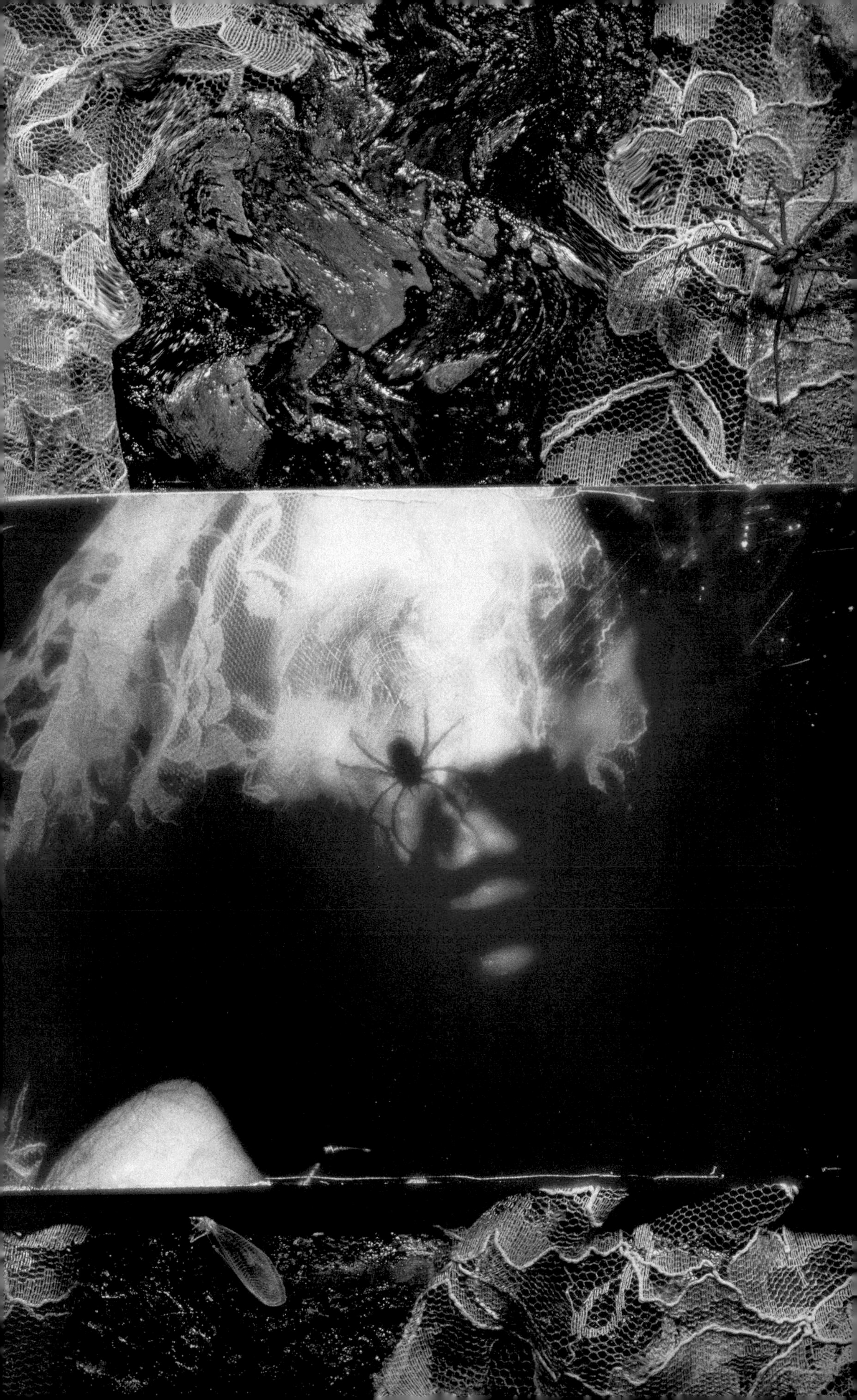

INTO THE NIGHT

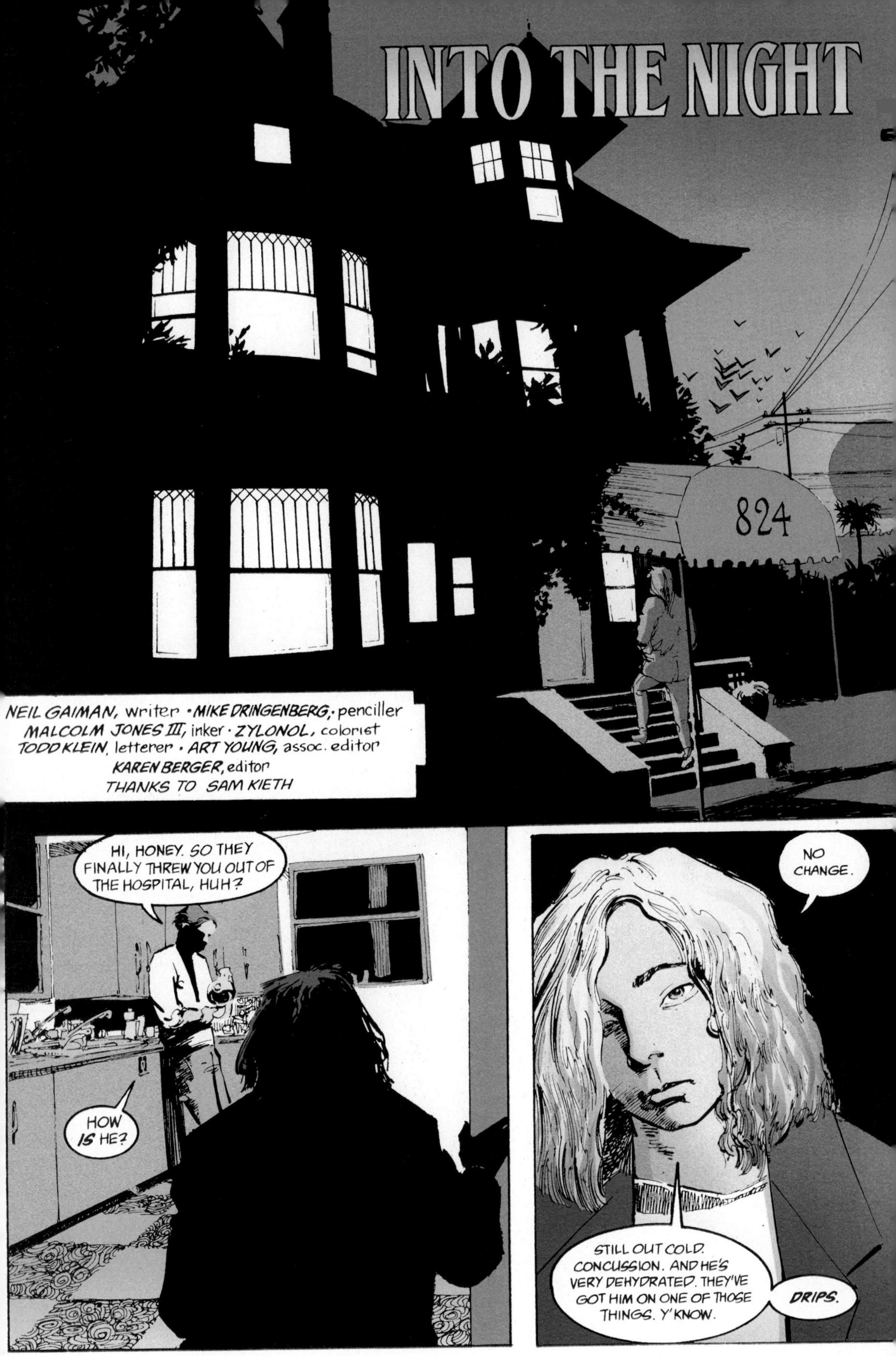

824
NEIL GAIMAN, writer • MIKE DRINGENBERG, penciller
MALCOLM JONES III, inker • ZYLONOL, colorist
TODD KLEIN, letterer • ART YOUNG, assoc. editor
KAREN BERGER, editor
THANKS TO SAM KIETH
HI, HONEY. SO THEY FINALLY THREW YOU OUT OF THE HOSPITAL, HUH?
HOW *IS* HE?
NO CHANGE.
STILL OUT COLD. CONCUSSION. AND HE'S VERY DEHYDRATED. THEY'VE GOT HIM ON ONE OF THOSE THINGS. Y'KNOW.
DRIPS.

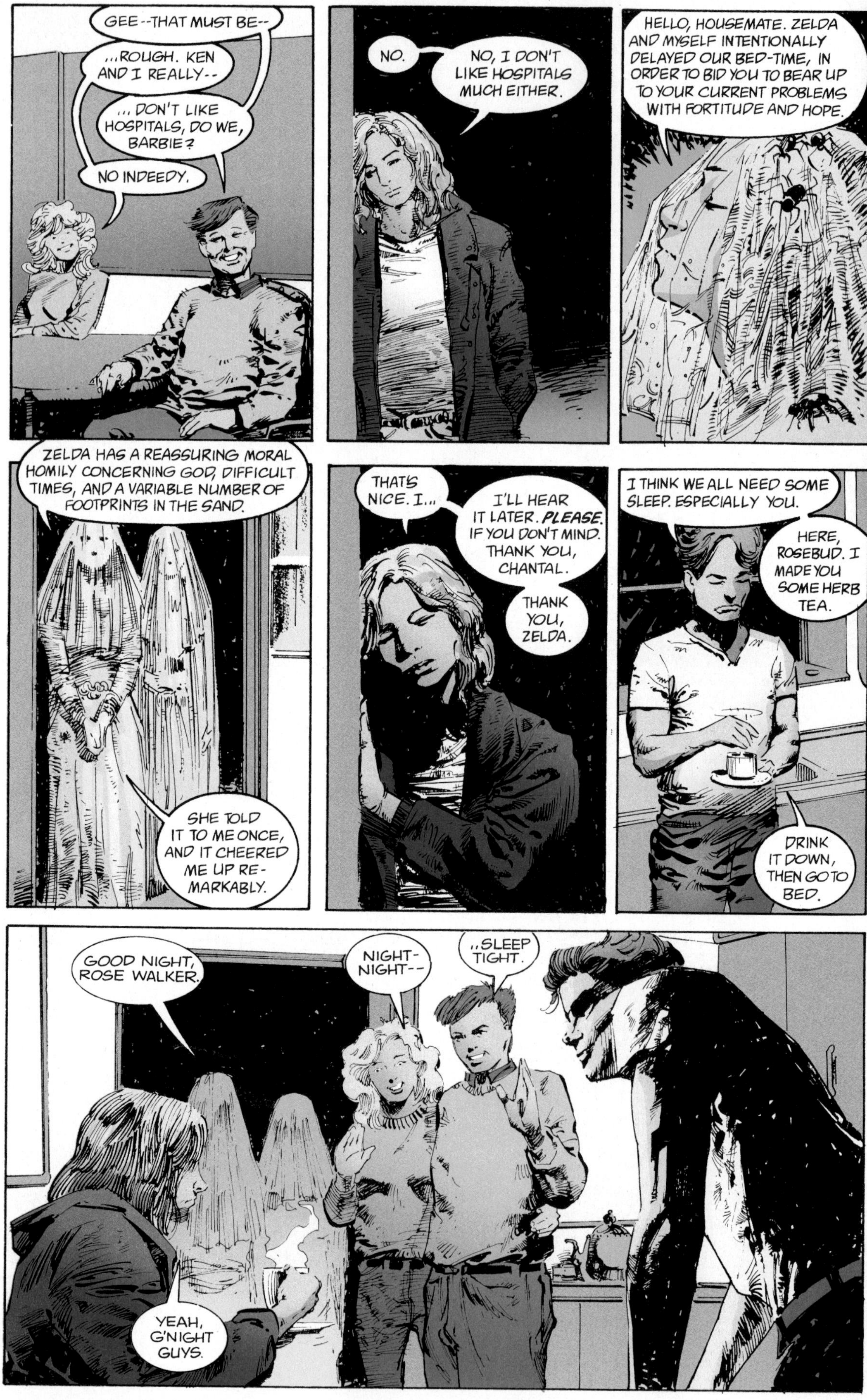
GEE--THAT MUST BE--
...ROUGH. KEN AND I REALLY--
...DON'T LIKE HOSPITALS, DO WE, BARBIE?
NO INDEEDY.
NO.
NO, I DON'T LIKE HOSPITALS MUCH EITHER.
HELLO, HOUSEMATE. ZELDA AND MYSELF INTENTIONALLY DELAYED OUR BED-TIME, IN ORDER TO BID YOU TO BEAR UP TO YOUR CURRENT PROBLEMS WITH FORTITUDE AND HOPE.
ZELDA HAS A REASSURING MORAL HOMILY CONCERNING GOD, DIFFICULT TIMES, AND A VARIABLE NUMBER OF FOOTPRINTS IN THE SAND.
SHE TOLD IT TO ME ONCE, AND IT CHEERED ME UP RE-MARKABLY.
THAT'S NICE. I...
I'LL HEAR IT LATER. **PLEASE.** IF YOU DON'T MIND. THANK YOU, CHANTAL.
THANK YOU, ZELDA.
I THINK WE ALL NEED SOME SLEEP. ESPECIALLY YOU.
HERE, ROSEBUD. I MADE YOU SOME HERB TEA.
DRINK IT DOWN, THEN GO TO BED.
GOOD NIGHT, ROSE WALKER.
NIGHT-NIGHT--
..SLEEP TIGHT.
YEAH, G'NIGHT GUYS.

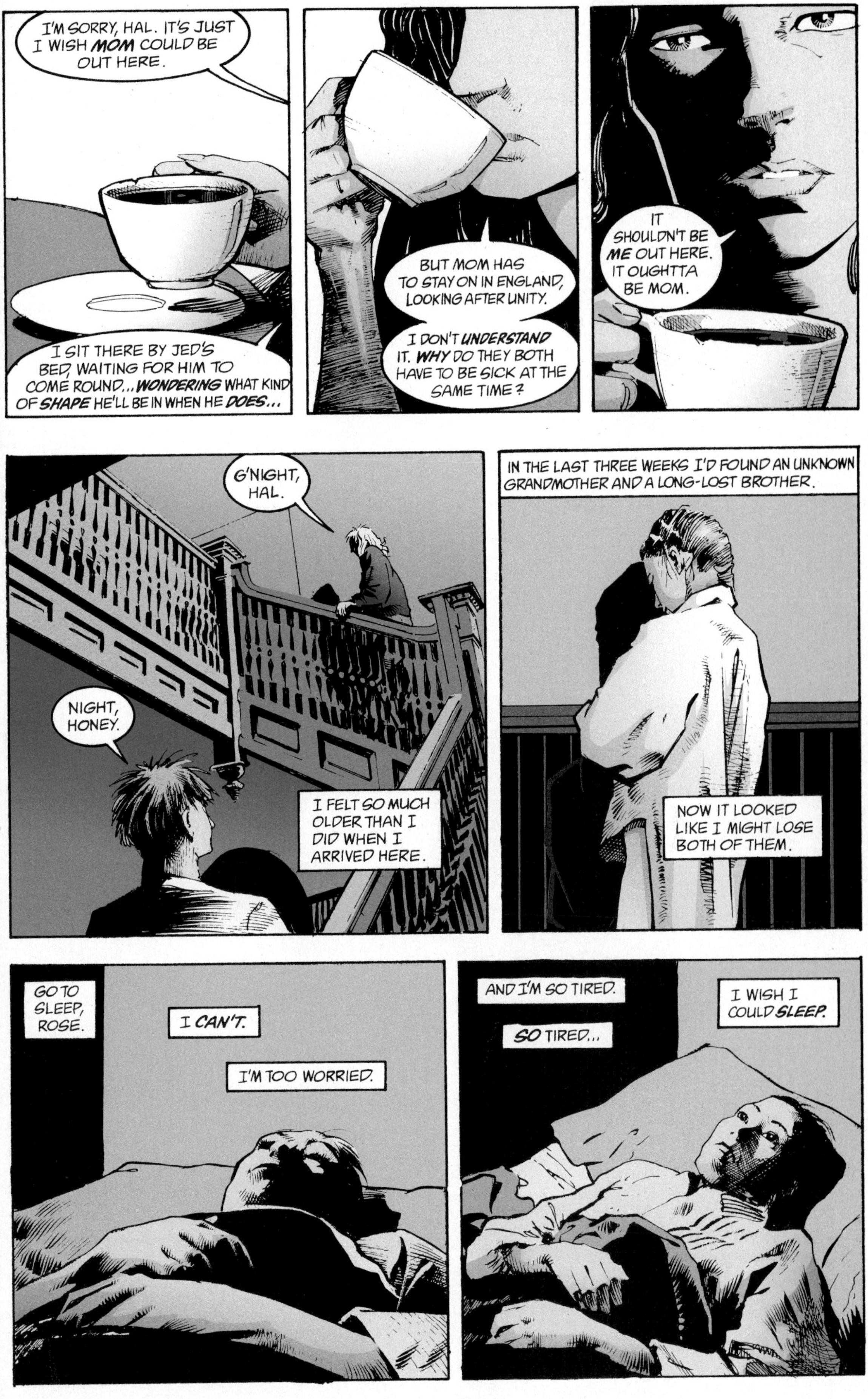
I'M SORRY, HAL. IT'S JUST I WISH MOM COULD BE OUT HERE.
I SIT THERE BY JED'S BED, WAITING FOR HIM TO COME ROUND... WONDERING WHAT KIND OF SHAPE HE'LL BE IN WHEN HE DOES...
BUT MOM HAS TO STAY ON IN ENGLAND, LOOKING AFTER UNITY.
I DON'T UNDERSTAND IT. WHY DO THEY BOTH HAVE TO BE SICK AT THE SAME TIME?
IT SHOULDN'T BE ME OUT HERE. IT OUGHTTA BE MOM.
G'NIGHT, HAL.
NIGHT, HONEY.
I FELT SO MUCH OLDER THAN I DID WHEN I ARRIVED HERE.
IN THE LAST THREE WEEKS I'D FOUND AN UNKNOWN GRANDMOTHER AND A LONG-LOST BROTHER.
NOW IT LOOKED LIKE I MIGHT LOSE BOTH OF THEM.
GO TO SLEEP, ROSE.
I CAN'T.
I'M TOO WORRIED.
AND I'M SO TIRED.
SO TIRED...
I WISH I COULD SLEEP.

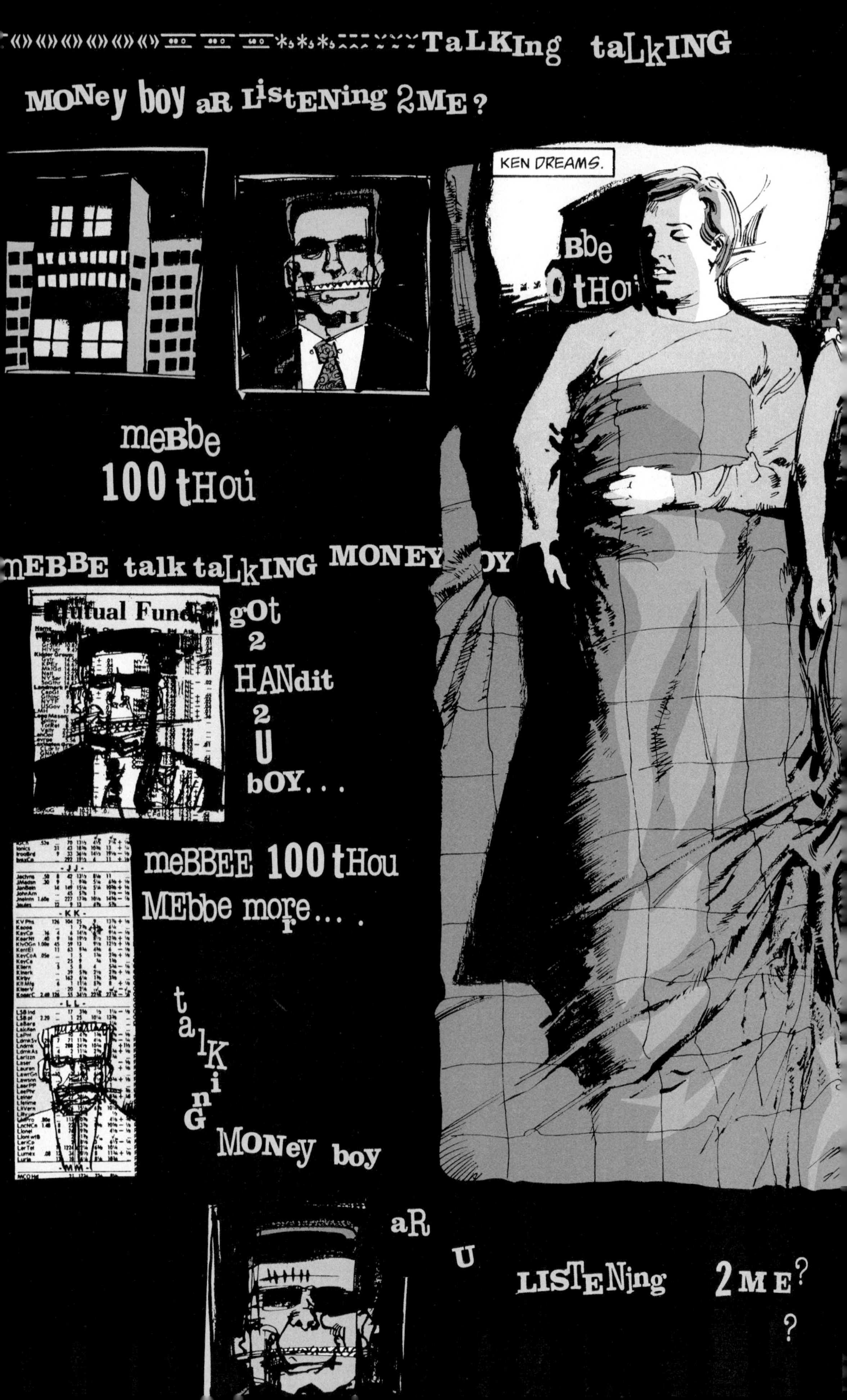
TaLKIng taLkING
MONey boy aR ListENing 2ME?
KEN DREAMS.
Bbe
tHou
mebbe
100 tHou
mEBBE talk taLkING MONEY
Mutual Funds
gOt 2 HANdit 2 U bOY...
meBBEE 100 tHou
MEbbe more....
talKinG MONey boy
aR U LISTENjng 2ME?
?

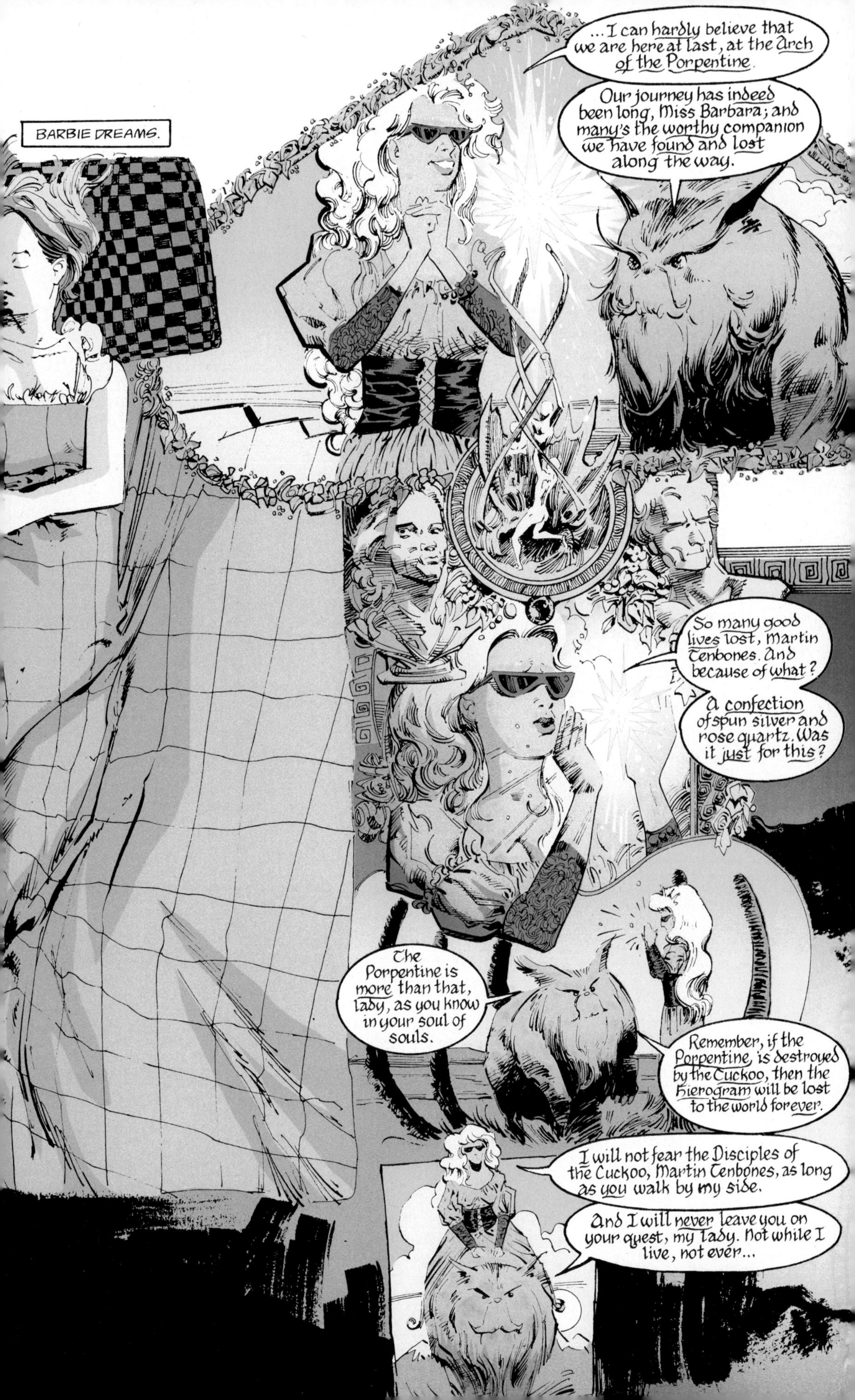
BARBIE DREAMS.
...I can hardly believe that we are here at last, at the Arch of the Porpentine.
Our journey has indeed been long, Miss Barbara; and many's the worthy companion we have found and lost along the way.
So many good lives lost, Martin Tenbones. And because of what?
A confection of spun silver and rose quartz. Was it just for this?
The Porpentine is more than that, lady, as you know in your soul of souls.
Remember, if the Porpentine is destroyed by the Cuckoo, then the Hierogram will be lost to the world forever.
I will not fear the Disciples of the Cuckoo, Martin Tenbones, as long as you walk by my side.
And I will never leave you on your quest, my lady. Not while I live, not ever...

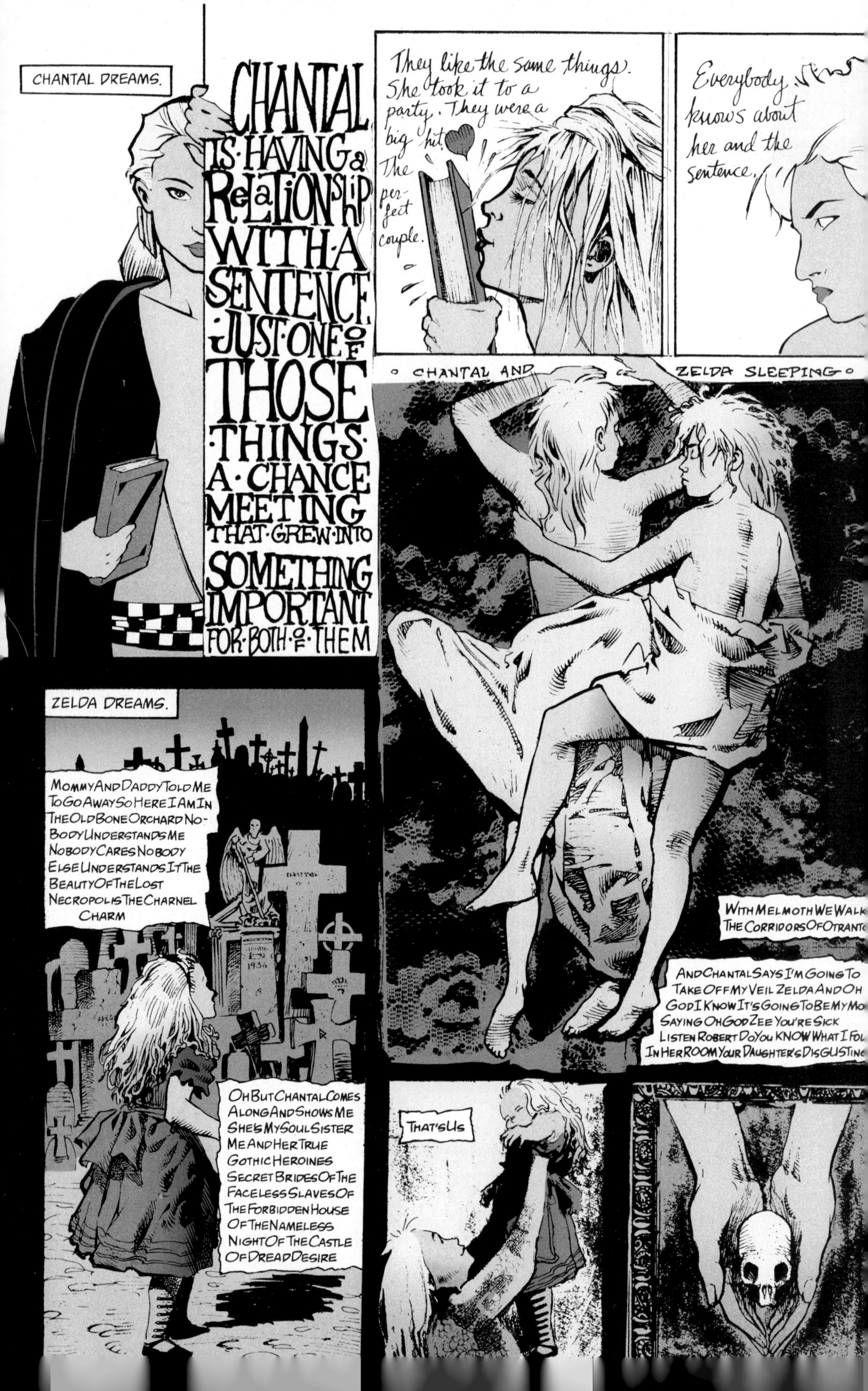

CHANTAL DREAMS.
CHANTAL IS HAVING A RELATIONSHIP WITH A SENTENCE. JUST ONE OF THOSE THINGS. A CHANCE MEETING THAT GREW INTO SOMETHING IMPORTANT FOR BOTH OF THEM
They like the same things. She took it to a party. They were a big hit. The perfect couple.
Everybody knows about her and the sentence.
CHANTAL AND ZELDA SLEEPING
ZELDA DREAMS.
MOMMY AND DADDY TOLD ME TO GO AWAY SO HERE I AM IN THE OLD BONE ORCHARD NOBODY UNDERSTANDS ME NOBODY CARES NOBODY ELSE UNDERSTANDS IT THE BEAUTY OF THE LOST NECROPOLIS THE CHARNEL CHARM
WITH MELMOTH WE WALK THE CORRIDORS OF OTRANTO
AND CHANTAL SAYS I'M GOING TO TAKE OFF MY VEIL ZELDA AND OH GOD I KNOW IT'S GOING TO BE MY MO
SAYING OH GOD ZEE YOU'RE SICK LISTEN ROBERT DO YOU KNOW WHAT I FO
IN HER ROOM YOUR DAUGHTER'S DISGUSTIN
OH BUT CHANTAL COMES ALONG AND SHOWS ME SHE'S MY SOUL SISTER ME AND HER TRUE GOTHIC HEROINES SECRET BRIDES OF THE FACELESS SLAVES OF THE FORBIDDEN HOUSE OF THE NAMELESS NIGHT OF THE CASTLE OF DREAD DESIRE
THAT'S US

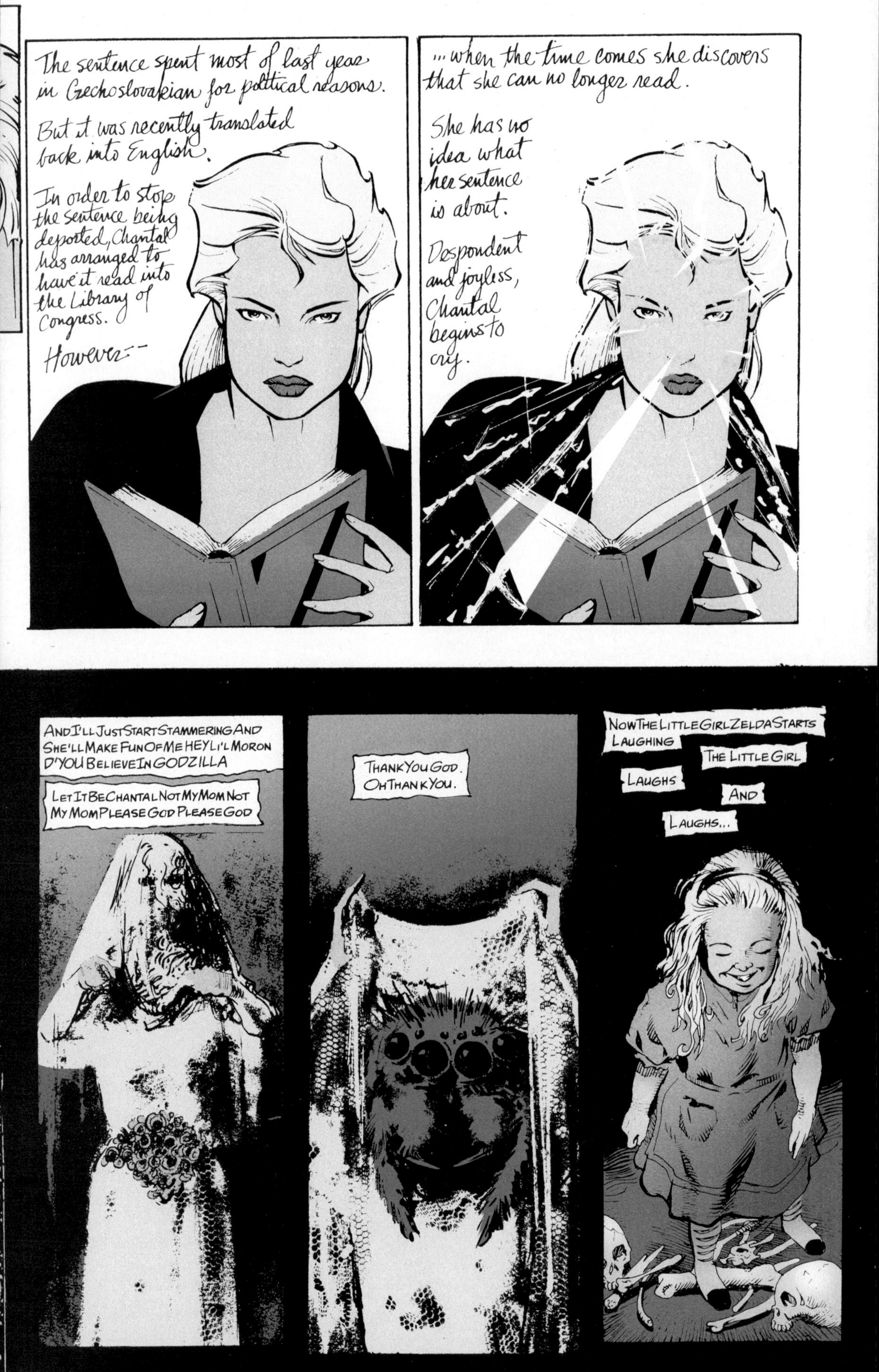
The sentence spent most of last year in Czechoslovakian for political reasons.
But it was recently translated back into English.
In order to stop the sentence being deported, Chantal has arranged to have it read into the Library of Congress.
However--
...when the time comes she discovers that she can no longer read.
She has no idea what her sentence is about.
Despondent and joyless, Chantal begins to cry.
AND I'LL JUST START STAMMERING AND SHE'LL MAKE FUN OF ME HEY LI'L MORON D'YOU BELIEVE IN GODZILLA
LET IT BE CHANTAL NOT MY MOM NOT MY MOM PLEASE GOD PLEASE GOD
THANK YOU GOD. OH THANK YOU.
NOW THE LITTLE GIRL ZELDA STARTS LAUGHING
THE LITTLE GIRL
LAUGHS
AND
LAUGHS...

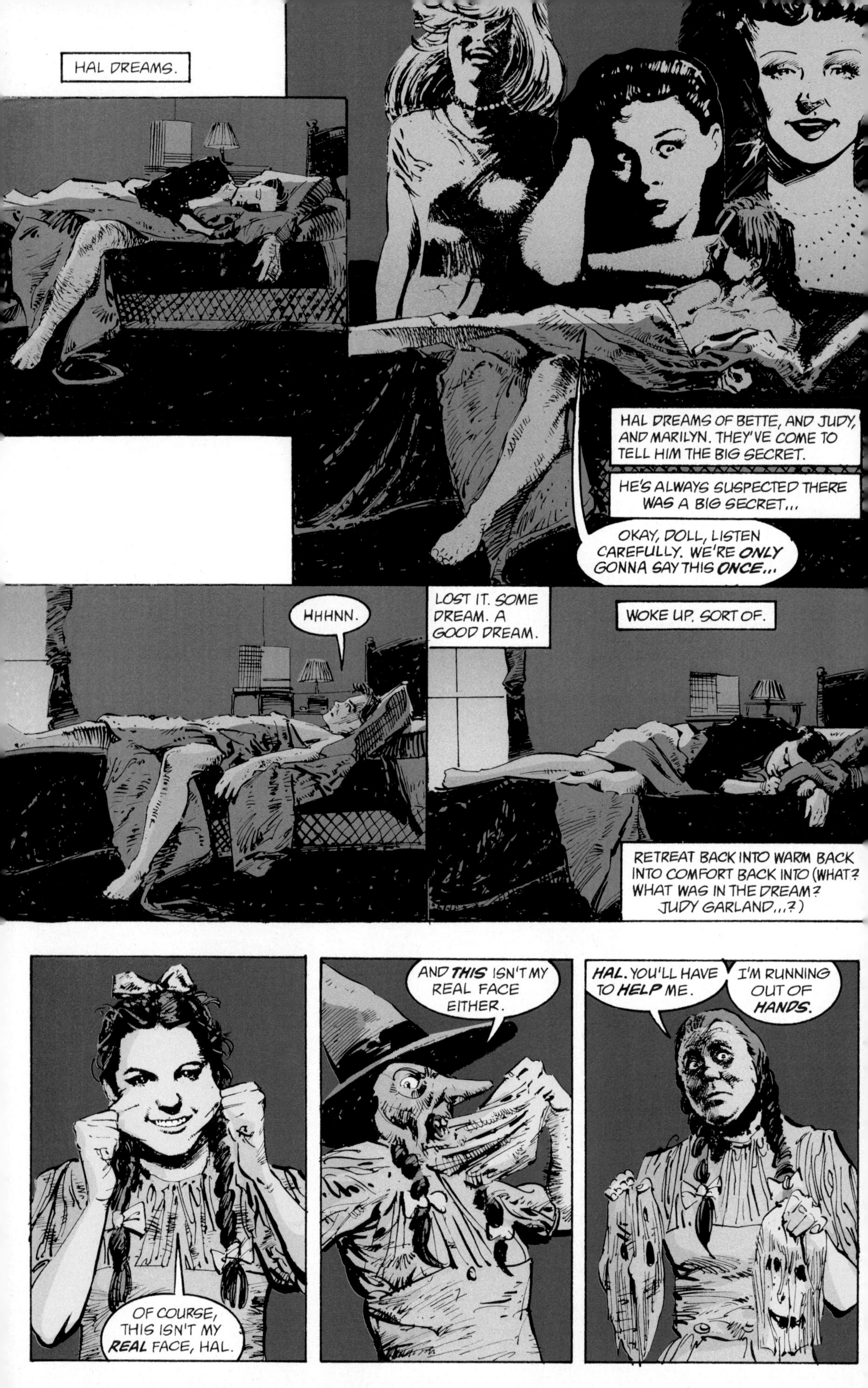
HAL DREAMS.
HAL DREAMS OF BETTE, AND JUDY, AND MARILYN. THEY'VE COME TO TELL HIM THE BIG SECRET.
HE'S ALWAYS SUSPECTED THERE WAS A BIG SECRET...
OKAY, DOLL, LISTEN CAREFULLY. WE'RE ONLY GONNA SAY THIS ONCE...
HHHNN.
LOST IT. SOME DREAM. A GOOD DREAM.
WOKE UP. SORT OF.
RETREAT BACK INTO WARM BACK INTO COMFORT BACK INTO (WHAT? WHAT WAS IN THE DREAM? JUDY GARLAND...?)
OF COURSE, THIS ISN'T MY REAL FACE, HAL.
AND THIS ISN'T MY REAL FACE EITHER.
HAL. YOU'LL HAVE TO HELP ME.
I'M RUNNING OUT OF HANDS.

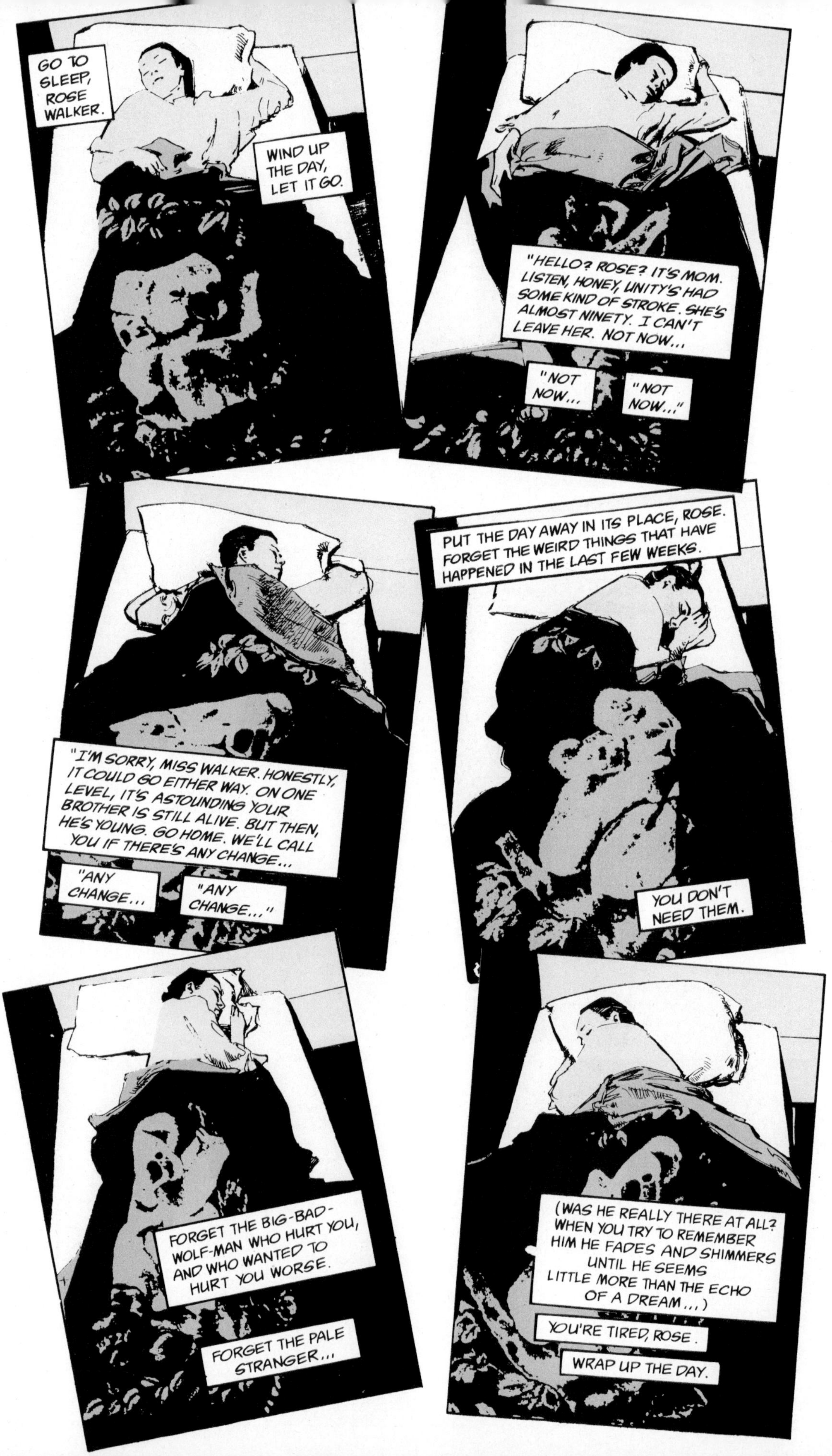
GO TO SLEEP, ROSE WALKER.
WIND UP THE DAY, LET IT GO.
"HELLO? ROSE? IT'S MOM. LISTEN, HONEY, UNITY'S HAD SOME KIND OF STROKE. SHE'S ALMOST NINETY. I CAN'T LEAVE HER. NOT NOW...
"NOT NOW...
"NOT NOW..."
"I'M SORRY, MISS WALKER. HONESTLY, IT COULD GO EITHER WAY. ON ONE LEVEL, IT'S ASTOUNDING YOUR BROTHER IS STILL ALIVE. BUT THEN, HE'S YOUNG. GO HOME. WE'LL CALL YOU IF THERE'S ANY CHANGE...
"ANY CHANGE...
"ANY CHANGE..."
PUT THE DAY AWAY IN ITS PLACE, ROSE. FORGET THE WEIRD THINGS THAT HAVE HAPPENED IN THE LAST FEW WEEKS.
YOU DON'T NEED THEM.
FORGET THE BIG-BAD-WOLF-MAN WHO HURT YOU, AND WHO WANTED TO HURT YOU WORSE.
FORGET THE PALE STRANGER...
(WAS HE REALLY THERE AT ALL? WHEN YOU TRY TO REMEMBER HIM HE FADES AND SHIMMERS UNTIL HE SEEMS LITTLE MORE THAN THE ECHO OF A DREAM...)
YOU'RE TIRED, ROSE.
WRAP UP THE DAY.

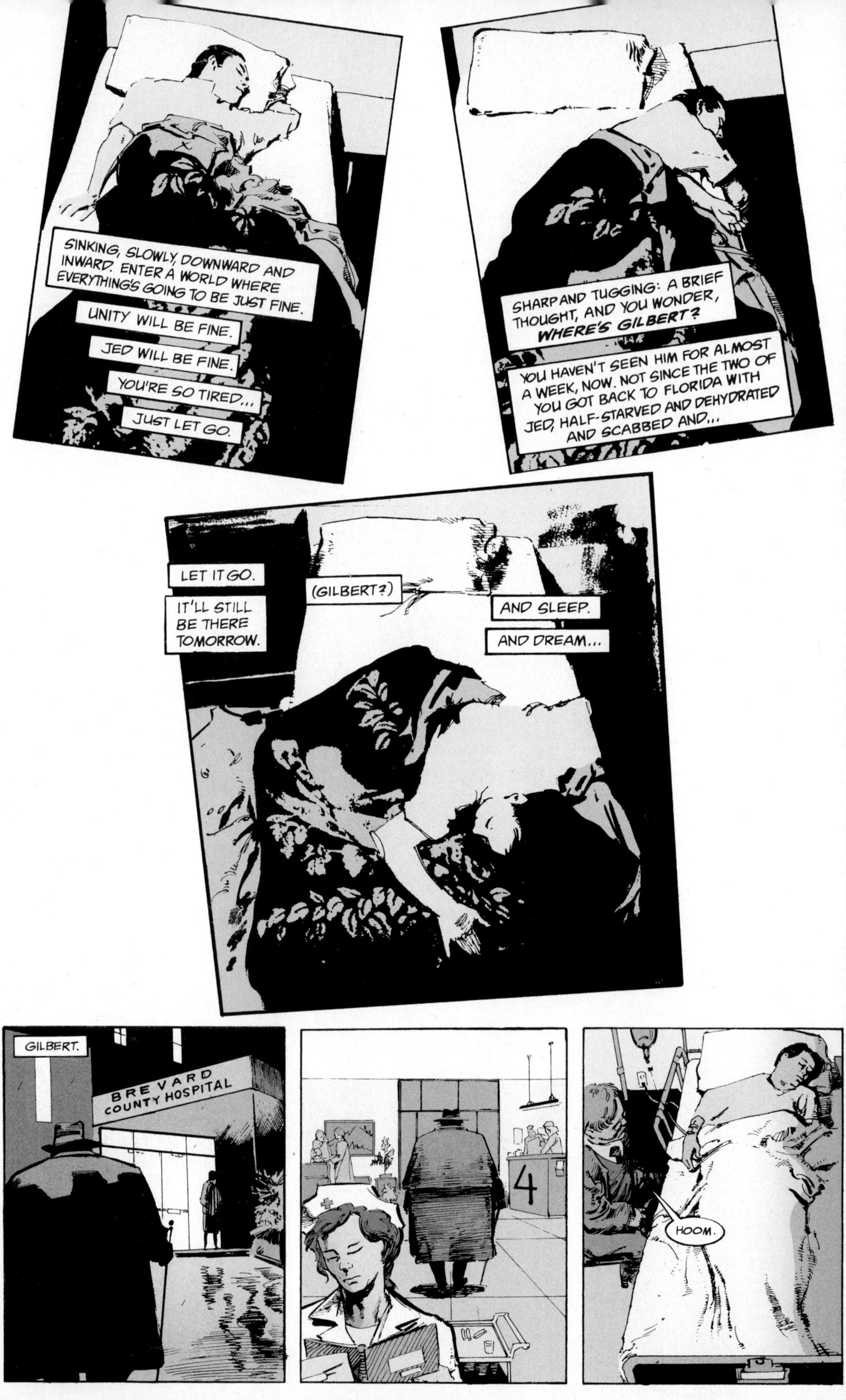
SINKING, SLOWLY, DOWNWARD AND INWARD. ENTER A WORLD WHERE EVERYTHING'S GOING TO BE JUST FINE.
UNITY WILL BE FINE.
JED WILL BE FINE.
YOU'RE SO TIRED...
JUST LET GO.
SHARP AND TUGGING: A BRIEF THOUGHT, AND YOU WONDER, WHERE'S GILBERT?
YOU HAVEN'T SEEN HIM FOR ALMOST A WEEK, NOW. NOT SINCE THE TWO OF YOU GOT BACK TO FLORIDA WITH JED, HALF-STARVED AND DEHYDRATED AND SCABBED AND...
LET IT GO.
IT'LL STILL BE THERE TOMORROW.
(GILBERT?)
AND SLEEP.
AND DREAM...
GILBERT.
BREVARD COUNTY HOSPITAL
4
HOOM.

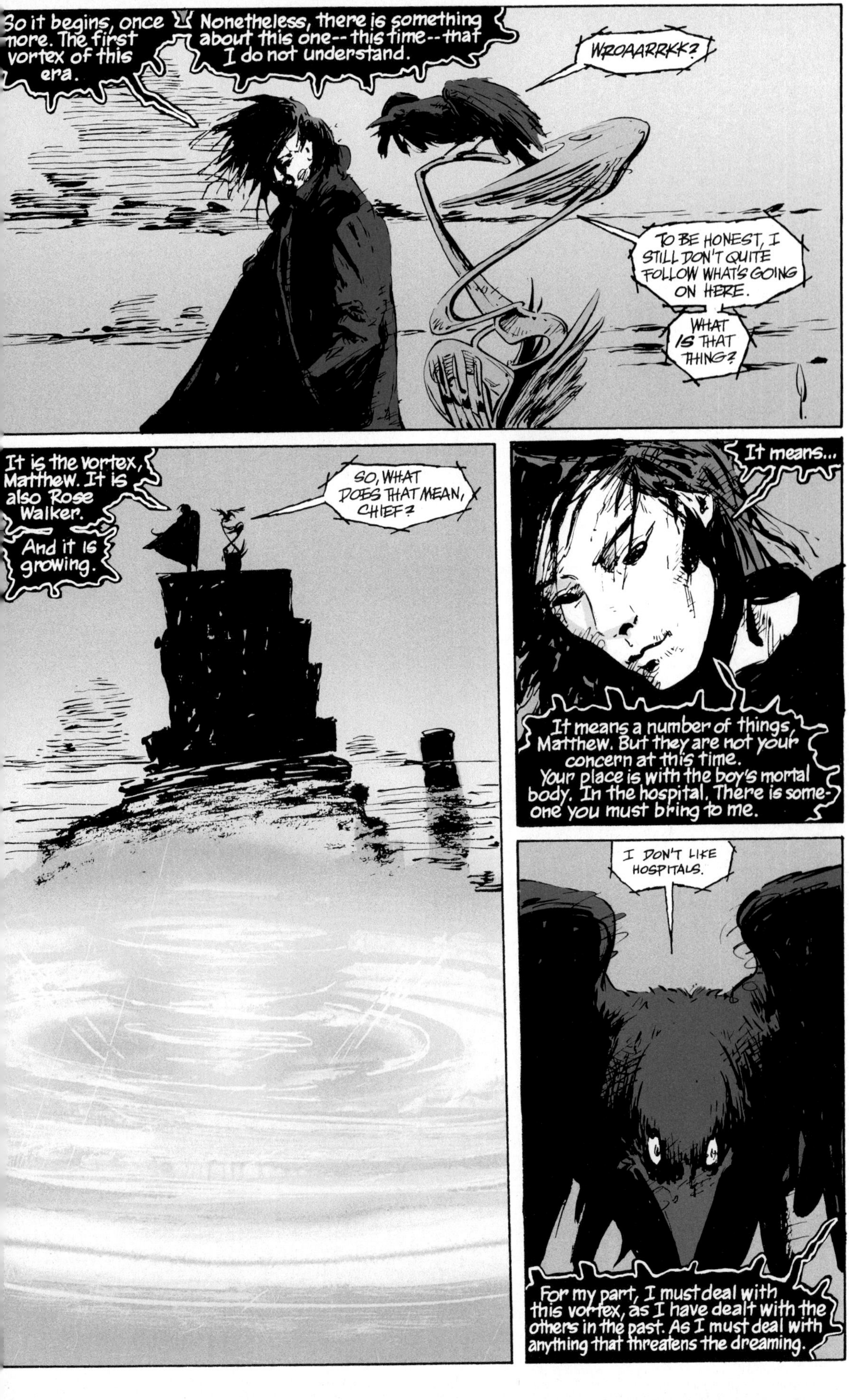

So it begins, once more. The first vortex of this era.
Nonetheless, there is something about this one-- this time-- that I do not understand.
WROAARRKK?
TO BE HONEST, I STILL DON'T QUITE FOLLOW WHAT'S GOING ON HERE.
WHAT IS THAT THING?
It is the vortex, Matthew. It is also Rose Walker.
And it is growing.
SO, WHAT DOES THAT MEAN, CHIEF?
It means...
It means a number of things, Matthew. But they are not your concern at this time. Your place is with the boy's mortal body. In the hospital. There is some-one you must bring to me.
I DON'T LIKE HOSPITALS.
For my part, I must deal with this vortex, as I have dealt with the others in the past. As I must deal with anything that threatens the dreaming.

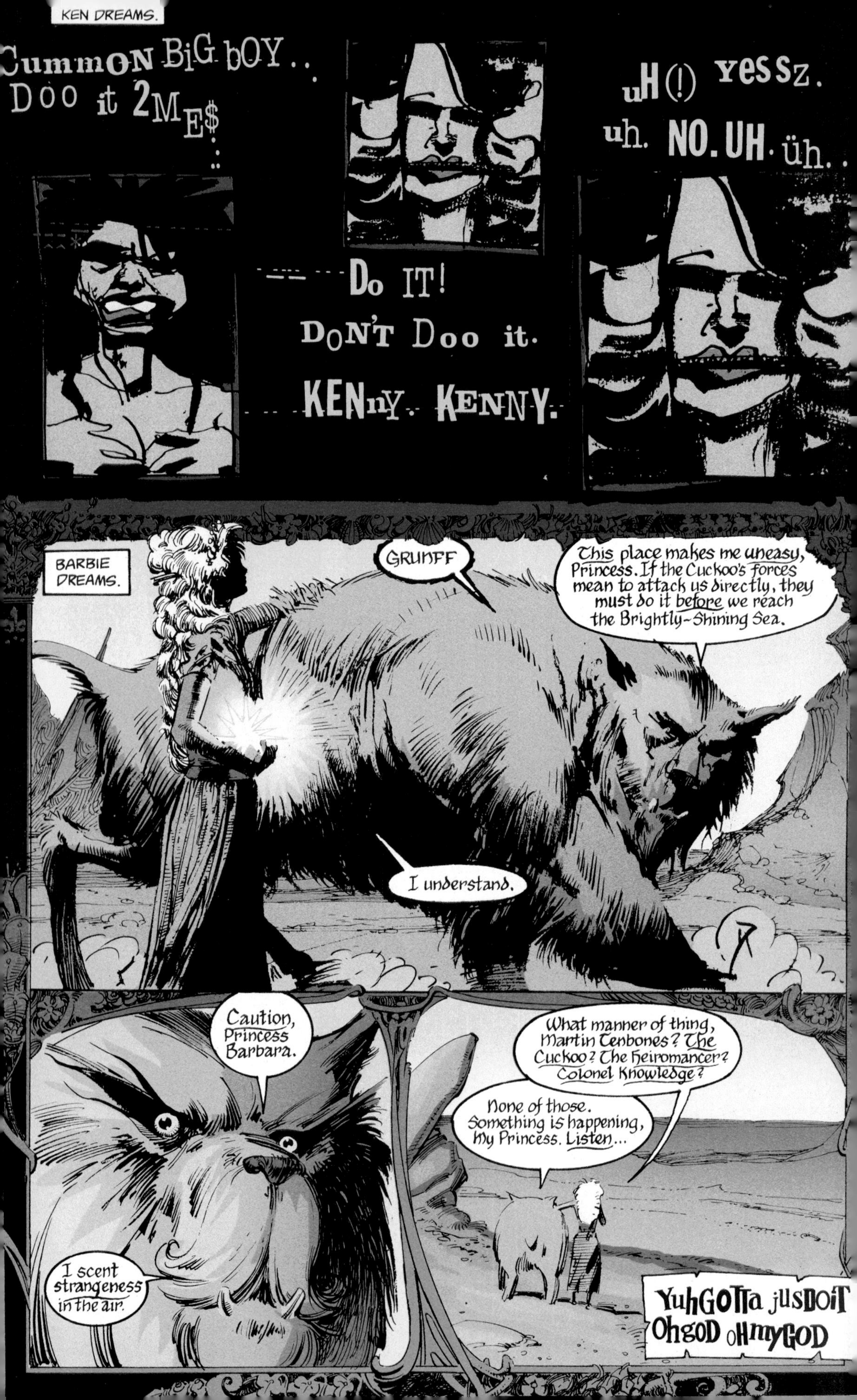
KEN DREAMS.
Cummon Big boy.. Doo it 2ME$..
uH(!) yessz. uh. NO.UH.üh..
Do IT!
DON'T Doo it.
KENny. KENNY.
BARBIE DREAMS.
GRUNFF
This place makes me uneasy, Princess. If the Cuckoo's forces mean to attack us directly, they must do it before we reach the Brightly-Shining Sea.
I understand.
Caution, Princess Barbara.
What manner of thing, Martin Tenbones? The Cuckoo? The Heiromancer? Colonel Knowledge?
None of those. Something is happening, My Princess. Listen...
I scent strangeness in the air.
YuhGOTTa jusDOiT OhgOD oHmyGOD

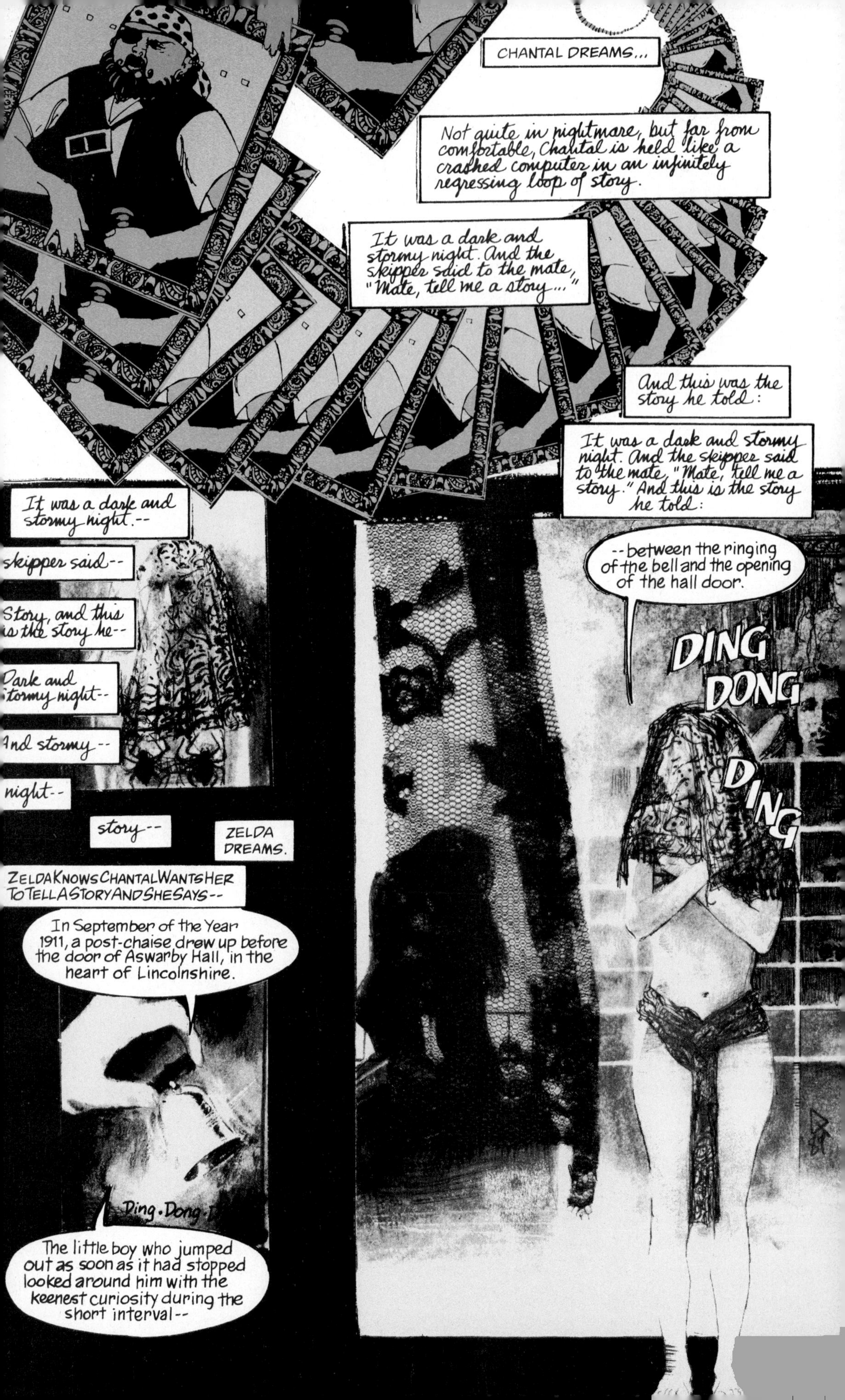
CHANTAL DREAMS...
Not quite in nightmare, but far from comfortable, Chantal is held like a crashed computer in an infinitely regressing loop of story.
It was a dark and stormy night. And the skipper said to the mate, "Mate, tell me a story..."
And this was the story he told:
It was a dark and stormy night. And the skipper said to the mate, "Mate, tell me a story." And this is the story he told:
It was a dark and stormy night.--
skipper said--
Story, and this is the story he--
Dark and stormy night--
And stormy--
night--
story--
ZELDA DREAMS.
ZELDA KNOWS CHANTAL WANTS HER TO TELL A STORY AND SHE SAYS--
In September of the Year 1911, a post-chaise drew up before the door of Aswarby Hall, in the heart of Lincolnshire.
Ding.Dong.
The little boy who jumped out as soon as it had stopped looked around him with the keenest curiosity during the short interval--
--between the ringing of the bell and the opening of the hall door.
DING DONG
DING

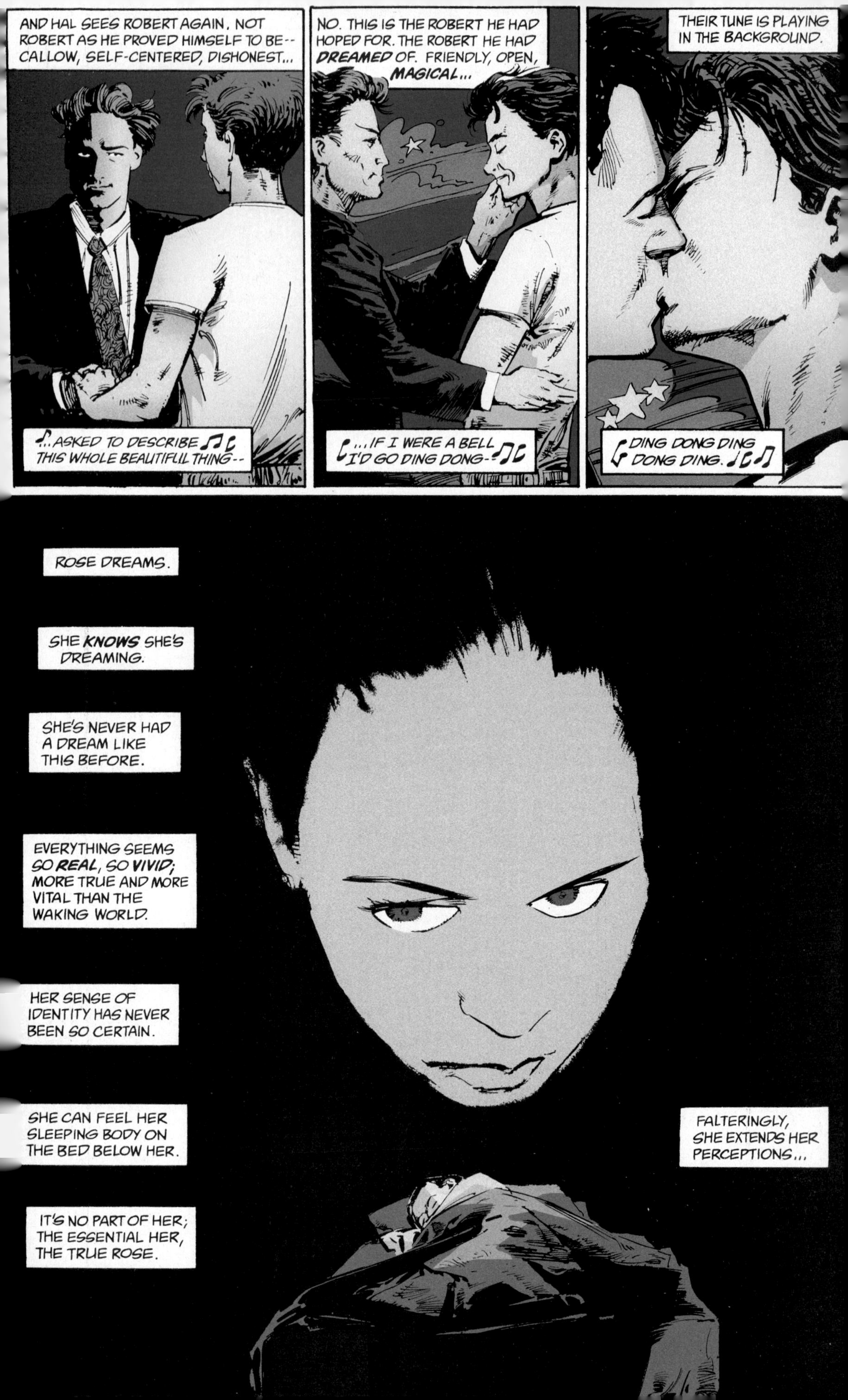
AND HAL SEES ROBERT AGAIN. NOT ROBERT AS HE PROVED HIMSELF TO BE-- CALLOW, SELF-CENTERED, DISHONEST...
♪...ASKED TO DESCRIBE ♫ THIS WHOLE BEAUTIFUL THING--
NO. THIS IS THE ROBERT HE HAD HOPED FOR. THE ROBERT HE HAD DREAMED OF. FRIENDLY, OPEN, MAGICAL...
...IF I WERE A BELL I'D GO DING DONG-- ♫
THEIR TUNE IS PLAYING IN THE BACKGROUND.
DING DONG DING DONG DING. ♪♫
ROSE DREAMS.
SHE KNOWS SHE'S DREAMING.
SHE'S NEVER HAD A DREAM LIKE THIS BEFORE.
EVERYTHING SEEMS SO REAL, SO VIVID; MORE TRUE AND MORE VITAL THAN THE WAKING WORLD.
HER SENSE OF IDENTITY HAS NEVER BEEN SO CERTAIN.
SHE CAN FEEL HER SLEEPING BODY ON THE BED BELOW HER.
IT'S NO PART OF HER; THE ESSENTIAL HER, THE TRUE ROSE.
FALTERINGLY, SHE EXTENDS HER PERCEPTIONS...

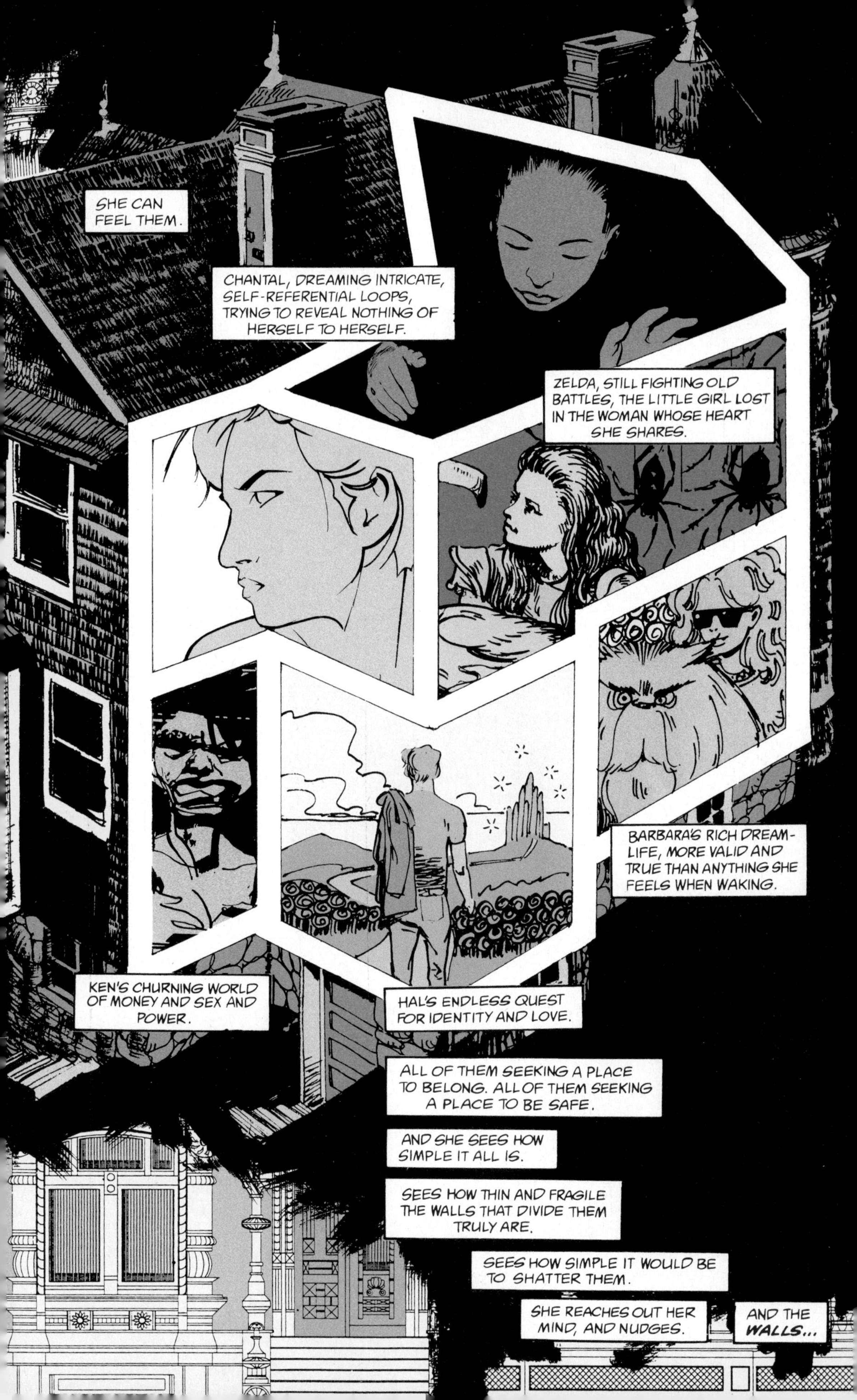

SHE CAN FEEL THEM.
CHANTAL, DREAMING INTRICATE, SELF-REFERENTIAL LOOPS, TRYING TO REVEAL NOTHING OF HERSELF TO HERSELF.
ZELDA, STILL FIGHTING OLD BATTLES, THE LITTLE GIRL LOST IN THE WOMAN WHOSE HEART SHE SHARES.
BARBARA'S RICH DREAM-LIFE, MORE VALID AND TRUE THAN ANYTHING SHE FEELS WHEN WAKING.
KEN'S CHURNING WORLD OF MONEY AND SEX AND POWER.
HAL'S ENDLESS QUEST FOR IDENTITY AND LOVE.
ALL OF THEM SEEKING A PLACE TO BELONG. ALL OF THEM SEEKING A PLACE TO BE SAFE.
AND SHE SEES HOW SIMPLE IT ALL IS.
SEES HOW THIN AND FRAGILE THE WALLS THAT DIVIDE THEM TRULY ARE.
SEES HOW SIMPLE IT WOULD BE TO SHATTER THEM.
SHE REACHES OUT HER MIND, AND NUDGES.
AND THE WALLS...

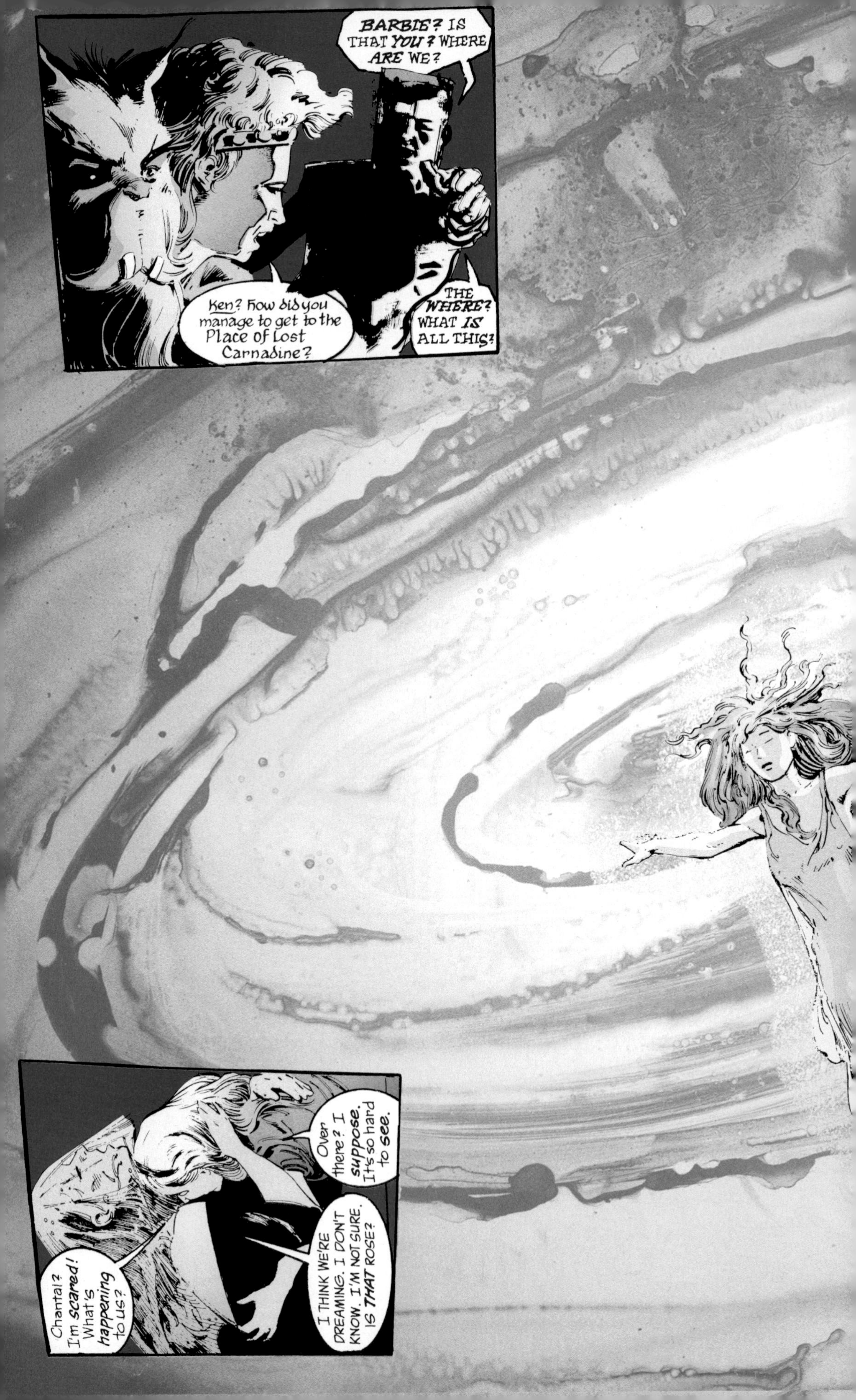
BARBIE? IS THAT YOU? WHERE ARE WE?
Ken? How did you manage to get to the Place of Lost Carnadine?
THE WHERE? WHAT IS ALL THIS?
Chantal? I'm scared! What's happening to us?
I THINK WE'RE DREAMING. I DON'T KNOW. I'M NOT SURE. IS THAT ROSE?
Over there? I suppose. It's so hard to see.

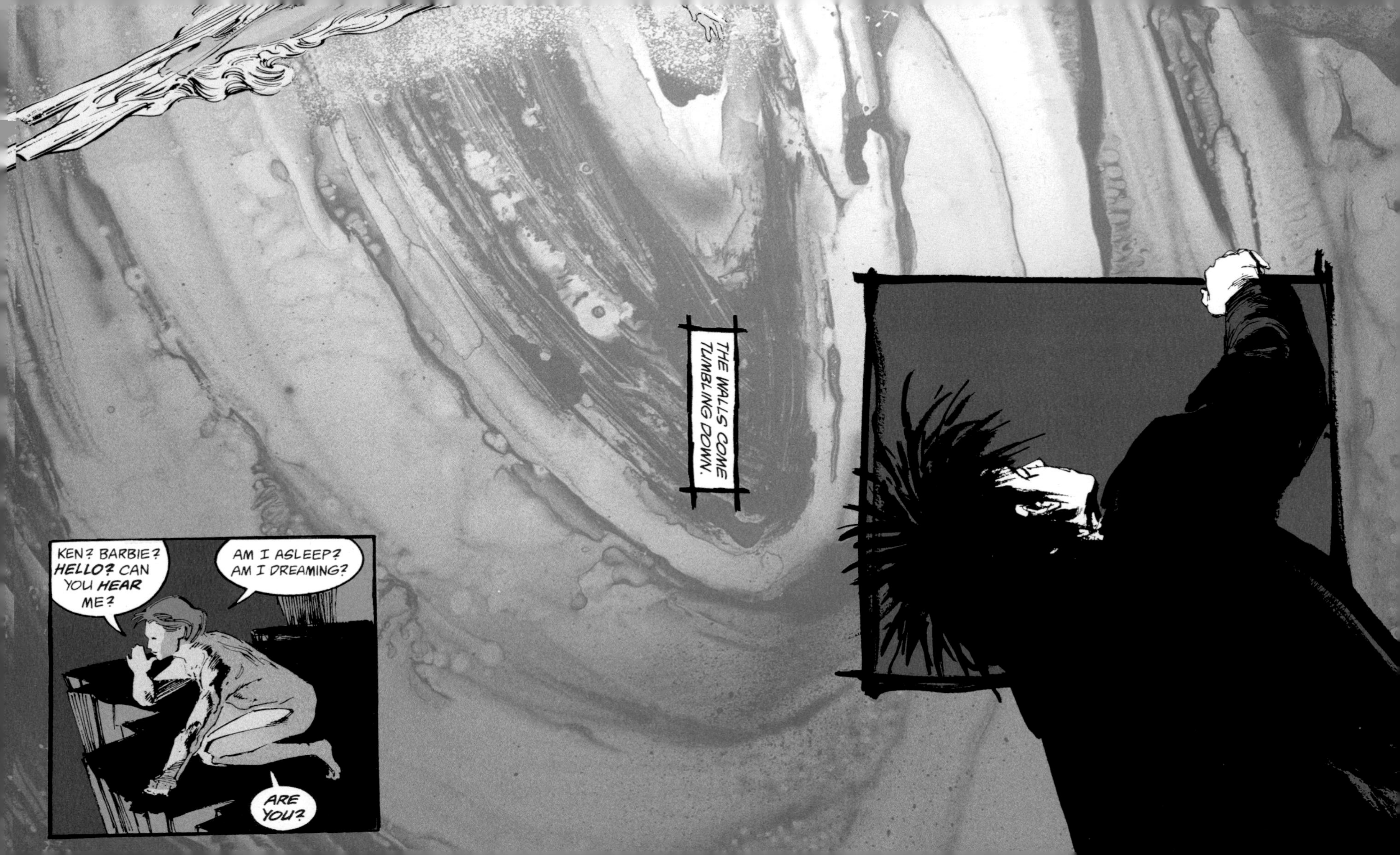

KEN? BARBIE? HELLO? CAN YOU HEAR ME?
AM I ASLEEP? AM I DREAMING?
ARE YOU?
THE WALLS COME TUMBLING DOWN.

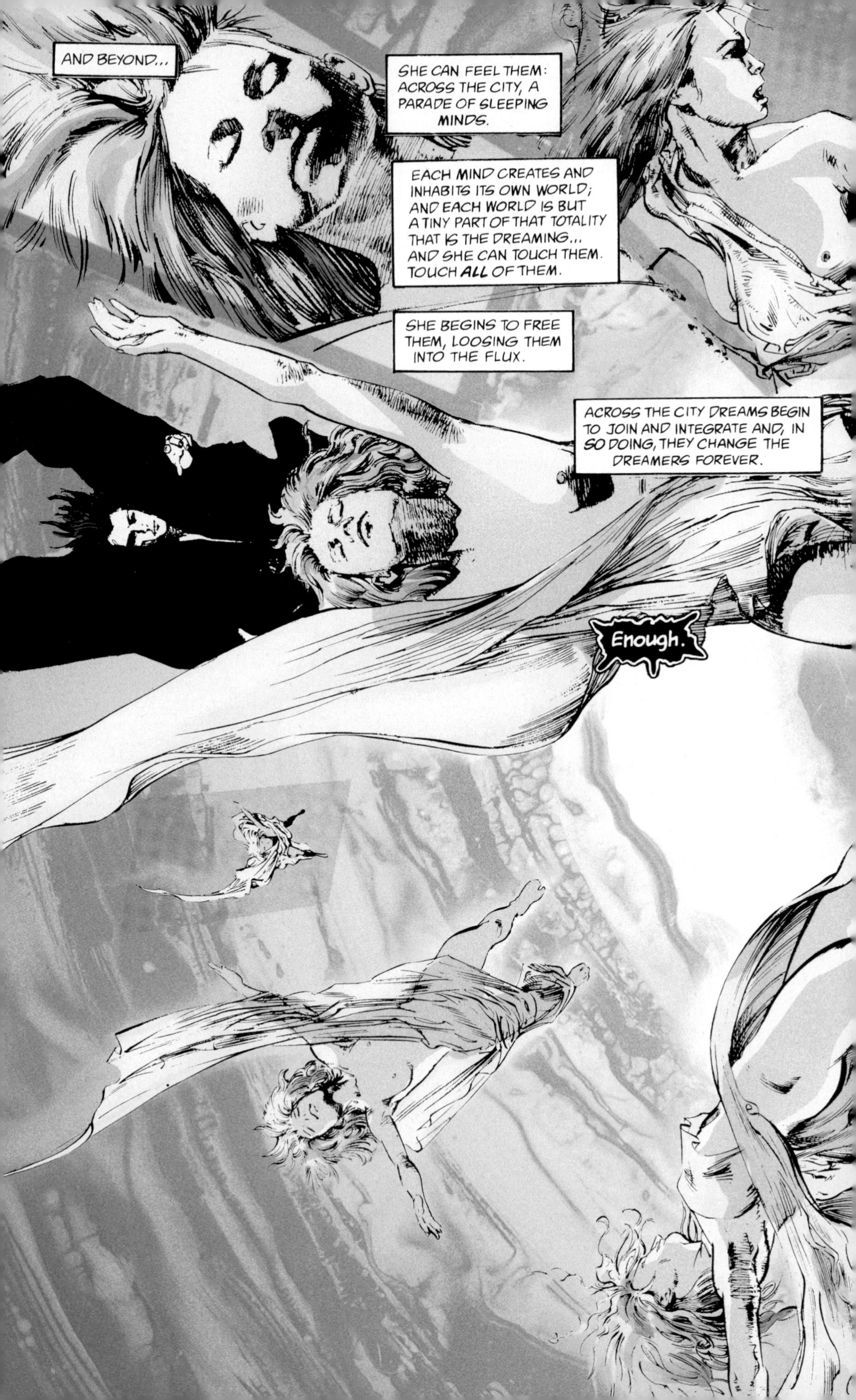
AND BEYOND...
SHE CAN FEEL THEM: ACROSS THE CITY, A PARADE OF SLEEPING MINDS.
EACH MIND CREATES AND INHABITS ITS OWN WORLD; AND EACH WORLD IS BUT A TINY PART OF THAT TOTALITY THAT IS THE DREAMING... AND SHE CAN TOUCH THEM. TOUCH ALL OF THEM.
SHE BEGINS TO FREE THEM, LOOSING THEM INTO THE FLUX.
ACROSS THE CITY DREAMS BEGIN TO JOIN AND INTEGRATE AND, IN SO DOING, THEY CHANGE THE DREAMERS FOREVER.
Enough.

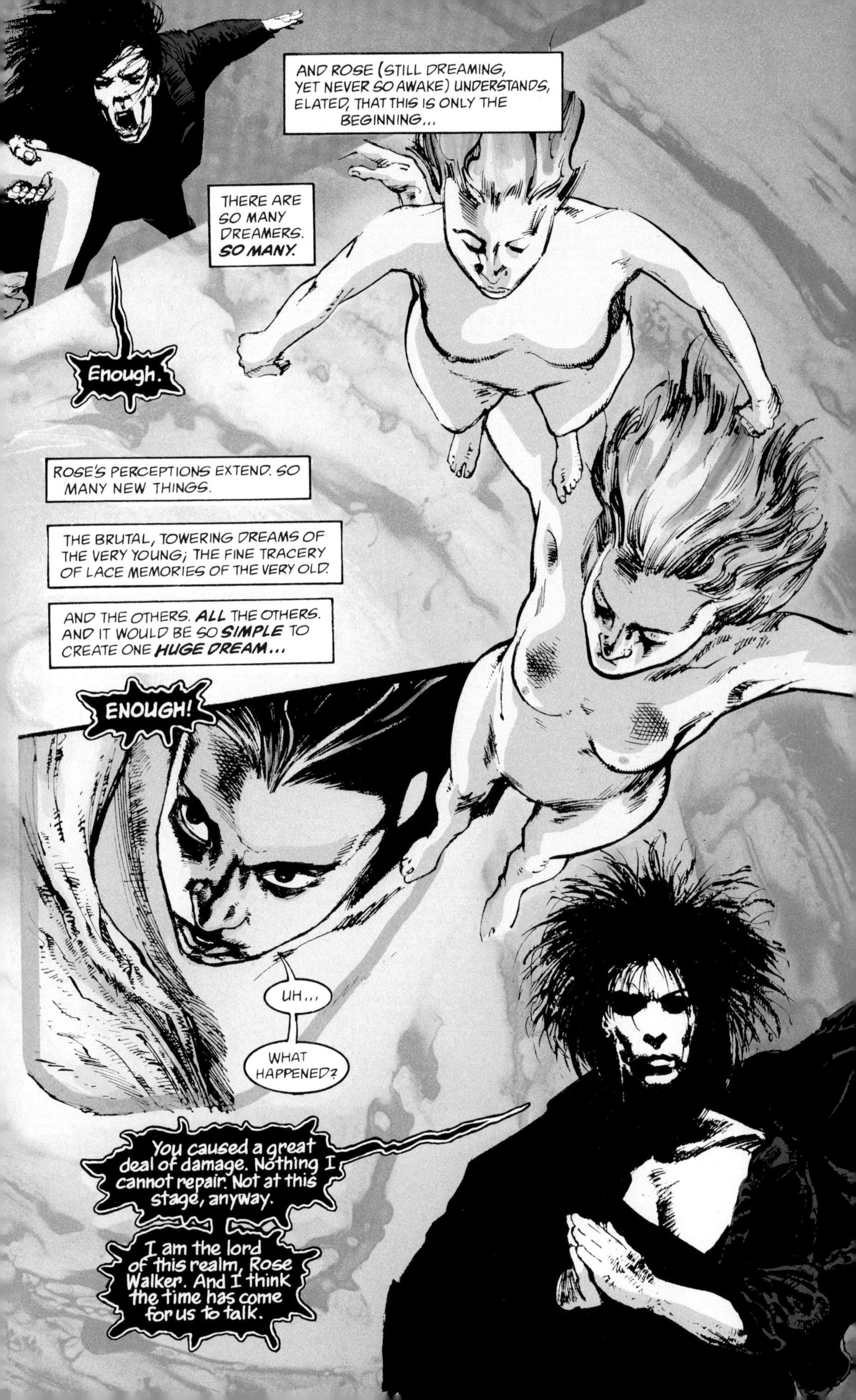
AND ROSE (STILL DREAMING, YET NEVER SO AWAKE) UNDERSTANDS, ELATED, THAT THIS IS ONLY THE BEGINNING...
THERE ARE SO MANY DREAMERS. SO MANY.
Enough.
ROSE'S PERCEPTIONS EXTEND. SO MANY NEW THINGS.
THE BRUTAL, TOWERING DREAMS OF THE VERY YOUNG; THE FINE TRACERY OF LACE MEMORIES OF THE VERY OLD.
AND THE OTHERS. ALL THE OTHERS. AND IT WOULD BE SO SIMPLE TO CREATE ONE HUGE DREAM...
ENOUGH!
UH...
WHAT HAPPENED?
You caused a great deal of damage. Nothing I cannot repair. Not at this stage, anyway.
I am the lord of this realm, Rose Walker. And I think the time has come for us to talk.

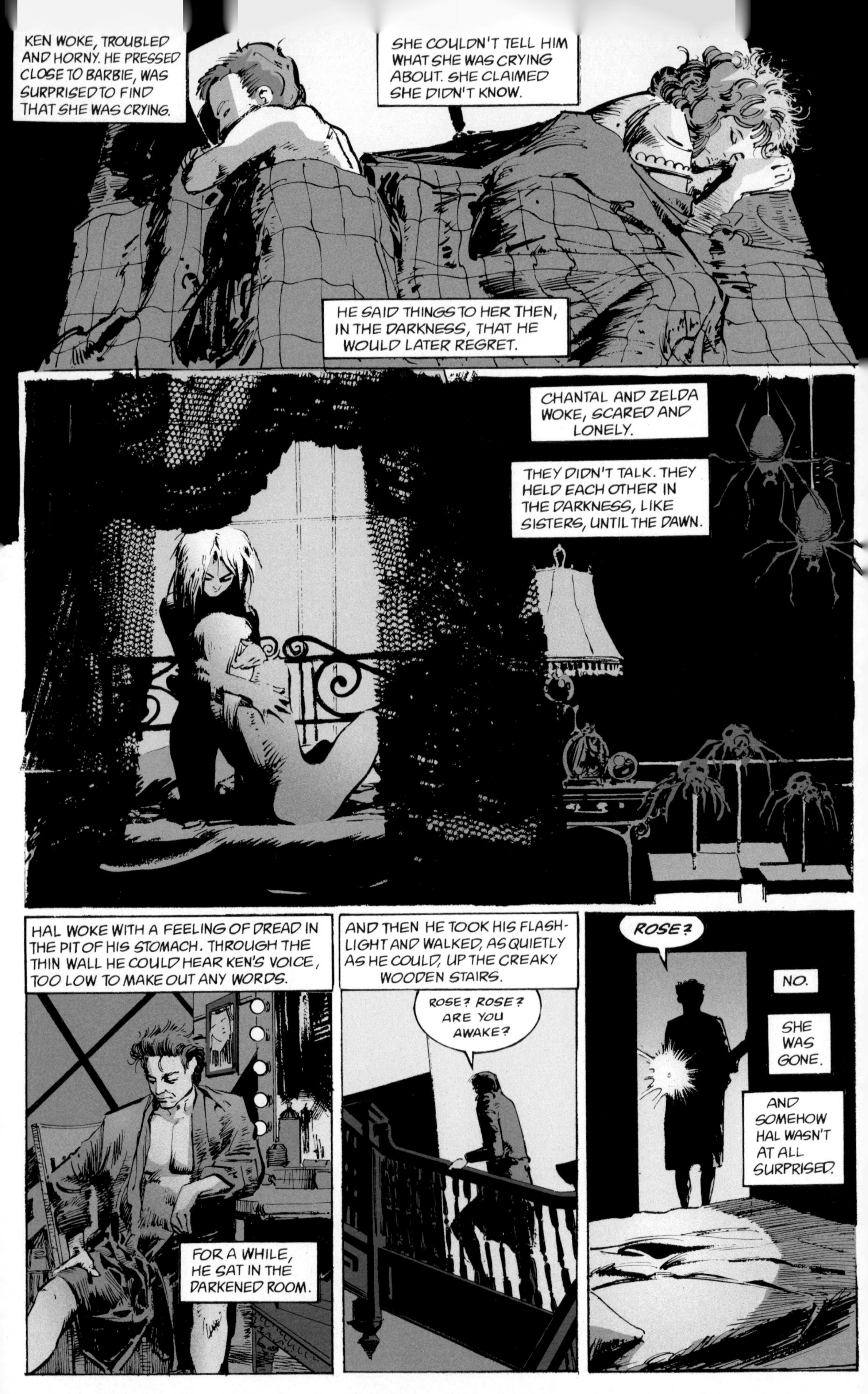
KEN WOKE, TROUBLED AND HORNY. HE PRESSED CLOSE TO BARBIE, WAS SURPRISED TO FIND THAT SHE WAS CRYING.
SHE COULDN'T TELL HIM WHAT SHE WAS CRYING ABOUT. SHE CLAIMED SHE DIDN'T KNOW.
HE SAID THINGS TO HER THEN, IN THE DARKNESS, THAT HE WOULD LATER REGRET.
CHANTAL AND ZELDA WOKE, SCARED AND LONELY.
THEY DIDN'T TALK. THEY HELD EACH OTHER IN THE DARKNESS, LIKE SISTERS, UNTIL THE DAWN.
HAL WOKE WITH A FEELING OF DREAD IN THE PIT OF HIS STOMACH. THROUGH THE THIN WALL HE COULD HEAR KEN'S VOICE, TOO LOW TO MAKE OUT ANY WORDS.
FOR A WHILE, HE SAT IN THE DARKENED ROOM.
AND THEN HE TOOK HIS FLASH-LIGHT AND WALKED, AS QUIETLY AS HE COULD, UP THE CREAKY WOODEN STAIRS.
ROSE? ROSE? ARE YOU AWAKE?
ROSE?
NO.
SHE WAS GONE.
AND SOMEHOW HAL WASN'T AT ALL SURPRISED.

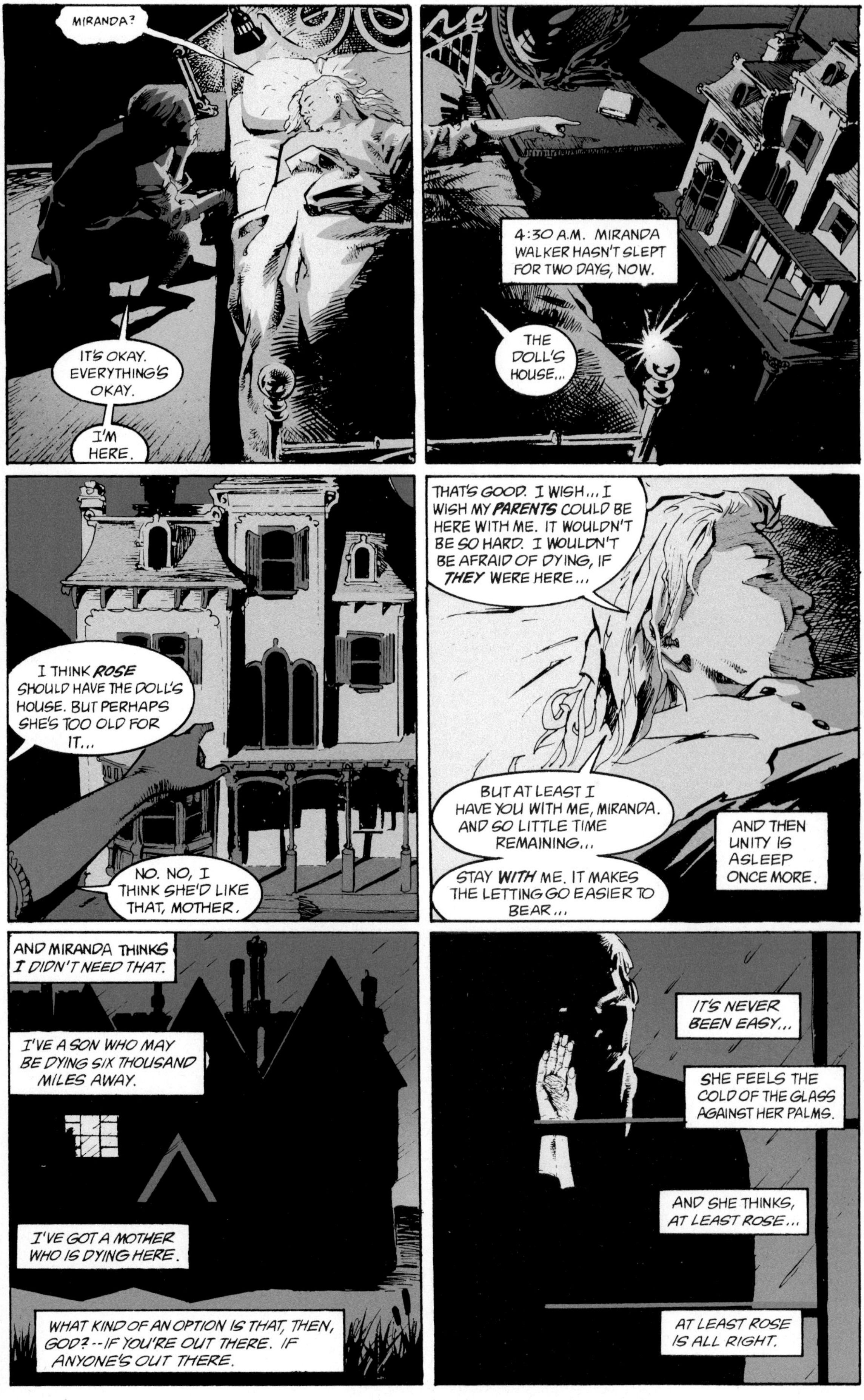
MIRANDA?
IT'S OKAY. EVERYTHING'S OKAY.
I'M HERE.
4:30 A.M. MIRANDA WALKER HASN'T SLEPT FOR TWO DAYS, NOW.
THE DOLL'S HOUSE...
I THINK ROSE SHOULD HAVE THE DOLL'S HOUSE. BUT PERHAPS SHE'S TOO OLD FOR IT...
NO. NO, I THINK SHE'D LIKE THAT, MOTHER.
THAT'S GOOD. I WISH... I WISH MY PARENTS COULD BE HERE WITH ME. IT WOULDN'T BE SO HARD. I WOULDN'T BE AFRAID OF DYING, IF THEY WERE HERE...
BUT AT LEAST I HAVE YOU WITH ME, MIRANDA. AND SO LITTLE TIME REMAINING...
STAY WITH ME. IT MAKES THE LETTING GO EASIER TO BEAR...
AND THEN UNITY IS ASLEEP ONCE MORE.
AND MIRANDA THINKS I DIDN'T NEED THAT.
I'VE A SON WHO MAY BE DYING SIX THOUSAND MILES AWAY.
I'VE GOT A MOTHER WHO IS DYING HERE.
WHAT KIND OF AN OPTION IS THAT, THEN, GOD? --IF YOU'RE OUT THERE. IF ANYONE'S OUT THERE.
IT'S NEVER BEEN EASY...
SHE FEELS THE COLD OF THE GLASS AGAINST HER PALMS.
AND SHE THINKS, AT LEAST ROSE...
AT LEAST ROSE IS ALL RIGHT.

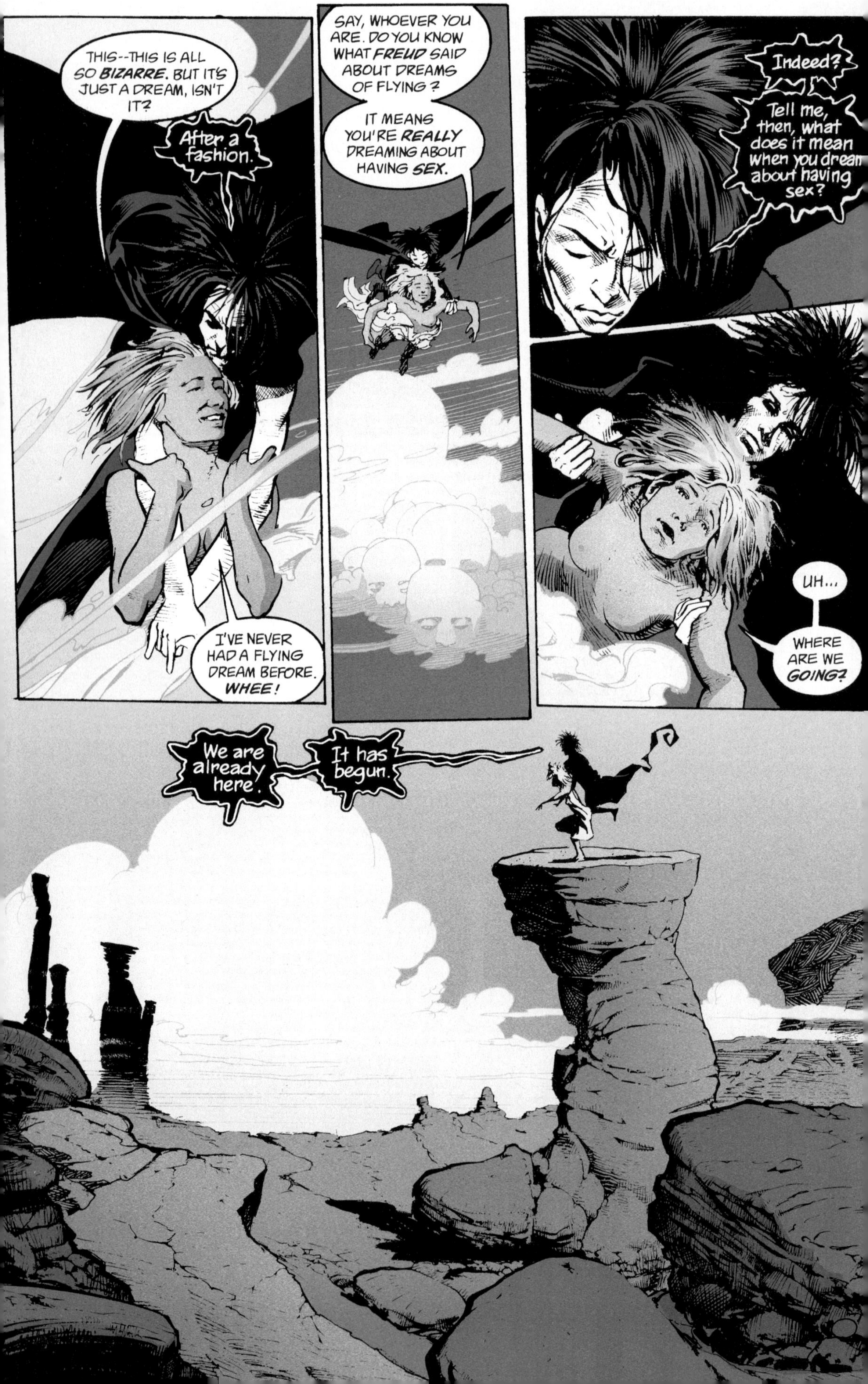

THIS--THIS IS ALL SO BIZARRE. BUT IT'S JUST A DREAM, ISN'T IT?
After a fashion.
I'VE NEVER HAD A FLYING DREAM BEFORE. WHEE!
SAY, WHOEVER YOU ARE. DO YOU KNOW WHAT FREUD SAID ABOUT DREAMS OF FLYING?
IT MEANS YOU'RE REALLY DREAMING ABOUT HAVING SEX.
Indeed?
Tell me, then, what does it mean when you dream about having sex?
UH...
WHERE ARE WE GOING?
We are already here.
It has begun.

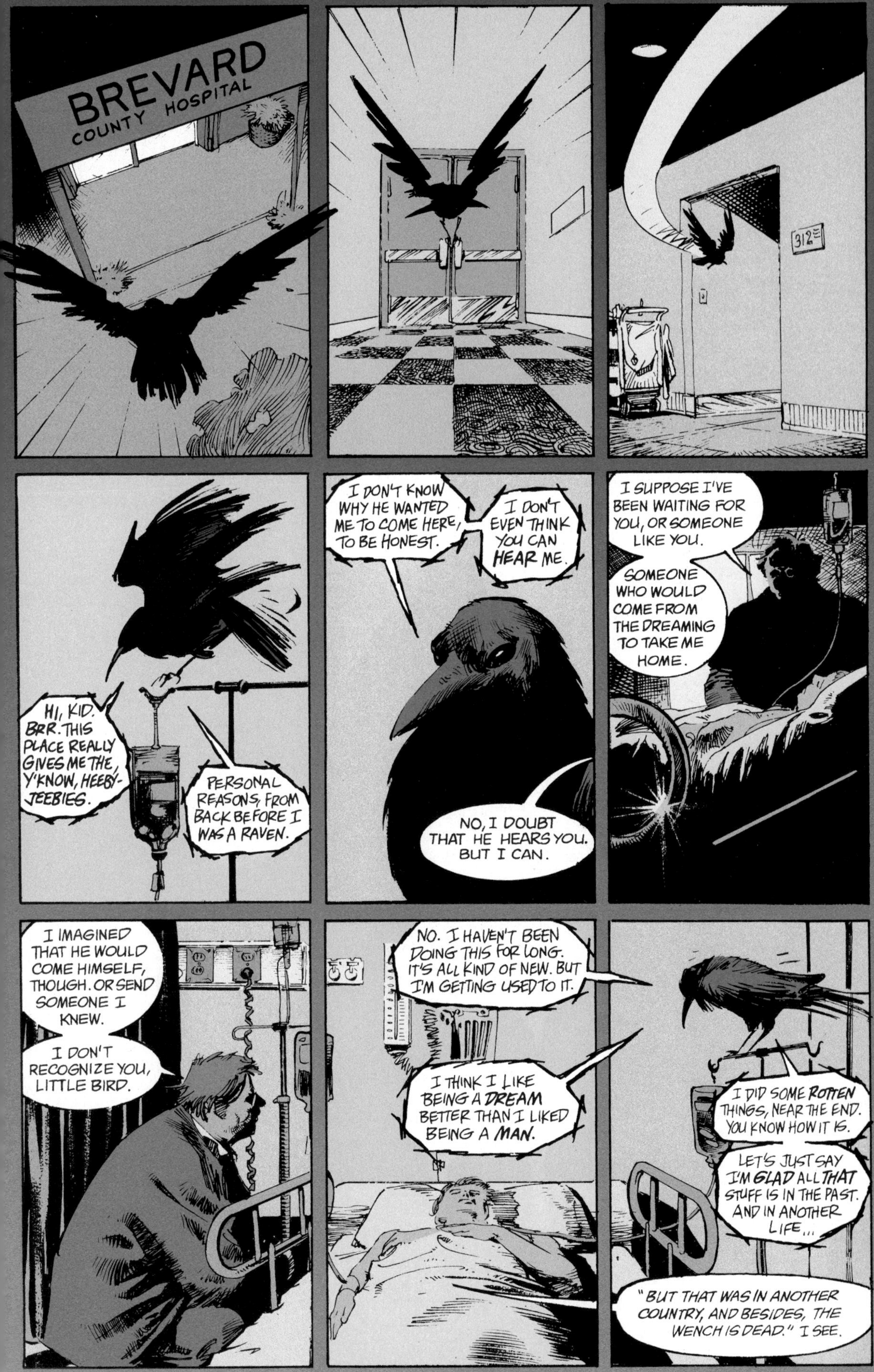
BREVARD COUNTY HOSPITAL
312
HI, KID. BRR. THIS PLACE REALLY GIVES ME THE, Y'KNOW, HEEBY-JEEBIES.
PERSONAL REASONS, FROM BACK BEFORE I WAS A RAVEN.
I DON'T KNOW WHY HE WANTED ME TO COME HERE, TO BE HONEST.
I DON'T EVEN THINK YOU CAN HEAR ME.
NO, I DOUBT THAT HE HEARS YOU. BUT I CAN.
I SUPPOSE I'VE BEEN WAITING FOR YOU, OR SOMEONE LIKE YOU.
SOMEONE WHO WOULD COME FROM THE DREAMING TO TAKE ME HOME.
I IMAGINED THAT HE WOULD COME HIMSELF, THOUGH. OR SEND SOMEONE I KNEW.
I DON'T RECOGNIZE YOU, LITTLE BIRD.
NO. I HAVEN'T BEEN DOING THIS FOR LONG. IT'S ALL KIND OF NEW. BUT I'M GETTING USED TO IT.
I THINK I LIKE BEING A DREAM BETTER THAN I LIKED BEING A MAN.
I DID SOME ROTTEN THINGS, NEAR THE END. YOU KNOW HOW IT IS.
LET'S JUST SAY I'M GLAD ALL THAT STUFF IS IN THE PAST. AND IN ANOTHER LIFE...
"BUT THAT WAS IN ANOTHER COUNTRY, AND BESIDES, THE WENCH IS DEAD." I SEE.

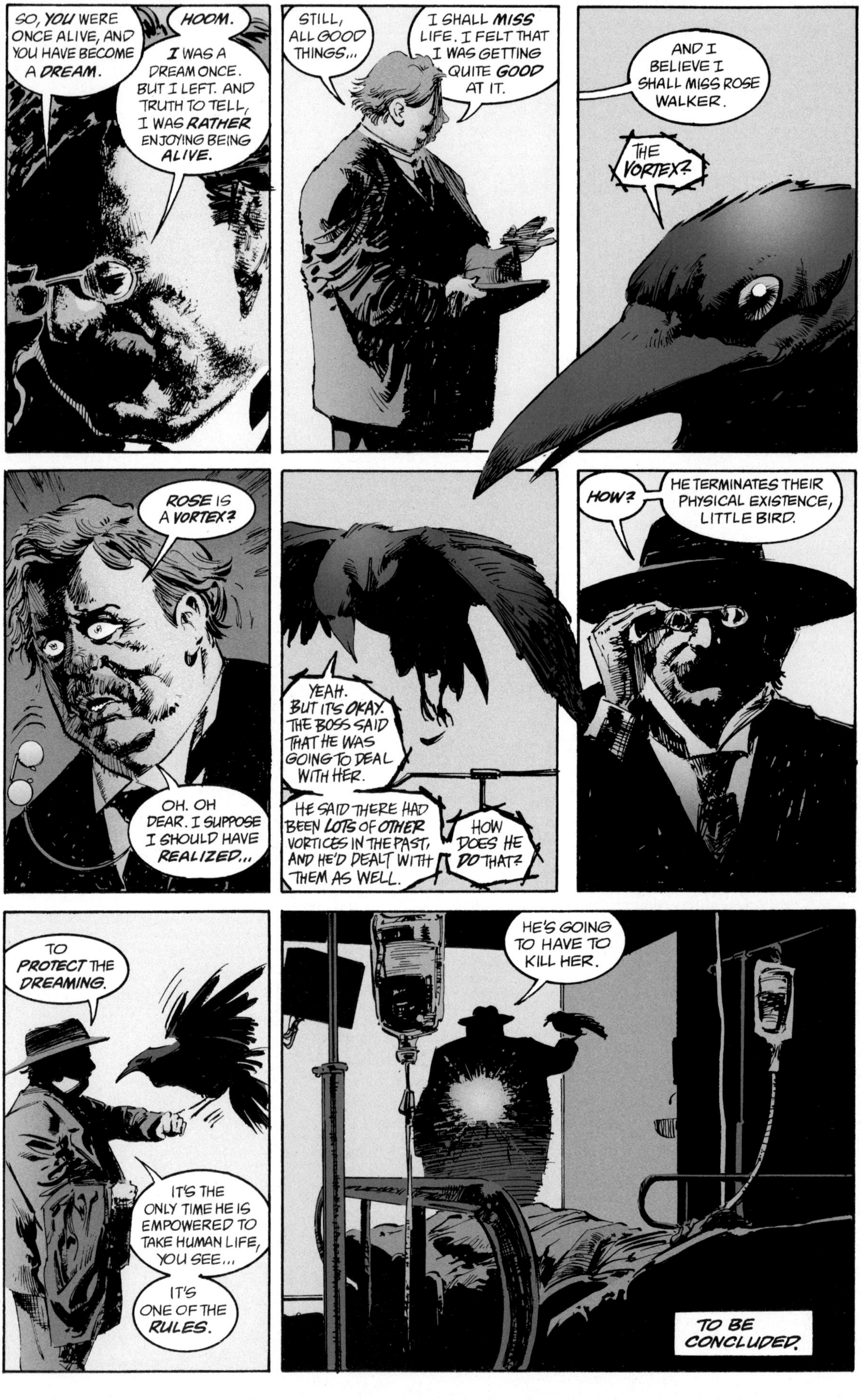
SO, YOU WERE ONCE ALIVE, AND YOU HAVE BECOME A DREAM.
HOOM.
I WAS A DREAM ONCE. BUT I LEFT. AND TRUTH TO TELL, I WAS RATHER ENJOYING BEING ALIVE.
STILL, ALL GOOD THINGS...
I SHALL MISS LIFE. I FELT THAT I WAS GETTING QUITE GOOD AT IT.
AND I BELIEVE I SHALL MISS ROSE WALKER.
THE VORTEX?
ROSE IS A VORTEX?
OH. OH DEAR. I SUPPOSE I SHOULD HAVE REALIZED...
YEAH. BUT IT'S OKAY. THE BOSS SAID THAT HE WAS GOING TO DEAL WITH HER.
HE SAID THERE HAD BEEN LOTS OF OTHER VORTICES IN THE PAST, AND HE'D DEALT WITH THEM AS WELL.
HOW DOES HE DO THAT?
HOW?
HE TERMINATES THEIR PHYSICAL EXISTENCE, LITTLE BIRD.
TO PROTECT THE DREAMING.
IT'S THE ONLY TIME HE IS EMPOWERED TO TAKE HUMAN LIFE, YOU SEE...
IT'S ONE OF THE RULES.
HE'S GOING TO HAVE TO KILL HER.
TO BE CONCLUDED.

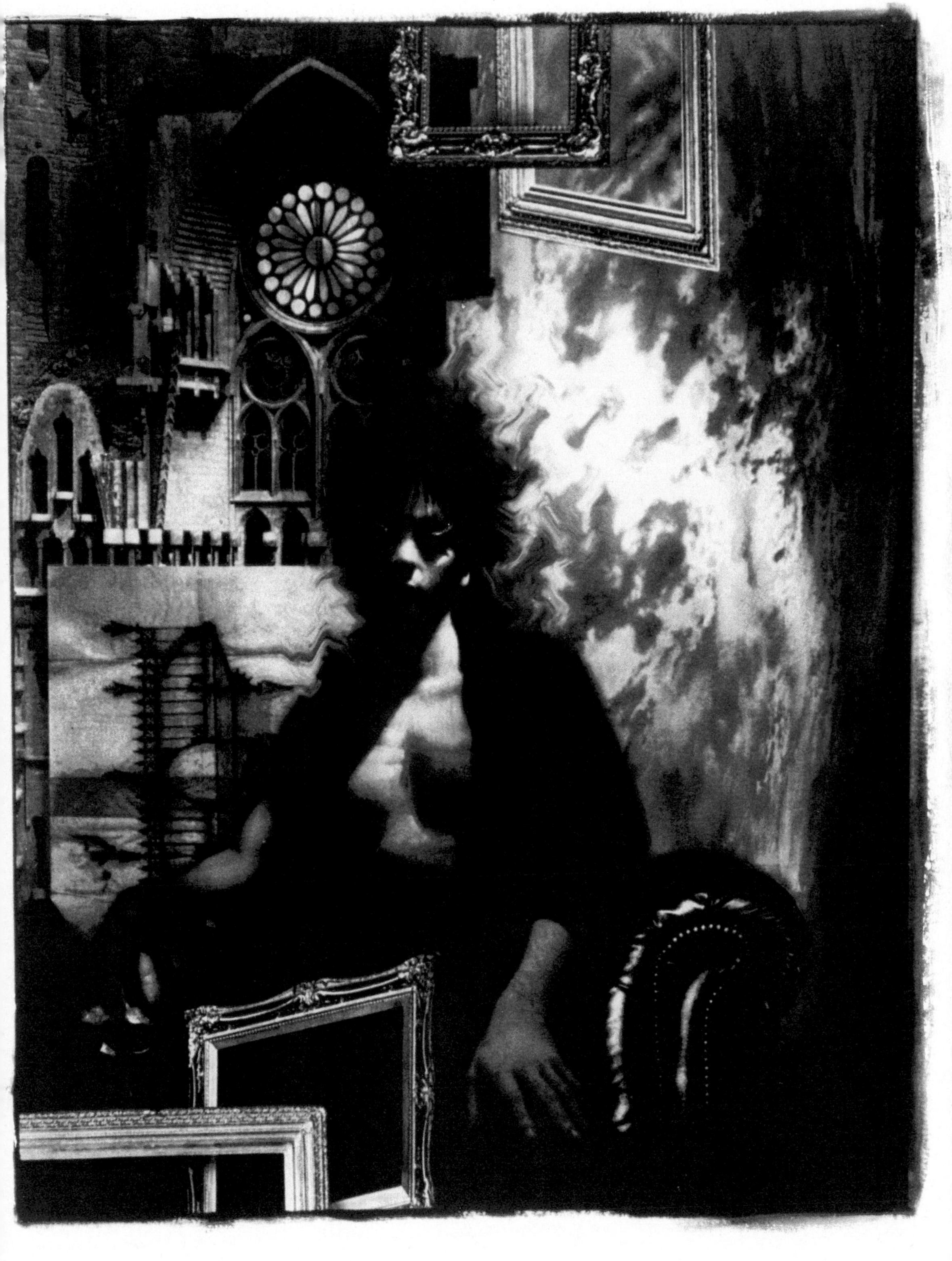

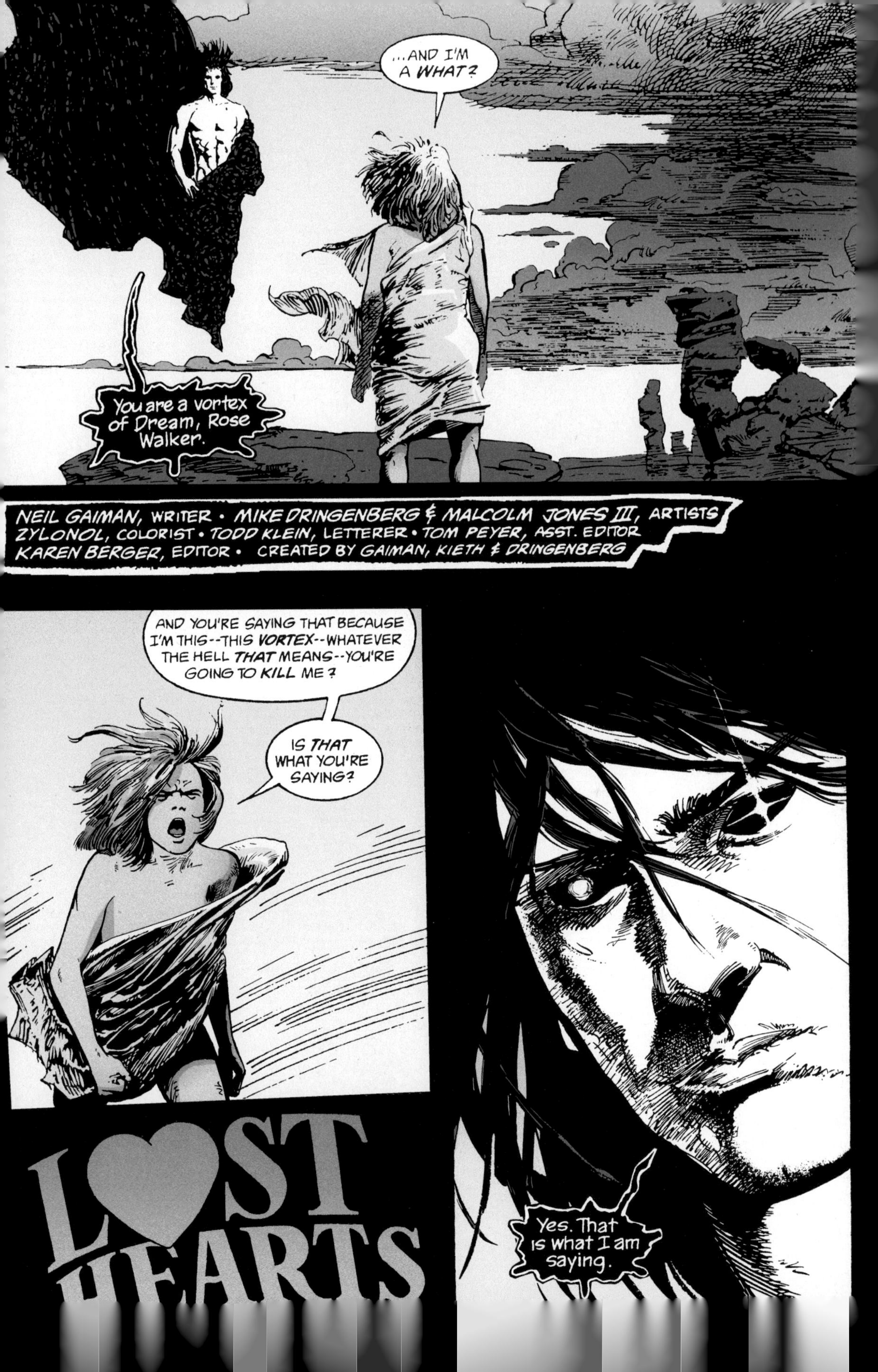
...AND I'M A WHAT?
You are a vortex of Dream, Rose Walker.
NEIL GAIMAN, WRITER • MIKE DRINGENBERG & MALCOLM JONES III, ARTISTS
ZYLONOL, COLORIST • TODD KLEIN, LETTERER • TOM PEYER, ASST. EDITOR
KAREN BERGER, EDITOR • CREATED BY GAIMAN, KIETH & DRINGENBERG
AND YOU'RE SAYING THAT BECAUSE I'M THIS--THIS VORTEX--WHATEVER THE HELL THAT MEANS--YOU'RE GOING TO KILL ME?
IS THAT WHAT YOU'RE SAYING?
Yes. That is what I am saying.
LOST HEARTS

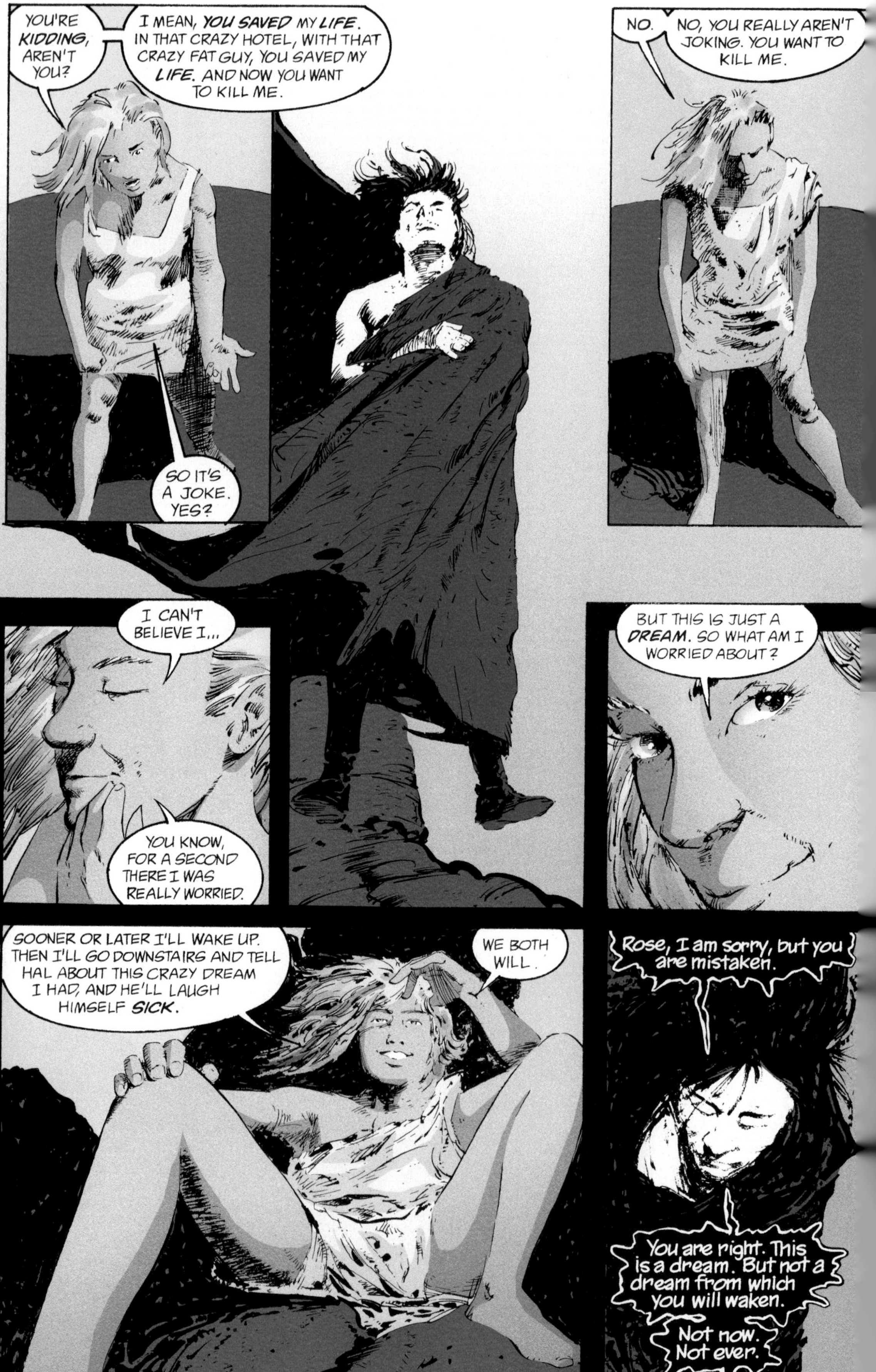
YOU'RE KIDDING, AREN'T YOU?
I MEAN, YOU SAVED MY LIFE. IN THAT CRAZY HOTEL, WITH THAT CRAZY FAT GUY, YOU SAVED MY LIFE. AND NOW YOU WANT TO KILL ME.
SO IT'S A JOKE. YES?
NO.
NO, YOU REALLY AREN'T JOKING. YOU WANT TO KILL ME.
I CAN'T BELIEVE I...
YOU KNOW, FOR A SECOND THERE I WAS REALLY WORRIED.
BUT THIS IS JUST A DREAM. SO WHAT AM I WORRIED ABOUT?
SOONER OR LATER I'LL WAKE UP. THEN I'LL GO DOWNSTAIRS AND TELL HAL ABOUT THIS CRAZY DREAM I HAD, AND HE'LL LAUGH HIMSELF SICK.
WE BOTH WILL.
Rose, I am sorry, but you are mistaken.
You are right. This is a dream. But not a dream from which you will waken.
Not now. Not ever.

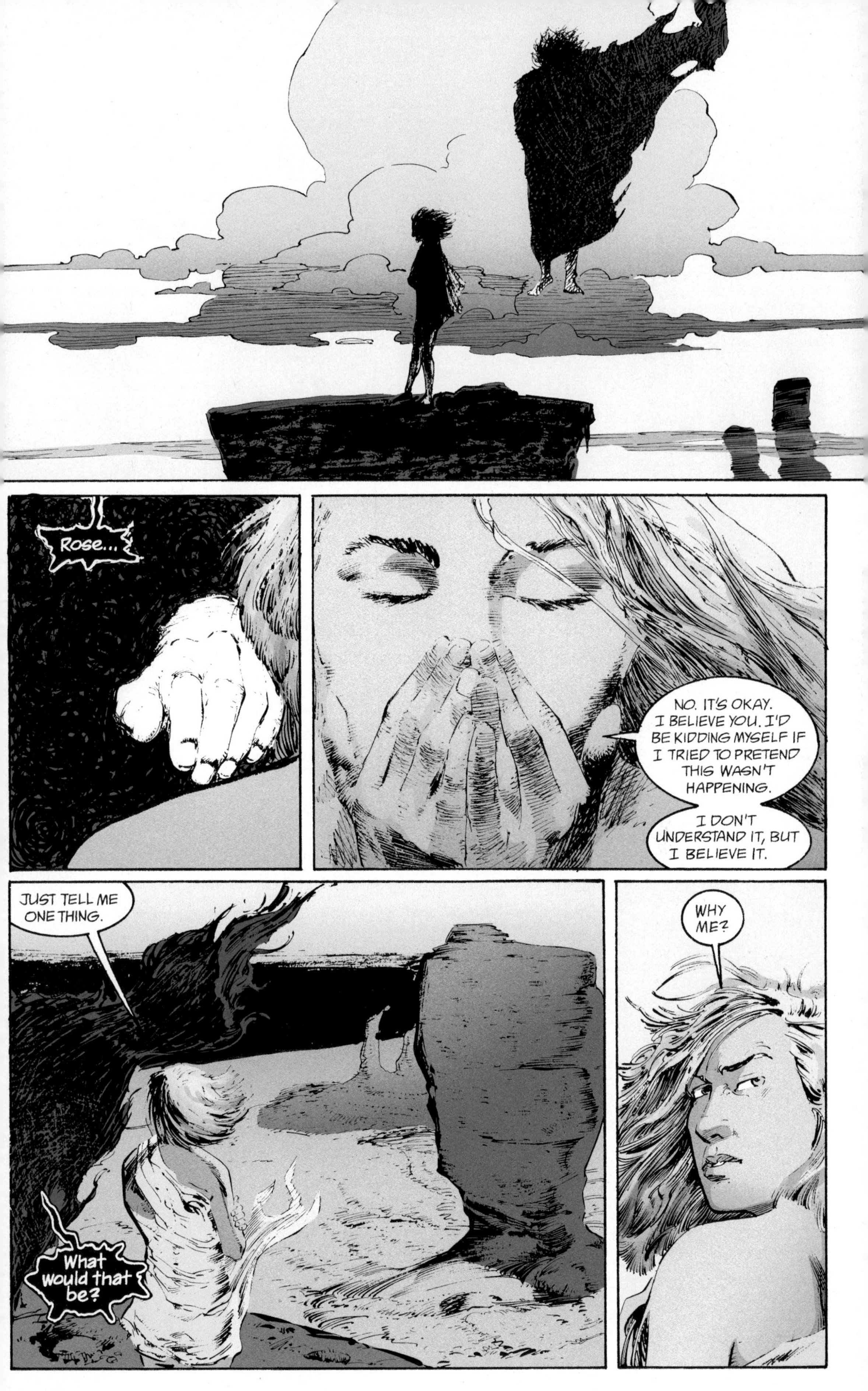
Rose...
NO. IT'S OKAY. I BELIEVE YOU. I'D BE KIDDING MYSELF IF I TRIED TO PRETEND THIS WASN'T HAPPENING.
I DON'T UNDERSTAND IT, BUT I BELIEVE IT.
JUST TELL ME ONE THING.
What would that be?
WHY ME?

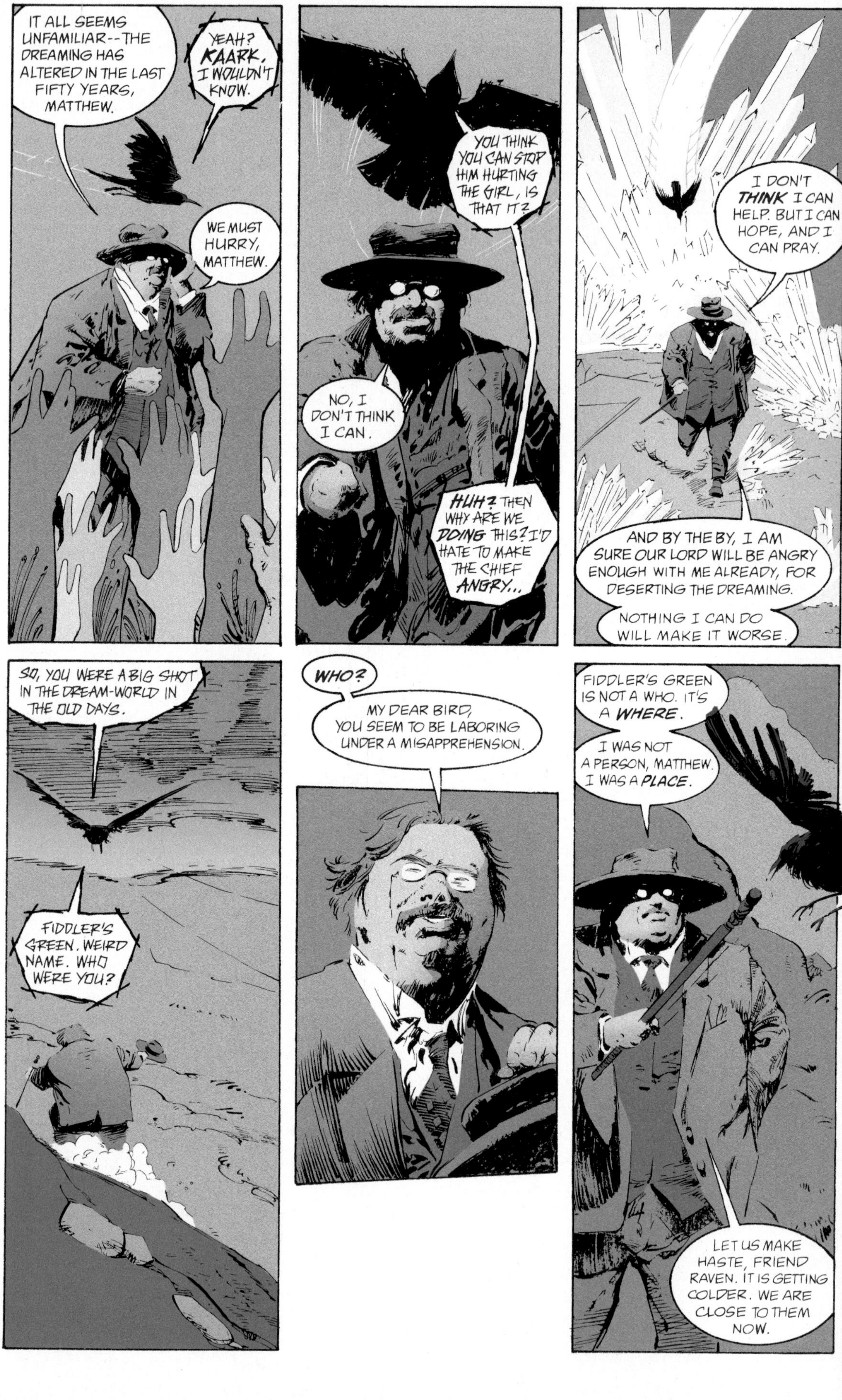
IT ALL SEEMS UNFAMILIAR--THE DREAMING HAS ALTERED IN THE LAST FIFTY YEARS, MATTHEW.
YEAH? KAARK. I WOULDN'T KNOW.
WE MUST HURRY, MATTHEW.
YOU THINK YOU CAN STOP HIM HURTING THE GIRL, IS THAT IT?
NO, I DON'T THINK I CAN.
HUH? THEN WHY ARE WE DOING THIS? I'D HATE TO MAKE THE CHIEF ANGRY...
I DON'T THINK I CAN HELP. BUT I CAN HOPE, AND I CAN PRAY.
AND BY THE BY, I AM SURE OUR LORD WILL BE ANGRY ENOUGH WITH ME ALREADY, FOR DESERTING THE DREAMING.
NOTHING I CAN DO WILL MAKE IT WORSE.
SO, YOU WERE A BIG SHOT IN THE DREAM-WORLD IN THE OLD DAYS.
FIDDLER'S GREEN. WEIRD NAME. WHO WERE YOU?
WHO?
MY DEAR BIRD, YOU SEEM TO BE LABORING UNDER A MISAPPREHENSION.
FIDDLER'S GREEN IS NOT A WHO. IT'S A WHERE.
I WAS NOT A PERSON, MATTHEW. I WAS A PLACE.
LET US MAKE HASTE, FRIEND RAVEN. IT IS GETTING COLDER. WE ARE CLOSE TO THEM NOW.

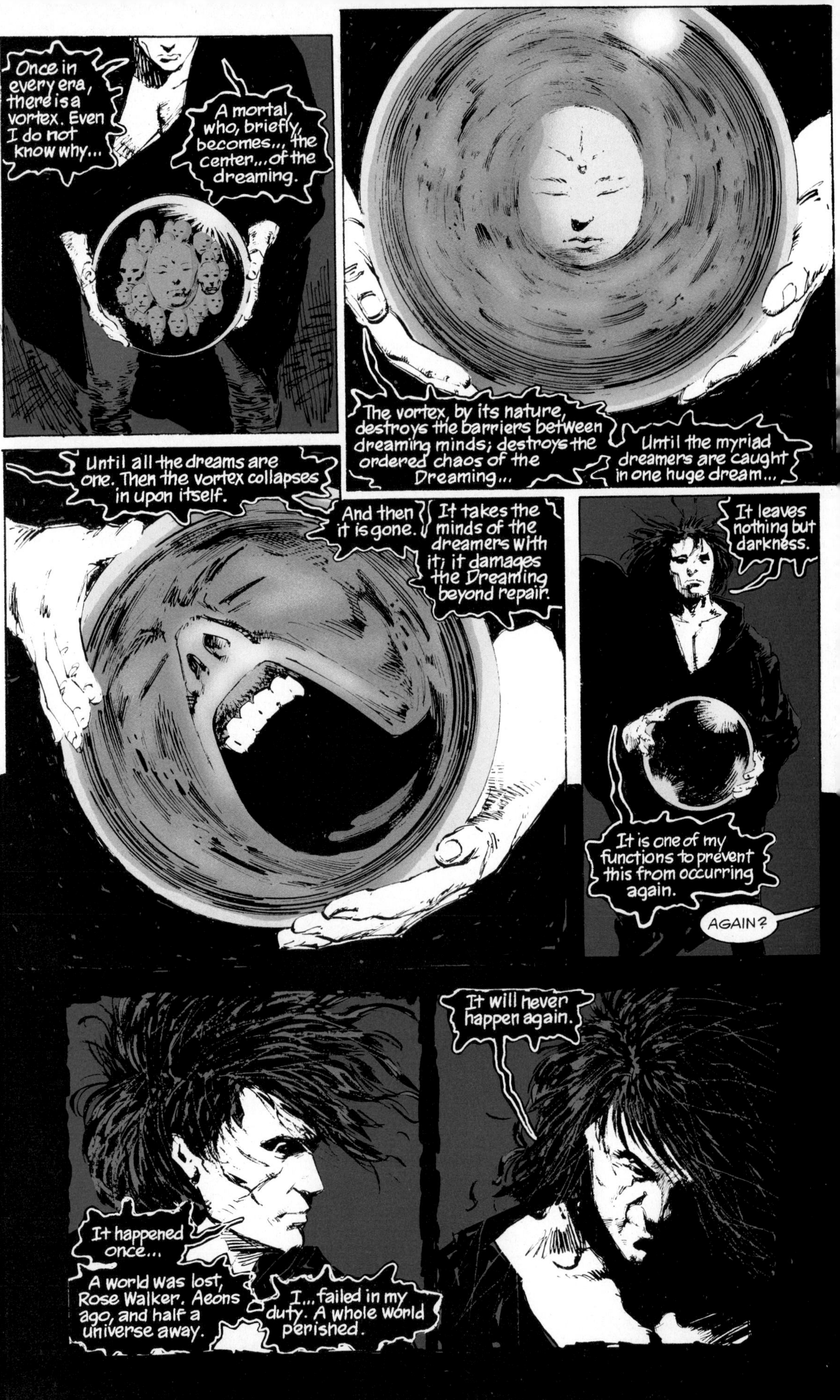
Once in every era, there is a vortex. Even I do not know why...
A mortal, who, briefly, becomes... the center... of the dreaming.
The vortex, by its nature, destroys the barriers between dreaming minds; destroys the ordered chaos of the Dreaming...
Until the myriad dreamers are caught in one huge dream...
Until all the dreams are one. Then the vortex collapses in upon itself.
And then it is gone.
It takes the minds of the dreamers with it; it damages the Dreaming beyond repair.
It leaves nothing but darkness.
It is one of my functions to prevent this from occurring again.
AGAIN?
It happened once...
A world was lost, Rose Walker. Aeons ago, and half a universe away.
I... failed in my duty. A whole world perished.
It will never happen again.

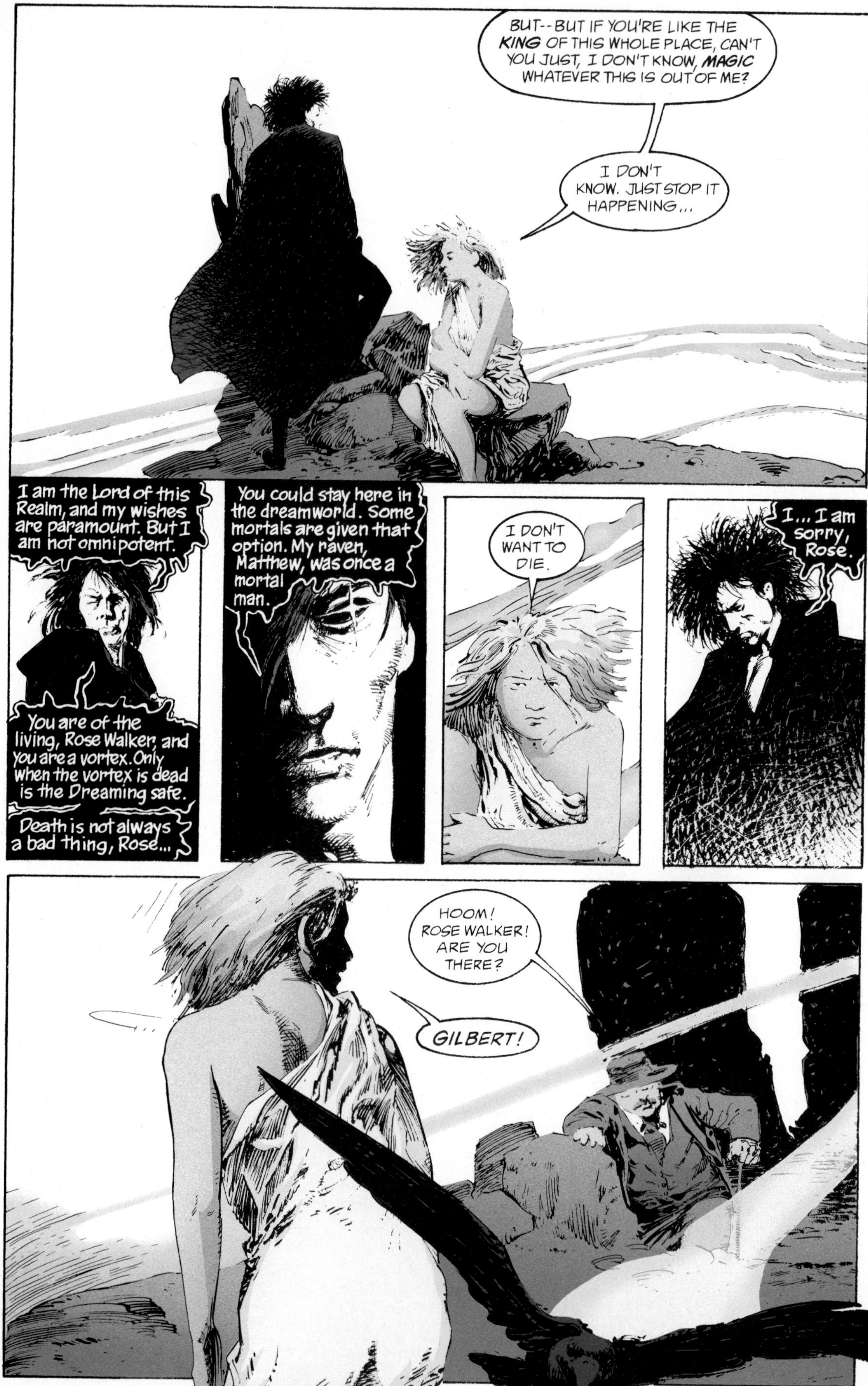
BUT--BUT IF YOU'RE LIKE THE KING OF THIS WHOLE PLACE, CAN'T YOU JUST, I DON'T KNOW, MAGIC WHATEVER THIS IS OUT OF ME?
I DON'T KNOW. JUST STOP IT HAPPENING...
I am the Lord of this Realm, and my wishes are paramount. But I am not omnipotent.
You are of the living, Rose Walker, and you are a vortex. Only when the vortex is dead is the Dreaming safe.
Death is not always a bad thing, Rose...
You could stay here in the dreamworld. Some mortals are given that option. My raven, Matthew, was once a mortal man.
I DON'T WANT TO DIE.
I... I am sorry, Rose.
HOOM! ROSE WALKER! ARE YOU THERE?
GILBERT!

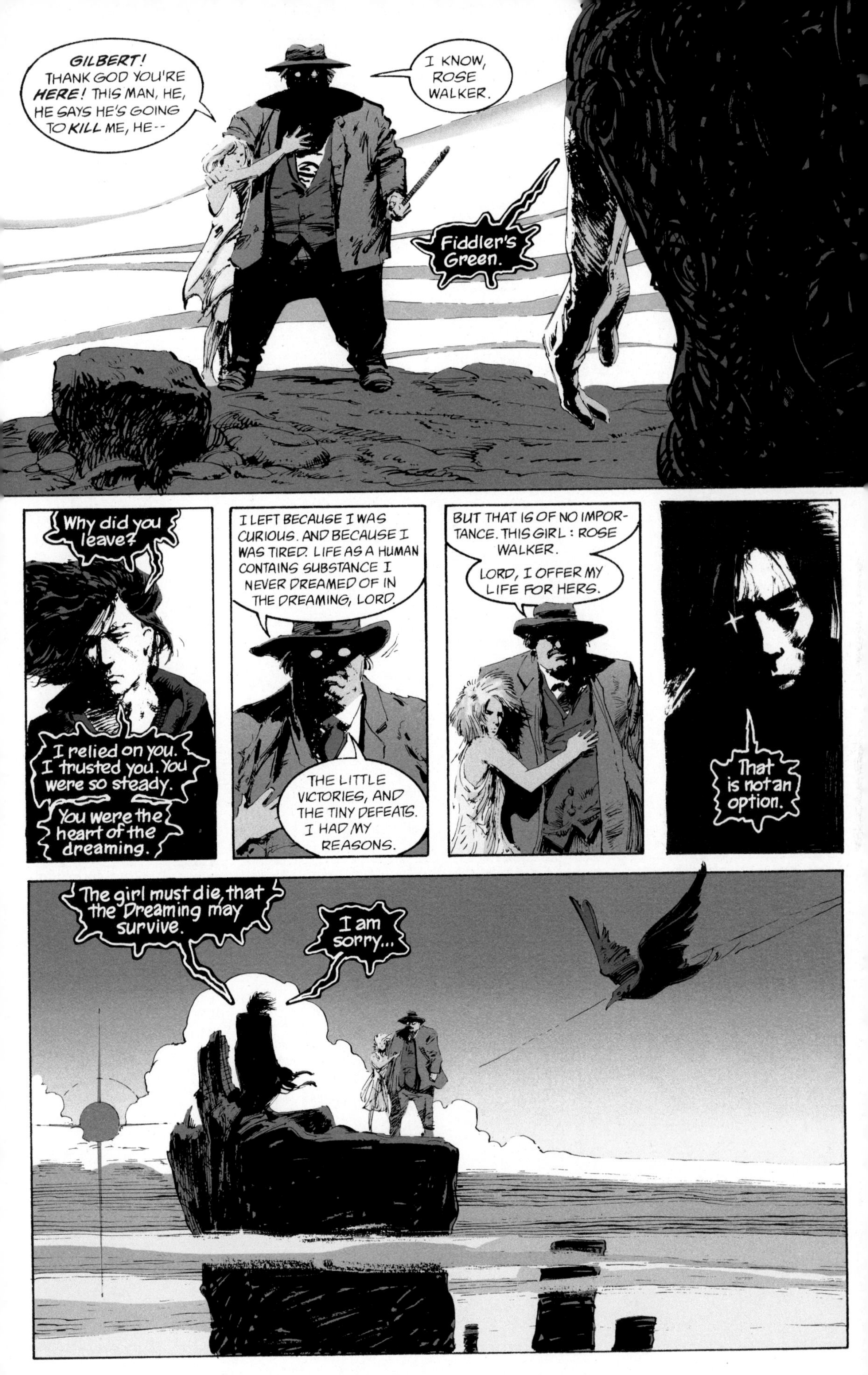

GILBERT! THANK GOD YOU'RE HERE! THIS MAN, HE, HE SAYS HE'S GOING TO KILL ME, HE--
I KNOW, ROSE WALKER.
Fiddler's Green.
Why did you leave?
I relied on you. I trusted you. You were so steady.
You were the heart of the dreaming.
I LEFT BECAUSE I WAS CURIOUS. AND BECAUSE I WAS TIRED. LIFE AS A HUMAN CONTAINS SUBSTANCE I NEVER DREAMED OF IN THE DREAMING, LORD.
THE LITTLE VICTORIES, AND THE TINY DEFEATS. I HAD MY REASONS.
BUT THAT IS OF NO IMPORTANCE. THIS GIRL : ROSE WALKER.
LORD, I OFFER MY LIFE FOR HERS.
That is not an option.
The girl must die, that the Dreaming may survive.
I am sorry...

"I'M SORRY, MIRANDA...

"I DON'T THINK I'VE BEEN A... VERY GOOD MOTHER...

DON'T THINK ABOUT IT, UNITY. MOTHER.

EVERYTHING'S GOING TO BE JUST FINE.

I... I THINK I'M GOING TO... HAVE TO SLEEP NOW.

UNITY KINKAID FINDS IT HARDER AND HARDER TO STAY ALIVE.

LIFE IS SO...

UNITY HEARS A VOICE, HER OWN VOICE, AND IT WHISPERS TO HER IN THE DARKNESS.

THE VOICE WHISPERS TO HER OF HER LIFE BEFORE THE LONG SLEEP. WHISPERS CHILDHOOD DREAMS OF A TALL, DARK MAN, WHOSE EYES DANCED LIKE TWIN STARS IN HER HEAD.

WHISPERS THE TRUTH.

AND THEN SHE GIVES IN TO SLEEP, HER BREATH SHALLOW AND HALT. DYING, IN A WORLD SHE FINALLY UNDERSTANDS...

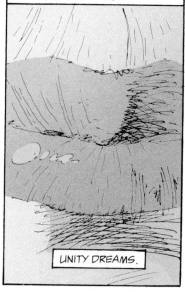

UNITY DREAMS.

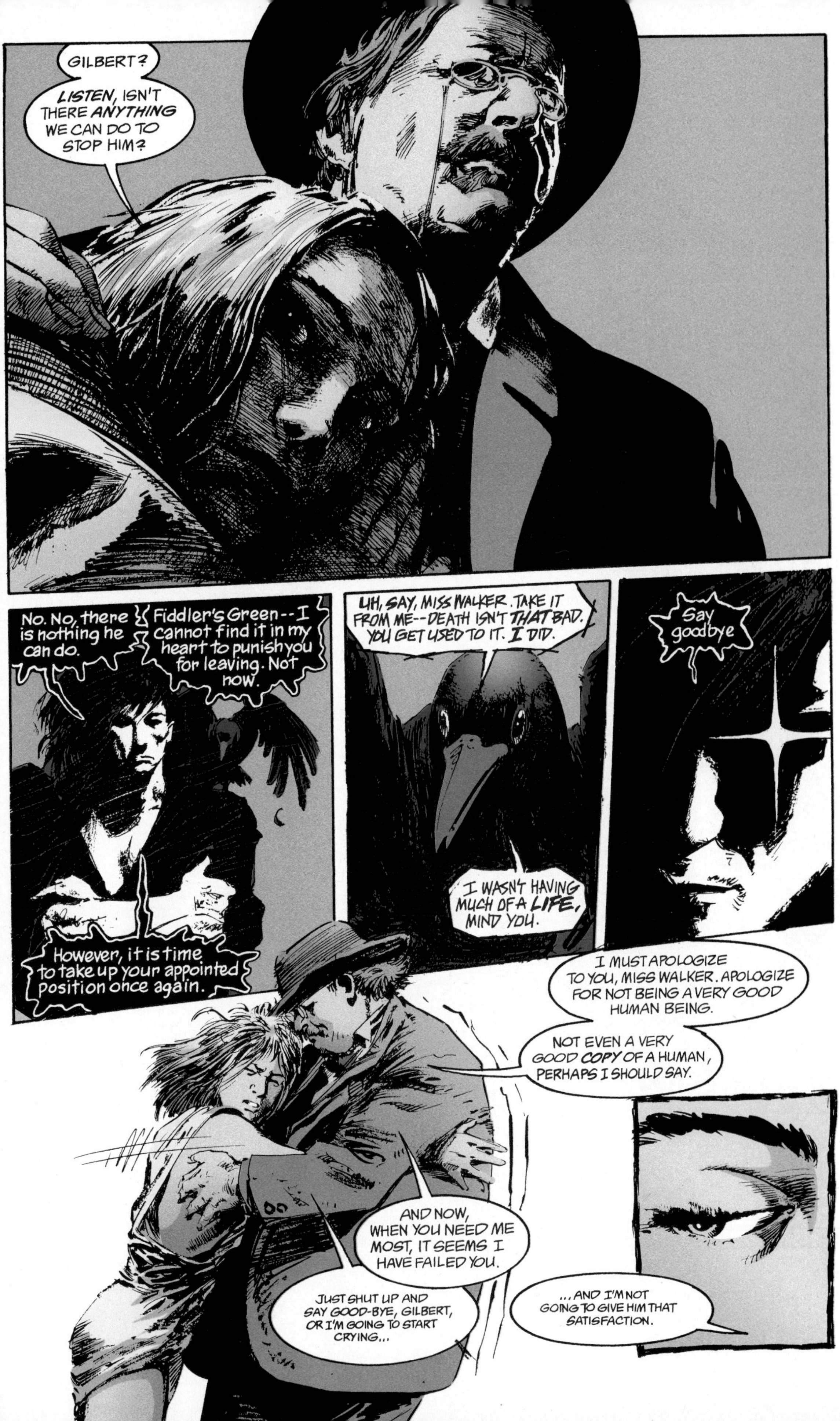
GILBERT?
LISTEN, ISN'T THERE ANYTHING WE CAN DO TO STOP HIM?
No. No, there is nothing he can do.
Fiddler's Green--I cannot find it in my heart to punish you for leaving. Not now.
However, it is time to take up your appointed position once again.
UH, SAY, MISS WALKER. TAKE IT FROM ME--DEATH ISN'T THAT BAD. YOU GET USED TO IT. I DID.
I WASN'T HAVING MUCH OF A LIFE, MIND YOU.
Say goodbye
I MUST APOLOGIZE TO YOU, MISS WALKER. APOLOGIZE FOR NOT BEING A VERY GOOD HUMAN BEING.
NOT EVEN A VERY GOOD COPY OF A HUMAN, PERHAPS I SHOULD SAY.
AND NOW, WHEN YOU NEED ME MOST, IT SEEMS I HAVE FAILED YOU.
JUST SHUT UP AND SAY GOOD-BYE, GILBERT, OR I'M GOING TO START CRYING...
...AND I'M NOT GOING TO GIVE HIM THAT SATISFACTION.

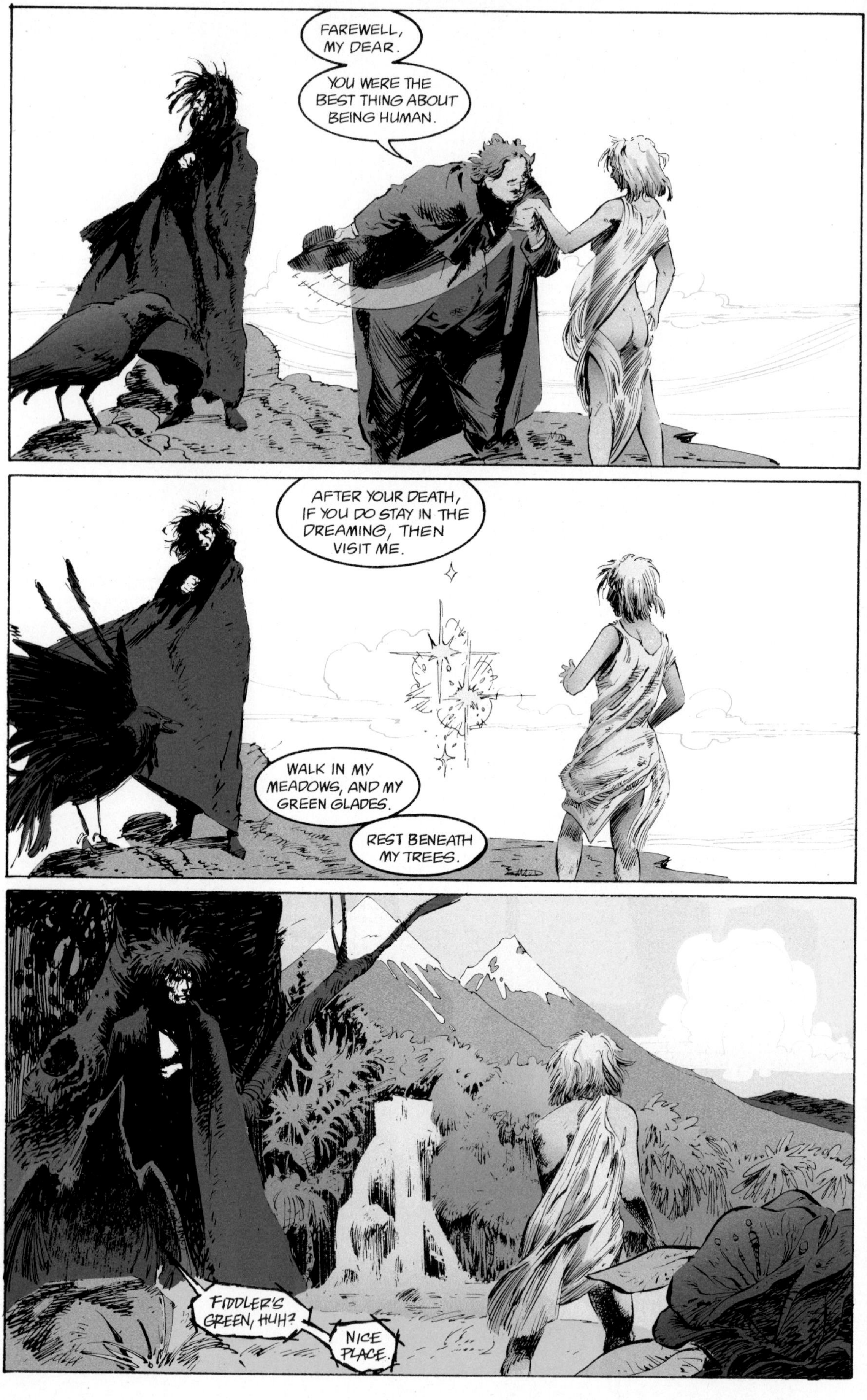
FAREWELL, MY DEAR.
YOU WERE THE BEST THING ABOUT BEING HUMAN.
AFTER YOUR DEATH, IF YOU DO STAY IN THE DREAMING, THEN VISIT ME.
WALK IN MY MEADOWS, AND MY GREEN GLADES.
REST BENEATH MY TREES.
FIDDLER'S GREEN, HUH?
NICE PLACE.

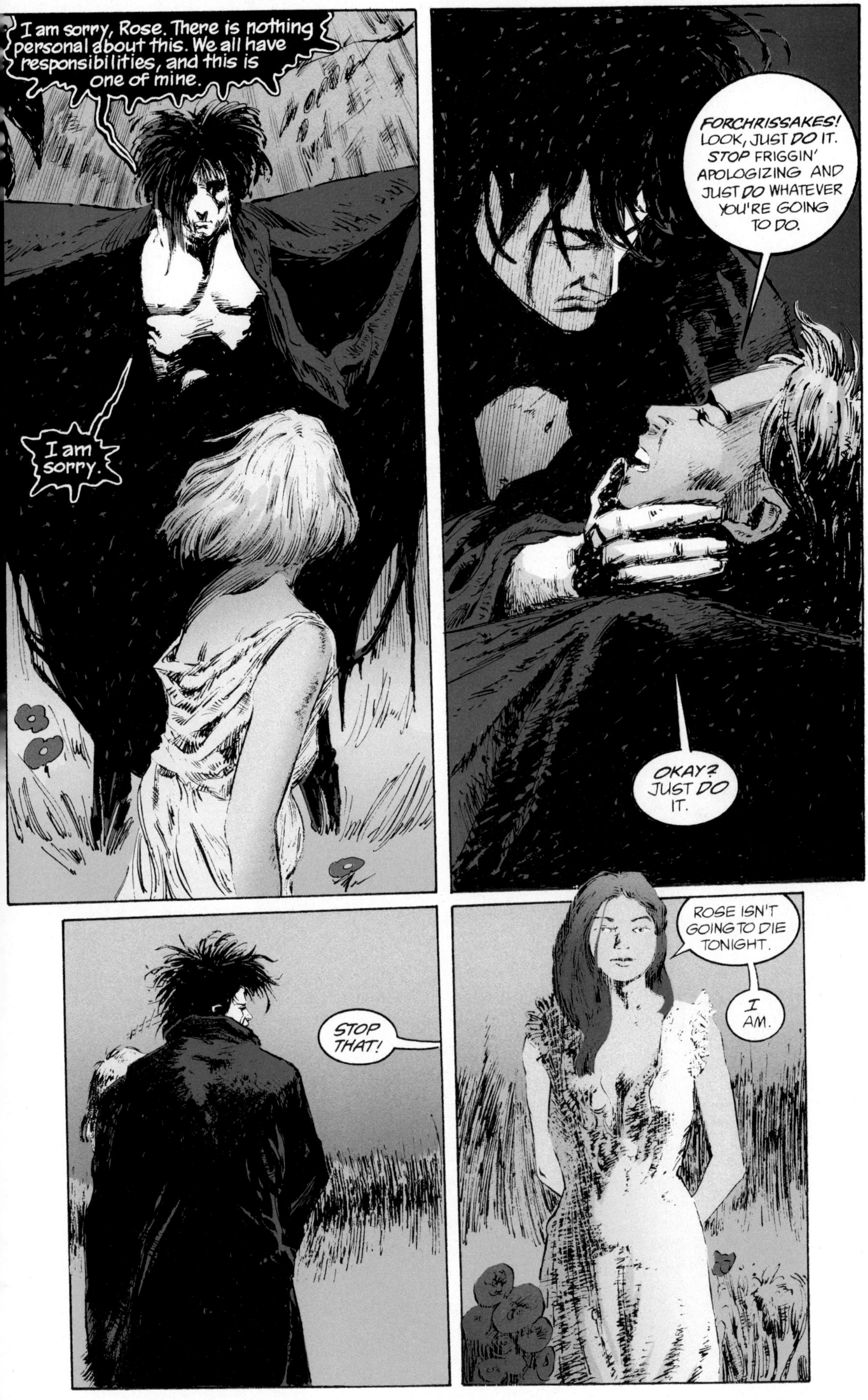
I am sorry, Rose. There is nothing personal about this. We all have responsibilities, and this is one of mine.
I am sorry.
FORCHRISSAKES! LOOK, JUST DO IT. STOP FRIGGIN' APOLOGIZING AND JUST DO WHATEVER YOU'RE GOING TO DO.
OKAY? JUST DO IT.
STOP THAT!
ROSE ISN'T GOING TO DIE TONIGHT.
I AM.

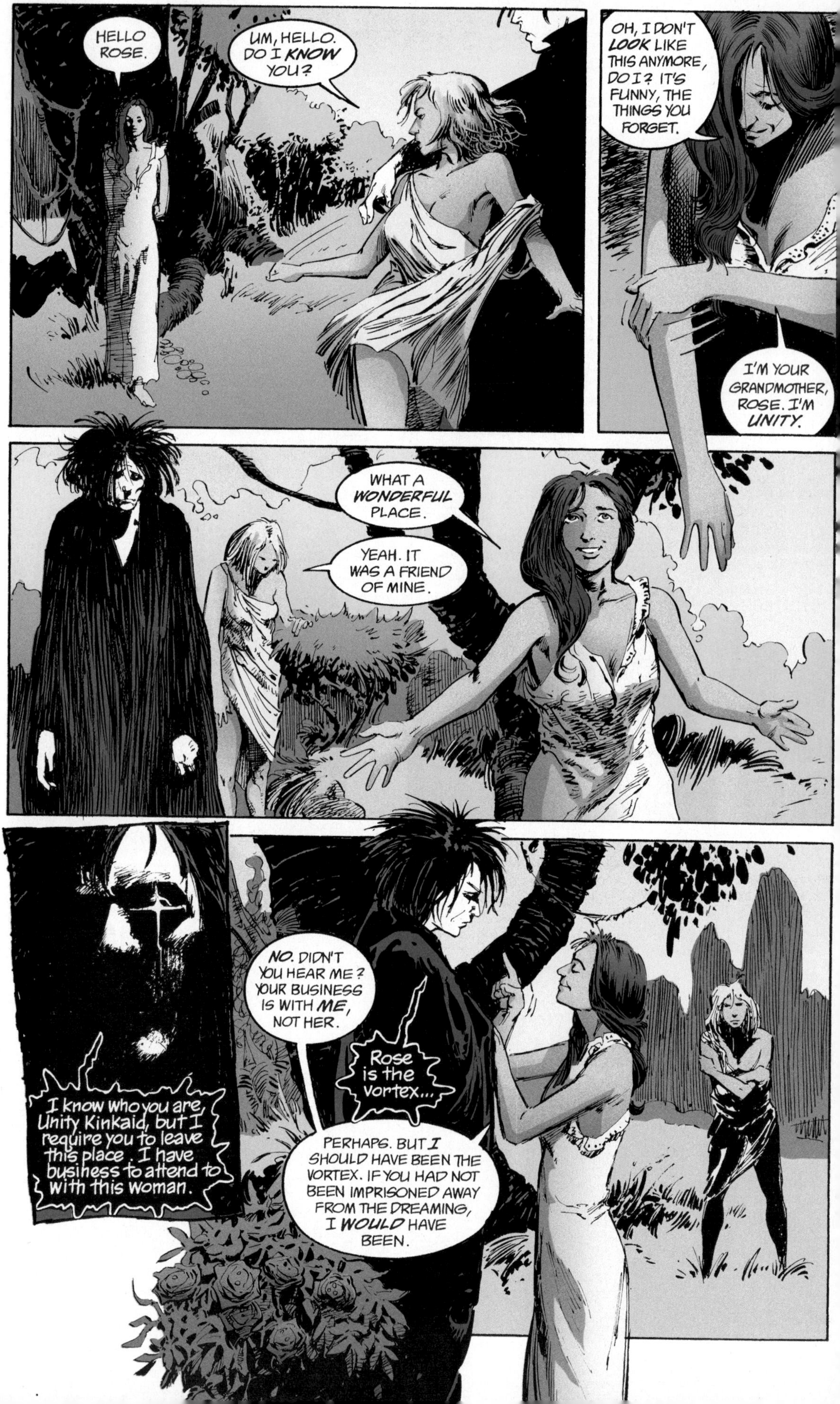
HELLO ROSE.
UM, HELLO. DO I KNOW YOU?
OH, I DON'T LOOK LIKE THIS ANYMORE, DO I? IT'S FUNNY, THE THINGS YOU FORGET.
I'M YOUR GRANDMOTHER, ROSE. I'M UNITY.
WHAT A WONDERFUL PLACE.
YEAH. IT WAS A FRIEND OF MINE.
I know who you are, Unity Kinkaid, but I require you to leave this place. I have business to attend to with this woman.
NO. DIDN'T YOU HEAR ME? YOUR BUSINESS IS WITH ME, NOT HER.
Rose is the vortex...
PERHAPS. BUT I SHOULD HAVE BEEN THE VORTEX. IF YOU HAD NOT BEEN IMPRISONED AWAY FROM THE DREAMING, I WOULD HAVE BEEN.

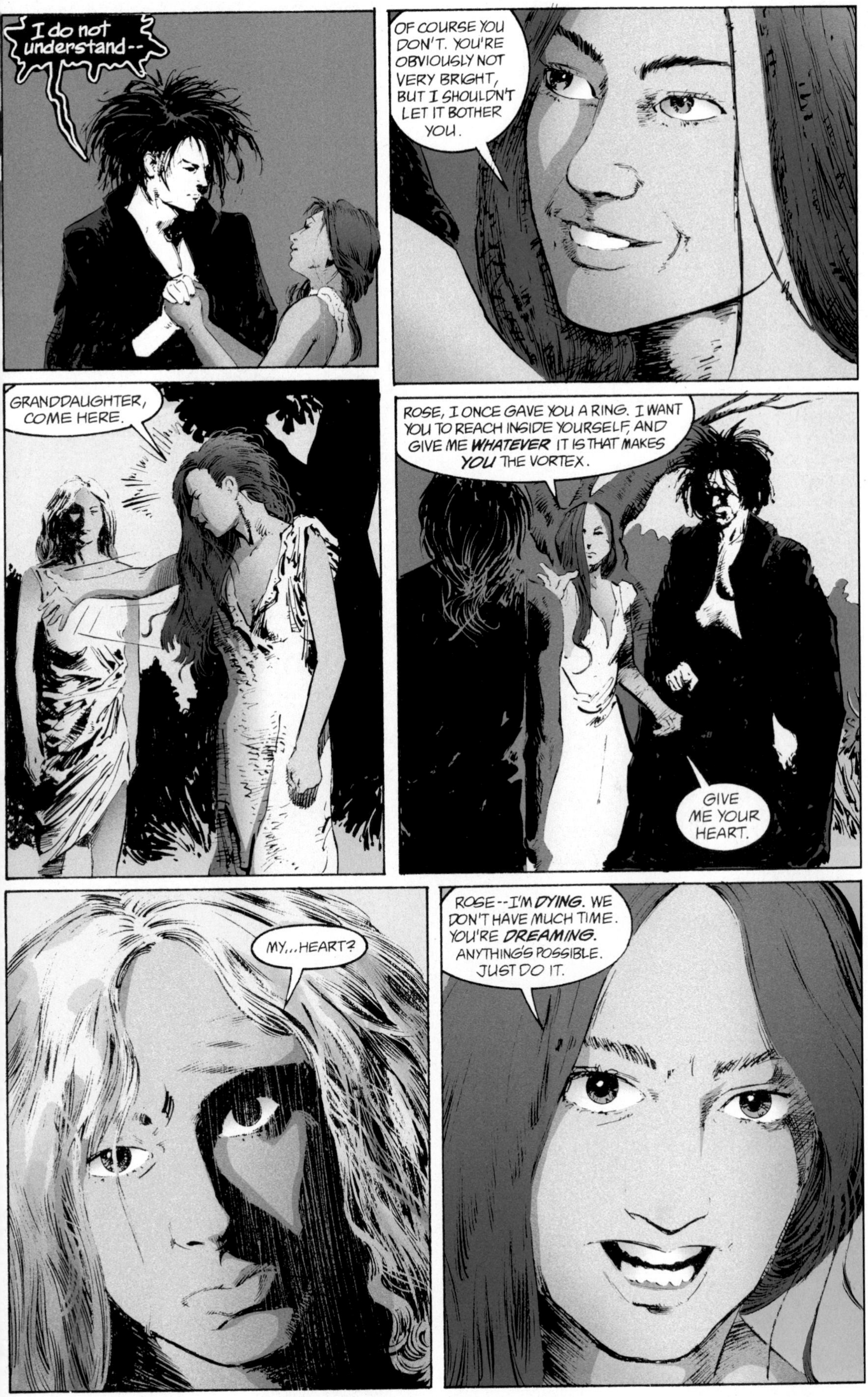
I do not understand--
OF COURSE YOU DON'T. YOU'RE OBVIOUSLY NOT VERY BRIGHT, BUT I SHOULDN'T LET IT BOTHER YOU.
GRANDDAUGHTER, COME HERE.
ROSE, I ONCE GAVE YOU A RING. I WANT YOU TO REACH INSIDE YOURSELF, AND GIVE ME WHATEVER IT IS THAT MAKES YOU THE VORTEX.
GIVE ME YOUR HEART.
MY... HEART?
ROSE--I'M DYING. WE DON'T HAVE MUCH TIME. YOU'RE DREAMING. ANYTHING'S POSSIBLE. JUST DO IT.

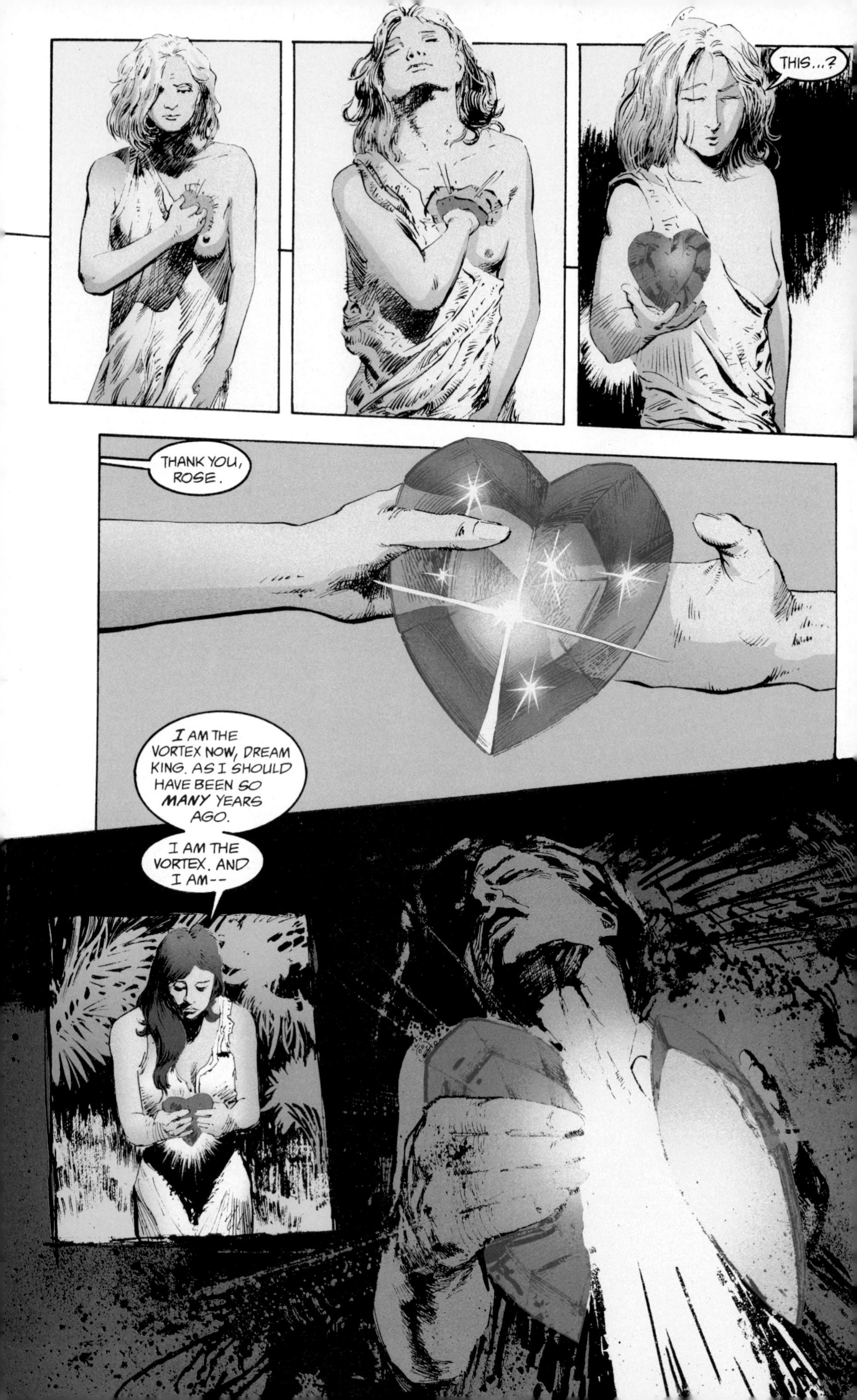
THIS...?
THANK YOU, ROSE.
I AM THE VORTEX NOW, DREAM KING. AS I SHOULD HAVE BEEN SO MANY YEARS AGO.
I AM THE VORTEX. AND I AM--

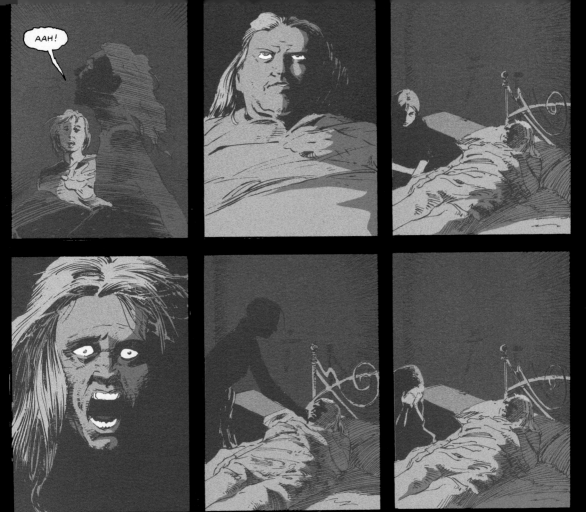

AAH!

WHAT...WHAT HAPPENED?

You died.

Let me help you up.

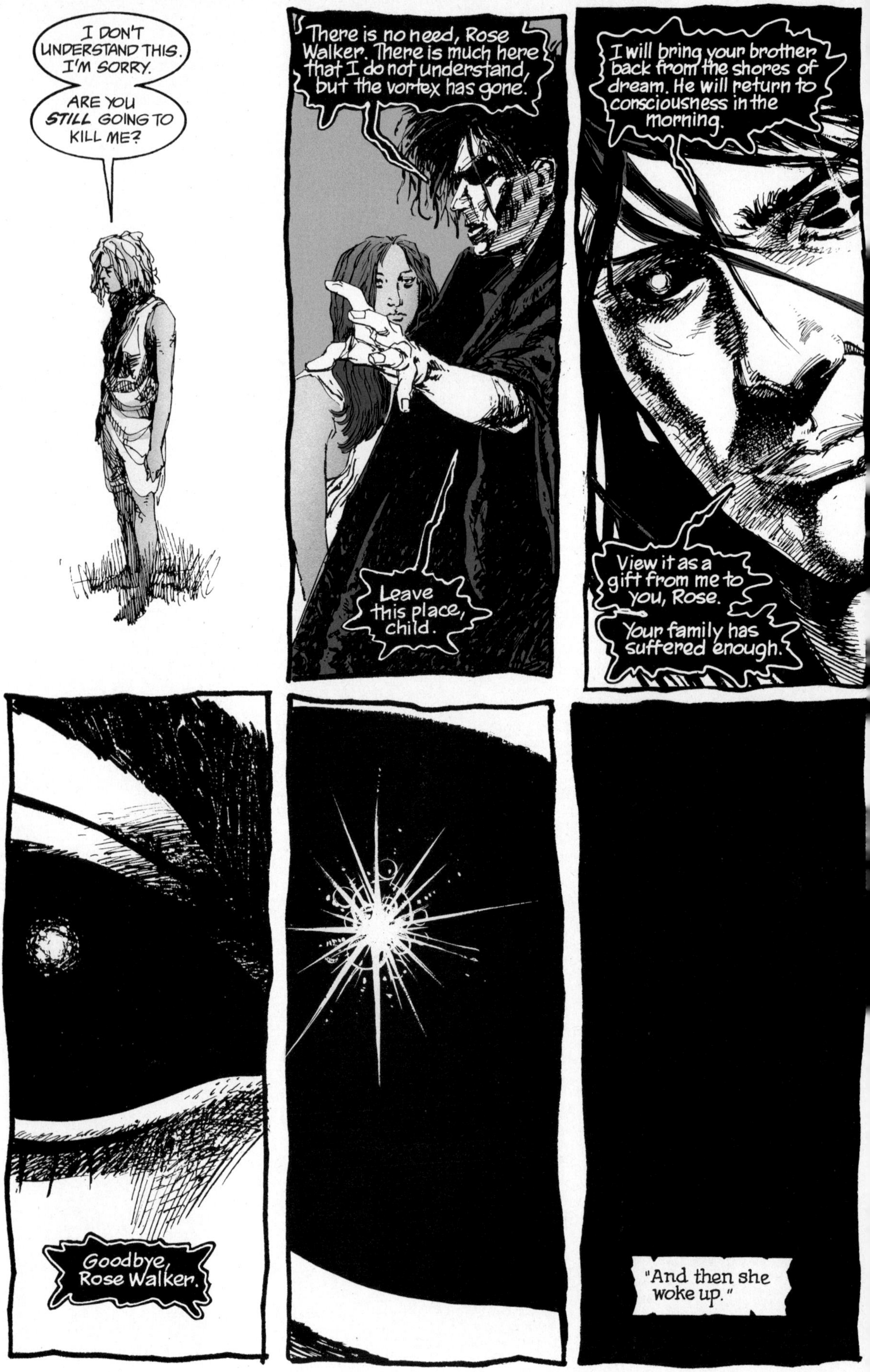
I DON'T UNDERSTAND THIS. I'M SORRY.
ARE YOU *STILL* GOING TO KILL ME?
There is no need, Rose Walker. There is much here that I do not understand, but the vortex has gone.
Leave this place, child.
I will bring your brother back from the shores of dream. He will return to consciousness in the morning.
View it as a gift from me to you, Rose.
Your family has suffered enough.
Goodbye, Rose Walker.
"And then she woke up."

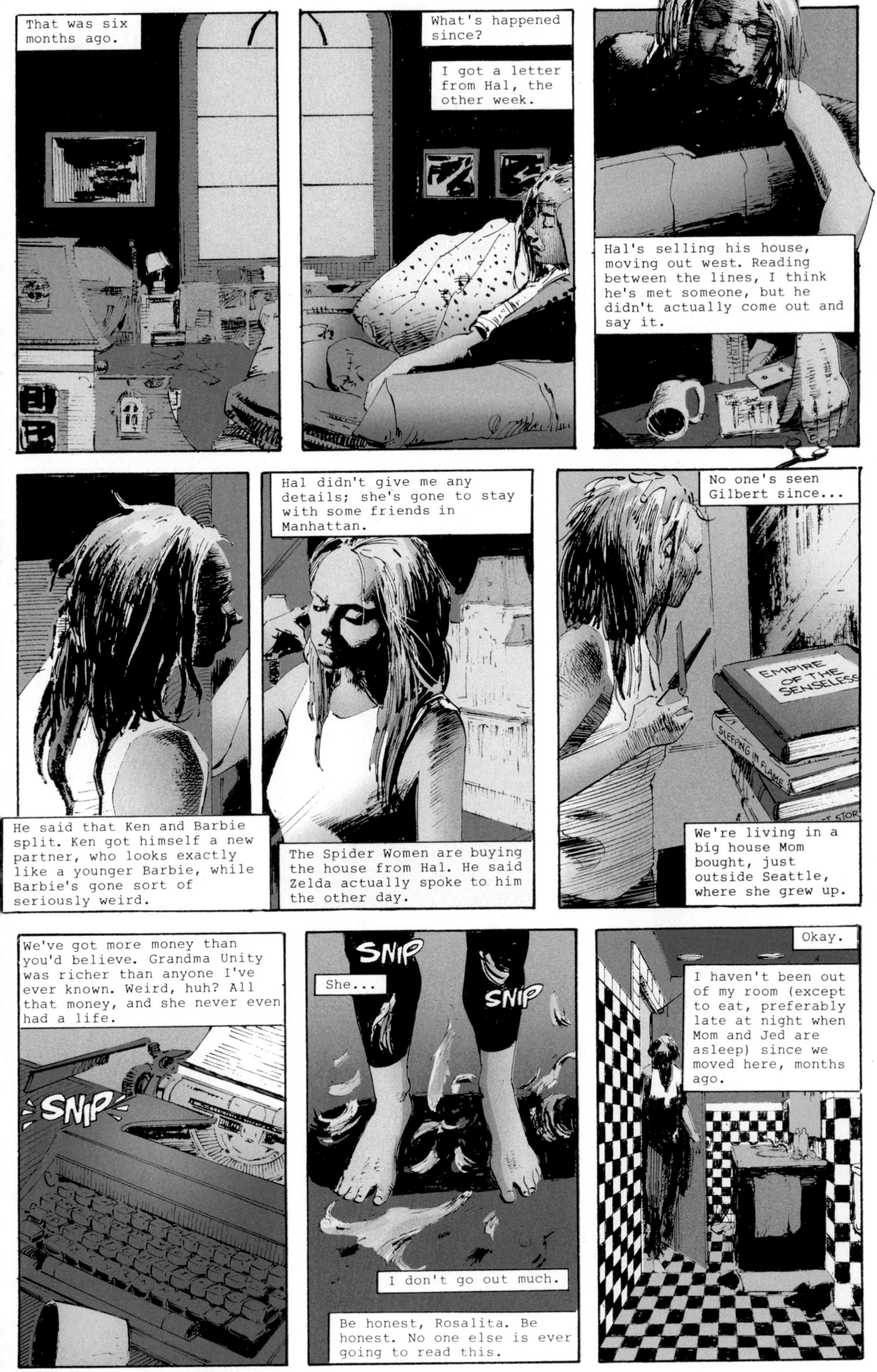
That was six months ago.
What's happened since?
I got a letter from Hal, the other week.
Hal's selling his house, moving out west. Reading between the lines, I think he's met someone, but he didn't actually come out and say it.
He said that Ken and Barbie split. Ken got himself a new partner, who looks exactly like a younger Barbie, while Barbie's gone sort of seriously weird.
Hal didn't give me any details; she's gone to stay with some friends in Manhattan.
The Spider Women are buying the house from Hal. He said Zelda actually spoke to him the other day.
No one's seen Gilbert since...
EMPIRE OF THE SENSELESS
SLEEPING IN FLAME
We're living in a big house Mom bought, just outside Seattle, where she grew up.
We've got more money than you'd believe. Grandma Unity was richer than anyone I've ever known. Weird, huh? All that money, and she never even had a life.
SNIP
SNIP
She...
SNIP
I don't go out much.
Be honest, Rosalita. Be honest. No one else is ever going to read this.
Okay.
I haven't been out of my room (except to eat, preferably late at night when Mom and Jed are asleep) since we moved here, months ago.

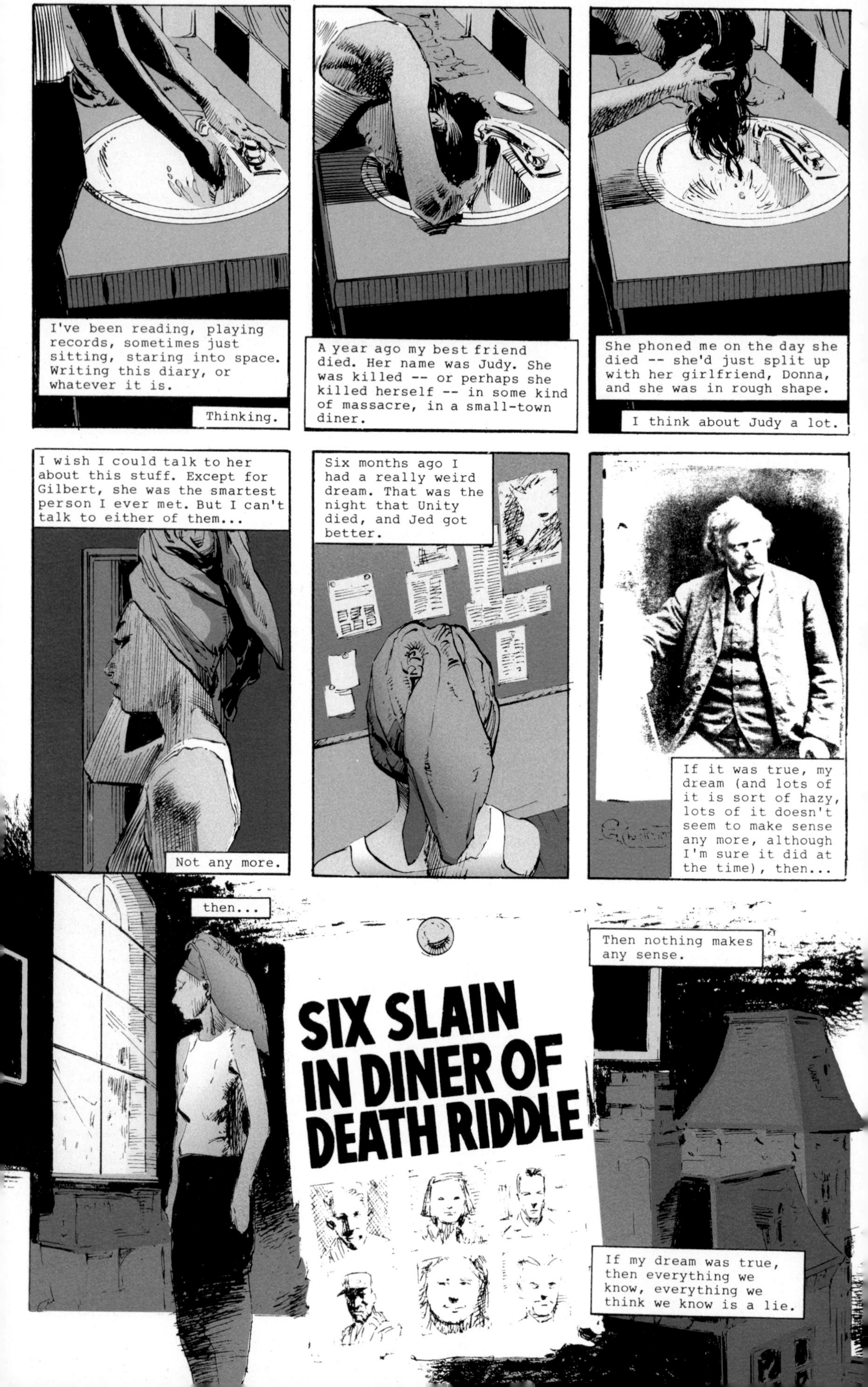
I've been reading, playing records, sometimes just sitting, staring into space. Writing this diary, or whatever it is.
Thinking.
A year ago my best friend died. Her name was Judy. She was killed -- or perhaps she killed herself -- in some kind of massacre, in a small-town diner.
She phoned me on the day she died -- she'd just split up with her girlfriend, Donna, and she was in rough shape.
I think about Judy a lot.
I wish I could talk to her about this stuff. Except for Gilbert, she was the smartest person I ever met. But I can't talk to either of them...
Not any more.
Six months ago I had a really weird dream. That was the night that Unity died, and Jed got better.
If it was true, my dream (and lots of it is sort of hazy, lots of it doesn't seem to make sense any more, although I'm sure it did at the time), then...
then...
SIX SLAIN IN DINER OF DEATH RIDDLE
Then nothing makes any sense.
If my dream was true, then everything we know, everything we think we know is a lie.

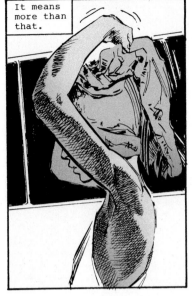

It means more than that.

It means the world's about as solid and as reliable as a layer of scum on the top of a well of black water which goes down forever, and there are things in the depths that I don't even want to think about.

It means that we're just dolls. We don't have a clue what's really going down, we just kid ourselves that we're in control of our lives **while a paper's** thickness away things that would drive us mad if we thought about them for too long play with us, and move us around from room to room, and put us away at night when they're tired, or bored.

In my dream, I could have destroyed everybody in the world.

In my dream, Gilbert wasn't even a person; he was a place.

In my dream, Grandma Unity gave up her life for me.

Dreams are weird and stupid and they scare me. I haven't slept properly for six months now.

It's a nice house. Too big, but that suits me. Means I don't have to see other people any more than I have to.

That's my story.

Okay.

It's even got a happy ending: Jed and Rose and their mother were finally reunited, and they all lived together in a big old house.

I've been brooding on that night for too long now. Six months.

And I've decided.

My dream. My weird dream. It was just a dream.

That's all. Just a dream.

"And then she woke up."

You know, I always hated stories that ended like that. I always felt cheated.

Six months is long enough to feel sorry for yourself. Isn't it?

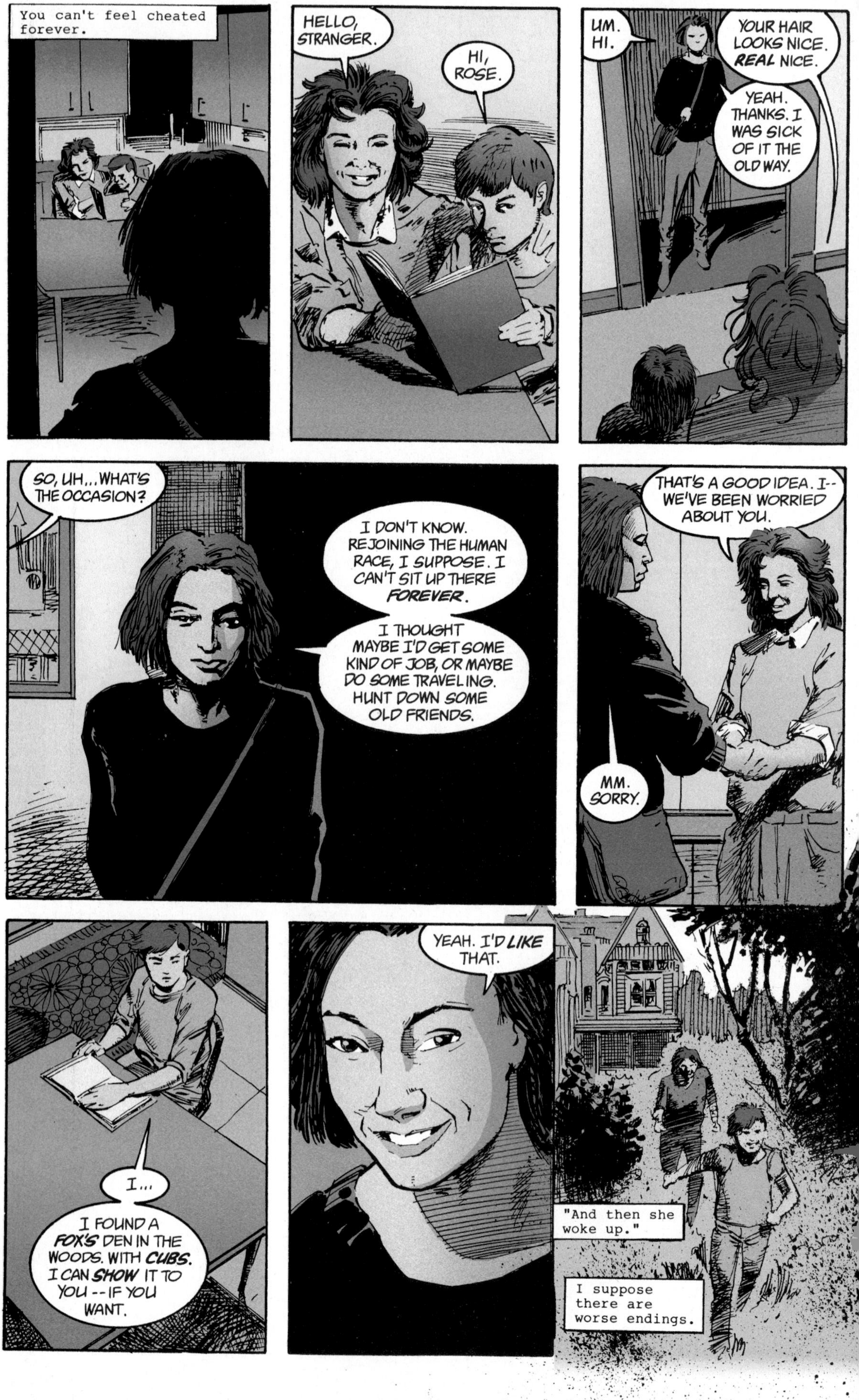
You can't feel cheated forever.
HELLO, STRANGER.
HI, ROSE.
UM. HI.
YOUR HAIR LOOKS NICE. REAL NICE.
YEAH. THANKS. I WAS SICK OF IT THE OLD WAY.
SO, UH... WHAT'S THE OCCASION?
I DON'T KNOW. REJOINING THE HUMAN RACE, I SUPPOSE. I CAN'T SIT UP THERE FOREVER.
I THOUGHT MAYBE I'D GET SOME KIND OF JOB, OR MAYBE DO SOME TRAVELING. HUNT DOWN SOME OLD FRIENDS.
THAT'S A GOOD IDEA. I-- WE'VE BEEN WORRIED ABOUT YOU.
MM. SORRY.
I...
I FOUND A FOX'S DEN IN THE WOODS. WITH CUBS. I CAN SHOW IT TO YOU -- IF YOU WANT.
YEAH. I'D LIKE THAT.
"And then she woke up."
I suppose there are worse endings.

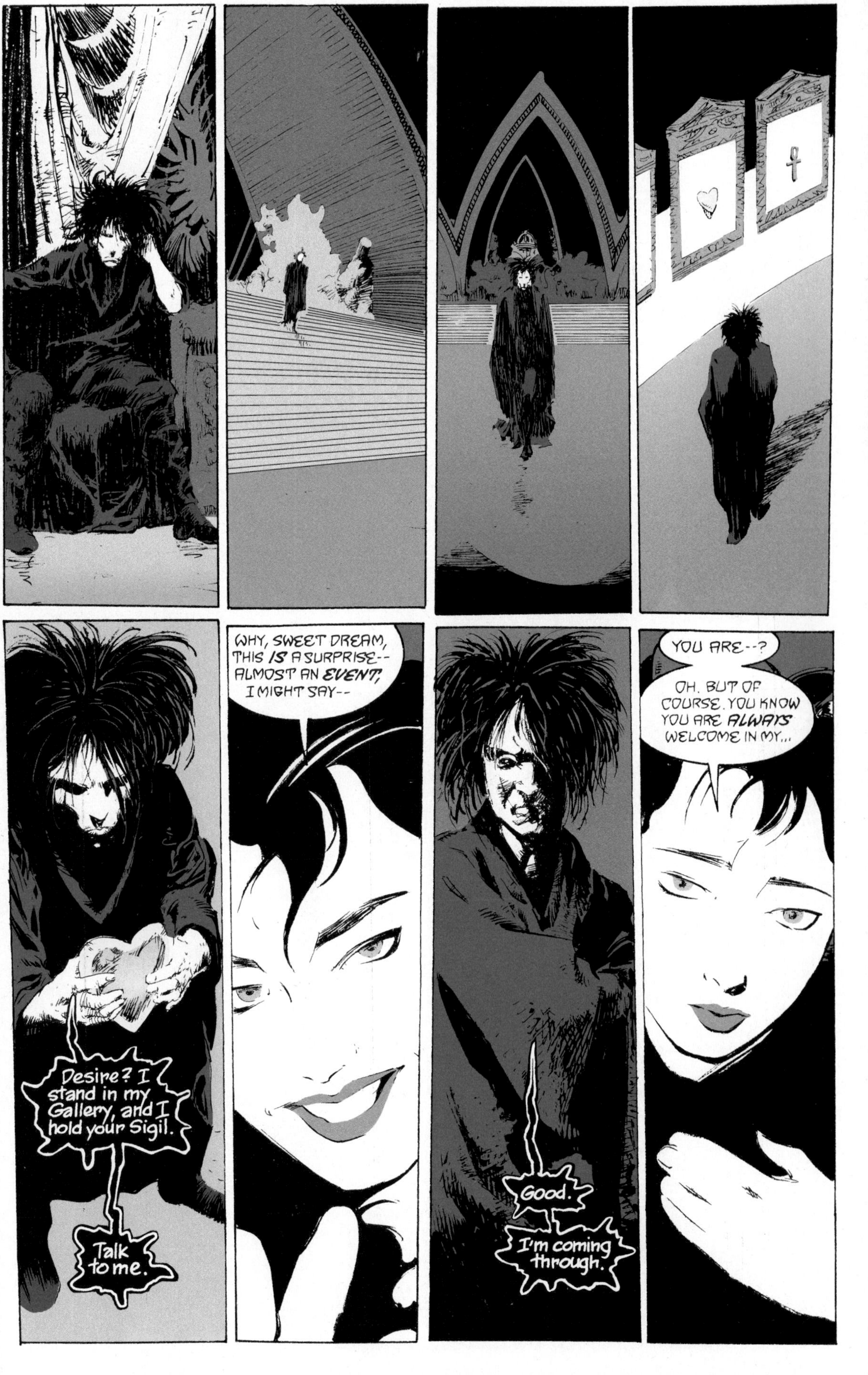
WHY, SWEET DREAM, THIS IS A SURPRISE-- ALMOST AN EVENT, I MIGHT SAY--
Desire? I stand in my Gallery, and I hold your Sigil.
Talk to me.
YOU ARE--?
OH. BUT OF COURSE. YOU KNOW YOU ARE ALWAYS WELCOME IN MY...
Good.
I'm coming through.

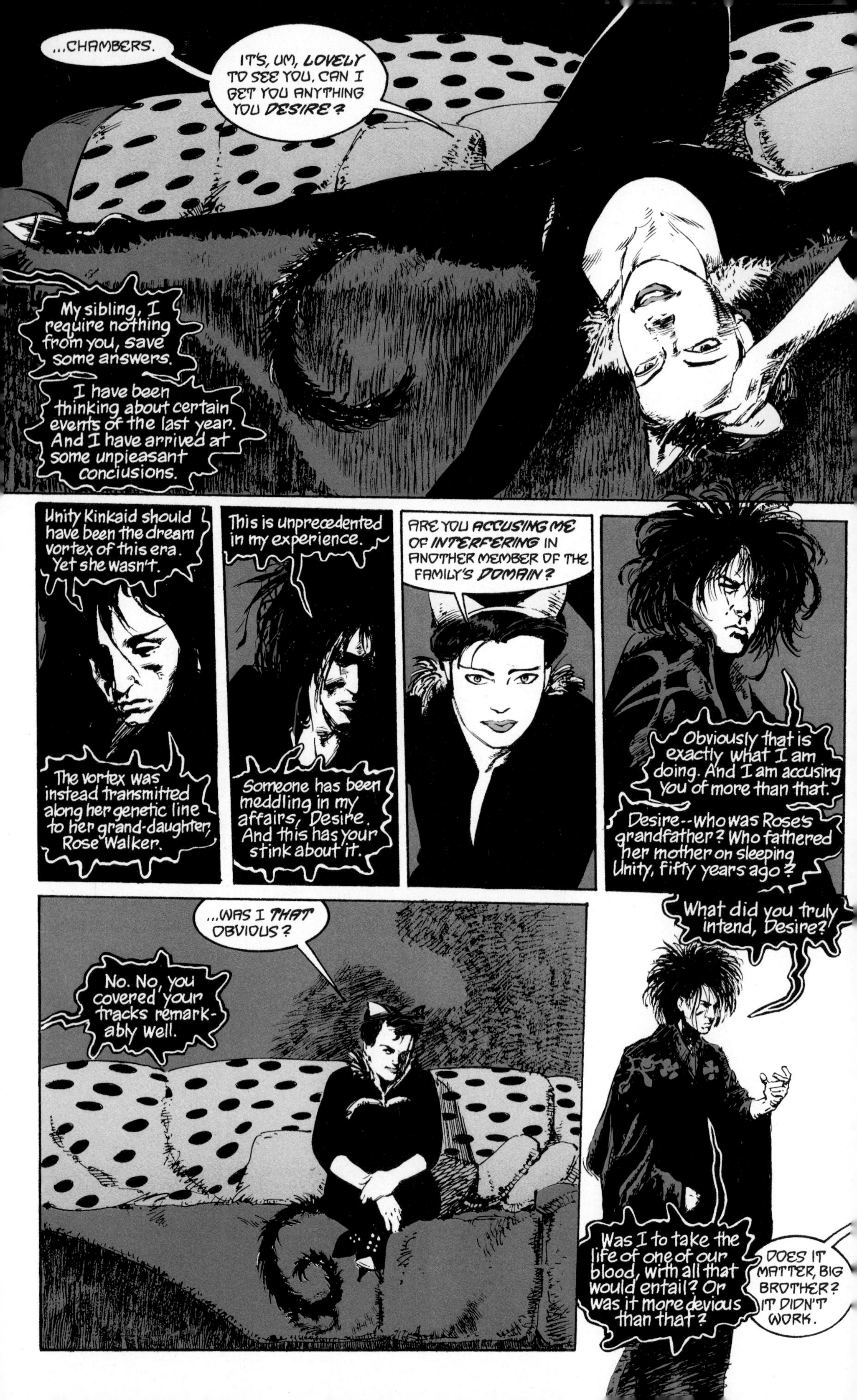
...CHAMBERS.
IT'S, UM, LOVELY TO SEE YOU. CAN I GET YOU ANYTHING YOU DESIRE?
My sibling, I require nothing from you, save some answers.
I have been thinking about certain events of the last year. And I have arrived at some unpleasant conclusions.
Unity Kinkaid should have been the dream vortex of this era. Yet she wasn't.
The vortex was instead transmitted along her genetic line to her grand-daughter, Rose Walker.
This is unprecedented in my experience.
Someone has been meddling in my affairs, Desire. And this has your stink about it.
ARE YOU ACCUSING ME OF INTERFERING IN ANOTHER MEMBER OF THE FAMILY'S DOMAIN?
Obviously that is exactly what I am doing. And I am accusing you of more than that.
Desire--who was Rose's grandfather? Who fathered her mother on sleeping Unity, fifty years ago?
...WAS I THAT OBVIOUS?
No. No, you covered your tracks remarkably well.
What did you truly intend, Desire?
Was I to take the life of one of our blood, with all that would entail? Or was it more devious than that?
DOES IT MATTER, BIG BROTHER? IT DIDN'T WORK.

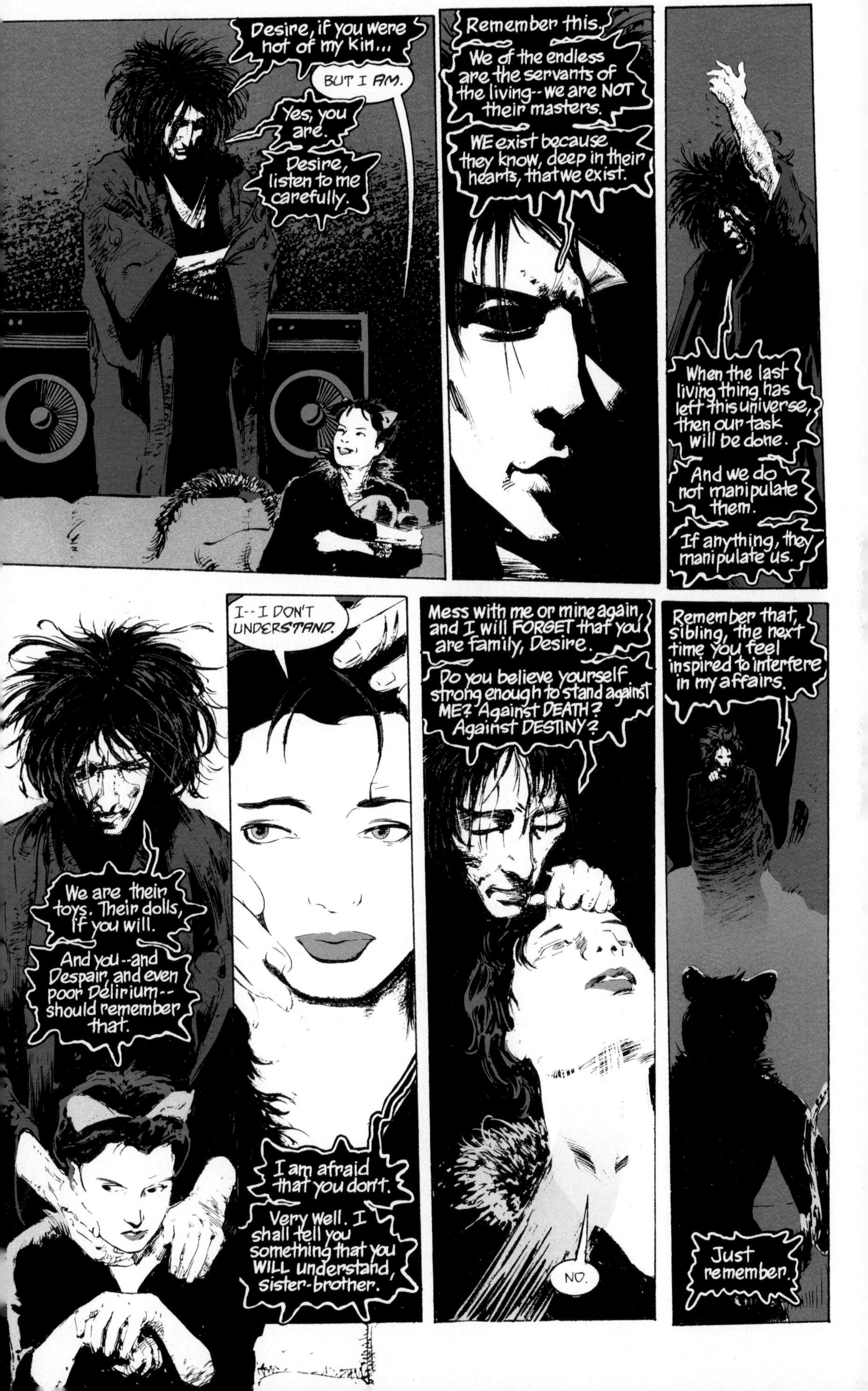
Desire, if you were not of my kin...
BUT I AM.
Yes, you are.
Desire, listen to me carefully.
Remember this.
We of the endless are the servants of the living--we are NOT their masters.
WE exist because they know, deep in their hearts, that we exist.
When the last living thing has left this universe, then our task will be done.
And we do not manipulate them.
If anything, they manipulate us.
We are their toys. Their dolls, if you will.
And you--and Despair, and even poor Delirium--should remember that.
I--I DON'T UNDERSTAND.
I am afraid that you don't.
Very well. I shall tell you something that you WILL understand, sister-brother.
Mess with me or mine again, and I will FORGET that you are family, Desire.
Do you believe yourself strong enough to stand against ME? Against DEATH? Against DESTINY?
NO.
Remember that, sibling, the next time you feel inspired to interfere in my affairs.
Just remember.

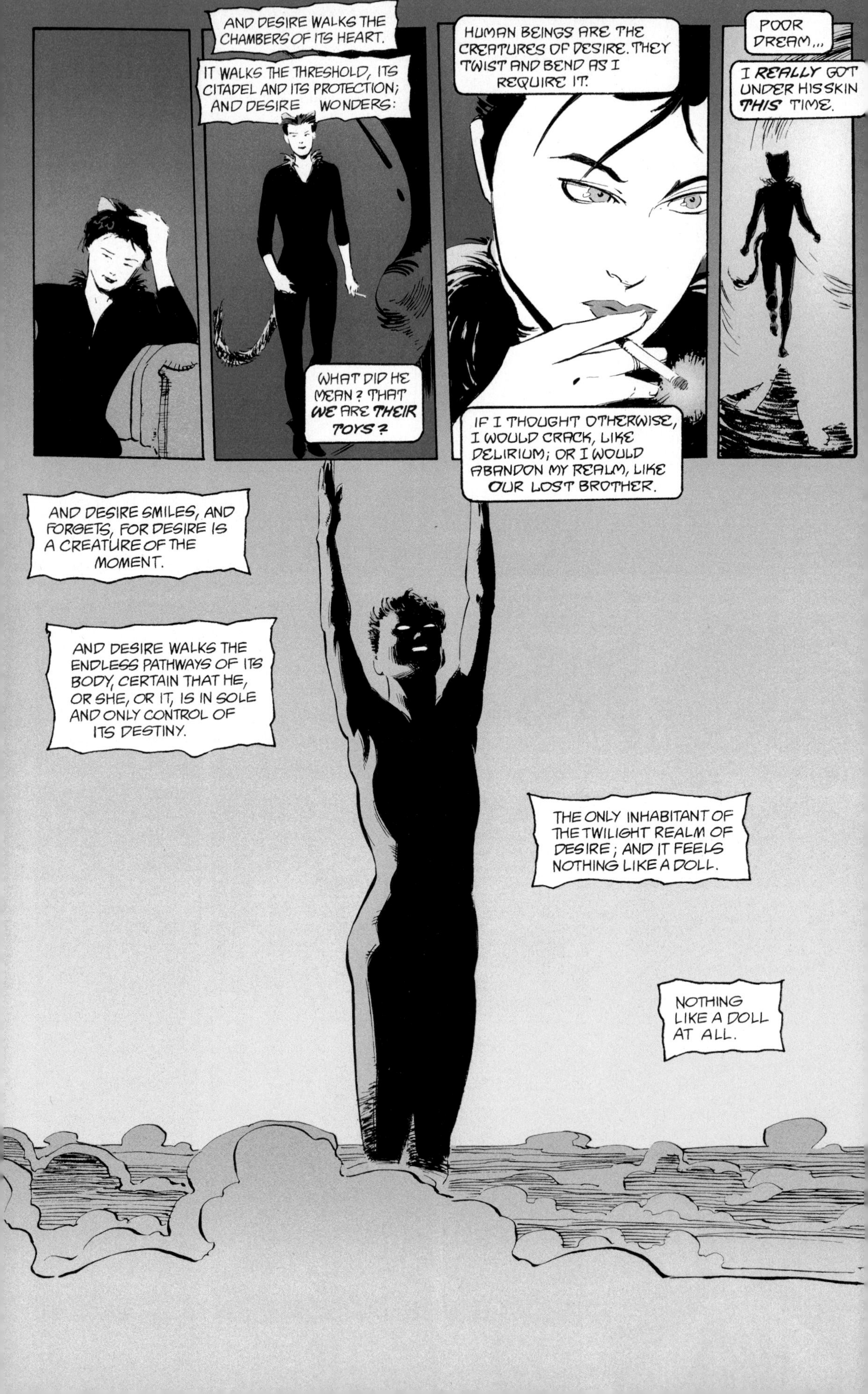

AND DESIRE WALKS THE CHAMBERS OF ITS HEART.
IT WALKS THE THRESHOLD, ITS CITADEL AND ITS PROTECTION; AND DESIRE WONDERS:
WHAT DID HE MEAN? THAT WE ARE THEIR TOYS?
HUMAN BEINGS ARE THE CREATURES OF DESIRE. THEY TWIST AND BEND AS I REQUIRE IT.
IF I THOUGHT OTHERWISE, I WOULD CRACK, LIKE DELIRIUM; OR I WOULD ABANDON MY REALM, LIKE OUR LOST BROTHER.
POOR DREAM...
I REALLY GOT UNDER HIS SKIN THIS TIME.
AND DESIRE SMILES, AND FORGETS, FOR DESIRE IS A CREATURE OF THE MOMENT.
AND DESIRE WALKS THE ENDLESS PATHWAYS OF ITS BODY, CERTAIN THAT HE, OR SHE, OR IT, IS IN SOLE AND ONLY CONTROL OF ITS DESTINY.
THE ONLY INHABITANT OF THE TWILIGHT REALM OF DESIRE; AND IT FEELS NOTHING LIKE A DOLL.
NOTHING LIKE A DOLL AT ALL.

I do not know whether you know all that is to be known
concerning small mirrors: but of this, silence.
—Arthur Machen, in a letter to James Branch Cabell, 17 February 1918

Writers are liars.
—Erasmus Fry, in conversation, 6 May 1986

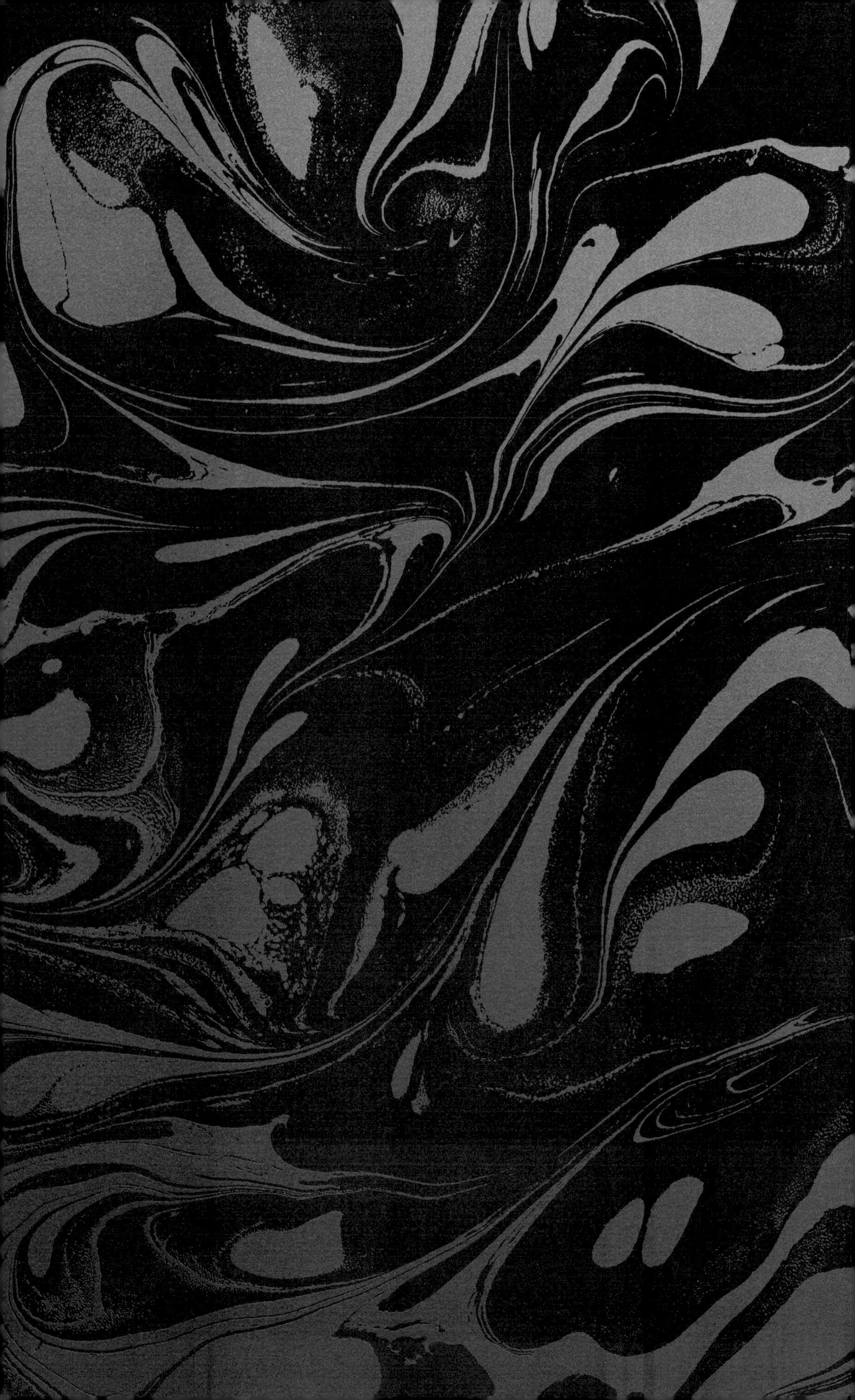

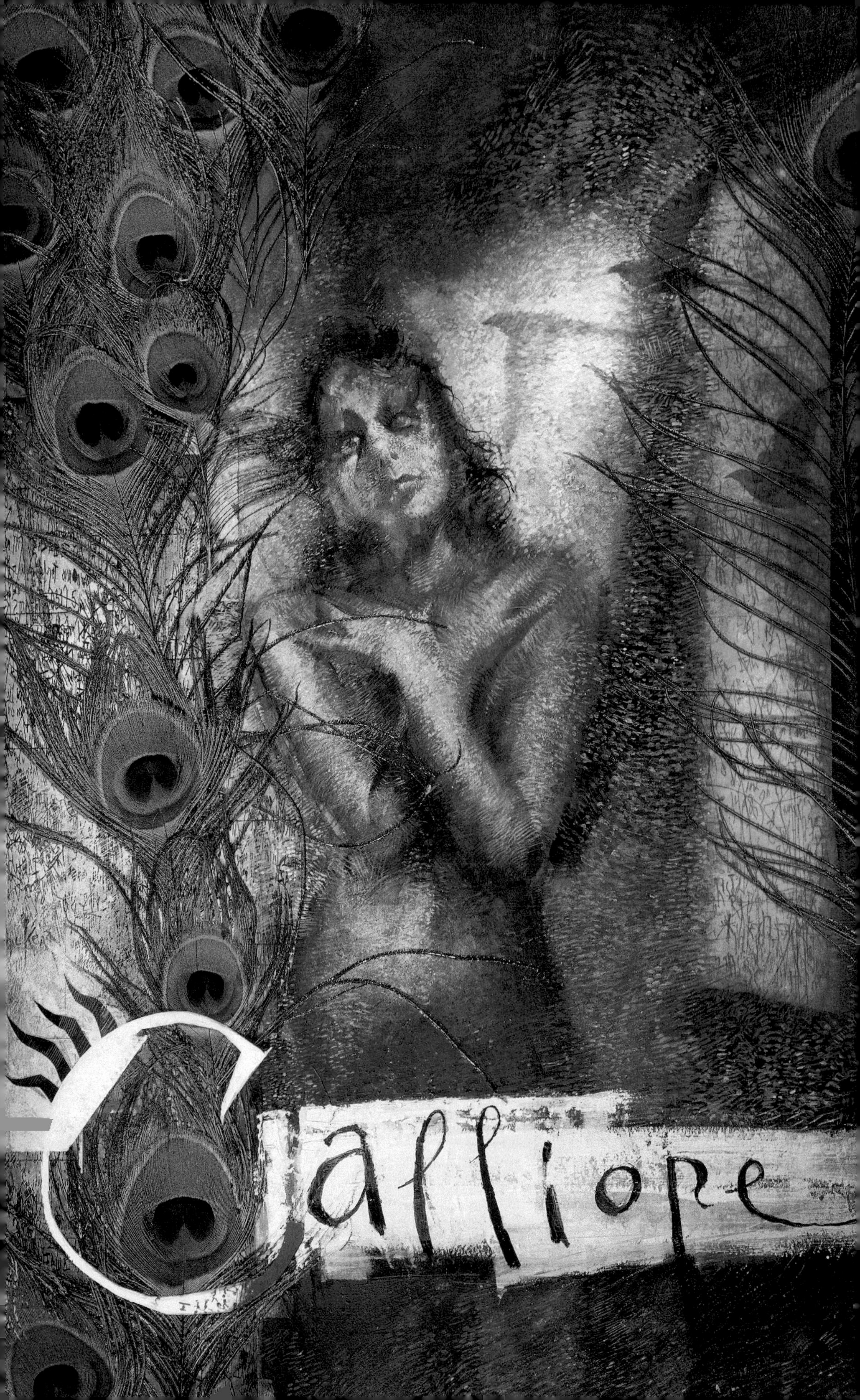
Calliope

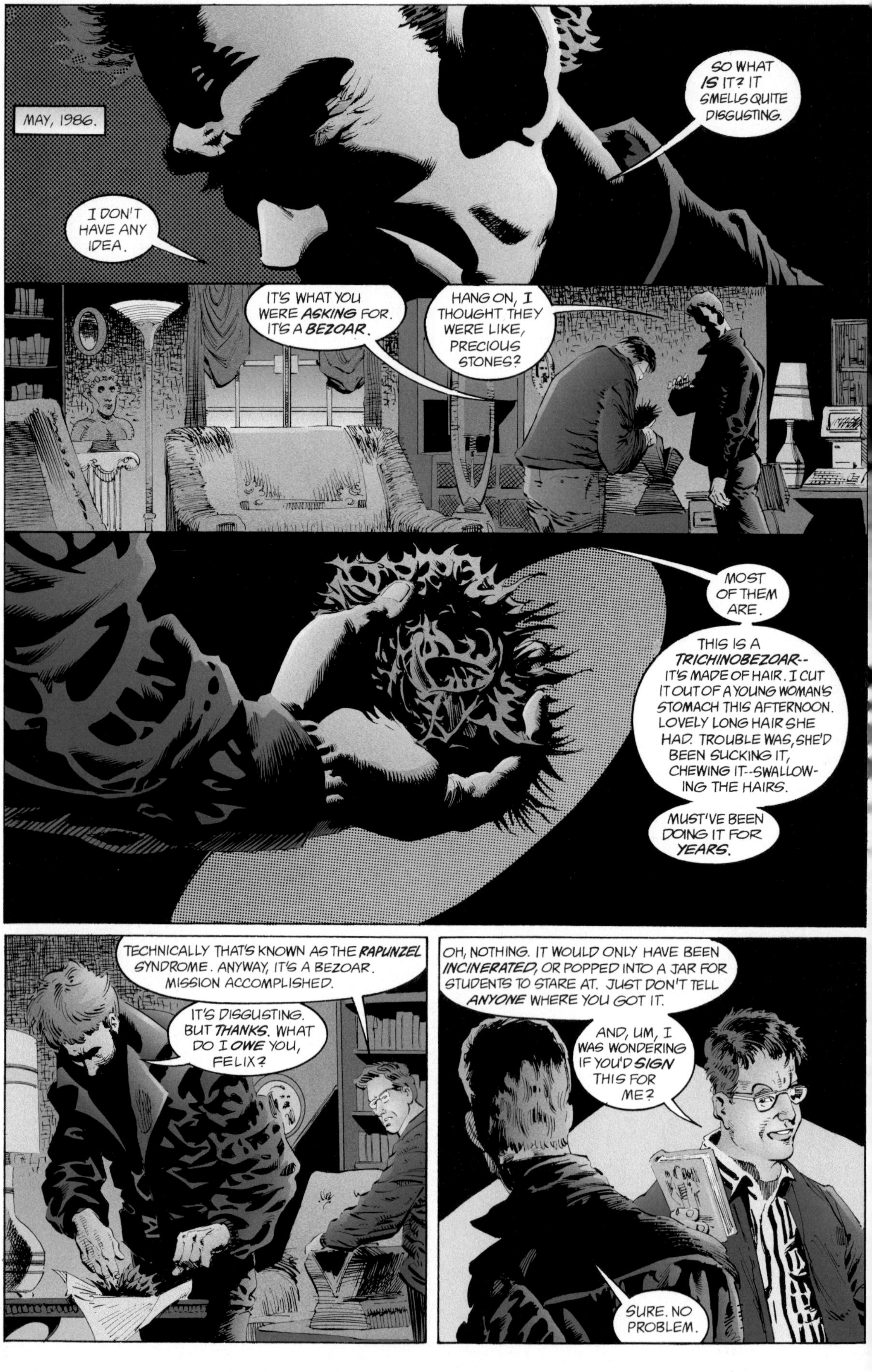
MAY, 1986.
SO WHAT IS IT? IT SMELLS QUITE DISGUSTING.
I DON'T HAVE ANY IDEA.
IT'S WHAT YOU WERE ASKING FOR. IT'S A BEZOAR.
HANG ON, I THOUGHT THEY WERE LIKE, PRECIOUS STONES?
MOST OF THEM ARE.
THIS IS A TRICHINOBEZOAR-- IT'S MADE OF HAIR. I CUT IT OUT OF A YOUNG WOMAN'S STOMACH THIS AFTERNOON. LOVELY LONG HAIR SHE HAD. TROUBLE WAS, SHE'D BEEN SUCKING IT, CHEWING IT--SWALLOWING THE HAIRS.
MUST'VE BEEN DOING IT FOR YEARS.
TECHNICALLY THAT'S KNOWN AS THE RAPUNZEL SYNDROME. ANYWAY, IT'S A BEZOAR. MISSION ACCOMPLISHED.
IT'S DISGUSTING. BUT THANKS. WHAT DO I OWE YOU, FELIX?
OH, NOTHING. IT WOULD ONLY HAVE BEEN INCINERATED, OR POPPED INTO A JAR FOR STUDENTS TO STARE AT. JUST DON'T TELL ANYONE WHERE YOU GOT IT.
AND, UM, I WAS WONDERING IF YOU'D SIGN THIS FOR ME?
SURE. NO PROBLEM.

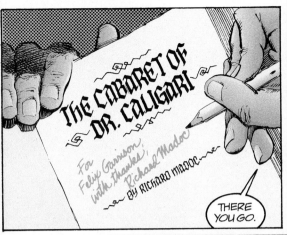

THE CABARET OF DR. CALIGARI

For Felix Garrison, with thanks, Richard Madoc
-- BY RICHARD MADOC

THERE YOU GO.

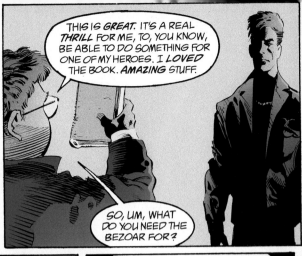

THIS IS *GREAT.* IT'S A REAL *THRILL* FOR ME, TO, YOU KNOW, BE ABLE TO DO SOMETHING FOR ONE OF MY HEROES. I *LOVED* THE BOOK. *AMAZING* STUFF.

SO, UM, WHAT DO YOU NEED THE BEZOAR FOR?

LIKE YOU WERE ASKING THE OTHER DAY-- WHERE DO WRITERS GET OUR CRAZY IDEAS? HEH.

IT'S RESEARCH, REALLY.

I HEARD YOU WERE WRITING A SEQUEL TO *THE CABARET*-- I'M REALLY EXCITED.

OH. GREAT.

UH, THAT'S THE PHONE. LISTEN, THANKS AGAIN FOR THE THING.

NO PROBLEM. I KNOW HOW *BUSY* YOU ARE. I'LL JUST LET MYSELF OUT, THEN. 'BYE.

BREEP BREEP

HELLO? RICHARD MADOC SPEAKING.

OH. HI, HARRY.

RICK? IT'S HARRY. LISTEN, WE HAVE TO *TALK.* YOUR PUBLISHERS WERE ONTO ME AGAIN TODAY.

LISTEN, THE NOVEL'S ALMOST NINE MONTHS OVERDUE, AND THEY'RE THREATENING TO CAUSE TROUBLE. YOU'RE IN BREACH OF CONTRACT, RICK. IS IT FINISHED *YET?*

NEARLY FINISHED.

WELL, *HOW* MUCH HAVE YOU GOT TO GO?

IT'S *ALMOST* FINISHED, HARRY. YOU CAN'T RUSH THESE THINGS. ANOTHER COUPLE OF WEEKS, MAYBE, OKAY?

LISTEN, I'M *REALLY* BUSY. I'LL GET BACK TO YOU. OKAY?

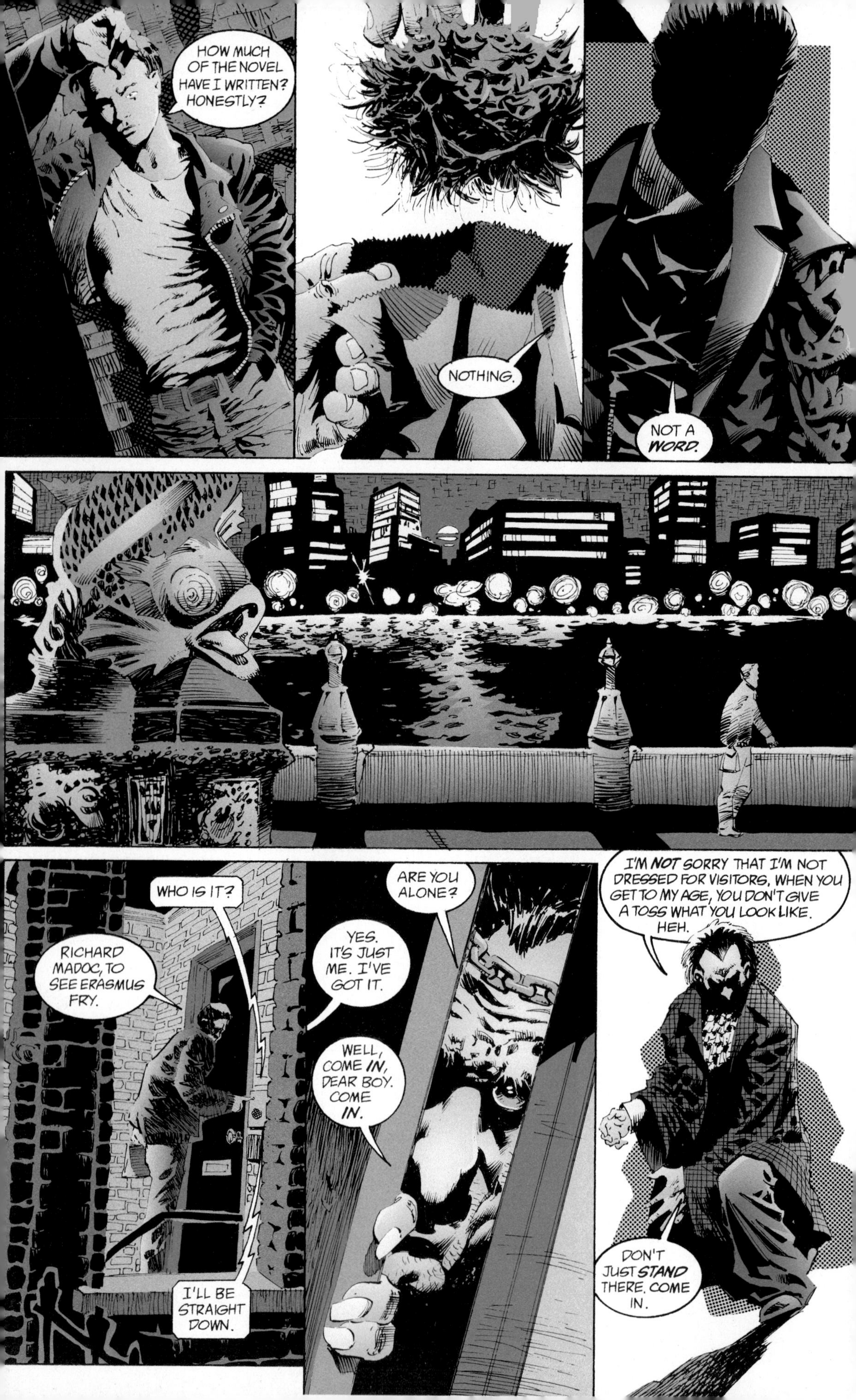
HOW MUCH OF THE NOVEL HAVE I WRITTEN? HONESTLY?
NOTHING.
NOT A WORD.
WHO IS IT?
RICHARD MADOC, TO SEE ERASMUS FRY.
I'LL BE STRAIGHT DOWN.
ARE YOU ALONE?
YES. IT'S JUST ME. I'VE GOT IT.
WELL, COME IN, DEAR BOY. COME IN.
I'M NOT SORRY THAT I'M NOT DRESSED FOR VISITORS, WHEN YOU GET TO MY AGE, YOU DON'T GIVE A TOSS WHAT YOU LOOK LIKE. HEH.
DON'T JUST STAND THERE. COME IN.

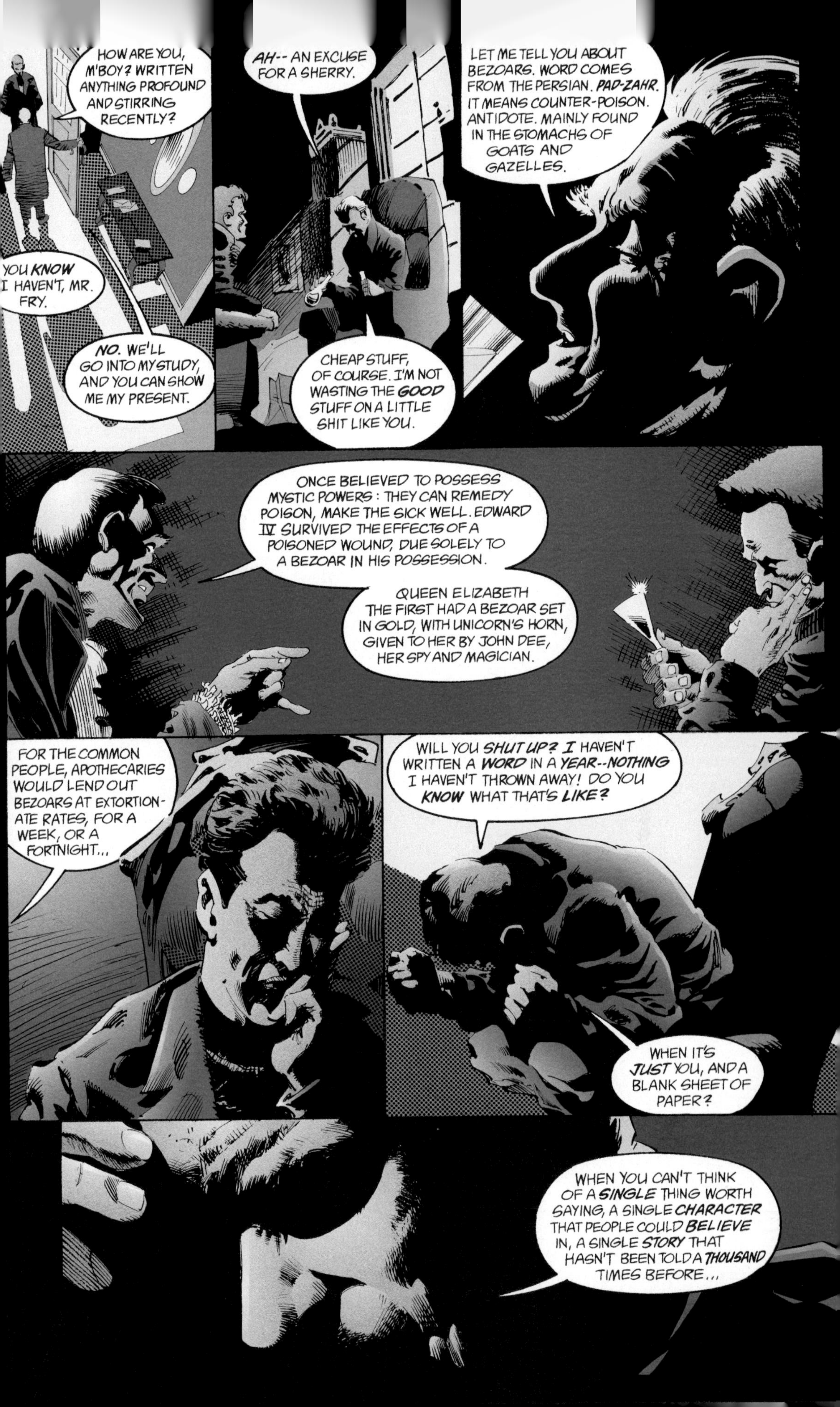

HOW ARE YOU, M'BOY? WRITTEN ANYTHING PROFOUND AND STIRRING RECENTLY?
YOU KNOW I HAVEN'T, MR. FRY.
NO. WE'LL GO INTO MY STUDY, AND YOU CAN SHOW ME MY PRESENT.
AH-- AN EXCUSE FOR A SHERRY.
CHEAP STUFF, OF COURSE. I'M NOT WASTING THE GOOD STUFF ON A LITTLE SHIT LIKE YOU.
LET ME TELL YOU ABOUT BEZOARS. WORD COMES FROM THE PERSIAN. PAD-ZAHR. IT MEANS COUNTER-POISON. ANTIDOTE. MAINLY FOUND IN THE STOMACHS OF GOATS AND GAZELLES.
ONCE BELIEVED TO POSSESS MYSTIC POWERS: THEY CAN REMEDY POISON, MAKE THE SICK WELL. EDWARD IV SURVIVED THE EFFECTS OF A POISONED WOUND, DUE SOLELY TO A BEZOAR IN HIS POSSESSION.
QUEEN ELIZABETH THE FIRST HAD A BEZOAR SET IN GOLD, WITH UNICORN'S HORN, GIVEN TO HER BY JOHN DEE, HER SPY AND MAGICIAN.
FOR THE COMMON PEOPLE, APOTHECARIES WOULD LEND OUT BEZOARS AT EXTORTION-ATE RATES, FOR A WEEK, OR A FORTNIGHT...
WILL YOU SHUT UP? I HAVEN'T WRITTEN A WORD IN A YEAR--NOTHING I HAVEN'T THROWN AWAY! DO YOU KNOW WHAT THAT'S LIKE?
WHEN IT'S JUST YOU, AND A BLANK SHEET OF PAPER?
WHEN YOU CAN'T THINK OF A SINGLE THING WORTH SAYING, A SINGLE CHARACTER THAT PEOPLE COULD BELIEVE IN, A SINGLE STORY THAT HASN'T BEEN TOLD A THOUSAND TIMES BEFORE...

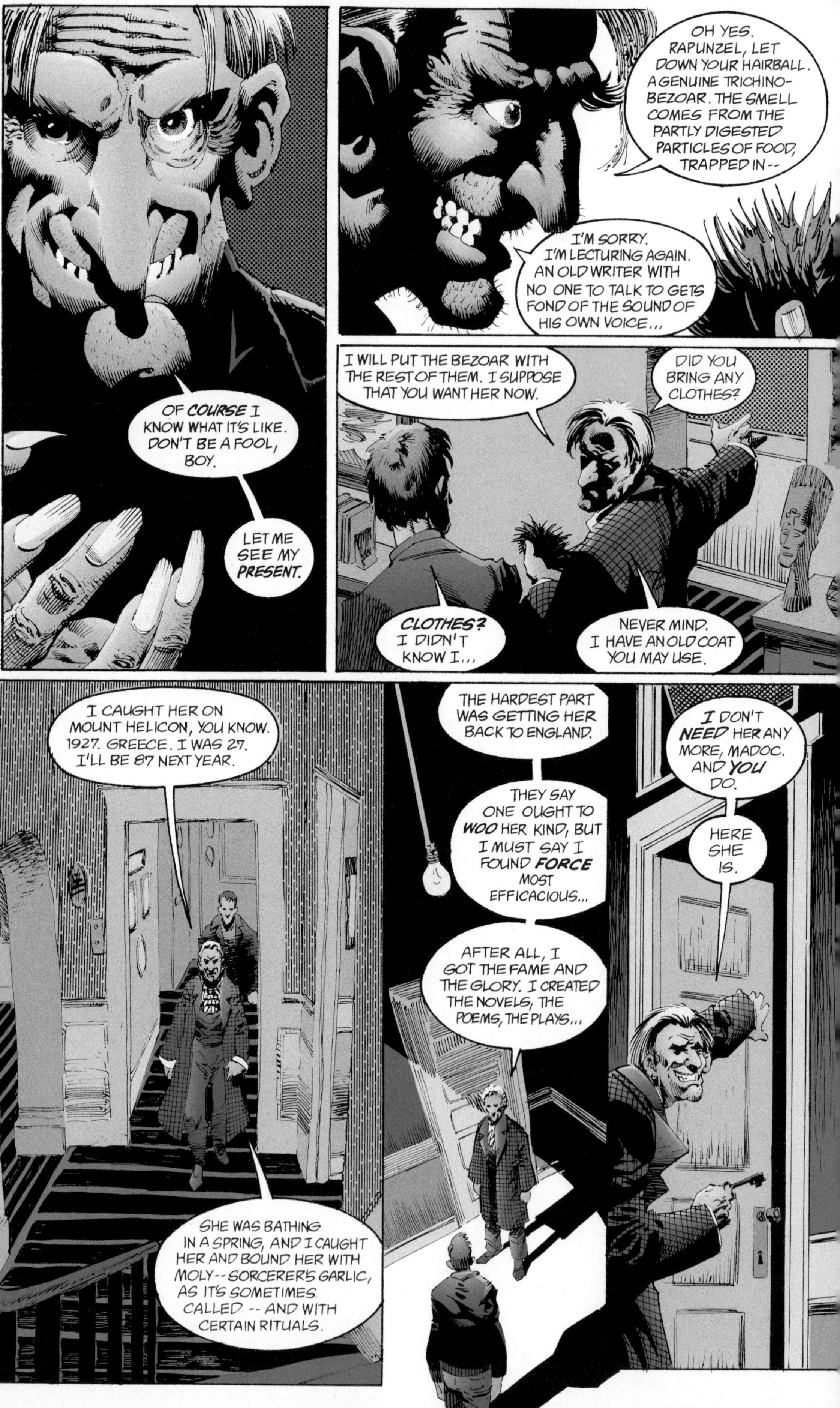

OF COURSE I KNOW WHAT IT'S LIKE. DON'T BE A FOOL, BOY.
LET ME SEE MY PRESENT.
OH YES. RAPUNZEL, LET DOWN YOUR HAIRBALL. A GENUINE TRICHINO-BEZOAR. THE SMELL COMES FROM THE PARTLY DIGESTED PARTICLES OF FOOD, TRAPPED IN--
I'M SORRY. I'M LECTURING AGAIN. AN OLD WRITER WITH NO ONE TO TALK TO GETS FOND OF THE SOUND OF HIS OWN VOICE...
I WILL PUT THE BEZOAR WITH THE REST OF THEM. I SUPPOSE THAT YOU WANT HER NOW.
DID YOU BRING ANY CLOTHES?
CLOTHES? I DIDN'T KNOW I...
NEVER MIND. I HAVE AN OLD COAT YOU MAY USE.
I CAUGHT HER ON MOUNT HELICON, YOU KNOW. 1927. GREECE. I WAS 27. I'LL BE 87 NEXT YEAR.
SHE WAS BATHING IN A SPRING, AND I CAUGHT HER AND BOUND HER WITH MOLY--SORCERER'S GARLIC, AS IT'S SOMETIMES CALLED --AND WITH CERTAIN RITUALS.
THE HARDEST PART WAS GETTING HER BACK TO ENGLAND.
THEY SAY ONE OUGHT TO WOO HER KIND, BUT I MUST SAY I FOUND FORCE MOST EFFICACIOUS...
AFTER ALL, I GOT THE FAME AND THE GLORY. I CREATED THE NOVELS, THE POEMS, THE PLAYS...
I DON'T NEED HER ANY MORE, MADOC. AND YOU DO.
HERE SHE IS.

HER NAME'S CALLIOPE.
CALLIOPE
NEIL GAIMAN WRITER
KELLEY JONES GUEST PENCILLER
MALCOLM JONES III INKER
DANIEL VOZZO COLORIST
TODD KLEIN LETTERER
TOM PEYER ASSIST. EDITOR
KAREN BERGER EDITOR
FEATURING CHARACTERS CREATED BY GAIMAN, KIETH & DRINGENBERG

RICHARD, **THIS** IS **CALLIOPE**. THE YOUNGEST OF THE NINE MUSES. SHE WAS **HOMER'S** MUSE, SO SHE **OUGHT** TO BE GOOD ENOUGH FOR YOU.

DON'T GET YOURSELF ALL WORKED UP, CALLIOPE.

NO, **THIS** IS RICHARD MADOC. HE'S A NOVELIST--OR AT LEAST, HE'S WRITTEN ONE **EXTREMELY** SUCCESSFUL FIRST NOVEL, AND HAS FOUND HIMSELF QUITE UNABLE TO WRITE ANYTHING ELSE.

WHAT WOULD YOU WITH ME NOW, ERASMUS? AM I NOW TO PERFORM FOR YOUR AMUSEMENT? IS THIS MAN TO BE OUR AUDIENCE?

CALLIOPE, I'M GIVING YOU TO RICHARD. YOU'RE **HIS** NOW.

BUT YOU SAID-- YOU TOLD ME, YOU **PROMISED** THAT YOU WOULD **FREE** ME BEFORE YOU DIED. YOU SAID I COULD HAVE MY FREEDOM...

PUT NOT YOUR TRUST IN PRINCES, MY DEAR.

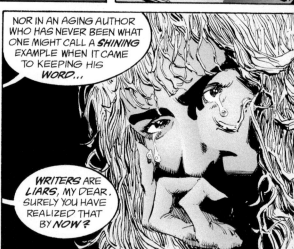

NOR IN AN AGING AUTHOR WHO HAS NEVER BEEN WHAT ONE MIGHT CALL A **SHINING** EXAMPLE WHEN IT CAME TO KEEPING HIS **WORD**...

WRITERS ARE **LIARS**, MY DEAR. SURELY YOU HAVE REALIZED THAT BY **NOW**?

TAKE THE LITTLE COW **AWAY**, MADOC. I NEVER WANT TO SEE **EITHER** OF YOU AGAIN.

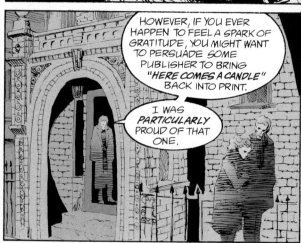

HOWEVER, IF YOU EVER HAPPEN TO FEEL A SPARK OF GRATITUDE, YOU MIGHT WANT TO PERSUADE SOME PUBLISHER TO BRING **"HERE COMES A CANDLE"** BACK INTO PRINT.

I WAS **PARTICULARLY** PROUD OF THAT ONE.

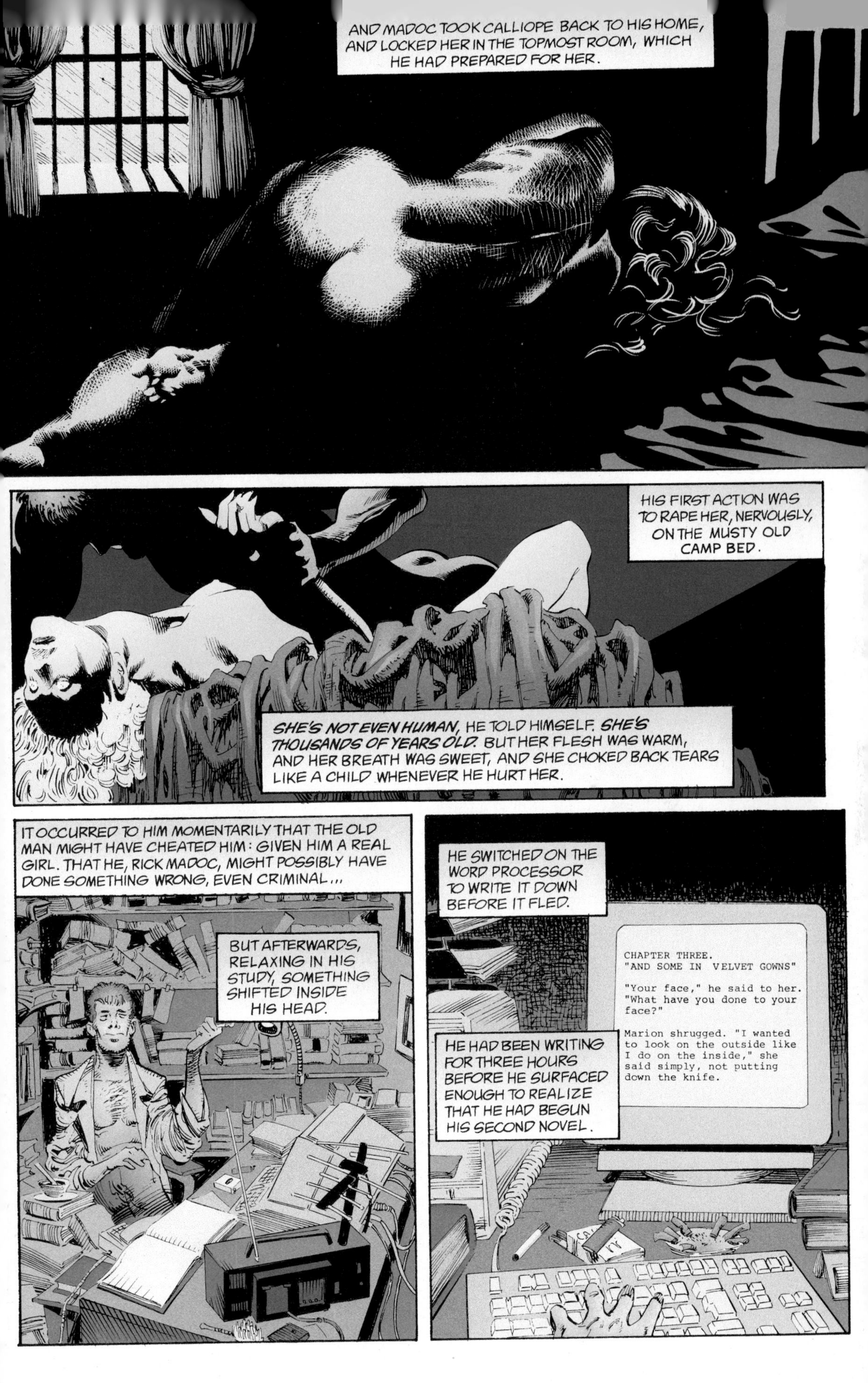
AND MADOC TOOK CALLIOPE BACK TO HIS HOME, AND LOCKED HER IN THE TOPMOST ROOM, WHICH HE HAD PREPARED FOR HER.
HIS FIRST ACTION WAS TO RAPE HER, NERVOUSLY, ON THE MUSTY OLD CAMP BED.
SHE'S NOT EVEN HUMAN, HE TOLD HIMSELF. SHE'S THOUSANDS OF YEARS OLD. BUT HER FLESH WAS WARM, AND HER BREATH WAS SWEET, AND SHE CHOKED BACK TEARS LIKE A CHILD WHENEVER HE HURT HER.
IT OCCURRED TO HIM MOMENTARILY THAT THE OLD MAN MIGHT HAVE CHEATED HIM: GIVEN HIM A REAL GIRL. THAT HE, RICK MADOC, MIGHT POSSIBLY HAVE DONE SOMETHING WRONG, EVEN CRIMINAL...
BUT AFTERWARDS, RELAXING IN HIS STUDY, SOMETHING SHIFTED INSIDE HIS HEAD.
HE SWITCHED ON THE WORD PROCESSOR TO WRITE IT DOWN BEFORE IT FLED.
CHAPTER THREE.
"AND SOME IN VELVET GOWNS"
"Your face," he said to her. "What have you done to your face?"
Marion shrugged. "I wanted to look on the outside like I do on the inside," she said simply, not putting down the knife.
HE HAD BEEN WRITING FOR THREE HOURS BEFORE HE SURFACED ENOUGH TO REALIZE THAT HE HAD BEGUN HIS SECOND NOVEL.

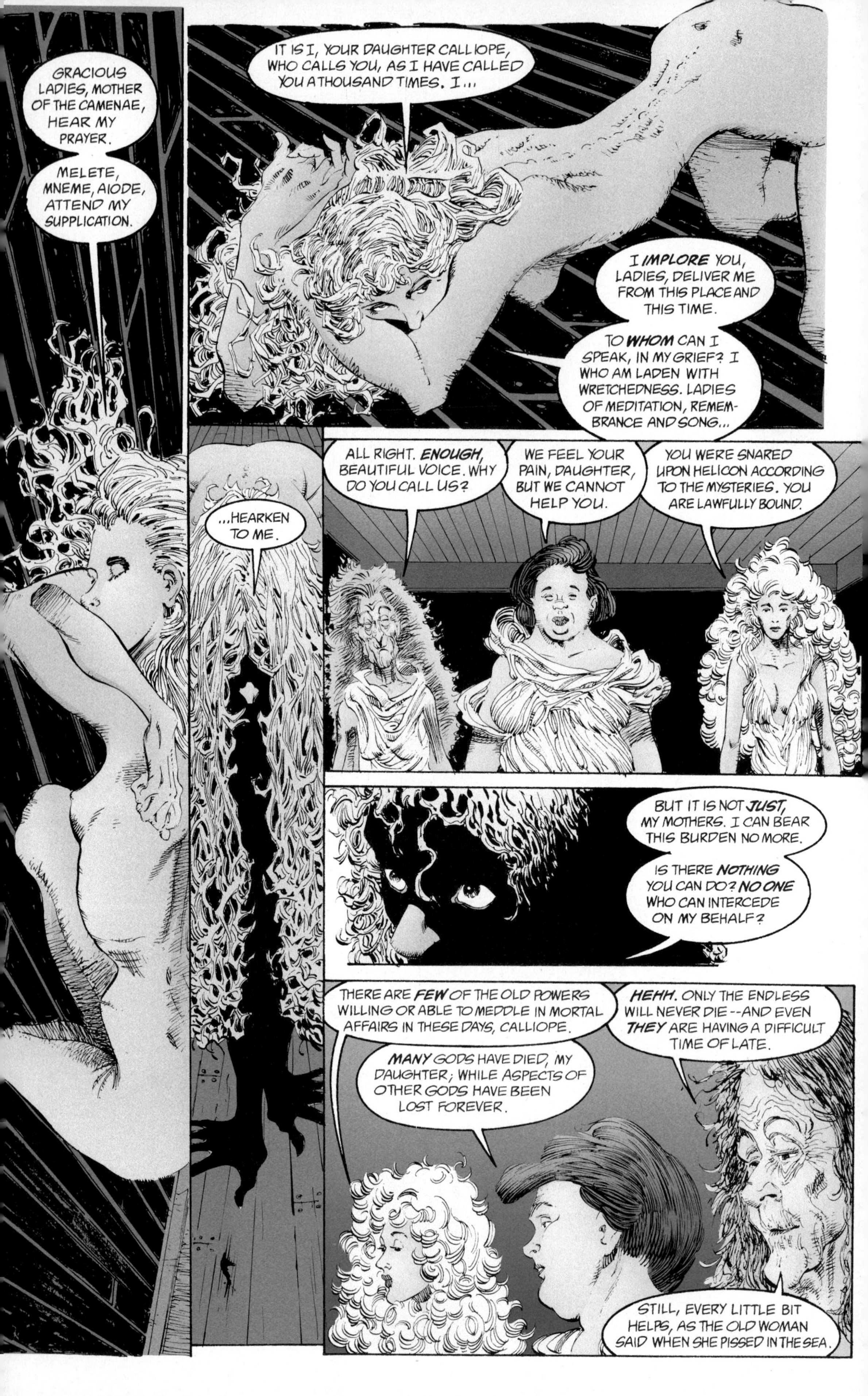

GRACIOUS LADIES, MOTHER OF THE CAMENAE, HEAR MY PRAYER.
MELETE, MNEME, AIODE, ATTEND MY SUPPLICATION.
IT IS I, YOUR DAUGHTER CALLIOPE, WHO CALLS YOU, AS I HAVE CALLED YOU A THOUSAND TIMES. I...
I IMPLORE YOU, LADIES, DELIVER ME FROM THIS PLACE AND THIS TIME.
TO WHOM CAN I SPEAK, IN MY GRIEF? I WHO AM LADEN WITH WRETCHEDNESS. LADIES OF MEDITATION, REMEMBRANCE AND SONG...
...HEARKEN TO ME.
ALL RIGHT. ENOUGH, BEAUTIFUL VOICE. WHY DO YOU CALL US?
WE FEEL YOUR PAIN, DAUGHTER, BUT WE CANNOT HELP YOU.
YOU WERE SNARED UPON HELICON ACCORDING TO THE MYSTERIES. YOU ARE LAWFULLY BOUND.
BUT IT IS NOT JUST, MY MOTHERS. I CAN BEAR THIS BURDEN NO MORE.
IS THERE NOTHING YOU CAN DO? NO ONE WHO CAN INTERCEDE ON MY BEHALF?
THERE ARE FEW OF THE OLD POWERS WILLING OR ABLE TO MEDDLE IN MORTAL AFFAIRS IN THESE DAYS, CALLIOPE.
MANY GODS HAVE DIED, MY DAUGHTER; WHILE ASPECTS OF OTHER GODS HAVE BEEN LOST FOREVER.
HEHH. ONLY THE ENDLESS WILL NEVER DIE--AND EVEN THEY ARE HAVING A DIFFICULT TIME OF LATE.
STILL, EVERY LITTLE BIT HELPS, AS THE OLD WOMAN SAID WHEN SHE PISSED IN THE SEA.

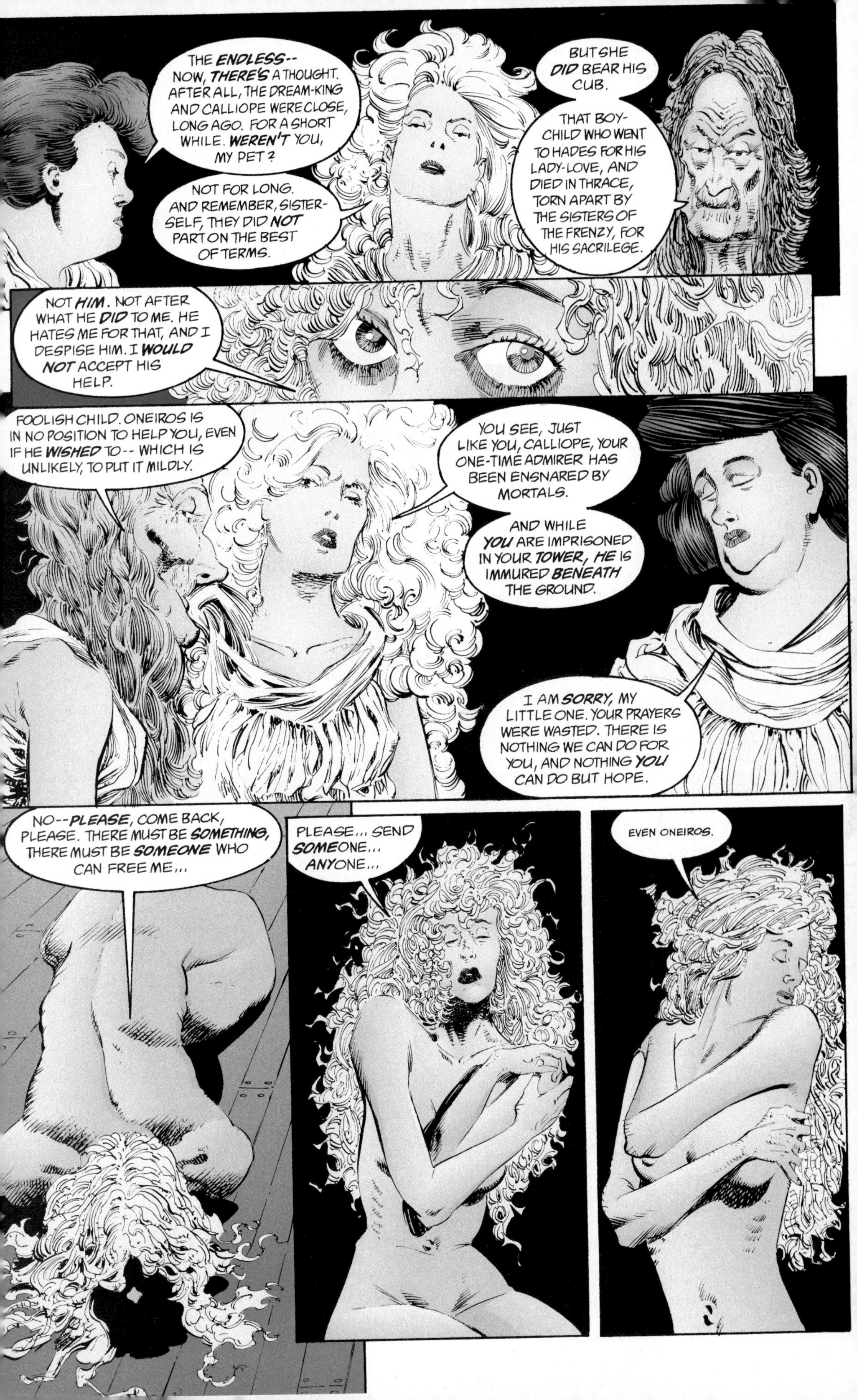
THE ENDLESS-- NOW, THERE'S A THOUGHT. AFTER ALL, THE DREAM-KING AND CALLIOPE WERE CLOSE, LONG AGO. FOR A SHORT WHILE. WEREN'T YOU, MY PET?
NOT FOR LONG. AND REMEMBER, SISTER-SELF, THEY DID NOT PART ON THE BEST OF TERMS.
BUT SHE DID BEAR HIS CUB.
THAT BOY-CHILD WHO WENT TO HADES FOR HIS LADY-LOVE, AND DIED IN THRACE, TORN APART BY THE SISTERS OF THE FRENZY, FOR HIS SACRILEGE.
NOT HIM. NOT AFTER WHAT HE DID TO ME. HE HATES ME FOR THAT, AND I DESPISE HIM. I WOULD NOT ACCEPT HIS HELP.
FOOLISH CHILD. ONEIROS IS IN NO POSITION TO HELP YOU, EVEN IF HE WISHED TO -- WHICH IS UNLIKELY, TO PUT IT MILDLY.
YOU SEE, JUST LIKE YOU, CALLIOPE, YOUR ONE-TIME ADMIRER HAS BEEN ENSNARED BY MORTALS.
AND WHILE YOU ARE IMPRISONED IN YOUR TOWER, HE IS IMMURED BENEATH THE GROUND.
I AM SORRY, MY LITTLE ONE. YOUR PRAYERS WERE WASTED. THERE IS NOTHING WE CAN DO FOR YOU, AND NOTHING YOU CAN DO BUT HOPE.
NO--PLEASE, COME BACK, PLEASE. THERE MUST BE SOMETHING, THERE MUST BE SOMEONE WHO CAN FREE ME...
PLEASE... SEND SOMEONE... ANYONE...
EVEN ONEIROS.

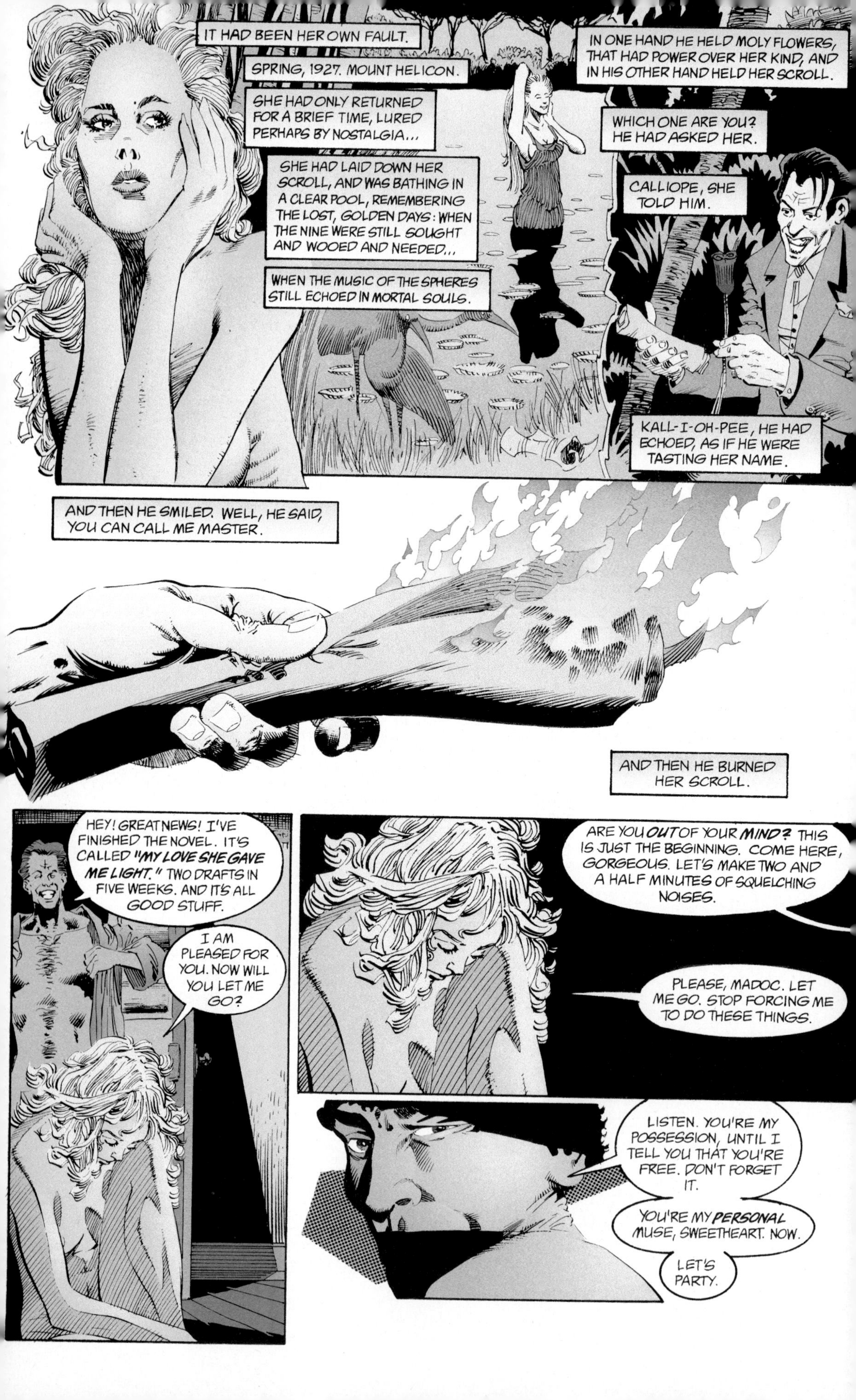
IT HAD BEEN HER OWN FAULT.
SPRING, 1927. MOUNT HELICON.
SHE HAD ONLY RETURNED FOR A BRIEF TIME, LURED PERHAPS BY NOSTALGIA...
SHE HAD LAID DOWN HER SCROLL, AND WAS BATHING IN A CLEAR POOL, REMEMBERING THE LOST, GOLDEN DAYS: WHEN THE NINE WERE STILL SOUGHT AND WOOED AND NEEDED...
WHEN THE MUSIC OF THE SPHERES STILL ECHOED IN MORTAL SOULS.
IN ONE HAND HE HELD MOLY FLOWERS, THAT HAD POWER OVER HER KIND, AND IN HIS OTHER HAND HELD HER SCROLL.
WHICH ONE ARE YOU? HE HAD ASKED HER.
CALLIOPE, SHE TOLD HIM.
KALL-I-OH-PEE, HE HAD ECHOED, AS IF HE WERE TASTING HER NAME.
AND THEN HE SMILED. WELL, HE SAID, YOU CAN CALL ME MASTER.
AND THEN HE BURNED HER SCROLL.
HEY! GREAT NEWS! I'VE FINISHED THE NOVEL. IT'S CALLED "MY LOVE SHE GAVE ME LIGHT." TWO DRAFTS IN FIVE WEEKS. AND IT'S ALL GOOD STUFF.
I AM PLEASED FOR YOU. NOW WILL YOU LET ME GO?
ARE YOU OUT OF YOUR MIND? THIS IS JUST THE BEGINNING. COME HERE, GORGEOUS. LET'S MAKE TWO AND A HALF MINUTES OF SQUELCHING NOISES.
PLEASE, MADOC. LET ME GO. STOP FORCING ME TO DO THESE THINGS.
LISTEN. YOU'RE MY POSSESSION, UNTIL I TELL YOU THAT YOU'RE FREE. DON'T FORGET IT.
YOU'RE MY PERSONAL MUSE, SWEETHEART. NOW.
LET'S PARTY.

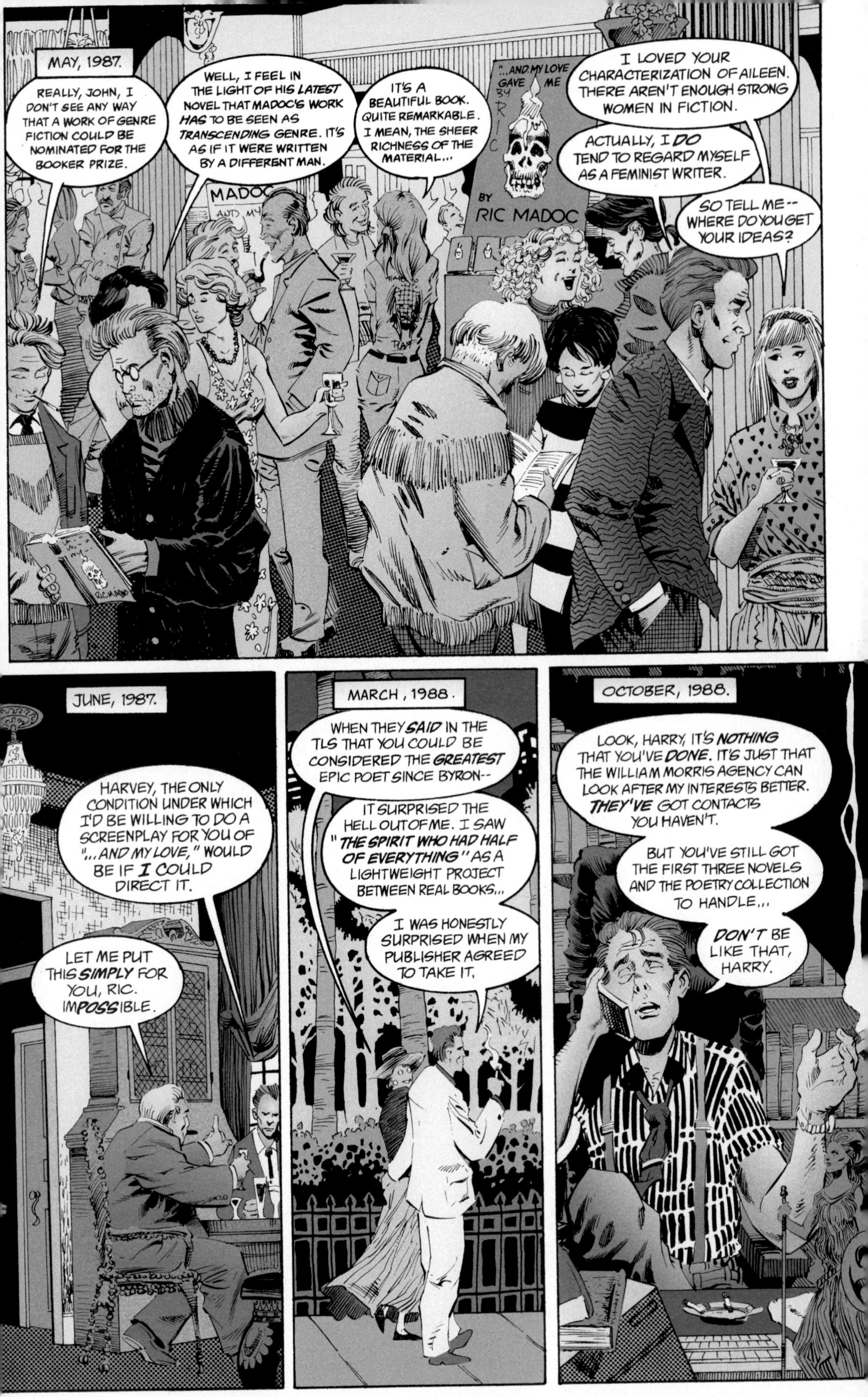

MAY, 1987.
REALLY, JOHN, I DON'T SEE ANY WAY THAT A WORK OF GENRE FICTION COULD BE NOMINATED FOR THE BOOKER PRIZE.
WELL, I FEEL IN THE LIGHT OF HIS *LATEST* NOVEL THAT MADOC'S WORK *HAS* TO BE SEEN AS *TRANSCENDING* GENRE. IT'S AS IF IT WERE WRITTEN BY A DIFFERENT MAN.
IT'S A BEAUTIFUL BOOK. QUITE REMARKABLE. I MEAN, THE SHEER RICHNESS OF THE MATERIAL...
"...AND MY LOVE GAVE ME"
BY RIC MADOC
I LOVED YOUR CHARACTERIZATION OF AILEEN. THERE AREN'T ENOUGH STRONG WOMEN IN FICTION.
ACTUALLY, I *DO* TEND TO REGARD MYSELF AS A FEMINIST WRITER.
SO TELL ME-- WHERE DO YOU GET YOUR IDEAS?
JUNE, 1987.
HARVEY, THE ONLY CONDITION UNDER WHICH I'D BE WILLING TO DO A SCREENPLAY FOR YOU OF "*...AND MY LOVE,*" WOULD BE IF *I* COULD DIRECT IT.
LET ME PUT THIS *SIMPLY* FOR YOU, RIC. IM*POSS*IBLE.
MARCH, 1988.
WHEN THEY *SAID* IN THE TLS THAT YOU COULD BE CONSIDERED THE *GREATEST* EPIC POET SINCE BYRON--
IT SURPRISED THE HELL OUT OF ME. I SAW "*THE SPIRIT WHO HAD HALF OF EVERYTHING*" AS A LIGHTWEIGHT PROJECT BETWEEN REAL BOOKS...
I WAS HONESTLY SURPRISED WHEN MY PUBLISHER AGREED TO TAKE IT.
OCTOBER, 1988.
LOOK, HARRY, IT'S *NOTHING* THAT YOU'VE *DONE*. IT'S JUST THAT THE WILLIAM MORRIS AGENCY CAN LOOK AFTER MY INTERESTS BETTER. *THEY'VE* GOT CONTACTS YOU HAVEN'T.
BUT YOU'VE STILL GOT THE FIRST THREE NOVELS AND THE POETRY COLLECTION TO HANDLE...
DON'T BE LIKE THAT, HARRY.

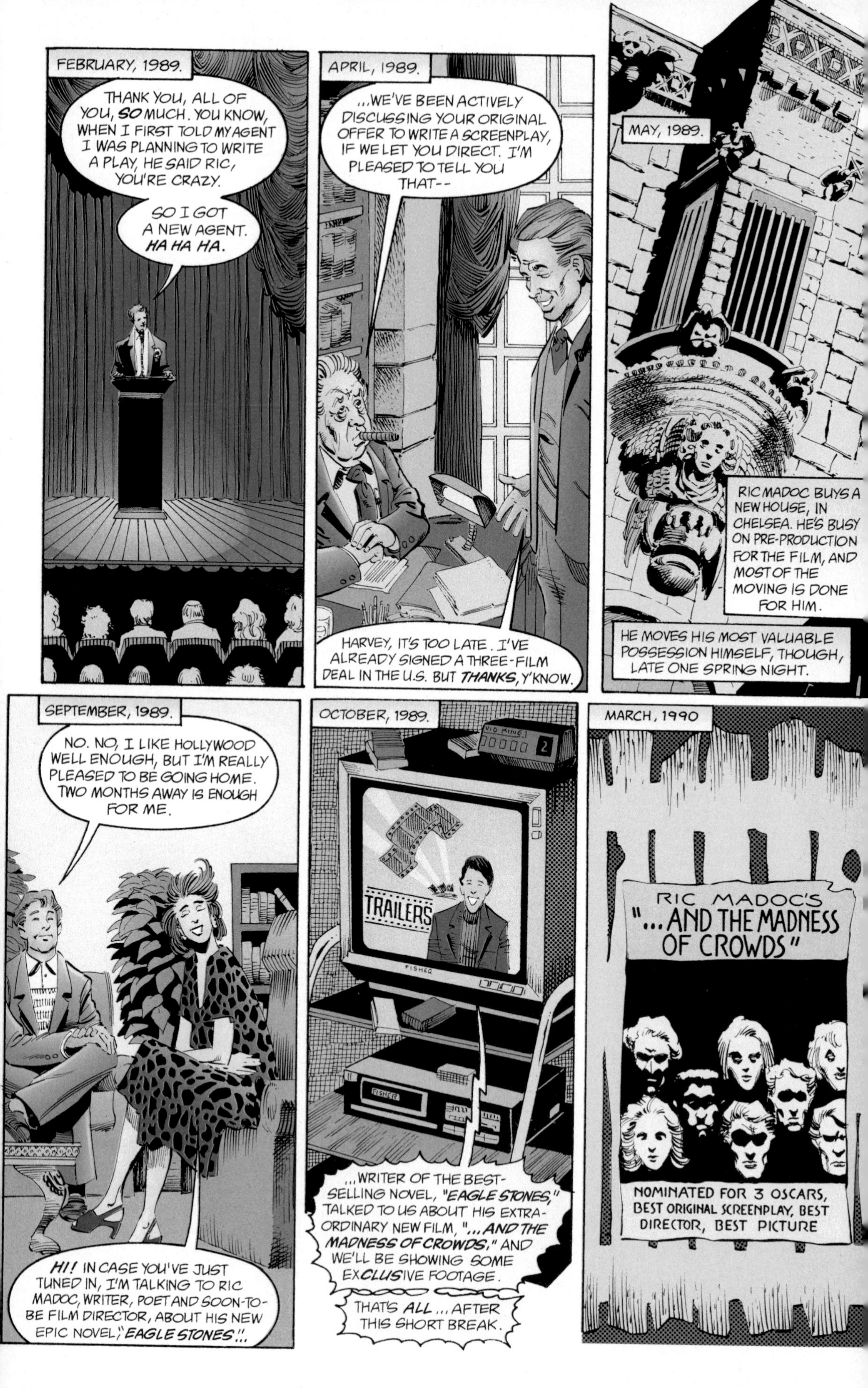
FEBRUARY, 1989.
THANK YOU, ALL OF YOU, SO MUCH. YOU KNOW, WHEN I FIRST TOLD MY AGENT I WAS PLANNING TO WRITE A PLAY, HE SAID RIC, YOU'RE CRAZY.
SO I GOT A NEW AGENT. HA HA HA.
APRIL, 1989.
...WE'VE BEEN ACTIVELY DISCUSSING YOUR ORIGINAL OFFER TO WRITE A SCREENPLAY, IF WE LET YOU DIRECT. I'M PLEASED TO TELL YOU THAT--
HARVEY, IT'S TOO LATE. I'VE ALREADY SIGNED A THREE-FILM DEAL IN THE U.S. BUT THANKS, Y'KNOW.
MAY, 1989.
RIC MADOC BUYS A NEW HOUSE, IN CHELSEA. HE'S BUSY ON PRE-PRODUCTION FOR THE FILM, AND MOST OF THE MOVING IS DONE FOR HIM.
HE MOVES HIS MOST VALUABLE POSSESSION HIMSELF, THOUGH, LATE ONE SPRING NIGHT.
SEPTEMBER, 1989.
NO. NO, I LIKE HOLLYWOOD WELL ENOUGH, BUT I'M REALLY PLEASED TO BE GOING HOME. TWO MONTHS AWAY IS ENOUGH FOR ME.
HI! IN CASE YOU'VE JUST TUNED IN, I'M TALKING TO RIC MADOC, WRITER, POET AND SOON-TO-BE FILM DIRECTOR, ABOUT HIS NEW EPIC NOVEL, "EAGLE STONES"...
OCTOBER, 1989.
VID KING
TRAILERS
FISHER
...WRITER OF THE BEST-SELLING NOVEL, "EAGLE STONES," TALKED TO US ABOUT HIS EXTRA-ORDINARY NEW FILM, "...AND THE MADNESS OF CROWDS," AND WE'LL BE SHOWING SOME EXCLUSIVE FOOTAGE.
THAT'S ALL ... AFTER THIS SHORT BREAK.
MARCH, 1990
RIC MADOC'S "...AND THE MADNESS OF CROWDS"
NOMINATED FOR 3 OSCARS, BEST ORIGINAL SCREENPLAY, BEST DIRECTOR, BEST PICTURE

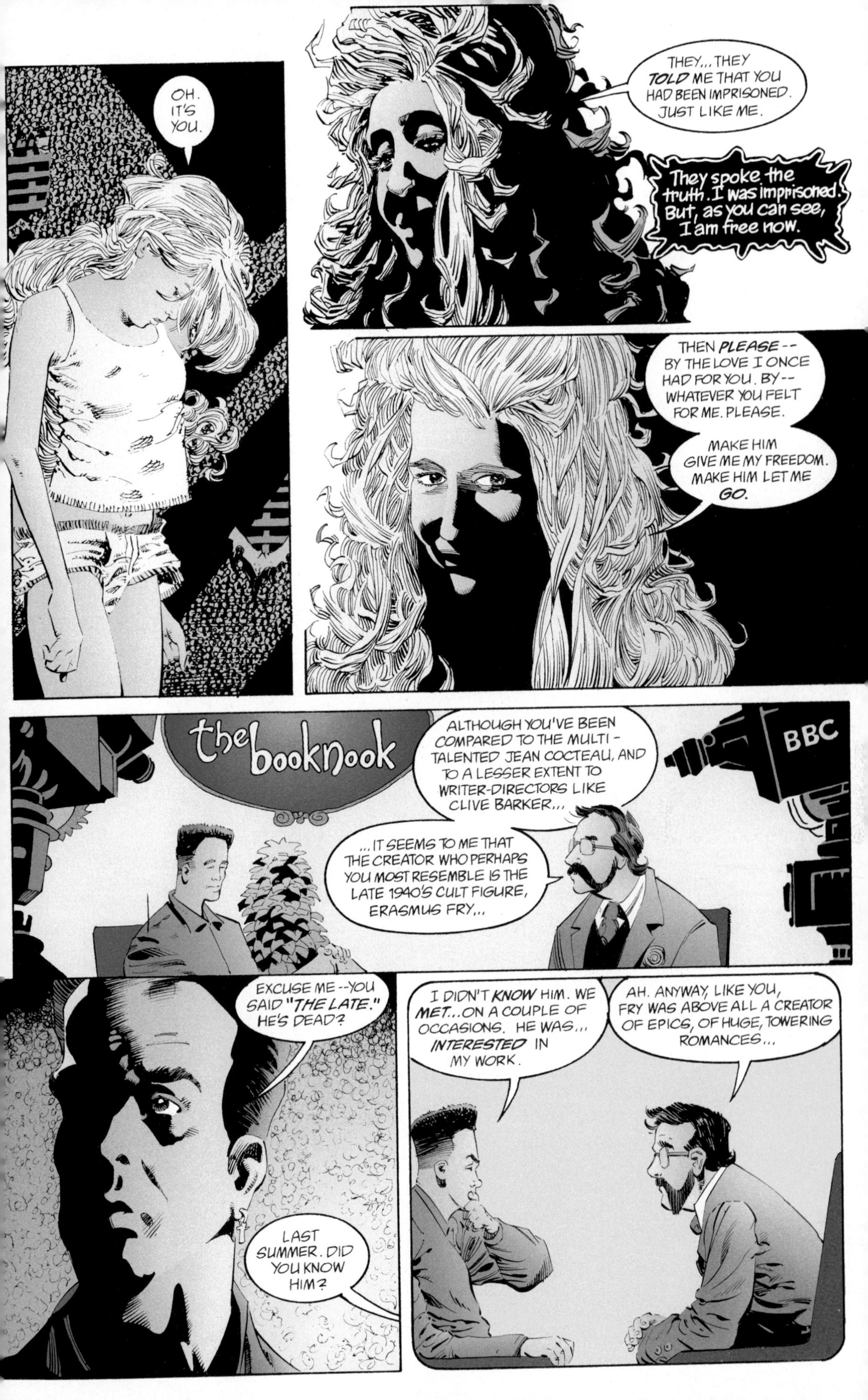

OH. IT'S YOU.
THEY... THEY TOLD ME THAT YOU HAD BEEN IMPRISONED. JUST LIKE ME.
They spoke the truth. I was imprisoned. But, as you can see, I am free now.
THEN PLEASE -- BY THE LOVE I ONCE HAD FOR YOU. BY -- WHATEVER YOU FELT FOR ME. PLEASE.
MAKE HIM GIVE ME MY FREEDOM. MAKE HIM LET ME GO.
the booknook
BBC
ALTHOUGH YOU'VE BEEN COMPARED TO THE MULTI-TALENTED JEAN COCTEAU, AND TO A LESSER EXTENT TO WRITER-DIRECTORS LIKE CLIVE BARKER...
...IT SEEMS TO ME THAT THE CREATOR WHO PERHAPS YOU MOST RESEMBLE IS THE LATE 1940'S CULT FIGURE, ERASMUS FRY...
EXCUSE ME --YOU SAID "THE LATE." HE'S DEAD?
LAST SUMMER. DID YOU KNOW HIM?
I DIDN'T KNOW HIM. WE MET... ON A COUPLE OF OCCASIONS. HE WAS... INTERESTED IN MY WORK.
AH. ANYWAY, LIKE YOU, FRY WAS ABOVE ALL A CREATOR OF EPICS, OF HUGE, TOWERING ROMANCES...

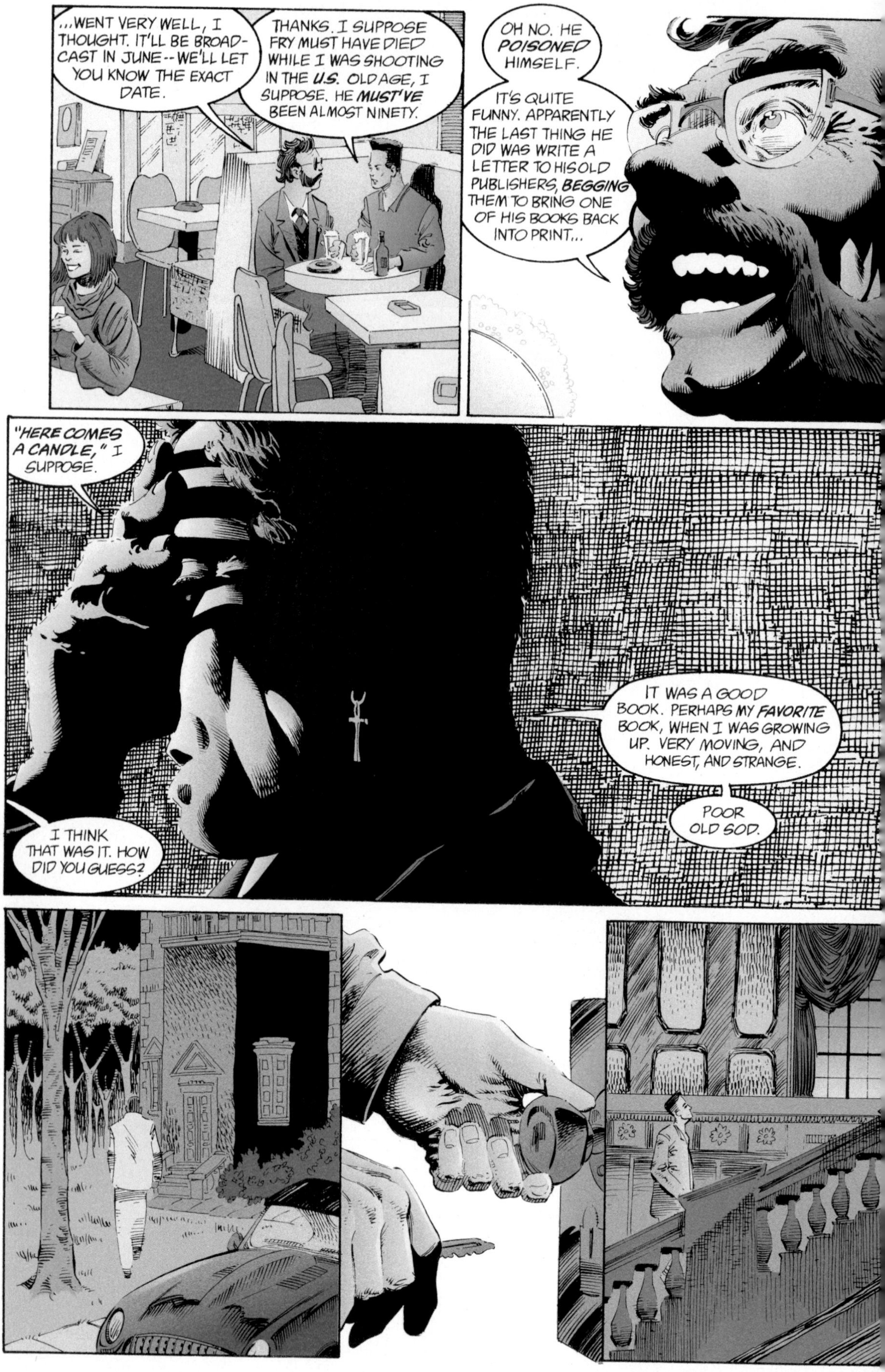
...WENT VERY WELL, I THOUGHT. IT'LL BE BROAD-CAST IN JUNE--WE'LL LET YOU KNOW THE EXACT DATE.
THANKS. I SUPPOSE FRY MUST HAVE DIED WHILE I WAS SHOOTING IN THE U.S. OLD AGE, I SUPPOSE. HE MUST'VE BEEN ALMOST NINETY.
OH NO. HE POISONED HIMSELF.
IT'S QUITE FUNNY. APPARENTLY THE LAST THING HE DID WAS WRITE A LETTER TO HIS OLD PUBLISHERS, BEGGING THEM TO BRING ONE OF HIS BOOKS BACK INTO PRINT...
"HERE COMES A CANDLE," I SUPPOSE.
I THINK THAT WAS IT. HOW DID YOU GUESS?
IT WAS A GOOD BOOK. PERHAPS MY FAVORITE BOOK, WHEN I WAS GROWING UP. VERY MOVING, AND HONEST, AND STRANGE.
POOR OLD SOD.

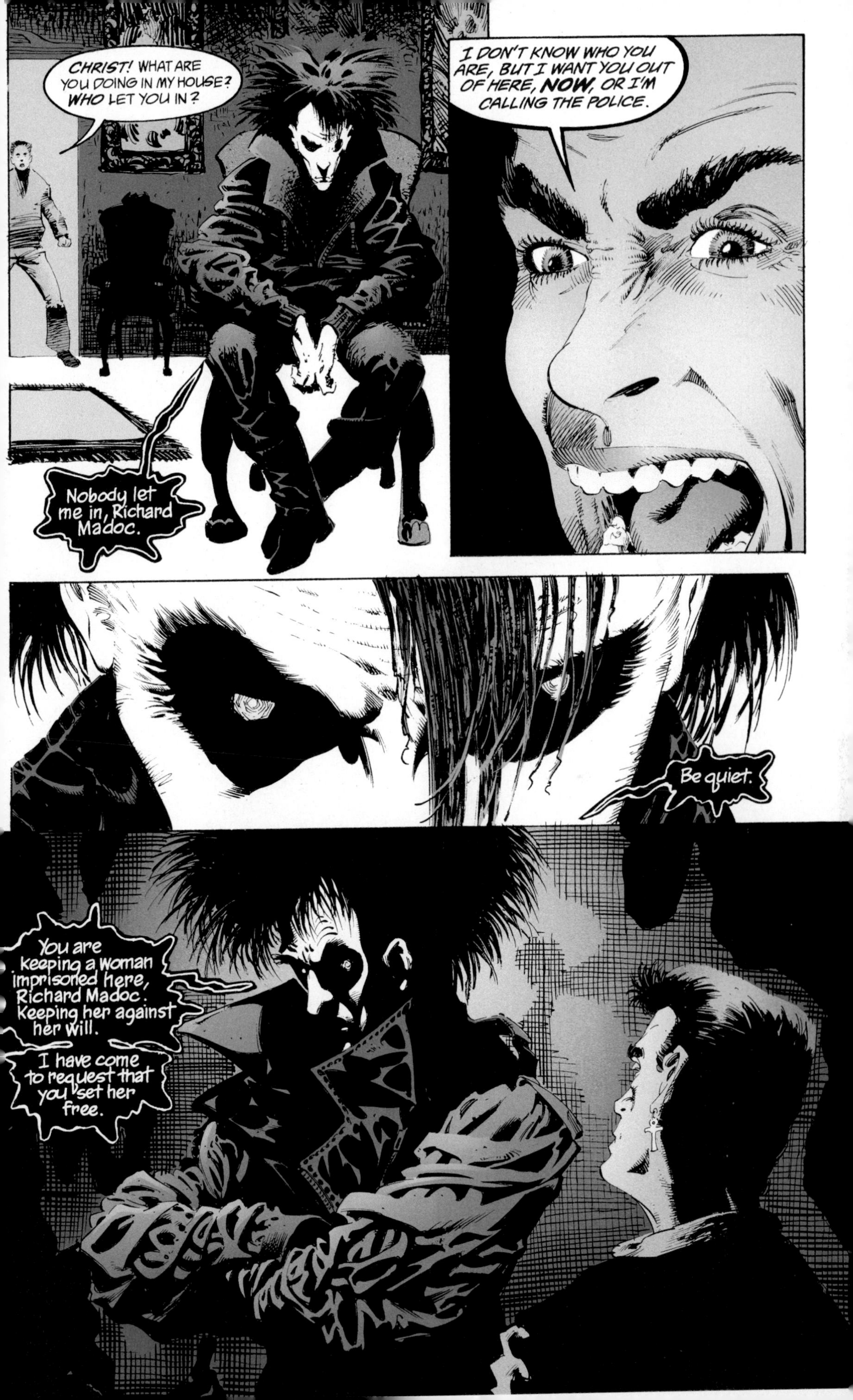
CHRIST! WHAT ARE YOU DOING IN MY HOUSE? WHO LET YOU IN?
Nobody let me in, Richard Madoc.
I DON'T KNOW WHO YOU ARE, BUT I WANT YOU OUT OF HERE, NOW, OR I'M CALLING THE POLICE.
Be quiet.
You are keeping a woman imprisoned here, Richard Madoc. Keeping her against her will.
I have come to request that you set her free.

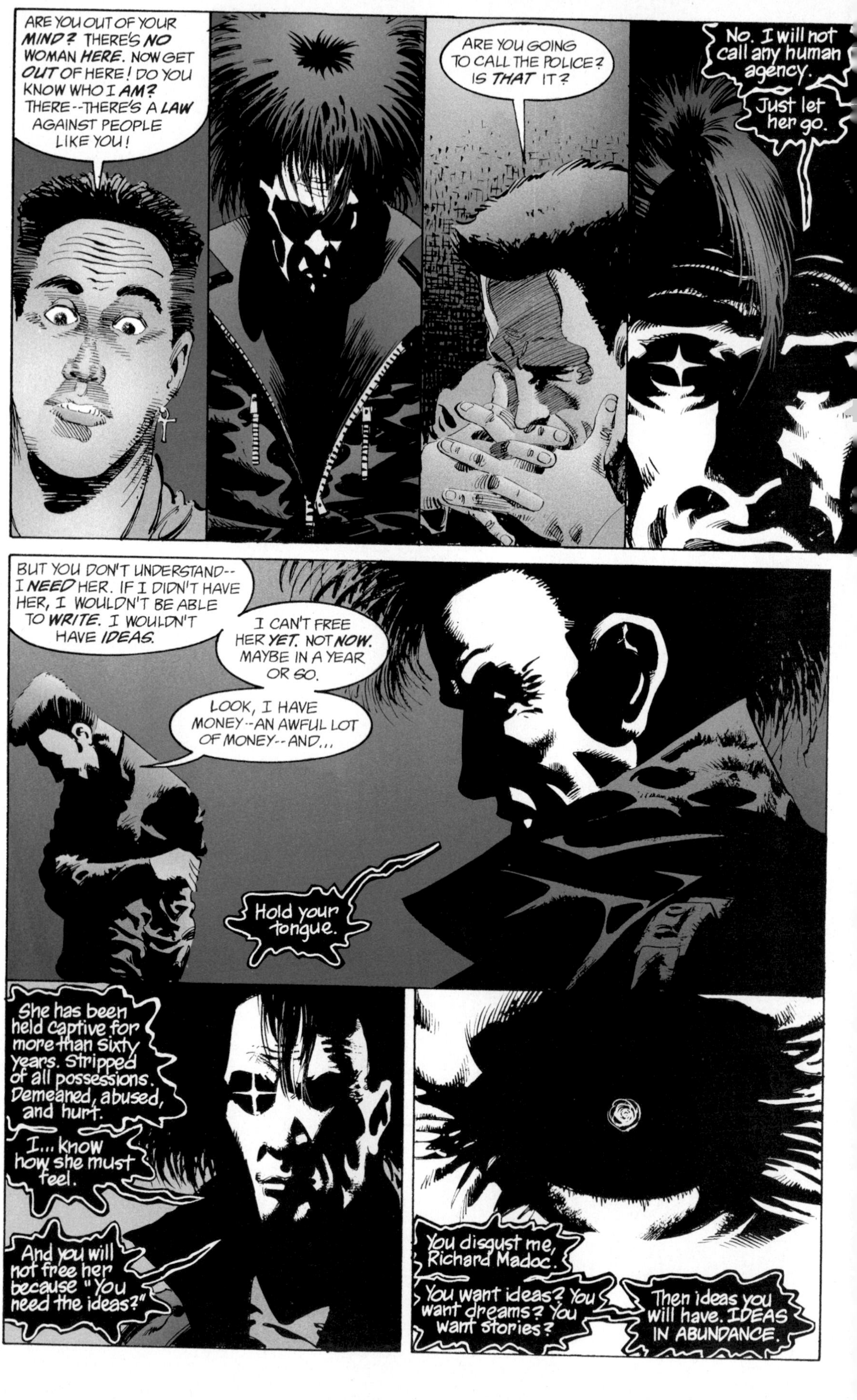
ARE YOU OUT OF YOUR MIND? THERE'S NO WOMAN HERE. NOW GET OUT OF HERE! DO YOU KNOW WHO I AM? THERE--THERE'S A LAW AGAINST PEOPLE LIKE YOU!
ARE YOU GOING TO CALL THE POLICE? IS THAT IT?
No. I will not call any human agency.
Just let her go.
BUT YOU DON'T UNDERSTAND-- I NEED HER. IF I DIDN'T HAVE HER, I WOULDN'T BE ABLE TO WRITE. I WOULDN'T HAVE IDEAS.
I CAN'T FREE HER YET. NOT NOW. MAYBE IN A YEAR OR SO.
LOOK, I HAVE MONEY--AN AWFUL LOT OF MONEY--AND...
Hold your tongue.
She has been held captive for more than sixty years. Stripped of all possessions. Demeaned, abused, and hurt.
I... know how she must feel.
And you will not free her because "You need the ideas?"
You disgust me, Richard Madoc.
You want ideas? You want dreams? You want stories?
Then ideas you will have. IDEAS IN ABUNDANCE.

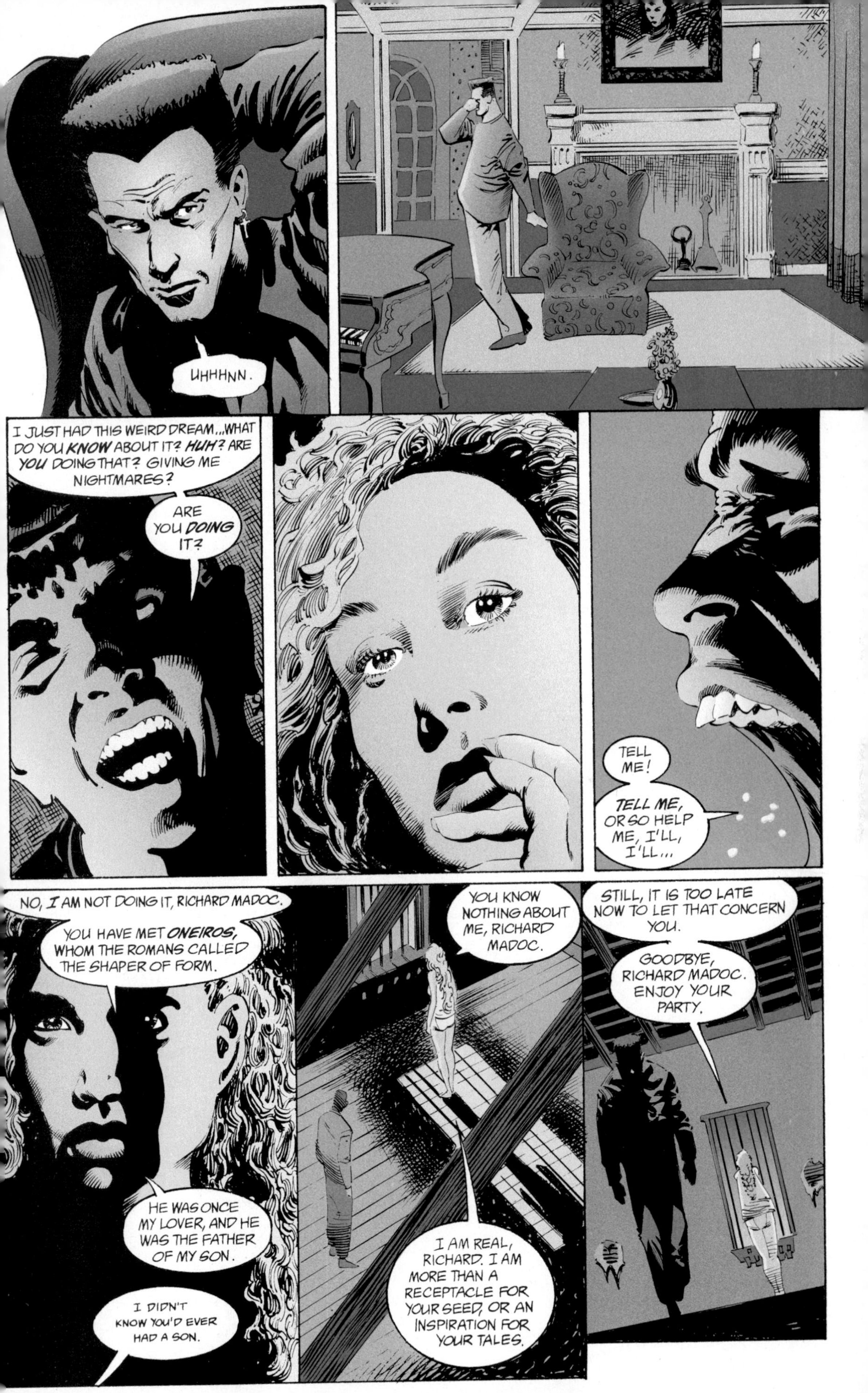
UHHHNN.
I JUST HAD THIS WEIRD DREAM...WHAT DO YOU KNOW ABOUT IT? HUH? ARE YOU DOING THAT? GIVING ME NIGHTMARES?
ARE YOU DOING IT?
TELL ME!
TELL ME, OR SO HELP ME, I'LL, I'LL...
NO, I AM NOT DOING IT, RICHARD MADOC.
YOU HAVE MET ONEIROS, WHOM THE ROMANS CALLED THE SHAPER OF FORM.
HE WAS ONCE MY LOVER, AND HE WAS THE FATHER OF MY SON.
I DIDN'T KNOW YOU'D EVER HAD A SON.
YOU KNOW NOTHING ABOUT ME, RICHARD MADOC.
I AM REAL, RICHARD. I AM MORE THAN A RECEPTACLE FOR YOUR SEED, OR AN INSPIRATION FOR YOUR TALES.
STILL, IT IS TOO LATE NOW TO LET THAT CONCERN YOU.
GOODBYE, RICHARD MADOC. ENJOY YOUR PARTY.

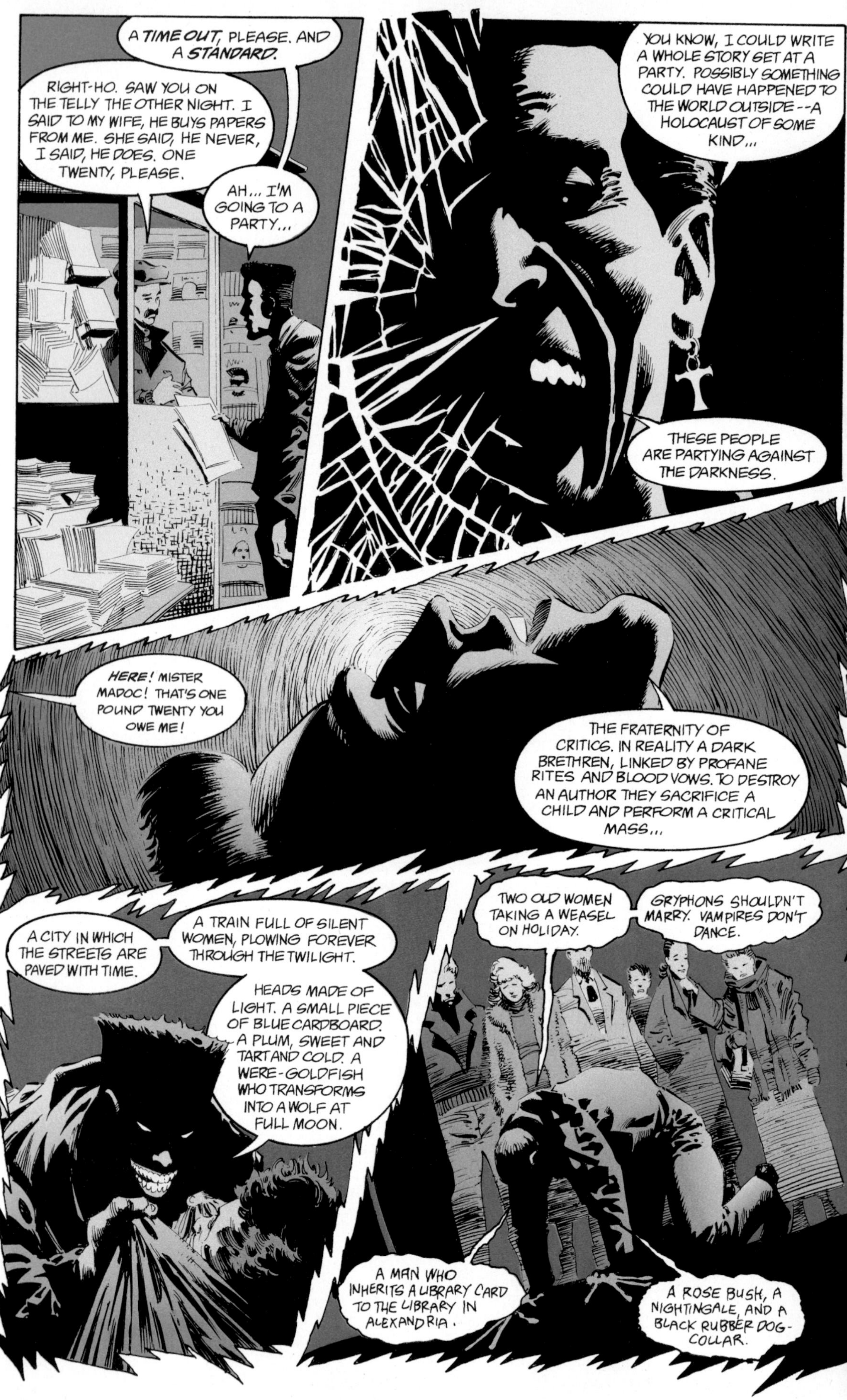
A TIME OUT, PLEASE. AND A STANDARD.
RIGHT-HO. SAW YOU ON THE TELLY THE OTHER NIGHT. I SAID TO MY WIFE, HE BUYS PAPERS FROM ME. SHE SAID, HE NEVER, I SAID, HE DOES. ONE TWENTY, PLEASE.
AH... I'M GOING TO A PARTY...
YOU KNOW, I COULD WRITE A WHOLE STORY SET AT A PARTY. POSSIBLY SOMETHING COULD HAVE HAPPENED TO THE WORLD OUTSIDE--A HOLOCAUST OF SOME KIND...
THESE PEOPLE ARE PARTYING AGAINST THE DARKNESS.
HERE! MISTER MADOC! THAT'S ONE POUND TWENTY YOU OWE ME!
THE FRATERNITY OF CRITICS. IN REALITY A DARK BRETHREN, LINKED BY PROFANE RITES AND BLOOD VOWS. TO DESTROY AN AUTHOR THEY SACRIFICE A CHILD AND PERFORM A CRITICAL MASS...
A CITY IN WHICH THE STREETS ARE PAVED WITH TIME.
A TRAIN FULL OF SILENT WOMEN, PLOWING FOREVER THROUGH THE TWILIGHT.
HEADS MADE OF LIGHT. A SMALL PIECE OF BLUE CARDBOARD. A PLUM, SWEET AND TART AND COLD. A WERE-GOLDFISH WHO TRANSFORMS INTO A WOLF AT FULL MOON.
TWO OLD WOMEN TAKING A WEASEL ON HOLIDAY.
GRYPHONS SHOULDN'T MARRY. VAMPIRES DON'T DANCE.
A MAN WHO INHERITS A LIBRARY CARD TO THE LIBRARY IN ALEXANDRIA.
A ROSE BUSH, A NIGHTINGALE, AND A BLACK RUBBER DOG-COLLAR.

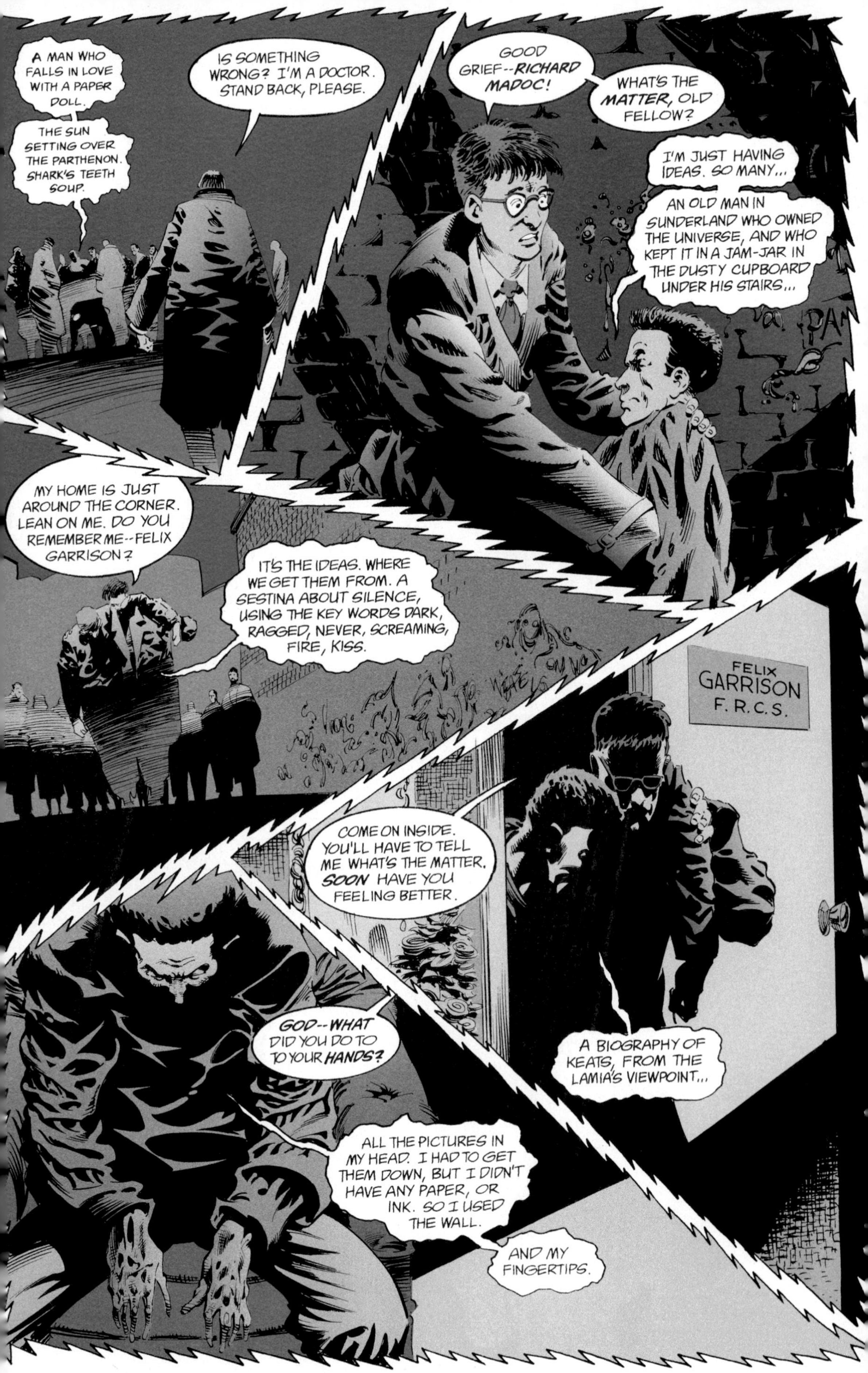
A MAN WHO FALLS IN LOVE WITH A PAPER DOLL.
THE SUN SETTING OVER THE PARTHENON. SHARK'S TEETH SOUP.
IS SOMETHING WRONG? I'M A DOCTOR. STAND BACK, PLEASE.
GOOD GRIEF--RICHARD MADOC!
WHAT'S THE MATTER, OLD FELLOW?
I'M JUST HAVING IDEAS. SO MANY...
AN OLD MAN IN SUNDERLAND WHO OWNED THE UNIVERSE, AND WHO KEPT IT IN A JAM-JAR IN THE DUSTY CUPBOARD UNDER HIS STAIRS...
MY HOME IS JUST AROUND THE CORNER. LEAN ON ME. DO YOU REMEMBER ME--FELIX GARRISON?
IT'S THE IDEAS. WHERE WE GET THEM FROM. A SESTINA ABOUT SILENCE, USING THE KEY WORDS DARK, RAGGED, NEVER, SCREAMING, FIRE, KISS.
FELIX GARRISON F.R.C.S.
COME ON INSIDE. YOU'LL HAVE TO TELL ME WHAT'S THE MATTER. SOON HAVE YOU FEELING BETTER.
A BIOGRAPHY OF KEATS, FROM THE LAMIA'S VIEWPOINT...
GOD--WHAT DID YOU DO TO YOUR HANDS?
ALL THE PICTURES IN MY HEAD. I HAD TO GET THEM DOWN, BUT I DIDN'T HAVE ANY PAPER, OR INK. SO I USED THE WALL.
AND MY FINGERTIPS.

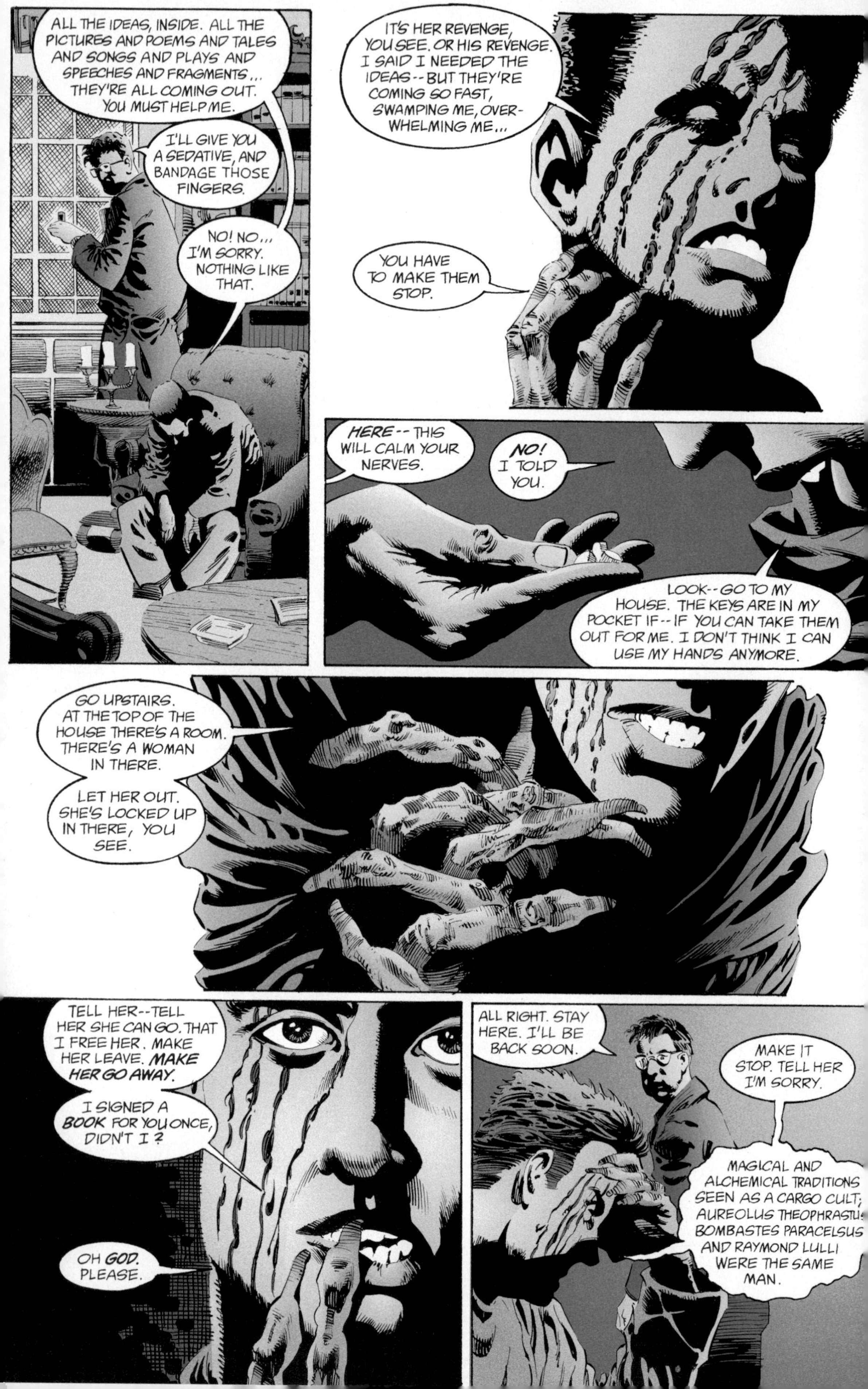
ALL THE IDEAS, INSIDE. ALL THE PICTURES AND POEMS AND TALES AND SONGS AND PLAYS AND SPEECHES AND FRAGMENTS... THEY'RE ALL COMING OUT. YOU MUST HELP ME.
I'LL GIVE YOU A SEDATIVE, AND BANDAGE THOSE FINGERS.
NO! NO... I'M SORRY. NOTHING LIKE THAT.
IT'S HER REVENGE, YOU SEE. OR HIS REVENGE. I SAID I NEEDED THE IDEAS--BUT THEY'RE COMING SO FAST, SWAMPING ME, OVER-WHELMING ME...
YOU HAVE TO MAKE THEM STOP.
HERE--THIS WILL CALM YOUR NERVES.
NO! I TOLD YOU.
LOOK--GO TO MY HOUSE. THE KEYS ARE IN MY POCKET IF--IF YOU CAN TAKE THEM OUT FOR ME. I DON'T THINK I CAN USE MY HANDS ANYMORE.
GO UPSTAIRS. AT THE TOP OF THE HOUSE THERE'S A ROOM. THERE'S A WOMAN IN THERE.
LET HER OUT. SHE'S LOCKED UP IN THERE, YOU SEE.
TELL HER--TELL HER SHE CAN GO. THAT I FREE HER. MAKE HER LEAVE. MAKE HER GO AWAY.
I SIGNED A BOOK FOR YOU ONCE, DIDN'T I?
OH GOD. PLEASE.
ALL RIGHT. STAY HERE. I'LL BE BACK SOON.
MAKE IT STOP. TELL HER I'M SORRY.
MAGICAL AND ALCHEMICAL TRADITIONS SEEN AS A CARGO CULT; AUREOLUS THEOPHRASTUS BOMBASTES PARACELSUS AND RAYMOND LULLI WERE THE SAME MAN.

UM. **HELLO?**

IS THERE, UM, ANYONE HERE? HE SAYS-- RIC, UH, SAYS YOU'RE FREE TO GO. **HELLO?**

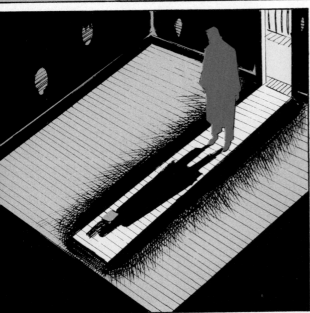

HERE COMES A CANDLE BY ERASMUS FRY

SHE WAS HIS MUSE-- AND THE SLAVE OF LUST?

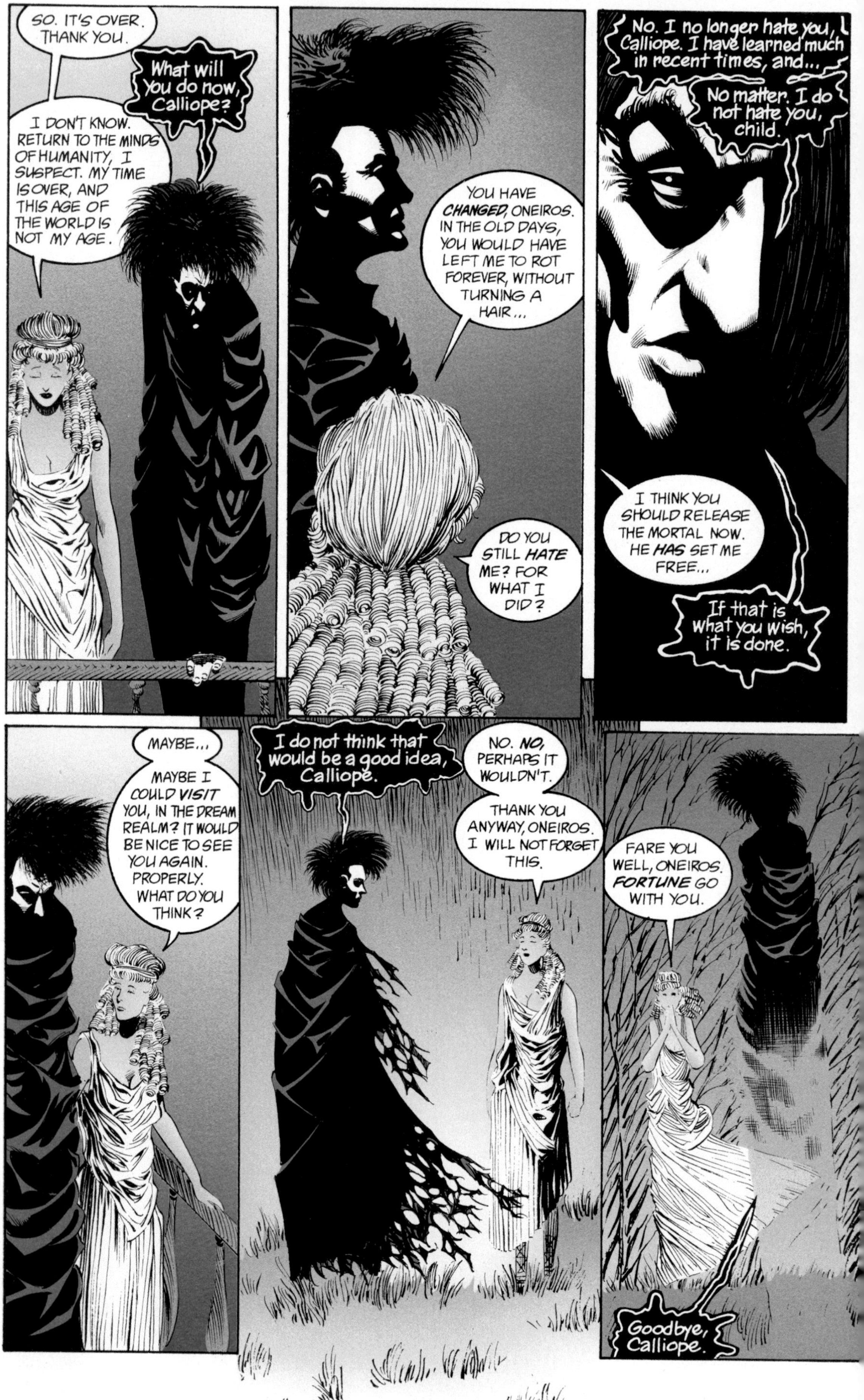

SO. IT'S OVER. THANK YOU.
What will you do now, Calliope?
I DON'T KNOW. RETURN TO THE MINDS OF HUMANITY, I SUSPECT. MY TIME IS OVER, AND THIS AGE OF THE WORLD IS NOT MY AGE.
YOU HAVE CHANGED, ONEIROS. IN THE OLD DAYS, YOU WOULD HAVE LEFT ME TO ROT FOREVER, WITHOUT TURNING A HAIR...
DO YOU STILL HATE ME? FOR WHAT I DID?
No. I no longer hate you, Calliope. I have learned much in recent times, and...
No matter. I do not hate you, child.
I THINK YOU SHOULD RELEASE THE MORTAL NOW. HE HAS SET ME FREE...
If that is what you wish, it is done.
MAYBE...
MAYBE I COULD VISIT YOU, IN THE DREAM REALM? IT WOULD BE NICE TO SEE YOU AGAIN. PROPERLY. WHAT DO YOU THINK?
I do not think that would be a good idea, Calliope.
NO. NO, PERHAPS IT WOULDN'T.
THANK YOU ANYWAY, ONEIROS. I WILL NOT FORGET THIS.
FARE YOU WELL, ONEIROS. FORTUNE GO WITH YOU.
Goodbye, Calliope.

I'VE DONE IT, RIC. UM, HOW ARE YOU FEELING NOW?

I...I DON'T KNOW ANY MORE. I KEEP TRYING TO THINK...ABOUT WHAT SHE SAID...

"THE SHAPER OF FORMS"... IT SEEMS LIKE IT SHOULD *MEAN* SOMETHING...

THERE WAS NO ONE THERE. IN THE ROOM. THERE WAS JUST A BOOK.

I DON'T KNOW... IT DOESN'T CONNECT WITH ANYTHING...IT'S A NAME...

I WISH I COULD REMEMBER.

IT'S SO HARD TO THINK...

...MORPHEUS? ...ORPHEUS?...ONE OF THOSE...

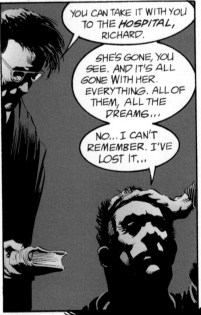

YOU CAN TAKE IT WITH YOU TO THE *HOSPITAL*, RICHARD.

SHE'S GONE, YOU SEE. AND IT'S ALL GONE WITH HER. EVERYTHING. ALL OF THEM, ALL THE DREAMS...

NO...I CAN'T REMEMBER. I'VE LOST IT...

IT'S GONE. I'VE GOT NO IDEA ANY MORE.

NO IDEA AT ALL.

NEXT...   A DREAM OF A THOUSAND CATS

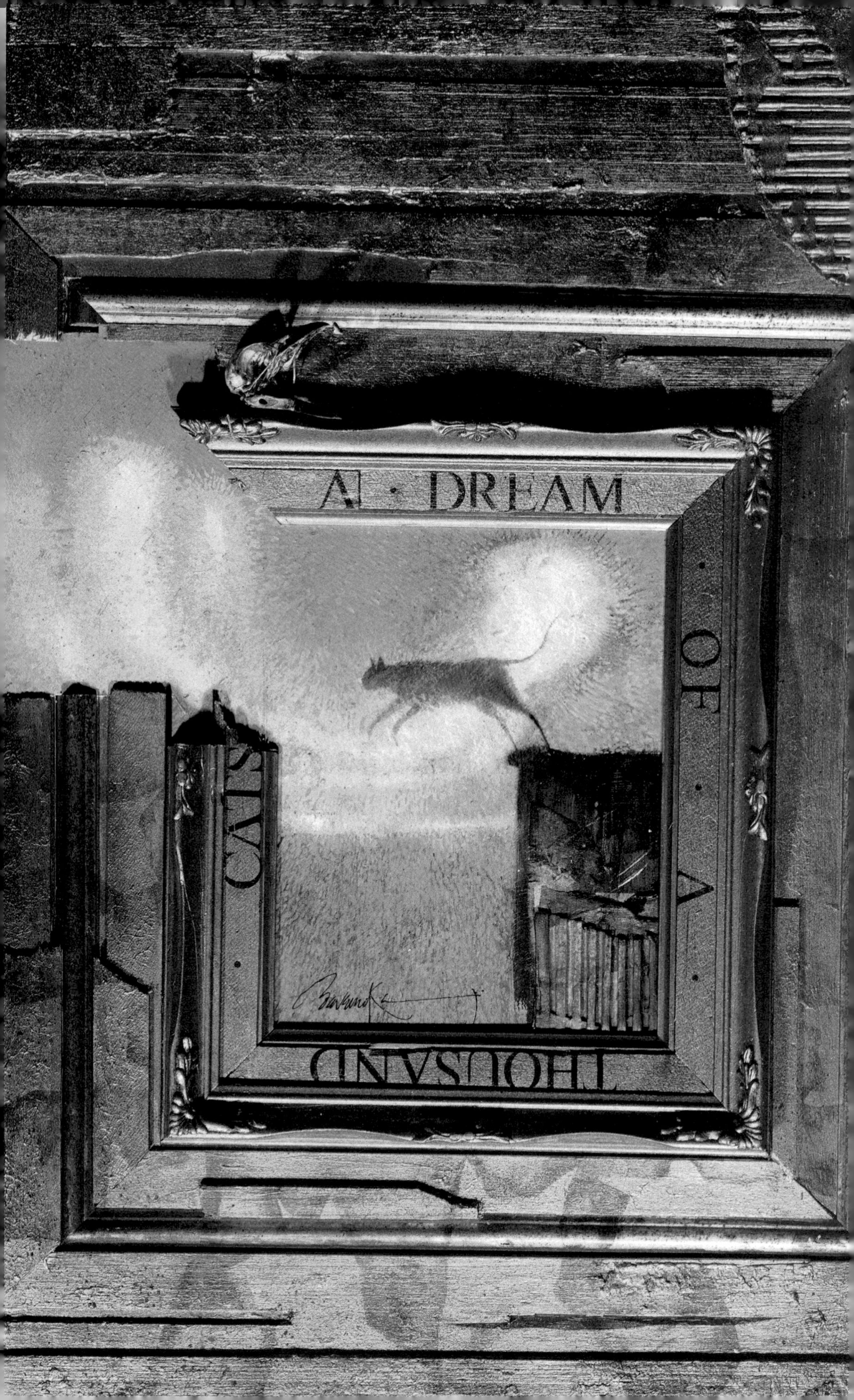
A · DREAM · OF · A · THOUSAND · CATS

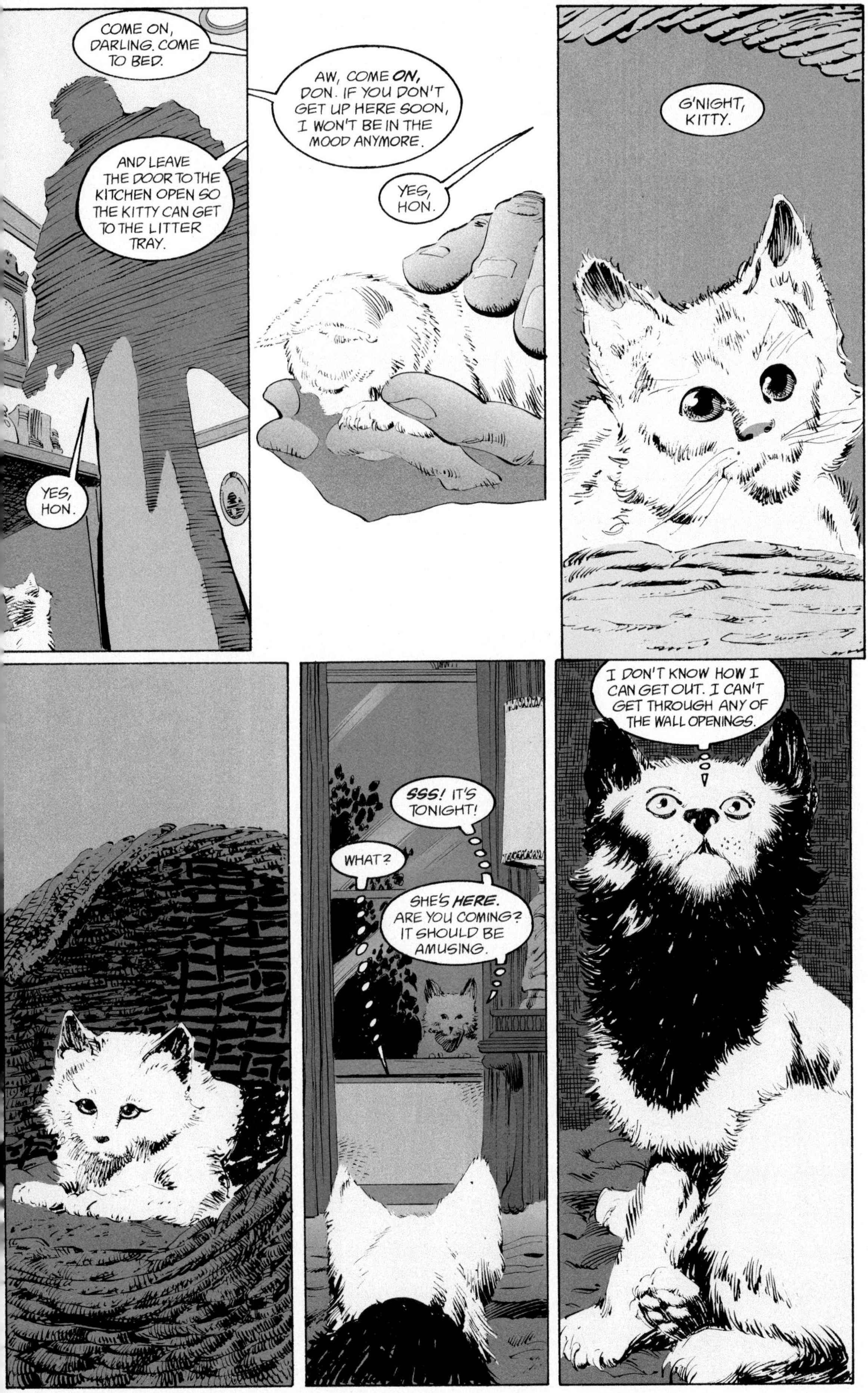
COME ON, DARLING. COME TO BED.
AND LEAVE THE DOOR TO THE KITCHEN OPEN SO THE KITTY CAN GET TO THE LITTER TRAY.
YES, HON.
AW, COME ON, DON. IF YOU DON'T GET UP HERE SOON, I WON'T BE IN THE MOOD ANYMORE.
YES, HON.
G'NIGHT, KITTY.
SSS! IT'S TONIGHT!
WHAT?
SHE'S HERE. ARE YOU COMING? IT SHOULD BE AMUSING.
I DON'T KNOW HOW I CAN GET OUT. I CAN'T GET THROUGH ANY OF THE WALL OPENINGS.

UP THERE. A CLEAR-HOLE IS PARTLY OPENED. YOU CAN GET OUT THROUGH THERE.

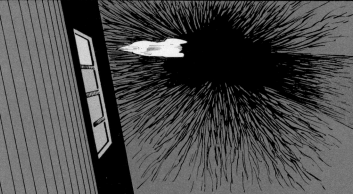

SHAKE YOUR TAIL, LITTLE ONE. WE MUSTN'T MISS THIS.

OHH. CAN YOU NOT *SCENT* IT, CHILD? THE CALL OF THE NIGHT?

HURRY. *HURRY.*

WAIT FOR ME. OH *WAIT* FOR ME, *PLEASE.*

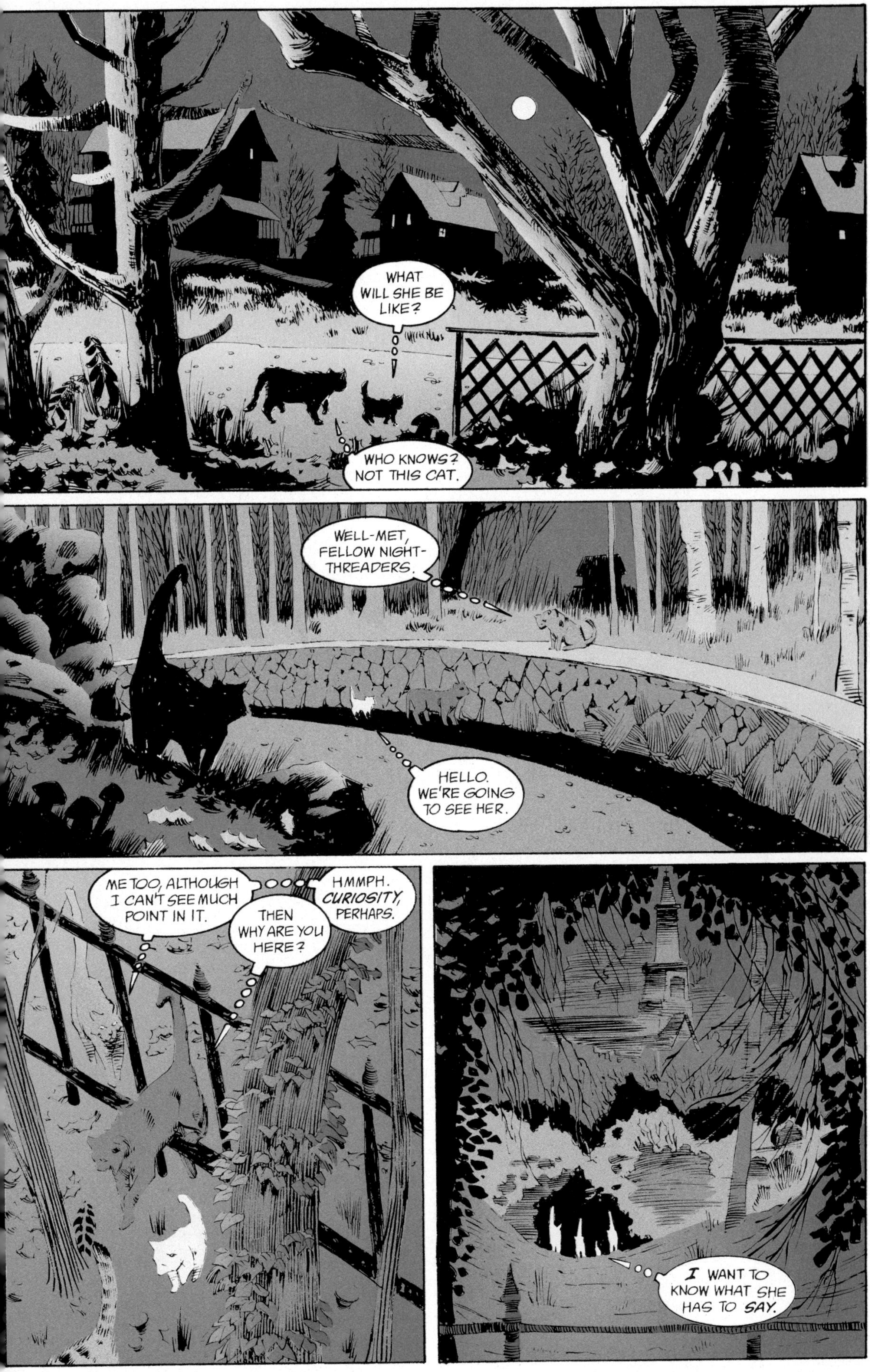
WHAT WILL SHE BE LIKE?
WHO KNOWS? NOT THIS CAT.
WELL-MET, FELLOW NIGHT-THREADERS.
HELLO. WE'RE GOING TO SEE HER.
ME TOO, ALTHOUGH I CAN'T SEE MUCH POINT IN IT.
THEN WHY ARE YOU HERE?
HMMPH. *CURIOSITY*, PERHAPS.
I WANT TO KNOW WHAT SHE HAS TO *SAY*.

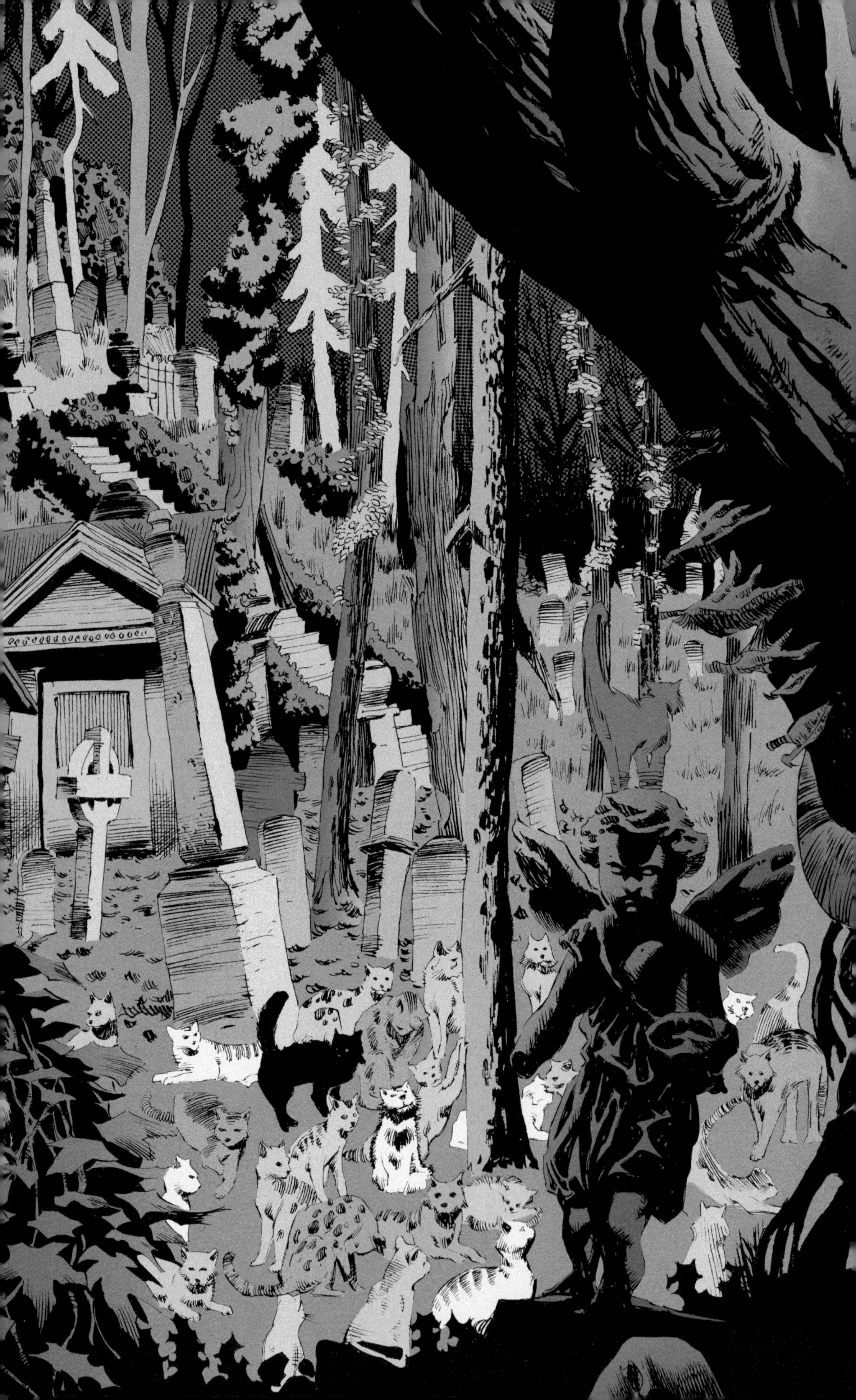

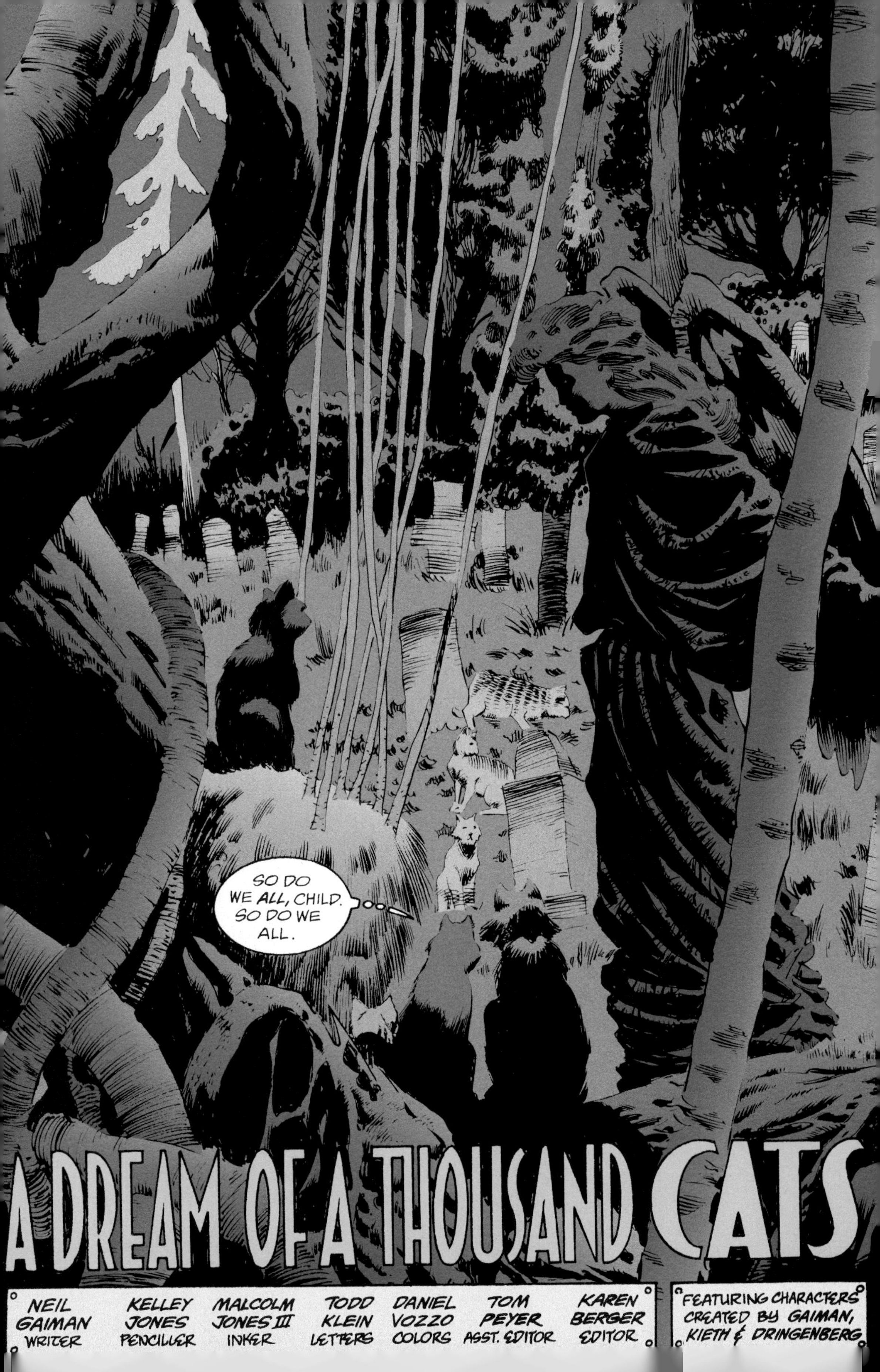
SO DO WE ALL, CHILD. SO DO WE ALL.
A DREAM OF A THOUSAND CATS
NEIL GAIMAN WRITER
KELLEY JONES PENCILLER
MALCOLM JONES III INKER
TODD KLEIN LETTERS
DANIEL VOZZO COLORS
TOM PEYER ASST. EDITOR
KAREN BERGER EDITOR
FEATURING CHARACTERS CREATED BY GAIMAN, KIETH & DRINGENBERG

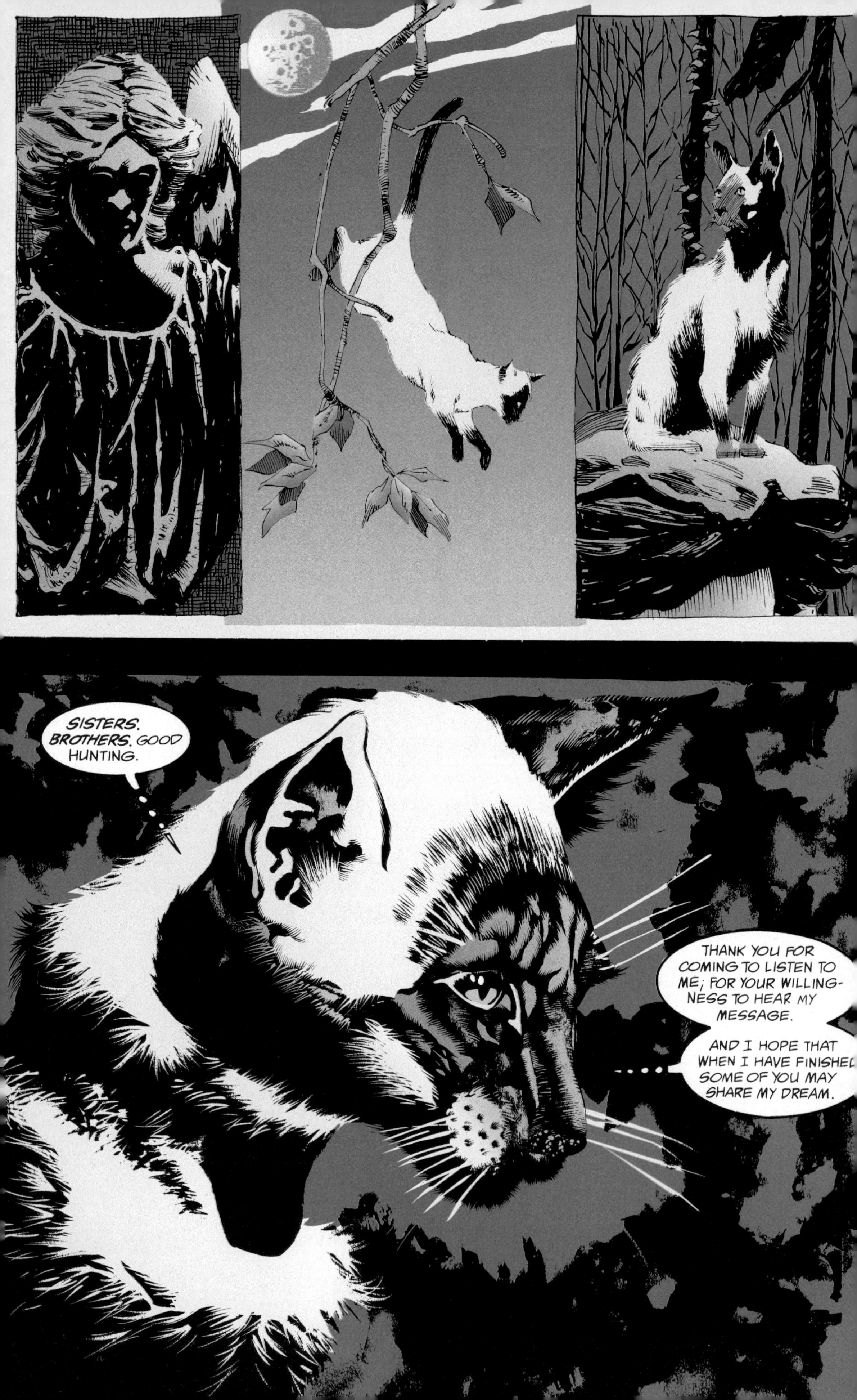
SISTERS. BROTHERS. GOOD HUNTING.
THANK YOU FOR COMING TO LISTEN TO ME; FOR YOUR WILLINGNESS TO HEAR MY MESSAGE.
AND I HOPE THAT WHEN I HAVE FINISHED SOME OF YOU MAY SHARE MY DREAM.

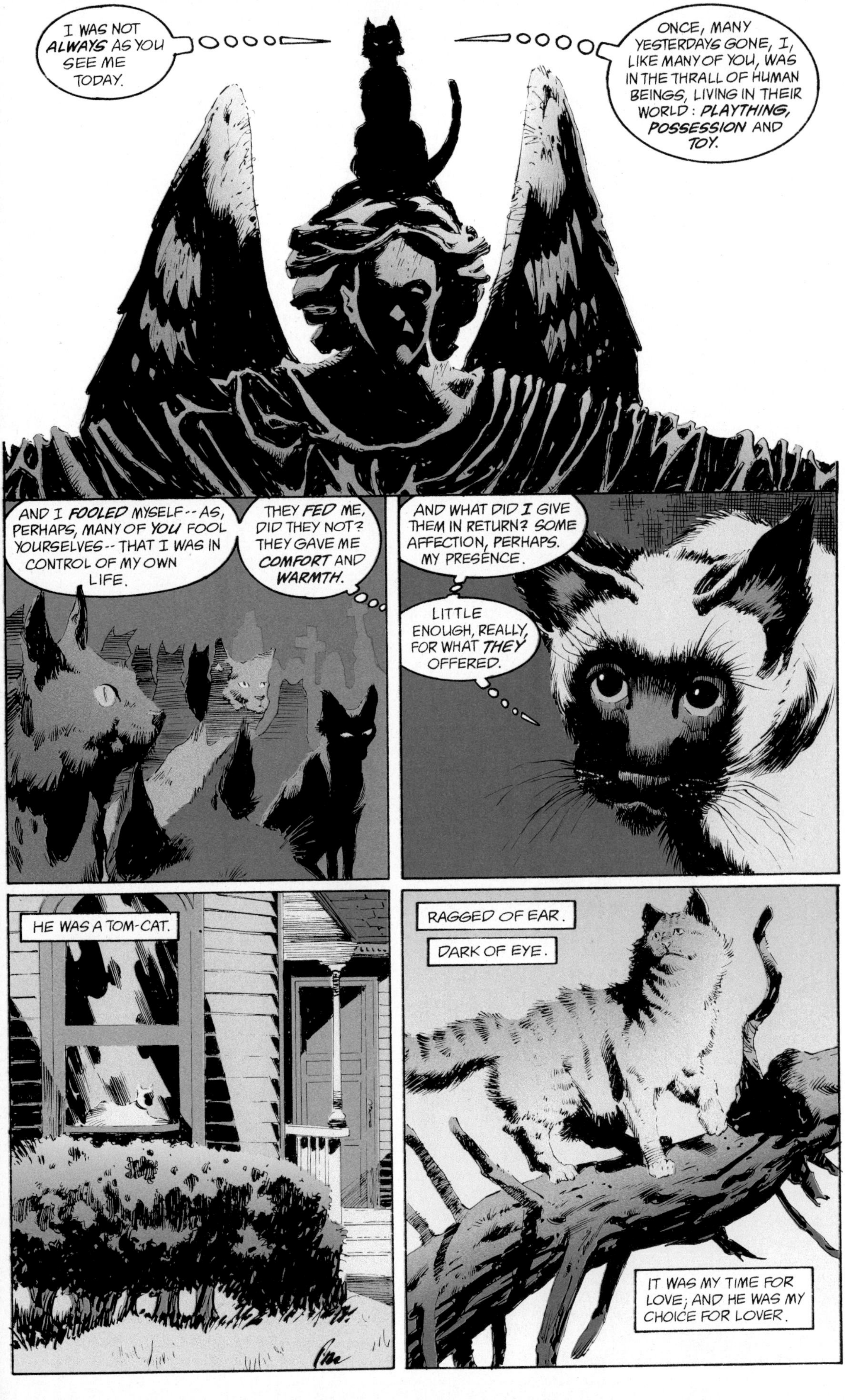
I WAS NOT ALWAYS AS YOU SEE ME TODAY.
ONCE, MANY YESTERDAYS GONE, I, LIKE MANY OF YOU, WAS IN THE THRALL OF HUMAN BEINGS, LIVING IN THEIR WORLD : PLAYTHING, POSSESSION AND TOY.
AND I FOOLED MYSELF -- AS, PERHAPS, MANY OF YOU FOOL YOURSELVES -- THAT I WAS IN CONTROL OF MY OWN LIFE.
THEY FED ME, DID THEY NOT? THEY GAVE ME COMFORT AND WARMTH.
AND WHAT DID I GIVE THEM IN RETURN? SOME AFFECTION, PERHAPS. MY PRESENCE.
LITTLE ENOUGH, REALLY, FOR WHAT THEY OFFERED.
HE WAS A TOM-CAT.
RAGGED OF EAR.
DARK OF EYE.
IT WAS MY TIME FOR LOVE; AND HE WAS MY CHOICE FOR LOVER.

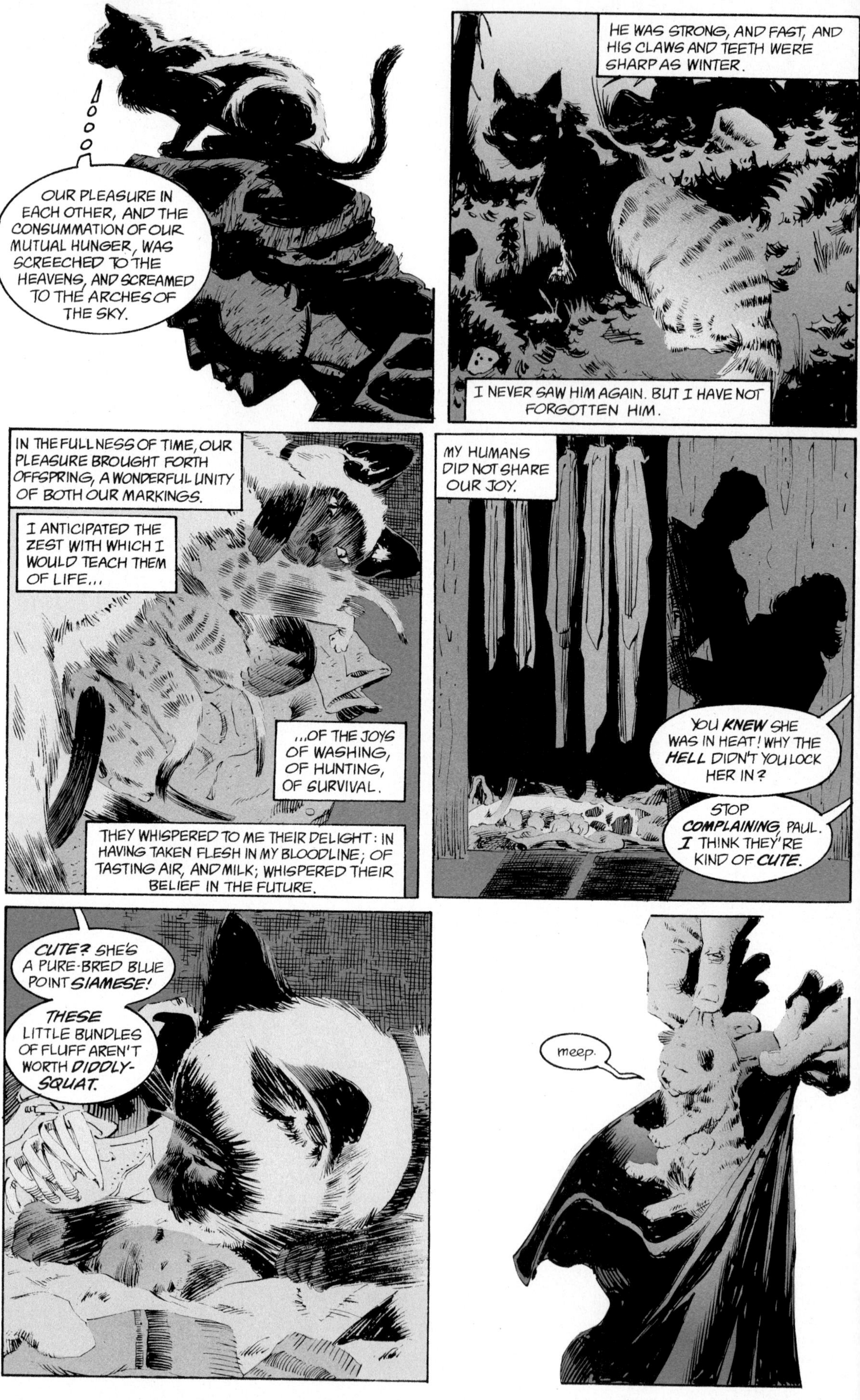
OUR PLEASURE IN EACH OTHER, AND THE CONSUMMATION OF OUR MUTUAL HUNGER, WAS SCREECHED TO THE HEAVENS, AND SCREAMED TO THE ARCHES OF THE SKY.
HE WAS STRONG, AND FAST, AND HIS CLAWS AND TEETH WERE SHARP AS WINTER.
I NEVER SAW HIM AGAIN. BUT I HAVE NOT FORGOTTEN HIM.
IN THE FULLNESS OF TIME, OUR PLEASURE BROUGHT FORTH OFFSPRING, A WONDERFUL UNITY OF BOTH OUR MARKINGS.
I ANTICIPATED THE ZEST WITH WHICH I WOULD TEACH THEM OF LIFE...
...OF THE JOYS OF WASHING, OF HUNTING, OF SURVIVAL.
THEY WHISPERED TO ME THEIR DELIGHT: IN HAVING TAKEN FLESH IN MY BLOODLINE; OF TASTING AIR, AND MILK; WHISPERED THEIR BELIEF IN THE FUTURE.
MY HUMANS DID NOT SHARE OUR JOY.
YOU KNEW SHE WAS IN HEAT! WHY THE HELL DIDN'T YOU LOCK HER IN?
STOP COMPLAINING, PAUL. I THINK THEY'RE KIND OF CUTE.
CUTE? SHE'S A PURE-BRED BLUE POINT SIAMESE!
THESE LITTLE BUNDLES OF FLUFF AREN'T WORTH DIDDLY-SQUAT.
meep.

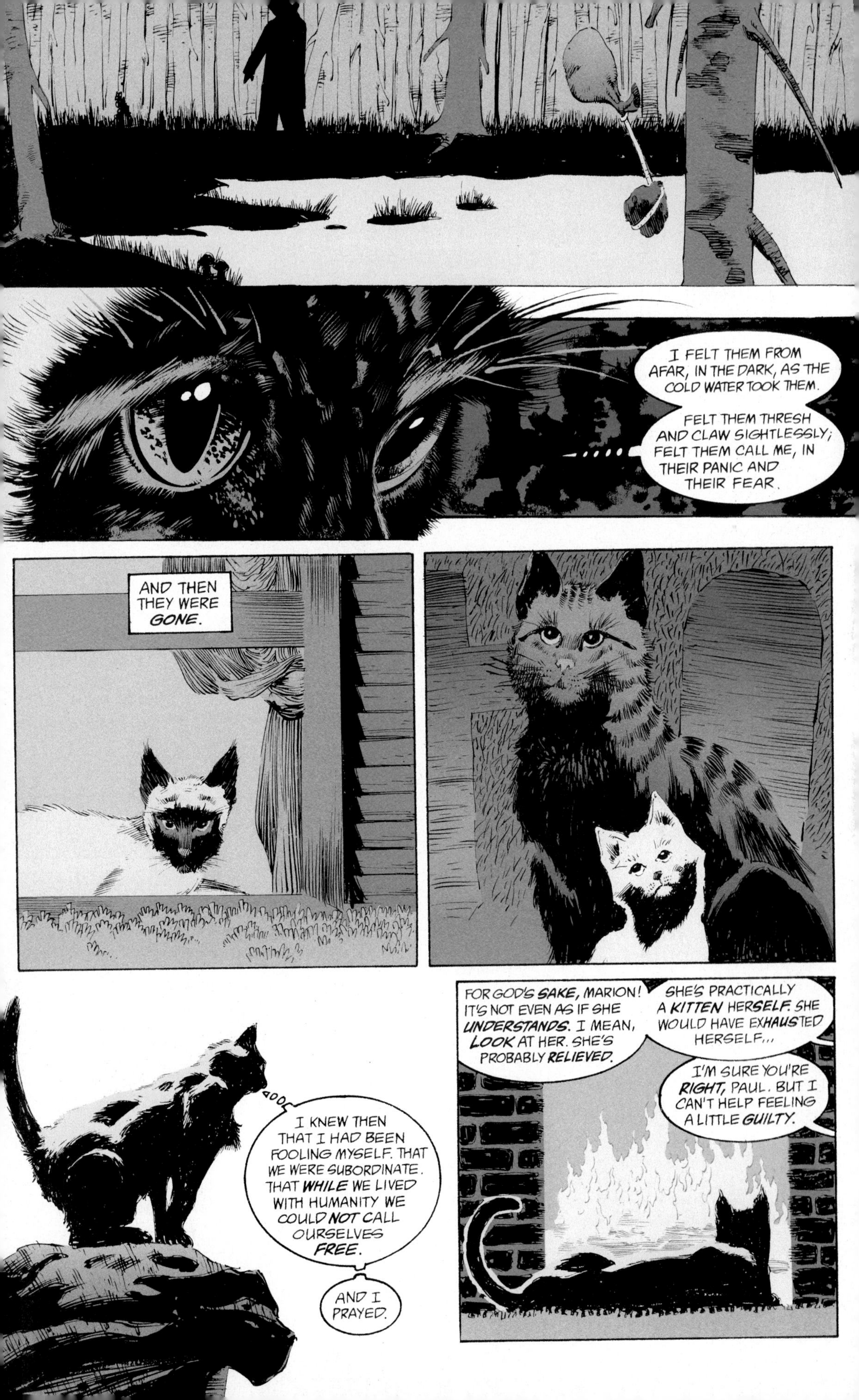
I FELT THEM FROM AFAR, IN THE DARK, AS THE COLD WATER TOOK THEM.
FELT THEM THRESH AND CLAW SIGHTLESSLY; FELT THEM CALL ME, IN THEIR PANIC AND THEIR FEAR.
AND THEN THEY WERE GONE.
I KNEW THEN THAT I HAD BEEN FOOLING MYSELF. THAT WE WERE SUBORDINATE. THAT WHILE WE LIVED WITH HUMANITY WE COULD NOT CALL OURSELVES FREE.
AND I PRAYED.
FOR GOD'S SAKE, MARION! IT'S NOT EVEN AS IF SHE UNDERSTANDS. I MEAN, LOOK AT HER. SHE'S PROBABLY RELIEVED.
SHE'S PRACTICALLY A KITTEN HERSELF. SHE WOULD HAVE EXHAUSTED HERSELF...
I'M SURE YOU'RE RIGHT, PAUL. BUT I CAN'T HELP FEELING A LITTLE GUILTY.

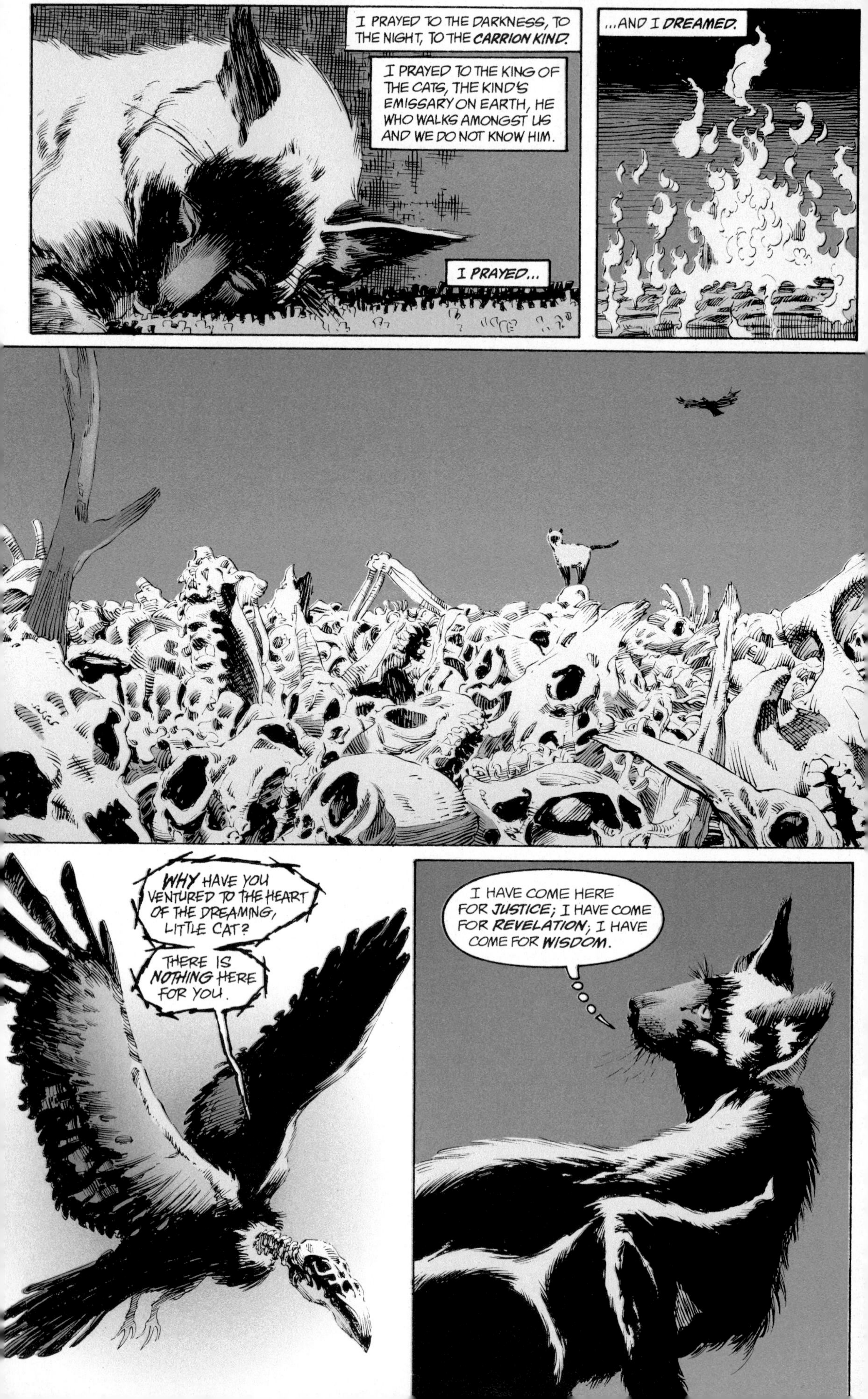

I PRAYED TO THE DARKNESS, TO THE NIGHT, TO THE CARRION KIND.
I PRAYED TO THE KING OF THE CATS, THE KIND'S EMISSARY ON EARTH, HE WHO WALKS AMONGST US AND WE DO NOT KNOW HIM.
I PRAYED...
...AND I DREAMED.
WHY HAVE YOU VENTURED TO THE HEART OF THE DREAMING, LITTLE CAT?
THERE IS NOTHING HERE FOR YOU.
I HAVE COME HERE FOR JUSTICE; I HAVE COME FOR REVELATION; I HAVE COME FOR WISDOM.

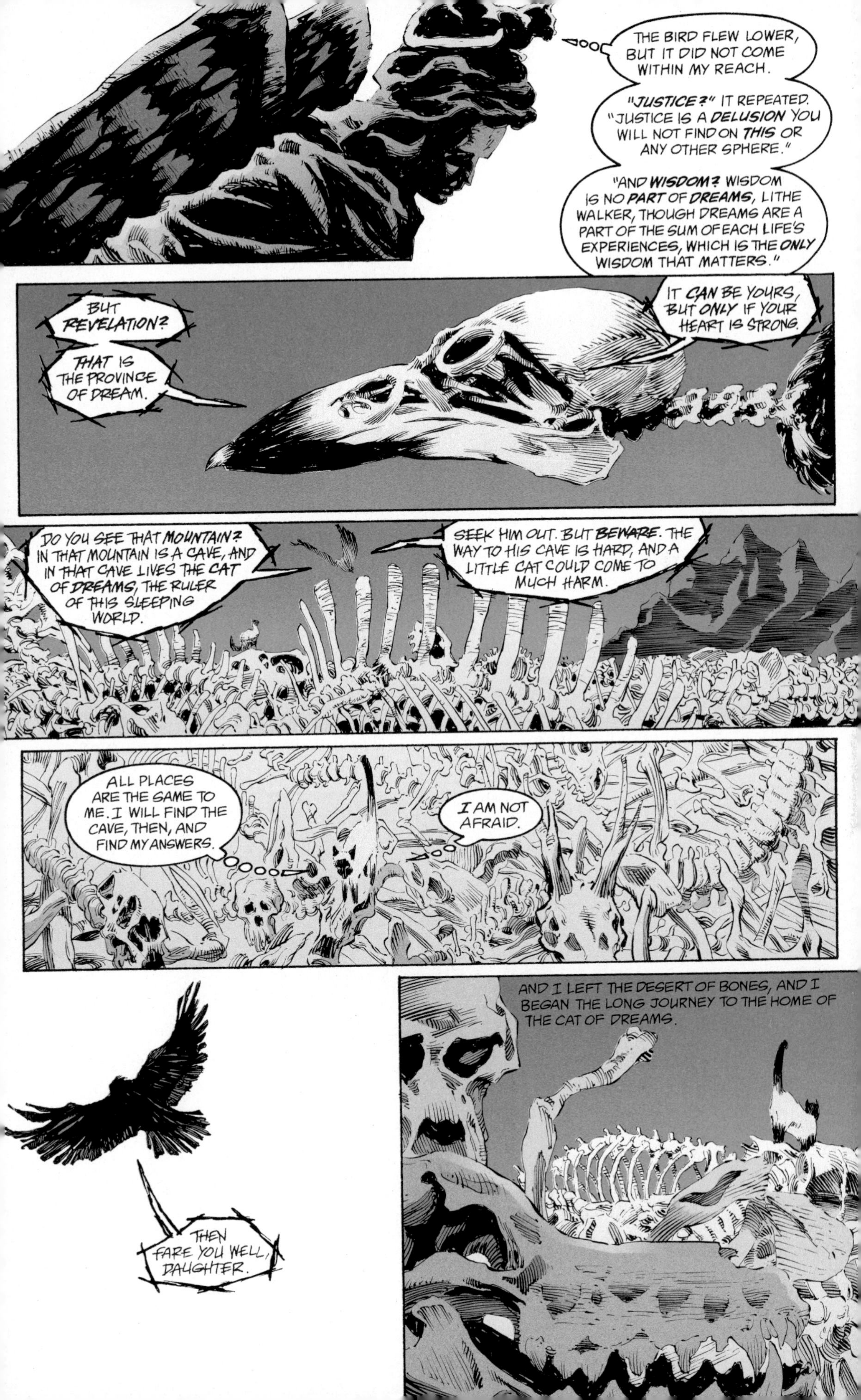
THE BIRD FLEW LOWER, BUT IT DID NOT COME WITHIN MY REACH.
"JUSTICE?" IT REPEATED. "JUSTICE IS A DELUSION YOU WILL NOT FIND ON THIS OR ANY OTHER SPHERE."
"AND WISDOM? WISDOM IS NO PART OF DREAMS, LITHE WALKER, THOUGH DREAMS ARE A PART OF THE SUM OF EACH LIFE'S EXPERIENCES, WHICH IS THE ONLY WISDOM THAT MATTERS."
BUT REVELATION?
THAT IS THE PROVINCE OF DREAM.
IT CAN BE YOURS, BUT ONLY IF YOUR HEART IS STRONG.
DO YOU SEE THAT MOUNTAIN? IN THAT MOUNTAIN IS A CAVE, AND IN THAT CAVE LIVES THE CAT OF DREAMS, THE RULER OF THIS SLEEPING WORLD.
SEEK HIM OUT. BUT BEWARE. THE WAY TO HIS CAVE IS HARD, AND A LITTLE CAT COULD COME TO MUCH HARM.
ALL PLACES ARE THE SAME TO ME. I WILL FIND THE CAVE, THEN, AND FIND MY ANSWERS.
I AM NOT AFRAID.
THEN FARE YOU WELL, DAUGHTER.
AND I LEFT THE DESERT OF BONES, AND I BEGAN THE LONG JOURNEY TO THE HOME OF THE CAT OF DREAMS.

I WALKED THROUGH THE WOOD OF GHOSTS, WHERE THE DEAD AND THE LOST WHISPERED CONTINUALLY, PROMISED ME WORLDS IF I WOULD ONLY STOP AND PLAY WITH THEM.

AT ONE POINT I THOUGHT I HEARD MY CHILDREN CALLING ME. BUT I STRAIGHTENED MY TAIL, AND I WALKED FORWARD.

I CLOSED MY EARS TO THEIR ENTREATIES.

I WALKED THROUGH THE COLD PLACES, HARD AND FROZEN, WHERE EVERY STEP WAS PAIN, EVERY MOVEMENT WAS TORMENT.

I WALKED ON.

I WALKED THROUGH THE WETNESS THAT NUMBED MY PAWS, DRENCHED MY FUR, TRIED TO WASH AWAY MY MEMORIES.

I WALKED THROUGH THE DARKNESS, THROUGH THE VOID, WHERE EVERYTHING WAS SUCKED FROM ME--EVERYTHING THAT MAKES ME WHAT I AM.

AND, AFTER A TIME, MY SELF RETURNED TO ME, AND I LEFT THAT PLACE, AND I FOUND MYSELF AT THE MOUNTAIN OF THE CAT OF DREAMS.

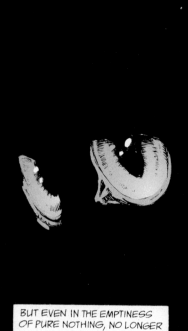

BUT EVEN IN THE EMPTINESS OF PURE NOTHING, NO LONGER KNOWING WHY I WAS WALKING OR WHAT I WAS SEEKING, I WALKED ONWARD.

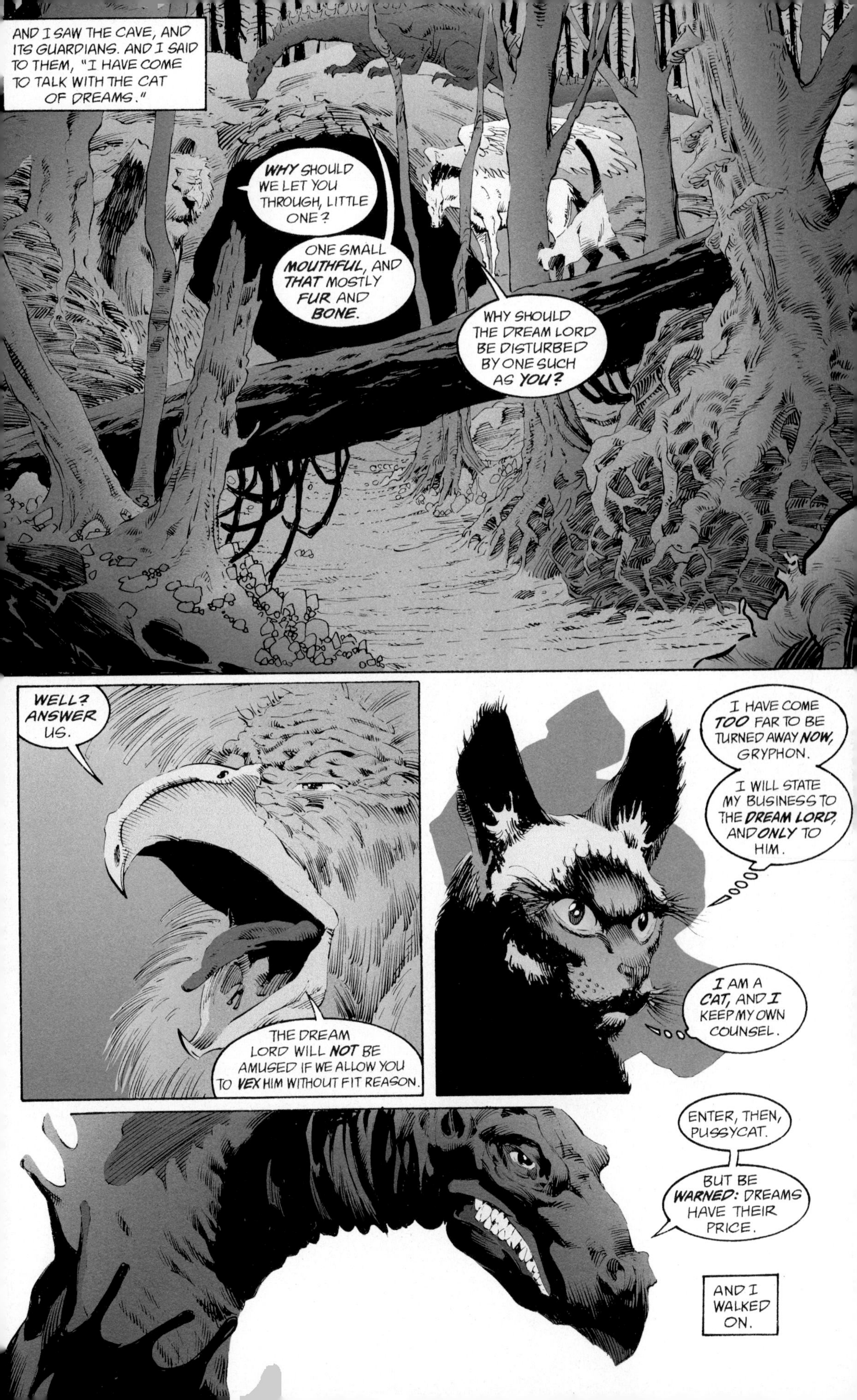
AND I SAW THE CAVE, AND ITS GUARDIANS. AND I SAID TO THEM, "I HAVE COME TO TALK WITH THE CAT OF DREAMS."
WHY SHOULD WE LET YOU THROUGH, LITTLE ONE?
ONE SMALL MOUTHFUL, AND THAT MOSTLY FUR AND BONE.
WHY SHOULD THE DREAM LORD BE DISTURBED BY ONE SUCH AS YOU?
WELL? ANSWER US.
THE DREAM LORD WILL NOT BE AMUSED IF WE ALLOW YOU TO VEX HIM WITHOUT FIT REASON.
I HAVE COME TOO FAR TO BE TURNED AWAY NOW, GRYPHON.
I WILL STATE MY BUSINESS TO THE DREAM LORD, AND ONLY TO HIM.
I AM A CAT, AND I KEEP MY OWN COUNSEL.
ENTER, THEN, PUSSYCAT.
BUT BE WARNED: DREAMS HAVE THEIR PRICE.
AND I WALKED ON.

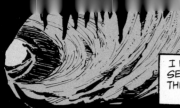

THE SCENT ON THE AIR WAS STRANGE, BUT STILL IT WAS CAT.

I WALKED FORWARD SLOWLY, EVERY SENSE SCREAMING AT ME TO FLEE THIS PLACE. MY FUR PRICKLED, MY CLAWS EXTENDED.

AND THEN I STOOD BEFORE HIM.

I AM HERE.

And who might you be?

A *CAT*. A WALKER IN NIGHT PLACES. A DEAD CROW SENT ME HERE, FOR REVELATION.

I HOPED I SOUNDED CONFIDENT, BUT TRULY I WAS SCARED.

Walk with me, then, little sister, and tell me why you have sought me out.

I... I WANT TO *UNDERSTAND*.

WHY COULD THEY TAKE MY CHILDREN FROM ME? *WHY* DO WE LIVE AS WE DO? I DON'T *UNDERSTAND*.

A cat may look at a king, or so they say.

Look into my eyes then, little sister.

Look into my eyes.

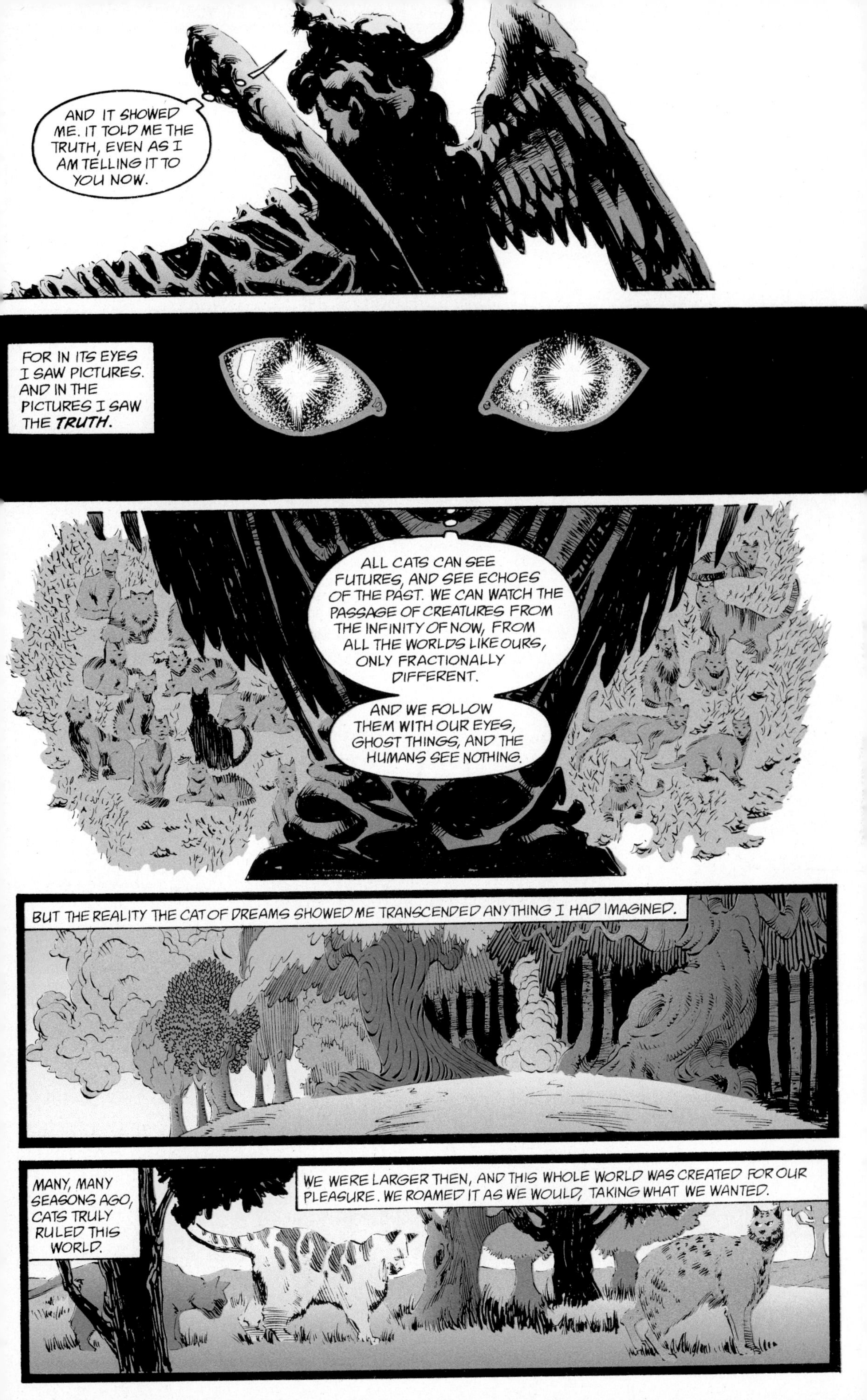
AND IT SHOWED ME. IT TOLD ME THE TRUTH, EVEN AS I AM TELLING IT TO YOU NOW.
FOR IN ITS EYES I SAW PICTURES. AND IN THE PICTURES I SAW THE **TRUTH**.
ALL CATS CAN SEE FUTURES, AND SEE ECHOES OF THE PAST. WE CAN WATCH THE PASSAGE OF CREATURES FROM THE INFINITY OF NOW, FROM ALL THE WORLDS LIKE OURS, ONLY FRACTIONALLY DIFFERENT.
AND WE FOLLOW THEM WITH OUR EYES, GHOST THINGS, AND THE HUMANS SEE NOTHING.
BUT THE REALITY THE CAT OF DREAMS SHOWED ME TRANSCENDED ANYTHING I HAD IMAGINED.
MANY, MANY SEASONS AGO, CATS TRULY RULED THIS WORLD.
WE WERE LARGER THEN, AND THIS WHOLE WORLD WAS CREATED FOR OUR PLEASURE. WE ROAMED IT AS WE WOULD, TAKING WHAT WE WANTED.

IN THOSE TIMES HUMANS WERE TINY CREATURES, NO LARGER THAN WE ARE NOW.

AND THE HUMANS WOULD GROOM US, AND FEED US, AND PET US.

AND WHEN THE MOON SHONE FULL, WE WOULD *HUNT* THEM, AND WE WOULD EAT *PART* OF THEM, BUT CHIEFLY WE WOULD HUNT THEM...

...FOR THEY WERE MORE DELIGHTFUL TO HUNT EVEN THAN BIRDS, AND BACK THEN, MICE WERE TOO SMALL AND INSIGNIFICANT FOR US TO DEIGN TO TOUCH.

OH, THE *JOY* OF THOSE HUNTING DAYS, BENEATH THE CAT'S MOON. THE *GAME* OF *CAT* AND *MAN*...

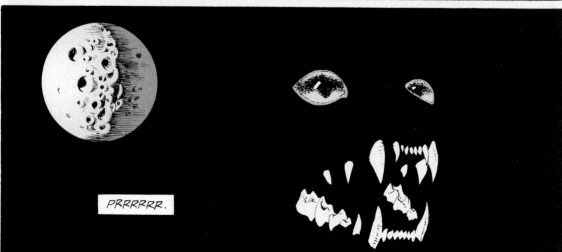

PRRRRRR.

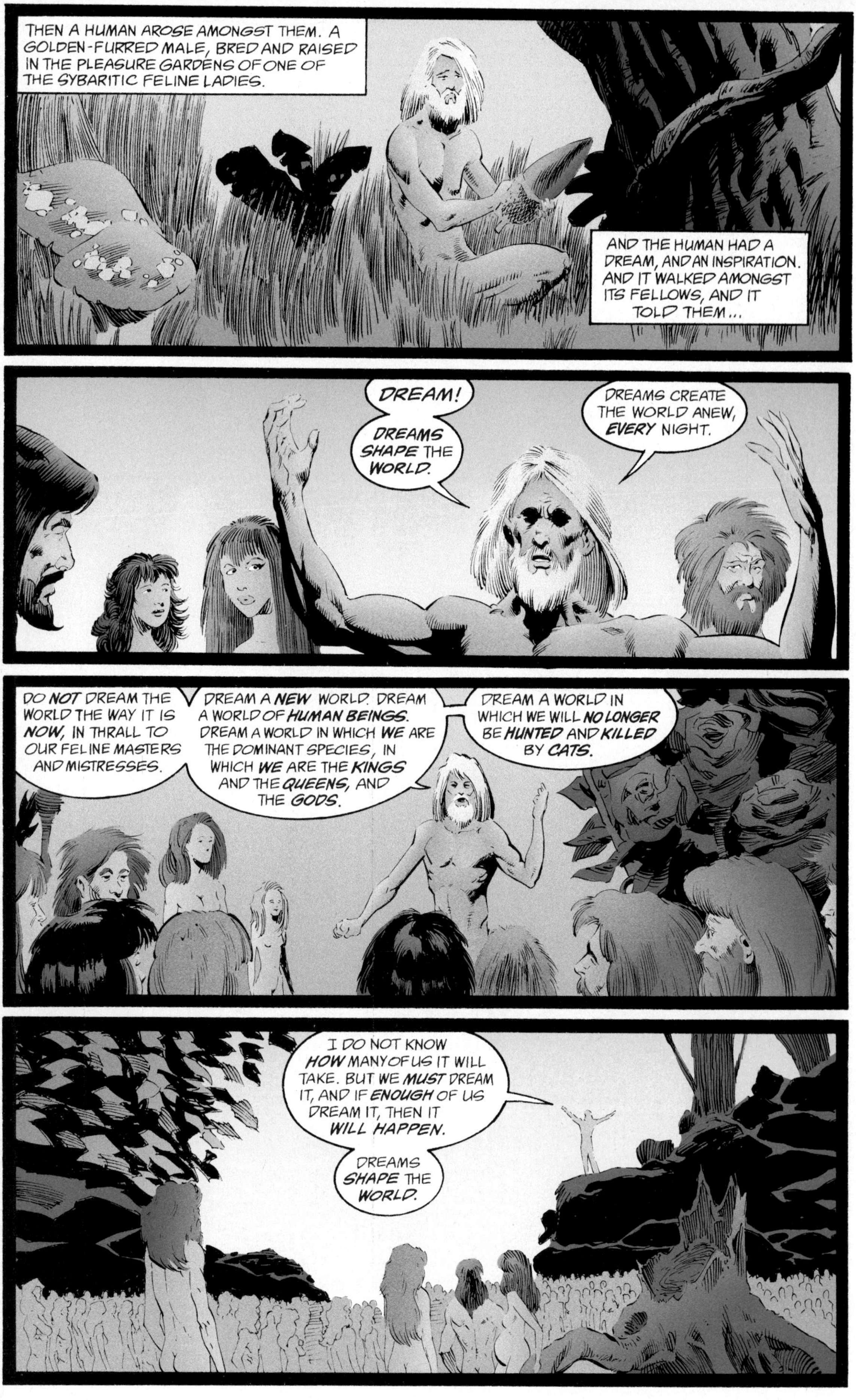
THEN A HUMAN AROSE AMONGST THEM. A GOLDEN-FURRED MALE, BRED AND RAISED IN THE PLEASURE GARDENS OF ONE OF THE SYBARITIC FELINE LADIES.
AND THE HUMAN HAD A DREAM, AND AN INSPIRATION. AND IT WALKED AMONGST ITS FELLOWS, AND IT TOLD THEM...
DREAM!
DREAMS SHAPE THE WORLD.
DREAMS CREATE THE WORLD ANEW, EVERY NIGHT.
DO NOT DREAM THE WORLD THE WAY IT IS NOW, IN THRALL TO OUR FELINE MASTERS AND MISTRESSES.
DREAM A NEW WORLD. DREAM A WORLD OF HUMAN BEINGS. DREAM A WORLD IN WHICH WE ARE THE DOMINANT SPECIES, IN WHICH WE ARE THE KINGS AND THE QUEENS, AND THE GODS.
DREAM A WORLD IN WHICH WE WILL NO LONGER BE HUNTED AND KILLED BY CATS.
I DO NOT KNOW HOW MANY OF US IT WILL TAKE. BUT WE MUST DREAM IT, AND IF ENOUGH OF US DREAM IT, THEN IT WILL HAPPEN.
DREAMS SHAPE THE WORLD.

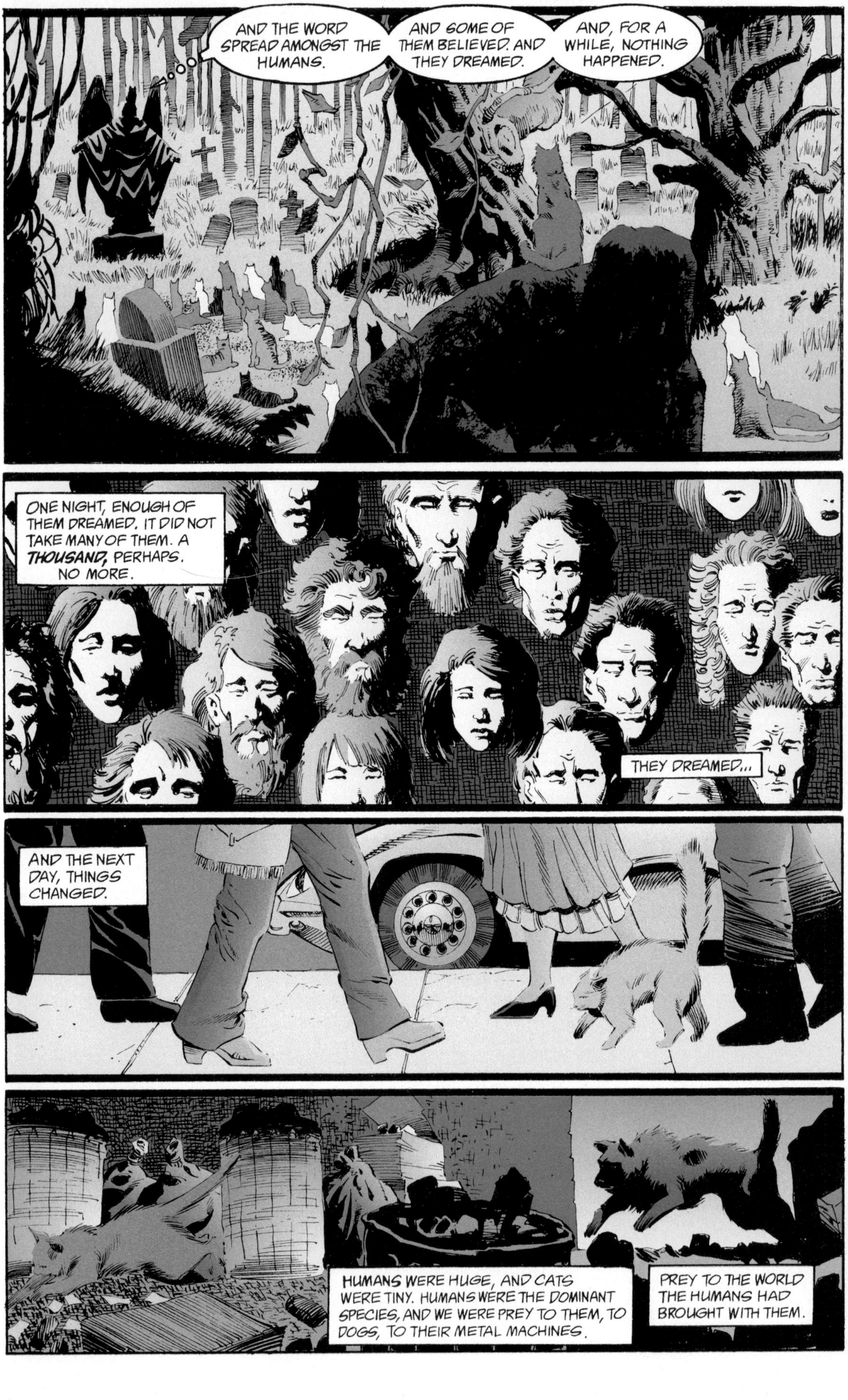
AND THE WORD SPREAD AMONGST THE HUMANS.
AND SOME OF THEM BELIEVED. AND THEY DREAMED.
AND, FOR A WHILE, NOTHING HAPPENED.
ONE NIGHT, ENOUGH OF THEM DREAMED. IT DID NOT TAKE MANY OF THEM. A THOUSAND, PERHAPS. NO MORE.
THEY DREAMED...
AND THE NEXT DAY, THINGS CHANGED.
HUMANS WERE HUGE, AND CATS WERE TINY. HUMANS WERE THE DOMINANT SPECIES, AND WE WERE PREY TO THEM, TO DOGS, TO THEIR METAL MACHINES.
PREY TO THE WORLD THE HUMANS HAD BROUGHT WITH THEM.

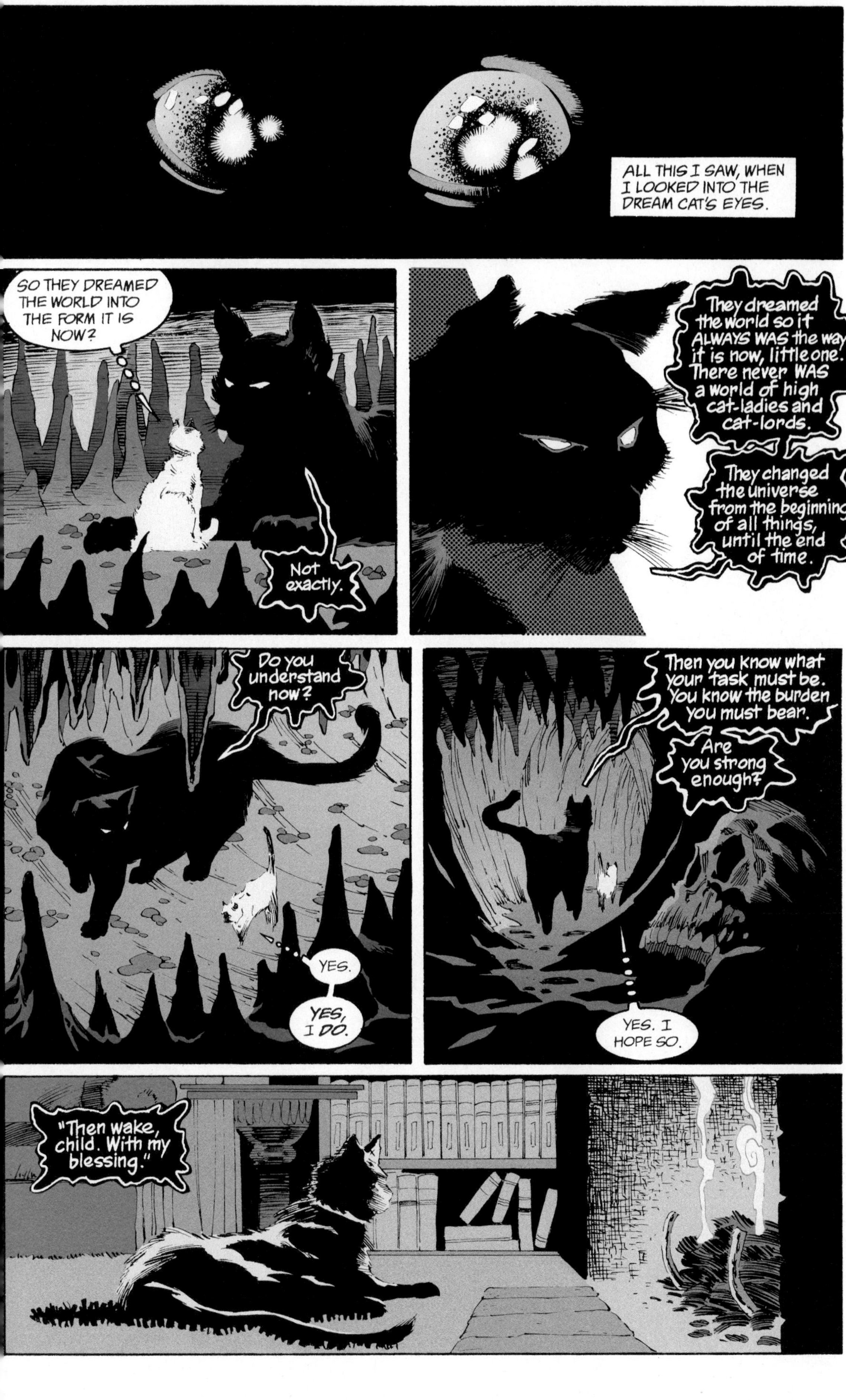

ALL THIS I SAW, WHEN I LOOKED INTO THE DREAM CAT'S EYES.
SO THEY DREAMED THE WORLD INTO THE FORM IT IS NOW?
Not exactly.
They dreamed the world so it ALWAYS WAS the way it is now, little one. There never WAS a world of high cat-ladies and cat-lords.
They changed the universe from the beginning of all things, until the end of time.
Do you understand now?
YES.
YES, I DO.
Then you know what your task must be. You know the burden you must bear.
Are you strong enough?
YES. I HOPE SO.
"Then wake, child. With my blessing."

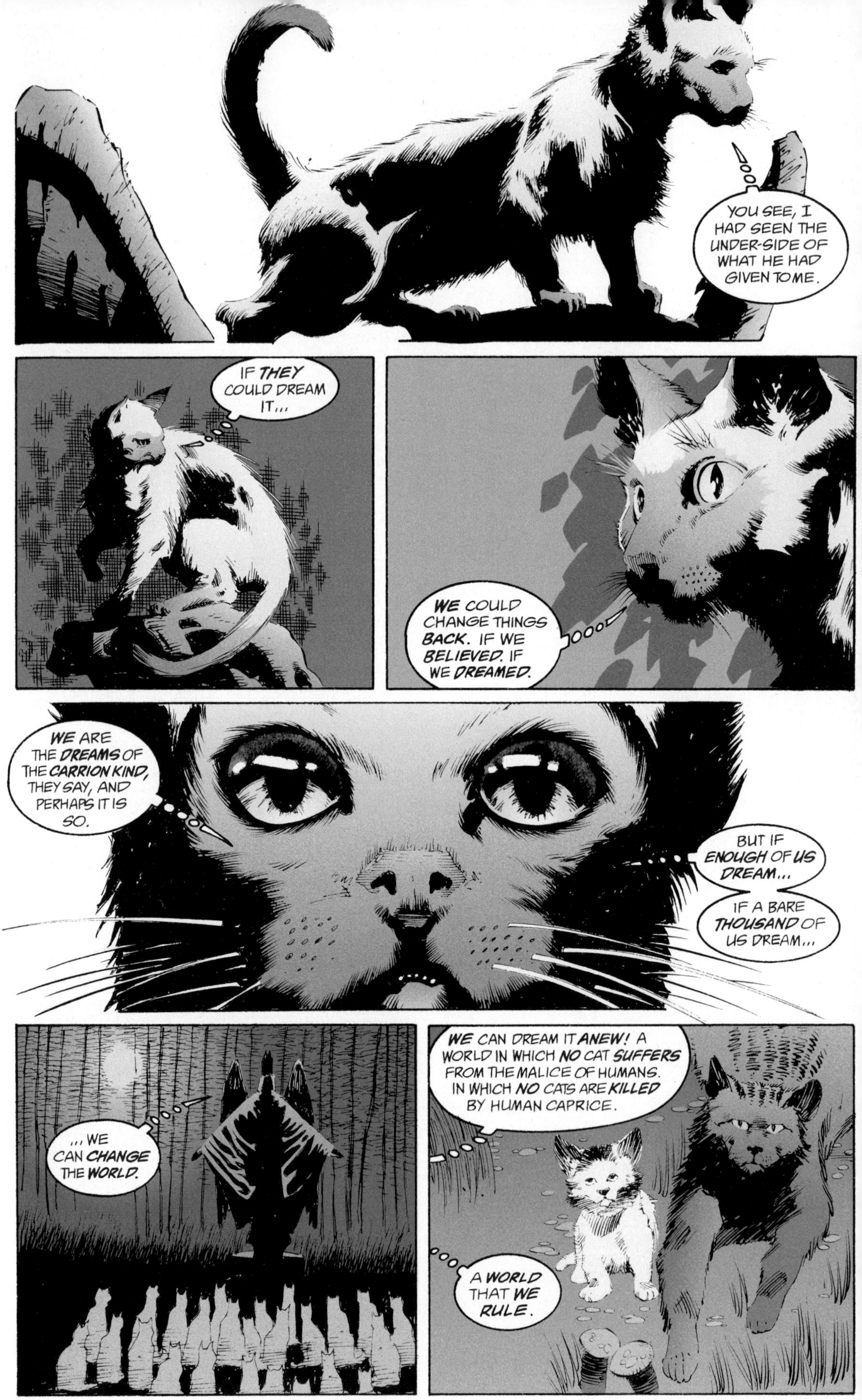
YOU SEE, I HAD SEEN THE UNDER-SIDE OF WHAT HE HAD GIVEN TO ME.
IF THEY COULD DREAM IT...
WE COULD CHANGE THINGS BACK. IF WE BELIEVED. IF WE DREAMED.
WE ARE THE DREAMS OF THE CARRION KIND, THEY SAY, AND PERHAPS IT IS SO.
BUT IF ENOUGH OF US DREAM...
IF A BARE THOUSAND OF US DREAM...
...WE CAN CHANGE THE WORLD.
WE CAN DREAM IT ANEW! A WORLD IN WHICH NO CAT SUFFERS FROM THE MALICE OF HUMANS. IN WHICH NO CATS ARE KILLED BY HUMAN CAPRICE.
A WORLD THAT WE RULE.

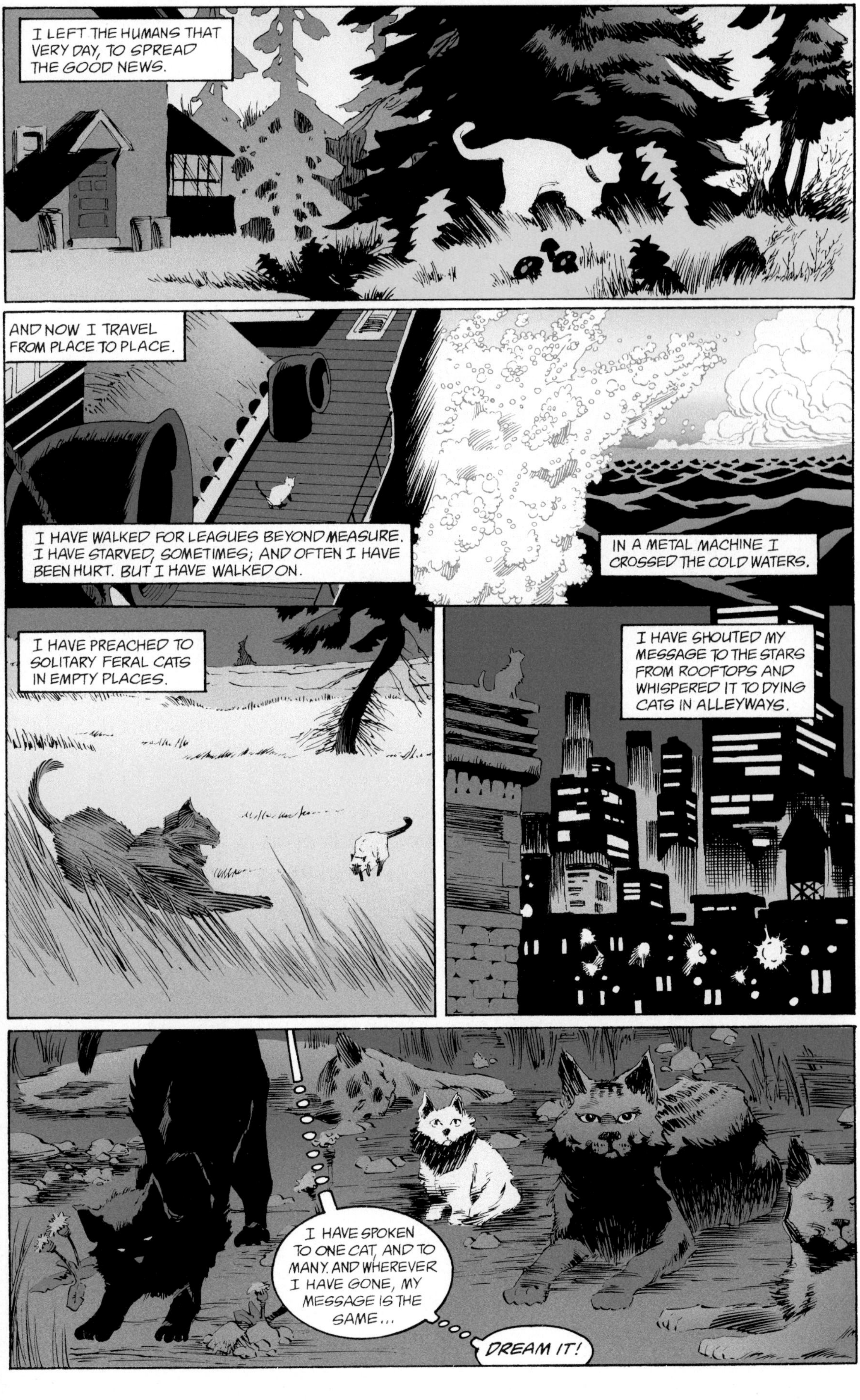
I LEFT THE HUMANS THAT VERY DAY, TO SPREAD THE GOOD NEWS.
AND NOW I TRAVEL FROM PLACE TO PLACE.
I HAVE WALKED FOR LEAGUES BEYOND MEASURE. I HAVE STARVED, SOMETIMES; AND OFTEN I HAVE BEEN HURT. BUT I HAVE WALKED ON.
IN A METAL MACHINE I CROSSED THE COLD WATERS.
I HAVE PREACHED TO SOLITARY FERAL CATS IN EMPTY PLACES.
I HAVE SHOUTED MY MESSAGE TO THE STARS FROM ROOFTOPS AND WHISPERED IT TO DYING CATS IN ALLEYWAYS.
I HAVE SPOKEN TO ONE CAT, AND TO MANY. AND WHEREVER I HAVE GONE, MY MESSAGE IS THE SAME...
DREAM IT!

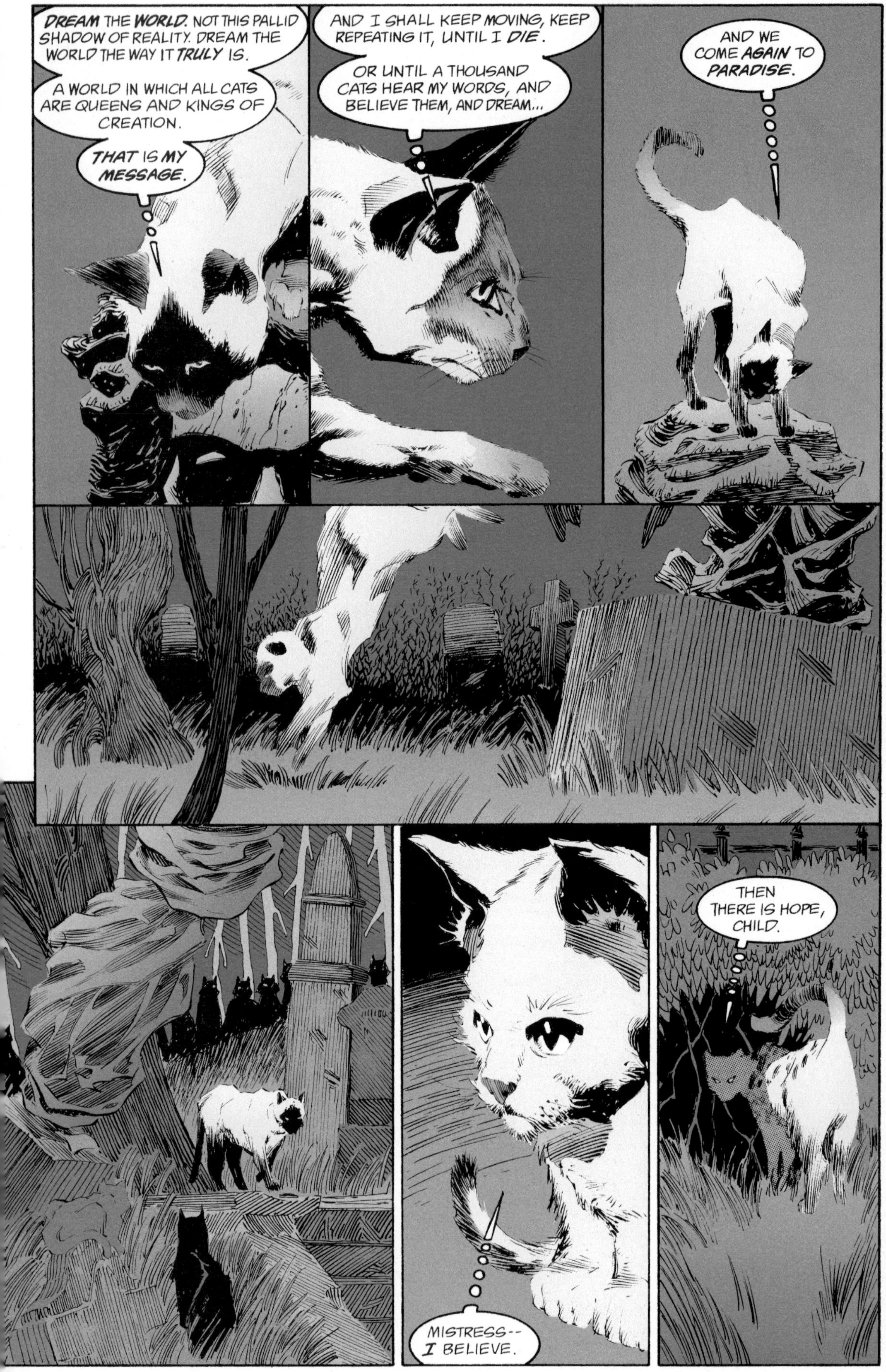

DREAM THE WORLD. NOT THIS PALLID SHADOW OF REALITY. DREAM THE WORLD THE WAY IT TRULY IS.
A WORLD IN WHICH ALL CATS ARE QUEENS AND KINGS OF CREATION.
THAT IS MY MESSAGE.
AND I SHALL KEEP MOVING, KEEP REPEATING IT, UNTIL I DIE.
OR UNTIL A THOUSAND CATS HEAR MY WORDS, AND BELIEVE THEM, AND DREAM...
AND WE COME AGAIN TO PARADISE.
MISTRESS-- I BELIEVE.
THEN THERE IS HOPE, CHILD.

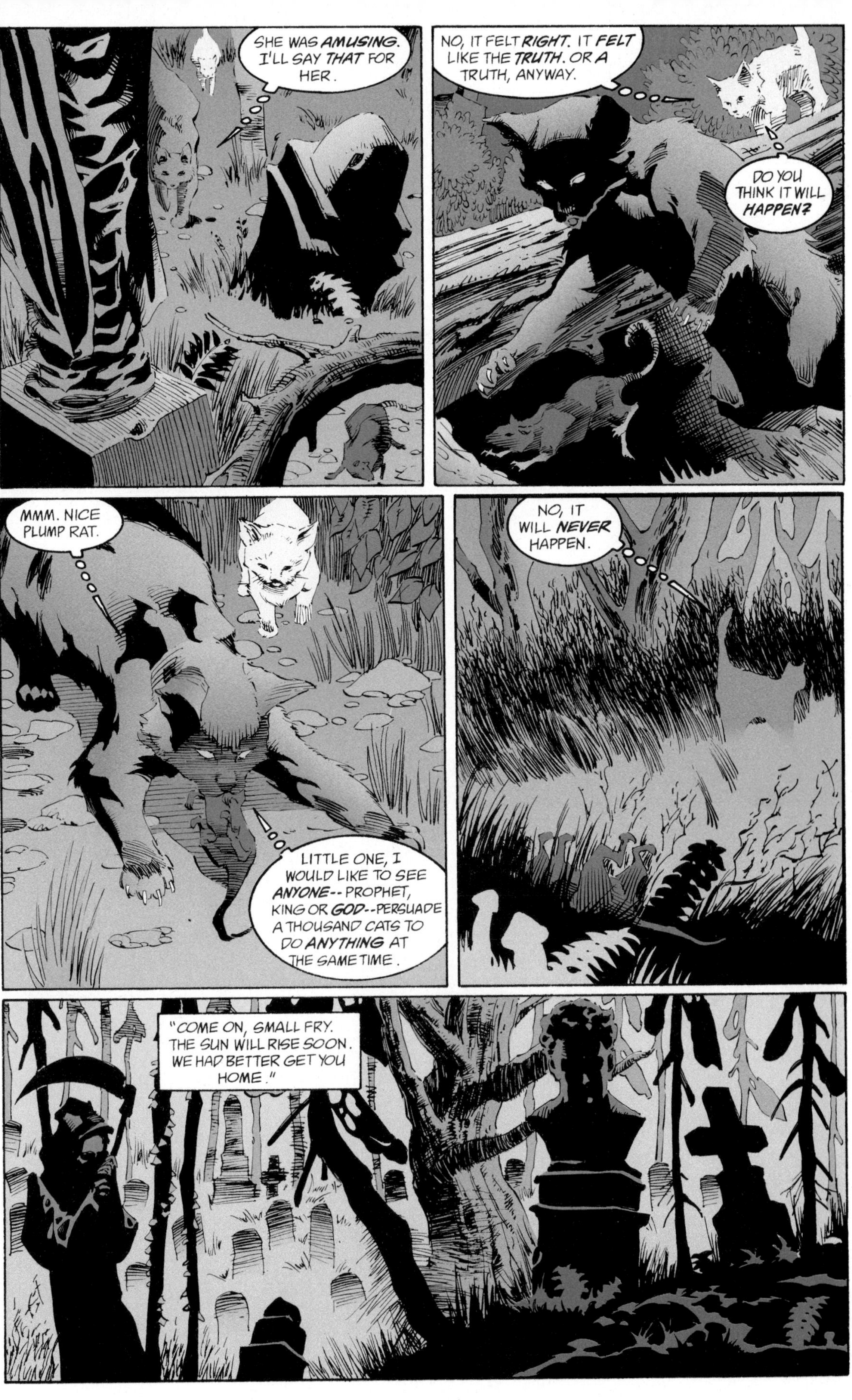
SHE WAS AMUSING. I'LL SAY THAT FOR HER.
NO, IT FELT RIGHT. IT FELT LIKE THE TRUTH. OR A TRUTH, ANYWAY.
DO YOU THINK IT WILL HAPPEN?
MMM. NICE PLUMP RAT.
LITTLE ONE, I WOULD LIKE TO SEE ANYONE-- PROPHET, KING OR GOD--PERSUADE A THOUSAND CATS TO DO ANYTHING AT THE SAME TIME.
NO, IT WILL NEVER HAPPEN.
"COME ON, SMALL FRY. THE SUN WILL RISE SOON. WE HAD BETTER GET YOU HOME."

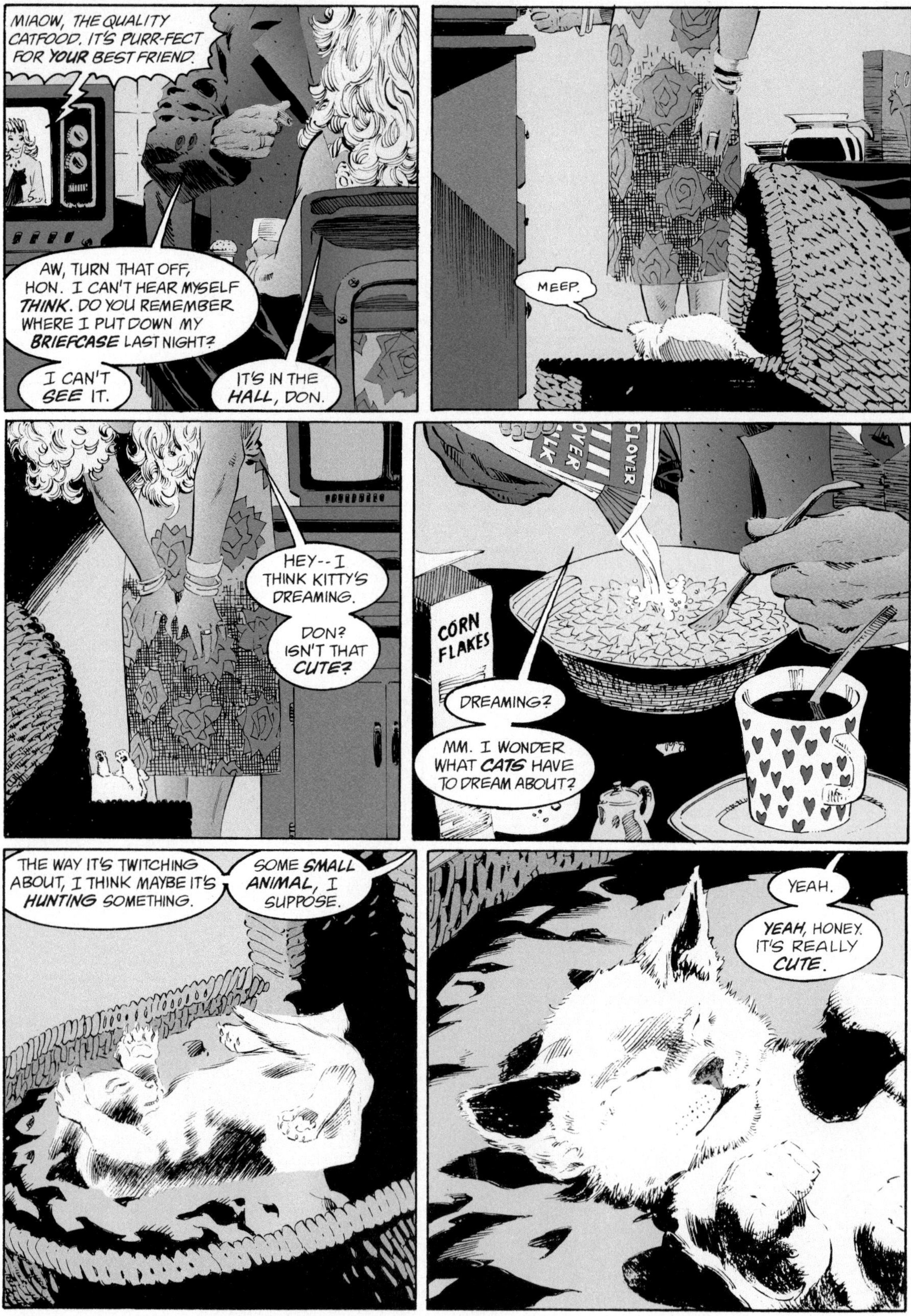
MIAOW, THE QUALITY CATFOOD. IT'S PURR-FECT FOR YOUR BEST FRIEND.
AW, TURN THAT OFF, HON. I CAN'T HEAR MYSELF THINK. DO YOU REMEMBER WHERE I PUT DOWN MY BRIEFCASE LAST NIGHT?
I CAN'T SEE IT.
IT'S IN THE HALL, DON.
MEEP.
HEY--I THINK KITTY'S DREAMING.
DON? ISN'T THAT CUTE?
CLOVER
CORN FLAKES
DREAMING?
MM. I WONDER WHAT CATS HAVE TO DREAM ABOUT?
THE WAY IT'S TWITCHING ABOUT, I THINK MAYBE IT'S HUNTING SOMETHING.
SOME SMALL ANIMAL, I SUPPOSE.
YEAH.
YEAH, HONEY. IT'S REALLY CUTE.

NEXT: A MIDSUMMER NIGHT'S DREAM...

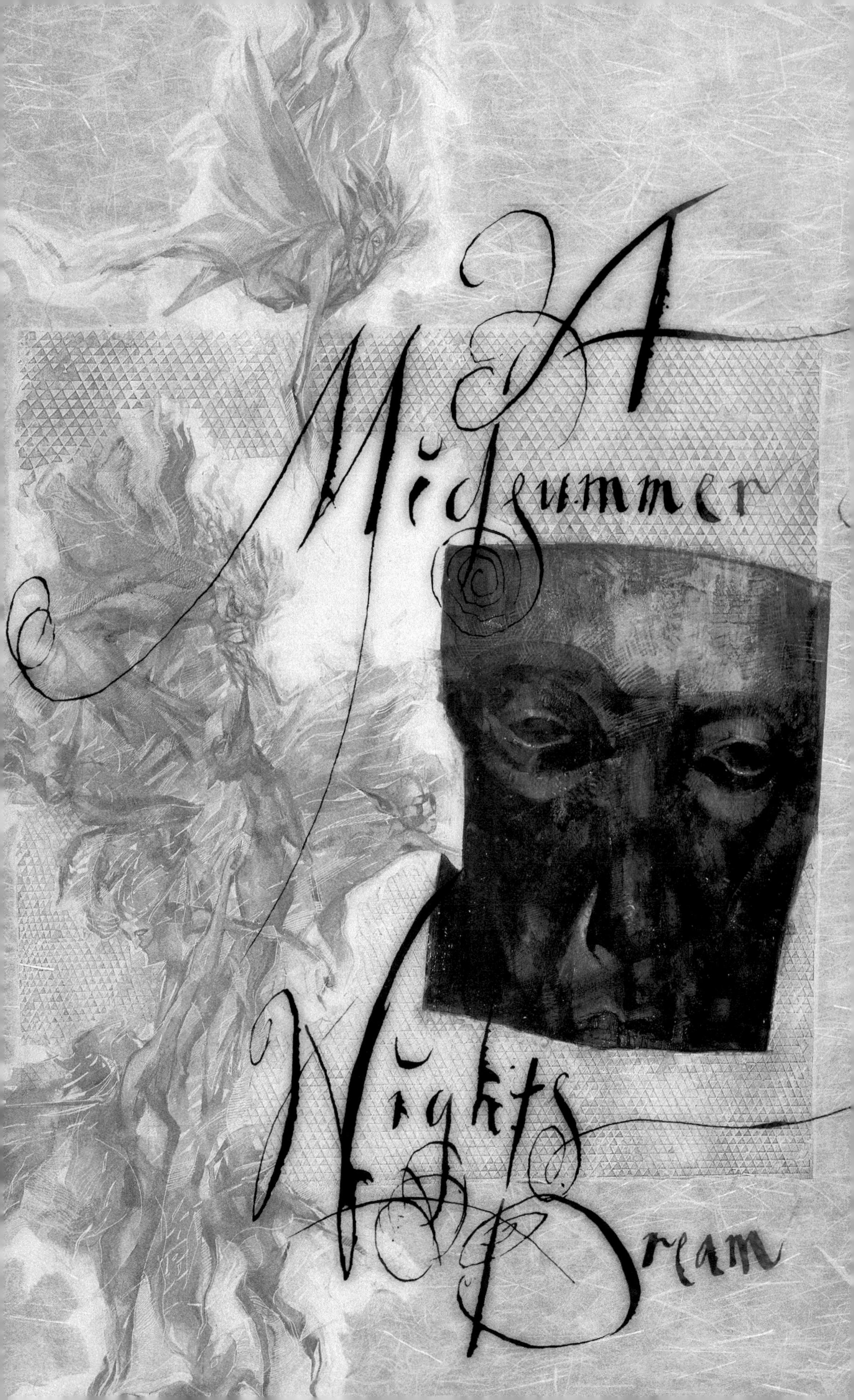
A
Midsummer
Nights
Dream

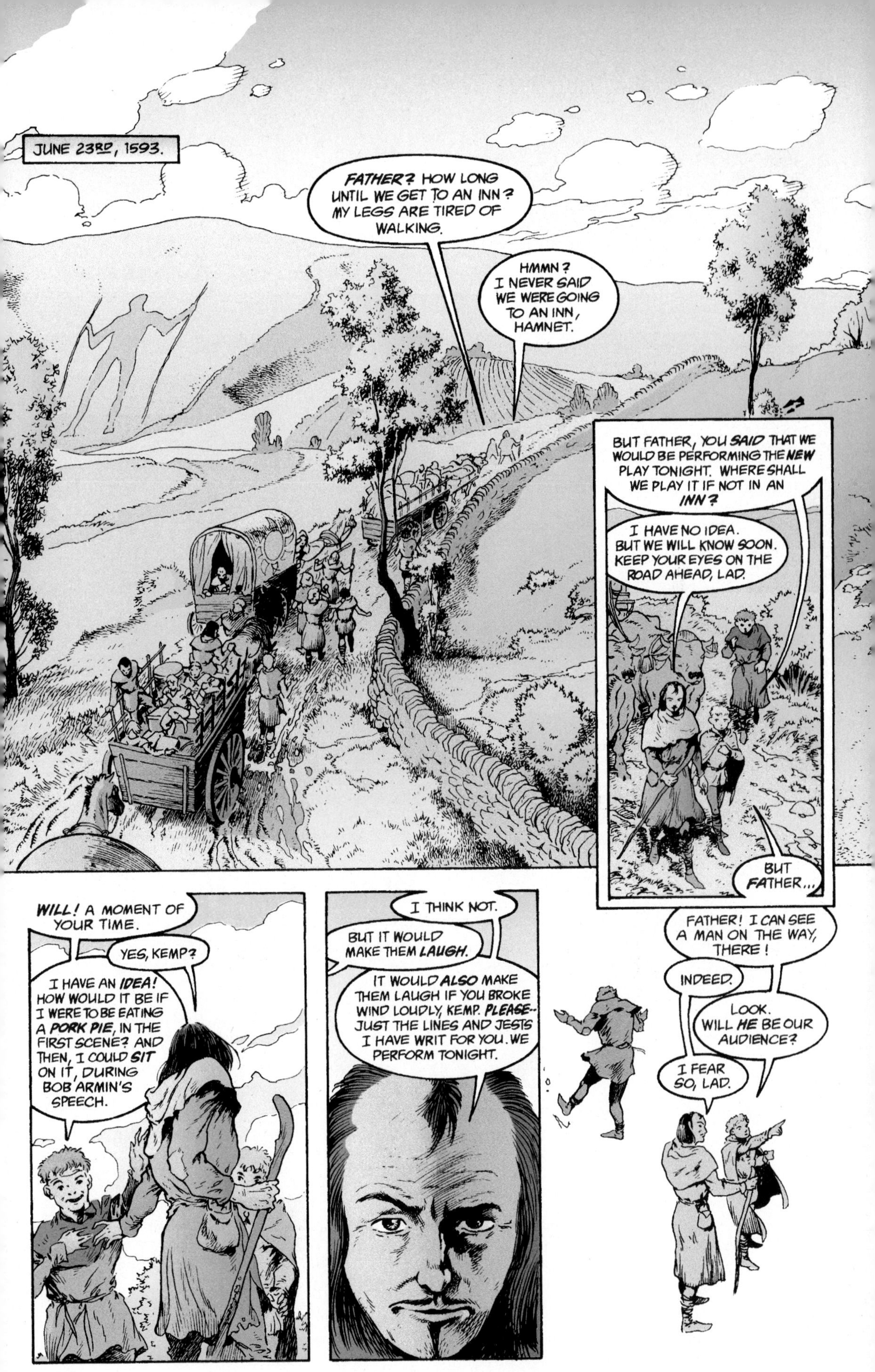

JUNE 23RD, 1593.
FATHER? HOW LONG UNTIL WE GET TO AN INN? MY LEGS ARE TIRED OF WALKING.
HMMN? I NEVER SAID WE WERE GOING TO AN INN, HAMNET.
BUT FATHER, YOU SAID THAT WE WOULD BE PERFORMING THE NEW PLAY TONIGHT. WHERE SHALL WE PLAY IT IF NOT IN AN INN?
I HAVE NO IDEA. BUT WE WILL KNOW SOON. KEEP YOUR EYES ON THE ROAD AHEAD, LAD.
BUT FATHER...
WILL! A MOMENT OF YOUR TIME.
YES, KEMP?
I HAVE AN IDEA! HOW WOULD IT BE IF I WERE TO BE EATING A PORK PIE, IN THE FIRST SCENE? AND THEN, I COULD SIT ON IT, DURING BOB ARMIN'S SPEECH.
I THINK NOT.
BUT IT WOULD MAKE THEM LAUGH.
IT WOULD ALSO MAKE THEM LAUGH IF YOU BROKE WIND LOUDLY, KEMP. PLEASE.. JUST THE LINES AND JESTS I HAVE WRIT FOR YOU. WE PERFORM TONIGHT.
FATHER! I CAN SEE A MAN ON THE WAY, THERE!
INDEED.
LOOK. WILL HE BE OUR AUDIENCE?
I FEAR SO, LAD.

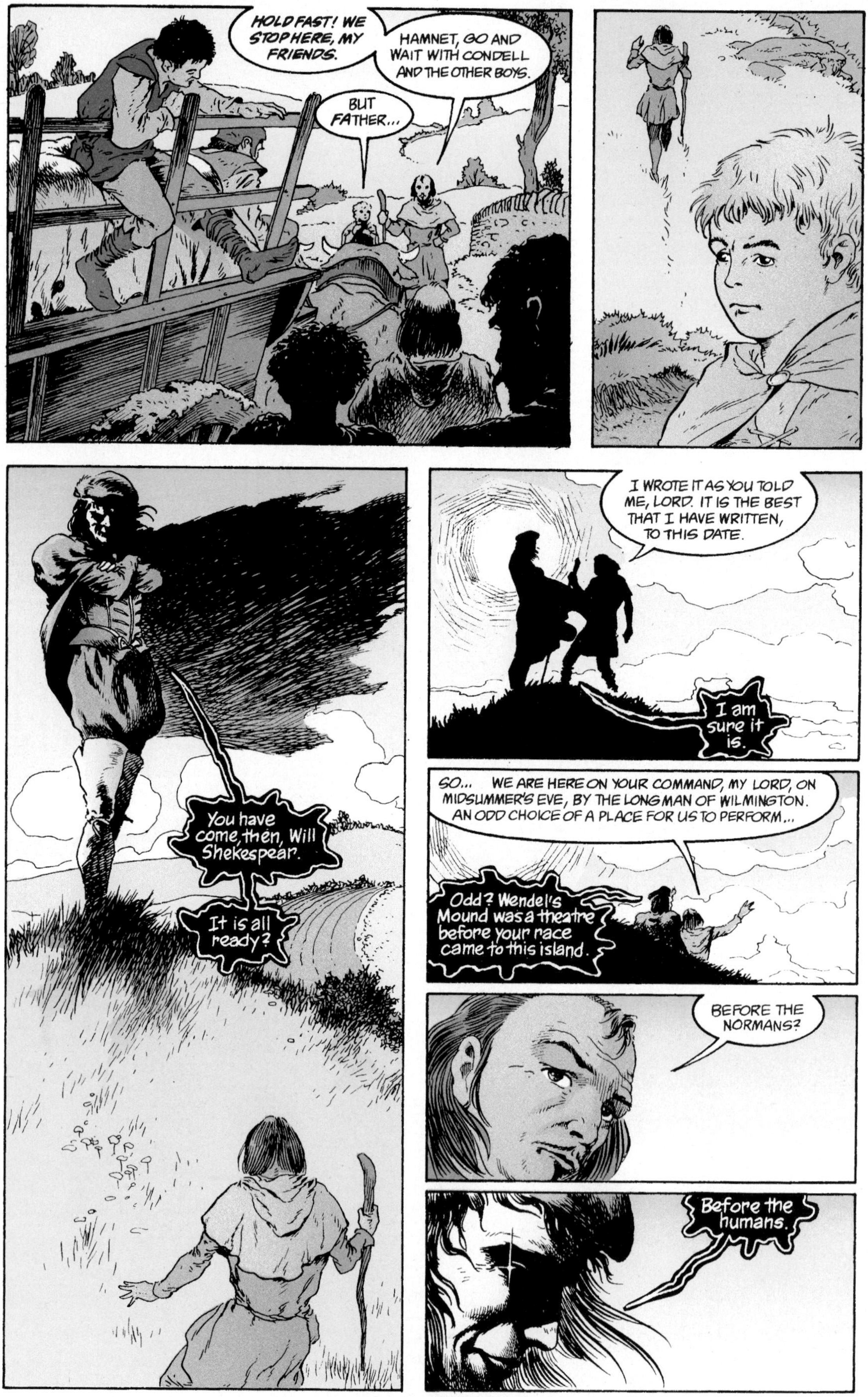
HOLD FAST! WE STOP HERE, MY FRIENDS.
HAMNET, GO AND WAIT WITH CONDELL AND THE OTHER BOYS.
BUT FATHER...
You have come, then, Will Shekespear.
It is all ready?
I WROTE IT AS YOU TOLD ME, LORD. IT IS THE BEST THAT I HAVE WRITTEN, TO THIS DATE.
I am sure it is.
SO... WE ARE HERE ON YOUR COMMAND, MY LORD, ON MIDSUMMER'S EVE, BY THE LONG MAN OF WILMINGTON. AN ODD CHOICE OF A PLACE FOR US TO PERFORM...
Odd? Wendel's Mound was a theatre before your race came to this island.
BEFORE THE NORMANS?
Before the humans.

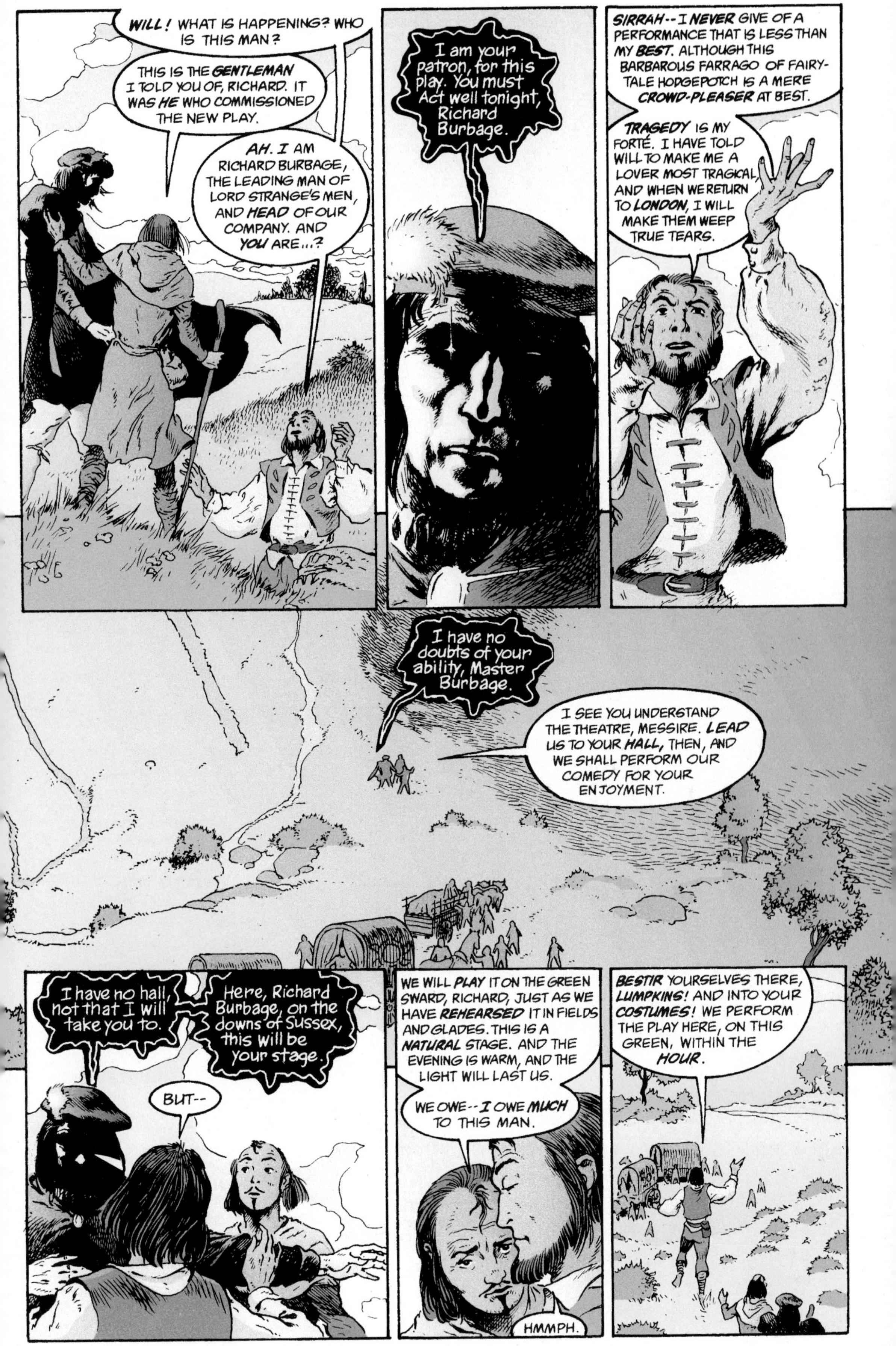
WILL! WHAT IS HAPPENING? WHO IS THIS MAN?
THIS IS THE GENTLEMAN I TOLD YOU OF, RICHARD. IT WAS HE WHO COMMISSIONED THE NEW PLAY.
AH. I AM RICHARD BURBAGE, THE LEADING MAN OF LORD STRANGE'S MEN, AND HEAD OF OUR COMPANY. AND YOU ARE...?
I am your patron, for this play. You must Act well tonight, Richard Burbage.
SIRRAH--I NEVER GIVE OF A PERFORMANCE THAT IS LESS THAN MY BEST. ALTHOUGH THIS BARBAROUS FARRAGO OF FAIRY-TALE HODGEPOTCH IS A MERE CROWD-PLEASER AT BEST.
TRAGEDY IS MY FORTÉ. I HAVE TOLD WILL TO MAKE ME A LOVER MOST TRAGICAL, AND WHEN WE RETURN TO LONDON, I WILL MAKE THEM WEEP TRUE TEARS.
I have no doubts of your ability, Master Burbage.
I SEE YOU UNDERSTAND THE THEATRE, MESSIRE. LEAD US TO YOUR HALL, THEN, AND WE SHALL PERFORM OUR COMEDY FOR YOUR ENJOYMENT.
I have no hall, not that I will take you to.
Here, Richard Burbage, on the downs of Sussex, this will be your stage.
BUT--
WE WILL PLAY IT ON THE GREEN SWARD, RICHARD, JUST AS WE HAVE REHEARSED IT IN FIELDS AND GLADES. THIS IS A NATURAL STAGE. AND THE EVENING IS WARM, AND THE LIGHT WILL LAST US.
WE OWE--I OWE MUCH TO THIS MAN.
HMMPH.
BESTIR YOURSELVES THERE, LUMPKINS! AND INTO YOUR COSTUMES! WE PERFORM THE PLAY HERE, ON THIS GREEN, WITHIN THE HOUR.

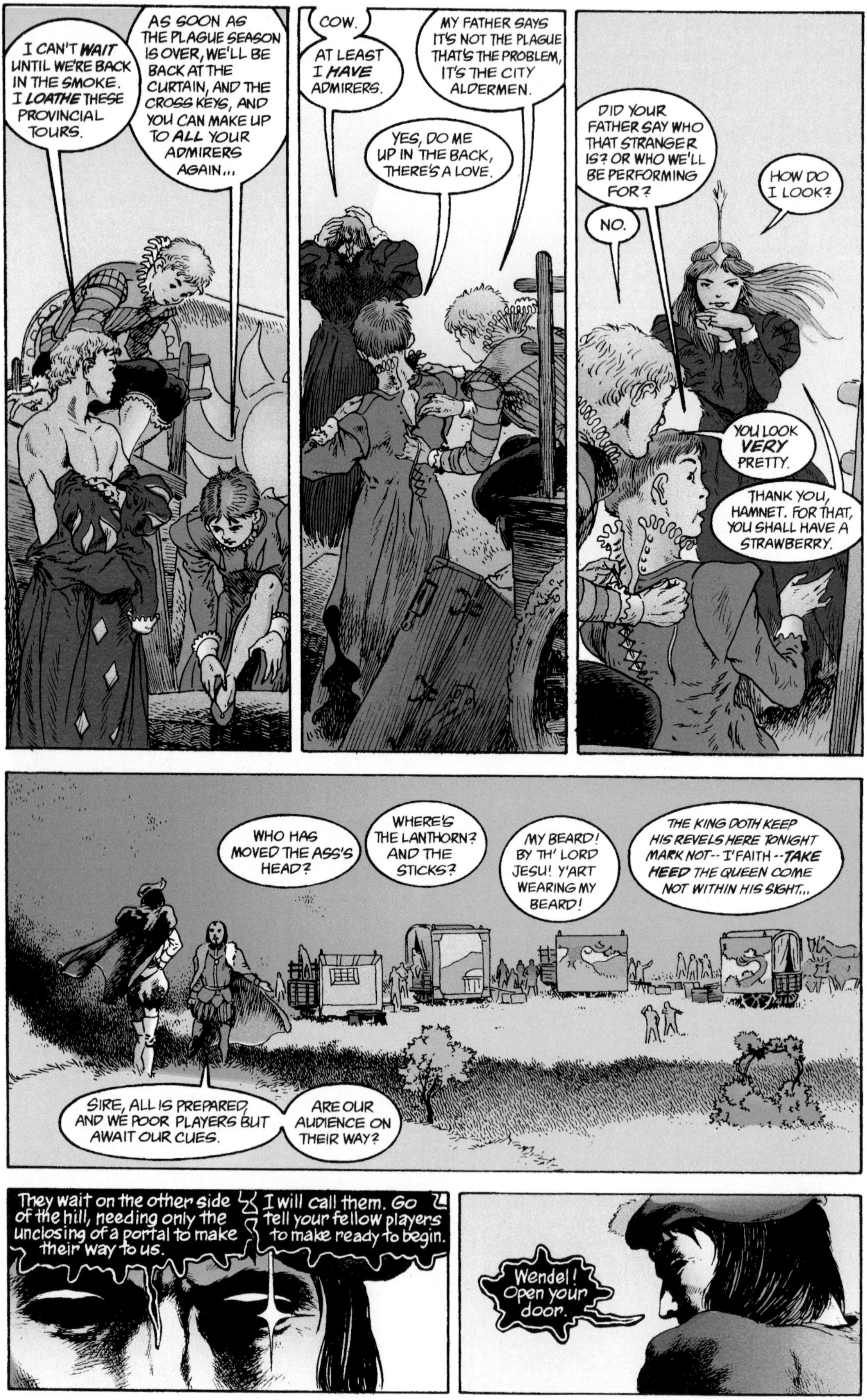
I CAN'T WAIT UNTIL WE'RE BACK IN THE SMOKE. I LOATHE THESE PROVINCIAL TOURS.
AS SOON AS THE PLAGUE SEASON IS OVER, WE'LL BE BACK AT THE CURTAIN, AND THE CROSS KEYS, AND YOU CAN MAKE UP TO ALL YOUR ADMIRERS AGAIN...
COW.
AT LEAST I HAVE ADMIRERS.
MY FATHER SAYS IT'S NOT THE PLAGUE THAT'S THE PROBLEM, IT'S THE CITY ALDERMEN.
YES, DO ME UP IN THE BACK, THERE'S A LOVE.
DID YOUR FATHER SAY WHO THAT STRANGER IS? OR WHO WE'LL BE PERFORMING FOR?
NO.
HOW DO I LOOK?
YOU LOOK VERY PRETTY.
THANK YOU, HAMNET. FOR THAT, YOU SHALL HAVE A STRAWBERRY.
WHO HAS MOVED THE ASS'S HEAD?
WHERE'S THE LANTHORN? AND THE STICKS?
MY BEARD! BY TH' LORD JESU! Y'ART WEARING MY BEARD!
THE KING DOTH KEEP HIS REVELS HERE TONIGHT MARK NOT-- I'FAITH --TAKE HEED THE QUEEN COME NOT WITHIN HIS SIGHT...
SIRE, ALL IS PREPARED, AND WE POOR PLAYERS BUT AWAIT OUR CUES.
ARE OUR AUDIENCE ON THEIR WAY?
They wait on the other side of the hill, needing only the unclosing of a portal to make their way to us.
I will call them. Go tell your fellow players to make ready to begin.
Wendel! Open your door.

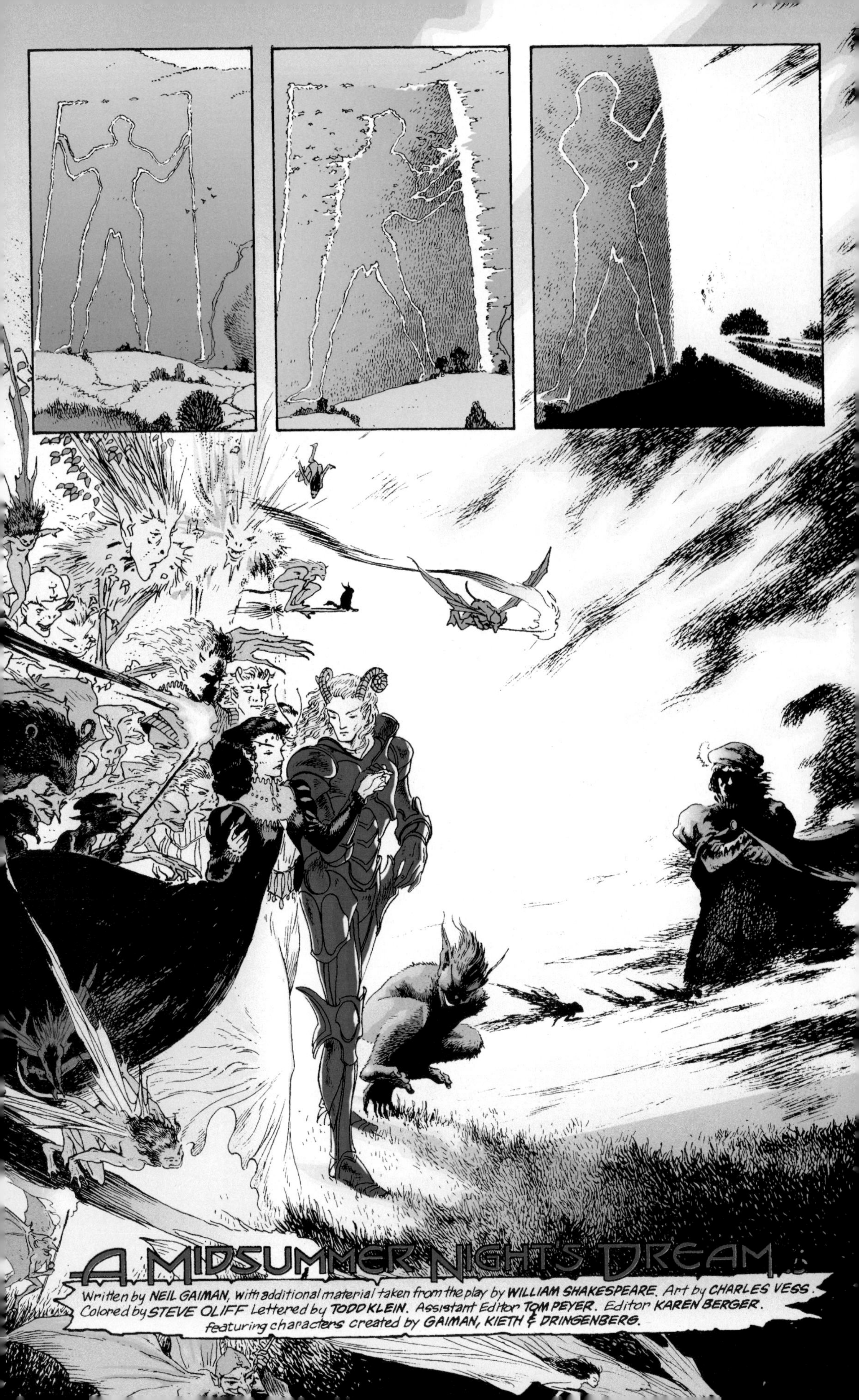
A MIDSUMMER NIGHT'S DREAM
Written by NEIL GAIMAN, with additional material taken from the play by WILLIAM SHAKESPEARE. Art by CHARLES VESS.
Colored by STEVE OLIFF Lettered by TODD KLEIN. Assistant Editor TOM PEYER. Editor KAREN BERGER.
featuring characters created by GAIMAN, KIETH & DRINGENBERG.

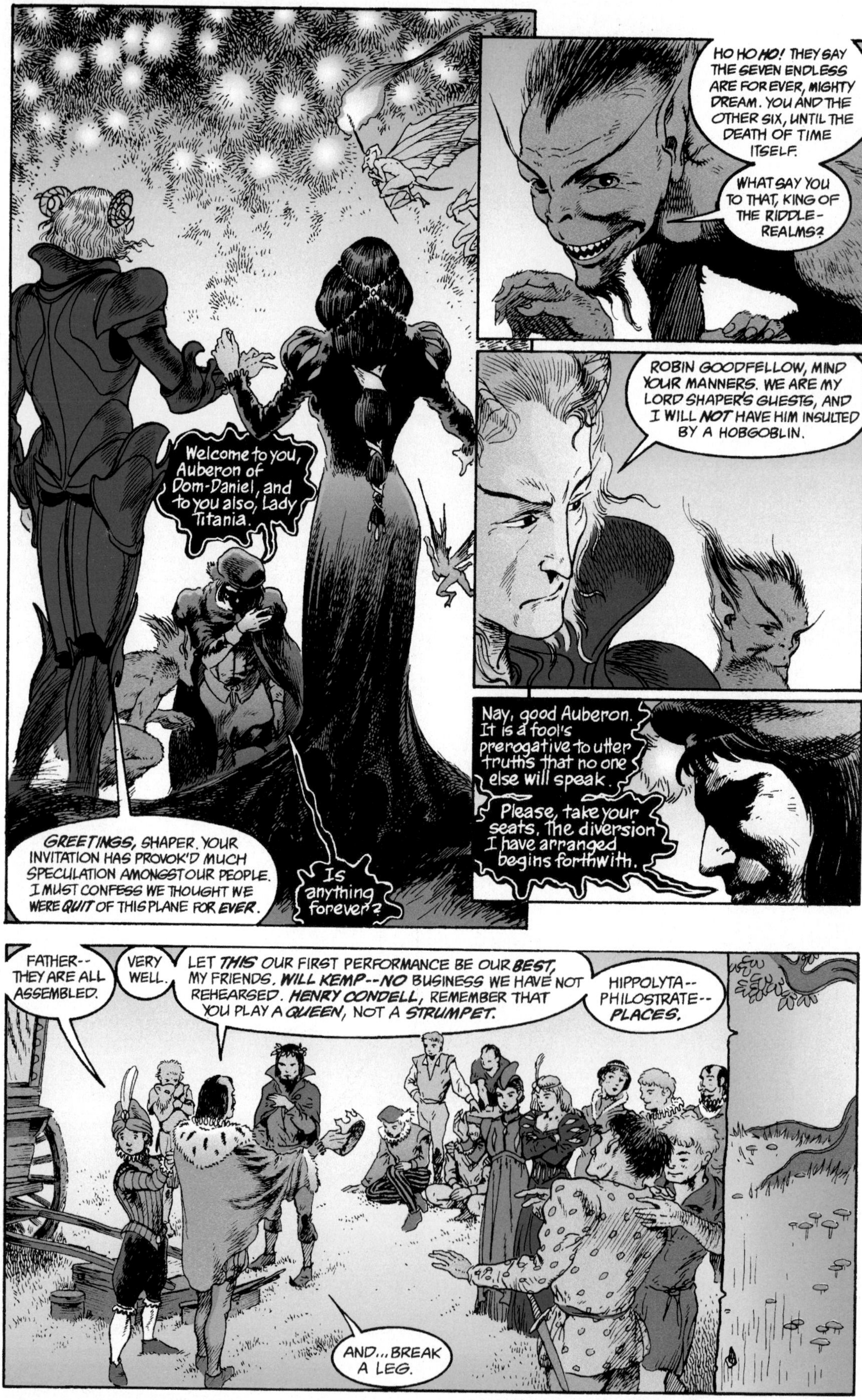
Welcome to you, Auberon of Dom-Daniel, and to you also, Lady Titania.
GREETINGS, SHAPER. YOUR INVITATION HAS PROVOK'D MUCH SPECULATION AMONGST OUR PEOPLE. I MUST CONFESS WE THOUGHT WE WERE QUIT OF THIS PLANE FOR EVER.
Is anything forever?
HO HO HO! THEY SAY THE SEVEN ENDLESS ARE FOR EVER, MIGHTY DREAM. YOU AND THE OTHER SIX, UNTIL THE DEATH OF TIME ITSELF.
WHAT SAY YOU TO THAT, KING OF THE RIDDLE-REALMS?
ROBIN GOODFELLOW, MIND YOUR MANNERS. WE ARE MY LORD SHAPER'S GUESTS, AND I WILL NOT HAVE HIM INSULTED BY A HOBGOBLIN.
Nay, good Auberon. It is a fool's prerogative to utter truths that no one else will speak.
Please, take your seats. The diversion I have arranged begins forthwith.
FATHER-- THEY ARE ALL ASSEMBLED.
VERY WELL.
LET THIS OUR FIRST PERFORMANCE BE OUR BEST, MY FRIENDS. WILL KEMP--NO BUSINESS WE HAVE NOT REHEARSED. HENRY CONDELL, REMEMBER THAT YOU PLAY A QUEEN, NOT A STRUMPET.
HIPPOLYTA-- PHILOSTRATE-- PLACES.
AND... BREAK A LEG.

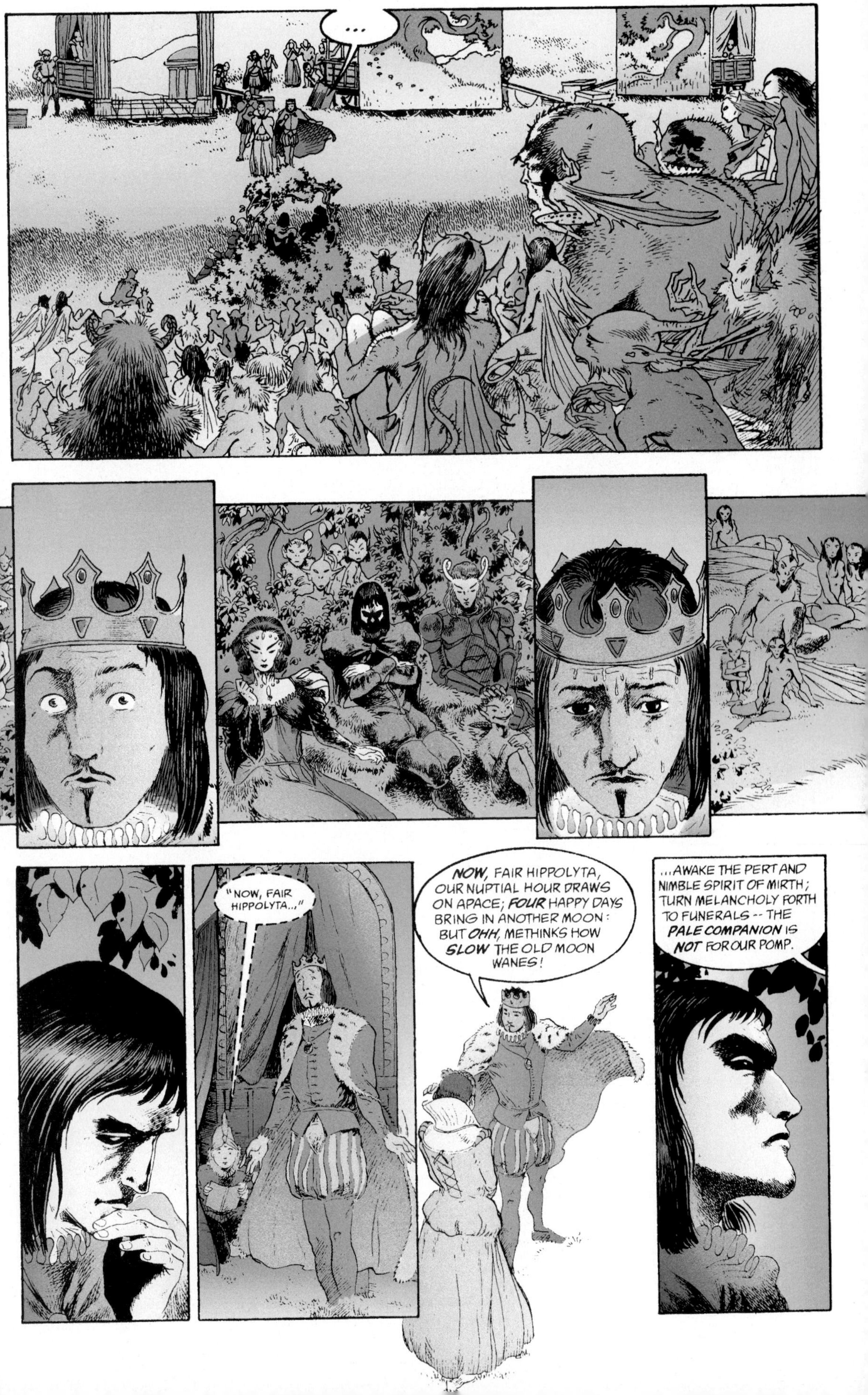
...
"NOW, FAIR HIPPOLYTA..."
NOW, FAIR HIPPOLYTA, OUR NUPTIAL HOUR DRAWS ON APACE; FOUR HAPPY DAYS BRING IN ANOTHER MOON: BUT OHH, METHINKS HOW SLOW THE OLD MOON WANES!
...AWAKE THE PERT AND NIMBLE SPIRIT OF MIRTH; TURN MELANCHOLY FORTH TO FUNERALS -- THE PALE COMPANION IS NOT FOR OUR POMP.

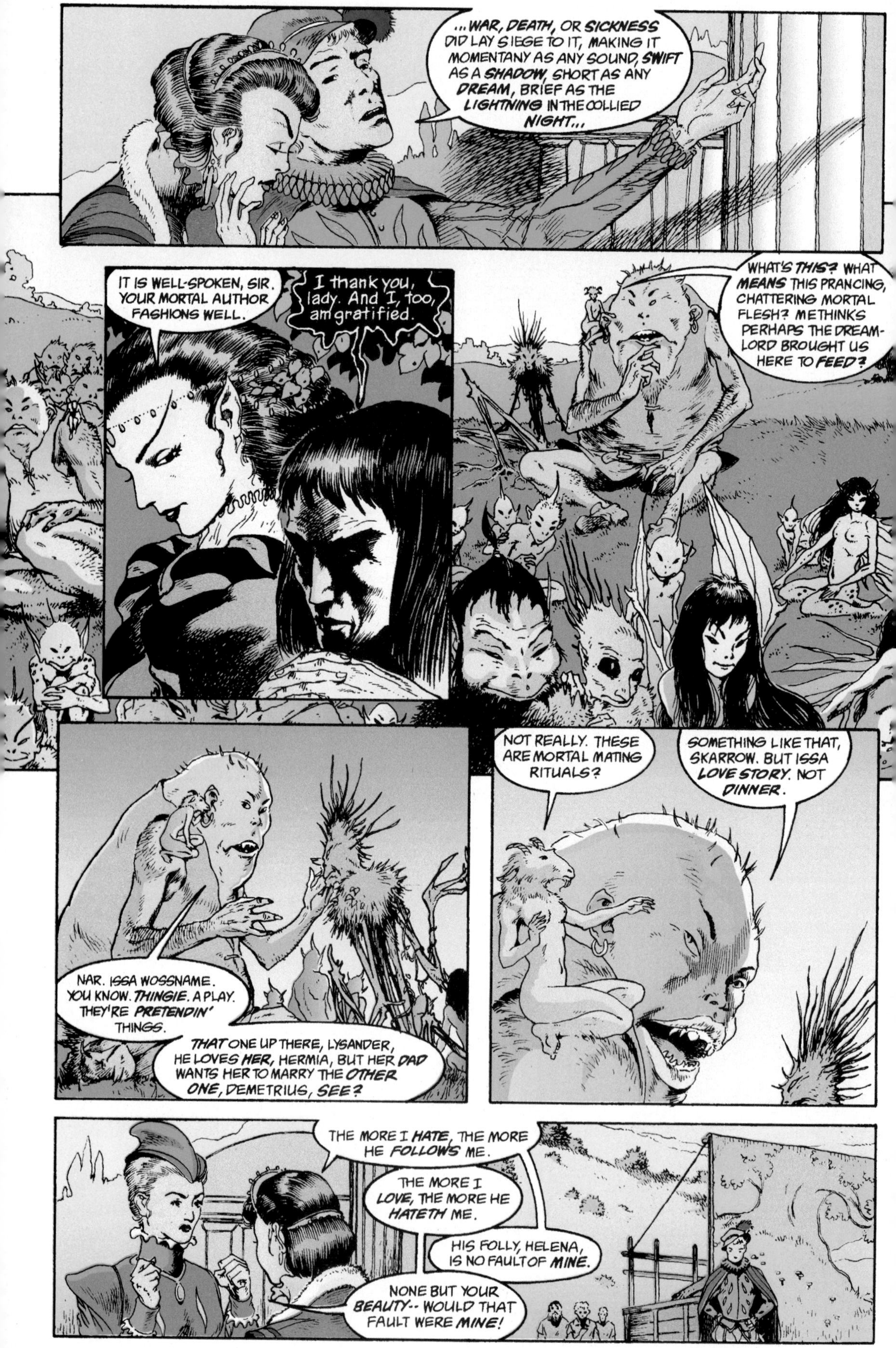
...WAR, DEATH, OR SICKNESS DID LAY SIEGE TO IT, MAKING IT MOMENTANY AS ANY SOUND, SWIFT AS A SHADOW, SHORT AS ANY DREAM, BRIEF AS THE LIGHTNING IN THE COLLIED NIGHT...
IT IS WELL-SPOKEN, SIR. YOUR MORTAL AUTHOR FASHIONS WELL.
I thank you, lady. And I, too, am gratified.
WHAT'S THIS? WHAT MEANS THIS PRANCING, CHATTERING MORTAL FLESH? METHINKS PERHAPS THE DREAM-LORD BROUGHT US HERE TO FEED?
NAR. ISSA WOSSNAME. YOU KNOW. THINGIE. A PLAY. THEY'RE PRETENDIN' THINGS.
THAT ONE UP THERE, LYSANDER, HE LOVES HER, HERMIA, BUT HER DAD WANTS HER TO MARRY THE OTHER ONE, DEMETRIUS, SEE?
NOT REALLY. THESE ARE MORTAL MATING RITUALS?
SOMETHING LIKE THAT, SKARROW. BUT ISSA LOVE STORY. NOT DINNER.
THE MORE I HATE, THE MORE HE FOLLOWS ME.
THE MORE I LOVE, THE MORE HE HATETH ME.
HIS FOLLY, HELENA, IS NO FAULT OF MINE.
NONE BUT YOUR BEAUTY-- WOULD THAT FAULT WERE MINE!

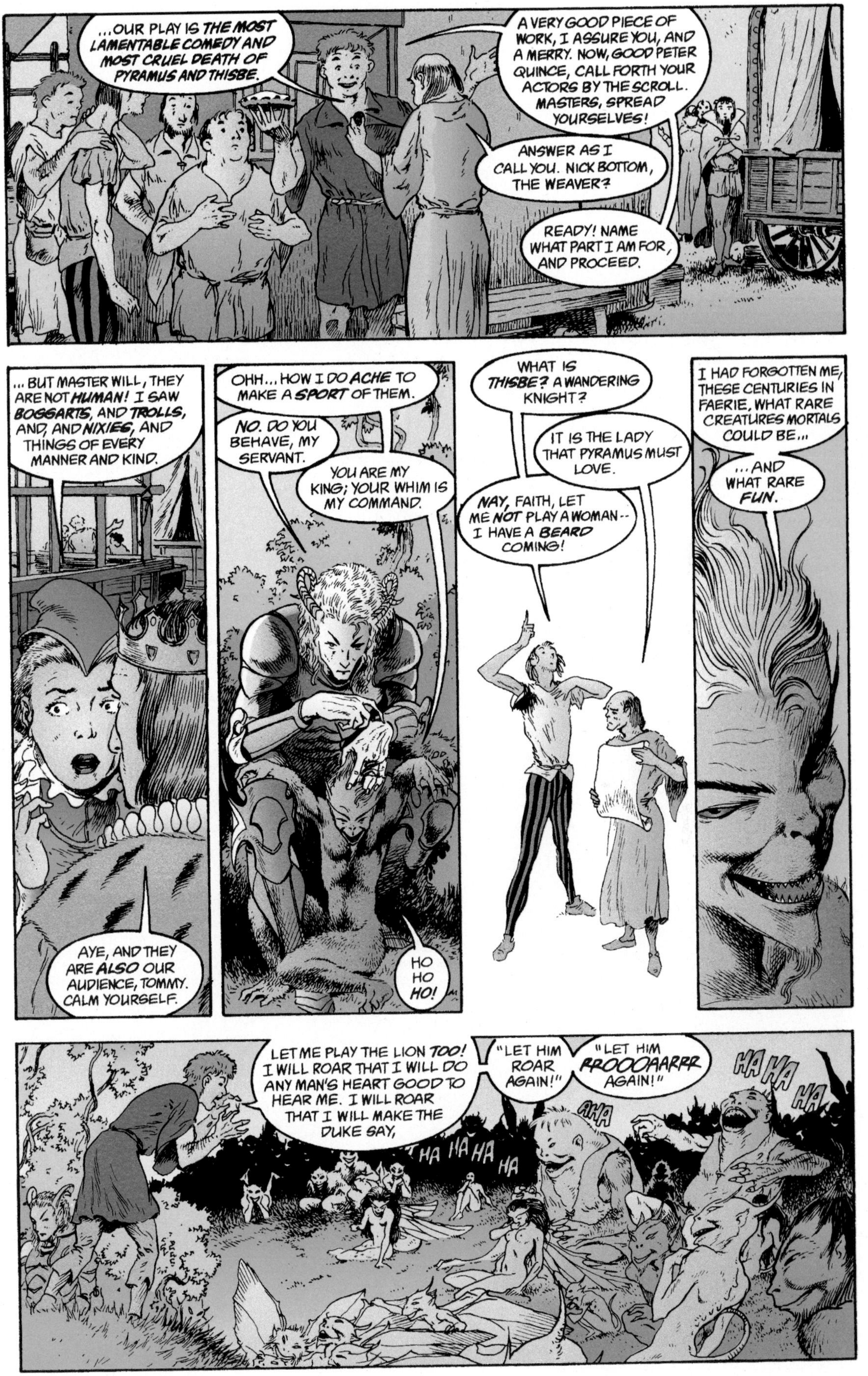
...OUR PLAY IS THE MOST LAMENTABLE COMEDY AND MOST CRUEL DEATH OF PYRAMUS AND THISBE.
A VERY GOOD PIECE OF WORK, I ASSURE YOU, AND A MERRY. NOW, GOOD PETER QUINCE, CALL FORTH YOUR ACTORS BY THE SCROLL. MASTERS, SPREAD YOURSELVES!
ANSWER AS I CALL YOU. NICK BOTTOM, THE WEAVER?
READY! NAME WHAT PART I AM FOR, AND PROCEED.
...BUT MASTER WILL, THEY ARE NOT HUMAN! I SAW BOGGARTS, AND TROLLS, AND, AND NIXIES, AND THINGS OF EVERY MANNER AND KIND.
AYE, AND THEY ARE ALSO OUR AUDIENCE, TOMMY. CALM YOURSELF.
OHH... HOW I DO ACHE TO MAKE A SPORT OF THEM.
NO. DO YOU BEHAVE, MY SERVANT.
YOU ARE MY KING; YOUR WHIM IS MY COMMAND.
HO HO HO!
WHAT IS THISBE? A WANDERING KNIGHT?
IT IS THE LADY THAT PYRAMUS MUST LOVE.
NAY, FAITH, LET ME NOT PLAY A WOMAN-- I HAVE A BEARD COMING!
I HAD FORGOTTEN ME, THESE CENTURIES IN FAERIE, WHAT RARE CREATURES MORTALS COULD BE...
...AND WHAT RARE FUN.
LET ME PLAY THE LION TOO! I WILL ROAR THAT I WILL DO ANY MAN'S HEART GOOD TO HEAR ME. I WILL ROAR THAT I WILL MAKE THE DUKE SAY,
"LET HIM ROAR AGAIN!"
"LET HIM RROOOOAARRR AGAIN!"
HA HA HA
AHA
HA HA HA
HA

EITHER *I* MISTAKE YOUR SHAPE AND MAKING *QUITE*, OR ELSE *YOU* ARE THAT *SHREWD* AND *KNAVISH* SPRITE CALLED *ROBIN GOODFELLOW*:

ARE YOU NOT *HE* THAT *FRIGHTS* THE MAIDENS OF THE *VILLAGERY...?*

IT'S *YOU!* HOBGOBLIN, THAT ACTOR PERSONATES *YOU!*

THOU SPEAK'ST *ARIGHT: I AM* THAT MERRY WANDERER OF THE NIGHT.

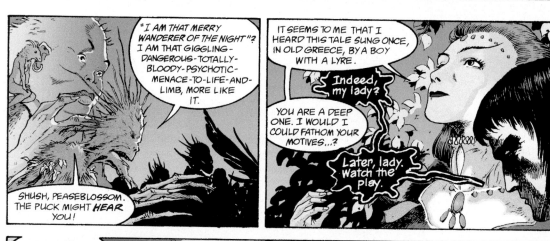

"I AM THAT MERRY WANDERER OF THE NIGHT"? I AM THAT GIGGLING- DANGEROUS-TOTALLY- BLOODY-PSYCHOTIC- MENACE-TO-LIFE-AND- LIMB, MORE LIKE IT.

SHUSH, PEASEBLOSSOM. THE PUCK MIGHT *HEAR* YOU!

IT SEEMS TO ME THAT I HEARD THIS TALE SUNG ONCE, IN OLD GREECE, BY A BOY WITH A LYRE.

Indeed, my lady?

YOU ARE A DEEP ONE. I WOULD I COULD FATHOM YOUR MOTIVES...?

Later, lady. Watch the play.

ILL-MET BY *MOONLIGHT*, PROUD TITANIA.

WHAT, JEALOUS OBERON? FAIRY, SKIP HENCE. I HAVE FORSWORN HIS *BED* AND *COMPANY*.

TARRY, RASH WANTON! AM I NOT THY LORD?

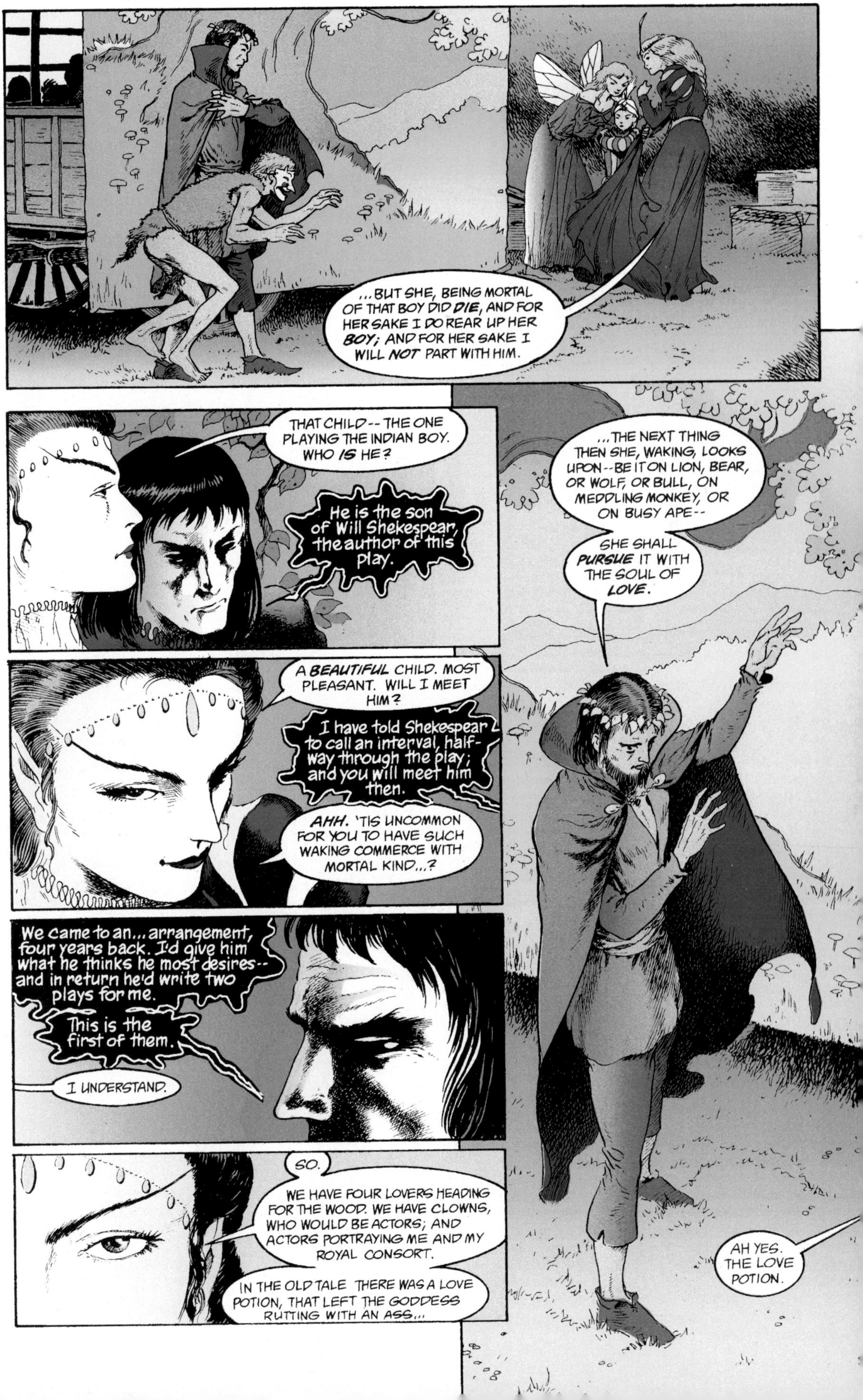
...BUT SHE, BEING MORTAL OF THAT BOY DID DIE, AND FOR HER SAKE I DO REAR UP HER BOY; AND FOR HER SAKE I WILL NOT PART WITH HIM.
THAT CHILD-- THE ONE PLAYING THE INDIAN BOY. WHO IS HE?
He is the son of Will Shekespear, the author of this play.
A BEAUTIFUL CHILD. MOST PLEASANT. WILL I MEET HIM?
I have told Shekespear to call an interval, half-way through the play; and you will meet him then.
AHH. 'TIS UNCOMMON FOR YOU TO HAVE SUCH WAKING COMMERCE WITH MORTAL KIND...?
We came to an... arrangement, four years back. I'd give him what he thinks he most desires-- and in return he'd write two plays for me.
This is the first of them.
I UNDERSTAND.
SO.
WE HAVE FOUR LOVERS HEADING FOR THE WOOD. WE HAVE CLOWNS, WHO WOULD BE ACTORS; AND ACTORS PORTRAYING ME AND MY ROYAL CONSORT.
IN THE OLD TALE THERE WAS A LOVE POTION, THAT LEFT THE GODDESS RUTTING WITH AN ASS...
...THE NEXT THING THEN SHE, WAKING, LOOKS UPON--BE IT ON LION, BEAR, OR WOLF, OR BULL, ON MEDDLING MONKEY, OR ON BUSY APE--
SHE SHALL PURSUE IT WITH THE SOUL OF LOVE.
AH YES. THE LOVE POTION.

STAY-- THOUGH THOU KILL ME, SWEET DEMETRIUS.

I CHARGE THEE HENCE-- AND DO NOT *HAUNT* ME THUS!

O, WILT THOU DARKLING LEAVE ME? DO *NOT* GO!

STAY, ON THY PERIL. I ALONE WILL GO.

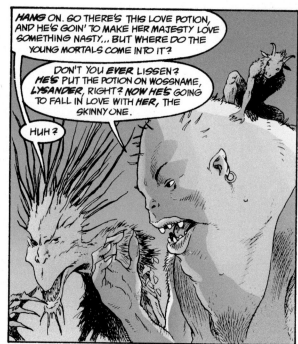

HANG ON. SO THERE'S THIS LOVE POTION, AND HE'S GOIN' TO MAKE HER MAJESTY LOVE SOMETHING NASTY... BUT WHERE DO THE YOUNG MORTALS COME INTO IT?

DON'T YOU *EVER* LISSEN? *HE'S* PUT THE POTION ON WOSSNAME, *LYSANDER*, RIGHT? *NOW HE'S* GOING TO FALL IN LOVE WITH *HER*, THE SKINNY ONE.

HUH?

YOU SEE, THE PUCK THOUGHT *HE* WAS THE OTHER ONE, SO WHEN--

CAN'T YOU BE QUIET? *SOME* OF US ARE TRYING TO LISTEN.

NOT HERMIA BUT HELENA I LOVE--WHO WOULD NOT CHANGE A RAVEN FOR A DOVE?

THE PLAY GOES *WELL*, WILL. *HOWEVER*, IT SEEMS TO ME THAT WE ARE PERFORMING FOR SIMPLE APPLAUSE. AND EVEN WE GLORIOUS VAGABONDS MUST *EAT*.

WE SHALL HAVE AN INTERVAL, AT THE END OF KEMP AND CONDELL'S FIRST SCENE. WE CAN TALK OF SILVER THEN.

AY ME! FOR *PITY!* WHAT A *DREAM* WAS *HERE!* LYSANDER, LOOK HOW I DO QUAKE WITH FEAR!

METHOUGHT A SERPENT ATE MY *HEART* AWAY, AND YOU STOOD *SMILING* AT HIS CRUEL PREY.

LYSANDER...?

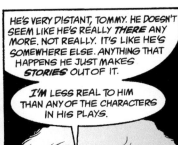

YOU MUST BE VERY PROUD OF YOUR FATHER, HAMNET.

PROUD? I SUPPOSE...

HE'S VERY DISTANT, TOMMY. HE DOESN'T SEEM LIKE HE'S REALLY *THERE* ANY MORE. NOT REALLY. IT'S LIKE HE'S SOMEWHERE ELSE. ANYTHING THAT HAPPENS HE JUST MAKES *STORIES* OUT OF IT.

I'M LESS REAL TO HIM THAN ANY OF THE CHARACTERS IN HIS PLAYS.

MOTHER SAYS HE'S *CHANGED* IN THE LAST FIVE YEARS, BUT I DON'T REMEMBER HIM ANY OTHER WAY. *JUDITH*-- SHE'S MY TWIN SISTER-- SHE ONCE JOKED THAT IF I *DIED*, HE'D JUST WRITE A *PLAY* ABOUT IT.

"HAMNET."

COME ON, LADDIE. I AM BACK *ON* IN A MINUTE!

MOTHER *ORDERED* HIM TO HAVE ME FOR THIS SUMMER. IT'S THE *FIRST* TIME I'VE SEEN HIM FOR *MORE* THAN A *WEEK* AT A TIME, THAT I REMEMBER.

BUT WE LIVE FIVE DAYS' RIDE FROM LONDON, UP IN WARWICKSHIRE, AND SEE HIM SELDOM.

ALL THAT MATTERS TO HIM... ...ALL THAT MATTERS IS THE STORIES.

I WOULD BE *PROUD* OF HIM, IF HE WERE *MY* FATHER.

I'LL FOLLOW YOU, I'LL LEAD YOU ABOUT, AROUND, THROUGH BUSH, THROUGH BRAKE, THROUGH BRIAR.

SOMETIME A *HORSE* I'LL BE, SOMETIME A *HOUND*--

--A *HOG*, A HEADLESS *BEAR*, SOMETIME A *FIRE*...

WHY DO THEY RUN AWAY?

THIS IS A *KNAVERY* OF THEM TO MAKE *ME* A-FEARED!

THIS IS *MAGNIFICENT*-- AND IT IS *TRUE*!

IT NEVER *HAPPENED*; YET IT IS *STILL* TRUE. WHAT MAGIC ART IS THIS?

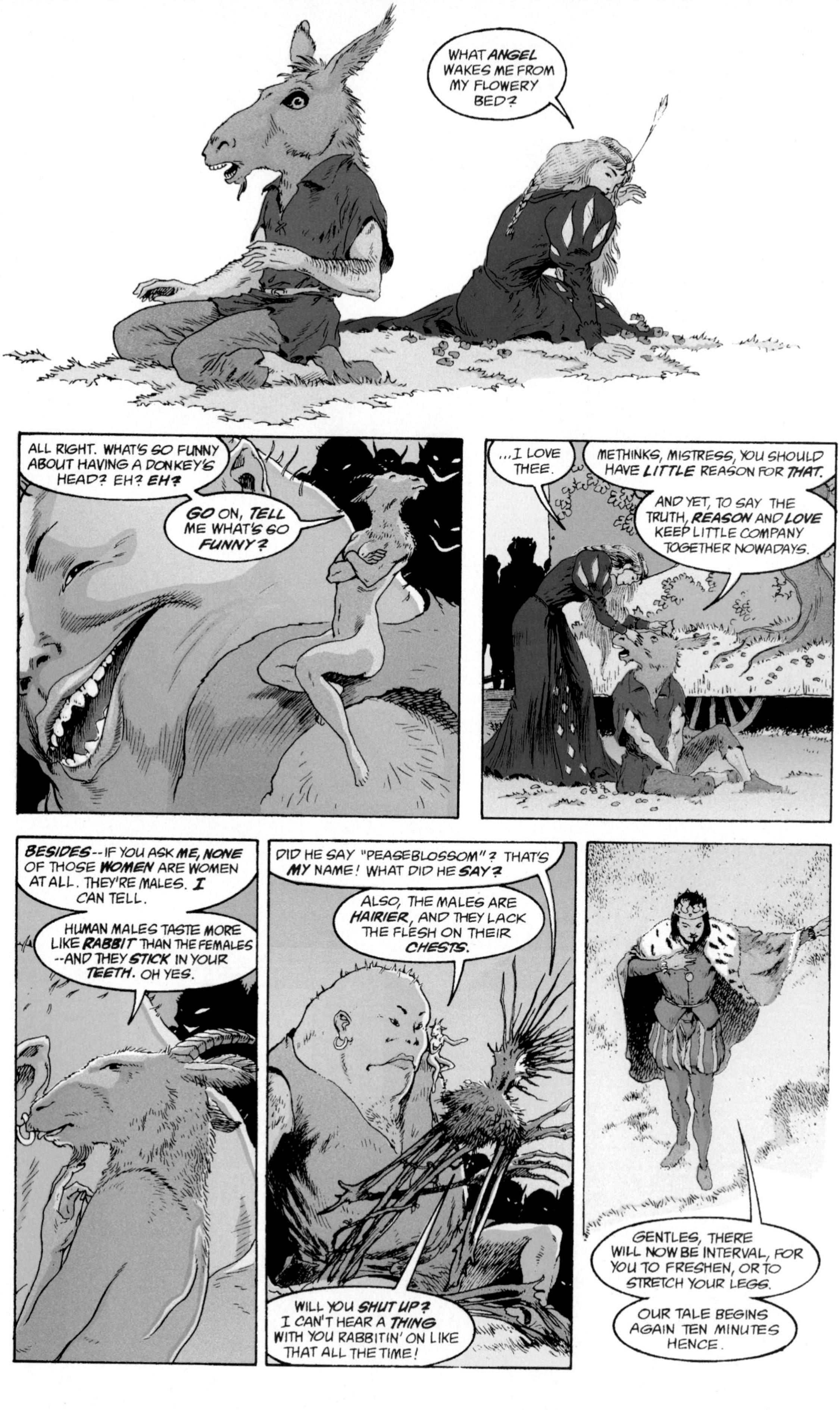
WHAT ANGEL WAKES ME FROM MY FLOWERY BED?
ALL RIGHT. WHAT'S SO FUNNY ABOUT HAVING A DONKEY'S HEAD? EH? EH?
GO ON, TELL ME WHAT'S SO FUNNY?
...I LOVE THEE.
METHINKS, MISTRESS, YOU SHOULD HAVE LITTLE REASON FOR THAT.
AND YET, TO SAY THE TRUTH, REASON AND LOVE KEEP LITTLE COMPANY TOGETHER NOWADAYS.
BESIDES--IF YOU ASK ME, NONE OF THOSE WOMEN ARE WOMEN AT ALL. THEY'RE MALES. I CAN TELL.
HUMAN MALES TASTE MORE LIKE RABBIT THAN THE FEMALES --AND THEY STICK IN YOUR TEETH. OH YES.
DID HE SAY "PEASEBLOSSOM"? THAT'S MY NAME! WHAT DID HE SAY?
ALSO, THE MALES ARE HAIRIER, AND THEY LACK THE FLESH ON THEIR CHESTS.
WILL YOU SHUT UP? I CAN'T HEAR A THING WITH YOU RABBITIN' ON LIKE THAT ALL THE TIME!
GENTLES, THERE WILL NOW BE INTERVAL, FOR YOU TO FRESHEN, OR TO STRETCH YOUR LEGS.
OUR TALE BEGINS AGAIN TEN MINUTES HENCE.

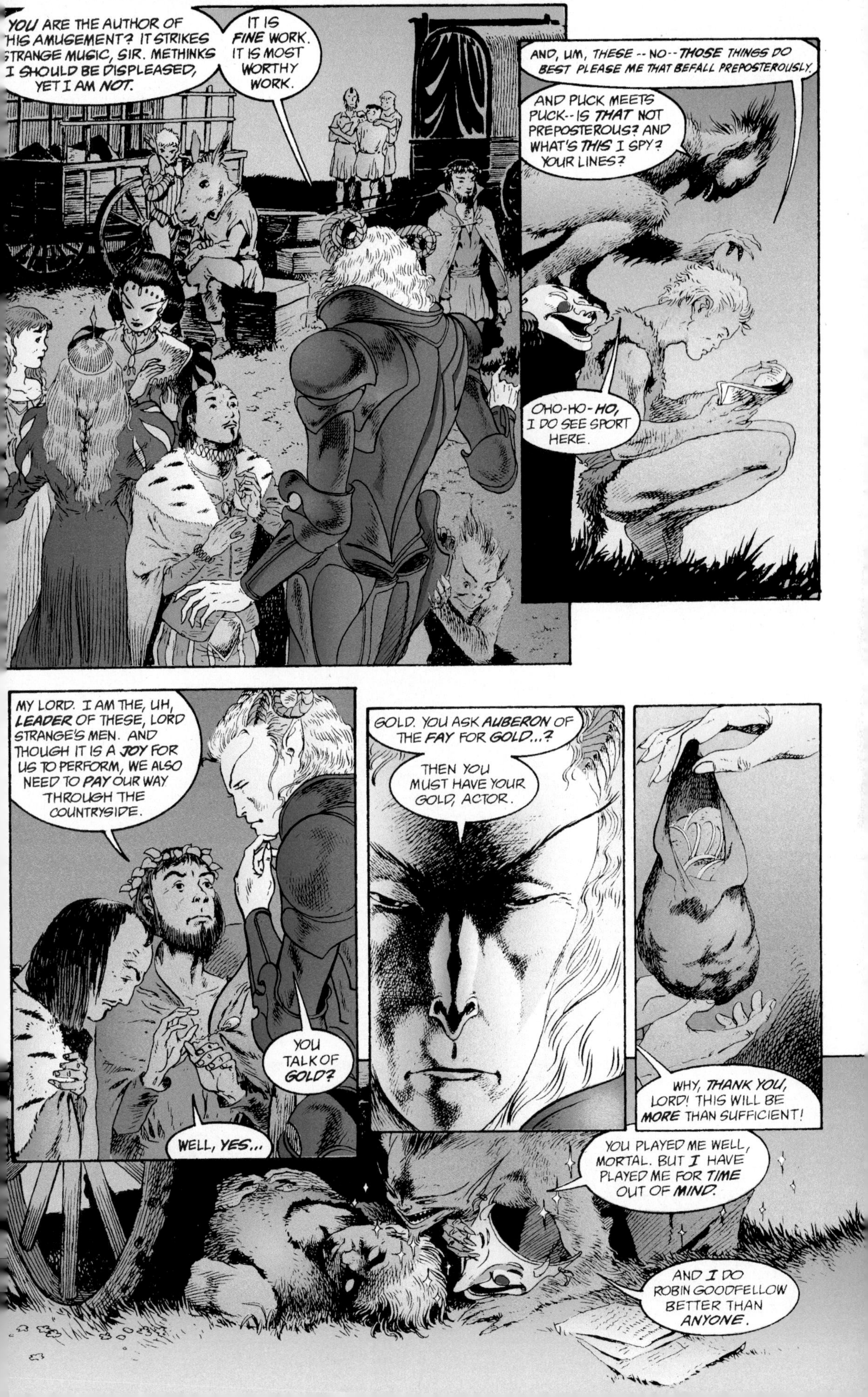

YOU ARE THE AUTHOR OF THIS AMUSEMENT? IT STRIKES STRANGE MUSIC, SIR. METHINKS I SHOULD BE DISPLEASED, YET I AM NOT.
IT IS FINE WORK. IT IS MOST WORTHY WORK.
AND, UM, THESE -- NO -- THOSE THINGS DO BEST PLEASE ME THAT BEFALL PREPOSTEROUSLY.
AND PUCK MEETS PUCK -- IS THAT NOT PREPOSTEROUS? AND WHAT'S THIS I SPY? YOUR LINES?
OHO-HO-HO, I DO SEE SPORT HERE.
MY LORD. I AM THE, UH, LEADER OF THESE, LORD STRANGE'S MEN. AND THOUGH IT IS A JOY FOR US TO PERFORM, WE ALSO NEED TO PAY OUR WAY THROUGH THE COUNTRYSIDE.
YOU TALK OF GOLD?
WELL, YES...
GOLD. YOU ASK AUBERON OF THE FAY FOR GOLD...?
THEN YOU MUST HAVE YOUR GOLD, ACTOR.
WHY, THANK YOU, LORD! THIS WILL BE MORE THAN SUFFICIENT!
YOU PLAYED ME WELL, MORTAL. BUT I HAVE PLAYED ME FOR TIME OUT OF MIND.
AND I DO ROBIN GOODFELLOW BETTER THAN ANYONE.

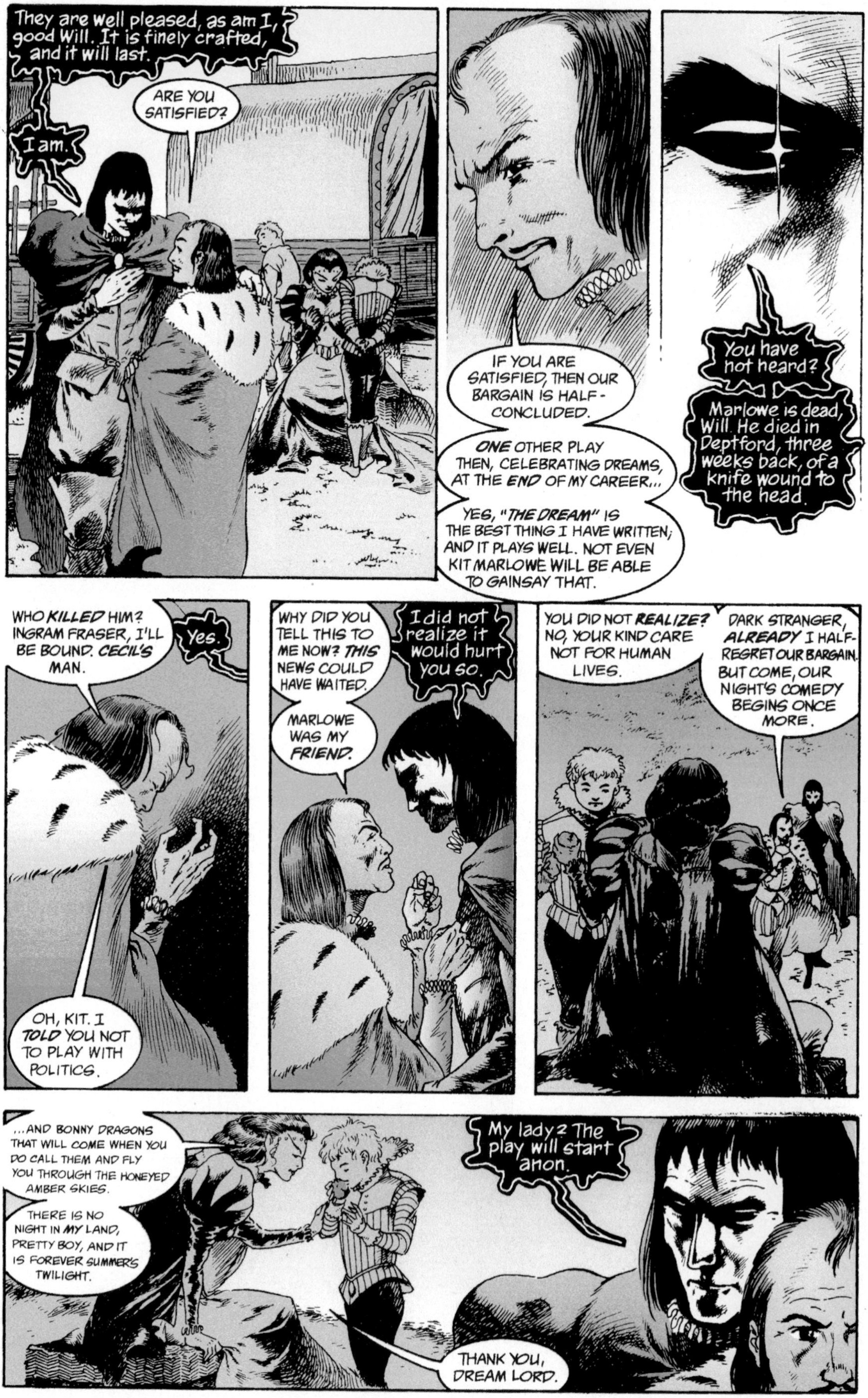
They are well pleased, as am I, good Will. It is finely crafted, and it will last.
ARE YOU SATISFIED?
I am.
IF YOU ARE SATISFIED, THEN OUR BARGAIN IS HALF-CONCLUDED.
ONE OTHER PLAY THEN, CELEBRATING DREAMS, AT THE END OF MY CAREER...
YES, "THE DREAM" IS THE BEST THING I HAVE WRITTEN; AND IT PLAYS WELL. NOT EVEN KIT MARLOWE WILL BE ABLE TO GAINSAY THAT.
You have not heard?
Marlowe is dead, Will. He died in Deptford, three weeks back, of a knife wound to the head.
WHO KILLED HIM? INGRAM FRASER, I'LL BE BOUND. CECIL'S MAN.
Yes.
OH, KIT. I TOLD YOU NOT TO PLAY WITH POLITICS.
WHY DID YOU TELL THIS TO ME NOW? THIS NEWS COULD HAVE WAITED.
I did not realize it would hurt you so.
MARLOWE WAS MY FRIEND.
YOU DID NOT REALIZE? NO, YOUR KIND CARE NOT FOR HUMAN LIVES.
DARK STRANGER, ALREADY I HALF-REGRET OUR BARGAIN. BUT COME, OUR NIGHT'S COMEDY BEGINS ONCE MORE.
...AND BONNY DRAGONS THAT WILL COME WHEN YOU DO CALL THEM AND FLY YOU THROUGH THE HONEYED AMBER SKIES.
THERE IS NO NIGHT IN MY LAND, PRETTY BOY, AND IT IS FOREVER SUMMER'S TWILIGHT.
My lady? The play will start anon.
THANK YOU, DREAM LORD.

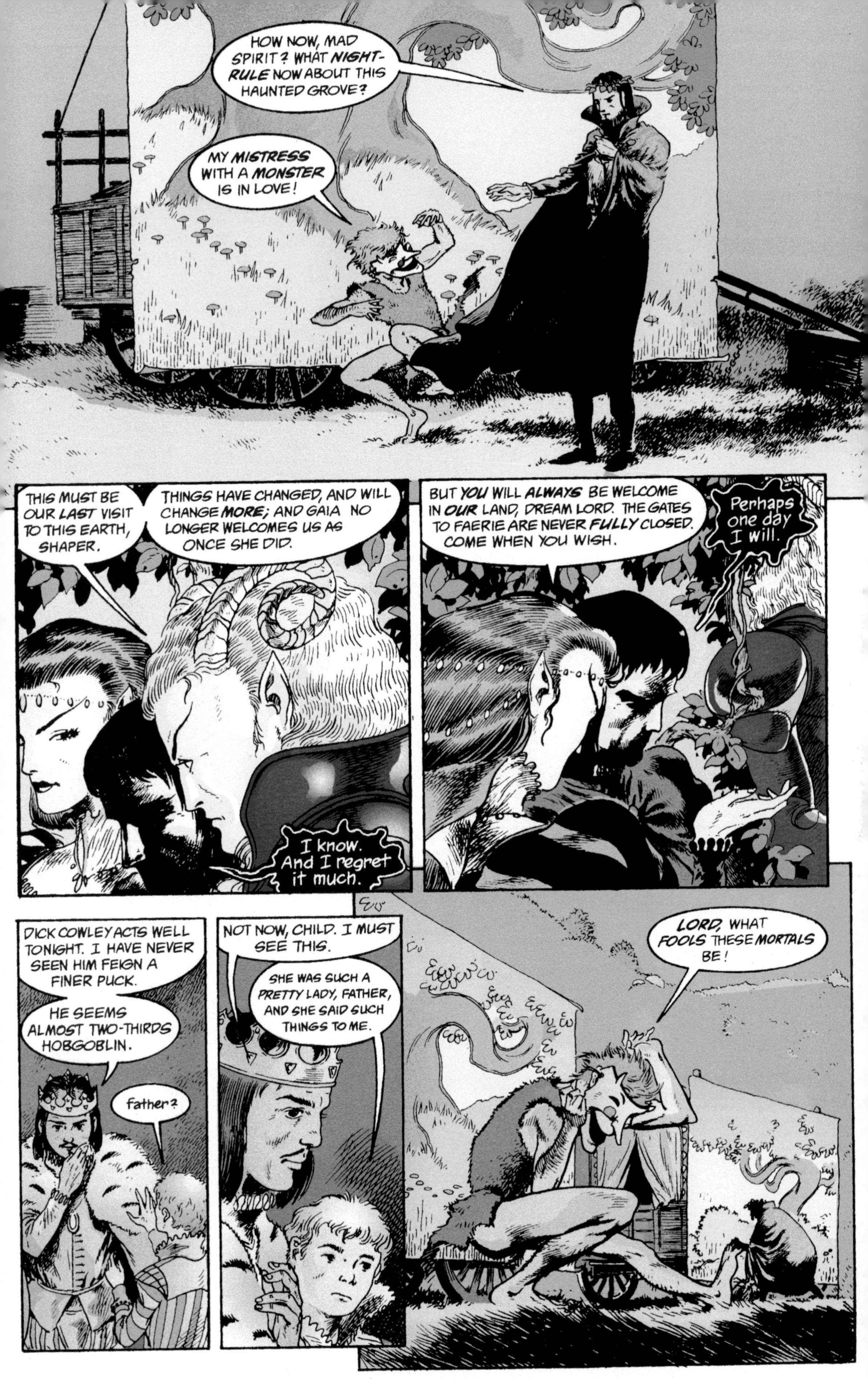
HOW NOW, MAD SPIRIT? WHAT NIGHT-RULE NOW ABOUT THIS HAUNTED GROVE?
MY MISTRESS WITH A MONSTER IS IN LOVE!
THIS MUST BE OUR LAST VISIT TO THIS EARTH, SHAPER.
THINGS HAVE CHANGED, AND WILL CHANGE MORE; AND GAIA NO LONGER WELCOMES US AS ONCE SHE DID.
I know. And I regret it much.
BUT YOU WILL ALWAYS BE WELCOME IN OUR LAND, DREAM LORD. THE GATES TO FAERIE ARE NEVER FULLY CLOSED. COME WHEN YOU WISH.
Perhaps one day I will.
DICK COWLEY ACTS WELL TONIGHT. I HAVE NEVER SEEN HIM FEIGN A FINER PUCK.
HE SEEMS ALMOST TWO-THIRDS HOBGOBLIN.
Father?
NOT NOW, CHILD. I MUST SEE THIS.
SHE WAS SUCH A PRETTY LADY, FATHER, AND SHE SAID SUCH THINGS TO ME.
LORD, WHAT FOOLS THESE MORTALS BE!

COME, SIT THEE DOWN UPON THIS FLOWERY BED, WHILE I THY AMIABLE CHEEKS DO COY, AND STICK MUSKROSES IN THY SLEEK, SMOOTH HEAD, --

--AND *KISS* THY FAIR LARGE EARS, MY GENTLE JOY.

WHERE'S *PEASEBLOSSOM?*

READY!

SCRATCH MY HEAD, PEASEBLOSSOM.

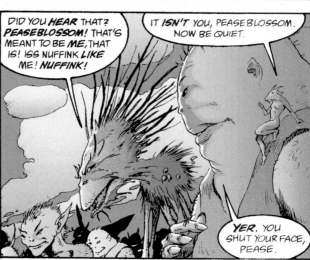

DID YOU *HEAR* THAT? *PEASEBLOSSOM!* THAT'S MEANT TO BE *ME*, THAT IS! ISS NUFFINK *LIKE* ME! *NUFFINK!*

IT *ISN'T* YOU, PEASE BLOSSOM. NOW BE QUIET.

YER. YOU SHUT YOUR FACE, PEASE.

ISSA *WOSSNAME.* TRAVELOGUE? NAH. *TRAVESTY.* THAT'S IT.

I'M THE ONLY PEASEBLOSSOM AMONG THE FAY. "SCRATCH HIS HEAD". *I'LL* GIVE HIM SCRATCH HIS BLEEDIN' HEAD!

PEASEBLOSSOM...

...AND *NOW* I HAVE THE BOY I WILL *UNDO* THIS HATEFUL IMPERFEC-TION OF HER EYES.

AND, GENTLE PUCK, TAKE THIS TRANSFORMED SCALP FROM OFF THE HEAD OF THIS ATHENIAN SWAIN.

MMMPH! MUMUMPH MM MPPH!

LIKE I SAID. I'M NOT HAVIN' YOU SPOILIN' IT FOR EVERYONE.

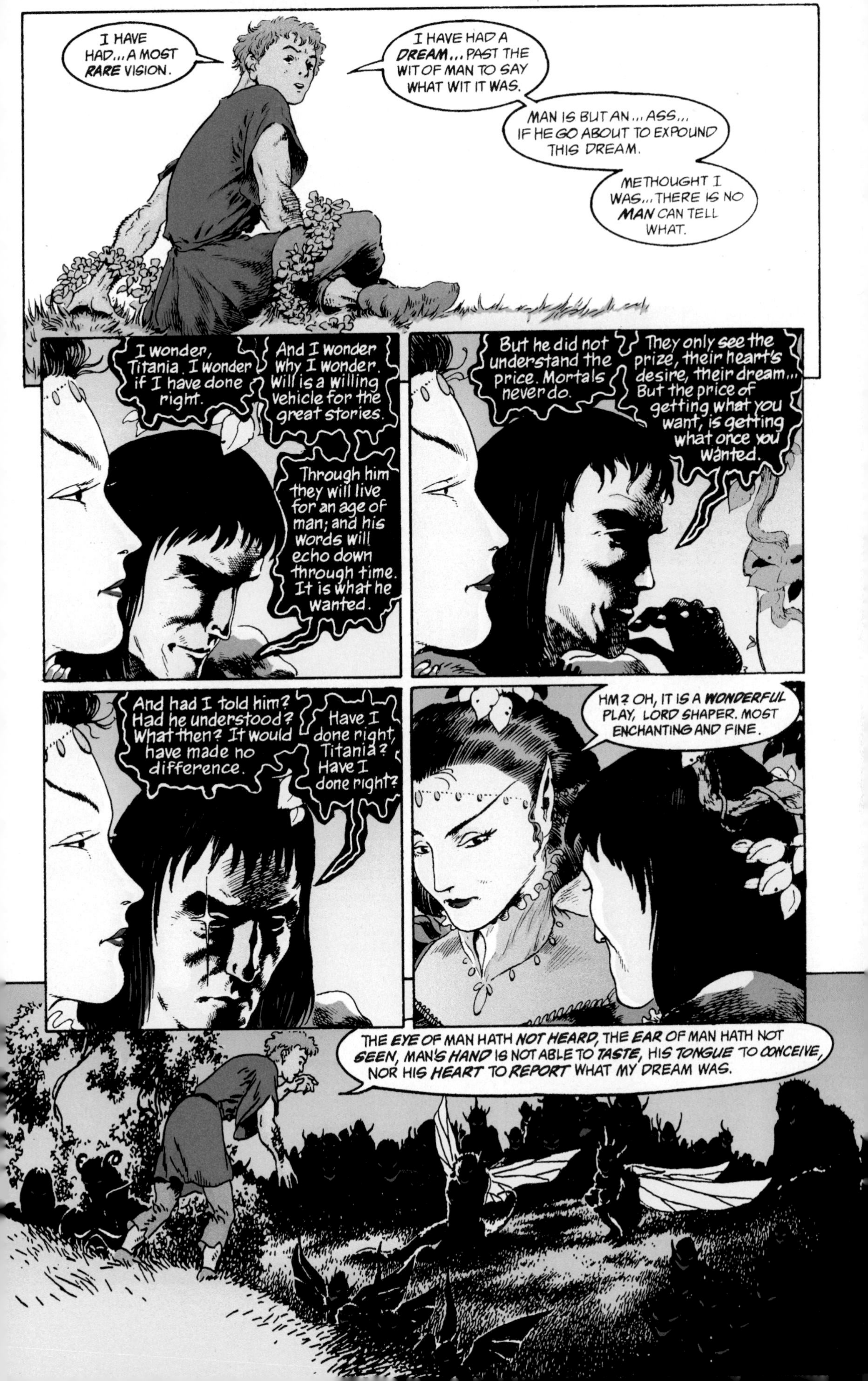
I HAVE HAD... A MOST RARE VISION.
I HAVE HAD A DREAM... PAST THE WIT OF MAN TO SAY WHAT WIT IT WAS.
MAN IS BUT AN... ASS... IF HE GO ABOUT TO EXPOUND THIS DREAM.
METHOUGHT I WAS... THERE IS NO MAN CAN TELL WHAT.
I wonder, Titania. I wonder if I have done right.
And I wonder why I wonder. Will is a willing vehicle for the great stories.
Through him they will live for an age of man; and his words will echo down through time. It is what he wanted.
But he did not understand the price. Mortals never do.
They only see the prize, their heart's desire, their dream... But the price of getting what you want, is getting what once you wanted.
And had I told him? Had he understood? What then? It would have made no difference.
Have I done right, Titania? Have I done right?
HM? OH, IT IS A WONDERFUL PLAY, LORD SHAPER. MOST ENCHANTING AND FINE.
THE EYE OF MAN HATH NOT HEARD, THE EAR OF MAN HATH NOT SEEN, MAN'S HAND IS NOT ABLE TO TASTE, HIS TONGUE TO CONCEIVE, NOR HIS HEART TO REPORT WHAT MY DREAM WAS.

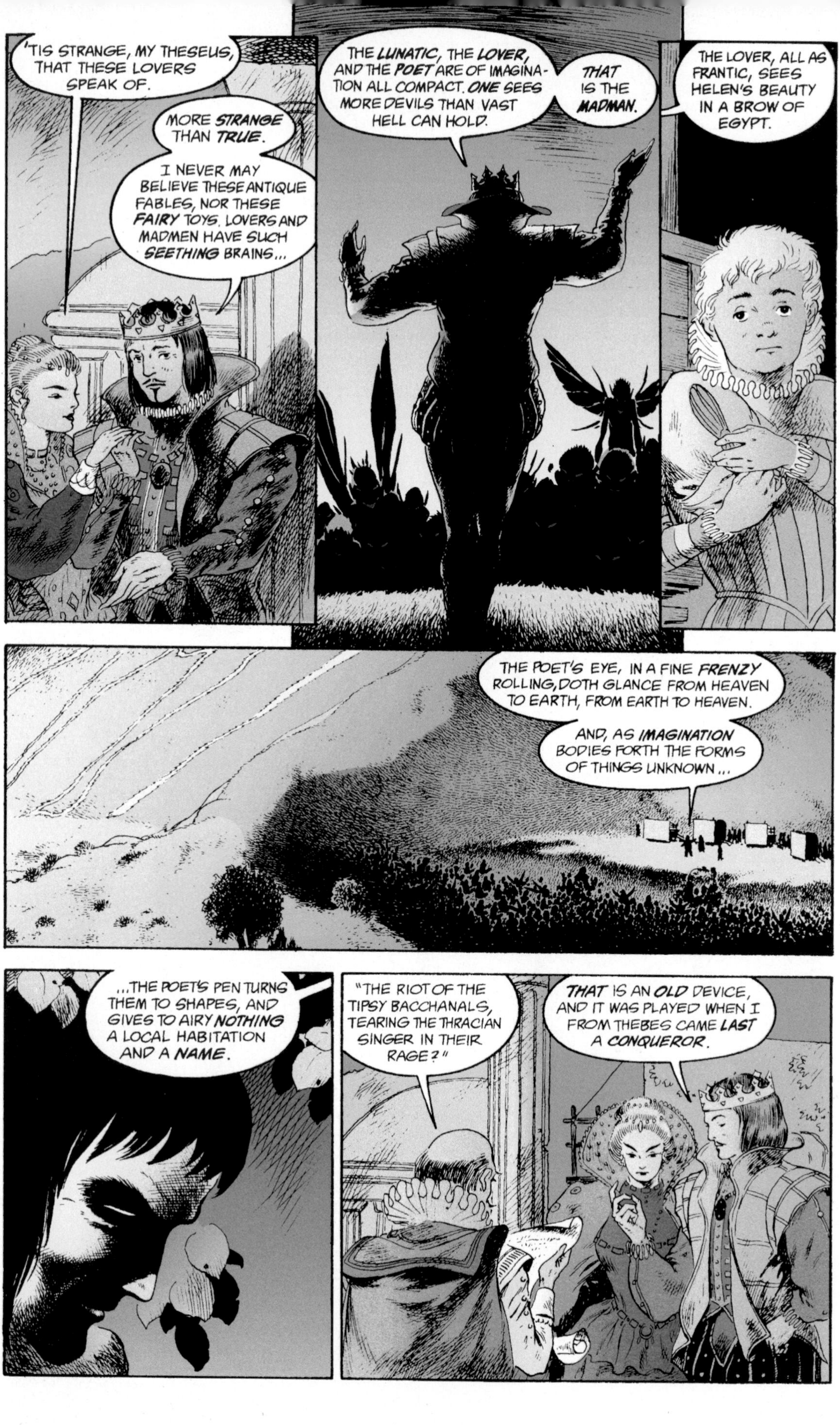
'TIS STRANGE, MY THESEUS, THAT THESE LOVERS SPEAK OF.
MORE STRANGE THAN TRUE.
I NEVER MAY BELIEVE THESE ANTIQUE FABLES, NOR THESE FAIRY TOYS. LOVERS AND MADMEN HAVE SUCH SEETHING BRAINS...
THE LUNATIC, THE LOVER, AND THE POET ARE OF IMAGINATION ALL COMPACT. ONE SEES MORE DEVILS THAN VAST HELL CAN HOLD.
THAT IS THE MADMAN.
THE LOVER, ALL AS FRANTIC, SEES HELEN'S BEAUTY IN A BROW OF EGYPT.
THE POET'S EYE, IN A FINE FRENZY ROLLING, DOTH GLANCE FROM HEAVEN TO EARTH, FROM EARTH TO HEAVEN.
AND, AS IMAGINATION BODIES FORTH THE FORMS OF THINGS UNKNOWN...
...THE POET'S PEN TURNS THEM TO SHAPES, AND GIVES TO AIRY NOTHING A LOCAL HABITATION AND A NAME.
"THE RIOT OF THE TIPSY BACCHANALS, TEARING THE THRACIAN SINGER IN THEIR RAGE?"
THAT IS AN OLD DEVICE, AND IT WAS PLAYED WHEN I FROM THEBES CAME LAST A CONQUEROR.

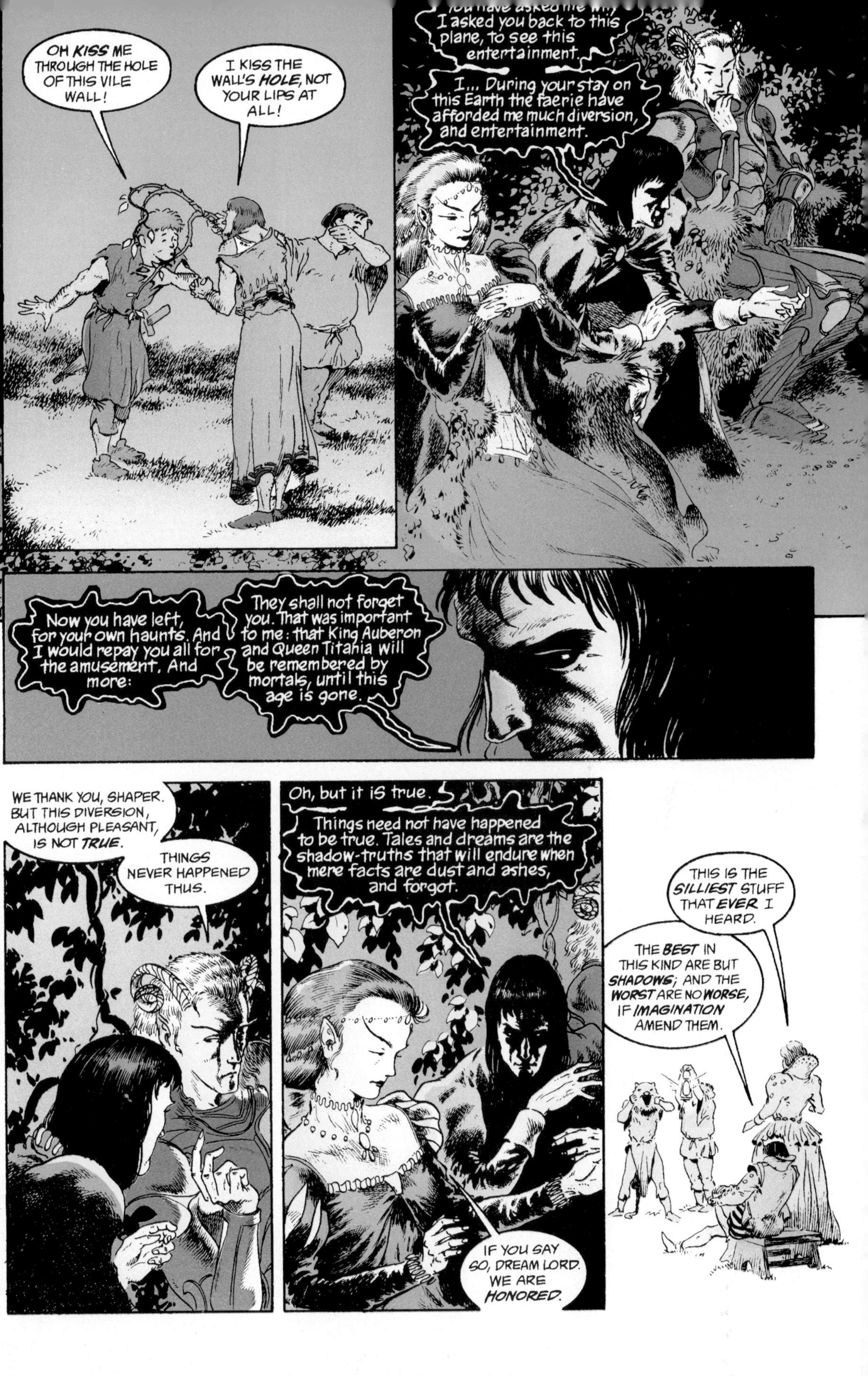

OH KISS ME THROUGH THE HOLE OF THIS VILE WALL!
I KISS THE WALL'S HOLE, NOT YOUR LIPS AT ALL!
I asked you back to this plane, to see this entertainment.
I... During your stay on this Earth the faerie have afforded me much diversion, and entertainment.
Now you have left, for your own haunts. And I would repay you all for the amusement. And more:
They shall not forget you. That was important to me: that King Auberon and Queen Titania will be remembered by mortals, until this age is gone.
WE THANK YOU, SHAPER. BUT THIS DIVERSION, ALTHOUGH PLEASANT, IS NOT TRUE.
THINGS NEVER HAPPENED THUS.
Oh, but it is true.
Things need not have happened to be true. Tales and dreams are the shadow-truths that will endure when mere facts are dust and ashes, and forgot.
IF YOU SAY SO, DREAM LORD. WE ARE HONORED.
THIS IS THE SILLIEST STUFF THAT EVER I HEARD.
THE BEST IN THIS KIND ARE BUT SHADOWS; AND THE WORST ARE NO WORSE, IF IMAGINATION AMEND THEM.

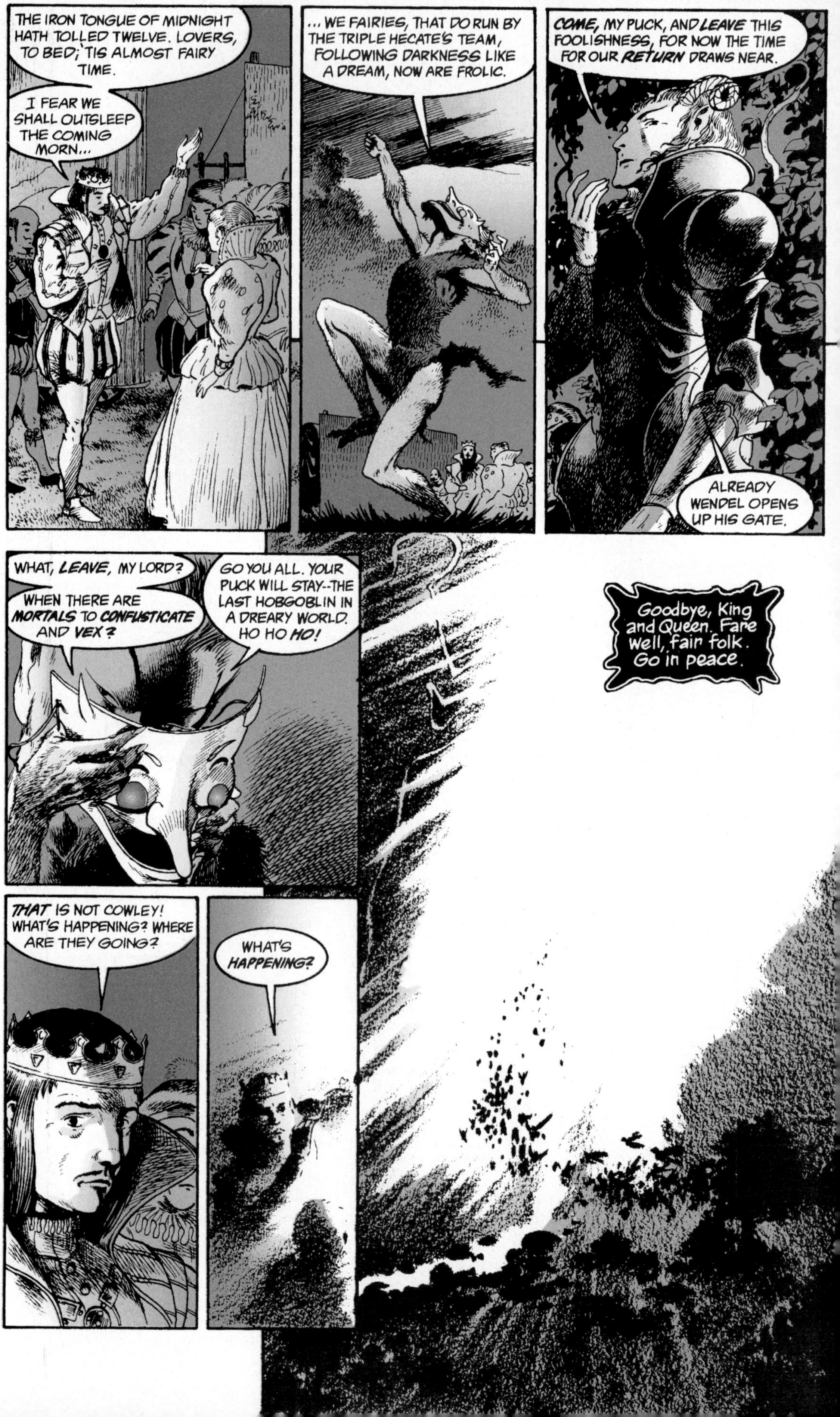
THE IRON TONGUE OF MIDNIGHT HATH TOLLED TWELVE. LOVERS, TO BED; 'TIS ALMOST FAIRY TIME.
I FEAR WE SHALL OUTSLEEP THE COMING MORN...
...WE FAIRIES, THAT DO RUN BY THE TRIPLE HECATE'S TEAM, FOLLOWING DARKNESS LIKE A DREAM, NOW ARE FROLIC.
COME, MY PUCK, AND LEAVE THIS FOOLISHNESS, FOR NOW THE TIME FOR OUR RETURN DRAWS NEAR.
ALREADY WENDEL OPENS UP HIS GATE.
WHAT, LEAVE, MY LORD?
WHEN THERE ARE MORTALS TO CONFUSTICATE AND VEX?
GO YOU ALL. YOUR PUCK WILL STAY--THE LAST HOBGOBLIN IN A DREARY WORLD. HO HO HO!
Goodbye, King and Queen. Fare well, fair folk. Go in peace.
THAT IS NOT COWLEY! WHAT'S HAPPENING? WHERE ARE THEY GOING?
WHAT'S HAPPENING?

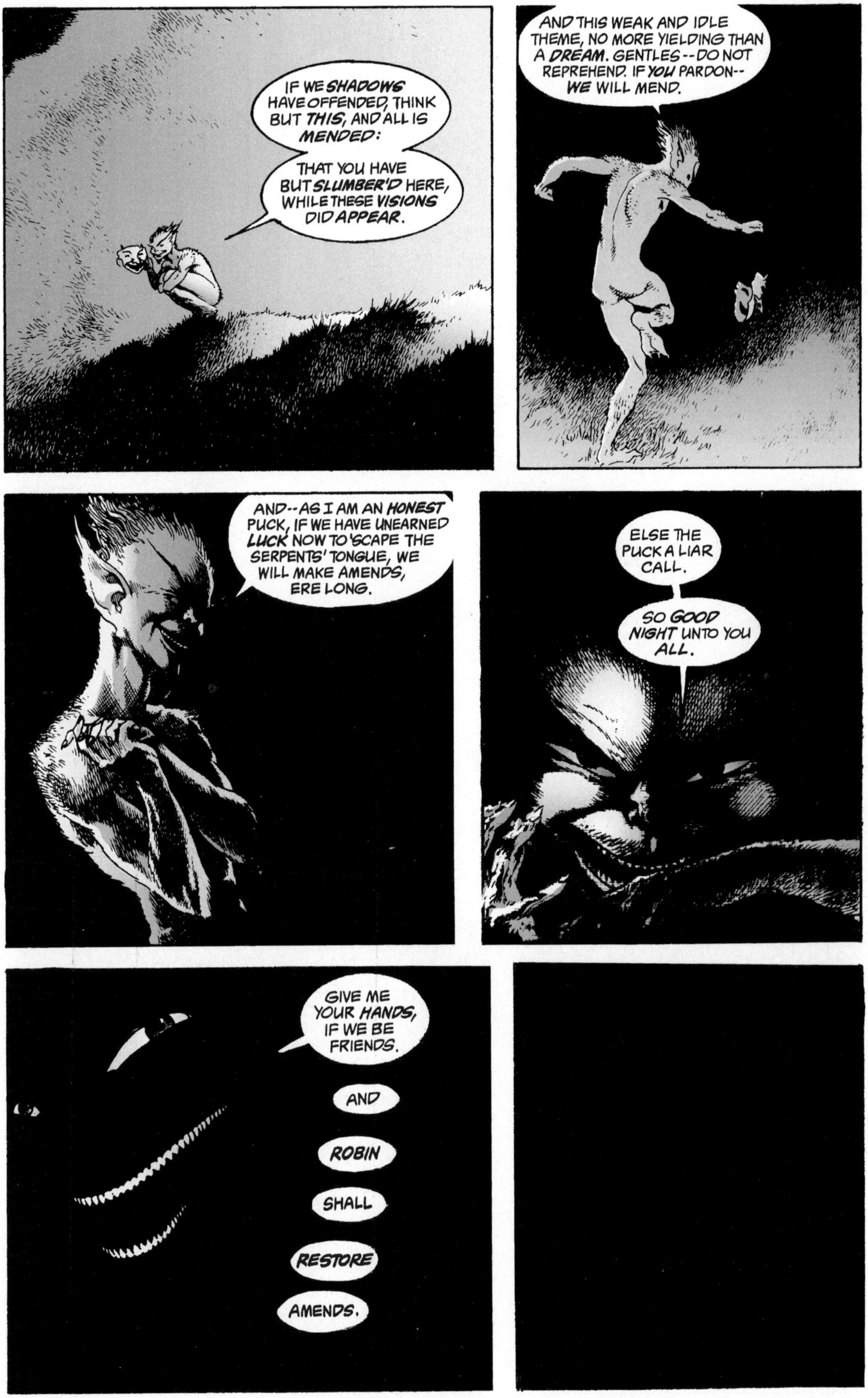
IF WE SHADOWS HAVE OFFENDED, THINK BUT THIS, AND ALL IS MENDED:
THAT YOU HAVE BUT SLUMBER'D HERE, WHILE THESE VISIONS DID APPEAR.
AND THIS WEAK AND IDLE THEME, NO MORE YIELDING THAN A DREAM. GENTLES--DO NOT REPREHEND. IF YOU PARDON--WE WILL MEND.
AND--AS I AM AN HONEST PUCK, IF WE HAVE UNEARNED LUCK NOW TO 'SCAPE THE SERPENTS' TONGUE, WE WILL MAKE AMENDS, ERE LONG.
ELSE THE PUCK A LIAR CALL.
SO GOOD NIGHT UNTO YOU ALL.
GIVE ME YOUR HANDS, IF WE BE FRIENDS.
AND
ROBIN
SHALL
RESTORE
AMENDS.

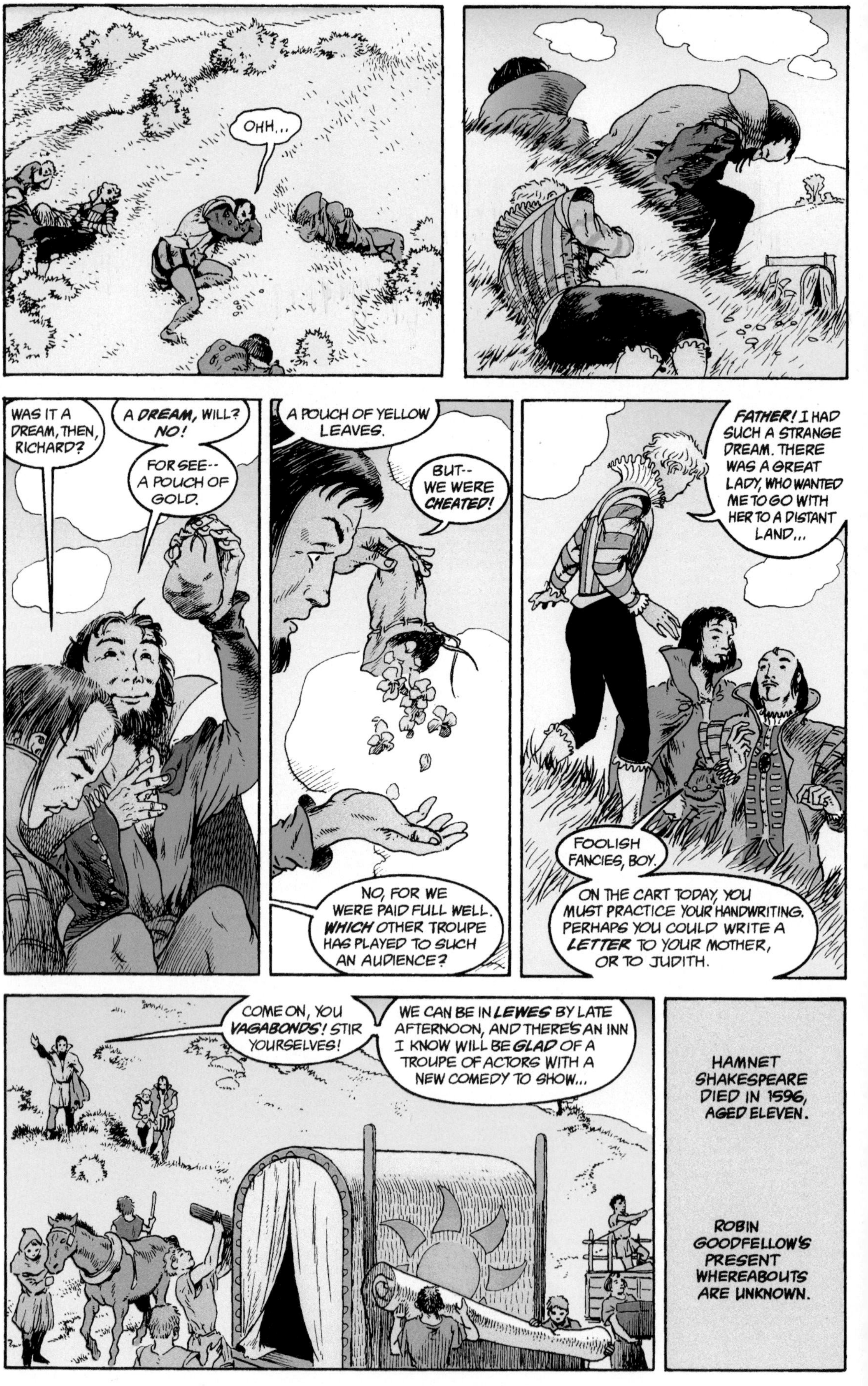
OHH...
WAS IT A DREAM, THEN, RICHARD?
A DREAM, WILL? NO!
FOR SEE-- A POUCH OF GOLD.
A POUCH OF YELLOW LEAVES.
BUT-- WE WERE CHEATED!
NO, FOR WE WERE PAID FULL WELL. WHICH OTHER TROUPE HAS PLAYED TO SUCH AN AUDIENCE?
FATHER! I HAD SUCH A STRANGE DREAM. THERE WAS A GREAT LADY, WHO WANTED ME TO GO WITH HER TO A DISTANT LAND...
FOOLISH FANCIES, BOY.
ON THE CART TODAY, YOU MUST PRACTICE YOUR HANDWRITING. PERHAPS YOU COULD WRITE A LETTER TO YOUR MOTHER, OR TO JUDITH.
COME ON, YOU VAGABONDS! STIR YOURSELVES!
WE CAN BE IN LEWES BY LATE AFTERNOON, AND THERE'S AN INN I KNOW WILL BE GLAD OF A TROUPE OF ACTORS WITH A NEW COMEDY TO SHOW...
HAMNET SHAKESPEARE DIED IN 1596, AGED ELEVEN.
ROBIN GOODFELLOW'S PRESENT WHEREABOUTS ARE UNKNOWN.

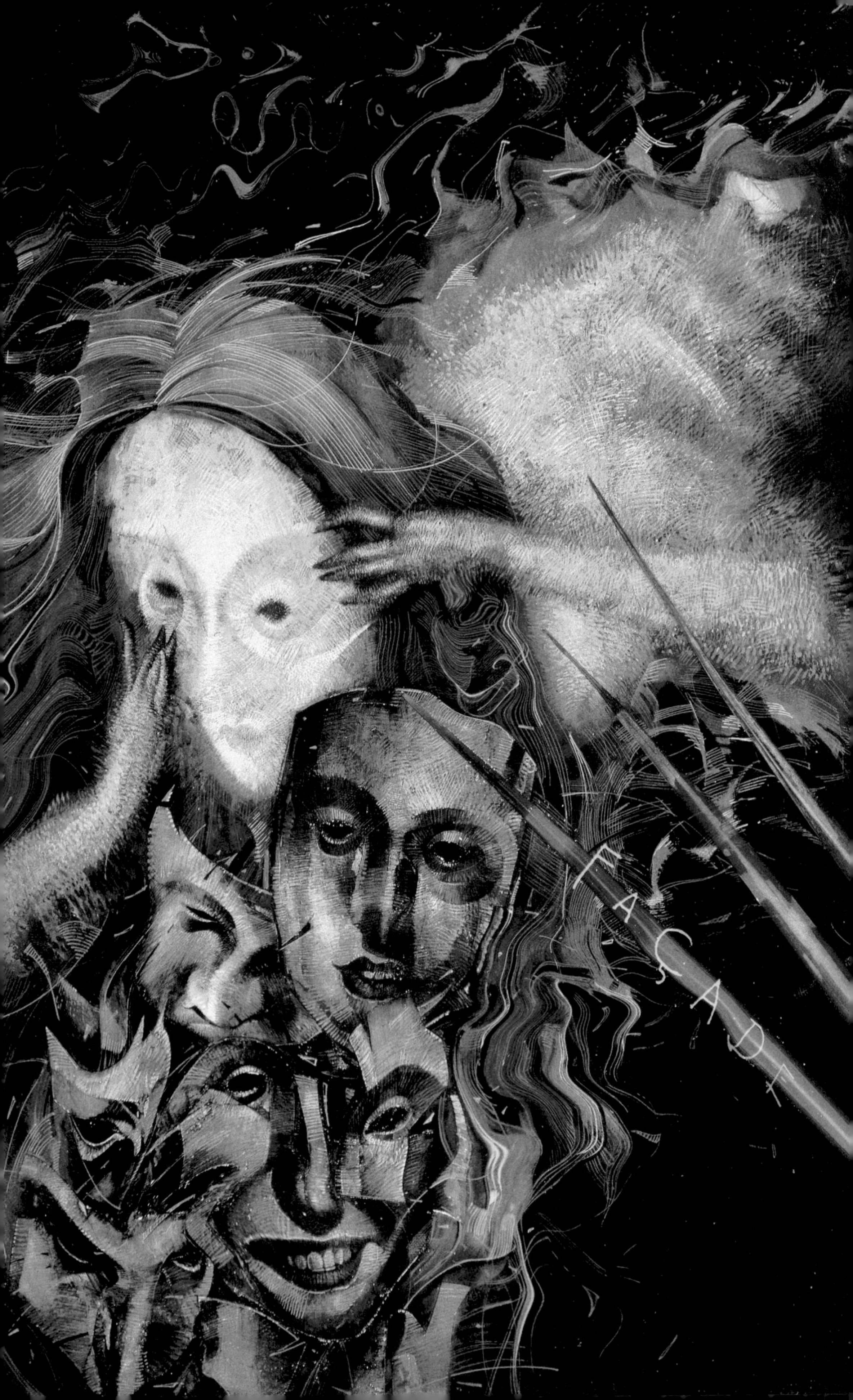
FAÇADE

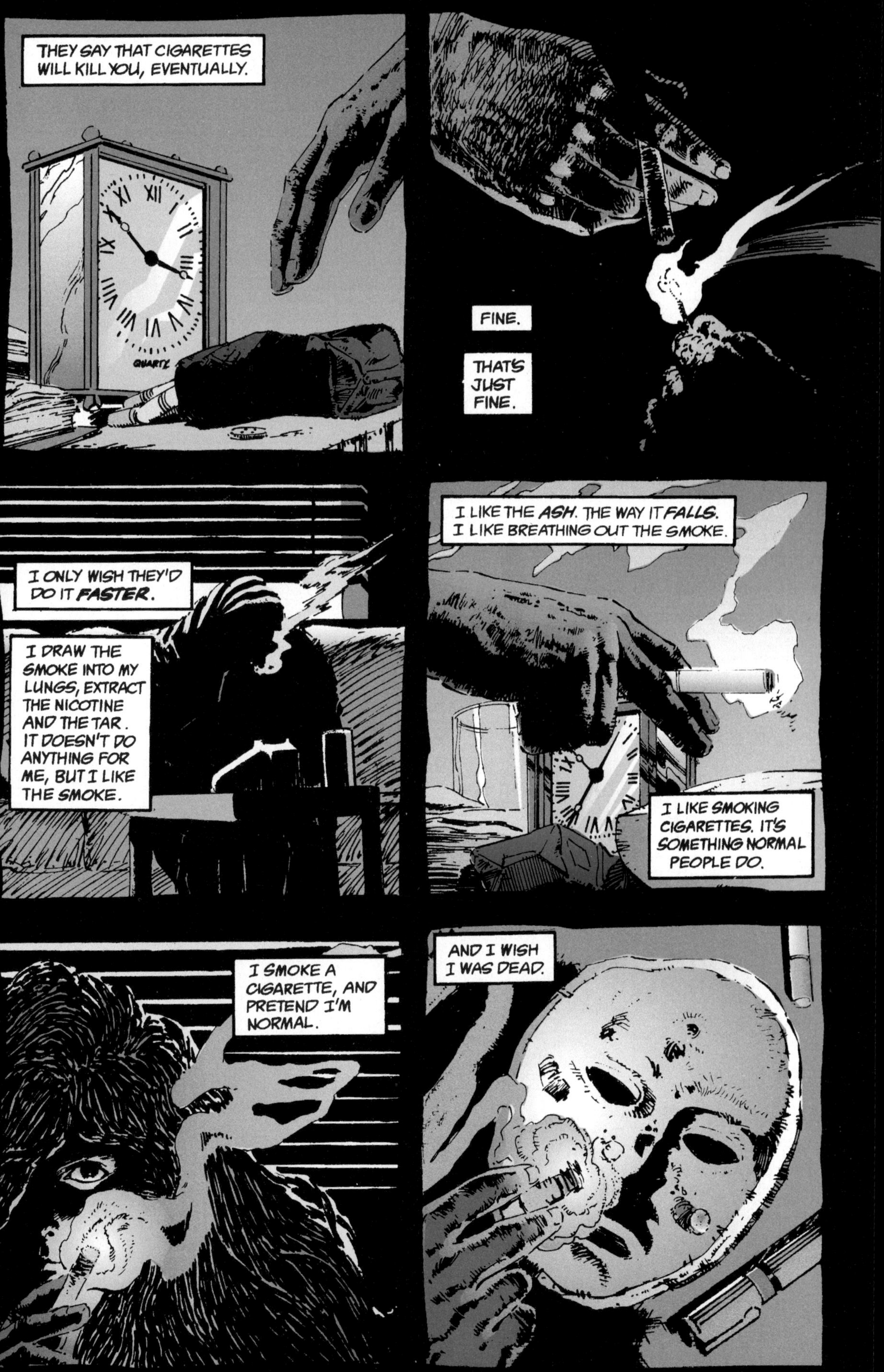
THEY SAY THAT CIGARETTES WILL KILL YOU, EVENTUALLY.
FINE.
THAT'S JUST FINE.
I ONLY WISH THEY'D DO IT FASTER.
I DRAW THE SMOKE INTO MY LUNGS, EXTRACT THE NICOTINE AND THE TAR. IT DOESN'T DO ANYTHING FOR ME, BUT I LIKE THE SMOKE.
I LIKE THE ASH. THE WAY IT FALLS. I LIKE BREATHING OUT THE SMOKE.
I LIKE SMOKING CIGARETTES. IT'S SOMETHING NORMAL PEOPLE DO.
I SMOKE A CIGARETTE, AND PRETEND I'M NORMAL.
AND I WISH I WAS DEAD.

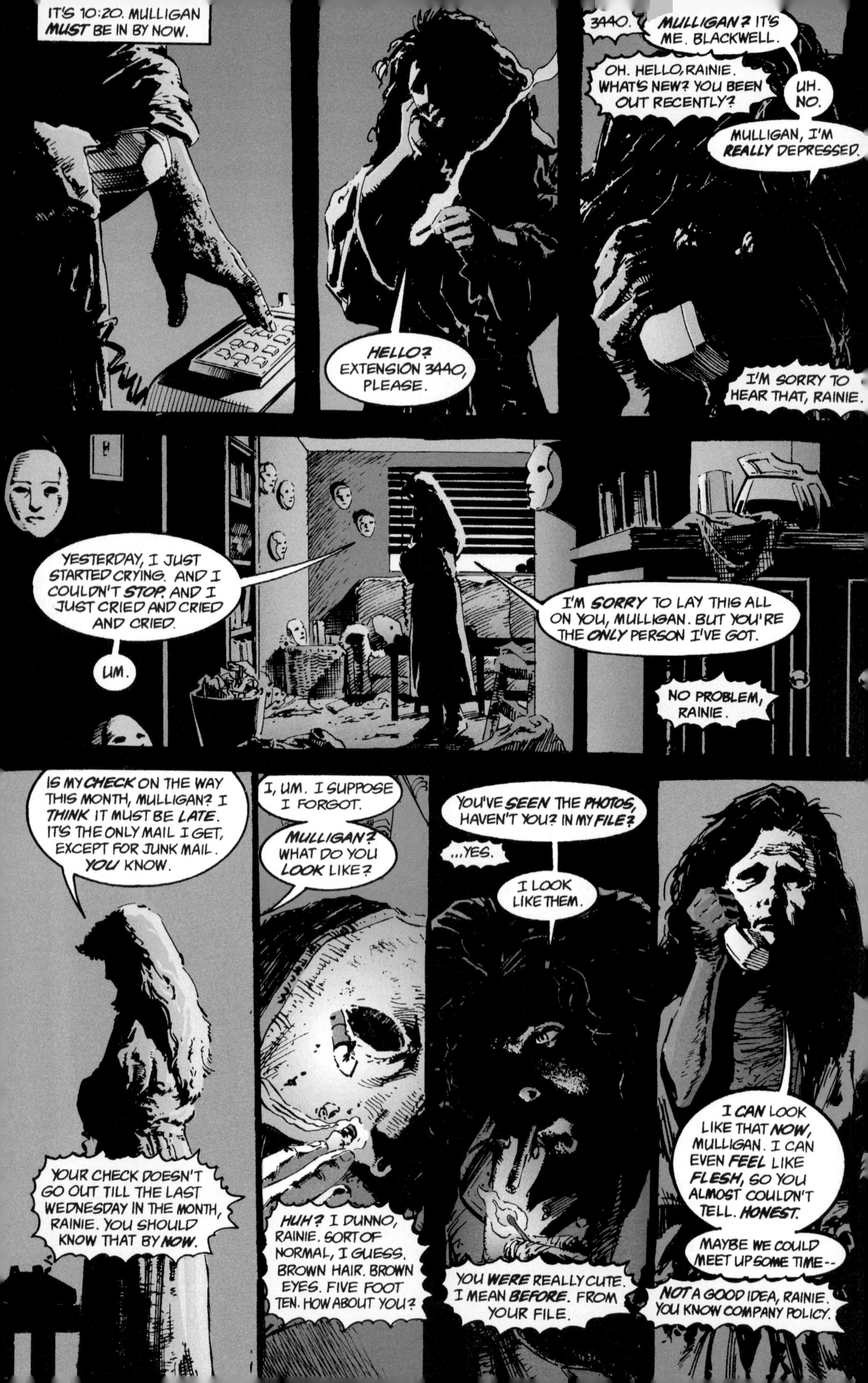
IT'S 10:20. MULLIGAN MUST BE IN BY NOW.
HELLO? EXTENSION 3440, PLEASE.
3440.
MULLIGAN? IT'S ME. BLACKWELL.
OH. HELLO, RAINIE. WHAT'S NEW? YOU BEEN OUT RECENTLY?
UH. NO.
MULLIGAN, I'M REALLY DEPRESSED.
I'M SORRY TO HEAR THAT, RAINIE.
YESTERDAY, I JUST STARTED CRYING. AND I COULDN'T STOP. AND I JUST CRIED AND CRIED AND CRIED.
UM.
I'M SORRY TO LAY THIS ALL ON YOU, MULLIGAN. BUT YOU'RE THE ONLY PERSON I'VE GOT.
NO PROBLEM, RAINIE.
IS MY CHECK ON THE WAY THIS MONTH, MULLIGAN? I THINK IT MUST BE LATE. IT'S THE ONLY MAIL I GET, EXCEPT FOR JUNK MAIL. YOU KNOW.
YOUR CHECK DOESN'T GO OUT TILL THE LAST WEDNESDAY IN THE MONTH, RAINIE. YOU SHOULD KNOW THAT BY NOW.
I, UM. I SUPPOSE I FORGOT.
MULLIGAN? WHAT DO YOU LOOK LIKE?
HUH? I DUNNO, RAINIE. SORT OF NORMAL, I GUESS. BROWN HAIR. BROWN EYES. FIVE FOOT TEN. HOW ABOUT YOU?
YOU'VE SEEN THE PHOTOS, HAVEN'T YOU? IN MY FILE?
...YES.
I LOOK LIKE THEM.
YOU WERE REALLY CUTE. I MEAN BEFORE. FROM YOUR FILE.
I CAN LOOK LIKE THAT NOW, MULLIGAN. I CAN EVEN FEEL LIKE FLESH, SO YOU ALMOST COULDN'T TELL. HONEST.
MAYBE WE COULD MEET UP SOME TIME--
NOT A GOOD IDEA, RAINIE. YOU KNOW COMPANY POLICY.

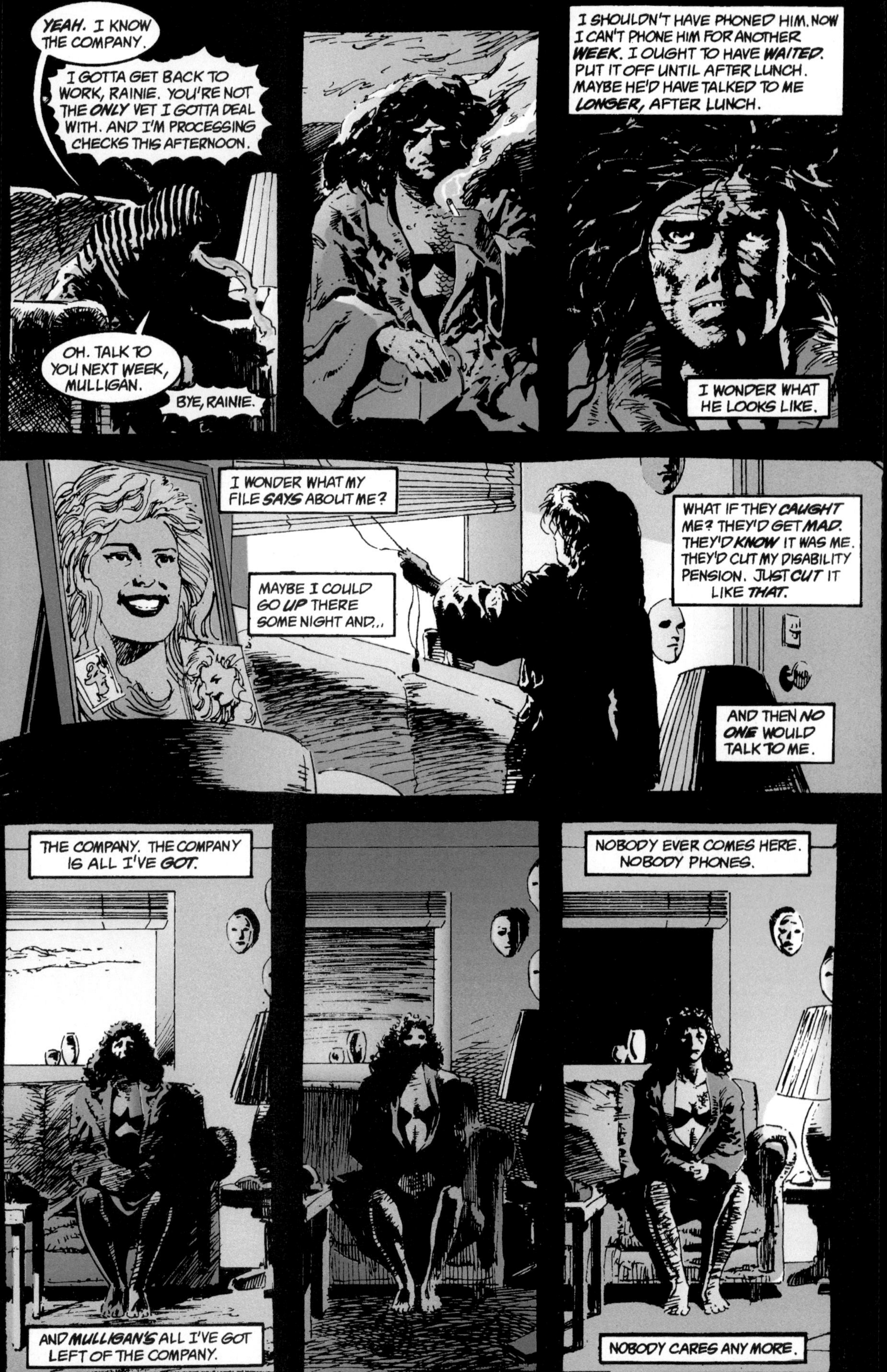
YEAH. I KNOW THE COMPANY.
I GOTTA GET BACK TO WORK, RAINIE. YOU'RE NOT THE ONLY VET I GOTTA DEAL WITH. AND I'M PROCESSING CHECKS THIS AFTERNOON.
OH. TALK TO YOU NEXT WEEK, MULLIGAN.
BYE, RAINIE.
I SHOULDN'T HAVE PHONED HIM. NOW I CAN'T PHONE HIM FOR ANOTHER WEEK. I OUGHT TO HAVE WAITED. PUT IT OFF UNTIL AFTER LUNCH. MAYBE HE'D HAVE TALKED TO ME LONGER, AFTER LUNCH.
I WONDER WHAT HE LOOKS LIKE.
I WONDER WHAT MY FILE SAYS ABOUT ME?
MAYBE I COULD GO UP THERE SOME NIGHT AND...
WHAT IF THEY CAUGHT ME? THEY'D GET MAD. THEY'D KNOW IT WAS ME. THEY'D CUT MY DISABILITY PENSION. JUST CUT IT LIKE THAT.
AND THEN NO ONE WOULD TALK TO ME.
THE COMPANY. THE COMPANY IS ALL I'VE GOT.
AND MULLIGAN'S ALL I'VE GOT LEFT OF THE COMPANY.
NOBODY EVER COMES HERE. NOBODY PHONES.
NOBODY CARES ANY MORE.

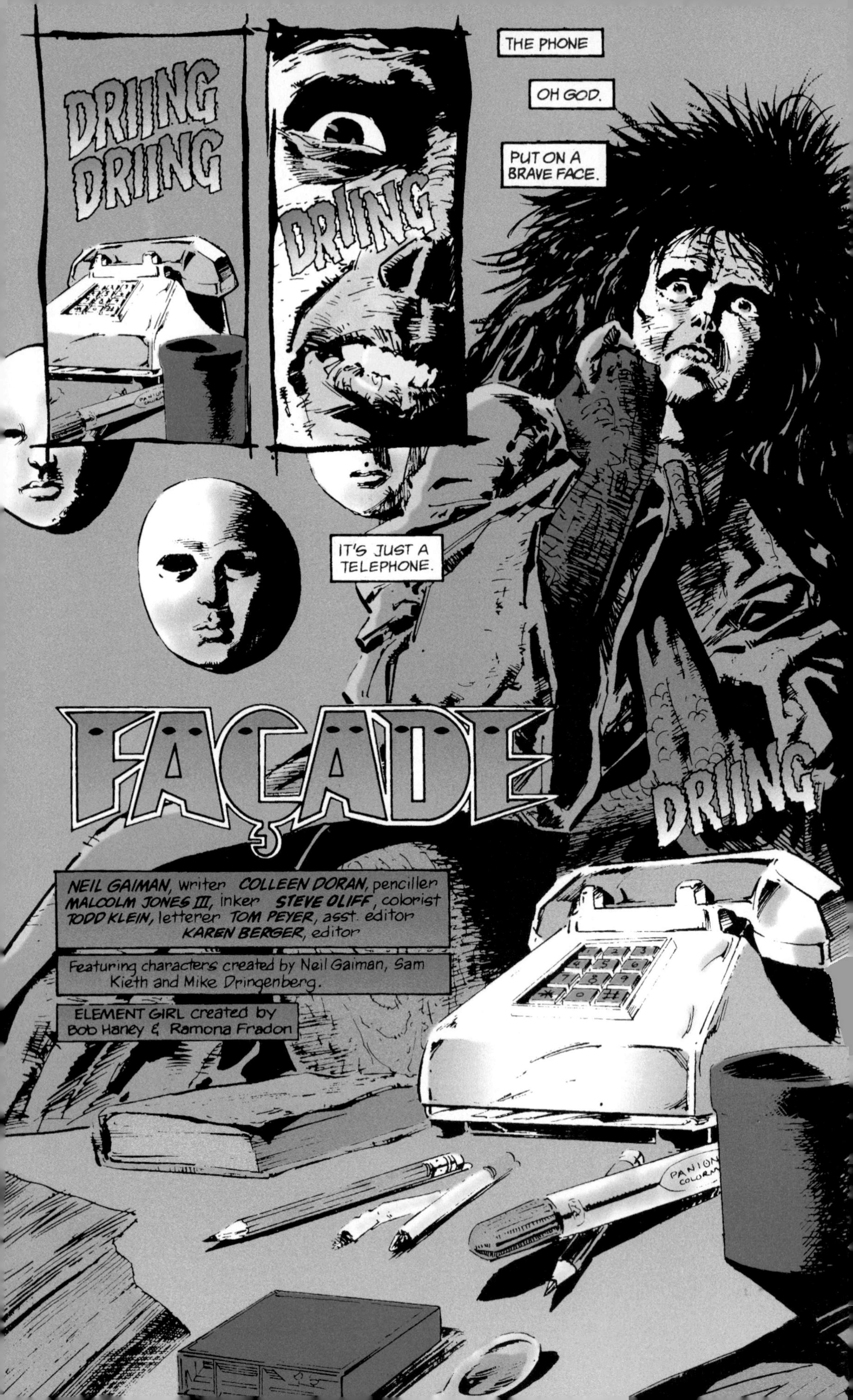
DRIING
DRING
DRING
THE PHONE
OH GOD.
PUT ON A BRAVE FACE.
IT'S JUST A TELEPHONE.
DRIING
FAÇADE
NEIL GAIMAN, writer COLLEEN DORAN, penciller
MALCOLM JONES III, inker STEVE OLIFF, colorist
TODD KLEIN, letterer TOM PEYER, asst. editor
KAREN BERGER, editor
Featuring characters created by Neil Gaiman, Sam Kieth and Mike Dringenberg.
ELEMENT GIRL created by Bob Haney & Ramona Fradon

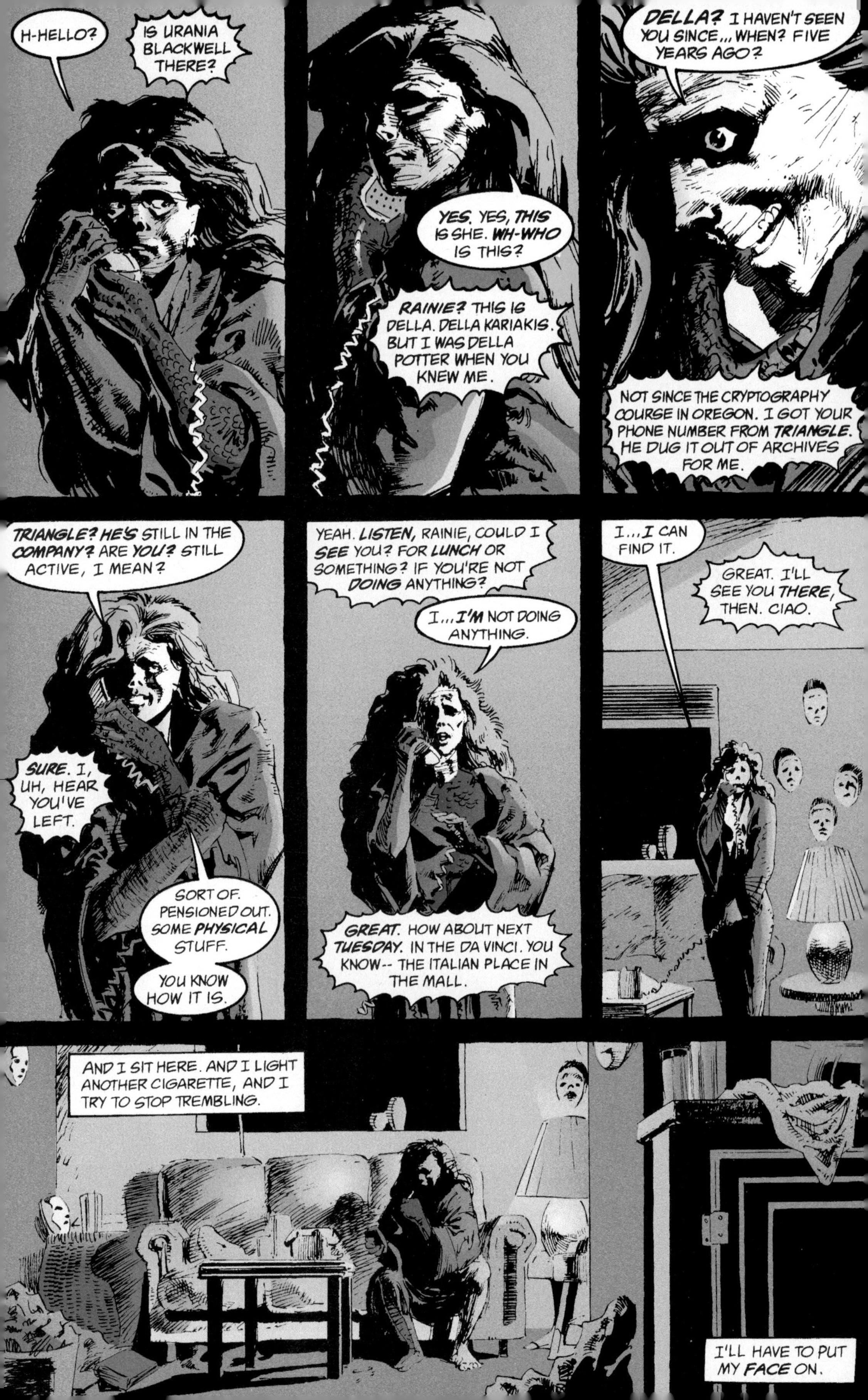
H-HELLO?
IS URANIA BLACKWELL THERE?
YES. YES, THIS IS SHE. WH-WHO IS THIS?
RAINIE? THIS IS DELLA. DELLA KARIAKIS. BUT I WAS DELLA POTTER WHEN YOU KNEW ME.
DELLA? I HAVEN'T SEEN YOU SINCE... WHEN? FIVE YEARS AGO?
NOT SINCE THE CRYPTOGRAPHY COURSE IN OREGON. I GOT YOUR PHONE NUMBER FROM TRIANGLE. HE DUG IT OUT OF ARCHIVES FOR ME.
TRIANGLE? HE'S STILL IN THE COMPANY? ARE YOU? STILL ACTIVE, I MEAN?
SURE. I, UH, HEAR YOU'VE LEFT.
SORT OF. PENSIONED OUT. SOME PHYSICAL STUFF.
YOU KNOW HOW IT IS.
YEAH. LISTEN, RAINIE, COULD I SEE YOU? FOR LUNCH OR SOMETHING? IF YOU'RE NOT DOING ANYTHING?
I... I'M NOT DOING ANYTHING.
GREAT. HOW ABOUT NEXT TUESDAY. IN THE DA VINCI. YOU KNOW-- THE ITALIAN PLACE IN THE MALL.
I... I CAN FIND IT.
GREAT. I'LL SEE YOU THERE, THEN. CIAO.
AND I SIT HERE. AND I LIGHT ANOTHER CIGARETTE, AND I TRY TO STOP TREMBLING.
I'LL HAVE TO PUT MY FACE ON.

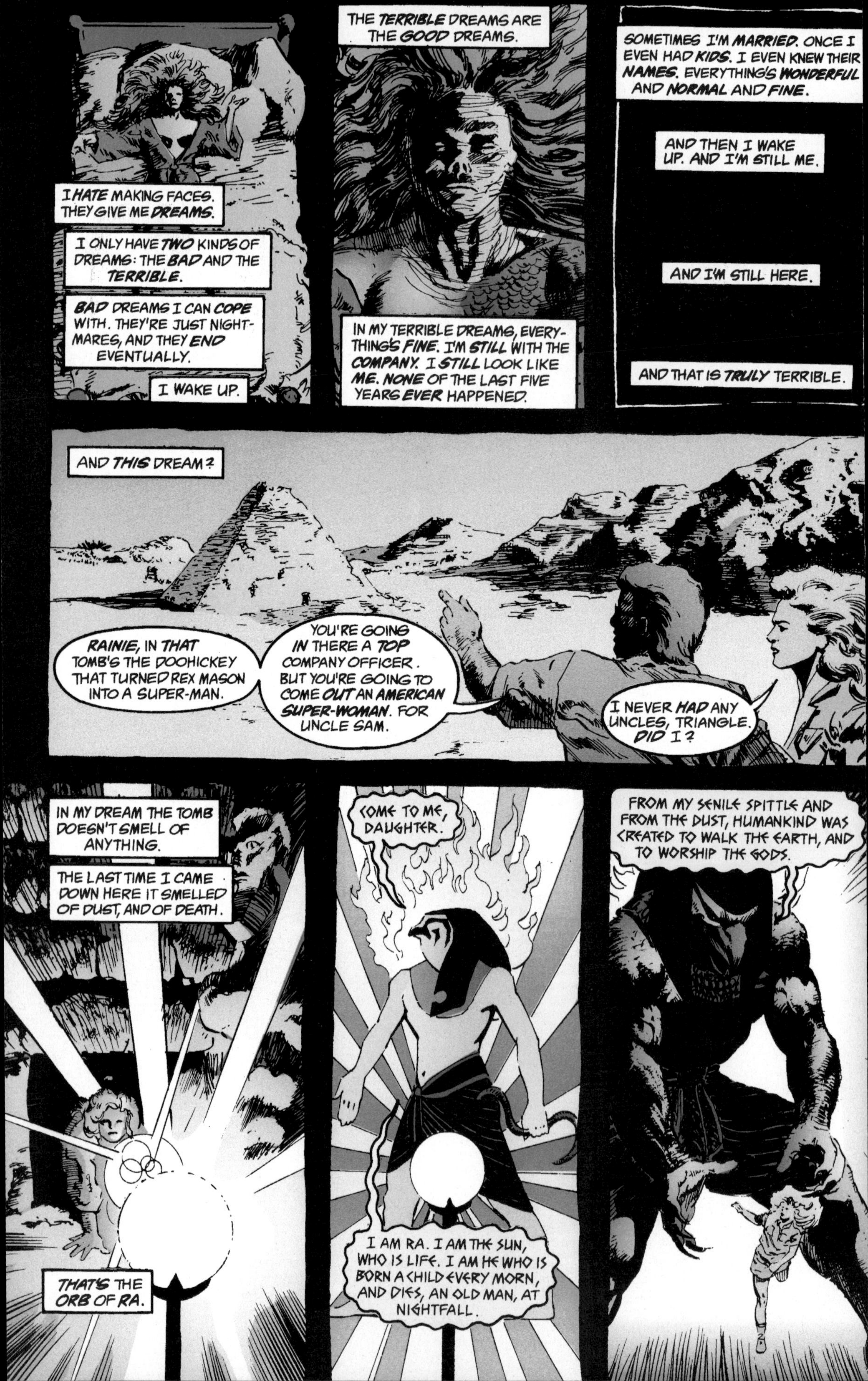
I HATE MAKING FACES. THEY GIVE ME DREAMS.
I ONLY HAVE TWO KINDS OF DREAMS: THE BAD AND THE TERRIBLE.
BAD DREAMS I CAN COPE WITH. THEY'RE JUST NIGHT-MARES, AND THEY END EVENTUALLY.
I WAKE UP.
THE TERRIBLE DREAMS ARE THE GOOD DREAMS.
IN MY TERRIBLE DREAMS, EVERY-THING'S FINE. I'M STILL WITH THE COMPANY. I STILL LOOK LIKE ME. NONE OF THE LAST FIVE YEARS EVER HAPPENED.
SOMETIMES I'M MARRIED. ONCE I EVEN HAD KIDS. I EVEN KNEW THEIR NAMES. EVERYTHING'S WONDERFUL AND NORMAL AND FINE.
AND THEN I WAKE UP. AND I'M STILL ME.
AND I'M STILL HERE.
AND THAT IS TRULY TERRIBLE.
AND THIS DREAM?
RAINIE, IN THAT TOMB'S THE DOOHICKEY THAT TURNED REX MASON INTO A SUPER-MAN.
YOU'RE GOING IN THERE A TOP COMPANY OFFICER. BUT YOU'RE GOING TO COME OUT AN AMERICAN SUPER-WOMAN. FOR UNCLE SAM.
I NEVER HAD ANY UNCLES, TRIANGLE. DID I?
IN MY DREAM THE TOMB DOESN'T SMELL OF ANYTHING.
THE LAST TIME I CAME DOWN HERE IT SMELLED OF DUST, AND OF DEATH.
THAT'S THE ORB OF RA.
COME TO ME, DAUGHTER.
I AM RA. I AM THE SUN, WHO IS LIFE. I AM HE WHO IS BORN A CHILD EVERY MORN, AND DIES, AN OLD MAN, AT NIGHTFALL.
FROM MY SENILE SPITTLE AND FROM THE DUST, HUMANKIND WAS CREATED TO WALK THE EARTH, AND TO WORSHIP THE GODS.

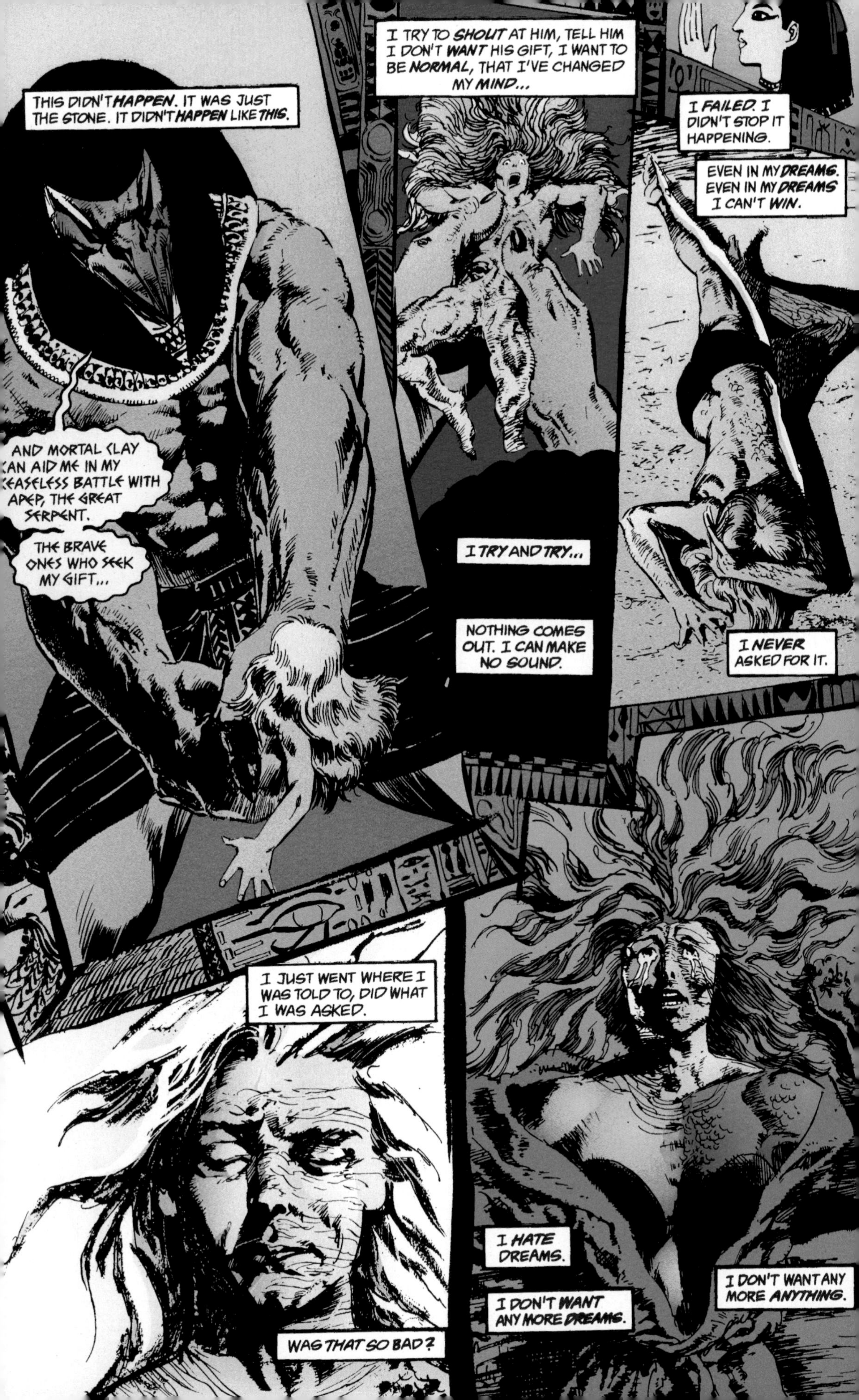

THIS DIDN'T HAPPEN. IT WAS JUST THE STONE. IT DIDN'T HAPPEN LIKE THIS.
AND MORTAL CLAY CAN AID ME IN MY CEASELESS BATTLE WITH APEP, THE GREAT SERPENT.
THE BRAVE ONES WHO SEEK MY GIFT...
I TRY TO SHOUT AT HIM, TELL HIM I DON'T WANT HIS GIFT, I WANT TO BE NORMAL, THAT I'VE CHANGED MY MIND...
I TRY AND TRY...
NOTHING COMES OUT. I CAN MAKE NO SOUND.
I FAILED. I DIDN'T STOP IT HAPPENING.
EVEN IN MY DREAMS. EVEN IN MY DREAMS I CAN'T WIN.
I NEVER ASKED FOR IT.
I JUST WENT WHERE I WAS TOLD TO, DID WHAT I WAS ASKED.
WAS THAT SO BAD?
I HATE DREAMS.
I DON'T WANT ANY MORE DREAMS.
I DON'T WANT ANY MORE ANYTHING.

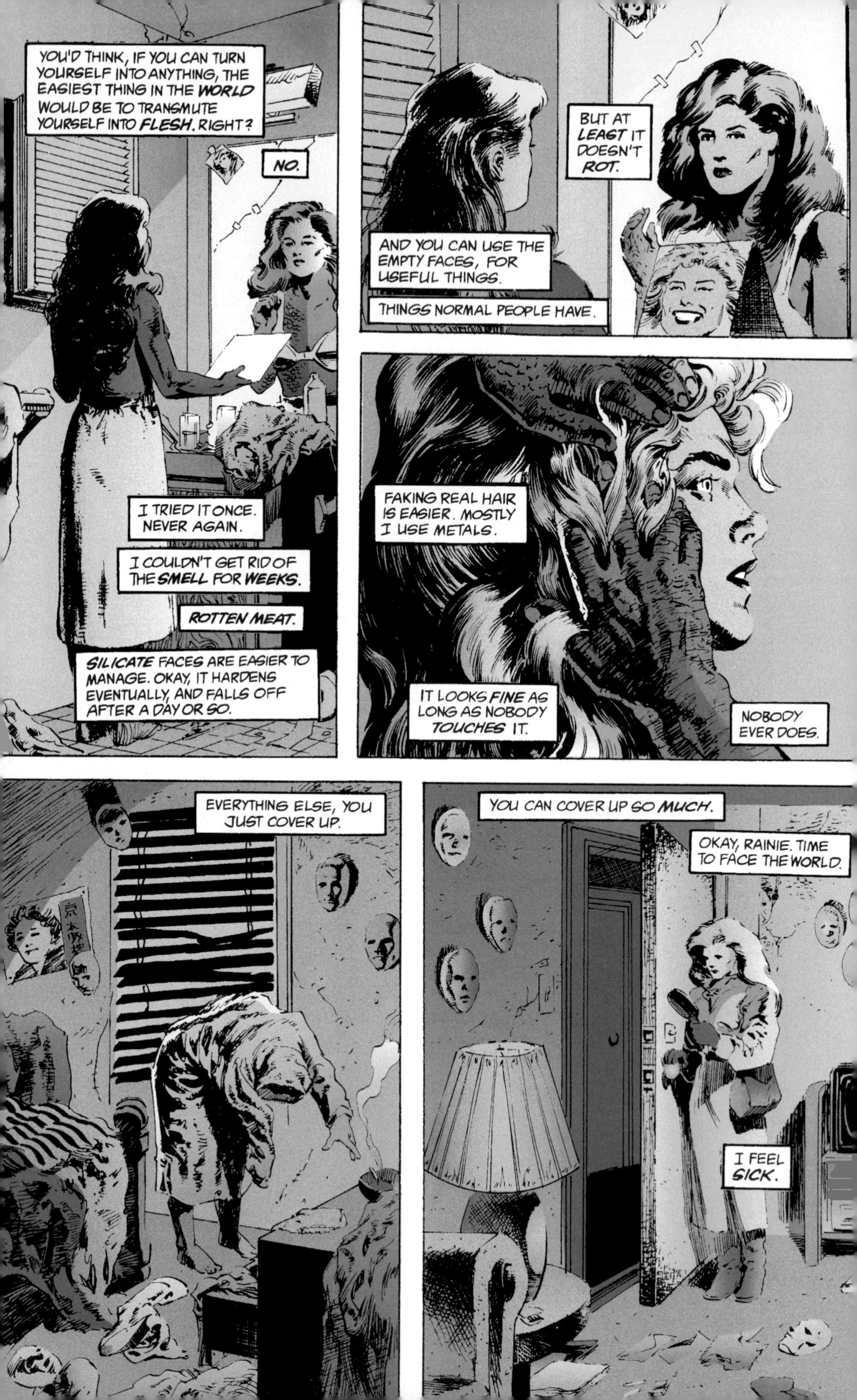

YOU'D THINK, IF YOU CAN TURN YOURSELF INTO ANYTHING, THE EASIEST THING IN THE WORLD WOULD BE TO TRANSMUTE YOURSELF INTO FLESH. RIGHT?
NO.
I TRIED IT ONCE. NEVER AGAIN.
I COULDN'T GET RID OF THE SMELL FOR WEEKS.
ROTTEN MEAT.
SILICATE FACES ARE EASIER TO MANAGE. OKAY, IT HARDENS EVENTUALLY, AND FALLS OFF AFTER A DAY OR SO.
BUT AT LEAST IT DOESN'T ROT.
AND YOU CAN USE THE EMPTY FACES, FOR USEFUL THINGS.
THINGS NORMAL PEOPLE HAVE.
FAKING REAL HAIR IS EASIER. MOSTLY I USE METALS.
IT LOOKS FINE AS LONG AS NOBODY TOUCHES IT.
NOBODY EVER DOES.
EVERYTHING ELSE, YOU JUST COVER UP.
YOU CAN COVER UP SO MUCH.
OKAY, RAINIE. TIME TO FACE THE WORLD.
I FEEL SICK.

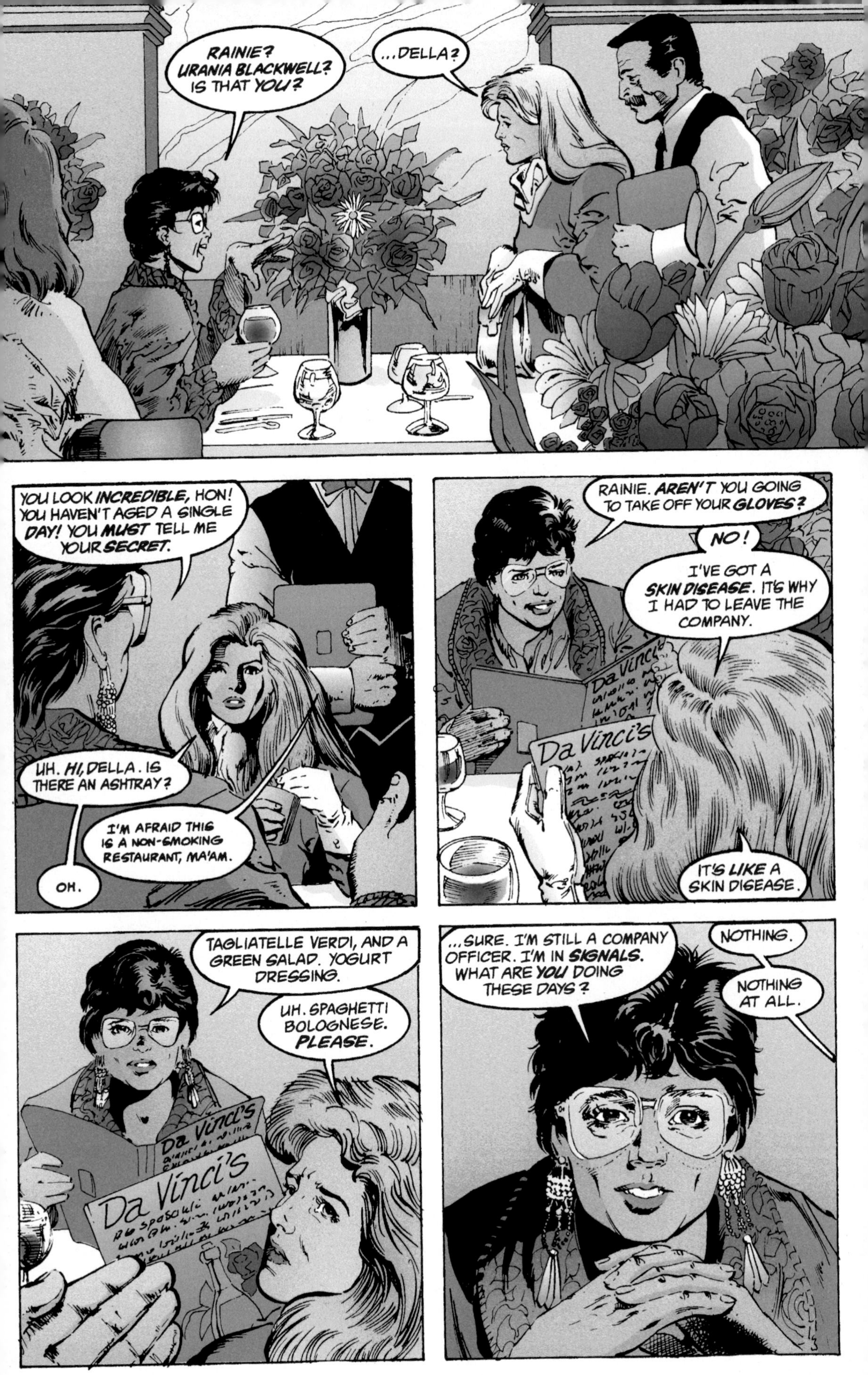
RAINIE? URANIA BLACKWELL? IS THAT YOU?
...DELLA?
YOU LOOK INCREDIBLE, HON! YOU HAVEN'T AGED A SINGLE DAY! YOU MUST TELL ME YOUR SECRET.
UH. HI, DELLA. IS THERE AN ASHTRAY?
I'M AFRAID THIS IS A NON-SMOKING RESTAURANT, MA'AM.
OH.
RAINIE. AREN'T YOU GOING TO TAKE OFF YOUR GLOVES?
NO!
I'VE GOT A SKIN DISEASE. IT'S WHY I HAD TO LEAVE THE COMPANY.
IT'S LIKE A SKIN DISEASE.
Da Vinci's
TAGLIATELLE VERDI, AND A GREEN SALAD. YOGURT DRESSING.
UH. SPAGHETTI BOLOGNESE. PLEASE.
Da Vinci's
...SURE. I'M STILL A COMPANY OFFICER. I'M IN SIGNALS. WHAT ARE YOU DOING THESE DAYS?
NOTHING.
NOTHING AT ALL.

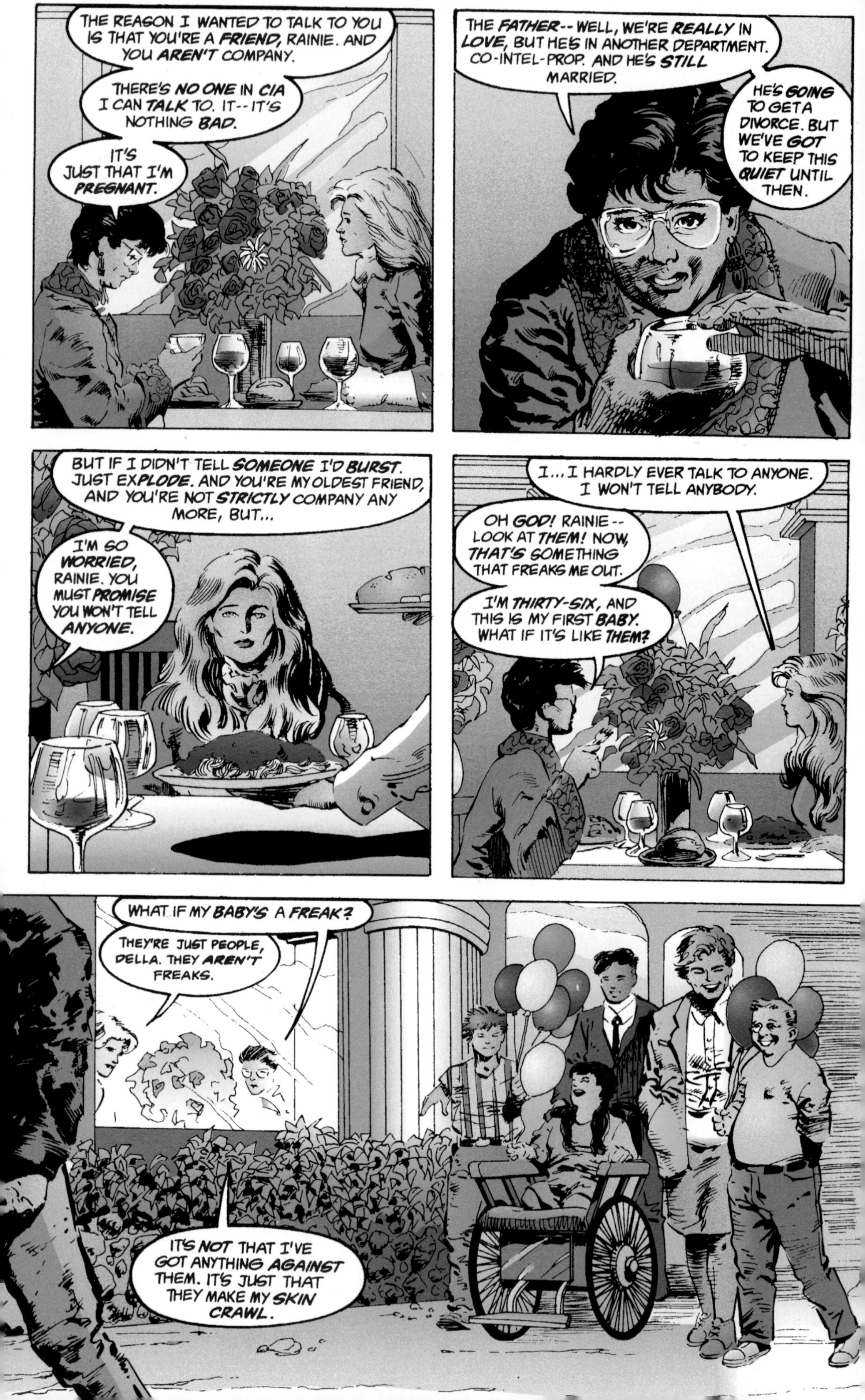
THE REASON I WANTED TO TALK TO YOU IS THAT YOU'RE A FRIEND, RAINIE. AND YOU AREN'T COMPANY.
THERE'S NO ONE IN CIA I CAN TALK TO. IT--IT'S NOTHING BAD.
IT'S JUST THAT I'M PREGNANT.
THE FATHER--WELL, WE'RE REALLY IN LOVE, BUT HE'S IN ANOTHER DEPARTMENT. CO-INTEL-PROP. AND HE'S STILL MARRIED.
HE'S GOING TO GET A DIVORCE. BUT WE'VE GOT TO KEEP THIS QUIET UNTIL THEN.
BUT IF I DIDN'T TELL SOMEONE I'D BURST. JUST EXPLODE. AND YOU'RE MY OLDEST FRIEND, AND YOU'RE NOT STRICTLY COMPANY ANY MORE, BUT...
I'M SO WORRIED, RAINIE. YOU MUST PROMISE YOU WON'T TELL ANYONE.
I... I HARDLY EVER TALK TO ANYONE. I WON'T TELL ANYBODY.
OH GOD! RAINIE--LOOK AT THEM! NOW, THAT'S SOMETHING THAT FREAKS ME OUT.
I'M THIRTY-SIX, AND THIS IS MY FIRST BABY. WHAT IF IT'S LIKE THEM?
WHAT IF MY BABY'S A FREAK?
THEY'RE JUST PEOPLE, DELLA. THEY AREN'T FREAKS.
IT'S NOT THAT I'VE GOT ANYTHING AGAINST THEM. IT'S JUST THAT THEY MAKE MY SKIN CRAWL.

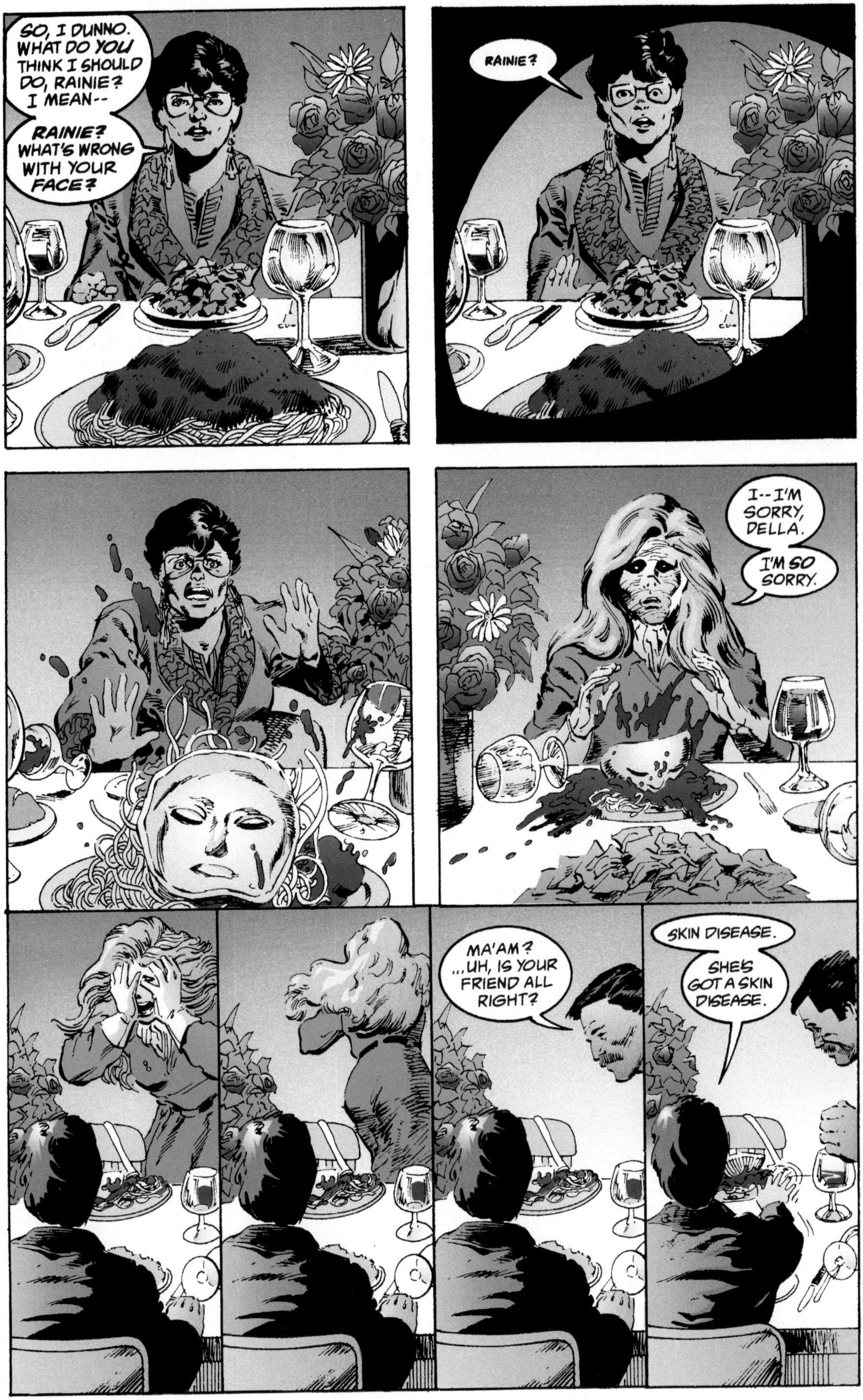
SO, I DUNNO. WHAT DO YOU THINK I SHOULD DO, RAINIE? I MEAN--
RAINIE? WHAT'S WRONG WITH YOUR FACE?
RAINIE?
I--I'M SORRY, DELLA.
I'M SO SORRY.
MA'AM? ...UH, IS YOUR FRIEND ALL RIGHT?
SKIN DISEASE.
SHE'S GOT A SKIN DISEASE.

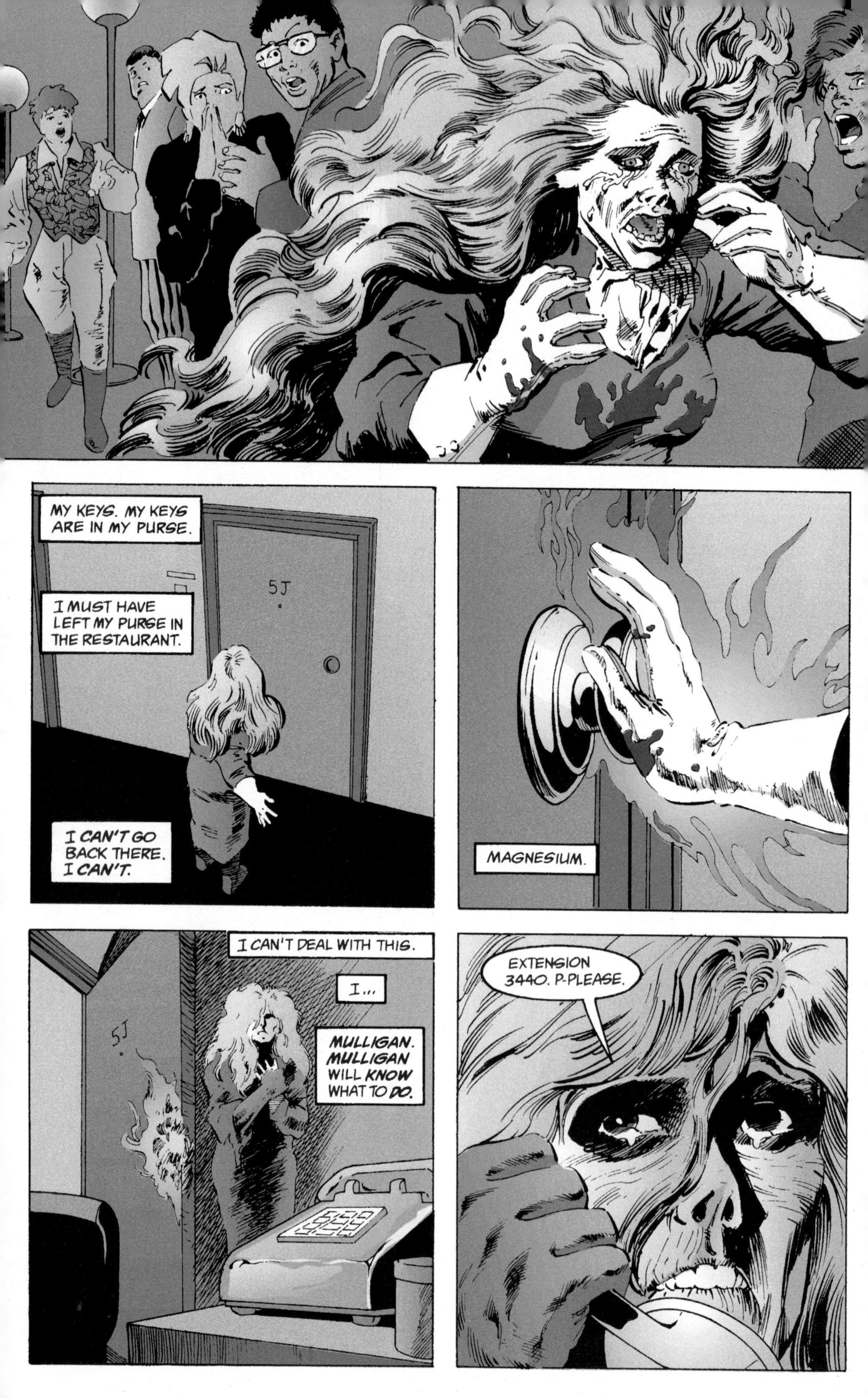
MY KEYS. MY KEYS ARE IN MY PURSE.
5J
I MUST HAVE LEFT MY PURSE IN THE RESTAURANT.
I CAN'T GO BACK THERE. I CAN'T.
MAGNESIUM.
I CAN'T DEAL WITH THIS.
I...
MULLIGAN. MULLIGAN WILL KNOW WHAT TO DO.
5J
EXTENSION 3440. P-PLEASE.

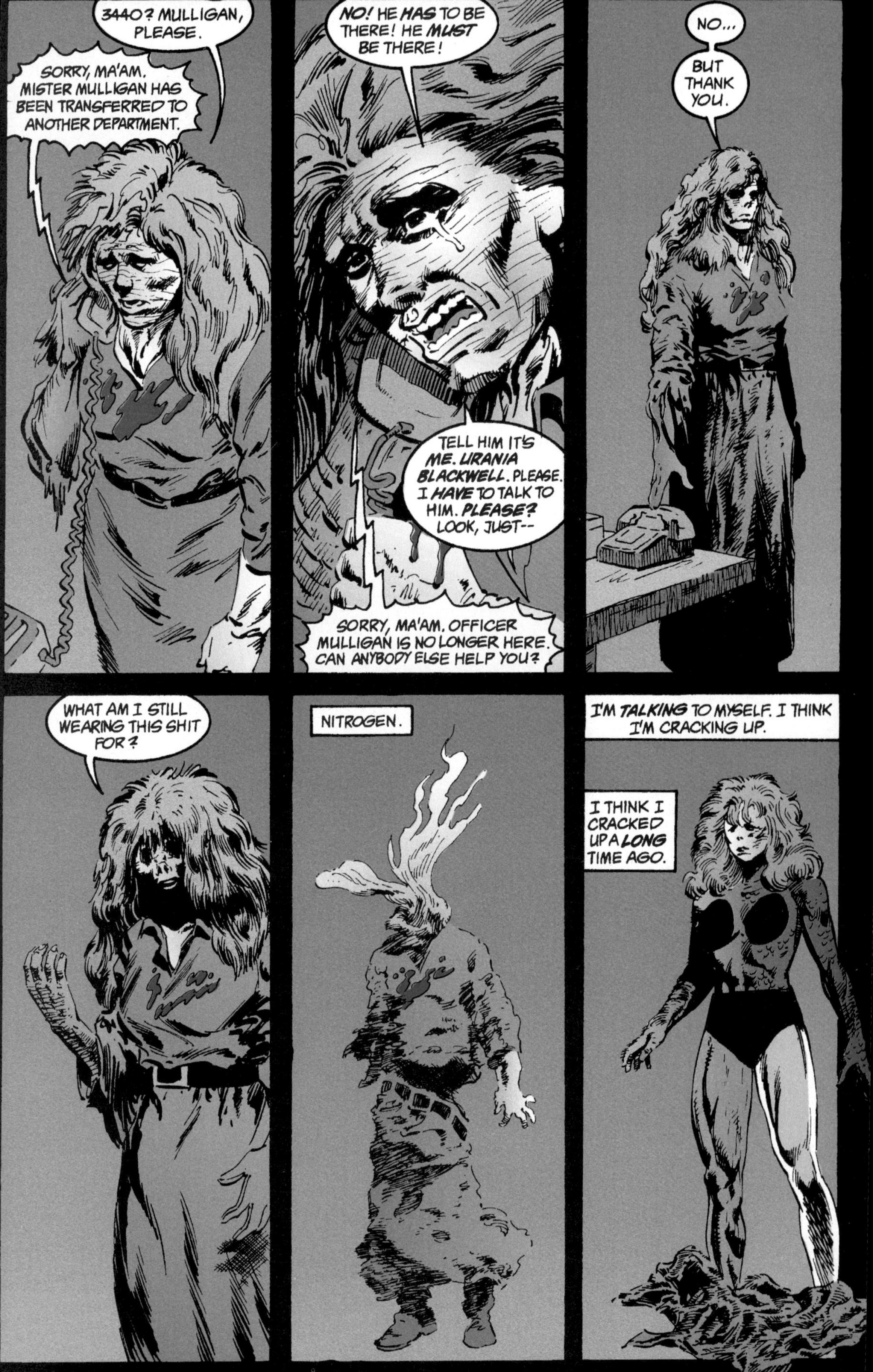
3440? MULLIGAN, PLEASE.
SORRY, MA'AM. MISTER MULLIGAN HAS BEEN TRANSFERRED TO ANOTHER DEPARTMENT.
NO! HE HAS TO BE THERE! HE MUST BE THERE!
TELL HIM IT'S ME. URANIA BLACKWELL. PLEASE. I HAVE TO TALK TO HIM. PLEASE? LOOK, JUST--
SORRY, MA'AM. OFFICER MULLIGAN IS NO LONGER HERE. CAN ANYBODY ELSE HELP YOU?
NO...
BUT THANK YOU.
WHAT AM I STILL WEARING THIS SHIT FOR?
NITROGEN.
I'M TALKING TO MYSELF. I THINK I'M CRACKING UP.
I THINK I CRACKED UP A LONG TIME AGO.

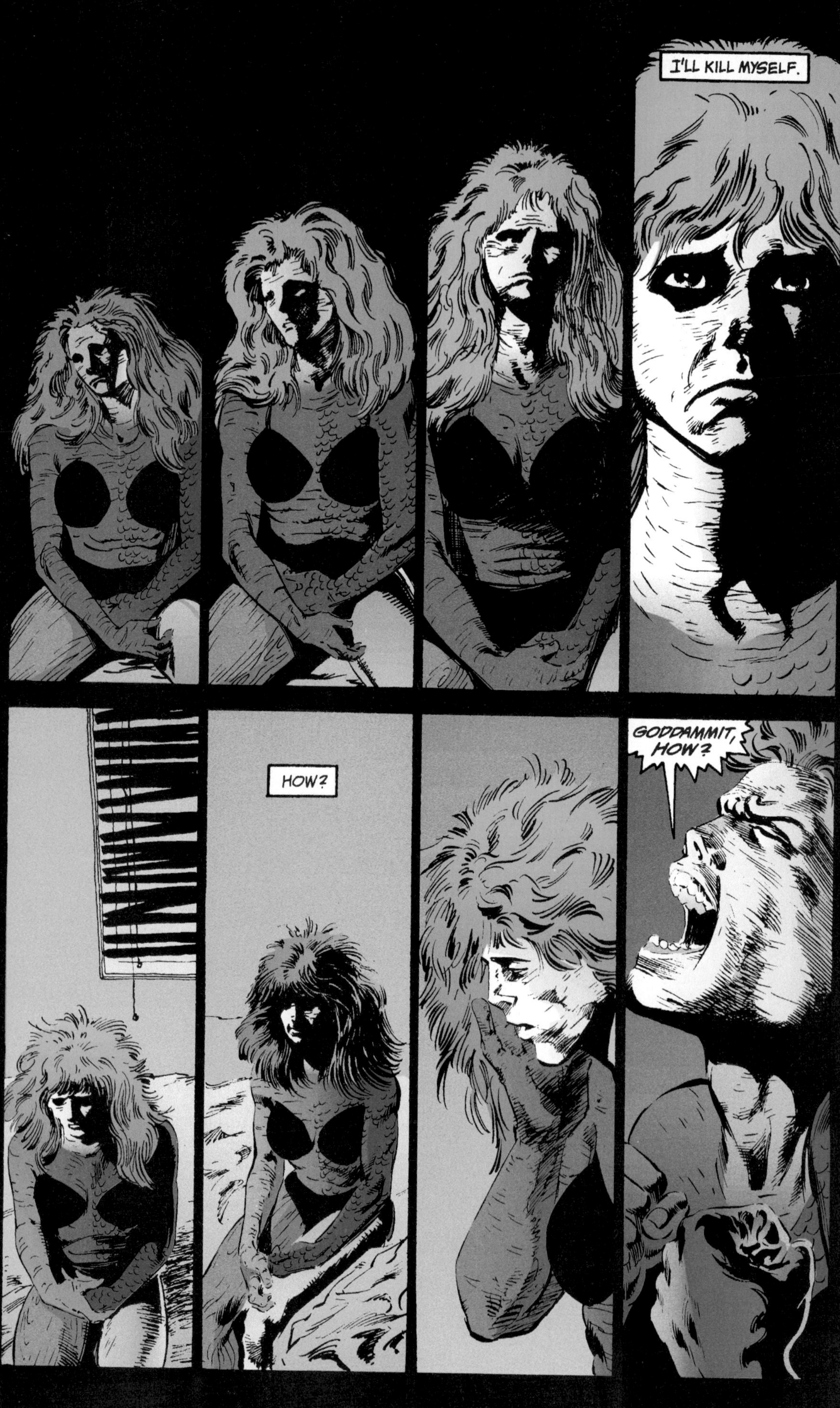
I'LL KILL MYSELF.
HOW?
GODDAMMIT, HOW?

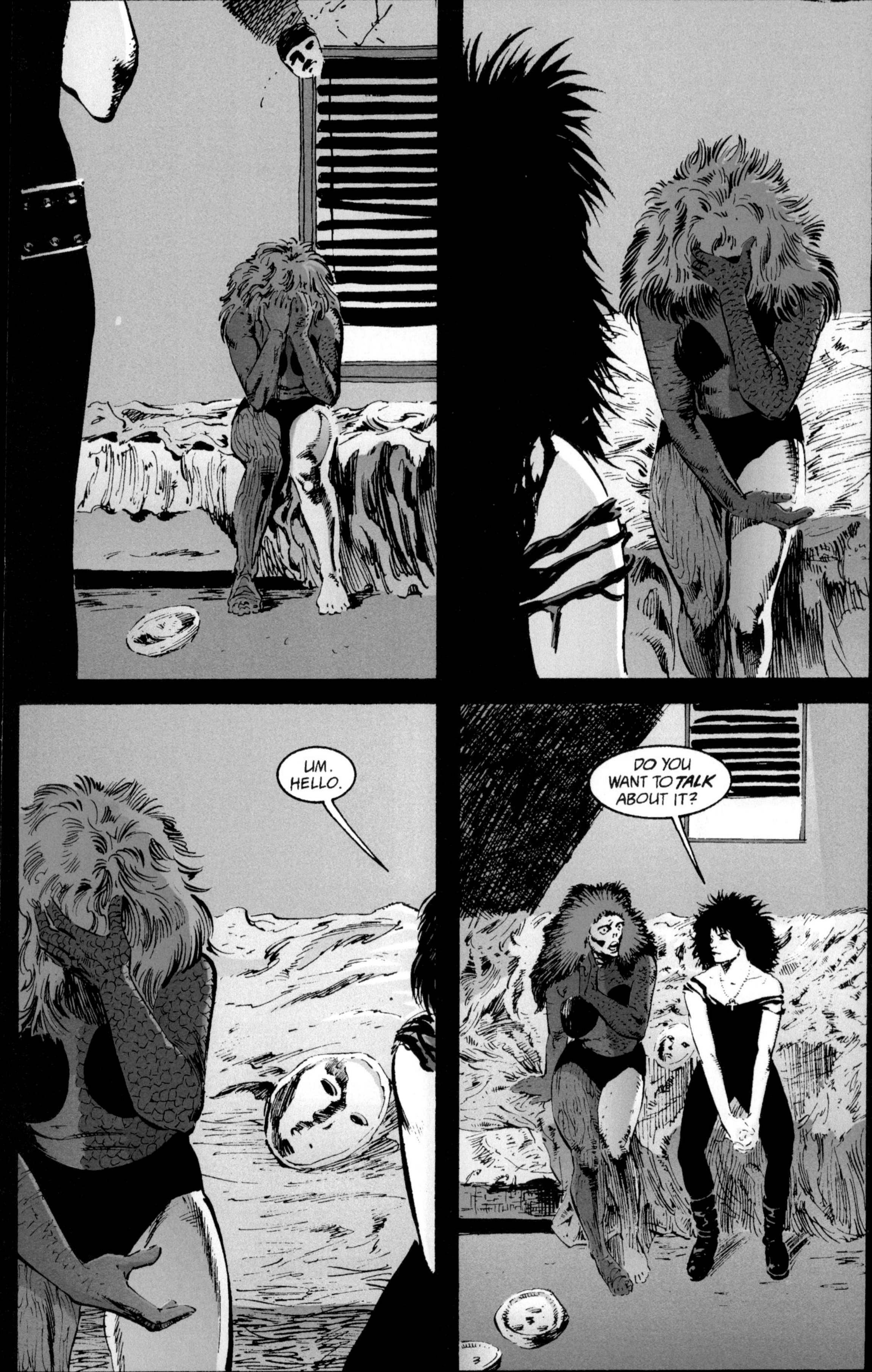
UM. HELLO.
DO YOU WANT TO *TALK* ABOUT IT?

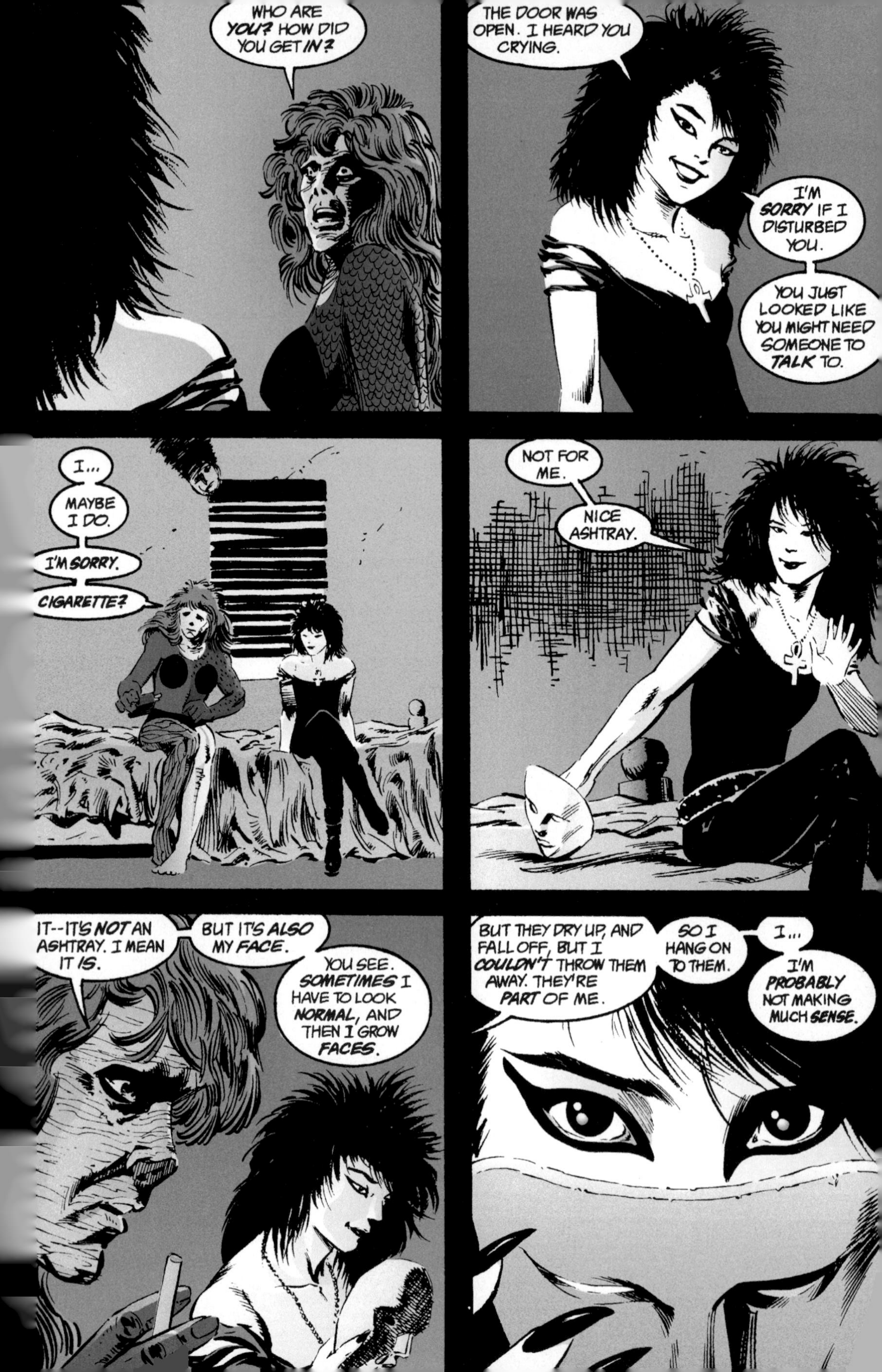
WHO ARE YOU? HOW DID YOU GET IN?
THE DOOR WAS OPEN. I HEARD YOU CRYING.
I'M SORRY IF I DISTURBED YOU.
YOU JUST LOOKED LIKE YOU MIGHT NEED SOMEONE TO TALK TO.
I...
MAYBE I DO.
I'M SORRY.
CIGARETTE?
NOT FOR ME.
NICE ASHTRAY.
IT--IT'S NOT AN ASHTRAY. I MEAN IT IS.
BUT IT'S ALSO MY FACE.
YOU SEE. SOMETIMES I HAVE TO LOOK NORMAL, AND THEN I GROW FACES.
BUT THEY DRY UP, AND FALL OFF, BUT I COULDN'T THROW THEM AWAY. THEY'RE PART OF ME.
SO I HANG ON TO THEM.
I...
I'M PROBABLY NOT MAKING MUCH SENSE.

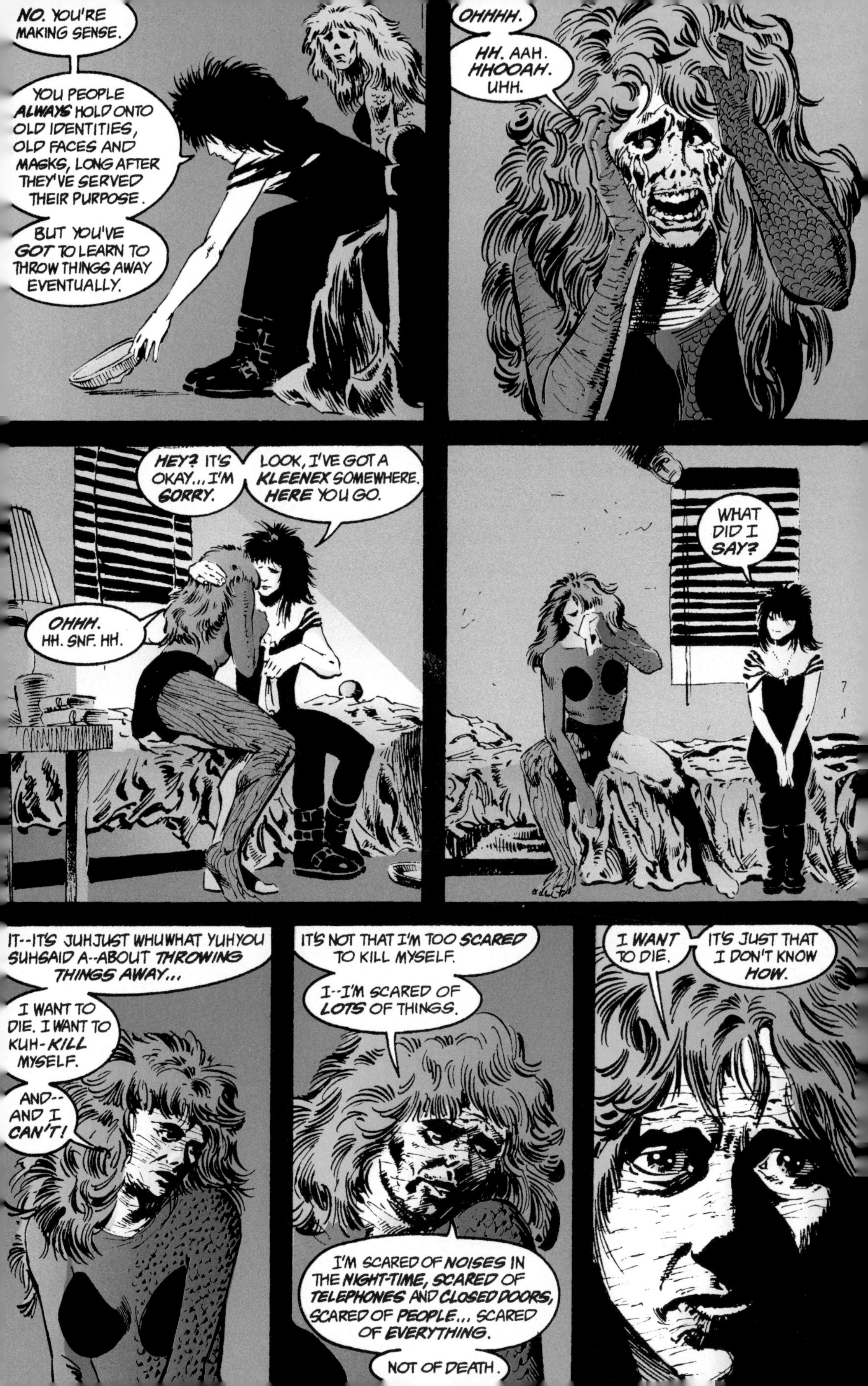
NO. YOU'RE MAKING SENSE.
YOU PEOPLE ALWAYS HOLD ONTO OLD IDENTITIES, OLD FACES AND MASKS, LONG AFTER THEY'VE SERVED THEIR PURPOSE.
BUT YOU'VE GOT TO LEARN TO THROW THINGS AWAY EVENTUALLY.
OHHHH.
HH. AAH. HHOOAH. UHH.
HEY? IT'S OKAY... I'M SORRY.
LOOK, I'VE GOT A KLEENEX SOMEWHERE. HERE YOU GO.
OHHH. HH. SNF. HH.
WHAT DID I SAY?
IT--IT'S JUHJUST WHUWHAT YUHYOU SUHSAID A--ABOUT THROWING THINGS AWAY...
I WANT TO DIE. I WANT TO KUH-KILL MYSELF.
AND-- AND I CAN'T!
IT'S NOT THAT I'M TOO SCARED TO KILL MYSELF.
I--I'M SCARED OF LOTS OF THINGS.
I'M SCARED OF NOISES IN THE NIGHT-TIME, SCARED OF TELEPHONES AND CLOSED DOORS, SCARED OF PEOPLE... SCARED OF EVERYTHING.
NOT OF DEATH.
I WANT TO DIE.
IT'S JUST THAT I DON'T KNOW HOW.

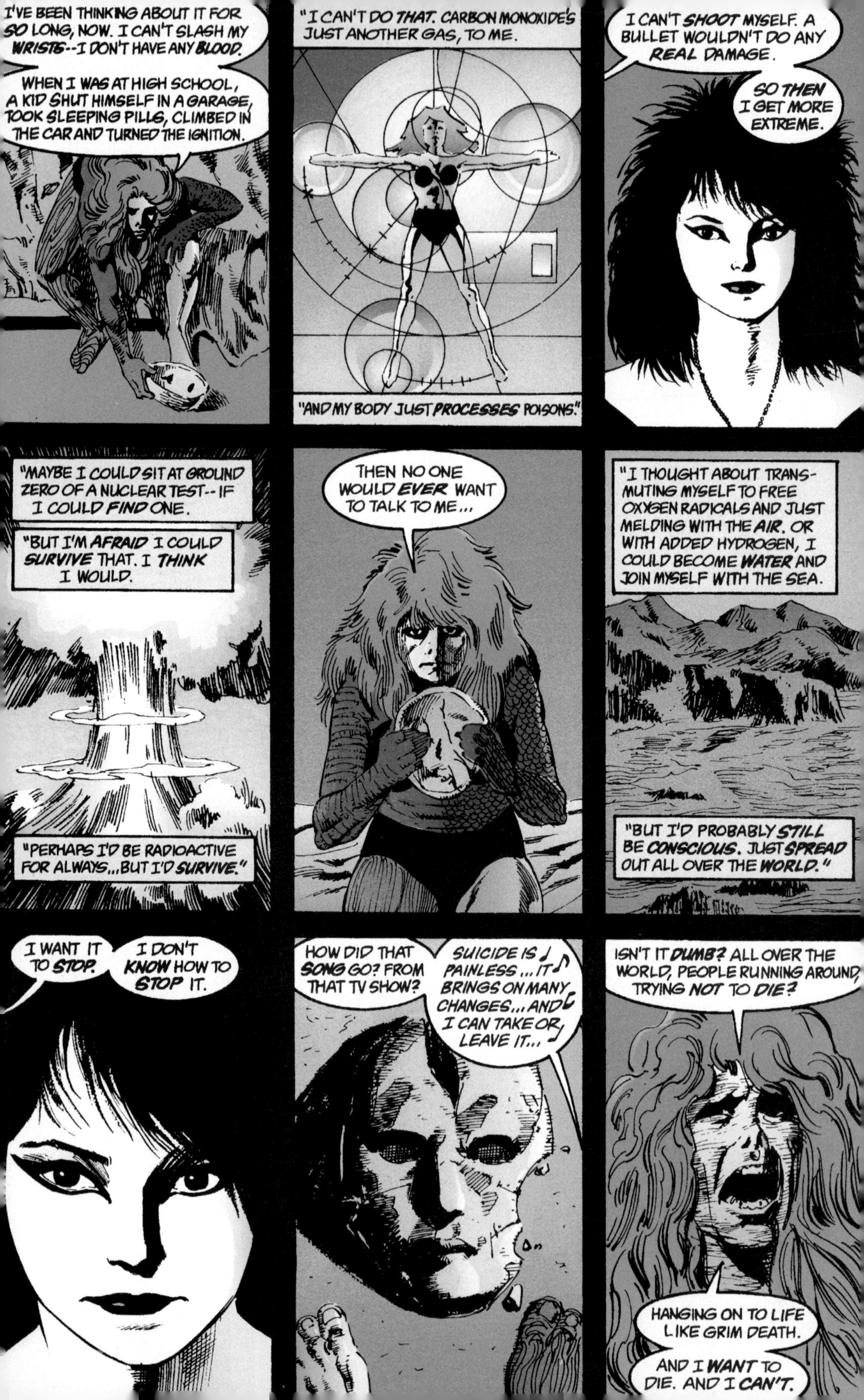
I'VE BEEN THINKING ABOUT IT FOR SO LONG, NOW. I CAN'T SLASH MY WRISTS--I DON'T HAVE ANY BLOOD.
WHEN I WAS AT HIGH SCHOOL, A KID SHUT HIMSELF IN A GARAGE, TOOK SLEEPING PILLS, CLIMBED IN THE CAR AND TURNED THE IGNITION.
"I CAN'T DO THAT. CARBON MONOXIDE'S JUST ANOTHER GAS, TO ME.
"AND MY BODY JUST PROCESSES POISONS."
I CAN'T SHOOT MYSELF. A BULLET WOULDN'T DO ANY REAL DAMAGE.
SO THEN I GET MORE EXTREME.
"MAYBE I COULD SIT AT GROUND ZERO OF A NUCLEAR TEST-- IF I COULD FIND ONE.
"BUT I'M AFRAID I COULD SURVIVE THAT. I THINK I WOULD.
"PERHAPS I'D BE RADIOACTIVE FOR ALWAYS...BUT I'D SURVIVE."
THEN NO ONE WOULD EVER WANT TO TALK TO ME...
"I THOUGHT ABOUT TRANS-MUTING MYSELF TO FREE OXYGEN RADICALS AND JUST MELDING WITH THE AIR. OR WITH ADDED HYDROGEN, I COULD BECOME WATER AND JOIN MYSELF WITH THE SEA.
"BUT I'D PROBABLY STILL BE CONSCIOUS. JUST SPREAD OUT ALL OVER THE WORLD."
I WANT IT TO STOP.
I DON'T KNOW HOW TO STOP IT.
HOW DID THAT SONG GO? FROM THAT TV SHOW?
SUICIDE IS PAINLESS... IT BRINGS ON MANY CHANGES... AND I CAN TAKE OR LEAVE IT...
ISN'T IT DUMB? ALL OVER THE WORLD, PEOPLE RUNNING AROUND, TRYING NOT TO DIE?
HANGING ON TO LIFE LIKE GRIM DEATH.
AND I WANT TO DIE. AND I CAN'T.

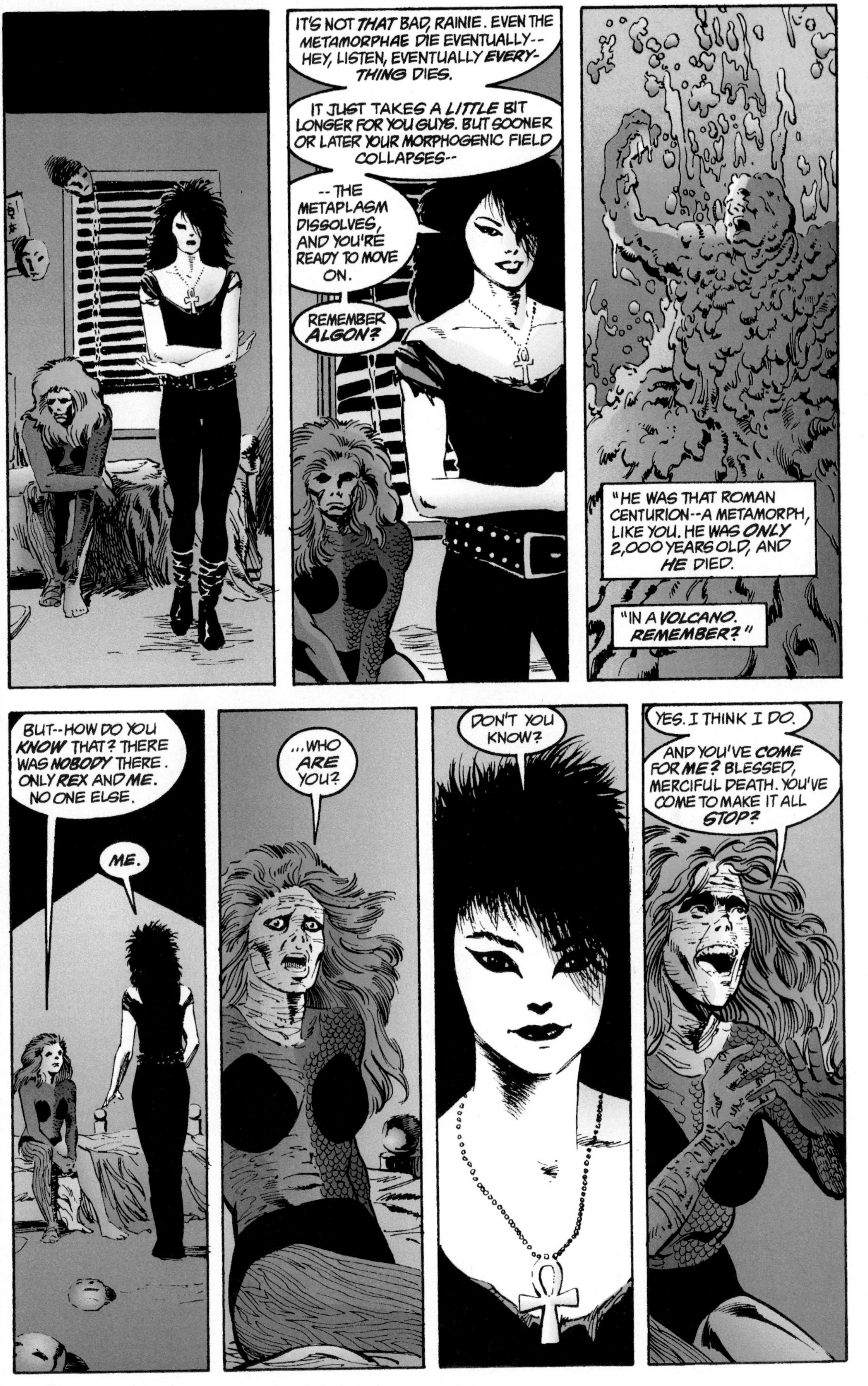
IT'S NOT THAT BAD, RAINIE. EVEN THE METAMORPHAE DIE EVENTUALLY-- HEY, LISTEN, EVENTUALLY EVERYTHING DIES.
IT JUST TAKES A LITTLE BIT LONGER FOR YOU GUYS. BUT SOONER OR LATER YOUR MORPHOGENIC FIELD COLLAPSES--
--THE METAPLASM DISSOLVES, AND YOU'RE READY TO MOVE ON.
REMEMBER ALGON?
"HE WAS THAT ROMAN CENTURION--A METAMORPH, LIKE YOU. HE WAS ONLY 2,000 YEARS OLD, AND HE DIED.
"IN A VOLCANO. REMEMBER?"
BUT--HOW DO YOU KNOW THAT? THERE WAS NOBODY THERE. ONLY REX AND ME. NO ONE ELSE.
ME.
...WHO ARE YOU?
DON'T YOU KNOW?
YES. I THINK I DO.
AND YOU'VE COME FOR ME? BLESSED, MERCIFUL DEATH. YOU'VE COME TO MAKE IT ALL STOP?

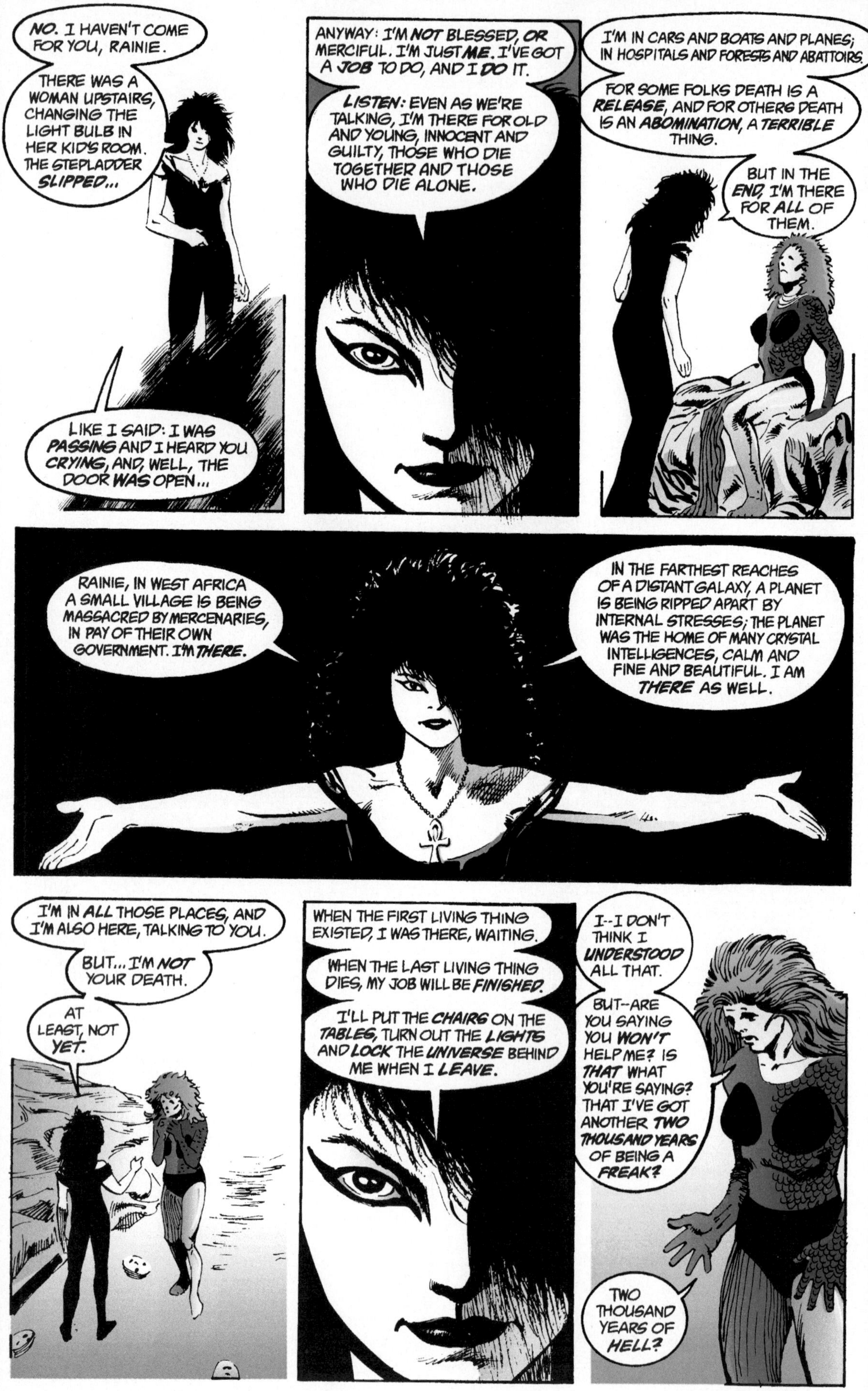
NO. I HAVEN'T COME FOR YOU, RAINIE.
THERE WAS A WOMAN UPSTAIRS, CHANGING THE LIGHT BULB IN HER KID'S ROOM. THE STEPLADDER SLIPPED...
LIKE I SAID: I WAS PASSING AND I HEARD YOU CRYING, AND, WELL, THE DOOR WAS OPEN...
ANYWAY: I'M NOT BLESSED, OR MERCIFUL. I'M JUST ME. I'VE GOT A JOB TO DO, AND I DO IT.
LISTEN: EVEN AS WE'RE TALKING, I'M THERE FOR OLD AND YOUNG, INNOCENT AND GUILTY, THOSE WHO DIE TOGETHER AND THOSE WHO DIE ALONE.
I'M IN CARS AND BOATS AND PLANES; IN HOSPITALS AND FORESTS AND ABATTOIRS.
FOR SOME FOLKS DEATH IS A RELEASE, AND FOR OTHERS DEATH IS AN ABOMINATION, A TERRIBLE THING.
BUT IN THE END, I'M THERE FOR ALL OF THEM.
RAINIE, IN WEST AFRICA A SMALL VILLAGE IS BEING MASSACRED BY MERCENARIES, IN PAY OF THEIR OWN GOVERNMENT. I'M THERE.
IN THE FARTHEST REACHES OF A DISTANT GALAXY, A PLANET IS BEING RIPPED APART BY INTERNAL STRESSES; THE PLANET WAS THE HOME OF MANY CRYSTAL INTELLIGENCES, CALM AND FINE AND BEAUTIFUL. I AM THERE AS WELL.
I'M IN ALL THOSE PLACES, AND I'M ALSO HERE, TALKING TO YOU.
BUT... I'M NOT YOUR DEATH.
AT LEAST, NOT YET.
WHEN THE FIRST LIVING THING EXISTED, I WAS THERE, WAITING.
WHEN THE LAST LIVING THING DIES, MY JOB WILL BE FINISHED.
I'LL PUT THE CHAIRS ON THE TABLES, TURN OUT THE LIGHTS AND LOCK THE UNIVERSE BEHIND ME WHEN I LEAVE.
I--I DON'T THINK I UNDERSTOOD ALL THAT.
BUT--ARE YOU SAYING YOU WON'T HELP ME? IS THAT WHAT YOU'RE SAYING? THAT I'VE GOT ANOTHER TWO THOUSAND YEARS OF BEING A FREAK?
TWO THOUSAND YEARS OF HELL?

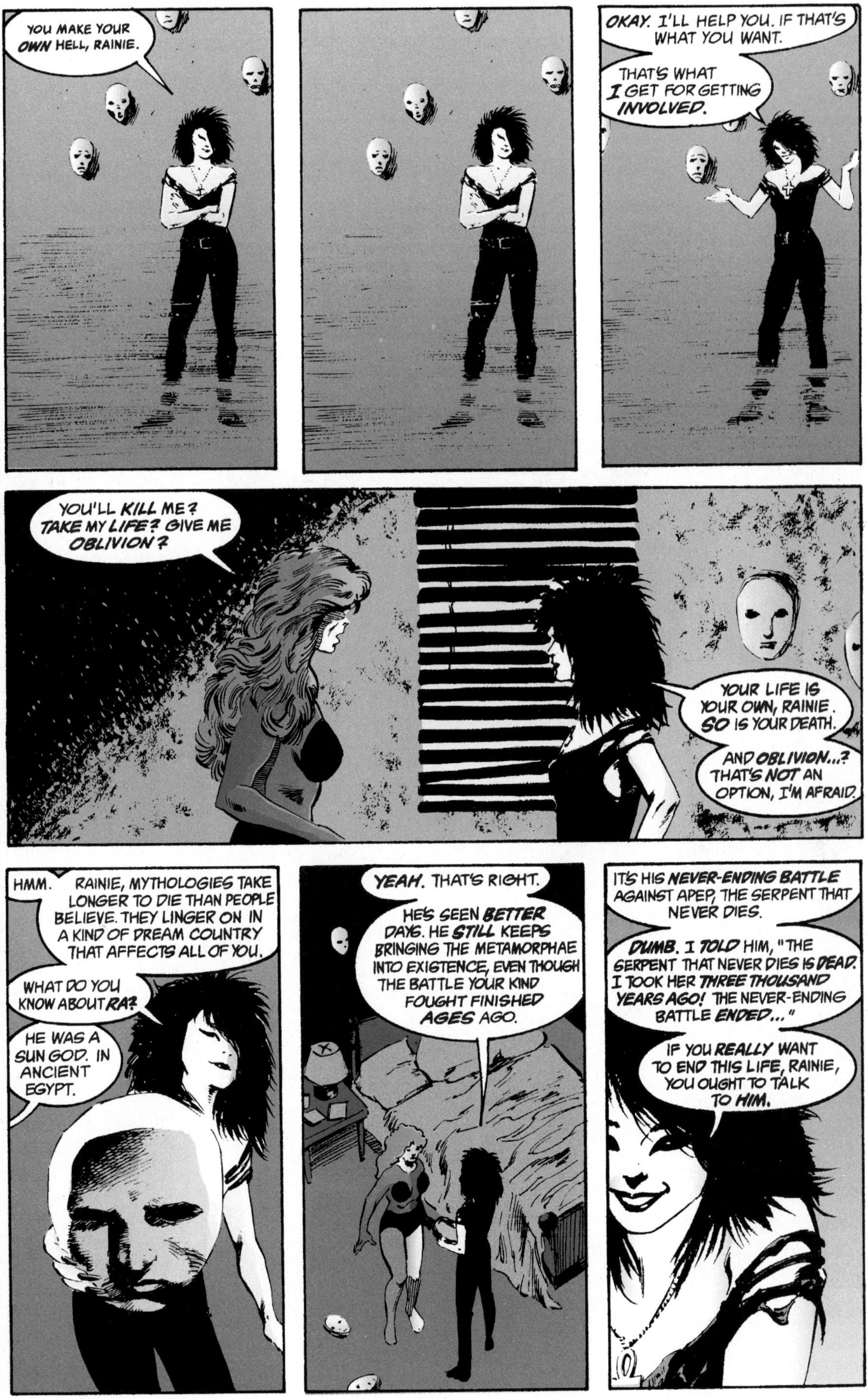

YOU MAKE YOUR OWN HELL, RAINIE.
OKAY. I'LL HELP YOU. IF THAT'S WHAT YOU WANT.
THAT'S WHAT I GET FOR GETTING INVOLVED.
YOU'LL KILL ME? TAKE MY LIFE? GIVE ME OBLIVION?
YOUR LIFE IS YOUR OWN, RAINIE. SO IS YOUR DEATH.
AND OBLIVION...? THAT'S NOT AN OPTION, I'M AFRAID.
HMM.
RAINIE, MYTHOLOGIES TAKE LONGER TO DIE THAN PEOPLE BELIEVE. THEY LINGER ON IN A KIND OF DREAM COUNTRY THAT AFFECTS ALL OF YOU.
WHAT DO YOU KNOW ABOUT RA?
HE WAS A SUN GOD. IN ANCIENT EGYPT.
YEAH. THAT'S RIGHT.
HE'S SEEN BETTER DAYS. HE STILL KEEPS BRINGING THE METAMORPHAE INTO EXISTENCE, EVEN THOUGH THE BATTLE YOUR KIND FOUGHT FINISHED AGES AGO.
IT'S HIS NEVER-ENDING BATTLE AGAINST APEP, THE SERPENT THAT NEVER DIES.
DUMB. I TOLD HIM, "THE SERPENT THAT NEVER DIES IS DEAD. I TOOK HER THREE THOUSAND YEARS AGO! THE NEVER-ENDING BATTLE ENDED..."
IF YOU REALLY WANT TO END THIS LIFE, RAINIE, YOU OUGHT TO TALK TO HIM.

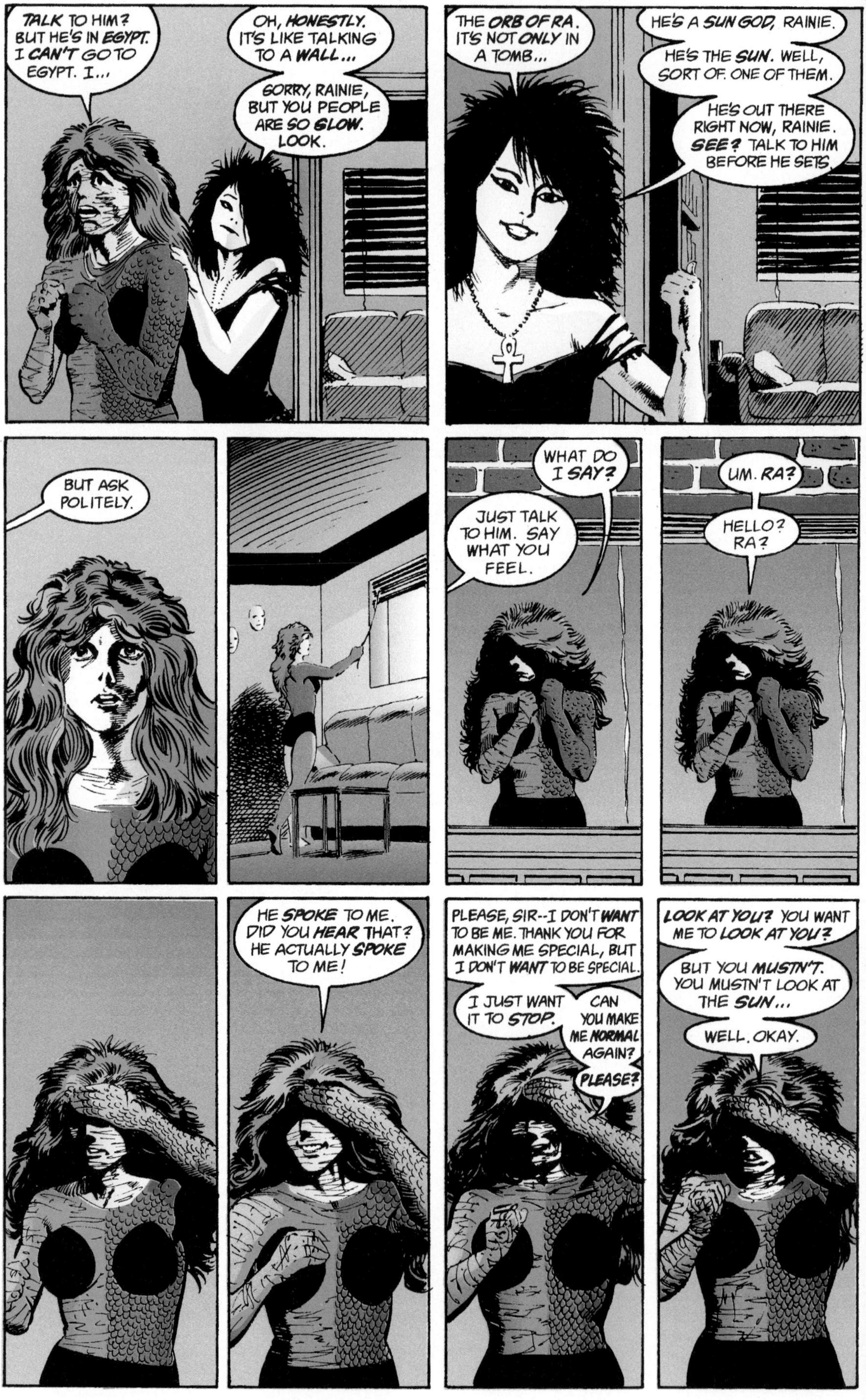
TALK TO HIM? BUT HE'S IN EGYPT. I CAN'T GO TO EGYPT. I...
OH, HONESTLY. IT'S LIKE TALKING TO A WALL...
SORRY, RAINIE, BUT YOU PEOPLE ARE SO SLOW. LOOK.
THE ORB OF RA. IT'S NOT ONLY IN A TOMB...
HE'S A SUN GOD, RAINIE.
HE'S THE SUN. WELL, SORT OF. ONE OF THEM.
HE'S OUT THERE RIGHT NOW, RAINIE. SEE? TALK TO HIM BEFORE HE SETS.
BUT ASK POLITELY.
WHAT DO I SAY?
JUST TALK TO HIM. SAY WHAT YOU FEEL.
UM. RA?
HELLO? RA?
HE SPOKE TO ME. DID YOU HEAR THAT? HE ACTUALLY SPOKE TO ME!
PLEASE, SIR--I DON'T WANT TO BE ME. THANK YOU FOR MAKING ME SPECIAL, BUT I DON'T WANT TO BE SPECIAL.
I JUST WANT IT TO STOP.
CAN YOU MAKE ME NORMAL AGAIN?
PLEASE?
LOOK AT YOU? YOU WANT ME TO LOOK AT YOU?
BUT YOU MUSTN'T. YOU MUSTN'T LOOK AT THE SUN...
WELL. OKAY.

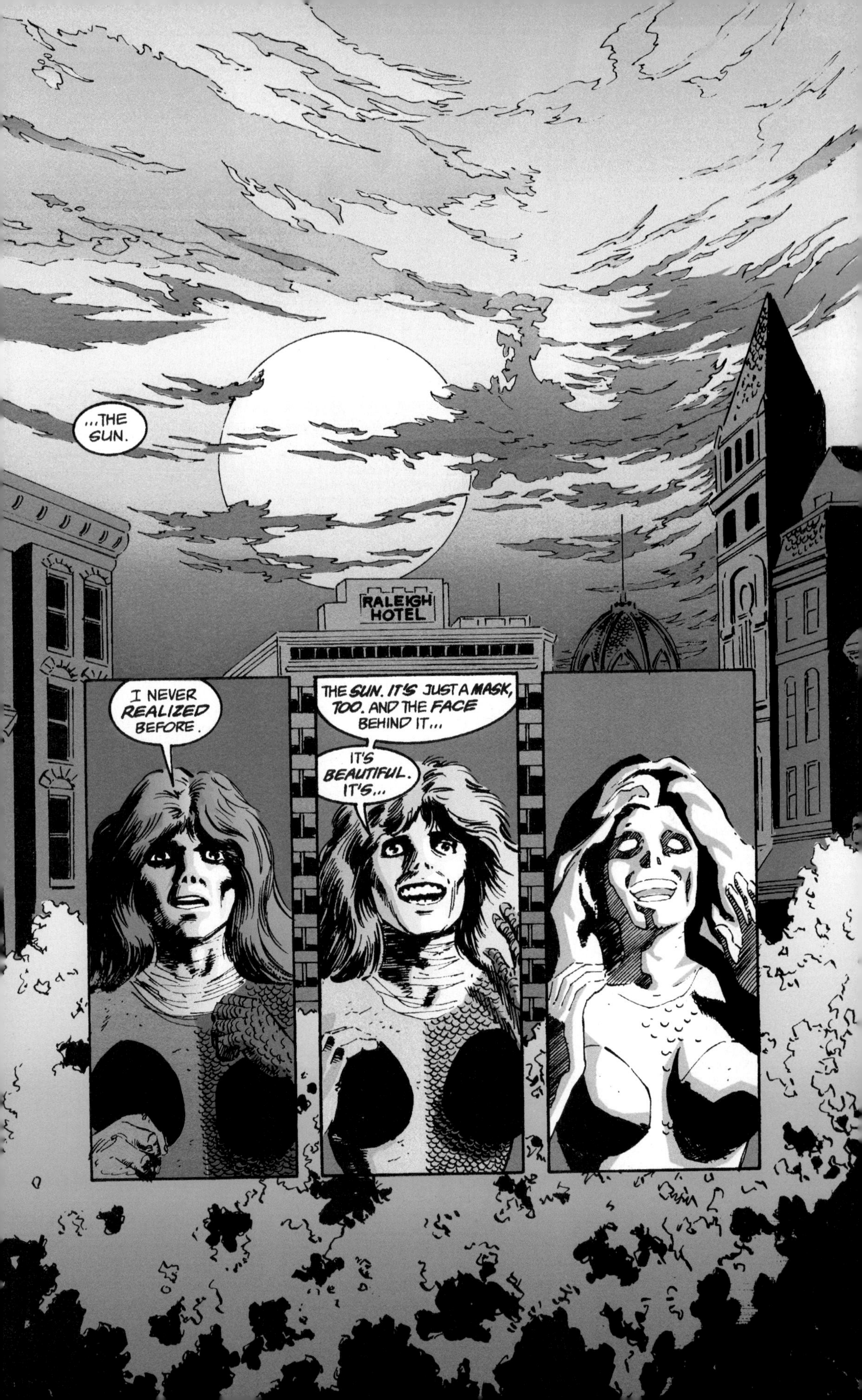
...THE SUN.
RALEIGH HOTEL
I NEVER REALIZED BEFORE.
THE SUN. IT'S JUST A MASK, TOO. AND THE FACE BEHIND IT...
IT'S BEAUTIFUL. IT'S...

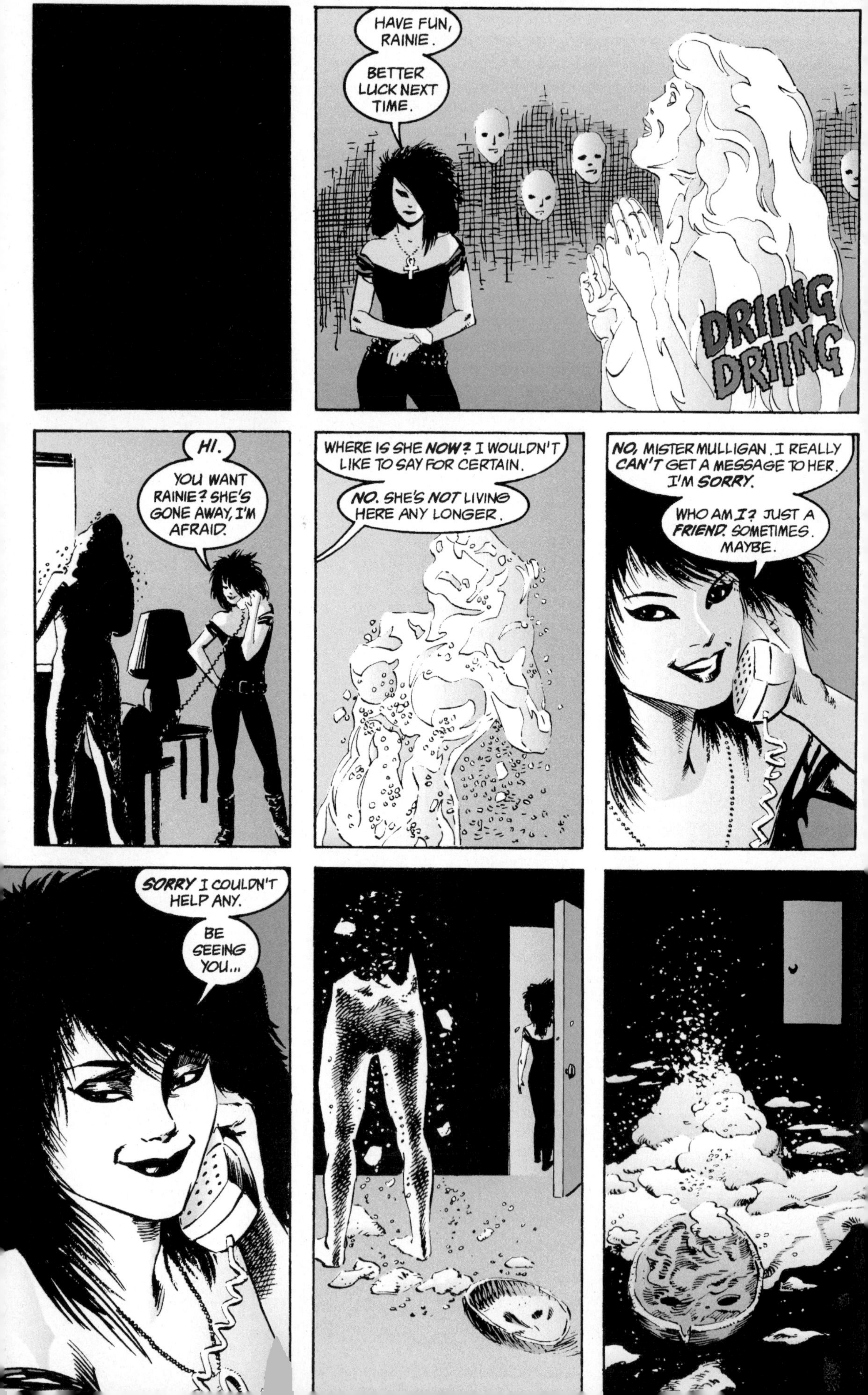
HAVE FUN, RAINIE.
BETTER LUCK NEXT TIME.
DRIING DRIING
HI.
YOU WANT RAINIE? SHE'S GONE AWAY, I'M AFRAID.
WHERE IS SHE NOW? I WOULDN'T LIKE TO SAY FOR CERTAIN.
NO. SHE'S NOT LIVING HERE ANY LONGER.
NO, MISTER MULLIGAN. I REALLY CAN'T GET A MESSAGE TO HER. I'M SORRY.
WHO AM I? JUST A FRIEND. SOMETIMES. MAYBE.
SORRY I COULDN'T HELP ANY.
BE SEEING YOU...

THE SANDMAN: A READING GUIDE

Originally published as a 75-issue run of comic books from 1988 to 1996, *The Sandman* was one of the first comics series to find a new and continuing audience as a series of collected books. As a result, its publication history in various forms in the ensuing decades has become somewhat complex.

In 2022, DC is undertaking a new effort to streamline this library, collapsing the series from 10 individually titled books to four volumes; we hope that this reading guide will clarify how to follow the story of *The Sandman* through both its original run and the follow-up works that have expanded this mythos.

THE SANDMAN BOOK ONE

Collecting issues #1-20 of the original series, this volume encompasses the story arcs previously published individually as *Preludes & Nocturnes*, *The Doll's House*, and *Dream Country*.

THE SANDMAN BOOK TWO

Collecting issues #21-37, *The Sandman Special* #1, and stories from the three *Winter's Edge* anthologies, this volume contains the story arcs *Season of Mists* and *A Game of You*, along with a portion of the material from the short-story collection *Fables & Reflections*.

THE SANDMAN BOOK THREE

Collecting issues #38-56 and a story from *Vertigo Preview* #1, the balance of *Fables & Reflections* appears here, along with *Brief Lives* and *Worlds' End*.

THE SANDMAN BOOK FOUR

Collecting issues #57-75 and stories from *Vertigo Jam* #1 and *Dust Covers*, this volume concludes the original series run, combining the epic story arcs *The Kindly Ones* and *The Wake*.

NEIL GAIMAN
THE SANDMAN
THE DELUXE EDITION • BOOK ONE
audible

Neil Gaiman
the SANDMAN
OMNIBUS
VOLUME
I

SANDMAN
NEIL GAIMAN

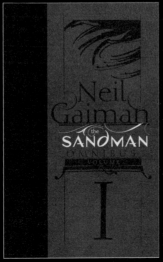

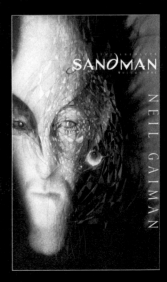

If you wish to collect *The Sandman* in a hardcover format, rather than softcover, three options are available: five Deluxe Editions, which collect the series at a slightly larger trim size; three Omnibus Editions, with handsome faux-leather covers and thousand-plus page counts; and the Absolute Editions, five top-of-the-line premium slipcase editions at an even larger physical scale. These editions also include material from the "Further Reading" section on the following page.

THE SANDMAN: FURTHER READING

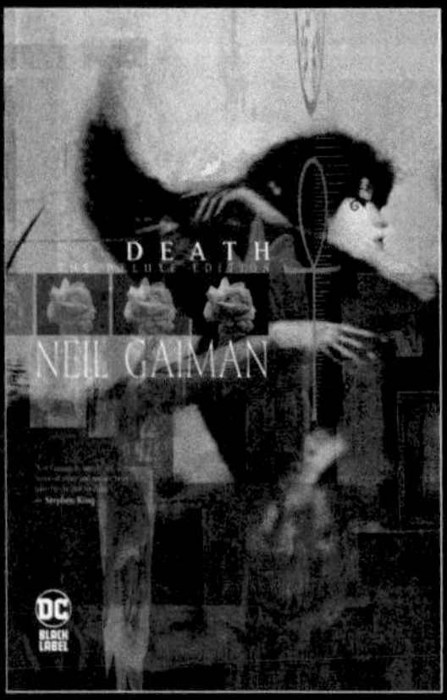
DEATH
NEIL GAIMAN

After the conclusion of the original 75-issue run of *The Sandman* in 1996, Neil Gaiman returned to its world for several follow-up volumes, extending the mythos with events that took place during, shortly after, and long before the events of the series.

DEATH: THE DELUXE EDITION

The most beloved member of the Endless, Death has starred in two stand-alone miniseries, *The High Cost of Living* and *The Time of Your Life*, both drawn by Chris Bachalo. This volume collects both, along with the short story "Death Talks About Life"—a public health message produced at the height of the AIDS crisis—and a gallery of pinups by renowned illustrators.

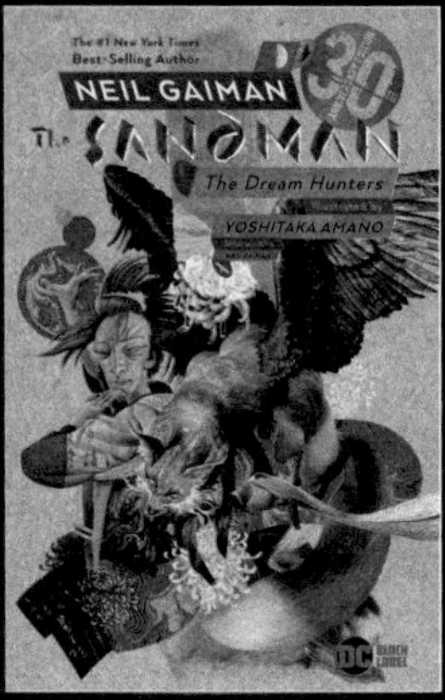
NEIL GAIMAN
The SANDMAN
The Dream Hunters
YOSHITAKA AMANO

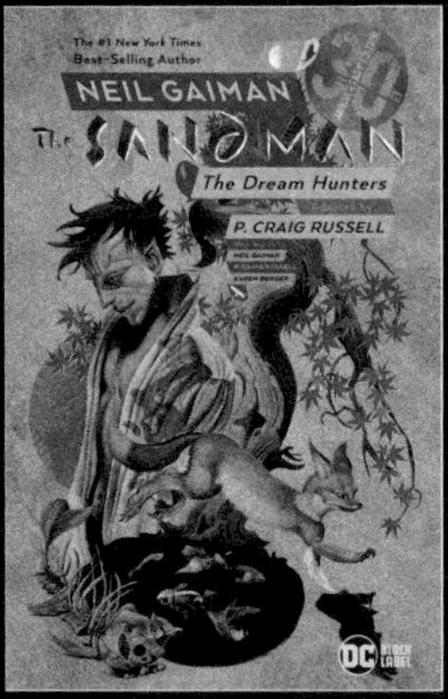
NEIL GAIMAN
The SANDMAN
The Dream Hunters
P. CRAIG RUSSELL

THE SANDMAN: THE DREAM HUNTERS

The first published follow-up to *The Sandman*, the tale of a Buddhist monk, a fox spirit, and their encounter with Dream is a story that has now been told in two formats: in its original 1998 form, a prose novella with gorgeous illustrations by Japanese legend Yoshitaka Amano; and in a 2009 comic book adaptation by "Ramadan" artist P. Craig Russell.

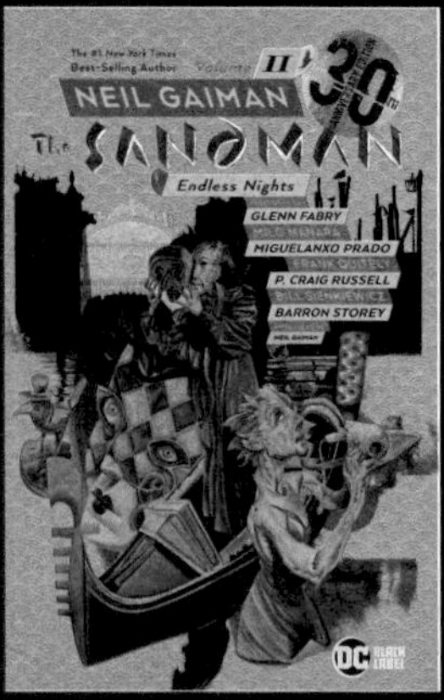
NEIL GAIMAN
The SANDMAN
Endless Nights
GLENN FABRY
MIGUELANXO PRADO
P. CRAIG RUSSELL
BARRON STOREY

THE SANDMAN: ENDLESS NIGHTS

A collection of short stories in collaboration with some of the finest artists in the comics medium, each chapter of this 2003 volume deepens our understanding of a different member of the Endless, jumping time periods from the modern day to the cosmic era before the formation of the Earth.

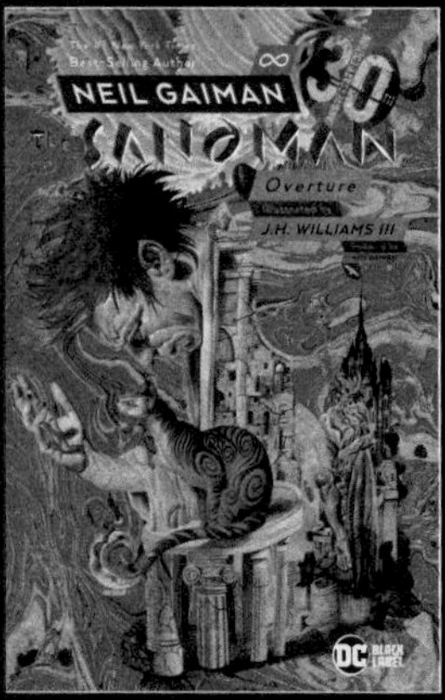
NEIL GAIMAN
The SANDMAN
Overture
J.H. WILLIAMS III

THE SANDMAN: OVERTURE

A dazzling formal experiment in both its structure and its unbelievable art by superstar J.H. Williams III, this 2015 follow-up to *The Sandman* tells a story of Desire and Dream, eternal rivals but still entangled siblings, as they confront the only beings more powerful than themselves: their own parents. As impossible as it sounds, this story manages to serve as both an epilogue and a prelude to *The Sandman*'s original run—and therefore it can be read in either order, enriching the reading experience either way.

THE SANDMAN UNIVERSE

In 2018, Neil Gaiman curated a collection of follow-up series, written and drawn by a new generation of comics talent, which continued the story of *The Sandman* in the modern era, explicitly set as many years later as had elapsed since the original run's conclusion. The one-shot that launched this new era is collected at the start of each Volume One, allowing each series to be read individually or as part of a whole.

Sandman Universe
The Dreaming
Sandman Universe
The Dreaming
Sandman Universe
The Dreaming

THE DREAMING

Just as *The Sandman* begins with Dream exiled from his realm, *The Dreaming* tells the story of what happens to Dream's subjects when he seemingly leaves his kingdom for good—this time, of his own volition.

The Dreaming Vol. 1: Pathways and Emanations / *The Dreaming Vol. 2: Empty Shells* / *The Dreaming Vol. 3: One Magical Movement*

Neil Gaiman
The Books of Magic
Sandman Universe
Books of Magic
Sandman Universe
Books of Magic
Sandman Universe
Books of Magic

BOOKS OF MAGIC

In 1990, as *The Sandman* was being published, Neil Gaiman wrote the miniseries *The Books of Magic* to organize DC's magical characters into one coherent world while also introducing the boy wizard Timothy Hunter—a child so powerful he would one day either lead them or destroy them. The Sandman Universe continues his story, now updated for our times.

The Books of Magic (Original Miniseries) / *Books of Magic Vol. 1: Moveable Type*
Books of Magic Vol. 2: Second Quarto / *Books of Magic Vol. 3: Dwelling in Possibility*

Sandman Universe
House of Whispers
Sandman Universe
House of Whispers
Sandman Universe
House of Whispers

HOUSE OF WHISPERS

Expanding the Sandman Universe with the tales and traditions of the Afro-Latino diaspora, this series also introduces the goddess Erzulie and the Houses of Whispers and Watchers, twins to Cain and Abel's Houses of Mysteries and Secrets.

House of Whispers Vol. 1: The Power Divided / *House of Whispers Vol. 2: Ananse* / *House of Whispers Vol. 3: Watching the Watchers*

LUCIFER

The devious devil who challenged Dream in *The Sandman* continues his quest for the ultimate escape: first, from a complex prison seemingly designed to entrap him, and then from the prison of his own creation and his divine purpose.

Lucifer Vol. 1: The Infernal Comedy / *Lucifer Vol. 2: The Divine Tragedy* / *Lucifer Vol. 3: The Wild Hunt* / *Lucifer Vol. 4: The Devil at Heart*

Sandman Universe
Lucifer
The Infernal Comedy
WILL SIN FOR FOOD

Sandman Universe
Lucifer
The Divine Tragedy

Sandman Universe
Lucifer
Volume Three
The Wild Hunt

Sandman Universe
Lucifer
The Devil at Heart

Sandman Universe
Dreaming
Waking Hours

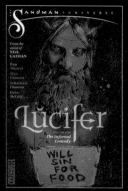

THE DREAMING: WAKING HOURS

This standalone volume introduces a new set of characters to the Sandman Universe—including Ruin, a nightmare in love with a human being, and Heather After, a sorceress with a startling connection to Dream's darkest hour—and puts them on a collision course with William Shakespeare himself.

Sandman Universe
John Constantine
Hellblazer

Sandman Universe
John Constantine
Hellblazer
Volume Two
The Best Version of You
Simon Spurrier
Aaron Campbell
Matías Bergara
Jordie Bellaire

JOHN CONSTANTINE, HELLBLAZER

The original Thatcher-era tales of John Constantine were an inspiration for *The Sandman*; here, the character is reborn in a new and more modern era—which he refuses to admit might be doing its best to leave him behind.

John Constantine, Hellblazer Vol. 1: Marks of Woe

John Constantine, Hellblazer Vol. 2: The Best Version of You

Sandman Universe Classics
the Books of Magic
Omnibus
Volume One

Sandman Universe Classics
the Books of Magic
Omnibus
Volume Two

Sandman Universe Classics
Lucifer
Omnibus
Volume One
Mike Carey
Peter Gross
Ryan Kelly
Dean Ormston

Sandman Universe Classics
Lucifer
Omnibus
Volume Two
Mike Carey
Peter Gross
Ryan Kelly
Dean Ormston

And while the volumes under the Sandman Universe banner are the currently published continuations of the *Sandman* story, which continues to develop and grow, prior long-running spinoffs from the 1990s and 2000s are also available as "The Sandman Universe Classics," collecting the previous iterations of *Lucifer* and *The Books of Magic* in hardcover omnibus form.

The Books of Magic Omnibus Vol. 1 / *The Books of Magic Omnibus Vol. 2* / *Lucifer Omnibus Vol. 1* / *Lucifer Omnibus Vol. 2*